Educational Research

An Introduction

Eighth Edition

Meredith D. Gall
University of Oregon

Joyce P. Gall
University of Oregon

Walter R. Borg

PEARSON

Boston   New York   San Francisco
Mexico City   Montreal   Toronto   London   Madrid   Muncih   Paris
Hong Kong   Singapore   Tokyo   Cape Town   Sydney

KH

Senior Editor: Arnis E. Burvikovs
Editorial Assistant: Erin Reilly
Marketing Manager: Tara Kelly
Production Editor: Gregory Erb
Editorial Production Service: Tom Conville for Nesbitt Graphics, Inc.
Composition Buyer: Linda Cox
Manufacturing Buyer: Megan Cochran
Electronic Composition: Nesbitt Graphics, Inc.
Interior Design: Nesbitt Graphics, Inc.
Cover Administrator: Kristina Mose-Libon
Permissions Manager: Robert Tonner

For related titles and support materials, visit our online catalog at www.ablongman.com.

Between the time website information is gathered and then published, it is not unusual for some sites to have closed. Also, the transcription of URLs can result in typographical errors. The publisher would appreciate notification where these errors occur so that they may be corrected in subsequent editions.

Library of Congress Cataloging-in-Publication Data
Gall, Meredith D.
    Educational research: an introduction / Meredith D. Gall, Joyce P. Gall, Walter R. Borg.—8th ed.
        p. cm.
        Includes bibliographical references and index.
        ISBN 0-205-48849-8
        1. Education—Research. 2. Education—Research—United States. I. Gall, Joyce P. II. Borg, Walter R. III. Title.
    LB1028.B6 2007
    370.7'2—dc22   2005056474

Printed in the United States of America

10 9 8 7 6 5 4 3 2 1   RRD-VA   10 09 08 07 06

7/12/06

Dedicated to Mark and Joy's son, Jon

BRIEF CONTENTS

CONTENTS

Part IV: Quantitative Research Design   297

10. Nonexperimental Research: Descriptive and Causal-Comparative Designs   298

Part V: Approaches to Qualitative Research   445

14. Case Study Research   446

PART VI: Applications of Research   557

This is the seventh revision of *Educational Research: An Introduction* since it was first published in 1963. Does research methodology change rapidly enough to warrant so many revisions?

Our answer is yes. The seventh edition was published 5 years ago, but since then we have seen important new developments in the research enterprise that education professionals should know about. For example, the U.S. government created the Institute of Education Sciences in 2002, which reflects a growing belief that educational practice can be put on a more scientific grounding, similar to what we find in medical practice. We discuss this institute and its potential impact on educational research in Chapter 1.

The role of electronic resources in educational research becomes more important each year. Electronic versions of databases for searching the research literature are rapidly making hard-copy versions obsolete. New online research journals keep appearing, and many traditional hard-copy journals now have an electronic counterpart. Another impressive development is that educators can now view many articles and documents in full-text format on their computer screens and print them, if they wish, without the need to make time-consuming trips to the library. We discuss all these developments in Chapter 4.

The fields of quantitative research design, measurement, and statistics were already well developed when we prepared the first several editions of this book, but they keep evolving in important ways. In particular, research methodologists are continuing to refine item response theory, measurement of effect size, use of computers and the Internet to collect and analyze data, and multilevel modeling as ways to portray the complexities of teaching, learning, and schooling. These methodological techniques and others are treated in Parts III and IV.

The problems of interest to quantitative researchers change as new problems of educational practice come to the fore. The accountability movement and No Child Left Behind (NCLB) legislation have heightened concerns about the achievement gap between white students and students of color, leading to an increased focus on research to discover the reasons for the gap and ways to overcome it. Basic research on teaching and learning processes involved in the acquisition of core academic skills (reading, writing, and mathematics) is also thriving. We have replaced older examples of educational research studies with many new examples, most published after 2000, that reflect these new research priorities.

Qualitative research design, the focus of much of Parts V and VI, is undergoing rapid evolution as well. Increased variety in the research methods and contributors clustered under the qualitative research umbrella is represented in the literature. In a continuing nod to the postmodern, many voices are heard but few are privileged. Rejection of essentialist perspectives, certainly of any from the positivist–quantitative research orientation, but also of those from within its own interpretive research orientation, is a pervasive theme that we highlight in this new edition.

Qualitative research reports still tend to be almost twice as long as quantitative research reports and do not follow a standard format. Much time and considerable skill are required not only to conduct and report such research, but also to read and summarize it in a way that does justice to its rich variety of topics, approaches, participants, and authors. Furthermore, an increasing percentage of qualitative-research citations accessed by preliminary sources involve opinion pieces or essays, rather than reports involving traditional methods of data collection.

Chapter 1 of this book describes description, prediction, improvement, and explanation as the general goals of research. We venture to characterize the more specific goals of qualitative researchers as to (1) utilize and enjoy the widest range of genres in constructing and communicating the research act; (2) give voice to culturally diverse individuals and groups, particularly indigenous peoples and others living under oppression; (3) expose the unintended or hidden and sometimes negative side of much past and current educational and cultural practice; and (4) remake social contracts, and indeed society as a whole, toward greater equity, harmony, and joy for all.

In response to these trends, we have taken care in this new edition to present many new examples of qualitative research that reflect the goals, diverse genres, and justice-seeking perspectives typical of this body of research and also the quality and rigor that are possible with qualitative research. Also, we have sought to help our readers embrace the complexities, possibilities, and varied approaches to disciplined inquiry in qualitative research.

Overview of the Book's Content and Organization

Educational Research: An Introduction, Eighth Edition has six parts, each preceded by a brief introduction.

Part I includes one chapter that provides an overview of the field of educational research. We recommend it as a starting point to help students develop an initial understanding of the nature of research before they start learning the specifics of research methodology.

The remaining chapters are ordered to correspond to the order of the research process, for the most part. We recommend that students consider research questions and possible research designs, but not actually undertake a formal investigation until they have read and mastered all the chapters that are relevant to it. Generally, this means first reading all the chapters in Parts I, II, and III, and then those chapters in Parts IV, V, and VI that cover the type of research that the student wishes to undertake.

Part II describes the process of planning a research study: developing a research proposal (Chapter 2); dealing with ethics and site relations issues (Chapter 3); and reviewing the literature (Chapter 4). Because a good research proposal anticipates the final report, Chapter 2 also describes the last stage of a research study: writing a dissertation, thesis, or other type of final report.

Part III covers the general methodological procedures used in research studies. These include various statistical techniques for analyzing research data (Chapter 5) and procedures for selecting the research sample (Chapter 6). Next are three chapters on how to collect research data using tests and self-report measures (Chapter 7), questionnaires and interviews (Chapter 8), and observation and content analysis (Chapter 9).

Part IV covers the major research designs used in quantitative research. Nonexperimental designs are discussed first: descriptive and causal-comparative designs in Chapter 10, and correlational designs in Chapter 11. Experimental designs are discussed in Chapters 12 and 13.

Part V focuses on approaches to qualitative research in education. Chapter 14 describes a basic qualitative method, the case study, and Chapter 15 describes qualitative research traditions and their specialized approaches. Chapter 16 provides in-depth coverage of one of these traditions, historical research.

Part VI includes two chapters about how research methods can be applied for purposes beyond the generation of scientific knowledge and theory. Chapter 17 describes how research methods are used in program evaluation and R&D projects. Chapter 18 concerns action research, which has the goal of generating knowledge to improve local professional practice.

Learning Aids

The information load in a book of this type is considerable, so each chapter contains learning aids to help the student master its content. These aids include the following:

- A brief *overview* at the start of each chapter sets the stage for what the student will read.
- *Chapter objectives* at the start of each chapter identify major concepts and techniques that will be covered.
- *Technical terms* are boldfaced in the text when they appear for the first time in the chapter, and defined in the Glossary at the end of the book.
- *Touchstones in Research* are marginal citations throughout each chapter that guide students to more information and resources.
- *Recommendations* at the end of each chapter help students apply the chapter content to their own research study.
- A *Self-Check Test* concludes each chapter (answers appear at the back of the book).

Instructor's Manual

The *Instructor's Manual* provides various resources that facilitate teaching a course on research methods using *Educational Research: An Introduction, Eighth Edition.* These resources include: suggestions pertaining to various course elements, such as content coverage, content sequence, teaching activities, and homework; an example of a course syllabus; a form for outlining a research proposal, which can be used as a course project; and a test-item file for each chapter containing closed-form items, short-answer items, and application items based on situations that arise when conducting educational research.

Acknowledgments

Whatever success this book has enjoyed is due in large measure to Walter Borg, who wrote the first edition. He invited one of us (Mark Gall) to become his co-author for the second through fifth editions. Walter died in 1990 after a long, distinguished career as a professor and researcher. Mark's colleague and spouse, Joy Gall, has co-authored subsequent editions.

We wish to acknowledge our colleagues at the University of Oregon and elsewhere who continue to stimulate our thinking about educational research and practice. Among these gifted professionals, we wish to single out for this edition Dr. Martin Kaufman, professor and former dean of the University of Oregon's College of Education. His support for our work on this book and other endeavors has been unfailing. In addition, his commitment to research as an essential foundation for improving educational practice is a continual source of inspiration for us and others who work with him.

Finally, we thank Arnis Burvikovs at Allyn & Bacon for his expertise and encouragement during the developmental and production phases of this edition. We wish to acknowledge, too, other editors who helped us over the years, including Ed Artinian, Ginny Blanford, Art Pomponio, Ray O'Connell, and Mary Kriener.

Meredith "Mark" Gall
Joyce P. (Joy) Gall

Meredith "Mark" Gall is a professor in the College of Education at the University of Oregon. He is also the author of *Applying Educational Research: A Practical Guide*, Fifth Edition (with Joyce P. Gall and Walter R. Borg) published by Pearson/Allyn & Bacon and *Clinical Supervision and Teacher Development: Preservice and Inservice Applications*, Fifth Edition (with Keith A. Acheson), published by John Wiley & Sons.

Joyce "Joy" Gall is a courtesy assistant professor in the College of Education at the University of Oregon. She is also the author of *Applying Educational Research: A Practical Guide*, Fifth Edition (with M. D. Gall and Walter R. Borg) published by Pearson/Allyn & Bacon.

Walter R. Borg, late professor emeritus at Utah State University, was one of the major developers of microteaching, a widely used method of teacher education. He was the senior author of *Educational Research: An Introduction* through its first five editions, starting in 1963.

Introduction

Part I provides an overview of educational research as an organized, professional approach to inquiry. You will find that educational research is not a simple matter of discovering facts about education, but rather that it has diverse goals, including the development of theories to explain educational phenomena.

You also will find that educational researchers must deal with important, but still unresolved, philosophical issues having to do with the nature of social reality and how to acquire knowledge about it. Different researchers have taken opposing positions on these issues, and consequently, they have developed quite different approaches to the investigation of education. We introduce you to the two main approaches, commonly known as quantitative and qualitative research. Other parts of the book provide detailed explanations of how to conduct research studies using one or the other approach. You should study this part of the book first, though, so that you understand why these different approaches evolved.

In reading Part I, you will find that research plays an important role in improving educational practice. At the same time, educational research is a very human process and, therefore, is prone to error and bias. Researchers have developed procedures to minimize the influence of error and bias on their findings. In this respect, the approach to educational inquiry that involves conducting research is different from other approaches to learning about education and improving it.

CHAPTER 1

The Nature of Educational Research

OVERVIEW

What does it mean to do educational research, and how can it contribute to the improvement of educational practice? These are the questions that we address in this chapter. We explore issues of concern to philosophers of science and show how their insights have opened up new lines of inquiry about educational phenomena. We also respond to recent criticisms of science by showing how educational research and other types of social science inquiry contribute to the search for truth about the human condition.

OBJECTIVES

After studying this chapter, you should be able to

1. Describe the four types of knowledge yielded by educational research.
2. Explain the elements of a theory and the steps that are involved in testing a theory.
3. State several reasons why it is difficult to apply research findings to educational practice.
4. Explain why basic research is worth supporting, even when it does not lead to direct improvements in educational practice.
5. State six features of postpositivist inquiry that characterize its approach to the search for truth.
6. Explain why constructivist researchers are careful to distinguish between the perspectives of the researcher, the research participants, and the readers of research reports.
7. Explain how the search for general laws is affected by a researcher's decision to study either cases or populations.
8. Describe several limitations of both quantification and verbal data in social science research.
9. Explain the difference between the mechanical, the interpretive, and the structural views of causation in social reality.
10. Describe how postmodernists view social science research.
11. State the main differences between quantitative and qualitative researchers in their epistemological assumptions and methodology.
12. Provide a definition of research that you can defend.

Contributions of Research to Knowledge about Education

A colleague once speculated that if doctors were to lose their base of medical research knowledge, most of them would have to stop working. They would have no idea how to treat anything except common ailments. Surgeons, for example, could not perform open-heart surgery if they lacked research-based knowledge about heart functions, anesthesia, the meaning of symptoms, and the likely risks of particular surgical procedures. In contrast, if educators suddenly were to lose the body of knowledge that has been gained thus far from educational research, their work would be virtually unaffected. Schools would continue to operate pretty much as they do now. It is difficult to imagine teachers who would refuse to teach students because they did not possess sufficient research-based knowledge about the learning process or the effectiveness of different instructional methods.

Touchstone in Research

Gage, N. L. (1996). Confronting counsels of despair for the behavioral sciences. *Educational Researcher, 25*(3), 5–15, 22.

The point of this comparison of medicine and education is that, in the opinion of this colleague, research still has relatively little influence on the day-to-day work of educators. Whether true or not, his assessment of educational practice raises an important question: Why should one do educational research?

The usual answer to this question is that educational research develops new knowledge about teaching, learning, and educational administration. This new knowledge is of value because it will lead eventually to the improvement of educational practice. However, if you examine this answer, it raises new questions, especially, What do we mean by *research*? and How does research get translated into practice?

The purpose of this chapter is to explain how various educators and philosophers of science have answered these questions. Hopefully, the ideas that we present will cause you to examine your present notions about educational research. At the least, you should develop a better understanding of why thousands of educational researchers throughout the world believe in the value of their work.

In the next sections, we consider four types of knowledge that research contributes to education: (1) description, (2) prediction, (3) improvement, and (4) explanation.

Description

Many research studies involve the description of natural or social phenomena—their form, structure, activity, change over time, relationship to other phenomena, and so on. Many important scientific discoveries have resulted from researchers making such descriptions. For example, astronomers have used their telescopes to develop descriptions of different parts of the universe. In the process they have discovered new galaxies and have determined the structure of the universe. These discoveries in turn have shed light on questions concerning the origins of the universe and where it is headed.

The descriptive function of research is heavily dependent upon instrumentation for measurement and observation. Researchers sometimes work for many years to perfect such instruments—for example, electron microscopes, galvanometers, and standardized tests of intelligence. Once instruments are developed, they can be used to describe phenomena of interest to the researchers. For this reason, we include several chapters (7, 8, and 9) that describe the various data-collection instruments used in educational research.

Descriptive studies have greatly increased our knowledge about what happens in schools. Some of the most important books in education, such as *Life in Classrooms* by

Philip Jackson, *The Good High School* by Sara Lawrence Lightfoot, and *Amazing Grace* by Jonathan Kozol, have reported studies of this type.[1]

Some descriptive research is intended to produce statistical information about aspects of education of interest to policy makers and educators. The National Center for Education Statistics specializes in this kind of research. Many of its findings are published in an annual volume called the *Digest of Educational Statistics*. This center also administers the National Assessment of Educational Progress (NAEP), which collects descriptive information about how well the nation's youth are doing in various subject areas.[2] This information sometimes makes its way into newspapers, thereby influencing the way community members and policy makers think about the quality of the educational system.

Prediction

Another type of research knowledge involves prediction, which is the ability to predict a phenomenon that will occur at time *Y* from information available at an earlier time *X*. For example, lunar eclipses can be predicted accurately from knowledge about the relative motion of the Moon, Earth, and Sun. The next stage of an embryo's development can be predicted accurately from knowledge of the embryo's current stage. A student's achievement in school can be predicted fairly accurately by an aptitude test administered a year or two earlier.

Educational researchers have done many prediction studies to acquire knowledge about factors that predict students' success in school and in the world of work. One reason for doing such research is to guide the selection of students who will be successful in particular educational settings. For example, the Scholastic Aptitude Test (SAT) and similar measures are administered to millions of high school students annually. Universities and colleges use the test results, along with other data, to select students who have the best chance of success in the institution's academic programs. Prediction research continues to be needed in order to acquire more knowledge about how well these tests predict, whether they predict equally well for different groups of students (such as ethnic-minority students), and whether new instruments can improve the predictability of success in particular settings.

Another purpose of prediction research is to identify students who are likely to be unsuccessful as their education progresses so that prevention programs can be instituted. For example, there is much concern about the high number of school dropouts nationally.[3] By collecting different types of information about students in the sixth grade, for example, and following those students until they graduate from high school or drop out, researchers can determine which information provides the best predictions. This predictive knowledge can be used to identify sixth graders who are at risk of becoming high school dropouts. With this knowledge, it is possible to develop programs specifically for these students in order to increase their chances of success in school.

Educational research has generated a large body of knowledge about factors that predict various outcomes that have social importance (e.g., academic success, career success, criminal conduct). Procedures for doing research for the purpose of prediction are presented in Chapters 10 and 11.

1. Jackson, P. W. (1968). *Life in classrooms*. New York: Holt, Rinehart & Winston; Lightfoot, S. L. (1983). *The good high school*. New York: Basic Books; Kozol, J. (1995). *Amazing grace: The lives of children and the conscience of a nation*. New York: Crown.
2. Jones, L. V. (1996). A history of the National Assessment of Educational Progress and some questions about its future. *Educational Researcher, 25*(7), 15–22.
3. Kaufman, P., Alt, M. N., Klein, S., & Chapman, C. D. (2004). *Dropout rates in the United States: 2001*. (Statistical Analysis Report NCES 2005-046). Washington, DC: National Center for Education Statistics. (ERIC Document Reproduction Service No. ED483073)

Improvement

The third type of research knowledge concerns the effectiveness of interventions designed to improve practice. Examples of interventions in different professions are drug therapies in medicine, construction materials in engineering, and marketing strategies in business. Many educational research studies are done to identify interventions, or factors that can be transformed into interventions, for improving students' academic achievement.

Various syntheses of intervention-oriented research are available, including one by Jere Brophy on generic features of good teaching.[4] His list of effective interventions was derived from empirical research on teaching practices that are associated with improvements in student learning outcomes. He also reviewed the literature on instructional design, theories of teaching and learning (e.g., social constructivism), and curriculum standards developed by professional organizations and committees. The features of good teaching are listed in Table 1.1.

Brophy's synthesis of research shows that educational researchers and theorists have discovered many effective interventions for improving students' academic achievement.

TABLE 1.1

Generic Features of Good Teaching Identified by Educational Researchers

1. *Supportive classroom climate:* Students learn best within cohesive and caring learning environments.
2. *Opportunity to learn:* Students learn more when most of the available time is allocated to curriculum-related activities and the classroom management system emphasizes maintaining students' engagement in these activities.
3. *Curricular alignment:* All components of the curriculum are aligned to create a cohesive program for accomplishing instructional purposes and goals.
4. *Establishing learning orientations:* Teachers can prepare students for learning by providing an initial structure to clarify intended outcomes and cue desired learning strategies.
5. *Coherent content:* To facilitate meaningful learning and retention, content is explained clearly and developed with emphasis on its structure and connections.
6. *Thoughtful discourse:* Questions are planned to engage students in sustained discourse structured around powerful ideas.
7. *Practice and application activities:* Students need sufficient opportunities to practice and apply what they are learning and to receive improvement-oriented feedback.
8. *Scaffolding students' task engagement:* The teacher provides whatever assistance students need to enable them to engage in learning activities productively.
9. *Strategy teaching:* The teacher models and instructs students in learning and self-regulation strategies.
10. *Cooperative learning:* Students often benefit from working in pairs or small groups to construct understandings or help one another master skills.
11. *Goal-oriented assessment:* The teacher uses a variety of formal and informal assessment methods to monitor progress toward learning goals.
12. *Achievement expectations:* The teacher establishes and follows through on appropriate expectations for learning outcomes.

Source: Based on research findings reported in: Brophy, J. (2001). Introduction. In J. Brophy (Ed.), *Advances in research on teaching* (Vol. 8, pp. 1–23). Oxford: JAI Elsevier.

---

4. Brophy, J. (2001). Introduction. In J. Brophy (Ed.), *Advances in research on teaching* (Vol. 8, pp. 1–23). Oxford: JAI Elsevier.

Further research is needed to refine these interventions and determine their effectiveness across different educational settings and for different types of students. Also, research is needed to turn generally stated interventions into actual interventions. For example, curricular alignment is one feature of effective teaching. Essentially, curricular alignment is a construct that refers to similar, but different interventions in different research studies; the construct of curricular alignment needs to be developed into a set of operational procedures that educators can use reliably and efficiently to improve student learning. As these procedures are developed, research will be needed to validate their effectiveness. Various research designs are available for this purpose, but particularly those described in Chapters 12 and 13 on experimental research, Chapter 17 on evaluation research, and Chapter 18 on action research.

Another approach to improving education through inquiry has become prominent in recent years. Cultural studies, a branch of critical theory, is a type of social science inquiry that investigates the power relationships in a culture in order to help emancipate its members from the many forms of oppression that are perceived to operate in the culture. Researchers who engage in this approach to inquiry would be inclined to state their purpose not as the improvement of education, but as the emancipation of the members of the educational system who are oppressed in some manner. A branch of historical research, called *revisionist history,* also examines power relationships, particularly those that are oppressive, as they occurred in the past. These power relationships reflect large-scale societal and cultural forces that affect students' learning. In contrast, Table 1.1 mostly lists interpersonal interventions at the level of classroom instruction. We discuss critical theory and cultural studies in Chapter 15 and revisionist history in Chapter 16.

Explanation

Touchstone in Research

McInerney, D. M., & Van Etten, S. (Eds.). (2004). *Big theories revisited.* Greenwich, CT: Information Age Publishing.

The fourth type of research knowledge—explanation—is the most important in the long term. In a sense, this type of knowledge subsumes the other three. If researchers are able to explain an educational phenomenon, it means that they can describe it, can predict its consequences, and know how to intervene to change those consequences.

Researchers ideally frame their explanations as theories about the phenomena being investigated. Because education encompasses so many different kinds of phenomena, it is not surprising that a substantial number of theories have been developed to explain them, for example, attribution theory, self-determination theory, expectancy value theory, sociocultural theories of knowing and learning, critical race theory, feminist theory, and theory of knowledge. As you become conversant with lines of research in your areas of interest, you generally will find that a few key theories guide this research. You will need to develop an understanding of these theories and consider them in designing your own research studies.

A **theory** is an explanation of a certain set of observed phenomena in terms of a system of constructs and laws that relate these constructs to each other. To illustrate what this definition means, consider Jean Piaget's theory of intellectual development. Piaget's theory is familiar to most educators and has had a substantial influence on American curriculum and instruction.

First, Piaget's theory is a *system,* in that it consists of a set of constructs and their relationship to each other. The system is loose in that the constructs were developed and changed in the many treatises that Piaget and his colleagues wrote over a period of decades. Other researchers have attempted to pull the theory together by writing concise descriptions of it. These concise descriptions are representations of the theory-as-system.

The theoretical system is designed to explain a set of phenomena: the behavior of infants and children with respect to their environment. For example, Piaget observed how children of different ages responded to a particular task. The children's responses constituted phenomena to be explained by the theory.

The theory provides an explanation of phenomena by first specifying a set of theoretical constructs. A **theoretical construct** is a concept that is inferred from observed phenomena. It can be defined constitutively or operationally. A **constitutively defined construct** is one that is defined by referring to other constructs. For example, the Piagetian construct of conservation can be defined as the ability to recognize that certain properties of an object remain unchanged when other properties of the object (e.g., substance, length, or volume) undergo a transformation. Note that in this definition *conservation* is defined by referring to other constructs (e.g., *property, transformation,* or *length*). Keep in mind that constitutively defined constructs are descriptive labels that refer to phenomena of interest to a theorist. For example, the term *conservation* is not the same thing as the phenomena to which that term refers. Therefore, it is possible for different theorists to invoke the same construct to refer to different phenomena, or for different theorists to invoke different constructs to refer to similar phenomena. In fact, conflicting research findings sometimes occur because a set of studies purports to have investigated a particular construct, when actually the researchers have used the same construct (e.g., computer-assisted instruction), but investigated quite different phenomena.

An **operationally defined construct** is one that is defined by specifying the activities used to measure or manipulate it. For example, the construct *conservation* (defined constitutively above) could be defined operationally by referring to a particular task, for example, pouring a constant amount of liquid into different-sized containers and then asking a child whether the amount of liquid remains the same. Operationally defined constructs have the serious weakness that the construct is defined in terms of its measurement. For example, one might define the construct of intelligence as that which is measured by an intelligence test such as the Wechsler Adult Intelligence Scale (WAIS). This definition does not identify the phenomena to which the construct *intelligence* refers, and it does not allow us to critically analyze whether the WAIS provides valid measurement of those phenomena. Thus, constitutively defined constructs are preferred as long as the phenomena to which each such construct refers are carefully delineated and described.

In conducting investigations, some researchers use the term *variable* rather than *construct.* A **variable** is a quantitative expression of a construct. Variables usually are measured in terms of scores on an instrument such as an achievement test or an attitude scale or in terms of categories of a construct (e.g., public vs. private schools).

As we stated above, a theory specifies laws relating constructs to each other. A **law** (also called a *scientific law*) is a generalization about the causal, sequential, or other relationship between two or more constructs. Theorists can posit these generalized relationships and then subject them to empirical verification, or they can take generalized relationships first discovered by researchers and incorporate them in their theory. An example of a theoretical law can be found in Piaget's theory of the stages of intellectual development: sensorimotor, preoperational, concrete operations, and formal operations. Each of these stages is a construct. Piaget proposed the law that these constructs are related to each other as an invariant sequence: The sensorimotor stage always is followed by the preoperational stage; the preoperational stage always is followed by the concrete operations stage; and the concrete operations stage always is followed by the formal operations stage.

The soundness of a theory depends not only on the specification of laws that relate constructs to each other, but also on specification of the relationship between each construct and its measurement. As Jeffrey Edwards and Richard Bagozzi put it, "A theory can be divided into two parts: one that specifies relationships between theoretical constructs and another that describes relationships between constructs and measures."[5] Some specifications involve assumptions about how a construct and measurements of it are causally related. Others have to do with the nature of constructs as we described them above: technically, scores on measurement tools such as tests and attitude scales do not measure the construct; rather the scores measure the phenomena named by the construct. Thus, in testing a theory, one needs to check a measure carefully to ensure that it encompasses the phenomena of theoretical interest. Just because a measurement tool has the construct as part of its name does not mean necessarily that it measures the phenomena to which the researcher's theoretical construct refers.

The relationship between constructs and their measurement is discussed further in Chapter 7 in the section on test validity and also in Chapter 11 in the sections on structural equation modeling and factor analysis.

Uses of Theory

Theories serve several useful purposes. First, theoretical constructs identify commonalities in otherwise isolated phenomena. Piaget's theory, for example, identifies many isolated infant behaviors as instances of sensorimotor intelligence. In other words, theoretical constructs identify the universals of experience so that we can make sense of experience. Second, the laws of a theory enable us to make predictions and to control phenomena. Because astronomers have a well-developed theory, they can make very accurate predictions about the occurrence of eclipses and other phenomena in the universe. Because professionals in special education work from a well-developed theory of learning (sometimes called *behavioral theory*), they can make instructional interventions that dependably lead to positive changes in student behavior.

Scientists sometimes speak of "small" and "large" theories. A small theory might be developed to account for a limited set of phenomena (e.g., antecedents and consequences of teacher morale). A large theory might account for many phenomena (e.g., behavioral theory and social–cognitive theory). Also, a theory might grow as it is shown to explain more phenomena or as it incorporates more constructs to explain phenomena. A researcher might start with a small theory of academic achievement. As more determinants of achievement are discovered, the researcher can enlarge the theory to accommodate them.

Approaches to Theory Development

We describe two approaches to theory development in this book. The **grounded theory** approach involves deriving constructs and laws directly from the immediate data that one has collected rather than from prior research and theory. In other words, the constructs and laws are "grounded" in the particular set of data that the researcher has collected. The usefulness of the constructs and laws can be tested in subsequent research. We discuss this approach to theory development in Chapter 14.

The other approach to developing a theory is to start by formulating a theory and then submit it to a test by collecting empirical data. The process of testing has three steps:

1. the formulation of a hypothesis,
2. the deduction of observable consequences of the hypothesis, and
3. the testing of the hypothesis by making observations (that is to say, by collecting and analyzing research data).

This process is commonly thought of as the scientific method, although some philosophers of science doubt that there is any such thing as *the* scientific method. Paul Feyerabend,

---

5. Edwards, J. R., & Bagozzi, R. P. (2000). On the nature and direction of relationships between constructs and measures. *Psychological Methods, 5*(2), 155–174. Quote appears on p. 155.

for example, states, "The idea of a method that contains firm, unchanging, and absolutely binding principles for conducting the business of science meets considerable difficulty when confronted with the results of historical research [i.e., research on the history of science]."[6]

Example of Theory Testing

The three steps for testing a theory empirically are illustrated in a research study of discourse theories by Matthew McCrudden, Gregory Schraw, and Gretchen Kambe.[7] These theories provide explanations for how readers generate meaning from text. There is no unified discourse theory as yet, but most include three major constructs (goals, inferential processes, and learning) that are related to each other sequentially: (1) the reader develops a set of goals for reading, (2) the goals facilitate inferential processes, and (3) the inferential processes facilitate learning.

McCrudden and colleagues focused on the constructs of *goal* and *relevance*. They defined relevance as the extent to which text elements are related to the reader's specific goals and purposes for "reading."[8] They reasoned that readers comprehend text by searching for information in text that is relevant to their goals. One way to create goal relevance is to give "relevance instructions" to the reader by such means as inserted questions or instructions to focus on particular segments of the text.

How can these researchers test whether their theory is valid? The first step is to formulate a **hypothesis,** which is a tentative proposition about the relationship between two or more theoretical constructs. Focusing on the construct of relevance, McCrudden formulated two hypotheses to test the theory that the readers' goals influence inferential processes that cause them to focus on relevant text, and these processes in turn facilitate learning. One hypothesis was what they called the "increased effort hypothesis," which states that relevance instructions prior to reading increases the amount of time that readers attend to relevant sections of the text, thereby facilitating learning of those parts of the text that are goal relevant. The competing hypothesis was the "no increased effort hypothesis," which makes the same prediction about learning of goal-relevant text, but which predicts that relevance instructions do not increase reading time. The rationale is that relevance instructions, if highly specific, tell readers in advance which text segments are relevant; therefore, readers do not need to spend time deciding whether the text is relevant or irrelevant.

The next step in testing a theory is to deduce observable consequences of the hypothesis. McCrudden and colleagues followed this step by designing an experiment in which college students would read passages from a science text that describes the effects of space travel on the human body. The experiment allowed for testing of the hypotheses and investigation of other variables of interest. (The experimental design, which was repeated in a replication experiment, was more complex than described here.) Basically, some students (the control group) would receive no prereading relevance instructions, whereas others (the experimental group) would receive such instructions. The latter group of students would be asked to read six questions whose answers could be found in the text and to rate how interesting they found each question; they also would be told to focus on these questions as they read the passage. All students in the control and experimental groups then would read the passage individually on a computer screen. McCrudden and colleagues predicted the groups would act in certain ways if the hypotheses were valid.

6. Feyerabend, P. (1978). *Against method*. London: Verso. Quote appears on p. 23.
7. McCrudden, M. T., Schraw, G., & Kambe, G. (2005). The effect of relevance instructions on reading time and learning. *Journal of Educational Psychology, 97*(1), 88–102.
8. Ibid., p. 88.

The third step in testing a theory is to collect empirical data and determine whether they correspond to the hypotheses. McCrudden and colleagues recruited college students and assigned them randomly to the conditions in the experimental design. Students' learning was measured by having them write as much as they could recall from the text. Their reading time was measured by computing their reading time for each sentence on the computer screen to the nearest millisecond.

Statistical analyses allowed for several tests of the hypotheses. The analyses supported both hypotheses, in that students recalled more goal-relevant text than goal-irrelevant text. The analyses also found that students did not spend more time reading goal-relevant text, thereby supporting the no-increased-effort hypothesis and disconfirming the increased-effort hypothesis.

This study by McCrudden and colleagues illustrates the process of testing a theory. The parts of discourse theory to which the hypotheses relate is strengthened. We can have more confidence that discourse theory provides a good explanation of the reading process: individuals focus their reading based on their goals; the goals cause them to attend to goal-relevant text during the reading process and to recall the content of the goal-relevant text better at later points in time. The theory also has practical implications by suggesting to teachers that they can influence how their students read text and recall it later by shaping the students' reading goals prior to the actual reading of the text.

Despite the power of the so-called scientific method to test the validity of hypotheses, it has several weaknesses. One of them is that the researcher may deduce inappropriate observable consequences from the hypothesis, and thus make an inappropriate test of the hypothesis. For example, McCrudden and colleagues assumed that prereading of text-relevant questions improves students' goal-focusing behavior when it comes time to read the text passage. However, students possibly would find the questions confusing and not see their relevance to the actual reading task. Also, the no-increased-effort hypothesis might not have held up if there were significant consequences to students for their performance on the recall test. Therefore, other theorists and researchers need to check each study carefully to determine whether appropriate measures and situations were used. It is especially important to make these checks when the empirical results do not support the hypothesis. One would not want to reject a hypothesis, and with it a basically sound theory, simply because it was put to an inappropriate test.

The other weakness of the scientific method is more difficult to overcome: Any observable result potentially can support multiple, sometimes conflicting, theories. For this reason, a researcher can never prove a theory, but can only support it, as we explain later in the chapter.

Application of Research to Educational Practice

Touchstone in Research

Burkhardt, H., & Schoenfeld, A. H. (2003). Improving educational research: Toward a more useful, more influential, and better-funded enterprise. *Educational Resarcher, 32*(9), 3–14.

In the preceding section, we observed that the goal of educational research is to generate knowledge that describes, predicts, improves, and explains processes and practices related to education. The knowledge base keeps growing, but this does not mean necessarily that educational practitioners know about it, value it, or apply it in their work. For example, some individuals argue that the monies spent on research might be better used to improve school programs, educators' salaries, and other aspects of schooling. Others argue that teaching is an art, not a science, and therefore research is irrelevant. Still others claim that, as busy practitioners, they do not have the time to study research and think about its practical implications.

To understand the connection between research and practice, a good starting point is to consider that schools, colleges, and universities were not built on a scientific knowledge base about teaching, learning, the role of culture and family in students' development, and other such matters. In fact, the research enterprise came after and evolved more slowly than the schooling enterprise.[9] This may explain why practitioners typically do not look to research for answers to their questions and problems. Given this situation, researchers in education and other service professions have initiated efforts to show practitioners, policy makers, and the general public how scientific knowledge can improve practice.

One example of this effort comes from psychology. In a recent publication, the American Psychological Association provided a variety of examples of how psychological research knowledge can and does improve society and the lives of individuals.[10] The range of examples includes practical applications of research to improve roadway safety, help individuals with debilitating medical conditions, prevent violence, overcome prejudice, and use eyewitness evidence appropriately in the criminal justice system.

Closer to home, the practice of education has benefited greatly from the contributions of educational researchers who specialize in test development. As we explain in Chapter 7, the development of tests of academic achievement, aptitudes, interests, and school-related personality characteristics relies heavily on test theory and test validation research. These tests are so prevalent in educational practice that it is easy to forget their origins in the work of a great many educational researchers over a period of many decades. It is also easy to overlook the fact that some of the most important problems and policies in educational practice revolve around the results of researcher-developed tests. For example, the achievement gap between white students and certain groups of ethnic-minority students has received widespread attention in recent years. This serious problem in educational practice might not have come to light in such a compelling manner without the documentation provided by these tests. National policies, such as the No Child Left Behind Act, have been enacted to close this achievement gap. Consequently, the daily work of educational practitioners is increasingly being shaped by accountability standards to improve student academic performance, as measured by research-validated tests. In the area of student testing, then, it seems fair to say that educational research is a driving force in educational practice.

The U.S. government has made significant efforts in recent years to develop a more coordinated and systematic approach to educational research that can be applied to schooling. The key agency for these efforts is the Institute of Education Sciences (IES), which is housed in the U.S. Department of Education.[11] This agency began operating in 2002; its predecessor agency was the Office of Educational Research and Improvement (OERI). The mission statement for IES is as follows:

> Established by the Education Sciences Reform Act of 2002, the Institute of Education Sciences is the research arm of the Department of Education. Its mission is to expand knowledge and provide information on the condition of education, practices that improve academic achievement, and the effectiveness of Federal and other education programs. Its goal is the transformation of education into an evidence-based field in which decision makers routinely seek out the best available research and data before adopting programs and practices that will affect significant numbers of students.[12]

This mission statement highlights the importance of increasing research knowledge, but a particular kind of knowledge, namely, knowledge that directly affects educational

---

9. The history of the relationship between school practice and research is traced in: Lagemann, E. C. (2000). *An elusive science: The troubling history of education research.* Chicago: University of Chicago Press.
10. American Psychological Association. *Behavior matters: How research improves our lives.* Retrieved January 5, 2006, from http://www.decadeofbehavior.org/BehaviorMattersBooklet.pdf
11. Information about the Institute of Education Sciences is available at http://www.ed.gov/offices/IES/
12. Ibid., home page.

practice. From the perspective of educators, this means adopting *evidence-based* practices, which may or may not be the same practices that they would adopt based on their own experiences and beliefs about what is best for students. In this respect, education is following the trend toward evidence-based medicine in healthcare. Increasingly, insurers and governmental programs such as Medicare are approving treatments for patients only if they are evidence-based, and they are compelling hospitals and healthcare providers to use evidence-based practices.[13]

IES has created the What Works Clearinghouse (WWC) to help practitioners identify evidence-based practices.[14] This agency reviews research studies of the effectiveness of educational interventions, which include programs, products, practices, and policies. The review process is rigorous and standardized in order to draw conclusions about which interventions have evidence to support their effectiveness. The interventions fall into such topic areas as middle school mathematics curriculum, character education, dropout prevention, adult literacy, and peer-assisted learning in elementary school. WWC has the challenge of addressing researchers and their methodological issues and preferences, while also addressing the community of educational practitioners, who must take evidence-based practices and turn them into operational realities at the local level.[15]

Limitations of Research Knowledge

Has research knowledge influenced the practice of education, and if so, how has it influenced practice? What is the proper relationship between research knowledge and educational practice? These are difficult questions to answer. Rather than attempting to do so, we will make several observations that may help you form your own answers. The first is that research knowledge and the practice of education have different goals, as D. C. Phillips observes:

> Research findings take the form, roughly, of "X is Y" or "the probability of an X having the feature Y is p"; in other words, they are statements of the "is" form. On the other hand, implications for practice take the form such as, "person A ought to do Z to person B." In other words, they are statements involving an "ought" or "should" or some other locution involving the passing of a value judgment. But it is a point of logic that from statements only involving the use of "is," a conclusion involving "ought" or one of its locutions cannot validly be deduced.[16]

Questions involving *is* can be answered objectively by well-designed research. Questions involving *ought* are value laden and can be resolved only through dialogue and a decision-making process that includes various constituencies. Researchers should not expect their findings about *is* to result in educational change immediately, and without critical appraisal. Likewise, practitioners should not look to research for prescriptive advice. It seems much more sensible to use research knowledge about what *is* to inform dialogue about what *ought* to be—a dialogue that should be informed by other considerations as well.

Although research discovers what *is,* it does so with several important limitations. One is that research findings have limited generalizability. For example, in conducting a study, many researchers select a sample that represents one defined population (e.g., elementary teachers in urban schools). Depending on how well the sampling is done, the results of the

---

13. A large number of books and articles about evidence-based medicine have appeared recently, including: Sayer, L. (2005). *Evidence-based medicine guidelines.* Hoboken, NJ: Wiley.
14. Information about the What Works Clearinghouse is available at http://www.whatworks.ed.gov
15. WWC has issued an online publication to help practitioners understand and apply evidence-based practices: U.S. Department of Education. *Identifying and implementing educational practices supported by rigorous evidence: A user friendly guide.* http://www.ed.gov/rschstat/research/pubs/rigorousevid/index.html
16. Phillips, D. C. (1980). What do the researcher and the practitioner have to offer each other? *Educational Researcher, 9*(11), 19.

study can be generalized to that particular population, but not beyond. Even within the defined population, most likely there will be teachers for whom the generalization does not hold. In other studies, the researcher may study only one or a few cases, albeit intensively. Generalization to other cases can be done, but it must be done on a case-by-case basis. Therefore, it seems that practitioners can look to research knowledge for guidance, but they need to ask themselves, "Are these findings likely to apply to my situation?"

Another limitation of research knowledge is that while it discovers what is, it always does so within a certain worldview and set of values. As we explain later in the chapter, theories and research are value laden; there is no such thing as purely objective research. Therefore, putting a research finding into practice also means putting a particular set of values into practice. For example, the interventions shown in Table 1.1 are more or less effective in improving students' academic achievement, usually as measured by performance on standardized achievement tests. Using this research knowledge as evidence for advocating one or more of the interventions, then, means also advocating high test performance as a valued outcome of schooling. There are other valued outcomes of schooling, however, such as curiosity, self-reliance, and humanitarian attitudes, that may not be promoted by these interventions. Also, the investigations that produced this research knowledge imply a certain view of teachers, as Magdalene Lampert observes:

> They . . . assume that *the teacher is a technical-production manager* who has the responsibility for monitoring the efficiency with which learning is being accomplished. In this view, teaching can be improved if practitioners use researchers' knowledge to solve classroom problems. The teacher's work is to find out what researchers and policymakers say should be done with or to students and to do it. How much time should be spent on direct instruction versus seatwork? How many new words should be in stories children are required to read? If the teacher does what she is told, students will learn.[17]

Lampert advances a different view of teachers, namely, teachers as dilemma managers. This view emerged from her own research studies, which revealed that classroom teaching involves many problematic situations involving competing interests that the teacher must resolve.

Lampert's view of teaching is consistent with the views of others who have studied professional practice. One of the most influential of these individuals is Donald Schön.[18] He claims that a flawed model of *technical rationality* dominates thinking about the relationship between research and practice. He describes the model in these terms:

> According to the model of Technical Rationality—the view of professional knowledge which has most powerfully shaped both our thinking about the professions and the institutional relations of research, education, and practice—professional activity consists in instrumental problem solving made rigorous by the application of scientific theory and technique.[19]

According to Schön, this model is flawed because research, especially research in the positivist tradition, assumes a stable, consistent reality about which generalizations can be made and applied, whereas professional practice involves "complexity, uncertainty, instability, uniqueness, and value-conflict."[20]

Schön and many others claim that practitioners need to engage in reflection-in-action, not in the application of research knowledge, in order to deal with the "messiness"

17. Lampert, M. (1985). How do teachers manage to teach? Perspectives on problems in practice. *Harvard Educational Review, 55,* 178–194.
18. Schön, D. A. (1983). *The reflective practitioner.* New York: Basic Books.
19. Ibid., p. 21.
20. Ibid., p. 39.

of their work. Reflection-in-action has various elements, but chief among them is a kind of experimentation based on practitioners' analysis of each unique situation they confront. (We discuss Schön's views about reflection in more detail in Chapter 18.)

In our view, Schön's model of reflection-in-action does not preclude research knowledge as a basis for professional action. The model only implies that research knowledge cannot be the sole basis for professional action. In fact, researchers have found that the primary venue for professional practice in education, the classroom, is marked more by sameness of practice than by diversity and uniqueness.[21] One might argue that if practitioners were more aware of research knowledge, they might actually be in a better position to accommodate the great individual and group differences found among their clients and constituencies.

The Importance of Basic Research

Some practitioners believe that educational research is too theoretical and too focused on basic processes of learning (e.g., brain functions underlying memory, or eye movements during reading). They believe that instead of such basic research, priority should be given to applied research that addresses actual problems as perceived by practitioners. This argument raises questions about the relative value of basic and applied research in education.

While applied research, virtually by definition, seems more likely to contribute to the improvement of educational practice, an important study in the field of medicine gives us reason to reconsider.[22] Julius Comroe and Robert Dripps started their study by identifying the most important clinical advances since the early 1940s in the treatment of cardiovascular and pulmonary diseases, which account for more than half of all deaths in the United States each year.

With the assistance of 140 consultants, Comroe and Dripps identified the bodies of knowledge that needed to be developed through research before the 10 clinical advances could reach their present state of achievement. A total of 137 essential bodies of knowledge were identified, such as the anatomy of cardiac defects, blood typing, the monitoring of blood pressure, and the management of postoperative infection.

The next step in Comroe and Dripps's investigation was to identify key scientific reports that contributed to these bodies of knowledge. Each report was classified into one of six categories:

1. Basic research unrelated to the solution of a clinical problem (36.8%)
2. Basic research related to the solution of a clinical problem (24.9%)
3. Studies not concerned with basic biological, chemical, or physical mechanisms (21.2%)
4. A review and critical analysis of published work and the synthesis of new concepts without new experimental data (1.8%)
5. Developmental work or engineering to create, improve, or perfect apparatus or a technique for research use (3.9%)
6. Developmental work or engineering to create, improve, or perfect apparatus for use in diagnosis or care of patients (11.4%)

The numbers in parentheses show the percentage of reports assigned to each category.

The remarkable finding is the high percentage of basic research studies (36.8% + 24.9% = 61.7%) that were essential to the development of current treatment of cardiovascular and pulmonary disease. Equally remarkable is the high percentage (36.8%) of basic research

21. Sirotnik, K. A. (1983). What you see is what you get—Consistency, persistency, and mediocrity in classrooms. *Harvard Educational Review, 53*(1), 16–31.
22. Comroe, J. H., Jr., & Dripps, R. D. (1976). Scientific basis for the support of biomedical science. *Science, 192*, 105–111.

studies that were not even related to the practice of cardiovascular-pulmonary medicine. These results suggest that research can influence practice even when this is not its purpose and even if practitioners are unaware of the research.

Funding for Educational Research

Research has demonstrated its ability to improve not only medicine but other fields of professional practice as well. We can think of no reason why education should be an exception. Yet the surprising fact is that there is relatively little financial support for educational research. Of the federal funding for public schools, less than 1 percent has been allocated for research each year between 1975 and 2003; by contrast, in the same time period about 10 percent of the federal funding for defense and about 6 percent of the federal funding for health have been allocated for research.[23] Why educational research receives so little funding and what might happen to educational practice if funding increased dramatically are questions well worth contemplating.

Epistemological Issues in Educational Research

As you learn more about educational research, you will find that it is not a unified enterprise. For example, you will find that the approaches to educational research described in Part IV of this book involve the study of samples and populations, and that they rely heavily on numerical data and statistical analysis. In contrast, the approaches described in Part V involve the study of cases; they make little use of numerical data or statistics, relying instead on verbal data and interpretive analysis.

Touchstone in Research Crotty, M. (2003). *The foundations of social research: Meaning and perspective in the research process.* Thousand Oaks, CA: Sage.

Why does educational research involve such diverse approaches? To answer this question, we need to review the epistemological issues that underlie scientific inquiry. **Epistemology** is the branch of philosophy that studies the nature of knowledge and the process by which knowledge is acquired and validated. Some epistemologists have a particular interest in the nature of inquiry and knowledge in the natural sciences and the social sciences. These philosophers (sometimes called *philosophers of science*) have sought answers to such questions as: Are the objects that researchers study (e.g., neutrons and self-concept) real? How is research knowledge different from other forms of knowledge, and does it have any special authority? What is a theory, and how can it be validated? What does it mean to find "laws" that enable us to predict individual and group behavior? Is inquiry in the social sciences fundamentally different from inquiry in the natural sciences?

As philosophers have investigated these and related questions over a period of many centuries, they have developed different schools of thought. Social science researchers have been influenced by these schools of thought (e.g., positivism, constructivism, phenomenology), and in addition they have staked out their own epistemological positions about how research in their respective disciplines (e.g., anthropology, psychology, and sociology) should be done. Below we focus on key epistemological issues as viewed by educational researchers at the present time. Following this discussion, we show how different researchers take different positions on these issues, and, as a consequence, how they advocate and conduct quite different types of educational research.

Positivism and Postpositivism

Some researchers assume that features of the social environment have an **objective reality,** which means that these features exist independently of the individuals who created

23. Kuncl, R. W. (2004). Federal underinvestment in education research. *Academe, 90*(4), 44–50.

Touchstone in Research

Phillips, D. C., & Burbules, N. C. (2000). *Postpositivism and educational research.* New York: Rowman & Littlefield.

them or who observe them. Suppose, for example, that a teacher pastes a gold star on a student's paper. Under the assumption of an objective reality, this gold star has an existence that is independent of the teacher who assigned it and also independent of the researcher who notices the gold star while studying the teacher's feedback to students. Thus, to the extent that the researcher is free of subjective bias, he can collect data that accurately represents the gold star as it really is.

Researchers who subscribe to a positivist epistemology make this assumption of an objective social reality. Sally Hutchinson, for example, states, "Positivists view the world as being 'out there,' and available for study in a more or less static form."[24] The task of positivist scientific inquiry, then, is to make bias-free observations of the natural and social world "out there." We define **positivism** as the epistemological doctrine that physical and social reality is independent of those who observe it, and that observations of this reality, if unbiased, constitute scientific knowledge.[25]

Behavioral researchers in education and psychology exemplify an approach to scientific inquiry that is grounded in positivist epistemology. They focus on the study of observable behavior as the basis for building scientific knowledge. Although behavioral researchers use abstract concepts such as *reinforcement* and *punishment,* they define these concepts in terms of the procedures that are used to observe and measure their behavioral manifestations. Many other researchers besides behaviorists also subscribe to a positivist view of reality and its study. For example, many researchers who study intelligence define this concept as an individual's performance (an observable event) on a particular type of test. The individual's performance is measured as an IQ score, which then can be related to possible antecedents and consequences of intelligence. Much of the research that has been done, and that continues to be done, in education and the social sciences is based on positivist epistemology.

Various weaknesses of the positivist approach to social science research became apparent over the last century, resulting in a modified form of positivism called **postpositivism.** Postpositivism is an epistemology that assumes an objective reality, but that this objective reality can only be known imperfectly. According to postpositivism, theories about objective reality cannot be validated in an absolute sense, but their validity can be strengthened through their resistance to research efforts to refute them.

To understand the weaknesses of positivism that led to postpositivism, we will start with a hypothetical research problem. Suppose a researcher observes informally that some teachers are able to keep their classrooms under better control than other teachers. Proceeding from this observation, the researcher decides to undertake a program of research to document the fact that some teachers are better classroom managers than others, to discover the techniques that the better managers use to keep their classes under control, and eventually to develop a theory of classroom management. (In actuality, many researchers already are involved in this program of research.)

Some critics would claim that the proposed research is biased by the researcher's values. To conduct the studies, the researcher will need to define what she means by the term *classroom control.* The researcher's definition might involve notions about students doing what the teacher expects them to do rather than acting on their own initiative, being quiet rather than unruly, avoiding nonacademic engagement with other students, and not giving the teacher reason to discipline them for misbehavior. If we take the analysis further,

24. Hutchinson, S. A. (1988). Education and grounded theory. In R. R. Sherman & R. B. Webb (Eds.), *Qualitative research in education: Focus and methods* (pp. 123–140). London: Falmer. Quote appears on p. 124.
25. Several variants of positivist epistemology are described in Chapter 4 of: Phillips, D. C. (1987). *Philosophy, science, and social inquiry.* New York: Pergamon.

we probably will find that the researcher's definition of classroom control is grounded in more fundamental beliefs about what should be taught in the curriculum and what the goals of schooling should be.

What the researcher is able to discover about classroom management will be largely determined by her conception of *classroom control* and of other key concepts involved in her formulation of the research problem. If the researcher eventually develops a theory of classroom control, testing the theory will require empirical tests using data-collection measures that correspond to her definitions of *classroom control* and other constructs. Thus, research observations are *theory laden*. One really cannot collect data that are independent of the theory, as is required by the tenets of positivism.

Who is to say that the researcher's definition of classroom control is the right one? All we can say is that her definition reflects her particular values and experiences, and perhaps her personal biases as well. Other researchers with different values and experiences might develop other definitions, for example, that classroom control is the teacher's ability to create a situation in which students take responsibility for their own learning, engage in independent learning, and share with the teacher the task of creating reasonable classroom rules. This definition of classroom control will lead these researchers to undertake programs of research that will yield different findings about classroom management.

As critics see it, this situation creates a major problem for scientific inquiry. There is no absolute basis for determining the truth about classroom management. Scientific inquiry, which should be objective (i.e., unbiased), is revealed to be biased by the researcher's values. Thus, critics claim that researchers cannot conclude that one theory about classroom management is more valid than another theory because the research supporting each theory is inherently biased, albeit in different ways. If this is true, then, as the philosopher of science Denis Phillips observes, we would have to give equal weight to, or at least tolerate, "Nazis, flat-earthers, astrologers, paranoics, Freudians, Skinnerians, and anyone else who ever strongly believed in a theory."[26] The physical and social science of past centuries can be dismissed or cherished, depending on our biases, as the work of "dead white males."

The value-laden character of research has become a matter of considerable concern among educators who study racism in society and education. For example, ethnic-minority students were conceptualized as "culturally disadvantaged" or "culturally deprived" in some educational research studies in the recent past. These terms reveal explicit racial bias, but other forms of racial bias in educational research may be more implicit and more pervasive. For example, James Scheurich and Michelle Young make the following claim:

> In a very important sense, we White researchers are unconsciously promulgating racism on an epistemological level. As we teach and promote epistemologies like positivism to postmodernism, we are, at least implicitly, teaching and promoting the social history of the dominant race at the exclusion of people of color, scholars of color, and the possibility for research based on other race/culture epistemologies.[27]

Scheurich and Young observe that other, race-based epistemologies are as deserving of consideration for educational research as those grounded in Eurocentric views of reality and knowing. For example, they cite Patricia Hill Collins's Afrocentric feminist epistemology as a fruitful counter to prevailing epistemologies in educational research.[28] Collins's epistemology gives

26. Phillips, *Philosophy, science, and social inquiry*, p. 89.
27. Scheurich, J. J., & Young, M. D. (1997). Coloring epistemologies: Are our research epistemologies racially biased? *Educational Researcher, 26*(4), 4–16. Quote appears on p. 11.
28. Collins, P. H. (1991). *Black feminist thought: Knowledge, consciousness, and the politics of empowerment.* New York: Routledge.

precedence to concrete experience, dialogue between researcher and informants, and the ethics of caring and personal accountability.

Weaknesses of positivism as an epistemology have caused social science researchers, including educational researchers, to rethink their claims to authority. Many of them have adopted the epistemology of postpositivism. The following is a list of research practices characteristic of a postpositivist stance toward inquiry.

1. *The creation of concepts and procedures that are shared and publicly accessible.* Social science researchers have developed specialized concepts (e.g., validity and reliability) and procedures (e.g., random assignment of individuals to groups in experiments) to help them conduct investigations of high quality. These concepts and procedures are embodied in terminology that allows researchers to communicate with each other and their various constituencies. Ambiguities in existing terms are noted and clarified. New terms come into being to describe new concepts and procedures. This terminology is defined formally in dictionaries, in textbooks such as the one you are reading, and in other publications.[29] The professional community of researchers takes on this responsibility for clarifying, updating, and making public their terminology.

Everyone is free to learn and use this terminology and the concepts and procedures it embodies. There are no secret societies of researchers (at least none that we know of!), and no special initiation is required for access to the research process. Anyone is free to conduct scientific inquiry, as evidenced by the fact that research manuscripts submitted to journals for publication are judged "blind," meaning that reviewers do not have access to the names of the authors or other identifying information about them. In this way, no researcher is privileged over another. Of course, there are power struggles in the arenas of funding and publicity for research findings, but it seems highly unlikely that important theories and findings could be suppressed over the long term.

2. *The replicability of findings.* When researchers publish their findings, they also must make public the procedures by which these findings were obtained. Otherwise, the results will not be published. By making their procedures public, researchers enable other researchers to conduct replication studies to determine whether the use of the same or similar procedures as the original researcher will yield the same results. In fact, some researchers conduct their own replication studies, and only publish the findings if their original findings are replicated. We discuss replication as a research strategy further in Chapter 2.

3. *The refutability of knowledge claims.* Karl Popper proposed a standard for testing knowledge claims that has won general acceptance among social science researchers.[30] Popper, a philosopher of science, argued that science advances by submitting its knowledge claims (theories, predictions, hunches) to empirical tests that allow for their refutation. As we explained earlier in the chapter, a researcher tests a theory by formulating a hypothesis and then collecting data relating to the hypothesis. If the data are inconsistent with the hypothesis, we can say that the hypothesis is refuted. As a result, the theory from which the hypothesis was derived must be abandoned or modified to accommodate the negative findings. If the data are consistent with the hypothesis, we can conclude that the theory is supported, but not that it is correct. The reason is that another empirical test of the theory may yet refute it. In Popper's view of science, then, we can say that the flat-earth theory has proved to be wrong, but not that the round-earth theory has proved to be correct. We can say only that this theory has thus far withstood all attempts to disprove it.

---

29. Examples of such dictionaries are: Coleman, A. M. (2001). *A dictionary of psychology.* New York: Oxford University Press; Vogt, W. P. (1995). *Dictionary of statistics and methodology* (2nd ed.). Thousand Oaks, CA: Sage.
30. Popper, K. (1968). *Conjectures and refutations.* New York: Harper.

The refutation test of knowledge claims provides an indirect method for determining whether Theory X is more valid than Theory Y. While the concepts and methods of observation used to test each theory reflect the values implicit in the theory, each theory nonetheless can be falsified by empirical tests of hypotheses derived from the theory. In other words, data-collection instruments are not so value-laden that they are incapable of falsifying the theory from which the instruments were derived. Thus, Theory X or Theory Y can be falsified. If both theories survive efforts to refute them, they can co-exist as alternative explanations of social reality. For example, both behavioral and cognitive theories of human behavior have a large body of empirical evidence to support them, and so both continue to survive and to influence educational practice. In fact, there has been cross-fertilization between the two theories. Some researchers call themselves *cognitive behaviorists*.

The refutation test of knowledge claims is more rigorous than the way we test everyday knowledge claims. For example, suppose that a university professor decides one term to let his students call him at home or the office for appointments rather than only letting them contact him during posted office hours. The professor notices that the students' evaluations of his course are higher than usual for that term. From this observation, he claims to have proved that allowing students greater access to a professor will cause students to evaluate the professor's instruction more positively. The "proof" rests on shaky grounds, however, because the professor has not demonstrated that all instances of increased access will produce this result. It is possible that we can find other professors, or other occasions when that professor teaches, where the connection between access and improved evaluations does not hold.

Superstitious thinking and fields of knowledge such as astrology are susceptible to this flaw in reasoning. Suppose a person uses her spouse's birthday to select numbers for a lottery ticket, and she wins. From this event she concludes that if she selects numbers from the birthday of her spouse or other family members, she will increase her chances of winning the lottery in the future. Similarly, astrologists may conclude that because certain things have happened to someone born on a certain day, these things are likely to happen to other people born on that day. In other words, they make an observation first and then make a broad knowledge claim. In contrast, researchers who follow Popper's logic make a knowledge claim first and then test it by making observations. The tests are cautious in that contrary data can disprove the knowledge claim, but confirmatory data do not prove it. Instead, if the data are confirmatory, we conclude that the knowledge claim has withstood efforts to refute it.

4. *Control for errors and biases*. Researchers acknowledge the propensity for error and bias in data collection. Thus, they design their studies to minimize the influence of such factors. For example, in making quantitative observations, researchers attempt to use multiple observers and to train them carefully in the system for collecting data on observational variables. Statistical procedures are available for estimating the observers' accuracy.

While observations rarely are completely accurate, they usually are accurate enough for research purposes. With respect to qualitative data, case study researchers typically *triangulate* their data from one method of observation by seeking corroboration from other types of data that they have collected. In this respect, Biddle and Anderson make an important distinction between *case studies* and *case stories*:

> The former [case study] is an inquiry conducted according to rules of evidence. It is rigorous in its observations. Its objective is not to confirm the investigator's commitments but to investigate a problem. The latter [case story] is designed to illustrate conclusions to which the author is already committed.[31]

---

31. Biddle, B. J., & Anderson, D. S. (1986). Theory, methods, knowledge, and research on teaching. In M. C. Wittrock (Ed.), *Handbook of research on teaching* (3rd ed., pp. 230–252). New York: Macmillan. Quote appears on p. 239.

In the same vein, Thomas Good and Joel Levin criticize the recent emphasis on personal story and personal voice as a self-sufficient type of knowledge for improving education:

> . . . when story is used to supplant research, theory, and empirical evidence, rather than to supplement it, we have serious reservations about its value . . . . Some stories are knowingly distorted and used for self-justification and self-enhancement.[32]

It is important to note that Good and Levin do not reject personal story and voice entirely. They can provide valuable perspective and insights when considered in relation to relevant research and theory.

The procedures we describe in Chapter 14 are designed to help you do case study research rather than tell case stories. Similarly, the procedures we describe for other research designs and approaches are primarily intended to minimize researcher errors and biases.

5. *Boundedness of knowledge claims.* Researchers have developed procedures to ensure that they do not generalize their knowledge claims beyond what can be supported by their empirical findings. These procedures involve sampling logic, which is explained in Chapter 6. For example, quantitative researchers typically define a population (e.g., fifth-grade teachers in urban school systems) and study a sample that is representative of the population. Findings based on data collected from the sample are generalized only to that population. The amount of possible error in the generalizations is estimated in a manner similar to what we read about in national polls (e.g., "This candidate is viewed positively by 62 percent of American voters, with a ± 6 percent margin of error"). The generalization of knowledge claims beyond the defined population is considered speculative until supported by evidence from new studies involving other populations.

6. *A moral commitment to progressive discourse.* Carl Bereiter observed that, "what makes science special is that scientists have done a better job than most other groups of practicing certain virtues."[33] These virtues involve a commitment to **progressive discourse,** which means that anyone at any time can offer a criticism about a particular research study or research methodology, and if it proves to have merit, that criticism is listened to and accommodated. The process of criticism, debate, and resolution assumes that researchers have made a moral commitment to listen to each other, remain open to new research findings, and change their views when it is appropriate to do so. In this way, the research community progresses in its understanding of the phenomena that are within its scope of inquiry.

If you examine issues of *Educational Researcher, American Educational Research Journal,* and *Review of Educational Research,* you will find many examples of critical commentaries on research methodology, research epistemology, and reports of research findings. (These three journals are official publications of the American Educational Research Association.) These commentaries have a cumulative impact on the educational research enterprise, advancing our understanding both of what educational researchers are discovering and how they are discovering it.

The preceding analysis demonstrates that educational research and other social science disciplines make no claims about an absolute, objective standard of truth. (Some researchers may think differently, but they are exceptions.) At the same time, the social sciences do lay claim to a special sort of authority—the authority that derives from its practice of self-criticism, acknowledgement of the refutability of knowledge claims, and the

---

32. Good, T. L., & Levin, J. R. (2001). Educational psychology yesterday, today, and tomorrow: Debate and direction in an evolving field. *Educational Psychologist, 36,* 69–72. Quote appears on pp. 69–70.

33. Bereiter, C. (1994). Implications of postmodernism for science, or, science as progressive discourse. *Educational Psychologist, 29,* 3–12. Quote appears on p. 6.

submission of each researcher's findings to replication tests by other researchers. Through the exercise of this authority, educational researchers also make claim to progress of a certain sort. That progress involves successively more comprehensive understanding of educational phenomena, based on the open discussion and resolution of issues and the development of theories that have withstood or have been modified in response to refutability tests.

Constructivism

An opposing epistemological position to positivism is based on the assumption that social reality is constructed by the individuals who participate in it. These "constructions" take the form of interpretations, that is, the ascription of meanings to the social environment. Features of the social environment are not considered to have an existence apart from the meanings that individuals construct for them.

To guide our discussion of constructivism, we will make reference to the simple model shown in Figure 1.1. One of the elements in the figure is the individual person (designated A), let's say, a teacher. The teacher interacts with an environment that is both physical (B) and social (C). For example, most teachers use textbooks. At the level of physical reality, a textbook consists of paper and ink, whose reality is constituted by particular biochemical properties. At the level of social reality, the teacher refers to this object by a label *textbook,* which is used as well by other individuals who are members of a particular group (English-language speakers). The teacher uses the textbook to perform a particular social function (instruction) with a particular type of individual (students). The roles of both teacher and

FIGURE 1.1

The Elements of Social Science Inquiry

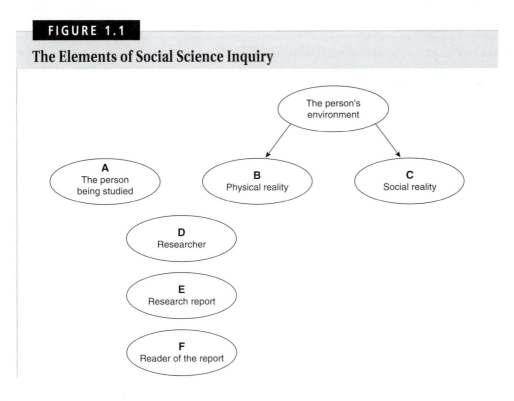

student are dictated in large part by society. Thus, all these aspects of the social environment are socially defined, and in this sense they constitute a social reality.

Educational researchers (D in Figure 1.1) and other social scientists (e.g., anthropologists, psychologists, and sociologists) conduct investigations to learn about individual persons (or groups of persons), about aspects of their social environment, or about the interaction between the two (e.g., how teachers use textbooks during instruction). Social scientists generally do not study physical reality, although an increasing number of researchers are investigating the relationship between brain functions (a physical reality) and cognitive processes (e.g., attention and problem solving) that occur while individuals work on intellectual tasks (a social reality).

After conducting a study, the researcher writes a report of her findings (E in Figure 1.1), which then is read by other individuals (F). The readers might be other researchers, educational practitioners, policy makers, staff members of the agency that funded the study, and members of the general community. Different reports about the same study might be written for different audiences.

To return to our example of the gold star on a student's paper in the previous section, the researcher might consider it as an instance of teacher feedback to students. The teacher might view the gold star as a symbolic message to the student that he has written a good paper relative to other papers he has written. The student might view the gold star as a symbolic message that he has written a better paper than most other papers in the class. Still another student might view the gold star as a sign that the teacher was too busy to provide written feedback and therefore used the gold star as a substitute. Thus, the gold star constitutes different social realities (C in Figure 1.1), not a fixed, independent reality.

This view of social reality is consistent with the constructivist movement in cognitive psychology, which posits that individuals gradually build their own understanding of the world through experience and maturation.[34] Formal instruction has some influence, but children do not assimilate it directly. Their minds are not like the philosopher John Locke's *tabula rasa* (meaning "blank slate") upon which knowledge is written. Piaget's theory of intellectual development in children exemplifies the constructivist movement in cognitive psychology.

Educational researchers who subscribe to this constructivist position believe that scientific inquiry must focus on the study of multiple social realities, that is, the different realities created by different individuals as they interact in a social environment. They also believe that these realities cannot be studied by the analytic methods of positivist research. As Yvonna Lincoln and Egon Guba state, "There are multiple constructed realities that can be studied only holistically. . . ."[35] This constructivist position in large part was developed in reaction to the positivist and postpositivist approaches to social science inquiry; it sometimes is called *constructionism*. We define **constructivism** as the epistemological doctrine that social reality is constructed, that it is constructed differently by different individuals, and that these constructions are transmitted to members of a society by various social agencies and processes. Thus, if we consider a concept such as intelligence, the constructivist assumption of multiple constructed realities would lead us to the conclusion that intelligence has no objective reality. Rather, intelligence is a socially constructed label that has different meanings for different individuals and that, if measured, would be measured in different ways by different researchers.

Our above examples involved instances in which individuals (A in Figure 1.1) construct the features of their social environment (C). An extension of this epistemological

34. Bruner, J. (1986). *Actual minds, possible worlds.* Cambridge, MA: Harvard University Press.
35. Lincoln, Y. S., & Guba, E. G. (1985). *Naturalistic inquiry.* Beverly Hills, CA: Sage. Quote appears on p. 37.

doctrine is that individuals also construct themselves. According to this view, we do not have an objectively real self. Each of us constructs a self.[36] In fact, we construct multiple selves, for example, a created self that is totally private to us, and a social self that is created through our style of dress, mannerisms, and other devices displayed to others. This social self forms multiple selves, because we dress and act differently for different groups and on different occasions.

Constructivism, together with positivism and postpositivism, do not exhaust the epistemological orientations to research. We will describe postmodern and interpretive epistemological orientations later in this chapter, and still other orientations in Chapters 14 and 15.

Objective and Constructed Realities

There are several methodological consequences of the constructivist assumption that individuals construct their selves and the features of their social environment. One is that the researcher (D in Figure 1.1) must find ways to get individuals to reveal their constructions of social reality. Using the labels of Figure 1.1, we can depict these constructions as A → C (to be read, "A's construction of C"). To determine A → C, researchers typically interview A (generally called a *research participant*, or in the case of ethnographic fieldwork, an *informant*). In talking with the researcher, an informant (A) creates a construction (A → C) that depends upon her view of the researcher and her ability and willingness to communicate with the researcher. In other words, A → C depends upon A → D. Problems can occur as a consequence of this dependency. For example, Paul Stoller and Cheryl Olkes did ethnographic fieldwork among the Songhay people of Niger.[37] Stoller subsequently realized that

> [E]veryone had lied to me and . . . the data I had so painstakingly collected were worthless. I learned a lesson: Informants routinely lie to their anthropologists.[38]

This statement reflects Stoller's appraisal, that is, his construction, of what his informants told him. Thus, just as research participants construct views about the researcher (A → D), so the researcher constructs views about the research participants (D → A).

The situation becomes further complicated when we realize that researchers eventually write reports of their studies and submit them to an audience of readers. The report itself (E in Figure 1.1) is a construction by the researcher (D → E). It represents what the researcher chooses to report and how he chooses to report it. Furthermore, no matter what the report states, the reader (F in Figure 1.1) will construct her own interpretation of what the findings mean. Norman Denzin describes the process in this manner:

> The researcher creates a field text consisting of field notes and documents from the field. From this text he or she creates a research text, notes and interpretations based on the field text, what David Plath (1990) calls "filed notes." The researcher then re-creates the research text as a working interpretive document. This working document contains the writer's initial attempts to make sense out of what has been learned . . . The writer next produces a quasi-public text, one that is shared with colleagues, whose comments and suggestions the writer seeks. The writer then transforms this statement into a public document, which embodies the writer's self-understandings, which are now inscribed in the experiences of those studied. This statement, in turn, furnishes the context for the understandings the reader brings to the experiences described by the writer.[39]

---

36. For an example of this view of self, see: Sampson, E. E. (2000). Reinterpreting individualism and collectivism: Their religious roots and monologic versus dialogic person–other relationship. *American Psychologist, 55,* 1425–1432.
37. Stoller, P., & Olkes, C. (1987). *In sorcery's shadow: A memoir of apprenticeship among the Songhay of Niger.* Chicago: University of Chicago Press.
38. Ibid., p. 229.
39. Denzin, N. K. (1994). The art and politics of interpretation. In N. K. Denzin & Y. S. Lincoln (Eds.), *Handbook of qualitative research* (pp. 500–515). Thousand Oaks, CA: Sage. Quote appears on pp. 501–502.

Constructivist researchers deal with these multiple layers of construction (i.e., interpretation) in various ways. For example, some researchers make explicit their constructivist role in scientific inquiry by writing research reports in which they play a key role alongside their research participants. They describe their personal experiences and reactions in the field, and how their approach to data collection affected the types of findings that resulted. This focus on the researcher's self as an integral constructor of the social reality being studied is called **reflexivity.** In the following statement, David Altheide and John Johnson advocate reflexivity in ethnographic research (we describe this type of research in Chapter 15):

> Good ethnographies show the hand of the ethnographer. The effort may not always be successful, but there should be clear "tracks" indicating the attempt has been made. We are in the midst of a rediscovery that social reality is constructed by human agents—even social scientists!—using cultural categories and language in specific situations or contexts of meaning. This interest is indeed welcome, because it gives us license to do yet another elucidation of the "concept of knowing."[40]

Reflexivity in scientific inquiry has become an important movement not only in ethnography, but also in other social science disciplines. The movement sometimes is called the *reflexive turn* in the social sciences. Positivist researchers in these sciences reject reflexivity, however. Their goal is to keep the self out of the processes of collecting data and reporting their findings as much as possible.

The objective orientation of positivist researchers is reflected in the *Publication Manual of the American Psychological Association,* a guide for reporting psychological research, which for most of its history has been grounded in positivist epistemology.[41] (The *Manual* also is widely used in the reporting of educational research and research in other social science disciplines.) Robert Madigan, Susan Johnson, and Patricia Linton did an analysis of reporting recommendations in the *Manual* (fourth edition). The following are two of their conclusions:

> In APA style, language use is not allowed to call attention to itself. Dillon (1991) described this as the "rhetoric of objectivity" that has evolved to create the impression of neutrality or impersonal detachment and that is generally characteristic of the empirical disciplines. This effect is enhanced by giving the persona of the writer a low profile in the text, keeping the focus on the phenomena under study . . .
>   APA style [leads] toward practices that make language appear as a transparent medium for conveying objective information about a fixed external reality.[42]

We see, then, that the standard format for writing reports of positivist research is consistent with its epistemology of scientific inquiry, which is objective rather than reflexive in nature.

Cases and Populations

Researchers who subscribe to constructivist epistemology believe that the study of individuals' interpretations of social reality must occur at the local, immediate level. For example, suppose that a constructivist researcher is interested in teachers' interpretations of the act of teaching, that is, the meanings they ascribe to various features of teaching (e.g., lesson planning, student misbehavior in class, and homework assignments). To determine

---

40. Altheide, D. L., & Johnson, J. M. (1994). Criteria for assessing interpretive validity in qualitative research. In N. K. Denzin & Y. S. Lincoln (Eds.), *Handbook of qualitative research* (pp. 485–499). Thousand Oaks, CA: Sage. Quote appears on pp. 493–494.
41. *Publication Manual of the American Psychological Association* (5th ed.). (2001). Washington, DC: American Psychological Association.
42. Madigan, R., Johnson, S., & Linton, P. (1995). The language of style: APA style as epistemology. *American Psychologist, 50,* 428–436. Quote appears on pp. 433–434.

these meanings, the researcher needs to study particular teachers (local) rather than teachers in general (distant). Also, the researcher needs to identify a particular time frame for study. The way that a teacher constructs meanings at one point in time (immediate) may not be the way he constructs meanings at another point in time (past and future). The epistemological assumption about the local, immediate character of meanings implies, then, that the researcher must study particular cases, that is, particular instances of the phenomenon that interests him.

Researchers who subscribe to positivist epistemology believe that features of the social environment retain a high degree of constancy across time and space, just as physicists believe that neutrons and protons have objective features that do not vary from one laboratory setting to another or from one day to the next. For example, in reviewing positivist research on teaching, Frederick Erickson states,

> Positivist research on teaching presumes that history repeats itself; that what can be learned from past events can generalize to future events—in the same setting and in different settings.[43]

This assumption of constancy justifies their search for what is generally true of the social environment. Local variations are considered to be "noise." For example, a positivist researcher might be interested in whether an emphasis on higher-cognitive questions in instruction would improve student learning. In doing a research study, this researcher would not be interested in whether the higher-cognitive questions of a particular teacher make a difference. Instead, she would want to determine general trends for a defined population of teachers. If she found that higher-cognitive questions generally promote student learning, she would claim to have discovered a "law," a "principle," a "rule," or a similar term. The fact that the law does not hold for a particular teacher would be considered "noise," that is, an unexplained variation. We see, then, that positivist researchers study samples and populations, not cases.

The epistemological assumptions that lead to the study of cases or populations also have implications for how findings of a particular research study are generalized. In the study of cases, the critical question for generalizing findings is this: Have we learned something about this case that can inform us about another case? Generalization of case study findings must be made on a case-by-case basis.

This approach to generalization is analogous to how we often think in our everyday life. Suppose you are a teacher and you observe another teacher who uses a particular teaching technique successfully. You probably will proceed to study the teacher's work situation (the grade level, the social class of the students, the curriculum, etc.) and decide whether it is similar to your own work situation. If you decide that it is similar, you probably will conclude that the technique has a good chance of being effective in your situation, too. Thus, you generalize from a given case to another case.

The process of generalization is different in positivist research. The researcher starts by defining a population of interest. The population typically includes too many members to study all of them, so the researcher attempts to select a manageable sample, but one that is representative of the population. He then attempts to generalize to the larger population the findings obtained from studying the sample. Statistical techniques are available to determine the likelihood that sample findings (e.g., students in the sample who received Method A earned higher test scores than students who received Method B) are likely to apply to the population.

---

43. Erickson, F. (1986). Qualitative methods in research on teaching. In M. C. Wittrock (Ed.), *Handbook of research on teaching* (3rd ed., pp. 119–161). New York: Macmillan. Quote appears on p. 129.

The physical sciences have achieved prominence among the academic disciplines because of their demonstrated ability to discover highly generalizable laws that explain features of physical reality. The social sciences and related professional disciplines such as education have not achieved the same level of respect and authority because their ability to discover general laws remains in doubt. If one subscribes to the assumption of constructivist epistemology that meaning is embedded in local, immediate contexts, it follows that generalizations about features of social reality necessarily will be difficult and tentative. The positivist assumption of an objective, relatively constant social reality leads to the more optimistic view that general laws governing social reality can be discovered.

Numerical and Verbal Representations of Social Reality

Alford Crosby claims that the great achievements of Western civilization starting during the Renaissance were the result of a shift away from the qualitative worldview that had dominated society up to then.[44] In that qualitative worldview, symbolism, mythology, and religion were used to explain human events and physical phenomena. For example, time "was envisioned not as a straight line marked off in equal quanta, but as a stage for the enactment of the greatest of all dramas, Salvation versus Damnation."[45]

With the shift toward a quantitative worldview, reality was viewed differently:

> In practical terms, the new approach was simply this: reduce what you are trying to think about to the minimum required by its definition; visualize it on paper, or at least in your mind, be it the fluctuation of wool prices at the Champagne fairs or the course of Mars through the heavens, and divide it, either in fact or in imagination, into equal quanta. Then you can measure it, that is, count the quanta.[46]

Quantitative thinking generated many inventions, including mechanical clocks that break time into ticks of equal length; geometrically precise maps in which gridlines mark off equal units of the earth's surface; double-entry bookkeeping in which goods and services are represented as monetary units; and the use of algebraic notation to indicate known and unknown quantities.

The analysis of reality into quanta is so embedded in contemporary society that we take it for granted. The computer, digital sound, and digital video represent reality in the simplest of quanta—1s and 0s. Western capitalism depends on the capacity to create quantitative representations of property, goods, and services. (Hernando De Soto found that underdeveloped countries have an enormous amount of capital, but cannot access it because they lack this capacity.[47]) Most research advances in the physical and social sciences that we read about in the news involve the quantification of reality and mathematics, especially statistical analysis. In education, too, much of the research that is considered newsworthy involves students' performance on tests, which represents quantification of learning and aptitude.

The use of quantification to represent and analyze features of social reality is consistent with positivist epistemology. Because this epistemology assumes that features of social reality have a constancy across time and settings, a particular feature can be isolated and it can be conceptualized as a variable, that is, as an entity that can take on different values. These values can be expressed as a numerical scale. For example, a typical achievement test is assumed to yield scores that form an interval scale.

44. Crosby, A. W. (1997). *The measure of reality: Quantification and Western society, 1250–1600.* New York: Cambridge University Press.
45. Ibid., p. 28.
46. Ibid., p. 228.
47. De Soto, H. (2000). *The mystery of capital: Why capitalism triumphs in the West and fails everywhere else.* New York: Basic Books.

Suppose that we, as positivist researchers, select class size as a feature of the classroom environment to study. We decide to operationally define class size as the average number of students who are enrolled in a teacher's classroom over the course of the school year. We then can observe a sample of teachers' classrooms and make this count. The resulting data consist of numerical scores: Teacher A's classroom has 23 students, Teacher B's classroom has 37 students, and so on. A comparison of the scores would lead us logically to the conclusion that Teacher A's class size is smaller than Teacher B's class size. The scores for all the teachers can be averaged to yield a mean class size for the sample. Also, by collecting additional data, we can determine whether the variable of class size is related to other variables. For example, we can conceptualize a variable called *student off-task behavior,* develop a measure of it, and collect data in the classroom of each teacher in the sample. The two sets of numerical data (class size and student off-task behavior) then can be analyzed to determine whether they are related in some way (e.g., larger class sizes might tend to be associated with higher off-task rates). The great majority of educational research studies have represented and analyzed features of the social environment in just this way.

Some researchers and philosophers of science have questioned this use of quantification in social science research. Marx Wartofsky, for example, raises this issue:

> The question of the limited scope of such techniques as are directly quantitative (in terms of interval or ratio scales) raises the problem of "importance" and "triviality" in social-science research strategy. For it may increasingly become the case that central societal facts which do not lend themselves to such analysis will tend to be overlooked or de-emphasized on such narrowly methodological grounds, by virtue of the easy quantification of other, perhaps marginal facts. Social-science research oriented toward empirical-quantitative studies may very well then take the path of least resistance. But the path of least resistance to quantification may be the path of least significance as well, so that data analysis may proliferate precisely where it is least important.[48]

As applied to our example, Wartofsky's analysis raises the question of whether class size and student off-task behavior are features of the social environment that can be quantified, but that are not particularly significant for understanding how classrooms work and what makes them work well or poorly as arenas for instruction.

Constructivist epistemology raises another concern about quantification. The operational definition of class size as a count of the average number of students enrolled in a class over the course of a school year assumes that values of this variable have the same meaning across classrooms. Constructivist researchers, however, would question this assumption. Two teachers both may have 25 enrolled students. In Teacher A's class, though, some of these students may have behavior disorders and may have been assigned to the teacher without her consent. In Teacher B's class, all the students may be able learners, whose presence in class the teacher welcomes. Thus, the number *25* has two different meanings in these situations. For Teacher A, *25* may represent an oppressive teaching situation, whereas for Teacher B, *25* may represent a comfortable teaching situation. If researchers conduct an investigation to determine whether increases in class size make instruction more difficult, they may be misled because a particular value of the variable *class size* may not have the same meaning for the teachers in all the classes having that value.

Constructivist researchers attempt to avoid the problems created by quantification of features of the social environment by focusing their investigations on the study of individual cases and by making "thick" verbal descriptions of what they observe. If possible, they also make video or audio recordings, which preserve the events in a fairly authentic

---

48. Wartofsky, M. W. (1968). *Conceptual foundations of scientific thought: An introduction to the philosophy of science.* New York: Macmillan. Quote appears on p. 393.

manner for subsequent data analysis. The data analysis, too, is primarily verbal rather than statistical. The researcher searches for just the right words to represent the themes and patterns that she discovers in the data.

Analytic induction is involved in this process of discovery. **Analytic induction** means that the researcher searches through the data bit by bit and then infers that certain events or statements are instances of the same underlying theme or pattern. Thus, themes and patterns are induced from the data. In contrast, a deductive approach would involve identifying themes and patterns prior to data collection and then searching through the data for instances of them.

This verbal, visual, inductive approach corresponds to how people in general get to know a person or a situation. In our society, we ask lots of questions (a verbal technique) and get lots of answers (verbal data) in return. We also may take photographs or make a videotape for later reflection. Later, if someone asks what the person or situation we studied is like, we give a verbal description that attempts to be faithful to the original situation. If we are describing a person, we may recount things she said and stories she told about herself. If we have a photograph of the person, we may show it. As you will find in Chapter 14, case study research in education uses similar methods.

Though verbal and visual methods of representation and data analysis appear to avoid the problems with quantification noted above, they have several drawbacks. The words and form of speech that a researcher uses to interview an informant in the field setting being studied may not have the same meaning for the informant as for the researcher. Furthermore, one informant may use the same words as another informant, but with different meanings. In addition, although language is highly versatile, it does not represent all the important features of a social environment. For example, some social science researchers have theorized that certain important features of social life are invisible:

> "What is happening here?" may seem a trivial question at first glance. It is not trivial since everyday life is largely invisible to us (because of its familiarity and because of its contradictions, which people may not want to face). We do not realize the patterns in our actions as we perform them. The anthropologist Clyde Kluckhohn illustrated this point with an aphorism: "The fish would be the last creature to discover water."[49]

If it is true that certain features of the social environment are invisible to those who participate in it, then they, and the researcher as well, may lack the language to make them visible.

Mechanical, Interpretive, and Structural Views of Causation

Explanation is a major goal of scientific inquiry. As researchers, we want to know not only what happened, but why. Also, we want to understand the consequences of alterations in the social environment. That is, we want to understand the causal connections among social phenomena. For example, what factors cause some students to do well in reading and others to do poorly? What are the effects of learning to read well or poorly?

Different researchers make different epistemological assumptions about the nature of causality, and these assumptions affect their approach to the study of cause-and-effect relationships among educational phenomena. Positivist researchers have what may be described as a "mechanical" view of causation. In Newtonian physics, mechanical causation involves force and matter. For example, when a pool player strikes a ball in a game of pool, this action creates a force that starts the ball rolling toward another ball. The force is transmitted into the second ball, which causes it to start rolling, too.

---

49. Erickson, *Qualitative methods*, p. 121.

A similar view of causation permeates positivist research in the social sciences, if only metaphorically. For example, intelligence is thought to cause some students to do well at academic tasks and others to do poorly. Academic success is thought to affect an individual's choice of career and income. In this example, intelligence, academic success, career, and income are viewed somewhat like matter (i.e., real social objects) that can exert force on, or can be affected by the force of, other matter. The research designs that you will study in Chapters 10 through 13 are used by positivist researchers in a search for causal connections of this type. Some designs are more sophisticated than others in enabling a researcher to investigate multiple causes of a particular outcome (e.g., test performance) and the relative "weight" or "force" of each presumed cause.

Constructivist researchers view causation much differently. They assume that people develop interpretations of the social environment that affect their subsequent actions. For example, constructivist researchers do not view intelligence as a real entity that causes children to do well or poorly in school. Rather, the child and the people in his life (e.g., parents, teachers, classmates) develop interpretations of the child's intelligence that affect his subsequent school performance. Thus, our interpretations, and especially the intentions we form on the basis of these interpretations, are the true causal agents in the social environment. Therefore, to discover causal patterns in social phenomena, constructivists investigate individuals' interpretations of social reality.

Some positivist researchers examine individuals' interpretations as causal factors, but these causal factors are conceptualized as personality characteristics rather than as interpretations embedded in transitory, local events. For example, there are quantitative measures of *locus of control,* which refers to whether the individual believes that he personally controls his destiny or whether external forces do. A constructivist would be more inclined to see these beliefs as situational perceptions: An individual might believe at one time and in one situation that he is in control of what is happening, whereas at another time and in another situation, he might see himself as a "victim" of external forces.

Another epistemological perspective on causation, called *scientific realism,* has influenced research in the physical and social sciences.[50] **Scientific realism** is the philosophical doctrine that the real world consists of layers of causal structures, some of them hidden from view, that interact to produce effects that may or may not be observable. To explain what this means, we will refer again to the example of the pool game. There is more to the story than the first ball causing the second ball to move. To understand the full causal pattern at work, we need to know what the pool player was intending when she hit the first ball (e.g., her intentions about how hard to hit the first ball and in what direction), the idiosyncrasies of the pool table (e.g., perhaps the table has a slant that affects each ball's action), the idiosyncrasies of the cue stick, and so forth. All these factors are causal structures that can interact to produce the observed effect. The goal of inquiry, according to scientific realists, is to discover how these causal structures work.

As applied to education and other social science disciplines, scientific realism postulates that the real causes of human behavior are underlying causal structures. Discovering what these structures are is difficult because they may or may not have observable effects in particular situations. For example, suppose a teacher thinks about how to react to a student who is inattentive. He considers various alternatives and, in the end, rejects them all. There is no observable behavior that tells the researcher what causal entities might have been at work. Examples of possible entities might be: the teacher's decision-making

---

50. For a more complete explanation of scientific realism, see: House, E. R. (1991). Realism in research. *Educational Researcher, 20*(6), 2–9, 25.

process in such situations, the teacher's store of knowledge about consequences of past responses to student inattention, the interpersonal dynamics of this particular classroom, and the teacher's knowledge of the student's home environment and academic performance. Each of these is a potential causal structure that can interact with the other causal structures to produce an effect. Because of the complexity of possible interactions, researchers will not be able to make precise predictions of human behavior. They only will be able to determine trends and probabilities. The various research traditions that have developed in qualitative inquiry seem particularly well suited for discovering what these causal structures might be in educational environments. In fact, research traditions such as structuralism and cognitive psychology (both discussed in Chapter 15) make explicit reference to structures that underlie behavior and influence it.

To summarize, positivist epistemology assumes a mechanistic causality among social "objects." Constructivist epistemology assumes that individuals' interpretations of situations cause them to take certain actions. Scientific realism assumes that there are multiple layers of causal structures, which are real entities that interact with each other to cause people to take certain actions or, in some cases, to take no action.

Postmodernism

Touchstone in Research

St. Pierre, E. A. (2000). The call for intelligibility in postmodern educational research. *Educational Researcher, 29*(5), 25–28.

Just as postpositivism can be seen as a reaction against positivism, so too can postmodernism be seen as a reaction against modernism. Modernism has its roots in the Enlightenment, which promoted the advancement of knowledge through scientific observation and the belief that, "under the seeming surface chaos of the world, of society, there exists a rationality, a basic truth that can be identified and harnessed for human good."[51] Positivist science is a prominent manifestation of the modernist spirit. Kenneth Gergen, a leader in the postmodernist movement, makes the point more bluntly: "In the modernist tradition, one is taught to take marching orders from reality—to observe the world for what it is and to report accordingly."[52]

Postmodernism, which developed as a reaction against modernism, is a broad social and philosophical movement that questions the rationality of human action, the use of positivist epistemology, and any human endeavor (e.g., science) that claims a privileged position with respect to the search for truth or that claims progress in the search for truth. Laurel Richardson put the matter this way:

> The core of postmodernism is the *doubt* that any method or theory, discourse or genre, tradition or novelty, has a universal and general claim as the "right" or the privileged form of authoritative knowledge. Postmodernism *suspects* all truth claims of masking and serving particular interests in local, cultural, and political struggle.[53]

Thus, postmodernists not only would question the possibility that social scientists could prove that Theory X is valid and Theory Y is not, but they would question whether social science inquiry into Theory X and Theory Y is superior to any other form of inquiry, such as literary studies or astrology. In postmodern thinking, too, all cultures have equal claim to the truth of things. According to postmodernists, the search for truth should be replaced by a "conversation" among "many voices."[54]

---

51. Graham, E., Doherty, J., & Malek, M. (1992). Introduction: The context and language of postmodernism. In Doherty, J., Graham, E., & Malek, M. (Eds.), *Postmodernism and the social sciences* (pp. 1–23). Basingstoke, England: Macmillan. Quote appears on p. 8.
52. Gergen, K. J. (2001). Psychological science in a postmodern context. *American Psychologist, 56*(10), 803–813.
53. Richardson, L. (1994). Writing: A method of inquiry. In N. K. Denzin & Y. S. Lincoln (Eds.), *Handbook of qualitative research* (pp. 516–529). Thousand Oaks, CA: Sage. Quote appears on p. 517.
54. Doherty, Graham, & Malek, *Postmodernism and the social sciences,* pp. 17–18.

Postmodernists make a strong case in arguing that other forms of inquiry, such as literature and the arts, also may lay claim to authority. In fact, some educational researchers have made strong cases for literature and art as forms of inquiry.[55] However, they generally do not argue that literature and art are superior to social science inquiry, only different. You can gain some insight into the differences for yourself if you compare literature and art with each of the six characteristics of social science inquiry described in the section on positivism and postpositivism in this chapter. For example, writers and artists do not subject their "knowledge claims" to the tests of refutability to which social scientists subject their knowledge claims. While postmodernists may claim that "anything goes," all forms of inquiry do not "go" the same way or justify their authority in the same way.

Quantitative and Qualitative Research

In the preceding discussion, we demonstrated that different researchers make different epistemological assumptions about the nature of scientific knowledge and how to acquire it. If you favor one set of assumptions, you will conduct one type of educational research. If you favor another set of assumptions, you will conduct a different type.

While the terms *positivist research* and *constructivist research* appear in the literature, it is more common to see the terms *quantitative research* and *qualitative research,* respectively, used to refer to the distinctions we made above. Because these terms are in common use, we employ them throughout the rest of the book, especially in Parts IV and V. These terms emphasize the fact that the two types of research differ in the nature of the data that are collected. **Quantitative research** is virtually synonymous with positivist research. For a definition of **qualitative research,** we refer to the one offered by Norman Denzin and Yvonna Lincoln:

> Qualitative research is multimethod in its focus, involving an interpretive, naturalistic approach to its subject matter. This means that qualitative researchers study things in their natural settings, attempting to make sense of, or interpret, phenomena in terms of the meanings people bring to them.[56]

Table 1.2 provides a further elaboration of the distinguishing characteristics of quantitative and qualitative research.

The label *interpretive research* sometimes is used instead of *qualitative research.* Erickson defines **interpretive research** as the study of the immediate and local meanings of social actions for the actors involved in them.[57] This definition is consistent with the definition of *qualitative research* offered above. It is also similar to constructivist epistemology.

Another term that sometimes is used instead of *qualitative research* is *case study research.* This term emphasizes the fact that qualitative research focuses on the study of cases rather than of populations and samples. As we explain in Chapter 14, much of the methodology used in case studies evolved along lines suggested by interpretive epistemology and therefore is consistent with the qualitative research traditions described in Chapter 15. However, some case study researchers subscribe to positivist epistemology. In Chapter 14, we note these exceptions to the general qualitative, constructivist orientation of case study research.

---

55. For example, see: Eisner, E. W. (1979). *The educational imagination: On the design and evaluation of school programs.* New York: Macmillan; Greene, M. (1988). Qualitative research and the uses of literature. In R. R. Sherman & R. B. Webb (Eds.), *Qualitative research in education: Focus and methods* (pp. 175–189). London: Falmer.
56. Denzin, N. K., & Lincoln, Y. S. (1994). Introduction: Entering the field of qualitative research. In N. K. Denzin & Y. S. Lincoln (Eds.), *Handbook of qualitative research* (pp. 1–17). Thousand Oaks, CA: Sage. Quote appears on p. 2.
57. Erickson, *Qualitative methods.*

TABLE 1.2

Differences between Quantitative and Qualitative Research

Quantitative Researchers	Qualitative Researchers
Assume an objective social reality.	Assume that social reality is constructed by the participants in it.
Assume that social reality is relatively constant across time and settings.	Assume that social reality is continuously constructed in local situations.
View causal relationships among social phenomena from a mechanistic perspective.	Assign human intentions a major role in explaining causal relationships among social phenomena.
Take an objective, detached stance toward research participants and their setting.	Become personally involved with research participants, to the point of sharing perspectives and assuming a caring attitude.
Study populations or samples that represent populations.	Study cases.
Study behavior and other observable phenomena.	Study the meanings that individuals create and other internal phenomena.
Study human behavior in natural or contrived settings.	Study human actions in natural settings.
Analyze social reality into variables.	Make holistic observations of the total context within which social action occurs.
Use preconceived concepts and theories to determine what data will be collected.	Discover concepts and theories after data have been collected.
Generate numerical data to represent the social environment.	Generate verbal and pictorial data to represent the social environment.
Use statistical methods to analyze data.	Use analytic induction to analyze data.
Use statistical inference procedures to generalize findings from a sample to a defined population.	Generalize case findings by identifying other similar cases.
Prepare impersonal, objective reports of research findings.	Prepare interpretive reports that reflect researchers' constructions of the data and an awareness that readers will form their own constructions from what is reported.

Given that both quantitative research and qualitative research are conducted to investigate education, several questions arise. Is one approach better than the other? Do they complement each other in some way? Do they produce conflicting findings?

Mixed-Methods Research

Touchstone in Research

Taskakkori, A., &
Teddlie, C. (Eds.)
(2003). *Handbook of
mixed methods in
social & behavioral
research*. Thousand
Oaks, CA: Sage.

There is a growing consensus among researchers that qualitative and quantitative research can complement each other. A review of quantitative studies about a particular phenomenon combined with a review of qualitative studies about the same phenomenon can provide richer insights and raise more interesting questions for future research than if only one set of studies is considered. Increasingly, though, we find researchers who combine both quantitative and qualitative methods in the design of a single study. This approach has come to be known as *mixed-methods research*.

As defined by R. Burke Johnson and Anthony Onwuegbuzie, mixed-methods research is "the class of research where the researcher mixes or combines quantitative and qualitative research techniques, methods, approaches, concepts or language into a single study."[58] These authors draw on the philosophy of pragmatism to argue that quantitative and qualitative approaches can coexist productively within a single study. Pragmatists such as Charles Sanders Pierce, William James, and John Dewey argued that the truth value of a concept, idea, method, or other entity is determined by whether it has pragmatic—that is, useful—consequences. Thus, although quantitative research and qualitative research generally are grounded in different and seemingly incompatible epistemologies, they both can be "true" within the philosophy of pragmatism if their joint deployment in a mixed-methods study results in useful findings.

Various mixed-methods designs have been used by educational researchers.[59] One approach is to use quantitative methods to answer research questions or test hypotheses when the constructs and their measures can be specified in advance of data collection, but also to use qualitative methods to discover additional constructs that are relevant to the study's goals. An example of this type of mixed-methods design is a study of international students conducted by Stephen Stoynoff.[60] English was the second language for the 77 students in his sample, and they had just started their freshman year at a U.S. university. Stoynoff conducted a quantitative research study to determine how well their scores on the Test of English as a Foreign Language (TOEFL) and the Learning and Study Strategies Inventory (LASSI) predicted their first-term grade point average (GPA). The results indicated that TOEFL and LASSI scores yielded only modest predictions of GPA. Stoynoff then conducted qualitative case studies of selected members of his sample to determine whether other factors might be more important to the academic success of international students. Stoynoff made the following discovery from the case studies:

> The LASSI does not measure the compensatory methods that students use to help them negotiate the system. Interviews revealed that students sought social assistance from a wide variety of persons. They used tutors and roommates to explain and review homework. They borrowed lecture notes, previous tests, and papers from classmates and friends. They asked teachers for extra help. Students also learned to carefully select their courses based on the recommendations of others. These compensatory methods are not measured by the LASSI . . . .[61]

These insights could be used to conceptualize what a "compensatory strategy" means. An instrument (e.g., a self-report inventory) then could be developed to measure the observable manifestations of this conceptualization. The instrument could be administered to a sample in a quantitative research study to test—and hopefully to confirm—Stoynoff's insights. Depending on the results, new qualitative studies might be done, yielding new insights that could be tested in subsequent quantitative studies.

Madhabi Chatterji proposed a different mix of quantitative and qualitative research for use in evaluating the effects of educational programs and other interventions.[62] Quantitative methods alone might be sufficient if the intervention is very brief (typically, an hour or less) and can be administered in a laboratory-like setting. However, real-life educational programs tend to extend over months or years, and they must be adapted to various organizational structures and the values and preexisting beliefs of the educators who will implement them.

58. Johnson, R. B., & Onwuegbuzie, A. (2004). Mixed methods research: A research paradigm whose time has come. *Educational Researcher, 33*(7), 14–26. Quote appears on p. 17.
59. A typology of mixed-methods designs can be found in Johnson & Onwuegbuzie, op. cit.
60. Stoynoff, S. J. (1990). English language proficiency and study strategies as determinants of academic success for international students in U.S. universities. *Dissertation Abstracts International, 52*(01), 97A. (UMI No. 9117569)
61. Ibid., p. 112.
62. Chatterji, M. (2004). Evidence on "What Works": An argument for extended-term mixed-method (ETMM) evaluation designs. *Educational Researcher, 33*(9), 3–13.

Moreover, the programs are likely to have both intended and unintended effects on the students or other clients for whom the programs are designed.

Chatterji argues for the use of extended-term mixed-method (ETMM) designs to conduct experiments on the effects of these real-life educational interventions. The general form of these designs is as follows:

> ETMM designs follow life-spans of individual programs/policy initiatives within particular environments, employing appropriate descriptive research methods in the early stages of program adoption and implementation followed by timely and judicious implementation of experimental designs at a subsequent stage.[63]

The data-collection methods can be quantitative, qualitative, or both, at either the descriptive phase or the experimental phase of the study or at both phases.

Chatterji describes an application of the ETMM approach to the study of an extended-day supplemental program for elementary schoolchildren. In the first phase, during the summer and first semester of the school year, the researchers collected qualitative descriptive data by conducting informal interviews with school leaders and making qualitative observations of school and classroom activities and orientation and training sessions. During the first semester, they also initiated an experiment with a group of teachers who volunteered to try the new program (the experimental group) and another group of teachers who did not use the new program (the control group).

The rich qualitative data that they collected in the descriptive phase led them to discover that student misbehavior and associated management problems interfered with the designed delivery of the experimental program. Various stakeholders worked to solve these problems and, in the second semester, the experiment was continued. Whereas the extended-day supplemental program was found to have either zero or negative effects on students' learning of basic skills in the first semester, positive learning effects relative to the control group of students were found in the second semester.

In a traditional experiment, the experimental and control groups would have been formed, the program would have been put in place, and student learning gains from preexperiment to postexperiment would have been measured. The experiment likely would have demonstrated that the program was ineffective. However, the mixed-method design that Chatterji and colleagues used made it possible to study the program's implementation over time, to collect qualitative data to identify and solve implementation problems, and then to conduct an experiment that provided a fair test of the program. From the perspective of pragmatist philosophy, the extended-term mixed-method approach was a valid approach for this study because it yielded useful results.

A Definition of Research

To define the term *research*, we need to consider two related terms, *science* and *scientific research*. There are no authoritative definitions for or distinctions between these terms, but some emerge in practice. People usually speak of the sciences as specialized disciplines of inquiry. At the broadest level, they speak of the natural sciences and the social sciences, with biology, physics, and chemistry as examples of the former and psychology, sociology, and anthropology as examples of the latter.

The term *research* is more indeterminate in that it is not necessarily tied to a particular specialized discipline. Thus, individuals may speak of doing their own research, for example, to collect information for a family genealogy or to decide on a location for their business.

---

63. Ibid., p. 4.

When we use the term *research* in this book, we are not referring to this kind of inquiry, whose purpose is to satisfy an individual's needs. Rather, we are referring to research whose purpose is to contribute knowledge that improves our collective understanding of education.

Our formal definition of *research* would be this: a form of inquiry in which (1) key concepts and procedures are carefully defined in such a way that the inquiry can be replicated and possibly refuted, (2) controls are in place to minimize error and bias, (3) the generalizability limits of the study's results are made explicit, and (4) the results of the study are interpreted in terms of what they contribute to the cumulative body of knowledge about the object of inquiry.

You will note that this definition makes no reference to theory. This is because many research studies in education contribute to knowledge, but are not theory-based. These studies might have made a more substantial contribution if they had been grounded in a theory and designed to test it. However, in our view at least, theory testing is not an essential element of research.

Some might argue that this definition of research privileges postpositivist research over constructivist research or quantitative research over qualitative research. Our response is that the wording of the definition has a postpositivist slant, but that many, if not most, constructivist and qualitative researchers share the same concerns (e.g., control for error and bias), although they think about them differently.

In an influential book, a group of educational researchers offered their view of what constitutes *scientific research*.[64] Their core definition is this: "Scientific research, whether in education, physics, anthropology, molecular biology, or economics, is a continual process of rigorous reasoning supported by a dynamic interplay among methods, theories, and findings."[65] They elaborated on this definition by asserting that scientific research in education and other disciplines follows six guiding principles. Scientific research

1. poses significant questions that can be investigated empirically,
2. links research to relevant theory and continually generates and refines theories,
3. uses methods that permit direct investigation of the questions,
4. provides a coherent and explicit chain of reasoning from an investigation's empirical results to inferences based on these results,
5. calls for replication studies to validate, generalize, and synthesize the results of individual studies, and
6. discloses a study's findings to encourage professional scrutiny and critique.

These principles are, for the most part, incorporated in the definition of *research* that we offered above.

The book in which these principles appear, *Scientific Research in Education*, has had a major impact on the shaping of national policy for the funding of educational research, especially on the policies of the No Child Left Behind Act and the Institute of Education Sciences. For some in the research community, the book was read as privileging postpositivism and experiments over other epistemologies and research methods.[66] For others, it was seen as an outright rejection of postmodernism, the qualitative research traditions presented in Chapter 15 of this book, and action research, which is presented in Chapter 18.[67]

The controversy aroused by *Scientific Research in Education* indicates that there is no universally accepted, authoritative conception of the epistemological underpinnings of

64. Shavelson, R. J., & Towne, L. (Eds.). (2002). *Scientific research in education.* Washington, DC: National Academy Press.
65. Ibid., p. 2.
66. Eisenhart, M., & Towne, L. (2003). Contestation and change in national policy on "scientifically based" education research. *Educational Researcher, 32*(7), 31–38.
67. St. Pierre, E. A. (2002). "Science" rejects postmodernism. *Educational Researcher, 31*(8), 25–27.

research or of its methods and goals. Our own position perhaps can be summarized as pragmatic: Let different researchers, from the most positivist to the most postmodern, pursue their lines of inquiry and then determine which bear fruit in terms of useful, persuasive knowledge and theory. Educational research, in particular, is too young a scientific enterprise for anyone to draw definitive conclusions about which epistemology and methods are best. For this reason, we have been eclectic in our presentation of the various facets of contemporary educational research throughout this book.

Learning How to Do Educational Research

Touchstone in Research

Larabee, D. F. (2003). The peculiar problems of preparing educational researchers. *Educational Researcher,* *32*(4), 13–22.

The purpose of this chapter is to help you understand *why* educational research is worth doing. The following chapters describe *how* to do educational research. However, "book knowledge" of these tools and concepts will not turn you into a competent researcher. To achieve this goal, it is essential that you acquire experience both in reading research reports and in doing your own research. As you read the chapters of this book, we recommend that you also read published research studies in your areas of interest in order to put "flesh and blood" on the ideas that we present. Chapter 4 explains how the research literature is organized and how to access it to identify research studies on particular topics.

As for learning how to do research, the best way—perhaps the only way—is to apprentice yourself to an experienced researcher. You might identify such an individual among the faculty of a university school of education or a research institute. Researchers generally are happy to advise others on their research projects, and they are likely to welcome novices willing to volunteer as assistants on their projects. In addition, you can learn from the larger community of educational researchers by joining their professional association, which is the American Educational Research Association (AERA) and its various divisions and special interest groups.[68] Another major association is the American Psychological Association (APA) and its Division 15 (Educational Psychology).[69] APA's Division 15 published a book that describes the contributions of important educational researchers over the past century.[70] These researchers can serve as models for all of us about the spirit of educational research and how research agendas are set and maintained by dedicated researchers over the course of a career.

In reading this text, you should reflect on your personal orientation to the various research methods presented in it. You may find that you are more sympathetic to the perspectives and methods of quantitative research, or that your bent is toward qualitative research. It is perfectly acceptable to specialize in a particular approach to research. Most educational researchers do so. At the same time, it is important to become familiar with the full range of research approaches. This is true for several reasons. First, you will find, when you study a particular problem in education, that different researchers are likely to have used different epistemological and methodological approaches to shed light on it; if you don't understand these approaches, you will not be able to develop a comprehensive understanding of the problem and what is known about it. Second, a breadth of understanding is needed in order to communicate, and possibly collaborate, with individuals in the entire research community, not just those who share your views. Finally, as we observed earlier in the chapter, mixed-methods designs are becoming increasingly popular and valid. Unless you are conversant with a range of quantitative *and* qualitative methodologies, these designs will not be an option for you.

---

68. The Web home page for AERA is http://www.aera.net
69. The Web home page for APA is http://www.apa.org
70. Zimmerman, B. J., & Schunk, D. H. (Eds.). (2003). *Educational psychology: A century of contributions.* Mahwah, NJ: Erlbaum.

SELF-CHECK TEST

Circle the correct answer to each of the following questions.
An answer key is provided at the back of the book.

1. Educational research findings tend not to affect practice directly because
   a. research findings are too neutral.
   b. research findings derive almost entirely from basic research.
   c. policy makers tend to see no value in research findings.
   d. policy makers view research findings as only one basis for decision making.

2. A constructivist researcher would view the concept of learning disorder as
   a. generalizable across cultures.
   b. theory free.
   c. value-laden.
   d. value-free.

3. The use of standardized tests, detachment from the persons being studied, and interest in finding general laws are characteristics of
   a. postpositivist research.
   b. constructivist research.
   c. interpretive research.
   d. postmodern research.

4. The statement, "Aptitude will be measured by the quantitative scale of the Scholastic Aptitude Test (SAT)," is an example of
   a. a theoretical law.
   b. an operationally defined construct.
   c. a constitutively defined construct.
   d. a hypothesis.

5. A study that tested a hypothesis derived from a theory about how brain chemistry affects short-term memory would be an example of
   a. basic research.
   b. applied research.
   c. postmodern research.
   d. descriptive research.

6. Case study findings
   a. have no generalizability.
   b. can be generalized to the defined population that they represent.
   c. can be generalized to a population defined by the researcher, but not to a population defined by readers of the research report.
   d. can be generalized to other similar cases.

7. Constructivist researchers would question the practice of quantification in the social sciences on the grounds that
   a. quantifiable aspects of social phenomena tend to be unimportant.
   b. numerical values of a variable can have different meanings for different individuals.
   c. quantification of social phenomena assumes that these phenomena are constant across time and settings.
   d. all of the above.

8. Of the following claims, the one that postmodernists most likely would endorse is that
   a. scientific research is a more valid form of inquiry than literature for understanding the human condition.
   b. scientific research is not a more valid form of inquiry than literature for understanding the human condition.
   c. collaboration by scientists and artists will yield genuine progress in understanding the human condition.
   d. non-Western cultures are more likely to advance understanding of the human condition because they are not grounded in positivist assumptions.

9. According to the refutability standard proposed by Karl Popper, knowledge claims
   a. can be disproved, but not proved.
   b. can be proved, but not disproved.
   c. can be proved only by hypothesis testing.
   d. can be proved or disproved, but only if the knowledge claim is not value-laden.

10. Scientific realists believe that
    a. interpretations are the primary causal agent in social reality.
    b. social reality consists of layers of causal structures.
    c. Newtonian physics provides the best model for understanding causation in social reality.
    d. causation is an unnecessary concept in developing theories of social behavior.

PART II

Planning a Research Study

Reduced to its most essential elements, research is a process of identifying something unknown and then collecting data to make it known. Chapter 2 helps you with the first step of that process: identifying something unknown that, if investigated, would contribute significantly to the knowledge base of education. We show you how to frame the something unknown, called a *research problem*, as an explicit set of research hypotheses, questions, or objectives that you will investigate.

After identifying a research problem, you will need to develop a plan for investigating it. The plan should cover such matters as selection of a sample or case, administration of tests or other measures, and choice of statistics for data analysis. If you are doing the study as a requirement for an advanced degree, the plan must be written as a formal research proposal and submitted to your thesis or dissertation committee for its approval. Chapter 2 shows you how to write the proposal and how to use it as the basis for writing a final report—a thesis, a dissertation, a journal article, or a professional paper—of the completed study.

You have a legal and ethical obligation to use certain procedures to ensure that the persons whom you plan to study are protected from physical and psychological harm. Chapter 3 describes these procedures, which typically must be planned and approved before you start collecting data. It also describes steps you can take to solicit and maintain the cooperation of research participants and to build a positive relationship with the site where you will conduct research.

Educational researchers contribute their findings to build a collective knowledge base that informs professional practice and theory development. Chapter 4 shows you how to conduct a comprehensive review of the literature about a research problem in order to determine the existing knowledge base and unresolved issues. The findings of the literature review will constitute a significant part of your research proposal.

CHAPTER 2

The Research Process: From Proposal to Final Report

OVERVIEW

Careful planning is the key to conducting a worthwhile, sound research study. In this chapter, we describe how to identify a research problem that is likely to contribute to knowledge about education, and how to develop the problem into a detailed proposal that will be accepted by your thesis or dissertation committee, a funding agency, or other reviewers. We also illustrate how a well-written proposal serves as the initial draft of several chapters of a thesis or dissertation. Finally, we explain how to report a completed study as a journal article or paper at a professional meeting.

OBJECTIVES

After studying this chapter, you should be able to

1. Distinguish between the desire to contribute to personal knowledge and the desire to contribute to research knowledge in selecting a problem for a research project.
2. Describe the characteristics of a theory-based research project.
3. Describe possible reasons for doing a study that replicates and extends previous research.
4. Explain the advantages of doing a thesis or dissertation study as part of a team project.
5. List the sections of a typical research proposal, and describe the topics included in each section.
6. Distinguish between directional hypotheses, null hypotheses, research questions, research objectives, and statements of purpose in a proposal.
7. Explain why it is advantageous to conduct a pilot study prior to a full-scale, formal study.
8. List the chapters of a typical thesis or dissertation, and describe the topics covered in each chapter.
9. State the factors involved in selecting a journal to which to submit your research study for publication.
10. Explain why and how one might submit a research paper for presentation at a professional meeting.

Introduction

A research study typically has five major stages.

Stage 1: Identifying a significant research problem. Problems to study may come readily to mind, but they may not be ones that contribute significantly to research knowledge or to the improvement of practice. Another possibility is that the problem you identify is significant, but you lack the resources or expertise necessary to study it. In the next section of this chapter, we describe several methods for identifying a research problem that is both significant and feasible to study.

Stage 2: Writing a research proposal. The purpose of a research proposal is to describe the problem you wish to study and how you plan to study it. This process compels you to think through and record on paper your research design (e.g., conducting an experiment or doing a case study) and the procedures that you will use to select a sample, collect data, and analyze the data. It is much easier to find flaws in a written proposal and correct them than it is to discover and correct flaws after you start collecting data. Also, university and college faculty generally require you to write a proposal for thesis or dissertation research. They must approve the proposal before you can start collecting data. If you are seeking financial support from a funding agency, a formal proposal almost certainly will be required. Much of this chapter concerns the proposal-writing process.

Stage 3: Conducting a pilot study. The purpose of a pilot study is to develop and try out data-collection methods and other procedures (e.g., training procedures to be used in an experiment). Problems can be identified and solved now more easily than when the main study is underway. We describe the features of a pilot study later in the chapter.

Stage 4: Conducting the main study. In the main study, you collect and analyze the actual data that you will report in your dissertation or other document. This process is challenging, but you should be able to complete it successfully if you have prepared a good research proposal, conducted a pilot study, and revised the proposal based on what you have learned from this work.

Stage 5: Preparing a report. If you are a graduate student, this report most likely will constitute your master's thesis or doctoral dissertation. (Hereafter, we refer to both types of reports as *dissertations* because they are similar in essential respects.) In addition, you may wish to report your findings in a journal article or in a presentation at a professional meeting. We describe how to prepare these reports at the end of the chapter.

Depending on the study, the five stages delineated above may overlap, or might occur in a different order. For example, many qualitative studies involve an emergent research design: Some data are collected (the fourth stage), and analyses of these data are used to further develop the proposal (the second stage). Another variation is for a pilot study (third stage) to be done prior to writing the research proposal (second stage), or not at all.

Reading this chapter alone will not prepare you to identify your research problem and write a proposal. First you will need to develop an understanding of the research methods and designs covered in this book. Studying this chapter will contribute to this understanding because it provides an overview—an advance organizer, as it were—for the entire educational research enterprise.

Identifying a Research Problem

The imagination and insight that goes into defining the research problem usually determines the ultimate value of a research study more than any other factor. For this reason, you should devote a substantial amount of time to selecting the research problem that you will investigate in your dissertation study. It is entirely reasonable to spend several months or longer thinking about potential problems to study, talking to others about them, and reviewing relevant literature before you reach closure on your research problem and the methods for studying it.

The very process of seeking a research problem to study is an important step in your professional development. At the outset, you may not be able to generate any problems, or you may conclude from your initial exploration of the literature that research has already solved all the problems in education. Your first ideas for research may appear naive after you study the sophisticated formulations of experienced researchers. As you continue reading, though, your own thinking will become more sophisticated, and the problems you frame for study will be better grounded in the existing knowledge base and more likely to advance it.

One reason that students often seize upon a trivial or vague research problem is that they spend too long a time in their graduate program before starting the search for a suitable research problem. They have had years of experience in taking courses; thus the coursework involved in graduate school is familiar, and they are confident that they can complete it successfully. In contrast, the research training component of a graduate program generally is new and often difficult. In fact, every university has a lengthy list of "all-buts," or as they sometimes are called, *Ab.Ds*—students who have completed "All but Dissertation." To avoid being an "all-but," you should gain some insight into research and begin your search for a suitable problem as soon as possible after starting graduate work, even if you do not plan to carry out the study until after you finish your coursework and comprehensive examinations.

In looking for a research problem, bear in mind some of the possible benefits of conducting your research study to prepare you for your profession. Because of the extensive reading you must do for your study, you will be building a sizable fund of knowledge. Therefore, it makes sense to develop a research study in an area that is directly related to your professional goals. For example, if you are attracted to staff development as a possible career, you might consider identifying a research problem having to do with this aspect of educational practice. Also, consider the fact that if you conduct a study on a significant problem, you may be able to publish your findings in a refereed journal or present them at a professional meeting. These contributions to the field will enhance your professional status and your qualifications for position openings.

Reading the Research Literature

Some beginning researchers select a problem to study simply because it is of interest to them and they want to learn more about it. They might consider these reasons to be sufficient justification for doing the study. However, there is another criterion to consider: the likely contribution of the proposed study to research knowledge.

Research knowledge is not the same thing as personal knowledge. Both types of knowledge are valuable, but they serve different purposes and must satisfy different standards. Research knowledge is represented in journals, books, and other publications that are judged to be reputable by professional researchers, including the professors who are charged with the responsibility of approving dissertations. Also, research knowledge is cumulative, in the sense that readers of research are interested in determining how a given study relates to and contributes to what is already known about the problem that was studied. Therefore, if a researcher grounds her study only in her personal interests and goals and ignores the research literature, the "gatekeepers" (e.g., professors on dissertation committees and journal editors) will not be able to judge whether and how the study contributes to research knowledge.

It is perfectly acceptable to start the process of identifying a research problem by examining your personal interests and goals. Once you have done so, though, you must make an extensive study of the literature. In the process, you should ask and answer such questions as, Has research on this problem been conducted previously? If so, what has been learned? What more can I contribute to what is already known? Are the methods that I intend to use worse than, as good as, or better than the methods used by other researchers? Is my research problem significant, or are there more compelling research problems that should be addressed?

Prior to studying the literature in a problem area that interests you, you will need to know how the educational literature is organized and how to access it. Chapter 4 provides this information. For example, we list various sources of existing reviews of the literature. If you can locate a published review in your area of interest, it will help you develop an initial understanding of what types of research have been done and how the resulting knowledge is organized. We also list indexes that will help you identify relevant primary sources, that is, reports of research and of theory development by the original investigators.

In reading the literature, keep in mind that researchers often mention problems in need of investigation at the end of their reports. For example, consider these statements in published research articles:

1. From a study to determine whether programs offering support, guidance, and orientation for beginning teachers have a positive effect on the retention of these teachers in the schools that employed them and in the teaching profession:

   There are many pressing policy questions that warrant investigation and for which existing research has of yet shed little light. Is there a significant difference in effectiveness between induction and mentoring programs depending upon how the mentors are selected, kind of training they are given, and the degree to which they are compensated for their participation? How does the quantity and timing of contact between new teachers and their mentors impact the effectiveness of the mentorship experience? Is there an optimum program length for induction and mentoring programs, beyond which additional time is of diminishing value? Are induction and mentoring programs particularly helpful for new teachers whose formal preparation is relatively weak, or are they helpful regardless of the quality of preclassroom preparation?[1]

2. From a study of what Japanese and U.S. teachers think about as they construct mathematics lessons for students in fifth- to eighth-grade classrooms:

   In this study, the Japanese contrast enabled us to clarify the foci of U.S. teachers' lesson construction (i.e., content over process), something that would have been difficult to do if we had examined U.S. teachers only. Using a cross-national approach in future research, which does not have to be limited to comparing U.S. and Japanese teachers, seems important.[2]

3. From a study of public school choice from the perspective of parents:

   This study showed that there is a parent standpoint from which to research educational institutions and parent involvement practices . . . . I do recognize that in many ways, the parent standpoint presented in this one analysis is not inclusive enough. There are many parent voices and stories left unstudied that if heard would add to an even deeper understanding of our educational institutions.[3]

1. Smith, T. M., & Ingersoll, R. M. (2004). What are the effects of induction and mentoring on beginning teacher turnover? *American Educational Research Journal, 41*(3), 681–714. Quote appears on p. 707.
2. Fernandez, C., & Cannon, J. (2005). What Japanese and U.S. teachers think about when constructing mathematics lessons: A preliminary investigation. *Elementary School Journal, 105*(5), 481–498. Quote appears on p. 495.
3. André-Bechely, L. (2005). Public school choice at the intersection of voluntary integration and not-so-good neighborhood schools: Lessons from parents' experiences. *Educational Administration Quarterly, 41*(2), 267–305. Quote appears on p. 301.

Any one of these statements can be the stimulus for a research study. Some of our students have identified their idea for a dissertation project by coming across just such a statement in the course of reading the literature in their area of interest. Furthermore, by reading the literature, they have obtained excellent ideas for suitable research designs and procedures to address the problem that they selected for study.

Doing Theory-Based Research

An approach that is likely to produce an outstanding research study is to formulate a research problem that will test a theory that you or someone else developed. As we explained in Chapter 1, a theory is an explanation of observed events in terms of constructs and laws that specify how the constructs are related to each other. When a construct is thought of as a characteristic that can vary in quantity or quality, it is called a *variable*.

Theory-based research usually consists of testing a hypothesis (a speculation about the relationship between two or more variables) that is derived from a theory. A **hypothesis** is a testable prediction about observable phenomena that is based on a theory's constructs and their presumed relationships.

Example of Theory-Based Research

Roger Goddard, Scott Sweetland, and Wayne Hoy used theory to guide their research on factors affecting student achievement in urban elementary schools.[4] The primary factor of interest was academic emphasis, which they defined as "the extent to which the school is driven by a quest for academic excellence."[5] The researchers drew upon social cognitive theory to predict how a school's level of academic emphasis would affect students' academic achievement.[6]

Essentially, social cognitive theory seeks to explain how particular factors shape individual and group perceptions, and how these perceptions, in turn, shape individual and group behavior. An important construct in the theory is *agency*, which refers to the tendency of individuals to pursue a course of action to achieve particular goals. For example, a school principal might have a sense of agency that drives her to pursue academic excellence. According to social cognitive theory, certain kinds of experiences can influence the principal's perceptions and thereby change her sense of agency and self-efficacy. Goddard, Sweetland, and Hoy use the example of a school staff that perceives another school experiencing success with a program for at-risk students. The staff can learn vicariously from this experience and can engage in self-regulation by changing their previous practices to those of the successful program. (Vicarious learning and self-regulation are central constructs of social cognitive theory.) These perceptual and behavioral changes, in turn, can produce improvements in students' academic achievement.

Reasoning in this way from social cognitive theory, the researchers hypothesized that teachers' perceptions of school norms and expectations involving academic emphasis will influence their work behavior and, subsequently, student learning. In the researchers' own words: "we hypothesize that the academic emphasis of a school is positively associated with differences between schools in student-level achievement in both reading and mathematics."[7] They tested the hypothesis with a sample of 45 elementary schools. Teachers

---

4. Goddard, R. D., Sweetland, S. R., & Hoy, W. K. (2000). Academic emphasis of urban elementary schools and student achievement in reading and mathematics: A multilevel analysis. *Educational Administration Quarterly, 36*, 683–702.
5. Ibid., p. 686.
6. Bandura, A. (1986). *Social foundations of thought and action: A social cognitive theory.* Upper Saddle River, NJ: Prentice Hall.
7. Goddard et al., Academic emphasis. p. 690.

completed a measure of academic emphasis, and the school district provided data on student achievement in mathematics and reading.

As hypothesized, Goddard, Sweetland, and Hoy found that academic emphasis was a significant predictor of between-school differences in student achievement in both mathematics and reading. The findings also provided support for social cognitive theory:

> The results provide initial support for Bandura's (1986, 1997) suggestion that the concepts and assumptions of social cognitive theory can be extended to organizations and are useful in examining school outcomes. We hasten to add that further testing of social cognitive theory in the schools is needed, but the current results are encouraging because our hypothesis was driven by this theory. We hope that the identification of the theoretical underpinnings of academic emphasis illuminates pathways to future research on school improvement and that school leaders can apply these ideas to make their schools better places for students to learn.[8]

Thus, a hypothesis derived from theory guided the design of the research study, the findings of which both improved educators' understanding of factors that improve student learning and strengthened the theory.

It is worth noting that the researchers stated their findings *supported* social cognitive theory, not *proved* it. Even if a number of studies produce evidence supporting a theory and no disconfirming evidence is found, a theory is never proved. As we explained in Chapter 1, researchers generally accept the argument of Karl Popper (a philosopher of science) that the possibility of disconfirming evidence in the future always exists. On the other hand, one study that produces disconfirming evidence calls for revision or rejection of the theory.

Advantages of Theory-Based Research

Theory-based research on educational phenomena has several advantages, irrespective of whether it involves the use of quantitative or qualitative methods. First, theory-based research usually yields important findings. Without a theory as the starting or end point, many studies address trivial questions or contribute nothing to the slow accumulation of knowledge needed for the advancement of a science of education. Second, a theory can provide a rational basis for explaining or interpreting the results of research. Studies without a theoretical foundation often produce results that the investigator is at a loss to explain. Such studies still can help in the development of a theory, but their impact on our understanding of the phenomena being studied is much less clear and immediate than that of research that is firmly based on existing theory or that discovers theory.

Replicating and Extending Previous Research

Another strategy for identifying a research problem is to replicate and extend the study of a problem that was investigated by other researchers. In the physical sciences, important studies always are replicated before their findings are accepted by the scientific community.

The importance of this strategy is illustrated by a study of replication research on the effectiveness of medical interventions.[9] J. P. Ioannidis examined 45 highly publicized, original-research studies published between 1990 and 2003 that claimed to have found evidence that a drug or other treatment worked. Nearly one-third of these drugs or treatments were not found to have the same effectiveness in subsequent replication studies: For 7 of the drugs or treatments, the replication studies obtained results contradictory to the original research study; and for another 7, the results were not as strongly positive as those found

---

8. Ibid., p. 699.
9. Ioannidis, J. P. (2005). Contradicted and initially stronger effects in highly cited clinical research. *Journal of the American Medical Association, 294*(2), 218–228.

in the original research study. Without replication research, some drugs or treatments might make their way into medical practice with no beneficial effects and possible harm to patients.

The need for replication is even more critical in education and other social science disciplines because studies often have weaknesses in methodology or very limited generalizability. Therefore, you might be able to make a valuable contribution by repeating, and improving upon, a research study that other researchers conducted.

We do not advocate a literal replication as a project for your dissertation, however. Dissertation committees generally expect students to carry out a research study that is original in some respect. Therefore, you should extend the study to be replicated in some significant way. The following are types of extensions that are likely to be worthwhile:

1. *To check the findings of a "breakthrough" study.* Occasionally a study is reported that produces new and surprising evidence, that reports findings which conflict with previous research, or that challenges a generally accepted theory. Research involving replication of such studies is useful because it helps support or disconfirm the validity of their findings and interpretations. If supported by replication, such studies often open up a new area of investigation or have a major impact upon educational practice.

An example of a breakthrough study that had a major impact on the educational community is one conducted by David Wiley and Annegret Harnischfeger.[10] They concluded from their data analyses that lengthening the school year by 10 days, increasing the school day to six hours, and raising the average daily attendance to 95 percent would bring about major achievement gains, including a 65 percent gain in reading comprehension and a 34 percent gain in mathematics achievement. Considerable controversy developed over the validity of Wiley and Harnischfeger's findings, thus creating an ideal situation for replication research. One such replication study was conducted by A. Daniels and E. Haller.[11] Daniels and Haller's analysis of data from one high school over a 10-year period suggested that students' mathematics achievement was negatively affected by the school's deliberate reduction in the amount of available classroom time, but that English achievement was not similarly affected.

2. *To check the validity of research findings across different populations.* The typical research study in education is carried out with a small sample of individuals representing a limited population. Without replication, the degree to which the findings from that study apply to other populations cannot be determined. For example, Charles Fisher and his colleagues studied the relationship between specific teacher behaviors and the achievement of second- and fifth-grade students in mathematics and reading.[12] These researchers found that teachers' use of academic monitoring was negatively related to reading achievement but positively related to mathematics achievement. They also found several teaching behaviors that were positively related to the achievement of fifth-grade students but negatively related to second-grade achievement.

These findings demonstrate the hazards of generalizing research findings across settings. Replication studies are necessary to determine the limits of generalizability. As evidence accumulates about situations where the findings generalize and where they

---

10. Wiley, D. E., & Harnischfeger, A. (1974). Explosion of a myth: Quantity of schooling and exposure to instruction: major educational vehicles. *Educational Researcher, 3*(4), 7–12.
11. Daniels, A. H., & Haller, E. J. (1981). Exposure to instruction, surplus time, and student achievement: A local replication of the Harnischfeger and Wiley research. *Educational Administration Quarterly, 17*, 48–68.
12. Fisher, C. W., Filby, N. N., Marleave, R., Cahen, L. S., Dishaw, M. M., Moore, J. E., & Berliner, D. C. (1978). *Teaching behaviors, academic learning time and student achievement: Final report of Phase III-B, Beginning Teacher Evaluation Study.* San Francisco: Far West Laboratory for Educational Research and Development.

do not, it may be possible to develop a theory to explain the pattern. For example, Fisher and colleagues found a situation where academic monitoring affected learning and a situation where it did not. With continued replication studies across different situations, a pattern of positive and negative findings might develop that would help us better understand the nature of academic monitoring. This understanding eventually could lead to the development of a formal theory of academic monitoring or to the strengthening of an existing theory.

3. *To check trends or change over time.* Many research results in the social sciences depend on particular historical circumstances. Thus, research findings that were valid 20 years ago may be invalid today. Replication is a useful tool for checking earlier findings and identifying trends. For example, James Baumann, James Hoffman, Ann Duffy-Hester, and Jennifer Ro conducted a modified replication of a major 1963 study of the status of reading instruction in U.S. public elementary schools.[13] They found some similarities. For example, teachers in both the 1960s and today provide explicit instruction in phonic analysis and also report that their greatest challenge is accommodating struggling and underachieving readers. However, they also found some differences. For example, today's teachers have an eclectic perspective about reading instruction, in contrast to the strong skills-based emphasis of the 1960s, and school and classroom libraries are more prevalent and better equipped now. According to the researchers, these changes represent a certain amount of progress, but challenges in reading instruction still remain. New replication studies will be needed in the years to come to determine how well these challenges have been met.

4. *To check important findings using different methodology.* In any research study, the soundness of the findings might be compromised by methodological flaws, such as the use of measures that yield scores having weak validity or reliability; experimental interventions of too brief duration; or uncontrolled variables. Thus, it is important to replicate studies using better methodology. This was the case in Thomas Goolsby's research study of differences between expert and novice music teachers at the middle- and high-school level.[14] Goolsby had conducted two previous studies of expert and novice music teachers to determine how they rehearsed students to play a band composition. However, he had not controlled for the composition the band rehearsed. Therefore, observed differences between expert and novice teachers could have been a function of the composition the teachers selected for rehearsal rather than a function of their teaching expertise.

In the replication study, all teachers rehearsed the same band composition. Thus, any observed differences between expert and novice teachers could not be attributed to differences in the band composition that was selected for rehearsal. The findings of the replication study generally were similar to the two previous studies, but several interesting disparities were also found.

5. *To develop more effective or efficient interventions.* Educators continually are searching for more effective and efficient versions of instructional programs or procedures. Thus, once researchers have demonstrated that a program or procedure has beneficial outcomes, they or other researchers often do replication-and-extension studies to determine whether it can be further improved. This was the case in a study conducted by David Arnold and his

13. Baumann, J. F., Hoffman, J. V., Duffy-Hester, A. M., & Ro, J. M. (2000). *The First R* yesterday and today: U.S. elementary reading instruction practices reported by teachers and administrators. *Reading Research Quarterly, 35,* 338–377.
14. Goolsby, T. W. (1999). A comparison of expert and novice music teachers' preparing identical band compositions: An operational replication. *Journal of Research in Music Education, 47,* 174–187.

colleagues.[15] The abstract of the published article explains the replication-and-extension process:

> G. J. Whitehurst et al. (1988) taught mothers specific interactive techniques to use when reading picture books with their preschool-age children. This intervention program, called *dialogic reading,* produced substantial effects on preschool children's language development. However, the costs of one-on-one training limit the widespread use of dialogic reading techniques. In this study the authors aimed to replicate and extend the results of the original study of dialogic reading by developing and evaluating an inexpensive videotape training package for teaching dialogic reading techniques. Mothers were randomly assigned to receive no training, traditional direct training, or videotape training. Results supported the conclusions of Whitehurst et al.: Dialogic reading had powerful effects on children's language skills and indicated that videotape training provided a cost-effective, standardized means of implementing the program.[16]

Many instructional interventions have been developed and tested in an expensive format. Replication-and-extension research is needed to further develop and test them to ensure that they are feasible, yet cost-effective in actual work settings.

Working on a Team Project

Some professors and research directors receive financial support to conduct educational research in the form of contracts and grants from federal agencies and private foundations. Their projects may be large enough to require a research team, in which case there might be an opportunity for a graduate student to be a team member. As a rule, the project director provides overall direction, but graduate students can conduct studies that fall within the project's scope of inquiry. For example, one of the authors (M. Gall) codirected a project that investigated the relationship between teachers' instructional practices in algebra classes. Two doctoral students participated in the design of the study and collected data for it. They framed their own research questions within the study, analyzed the database to answer them, and presented their findings as dissertations.[17]

Working on team projects has both advantages and disadvantages. Perhaps the most important advantage is that financial support usually is available for working on the project. This support might only cover paying for test administration or providing needed materials or clerical assistance. However, it might involve receiving a scholarship or research assistantship that is sufficient to meet your major expenses while you complete your graduate work. A team project also offers you an opportunity to participate in a larger, more sophisticated study than would be the case if you were working independently. You also have a chance to learn something about the dynamics of team research. This experience will help you if you have subsequent opportunities to direct, or to be a team member on, other research projects. You also can learn much from other members of the research team because each team member brings a different background of training and experience to the project.

Team research projects involve interdependency, which can be a disadvantage if one or more project members are uncooperative or irresponsible. Also, project members might

---

15. Arnold, D. H., Lonigan, C. J., Whitehurst, G. J., & Epstein, J. N. (1994). Accelerating language development through picture book reading: Replication and extension to a videotape training format. *Journal of Educational Psychology, 86,* 235–243.
16. Ibid., p. 235.
17. Erickson, D. K. (1986). The differential effects of teacher behavior on girls' and boys' achievement, attitudes, and future coursework plans in high school algebra classes. *Dissertation Abstracts International, 47*(11), 3960A. (UMI No. 8629554); Grace, D. P. (1986). Patterns of effective mathematics teaching for low-achieving high school students in beginning algebra classes: An aptitude-treatment interaction study. *Dissertation Abstracts International, 47*(11), 4010A. (UMI No. 8629557)

have incompatible goals. For example, it might be important for you to be finished by a certain date, but other members might have looser time lines. Disagreements about ownership of data and authorship of reports resulting from the study can arise, too. These and other problems can be avoided if you check the team's level of collegiality beforehand and if you reach agreements at the outset (preferably in writing) about how the project will be conducted and how conflicts will be resolved.

Preparing a Research Proposal

If you are ready to do dissertation research, your faculty committee most likely will require you to write a formal proposal, which they must approve before you can start collecting data. In the case of a quantitative research study, the proposal might need to be a highly detailed plan, in effect, a blueprint for the study. Once the proposal is approved, you can conduct the study, secure in the knowledge that if you execute the specified plan and write a technically sound report, the committee will approve the thesis or dissertation.

> ## Touchstones in Research
>
> Krathwohl, D. R., & Smith, N. L. (2004). *How to prepare a dissertation proposal: Suggestions for students in education and the social and behavioral sciences.* Syracuse, NY: Syracuse University Press.
>
> Locke, L. F., Spirduso, W. W., & Silverman, S. J. (1999). *Proposals that work: A guide for planning dissertations and grant proposals* (4th ed.). Thousand Oaks, CA: Sage.

If you plan to do a qualitative research study, it is unlikely that you will want or need such a detailed research proposal. In qualitative research, certain aspects of the research design are likely to be emergent, meaning that your initial experiences in the field will affect your plans for subsequent data collection. In our experience, dissertation committees have handled the emergent nature of qualitative studies by asking the student to prepare an initial proposal that is as complete as possible. If the proposal is approved, the student can collect data, but then must meet again with the committee at critical junctures during the fieldwork. In this way, the committee fulfills its supervisory role, and the student is protected from unanticipated criticism when submitting the final dissertation for the committee's approval.

Writing a thorough, carefully reasoned research proposal has several advantages. First, it compels you to state all your ideas in written form so they can be evaluated and improved upon by you and others. Second, the proposal can serve as a guide when you conduct the study. Otherwise, you will need to rely on memory and might forget important procedural details. Finally, a well-written, comprehensive proposal provides a head start on writing the dissertation. As we explain later in the chapter, a typical dissertation has much the same organization and content as a research proposal.

A research proposal typically contains the following sections: introduction, review of the literature, research design, research method, data analysis, human subjects protection, and time line. You should check with your faculty advisor or other source to determine whether your university department requires a different format.[18]

Introductory Section

Research proposals usually start with an introductory section that (1) states the research problem, (2) explains how the proposed study is grounded in the research literature, (3) suggests its potential contribution to research knowledge and educational practice, and (4) lists the research hypotheses, questions, or objectives that the study is designed to address. In short, the introductory section of the proposal should *sell* the reader on the idea that the study is worth doing.

---

18. Various software tools are available to help you in preparing a research proposal, dissertation, or other research report, including: *Methodologist's Toolchest* (http://www.ideaworks.com); *Endnote* (http://www.endnote.com); and *ProCite* (http://www.procite.com)

Research Hypotheses in Quantitative Research

As we explained earlier in the chapter, a hypothesis is a theory-based prediction about observed phenomena. If your study will test hypotheses, they should be stated in the introductory section of the proposal. Each hypothesis should be accompanied by a rationale that explains why it is plausible given the theory from which it was derived. For example, Donna Sundre and Anastasia Kitsantas conducted an experiment to determine the power of two theories to predict college students' performance on different test formats under different testing conditions.[19] The first theory, the self-regulation theory, specifies self-monitoring, motivational-belief, learning-strategy, and attribution constructs and their relationship to learning outcomes. The second is expectancy-value motivational theory, which specifies expectancy-of-success, goal-value, and affective constructs and their relationship to learning outcomes. (Because this theory was applied to a test-taking situation, the constructs were considered as aspects of "test-taking motivation.")

Sundre and Kitsantas developed four hypotheses about how students who varied in self-regulation and expectancy-value processes would perform on essay and multiple-choice tests under two different conditions: consequential (test score counts toward a course grade) and nonconsequential (does not count). A rationale for each hypothesis was carefully developed from the theories of self-regulation and expectancy-value motivation and then summarized in the statement of the two hypotheses. Their two hypotheses, involving predictions of student performance on the essay test under the two consequence conditions, are described below:

> Moving to the essay test conditions, it was predicted in the consequential essay condition that self-regulated strategies would predict significant variance but motivation would not. Previous research indicates that a complex task, such as writing an essay, benefits greatly from the use of self-regulation strategies. Test-taking motivation is not expected to predict performance in the consequential condition, because all students would be highly motivated and would react positively to the task. The fourth hypothesis indicated that in the non-consequential essay test performance, self-regulation strategies and test-taking motivation would explain significant variability in test performances. In this condition, despite the greater task demand of an essay performance, self-regulated learners would have greater opportunity to demonstrate learning, and those with higher test-taking motivation would react positively to the task, triggering willingness to display learning.[20]

In this example, the reader is provided two explicit hypotheses that can be supported or refuted by empirical data analysis. If supported, the hypotheses strengthen the theories as explanations and predictors of student learning in other instructional situations.

Hypotheses can be stated in two forms, directional and null. The **directional hypothesis** states the researcher's expectations about what the data will show, for example, which of two experimental treatments will yield superior results on an outcome measure. The following are examples of directional hypotheses:

1. There is a *positive* relationship between the number of older siblings and the social maturity scores of six-year-old children.
2. Children who attend preschool will make *greater* gains in first-grade reading achievement than comparable children who do not attend preschool.

19. Sundre, D. L., & Kitsantas, A. (2004). An exploration of the psychology of the examinee: Can examinee self-regulation and test-taking motivation predict consequential and non-consequential test performance? *Contemporary Educational Psychology, 29*(1), 6–26.
20. Ibid., pp. 11–12.

In contrast to the directional hypothesis, the **null hypothesis** states that no relationship exists between the variables studied, or no difference will be found between the experimental treatments. For example, in null form the aforementioned hypothesis could be stated thus: There will be no significant difference between children who attend preschool and children who do not attend preschool in their first-grade reading achievement gain scores. The null hypothesis usually does not reflect the researcher's expectations. It is used principally because it fits the logic of inferential statistics (described in Chapter 5).

Readers may be confused by the null hypothesis because it appears senseless to hypothesize the exact opposite of one's expectations. This is a disadvantage of the null form because the researcher's expectations, based as they are upon considerable insight into other research and theory, often make the study clearer to the person reading the research report. Some researchers overcome this problem by stating both a directional hypothesis, which reflects their expectations based on theory or previous research, and a null hypothesis, which is used in performing tests of statistical significance.

Research Hypotheses in Qualitative Research

As stated above, a quantitative researcher who is doing a theory-driven study will use hypotheses as the starting point for designing the research methodology. Qualitative research studies might be informed by a theoretical or epistemological framework, but formal hypotheses are not typically used to frame the study. An exception of a sort is qualitative research that is framed within grounded-theory methodology, which we explain in Chapters 1 and 14. In this qualitative research tradition, hypotheses are the outcome of the study rather than the initiators of it.

An example is a study by Patricia Cranton and Ellen Carusetta, who sought to understand what university faculty mean by the concept of "authentic teaching."[21] They collected observations and interviews of 22 faculty members over several years and then analyzed transcripts of what they observed and heard.

Cranton and Carusetta found five main categories into which the transcript data could be grouped: self, other, relationship, context, and critical reflection. Using these categories, they framed several hypotheses about authenticity in teaching, for example:

> . . . we would hypothesize that as an individual develops self-awareness, which continues for the course of a career, authenticity also develops.
> . . . we would hypothesize that a person who articulates a good awareness of others as human beings is more likely to show authenticity in teaching and that as this awareness develops, so does authenticity.
> . . . we hypothesize that a teacher who engages in critical reflection on self, other, relationships, and context is more likely to be working toward becoming authentic.[22]

The researchers conclude their report by stating, "We hope that the tentative hypotheses we have raised here about authenticity in teaching will both guide practice and suggest areas for research, development, and theorizing."[23] This statement illustrates how hypotheses are the end point—not the starting point, as in quantitative research—for a qualitative study using grounded-theory methodology.

---

21. Cranton, P., & Carusetta, E. (2004). Perspectives on authenticity in teaching. *Adult Education Quarterly, 55*(1), 5–22.
22. Ibid., pp. 19–21.
23. Ibid., p. 21.

Research Questions and Purposes

If a study is not designed to test hypotheses derived from a theory, you instead can state research questions, purposes, objectives, or goals. Depending on the study, it may be appropriate to use several of these formats. As with hypotheses, each question, purpose, or objective should be supported by a rationale. The reader needs to know why the researcher framed the question or purpose, and how research findings relating to it are likely to advance knowledge and improve educational practice.

An example of the use of research questions to frame a study is found in an investigation conducted by Joe Nichols.[24] The purpose of his study was to determine whether *block scheduling* in high schools would improve students' grade-point average (GPA). High schools traditionally have 6 to 8 classes, each covering a different subject, each day. In contrast, a 4-by-4 block schedule would have 4 classes per day, each for a longer period of time than the traditional 6 to 8 classes. Several variants of the 4-by-4 block schedule also can be tried. Nichols followed a group of high schools for a period of years before and after they adopted block scheduling. After reviewing the literature on block scheduling, Nichols stated:

> Specifically, the research questions guiding this study were:
>
> 1. Did student GPAs in English and language arts courses increase significantly when schools adopted block format scheduling structures?
> 2. Were GPAs for high- and low-income students affected differently after block-scheduling structures were implemented?
> 3. Were GPAs of minority and majority students affected differently after block-scheduling structures were implemented?[25]

Nichols's data analyses were directed to answering each of these three research questions.

Research questions can be phrased instead as objectives, goals, or purposes. Phrasing is more a matter of personal preference than anything else. An example of a goal statement used to frame a research investigation can be found in a study conducted by Mark Chapell and six co-researchers.[26] The goal statement is preceded by a brief summary of a literature review documenting the need for the study:

> On the basis of the empirical literature, it is clear that test anxiety is associated with reduced grade point average (GPA), but there are few large-scale studies reporting the relationship between test anxiety and GPA in undergraduates and none in graduate students. The main goal of this study, therefore, was to investigate the relationship between test anxiety and GPA in large samples of undergraduate and graduate students.[27]

The researchers also stated another goal for the study, but phrased it differently:

> Studies have consistently found that female students have significantly higher test anxiety than male students . . . . Given this consistent difference, this study also investigated sex differences in academic performance related to test anxiety.[28]

Chapell and his co-researchers used these goals to frame their research methodology and data analyses.

---

24. Nichols, J. D. (2005). Block-scheduled high schools: Impact on achievement in English and language arts. *Journal of Educational Research, 98*(5), 299–309.
25. Ibid., p. 301.
26. Chapell, M. S., Blanding, Z. B., Silverstein, M. E., Takahashi, M., Newman, B., Gubi, A., & McCann, N. (2005). Test anxiety and academic performance in undergraduate and graduate students. *Journal of Educational Psychology, 97*(2), 268–274.
27. Ibid., p. 268.
28. Ibid., pp. 268–269.

Literature Review Section

Although you might review many research reports and theoretical writings in developing your research problem, you typically will identify a few as most critical. These publications should be described in the introductory section of the research proposal as part of the rationale for the project. They can be discussed at greater length in the literature review section of the proposal, together with other relevant material, such as

1. The findings of other studies in the line of research that includes each critical study
2. The findings of studies in lines of research that have some degree of relevance to the proposed study
3. A critique of methods used in previous research
4. The conclusions drawn by researchers who previously have reviewed the literature relevant to your proposed study
5. Applications, if any, of previous research findings to professional practice

A thorough literature review that includes the topics listed above could be as long as, or longer than, the combined length of all the other sections of the proposal. This length is justified by the need to ground your research problem and methodology in a deep understanding of the existing knowledge base, as represented in the literature. It would be embarrassing to find after you have completed a study that you had overlooked previous research that, had you known about it beforehand, would have changed the way you framed your research problem or designed your methodology.

The process of conducting the review and writing a report of your findings in the research proposal is time-consuming. Your dissertation must include a substantial literature review, typically in its own chapter. By writing the review at the proposal stage, you will already have completed a significant part of the writing of the dissertation. Detailed procedures for reviewing the literature are described in Chapter 4.

Part IV of this book covers the major quantitative research designs: descriptive, causal-comparative, correlational, and experimental. Part V describes case study design and qualitative research designs grounded in various academic disciplines such as anthropology, philosophy, psychology, and sociology. You will need to propose a design for your study and describe how you will implement it in the particular setting that you have chosen to investigate. If you did not explain why you selected that design in the introductory section of the proposal, you should do so in the research design section.

Research Design Section

An example of a research design statement can be found in Jennifer Booher-Jennings's study of the Texas accountability system for student achievement.[29] Her qualitative research study sought to understand how teachers in one Texas school and the school district as a whole changed their policies and practices in response to the Student Success Initiative, which requires third-grade students to pass a state-mandated reading test to be promoted to the fourth grade. The Student Success Initiative is one element of the Texas accountability system.

29. Booher-Jennings, J. (2005). Below the bubble: "Educational triage" and the Texas Accountability System. *American Educational Research Jornal, 42*(2), 231–268.

To address her research question, Booher-Jennings needed a flexible research design that would enable her to identify the various interacting forces that influenced changes in the school's policies and practices, as she explains here:

> According to Yin (1994), the case study research strategy is fitting in circumstances in which "the boundaries between phenomenon and context are not clearly evident" (p. 13). Because the history, culture, and unique circumstances of a school mediate its response to external contingencies such as those associated with the Texas Accountability System, I used a case study design, enabling the school and district context to be taken into account.[30]

We describe Robert Yin's approach to case study design in Chapter 14. Specification of the research design influences in large part the researcher's choice of methods, which are described in the next section of the proposal.

Research Methods Section

The section on research methods should describe your sampling procedures, data-collection procedures, and any other procedures that are critical to your study.

Sampling procedures are described in Chapter 6. We explain there that it would be a mistake to select a sample (for a quantitative study) or case (for a qualitative study) simply because it is convenient to recruit for participation in the study. You need to use sound sampling logic instead. If you are proposing a quantitative study, you should explain how your sample is representative of a defined population. If you are proposing a qualitative study, you should explain why the case, or cases, that were selected are likely to yield significant insights about the phenomenon of interest.

In describing your data-collection procedures, you should identify each instrument (e.g., a test, a questionnaire, or an interview schedule), the variables it is designed to measure, its validity and reliability, and the steps that you will follow in using it. These matters are discussed in Chapter 7 (tests and self-report measures), Chapter 8 (questionnaires and interviews), and Chapter 9 (observation and content analysis). A common mistake is to mention a variable in the introductory section of the proposal but not to indicate how it will be measured when describing your data-collection procedures. The converse mistake is to introduce in the research method section a variable to be measured that was not mentioned in the introductory section.

If you are proposing a qualitative study, other data-collection procedures are relevant and should be described. We explain these procedures in Chapter 14. They include defining the focus of your data-collection efforts and checking your data for credibility, authenticity, and representativeness.

Any special procedures that you intend to use should be described in this section of the proposal. For example, if you plan to do an experiment that tests the effectiveness of an instructional method, you should describe the method in detail, how you propose to train the sample to use it, and how you plan to check whether the sample implemented it as intended. If you plan to do a qualitative study, you might find it necessary to specify your procedures for gaining entry into a field setting and for obtaining the cooperation of informants and other participants.

Data Analysis Section

You should develop a tentative plan for data analysis because it will have considerable bearing on the sample size you will need, the procedures for scoring tests or other measures, and the procedures for creating computer data files. If you give no thought to analysis until after

---

30. Ibid., p. 236.

the data are collected, you may find that it is impossible to analyze them in the way that you wish.

In writing this section of the proposal, you should consider listing all your hypotheses, questions, objectives, or purposes. Then you should indicate the data that will be needed to address each one, and the measures that will yield these data. Finally, describe the method that you will use to analyze the data. This process will serve as a useful check that you actually will be able to test your hypotheses, answer your questions, or accomplish your objectives or purposes when you move from planning to conducting the study.

Protection of Human Subjects Section

As we explain in Chapter 3, any research project involving the participation of human beings must be reviewed by an institutional review board (IRB). The purpose of the board's review is to ensure that the rights of research participants to confidentiality and freedom from harm are protected. The board may ask you to complete a separate set of forms on which you provide the requested information. You might find it necessary to append these forms to your research proposal and, in addition, to include a brief summary of your protection procedures in the body of the proposal.

If the research study involves significant risks to participants or involves vulnerable populations (e.g., handicapped children), the board probably will want to review the entire proposal in detail. We know of instances where the researcher needed to revise the proposal significantly because it contained insufficient information for the board to determine whether the potential benefits of the study outweighed its potential risks. (The risk–benefit ratio is an important criterion in reviewing a research proposal for human-subjects protection.)

Time Line Section

Your research proposal should include a time line that states each step of the study, the approximate date when it will be completed, and the estimated number of hours or days it will require. Creating this time line will help you think through the entire research process and alert you to possible problems, such as the following:

1. The institutional review board takes longer than expected to evaluate your plan for protecting human subjects or asks you to make time-consuming revisions that you did not anticipate.
2. To start your study in October, school officials must be contacted during the summer when they might be unavailable for various reasons.
3. The collection of pretest data for your study needs to occur before the experiment begins, but teachers and students are busy with state-mandated testing during the period of time that works best for you.
4. Several of the key informants that you identified for your study will only be available within certain time windows.
5. If you do not complete the thesis or dissertation by a given date, you might have to wait weeks or months to assemble the faculty committee that will evaluate it.

As you identify such problems and constraints in your time line, you can make appropriate adjustments in your planning. This is far easier than trying to solve these problems after data collection has begun.

A time line that includes only the major steps of the planned study might be adequate. The following is an example (anticipated completion dates in parentheses):

1. Faculty committee reviews proposal. (early September)
2. IRB reviews proposal. (late September)

3. Proposal is revised based on feedback from the faculty committee and IRB. (mid-October)
4. Final approval to start data collection is obtained from the faculty committee and IRB. (end of October)
5. Data are collected. (middle of January)
6. Data are analyzed. (late February)
7. First draft of report is completed and submitted to faculty committee for feedback. (end of April)
8. Final draft of report is completed and defended before the faculty committee. (late May)
9. Final revisions are completed, and the dissertation is submitted to the Graduate School. (early June)

Some research procedures are sufficiently complex that it pays to create a time line for them to ensure that you do not omit a step or run out of time. For example, the development of a psychometrically sound test, attitude scale, or other measure involves many steps (see Chapter 7). Creating a time line for the development process will help to ensure that you do not omit a step or allot insufficient time to complete it.[31]

Conducting a Pilot Study

Whenever possible, you should include a pilot study as part of your research project. A **pilot study** involves small-scale testing of the procedures that you plan to use in the main study, and revising the procedures based on what the testing reveals. For many quantitative and qualitative research studies, two or three participants may be sufficient. An exception would be a pilot study for the purpose of developing an instrument such as an achievement test or attitude scale. Several hundred participants may be necessary in order to develop and refine the instrument to the point that it has satisfactory measurement properties.

In some cases, the pilot study can be carried out after the research proposal has been approved by the dissertation committee. In this case, a brief description of the planned pilot study in the proposal should be sufficient. In other cases, you will want to conduct the pilot study first and describe what you learned from it in your research proposal.

For example, suppose your research problem involves trying out a new procedure for improving students' reading comprehension. You have derived the procedure from a theory of reading comprehension, but there is no precedent for the procedure in the research literature. A dissertation committee might question whether the effort of a full-scale, formal study is necessary as an initial tryout. A pilot study can be done to determine whether the procedure has merit and to correct obvious flaws. If the pilot study indicates that the procedure has merit, this finding and the evidence supporting it can be included in the research proposal as part of the justification for conducting a formal, full-scale study of its effectiveness.

Using the Proposal in Writing the Dissertation

If you have written a detailed research proposal, you will have done much of the work of writing the dissertation. (As we stated above, thesis research generally is similar to dissertation research, so our remarks about writing a dissertation also apply to writing a thesis.)

Touchstones in Research

Meloy, J. M. (2001). *Writing the qualitative dissertation: Understanding by doing* (2nd ed.). Mahwah, NJ: Erlbaum.

Rudestam, K. E., & Newton, R. R. (2000). *Surviving your dissertation: A comprehensive guide to content and process* (2nd ed.). Thousand Oaks, CA: Sage.

---

31. PERT (Program Evaluation and Review Technique) is a sophisticated technique for time planning. An example of its use is presented in: Foster, C., & Lent, J. R. (1986). Application of Program Evaluation and Review Technique (PERT) within a curriculum development project. *Journal of Special Education Technology, 8,* 47–58.

FIGURE 2.1

Organization of a Dissertation Reporting an Educational Research Study

Front Matter

Title page
Preface and Acknowledgments
Table of contents
List of tables
List of figures

Body of the Dissertation

Chapter 1. Introduction
    a. General statement of the problem
    b. Significance of the study
    c. Research hypotheses, questions, objectives, or purposes
Chapter 2. Review of the literature
    a. Review of previous research and opinion
    b. Interpretive summary of the current state of knowledge
Chapter 3. Research method
    a. Research design
    b. Sample selection and procedures for human subject protection
    c. Measures
    d. Other procedures (e.g., description of treatment conditions)
    e. Time line
Chapter 4. Results
    a. Overview of statistical procedures
    b. Description of results for each hypothesis, question, objective, or purpose
    c. Supplemental analyses
Chapter 5. Discussion
    a. Interpretation of each result
    b. Limitations of the study
    c. Implications for future research
    d. Implications for practice (if applicable)

Back Matter

Bibliography
Appendixes

The similarity between the proposal and the dissertation is evident in the dissertation outline shown in Figure 2.1. The first three chapters correspond to the topics and organization of a research proposal.

You should check with your dissertation committee to determine whether they wish you to use a different format or different chapter labels from what is shown in Figure 2.1. Also, keep in mind that the organization of a dissertation reporting a qualitative study may vary somewhat from that shown in Figure 2.1. (We discuss reporting style for qualitative research in Chapter 14.) For example, you may wish to report the findings for each case in a separate chapter, rather than combining all the findings into one chapter, which is the standard format for a quantitative research study.

It is not desirable or necessary to wait until all data have been collected and analyzed before starting to write the dissertation. There are likely to be some periods of time when you are extremely busy collecting or analyzing data, and other periods of time when you must sit and wait. These lulls can be used to revise the research proposal so that they form the first three chapters of the dissertation.

It may seem premature to learn about writing dissertations, journal articles, and papers (discussed below) before you have written your first research proposal. However, this learning process is worthwhile because it gives you a picture of the complete research process—from identifying a problem to reporting your findings. Thus, your initial steps are more likely to be pointed in a direction that will lead to your ultimate goal, that is, making a contribution to research knowledge about education.

We consider general format considerations below and then describe each section of the dissertation. We emphasize issues and problems that, in our experience, commonly arise in dissertation writing.

Format

Touchstones in Research

Publication Manual of the American Psychological Association, (5th ed.). (2001). Washington, DC: American Psychological Association.

APA Style Helper (Version 3.0) [CD-ROM]. (2001). Washington, DC: American Psychological Association.

Publication Manual of the American Psychological Association Web site: http://www.apastyle.org

Some universities prepare a special style manual for graduate students, whereas others refer students to a standard style manual. The most commonly used of the standard manuals is the *Publication Manual of the American Psychological Association.* You should follow carefully whatever manual you are asked to use. It reflects poorly on your scholarship to make errors in style, especially in your citations. If you hire someone to type your dissertation, you should check that this person knows the style that you are required to use.

It is helpful to ask your dissertation chairperson to identify several outstanding dissertations recently completed at your institution. An examination of these dissertations, together with the prescribed style manual, will give you most of the information needed to satisfy dissertation requirements. Also, study of the dissertations will give you an idea of your chairperson's standards and expectations.

A common problem in writing a dissertation or other research report is determining the proper tense to use. The general rule is to use the past tense to describe events that occurred at a point in time prior to the writing of the report. For example, you might write: "Sixty students were selected from a local school district . . ."; "Harber (1968) found in her study that . . ."; "The Stanford Achievement Test was developed to measure . . ."; "A *t* test was done. . . ." Each statement refers to an event or activity that occurred prior to the writing of the report.

The present tense is used to refer to assertions that continue to be true at the time the report is written. For example, you might write: "Research has shown consistently that inserted questions in text facilitate retention of the text content." The research has already occurred; hence, the past tense ("has shown") is used. We can presume that the relationship between inserted questions and retention continues to be true beyond the observations made by the researchers; hence, the present tense ("facilitate") is used. Similarly, you would write, "the Stanford Achievement Test measures various aspects of academic performance" because this feature of the test continues to be true at the time the report is written. Also, you would state that "Table 2 shows that . . ." because the table continues to perform a function. The table did not show a set of results just at one point in time. By the same logic, you would state that "this *t* value is statistically significant" because the results of a statistical significance test continue to be true beyond the point that the test was performed.

Front Matter

As shown in Figure 2.1, the front matter includes the title page, the preface and acknowledgments, a table of contents, a list of tables, and a list of figures.

The dissertation title should be brief, yet descriptive. It should incorporate words that other researchers are likely to use as descriptors in searching ERIC or other indexes to the literature (see Chapter 4). Suppose, for example, that a researcher has done an experiment comparing the achievement gains of sixth-grade students who used computers while learning American history with the achievement gains of a matched group of students who did not use computers. An appropriate title would be *An Experiment Comparing Conventional and Computer-Augmented Instruction in a Sixth-Grade American History Curriculum.* This title is brief, yet it gives the reader a good sense of the study's purpose. Furthermore, someone who is using such literature-search descriptors as *computer instruction, history instruction, history curriculum, elementary school,* or *experiment* would be likely to come across it.

Introductory Chapter

If the introductory section of the research proposal is well written, it can be elaborated into the first chapter of the dissertation. Both pieces of writing cover essentially the same topics.

Some dissertations start with pages of background information before stating the research problem. This information is meaningless to readers, because they do not know why they are expected to read it. We recommend instead that you state the research problem within the first two paragraphs and then proceed to present relevant background material.

The introductory chapter of some dissertations includes a separate section that presents definitions of technical terms that are central to the study. One problem with this approach is that the terms are defined out of context. Another problem is that if this section comes at the end of the chapter (as it often does), the reader is deprived of these definitions while reading the earlier parts of the chapter. We recommend that you define each term the first time it is used in the dissertation. There is no harm in repeating the definitions again if you wish to present all technical terms in one location, possibly in a glossary that appears as a dissertation appendix.

Literature Review Chapter

If you write a comprehensive review of the literature as part of your research proposal, you can use it as the literature review chapter of the dissertation.

Some dissertations fail to make a connection between the studies that are reviewed and the researcher's study. You do not want the reader wondering how the reviewed studies relate to your study. Therefore, you need to continually show how each set of studies, each theory, or each methodological flaw in previous research influenced the design of your study. Some researchers make these connections at the very end of the chapter, but that is too late.

Another pitfall to avoid in writing a literature review is that of presenting each study in essentially the same way. For example, some researchers treat each article in a separate paragraph and start each article with the name of the researchers who wrote it. Also, they devote the same amount of space to each study without regard to its importance or relevance. This type of review is tiresome to read and usually does not provide a good understanding of what is known about the research problem.

If you are reviewing many studies on the same problem or topic, it is helpful to organize them into a table. The first step is to decide which features of the studies to abstract, for example: nature of the sample, procedures or treatments, dependent variables, and statistical results for each variable. The next step is to review each study and write a capsule description of each feature. Finally, these descriptions are organized into a table. The advantages of this method are its concise presentation style and the ease with which studies can be compared. Table 2.1 presents a section from a large table of this type that was prepared by Ron Thorkildsen for a literature review in a dissertation study of social skills

TABLE 2.1

Summary of Research on Social Skills Training Programs for Mildly Handicapped Children

Study Number/ Authors	Social Skills Taught	Subjects/ Design	Type of Assessment	Training Techniques	Maintenance Training/ Assessment	Generalization Training/ Assessment	Results
(1) Ballard, Corman, Gottlieb, & Kauman (1977)	Cooperative interaction	N = 37 EMR grades 3, 4, & 5 Group design	Sociometric nomination	Cooperative groups formed	No training specified	In natural environment with nonhandicapped peers	1. Peer acceptance of experimental group increased and peer rejection decreased more than controls 2. Acceptance of controls decreased and rejection increased 3. Acceptance of experimental subjects was higher and rejection was lower by peers in second activity group than controls 4. Acceptance of experimental subjects by classmates who did not participate with them in group activity was higher after intervention than acceptance of controls by classmates
(2) Berler, Gross, & Drabman (1982)	1. Eye contact 2. Initiating social interactions 3. Praising 4. Responding to criticism 5. Making requests	N = 3 LD 8–10 years Single-subject design	1. Sociometric rating 2. Behavior observation 3. Role-play tests	1. Coaching 2. Modeling (videotape) 3. Behavioral rehearsal 4. Feedback	No training One-month follow-up	Natural role-playing situations	1. Increased use of appropriate skills during role playing 2. Performance maintained above baseline levels during follow-up 3. Performance did not generalize to natural school setting 4. Peer acceptance did not change

Source: Adapted from Table 1 on p. 14 in: Thorkildsen, R. J. (1984). An experimental test of a microcomputer/videodisc program to develop the social skills of mildly handicapped elementary students. *Dissertation Abstracts International, 45*(12), 3614A. (UMI No. 8502026)

training for mildly handicapped children. (Thorkildsen's table includes 18 studies, two of which are shown in Table 2.1.) Note that the table concisely presents a great deal of information about each study, and it facilitates comparisons between studies.

Research Method Chapter

In a good research proposal, the research methods will be described in detail. If so, it will be easy to expand this section of the proposal into a chapter of the dissertation. Of course, if the research design and procedures change once the study is underway, the research methods section needs to be revised to reflect what actually occurred.

In the research method chapter of dissertations, the main problems we have seen are insufficient detail and vagueness. Your description should be such that the reader has a clear, complete picture of all your procedures during the course of the study. This is a difficult goal to accomplish because, as the researcher, you are close to the study and may not see clearly all that needs to be made explicit. Therefore, it is advisable to give a draft of this chapter to a few colleagues and to ask them to identify anything they find to be confusing or incomplete.

Results Chapter

The results chapter of a dissertation presents the research findings, but does not discuss them; this task is left for Chapter 5.

General procedures for processing and analyzing the research data can be described at the beginning of the chapter. For example, you may have decided to remove some of the research participants from the database because they had missing data on too many variables. This decision affects some or all of the data analyses, and so it is appropriate to discuss it at the outset of the chapter. Other matters of general relevance are the computer programs used to analyze the data, transformations of scores to make them amenable to statistical analysis, and the organization of the chapter.

One of the best ways to present the results of statistical or qualitative analyses is to organize them around the study's hypotheses, questions, or objectives. Each hypothesis, for example, would be stated in the same form as it was presented in the introductory chapter of the dissertation. Then all findings pertinent to this hypothesis would be presented. If the study tested five hypotheses, there would be five sections of the chapter, each dealing with a separate hypothesis.

A useful approach to preparing the results chapter is to start by putting the results for each hypothesis, question, or objective in a table or figure. These graphic displays present results more clearly and economically than is possible in text presentation. After studying each table or figure, you can write a paragraph or two explaining what it contains and drawing the reader's attention to noteworthy findings.

You should avoid discussing every entry in the table or figure, whether significant or not. This style of presentation is boring, and it defeats the purpose of using tables and figures. The *Publication Manual of the American Psychological Association* explains the distinguishing features of tables and figures, and provides detailed instructions for constructing them.

Often the results of the planned analyses will suggest questions or hypotheses that were not part of the original dissertation proposal. If the available data can be used to address them, it is entirely appropriate to do supplemental analyses and to report them in a separate section of the results chapter. In certain situations, it even is appropriate to report supplemental analyses in the discussion chapter. For example, you may suggest an alternative explanation for one of your results in this chapter, and you may find that you can analyze some of your data to determine whether the explanation is viable.

Similar principles of presentation apply to the analysis of qualitative data. The results of the analyses can be organized according to the study's hypotheses, questions, or objectives. If the study involved a set of case studies, the analyses for each case can be presented separately. If possible, each case presentation should be organized similarly in order to facilitate comparisons between them.

The results of a statistical analysis can be presented concisely in a table and a few paragraphs of text. In a qualitative research study, however, the analysis of a case may require many pages of text. If you have studied multiple cases, you should consider making each the subject of a separate chapter. For example, Jane Njoora conducted a study of teenage mothers attending a high school that had a special program designed for their needs.[32] She described each of her sample of seven students in a separate chapter, with each student presented as a separate case in approximately 9 pages. A separate chapter was devoted to "lessons" that Njoora learned from the program director.

A different reporting style is used for case study findings than for statistical findings. The style relies on literary conventions such as story telling, vivid description, and a subjective point of view. For example, Njoora states, "I tell the teenage mothers' stories as they narrated them to me."[33] In presenting each mother as a separate case, she starts by sharing her own impressions of them. She then presents her observational and interview results within categories that are similar across cases. For example, the first case has these categories: early upbringing, early school experiences, school experiences in the teenage-mothers program, relationship with her boyfriend, the student's reflections as a young mother, and her needs, supports, and interpretation of the supports she is receiving. We discuss this type of reporting style in Chapter 14.

Discussion Chapter

The last chapter of a dissertation usually includes a brief summary of the research problem and method, an interpretation of each result, and a discussion of the limitations of the study and the implications of the findings.

A key task in writing the discussion chapter is to identify and interpret the important results. In examining each result, you should ask yourself such questions as: Is this an important result, and if so, why? Is it consistent with the results of previous research? If not, why not? Is there an existing theory that can explain the result? Does the result suggest the need to modify an existing theory? Are there alternative explanations of the result? Is one alternative explanation more plausible than others? Does the result merit further investigation to clarify it? If so, what form might such investigation take?

Your answers to these questions will be of great interest to other researchers for several reasons, including the fact that you were an eyewitness to the data-collection process. As an eyewitness, you have a better feeling for what the data mean than do other researchers, who must rely on your report for an understanding of what happened.

In discussing the study's methodological limitations, you should note problems that occurred in sampling procedures, instrumentation, data collection, and data analysis. Some of the problems might be inherent in the research design, whereas others might have

32. Njoora, J. G. (2003). Listening to the voice of school-going teenage mothers: A case study of their needs and supports (doctoral dissertation, University of Oregon, 1993). *Dissertation Abstracts International, 64* (08A). 2837
33. Ibid., p. 91.

occurred in the execution of the study. If an observed result was contrary to prediction, you should consider whether it was due to methodological flaws.

It is desirable to add a section on the implications of the findings for practice, if there are such implications. You can present speculations here that would be out of place in the results chapter.

Also desirable is a section that suggests questions for further research. The reason for this recommendation is that your experience in doing a study has put you in a good position for identifying the important questions that should be investigated next. Other researchers can combine your judgments with their own in order to design studies with the best likelihood of yielding important new knowledge.

Back Matter

The back matter of a dissertation usually consists of the bibliography and one or more appendixes.

The bibliography must list all the references that were cited in the body of the dissertation. Depending upon your institution, it may be permissible also to include pertinent references that were not cited. Whatever style manual you use, your citations should be accurate down to the last comma.

Appendixes are used to present information that is not critical to the study, but will be of interest to some readers. For example, appendixes are appropriate for statistical results that are not essential to the study (e.g., psychometric data for the research measures) and presentation of locally developed research measures (e.g., interview schedules and training materials).

Preparing a Journal Article

You have much to gain by preparing one or more journal articles based on your dissertation as soon as you have completed it. Many employers who have an open position for an educator with an advanced degree are interested in the publications of applicants. If you are able to list one or more publications (especially research publications) on your vita or resume, this will be to your advantage in obtaining a position.

The first step in preparing a research article is to decide what journal is most likely to publish studies on the problem that you investigated. The best candidates can be identified by checking the bibliography of your dissertation. You are likely to find that a few journals published the majority of studies that you cited as pertinent to your research problem. These journals are the ones most likely to accept your article for publication.

Another factor to consider in selecting a journal is its reputation. Some education journals are more widely read and more influential than others. Also, refereed journals generally are regarded more highly than nonrefereed journals. A **refereed journal** is one in which articles are evaluated by a panel of acknowledged experts to determine whether they merit publication. Most refereed journals prominently display their panel of reviewers at the front of each issue.

Once you decide upon the journal in which you wish to publish, you should examine the typical length and format of recently published articles in it. You also should check whether the journal follows the publication guidelines of the American Psychological Association (APA). In fact, most journals that publish educational research do follow these guidelines, which appear in the *Publication Manual of the American Psychological Association*. This publication provides detailed instructions on manuscript organization, content, and reporting style.

Touchstones in Research

Cabell, D. W. E., & English, D. L. (Eds.). (2005). *Cabell's directory of publishing opportunities: Educational set* (7th ed.). Beaumont, TX: Cabell Publishing.

Lounds, J., Oakar, M., & Knecht, K. (2002). Journal editors' view on the criteria a paper must meet to be publishable. *Contemporary Educational Psychology, 27*(2), 338–347.

A study by Bruce Hall, Ann Ward, and Connie Comer provides insight about criteria that affect a study's publishability in a research journal.[34] They selected a random sample of 128 educational research articles published in 1983 and had them rated by a panel of experienced researchers. The panel judged that 54 of the articles (about 43 percent) should have been rejected or accepted only after major revisions. Hall and his colleagues asked the panel to indicate the specific shortcomings that led them to make these judgments. Table 2.2 shows the most frequently cited shortcomings. Most involved flaws in research methodology (e.g., not establishing the validity and reliability of the measures used) or problems in how it was reported (e.g., not clearly describing the study's limitations). Before submitting an article to a journal, you may find it helpful to check it against this list of shortcomings.

The list shown in Table 2.2 is helpful, but it omits one criterion of research publishability that we believe is particularly important. Ronald Good and James Wandersee allude to this criterion in their statement, "The most challenging and important job that a reviewer or an editor has to perform is deciding whether or not a particular study was worth doing. . . ."[35]

As journal editors ourselves, we have rejected research manuscripts because we could not figure out why the study was worth doing, or in other words, why it was important. Conversely, we have accepted research manuscripts for publication because the study was important—despite flaws in methodology. For this reason, we emphasize the

TABLE 2.2

Specific Shortcomings Cited by Judges to Substantiate Decisions to Reject or Require Major Revisions in Educational Research Articles

Specific Shortcoming	Percentage of the 54 Articles Cited
1. Validity and reliability of data-gathering procedures not established	43
2. Research design not free of specific weaknesses	39
3. Limitations of study not stated	31
4. Research design not appropriate to solution of the problem	28
5. Method of sampling inappropriate	28
6. Results of analysis not presented clearly	28
7. Inappropriate methods selected to analyze data	26
8. Report not clearly written	26
9. Assumptions not clearly stated	22
10. Data-gathering methods or procedures not described	22

Source: Adapted from table 8 on p. 188 in: Hall, B. W., Ward, A. W., & Comer, C. B. (1988). Published educational research: An empirical study of its quality. *Journal of Educational Research, 81*(3), 182–189. Reprinted with permission from the Helen Dwight Reid Educational Foundation. Published by Heldref Publications, 1319 Eighteenth St., NW, Washington, DC 20036-1802. Copyright © 1988.

34. Hall, B. W., Ward, A. W., & Comer, C. B. (1988). Published educational research: An empirical study of its quality. *Journal of Educational Research, 81*(3), 182–189.
35. Good, R. G., & Wandersee, J. H. (1991). No royal road: More on improving the quality of published educational research. *Educational Researcher, 20*(8), 24–25. Quote appears on p. 24.

need to ground your study first and foremost in the research literature. Your awareness of what is known and not known about the problem you wish to investigate allows you to create a case for the importance of your study by showing how it contributes to the research literature.

Preparing a Paper for a Professional Meeting

It is a rewarding experience to present a paper based on your dissertation at a professional meeting. You can list it on your vita or resume as a professional accomplishment. Also, it helps you become better known to your colleagues.

Educational associations such as the American Educational Research Association (AERA) and the Association for Supervision and Curriculum Development (ASCD) announce a "call for papers" many months in advance of their annual meeting. The call for papers will appear in one of the association's publications, which are sent to all members. Its purpose is to invite members to submit proposals for papers to be delivered at the meeting. If your proposal is accepted, you usually are obligated to attend the meeting in order to deliver the paper in person. Therefore, it is inadvisable to submit a paper proposal unless you are reasonably certain that you (or a research colleague with whom you have worked) will be able to attend the meeting.

Papers presented at professional meetings generally are similar in form to articles published in research journals. You may have occasion, however, to present your study at a meeting of policy makers or practitioners who have limited understanding of research methodology. Patricia Haensly, Ann Lupkowski, and James McNamara developed a method called a **chart essay** that meets this need for a less technical presentation style.[36] The chart essay simplifies the elements of a research study by using charts to focus the audience's attention on aspects of the study that are most relevant to policy making.

Haensly and her colleagues illustrated the method using a study that determined the impact of students' participation in extracurricular activities on their high school grades. A chart essay format was used to present the findings to a conference of educators of gifted children. One of the charts is reproduced in Figure 2.2. The chart's banner states one of the study's research questions. The findings relevant to the question are stated in a form that does not require special expertise in statistics.

The "Trends" stated at the bottom of the chart are concise, nontechnical, and descriptive of the statistical findings. Trends statements are one of the most important elements of the chart essay:

> Taken collectively these trends statements provide the executive summary. At any point in the conference briefing session, they can be easily referenced . . . [We] have found that trends statements are often quoted directly in press releases, administrative reports, and public meetings.[37]

A feature of the chart essay format that helps readers understand complex research results is that each aspect of a study—for example, each research question—is shown on a separate one-page chart.

Touchstone in Research

Smith, M. C., & Carney, R. N. (1999). Strategies for writing succesful AERA proposals. *Educational Researcher, 28*(1), 42–45.

---

36. Haensly, P. A., Lupkowski, A. E., & McNamara, J. F. (1987). The chart essay: A strategy for communicating research findings to policymakers and practitioners. *Educational Evaluation and Policy Analysis, 9,* 63–75. See also: Jones, B. K., & Mitchell, N. (1990). Communicating evaluation findings: The use of a chart essay. *Educational Evaluation and Policy Analysis, 12,* 449–462.

37. Ibid., p. 70.

FIGURE 2.2

Sample Chart Essay from a Presentation on a Study of Extracurricular Activities in High School

Research Question Eleven

Does participation in student government contribute significantly to academic success in high school?

	High Involvement %	Moderate Involvement %	Some Involvement %	No Involvement %
Very High Grades 'A'	100.00	64.7	38.6	18.0
High Grades 'B'	—	35.3	26.5	39.2
Moderate Grades 'C'	—	—	33.7	39.9
Low Grades 'D'	—	—	1.2	2.9

Trends

- All high school students highly involved in student government (100%) earned very high grades.
- All high school students with moderate involvement in student government (64.7 plus 35.3 or 100%) earned very high or high grades.
- Most high school students with some involvement in student government (38.6 plus 26.5 or 65.1%) earned very high or high grades.
- High school students not involved in student government were least likely to earn high or very high grades.

Source: Figure 4 on p. 71 in: Haensly, P. A., Lupkowski, A. E., & McNamara, J. F. (1987). The chart essay: A strategy for communicating research findings to policymakers and practitioners. *Educational Evaluation and Policy Analysis, 9*, 63–75. Copyright © 1987 by the American Educational Research Association.

RECOMMENDATIONS FOR

Planning and Reporting Research

1. Select a research problem early in your program of study.
2. Ground your research problem in existing literature related to the problem.
3. Allow sufficient time to plan the study (typically several months or longer) so that it is well designed and likely to contribute to knowledge about education.
4. Conduct a pilot study of the research procedures in order to identify and correct flaws before the main study.
5. Create a realistic time line for completing the various stages of the study.
6. In writing the research proposal and final report, include a sound rationale for each of the study's hypotheses, questions, or objectives.
7. In writing the research proposal and final report, show how the studies included in the literature review relate to the present study.
8. In reporting the results of data analyses, relate them explicitly to the study's hypotheses, questions, or objectives.
9. Consider alternate explanations of the findings in the discussion section of the final report.
10. Study journal style requirements before submitting a research manuscript for publication.

SELF-CHECK TEST

Circle the correct answer to each of the following questions.
The answers are provided at the back of the book.

1. "There will be no significant difference between the scores on a measure of achievement of high- and low-anxious students" is a hypothesis written in _____ form.
   a. directional
   b. interrogative
   c. null
   d. objective

2. When a construct is thought of as a characteristic that can take on more than one value, it is called a
   a. variable.
   b. replicable construct.
   c. hypothetical construct.
   d. theoretical entity.

3. Replication research is particularly useful for
   a. identifying new variables that correspond to a construct.
   b. determining the social significance of a research finding.
   c. testing a hypothesis derived from theory.
   d. determining whether a research finding generalizes to other populations.

4. A pilot study generally should be conducted
   a. after the research proposal has been approved by the dissertation committee.
   b. whenever the research study involves testing the effects of a new instructional procedure.
   c. whenever the research study involves replication and extension.
   d. after development of the measures to be used in the research study.

5. Limitations of a study's research design and method are discussed in the _____ chapter of a thesis or dissertation.
   a. research findings
   b. research method
   c. discussion
   d. introductory

6. A thesis or dissertation
   a. is similar to a research proposal except for the research findings and discussion chapters.
   b. is similar to a research proposal except for the literature review chapter.
   c. is organized very differently from a research proposal.
   d. is organized very differently from research articles in journals.

7. A chart essay is
   a. a type of research article written for a practitioner journal.
   b. a commentary on the direction that research on a particular problem should take.
   c. a nontechnical format for presenting research findings.
   d. a presentation format specifically intended for reporting qualitative research findings.

CHAPTER 3

Ethics and Site Relations in Educational Research

OVERVIEW

If your proposed study involves collecting data from human participants, you will need to describe how you plan to protect them from possible harm, and submit this information to an institutional review board at your university or research agency. In this chapter we suggest strategies for designing a research study that conforms to ethical standards and legal regulations for protecting research participants from various types of harm. We also describe how to build a positive relationship with individuals whose cooperation and involvement you will need throughout your research study.

OBJECTIVES

After studying this chapter, you should be able to

1. Identify issues in the planning, conduct, and reporting of research that often raise ethical concerns.
2. Describe the purpose and focus of government regulations and codes of ethics developed by professional associations concerning research with human participants.
3. Describe two approaches for debriefing participants following research that involves deception.
4. Describe the purpose and procedures of an institutional review board.
5. Give examples of research situations involving legal, ethical, or human relations issues, and describe how such issues can be handled effectively.
6. Describe the procedures that should be included in a proposal for a research study to ensure that participants are protected from harm.
7. Describe several methods that researchers can use to ensure the privacy and confidentiality of research data.
8. Describe four aspects of site research that require positive human relations.

The Importance of Ethics and Site Relations in Educational Research

Ethics is a branch of philosophy concerned with questions of how people ought to act toward each other, which pronounces judgments of value about actions and develops rules to guide ethical choices.[1] Educational researchers have long relied on the philosophy of ethics, along with other bodies of knowledge including legal policies and regulations, to help identify and resolve the many value-laden issues involved in the proper conduct of research.

---

1. Kitchener, K. S. (2000). *Foundations of ethical practice, research, and teaching in psychology.* Mahwah, NJ: Erlbaum.

In a typical school today, an educational researcher is likely to encounter individuals with a range of talents and unique experiences, people from a wide range of ethnic backgrounds, students from wealthy and impoverished homes and homeless students, children being raised by grandparents or foster parents, people who have experienced abuse, and individuals with varied emotional, physical, or learning disabilities. Every researcher thus needs to consider carefully—before, during, and after the conduct of a research study—the ethical concerns that can affect their research participants. By understanding and addressing such ethical concerns, some of which are embedded in governmental regulations, educational researchers show respect for research participants, protect them from avoidable harm, and honor their contributions to research knowledge.

Marcel LaFollette conducted a survey of professional scientists in which they were asked whether they had direct knowledge of research fraud (data falsification, incorrect reporting of findings, and plagiarizing).[2] Nineteen percent of the scientists reported they knew of such fraud. Some cases of fraud or unethical behavior have been widely reported, such as the so-called Tuskegee study which withheld medical treatment for African American men with syphilis in order to study the progression of the disease.[3]

The fields of cultural studies and critical theory (see Chapter 15) also give us reason to pay more attention to ethical issues in the design and conduct of research. An essential assumption of these fields of inquiry is that all individuals are enmeshed in relationships of power with other individuals. No one is truly free; rather, we are dominated by other individuals or institutions, often in subtle ways. This is no less true of research. Researchers are in a position of power in relation to the individuals whom they study. Thus it is important for researchers to avoid, or minimize, misuse of that power.

One manifestation of this concern is the shift in terminology used to refer to the individuals whom researchers study. The traditional term was *subjects*. Now the preferred term when reporting about individuals who were studied in a research project is *participants* or their customary designation in society (e.g., *students, teachers,* or *administrators*).[4] Use of such terms conveys a sense of individuals' role as active, willing participants in a research study. We use that terminology in this chapter. However, some of the literature on protection of research participants, including federal regulations (described below), refers to such individuals as *human subjects,* so we occasionally use this term as well.

Typical Aspects of Educational Research That May Raise Ethical Concerns

It is important for you to know the ethical issues that can occur at various points in the research process so that you can anticipate them and employ appropriate strategies to resolve them. In this section we discuss aspects of the design, conduct, and reporting of research that often raise ethical concerns in research studies. Although these issues apply to both quantitative and qualitative research, some of them take on a different face in the two paradigms. Quantitative studies generally are guided by positivist epistemology (see Chapter 1), which tends to create an impersonal, detached relationship between researchers and participants. Ethical misjudgments are possible in this type of relationship, but they tend to be more obvious at the design stage of the research and thus more

Touchstone in Research

Howe, K. R., & Moses, M. S. (1999). Ethics in educational research. In A. Iran-Nejad & P. D. Pearson (Eds.), *Review of research in education:* vol. *24* (pp. 21–59). Washington, DC: American Educational Research Association.

Touchstones in Research

Christians, C. G. (2005). Ethics and politics in qualitative research. In N. K. Denzin & YS. Lincoln (Eds.), *The handbook of qualitative research* (3rd ed., pp. 139–164). Thousand Oaks, CA: Sage.

Sales, B. D., & Folkman, S. (Eds.). (2000). *Ethics in research with human participants.* Washington, DC: American Psychological Association.

---

2. LaFollette, M. C. (1994). Research misconduct. *Society, 31*(3), 6–10.
3. Jones, J. H. (1993). *Bad blood: The Tuskegee syphilis experiment.* New York: Free Press.
4. See p. 65 of: American Psychological Association (2001). *Publication manual of the American Psychological Association* (5th ed.). Washington, DC: Author.

easily corrected. In contrast, qualitative studies require a particular kind of intimacy between researchers and participants in order to discover the meanings and settings that define the participants' lived experiences. These meanings and settings might be secret or highly private in nature, and thus ethical issues concerning deception and obtaining access to data loom large. Qualitative research also tends to be more open-ended than quantitative research, "because parameters and a mapped research direction . . . unfold during the course of the investigation."[5] Thus the prior weighing of research risks and benefits and obtaining informed consent from research participants can pose a particular problem.

Planning and Design of Research

Researcher Qualifications

Because poorly designed research can cause harm to participants, the competence, perspective, and character of the researcher himself is an ethical issue. In discussing the ethics of research involving children, Gerald Koocher and Patricia Keith-Spiegel argue that researchers should study only those problems that they are fully competent to address.[6] They also recommend that researchers consult with colleagues for feedback on their competence to do the study and on whether their values and biases might compromise the integrity of the research design or the welfare of research participants.

Conflict of Interest

A conflict of interest arises when a researcher's choice of a data-collection instrument or intervention (e.g., use of particular curriculum materials) has financial implications for the researcher. For example, Grisso and his colleagues described cases in which researchers working in the field of biotechnology were in a position to gain financial advantage from research decisions in which they or their colleagues participated. Efforts are currently being made to establish legal guidelines to govern such cases.[7]

Neglect of Important Topics

Experts on research ethics have identified various problems that can arise for research participants or other groups when particular phenomena are studied. However, the neglect of certain topics by researchers is also an ethical issue. Luis Laosa, for example, noted a tendency among some researchers to generalize their findings to populations to which the findings may not apply.[8] Laosa discussed research findings about the use of students' scores on the Home Observation for Measurement of the Environment (HOME) Inventory to predict their intellectual performance. In one study, HOME scores significantly predicted intellectual performance for non-Hispanic white and African American samples, but the corresponding coefficients for the Mexican American sample were nonsignificant and near zero. Ignoring ethnic differences creates the possible risk of making inappropriate generalizations from one's research findings.

Another example of neglect is found in the field of health. For many years, thousands of school secretaries and teachers—most of them female—used ditto sheets and ditto fluid

5. Howe, K. R., & Dougherty, K. C. (1993). Ethics, institutional review boards, and the changing face of educational research. *Educational Researcher, 22*(9), 16–21.
6. Koocher, G. P., & Keith-Spiegel, P. C. (1990). *Children, ethics, & the law.* Lincoln, NE: University of Nebraska Press.
7. Grisso, T., Baldwin, E., Blanck, P. D., Rotheram-Borus, M. J., Scooler, N. R., & Thompson, T. (1991). Standards in research: APA's mechanism for monitoring the challenge. *American Psychologist, 46,* 758–766.
8. Laosa, L. M. (1991). The cultural context of construct validity and the ethics of generalizability. *Early Childhood Research Quarterly, 6,* 313–321.

to run copies of school materials. However, the 1985–86 *Registry of Toxic Effects of Chemical Substances,* published by the U.S. Department of Health and Human Services, included very few studies on the toxicity of methanol, the main chemical in ditto fluid.[9] Five animal studies had been conducted with mice and rats, but none examined possible effects on reproduction. As of that date, there were no studies of the effects of methanol on human beings in general, or on pregnant women in particular.

Research Methodology

Control Group Experience

Participants in experimental research are placed in different treatment conditions, and thus are not treated equally. The treatment group is likely to receive special training or the opportunity to participate in an innovative program, while the control group receives either nothing or a conventional program. An ethical dilemma exists here because the control group can be viewed as having been treated unfairly by not receiving the special training or innovative program. For example, Carolyn Evertson described an experiment in which treatment-group teachers attended classroom management workshops at the beginning of the school year.[10] School personnel expressed concern because control-group teachers did not participate in the training program and thus were deprived of its perceived benefits. The researchers dealt with this concern by scheduling the control-group teachers for the same workshops soon after data collection was completed.

Use of Deception

Deception is the act of creating a false impression in the minds of research participants through such procedures as withholding information, establishing false intimacy, telling lies, or using accomplices. Deception has been used frequently in laboratory studies conducted by psychologists in order to investigate phenomena that otherwise could not be studied. For example, suppose a researcher is interested in how students respond to another student's cheating. It would be difficult to find sufficient natural occurrences of this situation and to develop an unobtrusive method for collecting data on it. However, the situation could be created frequently and observed reliably by using an *accomplice* (also called a *confederate*), that is, an individual recruited by the researcher to engage in deception. The deception would involve having the accomplice "cheat" in the presence of other students so that the researcher can observe these students' reactions.

Another approach to research on this problem would be to conduct ethnographic fieldwork. The researcher might make explicit his role as a researcher and seek certain students at a school to act as informants. In order to get the informants to reveal secretive information about cheating incidents at the school, the researcher might attempt to engage them in a buddy relationship, a false intimacy that could be viewed as a form of deception.[11] Alternatively, the researcher might "go native" by pretending to be a student himself. (In fact, there are cases of adults who have disguised their identity and enrolled as high school students.) The disguise is clearly a deception, but one that is likely to unearth insider data about cheating in school.

Touchstone in Research

Korn, J. H. (1997). *Illusions of reality: A history of deception in social psychology.* Albany, NY: State University of New York Press.

 9. National Institute of Occupational Safety and Health (1985–86). *The registry of toxic effects of chemical substances.* Washington, DC: U.S. Department of Health and Human Services.
10. Evertson, C. M. (1989). Improving elementary classroom management: A school-based training program for beginning the year. *Journal of Educational Research, 83,* 82–90.
11. The use of seduction and related techniques in research is discussed in: Wong, L. M. (1998). The ethics of rapport: Institutional safeguards, resistance, and betrayal. *Qualitative Inquiry, 4,* 178–199.

Some people are opposed to the use of deception in any research because they believe that it is morally wrong. Others oppose deception for practical reasons as well. For example, Yvonna Lincoln and Egon Guba, two proponents of the constructivist paradigm in qualitative research, argue that "if the inquirer is interested in [respondents'] constructions, then it is pointless to lie to or deceive" them.[12]

Suppose that the use of deception in a particular study can be justified through analysis of its benefits relative to its risks. In this case, legal regulations require that researchers debrief subjects as soon as possible after the deception. Two different types of debriefing can be used: dehoaxing and desensitization.

In **dehoaxing** participants, the researcher must convince everyone who was deceived during a research study that deception was in fact involved. The purpose is to ensure that the false information will do no future harm to any participant. For example, students participating in a research study might be given fraudulent test scores in order to measure the effect of these scores on their level of aspiration. After the data have been collected, the researcher has a responsibility to inform them that the scores were not an accurate measure of their ability. If the students continued to believe that the false scores were correct, this belief might do long-lasting damage to their self-esteem or academic aspirations.

In some situations, simply telling participants that deception was used is not sufficient. Instead, it is necessary to engage in **desensitization,** which is a process of convincing participants of the deception and thus removing its undesirable effects. For example, suppose a researcher used deception in an experiment on conformity to college social norms. During the experiment, some students may have exhibited inappropriate behavior more frequently when other people (who are confederates) exhibit the behavior. For example, in the presence of a confederate whom they observed reading a newspaper during a college lecture, some students (unaware that they were being observed as part of an experiment) also might have ignored the professor and done something else unrelated to the class. The knowledge that they were observed engaging in such behavior might lead to concerns about their commitment to their studies.

Douglas Holmes suggested two approaches for desensitizing research participants in such situations.[13] One approach is to suggest that the participants' behavior resulted from the circumstances of the experiment and was not due to defects in their character or personality. A second approach is to point out that the participants' behavior is not abnormal or unusual. In effect, these approaches provide research participants with rationalizations that make it possible for them to accept the fact that they engaged in behavior that may be in conflict with their own self-perceptions or moral code. Still, some researchers or ethicists might argue that such a procedure actually promotes unethical behavior on the part of participants, rather than protecting them from such risk.

Use of Tests

The use of tests in research raises many ethical issues. For example, many individuals suffer from anxiety in testing situations. Thus, whenever a researcher administers a test as part of the data-collection process, some or all of the participants may be at risk for test anxiety. If you plan to administer tests in your research study, you should consider ways to elicit participants' best performance while minimizing their anxiety.

Personality inventories, attitude scales, and other self-report measures raise a different ethical issue. These measures require self-disclosure, which may be threatening to

---

12. Lincoln, Y. S., & Guba, E. G. (1989). Ethics: The failure of positivist science. *Review of Higher Education, 12,* 221–240. Quote appears on p. 230.
13. Holmes, D. S. (1976). Debriefing after psychological experiments: I. Effectiveness of postdeception dehoaxing. *American Psychologist, 31,* 868–875.

some individuals. Therefore, you will need to determine how to elicit valid responses to self-report measures while minimizing threats caused by self-disclosure. Assurances of the anonymity and confidentiality of the data are recommended procedures for this purpose.

Advances in computer-based test interpretation have added new ethical concerns to those traditionally associated with test taking. For example, some individuals may experience discomfort while taking a computer-administered test and may feel threatened by the knowledge that computer software will interpret their performance or self-report responses. There also is the potential for violation of privacy when test results are stored in computer files. The American Psychological Association has developed ethical guidelines for testing practices in general and for computer-based testing in particular.[14]

Termination of Treatment Conditions

The time frame for terminating an experimental program offered to participants as part of a research study may not coincide with the ideal time to end it in terms of participants' needs. Termination of the experimental treatment may be especially difficult for individuals if they have developed a good relationship with the research team, or if the baseline condition in a single-case experimental design is re-established. (Single-case experiments are described in Chapter 13.) To avoid harm to participants in such situations, researchers must weigh the planned schedule of research activities against the needs of participants. They may find it necessary to redesign the activities to minimize potential harm to participants when the treatment condition is terminated.

Data Collection and Analysis

The collection and analysis of empirical data is the heart of the research enterprise. Unfortunately, ethical misconduct is known to have occurred in the conduct of these activities. Researchers have fabricated data or statistical analyses. Also, they have misrepresented their findings by "massaging" the data through such methods as deleting selected data from analyses or failing to report results that do not support their research hypotheses. The most highly publicized cases of these types of misconduct have occurred in fields other than educational research but there is no reason to believe that educational research is immune to such problems.

Jeffrey Kromrey notes the "publish or perish" stress on research faculty and the unfortunately common view that only statistically significant results count as reasons for unethical practices involving data analysis.[15] Such ethics breaches range from naive or erroneous analyses of data, through deliberate selection of questionable methods of data analysis, to actual falsification of results. Researchers are also attempting to address the ethical conundrums specific to online experiments.[16]

It may be difficult or impossible to monitor researchers' behavior in collecting and analyzing data or to detect all instances of misconduct. Nonetheless, all researchers have a responsibility to develop an understanding of the great harm that results to the education profession and its clients if inaccurate "knowledge" is generated through ethical misconduct. We also must work with other members of the education community to ensure that ethical standards for research exist and are upheld.

14. Fremer, J., Diamond, E. E., & Camara, W. J. (1989). Developing a code of fair testing practices in education. *American Psychologist, 44,* 1062–1067; American Psychological Association (1987). *Guidelines for computer-based tests and interpretations.* Washington, DC: Author.
15. Kromrey, J. D. (1993). Ethics and data analysis. *Educational Researcher, 22*(4), 24–27.
16. Azar, B. (2000, April). Online experiments: ethically fair or foul? *Monitor on Psychology,* pp. 50–52. The National Institutes of Health's Office for Protection from Research Risks has prepared guidelines for institutional review boards that review studies conducted on the Internet; available at http://www.grants.nih.gov/grants/oppr/oppr.htm

Reporting of Research

Authorship

Various ethical issues arise in decisions about who is to be the author or co-author of a research report. For example, suppose an individual made significant contributions to a study by designing and conducting the statistical analyses, but did not write the final report. Should this individual be considered a co-author of the report? Suppose the principal researcher includes co-authors in one publication resulting from a research study (e.g., a presentation at a professional meeting), but not in another publication (e.g., a subsequent journal article). Is this ethical? Suppose several researchers do a study and co-author a report. One of these researchers later writes an article for a journal in which he explores implications of the study's findings for improving educational practice. Is it ethical for the researcher not to include his co-investigators as co-authors of this article? If there are several co-authors, how is order of authorship to be determined?

The first step in answering questions such as these is for all co-investigators to read the *Ethical Standards of the American Educational Research Association*, which we describe below. We recommend that all co-investigators then meet to discuss their preferences concerning the authorship of any reports resulting from the study. One of us (M. Gall) co-directed a large project in which he put in writing the agreements reached at such a meeting. All those involved in the project were able to express their preferences in the process of reaching consensus, and everyone received a copy of the written statement.

If you are a student who is doing research under the guidance of a university faculty member, you might check to determine whether the university has a policy for handling the various authorship issues that can arise in this situation. These issues can be especially difficult when graduate students are doing research with or under the direction of faculty members on whom they rely for completion of their degree programs. Such students are vulnerable because of the power differential between them and these faculty members.

An informal policy that one of us (M. Gall) has found to work well over a period of many years is this: Be generous about including co-investigators as co-authors. If there is any doubt, give the collaborator the benefit of the doubt, as when a statistician makes a significant professional contribution to your data analysis but does not write any of the final report except for several statistical tables. Regarding order of authorship, his policy—consistent with AERA's *Ethical Standards*—is that the order should be determined strictly by the amount of work of a professional nature done by each co-investigator, not by the co-investigator's reputation or seniority.

Sometimes an even more equitable strategy is used in listing authors. For example, Maria Ham and co-researchers (2004) describe their efforts to gain ethical approval for a participatory research study concerning how people with intellectual disabilities think about and maintain their health. The six authors, who include both nondisabled researchers and their colleagues with intellectual disabilities, played various roles in carrying out and reporting the study. They agreed that the authors should be listed alphabetically "in recognition of the fact that people had made different, but equally valuable contributions."[17]

17. Ham, M., Jones, N., Mansell, I., Northway, R., Price, L., & Walker, G. (2004). "I'm a researcher!" Working together to gain ethical approval for a participatory research study. *Journal of Learning Disabilities, 8*(4), 397–407. Quote appears on p. 398.

Plagiarism

An editorial in the *Journal of Educational Psychology* identifies **plagiarism** (the direct lifting of others' words for use in one's own publications) as an ethical issue of growing concern.[18] Plagiarism, perhaps even more than partial or dual publication (described below), damages an author's colleagues and the profession as a whole because it involves taking undeserved credit for something that another professional has written.

The journal editors, Joel Levin and Hermine Marshall, also argue that paraphragiarism is just as serious an offense as plagiarism. **Paraphragiarism** involves close copying of another writer's words or ideas, for example, extended paraphrases of another's words, one-to-one correspondence in the expression of ideas, and structural similarities in writing. Levin and Marshall make two suggestions to avoid this offense: First, cite the author of the original words, ideas, or structures. Second, do not attempt to paraphrase someone else's thoughts while looking directly at the source; instead, "close the book and then paraphrase (with appropriate referencing)."[19]

Partial or Dual Publication

Some research practices are ethically unacceptable because they are harmful to one's colleagues or to the profession as a whole. Several of these practices involve the manner in which the findings of research are reported. **Partial publication** involves disseminating research results in the "least publishable unit" rather than as a coherent whole. This situation can arise if a study involves different types of variables. For example, suppose an experiment is done to determine the effects of an instructional method on cognitive and attitudinal learning outcomes, involving students from different ethnic backgrounds. Partial publication would occur if the researcher published the results for the cognitive learning outcomes in one article, the results for the attitudinal outcomes in a second article, and the results for ethnic differences in a third article. An even more serious ethical lapse is **dual publication,** which involves publishing the same research results in more than one publication.

Grisso and his colleagues identified the ethical problems created by these practices.[20] For example, readers of the research literature may not be able to distinguish how several different reports of the same research study differ in focus, scope, or recency, which complicates their ability to grasp the overall pattern of the findings concerning a research problem. An even more serious ethical problem is that professors who engage in partial or dual publication may gain credit for numerous publications from the same study, and thus may receive tenure or promotion more readily than professors who report their findings in the form of fewer, more comprehensive publications. Also, partial and dual publication consumes scarce journal space or slots for presentations at professional conferences, and thus may prevent other deserving researchers from reporting their studies.

Another ethical issue involves the submission of research manuscripts for publication. We know of cases in which a researcher has submitted a manuscript to more than one journal without informing the journals that that this was being done. Each journal conducted an editorial review of the manuscript, and both accepted it for publication. Only then were the respective journal editors informed of the dual submission. In this case, the hard work of the editors of the journal rejected by the authors was for naught. For this reason, a researcher should submit a manuscript to one journal and await an editorial decision. If the decision is negative, the researcher then is free to submit it to another journal.

18. Levin, J. R., & Marshall, H. H. (1993). Publishing in the *Journal of Educational Psychology:* Reflections at midstream. *Journal of Educational Psychology, 85,* 3–6.
19. Ibid., p. 6.
20. Grisso et al., Standards in research.

Formal Regulation of Research Ethics

Your decisions regarding ethical questions and dilemmas that arise in a research study will reflect the depth of your moral reasoning and values. They also will reflect your understanding of ethical policies and procedures that have been put into place by the government and by professional associations.

Statements of Ethical Principles

Certain governmental regulations on the ethical conduct of research are legally binding. In addition, some professional associations whose members carry out educational research have produced general codes of ethics to guide such research. Some associations have also developed specialized ethical standards to guide testing (see Chapter 7) and program evaluation (see Chapter 17), activities in which many educational researchers are involved. Below we summarize the key government regulations and describe two general codes of ethics that are perhaps most relevant to educational research.

Government Regulations

Touchstone in Research

Jacob, S., & Hartshorne, T. S. (2003). *Ethics and law for school psychologists* (4th ed.). Hoboken, NJ: Wiley.

Governmental concern for protecting the rights of individuals from unethical research practices grew enormously following the Nazi regime in Germany, which ended after World War II. The Nuremberg Code was adopted after 23 Nazi physicians were tried for crimes against humanity. It provided a statement of the rights of individuals to understand and freely choose whether to participate in research.

The Nuremberg Code greatly influenced the development of medical ethics, which in turn influenced the development of ethical policies by social scientists (see preceding section) and national governments. In the United States in the 1960s and early 1970s, the federal government established definitions and regulations governing research performed with funding from federal agencies.

Current definitions and regulations can be found in the U.S. Government Office for Human Research Protections' (OHRP) Code of Federal Regulations for the Protection of Human Subjects.[21] The policy extends legal regulations previously in force and requires any institution that conducts research funded by a U.S. government agency to establish an institutional review board (IRB). Because of the importance of an IRB to the conduct of educational research, we describe it in depth in the next section.

Legal requirements for the protection of research participants in the United States and other countries undoubtedly will change as new issues arise. Therefore, the information we present in this chapter may no longer be current at the time you conduct your research study. Universities and large research agencies typically have a human-subjects compliance office that can inform you of regulations that are in effect for the type of study you plan to do.

Ethical Standards of the American Educational Research Association

Touchstone in Research

American Educational Research Association. (1992). Ethical standards of the American Educational Research Association. *Educational Researcher, 21*(7), 23–26.

The American Educational Research Association has published *Ethical Standards of the American Educational Research Association,* containing 45 standards organized under six main topics. Table 3.1 reproduces the preamble and an illustrative standard for each topic. We recommend that you obtain a copy of the *Ethical Standards* and study it carefully. You will find that some of the standards deal with ethical issues of special concern to beginning researchers.

21. Office for Protection from Research Risks, Protection of Human Subjects. Protection of human subjects: Title 45, Code of Federal Regulations, Part 46 (Office for Human Research Protections, Revised November 13, 2001). Available at http://www.hhs.gov/ohrp/humansubjects/guidance/45cfr46.htm

TABLE 3.1

Preambles and Illustrative Standards from the *Ethical Standards of the American Educational Research Association*

I. *Responsibilities to the Field*
Preamble. To maintain the integrity of research, educational researchers should warrant their research conclusions adequately in a way consistent with the standards of their own theoretical and methodological perspectives.
Illustrative standard. Educational researchers must not fabricate, falsify, or misrepresent authorship, evidence, data, findings, or conclusions.

II. *Research Populations, Educational Institutions, and the Public*
Preamble. Educational researchers conduct research within a broad array of settings and institutions, including schools, colleges, universities, hospitals, and prisons. It is of paramount importance that educational researchers respect the right, privacy, dignity, and sensitivities of their research populations and also the integrity of the institutions within which the research occurs.
Illustrative standard. Educational researchers should communicate their findings and the practical significance of their research in clear, straightforward, and appropriate language to relevant research populations, institutional representatives, and other stakeholders.

III. *Intellectual Ownership*
Preamble. Intellectual ownership is predominantly a function of creative contribution. Intellectual ownership is not predominantly a function of effort expended.
Illustrative standard. Authors should disclose the publication history of articles they submit for publication; that is, if the present article is substantially similar in content and form to one previously published, this fact should be noted and the place of publication cited.

IV. *Editing, Reviewing, and Appraising Research*
Preamble. Editors and reviewers have a responsibility to recognize a wide variety of theoretical and methodological perspectives and, at the same time, to ensure that manuscripts meet the highest standards as defined in the various perspectives.
Illustrative standard. Fairness requires a review process that evaluates submitted works solely on the basis of merit. Merit shall be understood to include both the competence with which the argument is conducted and the significance of the results achieved.

V. *Sponsors, Policy Makers, and Other Users of Research*
Preamble. Researchers, research institutions, and sponsors of research jointly share responsibility for the ethical integrity of research, and should ensure that this integrity is not violated. While it is recognized that these parties may sometimes have conflicting legitimate aims, all those with responsibility for research should protect against compromising the standards of research, the community of researchers, the subjects of research, and the users of research.
Illustrative standard. Educational researchers should disclose to appropriate parties all cases where they would stand to benefit financially from their research or cases where their affiliations might tend to bias their interpretation of their research or professional judgments.

VI. *Students and Student Researchers*
Preamble. Educational researchers have a responsibility to ensure the competence of those inducted into the field and to provide appropriate help and professional advice to novice researchers.
Illustrative standard. Educational researchers should inform students and student researchers concerning the ethical dimensions of research, encourage their practice of research consistent with ethical standards, and support their avoidance of questionable projects.

Source: Adapted from: American Educational Research Association. (1992). Ethical standards of the American Educational Research Association. *Educational Researcher, 21*(7), 23–26.

Touchstone in Research

American Psychological Association. (2002). Ethical principles of psychologists and code of conduct. *American Psychologist, 57,* 1060–1073. Also available at: http://www.apa.org/ethics/code.2002.html

Ethical Principles of the American Psychological Association

Many educational researchers belong both to AERA and APA. APA published a document, *Ethical Principles of Psychologists and Code of Conduct,* to guide its members, state psychology boards, courts, and other agencies. The current version includes five foundational ethical principles (A. Beneficence and Nonmaleficence, B. Fidelity and Responsibility, C. Integrity, D. Justice, and E. Respect for People's Rights and Dignity) and specific ethical standards for (1) resolving ethical issues, (2) competence, (3) human relations, (4) privacy and confidentiality, (5) advertising and other public statements, (6) record keeping and fees, (7) education and training, (8) research and publication, (9) assessment, and (10) therapy. Most of these standards are relevant to the conduct of research with human participants. APA also has a set of ethical standards for research involving animals.[22]

Institutional Review Boards' Role in Ensuring Research Ethics

An **institutional review board (IRB)** is a group of individuals who are authorized by an institution to determine whether research studies by colleagues affiliated with the institution comply with institutional regulations, professional standards of conduct and practice, and—most critically—the human-subjects provisions of the Code of Federal Regulations for the Protection of Human Subjects (hereafter, Federal Code).

The Design and Purpose of an IRB

An IRB has at least five members, and their qualifications must satisfy criteria specified in the Federal Code.[23]

Much of an IRB's work focuses on provisions for protection of human subjects in proposed projects, but it also is authorized to review research in progress. In addition, an IRB might oversee provisions for human-subjects protection in the collection of data in a foreign country by researchers affiliated with the institution, and the use of data that were collected in a previous project.[24]

The Federal Code specifies that certain types of educational research are exempt from the human-subjects provisions specified in the Code, including IRB review. However, it is our experience that many institutions will require all proposed research projects, including those to be conducted in educational settings, to undergo IRB review. Because the risks to participants in educational research studies typically are minimal, the IRB might expedite the review process. An IRB may use an expedited review procedure (review by the IRB chairperson or by just one or more of the IRB members) for research considered to involve no more than minimal risk or for minor changes in a previously approved research proposal.[25]

As with any government regulations, the Federal Code and IRB procedures are subject to different interpretations. In our experience, one of the main issues involves student-generated research, conducted either out of personal interest or as a course requirement. For example, if a course instructor asks students to develop an interview schedule and test

---

22. American Psychological Association. (2005). *Guidelines for ethical conduct in the care and use of animals.* Washington, DC: Author. Available at http://www.apa.org/science/anguide.html
23. Office for Protection from Research Risks, Protection of Human Subjects. Protection of human subjects, Paragraph 46.107.
24. Ibid., Paragraph 46.101.
25. Ibid., Paragraph 46.110.

it by using it to collect and analyze data from a small number of individuals, does this constitute a research project that must be proposed and submitted to an IRB for approval?

The Federal Code defines *research* as "a systematic investigation, including research development, testing and evaluation, designed to develop or contribute to generalizable knowledge."[26] In this context, *generalizable knowledge* has come to mean empirical findings that are reported in a formal manner (e.g., in a conference paper, technical report, or journal article) and that the investigator claims to be a contribution to research knowledge. It therefore includes both quantitative and qualitative research, even though some qualitative researchers claim that their research is case-specific and therefore not meant to be generalized. (See Chapter 14.)

By this definition, a research project conducted by a student as a course requirement does not constitute research that needs to be submitted to an IRB for approval at the proposal stage. Neither would a study conducted by a school district (e.g., a questionnaire survey of teachers' staff development needs or an analysis of student achievement scores across several school years) so long as the study's findings are used internally and not reported as knowledge about school districts in general. However, doctoral dissertation research requires IRB approval because the dissertation constitutes a publication of generalizable knowledge: The dissertation abstract is published in *Dissertation Abstracts International,* and anyone can secure a copy of the dissertation itself.

If you have any doubt about whether your proposed study conforms to the Federal Code's definition of research, you should submit it to an IRB for an opinion. One situation in particular requires special consideration. Suppose you are doing a research study as a course or degree requirement, and the faculty does not require IRB review because there is no expectation that the study will produce generalizable knowledge. However, suppose that you hope to do an excellent study that merits publication in some form. (We have come across undergraduate honor's theses and master's theses of high research quality.) If you have not obtained prior IRB approval for the study, there are likely to be serious adverse consequences if you try to publish it in a journal or report it at a conference. Therefore, if you have any aspiration to report your research findings in a formal setting outside your institution, you should discuss the need for advance IRB approval with your faculty advisors or local IRB members.

Examples of Research Situations That Call for IRB Review

Unless educational researchers carefully consider in advance the kinds of potential harm that can arise for participants in a research study, serious ethical problems can arise in the design, conduct, and reporting of their research. Below we describe five such problems, all based on actual cases.

Researcher A collects data about the personality characteristics of certain students and tells the students' teachers the results. This information influences one teacher to interpret the behavior of certain students in a more negative light than if he had not known the information.

Researcher B presents second graders with a large stack of cards to sort into piles according to shape and color.[27] The task proves overwhelming and unpleasant to some students. One student begins to look around the room and pays less attention to the task, while another becomes tense and begins sorting so fast that her error rate becomes extremely high.

---

26. Ibid., Paragraph 46.102.d.
27. This example is taken from p. 121 in: Koocher & Keith-Spiegel, *Children, ethics, & the law.* NE.

Researcher C wants to try out a computerized video game designed to promote a reduction in aggressive behavior and an increase in cooperative behavior among middle-school-age students. The researcher asks a teacher friend to identify the most popular students in her class. The researcher plans to take these students to a computer lab where he will observe them playing the video game as a group.

Researcher D does research using a new machine she just developed that measures muscle activity during certain sports movements by creating electrical fields around the arms and legs. The machine causes temporary tingling in some individuals' extremities. One of these individuals expresses concern that the machine has caused permanent muscle damage to his arm.

Researcher E sends bilingual research assistants to interview poor Chicano families in Texas about their attitudes toward their children's schools.[28] Her goal is to provide the schools with information to help them meet the needs of children whose families have recently moved to the area. The researcher is not aware that many of the interviewees would be considered illegal aliens by the U.S. government and may suspect that U.S. immigration authorities are involved in the research. Some research participants fabricate answers to conceal their citizenship status, and others avoid participation, thus ruining the random sample design.

If problems like these occur in a research study, they can create harm or inconvenience for the individuals being studied, as well as for others. They can also hamper future research, because the individuals whose permission is needed for conducting specific research studies might decline out of fear of possible complaints, protests, or even lawsuits.

Criteria for IRB Approval of a Research Project

Institutional review boards use specific criteria, based on the Federal Code, that a proposed research study must satisfy to provide adequate protection to research participants. An abbreviated version of these criteria as they appear in the Federal Code is shown in Table 3.2. Below we describe the most common procedures required by an IRB to ensure that these criteria are met.

Assessment of the Risk–Benefit Ratio

In reviewing the protocol for a planned study, the IRB considers carefully the study's risk–benefit ratio. A **risk–benefit ratio** is the balance between how much risk the participants will be exposed to and how much good is likely to result from the study. Risk to participants might be physical, psychological, or legal. Benefits can be considered in terms of how helpful the study is to participants, to some other group (e.g., the population to which the results will be generalized), or to the advancement of research knowledge. If risks are more than minimal, an assessment is made of the benefits to be expected from carrying out the study. Then the risks and benefits are subjectively compared to determine whether the latter sufficiently outweigh the former.

To illustrate, consider the example of Researcher D. The proposed research involved physical risk because of the unknown side effects of the newly developed machine for exciting muscles used by the researcher. To deal with this risk ethically, the researcher first should do an extensive review of the literature. The review should seek to determine that no adverse direct effects or side effects have been discovered from use of the type of equipment involved in the proposed research. If any adverse effects are found or suspected, the

---

28. This example is taken from page 3 in: Sieber, J. E. (1992). *Planning ethically responsible research.* Thousand Oaks, CA: Sage.

TABLE 3.2

Criteria for Institutional Review Board Approval of Research

1. Risks to subjects are minimized: (i) by using procedures which are consistent with sound research design and which do not unnecessarily expose subjects to risk, and (ii) whenever appropriate, by using procedures already being performed on the subjects for diagnostic or treatment purposes.
2. Risks to subjects are reasonable in relation to anticipated benefits, if any, to subjects, and the importance of the knowledge that may reasonably be expected to result.
3. Selection of subjects is equitable.
4. Informed consent will be sought from each prospective subject or the subject's legally authorized representative.
5. Informed consent will be appropriately documented.
6. When appropriate, the research plan makes adequate provision for monitoring the data collected to ensure the safety of subjects.
7. When appropriate, there are adequate provisions to protect the privacy of subjects and to maintain the confidentiality of data.
8. When some or all of the subjects are likely to be vulnerable to coercion or undue influence, such as children, prisoners, pregnant women, mentally disabled persons, or economically or educationally disadvantaged persons, additional safeguards have been included in the study to protect the rights and welfare of these subjects.

Source: Adapted from Paragraph 46.111 of: Office for Protection from Research Risks, Protection of Human Subjects. Protection of human subjects: Title 45, Code of Federal Regulations, Part 46 (Office for Human Research Protections, Revised November 13, 2001). Available at http://www.hhs.gov/ohrp/humansubjects/guidance/45cfr46.htm#46.111

researcher should note their severity and incidence of occurrence and describe the procedures that would be used to minimize and treat them.

Once the risks are assessed, the benefits of the proposed research should be determined. Is this study really necessary? What new knowledge is it likely to yield? For example, suppose the machine that Researcher D wishes to use proves to be more effective for measuring the speed of muscle recovery after exercise than machines currently in use. This potential benefit still might not outweigh the risk of physical harm to which research participants would be exposed. However, suppose that the machine, if proved accurate, could be used to detect the onset of neuromuscular disease more quickly than existing machines, as well as to measure the effectiveness of different physical education training procedures. In this case, IRB members might judge that the potential benefits of the study outweigh the physical risks to which research participants will be exposed.

Although the risk–benefit ratio appears to be a sound ethical approach, it puts the IRB in a position of ultimate authority over other people's lives. One can argue that individuals have absolute rights that an IRB cannot dismiss simply because of a favorable risk–benefit ratio. In fact, these absolute rights are protected through provisions for informed consent, privacy, and confidentiality, which we describe below. Thus, even if an IRB approves a research proposal, it cannot take away the rights of individuals to be informed of the study's purpose and to freely choose to decline participation without penalty.

Selection of Participants

If the researcher's sample includes minors or members of vulnerable populations (e.g., disabled students), he is expected to take special precautions to protect them from risk. In addition, participants must be selected equitably, such that any individual in the available population has a reasonable chance of being in the sample. For example, this guideline would prohibit a researcher from asking a teacher to select a group of students from her classroom to participate in an out-of-classroom experiment. This procedure is unacceptable because the teacher might view participation in the experiment as a special privilege, and therefore choose students whom she wishes to reward for one reason or another. Students who are not selected might feel resentment or a loss of self-esteem. Researcher C has violated this criterion by asking the teacher to select only the most popular students to participate in the tryout of the computerized video game. Not only might other students feel left out, but the researcher will not obtain information on the effects of playing the video game on the aggressive or cooperative behavior of these students. To avoid this potential harm to students, the researcher is expected to take steps to ensure that students are selected equitably. Selecting students by a random drawing would be one way to satisfy this requirement.

Obtaining Informed Consent

Researchers must inform each individual about what will occur during the research study, the information to be disclosed to the researchers, and the intended use of the research data that are to be collected. If adults are the participants, they must give their consent. In the case of minors, researchers must obtain only their assent (that is, apparent willingness) because minors cannot legally give consent. However, in most cases, written consent is needed from the child's main caretaker (usually a parent), and also from appropriate school personnel if the research is carried out in the schools.

Each participant should receive an explanation of the tests and experimental procedures to be used. This explanation must satisfy the participant that participation is important and desirable and that it is to his or her advantage to cooperate. Participants also must be informed that they can withdraw from participation at any time, and their requests to do so must be honored. If they are promised payments, rewards, or grade credits for participation, they must be offered these incentives even if they subsequently withdraw from the study. To do otherwise would be to give the impression that there is a penalty associated with leaving the study.

The IRB requires that each prospective research participant receive a letter describing the research and the conditions of their participation. The letter must be written in language that is understandable to them. Individuals who agree to participate in the study need to sign and return a copy of the letter, and keep a copy for themselves. Figure 3.1 shows an informed-consent letter from a qualitative research study carried out by Judy Cape at the University of Oregon as part of the requirements for completing her doctoral dissertation.[29] Cape was interested in how adults use writing in their work. She studied the writing skills of police officers in a local community. Four patrol officers, selected from a pool of 28 patrol officers employed in the community, served as her primary research participants. Because of the sensitive nature of the study (e.g., police reports are admissible as evidence in courts of law), the informed-consent letter needed to be particularly thorough.

As we noted above, informed consent includes participants' understanding that they have the right to withdraw from the research investigation at any time, and their freedom to exercise that right. The case of Researcher B at the beginning of this chapter involves a potential violation of this aspect of informed consent. According to Koocher and Keith-Spiegel, children rarely make clear requests to withdraw from research. However, they can exhibit implicit signs of "wanting out," such as the off-task or inappropriate behavior exhibited by the children studied by Researcher B. For this reason, Koocher and Keith-Spiegel recommend that investigators be alert to such cues and assist children in determining

---

29. Cape, J. E. (1993). The composing process of police officers: Writing police reports. *Dissertation Abstracts International 54*(08), 3000A. (Accession No. AAG 9402011)

FIGURE 3.1

Letter to Obtain Informed Consent from Participants in a Research Study

Dear . . . Patrol Officer:

I am a student at the University of Oregon working on my doctoral degree in teacher education. I am particularly interested in teaching writing. There is a large body of research that describes how students write various types of assignments, but very little about how people write once they leave school and enter a profession. I suspect that writing in the professions is, in some ways, quite different from writing in school. This study is my initial effort to discover what differences exist. I have chosen to study the way patrol officers write reports, not only because it is a large part of your job, but also because of the legal importance of those reports. I am seeking volunteers for my study, and I am hoping you will consider being one of those volunteers.

What we know about student writers includes: (a) how they plan/organize, (b) how they get their thoughts on paper (i.e., how many words they write in each burst, how much re-reading they do as they write, etc.), and (c) how much revising, crossing out, or changing they are likely to do. We also know something about how word processors have affected the writing process. These are the things I would like to study among patrol officers, and eventually people in other professions as well.

My study is descriptive, not evaluative. It does not deal with the content of your reports, but merely the process you use to write them. I want to capture realistic scenarios including breaks, interruptions, and any environmental influences on your writing.

If you decide to participate in my study, here is what would happen:

1. I will interview you to find out about your writing style, any writing instruction or assistance you've received, and the writing expected of you as a patrol officer. This interview will likely last 45–60 minutes. I will tape record the interview and transcribe your comments for future reference.

2. I will accompany you in the patrol car during at least 1 shift to learn more about the context in which you write.

3. I will videotape you as you write at least 2 reports. One camera will be focused on the report form you are writing. A second camera will film you at a distance to capture your writing environment.

4. After videotaping the writing of your report, you and I will view the tape together. I will ask you questions about your writing and will tape record your responses. I might ask you how you use your notes, which parts of the report were the easiest or hardest and why, why you chose a particular word, or what you were thinking during pauses. I will obtain a copy of your final report and your notes to use during the analysis phase of my study.

5. After collecting data for my study, I will analyze the results. You will be given the opportunity to read the portion of my dissertation that pertains to you. A copy of the completed dissertation will be given to the . . . Police Department.

Participation in this study is voluntary. Your decision whether or not to participate will not affect your relationship with the . . . Police Department. Furthermore, your captain has guaranteed that the results of the study will not affect your employment or status in the department. If you decide to participate, you are free to withdraw your consent and discontinue participation at any time without penalty. This study will be conducted during your regular working hours. Your Chief and your Captain have agreed to the terms of this study and are willing to be flexible in terms of the time needed to conduct interviews and post-taping interviews.

All data collected for this study become the property of the researcher. Any information that is obtained in connection with this study and that can be identified with you will remain confidential and will be disclosed only with your permission. Data will be handled according to the guidelines specified by the American Psychological Association. Although all possible safeguards will be used to protect your anonymity, the methodology of the study prevents complete anonymity in all situations. The use of pseudonyms will protect your identity from outsiders, but your superiors and perhaps some of your fellow officers will know of your involvement in the study.

(Continued)

FIGURE 3.1

(Continued)

By participating in this study, you are contributing to primary research on the nture of police writing. If schools are to adequately prepare students for the demands of writing in various professions, it is essential that researchers document the nature of writing within those professions. This will be the first study to look at the process of patrol officers' report writing and, as such, will offer a realistic description of the writing demands of your job and the various influences upon your writing. It will give each person who reads my final report a clear idea of how patrol officers write and the conditions under which such writing is accomplished.

Ideally, I would like four volunteers for my study. It would be helpful if these volunteers represent different lengths of service a patrol officers. I will include both female and male officers, and officers with varying degrees of expertise in the use of computers.

If you have any questions, please feel free to contact me (Judy Cape, [phone number]) or my university advisor (Lynn Anderson-Inman, [phone number]). If you have questions regarding your rights as a research subject, contact the Research Compliance Office, University of Oregon, Eugene, OR 97403, (phone number). Youwill be offered a copy of this form to keep.

Your signature indicates that you have read and understand the information provided above, that you willingly agree to participate, that you may withdraw your consent at any time and discontinue participation without penalty, that you will receive a copy of this form, and that you are not waiving any legal claims, rights or remedies. Volunteers will be selected by the researcher from among the applicants submitting this form. You will be notified of your selection by ___(date)___.

Signature   Date

Please return this form to Judy Cape before ___(date)___ by using the attached self-addressed, stamped envelope. Thank you.

Source: Reprinted with permission of Cape, J. E. (1992). The composing process of parol officers (Protocol #X26-93). Eugene, OR: University of Oregon, Office of Research Compliance.

---

whether they wish to withdraw. For example, they might ask, "Would you like to stop now?" They note that it is important to respect a participant's rights for autonomy even if she does not clearly state her apparent wishes, and that results based on data from unhappy, bored, or inattentive children are suspect.[30]

In some types of research, the findings could be invalidated if participants know beforehand the purpose of the study and the specific experiences in which they will be involved during data collection and experimental treatments. For example, some experiments involve deception, which is discussed further below. Deception might involve giving students false information about their performance to determine the effects of changes in their motivational level on subsequent task performance. Even in such situations, the researcher should obtain the individual's consent to be in the experiment and should tell participants that they will be informed of the experiment's purpose after the study is completed.

Maintenance of Privacy and Confidentiality

The case of Researcher A at the beginning of the chapter involved a violation of confidentiality. The researcher should not have given the teacher information about the personality characteristics of certain students. When a teacher has such information, students are put at risk because the teacher now has expectations that can influence the teacher's

---

30. Koocher & Keith-Spiegel, *Children, ethics, & the law.*

future behavior toward these students. For example, the teacher might relate to a student described as "emotionally disturbed" in a more guarded way during class. Or the teacher might have lowered expectations about a student's ability once the teacher learns that the student has been classified as having an "external locus of control."

The case of Researcher C also involves a violation of confidentiality. In this instance, the confidentiality of teachers is violated when a school administrator obtains data concerning teachers' effectiveness based on research criteria and classroom observations. Teachers identified as ineffective can suffer severe risks in terms of subsequent decisions made about them by the administrator who obtained this information.

Research participants should be told at the outset of the study who will have access to data. Once research data have been collected, the researcher must ensure that no unauthorized persons have access to them, and that the privacy of individuals to whom the data apply is protected.

A good rule to follow is to minimize the number of individuals who know the identity of research participants. In most studies, even assistants who help you collect and analyze research data do not need to know the participants' identity. In fact, it may be possible to collect research data so that no one, including the researcher, can link the data to specific individuals. Otherwise, some sort of linkage system, such as substituting numbers for names, can be used so that only a person who has access to a closely guarded code can identify data for a specific individuals.

In some projects, the researcher must retain some means of identifying participants by name. For example, in longitudinal studies the researcher must retain the names and current addresses of the research participants so she can follow them over time. In other research studies, data are gathered from a variety of sources. These data often need to be linked in order to have a clear picture of the phenomenon being studied. Such linkage is difficult unless some means of identifying specific individuals is retained for at least a short period of time.

When a research study deals with controversial or sensitive topics, confidentiality is extremely important. Researchers must take particular care with data that conceivably could be subpoenaed. In most states educational research data do not have privileged status (as does, for example, communication between husband and wife or between lawyer and client). Confidentiality must be further protected by not using the names of individuals or locations in any publications that result from the research project, unless agreed to by all parties.

While confidentiality always should be protected if research participants have been led to expect it, there are some situations where research ethics may require that their identity be revealed. Judith Shulman carried out collaborative research with beginning teachers who helped develop a casebook on mentoring for use in training new teachers.[31] These teachers told stories about their early experiences in teaching, and they asked that their names be kept on their own case reports. Administrators who reviewed the reports initially insisted on various substantive changes, including that the teacher-authors not be identified by name. Shulman described the careful negotiations between the researchers and school personnel that were necessary to accommodate the school district's major objections, and the argument that was used to convince the district to allow the teachers to be identified:

> The question of identifying teacher informants/collaborators can no longer be automatically answered on the side of anonymity. The ethnographer's traditions of rendering informants invisible were produced in an era when informants were seen as powerless and in need of protection. In our day, research on teaching has become one of the vehicles for the professionalization

---

31. Shulman, J. (1990). Now you see them, now you don't: Anonymity versus visibility in case studies of teachers. *Educational Researcher, 19*(6), 11–15.

and empowerment of teachers. The anonymous teacher may no longer be an appropriate focus for all studies of teaching.[32]

If the researcher has determined that confidentiality is essential to protect research participants, it can be provided in various ways, including

1. asking participants to furnish information anonymously;
2. using a third party (i.e., someone who is neither part of the research team nor affiliated with the institution from whom participants are drawn) to select the sample and collect data;
3. using an identifier (e.g., a detachable section of a questionnaire with a preprinted code) that can be destroyed as soon as the individual's response is received, so that the researcher can tell which participants responded but cannot associate particular responses with the individual who gave them;
4. if data from more than one administration must be matched for each participant, having participants make up an alias or code number (e.g., the birth dates of one's parents or every other digit in one's Social Security number); and
5. disposing of sensitive data at a designated time after the study is completed.

Treatment of Vulnerable Populations

The case of Researcher E at the beginning of the chapter involved a violation of ethical principles in conducting research with a vulnerable population, Hispanic families living in the United States without citizenship. Joan Sieber, who described this case in a book on research ethics, commented that a scientist with an understanding of community-based research would have enlisted community leaders in formulating the research procedures, would have trained community representatives to conduct the interviews, and would have closely supervised the entire research process.[33]

In describing the ethics code of the American Psychological Association, Grisso and his colleagues identified as examples of **vulnerable populations** individuals in poverty or "vulnerable people in transition" (e.g., people with profound mental retardation or serious mental illness who are moving from large institutional settings to community-based settings).[34] Other vulnerable populations were identified by Frederick Erickson.[35] He noted that any individuals who are the focus of a research study are especially vulnerable in relation to other individuals within their institution or community, and that those who are single occupants of an institutional status (such as the lone kindergarten teacher in a school or the school's principal) are particularly vulnerable. Vulnerability is often accentuated in qualitative research because the methodology typically involves intensive study of one case or a small number of cases over a substantial period of time.

Educational researchers may be very dissimilar in intellectual attainments, lifestyles, or values from the individuals whom they wish to study. This dissimilarity can expose the individuals to risk because of the researcher's lack of knowledge about their particular vulnerabilities. We already have mentioned one strategy that researchers can use to minimize risk, namely consulting with experts who have worked closely with individuals like those the researcher plans to study. Another approach is to involve representatives of the population in designing the research study. For example, Murray Wax reflected on the unique

---

32. Ibid., p. 14.
33. Sieber, *Planning ethically responsible research.*
34. Grisso, Standards in research.
35. Erickson, F. (1986). Qualitative methods in research on teaching. In M. C. Wittrock (Ed.), *Handbook of research on teaching* (3rd ed., pp. 119–161). New York: Macmillan.

ethics of research in American Indian communities. He claimed that joint planning between the investigator and the tribe

> would encourage researchers to think more deeply about both benefits and potential harms, as viewed by the tribal members. Rather than regarding themselves as the exploited victims of careerist scientists, they might come to define themselves as co-participants with correlative status, responsibilities, and privileges.[36]

This type of joint planning is becoming increasingly common in educational research, especially in qualitative research and in evaluation studies.

Site Relations in Educational Research

You should have a specific plan to establish and maintain positive human relations with the individuals who participate in your research study. Often these individuals are contacted through a particular site. Thus, you also need to build a positive relationship with the administrators and other members of the site from which you will select your research participants. Below we describe four aspects of field research that require positive site relations: (1) locating a satisfactory research site, (2) securing permission and cooperation for carrying out the research, (3) building a relationship with the site, and (4) dealing with possible human relations issues.

Location of a Research Site

Careful selection of a research site will help to ensure the success of your research study. If you wish to conduct a laboratory study, you may be able to carry it out at your university without much difficulty. For example, the initial research study of one of the authors (J. Gall, working at that time under her maiden name, Joyce Pershing) was conducted in a psychophysiology laboratory at the University of California at Berkeley, where she did her graduate work.[37] She investigated gender differences in grief and sadness, using undergraduate students enrolled in psychology courses as the research participants. The study involved students individually watching a film about the life and death of President John Kennedy, who was assassinated at the age of 46 while in office. While viewing the film, the student was attached to devices that measured skin conductance and heart rate. After the film, the student filled out a self-report measure of emotions. The use of a laboratory setting allowed the researcher to use experimental controls and data-collection methods that would have been virtually impossible in a field setting.

Field settings—such as schools, homes, and community centers—are more appropriate than laboratory settings for many of the problems that interest educational researchers. It is a major challenge, however, to locate a field setting and enlist the cooperation of the individuals within it whom you wish to study. Geoffrey Maruyama and Stanley Deno suggested several strategies for this purpose.[38] One of them is to contact a state or regional department of education where you might be able to find out about schools with educational facilities or demonstration programs that are consistent with your research interests.

If you currently are employed by an educational institution, you might consider conducting your research study there. In fact, the majority of doctoral dissertations with which we have been associated were conducted at the institution where the student was currently employed.

Touchstone in Research

de Laine, M. (2000). *Fieldwork, participation and practice: Ethics and dilemmas in qualitative research.* Thousand Oaks, CA: Sage.

---

36. Wax, M. L. (1991). The ethics of research in American Indian communities. *American Indian Quarterly, 15,* 431–456. Quote appears on pp. 453–454.
37. Pershing, J. C., & Averill, J. A. (1968). Sex differences in psychophysiological reactions to a sadness-inducing film. Paper presented at the Western Psychological Association convention, San Diego, CA.
38. Maruyama, G., & Deno, S. (1992). *Research in educational settings.* Thousand Oaks, CA: Sage.

Conducting a research study at your own institution has both advantages and disadvantages. On the positive side, you may find it easier to obtain approval for your study because you have access to the decision makers in your institution. Furthermore, you are familiar with the normal routines of the institution, such as how schedules are arranged, or what the best procedure is for setting up a meeting of key staff. On the negative side, your particular position within the institution may cause some members of the institution to conceal concerns that might affect your research. Furthermore, you could be hindered in carrying out your study, or vulnerable to certain sanctions, because of your relationship with particular individuals in the institution.

Securing Permission and Cooperation

When conducting research in institutions, you must follow certain procedures in order to obtain permission for your study and to gain cooperation from the individuals who will be affected by it. As a first step, you need a brief, clear, written description of your research design, which you can use to explain your proposed research. The human-subjects protocol that you prepare for your IRB, including letters of informed consent and a description of the measures that you plan to administer, can serve as this description. Having these documents available demonstrates your professionalism, which is essential to obtaining the support of an institution's administrators. Also, they are more likely to give their permission if they know exactly what is required of the institution and of individual participants, what problems might arise, and how the problems would be handled.

Some school administrators are negative about educational research because of their concern about its possible costs and inconvenience to their institution. For example, a superintendent might worry about staff time taken up by a research study conducted in schools, inconvenience to teachers and students, or possible objections from community members. Thus, before approaching anyone whose permission you will need, you should have prepared convincing answers to questions about such matters.

Of special concern to administrators is whether the research results will negatively reflect on their institution. They may be reluctant to voice this concern, however, so you should bring it up early in the negotiations and discuss it objectively. School administrators, in particular, need reassurance when your study involves assessment of students' or teachers' abilities. You can make the point that you will present your findings in such a way that they do not reflect unfavorably upon the sites used in the study. For example, you can note that research journal articles generally do not identify the sites where data were collected, and that you will follow this practice.

William Eiserman and Diane Behl outlined the types of questions that teachers of special education might ask to determine whether to become involved in a research study.[39] These questions, which are summarized in Table 3.3, are a useful guide to the types of questions you should be prepared to answer when communicating with representatives of your prospective research site. We believe that they are relevant not only to special education, but to other situations as well.

When working with any administrative hierarchy, you must take care to follow appropriate channels of authority. For example, say that you plan to select research participants from more than one school within a school district. Usually you must begin by obtaining approval from the superintendent, or from an authorized representative of this individual. Perhaps you already have spoken with a teacher within a school about your project, and

---

39. Eiserman, W. C., & Behl, D. (1992). Research participation: Benefits and considerations for the special educator. *Teaching Exceptional Children, 24,* 12–15.

TABLE 3.3

Questions That Educators Should Ask in Determining Whether to Become Involved in a Research Study

A. Conceptual Soundness of the Research
   1. What is the research question, and what type of research (e.g., descriptive, causal-comparative, correlational, experimental, qualitative) does it require?
   2. Is the research question important, that is, (a) does it address issues pointed out in recent literature as needing attention, (b) do policy concerns demand scientific attention to the question, and (c) is this question of particular interest to the teacher whose participation is being requested?
   3. Is the proposed evaluation plan likely to provide an answer to the question being addressed, and in particular, do the proposed duration for the study and the frequency or intensity of the treatment make sense in light of the expected results?

B. Feasibility of the Research
   1. At what point in the day will the research procedures occur, and how will they affect the current schedule?
   2. How disruptive of other activities will the research be?
   3. How will unavoidable changes in routines, such as special school events or holidays, affect the research?
   4. If student testing is to be conducted, how much time will be required?
   5. How much additional time will the teacher need to devote to the research?

C. Ethical Concerns
   1. Does the study in any way suggest an unreasonable compromise of any principle or value or place any of the subjects in the study at risk, and what safeguards will be in place to protect the rights of those involved in the study?
   2. Does the proposal clearly specify the obligations and responsibilities of all participating?
   3. How will informed consent be obtained from study participants?

Source: Adapted from: Eiserman, W. D., & Behl, D. (1992). Research participation: Benefits and considerations for the special educator. *Teaching Exceptional Children, 24,* 12–15. Copyright © 1992 by the Council for Exceptional Children. Reprinted with permission.

she has expressed support. In this case, that teacher might be willing to be an advocate in suggesting to the superintendent that the research project be approved. After obtaining approval, you should visit each school and present your ideas to the principal, or the individual authorized to represent the principal.

Suppose you have obtained permission from the superintendent, but run into difficulty with a specific principal. If the principal objects to the study being carried out in her school, the superintendent usually will support the principal, even if he previously gave tentative approval for the project. If the superintendent were inclined to force the principal to cooperate, it would make it very difficult to carry out effective research. The interest and cooperation of all persons concerned with the research study is necessary if it is to be carried through to a successful conclusion.

After the principal and superintendent have been briefed as to the purposes of the research and the procedures to be followed, you will need to meet with teachers in each participating school in order to obtain their interest and cooperation. Time usually can be arranged at a regularly scheduled faculty meeting for you to present your proposed study and, hopefully, to obtain the teachers' cooperation.

In most research involving children, parents also must be informed about the study and given an opportunity to express their opinions. Perhaps you can present your plans at a parent-teacher association (PTA) meeting. You also will need to prepare a letter of in-formed consent explaining the study and send it to the parents or guardians of all children whose participation is desired. Parents will need to sign the letter to signify approval of their child's participation in the study.

The degree of cooperation you receive from groups in the community that are served by the site depends on the nature of your research problem. For example, research dealing with academic achievement probably will not require a public relations program, because academics is generally regarded as a central mission of a school. However, a public rela-tions effort might be required for a school-based research study involving personality or social adjustment, in which the role of the school is less clear and when some of the mea-sures to be employed might be misunderstood by some community members.

Teachers, administrators, or others who represent the institution sometimes identify potential problems in the research design that you have overlooked. Whenever possible, you should solicit and follow their suggestions, unless doing so compromises ethical or sci-entific requirements of the study.

Building a Relationship with the Site

In discussing a proposed research project with site personnel, you need to ensure that all parties understand specifically what their responsibilities are. Try to bring up any ques-tions that could lead to future misunderstandings if not answered clearly at the outset. Keep careful notes during planning meetings. Once you feel that all parties understand their roles in the project, write a letter that spells out the agreement in specific terms, and send this letter to all individuals whose cooperation is critical to your research activities.

You will need to remain accessible to site personnel and interested in their input in order to maintain positive relationships with them while the study is in progress. For example, if problems or questions of teachers whose students are participating in your research study go unanswered, they may refuse to cooperate. Some teachers might even hamper your work, for example, by complaining to parents that your study is interfering with classwork or scheduling field trips for students on days when you had planned to do testing.

It is wise to keep individuals at the site informed of your progress and alerted to up-coming events in the research plan. When studying a single school, you should keep per-sonally in contact with participating teachers and administrators. When doing a larger project, you should send periodic reports and newsletters to teachers, parents, and other interested persons.[40] A sample letter, similar to one sent to teachers participating in a pro-ject conducted by one of the authors (W. Borg), is shown in Figure 3.2.

Most field research in education depends on warm personal relationships between the researcher and site personnel. Carrying out your research in a setting where you are known as a friend and colleague makes it much easier than if you are regarded as an out-sider with unknown motives. If you develop a sincere interest in the problems of practi-tioners and a respect for their ideas and viewpoints, you will gain insights that improve your research design and contribute to your findings. You probably also will receive a level of cooperation that makes it possible to complete your project even if the going gets rough.

An effective method for developing a good relationship with site personnel is to use your expertise to address some of their needs, for example, locating curriculum materials, conducting a literature search related to a current school problem, designing a questionnaire

---

40. This and other site relations procedures applicable to large research projects are described in: Paddock, S. C., & Packard, J. S. (1981). On the conduct of site relations in educational research. *Educational Researcher, 10*(3), 14–17.

FIGURE 3.2

Letter to Build Positive Site Relations with Participants in a School-Based Research Project

UTAH STATE UNIVERSITY • LOGAN, UTAH 84322–2810

DEPARTMENT OF PSYCHOLOGY
[phone number]

[date]

Dear Mrs. Oliver:

With your valued assistance we have just finished collecting data for the second year of the Utah ability-grouping study. I realize that this research has caused you inconvenience and has taken time from your classes. I assure you that we are aware of the problems that such a study causes in the cooperating schools and shall continue to try to reduce these problems during the remaining two years of the study. I'm afraid that it is inevitable that progressive school districts, such as your own, that choose to support research and strive to find better ways of educating our youth must pay for their leadership by accepting the problems that major research projects always bring.

I am pleased to tell you that we already have enough important results to indicate that this research is well worth the effort, the problems, and the inconveniences. Our work to date has yielded important new knowledge about ability grouping. The remaining two years of the study will certainly teach us more and will also give us a chance to check the results we have already obtained.

The work under way in the Utah study is one of the first extensive long-term evaluations of ability grouping, and I assure you that through your cooperation you are making a real and important contribution to the teaching profession.

Although I know you have been working closely with Mrs. Johnson from our staff, my deepest regret is that I have had little opportunity to meet personally with the teachers cooperating in this research. I know that many of you have questions about the study that I could answer. I am also sure that you have suggestions and ideas that would help us make this research better. I plan to visit each cooperating school before we start collecting data next year and hope that you will jot down ideas and suggestions so that we may discuss them at that time.

In closing, permit me to thank you again for your patience and cooperation. I am looking forward to meeting with you and exchanging ideas during the coming year.

Sincerely,

Walter Borg

Walter R. Borg

---

to obtain information they need, or helping prepare a research proposal for funding. Researchers who freely give assistance to site personnel create goodwill that helps ease some of the problems associated with doing research in institutions such as public schools.

Dealing with Human Relations Issues

In spite of your best efforts to establish good rapport with concerned groups, problems inevitably arise in conducting educational research in real-life institutional settings. Problems can range from accidental omission of a page from one's survey questionnaire to a flu epidemic that reduces one's sample at a critical point in the research design.[41] Each problem, whether your fault or not, can place a strain on your relationship with administrators and research participants. A helpful approach is to build time buffers into the research schedule, so that if problems occur you and the individuals whose cooperation you need can develop solutions that do not burden anyone involved in the study.

Probably the most serious human relations problem that can arise in educational research is a protest by members of the community. For example, some parents might object to particular items in a self-report measure or complain that participation in the research project is taking time away from their children's schooling. Such protests usually are made by a small, but vocal, group. In many cases, protests can be traced back to a failure to ensure that all individuals understand the procedures, measures, or intended application of the findings of the research.

If your research project is criticized by community members, make an attempt to provide them with your side of the story. You may find it helpful to point out the procedures that you used to obtain the informed consent of your research participants and the steps that you are taking to protect individual privacy and confidentiality. Also, stress the benefits that research participants will derive from being involved in the study.

RECOMMENDATIONS FOR

Ensuring That a Research Study Is Ethical, Legal, and Harmonious

1. Clarify the benefits of the proposed research study and how potential risks to research participants will be minimized.
2. Follow proper channels in setting up a study in a field setting.
3. Prepare answers for questions likely to be asked by site administrators about the research project.
4. Select research participants equitably.
5. Avoid compromising the integrity of the research design by making changes for the administrative convenience of the site from which research participants are to be drawn.
6. Follow correct procedures for obtaining informed consent from research participants or their parents or guardians.
7. Carry out effective debriefing of research participants following deception.
8. Develop adequate safeguards to ensure the privacy and confidentiality of research participants.
9. Use data-collection procedures and experimental treatments that can readily withstand possible criticisms of the research study.
10. Establish good rapport by maintaining ongoing communication with groups that have a stake in the research project.

---

41. Maruyama & Deno, *Research in educational settings.*

SELF-CHECK TEST

Circle the correct answer to each of the following questions.
The answers are provided at the back of the book.

1. To ensure confidentiality of research data collected from research participants, it is appropriate for the researcher to
   a. make certain that no unauthorized individuals have access to the data.
   b. inform the participants about who will have access to the data.
   c. remove the names of the research participants from data-collection instruments and replace them with a code.
   d. all of the above.

2. A graduate student is employed as a research assistant in a planned psychological experiment involving deception. In studying the research plan, she notices that no debriefing is planned. What is her most reasonable course of action?
   a. Because she is not in charge of the project, she has no ethical responsibility, and therefore she should do nothing.
   b. She should report the investigator to the institutional review board of the university immediately.
   c. She should talk with the investigator and suggest a debriefing procedure in order to protect participants from harm.
   d. She should resign her assistantship in order to protect her ethical position.

3. In experiments in which participants have been deceived, what is the ethical responsibility of the investigator?
   a. Inform participants before the study that the experiment involves deception, but do not identify what the deception is.
   b. At the end of the study give participants a written sheet that states that the study involved deception but does not describe the specific deception.
   c. Inform participants in writing at the end of the study of the specific nature of the deception.
   d. At the end of the study personally inform participants or carry out demonstrations to convince them that they were deceived and alleviate any continuing distress.

4. Naive or erroneous choices of data-analysis methods constitute a breach of ethics mainly because they can
   a. misrepresent questionable findings as research knowledge.
   b. discourage researchers from reporting their results.
   c. cause direct harm to research participants.
   d. reduce the likelihood of the research report's acceptance for publication.

5. Paraphragiarism involves
   a. listing as co-authors of a research report one or more prestigious individuals who were minimally involved in the research.
   b. disseminating research results in the "least publishable unit," rather than as a coherent whole.
   c. taking credit for research done by someone else.
   d. closely copying another writer's words or ideas in one's research report.

6. The main purpose of the Code of Federal Regulations for the Protection of Human Subjects is to
   a. protect research participants from unnecessary physical or psychological risk.
   b. inform individuals that they have the right to participate in research projects.
   c. protect individuals from invasion of privacy by the federal government.
   d. regulate the types of measures that can be used in collecting research data.

7. A risk-benefit ratio legitimately could involve the
   a. cost of doing the study relative to its potential for advancing the researcher's career.
   b. inconvenience to the research participants relative to the study's potential to improve the learning of the population whom they represent.
   c. probability that the study will yield nonsignificant results relative to the probability that it will yield significant results.
   d. all of the above.

8. If telling participants the purpose of the research study before data collection might invalidate

the results, the researcher's best course of action is to

a. refer participants to the institutional review board that is overseeing the study.

b. inform participants anyway, because regulations concerning informed consent require full disclosure.

c. tell participants that they will be informed of the purpose at the completion of the research.

d. give reasons other than the true reasons for the research.

9. If a college student agrees to participate in a research project and then drops out partway through the study,

a. the student should be informed that this is a violation of the ethics code of the American Psychological Association.

b. the student should be informed that he must contact the institutional review board that is overseeing the project.

c. nothing should be done, because participants have the right to withdraw at any time.

d. the student is legally committed to complete the project, and should be informed of this fact.

10. A potential disadvantage of conducting research in an educational institution at which the researcher is employed is that

a. his particular position may cause other members of the institution to conceal concerns that might affect his research.

b. he will probably have more difficulty obtaining permission to conduct the research than would an outsider.

c. he is biased about the best procedures for communication among staff of the institution.

d. all of the above.

11. Joint planning of research by researchers and research participants can reduce participants' vulnerability to risk because it tends to

a. lead to the selection of less vulnerable individuals as research participants.

b. take the focus off the research participants in relation to other individuals at the research site.

c. increase the number of research participants.

d. encourage the researchers to think more deeply about potential benefits and harms to research participants.

12. If a superintendent gives permission for research to be done in the school district,

a. it is not necessary to obtain clearance from an institutional review board.

b. it is not necessary to provide letters of informed consent to the research participants.

c. it still is necessary to obtain the cooperation of all individuals and groups that have a stake in the study.

d. it still is necessary to make any changes in the research design requested by the participants or by others who have a stake in the study.

13. If a teacher objects to students in the control group not receiving an experimental treatment that is viewed as desirable, the researcher's best course of action in order to maintain positive site relations is to

a. explain that the experimental design requires a control group that does not receive treatment.

b. provide the treatment to control-group students after data have been collected from the experimental group.

c. provide the treatment to both groups simultaneously in order to avoid conflict with the teacher.

d. use a different teacher's students to serve as the control group.

CHAPTER 4

Reviewing the Literature

OVERVIEW

To contribute to research knowledge in your area of interest, you first must review what other researchers have discovered. We show you how to do this type of review in this chapter. Much of our discussion involves the various types of documents that you will come across in a literature review: preliminary sources, which are hard-copy or electronic indexes to the literature; secondary sources, which are published reviews of particular bodies of literature; and primary sources, which are reports of research studies written by those who conducted them. Because your literature search may reveal both quantitative and qualitative research findings, we describe procedures for synthesizing and reporting both types.

OBJECTIVES

After studying this chapter, you should be able to

1. Explain the various ways that a literature review helps a researcher design a study.
2. Describe the four major steps involved in conducting a literature review.
3. Describe the difference between preliminary, secondary, and primary sources, and the role of each type of source in the literature-review process.
4. Locate relevant citations on an educational topic, using online versions of popular preliminary sources.
5. Describe several types of preliminary sources and their usefulness in doing a literature search.
6. Describe several major secondary sources and their usefulness in doing a literature search.
7. Describe a method for classifying the information contained in primary source documents that are identified through a literature search.
8. State several criteria that are useful in judging the merits of a quantitative or qualitative study.
9. Describe several flaws that weaken the reporting of a literature review.
10. Evaluate the relative advantages of narrative review, vote counting, chi-square, and meta-analysis for synthesizing quantitative research findings.
11. Explain the role of effect sizes in a meta-analysis.
12. Describe a method for synthesizing a body of literature that consists primarily of qualitative research studies.

Purposes of a Literature Review

Touchstone in Research

Reed, J. G., & Baxter, P. M. (2003). *Library use: Handbook for psychology* (3rd ed.). Washington, DC: American Psychological Association.

Unless your study explicitly builds on the work of other researchers in your area of inquiry, it is unlikely to contribute to research knowledge. Joel Levin and Hermione Marshall emphasized this point in commenting on their experience as editors of the *Journal of Educational Psychology:*

> For research to make a substantial contribution, it must be based on adequate knowledge of the field, and the study's introduction must reflect this knowledge. . . . Unfortunately, we sometimes receive manuscripts from investigators who base their research on early work that is now dated or from researchers who ignore current work. Reviewers may then be left questioning why the study was conducted, which usually leads to a recommendation of rejection.[1]

Despite the importance of a thorough review of the literature, this phase of the research process is slighted more often than any other phase. In our experience, it requires three to six months or more to do a good review of the literature, especially if you know little about the literature on your research problem at the outset. This time is well spent because a thorough review of the literature serves various important purposes, as we explain below.

1. *Delimiting the research problem.* Studies are doomed to failure if the researcher does not limit sufficiently the scope of the problem. Selecting a limited problem and investigating it in depth is far better than a superficial study of a broad problem. By reviewing the literature, you can find out how other researchers have formulated fruitful lines of focused inquiry within a broad field of interest.

For example, suppose you are doing research on instructional leadership. You might find that researchers have developed separate lines of inquiry about leadership as manifested by individuals in different roles—superintendents, principals, department heads, consultants, and so forth. You might find that some studies focus on describing the behavior of recognized instructional leaders, whereas others focus on the outcomes of effective and ineffective leadership. Also, you might find that different studies are framed by different theories. As you develop insight into how these delimited lines of inquiry arose and progressed, you will become more able to delimit your own problem for investigation.

2. *Seeking new lines of inquiry.* In doing a literature review, you should determine what research already has been done in your area of interest. Just as important, you should be alert to research possibilities that have been overlooked. Your unique experience and background may make it possible for you to see a facet of the problem that other researchers have not seen. These new viewpoints are most likely to occur in areas where little research has been done, but even in well-researched areas someone occasionally thinks of an approach that is unique and creative. For example, one of the authors (M. Gall) advised a doctoral student, Isabella Henderson, on a study of school improvement and change.[2] Henderson discovered that one line of research in this area had sought to understand the work of designated "change agents," that is, persons whose role is to facilitate a change process in an organization. She identified previous research studies of teachers, administrators, staff development specialists, and project coordinators in the role of change agent. However, her particular interest was department chairpersons in high schools who had been given the task of facilitating the implementation of a new social studies curriculum in one province in Canada.

1. Levin, J. R., & Marshall, H. H. (1993). Publishing in the *Journal of Educational Psychology:* Reflections at midstream. *Journal of Educational Psychology, 85,* 3–6. Quote appears on p. 3.
2. Henderson, I. M. (1993). The role of high school department heads as change agents in implementing a new social studies curriculum. *Dissertation Abstracts International, 54*(09), 3309A. (UMI No. 9405182)

In reviewing the literature, Henderson found little research on department chairpersons, and none on their possible role as change agents. She realized that conceptualizing this group as change agents and studying them with the methodology that had been developed in change-agent research would open a new line of inquiry. The research that resulted from the insights gained in Henderson's literature review led to new knowledge about department chairpersons. In addition, her findings provided a replication test of findings about change agents that had accumulated from previous research on other types of change agents in education.

3. *Avoiding fruitless approaches.* In reviewing the literature, be on the lookout for lines of inquiry in your area that proved to be fruitless. For example, literature searches sometimes identify several similar studies done over a period of years, all of which employed approximately the same research methodology and all of which failed to produce a significant experimental or correlational result. One or two further tests of an intervention or hypothesized relationship can be justified on the grounds that they confirm the previous finding of no significant effect. Additional studies, however, serve no useful purpose and suggest that the researcher has not done an adequate review of the literature.

4. *Gaining methodological insights.* In reviewing research reports, some individuals give scant attention to anything but the results reported. This is a mistake because other information in the report can help you in the design of your study. For example, a study conducted by one of the authors (W. Borg) tested a procedure for training inservice teachers to use specific classroom management skills.[3] Although the teachers could be taught to use a set of three specific skills in one week of instruction and practice, their use of the skills was awkward and unnatural. Because of this finding, the training program was revised to include four more weeks during which teachers practiced the skills they had learned earlier. This change resulted in much more effective teacher performance. The methodological insights gained in this study might be useful to other researchers who are interested in designing and testing programs to improve teachers' classroom skills.

5. *Identifying recommendations for further research.* Researchers often conclude their reports with a discussion of issues raised by their study and recommendations for other research that might be done. (Examples are provided in Chapter 2.) These issues and recommendations should be considered carefully because they represent insights gained by the researcher after considerable study of a given problem.

6. *Seeking support for grounded theory.* Many research studies are designed to test a theory that has been developed to explain the learning process or other educational phenomena. Barney Glaser, however, proposed that studies also can be designed such that data are collected first, and then a theory is derived from those data.[4] (Glaser's approach is described more fully in Chapters 2 and 14.) The resulting theory is called *grounded theory* because it is "grounded" in a set of real-world data.

Glaser advises researchers who plan to use the grounded theory approach not to conduct a review of the literature beforehand because they are likely to be exposed to other researchers' theories. As a result of this exposure, they might be unable to see their data with a fresh perspective. Glaser instead recommends this approach:

> [W]e collect the data in the field first. Then we start analyzing it and generating theory. When the theory seems sufficiently grounded and developed, *then* we review the literature in the

3. Borg, W. R. (1977). Changing teacher and pupil performance with protocols. *Journal of Experimental Education, 45*, 9–18.

4. Glaser, B. G. (1978). *Theoretical sensitivity: Advances in the methodology of grounded theory.* Mill Valley, CA: Sociology Press.

field and relate the theory to it through the integration of ideas. . . . Thus scholarship in the same area starts after the emerging theory is sufficiently developed so the theory will not be preconceived by preempting concepts.[5]

A literature review conducted in this fashion, that is, after researchers have developed grounded theory, might generate support for the theory, might lead them to question their own theory or the theories of others, or might cause them to refine their theory and develop ideas for further investigation.

Glaser qualified his position about the role of literature reviews in research by suggesting that researchers first read the literature on topics that are indirectly related to their area of investigation. The purpose of this reading is to help researchers develop ideas that will inform their fieldwork, without constraining their development of grounded theory.

Major Steps in a Literature Review

Touchstone in Research

Cooper, H. M. (1998). *Synthesizing research: A guide for literature reviews* (3rd ed.). Thousand Oaks, CA: Sage.

Prior to initiating a literature review, you should write a preliminary statement of your research problem. (Chapter 2 discusses this process in detail.) Having formulated a problem statement, you are now ready to initiate a literature review. The method that we recommend has four steps.

Step 1: Search preliminary sources. You will need to identify books, articles, professional papers, and other publications that are relevant to the problem statement. **Preliminary sources,** which are indexes to particular bodies of literature, are an essential aid for this task. They are similar to the subject index of a library catalog. By looking in the subject index for a particular topic (e.g., mathematics education), you can find all the books in the library that pertain to this topic. The preliminary sources that we describe below are much more comprehensive than a library index, however, because they index all sorts of publications—not just books—and they include publications wherever they may be located, not just the holdings of a particular library.

Step 2: Use secondary sources. In your examination of preliminary sources, you may find that other researchers already have written reviews of the literature that are relevant to your problem statement. Such reviews are examples of secondary sources. A **secondary source** is a document written by someone who did not actually do the research, develop the theories, or express the opinions that they have synthesized into a literature review. You can use preliminary sources to help determine whether relevant secondary sources are available.

Step 3: Read primary sources. Preliminary and secondary sources index or review research studies, respectively, but not in detail. For this reason, you will need to obtain and study the original reports of at least those studies that are most central to your proposed investigation. These original reports are called primary sources. A **primary source** is a document (e.g., journal article or dissertation) that was written by the individuals who actually conducted the research study or who formulated the theory or opinions that are described in the document.

Step 4: Synthesize the literature. Once you have read all the relevant primary and secondary sources, you will need to synthesize what you have learned in order to write a literature review. The purpose of the review is to inform the reader about what already is known, and what is not yet known, about the problems or questions that you plan to investigate. Also, you will need to make clear how your proposed study relates to, and builds upon, the existing knowledge base as represented in the literature.

5. Ibid., p. 31.

These four steps of the literature review process need not be done strictly in sequence. For example, as you review literature relevant to your problem statement, you may find that you want to reformulate the statement, which may take your literature search in a new direction. Also, you may find that the primary and secondary sources identified by your preliminary sources were only indirectly related to your problem statement. In this case, you will need to go back to the first step and attempt to find a more relevant preliminary source.

To conduct a thorough literature review, you need to know how to use preliminary, secondary, and primary sources. We describe each of them in the next sections.

Searching Preliminary Sources

Until the 1980s, most preliminary sources were in hard-copy format. This necessitated trips to a library that had these resources and the expenditure of many hours copying information from them. Still more hours were required to locate the documents that were identified in the preliminary sources.

All this has changed with the advent of the personal computer and the Internet. Online searching of electronic preliminary sources is now the norm. By *online*, we mean that a person can interact continuously with a preliminary source by connecting to the Internet using a Web browser (e.g., Internet Explorer, Safari) and then entering the Web address for the preliminary source. The delay between a search request and a response from the electronic preliminary source typically is a fraction of a second.

Because online searching has become so ubiquitous, our discussion of preliminary sources is based on this search format. For examples, we refer to the electronic library resources available at our university (the University of Oregon). You might find more or fewer resources at your university's library, and they might be organized a bit differently. Whenever possible, we emphasize features of online resources that are likely to be universal.

Types of Documents Indexed by Preliminary Sources

In doing a literature review in preparation for a new research study, you will search primarily for previous research studies. However, you also are likely to come across other reports of interest, including descriptions and evaluations of theories, educational practices, historical trends, and other such matters.

We use the term **document** to refer to any report you might come across in your literature search. Documents can take a variety of forms. For example, some educational journals are entirely electronic and available only on the Internet. Others are hard copy only. Some journals now have a hard-copy version and an electronic version. The latter is usually an Adobe Acrobat pdf file, which is an exact reproduction of the hard-copy version; the reproduction preserves the page layouts, pagination, fonts, and table and figure formatting of the hard-copy version. (We occasionally come across documents that are available as pdf files and an alternative electronic version.) If you examine the current edition of the *APA (American Psychological Association) Publication Manual,* you will find different citation formats for different types of documents.

Documents of relevance to education typically take the form of journal articles, books, and chapters in edited books. A substantial number of documents, however, take different forms and appear elsewhere, for example, dissertations, papers presented at education conferences, technical reports on studies sponsored by federal research programs, reports of projects conducted by school districts and other local agencies, and newsletters of professional organizations. Many of these reports constitute what is called

Touchstones in Research

Brem, S. K., & Boyes, A. J. (2000). Using critical thinking to conduct effective searches of online resources. *Practical Assessment, Research & Evaluation, 7*(7). Retrieved August 5, 2005 from http://pareonline.net/getvn.asp?v=7&n=7

Mardis, M. (2001). Uncovering the hidden Web, Part 1: Finding what the search engines don't. Retrieved January 5, 2006, from http://searcheric.org/digests/ed456863.html

fugitive literature or **gray literature** because they are not widely disseminated or easily obtained. It is important to be aware of these different types of documents, because if you wish to include them in your literature search, you might need to use particular preliminary sources.

Content and Coverage of Online Preliminary Sources

We will use *Education Abstracts* to illustrate the content and coverage of online preliminary sources. It is not as popular as the preliminary source maintained by ERIC (Education Resources Information Center), but ERIC was going through a major organizational restructuring at the time we are preparing this edition of the book. This preliminary source has not been updated for approximately a year, whereas *Education Abstracts* is current.

Before using a preliminary source like *Education Abstracts,* you should determine its coverage. By going to the online version of this preliminary source at our university library and clicking on several information buttons, we can learn about its coverage. As of mid-2005, it included more than 602,000 records. The term **record** (also called **citation**) refers to all the information that a preliminary source provides about a particular document, such as its author(s), title, the publication in which it appears, year of publication, and unique ID by which it is identified in the preliminary source.

The total collection of records in *Education Abstracts* is stored in electronic form. For this reason, the collection is called a *database*. Because the database is electronic, it needs to be accessed by a **search engine**, which is a type of specialized software that helps a user sift through the database to identify citations that satisfy particular criteria. In similar fashion, Google, Yahoo!, and other services rely on search engines to help you locate relevant Web sites throughout the Internet.

Information about *Education Abstracts* includes the fact that it covers English-language periodicals and yearbooks published in the United States and elsewhere. More specifically, it covers 659 sources (mostly periodicals), the titles of which we can examine on our computer screen. This examination reveals that *Education Abstracts* covers journals that we consider essential to our purposes and also that its coverage is broad with respect to both practitioner and research journals.

Other pertinent information is that the records cover documents published from 1983 to the present time. Thus, *Education Abstracts* would not be suitable if we wished to search for documents published prior to that year. Also, abstracts are available only for documents published since 1994. Because we are interested primarily in documents published from 2000 to the present time, these limitations are not of immediate concern to us.

Popular Online Preliminary Sources

Thousands of online preliminary sources have been developed to index the great array of scholarly disciplines and major topics within each discipline. To find out for yourself, try Google or another search engine and enter "literature database" and your topic as the search item. For example, suppose we're interested in research reports and other documents that focus on teaching strategies. We entered "teaching strategy literature database" in Google and came up with several million "hits" (i.e., Web sites that presumably are relevant to this search term). The first hit was the Web site http://www.ahceducation.umn.edu/OofE/Faculty/EBT.html, which listed a wide range of databases citing documents pertaining to teaching strategies.

Table 4.1 contains a list of online preliminary sources that are useful to educational researchers. It is by no means comprehensive, but it does serve to illustrate what is available.

TABLE 4.1

Examples of Online Preliminary Sources That Index the Education Literature

A. Bibliographies
Bibliographic index plus. Indexes more than 350,000 bibliographies, with many full-text downloads.

B. Book Reviews
Book review index. Indexes more than 4 million book reviews appearing in about 500 publications.
Education review. An open access electronic journal publishing reviews of books in education. Available at http://edrev.asu.edu.
PsycCRITIQUES. Indexes reviews of books in psychology, with full-text downloads. Replaces the hard-copy journal *Contemporary Psychology: APA Review of Books.*

C. Books
Books in print. Indexes approximately 2 million books in print, forthcoming books, and out-of-print books.
Childrens books in print. Indexes more than 550,000 books and multimedia materials for children and young adults. Available at http://www.childrensbooksinprint.com
Library of Congress online catalog. A comprehensive index of in-print and out-of-print books and other documents. Available at http://catalog.loc.gov

D. Directories
Directories in print. Indexes more than 15,000 directories in the United States and worldwide (hard copy only at present time).
Guide to American educational directories (hard copy only at present time).

E. Dissertations and Theses
Dissertation abstracts. Indexes dissertations in all academic subjects from 1861 to the present.
Master's theses directories (hard-copy only at present time).

F. Journal Articles, Papers, and Reports
Chicano database. Indexes publications relating to Mexican American, Latino, and Central American culture.
Education abstracts. Indexes English-language periodicals and yearbooks from 1983 to the present.
Educational administration abstracts. Indexes articles in approximately 100 journals.
ERIC. Indexes more than 850,000 documents in all areas of education published from 1966 to the present.
Government periodicals index. Indexes approximately 170 magazines and newsletters published by U.S. government agencies.
GPO monthly catalog of U.S. government publications. Indexes public documents issued by all branches of the U.S. government.
International index to black periodicals. Indexes approximately 150 journals and other sources relating to black studies, Africa, and the Caribbean.
JSTOR. Indexes more than 100 major research journals in a variety of academic disciplines, with full-text downloads.
Medline. Indexes publications relating to all areas of medicine.
PsycINFO. Indexes more than 1,900 journals in psychology and also doctoral dissertations and anthologies.
Sage family studies abstracts. Indexes publications relating to the family.
Sociological abstracts. Indexes publications in more than 1,500 journals and other sources on topics relating to sociology and related disciplines.
SPORTDiscus. Indexes approximately 300 journals about sports and physical education.
Web of science. Indexes publications that cite a particular publication.
Women's studies international. Indexes the interdisciplinary field of women's studies.

(Continued)

TABLE 4.1

(Continued)

G. Magazines and Newspapers
Magazines fulltext. Indexes more than 570 popular and technical magazines, with full-text downloads.
Newspaper source. Indexes more than 250 U.S. and international newspapers.
Ulrich's periodicals directory. Indexes more than 240,000 journals and magazines.

Note: With a few exceptions, all the preliminary sources listed here are available for online searching. Some are free, but most are subscription services. Many universities subscribe to these services for use by faculty, students, and others.

The list is organized into indexes to:

1. Bibliographies
2. Book reviews
3. Books in education and related fields
4. Directories
5. Dissertations and theses
6. Journal articles, papers, and reports
7. Magazines and newspapers

In addition to these preliminary sources, there are specialized preliminary sources that index tests and self-report measures. They are described in Chapter 7.

In the remainder of this section, we briefly describe several preliminary sources that are particularly useful or distinctive.

ERIC Since the 1960s, the Education Resources Information Center (ERIC) and its clearinghouses have maintained the most used preliminary source indexing education literature. Its database contains more than 1.1 million records dating back to 1966. More than 107,000 full-text nonjournal documents issued since 1993 are now available for free downloading directly from the Web site. As we prepare this edition of the book, the ERIC database is only up to 2004, but actions are being taken to bring it up to date and maintain it. For the current status of ERIC, go to its home page (http://www.eric.ed.gov/). Among other things, you will find a search engine for accessing ERIC records.

Dissertation abstracts Doctoral dissertations constitute a large body of research. Some doctoral graduates eventually publish their dissertations as a journal article or book, but for others the dissertation is the only document containing a report of the research study. For this reason, it is worthwhile to search this preliminary source. At the present time, this literature database includes more than 1.6 million dissertations and master's theses completed in North America and other parts of the world. The database is available from several vendors; you can check with your library to determine whether it has a subscription to one of them.

Google Scholar This source (http://scholar.google.com) is an ambitious undertaking by Google. It is both a search engine to a wide range of literature in all scholarly disciplines and a repository of that information. This means that *Google Scholar* can be used to download books and other documents that are in the public domain. An interesting and potentially important feature of its search engine is that it automatically extracts citations in articles and presents them as separate records. Some of these records may reference older documents, including seminal articles in edited books, that are not referenced by other preliminary sources.

PsycINFO This database is maintained by the American Psychological Association. It indexes a large number of pychology-related journals and other sources, more than 1,900 in total. Many of the journals and other document sources that it indexes are also covered by *ERIC* and *Education Abstracts.*

Web of Science This index has a unique function: to help researchers identify documents that cite a particular document of interest. It provides citation information for articles published in more than 13,000 journals in the physical and social sciences from 1975 to the present time. For example, Kenneth Sirotnik wrote an article, published in *Harvard Educational Review,* that presented findings from observations of over 1,000 elementary and secondary school classrooms in the United States.[6] Suppose we wish to know whether subsequent researchers cited this article and perhaps used it in designing their own study. Going to *Web of Science,* we enter Sirotnik's name, find his list of publications, and select the article in the *Harvard Educational Review.* We find that exactly 50 other documents have cited this article to date. Reviewing the abstracts for the documents, we develop a sense of how other researchers and practitioners have made use of this article in their own research and thinking about education.

Search Strategies in Using Preliminary Sources

Searching a preliminary source involves a certain amount of experimentation. To illustrate, suppose we are interested in research studies and recommended practices having to do with teachers' questioning techniques during classroom instruction.

We decide to start with *Education Abstracts* as our online preliminary source. Our library's version of this preliminary source is available from a company called OCLC First Search, which uses a common format for all the preliminary sources (called databases by OCLC) to which the library subscribes. The computer screen shows that *Education Abstracts* was updated July 25, 2005. If we did the same search 6 months later, we are likely to get a larger set of records. Therefore, if you do an initial search when designing a study and write the final report a year later, it is desirable to update the search accordingly.

The screen has a blank area in which to enter a keyword. A **keyword** is a word or phrase that the search engine for the preliminary source will look for in each record. Records typically contain a citation (authors, title, journal), abstract, and descriptors, so the search engine will look at each of these elements for the keyword.

Typing *teachers questioning techniques* in the keyword box and clicking the search button, we obtain 36 records. But is *techniques* the best word to use? Let's try *teachers questioning strategies.* This search yields 54 records. Now let's try a more general keyword: *questioning strategies.* This search yields 147 records. Which of these is the best keyword? It's probably best to try all of them and study the kinds of records retrieved.

As just stated, *teachers questioning techniques* yielded 36 records, and *teachers questioning strategies* yielded 54 records. We do not know whether the 54 records subsume the entire 36 records of the first keyword, a partial set, or a completely separate set. We can find this out by using a Boolean operator. A **Boolean operator** is a term that specifies a logical relationship among search terms; it is based on a branch of mathematics called Boolean logic. The three most common Boolean operators in online searching of preliminary sources are *or, and,* and *not.*

---

6. Sirotnik, K. A. (1983). What you see is what you get—Consistency, persistency, and mediocrity in classrooms. *Harvard Educational Review, 55,* 178–194.

If we are not certain whether *technique* or *strategies* is the best keyword, we can specify a keyword phrase that asks the search engine to find all records that contain either term. The computer screen for *Education Abstracts* allows us to enter *teachers questioning techniques,* select the Boolean operator *or,* and enter *teachers questioning strategies.* This search yields 77 records.

Suppose we are only interested in records for documents that are about elementary school teaching. We can use the Boolean operator *and* to limit the search to the subset of the 67 records that refer to elementary teaching. To do this, we enter *teachers questioning techniques,* select the Boolean operator *or,* enter *teachers questioning strategies,* select the Boolean operator *and,* and enter *elementary.* This search yields 11 records.

The Boolean operator *or,* which asks the search engine to look for records that contain one of two or more keywords, generally will increase the number of retrieved records. In contrast, the Boolean operator *and* generally will decrease the number of retrieved records.

Another Boolean operator is *not.* It is used when you can identify a keyword that you do not wish to be included in your search. Suppose we are interested in documents that are about teacher questions, but not those that involve college or university teaching. If we enter *teacher questions* as the keyword phrase, *Education Abstracts* returns 1,720 records. If we do the same search, but include *not college* and *not university,* the number of records is reduced to 1,444.

In a search for documents relevant to one's research topic, it is better to cast a wide net and discard irrelevant documents than it is to cast a small net that fails to retrieve relevant documents. With this principle in mind, we might ask whether the keywords *techniques* and *strategies* eliminate documents that are relevant to our interest in teachers' question-asking behavior. Why not simplify the keyword phrase to *teachers questions* or *teachers questioning*? We need to consider, though, whether the keyword *questions* is less restrictive than the keyword *questioning.* In fact, it is not necessary to choose between the two terms if we use a procedure known as truncation. **Truncation** is a procedure that is used to identify all records in a preliminary source that contain any keyword having a common root. The keyword *question* is a root word for other keywords like *questions, questioning,* and *question-asking.* Depending on the preliminary source, you would enter the word *question* to search for all keywords containing that root keyword or you would enter the word followed by an asterisk (*question**). The asterisk, sometimes called a *wildcard,* informs the search engine to look for all records that contain the root word or one of its extensions. Depending on the database, the wild card might be an asterisk, question mark, dollar sign, or other symbol.

We experimented by entering several keywords with and without the asterisk in *Education Abstracts* and obtained the following results:

teacher question (694 records)
teacher question* (3,116 records)
teacher* question* (5,654 records)

We see, then, that truncation makes a big difference in the number of retrieved records.

In searching the records retrieved by this search strategy, we find that many of them have the keyword *teacher** in one part of the record and *question** in another part of the record, but the document to which the record refers is not actually about teacher questions. We might find fewer, but more relevant, records by identifying only those in which the two keywords appear next to each other. This search can be done by placing quote marks around the desired keyword phrase. Entering *"teacher* question*"* as the keyword phrase, we obtain 144 records, a quick perusal of which indicates that most are highly relevant to our topic of interest. You can see, then, that the simple insertion of quotation marks around *teacher* question** reduces the retrieved records by a tremendous amount—from 5,654 to 144.

An online search of preliminary sources can be expanded or narrowed in other ways. For example, most allow the user to specify a range of publication years to be searched. Some allow the user to restrict the search to journal articles or books or to a particular country's publications. An important feature of certain preliminary sources is the coding of documents by professional indexers who use a category system. For example, consider PsycINFO, the online preliminary source maintained by the American Psychological Association. We entered the keyword *teacher questions* and selected an option that mapped it to the following subject categories:

- Teacher student interaction
- Elementary school students
- Questioning
- Teaching methods
- Teacher characteristics
- Elementary school teachers
- Group discussion
- Classroom behavior
- Science education
- High school students
- Reading education
- Conversation
- Discourse analysis
- Social studies education
- Mathematics education

PsycINFO allows us to search its database using any or all of these subject categories, including narrower terms for each category. Once again, experimentation is necessary to determine which search strategies are best for identifying documents that are relevant to one's research problem.

Displaying Records in Preliminary Sources

A typical online preliminary source will provide a basic citation (author, title, journal, publication date) for each record retrieved by the user's search request. The brevity of the citation makes it possible to scan a long list of records quickly. There usually is also the option of requesting a full record. One such record, which appears in ERIC, is shown in Figure 4.1.

You will see that most of the information in the record is useful for achieving an understanding of the study and judging its relevance to your own research problem. The abstract is particularly helpful, because it includes details of the study.[7] The descriptor terms also are helpful, because they can be used to generate new searches of the database for related documents.

Prior to personal computers, researchers needed to copy the information in a record by hand or make a photocopy from a hard copy of the preliminary source. All this has changed with the arrival of personal computers, the Internet, and sophisticated bibliographic software.

---

7. For an interesting article about abstracts and the "abstract of the future," see: Miech, E. J., Nave, B., & Mosteller, F. (2005). The 20,000 article problem: How a structured abstract can help practitioners sort out educational research. *Phi Delta Kappan, 86*(5), 396–400.

FIGURE 4.1

Example of a Record in the Preliminary Source *Educational Resources Information Center (ERIC)*

ERIC #:	EJ698924
Title:	Preservice Teachers' Self-Judgments of Test Taking
Authors:	Beghetto, Ronald A.;
Descriptors:	Economically Disadvantaged; Testing; Preservice Teachers; Achievement Tests;
Journal/Source Name:	Journal of Educational Research
Journal Citation:	v98 n6 p376 Jul 2005
Publisher:	Heldref Publications, Helen Dwight Reid Educational Foundation, 1319 Eighteenth Street, NW, Washington, DC 20036-1802. Web site: http://www.heldref.org
Publication Date:	2005-07-00
Pages:	5
Pub Types:	Journal Articles; Reports - Descriptive
Abstract:	The author examined potential differences between preservice teachers who held positive self-judgments of their test taking ability (positive self-judgers) and preservice teachers who held negative self-judgment of their test-taking ability (negative self-judgers). Preservice teachers (N = 87) enrolled in an introductory evaluation-for-decision-making course completed questions that measured views of testing. Significant differences in past experiences with testing, current views of testing, and future use of tests existed between positive and negative self-judgers. Positive self-judgers held significantly more favorable views regarding how accurately classroom and statewide assessments had measured their knowledge. On average, negative self-judgers attributed their poor test-taking performance to "bad tests," whereas positive self-judgers attributed their poor performance to a lack of preparation. Positive self-judgers were significantly more likely to agree that tests in general provide useful information. Negative self-judgers were significantly more likely to question the accuracy of information from statewide achievement tests and the fairness of classroom tests. Positive self-judgers intended to use tests in their classroom and to trust the results of classroom tests that they administered to a significantly greater degree than did negative self-judgers.

Source: ERIC database at http://www.eric.ed.gov

You can select any or all the records that you retrieve in your search and then exercise one of several options: Send them electronically to a computer printer, email them to yourself, or download them into bibliographic software such as Endnote or Procite. Many preliminary sources allow you to exercise these options for full records or for brief citations.

The most important advance in online searching in recent years is that many preliminary sources include a feature that allows you to download the actual document to which a record refers, or they will inform you how the document can be obtained from your local library or other source. We discuss this feature in the section on reading primary sources in this chapter.

Using Secondary Sources

Secondary sources in education are publications written by authors who were not direct observers of, or participants in, the events being described. These publications include most textbooks, scholarly books, encyclopedias, handbooks, and review articles in journals. For example, most history textbooks are secondary sources because the authors relied on the reports of others about past events rather than having observed the events themselves.

Some publications combine primary and secondary source information. For example, suppose an author writes an exhaustive review of the research literature on mathematics instruction for a handbook on this subject. If the author reports the results of her own research on mathematics instruction as part of the literature review, that portion of the review a primary source. The portion that reports the studies of other researchers, however, is a secondary source.

Secondary sources are useful because they combine knowledge from many primary sources into a single publication. For example, the *Encyclopedia of Educational Research* and the *International Encyclopedia of Education* contain short, readable articles on a wide variety of educational topics of general interest.[8] Among yearbooks devoted to literature reviews, one of the most useful is *Review of Research in Education,* sponsored by the American Educational Research Association. Among journals, the most comprehensive secondary source is *Review of Educational Research.*

Table 4.2 shows examples of these and other secondary sources that might prove useful to you in designing a research study. The list is by no means exhaustive, and some of the listed sources might have gone into new editions. Therefore, we recommend that you check the recency of a listed edition. You can do this by checking *Books in Print* or the Library of Congress catalog (see Table 4.1). Also, you can use these resources to search for other secondary sources. Combining the descriptor terms *handbook* or *encyclopedia* and a keyword term for your topic is a productive strategy.

A good secondary source is more than a compilation of research studies on a particular problem or topic. It organizes what is known about the problem or topic into a meaningful structure and shows how various research studies are connected to each other. Frank Murray and James Raths describe these purposes in the following manner:

> The scholarly literature . . . is like a wall that is built one stone at a time, each stone filling a hole previously unfilled, each one mortared and connected to those that came before and after it, each one providing a support for the subsequent ones, and each one being supported by those that came before. The review article attempts to describe the wall itself and to discover its mortar, its architecture and design; the wall's place in the architecture of the larger structure; its relation to the other elements in the structure; its significance, purpose, and meaning in the larger structure.[9]

---

8. American Educational Research Association. (2001). *Encyclopedia of educational research* (7th ed., Vols. 1–4). Farmington Hills, MI: Gale Group; Hustén, T., & Postlethwaite, T. N. (Eds.). (1994). *International encyclopedia of education* (2nd ed.). New York: Elsevier Science.
9. Murray, F., & Raths, J. (1996). Call for manuscripts. *Review of Educational Research, 64,* 197–200. Quote appears on p. 197.

> ### TABLE 4.2
> ## Examples of Secondary Sources: Published Reviews of the Education Literature

A. Annual Reviews
Annual review of psychology. (1950 to date). Stanford, CA: Annual Reviews.
Review of research in education. (1931 to date). Itasca, IL: Peacock.
Yearbook of the National Society for the Study of Education. (1910 to date). Chicago: National Society for the Study of Education.

B. Encyclopedias
American Educational Research Association. (2001). *Encyclopedia of educational research* (7th ed.). Farmington Hills, MI: Macmillan.
English, L. M. (Ed.). (2005). *International encyclopedia of higher education.* New York: Macmillan.
Grinstein, L., & Lipsey, S. I. (Eds.). (2001). *Encyclopedia of mathematics education.* New York: Routledge.
Guthrie, J. W. (Ed.). (2003). *Encyclopedia of education.* Farmington Hills, MI: Macmillan.
Hricko, M. (Ed.). (2005). *Encyclopedia of support services and distance education.* Hershey, PA: Idea Group Publishing.
Husén, T., & Postlethwaite, T. N. (Eds.). (1994). *International encyclopedia of education* (2nd ed.). New York: Elsevier. Entries relating to certain subjects (e.g., educational technology, economics of education, teaching and teacher education) have been cumulated and published as separate volumes.
Kazdin, A. E. (Ed.). (2000). *Encyclopedia of psychology.* Washington, DC: American Psychological Association; New York: Oxford University Press.
Levinson, D. L., Cookson, P. W., & Sadovnik, A. R. (Eds.). (2002). *Education and sociology: An encyclopedia.* New York: Garland.
Lopez, C. (Ed.). (2001). *World education encyclopedia: A survey of educational systems worldwide* (2nd ed.). Farmington Hills, MI: Macmillan.
Mitchell, B. M., & Salsburg, R. E. (Eds.). (1999). *Encyclopedia of multicultural education* (2nd ed.). Westport, CT: Greenwood.
Reynolds, C. R., & Fletcher-Janzen, E. (Eds.). (2004). *Concise encyclopedia of special education*: A reference for the education of the handicapped and other exceptional children and adults (2nd ed.). Hoboken, NJ: Wiley.

C. Journals Specializing in Literature Reviews
Psychological bulletin. (1904 to date). Arlington, VA: American Psychological Association.
Psychological review. (1894 to date). Washington, DC: American Psychological Association.
Review of educational research. (1931 to date). Washington, DC: American Educational Research Association.

D. Handbooks
Anfara, V. A. (Ed.). (2001). *Handbook of research in middle level education.* Greenwich, CT: Information Age Publishing.
Banks, J. A., & Banks, C. A. (Eds.). (2003). *Handbook of research on multicultural education.* (2nd ed.). Hoboken, NJ: Wiley.
Colwell, R., & Richardson, C. P. (Eds.). (2002). *The new handbook of research on music teaching and learning.* New York: Oxford University Press.
Eisner, E. W., & Day, M. D. (Eds.). (2004). *Handbook of research and policy in art education.* Mahwah, NJ: Erlbaum.
English, L. D. (Ed.). (2002). *Handbook of international research in mathematics education.* Mahwah, NJ: Erlbaum.
Heller, K., Mönks, F. J., Sternberg, R. J., & Subotnik, R. F. (Eds.). (2000). *International handbook of giftedness and talent.* Boston: Kluwer.
Jonassen, D. H. (Ed.). (2004). *Handbook of research for educational communications and technology* (2nd ed.). Mahwah, NJ: Erlbaum.

Linn, P. L., Howard, A., & Miller, E. (Eds.). (2004). *Handbook for research in cooperative education and internships.* Mahwah, NJ: Erlbaum.

MacArthur, C. A., Fitzgerald, J., Dunsmore, K., and others. (Eds.). (2005). *Handbook of writing research.* New York: Guilford.

Murphy, J., & Louis, K. S. (Eds.). (1999). *Handbook of research on educational administration* (2nd ed.). San Francisco: Jossey-Bass.

Neuman, S. B., & Dickinson, D. K. (Eds.). (2003). Handbook of early literacy research. New York: Guilford Press.

Pearson, P. D., Barr, R., Kamil, M. L., & Mosenthal, P. (Eds.). (1996–2000). *Handbook of reading research* (Vols. 1–3). Mahwah, NJ: Erlbaum.

Pinar, W. (Ed.). (2003). *International handbook of curriculum research.* Mahwah, NJ: Erlbaum.

Richardson, V. (Ed.). (2001). *Handbook of research on teaching* (4th ed.). Washington, DC: American Educational Research Association.

Smart, J. C. (Ed.). (2004). *Higher education: Handbook of theory and research.* New York: Kluwer.

Spodek, B., & Saracho, O. N. (Eds.). (2005). *Handbook of research on the education of young children* (2nd ed.). Mahwah, NJ: Erlbaum.

Teddlie, C., & Reynolds, D. (Eds.). (2000). *International handbook of school effectiveness research.* New York: Falmer.

Torres, C. A., & Antikainen, A. (Eds.). (2002). *The international handbook on the sociology of education: An international assessment of new research and theory.* Lanham, MD: Rowman & Littlefield.

A good secondary source, then, not only tells you what is known about the problem or topic you are investigating. It also provides a structure for positioning your proposed research so that others can appreciate its significance.

Secondary sources vary in quality. Therefore, you must read them with a critical eye. In a previous section of this chapter we described a literature review as a process consisting of four major steps. The author of a literature review can make errors and misjudgments at any of these steps. For example, you might find that relevant research reports were omitted or that the reviewer's interpretation of a study's findings is inconsistent with the findings as reported in the primary source.

To an extent, secondary sources reflect the biases, values, and agendas of the reviewer. As Patti Lather puts it:

> A review is gatekeeping, policing, and productive rather than merely mirroring . . . . A review is not exhaustive; it is situated, partial, perspectival.[10]

A review of the research literature, the type of secondary source about which Lather writes, is not, then, the "last word" about a research problem or topic. You might think of a literature review as a research study in itself with the studies being reviewed as the data that are analyzed and interpreted. As with any research investigation, the reviewer's findings are subject to refutation, replication efforts, and revision through progressive discourse (see Chapter 1).

This perspective on literature reviews reflects a postpositivist epistemology of educational research. Postmodern epistemologies, especially those embedded in critical theory (see Chapter 15), provide a different perspective, one that sees reviews of research studies published in journals as reflections of power relationships that exist in society and also as shapers of power relationships. A group of researchers, prominent in the field of educational critical theory, examined one of the preeminent sources of literature, *Review of Educational Research*, and their essays were published in an issue of that journal (Winter 1999). In summing up the essays, Thomas Popkewitz stated:

10. Lather, P. (1999). To be of use: The work of reviewing. *Review of Educational Research, 69,* 2–7. Quote appears on p. 3.

> The rules of knowledge expressed through the articles of *RER*, and more generally in profes-
> sional journals, embodied the political and moral agendas sanctified by these professional
> journals. Often, the question of the politics of education focuses on the struggles among differ-
> ent groups to define the Spencerian question, "What knowledge is of most worth?" But the pa-
> pers of this symposium point to a different politics of knowledge by looking at the rules and
> standards of school knowledge as governing systems and as the effects of power.[11]

This statement reflects the postmodern belief that there is no objective, privileged method
of inquiry. Instead, different groups assume control over knowledge production and the
use of this knowledge to shape school policy and practices. At the least, the views expressed
by Popkewitz and others compel us to ask whose voices are being heard in research studies and reviews of this research and whose voices are left out. Also, we need to ask how the
findings of literature reviews are being used to shape educational policies and what kinds
of values and forms of social control are embedded in these findings.

Reading Primary Sources

A primary source is a direct report of an event by an individual who actually observed or
participated in it. In educational research, a primary source generally is a report of a study
by one or more of the persons who conducted it, or a report by the authors of their own theory or opinions about educational phenomena.

As explained above, the research findings and theories reported in primary sources
often are reviewed in secondary sources. However, the authors of secondary source reviews may slant their interpretation of primary sources to agree with their own views, or
may omit some information that a reader wants to know. Thus, we recommend that you
do not rely entirely on secondary sources for your literature review, even if they appear
comprehensive and are recent. At the least, you should review for yourself the primary
sources that are most critical to your proposed study.

Primary sources are becoming increasingly available online. This means that you can
read primary sources on your computer screen, save them as pdf files, or print them. Many
university libraries now subscribe to journals in both hard-copy and online versions. Also,
your university library may have a version of an online preliminary source like *Education
Abstracts* that, for each identified research article or other document, tells you whether the
document can be downloaded and whether a hard copy is available at the library or an affiliated library.

An increasing number of scholarly electronic journals in the field of education are
available. Many are peer reviewed, full text, and accessible without cost.[12] If you identify
a document in one of these journals that you wish to access, you can go directly to its Web
site. In fact, you can "subscribe" to electronic journals in your field of interest just by
visiting them regularly.

As indicated above, ERIC has been one of the most important preliminary sources for
educators since 1966. ERIC is undergoing a restructuring as we prepare this edition of the
book. One of the new features of its online preliminary source will be full-text online documents for all or most of its citation records. At the end of 2005, there were more than
107,000 documents in the online collection, and this number is expected to grow dramatically in coming years.

---

11. Popkewitz, T. S. (1999). Reviewing reviews: *RER*, research, and the politics of educational knowledge. *Review of
    Educational Research, 69*(4), 397–404. Quote appears on p. 399.
12. For a list of electronic journals in education that is updated regularly, visit http://aera-cr.ed.asu.edu/links.html

Classifying Primary Sources

In reading primary sources, you should search for ways to classify them so that they do not remain an undifferentiated mass in your mind. The best method usually is to classify the documents according to the questions or objectives that are guiding your study. For example, one of the authors (M. Gall) served as the dissertation advisor for Douglas Herman, who did case studies of teachers who had been placed on a plan of assistance.[13] A plan of assistance is a remediation process for a teacher who is judged to be deficient in teaching performance or some other job responsibility.

Herman formulated six research questions:

1. What kinds of problems lead to teachers being placed on plans of assistance?
2. How are plans of assistance developed and, as written documents, what do they look like?
3. What kinds of remediation take place during plans of assistance?
4. Are plans of assistance effective?
5. Is the supervision of teachers on plans of assistance consistent with research findings and expert opinion about effective supervisory practice?
6. How can plans of assistance be improved?

He used these research questions to develop the following codes for classifying the documents that he identified in his literature search:

a. Documents containing information about why teachers get into difficulty, including difficulties that precipitate a plan of assistance.
b. Documents containing information about what happens during the various phases of a plan of assistance.
c. Documents containing information about whether plans of assistance are effective.
d. Documents containing information about effective supervisory practice.
e. Documents containing opinions about how teacher remediation and plans of assistance can be improved.

Each document was classified by one or more of these codes. Also, as Herman progressed in his literature review, he refined several of the codes. For example, code (d) was divided into three codes: (d-1) general supervisory practice; (d-2) supervisory practice for preservice teachers, and (d-3) supervisory practice for inservice teachers.

Using such a coding system is helpful in two ways. First, it stimulates you to actively read each document for its relevance to the major topics that underlie your research problem. Secondly, a coding system allows you to identify quickly the documents that concern a specific topic, and thus simplifies the job of writing your literature review.

Critical Evaluation of Research Studies

The first judgment you must make in studying a research report is its relevance to your research problem. If it proves to be relevant, your next judgment should concern the quality of the research described in the report. In making this judgment, keep in mind that the quality of published studies in education and related disciplines is, unfortunately, not high.

---

13. Herman, D. P. (1994). Teachers on plans of assistance: A descriptive study. *Dissertation Abstracts International, 54*(09), 3279A. (UMI No. 9405183)

This observation is based on our own experience and on a review by Bruce Tuckman of four studies that employed experts in research methodology to judge the quality of educational research published in journals and other sources.[14] On the basis of his review, Tuckman concluded that "much of the work in print ought not to be there."[15] The experts in the four studies concluded that between 40 and 60 percent of the research studies that they judged should have been extensively revised prior to publication or should not have been published at all.

Because both good and poor research is reported in the literature, you need to evaluate carefully the quality of each study that you identify as relevant to your problem. You should give more weight to the better research, and estimate how the results of a given study might have been affected by flaws in the research process.

This evaluation process requires a great deal of skill. Ideally, a researcher should master the entire research process before undertaking a literature review that will be disseminated to a professional audience. At the least, we recommend that you study the rest of this book *before* you conduct a literature review and initiate your own research plan. Most chapters, including this one, end with a section on recommendations for carrying out different types of research or different phases of the research process. These recommendations provide guidelines that can help you evaluate the quality of the research studies you read.

You may find it helpful to refer to Figure 4.2, which lists questions you should ask when evaluating a research report. Some of the questions apply to any research study, and others apply specifically to quantitative research or qualitative research. The questions are further elaborated in two forms contained in the Appendixes. The form in Appendix A is for your use in evaluating quantitative research reports, and the form in Appendix B is for your use in evaluating qualitative research reports. Each form lists the questions appropriate for that type of research, along with a description of the type of information you should look for in the report to answer each question and a sample answer.

Quantitative research reports that appear in journals usually are brief in order to meet the journals' space limitations. Their brevity and standardized format, however, make such reports less interesting to read than popular educational writing. Furthermore, you often must assume or guess about aspects of the study for which insufficient detail is provided. If important details about the study have been omitted, you can note this problem in your literature review. If a missing detail is critical to your planned study, you should consider writing the researcher to ask about it.

Synthesizing the Findings of Your Literature Review

Touchstone in Research

Dunkin, M. J. (1996). Types of errors in synthesizing research in education. *Review of Educational Research, 66,* 87–97.

Suppose you are at the point of having collected a large number of documents related to your research problem. These documents are likely to include literature reviews, opinion articles, theoretical essays, and many research studies. Your task now is to synthesize all this information into a coherent literature review. This is a complex process. It takes many weeks to synthesize a body of literature and write the review. Some parts of the process are creative and therefore defy precise analysis. The parts that can be made explicit are described below and in the next sections.

---

14. Tuckman, B. W. (1990). A proposal for improving the quality of published educational research. *Educational Researcher, 19*(9), 22–25. See also the study discussed in Chapter 2: Hall, B. W., Ward, A. W., & Comer, C. B. (1988). Published educational research: An empirical study of its quality. *Journal of Educational Research, 81*(3), 182–189.
15. Ibid., p. 22.

FIGURE 4.2

Questions to Ask When Evaluating a Report of a Quantitative or Qualitative Research Study

Introduction

1. Are the research problem, methods, and findings appropriate given the researchers' institutional affiliation, beliefs, values, and theoretical orientation?
2. Do the researchers express a positive or negative bias in describing the subject of the study (e.g., an instructional method, program, curriculum, person)?
3. Is the literature review section of the report sufficiently comprehensive? Does it include studies that you know to be relevant to the problem?
4. Are hypotheses, questions, or objectives explicitly stated, and if so, are they clear?
5. Do the researchers make a convincing case that each research hypothesis, question, or objective was important to study?
6. (Quantitative) Is each variable in the study clearly defined?
7. (Qualitative) Is the measure of each variable consistent with how the variable was defined?

Research Procedures

8. (Quantitative) Did the sampling procedures produce a sample that is representative of an identifiable population or of your local population?
9. (Quantitative) Did the researchers form subgroups that would increase understanding of the phenomena being studied?
10. (Qualitative) Did the sampling procedure result in a case or cases that were particularly interesting and from whom much could be learned about the phenomena of interest?
11. (Qualitative) Was there sufficient intensity of data collection?
12. Is each measure in the study sufficiently valid for its intended purpose?
13. Is each measure in the study sufficiently reliable for its intended purpose?
14. Is each measure appropriate for the sample?
15. Are the research procedures appropriate and clearly described so that others could replicate them if they wished?

Research Results

16. Were appropriate statistical techniques used, and were they used correctly?
17. (Qualitative) Did the report include a thick description that brought to life how the individuals responded to interview questions or how they behaved?
18. (Qualitative) Did the researchers triangulate their data sources and data-collection methods to test the soundness of their findings?
19. (Qualitative) Did clearly stated hypotheses or concepts emerge from the data that were collected?

Discussion of Results

20. Do the results of the data analyses support what the researchers conclude are the findings of the study?
21. Do the researchers provide reasonable explanations of the findings?
22. Do the researchers relate their findings to relevant theory and previous research?
23. Do the researchers appropriately qualify the generalizability of their findings?
24. Do the researchers reflect on their values and perspectives and how these might have influenced the study outcomes or steps that were taken to minimize their effect?
25. Do the researchers suggest further research to build on their findings or to answer questions that were raised by their findings?
26. Do the researchers draw reasonable implications for practice from the findings?

Note: Questions that apply specifically to quantitative research or to qualitative research are so noted. Otherwise questions apply to both types of research.

Source: Adapted from Appendixes 4 and 5 in: Gall, J. P., Gall, M. D., & Borg, W. R. (2005). *Applying educational research* (5th ed., pp. 534–543). Boston: Allyn & Bacon.

We recommend that you start by reading exemplary literature reviews, such as those found in the journal *Review of Educational Research* and in high-quality research articles and dissertations. They will give you a feeling for what a good literature review contains, and a mindset for undertaking the process of synthesizing and reporting the information that your literature search has revealed.

Some literature reviews have flaws that you should strive to avoid. Among them are the following:

1. The literature review stands alone from the other parts of the dissertation or article. In other words, the reader is not shown how the work of other researchers and theorists relates to the study being reported.
2. The review focuses on research findings without considering the soundness of the methodology used to generate the findings. Thus, the reader has no sense of how much confidence to place in the reviewer's conclusions.
3. The review does not include a description of the search procedures used to identify relevant literature. It is important to mention which preliminary and secondary sources were consulted, the descriptors used, and the time period covered.
4. The reviewer writes a literature review that consists of a set of isolated findings, opinions, and ideas. This flaw is most often manifested as a disconnected series of paragraphs—one paragraph for each document included in the review. You need to make a concerted effort to fit the findings, opinions, and ideas into a conceptual or theoretical framework developed by you or by other researchers. We think that this is what Richard Elmore had in mind when he stated:

> The most common defect of the literature reviews I have read is that they are pedestrian and mechanical in their judgment, even when they are comprehensive and rigorous in their method. They summarize the evidence, but they contribute nothing to the reader's understanding of it.[16]

To avoid these and other flaws, you should take time to reflect on how the information in the various documents you identified in the literature search relates to a theoretical or conceptual framework and to your proposed study. You also should take note of methodological problems in the studies you reviewed, comment on them in your report, and discuss how your proposed study will avoid them.

In the following sections, we focus on specific strategies for synthesizing research results reported in primary source documents. The strategies differ considerably depending on whether the research results to be synthesized are quantitative or qualitative in nature. Therefore, we describe them separately.

Synthesizing Quantitative Research Findings

The first step is to identify all the documents from your literature search that report statistical results relating to your research problem. Most of these documents will be primary sources. Having identified the relevant documents, you will need to determine how to synthesize the various statistical results reported in them. The following discussion explains several methods for performing this synthesis.

Touchstone in Research

Cooper, H., & Hedges, L. V. (Eds.). (1994). *The handbook of research synthesis.* New York: Russell Sage Foundation.

16. Elmore, R. (1991). Comment on "Towards rigor in reviews of multivocal literatures: Applying the exploratory case study method." *Review of Educational Research, 61,* 293–297. Quote appears on p. 295.

The Narrative Review

Prior to the landmark article by Gene Glass on meta-analysis in 1976, virtually all literature reviews in education were written in a narrative style.[17] These reviews emphasized better-designed studies, and organized their results to form a composite picture of the state of knowledge on the problem or topic being reviewed. The number of statistically significant results, compared with the number of nonsignificant results, may have been noted. Each study may have been described separately in a few sentences or a paragraph.

The major shortcoming of narrative reviews is their subjectivity. Reviewers seldom state their criteria for inclusion of studies in the review and often place too much emphasis on statistical significance in judging the practical or theoretical importance of a finding. (Statistical significance is explained in Chapter 5.) Richard Light and David Pillemer illustrated the subjectivity of narrative reviews by referring to two reviews of research on the effects of the environment on the IQs of adopted children.[18] Although the reviewers synthesized the *same* group of studies, they reached *opposite* conclusions!

Vote Counting

Gregg Jackson recommended a procedure for synthesizing research results that is sometimes called *vote counting*.[19] One version of this method involves classifying each statistical result into four categories: (1) a statistically significant positive result that is in the direction hypothesized; (2) a nonsignificant positive result; (3) a nonsignificant negative result that is opposite to the direction hypothesized; and (4) a statistically significant negative result.

It is possible that a set of research studies could yield many statistical results, none of which are statistically significant, but with all or most of them in the hypothesized direction. It is possible for no individual result to be statistically significant, but for the trend of of results across studies to be statistically significant.

A serious limitation of the vote-counting method is that a large number of statistical results is needed in order to detect reliable trends. Also, vote counting has the weakness that it considers only the direction of the effect, not its magnitude.[20] For example, suppose that one study finds that the experimental group exceeds the control group by 5 points on a criterion achievement test, and another study finds that the experimental group exceeds the control group by 10 points on the same test. If both results are statistically significant, both would be coded as "1" in the above-mentioned category system. The fact that the magnitude of the effect varied substantially from one study to the next would be ignored by the category system. This limitation is overcome by the method of meta-analysis described below.

The Chi-Square Method

An approach advocated by N. L. Gage takes into account the size of the sample and the magnitude of the relationship or difference reported in each study.[21] (The statistics used in the chi-square method are explained in Chapter 5.) The method is based on the fact that any p value can be transformed into a chi-square statistic with two degrees of freedom. This method involves first converting whatever inferential statistics are reported in each

17. Glass, G. V (1976). Primary, secondary, and meta-analysis of research. *Educational Researcher, 5*(10), 3–8.
18. Light, R. J., & Pillemer, D. B. (1984). *Summing up: The science of reviewing research.* Cambridge, MA: Harvard University Press.
19. Jackson, G. B. (1980). Methods for integrative reviews. *Review of Educational Research, 50,* 438–460.
20. See Chapter 4 in: Hedges, L. V., & Olkin, I. (1985). *Statistical methods for meta-analysis.* New York: Academic Press.
21. Gage, N. L. (1978). *The scientific basis of the art of teaching.* New York: Teachers College Press.

study (e.g., t, F, r) into exact probability (p) values by checking the appropriate statistical tables or using a computer program for this purpose. The probability values next are converted to chi-square values. Because chi-squares and degrees of freedom (df) are additive, the chi-squares and dfs for all studies then are summed. To determine the overall level of significance of the studies being combined, it is only necessary to check in a regular chi-square probability table for the summed values of chi-square and degrees of freedom.

The chi-square method has been largely supplanted by the method of meta-analysis, described below. However, meta-analysis generally requires many studies to yield a meaningful synthesis. The chi-square method should be considered when only a few statistical results are to be synthesized and when these results come from studies that are close replications of each other. For example, researchers sometimes do a study, and if they obtain interesting results, they replicate the study to determine whether the results are stable. In this situation, the statistical results of the two studies can be tested for their combined statistical significance with the chi-square method.

Meta-Analysis and Effect Size

Touchstones in Research

Hedges, L. V. (1998). *Statistical methods for meta-analysis.* San Diego: Academic Press.

Lipsey, M. W., & Wilson, D. B. (2000). *Practical meta-analysis.* Thousand Oaks, CA: Sage.

Since the late 1970s, meta-analysis has been the most widely used method for synthesizing the statistical results of a group of studies on the same problem. Therefore, when doing an online search of a preliminary source, you should consider entering the term *meta-analysis* and connecting it to your main topic descriptor with the *and* connector. If you can identify a relevant meta-analysis, it will greatly facilitate your literature review.

Meta-analysis has three major advantages over vote counting and the chi-square method for synthesizing quantitative results. To illustrate them, we will refer to a published meta-analysis on the relationship between parental involvement and the academic achievement of urban elementary school children. William Jeynes identified 41 research studies that had examined this relationship with a sufficient degree of quantitative data to allow for the use of meta-analytic techniques.[22] He found these studies through a systematic search of PsycINFO, ERIC, Dissertation Abstracts International, Sociological Abstracts, and other sources.

1. The first advantage of meta-analysis over vote counting and the chi-square method is that it focuses on the magnitude of the effect observed in each study, rather than on its statistical significance. For example, meta-analysis informs the reader not only whether the experimental group and control group obtained different scores on a criterion test, but also by how much they differed. In one part of Jeynes's meta-analysis, he examined the effects of an experimental condition in which schools instituted a parental-involvement program with a control condition involving no intervention or an alternative nonparental-involvement intervention. He found an average effect size of .27 across all the studies in his meta-analysis and across various outcome measures (children's grades, scores on standardized tests, and ratings of children's academic behavior and attitudes).

We explain the mathematical basis for an effect size in Chapter 5. Here it is sufficient to note that, in an experiment, effect sizes take the mean scores of two groups and indicate their percentile equivalent on the distribution of scores earned by the control group or the total score distribution across the two groups.[23] An effect size of .00 means that there is no

---

22. Jeynes, W. H. (2005). A meta-analysis of the relation of parent involvement to urban elementary school student academic achievement. *Urban Education, 40*(3), 237–269.

23. Effect sizes can be calculated in different ways. To simplify the discussion, we describe the magnitude of the effect size in terms of where the mean score of the experimental group falls on the distribution of scores earned by the control group. Depending on the data, however, the effect size can be based on the distribution of all the scores, that is, the combined scores of the experimental and control groups.

difference between the experimental and control groups: The average score of the experimental group is at the 50th percentile of the score distribution of the control group. In other words, the score distributions of the two groups are equivalent. The effect size of .27 found in Jeynes's meta-analysis means that the average academic achievement score of children whose parents participated in a parent-involvement program would be at the 61st percentile.

2. Another advantage of meta-analysis is that its metric, effect size, can be applied to any statistic and any measure. Some of the studies in Jeynes's meta-analysis appear to be experiments (a parental-involvement program was the intervention), whereas others are correlational research (examining the relationship between naturally occurring variations in parental school involvement and their children's academic outcomes). These different research designs generally involve different statistical analyses, and so it is not readily apparent whether the different statistics indicate the same magnitude of relationship between the presumed independent variable (participation in a parental-involvement program or parents' self-determined participation in their children's learning) and the dependent variable (measures of children's academic achievement).

Jeynes explains that "effect sizes from data in such forms as t tests, F tests, p levels, frequencies, and r values were computed via conversion formulas provided by Glass, McGaw, and Smith (1981)."[24] Thus, it was possible to compute a common metric, the effect size, for each study. This makes it possible, in turn, to determine whether different studies find different magnitudes of effect and also to determine the mean magnitude of effect across a set of studies.

3. The third advantage of meta-analysis is that it enables the reviewer to determine whether certain features of the studies included in the review affected the results obtained. For example, Jeynes was able to analyze the data in the 41 studies to determine whether parents' participation in their children's education had similar effects for boys and girls. This is an important analysis, because different research studies include different types of samples. If the sample includes mostly boys, one cannot infer with any confidence that the results would also apply to girls. By doing separate meta-analyses for boys and girls across the 41 studies, Jeynes obtained an effect size of .52 for girls and .62 for boys. These results indicate that parental involvement has moderately positive effects for both boys and girls and that the difference in effects is negligible.

Some features of a study have to do with the quality of the intervention and the quality of the research design. Depending on the focus of the meta-analysis, it might be worthwhile to code studies on these features and compare their effect sizes. For example, suppose we had reason to believe that parent-involvement programs had developed and improved over a period of decades. We would expect, then, that older studies that had experimented with prototype programs might have yielded lower effect sizes than recent studies, in which researchers had learned from the past and built stronger programs. With meta-analysis, it would be easy to test this supposition by computing an effect size for each study, recording the year in which the study was done, and then comparing the effect sizes of older studies with recent studies.

A meta-analysis is a time-consuming procedure, because you not only must conduct an exhaustive search for relevant primary source documents, but you must obtain and read them all. You cannot rely on abstracts and secondary source reviews, as you can in conventional literature reviews. You need the primary source documents in order to

24. Ibid., p. 244. Jeynes's citation refers to: Glass, G. V, McGaw, B., & Smith, M. L. (1981). *Meta-analysis in social research*. Beverly Hills, CA: Sage.

compute effect sizes and to code relevant features of the studies. For this reason, some students do a meta-analysis as their entire dissertation or thesis project.[25]

Synthesizing Qualitative Research Findings

Qualitative researchers study individual cases, making an effort to understand the unique character and context of each case. How, then, can the findings of case studies be synthesized? The challenge, as George Noblit and R. Dwight Hare explain, is to "retain the uniqueness and holism of accounts even as we synthesize them."[26]

Rodney Ogawa and Betty Malen suggested a method of synthesizing qualitative studies based on the principles and procedures of the exploratory case study method.[27] Their method applies to what they refer to as *multivocal literature,* which consists primarily of qualitative research but also may include some quantitative research and even non-research accounts of a phenomenon.

Because most qualitative research is exploratory, it is appropriate that a review of this research should be exploratory in nature, too. The purpose is to generate insights into the phenomena that were studied, and to develop hypotheses that can guide productive lines of research. In contrast, the method of meta-analysis has the purpose of drawing strong conclusions about whether an effect exists, and if so, how strong it is.

Our analysis of Ogawa and Malen's method suggests that it has eight essential steps.[28] The following description of these steps is not meant to imply that they are discrete, sequential, or applicable to all qualitative research reviews. Rather, our analysis is intended to provide a framework that you can use to develop your own approach to reviewing a body of literature that is primarily qualitative in nature.

Step 1: Create an audit trail. The term *audit trail* is used in qualitative research to refer to documentation about how a case study was conducted.[29] An **audit trail** could be included in a literature review to describe all the procedures and decision rules that were used by the reviewer. If such an account is included in the report of the literature review, readers can understand more fully how the review was done and can replicate the review, if they wish.

You should plan a procedure at the outset of the literature review for maintaining an audit trail of your activities, problems, and decisions. This early planning will ensure that the most important information guiding your decisions and discoveries is recorded. A diary format might work well because it records events in temporal order. In reviewing the diary, you can determine whether and how your thinking and procedures changed as the review progressed.

Step 2: Define the focus of the review. Qualitative research typically deals with complex social phenomena as they occur in a real-life context. For example, Ogawa and Malen described their own review of the literature on site-based school management. It is important that you conceptualize the social phenomenon of interest to you as a construct, and then develop a definition of this construct. For example, Ogawa and Malen developed this

---

25. Two examples of this type of dissertation are: Bennett, B. B. (1988). The effectiveness of staff development training practices: A meta-analysis. *Dissertation Abstracts International, 48*(07). 1739A (UMI No. 8721226); Rolheiser-Bennett, N. C. (1987). Four models of teaching: A meta-analysis of student outcomes. *Dissertation Abstracts International, 47*(11). 3966A (UMI No. 8705887)

26. Noblit, G. W., & Hare, R. D. (1988). *Meta-ethnography: Synthesizing qualitative studies.* Thousand Oaks, CA: Sage.

27. Ogawa, R. T., & Malen, B. (1991). Towards rigor in reviews of multivocal literatures: Applying the exploratory case study method. *Review of Educational Research, 61,* 265–286. See also four commentaries on this article in the same issue.

28. Our analysis generally follows the steps described by Ogawa and Malen, but for a few steps we developed our own elaborations and interpretations.

29. Guba, E., & Lincoln, Y. S. (1981). *Effective evaluation.* San Francisco, CA: Jossey-Bass.

definition of the construct of school-based management: "a form of decentralization that identified the school as the primary unit of improvement and the redistribution of decision-making authority as the primary means through which improvements may be stimulated and sustained."[30]

A definition of constructs is important because it defines the scope of the review. You should include documents about the phenomena that correspond to your definition and exclude documents that do not. To develop the definition, it first may be necessary to study a collection of potentially relevant documents. As you study them, you are likely to get clearer about what you wish to include in, and exclude from, your definition.

Step 3: Search for relevant literature. Many of the social phenomena of interest to qualitative researchers in education also are of interest to other individuals. Ogawa and Malen claim that the writings of these individuals should be included in the literature review because they shed light on the diverse meanings that people attribute to social phenomena and the context in which such phenomena occur. In the words of Glaser and Strauss, the writings of these individuals are "voices begging to be heard."[31]

If you accept Ogawa and Malen's position, your literature review could include not only qualitative research reports, but also nonresearch documents (e.g., newspaper articles, editorials, minutes of meetings, memos, program descriptions) and reports of informal investigations (e.g., internal program evaluations). Reports of quantitative research studies, if available, also could be included if they shed light on the meaning of the phenomena you are studying, but they would not be considered as inherently more valuable than the other documents to be reviewed.

Step 4: Classify the documents. After identifying and obtaining relevant documents, you will need to classify them in order to understand the types of data they represent. For example, Ogawa and Malen classified the documents relevant to school-based management that they examined into four types: project descriptions or status reports, position statements, systematic investigations, and related literature sources. Project descriptions reported efforts to institute or administer a school-based management project, whereas position statements built a case for such projects. Systematic investigations reported empirical data on the operation and outcomes of these projects. Related literature sources reported on topics related to school-based management, for example, the creation of community school boards and participatory decision-making arrangements.

Step 5: Create summary databases. Imagine that you have collected a wide range of documents pertinent to your topic, for example, case studies, program descriptions, minutes of meetings, newspaper accounts, scholarly books, and articles reporting quantitative research results. You cannot simply read all these documents, take casual notes, and then write a literature review. Instead, you will need to develop narrative summaries and coding schemes that take into account all the pertinent information in the documents. This process is iterative, meaning, for example, that you might need to develop a coding scheme, apply it to the documents, revise it based on this experience, and reapply it. In the words of Ogawa and Malen: "From the reams of raw materials [documents] collected, researchers must develop summations that can be (a) read and reread to be sure they are accurate reductions of the raw materials and (b) examined and reexamined to be sure that all pertinent information is taken into account throughout data analysis and reflected in the final report."[32] This qualitative approach to literature review is very similar to the process of data analysis in case study research (see Chapter 14).

30. Ogawa & Malen, Towards rigor in reviews, p. 277.
31. Ibid., p. 267.
32. Ibid., p. 280.

Step 6. Identify constructs and hypothesized causal linkages. In meta-analysis, the essential information in a quantitative research report is the statistical results, which are expressed as effect sizes. Reviewers of qualitative literature do not have the discovery of something equivalent to an effect size as their goal. As we stated above, their goals are to increase understanding of the phenomena being studied and to guide future research.

What, then, is to be understood in a review of qualitative literature? Ogawa and Malen claim that the reviewer should focus on identifying constructs that represent the major themes represented in the documents. For example, Ogawa and Malen identified *quality planning* as a major construct in their review of the literature on school-based management.

It is not necessary for the constructs to be explicitly labeled, defined, or frequently mentioned in the documents that are reviewed. In fact, different qualitative researchers and nonresearchers may use quite different language to describe a particular type of event or other phenomenon. The task of the reviewer is to search for themes (i.e., commonalities) in these different descriptions. If a theme seems important, the reviewer can generate a construct and an accompanying definition that represent the essence of the theme. The reviewer also has a responsibility to explain the relationship between the construct and its various manifestations in the literature being reviewed. An explanation is necessary in order to assure the reader that the construct is valid and emergent. The construct is valid if other individuals can use the reviewer's definition and indicators of the construct to identify or generate instances of the construct. The construct is emergent if it is clear to others that the construct was developed from the literature being reviewed and not just from the reviewer's idiosyncratic perceptions and biases.

In addition to identifying relevant constructs, the reviewer of qualitative literature also needs to develop hypotheses about causal linkages. For example, in their review of the literature on school-based management, Ogawa and Malen identified several hypotheses concerning causal linkages, for example: School-based management leads to renewed organizations, more academically successful schools, and restored confidence in schools. In addition to identifying these linkages, the reviewer needs to identify and evaluate the evidence presented in the documents to substantiate these claims of causal linkage. The reviewer also should judge the value and salience of the hypothesized linkages to the authors of the document and to stakeholders in the phenomena being studied.

Step 7: Search for contrary findings and rival interpretations. In reviews of quantitative research, it is common to find studies whose findings contradict each other. The reviewer might ignore the disparities and focus only on the general trend of findings, such as by computing a single effect-size statistic for all the studies. However, a better approach is to highlight striking disparities and attempt to interpret them.

Similarly, reviewers of qualitative studies need to be alert to the possibility of contrary findings and interpretations different from those that they reach. Ogawa and Malen provided an example of this need to be self-critical. In describing the process they followed in reviewing the literature on school-based management, they noted that their initial claim that this management approach did not improve staff morale was oversimplified:

> We ended, ultimately, by qualifying our assessment. Instead of concluding that site-based management had no effect, we suggested there is some evidence that site-based management may have initial, positive effects on the morale and motivation of some participants but that there is little evidence that site-based management produces sustained improvements in the morale or motivation of a substantial number of participants.[33]

33. Ibid., p. 282.

Step 8: Use colleagues or informants to corroborate findings. Ogawa and Malen recommend that reviewers of qualitative literature give drafts of their reports to colleagues for critique. Colleagues may be able to spot weaknesses in definitions, logic, and support for claims; they also can suggest alternative interpretations that should be considered. Authors of documents included in the literature review and participants in the events discussed in the review also can perform these functions.

The preceding discussion demonstrates that reviews of qualitative literature can, and should, be just as rigorous as reviews of quantitative literature. The two types of review differ only in the methods used to achieve that rigor.

RECOMMENDATIONS FOR

Reviewing Research Literature

1. Take sufficient time to identify the best descriptors and best preliminary, secondary, and primary sources in reviewing literature related to the research problem or topic.
2. Obtain and read at least the most important primary sources for your literature review rather than relying on abstracts in preliminary sources or summaries in secondary sources.
3. Examine critically all aspects of a study's research methodology before accepting a researcher's findings and interpretations as valid.
4. When appropriate, synthesize the statistical results of quantitative studies by meta-analytic or chi-square methods.
5. Consider contrary findings and alternative interpretations in synthesizing qualitative and quantitative literature.
6. Maintain a record or audit trail of the search procedures that were used in the literature review, and report them.
7. In writing the literature review, make explicit connections between the findings of your literature review and the research questions, hypotheses, or objectives that you plan to investigate.

SELF-CHECK TEST

Circle the correct answer to each of the following questions. The answers are provided at the back of the book.

1. A literature review need not be done prior to data collection when
   a. the researcher's list of keywords yields no citations in an online search of *Education Abstracts*.
   b. a relevant secondary source is available.
   c. a relevant meta-analysis is available.
   d. the researcher's goal is to develop grounded theory.

2. If the authors of a textbook report results of their own experiments, that portion of the text would be considered a
   a. secondary source.
   b. primary source.
   c. preliminary source.
   d. literature review.

3. Online preliminary sources vary primarily in
   a. the amount of information included in each record.
   b. the types of publications they index.
   c. the speed of their search engines.
   d. the amount of time it takes to index new publications.

4. The most comprehensive preliminary source for publications about education over the past 40 years is
   a. ERIC.
   b. PsycINFO.
   c. Web of Science.
   d. Google Scholar.

5. An example of a keyword search term that employs truncation is
   a. leadership.
   b. "school leadership."
   c. lead*.
   d. leadership not management.

6. Connecting two descriptors by *or* when conducting a computer search of the literature usually
   a. increases the number of records retrieved.
   b. reduces the number of records retrieved.
   c. retrieves only those records that include both descriptors.
   d. narrows the focus of your literature search.

7. The *Review of Educational Research*
   a. provides bibliographies of research completed in each calendar year.
   b. summarizes the research literature on a variety of educational topics.
   c. produces a current index to preliminary sources in education.
   d. provides brief digests of educational reports originally published in periodicals or newspapers.

8. The main weakness of narrative reviews is that they tend to:
   a. discuss too many marginally relevant studies.
   b. include too little detail about each study.
   c. be too subjective.
   d. focus more on theory than on actual statistical results.

9. Meta-analysis is a procedure for
   a. checking the thoroughness of a search for documents coded by ERIC descriptors.
   b. synthesizing the results of documents indexed by *CIJE* or *RIE*.
   c. synthesizing the statistical results of different studies about the same research problem.
   d. synthesizing the constructs identified in different qualitative studies about the same research problem.

10. An effect size is
    a. a limit field in a CD-ROM search of the literature.
    b. a criterion for judging the relevance of a primary source.
    c. a measure of the range of statistical results in a set of research studies.
    d. a measure of the magnitude of one statistical result.

11. An important purpose of a literature review of qualitative research is to:
    a. develop constructs and hypotheses that can guide further research.
    b. confirm or refute the reviewer's hypotheses.
    c. expose the commonalities in diverse educational phenomena.
    d. all of the above.

12. The rigor of a literature review of qualitative research can be enhanced by
    a. creating an audit trail.
    b. checking emergent constructs against the literature being reviewed.
    c. asking persons who are knowledgeable about the topic to critique the review.
    d. all of the above.

PART III

Research Methods

In designing a study, a researcher must develop a sound plan for selecting a sample, collecting data, and analyzing the data. If the plan is sound, the results of the study will be much easier to interpret. In this part of the book, you will learn sampling, data-collection, and data-analysis procedures that are appropriate for different types of research studies.

Chapter 5 provides an overview of the statistical techniques used in educational research. Some statistical techniques are used to check whether tests and other instruments yield valid, reliable measurements. Others are used to analyze the data in order to answer the questions or test the hypotheses that interest the researcher. Statistics play a central role in quantitative research, and they also have applications in qualitative research.

Chapter 6 presents procedures for selecting a sample. A research sample is most likely to consist of persons, but in some studies it is appropriate to sample documents, events, or other phenomena. The researcher's sampling logic depends upon whether a quantitative or qualitative study is being planned. In a quantitative study, the researcher attempts to select a sample that represents a defined population. In a qualitative study, the researcher selects a case, or cases, that will yield rich information about the phenomenon being studied. In either type of study, the researcher's choice of sampling procedure is important, because it affects the extent to which the study's findings can be generalized, or applied, to other situations.

Chapters 7 through 9 describe various methods for collecting either quantitative or qualitative data about the research sample or cases. Chapter 7 describes the use of tests and self-report measures to collect research data. Chapter 8 covers the collection of research data by using questionnaires and interviews. Chapter 9 discusses the use of observation and content analysis as data collection methods. We explain the advantages and limitations of each of these methods of data collection.

CHAPTER 5

Statistical Techniques

OVERVIEW

We begin this chapter by describing how statistics typically are used in quantitative and qualitative research. Next, we explain the different types of scores (ranks, percentiles, etc.) that can be generated from measurement data. We then provide an overview of three types of statistical techniques: (1) those used to describe educational phenomena, (2) those used to make inferences from samples to populations, and (3) those used to examine the properties of tests. We conclude with a discussion of three important issues in statistical analysis: the need for exploratory data analysis, the handling of missing data, and analysis of multilevel data.

OBJECTIVES

After studying this chapter, you should be able to

1. Describe how statistics are used in qualitative and quantitative research.
2. Distinguish between the various types of scores that are used in educational research.
3. Describe the purpose of each of the three types of descriptive statistics.
4. Describe situations in which the mean, median, or mode is the most appropriate measure of central tendency.
5. Interpret the meaning of the standard deviation in relation to the normal probability curve.
6. Describe the purpose of a test of statistical significance in educational research.
7. Define statistical power, and describe its four main determinants.
8. Explain how confidence limits, replication, and effect size can be used to

supplement tests of statistical significance in interpreting research findings.
9. Describe the use of stem-and-leaf displays and graphs in exploratory data analysis.
10. Explain procedures that can be used to handle missing data when carrying out a data analysis.
11. Explain how different units of statistical analysis (e.g., individual students, classrooms, or schools) can be incorporated in a research study and how they can affect one's research findings.
12. Explain how computers can be used to do statistical analyses and what steps can be taken to avoid computing errors and to retrieve data for further analysis at a later point in time.

The Use of Statistics in Educational Research

Statistics are mathematical techniques for analyzing numerical data to accomplish various purposes. For example, the calculation of a statistic known as the *mean* yields a single score that represents many scores, such as the scores of all the students who took a particular test.

Example of Statistical Analysis in a Research Study

Because quantitative research implies the use of numerical data, many people believe that statistics are the exclusive domain of quantitative research. In fact, statistics are used in virtually all quantitative studies, but in many qualitative studies as well. An example is the case study of one urban elementary school by Jennifer Booher-Jennings.[1] The purpose of the study was to determine how the school, its teachers, and the school district in which they were located were responding to a state mandate that required third-grade students to pass a state reading test (TAKS—Texas Assessment of Knowledge and Skills) to be promoted to the fourth grade.

As is typical of qualitative research, Booher-Jennings relied primarily on participant observation, interviews, and document review as methods of data collection. However, she also referred to quantitative data (primarily students' test scores) to form her interpretations of what was occurring at the school. In particular, she focused on the three practice TAKS tests that students take during the school year (October, December, and February), the official TAKS test (March), and a second official TAKS test (April) that gives nonpassers in March a second opportunity. Booher-Jennings found that if a student scores above 70 percent (the passing score), teachers and administrators refer to this student as a "passer." Students who score between 60 and 69 percent are referred to as "bubble kids," because they are in the bubble and have a reasonable chance of passing the official test with some instructional intervention. Students who score below 60 percent are labeled as "foundation kids" or "remedial kids." Students in special education programs form a separate category.

Booher-Jennings computed descriptive statistics to determine the percentage of children who fell into each category. These percentages are shown in Figure 5.1. In explaining this figure, she states:

> [A]s can be seen in Figure 1, only a small percentage of students in the third grade are in the bubble on any given assessment, while a sizable number remain at the bottom.[17] Notably, special education students who take the state's alternative test are not even given benchmark assessments and thus lose the opportunity to vie for resources in a system dominated by triage; they are, de facto, "hopeless cases."[2]

Elsewhere in her report, Booher-Jennings explains how typical teachers responded to her interview question about who the "bubble kids" are. For example, one teacher stated that they are "the ones that will pass with a little more help. With the pink ones [the remedial kids], it's really a lost cause. They must have fallen through the cracks somehow."[3] Other teacher comments are included throughout the article to illustrate the "bubble kid" phenomenon and educators' perceived pressure to raise the pass rate on the state test by allocating disproportionate resources to these children.

Touchstones in Research

Behrens, J. T., & Smith, M. L. (1996). Data and data analysis. In D. C. Berliner & R. C. Calfee (Eds.), *Handbook of educational psychology* (pp. 945–989). New York: Macmillan.

Vogt, W. P. (2005). *Dictionary of statistics and methodology: A nontechnical guide for the social sciences* (3rd ed.). Thousand Oaks, CA: Sage.

---

1. Booher-Jennings, J. (2005). Below the bubble: "Educational triage" and the Texas accountability system. *American Educational Research Journal, 42*(2), 231–268.
2. Ibid., p. 244. Footnote 17 in the quote explains a difference between the passing score established by the district and that established by the state.
3. Ibid., p. 241.

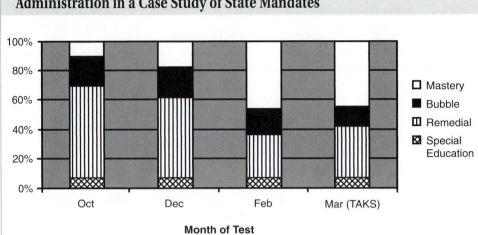

FIGURE 5.1

Third-Grade Scores on Reading Benchmark Tests and First TAKS Administration in a Case Study of State Mandates

Month of Test

Source: Figure 1 on page 244 in: Booher-Jennings, J. (2005). Below the bubble: "Educational triage" and the Texas accountability system. *American Educational Research Journal, 42*(2), 231–268. Copyright © 2005 by the American Educational Research Association.

This case study, predominantly qualitative in design, demonstrates that numerical data and statistical analysis are not the exclusive domain of quantitative research. The statistical analysis shown in Figure 5.1 is the only analysis of its type in the report, but it does serve as a useful supplement to the researcher's interpretive analysis of the interview and observational data. In this respect, case studies and other forms of qualitative research differ from quantitative research, in which statistical analysis plays the primary role.

The Need for Judgment in Statistical Analysis

Touchstone in Research

Wilcox, R. R. (1998). How many discoveries have been lost by ignoring modern statistical methods? *American Psychologist, 53*(3), 300–314.

Beginning researchers commonly assume that once numerical data have been collected, the application of statistical techniques is mechanical. In other words, they assume that for any set of research data there is a single *correct* statistical technique for analyzing it. In fact, statistical analysis requires a great deal of judgment—not unlike the kind of judgment required in qualitative research.

An illustration of the need for judgment in quantitative research is a dissertation study that one of the authors (M. Gall) advised.[4] The doctoral student, Ron Wolfe, administered a measure of personality and a questionnaire to 52 teachers in three overseas schools. The purpose of the study was to determine how well the teachers' scores on the predictor variables (their scores on the personality scales and responses to questionnaire items such as years of teaching experience) predicted their scores on criterion variables relating to job performance and cultural adjustment.

---

4. Wolfe, R. (1993). Experience, gender, marital status, and the 16PF questionnaire as predictors of American teachers' effectiveness in Southeast Asia schools. *Dissertation Abstracts International, 54*(09), 3407A. (UMI No. 9405241)

On the face of it, the correct statistical analysis in Wolfe's research study would be to calculate a correlation coefficient between each predictor variable and each criterion variable for the total sample. (As explained later in the chapter, a correlation coefficient provides a numerical expression of the strength of relationship between two variables.) Many previous research studies on the prediction of overseas teaching effectiveness had used precisely this method of statistical analysis. However, Wolfe decided to use his evolving understanding of the research setting to guide the statistical analysis.

Wolfe's first step was to re-examine how he had measured the criterion variables of job performance and cultural adjustment. The school principal had rated each teacher on seven items relating to different aspects of cultural adjustment (e.g., "This teacher accomplishes daily living tasks, such as shopping and laundry, with a minimum of difficulty") and five items relating to different aspects of job performance (e.g., "This teacher is able to maintain a classroom atmosphere conducive to student learning").

Wolfe next considered whether the ratings of the seven cultural adjustment items could be summed to yield a single score for cultural adjustment. By using a test statistic known as a reliability coefficient, he determined that five of the seven items were sufficiently consistent that they could be summed. By "consistent," we mean that teachers who get a high rating on one of the items are likely to get high ratings on the other four items; and teachers who get a low rating on one item are likely to get low ratings on the other four items. After examining the two inconsistent items, he decided that these items could be deleted for justifiable reasons, and that the other five items had enough in common that they could be summed to yield a single score that measured the construct of cultural adjustment. He used a similar reasoning procedure to determine that the five items measuring different aspects of job performance could be combined to yield a single score.

Besides obtaining the principals' ratings of each of the 52 teachers in the sample, Wolfe also obtained ratings from the teachers themselves because he wanted to know how teachers viewed their own cultural adjustment and job performance. He needed to perform the same item analysis for the teachers' ratings as he had for the principals' ratings in order to determine which items could be combined to form a total scale.

Wolfe then considered whether the total rating of the teacher's cultural adjustment made by the teacher and the total rating of that teacher made by the principal could be combined to form a single rating for that teacher, which would simplify the statistical analysis. However, he found that although the two sets of ratings correlated with each other, the correlation coefficient was not sufficiently large to warrant combining them. He reached a similar conclusion about the job performance ratings.

Wolfe next considered whether the teachers' self-ratings and the principals' ratings of the teachers should be given the same status as criterion variables. He decided that because principals hire the teachers, it is more important to be able to predict the principals' ratings. Therefore, statistical analyses involving principals' ratings were given precedence in reporting the statistical results.

At this point, Wolfe wondered whether the principals of the three schools actually discriminated in their ratings of different teachers. The reasoning was that, even though they were promised anonymity, the principals might have avoided the issue of evaluating their teachers' cultural adjustment and job performance by giving all or most of the teachers a high rating on each item. To check this possibility, Wolfe computed two statistics called the *mean* and *standard deviation* for each of the two total scores. There was sufficient variability in the scores between teachers to provide some assurance that the principals were making real discriminations between the teachers with respect to their job performance and cultural adjustment.

Having reached this point in the statistical analysis, Wolfe could have decided to correlate each predictor variable with the two criterion variables for the total sample of teachers from all three schools. However, he noted that the three overseas schools had substantially different emotional climates and value systems. For example, two of the schools were secular, but the third was a religious school; also, two of the schools were in the Philippines, but the other was in Malaysia. Therefore, Wolfe decided to calculate the correlation coefficients separately for the three schools. He found that, in fact, different personality scales correlated with ratings of cultural adjustment and job performance at the three schools. This statistical result means that teachers with one type of personality were more likely to do well in one of the schools, and teachers with another personality type were more likely to do well in another of the schools.

The magnitude of the correlation coefficients for the predictor and criterion variables was substantially greater than found in previous research on predicting the effectiveness of American teachers working overseas. Unlike Wolfe, the researchers who did these earlier studies had not taken into account the types of schools in their samples, and they had not done a detailed statistical analysis of their criterion measures. Wolfe obtained stronger and more interpretable results because his statistical analysis was guided by knowledge of a variety of statistical techniques, careful psychological reasoning, and extensive reflection on the context in which the numerical data were collected.

Acquiring Statistical Expertise

The preceding examples illustrate that you need to know about various statistical techniques whether you are doing quantitative or qualitative research. Also, you should know these techniques in sufficient depth that you can apply them thoughtfully rather than mechanically. In this chapter, we help you move toward this goal by providing an overview of the statistical techniques commonly used in educational research. The techniques are explained once again in Part IV, where they are discussed in the context of the research designs for which they are most appropriate.

By acquiring statistical expertise, you will be able to choose the most appropriate statistical techniques for your research problem and also to use these techniques correctly. You also will be able to judge the adequacy of the statistical techniques used in the research studies that you come across in your literature review.

Surprisingly, Kevin Kieffer, Robert Reese, and Bruce Thompson found many problems of commission and omission in their analysis of the statistical techniques used in articles published in two important research journals, *American Educational Research Journal* and *Journal of Counseling Psychology*.[5] Among the problems they found were the following:

- Only half the studies reported the reliability of scores obtained from tests and other measures administered to their sample. It is critical to assess and report reliability of scores, because low reliability will lead to incorrect estimates of the magnitude of observed effects. (Reliability of measures is discussed in Chapter 7.)
- Confidence intervals (explained in this chapter) were almost never reported, even though they help to estimate the plausible range of actual population scores when only a sample that represents the population has been measured.

---

5. Kieffer, K. M., Reese, R. J., & Thompson, B. (2001). Statistical techniques employed in AERJ and JCP articles from 1988 to 1997: A methodological review. *Journal of Experimental Education, 69*(3), 280–309.

- Effect sizes (explained in this chapter and Chapter 4) were both reported and interpreted in only a bit more than a third of the studies, even though this statistic is important in understanding the practical significance of a statistical result and in determining the consistency of findings across a set of studies on the same variables.

Kieffer, Reese, and Thompson also found that some statistical techniques in common use were applied inappropriately or incorrectly.

Statistical techniques have become more sophisticated over the past several decades. Furthermore, they have become more complex as researchers incorporate more variables and more complex environments (e.g., the simultaneous study of classroom, school, district, and state effects) in their research designs. Therefore, the acquisition of statistical expertise takes longer and requires more mathematical skills. For this reason, it is advisable to supplement your own statistical expertise with that of a recognized expert in statistics as you design a study and analyze its results, or when you come across studies in your literature review that employ statistical methods that raise questions for you.

Types of Scores

Individuals earn scores on tests and other measures, such as personality and attitude scales. The scores might be numerical or categorical. For example, a student's grade-point average is a numerical score, whereas the student's class standing in a high school is categorical (freshman, sophomore, junior, or senior).

Scores represent the possible values for a particular variable. For example, scores from 200 to 800 are the possible values on the SAT, a test that is an admission requirement at many universities. By themselves, scores—the values of a given variable—have no meaning. If I say that Bill Jones earned a score of 7 on the XYZ Test, the score would have no meaning unless I specify the construct that the XYZ Test measures. (The nature of constructs in research is explained in Chapter 1.) Specifying the construct only partially explains the meaning of a score. It is also necessary to specify the measurement scale that was used to generate the scores. As we explain later, measurement scales are of four types: nominal, ordinal, interval, and ratio.

We can define **scores**, then, as the set of possible values on a measurement scale for a particular variable that purports to represent a defined construct. Scores in educational practice and research take one of three forms: continuous scores, ranks, or categories. You need to understand the differences among these score forms, because the form in which the data are expressed usually determines your choice of a statistical analysis procedure. For example, if your research data consist of continuous scores on two groups, you most likely would analyze group differences by calculating mean scores and a statistic known as *t*. However, if the data are in the form of categories, you would analyze group differences by a chi-square (χ^2) test, which compares category frequencies between two or more groups.

The three types of scores used in educational research are explained below.

Continuous Scores

Continuous scores are values of a variable located on a continuum, ranging from high to low levels of the variable, and along which there are an indefinite number of points at which scores can occur. Intelligence tests, personality inventories, and most other standardized measures yield continuous scores.

Touchstone in Research

Harwell, M. R., & Gatti, G. G. (2001). Rescaling ordinal data to interval data in educational research. *Review of Educational Research, 71*(1), 105–131.

In practice, continuous scores usually are limited to whole numbers, but it must be possible, in theory, to compute fractional scores in order for the variable to be considered continuous. For example, IQ scores are considered continuous because an individual theoretically can obtain a score at any IQ point within the broad range of IQs possessed by human beings. Not only should it be possible for one individual to obtain a score of 101 while another obtains a score of 102, but it also should be possible to find an individual who would perform slightly higher than the individual with an IQ of 101 and slightly lower than an individual with an IQ of 102. In practice, however, IQ scores are reported only in whole number units.

Continuous scores can be contrasted with **discrete scores,** which are values of a variable that are distinct and separate from each other. For example, class size is a discrete score. We can say that a class has 15 students or 16 students, but we cannot say that a class has a fractional number of students between these two values.

Continuous scores are generated by tests and other measures that are interval or ratio scales. An **interval scale** is a measure that lacks a true zero point and for which the distance between any two adjacent points is the same. A **ratio scale** also is a measure for which the distance between any two adjacent points is the same, but it has a true zero point. For example, a thermometer is an interval scale because it has no true zero point, whereas a yardstick is a ratio scale because it has a true zero point.

Most educational tests and measures are treated as interval scales for purposes of statistical analysis, but in fact they lack the property of having the same distance between any two scores. On many academic achievement tests, for example, it takes less knowledge or skill to go from a score of 0 (no items answered correctly) to a score of 5 than it does to go from a near perfect score to a perfect score.

Tests typically have multiple items, and the individual's score on each item is summed to yield a total **raw score,** which is a form of continuous score. In the absence of other information, raw scores are difficult to interpret. For example, what does it mean that a student achieved a raw score of 30 items correct on a 50-item test? This raw score can represent good, poor, or average performance depending upon how other students scored or upon our expectations of how a particular student should have scored.

Because raw scores are difficult to interpret, they often are converted to derived scores, also a form of continuous score. **Derived scores** aid interpretation by providing a quantitative measure of each student's performance relative to a comparison group. Age equivalents, grade equivalents, standard scores, and percentiles (described in the next section) are examples of derived scores.

Age and Grade Equivalents

An **age equivalent** is the average score on a particular test earned by students of the same age. Similarly, a **grade equivalent** is the average score on the test earned by students of the same grade level.

Age and grade equivalents usually are determined at the time of test construction. The test developers will administer the new test to a large group of students (sometimes called the *standardization sample*) who represent a wide range of age and grade levels. The developers then determine the mean of the scores obtained by students at each age or grade level. These means are organized into tables of age and grade norms.

For example, suppose a researcher administers a test to a sample of beginning fifth graders (mean age of 11.3 years) and determines that they have a mean score of 56.7 on the test. Referring to the table of norms in the test manual, the researcher might find that in the standardization sample a score of 57 (56.7 would be rounded off to this number) was the average score earned by sixth graders and by students who were 12.7 years of age. On the basis of these norms, the researcher could conclude that the students in her sample were of above-average ability. This conclusion, of course, requires the assumption that the research sample was drawn from the same population as the standardization sample.

Standard Scores

A **standard score** is a form of derived score that uses standard deviation units (described later in the chapter) to express an individual's performance relative to the group's performance. The **z score** is a type of standard score frequently used in educational research. The first step in calculating a z score is to subtract the mean score of the total group from a person's raw score $(X - M)$. The next step is to divide the result by the standard deviation of the group's scores. For any distribution of raw scores, z scores have a mean of zero and a standard deviation of 1.00. Also, z scores are continuous and have equality of units. Thus, a person's relative standing on two or more tests can be compared by converting the raw scores to z scores.

Because z scores can yield negative numbers (e.g., a person who is one standard deviation below the group mean would earn a z score of -1.00), researchers sometimes convert raw scores to standard scores yielding only positive numbers. For example, **T scores** are standard scores that have a mean of 50 and a standard deviation of 10. The **stanine scale,** developed by the U.S. Air Force, is a standard score that has a mean of 5 and standard deviation of 2. The Stanford-Binet test of intelligence yields standard scores having a mean of 100 and a standard deviation of 16.

If you have administered a test for which age, grade, or percentile equivalents are available, it is advisable to report both the raw scores obtained by your research sample *and* the equivalents. The reason for this recommendation is that age and grade equivalents provide useful information about your research sample by showing how its performance compares to a standardization sample. Equivalents, however, should not be used in data analyses involving descriptive or inferential statistics. The reason for this caution is that equivalents have unequal units. Either raw scores or standard scores should be used instead.

Rank Scores

Some types of educational data are available as ranks, for example, a student's high school graduation rank. A **rank score** expresses the position of a person or object on a variable relative to the positions held by other persons or objects. This type of score is useful in situations where it is easier to rank individuals than to assign continuous scores to them.

Rank scores also are useful in situations where individuals might be reluctant to make discriminations. For example, suppose a researcher wants to ask a group of administrators to rate portfolios of twenty teachers completed for the purpose of demonstrating their professional competence. If the administrators used a 7-point rating scale, they might be inclined to give all or most of the teachers a high score on the scale. Consequently, there would be little discrimination between the teachers. To avoid this problem, the researcher could ask each administrator to rank the teachers on their professional competence as demonstrated in their portfolios. If this is done, each teacher would have a different rank, with the scores ranging from 1 to 20.

Percentiles are a commonly used type of rank score. **Percentiles** are obtained by computing the percentage of persons whose score falls below a given raw score. For example, if 50 percent of the sample obtains a raw score of 16 or below, then anyone obtaining a raw score of 16 would be at the 50th percentile. Manuals for published tests sometimes contain percentile equivalents for raw scores based on the standardization sample. Because percentiles are computed from raw scores, they are considered a form of derived score.

Rank scores are derived from measurements on an ordinal scale. An **ordinal scale** is a measure that represents an ordering of values of a variable, with no assumption of an equal interval between the values. For example, class rank based on grade-point average (GPA) is an ordinal scale. The student with the highest GPA in his or her class is ranked first, the student with the second highest GPA is ranked second, the student with the third highest GPA is ranked third, and so forth. It is possible for there to be only a slight difference between the highest ranked and second highest ranked student, but a moderate difference between the second highest ranked and third highest ranked student. Thus, the use of ranks as scores says nothing about the magnitude of the difference between the students' GPAs. We would need to refer to the students' actual GPAs, which form an interval scale, to determine the magnitude of the differences.

Categories

The term **category** refers to values of a variable that have no quantitative meaning. For example, gender is a categorical variable that has two values, male and female. We cannot say that one value of the variable is greater or less than the other; we can say only that they are different. Category values are measured by **nominal scales,** which can be defined as measures in which numerical scores can be used to represent categories, but the scores have no order or quantitative meaning. Using the example of gender, we can assign a score of 0 to individuals who are male and 1 to individuals who are female, but these scores are arbitrary; they do not indicate that males and females are ordered with respect to each other or that one gender is quantitatively greater than the other.

Descriptive Statistics

Descriptive statistics are mathematical techniques for organizing and summarizing a set of numerical data. To illustrate how descriptive statistics are used in educational research, we will refer to a study by Sandra Crosser concerning the relationship between children's age at the time of kindergarten entrance and their later school achievement.[6] Crosser was interested in providing empirical evidence to test the validity of the advice commonly given to parents that they should hold children back an additional year to mature before beginning kindergarten, particularly if the children are male.

Crosser obtained her research participants from seven public school districts in one state. Using school records, she identified all students with summer birthdates, which she defined as dates between June 1 and September 30. The variable of interest was the point at which these children entered kindergarten. The variable was dichotomous: early entrance (the autumn of the year when they were five years old), or late entrance (the autumn of the year when they were six years old). Of the total 253 potential participants, 190 had entered kindergarten at age five and 63 had entered at age six. First each of the students who had enrolled in kindergarten at age six (late entrant) was matched in gender and intelligence with a student who had enrolled in kindergarten at age five (early entrant). The matching process resulted in 45 pairs of students: 29 pairs of boys and 16 pairs of girls. Students for whom no satisfactory match could be found were eliminated from the sample. After completing the matching process, Crosser obtained the reading and mathematics test scores of these children when they were in the fifth or sixth grade.

---

6. Crosser, S. L. (1991). Summer birth date children: Kindergarten entrance age and academic achievement. *Journal of Educational Research, 84,* 140–146.

Measures of Central Tendency

A **measure of central tendency** is a single numerical value that is used to describe the average of an entire set of scores. For example, two groups of 45 children each (total $N = 90$) comprised the sample in Crosser's study of kindergarten entrance. We would have difficulty getting an accurate picture of each group's average performance on the reading and mathematics achievement measures by examining all 180 scores (90 children multiplied by 2 tests) one by one. However, Crosser was able to obtain an easily interpreted description of the typical or average performance of each group by calculating mean scores, which represent one measure of central tendency.

Table 5.1 shows the reading achievement mean scores for early-entry (age five) and late-entry (age six) kindergarten students in Crosser's study, separately by gender. The statistics in the column labeled M NCE are the mean scores for a test of students' reading achievement. This test gives each student a score that is a percentile rank, which Crosser converted to a type of standard score known as a **normal curve equivalent (NCE) score.** Like other types of standard scores, NCE scores make it possible to compare students' performance on tests that have different numbers of items and scoring procedures. Normal curve equivalent scores have a mean of 50 and a standard deviation of 21.06. These numbers were selected so that NCE scores would coincide with key percentiles in a score distribution. An NCE score of 1 corresponds to the 1st percentile; an NCE score of 50 corresponds to the 50th percentile; and an NCE score of 99 corresponds to the 99th percentile. Unlike percentiles, however, NCE scores have equal intervals between them.

By examining the descriptive statistics in Table 5.1, we see at a glance that children who enter kindergarten at age six have higher mean reading scores in later grades. We see also that this finding applies both to boys and girls. This difference in achievement would be much more difficult to detect if we had only the individual reading score of each child in the sample to examine.

TABLE 5.1

Reading Achievement Means at Fifth or Sixth Grade, Compared by Kindergarten Entrance Age

Kindergarten Entrance Age	n	M NCE[a]	SD	Dependent t Ratio	p
Boys	58			2.80	<.01
Age 5	29	49.03	18.49		
Age 6	29	58.17	19.96		
Girls	32			1.88	>.05 but <.10
Age 5	16	49.43	21.00		
Age 6	16	57.37	20.07		

[a]NCE = normal curve equivalent scores

Source: Adapted from table 6 on p. 145 in: Crosser, S. L. (1991). Summer birth date children: Kindergarten entrance age and academic achievement. *Journal of Educational Research, 84,* 140–146. Reprinted with permission from the Helen Dwight Reid Educational Foundation. Published by Heldref Publications, 1319 Eighteenth St., NW, Washington, DC 20036-1802. Copyright © 1991.

Mean, Median, and Mode

The mean, median, and mode are three different measures of central tendency. The **mean** is calculated by dividing the sum of all scores by the number of scores. The **median** is the middle point in a distribution of scores. The **mode** is the most frequently occurring score in a distribution. As noted earlier, the scores reported in the second column in Table 5.1 are mean scores of students' reading achievement. (The *M* in the top row of the table is an abbreviation for *mean*.)

The mean generally is considered the best measure of central tendency. One of its advantages over the median and mode is that it is more stable. This means that if we study several samples randomly drawn from the same population, the means are likely to be in closer agreement than the medians.

Skewness

When a distribution of scores is symmetrical, the mean and the median are located at the same point in the distribution. When the distribution has more extreme scores at one end than at the other—that is, when it is **skewed**—the mean always will be in the direction of the extreme scores. In this situation, the median will reflect more accurately the average performance of the sample, as can be seen by comparing the following two score distributions.

Distribution A	Distribution B
8	27
6	6
5	5
5	5
4	4
3	3
3	3
3	3
1	1
Mean = 4.2	Mean = 6.3
Median = 4.0	Median = 4.0

The two distributions differ by a single score. In the first distribution, both the mean and the median accurately represent average performance. In the second distribution, however, only the median provides an accurate representation of average performance. Just one person earned a score as high as or higher than the mean (6.3), even though the mean, as a measure of central tendency, is intended to represent average performance. As we shall discuss later in the chapter, this individual (whose score is 27) is called an *outlier*.

When a distribution is highly skewed, as in distribution B, both the mean and the median should be reported. Also, special statistics (presented in most textbooks of statistical methods) can be used to describe the amount of skewness and the shape of the score distribution. However, a visual presentation of the distribution of scores, as in the example in the preceding paragraph, usually is sufficient.

Categorical Data

Measures of central tendency can be calculated for continuous scores and for ranks. Categorical data, including dichotomies, are summarized by creating frequency distributions, as in the following example:

Category	Frequency	Percentage
Students earning letter in varsity sports	21	(11)
Students participating, but not earning letter	37	(20)
Students participating in intramural sports	115	(61)
Students not participating in athletics	16	(8)
	189	99

The most frequently occurring category is easily determined by inspecting the frequency distribution in this example. Also, the frequency of individuals or events in each category as a percentage of the total can be readily determined.

Measures of Variability

Variability is the amount of dispersion of scores about the mean score or other measure of central tendency. The desire to understand variability—also known as individual differences—motivates much of educational research. Thus, the measurement of variability plays a central role in research design and statistical analysis.

Standard Deviation

The **standard deviation** (usually abbreviated SD) is the measure of variability most often reported in research studies. Basically, the standard deviation is a measure of the extent to which scores in a distribution deviate from their mean. Thus, the first step in calculating the standard deviation is to subtract each score from the mean. The resulting deviation scores are then squared and entered into a formula to yield the standard deviation. Referring back to Table 5.1, you will find the standard deviations for students' reading achievement scores in the fourth column.

The standard deviation is the most commonly used measure of variability because it is stable. In other words, repeated samples drawn from the same population are likely to have similar standard deviations. Also, in analyses of research data, the standard deviation is needed in order to compute other statistics. The standard error of measurement, product-moment correlation, and many other statistics are based partly on the standard deviation. The standard deviation also forms the basis for the various types of standard scores described earlier in the chapter—z scores, T scores, stanine scores, and NCE scores.

The mean and standard deviation, taken together, usually provide a good description of how members of a sample scored on a particular measure. For example, if we know that a group of individuals has a mean score of 10 and a standard deviation of 2 on a test, and that the scores are distributed in the form of a normal curve (described in the next paragraph), we can infer that approximately 68 percent of them earned scores between 8 and 12, and that approximately 95 percent of them earned scores between 6 and 14.

Normal Curve

We can use the standard deviation to make these inferences because of the relationship between the standard deviation and the normal curve. The **normal curve** (also known as the

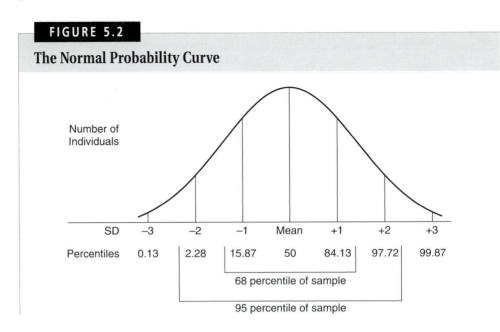

FIGURE 5.2

The Normal Probability Curve

Number of
Individuals

SD	−3	−2	−1	Mean	+1	+2	+3
Percentiles	0.13	2.28	15.87	50	84.13	97.72	99.87

68 percentile of sample

95 percentile of sample

normal probability curve) is a purely theoretical continuous probability distribution in which the height of the curve for each score point indicates the proportion of individuals who are expected to earn that score.

An example of a normal curve is shown in Figure 5.2. This curve shows that the scores of the majority of individuals tend to cluster close to the mean. As we move farther and farther from the mean, fewer cases occur. If the score distribution is normally distributed, approximately 68 percent of a sample will have scores within the range of plus or minus one standard deviation from the mean. Approximately 95 percent of such samples will have scores within the range of plus or minus two standard deviations from the mean. The curve for many measures of complex human characteristics and behavior has a shape similar to that shown in Figure 5.2.

Suppose that in one set of normally distributed scores, the mean is 3.0 and the standard deviation is 1.5. In another set of normally distributed scores, the mean is 25.0 and the standard deviation is 5.0. Even though the values of the mean and standard deviation of the two sets of scores vary, the properties of the normal curve can be used to infer the dispersion of scores. For example, Figure 5.2 indicates that approximately 16 percent of the scores in any normal score distribution will be one standard deviation or more above the mean (i.e., at the 84th percentile or higher). Thus, we can conclude that in the first set of scores in our example, approximately 16 percent of the scores will be 4.5 (i.e., 3.0 + 1.5) or larger. In the second set of scores, approximately 16 percent of the scores will be 30 (i.e., 25.0 + 5.0) or larger.

Other Measures of Variability

Occasionally the variance, rather than the standard deviation, is shown in research reports. The **variance** is the square of the standard deviation. For example, if the standard deviation is 4.0, the variance is 16.0. Calculation of the variance is an intermediate step in computing many complex statistics, such as analysis of variance. Another measure of variability that sometimes is reported is the **range.** This measure, as its name implies, is simply the lowest and highest scores in the distribution.

Correlational Statistics

The descriptive statistics presented in the preceding sections involve the description of scores on a single variable. In some types of research, however, we are interested in describing the relationship between two or more variables. Correlational statistics often are used for this purpose.

The **bivariate correlation coefficient** is a statistic that enables us to describe in mathematical terms the strength of the relationship between two variables (e.g., student attentiveness in class and academic achievement). There are many types of correlation coefficients. Selection of the appropriate coefficient depends upon the form of the scores (continuous, ranked, dichotomous, or categorical) that are to be related to each other.

Researchers increasingly are using **multivariate correlational methods.** These methods allow one to describe and explore the relationship between three or more variables at a time. This capability is important because the variables that are of most interest to educational researchers (e.g., academic achievement) usually are not affected by a single factor. Rather, they are affected by a complex of factors (e.g., home environment, personal characteristics, and prior school experience). Multivariate correlational methods enable researchers to study how these factors, both singly and in combination, affect outcome variables such as academic achievement.

The various types of correlational statistics and their use in research are discussed more fully in Chapter 11.

Inferential Statistics

Generalizing from a Sample to a Population

Rarely in educational research can we study every member of a specified population, for example, all sixth-grade students in the United States. Instead, data are collected from a sample of individuals who are randomly drawn from a defined population or who are assumed to be representative of some population. However, the research findings based on a sample are of little value unless they can be used to make *inferences* about the defined population.

Consider the study of kindergarten entrance by Crosser. As shown in Table 5.1, Crosser found that the later reading achievement of boys who started kindergarten at age six ($M = 58.17$) was 9.14 points higher than that of boys who started kindergarten at age five ($M = 49.03$). Crosser was interested not only in this sample of students, however. She wanted to know whether the finding would hold true of the population of students with characteristics similar to her sample.

Crosser's concern can be stated in the form of the following questions: Is this a chance finding? Is it possible that if we studied new samples we would find the same advantage for late entry to kindergarten? If we inferred from this sample that there is a true difference between the entire population of students entering kindergarten early and late, how likely is it that our inference is false?

Statisticians have developed a mathematical procedure, called *statistical inference*, that enables researchers to answer such questions. **Statistical inference** is a set of mathematical procedures for using probabilities and information about a sample to draw conclusions about the population from which the sample presumably was drawn. To understand these procedures, it is important to distinguish between a statistic and a parameter. A **statistic** is a mathematical expression that describes some aspect of a set of scores for a sample. A **parameter** is similar, but it describes some aspect of a set of scores for a population. For example, the mean of a set of scores for a population would be a parameter, whereas the mean of a set of scores for a sample would be a statistic. In using statistical inference techniques, we are attempting to use statistics computed from a sample to make inferences about population parameters.

The Null Hypothesis

Touchstone in Research

Wainer, H., & Robinson, D. H. (2003). Shaping up the practice of null hypothesis significance testing. *Educational Researcher, 32*(7), 22–30.

The initial step in testing whether an inference from a sample to the population that it represents is warranted is to establish a null hypothesis (described in Chapter 2). In the case of our example, the null hypothesis states that *no* difference will be found between the descriptive statistics compared in one's research study. For example, the null hypothesis for the boys in Crosser's study can be stated as follows:

> Reading-achievement mean scores in fifth or sixth grade for summer-birthdate boys who enter kindergarten at age five do not differ from the reading-achievement mean scores of summer-birthdate boys who enter kindergarten at age six.

After formulating the null hypothesis, the researcher carries out a test of statistical significance to determine whether the null hypothesis can be rejected (i.e., to determine whether there actually is a difference in the populations represented by the two groups). As we shall find in the next section, this test enables us to make statements of the type: "If the null hypothesis is correct, we would find this large a difference between sample means only once in a hundred experiments. Because we have found this large a difference, the null hypothesis quite probably is false. Therefore, we will reject the null hypothesis and conclude that the difference between sample means reflects a *true* difference between population means."

In educational research and practice, it is important to know not only whether the population means differ, but also the direction of the difference. In Crosser's study, for example, we want to know not only whether age five kindergarteners and age six kindergarteners differed in later reading achievement, but which of these two groups did better. The test of statistical significance can be done in a manner (two-tailed hypothesis testing, explained later in the chapter) that tests the probability of both directions of difference—in this case, the likelihood that age six kindergarteners perform better and the likelihood that age five kindergarteners perform better. Thus, the test of statistical significance yields two important results: It tells us whether the null hypothesis can be rejected and, if it is rejected, what the likely direction of difference between the two groups will be.

Tests of Statistical Significance

A **test of statistical significance** is done to determine whether the null hypothesis can be rejected. To illustrate the procedure, let us assume that the null hypothesis stated above is correct, meaning that the reading achievement scores of the population of summer-birthdate boys entering kindergarten early and the population of such boys entering kindergarten late are identical. (In reality, the null hypothesis is almost never true, because any two populations will differ, however slightly, on nearly any variable one might imagine.) Suppose that we select from these identical populations one sample of summer-birthdate boys entering kindergarten at age five and one sample entering at age six. Furthermore, assume that we repeat this procedure thousands of times. If each time we subtract the mean reading achievement score of the age six sample from the mean score of the age five sample, the difference scores will form a sampling distribution.

Suppose that the standard deviation (SD) of the sampling distribution for the reading achievement test for each population is 5.00. This means that 68 percent of the time the difference scores will have a value between $+5$ and -5 (one SD above and below the mean). About 95 percent of the time the difference scores will have a value between $+10$ and -10 (two SDs above and below the mean).

Now consider the fact that Crosser compared just one sample of boys who entered kindergarten early with one sample of boys who entered late. As stated above, a mean difference of 9.14 points was found on the reading achievement measure between the boys who entered early and boys who entered late. To test the null hypothesis, we need to pose and answer the question: How often would a difference score of this magnitude or larger be found between samples drawn from two populations whose means are the same?

Because we do not know the population means and standard deviations that are necessary to answer this question, we must estimate them using the sample means and standard deviations. These sample statistics are combined in such a way as to yield a critical ratio, also called a t value (or z value if the samples are large). Once a t value is obtained, we can determine how often a difference score of a given magnitude between samples of a given size will occur when there is no difference in the population. We make this determination by examining the p value associated with the t value. Tables of t values and their associated p values can be found in most statistics textbooks.

In Crosser's study, the t value for the reading achievement measure was 2.80 for boys (see the fifth column of Table 5.1). This large a t value indicates that if there was no difference in reading achievement between the population of summer-birthdate boys entering kindergarten early and the population of summer-birthdate boys entering kindergarten late, in every hundred samples studied, we would obtain this large or a larger difference less than once. This probability of occurrence is indicated by the p in Table 5.1. Next to p is "$<.01$," which means "less than .01" or "less than one time in a hundred." Because the observed difference of 9.14 points is an unlikely event, Crosser rejected the null hypothesis in favor of an alternative hypothesis, namely that there is a true difference in reading achievement between summer-birthdate boys entering kindergarten early and such boys entering kindergarten late.

Levels of Statistical Significance

The **t distribution** (or the **z distribution** if the sample is large) is used to determine the level of statistical significance of an observed difference between sample means. Generally, educational researchers choose to reject the null hypothesis if the t value reaches a significance level of $p < .05$.[7] Occasionally, the lower, that is, more stringent $p < .01$ level is chosen for rejecting the null hypothesis, while in exploratory studies the higher, that is, less stringent $p < .10$ level sometimes is used. You will note in Table 5.1 that Crosser indicated that the p value for the t test for the difference between early-entering girls and late-entering girls did not meet the usual probability level for rejecting the null hypothesis ($p = .05$ or less), but it did achieve the probability level sometimes used in exploratory studies ($p = .10$ or less).

When interpreting research results, remember that a *higher* level of significance corresponds to a *lower* p value. For example, $p < .05$ is a lower p value than $p < .10$, but a difference that is significant at the .05 p level is a more highly significant difference than a difference that is significant at the .10 p level.

Type I and Type II Errors

You should note that when the .10 level is chosen, there is one chance in 10 that the researcher will reject the null hypothesis when, in fact, the statistical evidence does not justify

---

7. For an explanation of the common use of the .05 level, see: Clowles, M., & Davis, C. (1982). On the origins of the .05 level of statistical significance. *American Psychologist, 37,* 553–558.

its rejection. If the significance level of .01 is chosen, however, there is only one chance in 100 that this will occur. The rejection of the null hypothesis when it is unwarranted is called a **Type I error.** Obviously, if we raise the significance level required to reject the null hypothesis (e.g., if we use $p < .01$ instead of $p < .05$), we reduce the likelihood of a Type I error. At the same time, we increase the likelihood of a **Type II error,** that is, the failure to reject the null hypothesis of no difference, when there is in fact a difference.

Interpretation of Significance Tests

Tests of statistical significance frequently are misinterpreted. Because these tests play such a large role in quantitative research design, we will consider common misinterpretations and the proper interpretation.

Alpha and Probability Values

Researchers commonly establish the level of significance (usually .10, .05, or .01) after the statistical analyses have been completed. A z or t value will be computed, and the researcher will refer to a significance table to determine how "significant" this value is. However, the logic of statistical inference dictates that the significance level be established *before* a z or t value is computed. You should make a decision at the outset of your study that if you find a difference between samples that exceeds a given significance level (for example, .05), the null hypothesis will be rejected. You cannot properly wait until after the statistical analysis to reject the null hypothesis at whatever significance level the t or z happens to reach.

The level of significance that is selected prior to data collection for accepting or rejecting a null hypothesis is called **alpha.** The level of significance actually obtained after the data have been collected and analyzed is called the **probability value,** and is indicated by the symbol p. For example, in her study of kindergarten entrance, Crosser properly interprets the p value for female students in Table 5.1: "Six-year-old female entrants scored higher in reading in fifth or sixth grade than did their five-year-old counterparts ($p < .10$), but not at the .05 alpha level set for the study."[8]

You will note in Crosser's statement that she did not indicate the precise probability level associated with the t value. Instead, she indicated that it was less than ($<$) .10. Until recently, this was common practice, because researchers needed to rely on statistical tables that only reported certain p values (typically $p = .10, .05, .01,$ and .001). Statistical packages for computers generally now report exact p values; therefore it is becoming customary to give the exact values in research reports.

Misinterpretation of p Values

1. The p value has been subject to various misinterpretations, which are explained here. Some people believe that the p value indicates the probability that the differences found between groups can be attributed to chance. For example, if you found that a mean difference of five IQ points between two groups was significant at the .01 level, it would be a misinterpretation to conclude that there is one chance in 100 that this is a "chance" difference. The proper interpretation of such a finding is that the null hypothesis was rejected (assuming that the .01 level of significance had been established beforehand); this is because the mean difference of five points exceeds the mean difference that we would find once in a hundred samples if the population mean difference was zero.

2. Another common misinterpretation of the level of significance is that it indicates how likely it is that your research hypothesis is correct. (The research hypothesis states

8. Crosser, p. 145.

that a difference between groups will be found, whereas the null hypothesis states that no difference will be found.) For example, suppose that you hypothesized that constructivist instruction will result in greater student achievement than conventional instruction. If the mean achievement score for students taught by the constructivist method is found to be significantly greater than the mean achievement score for students taught conventionally at the .01 level, you might conclude that the probability is 99 percent $(1.00 - .99 = .01)$ that your research hypothesis is correct. However, the level of significance only helps to make a decision about rejecting the null hypothesis; it has only an indirect bearing on confirmation of your research hypothesis. For example, you might find a significant difference between two groups but not for the reason that prompted your research hypothesis. Similarly, you might find too small a difference between groups to reject the null hypothesis, but your research hypothesis still might be correct. A Type II error could have occurred, the measures used to test the research hypothesis could have been inadequate, or some other flaw in the study occurred.

3. Still another misinterpretation of p values is to think that they indicate the probability of finding the same research results if a replication study was conducted. For example, you might think that if a difference between the means of two groups is significant at the .05 level, the same difference score will be found 95 times in every 100 replications of the study. However, even if the difference between mean scores that we obtained in our study is a true population difference and is highly significant, we still might find considerable variation in the magnitude of difference scores in a replication of the study. In short, the level of significance cannot be used to predict the results of future studies in which the conditions of the original study are replicated. It only can be used to make a decision about rejecting the null hypothesis.

4. The most common and most serious misinterpretation of the test of significance is to confuse the p value with the practical or theoretical significance of the research results. As we discuss later in the chapter, the level of statistical significance of obtained results is influenced to a considerable degree by the number of individuals included in the research sample. The larger the sample size, the smaller the result needed to reach a given level of statistical significance. For example, with a sample of 1,000 subjects, a correlation coefficient of .08 is significant at the .01 level. In contrast, a correlation coefficient of .42 with a sample of 22 subjects is significant only at the .05 level. However, the latter coefficient may have more significance for improving educational practice, because its magnitude is larger. Also, if the study was done to test a hypothesis derived from a theory, the latter coefficient has different implications for the theory than the former coefficient.

5. As we have already observed, the test of statistical significance is concerned with the inferences that we wish to make from sample statistics to population parameters. Thus, a test of statistical significance is done when we wish to determine how probable it is that the differences we have found between our samples also would be found in the populations from which they were drawn. Therefore, to use a test of statistical significance properly, we should use it only with samples that are randomly drawn from a specified population or, in the case of experiments, with samples that have been randomly drawn from a specified population *and* that have been randomly assigned to the various treatment and control conditions. However, researchers sometimes do not specify the population or do not use random sampling techniques, and thus the sample may not be representative. In these situations, the use of tests of statistical significance is questionable.

6. A test of statistical significance occasionally is done when the entire population has been studied. For example, suppose that a researcher defines all males and all females at a particular college as two populations. Then suppose the researcher finds, as hypothesized, that the females have a higher grade-point average than the males. In this situation

it is meaningless to do a test of statistical significance. The difference between grade-point averages is a *true* difference because the entire populations have been studied rather than samples drawn from their respective populations.

Criticisms of Significance Tests

The use of statistical significance in educational research has been criticized.[9] One criticism is that educational researchers seldom work with samples randomly drawn from defined populations, even though random sampling is a requirement for using statistical significance tests. Another criticism is that the tests often are misinterpreted, as we indicated above. The *p* value is taken as a measure of the worth of a study rather than for what it really is: a basis for rejecting the null hypothesis. The third criticism is that the *power* of statistical significance tests in educational research tends to be low. (The concept of statistical power is discussed after the next section.)

We believe that each of these criticisms is legitimate, yet they do not justify discontinuation of statistical significance testing. The tests are quite helpful under conditions of random sampling and high statistical power. Conversely, the tests should be used with caution, or not at all, under conditions of nonrandom sampling, nonrandom assignment, or low statistical power.

Our recommendation is for researchers to be wary of accepting an observed difference or relationship as real on the basis of one study, no matter how statistically significant the results are. A significant *p* value in a study is cause for optimism, but replications of the study should be done to get additional assurance that the observed result is real. Jacob Cohen makes this point well:

> The prevailing yes-no decision at the magic .05 level from a single research is a far cry from the use of informed judgment. Science simply doesn't work that way. A successful piece of research doesn't conclusively settle an issue, it just makes some theoretical proposition to some degree more likely. Only successful future replication in the same and different settings (as might be found through meta-analysis) provides an approach to settling the issue.[10]

Also, other indices should be calculated in each study to set *p* values in proper perspective. We discuss these indices—effect size, measures of correlation, and confidence intervals—later in the chapter.

Types of Significance Tests

Thus far in our discussion of inferential statistics, we have been concerned with how to determine whether the difference between two sample means reflects a population difference. A test of statistical significance based on the calculation of a *t* or *z* value is appropriate for this purpose. Other significance tests are available for answering other questions involving inferences from sample statistics to population parameters. They are discussed in Chapters 10 through 13.

Statistical Power Analysis

Researchers rarely want to confirm the null hypothesis. In other words, they do not intend for their research to demonstrate that there is no difference between groups, no correlation

9. For example, see: Harlow, L. L., Mulaik, S. A., & Steiger, J. H. (Eds.) (1997). *What if there were no significance tests?* Mahwah, NJ: Erlbaum; Schmidt, F. L. (1996). Statistical significance testing and cumulative knowledge in psychology: Implications for training of researchers. *Psychological Methods, 1*(2), 115–129.
10. Cohen, J. (1990). Things I have learned (so far). *American Psychologist, 45,* 1304–1312. Quote appears on page 1311.

between variables, or no effect of an experimental treatment. Instead, researchers usually conduct studies because they want to find differences, relationships, or effects. For example, researchers are more likely to become interested in investigating a method of instruction when they believe it will be superior to conventional practice than when they believe it is no more effective than conventional practice.

Given researchers' interest in discovering differences, relationships, and effects, they want to maximize the likelihood of rejecting the null hypothesis when in fact it is false. To help them, they use **statistical power analysis,** which is a procedure for studying the likelihood that a particular test of statistical significance will be sufficient to reject a false null hypothesis. In this context, the term **statistical power** refers to the probability that a particular test of statistical significance will lead to rejection of a false null hypothesis. The following is an overview of the four factors that are considered in statistical power analysis.

1. *Sample size.* It is a fact that statistical power increases automatically with *sample size*, assuming that the other factors described below are held constant. In other words, the larger the sample, the smaller the difference, relationship, or effect needed to reject the null hypothesis. For example, if you obtained a correlation coefficient of .25 between two variables in a sample of 47 students, you could not reject the null hypothesis at the .05 level of significance. If you obtained the same coefficient (.25) but with a larger sample ($N = 62$), you would be able to reject the null hypothesis at the .05 level of significance.

2. *Level of significance.* The second determinant of statistical power is the p value at which the null hypothesis is to be rejected. Statistical power can be increased by lowering the level of significance needed to reject the null hypothesis. Thus, a test of statistical significance with p set at .10 is more powerful than the same test with p set at .05. ("More powerful" means that it is easier to reject a false null hypothesis.) In practice, p usually is set at .05. However, as we explained above, some researchers feel that it is permissible to set p at .10 in exploratory studies in order to increase statistical power. A p of .10 increases the risk of a Type I error, but it might spotlight a potentially important difference, relationship, or effect that would have been overlooked had a lower p value been set.

3. *Directionality.* The third determinant of statistical power is whether *directionality* is specified in the research hypothesis. Directionality refers to the fact that observed differences and relationships can go in two directions. For example, in an experiment, treatment A can be better than treatment B (one direction), or treatment B can be better than treatment A (the other direction). However, we might be able to argue, on the basis of theory or previous research findings, that treatment B cannot possibly be better than treatment A.

If we can determine before doing the experiment that one direction is unlikely, we can increase statistical power by doing a *one-tailed test* of statistical significance. Some researchers, however, disagree with the use of one-tailed tests. They advocate instead the consistent use of two-tailed hypothesis testing, which they view as "more compatible with the growing meta-analytic view of social science as an incremental, cumulative, and shared enterprise."[11]

4. *Effect size.* The fourth determinant of statistical power is **effect size,** which is an estimate of the magnitude of the difference, relationship, or effect in the population being studied. (Effect size is discussed in Chapter 4 and later in this chapter.) To understand how effect size influences statistical power, you need to keep two facts in mind. First, it is a fact that greater observed differences, relationships, or effects will produce lower p values. For

Touchstones in Research

Cohen, J. (1988). *Statistical power analysis for the behavioral sciences* (2nd ed.). Mahwah, NJ: Erlbaum.

Murphy, K. R., & Myors, B. (2004). *Statistical power analysis: A simple and general model for traditional and modern hypothesis tests* (2nd ed.). Mahwah, NJ: Erlbaum.

11. Pillemer, D. B. (1991). One- versus two-tailed hypothesis tests in contemporary educational research. *Educational Researcher, 20*(9), 13–17. Quote appears on page 13.

example, a correlation coefficient (*r*) of .38 in a sample of 20 students is significant at the .10 level. In contrast, an *r* of .44 in the same size sample is significant at the .05 level. Thus, the null hypothesis can be rejected at the conventional significance level (.05) with an *r* of .44, but not with an *r* of .38.

Because the magnitude of an *r* affects the significance level, we need to ask what determines the magnitude of an *r*. This leads us to the second fact: A researcher is more likely to obtain a large effect size in a sample when there is a large effect size in the population. Returning to our example, suppose the value of *r* in the population from which the sample of 20 students was drawn is .65. It is likely, then, that samples drawn from this population will tend to yield similarly large values of *r*. Conversely, if the population value of *r* is small (for example, *r* = .30), samples drawn from this population will tend to yield similarly small values of *r*. In brief, if the population value of an *r* is large, it will be easier to reject the null hypothesis than if the population value is small.

The effect size in a population is beyond the researcher's control. For example, suppose one researcher decides to compare instructional method A with instructional method B. Suppose further that in the population, method A actually is much more effective than method B. Another researcher decides to compare method A and method C, which in actuality is just slightly better than method A. Both researchers do an experiment to compare the effectiveness of their two methods in improving student learning. If both researchers use the same sample size and significance level, the first researcher is more likely to reject his null hypothesis (A = B) than the second researcher, even though her null hypothesis (A = C) also is false. The reason is that method A is much better than method B in actuality, whereas method C is only slightly better than method A.

Stephen Olejnik created several tables to show the necessary sample sizes for different values of the various factors involved in statistical power analysis.[12] A condensed version of the tables is shown in Table 5.2. The table shows power analyses for a variety of commonly used tests of statistical significance.

To illustrate how to use this table, suppose that we are doing a research study to determine whether staff development specialists are more knowledgeable about curriculum than school principals. How many individuals do we need in our research sample? To answer this question using Table 5.2, we first need to select an appropriate test of statistical significance. We most likely will select the *t* test for independent samples, which is the first test shown in the first column. Next we decide that we wish to do a rigorous test of the null hypothesis to minimize the risk of a Type I error (rejecting the null hypothesis when it is true). Therefore, we select from among the sample sizes given for alpha = .05 in Table 5.2.

We see that there are six possible sample sizes for alpha = .05: 620, 386, 100, 64, 40, and 26. Our next step is to decide whether we think that there is a small, medium, or large effect size in the population that the sample is intended to represent. In other words, do we think it likely that the population of staff development specialists has much more (large effect size), somewhat more (medium effect size), or only a little bit more (small effect size) knowledge about curriculum than school principals? In examining Table 5.2, we see that we can get by with a much smaller sample (*N* = 40 or 26) if we are correct in thinking that the difference between the two populations is large. By contrast, we would need a much larger sample size (*N* = 620 or 386) if we thought the difference between the two populations is small.

12. Olejnik, S. F. (1984). Planning educational research: Determining the necessary sample size. *Journal of Experimental Education, 53,* 40–48.

TABLE 5.2

Minimal Total Sample Sizes for Different Hypothesis Tests with Alpha (α) at either the .05 or .10 Level of Significance and with Statistical Power at either the .7 or .5 Level

Hypothesis Test	Small Effect Size[1] Statistical Power		Medium Effect Size[1] Statistical Power		Large Effect Size[1] Statistical Power	
	.7 N	.5 N	.7 N	.5 N	.7 N	.5 N
Independent samples *t* test						
α = .05	620	386	100	64	40	26
α = .10	472	272	76	44	30	18
Related samples *t* test (matching variable *r* = .7)						
α = .05	188	118	32	22	14	10
α = .10	144	84	24	16	10	8
Related samples *t* test (matching variable *r* = .5)						
α = .05	310	194	52	32	22	14
α = .10	238	138	40	24	16	10
Analysis of variance, 3 groups						
α = .05	744	498	126	81	51	33
α = .10	600	357	96	60	39	24
Analysis of variance, 4 groups						
α = .05	884	580	144	96	60	40
α = .10	692	420	112	72	44	28
Analysis of covariance, 3 groups (covariate *r* = .7)						
α = .05	396	255	166	45	27	21
α = .10	309	186	51	33	21	15
Analysis of covariance, 3 groups (covariate *r* = .5)						
α = .05	579	375	96	63	39	27
α = .10	450	270	75	45	30	21
3 × 4 analysis of variance, 3-group main effect						
α = .05	780	504	132	96	60	36
α = .10	612	372	72	72	48	24
3 × 4 analysis of variance, 4-group main effect						
α = .05	888	588	156	108	72	48
α = .10	696	432	120	84	60	36
3 × 4 analysis of variance, interaction effect						
α = .05	1128	756	192	121	84	60
α = .10	900	564	156	96	72	48
Correlation coefficient (*r*)						
α = .05	616	384	66	42	23	15
α = .10	470	277	51	30	18	11
Partial correlation ($r_{vx.z}$)						
α = .05	312	195	44	29	21	14
α = .10	238	138	33	21	15	11

(Continued)

TABLE 5.2

(Continued)

Hypothesis Test	Small Effect Size[1]		Medium Effect Size[1]		Large Effect Size[1]	
	Statistical Power		Statistical Power		Statistical Power	
	.7 N	.5 N	.7 N	.5 N	.7 N	.5 N
Chi-square, 2 × 4						
$\alpha = .05$	879	576	98	64	35	23
$\alpha = .10$	688	418	76	46	28	17
Chi-square, 3 × 4						
$\alpha = .05$	1114	750	124	83	45	30
$\alpha = .10$	884	553	98	61	35	22

[1]For t tests, small, medium, and large effect sizes refer to .2, .5, and .8 standard deviations, respectively. For analysis of variance, analysis of covariance, and r, small, medium, and large effect sizes refer to 1 percent, 6 percent, and 13 percent explained variance in the dependent variable, respectively. For chi-square, small, medium, and large effect sizes refer to contingency coefficients of .1, .207, and .447, respectively.

Source: Adapted from tables 2 and 3 on pp. 44–45 in: Olejnik, S. F. (1984). Planning educational research: Determining the necessary sample size. *Journal of Experimental Education, 53*, 40–48. Adapted with permission from the Helen Dwight Reid Educational Foundation. Published by Heldref Publications, 1319 Eighteenth St., NW, Washington, DC 20036-1802. Copyright © 1984.

Suppose we think that the population difference is large, so now we have limited our necessary sample size to 40 or 26. The final step in selecting a sample size is to decide on the statistical power level, which refers to how certain we want to be about rejecting the null hypothesis if in actuality it is false. Table 5.2 shows two levels of certainty: .7 and .5. Because we want to be fairly certain to reject a false null hypothesis, we select the .7 power level. This means that we will need a total of 40 participants in our research sample. Because there are two groups in the research design, we will select 20 staff development specialists and 20 school principals.

Table 5.2 shows a small number of commonly used alpha levels, estimated effect sizes, and levels of statistical power. Tables that contain a wider range of values for these variables are available in other sources.

Supplements to Significance Tests

Tests of statistical significance should be supplemented by other approaches to explore further the statistical and practical significance of research data. Two of the approaches discussed below—calculation of confidence limits and replication studies—are concerned primarily with clarifying the statistical significance of research results. The other approach—calculation of effect size—is intended to clarify the practical significance of research results.

Confidence Limits

Confidence limits are used to estimate population values (i.e., parameters) based on what is known about sample values (i.e., statistics). More specifically, **confidence limits** define

Touchstones in Research

Thompson, B. (2001). Significance, effect sizes, stepwise methods, and other issues: Strong arguments move the field. *Journal of Experimental Education, 70*, 80–93.

DeVaney, T. A. (2001). Statistical significance, effect size, and replication: What do the journals say? *Journal of Experimental Education, 69*(3), 310–320.

the upper and lower value of a range of values for a sample statistic that is likely to contain a population parameter. (A **confidence interval** is the term used to refer to all the values within the range defined by the confidence limits.) Confidence limits are a branch of inferential statistics, because they enable researchers to make inferences from a sample statistic to a population parameter.

To illustrate confidence limits and intervals, suppose we know that the mean test score for a sample of research participants is 75. The sample mean and standard deviation can be used to estimate a range of values (the confidence interval) that are likely to include the true population mean. If our calculations reveal that the 95 percent confidence limits for the sample mean are 68 and 83, we can infer that there is a high likelihood that the true population mean lies between 68 and 83. Stated more precisely, we can infer that if we collected data on 100 research samples similar to the one we actually studied, only five of them would contain confidence limits that did not include the true population mean. In practice, we usually study a single research sample, but by calculating 95 percent confidence limits, we can be reasonably certain that ours is not in the 5 percent of sample means whose confidence limits do not contain the true population mean. Sometimes, 99 percent confidence limits are calculated instead.

A typical experiment will yield two posttreatment means—one for the experimental group and one for the control group. If we calculate confidence limits for each mean, we will have an easily interpreted measure of whether the observed difference between two means indicates a true difference between the populations represented by the samples. Suppose the experimental group mean is 24, with 95 percent confidence limits of 20 and 28. The control group mean is 15, with 95 percent confidence limits of 12 and 18. Given these limits, we can conclude that the true mean of the experimental population is unlikely to be lower than 20, and the true mean of the control population is unlikely to be higher than 18. Thus, it appears that the population represented by the experimental group sample actually outperformed the population represented by the control group sample in this hypothetical study.

Now consider what happens under a different set of conditions. Suppose the experimental group mean remains the same (24), but the 95 percent confidence limits are 17 and 31. The control group mean also remains the same (15), but the 95 percent confidence limits are 7 and 23. Thus, the true mean for the experimental population is likely to be as low as 17, and the true mean for the control population is likely to be as high as 23. Thus, we cannot disregard the possibility that the two population means are the same, with a likely value between 17 and 23.

Tests of statistical significance are almost always included in reports of quantitative research studies. Increasingly, researchers are recommending that confidence intervals for key statistics should be reported as well.[13] In fact, the *Publication Manual of the American Psychological Association* strongly recommends them: "Because confidence intervals combine information on location and precision and can often be directly used to infer significance levels, they are, in general, the best reporting strategy."[14] Procedures for calculating confidence intervals for different types of statistics are presented in various publications and software packages.[15]

13. Cahan, S. (2000). Statistical significance is not a "kosher certificate" for observed effects: A critical analysis of the two-step approach to the evaluation of empirical results. *Educational Researcher, 29*(1), 31–34; Cohen, J. (1994). The earth is round (*p* < .05). *American Psychologist, 49*, 997–1003.
14. *Publication manual of the American Psychological Association* (5th ed.). (2001). Washington, DC: American Psychological Association. Quote appears on p. 22.
15. See, for example: August 2001 issue of *Educational and Psychological Measurement* (various articles); *nQuery Advisor, Release 3* http://www.statsol.ie

Replication of Research Results

Touchstones in Research

Schaefer, W. D. (2001). Replication: A design principle for field research. *Practical Assessment, Research and Evaluation, 7*(15). Retrieved August 20, 2005 from http://pareonline.net/getvn.asp?v=7&n=15

Schneider, B. (2004). Building a scientific community: The need for replication. *Teachers College Record, 106*(7), 1471–1483.

Tests of statistical significance are used to help researchers draw conclusions about the validity of a knowledge claim on the basis of a single study. In other words, if the null hypothesis is rejected, we conclude that the knowledge claim (i.e., the research hypothesis) is true. If the null hypothesis is accepted, we conclude that the knowledge claim is false. As we explained earlier in the chapter, researchers should not draw such extreme conclusions. This warning applies even if the obtained level of statistical significance is extremely high (e.g., $p < .001$). One reason is that it is difficult to rule out all possible alternative explanations of the result. Another reason is that flaws in research design and execution creep into most studies. Thus, researchers should avoid extravagant claims about the validity of a knowledge claim on the basis of a single test of statistical significance from a single study. The significance test only serves to increase or decrease their confidence in their knowledge claims. They, or other researchers, should repeat the study in order to test further the validity of the knowledge claims.

Replication is the process of repeating a research study with a different group of research participants using the same or similar methods. Results of a study are more "significant"—in the sense of inspiring confidence that they represent true differences, relationships, or effects in the population—if a new study yields similar results, or if the present study repeats the findings of past research.

The importance of replication was emphasized by one of the early founders of research statistics and null hypothesis testing, Sir Ronald Fisher. He stated that a researcher:

> should only claim that a phenomenon is experimentally demonstrable when he knows how to design an experiment so that it will rarely fail to give a significant result. Consequently, isolated significant results which he does not know how to reproduce are left in suspense pending further investigation.[16]

Fisher's reference to reproducing of a result is equivalent to what we mean by replicating a result. Indeed, the replication of research findings, rather than reliance on a single study and null-hypothesis significance testing of its statistical results, is fundamental to research in any scientific or professional discipline, including education.

In fact, statistical significance is multiplicative across studies.[17] Two or more studies using the same methodology each can yield nonsignificant results, but if the results of each study are in the same direction, the p values from the statistical significance tests can be multiplied. For example, if the p value in each of two studies is .20, their combined probability is .04 (.20 $\times$ .20). Thus, the null hypothesis (which would be the same in both studies) can be rejected at the .04 level of significance.

If possible, you should attempt to replicate your research project, particularly if your findings show promise of making a substantial contribution to knowledge about education. If you are able to replicate your findings, they are much more impressive to other educational researchers than a statistically significant but weak finding (e.g., a correlation of .20 significant at the .01 level) obtained in the original study. A replicated finding is strong evidence against the possibility that a Type I error (rejection of the null hypothesis when it is true) occurred in the original study. Replication also provides other kinds of evidence, depending upon the type of replication study that is carried out.

16. Fisher, R. A. (1929). The statistical method in psychical research. *Proceedings of the Society for Psychical Research, 39*, 189–192. Quote appears on p. 189.
17. The combining of p values across studies also is discussed in Chapter 4 in the context of reviewing the results of quantitative research studies.

TABLE 5.3

Achievement of U.S. and Japanese Students on Posttests Measuring Curriculum Taught and Not Taught (Population: 8th Grade United States; 7th Grade Japan)

Achievement of Curriculum	United States (N = 5,459)		Japan (N = 7,643)		
	Mean Score[a]	SD	Mean Score[a]	SD	Effect Size[b]
Curriculum taught during target grade	40.4	29.9	63.6	27.8	.81
Curriculum not taught	27.7	34.2	38.2	29.4	.33

[a]Scores are percentage correct, corrected for guessing.

[b]Effect size $= \dfrac{\overline{X}_{Japan} - \overline{X}_{U.S.}}{SD_{weighted}}$.

Source: Adapted from table 1 on p. 19 in: Baker, D. P. (1993). Compared to Japan, the U.S. is a low achiever . . . really: New evidence and comment on Westbury. *Educational Researcher, 22*(3), 18–20. Copyright © 1993 by the American Educational Research Association.

Effect Size

We stated above that tests of statistical significance are inappropriate for making inferences about the practical significance of research results. What can be used in their place? The approach currently favored is to calculate confidence intervals and/or an effect size (ES) statistic. We discussed effect size earlier in the chapter with respect to its use in statistical power analysis. Also, the calculation and interpretation of ES were discussed in Chapter 4 as part of a method called *meta-analysis* for reviewing a set of quantitative research studies on a particular problem.

Another use of ES statistics is as an aid to interpreting the results of a single study. An example is a comparative analysis of the mathematics achievement of middle-school students in the United States and Japan by David Baker.[18] He used achievement test scores collected by the International Association for the Evaluation of Educational Achievement in a sample of U.S. and Japanese mathematics classes. The teacher of each class was asked to estimate whether he or she had taught the content needed to answer each item on the test. Students then were given two scores on the test: (1) for items having content taught by the teacher, the percentage that they answered correctly; and (2) for items having content *not* taught by the teacher, the percentage that they answered correctly. Baker believed that this analysis could solve the problem of how to determine whether U.S. or Japanese mathematics instruction is more effective, given that they include different content in their curricula. Comparing the two nations should be fair if their students' mathematical achievement is compared only on test items having content taught by the teacher.

Table 5.3 shows the results of Baker's analysis. Japanese students answered correctly an average of 63.6 percent of the test items having content taught by their teacher

18. Baker, D. P. (1993). Compared to Japan, the U.S. is a low achiever . . . really: New evidence and comment on Westbury. *Educational Researcher, 22*(3), 18–20.

Touchstones in Research

Kline, R. B. (2004). *Beyond significance testing: Reforming data analysis methods in behavioral research.* Washington, DC: American Psychological Association.

Vacha-Haase, T., & Thompson, B. (2004). How to estimate and interpret various effect sizes. *Journal of Counseling Psychology, 51*(4), 473–481.

(labeled "Curriculum taught during target grade"), whereas U.S. students answered correctly only an average of 40.4 such items. You will note that the last column also presents the ES for this difference (.81), and footnote b shows the formula used to calculate the effect size. The numerator of the formula is simply the Japanese mean score (63.6) minus the U.S. mean score (40.4), which equals 23.2. The denominator is a weighted standard deviation calculated by averaging the two standard deviations (SD) while taking into account the different sizes of the two samples. To estimate the denominator, we can ignore sample size differences and average the two SDs (29.9) and (27.8), for a result of 28.85. Dividing 23.2 by 28.85 yields .804, which is quite close to the ES of .81 stated in Table 5.3.

The larger the ES, the greater the difference between two groups. An ES of 1.00 means that the average student in one group scored at the 84th percentile of the other group's score distribution. In Table 5.3, the ES of .81 means that the average Japanese student (i.e., a student at the 50th percentile of the score distribution for his group) would be at the 79th percentile of the score distribution of the total sample (U.S. and Japanese students combined). These percentiles provide a better sense of how much U.S. and Japanese students differ in mathematics achievement than simply knowing their mean scores.

Another interesting finding reported in Table 5.3 is that Japanese students also performed better on items not taught by their teacher (labeled "Curriculum not taught" in the table) than did U.S. students. The ES of .33, however, is not large. It means that the average Japanese student scored at the 63rd percentile of the total score distribution.

The effect size statistic is helpful in judging the practical significance of a research result, but it is by no means an absolute index of practical significance. The magnitude of an ES is affected by the measures used, the absolute difference among group means, the shape of the score distribution, the individuals included in the sample, and possibly other factors. Also, an observed ES might be viewed as small or large depending on the outcome being studied (a small experimental effect on an important educational outcome is more impressive than a larger effect on an outcome of minor importance) and the population being studied (a small learning gain among students with learning disabilities might have just as much practical significance as a substantial learning gain among gifted students).

Effect sizes also can be calculated for statistical results obtained in theoretical research. Even a small effect can be viewed as important if it lends support to the theory being tested. Because many educational outcomes have multiple determinants, a theory might hypothesize what these determinants are, but not hypothesize the magnitude of their influence on the outcome of interest. In this case, small, moderate, and large effect sizes can contribute to the testing and refinement of the theory.

In sum, there is no simple answer to the problem of determining the practical or theoretical significance of research results. The ES is only an aid to interpretation, albeit an important one.

Psychometric Statistics

Statistics of various types can be used to explore and describe the psychometric properties of scores and the appropriateness of interpretations and uses of outcomes from tests and other measures. Selection of the appropriate statistics depends upon the type of psychometric information that is needed. As explained in Chapter 7, there are three types of psychometric information: test validity, test reliability, and item statistics.

Test validity refers to the appropriateness, meaningfulness, and usefulness of specific inferences made from test scores. Many different types of evidence can be collected to demonstrate the validity of these inferences. Much of this evidence is statistical in nature. For example, one type of validity evidence is predictive evidence, which demonstrates that the scores on a test can predict individuals' scores on a desired outcome measure such as grade-point average. This evidence is in the form of correlational statistics, which assess how well the test scores actually predict the outcome measure.

Test reliability refers to the consistency, stability, and precision of test scores. Any time we administer a test or other measure in which some characteristic is expressed in the form of a score, the obtained score always contains some measurement error. When the score has a large amount of measurement error, we say that it is unreliable. Conversely, a score with a small amount of measurement error is described as reliable. How reliable a score is can be described statistically using either a reliability coefficient or a standard error of measurement. There are numerous statistical approaches to estimating the reliability coefficient and the standard error of measurement for a given score on a measure.

Item statistics describe certain properties of individual items in a test or other measure. The most common item statistics are descriptors of item difficulty, the discrimination power of an item, and probability of guessing. Item statistics are used most frequently to revise a measure by identifying items that have a problem, such as poor discrimination power. As these items are revised to correct such problems or are replaced with better items, the measure will provide more reliable scores.

The various statistics involved in constructing and using tests are discussed in more detail in Chapter 7.

Problems in Statistical Analysis

The Need for Exploratory Data Analysis

A common mistake made by researchers is to calculate descriptive statistics (usually means and standard deviations) before carefully examining the individual scores collected in the study. The data in some research studies are "untouched by human hands" in the sense that they are entered immediately into the computer, and a statistical package generates the descriptive and inferential statistics specified by the researcher. The researcher in this situation has denied herself the opportunity to examine the raw data. Consequently, important patterns and phenomena revealed by the individual scores may be overlooked.

Statistical techniques for examining patterns and phenomena in individual scores have been developed. These techniques are not widely used, but they are worth studying because they have revealed new insights about the nature of data often collected in educational research. The techniques are known collectively as **exploratory data analysis,** which is a method for "discovering unforeseen or unexpected patterns in the data and consequently [for] gaining new insights and understanding of natural phenomena."[19]

Touchstones in Research

Hoaglin, D. C., Mosteller, F., & Tukey, J. (2000). *Understanding robust and exploratory data analysis.* New York: Wiley.

Tukey, J. W. (1977). *Exploratory data analysis.* Boston: Addison-Wesley Longman.

---

19. Leinhardt, G., & Leinhardt, S. (1980). Exploratory data analysis: New tools for the analysis of empirical data. In D. C. Berliner (Ed.), *Review of Research in Education* (Vol. 8, pp. 85–157). Washington, DC: American Educational Research Association.

Stem-and-Leaf Displays

Once the research data have been collected and quantified, exploratory data analysis can begin. An essential tool of exploratory data analysis is the **stem-and-leaf display,** which is a condensed graphical presentation of all the individual scores on a particular measure. Table 5.4 presents a conventional display of students' raw scores on a measure of silent reading, provided by a computer program. The scores are from a group of students with learning disabilities who participated in an experimental reading curriculum. The problem with such a display is that it is difficult to "see" the data. Patterns, and any departures from the patterns, are not easily detectable.

TABLE 5.4

Computer Printout of Raw Data

Student Number	Silent Reading Score	Student Number	Silent Reading Score
1	0.33	31	0.19
2	0.80	32	0.48
3	0.58	33	0.66
4	1.27	34	0.42
5	0.84	35	0.25
6	1.04	36	0.77
7	0.36	37	0.69
8	1.63	38	0.64
9	0.44	39	0.13
10	1.4	40	0.355
11	0.8	41	0.622
12	0.0	42	0.112
13	0.9	43	0.162
14	0.8	44	0.353
15	0.3	45	0.065
16	0.3	46	0.095
17	0.2	47	0.485
18	0.1	48	0.170
19	0.3	49	0.275
20	0.3	50	0.448
21	0.4	51	0.324
22	0.5	52	0.692
23	0.3	53	0.492
24	0.27		
25	0.23		
26	0.16		
27	0.17		
28	0.38		
29	0.75		
30	1.13		

Note: The first column is each student's identification (ID) code. The second column is students' scores on a measure of silent reading time.

Source: Adapted from table 2 on p. 91 in: Leinhardt, G. & Leinhardt, S. (1980). Exploratory data analysis: New tools for the analysis of empirical data. In D. C. Berliner (Ed.), *Review of Research in Education* (Vol. 8, pp. 85–157). Washington, DC: American Educational Research Association. Copyright © 1980 by the American Educational Research Association.

FIGURE 5.3

Stem-and-Leaf Display of Data Shown in Table 5.4

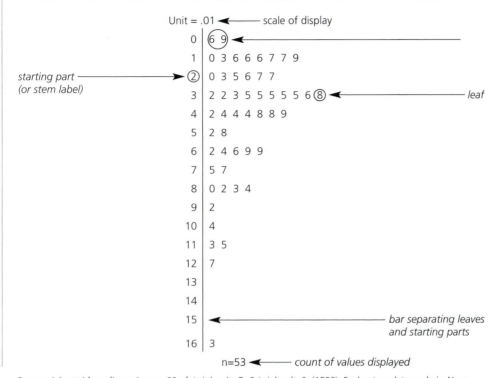

Unit = .01 ◄——— scale of display

```
         0 │ ⑥ ⑨ ◄————————————————————————————
         1 │ 0 3 6 6 6 7 7 9
         ② │ 0 3 5 6 7 7
         3 │ 2 2 3 5 5 5 5 5 6 ⑧ ◄——————————————— leaf
         4 │ 2 4 4 4 8 8 9
         5 │ 2 8
         6 │ 2 4 6 9 9
         7 │ 5 7
         8 │ 0 2 3 4
         9 │ 2
        10 │ 4
        11 │ 3 5
        12 │ 7
        13 │
        14 │
        15 │ ◄——————————————————————————— bar separating leaves
                                          and starting parts
        16 │ 3
```

starting part ——————————► (stem label) (or stem label)

n=53 ◄——— count of values displayed

Source: Adapted from figure 1 on p. 92 of: Leinhardt, G. & Leinhardt, S. (1980). Exploratory data analysis: New tools for the analysis of empirical data. In D. C. Berliner (Ed.). *Review of Research in Education* (Vol. 8, pp. 85–157). Washington, DC: American Educational Research Association. Copyright © 1980 by the American Educational Research Association.

Now examine the stem-and-leaf display in Figure 5.3. It is a display of the raw scores in Table 5.4. In a stem-and-leaf display, a bar separates starting parts, or *stem labels* (to the left of the bar) from each *stem* (to the right of the bar). Each *leaf* in the display can be converted to its original raw score by placing the stem label in front of it and multiplying by the *unit*, in this case, .01.

To understand how a stem-and-leaf display works, look at the stem label in the fourth row of the display, which is 3. This stem label is followed by a stem containing 11 leaves (2, 2, 3, 5, etc.). The third leaf in this stem is a 3. If we place the corresponding stem label in front of this leaf, we obtain the number 33. Multiplying this number by .01 gives us a score of .33, which is the score of the first student in Table 5.4. Now look at the bottom stem, which contains only one leaf (3). If we place the stem label (16) in front of this leaf, we obtain the number 163. Multiplying this number by .01 gives us a score of 1.63, which is the score of the eighth student in Table 5.4. You will note that there are no stems following the stem labels 13, 14, and 15 in Figure 5.3, which tells us that the score of 1.63 is quite discrepant from the other 52 scores in the display.

Touchstone in Research

Osborne, J. W., & Overbay, A. (2004). The power of outliers (and why researchers should ALWAYS check for them). *Practical Assessment, Research & Evaluation, 9*(6). Retrieved August 15, 2005 from http://pareonline.net/getvn.asp?v=9&n=6

Advantages of Stem-and-Leaf Displays

Stem-and-leaf displays have several advantages.

1. Stem-and-leaf displays make it easy to see the shape of the distribution of scores. It is apparent in Figure 5.3 that the scores do not form a normal distribution. Most of the scores are at the lower range of values, clustering around a value of approximately .30. Because the score distribution is skewed in this direction, the stem-and-leaf display would alert you to the possible need to use statistics that do not assume a normal curve distribution, for example, the median and range, and various nonparametric statistics.

2. Stem-and-leaf displays provoke questions about the data. For example, looking at Figure 5.3, you might speculate about the factors that caused most students to score at the lower end of the scale and a few students to score at the upper end of the scale. You might be able to formulate a research hypothesis about these factors and test it using available data, or your research hypothesis might provide the basis for designing a follow-up study.

3. Stem-and-leaf displays facilitate the detection of outliers. An **outlier** is an individual or other entity (e.g., one classroom out of a sample of 20 classrooms) whose score differs markedly from the scores obtained by other members of the sample. The student with a score of 1.63 in Figure 5.3 clearly is an outlier. If you identify an outlier, you first should check whether an error occurred in calculating the outlier's score. Some members of a sample show up as outliers simply because the researcher misplaced a decimal point or transposed the participant's score on another variable while preparing the data for computer analysis.

If the outlier's score is not attributable to a calculation or recording error, you need to search elsewhere for an explanation. Perhaps the outlier was not exposed to the same conditions as the other participants in the sample. A reading of the research report from which the raw data in Table 5.4 were taken indicates that such was the case in this study:

> In the actual research project from which these data were drawn, it was independently determined that the child on whom this outlier value was measured was, for administrative reasons, not under the control of the classroom teacher and was not, therefore, exposed to the same treatment as the other members of the class. He was ultimately removed from the study.[20]

The decision to eliminate outliers from a research study is problematic. Even one or two outliers can distort the results yielded by conventional statistics, unless the sample is large. You should not eliminate outliers for this reason, however. Outliers should be eliminated only for good cause, as in the case of the student described above. If outliers are left in the sample, consider analyzing the data using both parametric and nonparametric statistics. Comparison of the results yielded by these statistical techniques will yield information about how much the outliers are distorting the data.

In the example above, there would be little argument about the decision to call the score of 1.63 an outlier. But how about the student with a score of 1.27 in Figure 5.3, or the students with scores of 1.13 and 1.15? It is not clear that they should be considered outliers. Statistical techniques that yield quantitative decision rules for identifying outliers are available.[21] In reporting findings from your research study, you always should note the presence of outliers and explain how they were handled in the data analysis.

---

20. Ibid., pp. 153–154.
21. Ibid.

Graphical Displays

Graphs, such as those shown in Figures 5.1 through 5.4, are particularly helpful ways of displaying and understanding research findings. A **graph** is a diagram that shows the relationship between two variables. Indeed, Laurence Smith and his colleagues claim that the use of graphs is a major feature of scientific inquiry, especially in the "hard" sciences (e.g., chemistry, physics, and biology).[22] Among other things, they observe that graphs are persuasive: "They serve to convince other scientists of the validity of one's evidence, thereby aiding in the recruitment of allies to one's viewpoint. . . ."[23] For example, perhaps you will agree with us that Figure 5.1 provides a compelling, pictorial summary of Booher-Jennings's findings about how the triage system of resource allocation by teachers and administrators affects different groups of students in an accountability-by-assessment system.

At the least, you should consider the construction of graphs, such as stem-and-leaf displays, as a way to understand your data initially. In writing the report, you might use tables only or a combination of tables and graphs. In deciding which approach to use, you should consider a finding cited by Smith and his colleagues: "[S]ome experimental research on human perception suggests that tables are inferior to graphs for conveying trends in data, differing by nearly an order of magnitude on a standard measure of information transfer. . . ."[24]

The stem-and-leaf display shown in Figure 5.3 is a specific type of graph. In the case of Figure 5.3, we can think of the stem label as a variable with values ranging from 0 to 16. The second variable would be "stem length" (i.e., the number of leaves in the stem). Values of stem length can vary from 0 (e.g., stem label 13) to 11 (e.g., stem label 3). (Other examples of graphs are shown in Figure 11.1.)

The stem-and-leaf display could be converted, if we wished, into other types of graphs, for example, the one shown in Figure 5.4. Here each stem label is represented by a separate bar, and the height of the bar reflects the number of leaves in the stem. This figure is a **histogram,** which is a diagram that shows the relationship between two variables whose measures yield continuous scores. Note that the bars touch each other to indicate the continuous nature of the scores. In contrast, a **bar graph** is a diagram that shows the relationship between measures, one of which yields categorical scores. Each category (e.g., ethnicity) is represented by a separate bar, but the bars do not touch each other. This indicates that the categories are not in a "more" or "less" relationship to each other.

You will note that Figure 5.4 is simpler and easier to comprehend than Figure 5.3. However, it achieves those advantages by eliminating information. For example, if we look at stem label 3 in Figure 5.4, we know that more students earned scores between 3.0 and 3.9 than in any other stem, but we do not know how the scores are distributed within that range.

Figure 5.4 could be simplified still further by clustering stem labels within certain ranges, for example, 0–0.3, 0.4–0.7, 0.8–1.1, 1.2–1.6. We also could make the differences in frequency distributions between the ranges more dramatic by changing the scale of the graph (e.g., increasing the length of the unit used to represent each leaf). However, at some

Touchstone in Research

Wainer, H. (2004). *Graphic discovery: A trout in the milk and other visual adventures.* Princeton, NJ: Princeton University Press.

22. Smith, L. D., Best, L. A., Stubbs, D. A., Archibald, A. B., & Roberson-Nay, R. (2002). Constructing knowledge: The role of graphs and tables in hard and soft psychology. *American Psychologist, 57*(10), 749–761.
23. Ibid., p. 752.
24. Ibid., p. 753.

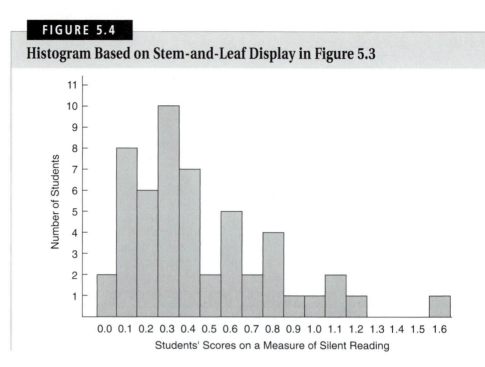

FIGURE 5.4

Histogram Based on Stem-and-Leaf Display in Figure 5.3

point in designing the graph, "dramatizing" differences can cross over into the realm of "distorting" differences. For this reason, researchers need to create displays that are informative and visually appealing, but not oversimplified or misleading. A stem-and-leaf display is well-suited for researchers' initial exploration of their data, but probably not for most research reports. Histograms, bar graphs (Figure 5.1 is an example), and other displays (e.g., pie graphs or the frequency polygon shown in Figure 5.2) are usually better suited for the latter purpose.

Missing Data

Touchstone in Research

Peugh, J. L., & Enders, C. K. (2004). Missing data in educational research: A review of reporting practices and suggestions for improvement. *Review of Educational Research, 74*(4), 525–556.

Missing data are items of information that the researcher intended to collect as part of the research design but are not available for the data analysis. Missing data can be the result of someone losing information through carelessness. In some research studies, for example, tests are administered to hundreds of students. Even though a particular student was present for the testing, her test might become lost in the course of handing it to the test administrator, returning it to the central data-collection center, attaching an ID code, or computer scoring of the test. This loss of data can complicate statistical analysis and weaken the study's contribution to research knowledge. Therefore, precautions should be taken to ensure that no data are lost through avoidable human error.

Missing data also can occur if an individual selected for the research sample refuses to or is unable to participate in part of the study. Even if an individual agrees to participate, he may be unavailable on particular occasions when data are collected. The likelihood of missing data increases as the number of data-collection sessions increases, simply because there are more opportunities for research participants to become ill or to be called away by other commitments.

TABLE 5.5

Missing Data in Two Tests Administered to an Experimental Group and a Control Group

	Test A				Test B			
	Experimental Group		Control Group		Experimental Group		Control Group	
Subject I.D.	Time 1	Time 2	Time 1	Time 2	Time 1	Time 2	Time 1	Time 2
001	5	7	4	5	—	37	38	40
002	4	—	4	4	42	63	—	51
003	8	12	—	7	53	71	45	43
004	—	17	15	—	36	63	55	55
005	6	—	4	3	15	17	38	50
006	10	13	8	10	52	—	63	64
007	3	5	5	7	49	45	—	36
008	7	5	5	5	38	—	50	48
009	—	10	10	—	47	65	36	40
010	12	17	9	—	50	54	47	51

Students frequently are subjects in educational research. Students often experience illnesses at the same time. If a substantial number of students are absent from school or are unavailable for a scheduled data-collection session, it probably is better to reschedule the session than to have incomplete data for the statistical analysis. This is not a rigid rule, however. In certain studies, the data might be uninterpretable unless they are collected at a specific time. In this situation, a better compromise might be to collect data from a partial sample, assuming that the resulting data still can yield interpretable findings.

Missing data are particularly challenging when several different tests have been administered on several occasions to the same groups of research participants. Consider the scores for two different tests administered at two intervals to an experimental and control group, depicted in Table 5.5. Missing data are indicated by a dash.

The researcher had planned to perform a separate analysis of covariance for each test. Time 1 scores are the *covariate,* and the difference between the experimental and control groups' mean scores at Time 2 is to be analyzed for statistical significance.[25]

How should missing data be handled? One solution is to eliminate incomplete cases, so that only research participants with both Time 1 and Time 2 data are included in the statistical analysis. This solution would entail the loss of four experimental participants and four control participants in analyzing Test A data, and the loss of three experimental participants and two control participants in analyzing Test B data. However, note that different participants would be eliminated across the two tests, and as a result the experimental and control

25. A covariate is an independent variable (in this case, Test A or Test B scores at Time 1) whose influence on the dependent variable (in this case, test A or test B scores at Time 2) is controlled by analysis of covariance.

groups would not have the same composition across the two samples. If we wished to include only those participants who have complete data for both tests and both test sessions, even more data would be lost. For example, the experimental group would include only three complete cases (003, 007, and 010)! Another solution is to estimate the missing data by plugging the group mean into each empty cell, or by using a form of regression analysis (explained in Chapter 11) known as *maximum likelihood estimation* to estimate more precisely the missing values. The decision to use one solution or another involves complex considerations. In this type of situation, we recommend that you consult an expert statistician.

The best solution obviously is to avoid missing data. Extra effort to ensure that all data required by the research design are collected will save effort later in the statistical analysis phase of the study. Note, too, that beyond a certain point, missing data can hopelessly compromise the research design. In that situation, the only alternatives are to abandon the study or to collect a new set of data.

The Unit of Statistical Analysis

Educational researchers can study individuals as they act in isolation, as they act independently but within a group setting, or as they act as a group. These distinctions are important to consider in deciding whether to use the individual research participant or a group of research participants as the unit of statistical analysis. The **unit of statistical analysis** is the sampling unit replicated within a research study. If the participant is the sampling unit, each participant added to the sample can be considered a replication of the phenomena to be described, correlated, or experimentally manipulated.

The effect of the statistical unit on research results is illustrated by the following example. Suppose the relative effectiveness of two teaching methods, A and B, is to be compared by having them used in different classrooms. Ten sixth-grade classrooms—two from each of five schools—are selected for the experiment. In each school one class is randomly assigned to teaching method A and the other to teaching method B for a period of two months. Hypothetical posttest scores of individual students following the experimental period are shown in Table 5.6. Elementary classrooms typically have 20 to 30 or more students, but to simplify the data presentation the table shows classes containing between 5 and 8 students.

In this experiment, the purpose of the statistical analysis is to determine whether the posttest scores of students who received teaching method A are significantly different from the posttest scores of students who received teaching method B. A *t* test can be done to test for statistical significance, but what is the best unit of statistical analysis—the individual student or the classroom group? If the unit is the individual student, there are 32 students instructed by teaching method A who can be compared with 34 students instructed by teaching method B. If the class is used as the unit, there are only five class means for teaching method A, to be compared with five class means for teaching method B.

Note, too, that the descriptive statistics vary as a function of the unit of analysis. The mean and standard deviation of scores for teaching method A are 23.6 and 5.42, respectively, when the student is the unit of analysis. In contrast, when the group is the unit of analysis, the mean and standard deviation of the group means (19.2, 24.2, 27.8, 20.2, 24.5) are 23.2 and 3.49, respectively.

This discussion of the unit of statistical analysis highlights the fact that education occurs at many levels, for example, individual students receiving tutorial instruction, small cooperative learning groups within classrooms, classrooms, schools, school districts, regions, states, and nations. You need to decide which levels include the phenomena of primary interest to you.

TABLE 5.6

Posttest Scores of Students Instructed by Two Different Teaching Methods

Method A (N = 32)

School I Class 1	School 2 Class 2	School 3 Class 3	School 4 Class 4	School 5 Class 5
18	25	28	17	22
22	18	27	19	24
27	29	29	23	30
15	30	30	18	15
9	19	24	24	27
24	M = 24.2	26	M = 20.2	21
M = 19.2		31		29
		27		28
		M = 27.8		M = 24.5

Method B (N = 34)

School 1 Class 6	School 2 Class 7	School 3 Class 8	School 4 Class 9	School 5 Class 10
25	16	19	22	21
22	25	21	20	29
18	18	28	24	18
18	23	16	19	14
20	15	15	18	22
22	9	21	21	M = 20.8
M = 20.8	22	14	15	
	M = 18.3	12	17	
		M = 18.3	M = 19.5	

Multilevel Analysis

Leigh Burstein argued that educational researchers should consider several levels at once in designing a study:

> Schooling activities occur within hierarchical organizations in which the sources of educational influence on students occur in the groups to which an individual belongs. These groups (learning groups within classrooms, classrooms within schools, schools within districts, families within communities, schools within communities) influence the thoughts, behavior, and feelings of their members. This hierarchical structure gives rise to multilevel data.[26]

By the term *multilevel data,* Burstein means data that can be analyzed at more than one level of grouping. For example, if a researcher collects data from three classrooms

Touchstone in Research

Schreiber, J. B., & Griffin, B. W. (2004). Review of multilevel modeling and multilevel studies in the *Journal of Educational Research* (1992–2002). *Journal of Educational Research, 98*(1), 24–33.

26. Burstein, L. (1980). Issues in the aggregation of data. In D. C. Berliner (Ed.), *Review of Research in Education* (Vol. 8, pp. 158–233). Washington, DC: American Educational Research Association. Quote appears on page 158.

within a school, the data can be analyzed at two levels: classroom (each classroom has a score, or set of scores, associated with it) and school (the mean score of the three classrooms on a variable yields some data about the school as a whole). Policy studies in education are concerned with even larger units of analysis. Researchers working on the National Assessment of Educational Progress (see Chapter 10) aggregate student data to the state level so that they can study differences among states in the educational attainments of their students. Researchers who are involved with the International Association for the Evaluation of Educational Achievement (see Chapter 10) have aggregated student data to the national level in order to examine differences among the nations of the world in their educational practices and outcomes.

Statistical procedures for analyzing multilevel data are being used increasingly as educational researchers become more interested in school, district, and other multilevel effects on students' learning and behavior. These statistical procedures typically are called *hierarchical linear modeling*, but occasionally the labels *hierarchical linear regression* or *multilevel modeling* are used. (see Chapter 11)

Hierarchical linear modeling is a statistical method for determining how several levels of grouping affect, either separately or in interaction with each other, the relationship between two or more variables. A "grouping" is a unit within which individuals are clustered (i.e., "nested") and influence each other, such as students in a classroom. Researchers sometimes wish to study several levels of grouping: for example, classrooms (each student is nested in a particular classroom), and classrooms across schools (each classroom is nested in a particular school).

To illustrate, suppose we hypothesize that: within individual students (non-nested factor), reading ability affects their math achievement; the relationship between these variables is affected by their teacher (nested factor), because we think that teachers vary in ability to individualize math instruction to accommodate different students' reading skills; this individualization is affected by the teachers' school (nested factor), because we think that principals vary in their emphasis on math instruction as a schoolwide priority. With a sufficiently large sample of students, teachers, and principals, hierarchical linear modeling can test these hypothesized nested and non-nested effects.

Processing Statistical Data

Computer Hardware

Most statistical analyses in educational research require complex computations. Therefore, researchers generally use a computer or other calculating machine to perform their statistical analyses.

If you have a large amount of data to analyze, you will need to use a mainframe computer, which has the capacity to perform many millions of calculations per minute. These computers are very expensive, and, therefore, they usually are only available at university and college computer centers. One mainframe computer can use its time-sharing features to serve the computing needs of an entire campus.

Most personal computers now have the capability to perform sophisticated statistical analyses on fairly large amounts of data. The main advantage of these computers over a mainframe computer is their convenience. A personal computer can be used when and where you wish. Use of the mainframe computer requires a trip to the computer center or a computer terminal linked to it. Also, there may be restrictions on its availability and charges for its use.

Some handheld calculators have the capability of performing statistical analyses by a simple press of an appropriate function key. Less sophisticated calculators also are useful if you have just a small amount of research data to be analyzed, and if the analyses are limited to simple descriptive and inferential statistics.

Computer Software

The most commonly used software for statistical analysis in educational research is SPSS, which is an acronym for Statistical Package for the Social Sciences (http://www.spss.com). SPSS is a comprehensive, integrated collection of computer programs for managing, analyzing, and displaying data. SPSS programs can perform the statistical procedures described in this chapter and in the following chapters. Most universities and colleges have SPSS available for their mainframe computers. A version of SPSS also is available for personal computers. SPSS is occasionally upgraded, so you should check whether you have the most current version.

Another widely available set of integrated statistical programs is SAS, an acronym for Statistical Analysis System (http://www.sas.com). It is more difficult to use than SPSS, but it has more capabilities.[27]

An increasing amount of statistical analysis software is available for personal computers. You should check the soundness of this software before using it. Some programs have not been fully tested for "bugs" (errors) or do not follow standard algorithms to arrive at a solution. Therefore, they may give spurious results.

Computer Consultants

Use of SPSS and similar computer software is fairly complicated. Many graduate students find it necessary to hire a computer consultant to assist them in analyzing the data for their thesis or dissertation. You should try to find a consultant who has a good understanding not only of computers but also of educational research methods and statistics. It is not advisable, however, to turn your data completely over to a consultant. Consultants are not likely to have the same "feel" for the data or methodology as you do, and therefore they may wind up doing inappropriate and inaccurate analyses.

These problems can be avoided by asking the consultant to explain each step of data file management and statistical analysis when it is executed. Also, you should specify the statistical techniques that are best to answer your research questions or test your hypotheses, rather than allow the consultant to choose them.

When possible, you should work alongside the consultant. For example, you can observe the consultant create the data entry program and enter some of the numerical data. When you understand how the process works, you can enter the remaining data on your own. Also, you can ask the consultant to use SPSS or related software in an interactive mode. As the consultant keyboards each set of commands, you can ask what they mean; you will be able to see on the computer screen the statistical results produced by the commands. This procedure is far better than trying to make sense of a stack of computer printouts generated by the consultant without your participation.

Touchstone in Research

Muijs, D. (2004). *Doing quantitative research in education: With SPSS.* Thousand Oaks, CA: Sage.

---

27. Andrews, F. M., Klem, L., O'Malley, P., Rodgers, W. L., Welch, K., & Davidson, T. N. (1998). *Selecting statistical techniques for social science data: A guide for SAS users.* Cary, NC: SAS Publishing.

Checking Data Analyses for Accuracy

Whether you use a calculator, personal computer, or mainframe computer, you should check continuously for accuracy. The first thing to check is the data file, which is your data as stored by the computer. Some calculators facilitate this check by making a paper tape of each data entry. This tape constitutes the data file. Computers show the data file on a screen or printout. Visual inspection of these displays can pick up obvious errors like unusually large or small values of a variable, or misaligned columns. A type of statistical software known as a data entry program also can pick up these errors.

The next task is to make spot checks of parts of the data file. If these checks reveal unacceptable errors, you will need to enter the data again. Data entry software programs allow you to keep the original data file and re-keyboard the new entries over it. The computer will signal whenever there is a discrepancy between the original entry and the new entry. You can check the discrepancy to determine which entry is in error.

The results of a statistical analysis can be checked in several ways. You can redo the analysis, or you can check the command file to ensure that the proper commands were used. A **command file** is a list of the computer software instructions that you used to perform your statistical analyses. Also, you can check part of the computer analysis by using a calculator. For example, if the computer program calculated a large number of correlation coefficients, you can compute one of them on a calculator. Generally, if the calculator result matches the computer result (within rounding errors), you can be confident that the computer computed all the other correlations without error.

If the results of a statistical analysis are implausible, you should consider the possibility of a computing error. Even if the results are plausible, however, they still should be checked.

Storing Research Data

After you have completed the data analyses for your study, you should file the raw data, hand computations, and computer printouts. The printouts should include the results of the statistical analyses, the data files, and the command files for major analyses. If you used a mainframe computer, an alternative is to store this information on a computer tape. A computer tape is more compact than a stack of printouts and is relatively inexpensive. A single tape is sufficient to store all the files for even a very large research study. If you used a personal computer, the various files can be saved on a storage device (e.g., a CD).

It is particularly important to retain the raw data, which are the test answer sheets, observation forms, recordings of interviews, and other research material as initially received from the research participants. For example, you might wish to refer back to the raw data to check a particular score that seems doubtful. Also, retaining the raw data makes it possible to use the data in future research. It is not uncommon to hit upon an idea for re-analyzing data after completion of the original study. The re-analysis may yield new and interesting information that would be lost if the raw data had been destroyed at the end of the original analysis. If any research findings are challenged, the raw data provide the only fully satisfactory source for rechecking them.

You should label all materials (e.g., printouts) involved in the data analysis and keep a record of all your steps. This takes time, but it is much less than the time that would be required to decipher unlabeled raw data or to redo lost calculations.

RECOMMENDATIONS FOR

Doing Statistical Analyses

1. Select the statistical techniques that are most appropriate for your data and goals.
2. Plan the major statistical analyses before conducting your study to ensure that the resulting data are analyzable.
3. Illuminate different aspects of a data set by using several statistical techniques, not just one.
4. Consider using nonparametric statistics when the data grossly fail to meet the necessary assumptions for parametric statistics.
5. In reporting p values for tests of statistical significance, take care to interpret their meaning correctly.
6. Use statistical power analysis to plan an adequate sample size for a study and to weigh the risks of Type I and Type II errors in tests of statistical significance.
7. Compute effect sizes and confidence limits in addition to tests of statistical significance.
8. Explore the characteristics of the raw scores obtained in a study before doing formal statistical analyses.
9. Adjust statistical analyses to account for missing data.
10. Consider the purpose of the research study and the data that were collected in deciding which unit(s) of statistical analysis to employ.

SELF-CHECK TEST

Circle the correct answer to each of the following questions. The answers are provided at the back of the book.

1. A type of score that is *not* appropriate for data analyses involving inferential statistics is
   a. raw scores.
   b. standard scores.
   c. percentile equivalents.
   d. continuous scores.

2. Category values are represented by:
   a. ordinal scales.
   b. nominal scales.
   c. interval scales.
   d. ratio scales.

3. The median is a better measure of central tendency to use than the mean when
   a. the researcher wishes to examine the raw scores.
   b. the score distribution is skewed.
   c. the scores are distributed normally.
   d. one score is obtained more frequently than any other.

4. An appropriate statement of a null hypothesis would be that
   a. the group receiving the experimental treatment will receive higher scores than the control group.
   b. the research sample will behave differently than the population from which it is drawn.
   c. the difference between sample means reflects a true difference between population means.
   d. no difference will be found between the groups being compared in one's research study.

5. A test of statistical significance is carried out when one wishes to determine
   a. the probability that the differences observed between two samples also will be found in the populations from which they were drawn.
   b. the probability of finding the same research results if one were to do a replication of the research study.
   c. whether the results have practical implications for educators.
   d. whether there is an actual difference between two populations in their scores on a variable of interest.

6. The power of a statistical significance test is increased by all of the following *except*
   a. greater sample size.
   b. use of a higher *p* value to reject the null hypothesis.
   c. estimated effect size.
   d. use of a nondirectional hypothesis.

7. Calculating confidence limits in a research study is a good idea because it
   a. provides a means for estimating population values.
   b. allows the researcher to explore the data for patterns and phenomena that otherwise might be missed.

   c. increases the probability of obtaining statistically significant results.
   d. provides a statistical method for replicating one's research study.

8. Effect size is a useful statistic to calculate in order to
   a. synthesize research findings from a number of studies of the same variable.
   b. study the likelihood that a particular *p* value will be sufficient to reject a false null hypothesis.
   c. assess the practical significance of research findings.
   d. all of the above.

9. Stem-and-leaf displays are useful for
   a. estimating missing data.
   b. detecting outliers.
   c. estimating effect size.
   d. estimating the probability of a Type I error.

10. A researcher is interested in the relationship between students' academic achievement and class size. The appropriate unit of analysis is
   a. the individual student.
   b. the classroom.
   c. the school.
   d. all of the above.

CHAPTER 6

Selecting a Sample

OVERVIEW

Educational researchers rarely can investigate the entire population of individuals, or other phenomena, that interest them. Instead, they must select a sample to study. In this chapter, we discuss how the logic of selecting this sample differs when doing quantitative and qualitative research. We explain the sampling strategies used in each type of research and the factors to be considered in deciding an optimum sample size. The chapter concludes with a discussion of issues involved in using volunteer samples. The sampling procedures described in the chapter apply not only to selection of research participants but also to the selection of events, curriculum materials, and other phenomena of interest to researchers.

OBJECTIVES

After studying this chapter, you should be able to

1. Compare the logic used in quantitative and qualitative research to apply research findings to other situations or cases.
2. Explain the relationship between a sample, the target population, and an accessible population.
3. Explain the relevance of population validity to sampling and two criteria for ensuring high population validity.
4. Describe the benefits and limitations of and procedures used in simple random sampling, systematic random sampling, stratified random sampling, cluster sampling, and convenience sampling in quantitative research.
5. Explain how probability sampling can be used to sample a phenomenon rather than a sample of individuals for a research study.
6. Identify three factors that should be considered in determining the sample size for a quantitative research study.

7. Explain the rationale for purposeful sampling in qualitative research.
8. Explain how replication logic can be applied in selecting cases for qualitative research.
9. Describe the various purposeful sampling strategies used in qualitative research and how they differ from each other.
10. Explain how the determination of the number of cases to study in qualitative research involves a trade-off between depth and breadth.
11. Describe typical differences between volunteers and nonvolunteers as research participants and how the influence of volunteers on research results can be tested.
12. Describe several techniques for improving the rate of volunteering for participation in a research study.

Sampling Logic in Research

This chapter describes the sampling techniques commonly used by educational researchers. Although we focus on how to select students, teachers, or other *individuals* for a research sample, the same sampling procedures and issues are involved in selecting a sample of *events* or *objects* to study. For example, a researcher might wish to select a sample of class periods to observe, or a sample of elementary reading textbooks to analyze. The class periods and textbooks can be selected using the same sampling techniques described in this chapter.

Suppose that a quantitative researcher wants to learn what educators think about school choice, that is, the funding of education to enable parents and students to choose among various schools more easily—public or private, religious or nondenominational, those adhering to one educational philosophy or another. The researcher would like to study every educator in the nation, but due to cost and time considerations must settle for administering a survey questionnaire to a small sample of perhaps 200 educators.

Now consider a different research situation. This researcher wishes to do a qualitative study of the views of former President Bill Clinton about school choice. He studies Clinton's speeches and writings about this subject over a period of time, and perhaps is even able to interview him.

The goals of sampling in these two studies are very different. In the first study, the sample is chosen with the intention that it represent a large population. In other words, the researcher is interested in the views of the entire population, not just those of the particular sample that she happened to select. The second researcher is interested primarily in his sample, which includes but a single case. He selected former President Bill Clinton because of his leadership and influence on the school-choice debate. It would not make sense to generalize his findings about this particular president to a larger population of presidents. Bill Clinton is a unique individual, and his views about school choice could not be construed as representative of other presidents or even of other government officials.

The preceding examples suggest that the logic for generalizing beyond one's sample is very different in quantitative and qualitative research. Later we will examine this difference more closely.

Sampling in Quantitative Research

Touchstones in Research

Henry, G. T. (1998). Practical sampling. In L. Bickman & D. J. Rog (Eds.), *Handbook of applied social research methods* (pp. 101–126). Thousand Oaks, CA: Sage.

Fink, A. (2003) *How to sample in surveys* (2nd ed.). Thousand Oaks, CA: Sage.

We turn now to specific procedures that quantitative researchers use to select a sample that represents a defined population.

Defining the Population of Interest

Quantitative researchers attempt to discover something about a large group of individuals by studying a much smaller group. The larger group that they wish to learn about is called a *population*, and the smaller group they actually study is called a *sample*. In quantitative research, **sampling** refers to this process of selecting a sample from a defined population with the intent that the sample accurately represent that population.

Target and Accessible Populations

Two types of populations are relevant to the sampling process in quantitative research. The first is the **target population,** which includes all the members of a real or hypothetical set of people, events, or objects to which researchers wish to generalize the results of their research. (Statisticians sometimes refer to the target population as a *universe.*) The advantage of drawing a small sample from a large target population is that it saves the time and expense of studying the entire population. If sampling is done properly, you can make inferences from the sample to an entire target population that are likely to be correct within a small margin of error. For example, in national surveys, researchers can use a random sample of 1,000 or so individuals to represent the views of the entire adult population (well over 100 million people) at a high level of accuracy.

The first step in sampling is to define the target population. Examples might include all school superintendents in Pennsylvania, all supervisors of student teachers in accredited teacher education programs in Canada, all bilingual children in the primary grades of the San Antonio School District, and students who have failed an algebra course in the New York City schools in the past three years. These examples illustrate how the target population can represent a large group scattered over a wide geographical area or a smaller group concentrated in a single area.

Few researchers have the resources to draw a sample from a very large, geographically dispersed target population, such as all first-grade students in U.S. public schools. Instead, they draw their samples from an **accessible population,** which is all the individuals who realistically could be included in the sample. For example, if you are planning to survey how high school students currently use computers at school and at home, your accessible population might be students in the school district in the neighborhood where you live, plus perhaps a few neighboring districts.

If the population is fairly large, you will need to find a way to identify all its members. Researchers generally rely on a published list, called a **sampling frame,** of the population that interests them. (A sampling frame typically is a published list, but in more general terms it is a set of directions for identifying the population.) For example, Kathy Green used a published list to select a random sample of teachers:

> [S]urvey forms were mailed in a rural western state to 700 teachers randomly selected from the State Department of Education list of all licensed educators.[1]

Appendix A includes directories of directories that can be used to locate some of these published lists. Of course, you should check to determine whether a relevant list is complete and fairly recent. School enrollment and memberships of organizations change constantly, so frequent updating of the population lists is necessary. Also, keep in mind that membership in most organizations is voluntary. Thus, the researcher who uses an organization's directory to define a population faces the risk of selecting a biased sample, because joiners of organizations might differ in important respects from nonjoiners. If this is the case, you need to define the accessible population as all members of a given organization rather than as all members of the profession or group that the organization serves.

Sampling frames can be very difficult to devise for certain populations of interest to educators. For example, suppose a researcher wishes to study homeless children. How can one identify a target or accessible population when these children typically are transient and often "hidden" from the community?[2] Victims of child abuse are another population that is difficult to identify. Different databases and data-collection methods have yielded different populations of these victims and different subpopulations based on racial classification.[3]

Researchers increasingly are using the Internet to collect data from research participants. This requires the identification of populations and methods of drawing samples to

1. Green, K. A. (1992). Differing opinions on testing between preservice and inservice teachers. *Journal of Educational Research, 86*, 37–42. Quote appears on p. 38.
2. Phelan, J. C., & Link, B. G. (1999). Who are "the homeless"? Reconsidering the stability and composition of the homeless population. *American Journal of Public Health, 89*, 1334–1338.
3. Ards, S., Chung, C., & Myers, Jr., S. L. (1998). The effects of sample selection bias on racial differences in child abuse reporting. *Child Abuse and Neglect, 22*, 103–115.

define the populations. These can be difficult tasks if members of the population have differential access to Internet capabilities, or if they do not provide accurate information (e.g., registering at a Web site but giving inaccurate information about themselves, such as an incorrect e-mail address).[4]

Inferential Leaps from a Sample to a Population

Even though most samples are selected from an accessible population, researchers usually want to know the degree to which the results can be generalized to the target population. This type of generalization requires two inferential leaps. First, the researchers must generalize the results for the sample to the accessible population from which the sample was selected. Second, they must generalize from the accessible population to the target population.

The inferential leap from the sample to the accessible population presents no problem if a **random sample** of the accessible population was obtained, that is, a sample in which all members of the accessible population had an equal chance of being selected. If the sample was not formed randomly, the researchers should compare the sample with the accessible population on characteristics critical to the study. Rarely will researchers be able to obtain data for all the characteristics they wish to compare, but they should try to obtain comparative information on at least the critical variables (usually such characteristics as gender, socioeconomic status, ethnicity, age, and academic ability). These data will demonstrate whether the sample is representative of the accessible population. If the sample is representative, you can safely generalize the results to the accessible population. If, however, the sample is biased (that is, not representative), researchers should report the nature of the bias and discuss how it might affect the research results.

In order to make the second inferential leap—from the accessible population to the target population—researchers must gather data to determine the degree of similarity between the two populations. Of course, it is possible to compare two populations on a great many variables. Nevertheless, if researchers are able to demonstrate that the accessible population is similar to the target population on a few variables that are particularly relevant to the study, they have done much to establish the population validity of their research results. Population validity is defined in the next section.

Resource limitations often limit researchers to drawing a random sample from a very small accessible population, as in a study of processes involved in reading by Richard Wagner and his associates:

> The subjects were 95 kindergarten and 89 second-grade students who were randomly selected from three elementary schools in Tallahassee, Florida.[5]

Studies based on a narrow accessible population are, of course, less generalizable than those based on broader populations. They still may have implications for other educators if it can be demonstrated that the accessible population—or a randomly drawn sample from it—is similar to a larger target population on critical variables. In the reading study Wagner and his associates described the sample with respect to age, gender distribution, ethnic distribution, and language fluency. Thus, readers of their report can determine whether the sample is similar to the target population of interest to them, and therefore whether the research findings are applicable to that target population.

4. Bradley, N. (1999). Sampling for Internet surveys: An examination of respondent selection for Internet research. *Journal of the Market Research Society, 41,* 387–395.
5. Wagner, R. K., Torgesen, J. K., Laughon, P., Simmons, K., & Rashotte, C. A. (1993). Development of young readers' phonological processing capabilities. *Journal of Educational Psychology, 85,* 83–103. Quote appears on p. 87.

How well do most researchers follow the logic of defining a target population and accessible population and drawing a representative sample from it? Steven Permut, Allen Michel, and Monica Joseph used four criteria to evaluate the sampling logic in 460 articles on marketing research.[6] The criteria were as follows:

1. A clear description of the *population* to which the results are to be generalized should be given.
2. The *sampling procedure* should be specified in sufficient detail that another investigator would be able to replicate the procedure. The details should include, at a minimum, (a) the type of sample (simple random, stratified random, convenience, etc.); (b) sample size; and (c) geographic area. Depending on the study, other descriptive data (e.g., gender, age, grade level, socioeconomic status) also should be included.
3. The *sampling frame*, that is, the lists, indexes, or other population records from which the sample was selected, should be identified.
4. The *completion rate*, which is the proportion of the sample that participated as intended in all of the research procedures, should be given.

Only 10 percent of the studies reviewed by Permut and his associates met all four criteria. In a similar analysis of 297 published studies in communications research, Dennis Lowry also found that only 10 percent met the four criteria.[7] In your own study, you should try, as a minimum, to satisfy the four criteria listed above.

Determining Population Validity

According to Glenn Bracht and Gene Glass, one of the criteria for judging experiments is population validity.[8] **Population validity** is the extent to which the results of an experiment can be generalized from the sample that participated in it to a larger group of individuals, that is, the population from which the sample was drawn. Bracht and Glass analyzed population validity with reference to quantitative research involving the experimental method. However, this concept applies just as well to the logic of sampling in other types of quantitative research.

To achieve good population validity, quantitative researchers must select the sample randomly from the defined population to which they wish to generalize their results. Also, this randomly drawn sample must be of sufficient size to reduce the probability that the sample, even though randomly drawn, has different characteristics than the population from which it was drawn.

Population validity is closely related to inferential statistics and statistical power analysis, which are explained in Chapter 5. Inferential statistics, which include tests of statistical significance and confidence intervals, enable researchers to make generalizations about population parameters on the basis of sample statistics. Therefore, inferential statistics contribute evidence to establish the population validity of a set of research results. Statistical power analysis also contributes relevant evidence, because it indicates the probability of Type I and Type II errors in drawing conclusions about population parameters.

Random samples and large sample sizes are difficult to achieve under the real-world conditions in which educational researchers typically collect data. In later sections of the

6. Permut, J. E., Michel, A. J., & Joseph, M. (1976). The researcher's sample: A review of the choice of respondents in marketing research. *Journal of Marketing Research, 13*, 278–283.
7. Lowry, D. T. (1979). Population validity of communication research: Sampling the samples. *Journalism Quarterly, 56*, 62–68, 76.
8. Bracht, G. H., & Glass, G. V. (1968). The external validity of experiments. *American Educational Research Journal, 5*, 437–474. The concept of population validity also is discussed in Chapter 12.

chapter we identify major difficulties in sampling that researchers encounter and compromises they can make to achieve an acceptable level of population validity for their studies.

Population validity can be quantified if we compute a statistic for a sample and know the actual parameter for the population from which the sample was randomly drawn. Suppose the statistic is the mean of the sample's scores on a test. Further suppose that the sample mean is 26.2 and the actual population mean is 29.4. The difference between the two means is 3.2. Thus, the population validity of the sample mean is less than perfect but still a fairly good approximation. In technical terms, this deviation of a sample mean (or other statistic, such as the standard deviation) from the population parameter is called **sampling error.**

Types of Probability Sampling

Samples can be drawn from accessible or target populations by various methods. Some of the methods involve **probability sampling,** which means that each individual in the population has a known probability of being selected. The probabilities are known because the individuals are chosen by chance. The following sections describe four types of probability sampling: (1) simple random sampling, (2) systematic random sampling, (3) stratified random sampling, and (4) cluster sampling.

Simple Random Sampling

A simple random sample is a group of individuals drawn by a procedure in which all the individuals in the defined population have an equal and independent chance of being selected as a member of the sample. By *independent* we mean that the selection of one individual for the sample has no effect on the selection of any other individual.

This definition of a simple random sample is adequate, but it does contain a slight flaw. In reality, each individual in the defined population cannot have an exactly equal chance of being selected into the sample. To understand why this is so, suppose there are 1,000 sixth-grade students in our accessible population, and we want to select a simple random sample of 100 students. When we select our first research participant, each student has one chance in 1,000 of being selected. Once this student has been selected, however, only 999 students remain; each student now has one chance in 999 of being selected as our second participant. Thus, as each student is selected, the probability of being selected next increases slightly because the population from which we are selecting has become one participant smaller.

The flaw in our initial definition of a **simple random sample** can be corrected by defining it as a sample selected from a population by a process that provides every sample of a given size an equal probability of being selected. In other words, suppose that your population has 1,000 members and you intend to draw a random sample of 50 participants from it. Now imagine every conceivable sample of 50 participants from this population. If you draw a random sample from the population, any one of these samples would have an equal chance of being the sample you select for your study.

The main advantage of randomly selected samples is that they yield research data that can be generalized to a larger population within margins of error that can be determined by statistical formulas. Random sampling also is preferred because it satisfies the logic by which a null hypothesis is tested with inferential statistics (see Chapter 5).

Random number generators Various techniques can be used to obtain a simple random sample. Suppose the research director of a large city school system wishes to obtain a random sample of 100 students from a population of 972 students currently enrolled in the ninth grade in School District A. First, he would obtain a copy of the district census for ninth-grade students and assign a number to each student. Then he would use a table of random numbers to draw a sample from the census list. Tables of random numbers usually consist of long series of five-digit numbers generated randomly by a computer.

Table 6.1 is a small portion of a typical table. To use the random numbers table, randomly select a column as a starting point, then select all the numbers that follow in that column. Because there are three digits in 972 (the number of cases in the accessible population, School District A), you only need to use the last three digits of each five-digit number. If more numbers are needed, proceed to the next column until sufficient numbers have been selected to make up the desired sample size.

In our example, suppose the researcher selects row 1 of column 5 in Table 6.1 as his starting point and uses the last three digits of each number in that column and each successive column. Thus, the researcher would select the 732nd student on the census list, skip the number 983 (there are only 972 cases in the population), select the 970th student, select the 554th student, and so on. This procedure would be followed (with a much larger table of random numbers, of course) until a sample of 100 pupils had been selected.

Another method for generating a sequence of random numbers is to use software with this capability. Also, at least one web site has this capability: (http://www.randomizer.org). (You might find other web sites by entering the keyword phrase "random number generator" in a generic search engine.)

Example of simple random sampling Simple random sampling is illustrated by a study involving the selection of a national random sample of secondary physics teachers.[9] The researchers responsible for this curriculum evaluation study (Wayne Welch, Herbert Walberg, and Andrew Ahlgren) wished to avoid a nonrandom sample of "volunteer" teachers. Use of volunteers, which is typical of many curriculum evaluation studies, makes it difficult to generalize the findings of the evaluation to other groups of teachers, especially nonvolunteers, who might be required to teach the new curriculum.

TABLE 6.1

Section from a Table of Random Numbers

					Column					
Row	1	2	3	4	5	6	7	8	9	10
1	32388	52390	16815	69298	82732	38480	73817	32523	41961	44437
2	05300	22164	24369	54224	35983	19687	11052	91491	60383	19746
3	66523	44133	00697	35552	35970	19124	63318	29686	03387	59846
4	44167	64486	64758	75366	76554	31601	12614	33072	60332	92325
5	47914	02584	37680	20801	72152	39339	34806	08930	85001	87820
6	63445	17361	62825	39908	05607	91284	68833	25570	38818	46920
7	89917	15665	52872	73823	73144	88662	88970	74492	51805	99378
8	92648	45454	09552	88815	16553	51125	79375	97596	16296	66092
9	20979	04508	64535	31355	86064	29472	47689	05974	52468	16834
10	81959	65642	74240	56302	00033	67107	77510	70625	28725	34191

9. Welch, W. W., Walberg, H. J., & Ahlgren, A. (1969). The selection of a national random sample of teachers for experimental curriculum evaluation. *School Science and Mathematics, 69,* 210–216.

The researchers first purchased a list of the names and addresses of 16,911 physics teachers compiled by the National Science Teachers Association. They commented in their report that this was the most comprehensive population list of high school physics teachers then available. It was not a complete list, however, because it was based on responses received from 81 percent of all secondary schools in the United States. Thus, their population was not "all high school physics teachers" but rather "all high school physics teachers on the 1966 NSTA list." Each teacher on the population list was assigned a number according to her ordinal position on the list. Then a table of random numbers was used to select a total of 136 teachers. These 136 teachers were sent letters inviting them to participate in the study, but it was possible to contact only 124 of them.

Eventually, 72 of the 124 teachers contacted agreed to participate in the study according to the conditions specified. Another 52 declined to participate—46 because of prior commitments and 6 because they were not interested. In order to determine whether their final sample was biased by its reliance on volunteers, the researchers decided to compare several characteristics of the 72 accepting teachers with those of the 46 who were unable to accept (hereafter referred to as nonacceptors). When this comparison was made, the researchers found that significantly more acceptors than nonacceptors worked in larger schools and taught the Physical Science Study Committee (PSSC) physics course. The researchers interpreted these differences as indicating that the accepting teachers were more likely to be those who taught in large schools where previous innovations had been accepted. Thus, although they attempted to obtain a truly random sample, their actual sample was somewhat biased in favor of teachers working in innovative schools and teachers who chose to volunteer as research participants. Nevertheless, the researchers' final sample probably was more representative than the samples used in most curriculum studies at that time. It was possible to generalize the study's findings to a national population of physics teachers, with certain qualifications.

Systematic Random Sampling

Systematic random sampling is easier than simple random sampling, if the sample to be selected is very large and a list of the accessible or target population is available. Suppose the population has 100,000 members and you wish to select a sample of 1,000 members from it. Further suppose the members are listed in a directory. If you were to use simple random sampling, you would need to number the members from 1 to 100,000 and then use a table of random numbers to select the sample of 1,000 members.

If you selected a systematic sample instead, you would first divide the population by the number needed for the sample (100,000 divided by 1,000 = 100). Then select at random a number smaller than the number arrived at by the division (in this example, a number smaller than 100, such as 36). Then, starting with the 36th member on the list, select every 100th name thereafter from the directory list. The time saved is substantial, because there is no need to assign a separate number to each member listed in the directory or to work back and forth between a table of random numbers and the directory.

Systematic random sampling should be avoided if there is any possibility of periodicity in the list (that is, if every nth person on the list shares a characteristic that is not shared by the entire population). For example, suppose you have 100 class lists, and you decide to select a sample by choosing the first name on each list. If the names are in alphabetical order, your sample most likely would include only students whose last name begins with A or B. This sample would underrepresent certain ethnic groups for whom a last name beginning with A or B is uncommon.

Stratified Random Sampling

A **stratified random sample** involves a sample selected so that certain subgroups in the population are adequately represented in the sample. For example, suppose that the population includes 10,000 students, of whom 100 are Laotian. If you draw a random sample of 200 students from this population, there is a strong likelihood that the sample would include no Laotian students or only a very few. Stratified random sampling ensures that a satisfactory representation of Laotian students is included in the sample, if this is important to your study.

In **proportional stratified random sampling,** the proportion of each subgroup in the sample is the same as their proportion in the population. Suppose we are comparing students with different ethnic backgrounds. Each ethnic background—Laotian, African American, Latino, and so forth—would be considered a separate *stratum*, that is, subgroup. Further suppose that Laotians are the smallest ethnic group in the population—100 students out of 10,000, which equals 1 percent of the population. We want to have at least 10 Laotian students in the sample. Therefore, we would randomly select 10 from all the Laotian students in the population. Because Laotian students comprise 1 percent of the population, the sample would need to include 1,000 students to be proportionally correct (10 students in the sample divided by .01). The size of other strata in the sample could then be determined. For example, if the population included 2,000 African-American students (which is 20 percent of the population), the sample should include 200 of them (20 percent of the predetermined sample size of 1,000 students).

A variant of this approach is **nonproportional stratified random sampling.** We might decide to select 20 students of each ethnic background in the population, regardless of their proportion in the population. This approach is quite acceptable, as long as we make generalizations only about the findings for students of each ethnic background. We cannot make generalizations from the total sample, because it does not represent accurately the proportional ethnic composition of the population.

Cluster Sampling

In **cluster sampling,** the unit of sampling is a naturally occurring group of individuals. Cluster sampling is used when it is more feasible to select groups of individuals (called clusters) rather than individuals from a defined population. For example, suppose you wish to administer a questionnaire to a random sample of 300 students in a population defined as all sixth graders in four school districts. The population includes a total of 1,500 sixth-graders in 50 classrooms, with an average of 30 students in each classroom.

One approach to sample selection would be to draw a simple random sample of 300 students using a census list of all 1,500 students. In cluster sampling, by contrast, you might draw a random sample of ten classrooms—assuming 30 students on average per classroom. Thirty students per classroom multiplied by ten classrooms equals 300 students, which is the desired sample size. Thus, you have achieved the efficiency of only having to access ten classrooms in order to administer a questionnaire to a random sample of 300 students. If you had used simple random sampling instead, you probably would have had to arrange for access to all 50 classrooms, even though some of these classrooms might include only one student in the random sample.

A variation of this method is **multistage cluster sampling,** which involves first selecting clusters and then selecting individuals within clusters. In the example we have been considering, suppose you wish to supplement the questionnaires with interviews of individual students. It is relatively easy to group-administer the questionnaire to every student in the ten classrooms. However, it would be very time consuming to interview all 300 students in them. Therefore, you could institute another sampling procedure (the second stage of multistage cluster sampling), in which you randomly select five students, for example, from each of the ten classrooms to interview. The interview sample, then, will include 50 students.

Conventional formulas for computing statistics on research data should not be used with samples chosen by cluster sampling. Special statistical formulas are available, but they are less sensitive to population differences. This disadvantage must be weighed against the possible savings in time and money that can result from cluster sampling.

In summary, you have a variety of sampling methods to consider in carrying out a quantitative research study. Sophisticated variants of the probability sampling methods we have described have been developed, primarily for use in large-scale survey research.[10] Therefore, if you plan to carry out a large-scale survey research study, you should investigate these methods further.

Example of Sampling a Phenomenon Rather Than Individuals

Mark Beeman, Geeta Chowdhry, and Karmen Todd carried out a research study that illustrates two important variants to the sampling strategies used in the other studies described in this chapter.[11] First, they sample not individual research participants, but instead a set of sociology textbooks used in university courses. Their research involved an analysis of the depth of coverage of the topic of affirmative action contained in such texts.

Second, the manner in which they selected their "sample" of texts suggests that they examined the entire accessible population of such textbooks and possibly the entire population that existed during the period of their study. The authors were thorough in identifying sociology textbooks: (1) They examined all the introductory texts that were sent to them by publishers to consider for adoption in the sociology courses they taught, and (2) they contacted any other publishers listed in *Books in Print, 1996–1997* who had listed an introductory text in the past five years. This process yielded a sample of 35 introductory sociology texts published from 1994 through 1997, which appears to be a very comprehensive set. The authors concluded that "for the majority of texts, affirmative action is neglected completely or discussions are limited to a couple of paragraphs or less."[12]

Nonprobability Sampling

In nonprobability sampling, individuals are not selected by chance, but by some other means. In the rest of this section, we describe a common method of nonprobability sampling used in quantitative research, usually called *convenience sampling*. Later we describe the various sampling methods used in qualitative research, which are grouped under the general heading of *purposeful sampling*. With one exception, called *purposeful random sampling*, all the sampling strategies used in qualitative research also are based on nonprobability sampling.

It is much more difficult to make valid inferences about a population from nonprobability sampling methods, but these methods are used in more than 95 percent of

---

10. For a description of these variants, see: Malhotra, N. K. (2003). *Marketing research: An applied orientation* (4th ed.). Upper Saddle River, NJ: Prentice Hall.
11. Beeman, M., Chowdhry, G., & Todd, K. (2000). Educating students about affirmative action: An analysis of university sociology texts. *Teaching Sociology, 28*(2), 98–115.
12. Ibid., p. 110.

research studies in the social sciences.[13] Undoubtedly, the reason for their prevalence is that it is much easier to select a nonprobability sample than a random sample when studying individuals in their natural environment.

Convenience Sampling

Each of the sampling methods described above involves a defined population and a sample of individuals or groups randomly drawn from that population. In actuality, many quantitative researchers do not use any of these methods to select a sample. Rather, the researcher selects a sample that suits the purposes of the study and that is convenient. The sample can be convenient for a variety of reasons: the sample is located at or near where the researcher works; the administrator who will need to approve data collection is a close colleague of the researcher; the researcher is familiar with the site and might even work in it; some of the data that the researcher needs already have been collected. In fact, many research studies that appear in journals involve college students, because the researcher is a professor and these students provide a convenient sample. In view of the fact that college students are not representative of the adult population in general, one would be justified in questioning the universality of certain principles of learning and instruction that appear in textbooks and other sources that are based on such research.

Researchers often need to select a convenience sample or face the possibility that they will be unable to do the study. Although a sample randomly drawn from a population is more desirable, it usually is better to do a study with a convenience sample than to do no study at all—assuming, of course, that the sample suits the purposes of the study.

If a convenience sample is used, the researchers and readers of their report must infer a population to which the results might generalize. The researcher can assist the inference process by providing a careful description of the sample. Although this recommendation seems obvious, it sometimes is violated in practice. For example, we came across this description of a sample (slightly paraphrased to mask the researcher's identity) in a journal issue: "The study involved 58 undergraduate seniors majoring in education at a southeastern university." That is the description in its entirety. There is insufficient information in this description to infer whether the results would generalize to all universities or to a limited subset (e.g., small private universities), and whether the results would generalize to all education majors or to a limited subset (e.g., education majors who have completed at least one school practicum, or those planning to teach at the high school level).

Example of a convenience sample A much fuller description of a convenience sample was provided by James Laney in the report of an experiment on two approaches to teaching economic concepts to young children:

> Transitional first-grade students were chosen as the population of interest for two reasons. First, because of his or her maturational age level, the transitional first grader is likely to have many misconceptions about basic economic concepts. Second, transitional first-grade classrooms make use of developmentally appropriate practices, and the treatment conditions used in this study were designed in accordance with such practices.
>
> All of the transitional first-grade students in one elementary school in north central Texas participated as subjects in the study. Thirty-one students made up the sample, including 25 Caucasians, 5 African-Americans, and 1 Hispanic student. Twenty of the students were boys, and 11 were girls. None of the students had received any instruction in economics prior to the study.

---

13. Ludbrook, J., & Dudley, H. (1998). Why permutation tests are superior to t and F tests in medical research. *American Statistician, 52,* 127–132.

Students' eligibility for placement in transitional first grade was determined at the end of their kindergarten year. Placement in the program was dependent on (a) the student's being 6 years of age by September 1 and (b) the student's having an approximate behavior age of 5 1/2 years as indicated by his or her score on an individually administered readiness test, the Maturational Assessment Test (Hull House Publishing Company, 1988), given by the school counselor. In addition to the two main selection criteria listed above, parents' and teachers' observations were also taken into account.[14]

This was most likely a convenience sample, because the school was located in north central Texas and the researcher worked at the University of North Texas. However, the researcher took care (1) to specify a population to which the results would likely generalize, (2) to describe pertinent characteristics of the sample, and (3) to provide a rationale for why the sample was well suited to the purpose of the study.

Inferential statistics often are used to analyze data collected from convenience samples, even though the logic of inferential statistics requires that the sample be randomly drawn from a defined population. Some researchers believe that inferential statistics for these samples cannot be interpreted meaningfully. Others believe that it is possible to conceptualize a population that the sample represents. They then reason that because the sample is representative of this population, the sample is equivalent to a sample randomly drawn from the population; therefore, the use of inferential statistics is justified.

Our position on the issue is that inferential statistics can be used with data collected from a convenience sample if the sample is carefully conceptualized to represent a particular population. Nevertheless, we believe that one should be cautious about accepting findings as valid and making generalizations from them on the basis of one study. Repeated replication of the findings is much stronger evidence of their validity and generalizability than is a statistically significant result in one study.

Determining Sample Size for a Quantitative Research Study

The general rule in quantitative research is to use the largest sample possible. The larger the sample, the more likely the research participants' scores on the measured variables will be representative of population scores. In addition to this general rule, researchers have developed rules of thumb for determining the minimum number of participants needed for different research methods. In correlational research, a minimum of 30 participants is desirable. In causal-comparative and experimental research, there should be at least 15 participants in each group to be compared. For survey research, Seymour Sudman suggested a minimum of 100 participants in each major subgroup and 20 to 50 in each minor subgroup.[15]

Mathematical procedures are available to make more precise estimates of the sample size needed to reject the null hypothesis when in fact it is false, and to determine the likely value of population parameters (typically, the population mean and standard deviation). These procedures involve statistical power analysis and are discussed in Chapter 5.

In addition to statistical power analysis, you should consider the following three factors in determining an optimal sample size for a quantitative research study:

1. *Subgroup analysis.* In many quantitative studies, it is desirable to break groups into subgroups for further analysis. For example, the primary data analysis for an experiment might involve a comparison of all research participants in the experimental group with all research participants in the control group. In addition, one might compare all male participants

14. Laney, J. D. (1993). Experiential versus experience-based learning and instruction. *Journal of Educational Research, 86,* 228–236. Quote appears on p. 14.
15. Sudman, S. (1976). *Applied sampling.* New York: Academic Press.

in the experimental group with all male participants in the control group, and similarly for female participants. This type of subgroup analysis sometimes is done as an afterthought, with the unfortunate consequence that the subgroup size is too small to produce adequate statistical power. Therefore, it is best to plan subgroup analyses at the design stage of a study so that an adequate sample size is selected.

2. *Attrition.* **Attrition** sometimes is a problem in research that extends over a substantial period of time. For example, in studies of school children, researchers often find that substantial numbers of them leave the school during the course of a school year; this is especially true of schools in low-income communities. Robert Goodrich and Robert St. Pierre estimate that 20 percent attrition per year is a realistic level for planning.[16] Attrition can be minimized by strategies such as developing research participants' commitment to the study and establishing good rapport with them. (See the section on site relations in Chapter 3.) Still, it is best to increase sample size by a certain percentage to account for possible attrition.

3. *Reliability of measures.* Measures with low reliability weaken the power of tests of statistical significance and estimates of population parameters. Therefore, if you must use measures with low reliability, you need to increase sample size accordingly. The converse is also true: If you must use a small sample, you should use measures with high reliability.

In many quantitative studies, there is a cost-benefit trade-off involving sample size. For example, in some studies it is desirable to use role playing, depth interviews, and other time-consuming measurement techniques. These techniques cannot be used in large-sample studies unless considerable financial support is available. The alternative is to obtain a large sample but to use relatively inexpensive measures such as questionnaires and standardized tests. However, a study that probes deeply into the characteristics of a small sample often provides more knowledge than a study that attacks the same problem by collecting only superficial data from a large sample.

In some research, very close matching of subjects on the critical variables concerned in the study is possible. Under these conditions, a small sample often will have good statistical power and can yield important results. The classic study by Horatio Newman, Frank Freeman, and Karl Holzinger on the intelligence of identical twins is a good example of such a study.[17] Because identical twins have the same genes, they are ideal for studying the relative influence of heredity and environment on various human characteristics. One phase of their research included only 19 pairs of separated identical twins, but this sample provided information about the relative influences of heredity and environment on intelligence that would have been difficult to obtain with large samples of less closely matched subjects.

Sampling in Qualitative Research

Now we turn to the procedures that qualitative researchers use to select cases to provide a basis for building or testing a theory.

Qualitative research is more flexible with respect to sampling techniques than quantitative research. This flexibility reflects the emergent nature of qualitative research design, which allows researchers to modify their research approach as data are collected. Therefore, the sampling techniques discussed in this section are suggestive rather than prescriptive, and they do not necessarily exhaust the possible ways in which a qualitative research sample might be selected.

16. Goodrich, R. L., & St. Pierre, R. G. (1979). *Opportunities for studying later effects of follow through.* Cambridge, MA: ABT Associates.
17. Newman, H. H., Freeman, F. N., & Holzinger, K. J. (1937). *Twins: A study of heredity and environment.* Chicago: University of Chicago Press.

Touchstone in Research

Stake, R. E. (2005). Qualitative case studies, their research approach. In N. K. Denzin & Y. S. Lincoln (Eds.), *Handbook of qualitative research* (3rd ed., pp. 443–466). Thousand Oaks, CA: Sage.

Rationale of Purposeful Sampling

The sample size in qualitative studies typically is small. The sample might be a single case. Let us consider specification of the *case* in case study research as Robert Yin views it.[18] (While Yin does not equate case studies with qualitative research, in the present authors' view the case study is a prototype for much of the qualitative research that is carried out.) The **unit of analysis** for a case study is the aspect of the phenomenon that will be studied in one or more cases. In a **single-case study design,** the unit of analysis could be a single individual (e.g., one teacher) or a single instance of a phenomenon (e.g., one occurrence of a school shooting), or it could be a number of similar individuals (e.g., several teachers involved in an innovative training program) or several instances of the same phenomenon (e.g., three schools that each experienced an incidence of school shooting within the past 5 years) that are collectively studied as one case. In a **multiple-case study design,** the unit of analysis needs to be at least two or more individuals or two or more instances of a phenomenon, selected either to be similar to each other or different from each other in some way that is of interest to the researchers. (We discuss multiple-case designs further in relation to replication logic.)

The purpose in selecting the case, or cases, is to develop a deeper understanding of the phenomena being studied. A related purpose often is to discover or test theories. For example, if researchers wish to understand how teachers attempt to implement a new curriculum, they might design a qualitative study that allows them to observe intensely a few teachers engaged in this activity for an entire school year. If the researchers also wish to understand how beginning and experienced teachers differ in implementing the new curriculum, they could deliberately select one teacher of each type for the study.

In this example, the two teachers are selected because they suit the purposes of the study. Michael Patton describes the type of sampling procedure used in qualitative research as *purposeful sampling*.[19] In **purposeful sampling** the goal is to select cases that are likely to be "information-rich" with respect to the purposes of the study. Thus, the researchers in our hypothetical example decided to identify at least one beginning teacher for a case study. Suppose there are five such teachers in the school district. In approaching the first teacher, they find that he is nervous, uncommunicative, and willing to participate in the study only if required to do so. The researchers decide not to pursue this teacher as a possible case. The next teacher is much more open and eager to participate, and is agreeable to the additional demands on his time that data collection will require. This teacher is selected for the study. At this point, the researchers decide that the intensity of data collection precludes the possibility of including another beginning teacher in the study. Thus, they settle for a sample of one beginning teacher. They would then go through a similar reasoning process to select one experienced teacher for the sample.

It is clear that purposeful sampling is not designed to achieve population validity. The intent is to achieve an in-depth understanding of selected individuals, not to select a sample that will represent accurately a defined population.

Applying Replication Logic

Robert Yin proposes a logic for sampling in case study research that is similar to the logic of Patton's purposeful sampling strategy.[20] Yin's logic, however, focuses specifically on the theory-building goal of case study research. When this is the goal, Yin argues

---

18. Yin, R. K. (2003). *Case study research: Design and methods* (3rd ed.). Thousand Oaks, CA: Sage.
19. Patton, M. Q. (2002). *Qualitative research & evaluation methods* (3rd ed.). Thousand Oaks, CA: Sage.
20. Yin, *Case study research.*

that the researcher should select a case study design that will enable her to develop or test a theory. The research findings about the case are then generalizable to the theory—not to a defined population. The critical test of whether this generalization is warranted is to determine whether the theory can be used to predict the findings that would be obtained through the study of other cases. For this purpose, the researcher would use a multiple-case study design to carry out **replications,** that is, studies with different research participants, but following similar research conditions, to increase the confidence in and extend the findings obtained with the original case or cases. Each multiple case thus would need to be carefully selected to predict either (1) similar results (a *literal replication*) or (2) contrasting results consistent with the theory (a *theoretical replication*). The replications based on a multiple-case design will thereby contribute to the underlying theoretical framework. In turn, the framework "later becomes the vehicle for generalizing to new cases. . . ."[21]

To illustrate this process, suppose a researcher is interested in how teachers can provide effective leadership in mathematics curriculum reform. He selects as a case to study a teacher who is recognized as a leader in this type of reform. From his findings about this case, the researcher develops a theory that the teacher is effective because she uses a particular leadership style. Furthermore, this leadership style is consistent with a particular theory of effective leadership. Now the researcher can use the theory to predict which other teachers would be effective leaders. He then identifies another teacher whose leadership style is consistent with the theory. If this teacher is effective as predicted, the findings of the first case study thus are replicated and the theory is further supported.

Yin refers to this process of generalizing findings from one case study to the next as replication logic. Specifically, **replication logic** is a strategy that uses theory to determine the other cases to which the findings for one case also apply. The validity of the theory is tested through a series of empirical replications based on a multiple-case design. If the theory is well supported by the replications, the theory will identify the population of individuals to whom a particular set of research findings will apply.

Yin distinguishes between two types of replication: literal and theoretical. If the researcher is doing a **literal replication,** she is predicting that the next case to be studied will yield results that are similar to those of similar cases that she or other researchers have studied. If the researcher is doing a **theoretical replication,** she is predicting that the next case to be studied will yield results that differ from those obtained for other cases that have been previously studied, in ways consistent with the theory that underlies the research. For example, suppose one does several case studies of cooperative learning groups and concludes that the opportunity for two or more students to explain concepts in the textbook to other group members enhances the group's learning. The researcher's interpretation of this finding is that multiple explanations provide different perspectives on what a concept means. These different perspectives are theorized to provide each student a richer basis for developing his or her own understanding of the concept than if only one perspective is presented. In a literal replication, the researcher would test the theory by selecting a case of another cooperative learning group in which students typically take turns offering explanations. In a theoretical replication, the researcher instead might select a case of a cooperative learning group in which one student dominates by explaining all the concepts or in which only a single student explains each concept.

21. Ibid., p. 48.

Yin's concept of replication logic is implied in the *grounded theory* approach to qualitative research developed by Anselm Straus and Juliet Corbin.[22] They, too, believe that case studies can be used to build theory, which, in turn, indicates the population to which the theory applies:

> [O]ne might study work in one organizational setting. Out of the study evolves the concept of "work flow." The phenomenon of work flow might be used to partially explain how work is carried out in the organization under investigation. However, the more general idea of work flow has possible application beyond this one organization. It might prove a valuable concept for explaining similar phenomena in other organizations. In doing further research, researchers will want to determine which parts of the concept apply to, or are valid in, these other organizations and what new concepts or hypotheses can be added to the original conceptualization.[23]

This statement implies the desirability of selecting a case, or cases, that will yield data from which a broadly applicable theory can be constructed. Piaget's theory of intellectual development was based on his observations of a small number of cases (primarily his own children), but the theory was formulated to apply to a very large population, namely, all human beings.

Types of Purposeful Sampling

Qualitative researchers use a variety of purposeful sampling strategies to select their cases for study. Table 6.2 summarizes 16 purposeful sampling strategies described by Patton. If the researchers are using a single-case design, only some of the strategies are appropriate, that is, the 12 strategies for which the entries in column 2 (Cases Selected) begin with the word *Cases*, rather than with the words *Multiple Cases*. If the researchers are using a multiple-case design, any of these sampling strategies can be used.

Strategies to Select Cases Representing a Key Characteristic

The sampling strategies we have numbered 1 to 7 in Table 6.2 all involve selection based on a key characteristic of the cases to be studied.

1. **Extreme or deviant case sampling** focuses on cases that are unusual or special. The findings of research on extreme cases can provide an understanding of more typical cases. An example is George Noblit's study of how teachers use caring in their instruction and the relation of caring to power.[24] To study these phenomena, he chose an exceptional case—an elementary teacher named Pam. Her exceptionality is conveyed in Noblit's description of her:

> She [Pam] was one of the opinion makers in the building, was revered by white and African American parents, and was the teacher who assumed charge of the school whenever the principal was out of the building. She was reputed to be the most effective teacher in the building, adept with "difficult" students and (I later concluded) with "difficult" parents. She never missed a chance to talk with parents and was frequently called by the school secretary to deal with parent complaints. Her power was such that she, in many ways, chose me to be in her classroom for the Caring Study, rather than the other way around.[25]

22. Strauss, A. L., & Corbin, J. M. (1998). *Basics of qualitative research: Techniques and procedures for developing grounded theory.* Thousand Oaks, CA: Sage. Grounded theory is discussed further in Chapters 2 and 14.
23. Ibid., p. 23.
24. Noblit, G. W. (1993). Power and caring. *American Educational Research Journal, 30,* 23–38.
25. Ibid., p. 27.

TABLE 6.2

Purposeful Sampling Strategies Used in Qualitative Research

SAMPLING STRATEGY	CASES SELECTED
Strategies to Select Cases Representing a Key Characteristic	
1. Extreme/deviant case	Cases that exhibit the characteristic to an extreme high or low extent
2. Intensity	Cases that exhibit the characteristic to a high or low, but not extreme, extent
3. Typical case	Cases that exhibit the characteristic to an average or typical extent
4. Maximum variation	Multiple cases that exhibit the entire range of variation in the characteristic
5. Stratified purposeful	Multiple cases that exhibit the characteristic at predefined points of variation
6. Homogeneous	Multiple cases that represent the characteristic to a similar extent
7. Random purposeful	Multiple cases selected at random from an accessible population
Strategies Reflecting a Conceptual Rationale	
8. Critical case	Cases that provide a crucial test of a theory, program, or other phenomenon
9. Theory-based/operational construct	Cases that manifest a particular theoretical construct
10. Confirming/disconfirming case	Cases that are likely to confirm/disconfirm findings from previous case studies
11. Criterion	Cases that satisfy an important criterion
12. Politically important case	Cases that are well known/politically important
Emergent Strategies	
13. Opportunistic	Cases that are selected during data collection to take advantage of unforeseen opportunities
14. Snowball/chain	Cases that are recommended by individuals who know other individuals likely to yield relevant, information-rich data
15. Combination/mixed purpose	Cases that are selected with more than one sampling strategy
Strategy Lacking a Rationale	
16. Convenience	Cases that are selected simply because they are available

Source: Adapted from Table 10.1 on p. 311 in Gall, J. P., Gall, M. D., & Borg, W. R. (2005). *Applying educational research: A practical guide*. Boston: Pearson. Published by Allyn and Bacon, Boston, MA. (5th ed.). Copyright © 2005 by Pearson Education, adapted with permission from the publisher.

The use of an exceptional case like Pam is helpful because the teacher characteristics to be studied are easy to detect and occur frequently. A possible problem with extreme cases is that educators might dismiss findings based on them simply because they are extreme or deviant.

2. **Intensity sampling** avoids this problem because it involves selecting cases that manifest the phenomenon of interest intensely but not extremely. As an illustration,

suppose a researcher was interested in the characteristics of inservice presenters. If an extreme-case sampling approach were used, the researchers might select star performers in the world of inservice education—the individuals who regularly make keynote presentations at national conferences and who consult nationally and internationally. These cases might be interesting, but of little relevance to educators who do inservice presenting on a much smaller scale. Therefore, the researcher might consider selecting educators who are highly respected as inservice presenters within their school district or local region. These educators still qualify as exceptional cases, but they are more like the vast majority of inservice presenters. By studying these less extreme cases, the researcher is more likely to obtain findings that deepen the understanding of most inservice presenters about ways in which they might improve. Also, the findings might enlighten administrators about reasonable qualifications and expectations for local staff who aspire to be inservice presenters.

3. **Typical case sampling,** as one might expect, involves the selection of typical cases to study. This strategy might be particularly useful in field tests of new programs. Developers and policy makers want their programs to be effective for the great majority of the individuals to be served by the program; otherwise, the program will not be considered cost-effective. Also, stories about typical cases might be useful for "selling" the program to various constituencies.

These first three sampling strategies—extreme or deviant case sampling, intensity sampling, and typical case sampling—complement one another. None is inherently superior to the others. Each serves important, but different purposes in qualitative research.

4. **Maximum variation sampling** involves selecting cases that illustrate the range of variation in the phenomena to be studied. For example, suppose a researcher wishes to study the experiences of different school districts that have received state-funded grants to develop innovative projects. In using a maximum variation sampling strategy, the researcher might select districts that vary widely in size, community setting (e.g., urban, rural), proximity to a university that has a college of education, and the type of project undertaken (e.g., curriculum development, staff development, services for a certain type of student). This strategy serves two purposes: to document the range of variation in the funded projects, and to determine whether common themes, patterns, and outcomes cut across this variation.

5. **Stratified purposeful sampling** is slightly different from maximum variation sampling. A stratified purposeful sample includes several cases at defined points of variation (e.g., average, above average, and below average) with respect to the phenomenon being studied. By including several cases of each type, the researcher can develop insights into the characteristics of each type, as well as insights into the variations that exist across types. In contrast, a researcher who uses maximum variation sampling is likely to have one case of each type, which might be insufficient for drawing conclusions about that type.

6. **Homogeneous sampling** is the opposite strategy of maximum variation sampling. Its purpose is to select a sample of similar cases so that the particular group that the sample represents can be studied in depth. For example, suppose a researcher is interested in orientation programs for incoming high school students. In doing pilot work, the researcher discovers that many high schools have orientation programs for all students, but only some high schools have a special orientation program for at-risk students. In planning the main study, the researcher might decide to limit the sample of cases to orientation programs for at-risk students. These programs can be the focus of intensive data

collection and study rather than being one aspect of a broader study of orientation programs in general.

7. **Random purposeful sampling** involves selecting a random sample using the methods of quantitative research. Nevertheless, the purpose of the random sample is not to represent a population, which would be its purpose in quantitative research. Rather, the purpose is to establish that the sampling procedure is not biased. For example, if a researcher is evaluating a program for which some constituencies are critical, the researcher can gain more credibility for his findings if he selects cases at random rather than looks for "success stories" to report.

Strategies Reflecting a Conceptual Rationale

The sampling strategies numbered 8 to 12 in Table 6.2 each reflect a particular conceptual rationale for the selection of cases. Strategies 8, 9, and 10 involve rationales related to the researchers' theoretical conceptions of the meaning of the case, whereas strategies 11 and 12 involve selection based on more practical criteria.

8. **Critical case sampling** involves selecting a single case that provides a crucial test of a theory, program, or other phenomenon. For example, Galileo provided a critical—and convincing—test of his theory of gravity by demonstrating that a feather fell at the same rate as a coin when both were placed in a vacuum.

Theories in education tend not to yield such precise predictions as are found in the physical sciences, and therefore a critical case sampling strategy might have less applicability. However, this sampling strategy could prove useful in studying educational programs and related phenomena. For example, a researcher might wish to evaluate a program by selecting a site in which it would be very difficult for the program to succeed. If a study of this case yielded positive results, one would be justified in claiming a strong generalization of the form: "If this program works here, it should work anywhere."

9. **Theory-based or operational construct sampling** is used when the purpose of the study is to gain understanding of real-world manifestations of theoretical constructs. To illustrate, we can consider Piaget's theory of intellectual development, which is widely used to interpret educational phenomena. One of the constructs of the theory is the concrete stage of development. A researcher might wish to develop further understanding of this construct by studying how it is manifested in particular settings. To achieve this purpose, the researcher would need to select a sample of children who are at this stage of development. Then she could do an intensive analysis of how they function intellectually in various situations of interest to her. In this example, then, the selection of cases is determined by a particular theoretical construct.

10. **Confirming and disconfirming case sampling** is done to validate findings of previous research. The validation process can be carried out in two ways. The first approach is to study cases that are likely to confirm patterns, themes, and meanings discovered in previous case studies. If the new case or cases are confirmatory, the validity and generalizability of the patterns, themes, and meanings are strengthened. The second approach is to look for cases that are good candidates for disconfirming previous research findings. If the findings from these cases replicate previous findings of patterns, themes, and meanings, their validity and generalizability are greatly strengthened. However, if the findings are, in fact, disconfirming, the researcher might develop new insights about the generalizability limits of previous findings.

One of the authors (M. Gall) has chaired the committee for several dissertations that involved case studies of various types of educational change agents: staff development specialists,[26] computer education specialists,[27] high school department chairpersons,[28] teachers trained to promote mathematics education reform,[29] and teacher-leaders in school restructuring efforts.[30] Following the first study (of staff development specialists), each of the other four has provided additional confirmatory cases. All the effective change agents possessed a combination of technical mastery and interpersonal skills (especially listening skills and the ability to exert influence indirectly). All the less effective change agents lacked one or both of these capabilities. What is needed now is a strong test of this pattern of results by seeking a disconfirming case. For example, as we look back over these dissertations, we see that all the change agents who served as cases worked within a primarily bottom-up model of educational change. A good disconfirming case, then, would be a change agent working within a top-down model of educational change. If effective change agents working within this model had both capabilities, the generalizability of the previous findings would be greatly strengthened. If the effective change agents lacked one or both of these capabilities, the meaning and generalizability of the previous findings would need to be reconsidered.

11. **Criterion sampling** involves the selection of cases that satisfy an important criterion. This strategy is particularly useful in studying educational programs. For example, suppose a researcher is planning to study a particular graduate program that prepares educational administrators. Using a criterion sampling strategy, the researcher might select two types of cases to study: (1) recent graduates who took more than ten years to obtain their doctorates; and (2) recent graduates who received their doctorates in three years or less. A study of cases that satisfied one or the other of these criteria most likely would yield rich information about aspects of the program that work well or poorly.

12. **Politically important case sampling** is a strategy that might serve a useful purpose for the researcher or funding agency. For example, if a researcher was interested in the educational methods used by cults, he might consider selecting as a case the Davidians (involved in the shoot-out in Waco, Texas in 1993), simply because that particular cult is so well known to a large group and the researcher's findings would be of widespread interest.

Emergent Strategies

We describe strategies 13, 14, and 15 as emergent because they all involve a change in the initial sampling strategy to better serve the purpose of studying the most information-rich cases possible.

13. **Opportunistic sampling** involves the use of findings from one case to inform the researcher's selection of the next case for study. In fact, the findings may alter the research design to be used in studying the next case.

Opportunistic sampling is one of the most important strategies in selecting qualitative research samples. Although Patton lists opportunistic sampling as a separate type of purposeful sampling, the principle underlying it applies to many of the strategies described above. For example, if you were to use the extreme or deviant case sampling strategy, you

26. Beaton, C. R. (1985). Identifying change agent strategies, skills, and outcomes: The case of district-based staff development specialists. *Dissertation Abstracts International, 47*(01), 65A. (UMI No. 8605828)
27. Strudler, N. B. (1987). The role of school-based computer coordinators as change agents in elementary school programs. *Dissertation Abstracts International, 48*(11), 2853A. (UMI No. 8800554)
28. Henderson, I. M. (1993). The role of high school department heads as change agents in implementing a new social studies curriculum. *Dissertation Abstracts International, 54*(09), 3309A. (UMI No. 9405182)
29. Rossi, M. A. (1993). The California mathematics project: Empowering elementary teachers to be leaders and change agents in mathematics reform. *Dissertation Abstracts International, 54*(09), 3314A. (UMI No. 9405218)
30. Fasold, Y. R. (1992). Case studies of teachers as leaders and change agents in school improvement and restructuring. *Dissertation Abstracts International, 54*(03), 794A. (UMI No. 9313288)

might start with the study of one case that you consider extreme. As you develop an understanding of this case, it may give you ideas about what to look for in selecting another extreme case, or it may cause you to switch to a typical case sampling strategy. Opportunistic sampling allows you the flexibility to make these switches.

Consider a typical problem that use of opportunistic sampling early in a research study might help the researcher avoid. We know of instances in which researchers have selected a multiple-case sample at the outset of the study. They secure the cooperation of the sample and their informed consent letters, and thus feel obliged to study all of them in depth. Unfortunately, the researchers sometimes discover after analyzing data from the first few cases that they would learn more by studying other cases than those to whom they have become obligated. By then, however, they may lack the resources to select new cases because of their commitments to the initially selected cases.

14. **Snowball or chain sampling** involves asking well-situated people to recommend cases to study. As the process continues, the researcher might discover an increasing number of well-situated people and an increasing number of recommended cases, all or some of whom can be included in the sample. Also, the names of a few individuals might come up repeatedly in talking to different well-situated people. If this type of convergence occurs, these individuals would make a highly credible sample.

15. **Combination/mixed purpose sampling** reflects a decision to change from one sampling strategy to another as data collection progresses in order to meet multiple research interests and needs or for triangulation of the results. As Patton describes it:

> For example, an extreme group or maximum heterogeneity approach may yield an initial potential sample size that is still larger than the study can handle. The final selection, then, may be made randomly—a combination approach. . . . Because research and evaluations often serve multiple purposes, more than one qualitative strategy may be necessary.[31]

Strategy Lacking a Rationale

16. **Convenience sampling,** as we discussed earlier in the chapter, is the strategy of selecting cases simply because they are available and easy to study. For example, researchers might select teachers at a school where they formerly worked, because they believe that it will be easy to obtain the teachers' agreement to participate in the study. Patton observes that convenience is the least desirable basis for selecting cases to study.[32] This strategy should be avoided because it is not purposeful in the same sense that the other 15 sampling strategies described above are purposeful.

Determining the Number of Cases for a Qualitative Research Study

In qualitative research, determining the number of cases is entirely a matter of judgment; there are no set rules. Patton suggests that selecting an appropriate sample size for a qualitative study involves a trade-off between breadth and depth:

> With the same fixed resources and limited time, a researcher could study a specific set of experiences for a larger number of people (seeking breadth) or a more open range of experiences for a smaller number of people (seeking depth). In-depth information from a small number of people can be very valuable, especially if the cases are information-rich. Less depth from a larger number of people can be especially helpful in exploring a phenomenon and trying to document diversity or understand variation.[33]

---

31. Patton, *Qualitative research & evaluation methods*, p. 242.
32. Ibid.
33. Ibid., p. 244.

Patton suggests that the ideal sampling procedure is to keep selecting cases until one reaches the point of redundancy, that is, until no new information is forthcoming from new cases.

Another reason for increasing the number of cases in a qualitative research study is consistent with Yin's replication logic.[34] As discussed above, Yin recommends selecting additional cases for the sample in order to provide replications. Each additional case that replicates the findings of the first case adds to the certainty of those findings.

Sample size obviously will be affected by the purposeful sampling strategy that you select in planning a qualitative study. If you are using a critical case strategy, a single, well-selected case might be sufficient; adding another one or two critical cases could serve as a replication of the first case. However, the decision to use a maximum variation strategy perhaps would require ten or more cases, even if the study was an initial exploration into the phenomenon of interest.

Volunteers in Research Samples

All research studies make demands on the individuals who are selected for the sample. For example, in planning an experiment, the researcher might select a random sample of teachers, but some of them might refuse to participate because they dislike the experimental intervention, do not wish to disrupt their normal schedule, or for some other reason. Some individuals may refuse to complete even a brief questionnaire because they are very busy or don't like following detailed directions. The remaining individuals no longer constitute a random sample, because individuals who agree to participate are likely to be different from those who do not.

A similar problem can arise in planning a qualitative study. The researchers might select several individuals to participate because they constitute interesting cases of the phenomenon they wish to investigate. However, one or more of the individuals might decline the offer to participate for a variety of reasons.

When individuals refuse to be members of a sample, there is very little that researchers can do to require their participation. As we explained in Chapter 3, ethical standards and informed consent requirements protect individuals' rights in research, including the right to refuse participation in a study or to cease participation at any point during the study.

If some individuals recruited for a study decline to participate, the remaining individuals in the sample should be considered "volunteer" participants. For example, if you send a questionnaire to 200 educators and 130 complete and return it, the 70 who did not return it are nonvolunteers and the 130 who did return it are volunteers. If you recruit a sample by such means as word of mouth or posted notices, all members of the resulting sample should be considered volunteers.

Characteristics of Research Volunteers

Touchstone in Research

Wainer, H. (2000). *Drawing inferences from self-selected samples.* Mahwah, NJ: Erlbaum.

Researchers have found that volunteer subjects are likely to be a biased sample of the target population. Robert Rosenthal and Ralph Rosnow reviewed this body of research to identify characteristics that have been found consistently to differentiate between volunteer and nonvolunteer subjects.[35] Some of the characteristics are supported by more research evidence than others. Table 6.3 lists the characteristics that Rosenthal and Rosnow believe are the best supported by research.

---

34. Yin, *Case study research.*
35. Rosenthal, R., & Rosnow, R. L. (1975). *The volunteer subject.* New York: Wiley.

TABLE 6.3

Characteristics of Research Volunteers

1. Volunteers tend to be better educated than nonvolunteers, especially when personal contact between investigator and respondent is not required.
2. Volunteers tend to have higher social-class status than nonvolunteers, especially when social class is defined by respondents' own status rather than by parental status.
3. Volunteers tend to be more intelligent than nonvolunteers when volunteering is for research in general, but not when volunteering is for somewhat less typical types of research, such as hypnosis, sensory isolation, sex research, small group research, or personality research.
4. Volunteers tend to be higher in need for social approval than nonvolunteers.
5. Volunteers tend to be more sociable than nonvolunteers.
6. Volunteers tend to be more arousal-seeking than nonvolunteers, especially when volunteering is for studies of stress, sensory isolation, and hypnosis.
7. Volunteers tend to be more unconventional than nonvolunteers, especially when volunteering is for studies of sex behavior.
8. Females are more likely than males to volunteer for research in general, but less likely than males to volunteer for physically and emotionally stressful research (e.g., electric shock, high temperature, sensory deprivation, interviews about sex behavior).
9. Volunteers tend to be less authoritarian than nonvolunteers.
10. Jews are more likely to volunteer than Protestants, and Protestants are more likely to volunteer than Roman Catholics.
11. Volunteers tend to be less conforming than nonvolunteers when volunteering is for research in general, but not when subjects are female and the task is relatively "clinical" (e.g., hypnosis, sleep, or counseling research).

Source: Adapted from Rosenthal, R., & Rosnow, R. L. (1975). *The volunteer subject.* New York: Wiley.

Note: Rosenthal and Rosnow list 11 other characteristics of volunteer subjects that are less well supported by research findings (pp. 195–196).

The degree to which the characteristics of volunteer samples are likely to affect the results of a research study depends on the specific nature of the study. Norman Bradburn and Seymour Sudman described as "really terrible sampling" those methods that depend entirely on respondents to volunteer in order to be included in the sample—for example, TV programs that ask viewers to telephone their yes or no vote on an issue that is proposed in a newspaper or on television.[36] They noted that the resulting requirement that all volunteers must make, and pay for, a telephone call creates substantial economic bias; that the responses generally come from individuals who are most committed to an issue; and that it becomes possible to "stuff the ballot box" by making multiple calls.

Volunteers in Research Requiring Parental Consent

In Chapter 3, we explained that researchers cannot ask school-age students ("minors") for their informed consent to participate in a study. Instead, consent is needed from the child's main caretaker, who typically is a parent. In other words, it is the parent or other caretaker who volunteers a child for a research study, not the child.

Researchers have conducted various studies to determine whether children having parental permission to participate in a research study differ from children not having

36. Bradburn, N. M., & Sudman, S. (1988). *Polls & surveys: Understanding what they tell us.* San Francisco, CA: Jossey-Bass.

parental permission. These studies have found that, in fact, the two groups differ from each other. In general, children having parental permission to participate in a research study are:

1. more academically competent.
2. more popular with their peers.
3. more physically attractive.
4. less likely to smoke cigarettes and marijuana.
5. more likely to be Caucasian.
6. more likely to come from two-parent households.
7. more likely to be involved in extracurricular activities.
8. less likely to be socially withdrawn.
9. less likely to be aggressive.[37]

These generalizations do not necessarily apply to all research studies requiring parental/caretaker consent. The particular age group of research participants and the nature of the research problem might affect whether children having parental consent have different characteristics from children not having parental consent.

Checking Volunteer Characteristics

The generalizations shown above and in Table 6.3 are sufficiently compelling that they warrant checking volunteer characteristics in any study in which there is a significant number of nonvolunteers in the selected sample.

An example of this type of comparison can be found in a study by Kathleen Mittag and Bruce Thompson.[38] They conducted a national survey of members of the American Educational Research Association (AERA) about several issues involving the use of statistics in research. The target sample, sampling frame, and sampling method were described as follows:

> We drew a stratified random sample of roughly 4% of the AERA members listed in the membership directory. The sample was stratified by AERA divisions to insure representativeness across the 12 divisions. A total of 1,127 surveys were mailed.[39]

Of these 1,127 surveys, 246 were returned. Thus, there were 246 volunteers and 881 nonvolunteers. (Twenty-one of the 246 volunteers returned unusable surveys, yielding a final volunteer sample of 225 individuals.) Mittag and Thompson were able to compare the volunteers and the target population on two variables—postal location and division membership. They found that the volunteers and target population were very similar on these variables, thus providing some evidence that the volunteers were representative of the population.

Mittag and Thompson went a step further to consider whether the volunteers might differ from the target population on other relevant variables:

> [I]t is conceivable that AERA members who were the most comfortable with and interested in statistical issues may have been most likely to respond to the survey. If this was the case, the results portray a more favorable picture than might apply in the full population.

---

37. This list of generalizations was developed from literature reviews and findings reported in: Anderson, C., Cheadle, A., Curry, S., Diehr, P., Shultz, L., & Wagner, E. (1995). Selection bias related to parental consent in school-based survey research. *Evaluation Review, 19,* 663–674; Noll, R. B., Zeller, M. H., Vannatta, K., Bukowski, W. M., & Davies, W. H. (1997). Potential bias in classroom research: Comparison of children with permission and those who do not receive permission to participate. *Journal of Clinical Child Psychology, 26,* 36–42.
38. Mittag, K. C., & Thompson, B. (2000). A national survey of AERA members' perceptions of statistical significance tests and other statistical issues. *Educational Researcher, 29*(4), 14–20.
39. Ibid., p. 14.

It must also be acknowledged that some AERA members do not use quantitative methods at all. These individuals may have been less likely to respond, as well.[40]

No data were available to compare the volunteers and nonvolunteers on these variables, but it is worthwhile for the researchers to bring them to the reader's attention. If other researchers become interested in the questions studied by Mittag and Thompson, they will be alert to issues concerning the volunteer rate and can make efforts to improve it and perhaps also to collect more data about volunteer and nonvolunteer characteristics.

Improving the Rate of Volunteering

Two typical situations arise in recruiting participants for a study. In one situation, you select a sample initially and then invite each member to participate. In the other situation, you write a description of the study and circulate or post this notice so that it is responded to by as many individuals as possible in the accessible population. In either situation, your goal is to design a recruitment process that minimizes the likelihood that only certain types of individuals will accept your invitation to participate in the study or respond to your notice.

In their research synthesis, Rosenthal and Rosnow identified eleven situational variables that tend to increase or decrease the rates of volunteering.[41] Their findings form the basis for the list of suggestions in Table 6.4. These are ways to increase the rate of volunteering and thus reduce sampling bias in a research study. Studying this list can help you design an effective recruitment process for your study, so that you minimize the likelihood of volunteer bias.

TABLE 6.4

Ways to Increase the Rate of Volunteering for a Research Study

1. Make the appeal for volunteers as interesting as possible to the group you are trying to enlist for the study.
2. Make the appeal for volunteers as nonthreatening as possible.
3. Make explicit the theoretical and practical importance of the study.
4. Make explicit how the group you are trying to enlist represents a target population that is particularly relevant to the study.
5. Emphasize that, by volunteering for the study, individuals have the potential to benefit others.
6. Offer to potential volunteers, when possible, not only payment for participation, but small courtesy gifts simply for taking time to consider whether they want to participate.
7. Have the request for volunteering made by a person of high status.
8. Try to avoid research tasks that can be psychologically or biologically stressful.
9. Try to communicate the idea that volunteering is the normal thing to do.
10. In situations where volunteering is regarded by the target population as the normal thing to do, ask each individual to make a public commitment to volunteer. Where nonvolunteering is regarded as the normal thing to do, create a situation where each individual can volunteer in private.
11. After a target population has been defined, have someone known to that population make the appeal for volunteers.

Source: Adapted from Rosenthal, R., & Rosnow, R. L. (1975). *The volunteer subject.* New York: Wiley.

---

40. Ibid., p. 18.
41. Rosenthal and Rosnow, *The volunteer subject.*

RECOMMENDATIONS FOR

Selecting a Research Sample

1. In reporting a study, describe in detail the target and accessible populations, sampling procedures, sampling frame, and volunteer rate.
2. In quantitative research, select a random sample rather than a convenience sample whenever possible.
3. If a convenience sample is selected, describe its characteristics in sufficient detail to enable others to infer the population it represents.
4. In quantitative research, select a sample size that maximizes the likelihood of rejecting the null hypothesis at a satisfactory level of statistical power and that, if appropriate, allows for subgroup analysis and sample attrition.
5. In qualitative research, consider which of the various types of purposeful sampling is most appropriate for studying the phenomenon of interest.
6. If any members of the selected sample choose not to volunteer, collect data to determine whether the volunteers are representative of the nonvolunteers or the accessible/target population on relevant characteristics.
7. Use various procedures to maximize the volunteer rate for the selected sample.

SELF-CHECK TEST

Circle the correct answer to each of the following questions. The answers are provided at the back of the book.

1. Qualitative researchers are similar to quantitative researchers in that they sometimes
   a. attempt to select samples that represent a population of interest.
   b. do research studies that involve a sample of a phenomenon, rather than a sample of individuals.
   c. base their sample selection on convenience.
   d. all of the above.
2. All the members of a real or hypothetical set of persons, objects, or events to which researchers wish to generalize research results are called a(n)
   a. target population.
   b. random sample.
   c. accessible population.
   d. volunteer subject pool.
3. If the researcher draws a sample from a narrow accessible population, the research results will probably be
   a. unreliable.
   b. generalizable to a limited population.
   c. generalizable to a broad population.
   d. of no theoretical value.
4. A simple random sample is best defined as a group of individuals
   a. each of whom had an equal and independent chance of being selected.
   b. who accurately represent the target population rather than the accessible population.
   c. who accurately represent the accessible population rather than the target population.
   d. who are selected by a process that provides every sample of a given size an equal probability of being selected.
5. The main advantage of random sampling is that the sample is more likely to
   a. include the correct number of subjects.
   b. agree to participate in the study.
   c. yield generalizable research data.
   d. yield statistically significant research findings.

6. Systematic sampling is most appropriate when
   a. a large sample must be selected from a nonperiodic list.
   b. a large sample must be selected from a periodic list.
   c. the target population is heterogeneous.
   d. the expected differences between the experimental and control groups are small.

7. Using inferential statistics with data collected from a convenience sample is justified if
   a. the sample is carefully conceptualized to represent a particular population.
   b. the researcher does not plan to generalize the findings of the study.
   c. the sample size is sufficiently large.
   d. the sample is composed of volunteers.

8. In cluster sampling the unit of sampling is
   a. the individual subject.
   b. the target population.
   c. a naturally occurring group of individuals.
   d. the proportion of subjects with extreme scores on the variable of interest.

9. Large samples should be used in quantitative research particularly when
   a. attrition is expected to be minimal.
   b. measures with low reliability are to be used.
   c. no subgroup analysis is planned.
   d. the population is highly homogeneous.

10. Theoretical replication differs from literal replication in that researchers select cases for study that
   a. yield results predicted to be similar to those of previous cases studied.
   b. yield results predicted to be different from those of previous cases studied.
   c. represent extreme or deviant cases.
   d. take advantage of unforeseen opportunities in the research.

11. Purposeful sampling involves
   a. selecting a sample that accurately represents a defined population.
   b. selecting as large a sample as possible within given cost constraints.
   c. selecting cases that are information-rich with respect to the study goals.
   d. all of the above.

12. Selecting a single case that provides a crucial test of a phenomenon is an example of _____ sampling in qualitative research.
   a. deviant case
   b. typical case
   c. critical case
   d. opportunistic

13. _____ sampling involves using the findings from the study of one case to inform the selection of the next case to be studied.
   a. convenience
   b. snowball
   c. criterion
   d. opportunistic

14. Compared to nonvolunteers, volunteers for research tend to be more
   a. authoritarian.
   b. conventional.
   c. antisocial.
   d. arousal-seeking.

15. To improve the rate of volunteering for a research study, it is desirable to
   a. emphasize the researcher's need to obtain a sufficient sample size.
   b. offer gifts for participation.
   c. have a male make the request for volunteering.
   d. explain in detail the risks that participation might entail.

CHAPTER 7

Collecting Research Data with Tests and Self-Report Measures

OVERVIEW

Administering tests and self-report measures is one of the main ways in which researchers collect data about individuals. These instruments can reveal information about aptitudes, academic achievement, and various aspects of personality. We start this chapter by describing the characteristics of a good test or self-report measure, with emphasis on validity and reliability criteria. We then discuss the wide range of measures that are available and how to obtain information about them. Computer technology has had a major impact on testing, so we discuss developments in this field. In the last part of the chapter, we explain how to develop your own tests and self-report measures and how to effectively administer them in a research study.

OBJECTIVES

After studying this chapter, you should be able to

1. Explain key similarities and differences between measures of performance and self-report measures used in educational research.
2. Explain four criteria for judging the quality of tests in research.
3. Explain what it means for a test to yield valid interpretations from test scores, and describe five types of evidence used to determine how valid such interpretations are.
4. Explain what it means for a test to yield reliable scores, and describe four approaches to determining test score reliability.
5. Explain what information about test score reliability is provided by generalizability theory and the standard error of measurement.

6. Describe the advantages of item response theory over classical test theory.
7. Describe the advantages of standardized tests over locally constructed tests in research studies.
8. Compare the distinctive advantages of norm-referenced, criterion-referenced, and individual-referenced measures.
9. Describe how computer technology is changing the development and use of tests.
10. Compare the distinctive advantages of individually administered and group-administered tests.
11. List five types of performance tests, and describe the primary characteristics of each type.

12. Describe procedures and criteria that have been proposed for determining the validity and reliability of performance assessment.

13. List seven types of personality measures, and describe the primary characteristics of each type.

14. Describe how *TestLink* and *TestReviewsOnline* can be used to find available tests and information about them.

15. Describe how to use the test manual, the test itself, and contact with the test developer to determine if a test

is appropriate for your research purposes.

16. Describe the steps involved in developing a test for use in research.

17. Describe at least three actions you can take if you encounter public or professional resistance to the tests that you wish to administer for a research study.

18. Describe several procedures that you can follow to obtain an individual's maximal effort on a performance test or honest responses on a personality measure.

Use of Tests and Self-Report Measures in Educational Research

The principles of measurement described in this chapter derive primarily from the quantitative tradition of educational research. In this tradition, researchers begin the process of measurement by defining the construct of interest to them, for example, mathematics achievement. They define the construct operationally, by specifying the activities used to measure it. Thus, mathematics achievement might be defined as the performance of individuals on a particular set of test items under specified conditions of administration. The testing situation is designed so that each individual's performance can be assigned a numerical score, such as a score of 0 to 50 on a 50-item test. In contrast, qualitative researchers typically do not place individuals in structured performance situations, preferring instead to study them in naturally occurring situations. Of course, quantitative or qualitative researchers might formulate problems for which data collection in both types of situation would be desirable. In this situation, tests would complement nicely two primary methods of data collection in qualitative research, namely, interviews (described in Chapter 8) and observation (described in Chapter 9).

The focus of this chapter is how to measure an individual's behavior by administering a test. A test is any structured performance situation that can be analyzed to yield numerical scores, from which inferences can be made about how individuals differ in the performance construct measured by the test. Examples of performance constructs are academic achievement in computer studies, verbal ability, and musical intelligence.

A **self-report measure** is a paper-and-pencil instrument whose items yield numerical scores from which inferences can be made about how individuals differ on various aspects of self, such as personality traits, self-concept, learning styles, attitudes, values, and interests. Unlike tests, these measures do not require individuals to "perform." Instead, self-report measures generally ask individuals to reveal whether they have the traits, thoughts, or feelings mentioned in the items. Despite this difference, self-report measures and tests are very similar in construction and administration. Therefore, although we frequently use the term *test* when explaining various measurement concepts and practices, the explanation generally applies to self-report measures as well.

Touchstones in Research

Keeves, J. P. (Ed.). (1997). *Educational research, methodology and measurement: An international handbook* (2nd ed.). New York: Pergamon.

Urbina, S. (2004). *Essentials of psychological testing.* Hoboken, NJ: Wiley.

Dwyer, C. A. (2005). *Measurement and research in the accountability era.* Mahwah, NJ: Erlbaum.

In conducting a review of the literature, you will read about researchers' use of various tests and self-report measures. Therefore, you need to understand these instruments and make judgments about their soundness. This chapter provides the basic knowledge that you will need for these purposes. This knowledge also will help you select or develop tests for your own study. In fact, some research studies focus entirely on test development or on investigating the soundness of already developed tests. If this is your purpose, the chapter will help you learn the fundamentals of measurement and testing, but you will need to obtain more extensive training in these fields.

Both practitioners and researchers rely heavily on tests and testing. For this reason, there is more collaboration between them in this area than in many other aspects of education. Practitioners need to continually improve the tests they develop, or their selection of tests to administer, in order to serve the best interests of students and various stakeholder groups. They often turn to researchers specializing in measurement to help them. Conversely, researchers need to use tests in their studies that will be judged by practitioners to be relevant and sound. Therefore, they must stay abreast of current trends in testing practice. In this chapter, you will find references not only to measurement research and theory, but also to testing practices in educational institutions.

Characteristics of a Good Test in Research

Criteria for Judging the Quality of Tests

In addition to its reliability and validity (discussed in later sections), four criteria are commonly used to judge whether a test is of sufficient quality to use in educational research. Each is explained below.

Objectivity

The **objectivity** of a test refers to whether its scores are undistorted by biases of the individuals who administer and score it. In fact, the development of a scientific discipline can be traced by the progress it has made in recognizing the possibility of personal errors in measurement and in ruling them out to an ever greater extent.

Certain tests, such as the Rorschach Inkblot Test or most essay tests, have low objectivity because the conditions of administration and scoring are highly flexible. Tester bias can occur easily under these conditions. In contrast, multiple-choice or other closed-form tests generally are much more objective, because they are mostly self-administered and all scorers can apply a scoring key, which allows them to agree perfectly. For this reason, multiple-choice tests often are called *objective tests*.

Standard Conditions of Administration and Scoring

As we suggested above, it is desirable for a test to have standard conditions of administration and scoring because these conditions increase its objectivity. Therefore, a well-developed test will include a manual that specifies the procedures that should be followed for any situation that might affect an individual's test performance. For example, the developers will specify how much time to allow for individuals to complete the test, whether instructions can be repeated, how to answer test-takers' questions, and how much personal interaction is permitted between the tester and test-takers. The developers also will specify scoring procedures, including those for special circumstances, such as when an individual marks two choices on a multiple-choice item.

A test that has procedures to ensure consistency in administration and scoring across all testing situations is called a **standardized test.** An important advantage of standardized tests is that they minimize measurement errors due to variations in administering and scoring them. Another advantage is that if you obtain significant findings in your research study, other researchers will be able to replicate and expand on them because they can create the same conditions of administration and scoring by consulting the test manual.

Standards for Interpretation

Objective test scores have no inherent interpretion, but are typically interpreted relative to something external to the test: either a criterion or a set of norms. For example, in criterion-referenced interpretation, scores are interpreted relative to some absolute performance standard, whereas scores on a norm-referenced test are interpreted relative to the performance of other individuals in a defined group. Standards for interpretation are explained in more detail later in the chapter.

Fairness

If a test is fair, two groups of equal ability with respect to the construct measured by the test (e.g., reading comprehension) should earn the same score on each item of the test. If the test is not fair, it is said to suffer from **differential item functioning,** which means that individuals of equal ability but from different subgroups (e.g., males and females) do not have the same probability of earning the same score on one or more of the test items. As part of the process of test construction, various procedures have been developed to detect and eliminate unfair test items.[1]

Test Validity

The 1999 *Standards for Educational and Psychological Testing* (hereafter referred to as the *Standards*) is an authoritative reference work on test validity and other test matters.[2] (Previous editions appeared in 1966, 1974, and 1985.) It was written by the Joint Committee on Educational and Psychological Tests, made up of representatives of the American Psychological Association, the American Educational Research Association, and the National Council on Measurement in Education. The *Standards* defines **validity** as the "degree to which evidence and theory support the interpretation of test scores entailed by proposed uses of tests."[3] This definition highlights the fact that test scores themselves are neither valid nor invalid. Rather, it is *interpretations* of the scores that are either valid or invalid.

For example, if we administer a history achievement test to a group of students, each student earns a score on the test. We then might *interpret* this score as representing how much each student has learned about history relative to other students. It is helpful to think about this interpretation as a "claim" that we make about the test scores. What evidence can we provide to support our interpretation of the scores yielded by administering a test? The *Standards* recognizes five main types of evidence for demonstrating the validity of test-score interpretations: evidence from (1) test content, (2) response processes, (3) internal structure, (4) relationship to other variables, and (5) consequences of testing. Each type is described below. Keep in mind, though, that these are not five types of validity. Validity is unitary in

Touchstones in Research

Sandoval, J., Frisby, C. L., Geisinger, K. F., Ramos-Grenier, J., & Scheuneman, J. D. (1998). *Test interpretation and diversity: Achieving equity in assessment.* Washington, DC: American Psychological Association.

Braun, H. I., Jackson, D. N., & Wiley, D. E. (2002). *The role of constructs in psychological and educational measurement.* Mahwah, NJ: Erlbaum.

1. Camilli, G., & Shepard, L. A. (1994). *Methods for identifying biased test items.* Thousand Oaks, CA: Sage; see also Chapters 3 and 7 of the 1999 *Standards for Educational and Psychological Testing* (described later in the chapter).
2. American Educational Research Association, American Psychological Association, and National Council on Measurement in Education (1999). *Standards for educational and psychological testing.* Washington, DC: American Educational Research Association.
3. Ibid., p. 9.

nature, but there are different ways to gather evidence about it. Another important point is that the current edition of the *Standards* uses different terms than the traditional terminology found in older research reports and books about measurement. The new terms emphasize the unitary nature of test validity and the fact that different kinds of empirical evidence can be synthesized to strengthen the case for the validity of a particular test.

Evidence from Test Content

Touchstone in Research

La Marca, P. M. (2001). Alignment of standards and assessments as an accountability criterion. *Practical Assessment, Research and Evaluation, 7*(21). Retrieved October 22, 2001 from http://pareonline.net/getvn.asp?v=7&n=21

Interpretations of test scores often refer to the relationship between a test's content and the construct that it claims to measure. As explained in Chapter 1, the term *construct* has a particular meaning in research: It is a concept that is inferred from commonalities among observed phenomena. For example, if a teacher gives students a Spanish test, the teacher is likely to claim that the test items represent the content that students were exposed to in the assigned textbook, supplementary curriculum materials, and the teacher's presentations in class.

Content-related evidence of test validity should not be confused with **face validity,** which involves only a casual, subjective inspection of the test items to judge whether they cover the content that the test purports to measure.[4] Content-related evidence typically is determined systematically by content experts, who define in precise terms the universe (also called *domain*) of specific content that the test is assumed to represent, and then determine how well that content universe is sampled by the test items. A test does not need to cover all the content in a given course of study for students' scores to be content-valid, but it must cover a representative sample of the content domain.

The importance of checking content-related validity evidence is illustrated by a study that compared the content of the four most popular mathematics textbooks with the four most commonly used standardized mathematics achievement tests.[5] The analysis showed an overlap of only 21 to 50 percent between textbook content and test content. This means that in the worst case, students had an opportunity to study only 21 percent of what was tested. With content-related validity this weak, this achievement test provides a highly inaccurate picture of what students learned in their mathematics course (assuming the teacher taught from the textbook).

Standards-based instruction is an important recent movement in education. This type of instruction requires alignment between curriculum content (typically determined by state-mandated standards), teachers' instruction, and assessment by standardized tests. Research by Gerald Tindal and Victor Nolet has found that this type of alignment is problematic for teachers.[6] Depending on the teacher, concepts that are included in the curriculum might, or might not, be included in instruction or on tests. Most troubling is the situation in which key concepts are tested, but were not taught well or were not represented adequately in the curriculum materials used in instruction. These findings suggest that researchers are not likely to find good evidence to support the validity of their test-score interpretations if they use test data collected in actual school settings.

Content-related validity evidence is particularly important in selecting tests to use in experiments involving the effect of instructional methods on achievement. For example, suppose that you are conducting research to determine whether the constructivist method

---

4. Nevo, B. (1985). Face validity revisited. *Journal of Educational Measurement, 22,* 287–293.
5. Porter, A. (1985, April) *Content determinants research: An overview.* Paper presented at the annual meeting of the American Educational Research Association, San Francisco. (ERIC Document Reproduction Service No. ED 274 510)
6. Tindal, G., & Nolet, V. (1996). Serving students in middle school content classes: A heuristic study of critical variables linking instruction and assessment. *Journal of Special Education, 29,* 414–432.

of teaching social studies is superior to lecture-based teaching. To enable a proper comparison, the achievement test administered at the end of instruction should be representative of the content covered during instruction. If the hypothesis states that the constructivist approach will lead to superior learning but the specific content taught by the teacher was not measured by the achievement test, the findings cannot be used either to support or reject the research hypothesis.

In many experiments, the treatment conditions being compared have different learning objectives. Therefore, it is advisable to select tests that yield content-valid interpretations for each treatment condition but to administer all the tests to the research participants in all the treatment conditions. We would expect research participants to do best on the test that has the best content-related evidence for their treatment condition, but if one of the treatment conditions is especially effective, the participants in that condition might do well on the less content-valid tests, too.

Evidence from Response Processes

Anyone who has taken or scored a test knows that the task engages particular cognitive and evaluative processes. These processes might, or might not, be relevant to the construct that the test purportedly measures. Therefore, the validity of test-score interpretations can be supported by evidence that the processes actually engaged by the test are consistent with a particular construct or constructs.

For example, suppose that judges are asked to rate college students' history essays on various scales, such as clarity of writing style and use of evidence to support conclusions. Further suppose that several of the judges assign higher ratings on the scales if the essay exhibits creativity, which they happen to value. If creativity is irrelevant to the scales, this process of looking for and valuing signs of creativity in students' writing compromises the validity of the test-score interpretations.

As another example, consider a test that purportedly requires students to use higher-order reasoning processes to solve certain types of problems. If students have received extensive instruction on these problem types and can solve them by applying algorithms rather than by reasoning, the validity of the test-score interpretations is compromised.

One procedure for collecting validity evidence related to response processes is to simply ask test-takers or judges to reflect aloud on the cognitive and evaluative processes they used during the task. These reflections can be recorded and then analyzed to determine their consistency with the construct measured by the test. The *Standards* describes additional procedures for collecting response-process evidence.

Evidence from Internal Structure

Nearly all tests have multiple items. Analysis of the relationship of these items to each other can provide evidence about the validity of test-score interpretations. For example, suppose a test is designed to measure one construct. If that is indeed the case, a correlational analysis (see Chapter 11) should demonstrate that an individual who answered a certain item a certain way (e.g., correctly) is more likely to answer other items the same way than an individual who answered it differently.

Some tests have subtests designed to measure different constructs (e.g., visual, spatial, verbal, and motor aptitudes) and provide a separate score for each one. Several kinds of correlational analysis, including factor analysis (see Chapter 11), enable the development of evidence to support the validity of interpretations based on individuals' scores on the various subtests.

Other analytic procedures based on the internal structure of a test are described in the *Standards.*

Evidence from Relationship to Other Variables

Researchers often explore the validity of a test by hypothesizing how a sample will perform on it in relation to their performance on measures of other variables. They then collect and analyze relevant data. If the data analysis supports the hypothesis, the researchers can use it as evidence of the test's validity.

One of the most common validity tests of this type is research on how well the test predicts a sample's scores on a predictive criterion. An example of this kind of research was carried out by Marvin Simner.[7] He developed an abbreviated version of the Printing Performance School Readiness Test (APPSRT), which is intended to identify at-risk or failure-prone children at the start of prekindergarten. He then sought to determine whether the shorter measure yielded predictions with sufficient predictive value that it could be used in place of the longer, original measure. Two samples of 171 children were tested early in prekindergarten and followed for three years. Scores on the APPSRT were then correlated with later measures of achievement: (1) students' grades in reading and arithmetic in first grade, and (2) their raw scores on two standardized achievement tests at the end of first grade. The scores on the APPSRT correlated between −.42 and −.58 with grades, and between −.40 and −.60 with achievement test scores. By using a cutoff score on the APPSRT, Simner was able to correctly identify 70 to 78 percent of the children who were later judged by their teachers as displaying poor performance, whereas the original, longer test (PPSRT) had correctly identified 81 percent of such children. Thus, he demonstrated that there was sufficient evidence of the predictive value of the APPSRT to support its use in place of the longer test.

Procedures for doing research on the predictive value of test score interpretations are described in Chapter 11.

The *Standards* describes several other types of test-criterion evidence that can be collected to support claims for the validity of test-score interpretations:

1. Evidence that a sample's test scores correlate positively with their scores on other measures that are hypothesized to measure the same construct. Evidence of this type is called **convergent evidence.**
2. Evidence that a sample's test scores correlate negatively with their scores on other measures that are hypothesized to measure a different construct. Evidence of this type is called **discriminant evidence.**
3. Evidence that scores on the test are distributed differently for two or more groups that are hypothesized to be different on the construct presumably measured by the test.
4. Evidence that a sample's test scores correlate positively with their scores on a measure of a criterion variable that was administered at approximately the same time. Evidence of this type, called **concurrent evidence,** comprises statistical results indicating how accurately test scores can predict criterion scores obtained at about the same point in time. Conversely, **predictive validity** comprises statistical results indicating how accurately test scores can predict criterion scores obtained at a later point in time. (The results of Simner's study, described above, yielded predictive evidence for the APPSRT.)

7. Simner, M. (1989). Predictive validity of an abbreviated version of the Printing Performance School Readiness Test. *Journal of School Psychology, 27,* 189–195.

No matter how well a validity study of a test is done, it yields evidence only for the sample of individuals who took it. This evidence might, or might not, apply to samples that represent other populations, or to other measures of the criterion variable. Also, it is possible that educational practice might change sufficiently over time that the evidence becomes outdated. Therefore, the *Standards* recommends ongoing validity studies to check the generalizability of existing evidence used to support validity claims.

Evidence from Consequences of Testing

The four types of evidence to support validity claims that we described above focus on the meaning of test scores, for example, the meaning of the construct that underlies the scores yielded by a particular test. However, Samuel Messick observed that there is more to test scores than their meaning.[8] He uses the term **consequential validity** to refer to the fact that test scores, the theory and beliefs behind the construct, and the language used to label the construct also embody certain values and have value-laden consequences when used to make decisions about individuals. These values and consequences need to be checked to determine whether our interpretations of test scores and the way we use these scores to make decisions are valid for particular uses.

A moment's reflection will reveal that the constructs measured by tests of intelligence, academic achievement, and personality are value-laden. The most obvious example is intelligence tests. Intelligence is not a neutral construct; it is valued by our society. The most commonly used tests of intelligence measure the kinds of ability required to do well in school, and therefore these tests imply that school performance is important. Other intelligence tests emphasize other abilities, such as creative talent, which is highly valued by some members of society but not others. The constructs measured by personality self-report instruments are equally value-laden. For example, there are measures of dominance, sociability, independence, depression, and anxiety, each of which has different value connotations for different members of society.

Just as the constructs measured by test scores are value-laden, so too are the social consequences of test score use. Test scores may be used appropriately or inappropriately, and they may have both intended and unintended consequences. Ability tests, for example, have the desirable and intended effect of identifying and advancing the academic careers of gifted students without regard to their social class or geographical location. However, ability tests also have had the unintended effect of creating large differences in the percentage of Caucasians who are promoted in certain work environments (e.g., police departments) compared with African Americans and Hispanics.

The *Standards* emphasizes that test validity and the social policies involving the use of tests are separate matters: "Although information about the consequences of testing may influence decisions about test use, such consequences do not in and of themselves detract from the validity of intended interpretations."[9] The distinction is important, because it implies, among other things, that one should not reject a test solely because of instances of misuse. For example, intelligence tests might be used to make judgments and decisions that are harmful to certain groups. However, scores from such tests might well be valid and useful for other purposes. Therefore, we need to consider carefully both test validity and test consequences in making use of tests in educational practice and research.

8. Messick, S. (1989). Validity. In R. L. Linn (Ed.), *Educational measurement* (3rd ed., pp. 13–103). New York: Macmillan.
9. American Educational Research Association et al., *Standards*, p. 16.

Test Reliability

Test reliability is essential in the selection of tests for use in research. Suppose that we administer the same essay test to a student on two occasions, and the student earns a slightly different score the second time. Or suppose that one of the student's essays is scored by five different raters. Three of the raters assign the same score, whereas the fourth rater assigns a somewhat higher score and the fifth rater assigns a somewhat lower score. What is the student's true score?

In classical test theory, this question is answered by making several assumptions. One assumption is that each person indeed has a **true score** on the test, which is her actual amount of the characteristic (e.g., ability, aptitude, knowledge) measured by the test. The second assumption is that any test of this characteristic is likely to have a certain amount of measurement error. The third assumption is that these errors of measurement are random. This means, for example, that if 100 raters scored the essay test mentioned above, their errors in scoring the test would be randomly distributed. Thus, some raters might assign higher scores to particular individuals, but they would be counterbalanced by raters who would assign lower scores to those individuals.

It follows from this analysis that any score obtained by administering a test will contain a true score component and an error score component. If a student's essay test was scored by 100 raters, the mean of those 100 scores would be her estimated true score. The standard deviation of the scores would provide an estimate of how much measurement error is present in the test. If the standard deviation was zero, it would mean that the person earned the same score on all 100 administrations. Thus, we could conclude that the test has no measurement error. However, suppose that the standard deviation was 5.0 and the mean score was 7.5. This is a large standard deviation relative to the mean score, and thus we would conclude that the test has considerable measurement error.

In classical test theory, the **reliability** of a test refers to the degree to which measurement error is absent from the scores yielded by the test. (Note in this definition that reliability is a property of a test's scores, not of the test itself.) We can define **measurement error** as the difference between an individual's true score on a test and the scores that she actually obtains on it over a variety of conditions. Both true score and measurement error are hypothetical constructs, meaning that we can estimate them by various procedures (described below), but we cannot measure them directly.

Each of the procedures for estimating true scores and measurement errors involves the computation of a reliability coefficient. Reliability coefficients vary between values of .00 and 1.00, with 1.00 indicating perfect reliability of the test scores (never attained in practice) and .00 indicating no reliability. In general, tests that yield scores with a reliability of .80 or higher are sufficiently reliable for most research purposes. Tests and self-report measures that are standardized can achieve reliabilities of .90 or better.

Although reliability is essential to validity, this does not mean that test scores with good reliability always yield valid score inferences. To understand this point, imagine that we have an instrument that uses strange scale units. It might yield highly consistent (i.e., reliable) measurements, but we would have no idea what these measurements mean. In other words, we are unable to draw valid inferences from the scores, reliable as they may be.

Reliability must be carefully considered in selecting tests for use in research. It always is desirable to have high test score reliability. In fact, you cannot make valid inferences from test scores if the scores have zero reliability. The reason should be obvious: Scores with zero reliability are all measurement error, and so there is no true score component. It is as if the individuals who took the test were assigned scores at random.

The minimum necessary level of test score reliability depends on the particular research study. For example, if you are planning to do an experiment with a small sample and you expect only a small mean score difference between the experimental and control groups on a particular variable, you will need to use a test that yields highly reliable scores. Conversely, if you are planning to do an experiment with a large sample and expect the mean scores of the experimental and control groups to differ substantially, even a test with scores of low reliability may be sufficient to detect the difference at the specified level of statistical significance.

Many tests yield subscores in addition to a total score. For example, an achievement test might yield a total score and subscores for reading, writing, and mathematics. However, reliability often is reported only for the total score. In such cases, the subscores must be used cautiously, because they generally have lower reliability than the total test score.

We can take our analysis of reliability a step further by considering the factors that might cause measurement error. These factors include the following:

1. A test's items are only a sample of the total domain of possible items that might be used to represent the ability, trait, attitude, or other construct being measured. Measurement error can result if different items on the test are not equivalent in how they sample the construct domain.
2. Test administrators may introduce measurement error by failing to administer the test consistently.
3. Test scorers may create measurement errors by not following consistent scoring procedures.
4. Testing conditions, such as a noisy or excessively warm room, may cause individuals to perform atypically on the test.
5. Variability in how individuals feel (e.g., being sick on test day) may cause atypical performance.

Classical test theory assumes that these measurement errors in obtained test scores are randomly distributed and unspecifiable. Measurement experts have developed different approaches to estimating test score reliability under these assumptions. We discuss each of these approaches below.

Types of Test Reliability

Alternate-form reliability is an approach to estimating test score reliability that involves examination of the particular *form* of the test that is administered. Suppose, for example, that two researchers each develop a specific form of a test, but with the intent of measuring the same construct. Each test has the same number of items, but they differ in content and style. In this case, there will be measurement errors in estimating individuals' true scores on the construct that the tests are designed to measure.

These errors can be estimated by determining alternate-form reliability. This is done by computing the correlation coefficient, called the **coefficient of equivalence,** between individuals' scores on two parallel forms of the same test. The two forms might be administered at a single sitting, or a prespecified interval might occur between the two administrations.

Because of the time and expense involved in constructing alternate forms of a test, alternate-form reliability is not commonly determined. The other types of reliability described below require only one test form.

Test–retest reliability is an approach to estimating test score reliability that involves examination of the occasion of test administration. To determine test–retest reliability, you would calculate a correlation coefficient, also called the **coefficient of stability,** between individuals' scores on the same measure on two different testing occasions. This is the most commonly determined type of reliability for tests for which alternate forms are not available.

The most critical issue in calculating test–retest reliability is to determine an appropriate delay between the two administrations of the test. If the second administration occurs too soon after the first, people will be able to remember their responses to many of the items, and the coefficient of stability will tend to be artificially high. On the other hand, if the second administration is delayed too long, people may go through an actual change in the magnitude of the variable measured by the test that they possess. In this case, measurement error arising from the occasion of test administration will be contaminated with true score changes, making it difficult to interpret the meaning of the obtained coefficient of stability.

Internal consistency is an approach to estimating test score reliability that involves examination of the individual items of the test. Several methods can be used to estimate a test's internal consistency. Each of them involves an analysis of scores from a sample of individuals on one administration of the test.

One method of estimating internal consistency involves calculating a split-half correlation coefficient, also called the **coefficient of internal consistency.** To calculate this coefficient, the developer administers the test to an appropriate sample. The test then is split into two subtests, usually by placing all odd-numbered items in one subtest and all even-numbered items in another subtest.

The coefficient of internal consistency represents the reliability of only half the test. Reliability tends to be lower as a test decreases in length. Therefore, the **Spearman–Brown prophecy formula** is used to make a correction to the reliability coefficient in order to obtain the reliability of the scores when the entire test is administered.

The method of **rational equivalence** is another method for estimating a test's internal consistency. The individual items are analyzed by one of several available formulas. Among the most common are the **Kuder–Richardson formulas,** after the authors of an article in which these formulas were first discussed.[10] The formulas in the article are numbered, and the two that are most widely used are K-R 20 and K-R 21. Formula K-R 21 is a simplified, easily calculated approximation of formula K-R 20. Items must be scored dichotomously (e.g., correct vs. incorrect, or yes vs. no) in order to use either K-R 20 or K-R 21. The Kuder–Richardson formulas usually yield lower reliability coefficients than those that would be obtained by the other methods of calculating reliability.

Cronbach's alpha coefficient (α) is a general form of the K-R 20 formula that can be used when items on a measure are not scored dichotomously. For example, some multiple-choice tests and essay tests include items that have several possible answers, each of which is given a different weight. Cronbach's alpha is a widely used method for computing test score reliability.

Intertester reliability is an approach to estimating a test's internal consistency that involves examination of the level of agreement between different administrators or scorers of a test. To obtain test scores, someone needs to administer the test and someone needs to score it. Both types of tester (i.e., the test administrator and the test scorer) can introduce measurement error into the test scores if they fail to follow the prescribed procedures exactly. The magnitude of test administration errors can be assessed by having several testers administer the test to a sample of individuals and then correlating their obtained scores with each other. Test-scoring errors can be assessed by a similar procedure.

---

10. Richardson, M. W., & Kuder, G. F. (1939). The calculation of test reliability coefficients based upon the method of rational equivalence. *Journal of Educational Psychology, 30,* 681–687.

Test administration errors are most likely if the testers have not been well trained or if the test is individually administered and requires interaction between the tester and examinee. Test scoring errors are most likely if the test items cannot be scored by a scoring key, but instead require judgment. Even with a scoring key, though, measurement errors can result if the person using the scoring key is careless. Machines that score tests can cause measurement errors, too, if they are calibrated inaccurately or if students have made pencil marks that the machine cannot detect.

Use of Generalizability Theory

While the approaches to estimating a reliability coefficient that we described above do not isolate sources of systematic measurement error in test scores, generalizability theory addresses this limitation.[11] Using generalizability theory, a researcher can design a study that systematically investigates several sources of measurement error (e.g., variations in items and variations in raters). **Generalizability theory** provides a way of conceptualizing and assessing the relative contribution of different sources of measurement error to the scores that you obtain from a sample of individuals. Analysis of variance is used to analyze the data in order to assess the effect of each source of measurement error and their interactions. (Analysis of variance is explained in Chapters 5 and 10.) Also, the researcher can calculate a **generalizability coefficient,** which is analogous to a reliability coefficient but reflects the combined measurement error due to all the sources that have been investigated.

Noreen Webb and her colleagues described a hypothetical study involving two sources of measurement error—items and occasions.[12] They explained how to calculate variance, error variance, and generalizability coefficients for making either relative decisions (e.g., rank ordering of individuals) or absolute decisions (e.g. pass-fail judgments) based on individuals' scores on a five-item vocational interest test. By calculating variance components and generalizability coefficients for different hypothetical study designs, Webb and her colleagues demonstrated how researchers can plan ahead to maximize the generalizability coefficient obtained in a research study by increasing the number of items or the number of measurement occasions. In their hypothetical study, adding items to the test was shown to increase reliability more than would administering the test on two occasions, and also would be less expensive.

Generalizability theory is not yet in common use, and, therefore, you are more likely to find reliability coefficients than generalizability coefficients for tests in print. Reliability coefficients should be sufficient for making a decision to select a particular test if you keep in mind that no single type of reliability coefficient can isolate all the possible sources of systematic measurement error.

Standard Error of Measurement

In both classical test theory and generalizability theory, an individual's obtained score on a test can be viewed as the combined result of his true score and measurement error. The **standard error of measurement** (also called the *standard error of the obtained score*) allows you to determine the probable range within which the individual's true score falls. For example, suppose the test manual for an algebra test reports that the alternate-form reliability coefficient (r_{11}) for a norm group of 300 ninth-grade students is .85, and the

11. Brennan, R. L. (2001). *Generalizability theory.* New York: Springer.
12. Webb, N. M., Rowley, G. L., & Shavelson, R. J. (1988). Methods, plainly speaking: Using generalizability theory in counseling and development. *Measurement and Evaluation in Counseling and Development, 21,* 81–90.

standard deviation of the test scores (s) is 14. The standard error of measurement (s_m) can be computed by the following formula:

$$s_m = s\sqrt{1 - r_{11}}$$

Substituting the given values into this equation we have

$$s_m = 14\sqrt{1 - .85}$$
$$= 14\sqrt{.15}$$
$$= 14 \times .387 = 5.42$$

Because s_m is normally distributed, we can estimate the probability that an error of a given size will occur. Given the properties of the normal distribution curve (see Chapter 5), we can assume that about two-thirds of all test scores will be within $\pm 1\ s_m$ (plus or minus one standard error of measurement) of the individuals' true scores, and about 95 percent will be within $\pm 2\ s_m$ (plus or minus two standard errors of measurement) of their true scores. Thus, in the above example, if a student obtained a score of 86 on the algebra aptitude test, the chances are about 2 in 3 that this student's true score is between 80.58 and 91.42 (i.e., 86 ± 5.42); the chances are about 95 in 100 that the student's true score lies between 75.16 and 96.84 (i.e., $86 \pm 2 \times 5.42$, or 86 ± 10.84).

It is clear from the formula that the size of s_m is inversely related to the level of the reliability coefficient. That is, as the reliability coefficient increases, the standard error of measurement becomes smaller. If the algebra test has a reliability of .96, the s_m would be 2.80; however, if the reliability is .57, the s_m would be 9.18. Thus, you can see that a low reliability coefficient for a test indicates large measurement errors in the obtained scores.

The standard error of measurement helps us to understand that the scores obtained on educational measures are only estimates and may be considerably different from individuals' presumed true scores. Therefore, we should avoid taking a test score at face value or overinterpreting the meaning of small differences between mean test scores. For example, there might be no true difference in intelligence between two students whose obtained scores are 97 and 102 on an IQ test with a large standard error of measurement. On another administration of the test the two students' scores might well be reversed.

Use of Item Response Theory

Touchstones in Research

Baker, F. B. (2002). *The basics of item response theory* (2nd ed.). College Park, MD: ERIC Clearinghouse on Assessment and Evaluation.

Embretson, S. E., & Reise, S. P. (2000). *Item response theory for psychologists.* Mahwah, NJ: Erlbaum.

Item response theory overcomes many of the major shortcomings on which the assumptions of classical test theory are based. As we have explained, classical test theory is based on the assumption that performance on a test reflects both the individual's true score on the ability, or other characteristic, measured by the test and measurement error randomly distributed around the true scores. Developers attempt to construct a test that is highly reliable (i.e., free of measurement error) and that is not too easy nor too difficult for the individuals being assessed.

A great many tests used in education have been developed within the framework provided by classical test theory. They are good tests but susceptible to the following problems:

1. The reliability estimates for the test and various item statistics (e.g., indices of item difficulty) depend on the sample from which they are derived. Thus, if a researcher or a practitioner uses the test with a sample that represents a different population from the one used in the test's development, its reliability and item characteristics might be different.

2. A test might be too easy or too difficult for some individuals. Under these conditions, the test will provide a poor estimate of their true score on the ability being measured.

3. Classical test theory assumes that the amount of measurement error is the same for all individuals taking the test. In reality, a particular test might have greater reliability (i.e., have less measurement error) for individuals at one level of ability measured by the test than for individuals at another level of ability.

4. According to classical test theory, the amount of measurement error in test items (as opposed to measurement error attributable to testing conditions, test scoring, and test takers) is determined by correlating test-takers' performance on an alternate, parallel form of the test. In practice, it is difficult to develop a strictly parallel form of a test, so this reliability check might not be done.

The shortcomings of test construction based on classical test theory are avoided by constructing tests using item response theory. For this reason, its influence on educational practice and research is increasing.

Item response theory (IRT) as an approach to test construction is based on the following assumptions:

1. An individual's performance on any single test item reflects a single ability.
2. Individuals with different amounts of that ability will perform differently on the item.
3. The relationship between the variables of ability and item performance can be represented by a mathematical function.

To describe IRT in simple terms, let us suppose that the ability being measured is reading ability. We will suppose further that there are five students (A, B, C, D, and E), each with a successively greater amount of this ability. Thus, student E has more reading ability than any other student, student D has more reading ability than student C, and so on.

Now suppose we administer a reading test item (I) that is very easy. All five students answer it correctly. This item tells us, then, that all the students have some minimal level of reading ability. We next administer another item (II) that students C, D, and E can answer, but students A and B cannot. This item is more difficult, and it serves to differentiate the reading ability of students C, D, and E from students A and B. We next administer an item (III) that only student E can answer. We now know that this item reflects a higher level of reading ability than the other two items, and it differentiates the reading ability of student E from the other four students.

The use of item response theory as an approach to item construction and analysis has two important features. First, it provides information about the amount of reading ability measured by each item. Second, students' performance on a given item provides information about how much reading ability each student has.

So far in our example we have described three test items, each reflecting a different level of reading ability. Suppose we construct 10 more items at each level (I, II, and III) by the same method (e.g., we would develop 10 more I-level items that all students can answer). This item bank would have several worthwhile uses:

1. We can customize testing for students of different ability levels. For example, suppose we give a student several I-level items to answer. If the student cannot answer any of them, we need not frustrate him, and extend the testing time unnecessarily, by administering II- and III-level items.

2. We can construct many different parallel tests, each of equivalent difficulty. For example, we can go into our item bank and randomly select two items of each level to construct a six-item test. We can then repeat the procedure and construct a parallel test of equivalent difficulty.

3. We can reduce measurement error for a particular individual by administering only items within the range of those she is likely to answer correctly. For example, if a student is like student C described above, we can administer many II-level items in order to determine the students' reading ability more precisely. (Increasing the number of items in a test reduces measurement error.) There is no point in administering I-level items, which are too easy for this student, or III-level items, which are too difficult.

Item response theory uses mathematical models to define the relationship between an observed behavior (i.e., performance on a given test item) and the ability that is presumed to underlie that performance. In practice, we do not know the true reading ability of individuals. It is a **latent trait,** that is, an unobservable characteristic that is hypothesized to explain observed behavior. For example, if we observe an individual reading a newspaper and answering questions about it with good comprehension, we infer from our observations that this person has good reading ability. We can observe the behavior of reading and answering questions, but not the underlying ability.

An **item characteristic curve** is a mathematical function that is created to show the relationship between test-item performance and the presumed underlying ability.

Two item characteristic curves are shown in Figure 7.1. Several features of the curves are worth noting:

1. The horizontal (x) axis represents the *underlying* ability (denoted by the symbol θ) measured by the items. The ability is measured in standard-score units (see Chapter 5), such that individuals with lesser amounts (minus values) have less of the ability than those with greater amounts (positive values).

2. The vertical (y) axis represents the probability (P) of answering a given item correctly. More precisely, P can be interpreted as the probability that an individual at a given level of ability, chosen at random from a sample of individuals at the same level, will answer the item correctly.

3. Item 2 is more difficult for students at most levels of the ability, because the probability of answering it correctly (P) is lower at most points of the x axis, which represents ability (θ).

4. Item 1 has more discriminating power, meaning that there is a greater difference in item performance between low-ability and high-ability students. For example, if we look at item 1, the probability is .45 that individuals at ability level 0 will answer it correctly, but .80 that individuals at ability level 1 will answer it correctly. For item 2, however, the probability is .35 that individuals at ability level 0 will answer it correctly, but only a slightly higher probability (.45) that individuals at ability level 1 will answer it correctly. We can express this finding by saying that item 1 has greater "information value" than item 2 for the range of ability under consideration.

5. Even individuals at the lowest level of ability (the left-most point of the x axis) have a probability greater than zero of answering the items correctly. This reflects the fact that the two items both allow for guessing.

FIGURE 7.1

Item Characteristic Curves

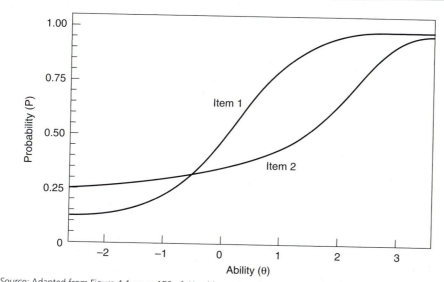

Source: Adapted from Figure 4.1 on p. 152 of: Hambleton, R. K. (1989). Principles and selected applications of item response theory. In R. L. Linn (Ed.), Educational measurement (3rd ed., pp. 147–200). New York: Macmillan. Copyright © 1989 by Macmillan. Reproduced with permission of Greenwood Publishing Group, Inc., Westport, CT.

In constructing tests using IRT, test developers use one of various possible item-characteristic-curve models to fit item-performance probabilities for pools of items to different ability levels. For example, different models are used depending on how the items are scored (e.g., correct–incorrect, partial-credit, multiple-choice), whether the items allow for guessing, or whether they vary in discrimination power (as do items 1 and 2 in Figure 7.1). One of the most commonly used models is the Rasch model (named after its original developer, Georg Rasch), because of its relative simplicity and power.[13] Users of the Rasch model are more likely to eliminate potential test items because they do not fit the model, whereas test developers not bound to the Rasch model are more likely to retain potential test items by searching for item characteristic curves that mathematically describe the data.

The variables that enter into the mathematical equations that describe item characteristic curves can be used in other equations to describe how much each item, and the test as a whole, contributes to precision of measurement and reliability. (The equations are called *item information functions* and *test information functions*.) In simple terms, if a test contains mostly items that are too difficult for individuals at a given level of ability, the test will have poor precision of measurement for those individuals. Also, if a test contains items that are at an appropriate level of difficulty (in general, items with *P* approximately 0.5) but

---

13. Andrich, D. (1988). *Rasch models for measurement.* Thousand Oaks, CA: Sage; Fischer, G. H., & Molenaar, I. W. (Eds.). (1995). *Rasch models: Foundations, recent developments, and applications.* New York: Springer-Verlag; Wright, B. D. (1999). Rasch measurement models. In G. N. Masters & J. P. Keeves (Eds.), *Advances in measurement in educational research and assessment* (pp. 85–97). Oxford: Pergamon.

very few of them, the test will have poor reliability. The ideal test from the perspective of IRT is one in which items are tailored to the ability of the individual: items that are not too easy or too difficult, and an adequate number of such items to minimize measurement error. Item response theory has other applications as well. For example, it has been used to rescale ordinal data to an interval scale.[14] Following this procedure, the scores on a measure of student performance are more likely to form a normal score distribution, which is a requirement of various statistical procedures used in educational research.

Test-development procedures based on item response theory are complex, and therefore few researchers are likely to use them to develop tests to measure variables of interest. However, they are being used increasingly in the construction of high-stakes tests, such as those used in standards-based education. As a researcher, you might find it desirable or necessary to use data from the prior administration of such tests in a study you plan to conduct. If so, it is essential that you understand at least the basics of item response theory and its associated procedures.

Approaches to Measurement

Educational tests can be used to assess how much students have learned or to evaluate the quality of educational programs designed to foster that learning. Tests also are used extensively to make selection and placement decisions in educational institutions and in the workplace. Below we consider three contrasting approaches to constructing tests for these purposes: (1) standardized and locally constructed measures; (2) norm-referenced, criterion-referenced, and individual-referenced measurement; (3) computer-based testing, and (4) individually administered and group-administered measures.

Standardized versus Locally Constructed Tests

Standardized tests typically are developed by commercial publishers or government agencies for use in a large number of sites. These tests have several advantages: The items generally are well written, standard conditions of administration and scoring have been established, and tables of norms are provided.

These advantages of standardized tests are offset by some drawbacks. Guessing, response sets, or random or careless answers can distort the scores. For example, because standardized tests usually impose a restricted time limit, they may not accurately reflect the characteristics of individuals who display a response set to respond more slowly, deliberately, or thoughtfully than their peers. Also, they are designed to permit comparison of individuals throughout a large population (e.g., all students currently in school in the United States), and therefore, the scores do not reflect the unique experiences of different types of individuals. Scores on standardized achievement tests, for example, tend to correlate highly with students' socioeconomic status, but minimally with any indicators of the instruction that students have received.[15] Another problem is that standardized tests have been accused of perpetuating bias against ethnic minorities and other groups,[16] and of neglecting to measure many personal and intellectual qualities that cannot easily be assessed in an objective, paper-and-pencil test format.

14. Harwell, M. R., & Gatti, G. G. (2002). Rescaling ordinal data to interval data in education research. *Review of Educational Research, 71*(1), 105–131.
15. English, F. W. (1992). *Deciding what to teach and test.* Newbury Park, CA: Corwin.
16. Cole, N. S., & Moss, P. A. (1989). Bias in test use. In R. L. Linn (Ed.), *Educational measurement* (3rd ed., pp. 201–219). New York: Macmillan.

The strengths of standardized tests usually outweigh their weaknesses, and for this reason they are commonly used in educational research.

Locally constructed tests are an alternative to standardized tests. They usually are developed by teachers for use with their own students. Such tests generally are inadequate for research purposes because teachers seldom are well trained in techniques for test construction and have difficulty applying what they do know about it.[17] For this reason you should be wary of using scores obtained from a teacher-made test in your study unless you first do an independent check of the test's validity and reliability. The test might be excellent for the teacher's instructional purposes, but test data must satisfy different criteria to be acceptable for use in research. These criteria, described at the beginning of the chapter, generally are better satisfied by standardized tests.

Referenced Test Scores

Suppose a student earns a score of 20 on a 30-item test. How should we interpret this score? Measurement experts have developed three different approaches to answering this question. Each involves a different frame of reference within which obtained test scores are given meaning. These different frames of reference are described below.

Norm-Referenced Measurement

Norm-referenced measurement involves the interpretation of an individual's test score by comparing it to the scores earned by other individuals. Norms are used for this purpose. A table of **test norms** is a set of scores from a large group that has previously taken that particular test, which typically have been converted to percentiles or another type of derived score. Such a table enables a researcher to relate an individual's score (or the mean score of her sample) to the scores of the defined population.

The sample used to create a table of test norms sometimes is called a *norming sample*. The norming sample's raw scores on the test typically are converted to percentile ranks. Given a particular raw score, a table of test norms based on percentile ranks enables us to determine the percentage of individuals in the norming sample who received the same or a lower score. Table 7.1 illustrates a table of test norms that converts raw scores to percentile ranks. To understand how the table works, suppose that we administered the hypothetical test to a research sample and found that their mean score was 33. Consulting the table of test norms, we find that the sample was at the 40th percentile on the distribution of the norming sample's scores. We could conclude, then, that our research sample performed somewhat below the average of individuals in the population represented by the norming sample.

A table of test norms also might include age and grade equivalents, which are explained in Chapter 5.

Norm-referenced measurement works best when the test includes items from a broadly defined domain of content and when it yields a wide distribution of scores. For example, a norm-referenced test in arithmetic achievement typically contains items on addition, subtraction, multiplication, and division. The items for each of these arithmetic operations will range from easy to difficult. This range of item difficulty makes it possible to distinguish between students who have mastered arithmetic at widely different levels.

A drawback of norm-referenced interpretation is that it tells us little about the student's specific strengths and weaknesses. For example, consider the test performance of

17. Campbell, C., & Evans, J. A. (2000). Investigation of preservice teachers' classroom assessment practices during student teaching. *Journal of Educational Research, 93,* 350–355; Fray, R. B., Cross, L. H., & Weber, L. J. (1993). Testing and grading practices and opinions of secondary teachers of academic subjects: Implications for instruction in measurement. *Educational Measurement: Issues and Practice, 12,* 23–30.

TABLE 7.1

Table of Test Norms

Raw Score	Percentile Rank	Raw Score	Percentile Rank
48		34	44
47		33	40
46		32	36
45	99+	31	30
44	96	30	22
43	93	29	18
42	90	28	15
41	87	27	11
40	81	26	7
39	76	25	4
38	71	24	3
37	65	23	1
36	56		
35	49		

these two students: Maria does very well on addition and subtraction, average on multiplication, and poorly on division; Carl performs at an average level in all four operations. These students differ greatly in their strengths and weaknesses, yet both could obtain exactly the same score on a norm-referenced test of arithmetic achievement.

A major problem that can occur with norm-referenced measurement is **test score pollution,** meaning that over time the performance of test takers may increase or decrease for various reasons, thus making the norms meaningless.[18] John Cannell carried out a study in the late 1980s showing that all states in the United States, as well as most school districts, had above-average scores on standardized achievement tests.[19] This phenomenon also has been referred to as *grade pollution* and *the Lake Wobegon phenomenon*. The obvious solution is to create a new table of norms for the test by administering it to a norming sample of students currently in school.

Because educators have great interest in individual differences between students that result from or affect instruction, much if not most research in education has relied on norm-referenced measurement. As we describe the next two measurement approaches, you might consider whether they are better suited to research questions that address other instructional phenomena.

Criterion-Referenced Measurement

Criterion-referenced measurement involves the interpretation of an individual's score by comparing it to a prespecified standard of performance. Achievement tests designed for criterion-referenced interpretation typically focus on a narrow domain of knowledge or skills. In mathematics, for example, one domain might be "all arithmetic problems involving the addition of three two-digit whole numbers." Note that this domain is much more narrow and precisely defined than is "arithmetic achievement on a norm-referenced test."

18. Test score pollution is described in: Haladyna, T. M., Nolen, S. B., & Haas, N. S. (1991). Raising standardized achievement test scores and the origins of test score pollution. *Educational Researcher, 20*(5), 2–7.
19. Cannell, J. J. (1988). Nationally normed elementary achievement testing in America's public schools: How all fifty states are above the national average. *Educational Measurement: Issues and Practice, 7,* 5–9.

A major purpose of criterion-referenced measurement is to estimate precisely the learner's level of performance and specific deficiencies in the domain covered by the test. Another purpose is to provide a sound rationale for making absolute (e.g., pass/no-pass) decisions based on test scores, as in mastery learning models of instruction. Once a domain has been defined and the items developed, a performance criterion can be established, such as, "Given a sample of problems requiring the addition of three two-digit whole numbers, all students will reach or exceed the 90 percent accuracy level."[20] Scores then can be interpreted in relation to this criterion.

Two subtypes of criterion-referenced measurement are called *domain-referenced* and *objectives-referenced measurement*. **Domain-referenced measurement** involves selection of a random sample of items drawn from an item pool that is representative of all possible test items for a well-defined content area. **Objectives-referenced measurement** provides information about how well the student performs on items measuring attainment of specific instructional objectives.

Several concerns arise in determining the reliability and validity of test scores based on criterion-referenced measurement. **Criterion-referenced measurement reliability** can be defined as the consistency with which the measure accurately estimates each individual's level of mastery of the test domain. The correlational methods used to determine the reliability of norm-referenced scores are not suitable for this purpose because they require sets of scores with considerable variability. Because the purpose of norm-referenced tests is to discriminate clearly among students at different achievement levels, items on such tests are selected to produce maximum scoring variability among individuals. In fact, items that nearly all students answer correctly are eliminated from norm-referenced tests. In contrast, even if everyone answers certain test items correctly, these items are appropriate in a criterion-referenced test.

Procedures for determining the reliability of criterion-referenced scores roughly parallel the split-half, test–retest, and alternate-form methods used with norm-referenced tests. You will recall that the test user's main concern in criterion-referenced measurement is whether students have achieved the established criterion. Reliability estimates compare different forms of the measure on their agreement in placing students into two groups: those who reached the criterion and those who did not. Reliability usually is reported in terms of percentage of agreement, rather than as a correlation coefficient.[21]

Individual-Referenced Measurement

Individual-referenced measurement involves comparing an individual's performance on a test at one point in time to that individual's performance on it at another point, or other points, in time. This approach can be used to track changes in a student's performance over time and how a student responds to specific instructional interventions. For example, if a student does poorly on a test, we could determine how well he does on the same test after a specific type of remedial instruction.

Individual-referenced measurement is particularly applicable to single-case experiments, which are described in Chapter 13. In this type of experiment, each research participant is studied individually as he or she responds to an intervention that might be introduced once or repeatedly. The individual can be asked to take the same test at different points in this process so that changes in performance can be measured.

---

20. Methods for establishing a performance criterion or standard in criterion-referenced measurement are described in: Berk, R. A. (1986). A consumer's guide to setting performance standards in criterion-referenced tests. *Review of Educational Research, 56*, 137–172; Kane, M. (1994). Validating the performance standards associated with passing scores. *Review of Educational Research, 64*, 425–462.

21. For specific procedures for computing the reliability of criterion-referenced tests, see: Berk, A consumer's guide.

Touchstone in Research

Van der Linden, W. J. (1999). Computerized educational testing. In G. N. Masters & J. P. Keeves (Eds.), *Advances in measurement in educational research and assessment* (pp. 138–150). Oxford: Pergamon.

Computer-Based Testing

The increasing availability and sophistication of computers are bringing many changes in measurement. We briefly summarize below how computers can facilitate various aspects of testing, from test development to test score interpretation. The particular situation that you wish to study may involve the use of computers for test administration, and therefore you need to understand how they work. Also, you may have access to a research center that has the computer capabilities described below. These capabilities can help you achieve significant efficiencies in test development, data collection, and data analysis.

Use of Computers in Test Development

The construction of tests is aided greatly by using a computer to store and manipulate potential test items. A word processing program can be used in test construction, but it does not solve the problem of renumbering test items. Testing software packages (e.g., BILOG, MULTILOG, RASCAL) not only add or revise items as needed, but can renumber items and put them in the desired test format. These packages also facilitate the use of alternate item stems, such as a graph that the test-taker must interpret or a brief audio presentation in a foreign language that the test-taker must translate. Further, testing software greatly speeds the process of item analysis, allowing the test developer to determine such aspects as the difficulty of each item and the percentage of a sample who chose each response option.

Computers play an essential role in adaptive testing. **Computer-adaptive testing** involves administration of a potentially different test to each test-taker by having the computer match the difficulty level of test items presented to each test-taker to his ability level as judged from his performance on earlier test items. Thus, as test administration progresses, an individual who answered all or most items correctly to that point will receive more difficult items in order to help determine her precise ability level, while an individual who answered all or most items incorrectly will receive less difficult items. This application of computer-adaptive testing is based on item response theory, which was described earlier.

Fritz Drasgow describes three avenues of emerging work that take computer-based testing well beyond merely the adaptive administration of traditional multiple-choice items: (1) visualization, involving the presentation of true color images with remarkable resolution, for example, for a dermatological disorder exam; (2) audition, for example, having examinees listen to musical recordings in the assessment of musical aptitude; and (3) interaction, in which full-motion video is presented on the computer to develop skills related to human interactions, such as conflict resolution and leadership.[22]

Use of Computers in Test Administration, Scoring, and Interpretation

Many standardized paper-and-pencil tests have been converted to computer format. The advantages include (1) the opportunity to randomize, or systematically vary, the order in which items are presented; (2) the opportunity to record or limit the amount of time that a test-taker spends on each item; (3) the elimination of opportunities for test-takers to look back or ahead to other sections of the test; (4) a reduction in scoring errors; and (5) faster scoring. It has even been suggested that a computerized test might be more effective than a paper-and-pencil test or interviewer in obtaining highly personal information (e.g., proneness to attempt suicide).

22. Drasgow, F. (2002). The work ahead: A psychometric infrastructure for computerized adaptive tests. In C. N. Mills, M. T. Potenza, J. J. Fremer, & W. C. Ward (Eds.), *Computer-based testing: Building the foundation for future assessments* (pp. 1–35). Mahwah, NJ: Erlbaum.

Despite the speed and efficiency of computer testing, it is important to consider whether computer testing would intimidate or hamper the performance of individuals who are unfamiliar with or dislike computers. For this reason, in some states the Division of Motor Vehicles has replaced the written driving test with a computer version, but will give a written version to individuals who request it.

Software packages can score and interpret individuals' test responses directly. For paper-and-pencil tests, optical scanners can read the test-taker's pencil marks on an answer sheet and organize them into a computer file. The software can generate raw scores, percentiles, and other scores for individuals; summary statistics for class groups, schools, and school systems; test subscores; and individual item analyses.

Testers also are making increasing use of computers to prepare narrative reports that interpret the numerical test scores. A catalog of statements is stored in the computer, and the computer is programmed so that a certain combination of scores or of responses to individual items calls up one or more of these statements. The report might be descriptive only (e.g., "John is somewhat above average in verbal reasoning") or it can involve interpretation, especially in the case of personality measures.[23]

Individual versus Group Testing

Many intellectual and personality characteristics can be measured by either a **group test,** which is administered at the same time to all the members of a group to be tested, or an **individual test,** which is administered to one individual at a time. For a group test, the test administrator distributes the test, reads the directions, and times it if it is a speed test. The test usually consists of objective items (e.g., yes–no, multiple-choice, or true–false). By contrast, some tests of intelligence and most projective tests of personality are individual tests.

Individual tests can make an essential contribution to a research project if the researcher is interested in studying process (e.g., how individuals respond to certain test items) in addition to product (e.g., what their total score is). If you are interested in such topics as the problem-solving strategies of fifth graders or typical reading comprehension problems of low-achieving students, you might wish to use individual tests in your research.

The nature of the sample also determines whether individually administered tests are necessary. Very young children, for example, usually should not be tested as a group because their attention span is limited and they do not have the reading skills required by group tests.

For many important educational constructs, standardized tests are available in both group-administered and individually administered format. The individual tests typically require more training to administer, and they also require more skill to interpret the scores properly.

Types of Tests and Self-Report Measures

In this section we describe ten types of tests that are commonly used in educational research. They are grouped into two categories: (1) performance tests, which include intelligence, aptitude, achievement, and diagnostic measures; and (2) personality measures, which include measures of personality traits, creativity, self-concept, attitudes, and interests. A large number of tests exists, and we describe only a few examples of each type. Some

Touchstone in Research

Saklofske, D. H., & Zeidner, M. (Eds.). (1995). *International handbook of personality and intelligence.* New York: Plenum.

---

23. For examples of research involving interpretations of students' conceptual understanding of mathematical or scientific phenomena based on their test responses, see Masters, G. N., Adams, R. J., & Wilson, M. (1999). Charting of student progress. In G. N. Masters, & J. P. Keeves (Eds.), *Advances in measurement in educational research and assessment* (pp. 254–267). New York: Pergamon.

were developed decades ago but still are in common use. If a test yields score inferences with the validity and reliability characteristics that you desire for your research project, its publication date should not deter you from considering it.

Measures of Performance

Many performance tests are available for use in research and practice. They vary widely in the constructs they measure, format items (e.g., short answer or true–false), and the type of scores they yield. (See Chapter 5 for an explanation of different types of scores.)

We describe the main types of performance tests below. You can find many examples of each type in the reference books and databases described later in the chapter.

Intelligence Tests

Intelligence tests provide an estimate of an individual's general intellectual level by sampling performance on a variety of intellectual tasks. These tests often include items on such tasks as vocabulary knowledge, mathematical problem solving, reading comprehension, and short-term memory of digits.

Most intelligence tests yield a single global score of intellectual performance, called the **intelligence quotient (IQ).** Some intelligence tests also yield subscores, such as verbal IQ and mathematical IQ. Subscores also may be provided for specific intellectual functions, such as spatial relationships, verbal ability, numerical reasoning, and logical reasoning. However, if you plan to make inferences from such subscores in your research study, you should check to determine whether the subscores are supported by sufficient evidence of construct validity and reliability.

In recent years a number of constructs have emerged that reflect personal or stylistic aspects of intelligence. They include *emotional intelligence,* which concerns an individual's emotional resiliency and expression of appropriate affect in interpersonal situations;[24] *multiple intelligences*, which attempt to measure diverse aspects of individual functioning, such as interpersonal, musical, and spatial intelligence, in addition to the more traditional areas of linguistic and logical–mathematical intelligence;[25] and *contextual intelligence*, which has been found to be of importance in sport psychology.[26] Such constructs exemplify the extensive middle ground that exists between performance measures and measures of personal characteristics, an area of considerable interest to educators.

Aptitude Tests

Aptitude tests are aimed at predicting an individual's future performance in a specific type of skill or area of achievement. Tests are available to measure aptitudes for many academic subjects, occupations, and areas of creative accomplishment. Because aptitude tests primarily are concerned with prediction of future behavior, evidence of their predictive validity is especially important.

Achievement Tests

Many standardized achievement tests are available. Some are intended to measure individuals' knowledge of specific facts, but the trend is to include more test items that assess higher-cognitive processes. The reason for this change is that recent curriculum standards

---

24. Wu, S. M. (2005). Development and application of a brief measure of emotional intelligence for vocational high school teachers. *Psychological Reports, 95*(3, Pt. 2), 1207–1218.

25. McMahon, S. D., Rose, D. S., & Parks, M. (2004). Multiple intelligences and reading achievement: An examination of the Teele Inventory of Multiple Intelligences. *Journal of Experimental Education, 73*(1), 41–52.

26. Brown, C. H., Gould, D., & Foster, S. (2005). A framework for developing contextual intelligence. *Sport Psychologist, 19*(1), 51–62.

at the state and national levels emphasize instruction in reasoning and problem-solving skills.

Administration time and content coverage for achievement tests vary greatly. For example, the Wide Range Achievement Test contains tests in reading, spelling, and arithmetic and requires less than 30 minutes to administer. In contrast, the intermediate level of the Metropolitan Achievement Test provides seven reading scores, six language scores, and eight mathematics scores and takes up to 10 hours to complete.

Evidence of validity based on test content is a major issue in selecting an achievement test. You should check to determine whether the content of test items parallels the content of the instructional program or intervention that is the subject of your research study. Selecting an achievement test with adequate content validity evidence usually is more difficult in areas such as social studies, where the content is highly varied, than in areas such as arithmetic, where the content and the curriculum learning sequence is more standard.

The administration of achievement tests has been found to be psychologically threatening to many teachers because it arouses concerns that poor performance on the test by their students would reflect negatively on their abilities as teachers.[27] Some teachers have been found to give students special preparation in areas covered by the test, and sometimes even on the specific test items covered.[28] To reduce the likelihood of teachers affecting students' scores through coaching or extra instruction, researchers can attempt to select a measure that differs from those that are routinely used to assess school achievement.

You also should consider the test ceiling when selecting an achievement test. A test with a **ceiling effect** is one that is too difficult or easy for some of the individuals to whom you plan to administer the test. Thus, a test with a low ceiling will not reflect gains made by these students following a research treatment designed to increase their achievement level. A test with too high a ceiling also would be inappropriate, because it would be too difficult for many of the individuals you plan to test and therefore would not discriminate among their actual levels of achievement.

Diagnostic Tests

Suppose that your research project involves remediation of individuals' learning difficulties, or evaluation of the effectiveness of a remedial program. In these situations, a diagnostic test might be helpful in identifying an appropriate research sample. A **diagnostic test** is a form of achievement test that is used to identify a student's strengths and weaknesses in a particular school subject. Diagnostic tests usually focus on the low end of the achievement spectrum and provide a detailed picture of each student's level of performance in the various skills that the subject involves.

A disadvantage of some diagnostic tests is that the subscores have low reliability, and often they are highly intercorrelated. For diagnostic purposes a criterion-referenced test covering the subject of interest might be a better choice, because it provides a measure of the learner's absolute level of performance in a precisely defined content area.

Performance Assessment

Performance assessment (also called *authentic assessment, alternative assessment,* and *performance testing*) is an approach to evaluating students by directly examining their performance on tasks that have intrinsic value. The tasks used in performance assessment are designed to represent complex, complete, real-life tasks. In contrast, the tasks on most paper-and-pencil tests, particularly multiple-choice items, do not have intrinsic value. Rather,

Touchstones in Research

Baker, E. L., O'Neil, H. F., & Linn, R. L. (1993). Policy and validity prospects for performance-based assessment. *American Psychologist, 48*(12), 1210–1218.

Cizek, G. J. (2001). *Setting performance standards: Concepts, methods, and perspectives.* Mahwah, NJ: Erlbaum.

27. Smith, M. L. (1991). Put to the test: The effects of external testing on teachers. *Educational Researcher, 20*(5), 8–11.
28. Haladyna et al., Raising test scores.

their value derives from their possible relationship to real-life tasks. A familiar example of performance assessment is the behind-the-wheel driving test required to obtain a license to drive an automobile. This performance assessment differs from the paper-and-pencil test (also available in computerized form) of knowledge of the "rules of the road," that is also required for a driver's license. Some people might demonstrate sufficient knowledge on the paper-and-pencil test but be unable or unwilling to demonstrate it in real-life driving situations.[29]

In performance assessment, researchers can evaluate either individual or group performance in completing a task, or the product resulting from such performance. Portfolio development also has become a popular form of performance assessment. A **portfolio** is a purposeful collection of a student's work that records her progress in mastering a subject domain (e.g., writing in multiple genres or solving math problems taken from different topic areas) and personal reflections on her own progress.[30] Instruction should be closely coordinated with this assessment process, and the teacher and students should collaborate in selecting the contents of a portfolio and criteria for judging it. The criteria are used to generate a **rubric,** a scoring guide that specifies criteria and a measurement scale for different levels of proficiency demonstrated by a portfolio. (Rubrics can also be used for other types of performance assessment besides portfolios.)

Robert Linn, Eva Baker, and Stephen Dunbar proposed a set of criteria for judging the validity of inferences drawn from performance assessments.[31] The criteria are shown in Table 7.2. Examination of these validity criteria suggests that performance assessments can be very useful to both practitioners and researchers, but that they have potential drawbacks, such as the difficulty of obtaining adequate content coverage. Interestingly, some of these drawbacks are the strengths of traditional paper-and-pencil tests. This observation suggests the desirability of using both paper-and-pencil tests and performance assessments in educational research studies, especially in experiments that evaluate the effects of instructional methods on student learning.

The reliability of a performance assessment is equally as important as its validity. As we explained earlier in the chapter, a test is reliable to the extent that its scores are free of measurement error, which is detected through repeated, independent measurements of the construct that is being assessed. Because of the complexity of most performance assessment tasks, it usually is not feasible, or necessary, to administer several parallel forms of them to students, as is done by including many items on a traditional standardized test. For example, individuals only take a driving test once if they pass it. They are not asked to take the test repeatedly in order to ensure that the pass-fail score is reliable. Similarly, a college student only needs to complete one honors thesis in order for a committee to judge whether he will graduate with honors.

Pamela Moss suggested another approach to reliability that legitimizes performance assessment without requiring demonstration of performance consistency across parallel forms of a task.[32] This approach is based on **hermeneutics,** which is a field of inquiry that seeks to interpret human phenomena by understanding how their different parts

---

29. The relative merits of traditional pencil-and-paper tests and performance assessment are discussed in Chapter 15 of: Worthen, B. R., Borg, W. R., & White, K. R. (1993). *Measurement and evaluation in the schools.* New York: Longman.

30. For more information about portfolios, see: Wolf, D., Bixby, J, Glenn, J., III, & Gardner, H. (1991). To use their minds well: Investigating new forms of student assessment. In G. Grant (Ed.), *Review of research in education* (Vol. 17, pp. 31–74). Washington, DC: American Educational Research Association; Forgette-Giroux, R., & Simon, M. (2000). Organizational issues related to portfolio assessment implementation in the classroom. *Practical Assessment, Research & Evaluation, 7*(4). Retrieved April 19, 2005 from http://pareonline.net/getvn.asp?v=7&n=4.

31. Linn, R. L., Baker, E. L., & Dunbar, S. B. (1991). Complex, performance-based assessment: Expectations and validation criteria. *Educational Researcher, 20*(8), 15–21.

32. Moss, P. A. (1994). Can there be validity without reliability? *Educational Researcher, 23*(2), 5–12.

TABLE 7.2

Criteria for Judging the Validity of Performance Assessments

1. *Consequences.* Are the consequences of using the performance assessment reasonable? For example, did some teachers provide more help to their students in assembling their portfolios such that students of other teachers are put at a disadvantage? Did the assembly of portfolios take an undue amount of time away from instruction?
2. *Fairness.* Did all students have an equal opportunity to acquire the expertise measured by the performance assessment? Did different judges apply different criteria in rating students' work?
3. *Generalizability.* Is there evidence that an individual's quality of work on one performance task will generalize to other similar tasks?
4. *Cognitive complexity.* If the performance assessment is designed specifically to measure students' proficiency in higher-order thinking skills, does it actually do so, or can students draw on their memory of how they have done similar tasks previously?
5. *Content quality.* Are the performance assessment tasks and scoring criteria authentic, that is, representative of real-life tasks and quality indicators?
6. *Meaningfulness.* Do groups other than the experts who designed the performance assessment task and scoring criteria view them as authentic?
7. *Content coverage.* Does the performance assessment adequately represent the content domain covered during instruction? Was the amount of content covered during instruction unduly constrained by the time required for performance assessment?
8. *Cost and efficiency.* Is the performance assessment too costly and cumbersome to administer? Cost and efficiency need to be considered when developing or selecting a performance assessment.

Source: Adapted from: Linn, R. L., Baker, E. L., & Dunbar, S. B. (1991). Complex, performance-based assessment: Expectations and validation criteria. *Educational Researcher, 20*(8), 15–21.

relate to the whole. (Hermeneutics is explained further in Chapter 15.) Consider the judging of the product of a performance task completed by a student in an art class. Let's say it is a watercolor painting. Different judges might rate the painting differently, thus raising concerns about the reliability of the scoring system. From a hermeneutic perspective, these differences are not necessarily a problem. The different judgments (the "parts") can be discussed and eventually reconciled until a consensual score ("the whole") is reached.

As Moss observed, this method often is used in real life. For example, members of a search committee meeting to fill a faculty position might disagree among themselves in how they rate different candidates for the position. They do not attempt to remove "unreliable" members of the search committee. Rather, they discuss their different viewpoints until they achieve an understanding that accounts for disagreements, and that process allows them to select the person whom they consider best for the position.

Hermeneutic principles can be used in similar fashion to handle differences in ratings of the student's various watercolor paintings, or differences between ratings of his paintings and, let's say, his sculptures. In traditional measurement, these differences would be taken as evidence of unreliability in performance, but a hermeneutic perspective would consider these differences as "parts" to be interpreted until they can be reconciled into a satisfactory overall interpretation (the "whole") that provides an understanding of the differences.

The hermeneutic perspective privileges the student's teachers in this interpretive process. This is because hermeneutic theorists believe that the "reader" of a phenomenon involving human behavior (viewed as the "text") is believed to bring her own preconceptions and prior knowledge to an interpretation of that phenomenon. Because teachers have more knowledge about their students than experts who only know students by the products that result from their work on a performance assessment task, the teachers' interpretations have special value. Moss used this tenet of hermeneutic theory to defend schools that use committees of teachers—or committees of teachers, parents, other students, and members of the community—to judge students' performance assessment products.

Measures of Personal Characteristics

We now shift to a discussion of **personality measures,** which assess individual differences in such aspects of personality as traits, needs, psychological disorders, values, and attitudes. Most of them are self-report measures in paper-and-pencil (or computerized) format that ask individuals to respond to items asking about the degree of occurrence of particular experiences, thoughts, or feelings in their life.

Personality Inventories

Personality inventories assess a variety of personality traits in a single self-report instrument, typically a paper-and-pencil measure. They have the advantages of low cost and ease of administration and scoring. Because many variables are measured at the same time, an inventory may contain a hundred or more items. The items usually are in objective form, such as yes-no or multiple choice, which allows for scoring to be done by computer or a template.

The major limitation of personality inventories is that they depend on the truthfulness and diligence of the individual's self-report. Many inventories contain a "lie scale" or "carelessness index" to detect individuals whose scores would show patterns that, if taken at face value, could lead researchers and practitioners to make invalid inferences. For example, J. W. O'Dell developed a carelessness index for the Sixteen Personality Factor Questionnaire that correctly selected 88 percent of randomly completed answer sheets.[33]

Another factor that can cause invalid responses to a personality inventory is a **response set,** which is the extent to which an individual's responses reflect a general predisposition rather than a careful analysis of the content of each item. Three types of response sets have been extensively researched: **social desirability set,** or the tendency to present oneself in a favorable light; **acquiescence bias,** or the set to agree with items irrespective of their content; and **deviance bias,** or the set to respond in ways that are different from typical or normal responses. If you believe that individuals in your sample are inclined to one of these response sets, you should not use a self-report inventory.

Personality inventories have been attacked as involving an invasion of privacy of the individuals taking the test. Therefore you should carefully review whether the personality inventory you are considering contains items that might cause a problem in your relationship with parents or community groups whose cooperation you will need. For example, administering an inventory to middle school students that contains questions about sexual experiences might raise objections from many people and thus jeopardize your entire study.

Projective Techniques

The term *projective technique* was popularized by Lawrence Frank.[34] A **projective technique** provides ambiguous visual stimuli and freedom of response, based on the assumption that such measures better reveal an individual's inner thoughts, fantasies, and unique structuring of reality than a test with more limited or structured response options.

33. O'Dell, J. W. (1971). Method for detecting random answers on personality questionnaires. *Journal of Applied Psychology, 55,* 380–383.
34. Frank, L. K. (1939). Projective methods for the study of personality. *Journal of Psychology, 8,* 389–413.

A presumed advantage of projective techniques is that they are less subject to faking than self-report inventories.

One of the most widely used projective techniques is the Thematic Apperception Test (TAT). This instrument consists of a set of drawings of individuals in various interpersonal situations; the respondent makes up a story in response to each situation. These stories presumably reveal the individual's inner world, and for this reason some qualitative researchers favor the use of the TAT and other projective techniques.[35]

Measures of Specific Personality Traits

Some personality measures focus on a single personality trait or a small set of related characteristics. If you are interested in a measure of only one personality trait, we recommend that you check reference works (described later in the chapter and in Appendix C) to see if a published measure is available. If you cannot find a suitable measure, check the general inventories to see if any of them include the personality trait that you wish to measure. If so, you can either administer the entire inventory or use the scoring key to extract the items that measure this trait and administer only those items. Before using the latter approach, though, you should obtain the publisher's permission. Also, if you administer only part of the inventory, use test norms with caution, because responses may be different when items measuring a single personality trait lack the context of the entire inventory.

Measures of Self-Concept

Self-concept is defined as the set of cognitions and feelings that each individual has about himself or herself. Many measures of self-concept include an assessment of self-esteem, which refers to how positively individuals feel about themselves generally or about specific aspects of the self, such as self as physical being, self as social being, or self as student.

While the construct of self-esteem has received a good deal of attention in education, research has shown mixed results as to its importance as an outcome or its relationship to other outcomes. For example, Richard Foxx and C. E. Roland report research that questions the impact of educational inclusion on the self-esteem of students with developmental disabilities.[36] By contrast, Elliot Aronson cites research showing that the use of multicultural "jigsaw groups," which encourage collaboration instead of competition, has a positive effect on both students' standardized test scores and their self-esteem.[37]

Measures of Learning Styles and Habits

Over a period of time, students develop characteristic ways of approaching learning tasks. As these become internalized, they constitute distinctive approaches to learning that are of interest to educators. For example, Ronald Schmeck used a measure that he developed, the Inventory of Learning Processes, to characterize students' learning as deep-elaborative or shallow-reiterative.[38] Deep-elaborative students are argumentative when reading or

35. For example, see: Gilligan, C., & Pollak, S. (1988). The vulnerable and invulnerable physician. In C. Gilligan, J. V. Ward, & J. M. Taylor (Eds.), *Mapping the moral domain: A contribution of women's thinking to psychological theory and education* (pp. 245–262). Cambridge, MA: Harvard University Press.
36. Foxx, R. M., & Roland, C. E. (2004). The self-esteem fallacy. In Jacobson, J. W., Foxx, R. M., & Mulick, J. A. (Eds.). *Controversial therapies for developmental disabilities: Fad, fashion and science in professional practice* (pp. 101–112). Mahwah, NJ: Erlbaum.
37. Aronson, E. (2005). How the Columbine High School tragedy could have been prevented. *Journal of Individual Psychology, 60*(4), 355–360.
38. Schmeck, R. R. (1988). Individual differences and learning strategies. In C. E. Weinstein, E. T. Goetz, and P. A. Alexander (Eds.), *Learning and study strategies: Issues in assessment, instruction, and evaluation* (pp. 171–191). San Diego, CA: Academic Press.

listening, and like to relate curriculum content to their personal life. Shallow-reiterative students process curriculum content superficially; they do not reflect on or personalize it.

Attitude Scales

An **attitude** can be defined as an individual's viewpoint or disposition toward a particular "object" (a person, a thing, an idea, etc.). Attitudes are considered to have three components: (1) an *affective* component, which consists of the individual's feelings about the attitude object; (2) a *cognitive* component, which is the individual's beliefs or knowledge about the attitude object; and (3) a *behavioral* component, which is the individual's predisposition to act toward the attitude object in a particular way.

Several procedures can be used to measure attitudes. A **Thurstone scale** requires individuals to express agreement or disagreement with a series of statements about the attitude object. A **Likert scale** asks individuals to rate their level of agreement (e.g., strongly agree, agree, undecided, disagree, or strongly disagree) with various statements. In the **semantic differential scale** technique, individuals rate an attitude object on a series of bipolar adjectives, such as fair–unfair, valuable–worthless, and good–bad.

Measures of Vocational Interest

Vocational interest inventories have proved to be of considerable value in educational research. They can be used to investigate how students come to develop specific vocational interests, and they also provide an indirect assessment of personality characteristics (e.g., an individual interested in banking is likely to have different personality characteristics from those of someone interested in becoming an artist). Vocational interest inventories typically require the individual to express their degree of interest in, or preference for, various types of activities, sports, hobbies, books, and other aspects of daily life that have been found to be typical among individuals in particular vocations.

Obtaining Information about Tests and Self-Report Measures

In planning a study, researchers sometimes select the first test they identify that appears to measure a construct that they wish to study. They might later encounter criticism that the test is invalid for that construct or inappropriate for the sample. This problem can be avoided by determining the range of tests that are available and collecting detailed information about each of them before selecting one. The following are questions that can guide your search for relevant information:

1. Is there evidence that the test is valid and reliable for the uses to which you want to put it?
2. Is the test's reading or task level appropriate for your sample?
3. Can the test be administered within the time constraints of your data-collection situation?
4. If the test measures achievement or aptitude, is it at an appropriate level of difficulty for the sample, that is, neither too simple nor too difficult?
5. Do the test's norms and validity and reliability evidence come from a population that is similar to the population from which your sample will be drawn?

The following section describes four sources of information to answer these questions: preliminary and secondary sources, the test manual, the test itself, and the test developer.

Searching Preliminary and Secondary Sources

Various reference books and online search engines are available to help you identify tests that measure the constructs you wish to study in your research. Some of them are indexes (which we call *preliminary sources*) that enable you to find tests that measure a particular construct. Others provide descriptions and critical reviews of particular tests.

Appendix C contains a list of these resources. In addition, you can search various specific databases (see Chapter 4) for publications about tests and constructs. Two particularly useful resources for identifying and getting information about tests for research use are described below. In most cases, you must contact the publisher to obtain the actual test materials.

Test Reviews Online allows researchers to access information on nearly 4,000 commercially available tests. Over 2,000 of these tests have been critically reviewed by the Buros Institute, publishers of the *Mental Measurements Yearbooks* (see Appendix C). You can obtain a listing of tests and reviews in 18 subject categories or purchase reviews of specific tests from the Test Reviews Online Web site (http://www.buros.unl.edu/buros/jsp/search.jsp). For example, we found a listing for a test measuring adaptive behavior, which gave the test title, authors, purpose, acronym, publisher, publisher address, and a review of the test from the 13th *Mental Measurements Yearbook*.

The Educational Testing Service maintains TestLink, the world's largest test collection database. It includes the Test Collection, an extensive library of 20,000 tests and other measurement devices, and Tests in Microfiche, a database of tests designed for research purposes and tests that are not commercially available. You can search the TestLink Web site (http://www.ets.org/testcoll/index.html). Tests from the Tests in Microfiche collection can be ordered directly from ETS.

Reading the Test Manual

A **test manual** is a booklet provided by the test publisher that provides information to help prospective test users determine whether the test is appropriate to their purposes and, if so, how to use the test. A good test manual will provide information about such matters as the theoretical constructs or rationale upon which the test is based, recommended uses of the test, evidence of validity and reliability, availability of norms, and availability of short and alternate forms of the test. The manual also should provide procedures for administering, scoring, and interpreting the test.

The *Standards for Educational and Psychological Testing* specify that the test developer is responsible for a poorly designed test or an inadequate test manual. However, researchers have the responsibility to determine whether the test is appropriate for use in their research project.

Examining the Test Itself

One of the most important types of information to use in evaluating a test for use in your research study is the test itself. Examination of the test is particularly important to answer questions about the face validity and content relevance of the test, and its appropriateness for your research sample. For example, the test manual may claim that a test is appropriate for fifth-grade students. However, when you examine a copy of the test, you may conclude that the required reading level is beyond that of the fifth graders whom you plan to study.

In addition to examining the test, you should consider taking it. This will increase your understanding of the test and possible problems in administering it.

Contacting the Test Developer

Because there is a considerable lag between the completion of research and its publication, the test developer often has information that has not yet been published, and also is likely to know of other researchers who have recently used the test. Thus, we advise you to contact the test developer directly to request test information. If you explain the purpose for which you wish to use the test, most developers will be cooperative. In fact, they may request a report of your research findings to add to those that already have been collected.

Using Tests or Self-Report Measures in a Research Project

Touchstone in Research

Wilson, M. (2004). *Constructing measures: An item response modeling approach.* Mahwah, NJ: Erlbaum.

Developing Your Own Test

Development of new tests is a complex and difficult process that requires considerable training in educational and psychological measurement. Therefore, we recommend that you make certain no suitable test is available before developing your own. Also, if you plan to develop a test for use in dissertation research, we advise that you design the study so that you only need to develop and validate one test. Otherwise the time-consuming process of test development might prevent you from reaching the point where you can use the tests you develop to answer your research questions. In fact, some theses and dissertations focus entirely on the development and validation of a new test.

The major steps of test development are shown in Table 7.3. Keep in mind, however, that each type of test also involves specialized development procedures.[39]

One of the most important activities in test development is item analysis, which is mentioned in step 5 of Table 7.3. An **item analysis** is a set of procedures for determining the difficulty, validity, and reliability of each item in the test. The specific procedures depend upon the nature of the test. For performance tests, it is customary to compute an **item-difficulty index,** which is a percentage for each item of the number of individuals who answered it correctly divided by the total number of individuals taking the test. For both performance and personality measures, it is common to compute a validity coefficient and reliability coefficient for each item. An **item-validity coefficient** is the correlation between individuals' responses to a particular item and their total score on a criterion measure taken either around the same time that the test is administered (concurrent validity) or at a later time (predictive validity). An **item-reliability coefficient** is the correlation between individuals' responses to a particular item and their total test score.

Dealing with Resistance to Tests

The testing movement has had a major impact on American society over the past 50 years. Millions of tests are administered each year for the purpose of making important decisions about individuals, for example, Who should be admitted to college, and to which college? Who should receive special commendation for their academic achievement? Who must repeat a class because of academic failure? The widespread use of tests to answer such questions has made them the subject of public scrutiny and criticism. Even if you intend to use tests only for a research project, negative attitudes of some groups and individuals toward testing in general might create problems for you.

---

39. Resources for test development include: DeVellis, R. F. (1991). *Scale development: Theory and applications.* Thousand Oaks, CA: Sage; Gronlund, N. E. (1997). *Assessment of student achievement.* Boston: Allyn & Bacon; Osterfind, S. J. (1998). *Constructing test items: Multiple-choice, constructed-response, performance and other formats.* Norwell, MA: Kluwer; Worthen, B. (1998). *Measurement and evaluation in schools* (2nd ed.). Boston: Addison-Wesley Longman.

TABLE 7.3

Steps in Developing a Test

STEP 1: **Define the constructs to be measured.** Give careful thought about the specific construct, or constructs, that the test will measure. Consider whether there is a theoretical basis for the constructs.

STEP 2: **Define the target population.** Characteristics of the target population must be considered in making many of the decisions involved in test construction. Therefore, define the target population in detail.

STEP 3: **Review related tests.** Review other tests that measure similar constructs to generate ideas about such matters as test format and methods for establishing validity.

STEP 4: **Develop a prototype.** Prepare a preliminary version of the test (i.e., a prototype). Several published sources provide guidelines on item writing.

STEP 5: **Evaluate the prototype.** Obtain a critical review of the prototype from experts in test development and the constructs being measured. Then, field-test the prototype with a sample from the target population, and do an item analysis on the resulting data.

STEP 6: **Revise the test.** Revise the prototype test based on the evaluations, and field-test the revised version. This cycle of field-test and revision may need to be repeated several times.

STEP 7: **Collect data on test validity and reliability.** Collect evidence to support the reliability of the test's scores and the validity of the inferences that you wish to make from these scores.

If the tests that you plan to administer come under attack, you should consider several points. First, some protesters may have a hidden agenda that is different from what is expressed. Second, representatives of the public at large lack the expertise needed to understand the function of many items used in psychological tests, so it probably is unwise to debate the merits of specific test items. Instead, you should explain how the test was developed and attempt to demonstrate that the test as a whole is valid and useful.

Third, it is important to take all actions that seem appropriate at the very outset of any challenge to your planned use of a test. If the research study is well designed, test-takers or other concerned individuals usually can be convinced of the value of the study. If newspaper reporters or other media personnel ask questions, be cooperative and acquaint them with the purpose and potential value of your study. Also, be willing to withdraw individuals from a study if they or their parents make a written request for withdrawal, even if they had earlier signed a letter of informed consent (see Chapter 3).

Finally, you should familiarize yourself with the guidelines stated in the *Standards for Educational and Psychological Testing,* which we described earlier in the chapter. You can indicate to protestors and other concerned individuals that professional standards for testing exist and that you have adhered to these standards.[40]

Testing in Field Sites

If you plan to administer tests in a school or other institution as part of your research study, you should come to an agreement with administrators about such questions as: What help will the institution provide for the testing program? How will make-up tests be scheduled, and who will administer them? What role will staff members play in the testing program?

40. Moreland, K. L., Eyde, L. D., Robertson, G. J., Primoff, E. S., & Most, R. B. (1995). Assessment of test user qualifications: A research-based measurement procedure. *American Psychologist, 50,* 14–23.

How will disciplinary problems that occur during testing be handled? Also, you should carefully schedule tests to fit the institution's routines. For example, schools usually have a fixed time schedule for each class period. If your testing extends beyond this class period, it is likely to cause problems for teachers.

If you are working with a large sample, testing the entire group at one time might make it difficult for the test administrator to answer questions or collect materials. Even a minor incident, such as a giggle, could disrupt the test situation for many people. Therefore, it might be advisable to break the sample into small groups and test each group separately. However, do not stretch out the testing over several weeks. Otherwise you face the risk that the testing situation will be significantly different for those individuals tested last compared to those tested first. Also, keep the testing conditions as nearly identical as possible for each group. This is especially important if you are conducting an experiment and the experimental and control groups are to be tested separately, which often is the case.

It is a good idea to avoid testing near major holidays or very close to the end of the school year. The excitement before an anticipated school break can make a significant difference in the attitude of many research participants.

Gaining the Cooperation of Test-Takers

The cooperation of research participants is essential to obtaining meaningful test scores. Before administering a test, ask yourself how you can maximize their cooperation and motivate them to perform at their highest level (in the case of ability tests) or in an honest manner (in the case of personality, attitude, or interest tests). If the test is for research purposes only, tokens that can be exchanged for small gifts or a positive experience (e.g., getting to play a video game after the test) can provide an incentive to participate.

To increase the likelihood that you are sampling individuals' maximal performance on tests of aptitude or achievement, attempt to make the testing a positive experience. One way to accomplish this goal with elementary and high school students is to ask the students' teacher to tell them that the test is important and that they should try to do their best on it. It is appropriate in some situations to have achievement tests for a research project also count as part of students' course grades.

To increase the cooperation of adults, a good approach is to tell them that you will reveal the purpose of the research study and its findings after the testing is completed. This appeals to their sense of curiosity and desire to contribute to research knowledge. Another useful strategy is to emphasize the official nature of the testing session by such methods as using a stopwatch, if appropriate, and carefully reading directions from a manual.

In administering personality measures, testers need to create an atmosphere in which test-takers feel comfortable about giving an honest picture of themselves, especially if some of the test items ask for sensitive information. One helpful procedure is to make clear before the testing session begins that under no circumstances will the test data be revealed to anyone, and that test scores will be reported in group form only (if this is true). Still another technique is to assign code numbers to all test-takers. If you plan beforehand, you should be able to arrange the test session so that test-takers can write a code number on their tests instead of their names.

A comfortable physical environment and consideration for the mental and physical state of the individuals taking the test are likely to increase cooperation. Testers also should master the test directions. It is annoying to be tested by someone who fumbles with materials, appears uncertain, or makes obvious errors.

RECOMMENDATIONS FOR

Using Tests and Self-Report Measures in Research

1. Before selecting a test for research, evaluate its objectivity, conditions of administration and scoring, and appropriateness for your sample.
2. Determine whether the available validity evidence supports the test-score interpretations you wish to make.
3. Determine whether the available reliability evidence supports your intended use of the test.
4. Consider whether a test based on item response theory is a suitable option.
5. Determine whether the referencing of the test's scores (e.g., availability of a table of test norms) is suitable for your purposes.
6. If possible, use a standardized test for your research rather than a locally constructed test.
7. Consider whether individual or group testing is most suitable for your purposes.
8. In designing research involving tests and self-report measures, consider using computer-based test development, administration, scoring, and interpretation.
9. Use good search strategies to identify available tests and self-report measures that are the best measure of the constructs you wish to study.
10. If using performance assessments in research, make sure that they are designed to meet the criteria that ensure the validity of inferences based on them.
11. When selecting an available test and again before administering it, thoroughly study the test itself, the test manual, and other sources of information.
12. Review available measures thoroughly before you decide to develop your own measure.
13. If you develop your own measure, do a thorough job of development, evaluation, revision, and collection of data on test validity and reliability.
14. Anticipate and plan for possible resistance to the test and testing procedures.

✓ SELF-CHECK TEST

Circle the correct answer to each of the following questions.
The answers are provided at the back of the book.

1. The objectivity of a test can be improved by
   a. providing a scoring key for all scorers to use.
   b. providing test norms to which a sample's scores can be compared.
   c. providing an absolute standard of performance to which a sample's scores can be compared.
   d. eliminating items on which different subgroups obtain different average scores.
2. An example of test-validity evidence based on relationship to other variables would be

   a. a comparison of the test content and the universe of content that the test is designed to measure.
   b. a comparison of the response processes used by test-takers and the response processes that the test is designed to elicit.
   c. the degree of correlation between the test scores and scores on a criterion variable.
   d. the degree of correlation between the items that make up the test.

3. In a test that yields subscores as well as a total score, test reliability generally is
   a. higher for certain subscores than for the total score.
   b. higher for the total score than for the subscores.
   c. equal for the subscores and the total score.
   d. lower than for a test without subscores.

4. To calculate the _____ of a measure, the measure is administered to a sample of individuals and then, after a delay, is again given to the same sample.
   a. alternate-form reliability
   b. test-retest reliability
   c. internal consistency
   d. reliability of subscores

5. Generalizability theory is useful for
   a. determining whether test-validity evidence generalizes to populations other than the ones on which it was collected.
   b. assessing the relative contribution of different sources of measurement error in a test.
   c. determining the degree of similarity across item characteristic curves.
   d. all of the above.

6. An important advantage of item response theory over classical test theory is that it
   a. speeds up the process of constructing a test.
   b. yields better validity generalizations.
   c. facilitates the construction of parallel tests of a construct.
   d. enables the measurement of more constructs in each item.

7. A typical advantage of a standardized test over a locally constructed test is its
   a. relatively lower cost.
   b. improved ability to assess individuals who complete tests more slowly.
   c. higher correlation with the instruction students have received.
   d. provision of tables of norms to which test takers' scores can be compared.

8. An important purpose of criterion-referenced measurement is to
   a. compare an individual's performance to the performance of other individuals.
   b. compare an individual's performance to an absolute standard of proficiency.
   c. extensively sample a broadly defined content domain.
   d. compare an individual's performance to his or her previous performance.

9. A good way to check the reliability of a performance assessment is to use
   a. alternate test forms.
   b. generalizability theory.
   c. hermeneutic theory.
   d. item response theory.

10. A potentially serious disadvantage of general personality inventories is that they usually are
    a. expensive to purchase.
    b. difficult to score.
    c. difficult to administer.
    d. based on self-report.

11. To obtain a copy of a commercially available test, a researcher generally should contact
    a. Test Reviews Online.
    b. Testlink.
    c. the test developer.
    d. the test publisher.

12. Computer-adaptive testing (CAT) differs most dramatically from traditional standardized tests with regard to
    a. the opportunity to randomize the ordering of item presentation.
    b. the feasibility of machine scoring.
    c. provision of interpretation of the numerical test scores.
    d. the potential for each test-taker to take a different version of the test.

13. The likelihood of eliciting honest responses to personality measures can be increased by
    a. assuring individuals that their answers will be kept confidential.
    b. telling individuals that they can see their results on the personality measure after it has been scored.
    c. using computer-adaptive testing.
    d. using principles drawn from hermeneutics.

CHAPTER 8

Collecting Research Data with Questionnaires and Interviews

OVERVIEW

This chapter describes the use of questionnaires and interviews as data-collection instruments in both quantitative and qualitative research. We describe the distinctive characteristics and compare advantages and drawbacks. Also, we present techniques for constructing and administering these types of instruments and for analysis of questionnaire and interview data.

OBJECTIVES

After studying this chapter, you should be able to

1. Describe the relative advantages and limitations of questionnaires and interviews in educational research.
2. Describe the steps in constructing and administering a research questionnaire.
3. Describe procedures providing anonymity to questionnaire respondents.
4. Describe the relative advantages and limitations of closed-form and open-form items in questionnaires.
5. Explain the effects of respondents' knowledge and the number of items on attitude measurement with questionnaires.
6. Explain the advantages of precontacting the sample to whom a questionnaire will be sent.
7. Describe several features of a cover letter that are likely to increase the response rate to a mailed questionnaire.
8. Describe several strategies for following up with nonrespondents in order to maximize the response rate to a questionnaire.
9. Describe the steps in preparing and conducting a research interview.

10. Describe the characteristics of key informant interviews, survey interviews, and focus group interviews.
11. Describe three levels of structure typical of quantitative research interviews and three levels of structure typical of qualitative research interviews.
12. Discuss the advantages of telephone interviews and computer-assisted telephone interviews.
13. Describe several factors that should be considered in selecting individuals to be research interviewers.
14. Describe two phases in the training of research interviewers.
15. Describe the tasks that are involved in conducting an interview.
16. Explain the respective advantages and limitations of note taking versus the use of a tape recorder or computer to record interview data.
17. Describe procedures for analyzing questionnaire or interview data with a quantitative research qpproach and with a qualitative research approach.

Questionnaires and Interviews as Data-Collection Methods

Questionnaires and interviews are used extensively in educational research to collect data about phenomena that are not directly observable: inner experience, opinions, values, interests, and the like. They also can be used to collect data about observable phenomena more conveniently than by direct observation. For example, it is much easier to use a questionnaire or interview to ask a principal how many teachers have at least one computer in their classroom than to walk around the school and make your own count. Of course, the advantage of ease is negated if the resulting data are inaccurate.

Questionnaires are printed forms that ask the same questions of all individuals in the sample and for which respondents record their answers in verbal form. (If the sample has subgroups, the questions asked of each subgroup may vary.) Respondents record a written or typed response to each questionnaire item. Also, the respondents typically control the data-collection process: They can fill out the questionnaire at their convenience, answer the items in any order, take more than one sitting to complete it, make marginal comments, or skip questions.

Interviews consist of oral questions asked by the interviewer and oral responses by the research participants. Interviews typically involve just one respondent at a time, but there is increasing interest in conducting group interviews. Respondents typically speak in their own words, and their responses are recorded by the interviewer, either in short-term memory for later note taking, verbatim on audiotape or videotape, or through handwritten or computer-generated notes. The interviewer is largely in control of the response situation, scheduling with the participant a mutually agreeable time and place to carry out the interview and then controlling the question pace and sequence to fit the circumstances of the situation.

Selecting between Questionnaires and Interviews

Questionnaires have two advantages over interviews for collecting research data: The cost of sampling respondents over a wide geographic area is lower, and the time required to collect the data typically is much less. However, questionnaires cannot probe deeply into respondents' beliefs, attitudes, and inner experience. Also, once the questionnaire has been distributed it is not possible to modify the items, even if they are unclear to some respondents.

The major advantage of interviews is their adaptability. Skilled interviewers make an effort to build trust and rapport with respondents, thus making it possible to obtain information that the individual probably would not reveal by any other data-collection method. They also can follow up a respondent's answers to obtain more information and clarify vague statements.

Robert Jackson and J. W. M. Rothney did an extensive follow-up study of 890 adults five years after their high school graduation.[1] The entire sample was sent a four-page mailed questionnaire, and a subsample of 50 individuals was selected for a personal interview that included the same questionnaire items. The researchers found that 83 percent of the questionnaires were returned, whereas 98 percent of the planned interviews were completed. Two experienced counselors rated each questionnaire or interview protocol for evidence

---

1. Jackson, R. M., & Rothney, J. W. M. (1961). A comparative study of the mailed questionnaire and the interview in follow-up studies. *Personnel and Guidance Journal, 39,* 569–571.

of personal problems. The mean number of problems yielded by the questionnaire data was 2.8, whereas the mean number of problems yielded by the interview data was 8.8.

Thus the interview yielded more complete information in Jackson and Rothney's study, particularly information concerning negative aspects of the self.[2] This advantage of the interview method is offset by some limitations, however. One is that it is difficult to standardize the interview situation so that the interviewer does not influence the respondent to answer questions a certain way. Another limitation is that interviews cannot provide anonymity for the respondents. In other words, the respondents must reveal their identities to the interviewer. Of course, the interviewer can analyze and report the interview data in a way that protects the identities of the participants.

The questionnaire is more commonly used than interviews in quantitative research, because its standardized, highly structured design is compatible with quantitative methods. The interview is more commonly used in qualitative research than questionnaires, because it permits open-ended exploration of topics and elicits responses that are couched in the unique words of the respondents. However, both methods can be used in either type of research. Robert Yin, for example, recommends using both methods when doing case study research, which typically involves a qualitative approach but can also generate quantitative data (see Chapter 14).[3] Thomas Huberty describes how to integrate data from interviews and questionnaires, as well as from observations and tests, in assessing youth with emotional behavior disorders.[4]

Validity and Reliability Issues

Questionnaires and interviews must meet the same standards of validity and reliability that apply to other data-collection measures in educational research. As we explain below, these standards are discussed at length elsewhere in the book. Therefore, do not interpret our brief treatment of validity and reliability here as an indication that they are tangential to good questionnaire and interview design.

If you are using a questionnaire or interview in a quantitative study, the validity and reliability standards described in the chapter on tests (Chapter 7) are relevant. For example, questionnaires often solicit respondents' opinions about particular topics and issues. If the researcher wishes to claim that these are the respondents' true opinions, she should collect evidence for demonstrating validity that the content of the items represents these constructs (evidence from test content). Another option is to determine whether the respondents express similar opinions on other measures of the same construct (evidence from relationship to other variables).

In practice, researchers tend to apply looser validity and reliability standards to questionnaires and interviews than to tests, because they typically are collecting information that is highly structured and more likely to be accurate (e.g., the respondents' years of schooling). Also they are usually interested in the average response of the total group rather than the response of a single individual. A lower level of item reliability is acceptable when the data are to be analyzed and reported at the group level than at the level of individual respondents.

2. These findings are generally supported by another study: Legacy, J., & Bennett, F. (1979). A comparison of the mailed questionnaire and personal interview methods of data collection for curriculum development in vocational education. *Journal of Vocational Education Research, 4,* 27–39.
3. Yin, R. K. (2002). *Case study research: Design and methods* (3rd ed.). Thousand Oaks, CA: Sage.
4. Huberty, T. J. (2003). Integrating interviews, observations, questionnaires, and test data relationships among assessment, placement, and intervention. In M. J. Breen & C. R. Fiedler (Eds.), *Behavioral approach to assessment of youth with emotional–behavioral disorders: A handbook for school-based practitioners* (2nd ed., pp. 587–633).

If you are using a questionnaire or interview in a qualitative study, the validity and reliability standards described in Chapter 14 are applicable. For example, the validity of a questionnaire or interview can be checked by using the method of triangulation described in that chapter.

Survey Research

Touchstones in Research

Fink, A., Bourque, L. B., Fielder, E. P., Oishi, S. M., & Litwin, M. (2002). *The survey kit* (2nd ed.). Thousand Oaks, CA: Sage; v. 1, The survey handbook; v. 2, How to ask survey questions; v. 3, How to conduct self-administered and mail surveys; v. 4, How to conduct telephone surveys; v. 5, How to conduct in-person interviews for surveys; v. 6, How to design survey studies; v. 7, How to sample in surveys; v. 8, How to assess and interpet survey psychometrics; v. 9, How to manage, analyze and interpret survey data; v. 10, How to report on surveys.

Fowler, F. J., Jr. (2001). *Survey research methods* (3rd ed.). Thousand Oaks, CA: Sage.

The term *survey* describes research that involves the administration of questionnaires or interviews. A **survey** is a method of data collection using questionnaires or interviews to collect data from a sample that has been selected to represent a population to which the findings of the data analysis can be generalized. This emphasis on generalization to a population is characteristic of quantitative research, but not of qualitative research. Because we consider both qualitative and quantitative research in this chapter, we do not use the term *survey* as a general label for the use of questionnaires and interviews in research. However, the chapter includes references to publications about surveys where appropriate.

The term **survey research** occasionally is used as if it were a particular type of research design. We think that it is less confusing if this term is used to refer to research studies that rely primarily on questionnaires or interviews for data collection. The reason is that either type of instrument can be used to achieve the purposes of various research designs (particularly, descriptive, causal-comparative, and case-study designs). For example, Table 8.2 on page 242 presents the results of a data analysis that is typical of a causal-comparative research design. The results shown in Table 8.4 on page 258, by contrast, are typical of a descriptive research design in quantitative research.

Steps in Constructing and Administering a Research Questionnaire

In this section we describe the major steps in carrying out a research study using a questionnaire: (1) defining research objectives, (2) selecting a sample, (3) designing the questionnaire format, (4) pretesting the questionnaire, (5) precontacting the sample, (6) writing a cover letter and distributing the questionnaire, (7) following up with nonrespondents, and (8) analyzing questionnaire data.

Step 1: Defining Research Objectives

Some researchers develop a questionnaire before they have thoroughly considered what they hope to obtain from the results. It is important that you first define your research problem and list the specific objectives to be achieved, or hypotheses to be tested, by the questionnaire. You might start with a broad topic (e.g., teachers' involvement in staff development), but you should sharpen its focus before beginning design of the questionnaire.

D. A. deVaus suggested five types of questions to help define the research objectives for a study involving questionnaires.[5] The questions are stated below in relation to the above-mentioned topic, teachers' involvement in staff development. (They also are relevant for studies involving interviewing.)

1. What is the *time frame* of your interest? Are you interested in teachers' current involvement in staff development, or do you want to study trends in their involvement over a period of years?

---

5. deVaus, D. A. (1992). *Surveys in social research* (3rd ed.). Boston: Allen & Unwin.

2. What is the *geographical location* of your interest? Do you want to study teachers in a particular state or region, or do you want to compare teachers from different locations?

3. Are you interested in a broad descriptive study or do you want to specify and compare different *subgroups*? For example, will you compare elementary, middle school, and high school teachers, or will you study teachers in general?

4. What *aspect* of the topic do you want to study? For example, are you interested in teachers' involvement in particular types of staff development activities, whether their involvement is mandatory or voluntary, or the amount of their involvement over a given time period?

5. How *abstract* is your interest? For example, are you interested in reporting facts, or do you want to interpret the information, relate it to a broad social context, or develop theory from the findings?

In describing the steps involved in conducting a questionnaire study, we shall refer to a study by Corrine Glesne and Rodman Webb.[6] These researchers were interested in tracking the growing emphasis on qualitative research in higher education in the United States. They wanted to determine who teaches qualitative research methods courses, the content of their courses, and their teaching methods. Their questionnaire was designed to obtain this information:

> The survey [questionnaire] asked about the training and academic background of qualitative research professors, content of courses, program requirements, and faculty perceptions of and interaction with students pursuing qualitative research dissertations.[7]

Glesne and Webb noted the irony of basing a study about the teaching of qualitative research methods courses on a quantitatively oriented questionnaire survey. The researchers chose to use questionnaires anyway, because of their usefulness in collecting both closed and open-ended information from a widespread sample.

Step 2: Selecting a Sample

Once your research objectives or hypotheses are clearly stated, you should identify the target population from which your sample will be selected. (This and other sampling techniques are described in Chapter 6.) If you do a sufficient background analysis, you can avoid the mistake of sending your questionnaire to a group that does not have the desired knowledge of the situation. For example, a graduate student seeking data on school financial policies in the 1980s sent questionnaires to principals of elementary and secondary schools. Many of the returned questionnaires were incomplete, and few specific facts of the desired sort were obtained. This questionnaire failed because at that time school superintendents and district specialists handled most matters concerning school finance. Because the principals who received the questionnaire had little specific knowledge about the topic, they were unable to supply the information requested.

The salience of the questionnaire content to the respondents (i.e., how important or prominent a concern it is for them) affects both the accuracy of the information received and the rate of response. A review of 181 studies using questionnaires rated by the reviewers as salient, possibly salient, or nonsalient to the respondents revealed that the return rate

6. Glesne, C., & Webb, R. (1993). Teaching qualitative research: Who does what? *International Journal of Qualitative Studies in Education, 6,* 253–266.
7. Ibid., p. 254.

averaged 77 percent for the salient studies, 66 percent for those judged possibly salient, and only 42 percent for those judged nonsalient.[8] These findings suggest the need to select a sample for whom your questionnaire items will be highly salient.

In the study by Glesne and Webb, the researchers gained access to a mailing list for the *International Journal of Qualitative Studies in Education*, a major journal publishing qualitative research studies. They sent a copy of their questionnaire to 360 professors whose names were on the journal's mailing list. The researchers commented:

> This was, admittedly, a fishing-net approach. Our assumption was that this readership would include people who teach qualitative research methods courses, and not everyone on the list taught such courses.[9]

Using this admittedly biased sampling approach, they received usable questionnaires from 73 respondents in 37 different states. The sample included 40 men and 33 women. Twenty-five held the title of professor, 28 the title of associate professor, 18 the title of assistant professor, and 2 the title of lecturer.

Step 3: Designing the Questionnaire

Touchstone in Research

Fowler, F. J., Jr. (1998). Design and evaluation of survey questions. In L. Bickman & D. J. Rog (Eds.), *Handbook of applied social research methods* (pp. 343–374). Thousand Oaks, CA: Sage.

Some research questionnaires appear to have been thrown together in an hour or two. The experience of receiving such haphazard questionnaires has led many educators to develop negative attitudes about the questionnaire as a data-collection instrument, so they deposit them in the recycling box with little more than a quick glance. You will need to overcome possible negative attitudes by careful construction and administration of your questionnaire. Table 8.1 summarizes guidelines for designing questionnaires. These guidelines are based on research findings about factors that influence questionnaire return rate.

Anonymity of Respondents

In most studies questionnaire respondents are asked to identify themselves, but anonymity might be necessary if highly personal or threatening information is requested. A questionnaire dealing with sexual behavior, for example, might receive more honest responses if the respondents can remain anonymous.

The major problem with anonymous questionnaires is that follow-ups to improve the return rate are more difficult. There are several solutions to this problem. One is to create a master code sheet that contains a code for each individual in the sample. The codes are put on the questionnaires. When an individual returns the questionnaire, the researcher can check off that person's name on the master code sheet. After a designated period of time, the researcher can determine which individuals have not returned their questionnaires and send them a new questionnaire.

This method is not completely anonymous, because the researcher can link the questionnaire (which has the code on it) to the individual's name by referring to the master code sheet. For complete anonymity, a variation of this approach can be used. The researcher sends each individual a prepaid postcard with the code on it and a questionnaire that contains no code. When the individual completes the questionnaire, she returns the questionnaire and the postcard separately. The postcard tells the researcher that this individual has completed the questionnaire, but he does not know which of the returned questionnaires came from that individual.

---

8. Heberlein, T. A., & Baumgartner, R. (1978). Factors affecting response rates to mailed questionnaires: A quantitative analysis of the published literature. *American Sociological Review, 43,* 447–462.
9. Glesne & Webb, Teaching qualitative research, p. 254.

TABLE 8.1

Guidelines for Designing a Questionnaire

1. Keep the questionnaire as short as possible.
2. Do not use technical terms, jargon, or complex terms that respondents may not understand.
3. Avoid using the words *questionnaire* or *checklist* on your form. Many persons are biased against these terms.
4. Make the questionnaire attractive; use high quality printing and brightly colored paper.
5. Organize the items so they are easy to read and complete.
6. Number the questionnaire pages and items.
7. Put the name and address of the individual to whom the questionnaire should be returned both at the beginning and end of the questionnaire, even if a self-addressed envelope is included.
8. Include brief, clear instructions, printed in bold type and in upper and lower case. Words that are all capital letters are hard to read.
9. Organize the questionnaire in a logical sequence. For example, you might group items with the same topic or items having the same response options together.
10. When moving to a new topic, include a transitional sentence to help respondents switch their train of thought.
11. Begin with a few interesting and nonthreatening items.
12. Put threatening or difficult items near the end of the questionnaire.
13. Do not put important items at the end of a long questionnaire.
14. Provide a rationale for the items so that the respondent understands their relevance to the study.
15. Include examples of how to respond to items that might be confusing or difficult to understand.
16. Avoid terms like *several, most,* and *usually,* which have no precise meaning.
17. State each item in as brief a form as possible.
18. Avoid negatively stated items, which are likely to be misread by respondents. The negative word tends to be overlooked, and respondents might give an answer that is opposite to their real opinion.
19. Avoid "double-barreled" items that require the subject to respond to two separate ideas with a single answer. For example: *Although labor unions are desirable in most fields, they have no place in the teaching profession.*
20. When a general question and a related specific question are to be asked together, it is preferable to ask the general question first. If the specific question is asked first, it tends to unnecessarily narrow the respondent's focus when answering the general question that follows.
21. Avoid biased or leading questions. If the respondent is given hints as to the type of answer that is preferred, there is a tendency to give that response.

Source: Adapted from: Berdie, D. R., Anderson, J. F., & Niebuhr, M. A. (1986). *Questionnaires: Design and use* (2nd ed.). Metuchen, NJ: Scarecrow.

Item Form

Writing items for questionnaires (and for interviews, too) may seem straightforward, but it actually demands great skill. You need to be able to write succinctly and clearly, which is no easy matter. More importantly, you need to have a good grasp of your respondents' characteristics so that you are able to use language that they understand, present items that engage their interests and willingness to respond honestly, and obtain all the information you need without exhausting their patience.

A major difficulty in constructing questionnaire items is that educational terms often have multiple meanings. For example, the terms *charter school, standards-based education,* and *teacher empowerment* may mean different things depending on the individual educator and the region in which one works. If you use such a term in a questionnaire item, it is highly advisable to include a definition that corresponds to your research objectives. For example, suppose a researcher is interested in educators' responses to the charter-school movement, not as it is occurring nationally but within the state being studied. Given this objective, the item might read: "The state department of education adopted a statute in 2001 that allows school districts to start charter schools, which are defined as schools that receive district funding but are administered independently, albeit with mandatory conformance to standards of the state department of education. What is the current status of charter schools of this type in your district?"

A questionnaire item can be in either **closed form,** meaning that the question permits only prespecified responses (e.g., a multiple-choice question), or **open form,** meaning that respondents can make any response they wish (e.g., an essay question). Which form to use is determined by the objective of the particular question. Evidence on the relative merits of closed- and open-form questions, however, suggests that the two formats produce similar information.[10]

The advantage of designing questions in closed form is that it makes quantification and analysis of the results easier. For example, suppose you wish to know the size of a teacher's home town. Probably the least useful way to ask the question is "What is your home town?" This question requires that you be able to read each teacher's response and then look it up in an atlas to determine the population. A somewhat better question would be "What is the population of your home town?" In this case you could classify the responses into population categories such as those used by the U.S. Census Bureau. A still better approach would be to ask "What is the population of your home town?" (Check one.), and provide the following response choices:

```
_____ Rural, unincorporated
_____ Incorporated, under 1,000
_____ 1,000 to 2,500
_____ 2,500 to 5,000
_____ 5,000 to 10,000
_____ 10,000 to 50,000
_____ 50,000 to 250,000
_____ Over 250,000
_____ Don't know
```

This item requires little of your effort to analyze the data, and also minimal effort from the respondents.

To determine the categories for a closed-form question, you can pilot-test the question by asking it in open form of a small number of respondents. Their answers can be used to develop the categories for the item. If you expect unusual responses, an "other" option can be provided.

In the questionnaire study on the teaching of qualitative research, Glesne and Webb began by interviewing several qualitative researchers about their training, teaching, and research. They used the interview information to develop an open-ended pilot questionnaire, and sent it to six professors of qualitative research. Feedback indicated that the open-ended questions were interesting but time consuming to answer. There was a concern that few professors would take the hour or more needed to complete the questionnaire. Based on this feedback, the researchers redesigned the questionnaire into a closed-form format,

---

10. Bradburn, N. M. (1982). Question-wording effects in surveys. In R. M. Hogarth (Ed.), *Question framing and response consistency* (pp. 65–76). San Francisco: Jossey-Bass.

with an open-ended option attached to most items for individuals who desired to respond more fully.

Use of Questionnaires in the Measurement of Attitudes

The individual items in a questionnaire each elicit a different bit of information. In effect, each item is a one-item test. The use of a one-item test is quite satisfactory when you are seeking a specific fact, such as number of years of full-time teaching experience, the number of wins and losses during a particular football coach's tenure, or proportion of students failing intermediate algebra. When questions assess attitudes, however, the one-item test approach is questionable with respect to both validity and reliability. A questionnaire that measures attitudes generally must be constructed as an attitude scale and must use a substantial number of items (usually at least 10) in order to obtain a reliable assessment of an individual's attitude.[11]

Touchstone in Research

Aiken, L. R. (2002). *Attitudes and related psychosocial constructs: Theories, assessment, and research.* Thousand Oaks, CA: Sage.

If you are planning to collect information about attitudes, you should first do a search of the research literature to determine whether a scale suitable for your purposes already has been constructed. (See Chapter 4 and Appendix C for information on locating such measures.) If a suitable scale is not available, you will need to develop one. **Likert scales,** which typically ask for the extent of agreement with an attitude item (for example, a five-point scale ranging from "strongly disagree" to "strongly agree") are a common type of attitude scale.

If you develop an attitude scale for your questionnaire study, you should pilot-test it in order to check its reliability and validity. Also, the pilot test should determine whether individuals in the sample have sufficient knowledge and understanding to express a meaningful opinion about the topic.

One method of dealing with the issue of respondents who lack familiarity with a topic is to include a "no opinion" option as a response alternative for each attitude item. Even so, individuals with little or no information about the topic might express an opinion in order to conceal their ignorance, or because they feel social pressure to express a particular opinion. Irving Allen conducted a questionnaire study of respondents attitudes' toward individuals and organizations that were the subject of considerable media attention at the time.[12] The respondents could express a favorable or unfavorable attitude by selecting among six Likert-type response categories, or they could select a seventh category to express no knowledge of a particular individual or organization. Ten percent of the sample expressed a favorable or unfavorable attitude toward a fictitious organization, about which it was impossible for them to have any knowledge! The individuals responding to the fictitious item were found to have less formal education than the rest of the sample. They also were more likely to express attitudes toward the other organizations and individuals contained in the questionnaire than to check the "don't know" category, and to express more favorable attitudes.

As we stated above, a "no opinion" option for each attitude item might alleviate the problem identified in Allen's study. Another strategy is to include several information questions at the beginning of an attitude questionnaire that can be used to screen out respondents who display little or no knowledge of the topics being studied.

---

11. For an expanded discussion of the measurement of attitudes by questionnaire, see: Schuman, H., & Presser, S. (1996). *Questions and answers in attitude surveys: Experiments on question form, wording, and context.* Thousand Oaks, CA: Sage.
12. Allen, I. L. (1966). Detecting respondents who fake and confuse information about question areas on surveys. *Journal of Applied Psychology, 50,* 523–528.

Web Questionnaires

Touchstone in Research

Mann, C., & Stewart, F. (2000). *Internet communication and qualitative research: A handbook for researching online.* Thousand Oaks, CA: Sage.

Researchers increasingly use the Internet to administer questionnaires. In a quantitative research study, Mike Carbonaro and Joyce Bainbridge administered a Web questionnaire to elementary school teachers concerning the use of Canadian children's literature in class.[13] Of 207 teachers nominated by their principals to participate, 110 teachers completed the questionnaire online. Distinctive features of the questionnaire design and administration used by these researchers include:

1. To avoid having any inappropriate person provide data, teachers logged onto the survey Web site with a designated ID and password. By logging on, they also recorded their consent to participate in the study.
2. Teachers responded to Likert-scale items and closed-form items by clicking on "radio buttons" (a Web-page feature). They responded to rank-order items by entering a number and to open-form items by typing a response.
3. After completing the questionnaire, teachers clicked a SUBMIT button, which transmitted their data to the researchers' Web server. If a teacher clicked this item without having completed the entire questionnaire, the Web software informed the teacher of which items still required completion.
4. The questionnaire data were secured in the researchers' Web server, so they were available only to them and the Web-server programmer.
5. Because the raw data were in electronic form, it was possible to import them directly into a statistical software program for analysis.

This approach to questionnaire design and administration has obvious advantages over conventional paper-and-pencil mailed questionnaires: Postal costs are eliminated; the possibility of missing data within questionnaires is reduced; and there is no need to transfer data manually from the questionnaire into an electronic format and check for possible errors in the transfer process. Also, Internet questionnaires can be designed to be interactive: Items can be tailored to the individual respondent, and respondents can be given feedback as they complete the items.

Web questionnaires are a powerful research tool, but they have costs and limitations that you should consider in deciding whether to use one in your research study. You will need to have access to a Web server and the ability to use specialized software to design the questionnaire, to process incoming data, and to guard against data-security breaches and multiple submissions from the same respondent or a submission from an individual not in the sample. Also, each respondent needs to have access to a Web browser and the ability to use it. Otherwise, the research study is vulnerable to sampling bias.[14]

Step 4: Pilot-Testing the Questionnaire

Touchstone in Research

Presser, S., Rothgeb, J. M., Couper, M. P., Lessler, J. T., Martin, E., Martin, J., & Singer, E. (2004). *Methods for testing and evaluating survey questionnaires.* Hoboken, NJ: Wiley.

You should carry out a thorough pilot test of the questionnaire before using it in your study. The pilot test should include a sample of individuals from the population from which you plan to draw your respondents. Also, the pilot-test form of the questionnaire should provide space for respondents to make criticisms and recommendations for improving the questionnaire. Another useful pilot-test strategy is to ask respondents to state in their own

---

13. Carbonaro, M., & Bainbridge, J. (2000). Design and development of a process for web-based survey research. *Alberta Journal of Educational Research, 46,* 392–394.
14. Bradley, N. (1999). Sampling for Internet surveys. An examination of respondent selection for Internet research. *Journal of the Market Research Society, 41,* 387–395.

words what they think each question means. The questions should be revised and retested until they are understood accurately by all or most members of the pilot-test sample.

In a study of this procedure, William Belson elicited answers from respondents to 29 questions that incorporated problems of interpretation frequently found in questionnaire items.[15] He then studied the respondents' interpretations of the questions in a second in-depth interview. On average, only 29 percent of the respondents interpreted the questions within permissible limits of the intended interpretation. This finding demonstrates the importance of questionnaire wording and the need to check it by a pilot test.

Questionnaires mailed to educators generally can be expected to yield a higher percentage of replies than questionnaires mailed to samples of the general population. The response rate is higher for an educational questionnaire because it usually is targeted at a homogeneous group, and this makes it possible to prepare a specific appeal for participation that is likely to be effective. If you have received responses from less than 66 percent of the pilot-test sample, you probably should make changes in the questionnaire or in the procedures for administering it before sending the questionnaire to the participants in your main study.

Apparently a pilot test of the questionnaire used by Glesne and Webb was not conducted. The authors state:

> Our interview and subsequent survey questions grew out of our own experiences and from reading the few available sources on teaching qualitative research. We realize now that we should have gathered more demographic data such as information on ethnicity, salary, years of service, and years at current rank. . . . If we had asked for more information about respondents, we would likely have had other questions as well.[16]

The researchers' comments reinforce the desirability of pilot-testing a questionnaire before distributing it.

Step 5: Precontacting the Sample

Researchers have found that contacting respondents before sending a questionnaire increases the rate of response. A **precontact** is an initial message in which the researchers identify themselves, discuss the purpose of the study, and request cooperation. The precontact can take the form of a letter, postcard, or telephone call, but some evidence suggests that telephone contacts are the most effective.[17] Respondents also can be asked to return a postcard mailed to them indicating their willingness to cooperate.

Precontacts probably are effective because they alert respondents to the imminent arrival of the questionnaire, thus reducing the chance that it will be thrown out as junk mail. Precontacts also put a more personal, human face on the research study. Finally, having once agreed to cooperate, the respondent is under some psychological pressure to do so when the questionnaire arrives.

Step 6: Writing a Cover Letter

An important objective in doing a questionnaire survey is to obtain a high return rate. We know of studies where the return rate was as low as 20 percent, which makes it virtually impossible to generalize from the sample's data to the population that it is intended to represent.

---

15. Belson, W. A. (1981). *The design and understanding of survey questions.* Lanham, MD: Lexington.
16. Glesne & Webb, Teaching qualitative research, pp. 254–255.
17. Linsky, A. S. (1975). Stimulating responses to mailed questionnaires: A review. *Public Opinion Quarterly, 39,* 82–101.

Because the cover letter accompanying the questionnaire strongly influences the return rate, it should be designed carefully. The letter should be brief, but it must convey certain information and impressions. The purpose of the study should be explained in order to persuade the respondents that the study is significant and that their answers are important. When using a questionnaire that includes sensitive or potentially threatening questions, you should provide a specific description of how confidentiality will be maintained. You also should explain the conditions that you have established for informed consent (see Chapter 3). A sample cover letter is shown in Figure 8.1.

Emphasizing the importance of the respondent can have a positive effect. If appropriate, you can mention the respondent's professional affiliation and the value of information that only members with this affiliation can supply. An offer to send the respondent a copy of the results also is effective. If such a promise is made, it should be honored. Failure to do so is unethical, and will lessen respondents' willingness to participate in other research studies.

It is desirable to associate your study with a professional organization with which prospective respondents might identify. For example, superintendents within a particular state might respond favorably to a letter signed by the state school superintendent or the president of a school administrators' association. If your study is well designed and deals with a significant problem, it usually is possible to have your cover letter co-signed by an individual whose endorsement represents a favorable symbol of authority to the respondents.

Responses to a questionnaire that is not aimed at a specific professional group tend to be more difficult to obtain, because specific appeals cannot be made. Even with a heterogeneous group, however, you might be able to phrase your appeal in terms of common values that you expect most individuals to have, such as the importance of education and community improvement.

Researchers have explored the effect of enclosing a small cash incentive with a questionnaire. Phil Edwards and his colleagues conducted a review of 292 studies that examined the effectiveness of strategies for influencing response to postal questionnaires designed to collect data in health research.[18] They concluded from statistical analyses of 75 such strategies that "the odds of response were more than doubled when a monetary incentive was used . . . and almost doubled when incentives were not conditional on response."[19] If you provide a cash incentive, it should be described as a token of appreciation rather than as payment for the respondent's time.

One of the items needed in the cover letter is a request that the questionnaire be returned by a particular date. Set this date so that the respondent will have sufficient time to fill out and return the questionnaire without rushing, but is not likely to put it aside until later. People tend to procrastinate if too generous a time allowance is given. A rule of thumb is to calculate the probable mailing time and allow the individual an additional week to complete the questionnaire and return it. You should include a stamped, self-addressed envelope with the questionnaire, so that individuals can respond with a minimum of inconvenience.

The design and neatness of your questionnaire and accompanying letter can improve the response rate. With up-to-date word-processing software, it is possible to produce a cover letter with personalized address information, and a handwritten signature of a different color can be scanned into the original. The questionnaire itself can be word

18. Edwards, P., Roberts, I., Clarke, M., DiGuiseppi, C., Pratap, S., Wentz, R., & Kwan, I. (2002). Increasing response rates to postal questionnaires: Systematic review. *British Medical Journal, 324*(7347), 1183–1185. Retrieved May 1, 2005, from http://bmj.bmjjournals.com/cgi/reprint/324/7347/1183
19. Ibid, p. 1.

FIGURE 8.1

Sample Cover Letter for a Mail Questionnaire

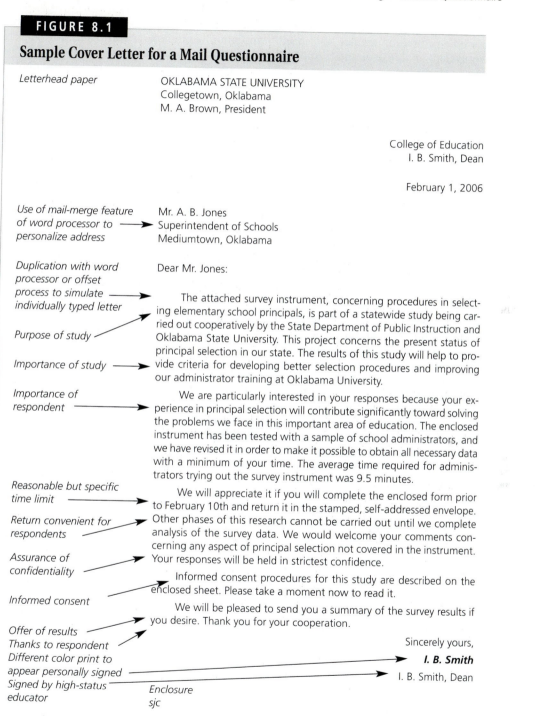

Letterhead paper

OKLAHAMA STATE UNIVERSITY
Collegetown, Oklahoma
M. A. Brown, President

College of Education
I. B. Smith, Dean

February 1, 2006

Use of mail-merge feature of word processor to personalize address →

Mr. A. B. Jones
Superintendent of Schools
Mediumtown, Oklahoma

Duplication with word processor or offset process to simulate individually typed letter →

Dear Mr. Jones:

Purpose of study

The attached survey instrument, concerning procedures in selecting elementary school principals, is part of a statewide study being carried out cooperatively by the State Department of Public Instruction and Oklahoma State University. This project concerns the present status of principal selection in our state. The results of this study will help to pro-

Importance of study →

vide criteria for developing better selection procedures and improving our administrator training at Oklahoma University.

Importance of respondent →

We are particularly interested in your responses because your experience in principal selection will contribute significantly toward solving the problems we face in this important area of education. The enclosed instrument has been tested with a sample of school administrators, and we have revised it in order to make it possible to obtain all necessary data with a minimum of your time. The average time required for administrators trying out the survey instrument was 9.5 minutes.

Reasonable but specific time limit →

We will appreciate it if you will complete the enclosed form prior to February 10th and return it in the stamped, self-addressed envelope.

Return convenient for respondents →

Other phases of this research cannot be carried out until we complete analysis of the survey data. We would welcome your comments concerning any aspect of principal selection not covered in the instrument.

Assurance of confidentiality →

Your responses will be held in strictest confidence.

Informed consent →

Informed consent procedures for this study are described on the enclosed sheet. Please take a moment now to read it.

Offer of results
Thanks to respondent →

We will be pleased to send you a summary of the survey results if you desire. Thank you for your cooperation.

Sincerely yours,

Different color print to appear personally signed →

I. B. Smith

Signed by high-status educator →

I. B. Smith, Dean

Enclosure
sjc

processed to include different font colors, photographs, and graphics. The originals can then be printed on a color laser printer and photocopied on a color copier with nearly equivalent quality to an offset print job, at a fraction of the cost. Quality can be further enhanced by the use of bond paper, which has more weight and texture than standard photocopy paper.

Step 7: Following Up with Nonrespondents

A few days after the time limit specified in the cover letter for return of questionnaires, it is desirable to contact nonrespondents by sending a follow-up letter, along with another copy of the questionnaire and another self-addressed envelope.[20] If the original cover letter did not succeed with the nonrespondent group, there is little point in sending the same letter again. Instead, you should try a different approach in your appeal for cooperation. For example, if you used a personal appeal in the initial letter, you might try a professional appeal in the first follow-up letter.

Successful follow-up letters usually take the approach that the researcher is confident the individual wished to fill out the questionnaire, but perhaps because of some oversight or an error on the researcher's part, it was overlooked. The follow-up letter then should repeat the importance of the study and the value of the individual's contribution, but with somewhat different language and emphasis from that in the original letter.

Postcard reminders have been tried also, and in some cases they have been found as effective as letters. However, Blaine Worthen and E. J. Brezezinski found that a form letter with another copy of the questionnaire obtained up to 7 percent more responses than a postcard with the same message.[21]

Figure 8.2 shows the pattern of responses reported in a review of 98 experimental studies on this problem. Although the reviewers point out that the results varied considerably across studies, these average percentages suggest what can be expected from different numbers of follow-ups. A few of the studies used four or more follow-ups, but this did not lead to a significant increase in returns over three follow-ups.

Suppose that you have a substantial percentage of nonrespondents after reaching the cutoff date for the return of the questionnaires to be included in your data analysis. You should ask yourself: How would the results differ if all respondents had returned the questionnaire? If only a small percentage of respondents did not respond, the answer is not critical. If more than 20 percent are missing, however, you need to pose this question, because the sample for whom data are available might not be representative of the population to which you wish to generalize your findings. Researchers have found that respondents and nonrespondents to questionnaires do not differ in most personality characteristics, but nonrespondents tend to have achieved less academic success than respondents.[22]

The ideal method to determine whether nonrespondents to your questionnaire differ from the respondents is to randomly select a small number of individuals from the nonresponding group. Then solicit their cooperation in letting you administer the questionnaire to them in an in-person or telephone-interview format. Individuals who are reluctant to complete a questionnaire may be more amenable to these approaches.

---

20. Heberlein, T. A., & Baumgartner, R. (1981). Is a questionnaire necessary in a second mailing? *Public Opinion Quarterly, 45*, 102–108.
21. Worthen, B. R., & Brezezinski, E. J. (1973, February). An experimental study of techniques for increasing return rate in mail surveys. Paper presented at the annual meeting of the American Educational Research Association, New Orleans.
22. For a summary of these findings, see the discussion of differences between volunteers and nonvolunteers in Chapter 6.

FIGURE 8.2

Synthesis of Research Findings on Response Rates for Initial Mailing and Different Numbers of Follow-ups

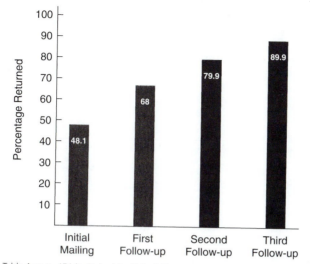

Source: Adapted from Table 1 on p. 451 in: Heberlein, T. A., & Baumgartner, P. (1978). Factors affecting response rates to mailed questionnaires: A quantitative analysis of the published literature. *American Sociological Review, 43*, 447–462. Reprinted with permission from the American Sociological Association and Thomas A. Heberlein.

A sample of 20 individuals should be sufficient to check the nonresponding group. A comparison of their responses to each item with the responses of those who replied initially will enable you to determine whether the nonresponding sample is biased. In this case, you should note these differences and discuss their significance in reporting the results of the responding sample.

Step 8: Analyzing Questionnaire Data

The researchers who studied the teaching of qualitative research in institutions of higher education in the United States followed a typical approach to analyzing questionnaire data:

> All forced-choice answers in the survey were coded and entered into the *Ecstatic* analysis program for quantitative data. This procedure allowed the easy generation of percentages, means, ranges, and cross tabulations. All comments and open-ended answers were entered in full into the *Ethnograph* text analysis program which assisted in coding and sorting respondents' words so that patterns could be ascertained.[23]

23. Glesne & Webb, Teaching qualitative research, p. 254. *Ecstatic* is a computer program for statistical analysis of data. *Ethnograph* is a computer program for analyzing documents and transcriptions. Cross-tabulations are statistical analyses that show the relationship between two variables.

TABLE 8.2

Formal Coursework in Qualitative Research Taken by Faculty Teaching Qualitative Methods Courses

Title	Coursework (%)	Little or No Coursework (%)	Total
Full Professors	6 (24%)	19 (76%)	25
Males*	2 (8%)	17 (68%)	19
Females	4 (16%)	2 (8%)	6
Associate Professors	16 (57%)	12 (43%)	28
Males	5 (18%)	7 (25%)	12
Females	11 (39%)	5 (18%)	16
Assistant Professors	15 (83%)	3 (16%)	18
Males	6 (33%)	1 (5%)	7
Females*	9 (50%)	2 (11%)	11

*Indicates that one respondent did not answer the question; the two lecturers were not included in the table.

Source: Table 1 on p. 255 in: Glesne, C., & Webb, R. (1993). Teaching qualitative research: Who does what? *International Journal of Qualitative Studies in Education, 6,* 253–266. Reprinted with permission of Taylor & Francis, Ltd. and Dr. Corrine Glesne.

The quantitative data were analyzed to yield frequencies and percentages of respondents checking each response category on particular closed-form questions. For example, Table 8.2 shows the degree to which professors teaching qualitative research methods courses had themselves taken formal coursework in qualitative research. Glesne and Webb concluded from these results that

> new faculty responsible for teaching qualitative methods courses generally have had more formal course work in qualitative methodology than older professors. . . . These percentages are not surprising, since the offering of qualitative research courses is fairly recent in most colleges of education. . . . What is surprising is that at each of the professorate levels, a higher percentage of women were trained in qualitative research than men.[24]

The results shown in Table 8.2 are consistent with the data obtained from a causal-comparative research design (see Chapter 10). None of the three variables—professorial rank, gender, and amount of qualitative-research coursework—was experimentally manipulated by the researchers. The three variables were related to each other in the data analysis in such a way as to reveal potential cause-and-effect relationships. In particular, the observed relationship between gender and coursework suggests (but by no means *proves*) that gender plays a causal role in whether an individual chooses to specialize in qualitative research methods. Further research would be necessary to determine whether and how these two variables are causally related to each other.

We emphasize this feature of Glesne and Webb's data analysis because it is commonly assumed that questionnaires and interviews are only suitable, or most suitable, for descriptive research. In fact, questionnaires and interviews can be used in various research designs.

Glesne and Webb also used a qualitative research approach in the analysis of their survey data. They included written comments from respondents, which provides an emic (i.e., the respondents') perspective, on the phenomenon being studied. They cite this

24. Glesne & Webb, Teaching qualitative research, p. 255.

comment from a respondent to an open-form question about what excites them about teaching qualitative research methods courses:

> I really enjoy and feel challenged to support students' research and their forays into what is often new territory—seeing their eyes light up when they see what research can be and when they move from "I thought it'd be easier" to "Wow, I never knew what was involved!"[25]

Quantitative data collected by questionnaires can be analyzed by the statistical methods described in Chapter 5. Methods for analyzing qualitative data are described in Chapter 14.

Steps in Preparing and Conducting Research Interviews

The steps involved in using interviews in educational research are similar to those involved in using questionnaires. The steps are (1) defining the purpose of the study, (2) selecting a sample, (3) designing the interview format, (4) developing questions, (5) selecting and training interviewers, (6) doing a pilot test of the interview procedures, (7) conducting the interviews, and (8) analyzing the interview data.[26]

Step 1: Defining the Purpose of the Interview

The first step in a study that will employ interviews to collect research data is to define the purpose of the study. Your purpose will determine the nature of the interview because different purposes require different levels of structure, types of questions, and interviewer qualifications.

The different interests and orientations of researchers have given rise to different types of interviews. Several have been developed for a particular purpose and context, but you may be able to adapt them for investigating your research problem. The following are three major types of research interviews: key informant interviews, survey interviews, and group interviews.

Key Informant Interviews

In a **key informant interview,** the interviewer collects data from individuals who have special knowledge or perceptions that would not otherwise be available to the researcher. Key informants often have more knowledge, better communication skills, or different perspectives than other members of the defined population.

A study by Eleanor Lynch, Rena Lewis, and Diane Murphy illustrates the use of key informant interviews in educational research.[27] The researchers described the purpose of their study as follows:

> The changing needs of children with chronic illnesses pose some serious questions:
>
> - How can school systems respond most effectively to the needs of children with chronic illness?
> - Should children be served under special education? If yes, how can procedures be adapted to allow for the week-to-week differences in children's educational needs?

Touchstones in Research

Fontana, A., & Frey, J. H. (2000). The interview: From neutral stance to political involvement. In N. K. Denzin & Y. S. Lincoln (Eds.), *Handbook of qualitative research* (3rd ed., pp. 695–727). Thousand Oaks, CA: Sage.

Gubrium, J. F., & Holstein, J. A. (Eds.). (2002). *Handbook of interview research: Context & method.* Thousand Oaks, CA: Sage.

25. Ibid., p. 262.
26. These steps are adapted from Stewart, C. J., & Cash, W. B., Jr. (1997). *Interviewing: Principles and practices* (8th ed.). Madison, WI: Brown & Benchmark.
27. Lynch, E. W., Lewis, R. B., & Murphy, D. S. (1992). Educational services for children with chronic illnesses: Perspectives of educators and families. *Exceptional Children, 59,* 210–220.

- How can we ensure that adequate information is available to teachers and other school personnel working with children with chronic illnesses?
- What do families want for their children with chronic illness and how can schools help support families' wishes?[28]

The researchers identified two groups of key informants from whom to collect interview data relating to these questions. One group was school district personnel who were in charge of services for children with chronic illnesses. This group could be expected to have expert knowledge about the research problem being investigated. The other group included parents of chronically ill children. The parents were key informants because they had direct knowledge of their family's needs with respect to the chronically ill child. We refer to this study by Lynch and her associates in the following sections to illustrate the various steps that are involved in using interviews in a research study.

Survey Interviews

Touchstone in Research

Singleton, R. A., Jr., & Straits, B. C. (2002). Survey interviewing. In J. F. Gubrium & J. A. Holstein (Eds.), *Handbook of interview research: Context & method* (pp. 59–82). Thousand Oaks, CA: Sage.

The purpose of **survey interviews** is to supplement data that have been collected by other methods. Margaret LeCompte, Judith Preissle, and Renata Tesch describe three types of survey interviews.[29] The first type is the **confirmation survey interview,** which is a structured interview that produces evidence to confirm earlier findings. These interviews are especially useful in large-scale questionnaire studies where in-depth interviewing cannot be carried out for all respondents.

The second type of survey interview is the **participant construct interview,** which is used to learn how informants structure their physical and social world. The result is a set of category systems used by the participant. For example, LeCompte conducted a research study in which she asked kindergarten children to tell her all the things they thought they and their teachers could do in kindergarten.[30] The responses were used to develop a typology of children's perceptions of student and teacher roles.

The third type of survey interview involves the interviewer's use of projective techniques to obtain responses from an interviewee. **Projective techniques** present ambiguous stimuli to elicit subconscious perceptions that would be difficult to observe in a natural setting or solicit through regular interviewing. Projective techniques are further explained in Chapter 7.

Focus Group Interviews

Touchstones in Research

Morgan, D. L. (1997). *Focus groups as qualitative research* (2nd ed.). Thousand Oaks, CA: Sage.

Williams, A., & Katz, L. (2001). The use of focus group methodology in education: Some theoretical and practical considerations. *International Electronic Journal for Leadership in Learning, 5*(3). Retrieved February 15, 2006, from http://www.ucalgary.ca/~iejll/volume5/katz.html

A group interview involves addressing questions to a group of individuals who have been assembled for this specific purpose. The individuals are selected because they are well informed about the research topic.

Group interviews have been used extensively by social science researchers and marketing researchers, who call them *focus group interviews,* or simply *focus groups.* Richard Krueger and Mary Anne Casey identified the following as characteristics of a **focus group:**

> [It is] a carefully planned discussion designed to obtain perceptions on a defined area of interest in a permissive, nonthreatening environment. It is conducted with approximately seven to ten people by a skilled interviewer. The discussion is relaxed, comfortable, and often enjoyable for participants as they share their ideas and perceptions. Group members influence each other by responding to ideas and comments in the discussion.[31]

28. Ibid., pp. 211–212.
29. LeCompte, M. D., Preissle, J., & Tesch, R. (1993). *Ethnography and qualitative design in educational research* (2nd ed.). San Diego, CA: Academic Press.
30. LeCompte, M. D. (1980). The civilizing of children: How young children learn to become students. *The Journal of Thought, 15,* 105–126.
31. Krueger, R. A., & Casey, M. A. (2000). *Focus groups: A practical guide for applied research* (3rd ed.). Thousand Oaks, CA: Sage. Quote appears on p. 18.

Qualitative researchers have become interested in the use of focus groups to collect data in recent years. These researchers are finding that the interactions among the participants stimulate them to state feelings, perceptions, and beliefs that they would not express if interviewed individually. Also, the focus group technique avoids putting the interviewers in a directive role. They ask questions to initiate discussion, but then allow participants to take major responsibility for stating their views and drawing out the views of others in the group.

Procedures for selecting a focus group are described in the next section.

Step 2: Selecting a Sample

A sample of respondents should be selected using one of the quantitative or qualitative sampling techniques described in Chapter 6. To study needed services for children with chronic illnesses, Lynch and her associates selected two samples: (1) a stratified random sample of school districts in California, and (2) a nonrandom sample of families with such children. Separate interview guides were developed for respondents in each sample.

Interviewers typically interview one respondent at a time, as in Lynch's study. It also is possible to conduct a focus group interview, as we explained in the preceding section. The focus group may consist of an established group, such as the teachers in a particular school. When using an established group, the researcher needs to be sensitive to pre-existing relationships among the group members. The focus group technique works best when all members are on an equal basis—for example, all the teaching staff of a preschool. If the school principal is included, the teachers may feel inhibited about sharing their actual perceptions of the phenomena being investigated.

Focus groups generally include seven to ten individuals. This group size encourages a wide sampling of views, but it is not so large that some individuals are deprived of an opportunity to speak.

When interviewing individuals, you can arrange to meet with each respondent at your mutual convenience. For a focus group, however, all respondents must be assembled at the same time and place. This is not an easy task, and so you will need to follow systematic procedures to ensure that it is accomplished successfully.[32]

Step 3: Designing the Interview Format

Quantitative and qualitative research interviews differ in whether the variables are pre-specified. In quantitative studies, the variables of interest to the researcher generally are prespecified. For example, suppose the researcher wishes to determine the factors that influence students to choose a particular major in college. Through a review of the literature, the researcher might discover that parents, parents' friends, relatives, teachers, and other students are possible sources of influence. In designing the interview the researcher would ask questions about each of these sources of influence, for example: "Did your father influence your choice of major?"

If a similar study were done from a qualitative research perspective, there might be little or no prespecification of variables. Instead, the interview questions might be broader in nature, for example: "How did you come to be an economics major?" At the stage of analyzing the data, the researcher might choose to identify quantifiable variables or broad themes and patterns.

Research interviews in quantitative and qualitative research also tend to differ in the degree of structure used in their designs. Quantitative research interviews usually are

---

32. Procedures for arranging a focus group meeting are described in Chapter 6 of Krueger & Casey, *Focus groups.*

somewhat structured so that all respondents are exposed to a nearly identical interview experience. In this case, structure involves carefully specifying in advance the opening statement, interview questions, and closing remarks to be used by all interviewers, to ensure that data from all respondents can be compared precisely.

Qualitative research interviews typically involve a format that is not as tightly structured, because the researcher's goal is to help respondents express their views of a phenomenon in their own terms. In both types of research, however, interviews can vary in the degree of structure they utilize. Below we describe three typical interview formats in quantitative research, followed by three typical interview formats in qualitative research, ordered in each case from the least to the most structured design.

Interview Formats in Quantitative Research

Interviews in quantitative research vary in structure. The three basic approaches are described below.

The **unstructured interview** does not involve a detailed interview guide. Instead, the interviewer asks questions that gradually lead the respondent to give the desired information. Usually the type of information sought is difficult for the respondent to express or is psychologically sensitive. For this reason the interviewer must adapt continuously to the respondent's perceived state of mind. This format is fairly subjective and time consuming.

The **semistructured interview** involves asking a series of structured questions and then probing more deeply with open-form questions to obtain additional information. For example, suppose a researcher is investigating the relationship between students' high school experiences and their subsequent achievement in college. In one part of the interview, the interviewer might try to elicit significant experiences in coursework by asking all respondents: "What course did you like best?" Suppose the respondent answers, "I liked chemistry best because the teacher made it interesting." At this point, the interviewer might probe by asking: "How did the teacher make it interesting?" Another respondent might say, "I liked my government class because we talked about real-life problems." The interviewer then might probe by asking such questions as: "What are some examples of these problems?" and "Why did you find these problems interesting?" In these two examples, the interviewer began with the same initial question but asked different probing questions based on the respondent's answer. This interview approach has the advantage of providing reasonably standard data across respondents, but of greater depth than can be obtained from a structured interview.

The study of children with chronic illness that we have been describing involved a semistructured telephone interview. When an appropriate respondent from each district was identified, this individual was sent an information packet that included the interview protocol. This procedure provided the respondent an opportunity to review the questions and prepare for the interview. Specific questions were drafted and formatted by the three researchers working as a team, reviewed and revised by state department of education personnel who had content and research expertise, and subjected to final review and revision by an advisory committee. In addition to experts, the advisory committee included representatives of the following groups: special educators, other teachers, parents of chronically ill children, and university students with chronic illnesses.

The **structured interview** involves a series of closed-form questions that either have yes-no answers or can be answered by selecting from among a set of short-answer choices. The respondents' answers are not followed up to obtain greater depth, and thus are similar to those obtained from a questionnaire. The advantage of an interview over a questionnaire in this case, however, is that the response rate can be increased, because the interviewer can interact with individuals to reduce the number of unusable or "don't know" responses.

Interview Formats in Qualitative Research

Michael Patton describes three basic approaches to collecting qualitative data through open-ended interviews, described below.[33]

The **informal conversational interview** relies entirely on the spontaneous generation of questions in a natural interaction, typically one that occurs as part of ongoing participant observation fieldwork. (Participant observation is explained in Chapter 9.) Because the conversation appears natural, the research participants may not even realize that they are being interviewed.

The **general interview guide approach** involves outlining a set of topics to be explored with each respondent. The use of an interview guide is based on the assumption that there is common information to be obtained from each respondent, but no set of standardized questions is written in advance. The order in which the topics are explored and the wording of the questions are not predetermined. They can be decided by the interviewer as the interview progresses.

The **standardized open-ended interview** involves a predetermined sequence and wording of the same set of questions to be asked of each respondent, in order to minimize the possibility of bias. This interview format is particularly appropriate when a large number of people are to conduct interviews on the same topic and the researcher wishes to reduce the variation in responses due to the fact that, left to themselves, different interviewers will ask questions on a single topic in different ways. The data obtained are thus systematic and thorough, but the process reduces flexibility and spontaneity for both the interviewer and the respondent.

Telephone Interviews

The telephone commonly is used for interviewing because it is much less expensive than face-to-face interviews, especially when the sample is geographically dispersed. Although its relatively lower cost is the greatest advantage of telephone interviews, they have other significant advantages as well:

1. You can select respondents from a broader accessible population than if interviewers needed to travel to the location of each respondent.
2. Because all interviewers can work from a central location, monitoring of interviews and quality control is easier.
3. Since little cost is incurred when no one answers, frequent callbacks are feasible.
4. Many groups, such as business people, school personnel, and parents, are easier to reach by telephone than by personal visits.
5. Telephone interviewing provides safe access to dangerous locations and access to restricted locations where interviewers might not be admitted.

There is some evidence that telephone interviews can be used to collect sensitive data. One study found that for nonthreatening questions respondents' distortions were slightly higher in telephone interviews than in face-to-face interviews.[34] For threatening questions, distortions were lower in telephone interviews. Although it would seem easier to

---

33. Patton, M. Q. (2002). *Qualitative research and evaluation methods* (3rd ed.). Thousand Oaks, CA: Sage.
34. Graves, R. M., & Kahn, R. L. (1979). *Surveys by telephone: A national comparison with personal interviews.* New York: Academic Press.

Touchstone in Research

Seidman, I. E. (1997). *Interviewing as qualitative research: A guide for researchers in education and the social sciences* (2nd ed.). New York: Teachers College.

Touchstones in Research

Bourque, L. B., & Fielder, E. P. (2002). *How to conduct telephone surveys.* Thousand Oaks, CA: Sage.

Lavrakas, P. J. (1998). Methods for sampling and interviewing in telephone surveys. In L. Bickman & D. J. Rog (Eds.), *Handbook of applied social research methods* (pp. 429–472). Thousand Oaks, CA: Sage.

establish rapport in a face-to-face interview, the physical presence of the interviewer might increase the perceived threat of questions about sensitive topics. Hanging up a phone obviously is easier than ejecting an interviewer from one's home or office. Nevertheless, some investigators have been successful in completing a very high percentage of telephone interviews, even when dealing with sensitive topics. In one study, completed interviews were obtained from 74 percent of the sample in personal interviews and 70 percent in telephone interviews.[35] Because the same items were used for the personal and telephone interviews, it was possible to compare the responses for the two methods. The results generally were very similar over a wide range of topics and item formats.

As we noted above, the study by Lynch and her associates concerning the educational needs of children with chronic illnesses was conducted by telephone.

When selecting a sample for a telephone interview, you will need the telephone number of each individual whom you select. If you use an organization's directory to select a sample, the members' telephone numbers may be listed. If not, you will need to determine the phone numbers by another procedure. The city telephone directory is useful, except for individuals who have unlisted numbers. (CD-ROMs and Web databases listing all telephone numbers in the United States are available as well.) Some individuals do not have telephones or have unlisted cell phones. There is currently no directory of cell phone numbers, and efforts to establish a national directory have met with resistance.[36] The National Do Not Call Registry lists phone numbers of individuals who do not wish to receive telephone calls from telemarketers, but telephone surveyors who are not offering goods or services are free of its restrictions.[37]

Keep in mind that if your telephone interview sample does not include individuals who have no telephone number, or whose number you cannot access, it represents a biased sample, which weakens the generalizability of your research results.[38]

Computer-Assisted Telephone Interviews

Computer-assisted telephone interviews involve the use of a computer to assist in gathering information from telephone interviews. This method virtually eliminates two major sources of common errors in interviews, that is, asking the wrong questions and recording data in the wrong place on the form. Most telephone interviews require the interviewer to jump to a different part of the form depending on the response of the person interviewed. For example, if the question is "Are you employed?" a "Yes" response might call for the interviewer to check this response on the interview guide and then turn three pages to a set of questions on mode of employment. If the interviewer does not turn the correct number of pages, inappropriate questions may be asked next, with the possible result of an incorrectly shortened interview.

This problem can be avoided by developing a computer program that not only records the individual's responses but also branches to the next question that should be asked. For example, as the interviewer types "Yes" (or a code like "Y") into the computer, the response will be recorded and the computer can be programmed to jump three pages in the computer file containing the interview guide and display the first question on mode of employment. The interviewer does not have to worry about turning pages, nor does she even

35. Ibid.
36. Information on the status of a national cell phone directory bill is available at the Web site http://www.wireless.weblogsinc.com/, retrieved May 26, 2005.
37. Information on the National Do Not Call Registry is available at the Web site https://www.donotcall.gov/, retrieved May 26, 2005.
38. For a review of changes in telephone survey response rates and their causes, see Curtin, R., Presser, S., & Singer, E. (2005). Changes in telephone survey nonresponse over the past quarter century. *Public Opinion Quarterly, 69*(1), 87–98.

see any inappropriate questions. The next question that appears is the one needed. Response accuracy generally increases with such computer-assisted interview techniques, because the interviewer can concentrate on responses rather than worry about what question to ask next. Also, because the interviewees' responses are entered into a computer file while the interview is in progress, the data are ready for statistical analysis by computer as soon as all the interviews are completed.

It obviously is difficult, however, for an interviewer to record lengthy open-form responses, which are typical in qualitative research. Web interviews help to overcome this difficulty, because the respondents can enter their responses themselves (see below). Another emerging strategy for transferring interview responses to computer files involves the use of voice-recognition software. The interviewer can record the responses (and probes, if any) into a hand-held recorder or mini-disk and then transcribe them later.

Web Interviews

Researchers are finding that through the use of the Internet they can interview types of respondents who would otherwise be difficult to reach. They can also design their interviews to take advantage of the unique opportunities of such communication approaches as email and chat rooms.

Nicole Shepherd conducted qualitative research interviews through computer-mediated communications (CMC) with young people suffering from depression.[39] The individuals who were interviewed responded to an invitation on a Web site that offers information and an online chat facility to support those suffering from depression.

Shepherd gave participants a choice of the medium in which she would interview them: face to face (for those who lived in the same city as the researcher), telephone, email, or through her own chat room.[40] Of 46 semistructured interviews, 13 were conducted by email and 7 by chat room. While she found the chat room interviews slow and frustrating, Shepherd discovered that "email lent itself to personal disclosure."[41]

With respect to the potential for online communication to enable distortion of individuals' true identity, the author notes, "Communicating online does enhance the ability of participants to lie about their embodied identities, but if the researcher is interested in exploring cultural themes or discourses this may not be of great importance."[42]

Step 4: Developing Questions

Whether questions are developed in advance of the interview or during the actual interview depends mainly on the type of interview. The unstructured interview in quantitative research and the informal conversational interview in qualitative research involve on-the-spot formulation of questions, based on a general plan and the interviewer's reading of relevant characteristics of each respondent (e.g., level of poise, talkativeness, and intelligence). The other interview formats make greater use of prespecified closed-form and open-form questions. For example, in the study of the needs of children with chronic illnesses, a series of open-form and closed-form questions was used.

The formulation of good questions in interviews at the unstructured end of the continuum depends more on the interviewer's ability to think on his feet during the interview

39. Shepherd, N. (2003). Interviewing online: Qualitative research in the network(ed) society. Paper presented at the Association of Qualitative Research Conference, July 17–19, Sydney, Australia; retrieved May 3, 2005, from http://eprint.uq.edu.au/archive/00001436/
40. For an explanation of chat rooms see: Fetterman, D. M. (2002). Web surveys to digital movies: Technological tools of the trade. *Educational Researcher, 6,* 29–37.
41. Ibid., Rapport and CMC, paragraph 1.
42. Ibid., Rapport and CMC, paragraph 6.

process. Developing questions for more structured interviews is best done by designing and trying out an interview guide. An **interview guide** specifies the questions, the sequence in which they are to be asked, and guidelines for what the interviewer is to say at the beginning and end of each interview. The interview guide should list the response options for each closed-form question and provide space for the interviewer to write down answers that do not fit prespecified response categories.

Figure 8.3 shows an interview guide from a study by Michael Ann Rossi. Her research project involved case studies of "teacher-leaders" in mathematics: teachers who had participated in a special mathematics institute and returned to their school district in a leadership role to improve mathematics instruction. Rossi was particularly interested in the strategies and skills of these teacher-leaders, and the outcomes that they effected. Her data-collection method involved interviewing each teacher-leader, the teacher-leader's supervisor, and teachers with whom the teacher-leader had worked. Separate interview guides were developed for each of these groups. The interview guide shown in Figure 8.3 was for interviewing teachers with whom the teacher-leader had worked.

Step 5: Selecting and Training Interviewers

You will need to decide how many interviewers to employ and whether they must have special qualifications. Probably, the most important selection criterion is the interviewer's ability to relate to respondents positively. An interviewer who might do a fine job of interviewing successful teachers might be totally unsuited to interview unmarried pregnant teenagers, for example.

Distinctive Respondents

Researchers have sought to determine how interviewers' personal characteristics (e.g., social class, age, race, gender) may affect the responses of individuals with similar or different characteristics.[43] Some researchers have tried matching interviewers and respondents on such variables in an attempt to improve research processes or outcomes. Something beyond matching, however, is necessary to ensure that individuals fitting any and every cultural category are treated respectfully and are truthfully represented in any research endeavor. Let us take gender as an example. While we conveniently treat gender as a dichotomous variable, this ignores the fact that some individuals identify as transgendered, gay, or otherwise nontraditional with respect to gender identification and/or sexual orientation. Thus researchers need to address, and yet also be sensitive to, the differences beyond those conveyed by traditional notions of gender, class, race, and so forth, in their relationships with research participants. They also need to pay attention to the fact that each individual has a unique location within the constellation of all such categories.[44]

Respondents as Interviewers

Some researchers recommend selecting interviewers from the respondent target population. An example of this approach is an investigation of at-risk students in urban high

43. For examples of research studies that have explored interviewer effects, see Rodgers, W., & Herzog, R. (1983). Interviewer effects on responses of younger and older respondents. Paper presented at the annual meeting of the Gerontological Society of America, San Francisco, November 20 (ERIC Accession No. ED241596); Nederhof, A. J. (1981). Impact of interviewer's sex on volunteering by females. *Perceptual and Motor Skills, 52*, 25–26; Shosteck, H. (1977). Respondent militancy as a control variable for interviewer effect. *Journal of Social Issues, 33*, 36–45.
44. For detailed discussions of challenges in and recommendations for interviewing children and adolescents, men, women, older people, elites, and the ill, as well as queering the interview and dealing with race in the interview process, see the eight chapters of Part II, Distinctive Respondents, in Gubrium, J. F., & Holstein, J. A. (Eds.). (2002). *Handbook of interview research: Context and method.* Thousand Oaks, CA: Sage.

FIGURE 8.3

Guide for Interviewing Teachers Who Worked with a Teacher-Leader

(Start by alluding to introduction from teacher-leader.) This is a visit to get acquainted. *It's not an evaluation of you,* of your school program, or of the teacher-leader. I would like to get a picture of mathematics teaching and learning in your school. My main focus is how you have worked with other people along the way regarding getting help with mathematics teaching and learning. I want to understand the story since _____ until now. I have a number of specific questions to ask.

1. Background
   a. Name
   b. Job title (or role)
   c. Thumbnail sketch of your job; what you do, who you work with.
   d. How long have you been teaching?
   e. How long have you been in this school?
2. I'm interested in the *flavor* or feeling in the school.
   a. Can you give me 3 or 4 adjectives that would describe that?
   b. Can you think back to when your school first got involved with changing mathematics teaching and learning?
      • when was that?
      • why did the school get involved?
      • how did you personally get involved?
      • what did you expect?
      • what do you think the teacher-leader expected?
   c. Could you give me a quick sketch of how mathematics teaching and learning is changing in your school right now?
      • are teachers involved as individuals?
      • how many are involved?
      • what is the role of the principal? is *she* supportive of change, or blocking it?
      • what is the purpose of the change?
      • what procedures or guidelines are followed, methods used?
      • what does the teacher-leader do?
3. a. Describe your involvement since that time.
   b. What contact have you had with others who are involved? (Especially PROBE for communication, cooperation, peer coaching)
   c. Are there stages or phases that can be identified regarding *your* involvement with the change? Your *school's* involvement?
4. Generally speaking, what do you see as the teacher-leader's main role?
   a. What's been *her* main contribution to your school's mathematics program?
   b. Can you give me a few adjectives to describe *her style,* way of working with people?
   c. What do you see as *her* special strengths?
   d. Could you tell me about a specific incident when ___ was *especially helpful?*
      • What did *she* do?
      • Why did you think this was helpful?
      • What skills did you see *her* using in this situation?
   e. Now let's take another incident.
      • What did *she* do, in detail?
      • Why did you think this was helpful?
      • What skills did you see *her* using in this situation?
   f. Do you think *her* skills and strengths have changed since you've known her? (GET ILLUSTRATIONS AND EXAMPLES)
   g. Ask questions d, e, and f except use *practical* rather than helpful.

(Continued)

FIGURE 8.3

(Continued)

5. I'm interested in the program's results. For (1) you, (2) other teachers, and (3) the students:
   a. What results have occurred?
   b. Why do you think these results happened?
   c. In your opinion, how did ___ contribute to these results?
6. a. What would you say are the necessary ingredients of success in this kind of program?
   b. Specifically, what recommendations do you have for how Math Project teacher-leaders work and who is selected?
7. Do you have anything else to add?

Source: Appendix F in: Rossi, M. A. (1993). The California Mathematics Project: Empowering elementary teachers to be leaders and change agents in mathematics reform. *Dissertation Abstracts International, 54* (09), 3314A (UMI No. 9405218)

schools by Edwin Farrell, George Peguero, Rasheed Lindsey, and Ronald White.[45] The study involved an ethnographic perspective, and interviewing was the primary method of data collection. In designing the study, the principal investigator (Farrell) noted the difficulty involved in him, "a white, middle class, middle-aged academic," collecting data in "a social setting made up, for the most part, of low-income black and Hispanic adolescents."[46] Farrell dealt with the problem by recruiting students from the target population (students identified as at risk of dropping out of high school) to serve as interviewers. Seven students collected the interview data and also participated in the data analysis. Three of the students who worked for the duration of the project were listed as co-authors of the journal article reporting the study's findings.

Training of Interviewers

Once interviewers are selected, all of them should be given training. The amount of training needed will be greater as its structure decreases and the depth of the interview increases. The training usually is carried out in two phases. In the first phase, the trainees study the interview guide and learn about the interview conditions (e.g., topics being investigated, logistics, necessary controls, and safeguards). The researcher's hypotheses or expected results should not be discussed with the interviewers at this point, because they are likely to bias the interviewers. Interviewers should become so familiar with the interview guide (wording, format, recording procedures, and allowable probes) that they can conduct the interview in a conversational manner without hesitating, backtracking, or needing to reread or study the guide.

In the second phase of training, trainees should conduct practice interviews and receive corrective feedback until their performance becomes polished and reaches the desired level of standardization or structure, objectivity, and reliability. Making a videotape recording of practice interviews provides effective models of acceptable interviewing techniques and corrective feedback. The videotape can be replayed several times so that trainees, preferably meeting as a group, can locate procedural errors, identify better procedures, and discuss alternative ways of dealing with problems that arise.

45. Farrell, E., Peguero, G., Lindsey, R., & White, R. (1988). Giving voice to high school students: Pressure and boredom, 'ya know what I'm sayin'?' *American Educational Research Journal, 25,* 489–502.
46. Ibid., p. 490.

Depending on the interview task, some trainees may not be able to achieve the criterion standards of performance. Other trainees may not be able to stay with the project for its duration. For example, in Farrell's study of at-risk students described above, four student interviewers left the project at various points in time. If you think that these problems are likely to arise in your study, you should consider recruiting and training more interviewers than you actually need.

In the study of children with chronic illnesses, one of the research team members, two graduate students, and a professional interviewer were trained in general techniques of telephone interviewing, use of the two interview guides, and procedures for recording responses. All interviewers were checked initially by a member of the research team to ensure that they were accurate, appropriate, and consistent in their approach. Periodic checks also were made throughout the study.

Interviewers who will conduct informal or unstructured interviews require special preparation. They should have access to senior researchers who can impart their artistry and experience. Also, senior researchers can model the interviewing process and supervise new interviewers as they practice the process.

Step 6: Pilot-Testing the Interview

Although interviews provide valuable data, they are quite susceptible to bias. Therefore, the interview guide and procedures should be pilot-tested to ensure that they will yield reasonably unbiased data. During the pilot interviews the researcher should be alert to communication problems, evidence of inadequate motivation on the part of respondents, and other clues that suggest the need for rephrasing questions or revising the procedure. The pilot test also can be used to identify threatening questions. Questionnaires containing questions of a sensitive nature have been found to be less likely to be returned.[47] Norman Bradburn and his associates defined a question as threatening when 20 percent or more of the respondents feel that most people would be very uneasy talking about the topic.[48] This criterion can be employed in the pilot test to identify such questions. If threatening questions are found, procedures should be developed to lower or eliminate their threat value. Randomized response measurement techniques have also been proposed as a way to overcome interviewees' unwillingness to answer embarrassing or threatening questions truthfully.[49]

Several methods of opening the interview should be tried to determine the one that establishes the best rapport and cooperation. Also, the researcher should evaluate methods of recording interview data to determine whether adequate information is being recorded, whether the recording method causes excessive breaks in communication during the interview, and whether methods for coding and analyzing the interview data are sound.

Even if a recorder will not be used during the regular interview procedure, recording pilot-test interviews is important. By playing back the interview or reading a transcript of it, interviewers can gain insights into their handling of the questions and become aware of problems that escaped them during the interview itself.

Interviewers also should consider selecting a subgroup from the pilot sample to check the wording of interview questions. As we discussed in the section on questionnaire pilot-testing, there is evidence that the same question can be interpreted differently by different

47. Edwards, et al., Increasing response rates.
48. Bradburn, N. M., Sudman, S., et al. (1981). *Improving interview method and questionnaire design.* San Francisco: Jossey-Bass.
49. Soeken, K. L. (1987). Randomized response methodology in health research. *Evaluation and the Health Professions, 10*(1), 58–66.

TABLE 8.3

Guidelines for Conducting a Research Interview

1. Assure respondents of absolute confidentiality before beginning the interview. If necessary, explain the procedures that will be used to assure confidentiality.
2. Build rapport by engaging in small talk before beginning the interview and using an everyday conversational style.
3. Explain the potential benefits of the study to the respondents.
4. The interviewer should talk less than the respondent. As a rule, the less the interviewer talks, the more information is produced.
5. Pose questions in language that is clear and meaningful to the respondent.
6. Ask questions that contain only a single idea.
7. In phrasing questions, specify the frame of reference you want the respondent to use in answering the question. For example, ask, "What do you think of the way your child's teacher handles parent-teacher conferences?" rather than "What do you think of the teacher your child has this year?" The latter question might be appropriate, however, if the goal is to determine the respondent's salient frames of reference.
8. Use simple probes when appropriate, for example, "Can you tell me more about that?"
9. Avoid contradicting or appearing to cross-examine the respondent.
10. Do not hint—either by specific comment, tone of voice, or nonverbal cues such as shaking the head—at preferred or expected responses to particular questions.
11. If a respondent seems threatened by a specific topic, move on to another one. Try returning to the topic later, with different phrasing.
12. Save complex or controversial questions for the latter part of the interview after rapport has been established.
13. When posing threatening or sensitive questions, ask the respondent about the behavior of friends as well as about the respondent's own behavior.
14. Do not ask many closed-form questions in succession.
15. Do not change interview topics too often.
16. Avoid leading questions. For example ask, "What is your opinion of federal aid to education?" instead of "Do you favor federal aid to education?" However, in some cases a leading question may be asked to elicit a particular type of information from the respondent.

respondents. If this happens, the validity of the interview is threatened. By pretesting questions, you can identify those that are ambiguous and revise them until all or most respondents interpret them similarly.

Step 7: Conducting the Interview

Researchers have discovered many interviewer behaviors that affect the quality of data yielded by the interview method. A list of recommended behaviors, compiled from various sources, is presented in Table 8.3. Most apply to interviews conducted in the context of either quantitative research or qualitative research.

Interviewing Tasks

Researchers should consider reviewing the list of interview guidelines shown in Table 8.3 to determine those that are important for the particular interviews that they will conduct or will train others to conduct. In addition, they should consider how they will handle the following interview tasks. This list is adapted from Andrea Fontana and James Frey's description of unstructured interviewing in qualitative research.[50] These authors note, however, that any list of steps cannot be followed as a how-to approach, because interviewing is an ambiguous process that must be constructed in context.

Accessing the setting   Gaining access involves such considerations as how the interviewers present themselves and how they phrase their requests for participation and respond to potential interviewees' questions. (Also see the section on gaining entry in Chapter 14.)

Understanding the respondents' language and culture   Interviewers should have a good understanding of the language and culture of their respondents, especially if nuances of language and culture are important to understanding the phenomena being investigated. For example, suppose the interviewer is collecting data from computer educators in a variety of institutional settings. In the course of an interview, a computer educator may use technical language and refer to various aspects of his workplace. If the interviewer does not understand that terminology and workplace, his ability to probe responses and take notes could be significantly impaired. This problem can be remedied to an extent if the interviewer realizes when he is not understanding the respondent's comments and is comfortable enough to ask for clarification.

The interviewer also must decide which aspects of the respondent's behavior to focus on during the interview. If possible, he should attend not only to what the respondent says, but also to the respondent's nonverbal communication. With respect to the latter, Raymond Gorden distinguished between four types of nonverbal communication:

> *Proxemic* communication is the use of interpersonal space to communicate attitudes, *chronemics* communication is the use of pacing of speech and length of silence in conversation, *kinesic* communication includes any body movements or postures, and *paralinguistic* communication includes all the variations in volume, pitch and quality of voice.[51]

In addition, the respondent's dress and any personal items present during the interview (e.g., hair style, makeup, jewelry, or the presence of a radio, guitar, laptop computer, book, etc.) can be regarded as aspects of communication. Any of these forms of nonverbal communication can be a significant source of research data. If desired, the interviewers can be trained to observe and take notes on their presence during the interview.

Deciding how to present oneself   The interviewer will need to decide what type of personal image to present to respondents. For example, suppose that the interviewer's respondents are teachers. The interviewer might decide to present herself as both a researcher and a teacher (assuming that she has had teaching experience). In opening the interview, then, she might say something about why she is a researcher and also describe her background in teaching. The latter information might help to establish trust and rapport with respondents.

Other aspects of the interviewer's image need to be considered as well, among them dress, institutional affiliation, and ethnicity. The researcher will need to consider the respondents carefully to determine which aspects of the interviewer's image are likely to be salient to them, and whether these aspects of image are likely to have an adverse or positive effect on the interview process.

50. Fontana, A., & Frey, J. H. (2005). The interview: From neutral stance to political involvement. In N. K. Denzin & Y. S. Lincoln (Eds.), *The Sage handbook of qualitative research* (3rd ed., pp. 695–727). Thousand Oaks, CA: Sage.
51. Gorden, R. L. (1980). *Interviewing: Strategy, techniques, and tactics* (3rd ed.). Homewood, IL: Dorsey. Quote appears on p. 335.

Locating an informant Researchers are advised to find an insider to translate the cultural mores and language of the group from whom interviewees are selected and perhaps to be present during the interviews.

Gaining trust Trust can be an important factor in the interview process if sensitive topics are to be discussed. For example, school administrators may be quite willing to divulge their views about the best way to improve school climate. It may be an entirely different matter to ask their opinion about whether schools should provide counseling for students who have been identified as having a nonconventional sexual orientation. If sensitive topics are the focus of the research study, the interviewer will need to establish a deep level of trust in order to obtain the desired data.

Establishing rapport The interviewer needs to decide how much rapport to establish with each respondent. Superficial rapport may be sufficient if the respondent appears comfortable with the interview process. Stronger rapport is necessary if the interviewer wishes the respondent to reveal deeply personal or sensitive information. Beyond a certain point, however, building rapport might work against the interviewer. For example, the respondent might feel so comfortable that he chooses to spend the interview time talking about matters that are irrelevant to the researcher's purposes.

Recording Interview Data

Note taking or tape recording are the usual methods for preserving the information collected in an interview. Before choosing one of these methods, the interviewer should consider carefully the advantages and disadvantages of each.

If an interview guide is used, the interviewer probably should take handwritten notes directly on a copy of the interview guide. An alternative is to use a laptop computer: As the respondent answers questions, the responses can be keyboarded directly into a computer file. The chief advantage of note taking is that it facilitates data analysis. The information is readily accessible and much of it might already have been classified into appropriate response categories by the interviewer.

A disadvantage of note taking is that it might disrupt the quality of communication between the interviewer and the respondent. When questions deal with simple factual information, respondents typically expect their answers to be written down, and may appear upset if they are not. On the other hand, if respondents are asked to reveal sensitive or confidential information, note taking may distract them and prevent them from giving information they otherwise might have given. In this case, the interviewer should consider delaying note taking until after the interview is completed and the respondent has left the setting. The risk is that the interviewer will forget important details, particularly those that disagree with the interviewer's expectations.

The use of audio recorders has several advantages over note taking in recording interview data for research. Most importantly, it reduces the tendency of interviewers to make an unconscious selection of data favoring their biases. The audio recording provides a complete verbal record, and it can be studied much more thoroughly than data in the form of interviewer notes. A recorder also speeds up the interview process, because there is no need for extensive note taking. Furthermore, if the interview is recorded, two or more individuals who are trained in the data analysis procedures can listen to the recording—or read the transcript—and code it independently. The reliability of their frequency counts or ratings can then be determined.

The main disadvantages of recording an interview are (1) the presence of the recorder changes the interview situation to some degree and (2) unless you have the appropriate tools, transcribing or accessing the information that has been recorded can be very time consuming. In interviews involving highly personal information, respondents might be reluctant to express their feelings freely if they know that their responses are being recorded. The interviewer should carefully explain the purpose of the recording and gain the confidence of the respondent, so as to minimize any undesirable effects of having the interview recorded.

In doing telephone interviews, you can purchase a duplex recording jack that connects the telephone and the tape recorder that you plan to use. As soon as the phone is picked up, the recorder will begin recording, and it will record until the phone is hung up. You must inform the person to whom you are speaking that the telephone interview is being recorded.

If you wish to transcribe the taped material using a word processor, you can purchase a foot pedal that is connected to the tape recorder with a jack. You can listen to the tape either with earphones or through the regular speaker, press the foot pedal to stop the tape while you record each segment, then press the foot pedal again to restart the tape.

Software is now available to turn a computer into an audio recorder. This capability is especially useful if you have a laptop computer that you can take to sites where you plan to conduct interviews. The software allows you to record the interview, make notations in the recording, and control the replay to facilitate transcription. Other software is available to convert an audio recording or dictation into text.[52]

Whichever recording method you use, practice usually is necessary. You should reach a level of automaticity in your recording skills so that you can focus your attention on the interview process rather than on the recording process. Also, practice might identify problems and issues that are best addressed prior to formal data collection.

Step 8: Analyzing Interview Data

The analysis of responses to closed-form interview questions is straightforward. It is typical to calculate the percentage of respondents who indicated each response option for each item. For example, in the study of children with chronic illnesses, Lynch and her associates computed the percentage of school district personnel ($N = 80$) and family members ($N = 72$) who mentioned barriers to services for this type of child. The percentages are shown in Table 8.4. Note that only barriers mentioned by at least five respondents in each sample are included in the table.

The analysis of responses to open-form questions requires the development of a category system. An example of this approach can be found in George Kuh's study of the impact of out-of-class experiences on students in college.[53] A total of 149 college seniors at twelve institutions were interviewed by eight trained interviewers using a semistructured

---

52. Specific tape-recording and dictation software programs are described in: Fetterman, D. M. (1998). Webs of meaning: Computer and internet resources for educational research and instruction. *Educational Researcher, 27*(3), 22–30; for an overview of the use of digital audio and video recording technology in education, see Barron, A. E., Orwig, G. W., Ivers, K. S., & Lilavois, N. (2002). *Technologies for education: A practical guide* (4th ed). Englewood, CO: Libraries Unlimited; and the Web site Planning Above and Beyond (section on Digital Audio) at Web address http://planningaboveandbeyond.com/LearningZone/OnTheMove/DigitalAudio/, accessed May 26, 2005.
53. Kuh, G. D. (1993). In their own words: What students learn outside the classroom. *American Educational Research Journal, 30*, 277–304.

TABLE 8.4

Barriers to Services for Chronically Ill Children Cited More Than Five Times by Districts or Families

Barrier	Percentage Cited	Number
District		
Lack of adequate funding	28.8	23
Lack of public and staff awareness	27.5	22
Inadequate services	12.5	10
Not enough teachers for these students	11.3	9
Children fall behind in their schoolwork	8.8	7
Children's absences	8.8	7
Uncooperative parents	8.8	7
Responsibility in the system for these students unclear	7.5	6
Family		
Teachers don't understand child's needs	9.7	7
School systems and teachers are misinformed about the illness	8.3	6

Source: Table 2 on p. 215 in: Lynch, E. W., Lewis, R. B., & Murphy, D. S. (1992–1993). Educational services for children with chronic illness: Perspectives of educators and families. *Exceptional Children, 59*, 210–220. Copyright © 1993 by the Council for Exceptional Children. Reprinted with permission from the Council for Exceptional Children.

interview guide. The interviews were transcribed and then analyzed to determine what types of outcomes were mentioned by students. The analysis involved a five-step procedure:

1. A doctoral student read all the transcripts and developed a set of eight categories of outcomes mentioned by the college students.
2. Another individual read a sample of the transcripts, and based on her analysis, the outcomes were revised and expanded to ten categories.
3. Four readers analyzed a transcript using the set of categories developed in step 2. Their work resulted in an expanded set of 13 outcome categories.
4. The four readers analyzed four more transcripts, using the set of categories developed in step 3. Their work resulted in several minor revisions to the categories and the addition of an "other" category for miscellaneous outcomes.
5. The researcher used the category system to code all 149 transcripts. In other words, each mention of an outcome in an interview was coded as an instance of a particular category.

The following three categories illustrate the types of outcomes mentioned by students: (1) self-awareness (includes self-examination, spirituality), (2) social competence (includes capacity for intimacy, working with others, teamwork, leadership, dealing with others, assertiveness, flexibility, public speaking, communication, patience), and (3) knowledge acquisition (includes academic and course-related learning, content mastery). Typical of a quantitative research approach, Kuh reported the mean number of times that each of these outcome categories was mentioned by the sample of 149 students, and the percentage of students who mentioned it 0, 1, 2, 3, 4, or 5 or more times. For example, the mean number of interview statements that were coded as the self-awareness outcome was 1.07 (standard deviation = 1.19). Forty percent of the sample did not mention it at all, 33 percent mentioned it once, 11 percent mentioned it twice, 11 percent mentioned it 3 times, 4 percent mentioned it 4 times, and 1 percent mentioned it 5 or more times.

Data similar to the data collected by Kuh could also be collected in a qualitative research study, but it would be analyzed and interpreted differently. For example, the grounded theory approach described in Chapter 14 could be used to generate categories, and counts could be made, as was done in Kuh's study. However, instead of reporting means and percentages, a researcher using grounded theory principles would use the method of constant comparison to compare entries within and across categories. He then would be likely to generate constructs, themes, and patterns from the categorical data. Perhaps he would invoke or develop a theory to explain the observed relationships between, for example, the lack of funding to serve chronically ill children and school systems' misunderstanding of such children's needs. Other approaches to qualitative data analysis are discussed in Chapters 14 and 15.

RECOMMENDATIONS FOR

Using a Questionnaire or an Interview Guide to Collect Research Data

1. Design questions that relate directly to your research objectives or hypotheses.
2. Pilot-test the questionnaire or interview guide to identify flaws in its design or administration procedures.
3. Use language that is comprehensible to the respondents.
4. Check that the respondents have sufficient knowledge of the topics covered by the questionnaire or interview guide.
5. Collect validity and reliability evidence relating to the constructs that the questionnaire or interview is designed to measure.
6. Avoid taxing the respondents' patience by including too many questions in the questionnaire or interview.
7. When mailing a questionnaire, include a persuasive cover letter.
8. In using mailed questionnaires, develop procedures for conducting several follow-ups of nonrespondents and for checking whether nonrespondents differ from respondents on factors critical to the study.
9. Select an interview format that is appropriate to the purposes of the study and the characteristics of the interviewees.
10. In conducting interviews, practice your interviewing and data-recording skills prior to formal data collection.

SELF-CHECK TEST

Circle the correct answer to each of the following questions.
The answers are provided at the back of the book.

1. In research, interviews differ from questionnaires in that for interview
   a. the respondent controls the response situation.
   b. the respondent is asked to provide personal information.
   c. the question sequence and wording can vary with each respondent.
   d. responses to factual questions tend to be more accurate.

2. The most basic consideration in selecting respondents for a questionnaire study is to
   a. determine the sample size.
   b. select a sample that has the desired knowledge.
   c. select the data-collection method that respondents prefer.
   d. study a population with which you are familiar.

3. In designing questionnaires, it is recommended that threatening or difficult items
   a. appear near the beginning of the questionnaire.
   b. appear near the end of the questionnaire.
   c. be eliminated from the questionnaire.
   d. be randomly spaced throughout the questionnaire.

4. A major problem with anonymous questionnaires, compared with questionnaires that identify the respondent, is that
   a. the return rate is much lower.
   b. respondents are less likely to provide valid information.
   c. follow-up procedures are more difficult.
   d. all of the above.

5. Individuals who express a favorable or unfavorable attitude toward a fictitious attitude item tend to
   a. express attitudes more consistently toward other attitude items in the questionnaire.
   b. express more favorable attitudes generally.
   c. have less formal education than other interviewees.
   d. all of the above.

6. Pretesting in questionnaire research can be used to
   a. determine if the individuals to be sampled have sufficient knowledge to give meaningful responses.
   b. determine the likely response rate to the questionnaire.
   c. revise the questionnaire items to reduce the possibility of misinterpretations.
   d. all of the above.

7. In writing a cover letter to accompany a mailed questionnaire, a researcher would be well advised to
   a. request that the questionnaire be returned by a certain date.
   b. avoid setting a time limit for return of the questionnaire.
   c. describe the consequences if the questionnaire is not returned by a certain date.
   d. avoid associating the research project with a professional institution.

8. Research studies generally indicate that the offer of small cash incentives to questionnaire respondents
   a. greatly increases the likelihood of individuals' return of a completed questionnaire.
   b. only slightly increases the likelihood of individuals' return of a completed questionnaire.
   c. only increases the likelihood of return of a completed questionnaire if the incentive is not conditional on response.
   d. slightly decreases the likelihood of individuals' return of a completed questionnaire.

9. Research has found that respondents who do not return the first questionnaire mailed to them
   a. do not respond to follow-ups unless accompanied by a cash reward.
   b. will respond in greater numbers if more than one follow-up mailing is done.
   c. have very different personality characteristics than individuals who do complete the first questionnaire mailed to them.
   d. have poor reading skills.

10. Compared with a mailed questionnaire, the principal advantage of the interview is the
    a. low cost of data collection.
    b. depth of information collected.
    c. ease of administration.
    d. high reliability of the obtained data.
11. An interview that uses ambiguous stimuli to elicit subconscious perceptions that would otherwise be difficult to assess is called a
    a. participant construct interview.
    b. confirmation survey interview.
    c. survey interview involving projective techniques.
    d. key informant interview.
12. Compared to a research questionnaire, a research interview has the following advantage(s):
    a. The cost of data collection is generally lower.
    b. It is possible to probe unclear responses.
    c. It is subject to interviewer bias.
    d. all of the above.
13. A focus group is a type of interview that
    a. involves response through e-mail or a chat room.
    b. is used to interview seven to ten individuals at the same time.
    c. involves response to audio or video presentations.
    d. puts interviewers in a directive role.
14. The use of interviews in quantitative research most closely resembles the use of from interviews in qualitative research with aspect to
    a. whether the variables to be measured are pre-specified.
    b. the degree to which all respondents are exposed to a nearly identical interview experience.
    c. the use of descriptive statistics to analyze the data.
    d. the necessity of careful training of interviewers.
15. An interview guide in research is
    a. an individual who trains and supervises interviewers.
    b. a document that helps interviewees interpret the questions they are being asked.

    c. a document that provides guidelines for the interviewer's verbalizations during the interview.
    d. a document that defines the expected answers to open-form questions.
16. In training interviewers, it is good practice for the researchers to
    a. explain the research hypotheses and expected results.
    b. videotape practice interviews to provide models and feedback for interviewers.
    c. require interviewers to memorize the interview guide.
    d. all of the above.
17. A form of nonverbal communications from respondents that interviewers would be wise to attend to is the respondents'
    a. body movements or postures.
    b. personal dress and grooming.
    c. variations in voice pitch and volume.
    d. all of the above.
18. The principal disadvantage of recording a research interview is the
    a. change that it produces in the interview situation.
    b. cost of the equipment that is required.
    c. superficiality of the obtained data.
    d. difficulty of obtaining factual information.
19. It is good interview technique to
    a. ask leading questions.
    b. avoid engaging in small talk before starting the formal interview.
    c. cross-examine respondents if they seem deceptive.
    d. make sure that respondents understand the purpose of each question asked.

CHAPTER 9

Collecting Research Data through Observation and Content Analysis

OVERVIEW

Rather than relying solely on others' self-reports of events, many researchers prefer to make their own observations. Much of this chapter describes how quantitative and qualitative researchers make systematic observations. We describe procedures for collecting observational data with, and without, research participants' awareness. In the last section of the chapter we explain content analysis, involving procedures by which various types of artifacts and written communications found in natural settings are analyzed to provide research data.

OBJECTIVES

After studying this chapter, you should be able to

1. State the advantages and limitations of observation compared to other data-collection methods.
2. Explain the differences between descriptive, inferential, and evaluative observational variables.
3. Explain the differences between duration, frequency-count, interval, and continuous procedures for recording observations.
4. State advantages and disadvantages of using a standard observation form in a research project.
5. Explain how video recorders, audio recorders, and computers can be used to record observational data.
6. Describe an effective procedure for selecting and training observers for a quantitative research study.
7. Explain the differences between criterion-related observer reliability, intra-observer reliability, and inter-observer reliability.
8. Describe various observer effects that weaken the validity and reliability of quantitative observational data, and procedures that can be used to minimize or avoid each effect.
9. Describe how observation in qualitative research differs from observation in quantitative research.
10. Describe the various roles that observers play in qualitative research.
11. Identify stages of observation in a qualitative research study.
12. Explain how observers in a qualitative research study prepare and gain entry into a field setting.
13. Describe various methods for recording observational data in qualitative research.

14. Describe observer effects in qualitative research and procedures that can be used to minimize each type of effect.

15. State the advantages and limitations of nonreactive observation and the study of material culture.

16. Describe the steps that a quantitative researcher follows in doing a content analysis.

17. Describe the steps that a qualitative researcher follows in analyzing documents and records.

Forms of Observation and Content Analysis

In Chapter 7 we reviewed tests and self-report measures, and in Chapter 8 we considered questionnaires and interviews as methods for collecting research data. All these methods of data collection rely on generation of research data by the research participants themselves. Although data from research participants usually are easy to obtain, many individuals bias the information they offer about themselves, or they cannot recall accurately the events of interest to the researcher.[1]

An alternative approach is to observe directly the behavior and the social and physical environment of the individuals being studied. Researchers using both quantitative and qualitative research approaches have developed systematic methods for these purposes. If used properly, these observational methods avoid the potential inaccuracy and bias of data generated by research participants. For example, Lee Sechrest suggested that social attitudes like prejudice are best studied through subtle observation in natural, real-life settings (called *naturalistic observation*), preferably without direct input from the individuals in the setting. Such observation provides more accurate data than that obtained from research participants, which often are biased by the set to give a socially desirable response.[2] Following this suggestion, some researchers have studied racial attitudes by observing such phenomena as the seating patterns of African American and Caucasian students in college classes.[3]

Even when bias is not present in self-report data, observational methods still may yield more accurate data. For example, educators have noted that most teachers dominate classroom talk at the expense of student participation. But what are the actual percentages of teacher and student talk in classrooms? Reports by teachers or students are unlikely to yield precise answers to this question, but an analysis of observations recorded on audio or video devices can do so.

Although observation is superior to data obtained directly from research participants for some research purposes, it is also more time-consuming. Behavior, or phenomena that result from and provide insights about behavior, must be observed over a period of time to obtain reliable data, whereas tests, self-report measures, questionnaires, and interviews usually can yield reliable data even when the data are collected only at one point in time. Also, if the observational method is used in a quantitative study, inter-observer reliability should be established by having independent observers record data on the situation being observed. This is not possible if the researcher must do all the observations himself.

1. In a review of six studies in which both observational and self-report data were collected on the same specific behaviors, none reported a clear relationship between the two types of data. See: Hook, C. M., & Rosenshine, B. V. (1974). Accuracy of teacher reports of their classroom behavior. *Review of Educational Research, 49,* 1–12.
2. Sechrest, L. (Ed.). (1979). *Unobtrusive measurement today.* San Francisco: Jossey-Bass.
3. Campbell, D. T., Kruskal, W. H., & Wallace, W. P. (1966). Seating aggregation as an index of attitude. *Sociometry, 29,* 1–15.

In this chapter we first describe **reactive observation,** which usually occurs in real-life contexts and in which individuals know they are being observed. We then cover **nonreactive observation,** which involves observations of behavior in which individuals do not know they are being observed, as well as the study of material objects to gain insights about individuals' behavior. Finally, we discuss the use of content analysis to study forms of written and spoken communication. We treat applications of each data-collection method in quantitative and qualitative research, aiming in the process to illustrate the different assumptions held by quantitative and qualitative researchers about the nature of the social reality being observed and about their roles as researchers.

These data-collection methods, along with those covered in Chapters 7 and 8, by no means exhaust the objects of study, nor ways of studying, the topics and phenomena of interest to educational researchers. Indeed, every material object or substance, every event, and every concept that someone can perceive, think about, or imagine is potential grist for the research mill.

Reactive Observation in Quantitative Research

Defining Observational Variables

Touchstones in Research

Bakeman, R., & Gottman, J. M. (1997). *Observing interaction: An introduction to sequential analysis* (2nd ed.). Cambridge: Cambridge University Press.

Waxman, H. C., Tharp, R. G., & Hilberg, R. S. (Eds.). (2004). *Observational research in U.S. classrooms: New approaches for understanding cultural and linguistic diversity.* Cambridge, UK: Cambridge University.

Pellegrini, A. D., with Symons, F. J., & Hoch, J. (2004). *Observing children in their natural worlds: A methodological primer* (2nd ed.). Mahwah, NJ: Erlbaum.

In a quantitative research study, the first step in observation is to define the variables that are to be observed. To illustrate this procedure, we will refer to a study by Hirokazu Sakaguchi.[4] The purpose of his research was to determine how the English language is taught in Japanese universities. As Sakaguchi explains:

> The present study examines what actually goes on in college-level English classes, and conclusions are drawn by means of empirical observation rather than by the application of linguistic theory. In the Japanese context, this approach is somewhat unusual. Research has been done in Japan into how to make classroom teaching more effective, but it has tended to proceed on a theoretical level, and very few researchers have used practical observation and analysis as a method of research. An important reason for this is the difficulty involved in gaining access to the classroom: professors have a tendency to regard their classroom activities as sacrosanct, perhaps partly because of sensitivity to outside criticism, and in general are highly reluctant to cooperate with researchers. In this respect, this study breaks new ground.[5]

Sakaguchi selected two types of English classes for observation: English literature classes taught by native Japanese instructors and English conversation classes taught by instructors whose native language was English.

After Sakaguchi decided to use direct observation as a method, he next decided to use an adaptation of the Flanders interaction analysis system, which is used to collect data on ten variables.[6] Sakaguchi used these variables and added 15 more. Brief definitions of them are shown in Table 9.1. More elaborate definitions, with examples of each variable, were used by Sakaguchi to train himself and another individual to make observations.

Next Sakaguchi needed a method for recording the observations. Following Flanders's procedures, he decided to code each three-second interval of a classroom lesson into one of the 25 behavior categories shown in Table 9.1. Thus, a 60-minute lesson would require 1,200 codings. (60 minutes = 3,600 seconds; 3,600 ÷ 3 = 1,200 intervals.)

4. Sakaguchi, H. (1993). A comparison of teaching methods in English-as-a-second-language conversation courses and reading courses in Japanese universities. *Dissertation Abstracts International, 54*(10), 3692A.(UMI No. 9405220)
5. Ibid., pp. 13–14.
6. Flanders, N. A. (1970). *Analyzing teaching behavior.* Reading, MA: Addison-Wesley.

TABLE 9.1

Observational Variables in a Study of English Classes at a Japanese University

Category 1 (Teacher accepts feelings). Teacher statements that reflect an awareness and unqualified acceptance of students' feelings.

Category 2 (Teacher encourages students). Praise and encouragement toward the students' questions, answers, and comments.

Category 2F (Teacher gives feedback). A quick, almost automatic response by the instructor that follows a student's statement, usually connoting approval or disapproval.

Category 3 (Teacher uses ideas of students). The instructor incorporates a student's idea into the lesson.

Category 4 (Teacher asks question). Questions asked by the teacher, except those that are directly related to the practice of English conversation.

Category 4C (Teacher asks conversational question). This applies to questions that are part of the dialogue or conversation practices.

Category 5 (Teacher lectures). This includes lecturing, expressing opinions, giving facts, interjecting thoughts, and off-hand comments.

Category 5Cr (Teacher corrects student's mistake). This consists of correcting errors in grammar, word usage, translations, pronunciation, rhythm, and intonation.

Category 5W (Teacher gives cues). Gives cues by word, expression, or sentence when a student gets stuck in the middle of an answer or translation.

Category 5C (Teacher answers conversation questions).

Category 6 (Teacher gives directions).

Category 7 (Teacher criticizes student).

Category 8 (Student responds). These are student responses to Category 4 questions.

Category 8C (Student gives conversational response). These are student responses to Category 4C questions, and to questions asked by one student to another.

Category 8R (Student engages in oral reading). This occurs mainly in literature classes when the instructor asks a student to read out loud a passage from the text.

Category 8SR (Student engages in silent reading).

Category 8D (Student draws picture).

Category 8T (Student translates).

Category 8S (Student gives summary). This occurs mainly in literature classes when the instructor asks the student to give the main idea in Japanese from one paragraph of the English text.

Category 9 (Student talks). These are questions, answers, comments, and utterances made voluntarily—as opposed to responses to teacher questions—by the students.

Category O (Silence or confusion). Moments of nonproductive confusion plus some productive silence, such as allowing students time to copy down information from the blackboard.

Category OS (Students engage in sheet work). This is time spent by students quietly working on their written exercises

Category OT (Teacher uses tape recorder). This occurs in literature classes when the instructor has students listen to tapes made by native English speakers.

Category OD (Teacher distributes handouts).

Category OB (Teacher or student writes on blackboard).

Source: Adapted from text on pp. 41–45 in: Sakaguchi, H. (1993). A comparison of teaching methods in English-as-a-second-language conversation courses and reading courses in Japanese universities. *Dissertation Abstracts International, 54*(10), 3692A. (UMI No. 9405220)

Finally, Sakaguchi had to decide how many lessons of each instructor to observe. Limiting observation to one lesson might yield an atypical picture of the instructor's teaching style. Sakaguchi chose to observe six lessons of each instructor in the sample. Observational data for all the instructors were collected at the same point in the university's academic year. We describe some of the findings from the analysis of these observational data below.

Types of Observational Variables

Three types of observational variables can be distinguished in quantitative research: descriptive, inferential, and evaluative. **Descriptive observational variables** are variables that require little inference on the part of the observer. They sometimes are called *low-inference variables* for this reason. One of their major advantages is that they generally yield reliable data. The variables shown in Table 9.1 would be considered descriptive observational variables.

Inferential observational variables are variables that require the observer to make an inference from behavior to a construct that is presumed to underly the behavior. For example, observers might be asked to record the confidence with which a teacher explains a mathematical concept. Some teachers might speak with a great deal of confidence, or emphasis, whereas others might appear uncertain or anxious in their explanation of the topic. Confidence, emphasis uncertainty, and anxiety are not behaviors but rather are psychological constructs that are inferred from behavior. For this reason they sometimes are called *high-inference variables*. It is much more difficult to collect reliable data on inferential observational variables than on descriptive observational variables.

Evaluative observational variables are variables that require not only an inference from behavior on the part of the observer but also an evaluative judgment. For example, we might be interested in obtaining ratings of the quality of each teacher's explanation of various mathematical concepts. Quality is not a behavior but rather a construct that is inferred from behavior. Also, it is a construct that is clearly evaluative in nature. Because it is difficult to make reliable observations of evaluative variables, we need to collect examples of explanations that define points along a continuum of excellent to poor explanations, and use these in training the observers.

Recording and Analyzing Observations

To ensure accurate recording, observers should record data on only one observational variable at a time. For example, most observers would find it quite difficult to record various aspects of a teacher's behavior while also recording the percentage of children who are paying attention to the teacher. In this situation, the reliability of both sets of observations probably would be low. A better approach would be to have different observers assigned to record each type of variable, or to have a single observer alternate between recording the teacher's behavior for a specified interval and then recording the students' behavior for the next interval.

Types of Recording Procedures

Procedures for making a recording of quantitative observations can be classified into four major types: (1) duration, (2) frequency-count, (3) interval, and (4) continuous.

Duration recording In **duration recording** the observer measures the elapsed time during which each target behavior occurs. A stopwatch generally is used for this purpose. It is easy to do duration recording for a single observational variable, such as the length of time a particular student is writing at her desk. An observer also can record different observational variables if they do not occur at the same time. For example, the observer can record the length of time that a particular student is on-task, off-task but not disruptive, mildly disruptive, or seriously disruptive.

Frequency-count recording In **frequency-count recording** the observer records each time a target behavior occurs. A tally sheet typically is used for this purpose. Frequency counts are most useful in recording behaviors of short duration and behaviors whose duration is not important. For example, one of the authors of this book (W. Borg) conducted a study in which each observer was trained to tally 13 teacher behaviors related to classroom management, such as goal-directed prompts, concurrent praise, and alerting cues.[7] The behaviors were of short duration, and no more than one behavior could occur at the same time. Interobserver reliabilities were satisfactory, ranging from .71 to .96 for the 13 behaviors.

Interval recording involves observing the behavior of an individual at given intervals. Sakaguchi's adaptation of Flanders's interaction analysis system is an example of this recording procedure. Every 3 seconds the instructor's, or a selected student's, behavior was coded into one of the 25 observational categories.

Once a sample of behavior has been recorded in this manner, the data must be summarized and reported to provide a meaningful description of what happened. In Sakaguchi's study, the primary research objective was to determine how the six instructors in his sample differed in their teaching style. For each observed lesson, his primary data were the number of 3-second intervals in which each observational variable in Table 9.1 occurred. For each variable, he divided the number of intervals in which it occurred by the total number of intervals that were recorded for all variables. The result of this calculation was a percentage, namely, the percentage of the total lesson time during which each variable was occurring. The final step in the analysis was to average the percentages for each variable across all six lessons that were observed for each instructor.

Table 9.2 shows a comparison of the results for two of the instructors in the sample—one a native-Japanese instructor of an English literature course, the other a native-English-speaking instructor of an English conversation course. Among the differences between the two instructors, we see that the conversation instructor spent 4.38 percent of class time encouraging students, whereas the literature instructor spent .62 percent of his time engaged in this activity. As would be expected, the students of the conversation instructor spent very little class time engaged in oral reading (13 percent) or translating (0 percent), whereas students of the literature instructor spent 19.58 percent of class time engaged in oral reading and 37.98 percent of class time engaged in translating passages from an assigned text.

The data analysis shown in Table 9.2 contributes to research knowledge about teacher and student use of instructional time in particular types of lessons. However, it does not tell us about *sequence,* that is, how the lessons unfolded over time. For example, we can surmise that each lesson started with one of the coded behaviors shown in Table 9.2, but we do not know which one. Also, we do not know what behavior was most likely to occur following, let's say, a student's engagement in oral reading (code 8R).

Various statistical techniques are available to address these questions about how observed behavior unfolds.[8] For example, in the study by Sakaguchi, if we wished to know which behavior was most likely to occur following an instance of a student engaged in oral reading, we could: (1) identify all instances of the 8R code; (2) identify which code occurred

---

7. Borg, W. R. (1977). Changing teacher and pupil performance with protocols. *Journal of Experimental Education, 45,* 9–18.

8. These techniques are described in Chapters 6–10 of: Bakeman, R., & Gottman, J. M. (1997). *Observing interaction: An introduction to sequential analysis* (2nd ed.). Cambridge: Cambridge University Press.

TABLE 9.2

Comparison of the Observed Teaching Style of Two English-Language Instructors at a Japanese University

Code	Category	Conversation Instructor (Percentage of Lesson)	Literature Instructor (Percentage of Lesson)
1	Instructor accepts feelings	.08	.04
2	Instructor encourages	4.38	.62
2F	Instructor gives feedback	3.65	1.56
3	Instructor uses student ideas	0	0
4	Instructor asks question	13.17	7.78
4C	Instructor asks conversational question	12.25	0
5	Instructor lectures	25.33	8.30
5Cr	Instructor corrects student mistake	1.85	4.58
5W	Instructor gives cues	.92	3.44
5C	Instructor answers conversational question	1.30	0
6	Instructor gives directions	2.53	3.44
7	Instructor criticizes student	1.03	1.44
8	Student responds	1.78	2.75
8C	Student gives conversational response	22.78	0
8R	Student does oral reading	.13	19.58
8SR	Student does silent reading	0	0
8D	Student draws picture	0	0
8T	Student translates	0	37.98
8S	Student summarizes	0	0
9	Student initiates talk	.20	2.08
O	Silence or confusion	2.05	5.20
OS	Students do worksheet	6.03	1.18
OT	Instructor uses tape recorder	0	0
OD	Instructor distributes handout	.39	0
OB	Instructor or student writes on blackboard	.22	0

Source: Adapted from Tables 1 and 4 on pp. 52 and 87, respectively, in: Sakaguchi, H. (1993). A comparison of teaching methods in English-as-a-second-language conversation courses and reading courses in Japanese universities. *Dissertation Abstracts International, 54*(10), 3692A. (UMI No. 9405220)

immediately after the end of each 8R code; (3) count the frequency of each of these codes; and (4) divide each code frequency count by the total frequency count for all codes to yield a percentage for each code. Using such a procedure, we might find that after a student finished oral reading, the most frequent next behavior was for the instructor to lecture.

Other statistical techniques for analyzing sequences of observed behavior are more complex. One of them is **time-series analysis,** which is a statistical technique for analyzing changes in an observed variable over time. For example, suppose Sakaguchi had counted the number of English words that a particular student spoke in class over a period of 50 class periods. Time-series analysis could be used to detect the presence of significant changes in the frequency count over this period of time.

Continuous recording involves recording all the behavior of the target individual or individuals for a specified observation interval. This method usually does not focus on a specific set of observational variables. Instead, the observer typically does a **protocol analysis,** which involves generating and interpreting a chronological narrative of everything that the individual does or everything that occurs in a particular setting. This method often is used in exploratory studies to help the researcher identify important behavior patterns, which subsequently are studied using one of the other methods of observational recording.

Because it is impossible to record everything in a protocol, the observer must focus on the events and contextual features that are most relevant to the research problem. To analyze the protocols, the researcher reads them, creates a content-analysis system that fits the data, and then rereads and classifies the recorded behavior into this system. This process corresponds to the steps used in quantitative content analysis of documents and other communication media, described later in the chapter.

Selecting an Observation Recording Procedure

Once you identify pertinent observational variables and their behavioral indicators, you need to select or develop a procedure for recording the observations. If a suitable procedure is not available, you might consider developing a paper-and-pencil observation form because it is fairly easy to construct and can accommodate a variety of observational variables.

A segment of an observation form is shown in Figure 9.1. The form requires the observer not only to record certain behaviors as they occur, but also to evaluate some of them on a rating scale. Item 2 of the observation form is of the latter type.

After developing a prototype of the observation form, you should try it out in a number of situations similar to those to be observed during data collection and correct any weaknesses you discover. For example, a common weakness of observation forms is that

FIGURE 9.1

Sample Observation Form

1. Check each question asked by the teacher into one of the following categories (observe for the first fifteen minutes of the class hour):

	Frequency	Total
a. asks student to solve a problem at blackboard	✓✓✓✓	4
b. asks student to solve a problem at his or her seat	✓✓✓✓✓✓✓	7
c. asks students if they have any questions or if they understand	✓✓	2
d. other	✓✓✓✓✓	5
	Grand Total	18

2. Each time the teacher asks a student to solve a problem, rate the problem's level of difficulty on a 5-point scale.

	Frequency	Total
1. difficult	✓✓✓	3
2.	✓	1
3. average	✓✓✓✓✓	5
4.	✓	1
5. easy	✓	1
	Grand Total	11[*]

[*]The sum here should equal the sum of categories *a* and *b* in item 1.

they require the observer to record more kinds of behavior or watch more individuals than can be done reliably. Various solutions to these problems are possible, such as employing different observers to record different behaviors or switching from the observation of one individual to another at designated intervals.

Standard Observation Forms

Instead of developing your own observation form for a research study, you may prefer to use one of the many standard observation forms that are available. These forms have several advantages. First, standard observation forms usually have reached a stage of development where they include evidence of their validity and reliability. Second, the use of a standard form saves you all the time that it would take to develop your own form. Third, most standard forms have been used in previous research studies, so you can compare your findings with theirs.

The obvious disadvantage of a standard observation form is that it may not include all the variables that you are interested in measuring. In this case you can use just the part of the form that you need and add your own procedures for assessing other variables. Keep in mind, however, that previously reported reliability and validity data may not apply if only part of an instrument is used.

Depending on your research interests, you might be able to find published collections of standard observation forms.[9] In addition, you can search the preliminary sources described in Chapter 4. To illustrate their use, we searched several electronic sources to identify standard forms for observing teaching behavior:

1. Entering the keywords *observation* and *teaching methods* in ERIC for the years 1999–2004 yielded 294 citations; the first journal article referred to an observation tool for assessing teachers' abilities to address diversity issues in the classroom.
2. Entering the keywords *observation* and *teaching methods* in PsycInfo for the years 1985–2005 yielded 29 results; one cited the book by Waxman and colleagues that is listed as a *Touchstone in Research* in this chapter.
3. Entering the descriptors *observation* and *teaching methods* in the ETS TestLink main ETS test site identified 956 documents, including a report on the Praxis III classroom performance assessment that includes a method for direct observation of teachers' classroom practice.

Studying the citations and instruments from these searches might help you identify a suitable observation form. If not, the search almost certainly will provide a conceptual basis for developing your own form.

Audio and Video Recording

It sometimes is impractical to collect observational data while the critical behavior is occurring. One such situation is when many of the behaviors to be recorded occur at the same time or closely together. If an audio or video recording of the events is made, it can be replayed several times for careful study and observers can count or rate the events at a convenient time. Another advantage of recording events is that it enables you to track behaviors that you did not anticipate at the outset of your study. For example, in a study of teacher praise, you might notice midway through your observations that teachers are using certain types of praise remarks that you did not include in your observation form.

---

9. For example, publications in the field of classroom research include: Borich, G. D., & Madden, S. K. (1977). *Evaluating classroom instruction: A sourcebook of instruments.* Reading, MA: Addison-Wesley Longman; Simon, A., & Boyer, E. G. (Eds.). (1974). *Mirrors for behavior III: An anthology of observation instruments* (3rd ed.). Philadelphia: Communication Materials Center (see also the 1st and 2nd editions); and Cangelosi, J. S. (1991). *Evaluating classroom instruction.* New York: Longman.

If you have recorded the original events, you can replay them and reclassify the praise statements so as to include the types of praise not listed on your original observation form.

If you decide to use an audio or video recording to collect observational data, keep in mind that technical competence is required to use such recording devices properly. For example, you may need to develop skills in using more than one microphone and frequently refocusing a video camera.

The study of Japanese university instruction by Sakaguchi that we described above involved the use of audiotape recordings. The audiotapes could be replayed as often as necessary to ensure reliable coding of the observational variables shown in Table 9.1.

Use of Computers and Other Electronic Devices

Various electronic devices (e.g., PalmPilots) and software programs are available for recording and analyzing observational data. The specific tasks that these devices can perform are as follows:

1. Recording and timing events and transcribing the data onto coding sheets.
2. Transferring the data from coding sheets into a computer file that then can be analyzed by a statistical package.
3. Cleaning up the data by locating coding errors and detecting "wild codes," which are codes that have no meaning in the coding system being used.
4. Interpreting the results of the data analysis. Computers have the capacity to produce a variety of graphic data representations, which can help in interpreting one's results.

If you are planning to collect observational data, you should first search the literature to determine whether a suitable device has been developed and used by other researchers. For example, Ned Flanders and his colleagues have developed computer technology to record data on the types of classroom interaction variables shown in Table 9.1.[10] The observer uses a pen-like device and special recording paper that contains a bar code for each interaction category and also for designated students, if that is desired. By moving the pen across the appropriate bar codes, the observer can record how long the teacher or student engaged in a particular type of behavior. This process is similar to the procedure used for charging items at the checkout counter in many stores.

After the observer has finished making observations he inserts the pen in a computer interface device, which stores the observations as a computer data file. A computer program is available for analyzing this data file and creating printouts that display the results in various formats, for example, the sequence of interactions during a lesson or the amount of time that each interaction category occurred.

Selecting and Training Observers

Researchers can make their own observations, train others to make them, or share the task with others. The advantage of using other individuals is that it allows for control of the observer bias that can occur when the same individual who designs the research study and frames its hypotheses also does the observing. In addition, if two or more similarly trained observers make independent observations, you can determine the level of inter-observer reliability of the observations. Researchers have found that the most reliable observers tend to be intelligent, verbally fluent, and motivated to do a good job.[11]

---

10. This type of computer-assisted observation is described on pp. 133–134 in: Acheson, K. A., & Gall, M. D. (2003). Clinical supervision and teacher development: Preservice and inservice applications (5th ed.). New York: Wiley.
11. Harter, D. P. (Ed.). (1982). *Using observers to study behavior*. San Francisco: Jossey-Bass.

The first step in training observers is to discuss the observation form with them. Describe each item sufficiently so that they develop a thorough understanding of what is to be observed and how it is to be recorded. Also, consider making video recordings of situations similar to those to be observed in the study, so that you can relate actual examples of each behavior to its definition.

The next step is to set up practice observations in which all observer trainees participate. If video recordings were made earlier, they can be used in the practice observations. Show a brief segment of the video, instructing trainees to record each behavior on the observation form as it occurs. Then check each trainee to determine if he correctly tallied the behaviors. If observers disagree with each other or with the criterion, replay the video, stopping at each behavior to discuss the most appropriate way to record it, and why. During these discussions, the observer's instruction sheet should be revised to include any necessary clarifications that arise during the training session. Special rules typically are needed to help observers decide how to record unusual behaviors that were not foreseen when the observation form was developed.

Determining Observer Agreement

Observational data are of no use unless they are collected by reliable observers. What does it mean for an observer to be reliable? Ted Frick and Melvyn Semmel answered this question by distinguishing between three types of observer reliability.[12] First, there is **criterion-related observer reliability,** which is the extent to which a trained observer's scores agree with those of an expert observer, such as the researcher who developed the observation instrument. This type of reliability is important because it provides assurance that the trained observer's understanding of the variables measured by the observation instrument is the same as that of an expert. Criterion-related observer reliability typically is established by first having an expert code a video or audio recording of events that include all the variables measured by the observation instrument. The trained observers then code the same recording, and their data are checked for agreement with the expert's data. Criterion-related observer reliability should be checked prior to data collection, and preferably during data collection as well.

The second type of observer reliability is **intra-observer reliability,** which is the extent to which the observer is consistent in her observational codings. This type of reliability can be established by having each observer twice code a video or audio recording of events similar to those that she will be asked to observe in the field. For example, observers might code a video recording on Monday and then code the same recording a few days later. This type of reliability is not commonly established, but you should check it if possible because it provides additional assurance that your observers are reliable. Intra-observer reliability should be checked before data collection begins, and if possible during data collection also.

The third type of observer reliability is **inter-observer reliability,** which is the extent to which observers agree with each other during actual data collection. To establish inter-observer reliability, you will need to have pairs of observers collect data on the same events. For example, suppose that you have trained 5 observers to collect data on 60 lessons taught by various teachers. For the sake of efficiency, you might have each observer collect data individually on 10 lessons. This procedure takes care of data collection for 50 of the 60 lessons. The other 10 lessons could be observed by all 5 observers for the purpose of determining inter-observer reliability.

---

12. Frick, T., & Semmel, M. I. (1978). Observer agreement and reliabilities of classroom observational measures. *Review of Educational Research, 48,* 157–184.

Frick and Semmel describe various procedures for calculating the level of criterion-related observer reliability and intra-observer reliability. These procedures involve calculating a percentage of agreement or a specialized correlation coefficient. The choice of procedure depends on the type of observational variable and the type of observer reliability to be determined.

Although determining observer reliability is important, it does not ensure that the final set of observational data will be reliable. Observers can agree perfectly in training or under particular field conditions, yet the typical situations that they observe may be very unstable, or they may differ so little from each other that accurate observation to distinguish between such small differences is not possible. In other words, observer reliability is a necessary but not sufficient condition for collecting reliable observational data.

Reducing Observer Effects

An **observer effect** is any action by observers that reduces the validity or reliability of the data they collect. Researchers should be aware of possible observer effects and take steps to avoid or minimize them.

Types of Observer Effects

Carolyn Evertson and Judith Green identified various types of observer effects.[13] We describe each type below and how it can be controlled.

Effect of the observer on the observed Unless concealed, the observer is likely to have an impact on the observed. For example, an observer entering a classroom for the first time probably will arouse the curiosity of the students and teacher. Their resulting inattentiveness may produce nonrepresentative observational data. One way to reduce this effect is for the observer to make several visits beforehand so that the students and the teacher take the observer's presence for granted and behave naturally.

A more serious problem occurs when the individuals being observed are influenced by the observer's intentions. For example, suppose the purpose of the research study is to record the number and length of dyadic interactions between the teacher and students in art classes. If they learn that this is the purpose of the study, teachers are likely to increase the frequency of their dyadic interactions, particularly if they believe that this is perceived as positive behavior. To avoid this problem, the researcher should tell the teachers at the outset that it is not possible to reveal the nature of the research project until it is completed. Also, the researcher should assure them that the data will be kept confidential and will not reflect unfavorably on the individuals who participate.

Observer personal bias **Observer personal bias** refers to errors in observational data that are traceable to personal characteristics of specific observers. One can argue that any observations made by human beings will contain some personal bias, because all of us are influenced by our experiences and beliefs. Nonetheless, the design of some research studies increases the potential for observer bias.[14]

Obvious sources of personal bias in observers should be looked for and eliminated if found. For example, to use an observer with a negative attitude toward certain ethnic

---

13. Evertson, C. M., & Green, J. L. (1986). Observation as inquiry and method. In M. C. Wittrock (Ed.), *Handbook of research on teaching* (3rd ed., pp. 162–213). New York: Macmillan. Evertson and Green identified ten types of observer effects reorganized here into seven types.
14. Salvia, J. A., & Mersel, C. J. (1980). Observer bias: A methodological consideration in special education research. *Journal of Special Education, 14,* 261–270. The authors reviewed 153 studies having a high potential for bias and found that only 22 percent reported adequate safeguards.

groups in a study involving observation of the creative endeavors of children from those ethnic groups and other children in a nursery school clearly would be inappropriate. The observer's bias almost certainly would lead to seeing more creative behavior among some children and either ignoring, misinterpreting, or minimizing the creative efforts of other children in this nursery school.

Observers have been found to produce biased data when research participants are given such labels as "emotionally disturbed" or "mentally retarded," are high or low in physical attractiveness, or have certain ethnic or socioeconomic backgrounds.[15] Researchers can reduce the influence of such factors on the observers who will collect data by avoiding the use of labels with positive or negative connotations.

Rating errors   When using observational rating scales, some observers form a response set that produces errors in their ratings on these scales. A **response set** is the tendency for an observer to make a rating based on a generalized disposition about the rating task rather than on the basis of the actual behavior of the individuals. The following are three response set errors of this sort:

1. The **error of leniency** is the tendency to assign high ratings to the majority of research participants, even when they differ markedly on the variable being measured.
2. The **error of central tendency** is the tendency for observers to rate all or most of the individuals whom they observe around the midpoint of the observational scales. Observers sometimes make such ratings to avoid difficult judgments.
3. The **halo effect** is the tendency for the observer's early impressions of the individual being observed to influence his ratings on all behaviors involving that individual. For example, if the observer forms an initially favorable impression of the person being observed, he may rate the individual favorably in subsequent observations.

When high-inference variables are being observed, the magnitude of these observer rating errors can be so large that the resulting ratings are virtually meaningless. For example, a study of the ratings of student teachers by cooperating teachers revealed so much halo effect and error of leniency that the validity of the entire rating system was called into question.[16] For example, the mean "attitude" rating of the 161 student teachers who were observed was 4.85 out of a possible 5.00, which suggests a strong error of leniency. If such response sets occur, you need to either reconceptualize the rating scale or select and train observers more carefully.

Observer contamination occurs when the observer's knowledge of certain data in a study influences the data that he records about other variables. For example, suppose that we are doing a study of the human relations skills of highly regarded elementary school principals. Poorly regarded and highly regarded principals could be identified by a composite of nominations made by teachers, parents, and school superintendents. Observers then are trained to observe the performance of the highly regarded and poorly regarded principals in faculty meetings and evaluate them on certain human relations skills. If the observers know beforehand which principals have been classified as highly regarded and which as poorly regarded, they almost certainly will be influenced by this knowledge when they collect

15. Ibid.
16. Phelps, L., Schmitz, C. D., & Boatright, B. (1986). The effects of halo and leniency on cooperating teacher reports using Likert-type rating scales. *Journal of Educational Research, 79,* 151–154.

observational data about the principals' behavior. The obvious solution to the problem is to keep possibly contaminating information from the observers.

Observer omission is the failure to record the occurrence of a behavior that fits one of the categories on the observation form. This failure can have several causes. One of them is personal bias, which we discussed above. Because of personal bias, the observer may overlook the occurrence of desirable behavior by an individual whom he perceives negatively. Another possibility is that the behaviors to be observed occur so close together that the observer cannot record all of them. The opposite situation also is possible: The behavior to be observed occurs so infrequently that the observer misses it.

Observation errors due to omissions can be detected during the development of the observation form or during observer training. You may find it necessary to simplify the observation or to assign multiple observers to a setting, with each observer responsible for recording data on different observational variables. In the case of infrequently occurring variables, you may need to provide cues and reminders to maintain observers' vigilance.

Observer drift   Once observers have been trained to the desired level of agreement and accuracy they should start collecting data promptly, because a delay can result in a decline in observer skills. Also, if the observations are to extend for more than one week, you should hold a weekly refresher training session for all observers. Otherwise, the observational data will become less reliable because of **observer drift,** the tendency for observers to gradually redefine the observational variables, which means that the data that they collect no longer reflect the definitions they learned during training.

Reliability decay   Research evidence suggests that observers should be checked frequently during the course of the study to keep them performing at a satisfactory level. Otherwise, the observational data are subject to **reliability decay,** which is the tendency for observational data recorded during the later phases of data collection to be less reliable than those collected earlier.

Paul Taplin and John Reid compared "decay" in reliability for three groups of observers: (1) those who were told they would not be checked, (2) those told they would be spot-checked at regular intervals, and (3) those told they would be checked on a random basis.[17] The randomly checked group maintained the highest level of reliability, followed by the spot-checked group; the not-checked group had the lowest reliability. The spot-checked group performed very well in the sessions when they knew they would be checked, and very poorly in the sessions when they thought they would not be checked. Therefore, the problem seems to be one of motivation, so you should do whatever possible to maintain observers' motivation. For example, you can try to convince observers of the importance of their task, schedule sessions so as to avoid observer fatigue, inform them that you will check their performance on a random basis, carry out frequent random checks, and give them frequent feedback on their reliability.

Reactive Observation in Qualitative Research

Observation in qualitative research differs from observation in quantitative research in many ways. Observers in a qualitative study do not seek to remain neutral or "objective" about the phenomena being observed and often include their own feelings and experiences in interpreting their observations. An example is Cathy Evans and Donna Eder's

17. Taplin, P. S., & Reid, J. B. (1973). Effects of instructional set and experimenter influence on observer reliability. *Child Development, 44,* 547–554.

Touchstone in Research

Angrosino, M. V. (2005). Recontextualizing observation: Ethnography, pedagogy, and the prospects for a progressive political agenda. In N. K. Denzin & Y. S. Lincoln (Eds.), *The Sage handbook of qualitative research* (3rd ed., pp. 729–745). Thousand Oaks, CA: Sage.

study of social isolation, which included in-depth observations of informal activities among middle school students during lunch.[18] The lunchroom observations included taking notes on the behavior of students who sat together while eating lunch toward students classified as isolates, who spent most of their lunch period alone.

The researchers observed many incidents involving ridicule of isolates, and all four observers "reported that witnessing such events was a source of emotional distress for them."[19] After one incident of this type, Evans wrote these field notes, which were included in the published research report:

> I was utterly and completely disgusted. I guess part of my problem was that I was disillusioned too—I thought Janice and Patty were above it. I didn't initiate conversation with Jenny because it would have targeted her more and I didn't reprimand the girls in my group because it would have possibly been more embarrassing to Jenny and I might as well witness what there is to witness, even if it's grossly unpleasant.[20]

Thus, these researchers sought to avoid criticizing or taking sides with specific participants, but still clearly considered their own reactions to events to be a legitimate part of the study, and worthy of reporting.

Another difference between quantitative and qualitative observation is that the focus of qualitative observation is much more emergent. Data collection in quantitative research generally is driven by a priori hypotheses, questions, or objectives. In contrast, at any point in the process qualitative observers are free to shift their attention to new phenomena and explore new research questions.

The third difference is that the focus of observation generally is much wider in qualitative research. In quantitative research, observers tend to concentrate on specific aspects of behavior and to ignore context. In qualitative research, however, observers look at behavior and its environmental setting from a holistic perspective.

Purpose of Observation in Qualitative Research

Two common methods of data collection in qualitative research—interviews and analysis of documents—involve words uttered or written by the participants in a natural setting. This information is limited by participants' knowledge, memory, and ability to convey information clearly and accurately, and being affected by how they wish to be perceived by outsiders. Observation, in contrast, allows researchers to formulate their own version of what is occurring and then check it with the participants. The inclusion of selected observations in a researcher's report provides a more complete description of phenomena than would be possible by just referring to interview statements or documents. Just as important, observations provide an additional source of data for verifying the information obtained by other methods.

An ethnographic study conducted by Katherine Rosier and William Corsaro provides an example of observation as one of several data sources.[21] Their study tested the validity of the common stereotype that the educational and economic problems of many African-American youth stem from deficiencies of the families in which they are raised. One aspect of the study involved interviewing parents and observing in the homes of children enrolled

---

18. Evans, C., & Eder, D. (1993). "NO EXIT": Processes of social isolation in the middle school. *Journal of Contemporary Ethnography, 22,* 139–170.
19. Ibid., p. 146.
20. Ibid.
21. Rosier, K. B., & Corsaro, W. A. (1993). Competent parents, complex lives: Managing parenthood in poverty. *Journal of Contemporary Ethnography, 22,* 171–204.

in Head Start. When visiting the homes, the researchers used direct observation to check the validity of parents' claims that despite their limited budgets, they regularly engaged their children in structured learning activities at home and provided educational toys and supplies. Considerable observational evidence was found to support such claims, including finished projects displayed on refrigerators and walls; tables cluttered with writing instruments, paper, and works in progress; and educational toys and books. Parents also presented the researchers with samples of their children's schoolwork.

The researchers describe a day that they spent observing Cymira, a child in Head Start, and four other children who were being cared for by Cymira's mother, Rhonda. While the children were playing outside, Rhonda got out a variety of both purchased and handmade educational materials, suited to varying ages. She then called all five children into the house. During the hour when they stayed indoors, Rhonda "checked and encouraged the children's work, and the older children assisted the younger ones."[22] Their careful, on-site observation helped the researchers confirm the validity of their finding from parent interviews that most parents of poor African-American children do seek to instill educational skills and values in their children at an early age.

In Chapter 15 we explain how qualitative research often utilizes various traditions, such as ethnography, cultural studies, and cognitive psychology. The purpose and form of observation vary across these traditions. In the following sections, we describe typical approaches that qualitative researchers use to collect observational data. If your proposed study follows a particular tradition of qualitative research, you should study the specific ways in which researchers working within that tradition have used observation as a data-collection method.

Defining the Observer Role

The observer role in qualitative research varies along a continuum from complete observer, through participant–observer and observer–participant, to complete participant.[23] As a **complete observer,** the researcher maintains a posture of independence from the setting being studied. As a **complete participant,** the researcher studies a setting in which she already is a member or assumes genuine membership during the course of the research. For example, David Hayano reported on his observations of fellow denizens of California's all-night card rooms.[24]

Between these two extremes are the observer–participant and participant–observer roles. In the **observer–participant role,** the researcher acts primarily as an observer, entering the setting only to gather data and interacting only casually and nondirectly with individuals or groups while engaged in observation. In the **participant–observer role,** the researcher observes and interacts closely enough with individuals to establish a meaningful identity within their group; however, the researcher does not engage in activities that are at the core of the group's identity. For example, Peter Adler, a sociologist and professor, played a participant-observer role in a study of college athletes at his university.[25] He maintained his researcher identity while actively participating with the basketball team and coaching staff in various roles, including insider, expert, and celebrity—but not in the core roles of coach, trainer, or player.

The researcher who designs a qualitative study most likely will be an observer during the data-collection phase. In some cases a team, which may include the researcher, makes

Touchstone in Research

Tedlock, B. (2005). The observation of participation and the emergence of public ethnography. In N. K. Denzin & Y. S. Lincoln (Eds.), *The Sage handbook of qualitative research* (3rd ed., pp. 467–481). Thousand Oaks, CA: Sage.

22. Ibid., p. 182.
23. Gold, R. L. (1958). Roles in sociological field observation. *Social Forces, 36,* 217–223.
24. Hayano, D. (1982). *Poker faces.* Berkeley, CA: University of California Press.
25. Adler, P. A., & Adler, P. (1991). *Backboards and blackboards.* New York: Columbia University Press.

observations in the field. Use of multiple observers lessens the burden on each observer and allows for more observation time overall. Furthermore, particularly if the observers are diverse in factors relevant to the phenomena being studied (e.g., gender and age), they can enhance the validity of observations by cross-checking each others' findings and eliminating inaccurate interpretations. In the study of peer treatment of social isolates described above, two other young adults served as lunchroom observers along with the two researchers.

Preparing for Observation

An observer in a qualitative research project can prepare by serving as an apprentice to an expert in the type of observation being planned. A period of apprenticeship is desirable because qualitative observation skills are complex and subtle; they do not lend themselves to the type of training procedures for quantitative observation that we described earlier in the chapter. By working alongside an expert, a novice observer gradually can develop an understanding of how to focus her observations and to shift the focus across the three stages (descriptive, focused, and selected) described below.

Although not a substitute for apprenticeship, some university programs provide courses in which you can develop particular skills needed in qualitative observation. These skills include the ability to write descriptions of observed events that are concrete rather than interpretive, to incorporate rich detail about observed events into field notes, and to convert rough, handwritten field notes into polished reports. Training in the use of video and audio recording equipment and in fieldwork techniques may be provided as well.

Once a qualitative research study is underway, you might encounter problems and issues unique to your field setting. It is helpful in such situations to maintain contact with an expert who can advise you. Such consultation maintains the integrity of the study, because in qualitative research the observation methodology is free to change as the researcher develops new insights into the phenomena being studied.

Determining the Focus of Observation

The focus of a qualitative researcher's observations is likely to shift from the early to later stages of a study. According to James Spradley, this process of shifting typically includes three stages.[26] First is the **descriptive stage,** when observations tend to be unfocused and general in scope, providing a base from which the observers can branch out in many directions. Second is the **focused stage,** when the observers have identified features of the phenomena under study that are of greatest interest and begin to direct their attention to collecting deeper information about this range of features. Finally, there is the **selective stage,** when research questions or problems have been defined and the observers' focus shifts to refining and deepening their understanding of the specific elements that have emerged as theoretically or empirically most essential. Observational data are gathered until enough data have been collected to achieve **theoretical saturation,** that is, when newly gathered findings essentially replicate earlier ones.[27]

The question of research focus also involves the decision as to what to observe at any given moment, and how to ensure that everything of potential interest is attended to. With respect to ensuring thorough coverage of the phenomena of interest, Norman Denzin suggests that all observational field notes should contain explicit reference to the following elements: participants, interactions, routines, rituals, temporal elements, interpretations,

26. Spradley, J. P. (1980). *Participant observation.* Fort Worth, TX: Harcourt.
27. Strauss, A. L., & Corbin, J. M. (1998). *Basics of qualitative research: Techniques and procedures for developing grounded theory* (2nd ed.). Thousand Oaks, CA: Sage.

and social organization of the participants.[28] Sharan Merriam presents a similar list, but also includes the setting (i.e., the physical environment, the context, and the kinds of behavior that the setting encourages, permits, discourages, or prevents) as well as subtle factors.[29] Subtle factors include informal and unplanned activities, symbolic and connotative meanings of words, nonverbal communication such as dress and physical space, and what does *not* happen, especially if it was expected.

A study by Robert Prophet and Patricia Rowell illustrates the features of a phenomenon on which observers might focus, and how the focus of observation shifts as the research project progresses.[30] Prophet and Rowell investigated teacher-student interaction in science classes in the African country of Botswana. The classes were at the junior secondary level and were taught in the English language. They describe the starting point for the study as follows:

> [We had] a desire to gain information and insights into the realities of life in science classrooms in the junior secondary schools. This goal was pursued using a conceptual framework in which teaching style and the use of knowledge exemplify power relationships in the classroom.[31]

Their descriptive stage of observation involves documenting classroom interactions by sitting discreetly at the back of the classroom and writing extensive notes. Excerpts from these field notes are included in the research report. The notes primarily document utterances by the teacher, by individual students, and by students speaking in unison. However, the observers also noted specific actions, such as when students raised their hands in order to be called on, when a student's comment was ignored by the teacher, or when the teacher wrote something on the board.

Prophet and Rowell state what their initial observations and interviews revealed:

> . . . the teachers generate learning experiences that are teacher-centered and which place the students in the role of passive recipients of knowledge. . . . The actual pedagogical principles underpinning teaching styles . . . appear to be based on rote learning. . . . These practices are so widespread and so taken for granted by all the participants that it is tempting to say simply, "This is what happens in schools."[32]

In their report, Prophet and Rowell express their growing sense of a major disparity between stated curriculum aims (i.e., that the teaching be situation be student-centered) and the actual authoritarian, teacher-centered classroom environment that they consistently observed.

Through their concurrent work at the University of Botswana, Prophet and Rowell realized that preservice teachers specializing in science education found "hands-on" science (e.g., laboratory experimentation) arduous and thus placed heavy reliance on rote learning in their own learning experiences as students. Because they had seen similar problems among secondary school students in their research study, Prophet and Rowell speculated that, "the seeds for future difficulties were being sown in the teacher education program."[33]

---

28. Denzin, N. K. (1989). *The research act* (3rd ed.). Englewood Cliffs, NJ: Prentice Hall.
29. Merriam, S. B. (1998). *Qualitative research and case study applications* (2nd ed.). San Francisco: Jossey-Bass.
30. Prophet, R. B., & Rowell, P. M. (1993). Coping and control: Science teaching strategies in Botswana. *International Journal of Qualitative Studies in Education, 6,* 197–209.
31. Ibid., p. 198.
32. Ibid., p. 201.
33. Ibid., p. 205.

During the final, selected-observation stage of their study, Prophet and Rowell paid particular attention to classroom activities designed to develop students' manipulative skills. Further observations, one of which is described in the research report, indicated that

> . . . the teaching of manipulative skills followed the same teacher-centered routine as described earlier, with students often not participating and teachers presenting instructions and information in an unclear verbal style. Very little student-based practical work was observed . . . .[34]

This teaching style was widely discrepant from the syllabus for the preservice teacher education program in science education.

As another part of the selected stage of their research, Prophet and Rowell developed a test of science skills and administered it to a small sample of students at each school. Students in general were found to perform poorly on the manipulative skills that were tested. In the conclusion of their research report, Prophet and Rowell summarize and interpret their findings in relation to their previously stated formulations concerning power relationships in classrooms.

We see in this research study how narrowing and deepening the focus of field observations can foster the emergence of qualitative interpretations, which constitute the primary findings of the study.

Gaining Entry into the Field Setting

As one would expect from the emergent nature of qualitative research, there are no strict rules about how to enter a field setting to make observations. You will need to develop a procedure based on the characteristics of the field setting and its members and on where you intend to situate yourself along the continuum of complete participant to complete observer.

You can gain insights into developing your procedure by consulting with expert qualitative researchers and by reading reports of their studies. For example, the study of social isolates in middle schools by Evans and Eders, described earlier in the chapter, is instructive. They describe their procedure for gaining entry into school lunchrooms as follows:

> Our strategy was to enter the lunchroom setting as peers rather than as authority figures. We wore jeans and other casual clothing as did most of the students. We made a point of never affiliating with teachers or other adults in this setting. This meant that some of us were sometimes included when teachers chastised our groups for initiating food fights and other disruptive activities! We initially entered the lunchroom environment as we imagined a new student in school would do, by sitting alone or next to a single person and starting conversations with students sitting nearby . . . although we informed everyone that we were from the local university and that we were studying adolescent friendship, we did not take notes openly . . . We did not inform the students of our ages, and although the age difference between the students and the researchers varied between 10 and 20 years, the students' consistent comments indicated they generally viewed us as . . . undergraduate students in our late teens . . . . The researchers' typical stance with groups to which we belonged was to become "a quiet member" of the group. We adopted a listening, receptive, nonjudgmental attitude toward other members . . . . When we did not report them for swearing or other school rule violations, their trust toward us increased dramatically and they assured other students that we were "okay."[35]

This description shows the researchers' insights about the need to present themselves to the adolescents under investigation as nonthreatening and friendly. If the same researchers

34. Ibid.
35. Evans & Eder, Processes of social isolation, pp. 145–146.

were to shift their research focus to teachers or administrators in the same school, one would expect them to adopt a more professional and mature appearance and manner, but to maintain the same level of neutrality and discretion with those groups as they had with the students, thereby demonstrating their trustworthiness.

Recording Observations

Qualitative researchers can make use of the same range of methods used by quantitative researchers to make a permanent record of their observations. For example, they can take written field notes using a laptop computer. Another option is to make an audio recording. A stenomask can be used for this purpose.[36] A **stenomask** is a sound-shielded microphone attached to a portable tape recorder that is worn on a shoulder strap. The observer can speak into the microphone while an activity is occurring without people nearby being able to hear the dictation. See the discussion of recording interview data in Chapter 8 for additional information about recording methods.

In some field settings, an observer taking notes on a tablet or in a notebook might distract participants or cause the observer to miss important aspects of events. It may be possible to take a few notes surreptitiously in such situations. Qualitative researchers have written field notes on toilet paper or inside matchbook covers in order to keep their role as observers from distracting research participants.

If you cannot take notes while in the field setting, you will need to remember what occurred and arrange to make notes soon after leaving the scene. Even if you cannot make complete field notes right away, you should at least try to write a summary of the sequence of events and noteworthy statements. You can use this summary later to stimulate your writing of a more extensive set of notes.

What Field Notes Should Include

The following are features of good field notes in a qualitative research study.

Field notes should be descriptive and reflective Descriptive information includes verbal portraits of the research participants, reconstruction of dialogue, description of the physical setting, accounts of particular events, and descriptions of the observer's behavior. Reflective information includes the researcher's personal account of the course of inquiry and may contain reflections on such elements as the methods of data collection and analysis, ethical dilemmas and conflict, and the observer's frame of mind, along with emerging interpretations. An example of field notes that include descriptive information, as well as reflections and interpretations, is shown in Figure 9.2. The notes that are reflective in nature are in italics.

Field notes should be detailed and concrete Observers should strive to write field notes that are detailed and concrete, not vague and overgeneralized. Table 9.3 shows an example of field notes at these two extremes.[36]

The excerpt on the right in Table 9.3 obviously is much more specific and descriptive than that on the left. Also, the language reflects low-inference observation, which is more helpful than high-inference observation when the researcher is ready to look for themes and patterns in the field notes and other data sources.

Field notes should include visual details when appropriate Field notes need not be limited to words. For example, an observer might draw a sketch of the layout of the physical

---

36. Stenomasks are described on pp. 248–249 in: Patton, M. (1990). *Qualitative evaluation and research methods* (2nd ed.). Thousand Oaks, CA: Sage.

FIGURE 9.2

Example of Field Notes with Observer Comments

B turned on the overhead projector and proceeded to show some examples. The first one was a colorful slide of the planets.

OC—B must like planets. There is a model of the solar system, in similar colors in B's office.

B pointed out that this particular slide would be useful in having students identify the planets and that the slide would not be very helpful in explaining planetary motion. The students were also shown an example of masking. (The names of the planets were masked by pieces of cardboard so that they could be revealed by the teacher, as required.)

OC—The students were attentive, but quiet, too quiet I thought. What's happening here is that the teacher is not asking enough questions. For example, B could have asked the students what the flaps were for, and why would you want to do such a thing. Instead of telling what the slide was good for, asking what it would be good for. Nice locus of control issue.

The second transparency's subject was the water cycle, a slide consisting of the main and two over-lays. B explained how an overhead of this kind could be used to describe a process.

OC—The students were quiet, no questions.

Note: Italicized field notes are reflective comments by the observer. OC is an abbreviation for observer comments.

Source: Segment from an unpublished report by R. Brandt, Observation of B's lesson on overhead transparencies, University of Georgia, April 30, 1987, published in: Merriam, S. B. (1988). *Case study research in education: a quali-tative approach.* San Francisco: Jossey-Bass (pp. 100–101). Reprinted with permission from Sharan B. Merriam.

setting in which the observed activities are occurring. If visual details are worthy of even more attention, the researcher can create a documentary-style visual record by making video recordings or taking photographs. Anthropologists and sociologists frequently generate visual representations based on photography, film, CD-ROMs, and other visual forms that can be presented, made available on the Internet, or examined as a data source. Douglas Harper describes the expanding role of visual information in anthropology and

TABLE 9.3

Example of Vague and Detailed Field Notes

Vague and Overgeneralized Field Notes	Detailed and Concrete Field Notes
The client was quite hostile toward the staff person.	When Judy, the senior staff member, told her that she could not do what she wanted to do, the client began to yell at Judy, telling her that she couldn't control her life, that she was on nothing but a "power trip," that she'd "like to beat the shit out of her," and that she could just "go to hell." She shook her fist in Judy's face and stomped out of the room, leaving Judy standing there with her mouth open, looking amazed.

Source: From p. 240 in: Patton, M. (1990). *Qualitative evaluation and research methods* (2nd ed.). Thousand Oaks, CA: Sage. Reprinted with permission of Sage Publications, Inc.

social science.[37] He also cautions social scientists to be aware that their selection and construction of such images can, and often do, reinforce cultural stereotypes. Qualitative researchers should thus analyze their motives and stance in selecting particular scenes and objects for preservation as recorded images.

A case study by Terry Wood, Paul Cobb, and Erna Yackel illustrates the use of video recordings in qualitative research.[38] The researchers examined how one elementary school teacher changed her approach to teaching mathematics while participating in an ongoing research project that involved constructivist views of learning. Every mathematics lesson taught by the teacher for an entire school year was videotaped, and two cameras were used to focus on four selected pairs of children during small-group activities. The video recordings, supplemented by field notes and copies of the children's classwork, were the main source of data used to document changes in students' mathematical understanding and social interaction in small groups.

Dealing with Observer Effects

As observers, qualitative researchers consider their biases and personal reactions to be part of the phenomenon that they are studying. They are therefore not as concerned as quantitative researchers with efforts to minimize observer bias or to control for observer effects. Instead they use procedures like those described below to deal with the possible effects of the observer on whom or what is observed. Chapter 14 provides a more general discussion of the criteria typically used by qualitative researchers to evaluate the soundness of their research findings.

Reactions of program participants and staff to the observer's presence Qualitative researchers strive neither to overestimate nor underestimate their effects on what is observed, but instead describe and analyze these effects as part of the research project.

Effects on the observer during the course of the study The goal is to realize that the observer will have reactions and to record them. The excerpt from Evans and Eder's field notes, in which the observer reported her distress at witnessing the mistreatment of social isolates by their middle school peers, typifies qualitative observers' attention to the effects of observations on themselves.

The observer's personal predispositions or biases To address this issue, qualitative researchers use established procedures for validating and verifying data analyses, so as to reduce any distortions that may have been introduced by their personal predispositions. These procedures include active efforts to test rival explanations for research findings, use of both qualitative and quantitative research approaches to examine a phenomenon, use of multiple observers and researchers, examination of findings from various theoretical perspectives, and reporting of the research project in sufficient detail that readers can "audit" the findings themselves.

Observer incompetence Qualitative observation data will be useless, and even misleading, if the observers have had insufficient preparation to do the type of data collection required by the research problem and approach. The solution to this problem is obvious. Observers should be thoroughly trained and otherwise prepared prior to collecting data in the field.

37. Harper, D. (2005). What's new visually? In N. K. Denzin & Y. S. Lincoln (Eds.), *The Sage handbook of qualitative research* (3rd ed., pp. 747–762). Thousand Oaks, CA: Sage.
38. Wood, T., Cobb, P., & Yackel, E. (1991). Change in teaching mathematics: A case study. *American Educational Research Journal, 28,* 587–616.

Analyzing Qualitative Observational Data

When the fieldwork phase of a qualitative research study is completed, the researchers are likely to have an extensive set of field notes and visual data that serve as a record of their observations. All these data need to be analyzed, interpreted, and reported. Michael Angrosino notes that observation-based research will be increasingly committed to "the ethnography of the particular . . . able to provide a rounded account of the lives of particular people, with the focus being on individuals and their ever-changing relationships rather than on the supposedly homogeneous, coherent, patterned, and . . . timeless nature of the supposed "group".[39] Angrosino argues that qualitative observation should focus on poor and marginalized individuals and be carried out not merely as a means of collecting data but as a form of service learning:

> Service learning, which begins with the careful observation of a community on the part of a committed student adopting a membership identity, is active engagment in and with the community in ways that foster the goals of a social justice-oriented progressive political and social agenda.[40]

Here the researcher's task in analyzing observational data involves not only becoming directly connected to the individuals being observed; it also involves using observation as a means of learning the needs of those individuals and doing practical and political work to address their needs.

Nonreactive Observation in Quantitative Research

Use of Unobtrusive Measures

Touchstone in Research

Webb, E. J., Campbell, D. T., Schwartz, R., & Sechrest, L. B. (1999). *Unobtrusive measures.* Thousand Oaks, CA: Sage.

We explained above how observer effects can weaken the validity and reliability of observational data. For example, the presence of an observer can affect the behavior of the observed individuals such that it becomes atypical. This and other observer effects can be avoided through the use of unobtrusive measures—sometimes called *nonreactive measures*. **Unobtrusive measures** are characterized by the fact that the data are collected in a natural setting, and the individuals are unaware that their behavior or its effects are being observed.

Suppose we are interested in students' use of computer technology in their studies. It would be difficult to observe students throughout the day, not knowing if and when they might use a computer. Unobtrusive measurement can help us with this problem. We could think of situations in which students would be likely to use a computer, and whether a product or "residue" would be produced that we could examine later. An obvious possibility is the use of computers for word processing of school assignments. We could ask teachers for permission to examine their students' assignments, observing which ones appear to be word-processed documents and which do not.

In this approach the students are unaware that their behavior or its effects are being observed, but their teachers are aware. Perhaps we can think of situations involving computer use that are unobtrusive for both groups. Suppose the schools that we are observing

---

39. Angrosino, M. V. (2005). Recontextualizing observation: Ethnography, pedagogy, and the prospects for a progressive political agenda. In N. K. Denzin & Y. S. Lincoln (Eds.), *The Sage handbook of qualitative research* (3rd ed., pp. 729–745).
40. Ibid., p. 741.

TABLE 9.4

Examples of Unobtrusive Measures in Research Studies

1. The floor tiles around the hatching-chick exhibit at Chicago's Museum of Science and Industry must be replaced every six weeks. Tiles in other parts of the museum need not be replaced for years. The selective erosion of tiles, indexed by the replacement rate, is a measure of relative popularity of exhibits.
2. One investigator wanted to learn the level of whiskey consumption in a town that was officially "dry." He did so by counting empty bottles in trash cans.
3. The degree of fear induced by a ghost-story-telling session can be measured by noting the shrinking diameter of a circle of seated children.
4. Chinese jade dealers have used the pupil dilation of their customers as a measure of the client's interest in particular stones. In 1872 Darwin noted this same variable as an index of fear.
5. Library withdrawals were used to demonstrate the effect of the introduction of television into a community. Fiction titles dropped, while nonfiction titles were unaffected.
6. The influence of the rate of interaction in managerial recruitment is shown by the overrepresentation of baseball managers who were infielders or catchers (high interaction positions) during their playing days.
7. Sir Francis Galton employed surveying hardware to estimate the bodily dimensions of African women whose language he did not speak.
8. Children's level of interest in Christmas was demonstrated by distortions in the size of their Santa Claus drawings.
9. Racial attitudes in two colleges were compared by noting the degree of clustering of African Americans and whites in lecture halls.

Source: Adapted from Webb, E. J., Campbell, D. T., Schwartz, R. D., Sechrest, L., & Grove, J. B. (1981). *Nonreactive measures in the social sciences* (2nd ed.). Boston: Houghton Mifflin.

make computers available for students in a technology center and in the school's library. We can obtain unobtrusive software that can be installed in these computers for the purpose of recording their duration of use, and even the users' keystrokes. Of course, this approach raises ethical questions, which we consider below.

Examples of unobtrusive measures that have been used in research studies are listed in Table 9.4. Measures of this type are especially useful when used in conjunction with conventional reactive measures, because they involve such a different approach to measurement. If we use several different kinds of instruments to measure the same variables, and they yield similar results, we can be much more confident that our results are valid.

Potential Limitations of Unobtrusive Measures

Validity The validity of some unobtrusive measures is uncertain. For example, the lost-letter technique has been used as an unobtrusive measure in research studies.[41] This technique involves making a large number of copies of various bogus letters, each of which is addressed to an organization that reflects a different opinion on an issue. The assumption is that an individual who finds a letter is more likely to mail it if the address represents an opinion that he or she supports. If this is true, the rate of return for letters representing different opinions will reflect the percentage of persons holding each opinion in the community under

41. For an interesting application of this technique, see: Farrington, D. P., & Knight, B. J. (1980). Stealing from a lost letter: Effects of victim characteristics. *Criminal Justice and Behavior, 7*, 423–435.

investigation. In several election studies, however, the proportion of letters returned failed to predict the election results, thus raising doubts about the validity of the technique.

Reliability The reliability of unobtrusive measures often is difficult to establish. Even for unobtrusive measures for which reliability can be computed, the data are of limited use to other researchers because most such measures are designed to study a very specific attitude or behavior pattern and are rarely used more than once. In contrast, conventional measures such as achievement tests, personality inventories, and attitude scales are used in many studies. Over a period of time, a useful body of knowledge about such measures is developed, and it is easier to obtain estimates of their reliability.

Ethical considerations The use of unobtrusive measures raises ethical issues involving informed consent and invasion of privacy. (These issues are discussed in Chapter 3.) Collection of nonreactive data in accessible locations usually is not regarded as an invasion of privacy. However, data collection in public areas where individuals nonetheless expect their behavior to be private, such as public restrooms, has been challenged as an invasion of privacy. Spying on an individual's private behavior (e.g., placing listening devices in the individual's home or office) clearly is an invasion of privacy.

Informed consent poses a difficult problem in unobtrusive measurement, because its main purpose is to collect data without the awareness of the individuals being studied. The act of requesting informed consent makes individuals aware that they will be studied and thus jeopardizes the nonreactivity of any subsequent measurement. Therefore, it is essential in some situations to forego informed consent.

An institutional review board (see Chapter 3) may look favorably on a request to forego informed consent if the the researcher can demonstrate the following conditions: The individuals being studied will incur no risk, the anonymity of the participants will be maintained, it is impossible to conduct the study under the condition of informed consent, and the study promises to produce significant benefits.

Nonreactive Observation in Qualitative Research

In practice, unobtrusive research typically involves quantitative observations, as shown by the examples in Table 9.4. For qualitative researchers, nonreactive observation typically involves the study of material objects and texts, from which information about individuals' behavior is inferred. Paul Atkinson and Sara Delamont argue that "the detailed investigation of objects, assemblages, and inventions demands a place in the general ethnographic study of social and cultural forms".[42] Qualitative researchers analyze such phenomena as expressions of how individuals and groups construct their social reality. Here we refer to such study as nonreactive qualitative observation.

Ian Hodder uses the term **material culture** to refer to the various objects created by different groups throughout history.[43] (Some researchers refer to them as *artifacts*.) He distinguishes between two types of material culture. First is material culture that serves a communicative, representational function. Text and signs are examples of this type of material culture. We discuss the study of text and signs by qualitative researchers later in the chapter.

The second type of material culture, which we call **practice-oriented material culture** is distinguished by its association with particular practices and meanings.

42. Atkinson, P., & Delamont, S. (2005). Analytic perspectives. In N. K. Denzin & Y. S. Lincoln (Eds.), *The Sage handbook of qualitative research* (3rd ed., pp. 821–840). Thousand Oaks, CA: Sage. Quote appears on p. 826.
43. Hodder, I. (2000). The interpretation of documents and material culture. In N. K. Denzin & Y. S. Lincoln (Eds.), *Handbook of qualitative research* (2nd ed., pp. 703–715). Thousand Oaks, CA: Sage.

For example, in his book *Reading the Past* Hodder describes his efforts to understand why only one tribe in the Baringo district in Kenya, Africa, the Ilchamus, decorate the calabashes (a type of gourd) that are used to hold milk for children and the meaning of this cultural practice.[44] Through historical analysis he traces the beginnings of the practice to around 1900, when the Ilchamus people gave up agriculture and began raising cattle as their main occupation. Now women no longer had to do the low-status work of growing food in the fields. They could bear more children, and they had more time to devote to decorative activity. Hodder traces how this activity reflects the extension of women's authority in the realm of reproduction (sexuality and the bearing of children) and beyond it into the realm of the provision of milk, which comes from cattle, which on the surface is considered a masculine domain. Hodder also notes that more recently women began decorating the hut interiors as well, which he ties directly to the growing movement of males to work in cities and reductions in family size and indirectly to an extension of women's areas of authority to the entire family dwelling. Furthermore, the women are now selling calabashes to tourists, which to Hodder represents their growing ability to become even more active participants in the outside world than the Ilchamus men.

Despite its importance, the use of practice-oriented material culture as a data source is problematic. The reason is that qualitative researchers usually cannot check the validity of their interpretations of the social reality that it represents by interviewing the individuals who produced it. Archaeologists have taken the lead in developing methods to deal with this problem, because they often find themselves in the situation of interpreting objects and fragments of objects from ancient cultures.

Practice-oriented material culture is worthy of observation by educational researchers. Many specialized materials have been developed or adopted by educators over time—among them, chalkboards, desks, classrooms, school buildings, computers, and video recorders. Students, too, use certain materials, such as notebooks, binders, pencils, staplers, calculators, and erasers. The study of such materials may provide valuable insights into how these groups construct the social context within which they cope with learning tasks and deal with other aspects of their public and private lives.

Content Analysis of Documents and Other Communication Media

Thus far in this chapter, our focus has been on methods for observing human behavior and features of the environment in which the behavior occurs. An important feature of human environments is the messages that people encode in various forms:

Written documents: Written materials include textbooks, students' completed homework assignments, tests, computer printouts of school data, newspapers, and memoranda.

Visual media: Photographs, posters, and drawings are examples of visual materials that may be analyzed.

Audio media: The researcher can analyze audiotape recordings, laser disc recordings, or radio programs.

Combinations of media: It may be desirable to analyze a variety of types of media, such as TV programs and CD-ROM discs that combine print, visual images, and sound.

---

44. Hodder, I. (1991). *Reading the past: Current approaches to interpretation in archaeology* (2nd ed.). New York: Cambridge University Press.

Touchstones in Research

Neuendorf, K. A. (2002). *The content analysis guidebook.* Thousand Oaks, CA: Sage. Also see *The content analysis guidebook online*, which supplements the text, available at Web site http://academic.csuohio.edu/kneuendorf/content

Stemler, S. (2001). An introduction to content analysis. ERIC Digest No. ED458218; retrieved June 2, 2005, from http://www.ericdigests.org/2002-2/content.htm

The content of these materials comprises forms of communication from one individual or group to another individual or group. These messages are the object of study in some research projects. Textbooks are of particular interest, because they convey much about the school curriculum. Textbooks and other written materials usually are called *documents* by researchers. We use the term *communication media* to refer both to documents and to materials whose messages are primarily visual or auditory.

If you plan to include communication media as a data source in your research, you will need to be systematic about identifying and analyzing them. In the following sections we describe appropriate procedures, depending on whether your research will be conducted from a quantitative or qualitative perspective.

Content Analysis in Quantitative Research

In quantitative research, the analysis of documents typically involves content analysis. **Content analysis** has been defined as "a generic name for a variety of means of textual analysis that involve comparing, contrasting, and categorizing a corpus of data to test hypotheses."[45] The raw material for content analysis can be any type of document or other communication medium.

Most content analyses in education involve collecting data on various aspects of the messages encoded in the communication product. These analyses generally involve fairly simple classifications or tabulations of specific information. Content analyses of student compositions for language arts classes, for example, could be used to develop a typology of students' grammatical and spelling errors and the frequency of different types of errors. This information can be used to revise language arts courses or develop remedial programs.

Steps in Content Analysis

In describing the steps involved in a content analysis, we refer to a research study of vocabulary instruction in social studies textbooks conducted by Janis Harmon, Wanda Hedrick, and Elizabeth Fox.[46] Although this example involves printed text, the procedures are equally appropriate for the analysis of other communication media, such as Web pages, film, and audio recordings.

Specify research questions, hypotheses, or objectives The researchers' study grew out of their appreciation of the important role that vocabulary instruction plays in students' ability to understand social-studies concepts presented in the upper-elementary and middle-school grades. Also, they were aware of effective research-based practices for promoting vocabulary development and wondered whether these practices were represented in the teachers' editions of social-studies textbooks.

These interests and concerns led Harmon and her colleagues to frame three research questions to guide their study:

1. What is the nature of the words or key terms selected by the social studies textbook publishers?
2. To what extent and how is vocabulary represented at each grade level and across series of published social studies programs for grades 4–8?
3. What vocabulary instructional supports do publishers provide for teachers?[47]

---

45. Schwandt, T. A. (2001). *Dictionary of qualitative inquiry* (2nd ed.). Thousand Oaks, CA: Sage. Quote appears on p. 34.
46. Harmon, J. M., Hedrick, W. B., & Fox, E. A. (2000). A content analysis of vocabulary instruction in social studies textbooks for grades 4–8. *Elementary School Journal, 100,* 253–271.
47. Ibid., p. 254.

Textbooks, especially teachers' editions, contain a great many content-related elements. By framing the research questions stated above, these researchers made explicit the scope of their investigation and also focused it sufficiently so that a manageable study could be designed.

Select a sample of documents to analyze The researchers selected teachers' editions of the social studies textbooks on the 1997–1998 Texas state adoption list for grades 4–8. The teachers' editions were selected because they contain both the text that students read and recommendations to teachers about how to teach this text. It was necessary to have documents that included these recommendations in order to address the third research question stated above.

Develop a category-coding procedure The essence of a content analysis is the coding of the document's messages into categories. Each category should represent a discrete variable that is relevant to your research objective. The categories should be mutually exclusive, such that any bit of communication can be coded by only one category in the category system.

If appropriate, consider employing a coding system that has been used in previous research. This option saves the time required to develop your own system. Also, the use of standard coding categories permits comparison with other studies that have used the same system. Consequently, the research project is more likely to make a contribution to theory and knowledge related to the topic you are researching.

In the vocabulary study that we are considering here, the researchers developed their own categories, but they represent standard features of textbooks, including teachers' editions. Among the categories are these: instructional objectives; instructional components (i.e., suggestions for tasks that teachers or students might complete in order to enhance instruction and learning); and key terms (i.e., words or phrases highlighted by the publishers), with subcategories for (1) general terms that might be found in any subject (e.g., *malady, revenge*), (2) technical multiple-meaning terms (e.g., *table, legend*), (3) technical, domain-specific words unique to social studies (e.g., *pueblo, colonist*), and (4) terms relating to specific persons, places, and events (e.g., *Bull Run, Dwight Eisenhower*).

After initial development of the content classification system, you should determine whether several raters can use it with a high degree of consistency. You can do this by calculating a correlation coefficient of inter-rater reliability for different raters' classifications.[48] If the inter-rater reliability is low, you will need to identify points of ambiguity in the content classification system and clarify them. To increase the reliability with which the classification system can be used, it is helpful to develop an explicit set of scoring rules.

A specific reliability check was not reported by the researchers who conducted the vocabulary study. There are repeated references to "we" in the report, so presumably the researchers checked each others' coding as the content analysis proceeded. Nonetheless, our confidence in the study findings would be strengthened by a reliability check.

Code the data A typical content analysis consists of making a frequency count of the occurrence of each coding category in each document in the sample. The general procedure is to create a computer file that reproduces the text of the document. (You can type the text or possibly use a scanning device that reads the text directly into a computer file.) Then read the computer file and type a code for each message that fits a particular category of

---

48. For information on calculating inter-rater reliability coefficients, see: Stemler, S. (2001). An overview of content analysis. *Practical Assessment, Research & Evaluation, 7*(17). Retrieved February 12, 2006, from http://www. pareonline.net/getvn.asp?v=7&n=17; Scott, W. (1955). Reliability of content analysis: The case of nominal scale coding. *Public Opinion Quarterly, 19*, 321–325.

the content-analysis system. A computer program can be used to count the frequency of each code, or to list together all the text messages that fit a particular code. Computer programs of this type are described in Chapter 14.

The frequency counts can be presented in the results section of the research report. Descriptive statistics also can be reported, for example, the mean number and standard deviation of the occurrences of each coding category across all the documents in the sample. Relationships between the variables represented by the different categories can be analyzed and reported, too.

In the vocabulary study, the researchers conducted several of these statistical analyses. For example, they calculated the mean percentage of key terms that fit each of their categories across the textbooks included in the content analysis. They found that 78 percent of the key terms were in the category of domain-specific words, with another 13 percent in the category of terms relating to specific persons, places, and events. In a related analysis, they asked three teachers to identify what they considered to be key terms in representative samples of text from the textbooks (the samples had been scanned so that the teachers could not identify which terms the publishers had marked as key). Surprisingly, there was only 48 percent agreement between the publishers' and teachers' lists.

Table 9.5 shows the results of an analysis of the instructional components involving key terms that were included in the teachers' editions of the textbooks. As you can see, the researchers classified the instructional components into three categories of tasks: instruction (i.e., teaching activities for the teacher); application (i.e., activities requiring students to use the key term); and review (i.e., activities in the review section of the textbook units, chapters, and lessons). For most of the textbooks, the vast majority of the instructional components involved application and review. A more fine-grained analysis of the components revealed an emphasis on surface-level vocabulary activities, for example, filling in blanks, doing crossword puzzles, and matching words with their definitions.

Interpret the results The final stage of a content analysis is to interpret the meaning of the results. The interpretive process will depend on the purpose of the study and its theoretical or conceptual framework.

In the vocabulary study, Harmon, Hedrick, and Fox used research knowledge about effective vocabulary instruction as a basis for evaluating publishers' practices as revealed by their content analyses. This research knowledge demonstrates the value of such instructional activities as word sorts, semantic mapping, and graphic organizers to help students make connections between their prior knowledge and new terminology. Harmon, Hedrick, and Fox found virtually no utilization of this research knowledge in the textbooks they analyzed:

> Our findings indicate that although publishers do give consideration to vocabulary in their programs, many activities are still grounded in vocabulary teaching and learning activities that are not supported by empirical evidence. Thus, publishers need to take a more aggressive stance to integrate current knowledge about vocabulary into their instructional procedures.[49]

The researchers also raise an important question for future research, based on their data analysis of teachers' and publishers' identification of key terms in social studies textbooks: "Disagreements between teachers and publishers over what should be highlighted as conceptually loaded terms raises questions concerning how publishers select key terms."[50] This is a good example of the principle that the value of a study often lies less with its findings and more in the questions it raises.

49. Harmon et al., A content analysis of vocabulary instruction, p. 269.
50. Ibid., p. 265.

TABLE 9.5

Categories of Vocabulary Tasks in the Teacher's Edition of Social Studies Textbooks

Series	Total	Instruction (%)	Application (%)	Review (%)
Harcourt Brace, grade 4	61	21	31	48
Harcourt Brace, grade 5	8	13	50	38
Harcourt Brace, grade 6	31	26	32	42
Houghton Mifflin, grade 4	64	25	36	39
Houghton Mifflin, grade 5	46	24	30	46
Houghton Mifflin, grade 6	135	23	36	41
Macmillan, grade 4	60	23	33	43
Macmillan, grade 5	108	27	33	40
Macmillan, grade 6	189	17	54	29
Silver Burdett Ginn, grade 4	40	15	55	30
Silver Burdett Ginn, grade 5	14	0	57	43
Silver Burdett Ginn, grade 6	41	2	49	49
Jarrett, grade 4	7	43	43	14
Benson, grade 7	7	29	0	71
Glencoe, grade 7	21	24	24	52
Holt, Rinehart & Winston, grade 7	6	17	33	50
Holt, Rinehart & Winston, grade 8	31	19	55	26
Prentice Hall, grade 8	17	6	12	82
Scott Foresman, grade 8	8	13	38	50

Source: Table 5 on p. 266 in: Harmon, J. M., Hedrick, W. B., & Fox E. A. (2000). A content analysis of vocabulary instruction in social studies textbooks for grades 4–8. *Elementary School Journal, 100,* 253–271. Copyright © 2000 by the University of Chicago Press. Reprinted with permission from the University of Chicago Press.

Analysis of Documents and Records in Qualitative Observation

Qualitative researchers often study written communications found in natural situations. These written communications are of various types. Yvonna Lincoln and Egon Guba define **documents** as written communications that are prepared for personal rather than official reasons.[51] In contrast, **records** are written communications that have an official purpose. For example, personal letters, personal diaries, and drafts of articles are documents, whereas legal contracts, commission reports for general circulation, tax statements, and newspaper articles are records.

Documents and records rely primarily on language to convey meaning. Other communications—for example, mathematics, music, and highway signs—rely on different types of sign systems to convey meaning. **Semiotics** is a field of inquiry that studies the meaning of these signs.[52] For example, Peter Manning and Betsy Cullum-Swan did a semiotic analysis of the various meanings conveyed by the different sign systems at McDonald's restaurants, among them, the menu board, lighting, arrangement of space, utensils and food wrappings, outdoor playgrounds, and the use of the "Mc" prefix to label various food items.[53] (Semiotics is explained further in Chapter 15.)

51. Lincoln, Y. S., & Guba, E. G. (1985). *Naturalistic inquiry.* Beverly Hills, CA: Sage.
52. Manning, P. K., & Cullum-Swan, B. (1994). Narrative, content, and semiotic analysis. In N. K. Denzin & Y. S. Lincoln (Eds.), *Handbook of qualitative research* (pp. 463–477). Thousand Oaks, CA: Sage.
53. Ibid.

In traditional quantitative research, the meaning of a text is assumed to be invariant across readers and across time. In other words, the meaning is in the text itself, and the meaning can be represented as discrete content variables and studied by the methods of content analysis. In contrast, qualitative researchers believe that the meaning of a text resides in the minds of its writer and its readers. Thus, the meaning of a particular document or record can change from reader to reader and from one historical period to another. Furthermore, a document or record can have different meanings at different levels of analysis. For example, the content of a textbook can be analyzed to determine what topics it covers. However, it also can be seen as a secondary source that is derived from primary sources. (Primary and secondary sources are explained in Chapter 4.) The relationship between the textbook and its primary sources thus can be the focus of a qualitative researcher's study.

To fully understand a document or record, therefore, the qualitative researcher needs to study the context in which it was produced—the author's purpose in writing it, the author's working conditions, the author's intended and actual audience, and the audience's purpose for reading it. The qualitative researcher also must realize that, in reading and analyzing the text, she creates her own meanings.

Documents and records from the distant past pose particular problems for the qualitative researcher because it is not possible to interview the author or readers from that time period. Also, the researcher cannot observe the situations in which these written communications were used originally or how they were made available for different audiences. Historians have developed various research methods to deal with these problems. Their methods are described in Chapter 16.

Qualitative researchers follow some of the same steps as quantitative researchers who use text and other communication media as data sources. They typically begin by identifying documents and records that are representative of the phenomenon that they plan to study. Once they have identified these materials, their next step is to determine which materials might be relevant to their research study. Then they determine how they can collect these materials for analysis within the guidelines for ethical conduct of research. If the materials cannot be removed from the natural setting, it may be possible to make photocopies and photographs of them in their setting for later analysis. Otherwise, the researchers will need to devise a method for analyzing them on site. Finally, they will need to consider the validity of the materials. Conceptions of validity that apply to historical documents and records (i.e., internal and external criticism) are described in Chapter 16.

The use of documents and records as data sources in qualitative research differs most from quantitative research in the analysis phase. In quantitative research, a set of variables is defined and applied uniformly to all the written communications in the sample. The variables are measured in such a way as to yield quantified data that can be analyzed by conventional statistics. In qualitative research, the analysis procedure is likely to be emergent. The same document or record can be analyzed at different points in the study, with each analysis yielding new constructs, hypotheses, and insights. The results of the analysis need not be expressed in quantified form. Furthermore, the same document or record can be analyzed from different perspectives and for different purposes.

The results of the qualitative researcher's analysis take the form of interpretations and hypotheses. Hodder proposes that these hypotheses and interpretations be weighed in relation to two different contexts—the context in which the documents and records were developed and the context in which they are now being interpreted for research purposes.[54] The researcher must take into account variations in meaning as they are studied

---

54. Hodder, The interpretation of documents.

across space, time, and cultures. Hodder suggests five criteria for confirming interpretations based on data obtained from documents and records:

1. internal coherence, meaning that different parts of the theoretical argument do not contradict one other and the conclusions follow from the premises;
2. external coherence, meaning that the interpretation fits theories accepted in and outside the discipline;
3. correspondence between theory and data;
4. the fruitfulness of the theoretical suppositions, that is, how many new directions, lines of inquiry, or perspectives are opened up; and
5. the trustworthiness, professional credentials, and status of the author and supporters of an interpretation.

An example of the use of documents, records, and signs in qualitative research is a study by G. Genevieve Patthey-Chavez concerning her perceptions of the cultural conflict between Latino students and their mainstream teachers in a Los Angeles high school.[55] Patthey-Chavez puts the high school in context by describing the neighborhood in which it was located. Her observations, carried out from 1986 to 1989, include various forms of public communications in the neighborhood:

> Area businesses now sport huge Spanish-language signs next to modest English-language ones; video stores advertise their Spanish-language collections; and several Spanish-language newspapers and radio and television stations compete very successfully with English-language media.[56]

She concludes from these observations that Salvadorean and Mexican cultural networks have been firmly and successfully established in this neighborhood.

Patthey-Chavez's observations of the school's curriculum focused on the English as a Second Language (ESL) program. In examining the text of ESL curriculum materials in use at the school, she found that they emphasized English grammatical structures. This emphasis, she notes, runs counter to current recommendations for ESL methodology, which emphasizes the development of students' oral communicative proficiency.

Patthey-Chavez draws upon a local newspaper article about the high school to illustrate what she perceives as its assimilationist mission, serving as "a port of entry for educational opportunity and the American way, a port of entry that students, but for a few miscreants, were eagerly passing through."[57] In her research report, Patthey-Chavez illustrates this theme by quoting the following excerpt from the newspaper article:

> Student Celia Toche, 17, came from El Salvador with her family five years ago, knowing no English. Now she is an honor student and hopes to go to college. She is usually so absorbed with physics tests, economic theory, trigonometry exercises and English literature that she rarely thinks anymore of such painful losses and frightening times as when armed guerillas perched on the roof of her school.
>
> Sometimes, however, she is reminded. "My parents didn't get a chance to get an education," she says. "It's a family treasure, to get an education here. I really value it a lot. So when I see people wasting the opportunities they've got here, the choices they have here, that's when I think about El Salvador. Here at Lima [High School], we know what we have—and we appreciate it."[58]

55. Patthey-Chavez, G. G. (1993). High school as an arena for cultural conflict and acculturation for Latino Angelinos. *Anthropology and Education Quarterly, 24,* 33–60.
56. Ibid., p. 40.
57. Ibid., p. 50.
58. Woo, E. (1986, September 28). Lima High makes a comeback. An inner city shows how it's done. *Los Angeles Times Magazine,* p. 14.

Patthey-Chavez claims that this student's experience represents a biased view of the high school's effectiveness. In working with other students from El Salvador, she found that some of them perceived El Salvadoran schools to be more rigorous and moral than American schools.

The use of a newspaper article as a data source for this study is significant for two reasons. First, it reveals information about one student's experience at the high school being studied. Second, the newspaper article creates meanings that are different from those created if the researcher had reported a personal interview with the student: An interview is a personal event, whereas a newspaper article provides a widely circulated public record of a conversation. The fact that the newspaper reporter chose to include this particular conversation supports Patthey-Chavez's claim that the school is supporting an assimilationist mission—a mission that the newspaper reporter apparently supports and wishes the public to know. In fact, one can speculate that the newspaper reporter is telling the readers what they want to hear, namely, that their public schools are striving to assimilate immigrants and succeeding in the task. The inclusion of the newspaper article as a data source widens the context of the study and provides a contrast with Patthey-Chavez's other data that question the assimilationist mission of schools.

RECOMMENDATIONS FOR

Using Observational and Content-Analysis Methods

1. Determine whether a mechanical or electronic device can facilitate your collection of observational data.
2. In making quantitative observations, provide adequate training for observers to minimize observer bias, response sets, contamination, drift, and reliability decay.
3. Check the validity and reliability of quantitative observational data that you obtain.
4. In designing a form for quantitative observation, include only as many variables as the observers can code reliably and avoid asking them to make overly precise discriminations.
5. In doing qualitative research, consider changing the focus of observation as data collection progresses in order to accommodate emerging findings and questions.
6. In making qualitative observations, consider carefully—and take data on—how you react to informants and others in the field setting, and how they react to you.
7. In making qualitative observations, prepare field notes that are rich in detail and in low-inference descriptions.
8. Consider whether it is possible to measure your research variables by collecting observational data on physical objects and "residues" of human behavior.
9. In doing a quantitative content analysis, include appropriate checks of validity and reliability.
10. In doing a qualitative analysis of communication media, consider the meaning of the text from different perspectives, including those of the author and intended audiences.

SELF-CHECK TEST

Circle the correct answer to each of the following questions.
The answers are provided at the back of the book.

1. Test anxiety is an example of
   a. a descriptive observational variable.
   b. an inferential observational variable.
   c. an evaluative observational variable.
   d. a nonintrusive variable.

2. Recording the number of times that a teacher calls on a student to answer a question about grammar in a Spanish class is an example of
   a. duration recording.
   b. frequency-count recording.
   c. interval recording.
   d. continuous recording.

3. Computers are used in observational research
   a. to time the duration of events.
   b. to detect observer errors in recording observational data.
   c. to make graphic representations of observational data.
   d. all of the above.

4. College students are trained to use a standard form when observing children's play behavior. They record their observations on this form, and their data are compared with those of an expert on child psychology. The purpose of this comparison is to check
   a. criterion-related observer reliability.
   b. intra-observer reliability.
   c. inter-observer reliability.
   d. internal reliability.

5. The same individuals are asked to record students' grade-point average by examining school records and also to observe the students' on-task behavior in three different classes. This procedure is most susceptible to
   a. reliability decay.
   b. the error of leniency.
   c. observer contamination.
   d. observer drift.

6. A researcher observes the meetings of a teachers union. She is a representative of this union, and therefore regularly attends the meetings. The researcher's role is that of
   a. complete observer.
   b. observer-participant.
   c. participant-observer.
   d. complete participant.

7. The selective stage of qualitative observation
   a. can achieve theoretical saturation.
   b. must involve a role shift from participant-observer to complete observer.
   c. precedes the focused stage.
   d. all of the above.

8. Field notes in qualitative research should
   a. emphasize high-inference observations.
   b. emphasize low-inference observations.
   c. avoid personal comments and reflections.
   d. have a highly selective focus.

9. Compared to reactive observation, data obtained from nonreactive observation is typically
   a. more reliable.
   b. easier to carry out.
   c. subject to ethical criticism.
   d. all of the above.

10. Qualitative researchers believe that material artifacts are
    a. expressions of how individuals and groups construct social reality.
    b. expressions of the dominant groups within a culture.
    c. outside the range of phenomena that they should study.
    d. useful to study only if they serve communicative, representational functions.

11. A qualitative researcher is analyzing the textbooks used in present-day Russian schools. To determine the meaning of the textbook content, the researcher is likely
    a. to study the authors of the textbooks.
    b. to study the teachers who use the textbooks.
    c. to study the students for whom the textbooks were written.
    d. all of the above.

PART IV

Quantitative Research Design

You need to design your research study so that it will answer the questions or test the hypotheses you have framed. To accomplish this task, you can refer to standard research designs that quantitative researchers have created and refined over time. These designs are described in Part IV. You need to become familiar with all of them in order to select the most appropriate one for your study and to understand quantitative research studies conducted by others.

Chapter 10 explains descriptive and causal-comparative research designs. A descriptive design is appropriate when your purpose is to create a detailed, quantitatively based description of a phenomenon: for example, people's opinions about educational issues or how teachers and students act in certain situations. In a causal-comparative design, the researcher forms two or more groups and compares them in order to explore possible causes or effects of a phenomenon.

Chapter 11 presents the major correlational research designs, which can be used to address questions and hypotheses similar to those addressed in a causal-comparative design. However, correlational research designs involve a different approach to sampling, measurement, and statistical analysis.

The common feature of descriptive, causal-comparative, and correlational research designs is that they involve the study of behavior, cognition, and other attributes of individuals without any intervention by the researcher. In other words, there is no attempt by the researcher to influence the individuals being studied.

In contrast, experimental research designs do involve researcher intervention. The researcher introduces an intervention, such as a new educational program or a new teaching method, and observes how the research participants react to it. The major experimental designs are described in Chapters 12 and 13.

As you read the chapters in Part IV, you will find that a major purpose of educational research is to discover and validate cause-and-effect relationships between variables. You also will learn that causal-comparative or correlational research can produce evidence about such relationships, but this evidence generally is not as convincing as that produced by a well-designed experiment.

CHAPTER 10

Nonexperimental Research: Descriptive and Causal-Comparative Designs

OVERVIEW

The descriptive method is the most basic of the quantitative research methods. It involves describing characteristics of a particular sample of individuals or other phenomena. We explain two major types of descriptive research: description of the characteristics of a sample at one point in time; and longitudinal research, in which changes in the characteristics of a sample over time are described. Next we discuss the causal-comparative method, which is used to explore possible causal relationships between variables. We explain the advantages and disadvantages of this research method and the steps involved in using it.

OBJECTIVES

After studying this chapter, you should be able to

1. Explain the relationship between descriptive research and causal-comparative research.
2. Describe the types of measurement tools and statistical techniques that are used commonly in descriptive research.
3. Explain the purpose of descriptive research studies in which a sample is studied at one point in time.
4. Explain the difference between trend, cohort, and panel studies, and the advantages of each type.
5. State two problems with the cross-sectional research design.
6. Describe three possible interpretations of a relationship between variable *A* and variable *B* that is discovered through causal-comparative research.

7. Explain the use of the extreme-groups sampling method in causal-comparative research.
8. Define suitable comparison groups, given an initially defined group in which a particular characteristic is present.
9. Explain how the *t* test is used in causal-comparative research.
10. Explain the situation in causal-comparative research in which a *t* test for correlated means should be used rather than a *t* test for independent means.
11. Interpret the *t* value resulting from a *t* test for a single mean, and describe how this test is used in causal-comparative research.
12. Describe how analysis of variance, analysis of covariance, and multivariate analysis of covariance are used in causal-comparative research.

13. Describe situations in causal-comparative research in which nonparametric tests of significance are more appropriate than parametric tests.

14. Describe how the chi-square test, the Mann-Whitney U test, the Wilcoxon signed rank test, and the Kruskal-Wallis test are used in causal-comparative research.

Introduction

Over time, quantitative researchers have developed various standard designs that facilitate the planning of their studies. These designs, which function somewhat like templates, involve standard nomenclature and procedures for organizing variables, selecting samples, establishing a schedule for data collection, and selecting appropriate techniques for statistical analysis.

Similarities among the research designs allow them to be classified. For example, we find it useful to classify research designs as either nonexperimental or experimental. Nonexperimental designs are similar in that the researcher studies phenomena as they exist. In contrast, the various experimental designs all involve researcher intervention. We describe nonexperimental designs (descriptive, causal-comparative, and correlational) in this chapter and Chapter 11. Experimental designs are described in Chapters 12 and 13.

Research designs also can be classified by their purpose. You will recall that, in Chapter 1, we stated that educational research is conducted for four primary purposes: description, prediction, improvement, and explanation.

Researchers whose purpose is description will employ one of two types of research design: *descriptive,* if the intent is to study phenomena as they exist at one point in time; and *longitudinal,* if the intent is to study phenomena as they change over time. These research designs are described in the next section of this chapter.

If the purpose of a research study is prediction, a correlational research design is used. Various designs of this type are described in the next chapter.

If the researcher's purpose is explanation, the focus of the study will be on understanding cause-and-effect relationships between variables. Causal-comparative designs, which are described in this chapter, can be used to discover and verify cause-and-effect relationships. However, correlational and experimental designs can be used as well. The choice of one type of design or another depends on several factors, which we explain in this and the next three chapters.

Finally, research can be done for the purpose of improving education by developing and testing interventions. Introducing an intervention and then observing its effects is, by definition, an experiment. Various experimental designs are described in Chapters 12 and 13.

An Example from Medical Research

The value of descriptive and causal-comparative research is illustrated by an example from medical practice, specifically, the treatment of cystic fibrosis, a life-shortening genetic disease that affects the entire body, but most seriously the lungs. Atul Gawande, who summarized this research for an article in *The New Yorker*, states:

> It used to be assumed that differences among hospitals or doctors in a particular specialty were generally insignificant. If you plotted a graph showing the results of all the centers treating cystic fibrosis—or any other disease, for that matter—people expected that the curve would look something like a shark fin, with most places clustered around the very best

Touchstones in Research

Campbell, D. T., & Stanley, J. C. (1981). *Experimental and quasi-experimental designs for research.* Boston: Houghton Mifflin.

Johnson, B. (2001). Toward a new classification of nonexperimental quantitative research. *Educational Researcher, 30*(2), 3–13.

outcomes. But the evidence has begun to indicate otherwise. What you tend to find is a bell curve: a handful of teams with disturbingly poor outcomes for their patients, a handful with remarkably good results, and a great undistinguished middle.[1]

The discovery of a bell curve in medical outcomes relating to cystic fibrosis is the result of careful descriptive research. Gawande notes that this research was conducted by the Cystic Fibrosis Foundation, which has collected performance data from American cystic-fibrosis treatment centers for over 40 years.

The next step in this type of research is to investigate what distinguishes the most effective treatment centers from the less effective ones. This is causal-comparative research, because it seeks to discover the *causes* (medical practices) for differential *effects* (medical outcomes for patients). Gawande does not describe a formal study, but his investigation follows this causal-comparative model. For example, sampling in causal-comparative research sometimes involves extreme groups (described later in this chapter). Gawande states that, in 2003, the life expectancy of cystic-fibrosis patients nationally was an average of 33 years, but the average life expectancy at the very best center was more than 47, a remarkable 14-year difference.

Gawande visited the very best center to learn possible causes of the difference between its patient outcomes and those achieved by lower-performing centers. What he found is that doctors and other staff at the best center have extremely high expectations for themselves and encourage patients to have the same expectations for themselves: "He [the center's director] and his colleagues aren't content if their patients' lung function is eighty per cent of normal, or even ninety per cent. They aim for a hundred per cent—or better."[2]

This remarkable example of research on medical practice has a parallel in research on educational practice. Researchers observe and document variations in important outcomes, such as academic achievement for each teacher's students or the teaching effectiveness of graduates of each teacher education program; and then they can attempt to discover the factors that cause these variations. Examples of this type of research are presented in the following sections of this chapter.

Descriptive Research Designs

The Purpose of Descriptive Research

Research in its most basic form involves the description of natural or man-made phenomena—their form, actions, changes over time, and similarities with other phenomena. Scientists have made many important discoveries through their efforts to describe phenomena. For example, astronomers have used telescopes to develop descriptions of different parts of the universe. This research has provided the basis for many other discoveries, such as the structure of our solar system and the ability to predict such stellar events as lunar eclipses.

Descriptive research is similarly important in education. **Descriptive research** is a type of quantitative research that involves making careful descriptions of educational phenomena. As you shall see in Part V, description—viewed as *understanding* what people or things mean—also is an important goal of qualitative research. For this reason, when planning a descriptive research study, you should be familiar with both quantitative and

---

1. Gawande, A. (2004, December 6). The bell curve: What happens when patients find out how good their doctors really are? *New Yorker*, 82–91. Quote appears on p. 83.
2. Ibid., p. 90.

qualitative approaches to description so that you can choose the approach best suited to your purposes.

Descriptive studies are concerned primarily with determining "what is." Examples of questions that might be studied in a descriptive research study are: How many teachers in our state hold favorable attitudes toward whole-language instruction? What kinds of activities typically occur in sixth-grade art classes, and how frequently does each one occur? What have been the reactions of school administrators to innovations in teaching physical science? Have first-grade textbooks changed in readability over the last 50 years?

Most educational research has a strong inclination toward discovering cause-and-effect relationships and testing new instructional methods and programs. However, unless researchers first generate an accurate description of an educational phenomenon as it exists, they lack a firm basis for explaining or changing it. Some of the most influential calls for reform of the educational system have used the findings of descriptive research, typically based on compelling observational data, to make their case. Books such as *Life in Classrooms* by Philip Jackson, *The Good High School* by Sara Lawrence Lightfoot, and *A Place Called School* by John Goodlad report studies of this type.[3]

Some descriptive studies involve primarily the administration of questionnaires or interviews to samples of research participants. This type of research (sometimes called *survey research*) has yielded much valuable knowledge about opinions, attitudes, and practices. This knowledge has helped shape educational policy and initiatives to improve existing conditions. Survey research is discussed in Chapter 8.

Measurement in Descriptive Research

Descriptive studies are limited by the types and quality of available measures. For this reason, many researchers work intensively on developing new measures or perfecting ones that already have been developed in order to describe precisely and accurately the phenomena of interest to them. These measures are of many types, including, for example, standardized achievement tests, classroom observation instruments, attitude scales, questionnaires, and interviews. If you are planning to do a descriptive study in the quantitative research tradition, you should be familiar with the various types of research measures discussed in Chapters 7 through 9.

Statistics in Descriptive Research

To describe a sample as a whole, a researcher typically will define variables, measure them, and for each measure compute one or more of the descriptive statistics mentioned in Chapter 5—that is, measures of central tendency (the mean, median, and mode) and measures of variability (standard deviation, variance, and range). The researcher also might calculate derived scores as an aid in interpreting the sample's scores on the variables that were measured. **Derived scores** aid interpretation by providing a quantitative measure of each individual's performance relative to a comparison group, for example, a normative sample. Age equivalents, grade equivalents, percentiles, and standard scores are examples of derived scores that commonly are used in descriptive research. (For additional explanation of derived scores, see Chapter 5.)

Some descriptive research is intended to produce statistical information about aspects of education that interest policy makers and educators. The National Center for Education Statistics specializes in this type of research.[4] Many of its findings are published in

3. Jackson, P. W. (1968). *Life in classrooms.* New York: Holt, Rinehart and Winston; Lightfoot, S. L. (1983). *The good high school.* New York: Basic Books; Goodlad, J. (1983). *A place called school.* New York: McGraw-Hill.
4. The Web homepage for the National Center for Education Statistics is http://www.nces.ed.gov

an annual volume called the *Digest of Educational Statistics.*[5] This center also administers the National Assessment of Educational Progress (NAEP), which collects descriptive information about the performance of youth at various ages in the subject areas that are taught in public school. A typical NAEP publication that appears periodically is the *Reading Report Card,* which reports descriptive statistics about the reading achievement of students at several grade levels.[6] On a larger scale, the International Association for the Evaluation of Educational Achievement (IEA) carries out descriptive studies of the academic achievement of students from many nations, including the United States.[7]

Two main types of descriptive research are found in the research literature, differing primarily in the time at which the variables of interest are measured. The first type involves measuring the characteristics of a sample at one point in time. The second type involves longitudinal research, in which a sample is followed over time. We discuss each of these types of descriptive research below.

Description of a Sample at One Point in Time

Descriptive research often involves nothing more than reporting the characteristics of one sample at one point in time. Opinion polls are an example of this type of research. Surveys of people's behavior is another example. For example, our local newspaper reported the results of a survey of freshmen on college campuses with high rates of drinking.[8] The researchers, located at the Harvard School of Public Health, found that more than a third of the freshmen engaged in binge drinking during their first week on campus. By the end of the first semester, 68 percent of the students had abused alcohol.

Descriptive studies in education, while simple in design and execution, can yield important knowledge. For example, it is commonly believed that each teacher has a unique teaching style. Yet a study of over 1,000 elementary and secondary teachers found little variety in actual teaching practices.[9] Teachers spend the majority of their time lecturing to the class or having students work on written assignments. On a smaller scale, two of the authors (W. Borg and M. Gall) once developed a training program to improve teachers' questioning skills. We were able to locate a study in which the researcher had made direct observations of the questioning practices of a sample of teachers.[10] The findings of this descriptive study helped us greatly in deciding which questioning techniques should be included in the initial version of the training program.

If you are planning to do a descriptive study, you should follow the usual steps involved in quantitative research: formulate a research problem; state research hypotheses, questions, or objectives; select an appropriate sample and measures; and collect and analyze the data.

Longitudinal Description of a Sample

A **longitudinal study** involves collecting data from a sample at different points in time in order to study changes or continuity in the sample's characteristics. Longitudinal research designs are difficult to implement, but they are essential for exploring problems in human

Touchstones in Research

Collins, L. M., & Sayer, A. G. (2001). *New methods for the analysis of change.* Washington, DC: American Psychological Association.

Singer, J. D., & Willett, J. B. (2003). *Applied longitudinal data analysis: Modeling change and event occurrence.* New York: Oxford University Press.

5. For an example of a *Digest* in electronic format, see http://www.nces.ed.gov/pubs2000/digest99/
6. For examples of the *Reading Report Card* in electronic format, see http://www.nces.ed.gov/nationsreportcard/reading/
7. Loxley, B. (1990). The International Association for the Evaluation of Educational Achievement. ERIC Digest. Retrieved January 7, 2006, from http://searcheric.org/digests.htm see also the Web homepage for IEA, http://www.iea.nl/
8. Hege, B. (1995, April 6). Binge drinking doesn't spare UO. *The Register-Guard,* pp. 1, 4.
9. Sirotnik, K. A. (1983). What you see is what you get—Consistency, persistency, and mediocrity in classrooms. *Harvard Educational Review, 53,* 16–31.
10. Floyd, W. D. (1960). An analysis of the oral questioning activity in selected Colorado primary classrooms. Unpublished doctoral dissertation, Colorado State College.

development, as David Magnusson, Lars Bergman, Georg Rudinger, and Bertil Torestad explain:

> The normal process in which an individual develops from birth through the life course is of interest in itself as a subject for research. Understanding and explaining that process is also fundamental for understanding what contributes to physical and mental health and for revealing the causes of mental, social and physical problems during the life course . . . the development of individuals cannot be adequately and effectively investigated without using a longitudinal research strategy.[11]

There are four main research designs in longitudinal research: trend, cohort, panel, and cross-sectional designs. They differ mainly in how the sample to be studied at different points in time is selected.

Trend Studies

Trend studies describe change by selecting a different sample at each data-collection point from a population that does not remain constant. For example, if you wanted to study trends in the use of graphing calculators in the teaching of high school mathematics, you could define the population as the members included in an annual directory of a national mathematics teachers association. Then you would select a sample of members from whom you would collect data about their use of graphing calculators. Next year's directory probably would include a somewhat different membership list, as new teachers join and existing members leave the association for various reasons. Thus, the population will have changed somewhat. You would select a new sample from this membership list and ask the teachers in the sample the same questions that you asked the previous year's sample. By repeating this process over a period of years, you would develop a picture of how teachers' use of graphing calculators has changed.

Trend studies are useful for studying changes in general populations that change constantly in terms of the individuals who are members of the population, for example, high school students or voters in school bond elections. A good example of trend research that has yielded important findings is that conducted by the National Assessment of Educational Progress (NAEP). The NAEP research team periodically administers achievement tests to national samples of students at different grade levels in order to determine whether the effectiveness of the nation's educational system is improving.

Cohort Studies

Cohort studies describe change by selecting a different sample at each data-collection point from a population that remains constant. For example, suppose that we wished to study the yearly work status of all elementary school teachers who received California teaching certificates in 1992. We would list the names of all members of this population, and at each data-collection point we would randomly select a sample from the list. Thus, the population would remain the same, but different individuals would be sampled each year. In contrast, in a trend study the population is likely to change at each data-collection point.

A report of research conducted at the Sandia National Laboratories by C. C. Carson, R. M. Huelskamp, and T. D. Woodall includes a cohort study of the high school completion rate of a single cohort of students (the class of 1982).[12] The study, based on data from the

Touchstone in Research

Glenn, N. D. (2005). *Cohort analysis* (2nd ed.). Thousand Oaks, CA: Sage.

---

11. Magnusson, D., Bergman, L. R., Rudinger, G., & Torestad, B. (Eds.) (1991). *Problems and methods in longitudinal research: Stability and change.* New York: Cambridge University Press. Quote appears on p. xiii.
12. Carson, C. C., Huelskamp, R. M., & Woodall, T. D. (1993). Perspectives on education in America: An annotated briefing. *The Journal of Educational Research, 86,* 259–311.

FIGURE 10.1

High School Completion for a National Sample of U.S. Students from the Class of 1982, Followed from 1980 to 1986

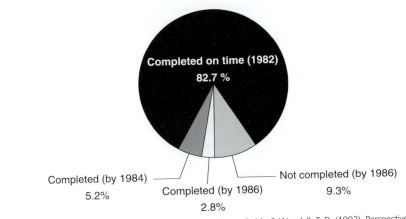

Source: Figure appears on p. 264 in: Carson, C. C., Huelskamp, R. M., & Woodall, T. D. (1993). Perspectives on education in America: An annotated briefing. *The Journal of Educational Research, 86,* 259–311. Published by Heldref Publications, 1319 Eighteenth St., NW, Washington, DC 20036-1802. Copyright © 1993.

National Center for Educational Statistics, involved a national sample of high school students who were projected to complete their senior year in 1982. The researchers followed the students from 1980 to 1986. The purpose of the study was to provide the most accurate measure possible of the current dropout rate of students from U.S. high schools.

The study's findings are summarized in Figure 10.1. The figure shows the percentage of the class of 1982 who had completed high school at three points in time—1982, 1984, and 1986. Only 82.7 percent of the students surveyed in 1982 had completed high school on time (by 1982). The percentage of students in this cohort who had completed high school by 1984 was 5.2 percent higher than in 1982, and the percentage who had completed high school by 1986 was 2.8 percent higher than in 1984. These students either had graduated from a regular high school or had earned the General Equivalency Degree (GED). Thus, less than 10 percent of this cohort would be classified as dropouts based on this expanded time frame. This is a substantially lower dropout rate than is reported in nonlongitudinal studies (typically, 25 to 30 percent).

Some trend and cohort studies are carried out using earlier data collected by other researchers. For example, suppose a survey of the vocational interests of seniors in Chicago high schools had been carried out in 1985. Another researcher could do a trend study by collecting comparable data in 2006 and comparing the two sets of data. In conducting replications of this type, the researchers should use the same questions and format as in the earlier surveys. There is some evidence and much practical experience to indicate that small changes in the wording of questions on a survey can produce large effects on answers (see Chapter 8).

Panel Studies

The third type of longitudinal research design is the **panel study.** A panel study involves selecting a sample at the outset of the study and then at each subsequent data-collection point surveying the same sample. Because panel studies follow the same individuals over time, you can note changes in specific individuals and also explore possible reasons why these individuals have changed. In contrast, individual changes cannot be explored in trend or cohort studies because different individuals make up the sample at each data-collection point.

Repeated measurements on a panel sample can have unintended side effects. Having been given the instrument or interview once, individuals have time to consider their answers for the next data collection. Furthermore, knowing that they are members of the panel may create expectations. For example, Terman's famous study of talent identified a panel of child geniuses and followed their development through childhood into adulthood.[13] The identification process itself may have created expectations that were self-fulfilling and thus changed the nature of the results.

Loss of subjects can be a problem in a panel study, especially when the study extends over a long period of time. For example, Anthony Winefield, Helen Winefield, and Marika Tiggemann conducted longitudinal surveys of a panel sample of young people (15 17-year-olds) over a period of 8 years.[14] The initial sample included 3,130 participants, but after 8 years, it had shrunk to only 484. Because of the problem of retaining an intact group over time, panel studies tend to be shorter in duration than other longitudinal studies.

Not only do the number of subjects in a panel study become smaller over time, but the subjects who remain in the sample tend to be a biased sample, because subjects who drop out are likely to be different from those who continue to participate in the study. In the study by Winefield and colleagues, dropouts tended to have lower academic ability, lower SES, and non-English backgrounds. (In Chapter 6 we discuss typical differences between research volunteers and nonvolunteers.)

Despite problems of attrition and repeated measurement, longitudinal research using a panel design has advantages over trend and cohort research. Because the same individuals are measured at each data-collection point, the panel design is sensitive to smaller changes than comparably sized samples in cohort or trend studies. Panel studies also have the advantage of identifying who is changing and in what way. We then can trace back to the events and characteristics of the individuals that might have contributed to the change.

Cross-Sectional Studies

Longitudinal research is difficult because of the extended time period during which data must be collected and the challenge of obtaining comparable subjects at each data-collection point. To counter these problems, researchers can simulate longitudinal research by doing cross-sectional research. In a **cross-sectional design** the data are obtained at one point in time, but from groups of different ages or at different stages of development. For example, suppose you were interested in how students' attitudes toward mathematics change from seventh grade to twelfth grade. To study this problem using a cross-sectional design, you could select a sample of students at each grade level and administer a questionnaire to all of them on the same date or within a narrow range of dates. Thus, the data-collection period is very short, and sample attrition is not an issue.

Cross-sectional research, however, has several limitations. A major problem is the effect of changes in the population that occur over time. For example, in the above example, the seventh-grade sample probably is representative of all students who are eligible to be in seventh grade because few students have dropped out of school at this grade level. However, because many students drop out before high school graduation, the twelfth-grade

---

13. The findings of Terman's study are reported in a series of books, including Terman, L. M., & Oden, M. M. (1959). *The gifted group at midlife* (Vol. 5). Stanford, CA: Stanford University Press.
14. Winefield, A. H., Winefield, H. R., & Tiggemann, M. (1990). Sample attrition bias in a longitudinal study of young people. *Australian Journal of Psychology, 42*(1), 75–85.

sample is unlikely to be representative of all students eligible to be in twelfth grade. Many of these students are no longer in school. Had a panel design been used instead, we would start with a sample of seventh graders and trace their attitude toward mathematics for a period of years. Some students in the sample might drop out of school over time, but changes in their attitudes for the period of time that they did remain in school could be analyzed.

Causal-Comparative Research Designs

The Study of Cause-and-Effect Relationships

As we explained at the start of the chapter, some quantitative research designs have the purpose of explaining educational phenomena through the study of cause-and-effect relationships. In these designs, the presumed cause is called the **independent variable,** and the presumed effect is called the **dependent variable.** For example, suppose we hypothesize that the introduction of state-mandated testing of all students will have a negative effect on teachers' morale. In this hypothesis, state-mandated testing is the independent variable (i.e., the presumed cause of a drop in teachers' morale), and teacher morale is the dependent variable (i.e., the presumed effect of the introduction of state-mandated testing).

In another hypothesis, this dependent variable (teacher morale) might become the independent variable. For example, we might hypothesize that teacher morale affects their rate of absenteeism from work. In this hypothesis, teacher morale is the independent variable, and absenteeism rate is the dependent variable.

In the rest of this chapter and the next, we consider research designs in which the researcher does not manipulate the independent variable in order to observe its effect on the dependent variable. These research designs do not permit strong conclusions about cause-and-effect, but are useful for initial exploratory investigations or in situations where it is impossible to manipulate the independent variable. For example, researchers might want to know whether teacher morale affects absenteeism. It would be virtually impossible for them to conduct a study in which they create work conditions that promote good morale among some teachers and poor morale among other teachers. Instead, they are limited to observing *naturally occurring* variations in teacher morale. These variations can be measured and related to *naturally occurring* variations in teacher absenteeism rates.

Research designs that rely on observation of relationships between naturally occurring variations in the presumed independent and dependent variables sometimes are called **ex post facto research.**[15] (*Ex post facto* is a Latin phrase meaning "operating retroactively.") In contrast, experiments involve actual manipulation of the independent variable by the researcher.

Causal-comparative research is a type of nonexperimental investigation in which researchers seek to identify cause-and-effect relationships by forming groups of individuals in whom the independent variable is present or absent—or present at several levels—and then determining whether the groups differ on the dependent variable. The critical feature of causal-comparative research is that the independent variable is measured in the form of categories. The categories can form a nominal scale (e.g., male versus female; American versus Asian versus European citizenship) or ordinal scale (e.g., nonemployed versus

---

15. A similar, but more detailed, definition is provided by Fred Kerlinger: "Ex post facto research is systematic empirical inquiry in which the scientist does not have direct control of independent variables because their manifestations have already occurred or because they are inherently not manipulable. Inferences about relations among variables are made, without direct intervention, from concomitant variation of independent and dependent variables." From Kerlinger, F. N. (1973). *Foundations of behavioral research* (2nd ed.). New York: Holt, Rinehart and Winston. Quote appears on p. 379.

employed part-time versus employed full-time). This approach to measuring the independent variable lends itself to particular statistical methods for analyzing the resulting data, which we describe in this chapter.

It is important to realize that an independent variable measured in categorical form might also be measurable as an interval or ratio scale. For example, consider the variable of employment. In designing a research study, we can choose to measure employment on a simple ordinal scale: the research participants are either employed or not employed. However, it is possible to measure employment more precisely as a ratio scale consisting of amount of hours of weekly employment—for example, 0 hours, 1.5 hours, 20 hours, 25 hours, 40 hours. In this case, a correlational research design (see Chapter 11) is more appropriate for organizing the independent and dependent variables and analyzing the resulting data.

In fact, any causal-comparative research design can be reconceptualized as a correlational research design by changing how the variables are measured or analyzed, or both. However, researchers sometimes prefer to use a causal-comparative design for two reasons: forming groups to measure the independent variable often is more consistent with how practitioners and other education stakeholders think about the world; and the statistical results typically are easier to comprehend and interpret.

The design of causal-comparative research studies can vary. The researcher can plan to include one independent variable or several in the design. Similarly, the researcher can choose to include one dependent variable or several. Also, the choice of statistics will vary depending on characteristics of the research data.

As you read about causal-comparative designs in this chapter, you will be laying the foundation for your study of experimental research designs in Chapters 13 and 14. This is because both causal-comparative research and experimental research involve the investigation of independent and dependent variables. You will find that experimental designs look similar to causal-comparative designs in terms of how the variables are organized and displayed. Also, you will find that some of the same statistical methods are used to analyze the resulting data.

Example of a Causal-Comparative Research Study

Leslie Vandevoort, Audrey Amrein-Beardsley, and David Berliner used a causal-comparative research design to investigate whether earning a certificate from the National Board for Professional Teaching Standards has a subsequent positive effect on students' academic achievement.[16]

The National Board was established in 1987 to determine standards of superior teaching and to develop a method of evaluating and certifying whether a teacher meets those standards. The evaluation process is time consuming and costs thousands of dollars, but teachers who meet the standards become board-certified, which is meant to confer prestige on them and assure school administrators and the community that they are highly effective in promoting students' learning. However, as Vandervoort and her colleagues note, there is little research to test the assumption that board-certified teachers actually bring about higher levels of student learning than teachers who are not board-certified. The purpose of the study was to empirically investigate this assumption.

As indicated above, causal-comparative research is nonexperimental. In an experiment, Vandevoort and colleagues would have formed a sample of teachers and randomly assigned half of them to prepare for, and go through, the National Board's evaluation

16. Vandevoort, L. G., Amrein-Beardsley, A., & Berliner, D. C. (2004, September 8). National Board certified teachers and their students' achievement. *Education Policy Analysis Archives, 12*(46). Retrieved August 25, 2005, from http://epaa.asu.edu/epaa/v12n46/

process and the other half to continue with their usual work patterns. However, it would be virtually impossible in the current schooling system to require any teacher to spend months preparing for the National Board evaluation and then submit to the demanding evaluation process, especially when there is a substantial risk of failure. Therefore, Vandervoort and her colleagues needed to look for natural, preexisting variations in the independent variable (holding or not holding National Board certification). For this reason, the researchers characterized their study as "an ex-post facto causal-comparative research design."[17]

Vandevoort and her colleagues were able to locate 35 board-certified teachers in early childhood or middle childhood education in Arizona, the state where the study was conducted. The comparison group consisted of nonboard-certified teachers working at the same grade levels in the same districts as the board-certified teachers.

The dependent variable in the research design was students' achievement gain over a period of 1 year on the SAT-9, a norm-referenced achievement test that measures skills in reading, math, and language. Gain was assessed by determining each student's SAT-9 scores in, let's say, 2002 and then again in 2003. Students were assigned to the board-certified condition if they had a nonboard-certified teacher in 2002 and a board-certified teacher in 2003. Students in the nonboard-certified condition had a nonboard-certified teacher both years. (In fact, the researchers created built-in replications of their research design by studying three school years, including 2002–2003.)

Because students were not randomly assigned to have, or not have, a board-certified teacher in 2003, it is possible that the two groups of students differed in initial academic achievement as measured by the SAT-9 in 2002. If so, this could compromise the research design: For example, if students of board-certified teachers had lower achievement than the comparison group in 2002, they might make greater achievement gains over the 1-year period simply because it is sometimes easier to go from a very low score to a moderate score than from a moderate score to a higher score (see Chapter 7). Thus, the greater gains of students having board-certified teachers could be attributed to their initial achievement level, not their exposure to superior teaching. To rule out this possibility, the researchers adjusted the gain scores using a statistical procedure known as analysis of covariance, which is described later in the chapter. In effect, analysis of covariance brings both groups of students to the same initial level of achievement on the SAT-9 so that any observed differences in gain scores can be attributed to the independent variable (National Board certification) rather than differences in initial achievement.

Table 10.1 shows the mean and standard deviation of adjusted gain scores for students at four different grade levels taught by National Board-certified teachers and nonboard-certified teachers. Separate adjusted gain scores are shown for students' performance on the reading, math, and language sections of the SAT-9. The table shows whether the difference between the mean scores of the two groups is statistically significant at the $p \leq .05$ level. In addition, the researchers present the effect size for each comparison, which is a measure of the practical significance of each observed difference between students of board-certified and nonboard-certified teachers. (See Chapter 5 for an explanation of effect sizes and tests of statistical significance.)

For example, we find in Table 10.1 that third-graders taught by board-certified teachers made an average adjusted gain of 38.6 points on the SAT-9 reading test, whereas third graders taught by nonboard-certified teachers made a smaller average adjusted gain of 31.2 points. The difference between the two mean gains (38.6 and 31.2) was statistically

17. Ibid., p. 22.

TABLE 10.1

Adjusted Gain Score Statistics for Students Taught by National Board-Certified Teachers or by Non National Board-Certified Teachers (2002–2003)

Grade 3

	Reading					Math					Language				
	N	Mean Gain*	S.D.	Sig.**	ES	N	Mean Gain	S.D.	Sig.	ES	N	Mean Gain	S.D.	Sig.	ES
Non-NBCT	15541	31.2	26.2	Yes	**1.191**	16275	27.3	29.4	Yes	**0.929**	16144	30.0	28.4	No	**1.056**
NBCT	105	38.6	25.3		**1.526**	118	33.7	27.9		**1.208**	117	34.6	28.9		**1.197**
Difference		7.4			**0.335**		6.4			**0.279**		4.6			**0.141**

Grade 4

	Reading					Math					Language				
	N	Mean Gain	S.D.	Sig.	ES	N	Mean Gain	S.D.	Sig.	ES	N	Mean Gain	S.D.	Sig.	ES
Non-NBCT	16103	28.0	24.1	Yes	**1.162**	16582	31.4	26.0	Yes	**1.208**	16529	19.6	25.8	Yes	**0.760**
NBCT	123	32.2	22.4		**1.438**	127	39.1	26.8		**1.459**	128	25.2	30.4		**0.829**
Difference		4.2			**0.276**		7.7			**0.251**		5.6			**0.069**

Grade 5

	Reading					Math					Language				
	N	Mean Gain	S.D.	Sig.	ES	N	Mean Gain	S.D.	Sig.	ES	N	Mean Gain	S.D.	Sig.	ES
Non-NBCT	16565	12.8	22.5	No	**0.569**	17020	25.3	24.3	No	**1.041**	16905	11.3	22.5	No	**0.502**
NBCT	40	14.4	25.0		**0.576**	41	24.1	29.7		**0.811**	43	6.8	20.9		**0.325**
Difference		1.6			**0.007**		−1.2			**−0.230**		−4.5			**−0.177**

Grade 6

	Reading					Math					Language				
	N	Mean Gain	S.D.	Sig.	ES	N	Mean Gain	S.D.	Sig.	ES	N	Mean Gain	S.D.	Sig.	ES
Non-NBCT	12743	12.1	19.8	No	**0.611**	12984	19.9	22.4	No	**0.888**	12914	13.3	22.1	No	**0.602**
NBCT	84	14.0	15.7		**0.892**	84	23.0	26.9		**0.855**	84	16.6	22.0		**0.755**
Difference		1.9			**0.281**		3.1			**−0.033**		3.3			**0.153**

*Adjusted gains scores calculated controlling for pretest scores.
**Difference between adjusted gain scores is significant at a $p < .05$ level.

Note: The researchers present similar tables for three other school years: 1999–2000, 2000–2001, and 2001–2002.

Source: Table 4 on p. 33 in: Vandevoort, L. G., Amrein-Beardsley, A., & Berliner, D. C. (2004, September 8). National Board-certified teachers and their students' achievement. *Education Policy Analysis Archives, 12*(46). Retrieved October 19, 2005, from http://epaa.asu.edu/epaa/v12n46/ Reprinted with permission of David C. Berliner.

significant, meaning that it is unlikely that the null hypothesis of no difference between the populations that these two groups represent (students of board-certified teachers and students of nonboard-certified teachers) is correct. In 10 of the 12 comparisons, students taught by board-certified teachers made greater gains than those taught by non-board-certified teachers. Also, the magnitude of the effect-size difference between the two adjusted mean gains (.335) is substantial. As Vandevoort and her colleagues state:

> In 75.0% (9/12) of the total cases, ESs were larger for students of NBCTs [National Board-certified teachers] than for students of non-NBCTs. The ES in favor of the students of the NBCTs averaged .225 in reading, about a two and a quarter months' advantage; .065 in mathematics, over a half month's advantage; and .047 in language, representing almost a half month's advantage.[18]

A disadvantage of causal-comparative research designs is that inferences about causality on the basis of the collected data are necessarily tentative. Therefore, we must be cautious about concluding from these results that the process of achieving National Board certification will make teachers more effective in promoting students' academic achievement. Alternative interpretations of the results are possible. For example, it might be that effective teachers (defined as teachers whose students make good gains on achievement tests) are more likely to seek and earn National Board certification. If so, we can say that a third variable C, teachers' initial teaching effectiveness, has a positive causal influence on variable A, the desire to seek and earn a National Board certificate, and variable B, their students' score gains on achievement tests. In this interpretation, which cannot be ruled out by the causal-comparative study described here, variable A does not have a causal influence on variable B. It only seems that way because a third variable, teachers' initial teaching effectiveness, influences the other two variables.

Another interpretation is that there is an actual causal relationship between National Board certification and student achievement gains, but the direction of causality is the reverse of what was hypothesized. How can this happen? It might be that board-certified teachers are assigned classes that have higher-achieving students initially. These students might make substantial achievement gains over the school year, thus making their teachers look good. Nonboard-certified teachers might be assigned classes with typical or lower-achieving students who would make lesser achievement gains. Vandevoort and her colleagues, to their credit, attempted to equalize the initial achievement level of students in both groups by a statistical technique, analysis of covariance. However, analysis of covariance does not always work as intended. In the present study, for example, it might equate students in the two groups on academic-achievement performance, but not on other critical variables.

The safest interpretation of this causal-comparative study is that it provides evidence *suggesting* that the process of preparing for and passing the assessments for National Board certification improves teachers' ability to help students learn. This tentative evidence is valuable, because it makes the case for investing in studies involving an experimental design (see Chapters 12 and 13), which typically are expensive, but that enable more definitive conclusions about the causal effect of National Board certification on student learning in school.

18. Ibid., p. 33.

Planning a Causal-Comparative Study

Statement of the Research Problem

The steps involved in causal-comparative research are illustrated in a study of the test-preparation processes used by college students. Anastasia Kitsantas investigated the relationship between students' use of self-regulatory processes before, during, and after a test (the presumed cause) and students' test performance (the presumed effect).[19]

The initial step in a causal-comparative study is to speculate about the causes or effects of the phenomenon that interests you. Your speculations can be based on previous research findings and theory, as well as on your own observations of the phenomenon. In the test-taking study, Kitsantas speculated that test performance might be influenced by self-regulation, which she defines as "self-generated thoughts, feelings, and actions for attaining goals."[20] Her literature review focused on research studies that identified the cognitive processes used by self-regulated learners and their relationship to academic performance. She noted that none of these studies examined specific self-regulatory processes during test preparation and test-taking.

After possible causes or effects of the phenomenon have been identified, they should be incorporated into the statement of the research problem. The research problem usually is stated in the form of research hypotheses, questions, or objectives. In the study we have been considering, the researcher formulated and tested the following hypotheses: "I hypothesized that high test scorers would use overall more self-regulatory processes while preparing for a test, taking a test, and following distribution of the test results than would low test scorers."[21]

In a causal-comparative study, the researcher should attempt to state and test alternative hypotheses about other factors that might explain observed differences between two groups. For example, Kitsantas focused on the effect of self-regulation on test performance, but one could argue that she should have considered alternative hypotheses as well. One such hypothesis that comes to mind is that students' academic ability influences both the use of self-regulatory processes and test performance. In other words, it might be that high-ability students, compared to lower-ability students, see more clearly the need to regulate their cognitive processes and also bring more knowledge and intellectual ability to the task of test-taking. If Kitsantas had wished, she could have incorporated a measure of academic ability in her study to test this alternative hypothesis.

Research results can confirm more than one alternative hypothesis. This is a common occurrence because complex behaviors, such as student learning, are determined by a variety of factors. The magnitude of difference between the two groups on each measure can be examined to make tentative inferences about how much each factor or set of factors affects the dependent variables (i.e., the presumed effects).

You can generate alternative hypotheses involving other variables using common sense or, more formally, by examining different theories that have been developed to explain the phenomena you are studying. This is preferable to the **shotgun approach,** which involves administering a large number of measures simply because they appear interesting or are available.

---

19. Kitsantas, A. (2002). Test preparation and performance: A self-regulatory analysis. *Journal of Experimental Education, 70*(2), 101–113. Our discussion of this study focused on the researcher's key variables, but we should note that her research design included additional variables relating to self-efficacy and students' perception of the importance of the test to a career as a psychologist.
20. Ibid., p. 101.
21. Ibid., p. 109.

Selecting Comparison Groups

After the research problem has been stated, the next step in causal-comparative research is to define the group that possesses the characteristic one wishes to study. The definition should be precise so that the results of the study can be interpreted meaningfully.

In the study of self-regulation described above, Kitsantas started with a sample of 77 students enrolled in an undergraduate psychology course. Some students dropped the course, and others did not complete all aspects of data collection, leaving a sample of 62 students.

The students took three in-class exams during the term. The first exam gave students the opportunity to become familiar with the exam structure and with their self-regulated strategies for dealing with it. The second exam was used to select a defined group, the students with high test performance. Kitsantas noted that students were expected to receive a grade of at least C+ to pass the course. She decided to define the group of high test scorers as those students who received an A on the second exam. Students who received a grade of B− or below were defined as low test scorers.

This approach to selecting comparison groups resulted in a sample of 14 high test scorers and 12 low test scorers. However, the original total sample included 62 students. It is evident, then, that Kitsantas eliminated the middle range of test scorers, a total of 36 students. This approach to selection of comparison groups is known as the **extreme-groups technique**, because it involves selecting the two extremes of a score distribution on one variable. An advantage of this approach is that the two extremes are more likely to reveal differences on the other variable of interest, in this case, use of self-regulatory strategies.

Another advantage of the extreme-groups technique becomes evident when data collection is labor intensive, as it was in this study. Data collection about self-regulatory processes involved time-consuming interviews. By focusing on the 26 highest and lowest test scorers, rather than the total sample of 62 students, the researcher saved quite a bit of time in data collection. However, the disadvantage of the extreme-groups technique is that we do not learn anything about the middle range of the sample. It might be that this range of students is relatively homogeneous in their use of self-regulation, or it might be that within this range of students the lower and higher test scorers differ in the same way that the extreme groups do. Another research study would be necessary to empirically test these speculations.

We see, then, that this researcher selected her comparison groups on the basis of the presumed effect, which is test performance. An alternative approach would have been to select comparison groups on the basis of the presumed cause, that is, use of self-regulatory strategies for test-taking. For example, Kitsantas could have formed two groups: (1) students who make substantial use of self-regulatory strategies and (2) students who make little use of self-regulatory strategies. Either approach—forming comparison groups on the basis of the presumed cause or the presumed effect—is acceptable.

The formation of comparison groups is a key factor that distinguishes causal-comparative research and experimental research. Kitsantas studied *naturally occurring variations* in student test performance. Had she used an experimental design, she might have *manipulated* conditions such that half of the students received training in self-regulatory strategies and half did not. If self-regulatory strategies affect test-taking performance and if the training actually worked, we would predict that the trained students would outperform the untrained students on subsequent tests.

The sample size for high test scorers ($n = 14$) and low test scorers ($n = 12$) was relatively small, although adequate. With a larger sample, formation of subgroups could have been considered. For example, suppose we had reason to hypothesize that self-regulation among males has different effects on test performance than self-regulation among females. This hypothesis could be tested by forming subgroups of males and females in the high-test-scoring group and subgroups of males and females in the low-test-scoring group.

Suppose the researcher found that the high test scorers and low test scorers differed on an extraneous variable. For example, suppose most of the students were juniors in college and most of the high test scorers had attended this college for all 3 years; in contrast, most of the low test scorers had attended a community college for the first 2 years and were still adjusting to the demands of starting a new college as juniors. Any observed difference between the high test scorers could be attributed to the difference in college attendance pattern, rather than the predicted differences in self-regulatory strategies.

One way to solve this problem would be to use a matching procedure. **Matching** is used to equate two groups on one or more extraneous variables so that these extraneous variables do not confound the study of causal relationships involving the variables of primary interest to the researcher. In the case of the self-regulation study, the researcher could take each student in the sample and match him or her with a student who had the same pattern of college attendance, that is, attending the same college for 3 years or transferring from a community college as a junior.

Matching procedures often create more problems than they solve. You cannot be certain that you have selected the most important variable or variables on which to match subjects. Also, you might not be able to find suitable matches for some members of the characteristic-present sample. Therefore, the preferred procedure is to try to select the characteristic-present and comparison samples randomly from the same population and then control for other variables through the use of analysis of covariance, which is described later in the chapter.

As we indicated earlier in the chapter, any causal-comparative design can be reconceptualized as a correlational design by changing how the variables are measured. To understand how this change can be made, consider that Kitsantas defined high test scorers as those students who received an A on the second exam and low test scorers as those students who received a B– or below. Also consider that these letter grades were derived from students' numerical score on the exam. (Kitsantas notes that students' mean score on the exam was 86.8, with a standard deviation of 6.06.)

Using the 62 students for whom complete data were available, we could determine each student's test score and his or her corresponding score on a measure of self-regulatory strategies. The two sets of scores can be analyzed by the correlational methods described in Chapter 11.

Numerical test scores are more precise than letter grades, because any letter grade typically represents a range of numerical scores (e.g., an A might be awarded to any student with a numerical test score between 90 and 100). However, the precision of individual numerical scores is offset by the fact that educators and community members could experience difficulty in interpreting the correlational statistics used to analyze them. Classifying a student as a high test scorer or low test scorer, as Kitsantas did, is less precise, but probably more meaningful to educators and others. Similarly, samples selected for other research

TABLE 10.2

Students' Self-Regulatory Strategies and Illustrative Behaviors

Strategy	Illustrative behaviors
Goal setting and planning	Set strategic goals and plan test preparation activities.
Keeping records and monitoring	Maintain daily records of studying progress.
Rehearsing and memorizing	Engage in overt and covert practice to memorize and remember test material.
Organizing and transforming	Rearrange and revise important lecture information
Seeking information and help	Obtain information from social and nonsocial sources.
Environmental structuring	Arrange optimal setting of study.
Self-consequencing	Reward oneself for completion of test preparation tasks.
Self-evaluation	Judge the quality or progress of test preparation.
Reviewing records	Review instructional material weekly.
Process of elimination	Use method of excluding multiple-choice distracters.

Source: Table 1 on p. 104 in: Kitsantas, A. (2002). Test preparation and performance: A self-regulatory analysis. *Journal of Experimental Education, 70*(2), 101–113. Reprinted with permission of the Helen Dwight Reid Educational Foundation. Published by Heldref Publications, 1319 Eighteenth St., NW, Washington, DC 20036-1802. Copyright © 2002.

studies might lend themselves to division into comparison groups that have established meanings. If so, this could be a strong basis for choosing a causal-comparative design over a correlational design.

Data Collection

Virtually any type of measuring instrument can be used in causal-comparative research. Standardized tests, questionnaires, interviews, and naturalistic observations all are useful for collecting data about presumed cause-and-effect relationships. In Kitsantas's study on self-regulatory strategies, her primary data-collection instrument was an interview schedule that measured students' self-regulatory strategies before, during, and after test-taking. The following is a sample interview question for each time frame:

- What do you do when you study for a personality test and find the theories difficult to understand? Are there any strategies you use to resolve the difficulty? If yes, what are they?
- When you are taking an essay personality test, do you use any strategies to help you recall key facts? If yes, what are they?
- When you receive your personality test results, what do you do with that information?[22]

The students' responses to these and 12 other interview questions were coded into categories derived from previous self-regulation research. The categories and illustrative examples are shown in Table 10.2. Two individuals coded each interview; there was 92 percent agreement on their coding. Students were given one point for each self-regulatory strategy that they mentioned using.

22. Ibid., pp. 103–104.

Data Analysis

The first step in an analysis of causal-comparative data is to conduct an exploratory data analysis and compute descriptive statistics for each comparison group in the study (see Chapter 5). These statistics generally will include the group mean and standard deviation. In the study of self-regulation, the mean and standard deviation for the number of times each group (high test scorers and low test scorers) mentioned a particular self-regulatory strategy were computed. These statistics are shown in Table 10.3. Examining this table, we see that the high test scorers made more mention of all but one of the coded self-regulatory strategies.

The next step typically is to do a test of statistical significance. The choice of significance test depends in part on whether the researcher is interested in comparing groups with respect to each group's mean score, variance, or median, or with respect to rank scores or category frequencies. Selection of an appropriate test also depends on whether the assumptions underlying the test being considered are satisfied, or at least not grossly violated.[23]

Various significance tests were introduced in Chapter 5 and are presented more fully here. Also, note that many of the same significance tests can be used to analyze data from experiments (see Chapters 12 and 13).

Statistical Analysis: The *t* Test

The t Test for the Difference between Means

The basic rationale for testing the significance of the difference between two sample means was explained in Chapter 5. It is appropriate to use the z distribution when large samples are studied ($N \geq 30$). When small samples are studied ($N \leq 29$), it is advisable to use the t test instead. In practice, researchers typically use t instead of z, irrespective of sample size.

Use of the *t* test in causal-comparative research depends on three assumptions about the obtained scores. The first assumption is that the scores form an interval or ratio scale of measurement. The second assumption is that scores in the populations under study are normally distributed. The third assumption is that score variances for the populations under study are equal. Statisticians have found that *t* tests provide accurate estimates of statistical significance even under conditions of substantial violation of these assumptions.[24] If you are concerned about score distributions in your data, you should consider doing both a *t* test and its nonparametric counterpart—either the Mann-Whitney *U* test or the Wilcoxon signed rank test (both described later in the chapter). If the two tests yield different results because the scores depart substantially from *t* test assumptions, you can report just the results of the nonparametric test.

The *t* tests for the self-regulatory strategies measured in Kitsantas's study are shown in Table 10.3. Using the conventional alpha level of .05 (see Chapter 5), we find that 7 of the 17 *t* tests were statistically significant and in the predicted direction; that is, high test scorers made more mention of using each self-regulatory strategy than did low test scorers.

---

23. For a discussion of common violations of assumptions underlying tests of statistical significance and methods for dealing with these violations, see: Keselman, H. J., Huberty, C. J., Lix, L. M., Olejnik, S., Cribbie, R. A., Donahue, B., Kowalchuk, R. K., Lowman, L. L., Petoskey, M. D., Keselman, J. C., & Levin, J. R. (1998). Statistical practices of educational researchers: An analysis of their ANOVA, MANOVA, and ANCOVA analyses. *Review of Educational Research, 68*, 350–386.
24. Boneau, C. A. (1960). The effects of violations of assumptions underlying the *t* test. *Psychological Bulletin, 57*, 49–64.

TABLE 10.3

Means, Standard Deviations, and *t* Tests of Self-Regulatory Processes Used by High versus Low Test Scorers Before, During, and Following Completion of the Test

Self-regulated strategies	Low test scorers (n = 12)		High test scorers (n = 14)		t	p
	M	SD	M	SD		
Self-regulated strategies implemented before test taking						
Goal setting and planning	.50	.52	1.00	.55	−2.35	<.05
Keeping records and monitoring	.42	.51	.71	.47	−1.54	>.14
Rehearsing and memorizing	.42	.79	.14	.36	1.16	>.27
Organizing and transforming	.33	.49	.86	.66	−2.25	<.05
Seeking information and help	.33	.49	1.07	.92	−2.49	<.05
Environmental structuring	.08	.29	.21	.43	−.90	>.37
Self-consequences	.00	.000	.07	.27	−.92	>.37
Self-regulatory strategies implemented during test taking						
Planning appropriate responses	.00	.00	.29	.47	−2.10	<.05
Keeping records and monitoring	.00	.00	.29	.61	−1.61	>.12
Organizing and transforming	.25	.62	.29	.47	−.17	>.87
Reviewing responses	1.75	1.66	3.07	1.59	−2.07	< .05
Process of elimination	.67	.49	.71	.82	−.18	>.86
Self-regulatory strategies implemented following test taking						
Goal setting and planning	.33	.89	1.14	1.02	−2.13	< .05
Keeping records and monitoring	.75	.62	1.64	1.28	−2.20	< .05
Reviewing notes of old test	.33	.78	.43	.51	−.37	>.71
Seeking information and help	.25	.87	.86	1.09	−1.54	>.13
Self-evaluation	.08	.29	.50	.86	−1.61	>.12

Note: Low test scorers received a grade of B− or below on the second test. High test scorers received a grade of A on the second test.

Source: Table 2 on p. 107 in: Kitsantas, A. (2002). Test preparation and performance: A self-regulatory analysis. *Journal of Experimental Education, 70*(2), 101–113. Reprinted with permission of the Helen Dwight Reid Educational Foundation. Published by Heldref Publications, 1319 Eighteenth St., NW, Washington, DC 20036-1802. Copyright © 2002.

A researcher might wish to compare two groups on many measured variables. Each comparison requires a separate *t* test. As shown in Table 10.3, high and low test scorers were compared on 17 self-regulatory strategies, requiring a total of 17 *t* tests. You can increase your chances of finding a significant difference between groups on a measured variable by comparing the groups on many measured variables. For example, suppose two groups are compared on 20 variables, resulting in 20 different *t* tests. Almost certainly one of the comparisons will yield a significant *p* (assuming alpha is set at .05) even if there is no difference between the populations represented by the samples on any of the variables. To understand how this happens, think about coin-tossing. On any given toss of a coin, your probability of the coin turning up heads is .50. But the probability is much higher that you will turn up a head at least once if you toss the coin 10 times.

As you increase the number of *t* tests, you also increase the risk of committing a Type I error. You can reduce this risk by setting the alpha level low (e.g., $p = .01$). If you find that the measured variables are intercorrelated, you can reduce the risk by using a statistical technique called *multivariate analysis of variance,* which is described later in the chapter.[25]

Use of multiple *t* tests is much less a problem if the direction of the group difference on each variable has been predicted on the basis of theory or previous research findings, prior to data collection. If a result is statistically significant and confirms a prediction, the alternative explanation that it was a chance result has low plausibility.

If a *t* test is appropriate for your data, you should consider whether you matched the two samples on some characteristic such that their scores on that characteristic vary systematically with their scores on the variable to be compared. If they are matched, the difference between the mean scores of the two groups on a measured variable can be tested by the **t test for correlated means.** For example, suppose the high-test-scoring student and low-test-scoring student had been matched on grade-point average. By this, we mean that for each high-test-scoring student there is a low-test-scoring student with a similar grade-point average. This matching variable would be used in the *t* test for correlated means when comparing the self-regulatory frequency counts for the two groups of students. If a matching variable is not available, the difference between the mean scores should be tested for statistical significance by the **t test for independent means.** The advantage of the *t* test for correlated means, if it can be used appropriately, is that it has greater statistical power than the *t* test for independent means.

Finally, in doing a *t* test, you will need to decide between a one-tailed or two-tailed test of significance. If you have hypothesized in advance of data collection which of the two mean scores will be greater, you can do a one-tailed test of significance. Otherwise, a two-tailed test is necessary. The advantage of the one-tailed test is that it has greater statistical power. In other words, the obtained difference between two sample scores is more likely to be statistically significant with a one-tailed *t* test than with a two-tailed *t* test.

The t Test for a Single Mean

In most causal-comparative studies, researchers compare the mean scores of two samples to determine whether they are significantly different from each other. Occasionally, though, they are interested in whether a sample mean differs significantly from a specified population mean. For example, suppose you investigate a sample of twelfth-grade students who share a particular characteristic (such as being college-bound). You administer the Wechsler Adult Intelligence Scale to each student and find that the mean IQ score is 109. As part of the data analysis, you might wish to determine whether this sample mean deviates significantly from the population mean. Assuming a population mean of 100, we can use the *t* test for a single mean to determine whether this difference (109 – 100) is

Touchstones in Research

Dunn, O. J., Clark, V. A., & Mickey, R. M. (2004). *Applied statistics: Analysis of variance and regression* (3rd ed.). Hoboken, NJ: Wiley.

Stevens, J. (2001). *Applied multivariate statistics for the social sciences* (4th ed.). Mahwah, NJ: Erlbaum.

---

25. Kitsantas conducted a multivariate analysis of variance in her study. Her first step was to sum the number of mentions of each group of self-regulatory strategies (before, during, and after the test). The results were a set of three variables and a tally for each student on each variable. The multivariate analysis of variance determined whether high and low test scorers differed significantly in their three tallies considered together.

statistically significant. The **_t_ test for a single mean** tests whether a sample mean differs significantly from a specified population mean.

Population means generally are not known in educational research. Some standardized tests provide norms based on very large samples, however. The means of these samples usually are close approximations of their respective population means. Also, population norms are available for many physical measures (e.g., height, weight, and strength) that are of interest to some educational researchers.

Statistical Analysis: Analysis of Variance

Comparison of More Than Two Means

Touchstone in Research

Lix, L. M., Keselman, J. C., & Keselman, H. J. (1996). Consequences of assumption violations revisited: A quantitative review of alternatives to the one-way analysis of variance F test. *Review of Educational Research, 66*, 579–619.

Some causal-comparative research designs involve the study of more than two groups. In a study by Louis Warren and Beverly Payne, three groups of middle-school teachers were compared.[26] Each group of teachers experienced a different form of school organization:

1. One group of teachers worked in interdisciplinary teams at their school, with each team including a small number of teachers from different academic disciplines. Each team was given a scheduled common planning time so that they could discuss the needs of their shared students and develop appropriate curriculum.
2. Like teachers in the first group, these teachers worked in interdisciplinary teams, but without a scheduled common planning time.
3. The third group of teachers worked in schools that had a traditional departmental organization: they were organized by subject area and had little opportunity to plan instruction with teachers in other subject areas.

The research question that guided the study was this: "Do these three organizational patterns have differential effects on teachers' efficacy and perceptions of their working environment?"[27]

To answer this question, the teachers in the three groups responded to several paper-and-pencil measures, including the Teacher Efficacy Scale. The scale has two subscales. A high score on the subscale for general teacher efficacy (maximum score = 36) means that the teacher believes that she can overcome external factors that might hinder students' learning. A high score on the subscale for personal teacher efficacy (maximum score = 54) means that the teacher believes that she knows and can use effective methods to help students learn.

Descriptive statistics for each of the three groups' scores on the two efficacy subscales are shown in Table 10.4. The difference between the mean scores for the three groups could be tested for statistical significance by performing three *t* tests, to compare the following: (1) Group 1 with Group 2; (2) Group 1 with Group 3; and (3) Group 2 with Group 3. The total number of *t* tests needed to compare all pairs of groups increases dramatically with each additional comparison group. For example, if the number of groups is five, a total of 10 comparisons would need to be made.

Instead of doing many *t* tests, researchers usually start by doing a simple analysis of variance. **Analysis of variance** (abbreviated as ANOVA) is a statistical procedure that compares the amount of between-groups variance in individuals' scores with the amount of within-groups variance. If the ratio of between-groups variance to within-groups variance

---

26. Warren, L. L., & Payne, B. D. (1997). Impact of middle grades' organization on teacher efficacy and environmental perceptions. *Journal of Educational Research, 90*, 301–308.
27. Ibid., p. 301.

TABLE 10.4

Teacher Efficacy in Middle Schools with Interdisciplinary Teams with Common Planning Time, Interdisciplinary Teams without Common Planning Time, or Traditional Departments

Teacher Efficacy Scale	Group 1	Group 2	Group 3	
	Interdisciplinary Teams, Common Planning Time (n = 31) M (SD)	Interdisciplinary Teams, No Common Planning Time (n = 25) M (SD)	Traditional Departments (n = 26) M (SD)	F(2,79)
Personal efficacy subscale	39.61 (4.36)	34.60 (5.26)	35.76 (4.69)	8.21 (p < .001)
General efficacy subscale	27.61 (6.05)	25.00 (3.83)	26.10 (3.84)	2.05 (p > .05)

Source: Adapted from Table 4 on p. 306 in: Warren, L. L., & Payne, B. D. (1997). Impact of middle grades' organization on teacher efficacy and environmental perceptions. *Journal of Educational Research, 90,* 301–308. Reprinted with permission of the Helen Dwight Reid Educational Foundation. Published by Heldref Publications, 1319 Eighteenth St., NW, Washington, DC 20036-1802. Copyright © 1997.

is sufficiently high, this indicates that there is more difference *between* the groups in their scores on a particular variable than there is *within* each group. If the analysis of variance yields a nonsignificant *F* ratio (the ratio of between-groups variance to within-groups variance), the computation of *t* tests to compare pairs of means is not appropriate. An exception to this rule occurs when the researcher, before data collection, hypothesized that a specific pair of means will differ significantly.

In the study by Warren and Payne, the analysis of variance shown in Table 10.4 indicates that the three groups of teachers differed significantly from each other on the personal efficacy subscale, but not on the general efficacy subscale. No further tests of statistical significance on the group means for the general efficacy subscale were done, because the *F* value for the analysis of variance was not significant. However, because the *F* value for the personal efficacy subscale was significant, the researcher should proceed to find which of the three pairs of means (1 versus 2, 1 versus 3, 2 versus 3) differed significantly from each other. Unless the researcher has planned to make specific comparisons *before* undertaking the study, a *t* test for multiple comparisons should be used. The **t test for multiple comparisons** is a test of the significance of the differences between more than two sample means. There are several types of *t* tests for multiple comparisons, including Duncan's multiple-range test and other techniques developed by Newman-Keuls, Tukey, and Scheffé. These special *t* tests adjust for the probability that the researcher will find a significant difference between mean scores simply because many comparisons are made on the same data.

In the study by Warren and Payne, the Tukey procedure, with the alpha level set at .05, was used to make the comparisons of the groups' mean score on the personal efficacy subscale. The researchers found that the mean score of teachers in interdisciplinary teams with common planning time (Group 1) was significantly higher than the mean score of teachers in interdisciplinary teams with no common planning time (Group 2). Also, the mean score of teachers in Group 1 was significantly higher than the mean score of teachers in traditional middle-school departments (Group 3). The mean scores of Group 2 and Group 3 did not differ significantly from each other. The researchers concluded that these statistical results "support the belief that common planning time can make middle grades schools a better and more beneficial place for teachers."[28]

Analysis of variance also allows researchers to compare subgroups that differ on more than one factor. In the study by Warren and Payne school organization is one factor. Another factor that could have been investigated is gender. For each organization separate groups of male and female teachers could have been formed, as shown below:

Type of Organization	Male Teachers	Female Teachers
Interdisciplinary and Common Planning	_____	_____
Interdisciplinary and No Common Planning	_____	_____
Traditional	_____	_____

Analysis of variance can be used to determine whether (1) the mean scores of teachers in these types of schools differ significantly, (2) the mean scores of male and female teachers differ significantly, and (3) the pattern of school differences is different for male and female teachers. This use of analysis of variance is similar to its use in analyzing data from two-factor and three-factor experiments (see Chapter 13).

Analysis of Covariance

In doing causal-comparative studies, researchers sometimes need to determine whether a difference between two groups on a particular variable can be explained by another difference that exists between the two groups. Suppose your hypothesis is that seventh-grade boys make more grammatical errors in writing class papers than seventh-grade girls. A sample of papers written by the two groups is scored for grammatical errors, and a t test shows that the mean number of errors is significantly greater for the boys than for the girls.

At this point you need to ask the question: Can this obtained difference be explained in terms of some other variable (besides gender) on which the groups might differ? In other words, alternative hypotheses need to be tested. You might consider the length of the students' papers as a possible explanatory variable. Suppose the sample of boys is found to have written significantly longer papers than the sample of girls, thus increasing their opportunity to make grammatical errors. You now need to determine whether controlling for initial differences in writing productivity eliminates the obtained difference in mean number of grammatical errors.

The statistical technique of **analysis of covariance** (ANCOVA) is used to control for initial differences between groups before a comparison of the within-groups variance and between-groups variance is made. The effect of ANCOVA is to make the two groups equal with respect to one or more control variables. If a difference still remains between the two groups, we cannot use the control variable to explain the effect. In our example, suppose you found that boys still made significantly more grammatical errors than girls after using analysis of covariance to control for initial differences in writing productivity. You would

28. Ibid., p. 307.

be able to conclude that the gender difference in grammatical errors was not due to the fact that boys write longer papers.

Analysis of covariance is useful in causal-comparative studies because the researcher cannot always select comparison groups that are matched with respect to all relevant variables except the one that is the main concern of the investigation. Analysis of covariance provides a post hoc method of matching groups on such variables as age, aptitude, prior education, socioeconomic class, or a measure of performance.

Research data need to satisfy certain statistical assumptions before analysis of covariance can be applied.[29] These assumptions, such as homogeneity of regression, can be checked empirically, but the computations are complex. Inexperienced researchers need to consult an expert statistician before using analysis of covariance.

Multivariate Analysis of Variance

Multivariate analysis of variance (MANOVA) is a statistical technique for determining whether groups differ on more than one dependent variable. The multivariate analysis of variance is similar to the *t* test and to analysis of variance. The major difference between the techniques is that the *t* test and analysis of variance can determine only whether several groups differ on one dependent variable.

Each research participant in a MANOVA will have a score on two or more dependent variables. These scores can be represented by a **vector,** which is a single mathematical expression representing the individual's scores on all the dependent variables. The mean of the vector scores for all the individuals in a given group is called a **centroid.** The purpose of MANOVA is to determine whether there are statistically significant differences between the centroids of different groups.

The concept of representing several dependent variables by a single vector can be understood in a nontechnical way. Consider the case of two groups—high- and low-achieving students—who have been measured on two dependent variables: attitude toward their present school and attitude toward engaging in further schooling. Imagine that one student has a score of 6 on her attitude toward her present school, and a score of 8 on her attitude toward engaging in further instruction. This student's scores can be expressed in the form (6, 8), indicating that she has a score of 6 on the first variable and a score of 8 on the second variable. The scores also can be represented on a graph, with each single point on the graph representing one student's scores on the two variables. Suppose the graph points (comparable to vector scores) for high-achieving students tend to occupy a different space on the graph than the points for the low-achieving students. The purpose of MANOVA, in a sense, is to determine whether these two spaces differ significantly from each other.

Our example is based on two dependent variables represented on a two-dimensional graph. You might try imagining the case of three dependent variables and how each individual's vector scores on them could be represented by a single point on a three-dimensional graph.

The first step in doing a MANOVA should be to test the assumption of the equality of group dispersions. If a nonsignificant *F* is obtained, we can conclude that the assumption is satisfied. (Researchers sometimes skip this step because MANOVA is robust, meaning that the assumption can be violated to an extent without violating the validity of the test.) The next step is to do a test of the statistical significance of the difference between group centroids. The most commonly used test for this purpose is Wilk's lambda (λ). This test

29. The assumptions are discussed in: Elashoff, J. D. (1969). Analysis of covariance: A delicate instrument. *American Educational Research Journal, 6,* 383–399.

yields an *F* value, which can be looked up in an *F* ratio table to determine its level of statistical significance. If a significant MANOVA *F* is obtained, we then can do an ANOVA on each dependent variable. The purpose of the ANOVAs is to determine which of the measured variables produce a statistically significant difference between the mean scores of the groups being studied. Although unlikely, it is possible to obtain a significant MANOVA *F* without finding a significant *F* in any of the ANOVAs.

A typical causal-comparative study includes a substantial number of dependent variables. This does not mean, however, that all the variables must be tested for statistical significance by a single MANOVA. You should group the variables into clusters (that is, vectors) that include variables that are educationally or psychologically related. Each cluster of variables can be analyzed by a separate MANOVA. If you wish to test a hypothesis involving a particular dependent variable, you can do an ANOVA directly without first including that variable in a MANOVA with other variables.

The use of MANOVA in causal-comparative research is illustrated by a study of college professor ratings conducted by Susan Basow and Nancy Silberg.[30] The main purpose of the study was to determine whether there is a bias in evaluations of professors such that female professors are given lower ratings than male professors. Each of 16 female professors at a private college in the northeastern United States was matched with a male professor of similar rank, teaching field, and years of experience at the college. (Matching procedures were described earlier in the chapter.)

The professors were evaluated by their students on six rating scales during the fifth or sixth week of the semester. The six scales are as follows: (1) scholarship, (2) organization/clarity, (3) instructor-group interaction, (4) instructor-individual student interaction, (5) dynamism/enthusiasm, and (6) overall teaching ability. The researchers also recorded the gender of each student who completed the rating scales.

The mean ratings of male and female professors on all six factors are shown in Table 10.5.

Basow and Silberg analyzed the group mean differences shown in Table 10.5 for statistical significance by the use of MANOVA. The six rating scales were considered to be a cluster of related variables. The *F* ratios for the MANOVA are shown in the first column of statistics in Table 10.6. The significant *F* for teacher gender (10.40) means that male and female professors had significantly different mean scores on the vector representing the six rating scales. The *F* ratios for the ANOVAs (analysis of variance) shown in the last six columns of Table 10.6 indicate which of the six rating scales yielded significantly different mean scores for male and female professors.

The MANOVA yielded a nonsignificant *F* for student gender (1.29), meaning that male and female students did not differ significantly in their mean score on the vector representing the six rating scales. Despite the nonsignificant MANOVA *F*, the researchers reported the *F* ratios for the ANOVAs performed on the individual rating scales. One of them—the *F* for scholarship—is significant. Because the MANOVA *F* was nonsignificant, however, one should be cautious about interpreting this gender difference in student ratings. It might be a spurious finding. As the number of *F* ratios that are calculated increases, so does the likelihood of obtaining a significant *F* by chance.

Finally, we see that the MANOVA *F* for the professor-gender by student-gender interaction (2.54) in Table 10.6 is statistically significant. This result means that the gender

---

30. Basow, S. A., & Silberg, N. T. (1987) Student evaluations of college professors: Are female and male professors rated differently? *Journal of Educational Psychology, 79,* 308–314.

TABLE 10.5

Descriptive Statistics for Ratings of Male and Female Professors by Male and Female College Students

	Male Student				Female Student			
	Male Professor (n = 275)		Female Professor (n = 278)		Male Professor (n = 284)		Female Professor (n = 243)	
Factors on Which Professors Were Rated	M	SD	M	SD	M	SD	M	SD
(1) Scholarship	11.7	3.1	12.9	3.1	12.0	3.1	11.9	3.2
(2) Organization/clarity	10.7	3.3	12.1	3.9	11.1	3.4	11.2	4.2
(3) Instructor-group interaction	11.8	3.2	12.5	3.5	12.1	3.2	11.9	3.6
(4) Instructor-individual student interaction	10.7	3.3	11.6	3.5	10.7	3.6	11.1	3.7
(5) Dynamism/enthusiasm	9.6	3.6	11.6	4.0	10.0	3.8	10.7	4.1
(6) Overall teaching ability	2.2	0.8	2.6	1.0	2.2	0.8	2.4	1.0

Note: Lower scores indicate more positive evaluations. Score range = 5–25, except for overall teaching ability, for which the range = 1–5.

Source: Adapted from Table 2 on p. 311 in: Basow, S. A., & Silberg, N. T. (1987). Student evaluations of college professors: Are female and male professors rated differently? *Journal of Educational Psychology, 79*, 308–314. Copyright 1987 by the American Psychological Association. American Psychological Association. Used with permission of the author, Dr. Susan A. Basow, Charles A. Dana Professor of Psychology, Lafayette College, Easton, PA.

TABLE 10.6

Multivariate Analysis of Variance Summary for Ratings of Male and Female Professors by Male and Female College Students

	Multivariate ANOVA[a]	Univariate ANOVA[b] Factors on Which Professors Were Rated					
Source	F	(1)	(2)	(3)	(4)	(5)	(6) Overall
Professor gender	10.40***	F 7.71**	10.63**	1.44	9.11**	34.64***	39.71***
Student gender	1.29	F 3.92*	1.15	0.45	1.85	1.12	3.72
Professor gender × Student gender	2.54*	F 9.67**	9.33**	4.62*	1.79	8.62**	7.10**

Note: Univariate analyses are on (1) Scholarship, (2) Organization/Clarity, (3) Instructor-Group Interaction, (4) Instructor-Individual Student interaction, (5) Dynamism/Enthusiasm, and (6) Overall teaching ability.
[a]dfs = 6,1071
[b]dfs = 1,1076
*p < .05 **p < .01***p < .001

Source: Adapted from Table 1 on p. 310 in: Basow, S. A., & Silberg, N. T. (1987). Student evaluations of college professors: Are female and male professors rated differently? *Journal of Educational Psychology, 79*, 308–314. Copyright 1987 by the American Psychological Association. Used with permission of the author, Dr. Susan A. Basow, Charles A. Dana Professor of Psychology, Lafayette College, Easton, PA.

difference in students' scores on the vector representing the six rating scales is dependent on the gender of the professor being rated. The nature of the interaction effect can be determined by examining Table 10.5. We see that male students rated female professors lower on all six scales, whereas female students did not differ systematically in their ratings of male and female professors.

Multivariate analysis of variance is a useful statistical technique because it helps the researcher see the data in a multivariate perspective. Groups that differ from each other on an important characteristic are also likely to differ from each other on other characteristics as well. Multivariate analysis of variance helps the researcher conceptualize and analyze the nature of these interrelated characteristics, and determine whether the groups being studied differ on them.

The correlational counterpart of MANOVA is canonical analysis, which is described in the next chapter. Either technique can be used to analyze data that consist of one or more independent variables and two or more dependent variables. Although one does find instances of MANOVA in the literature, canonical analysis is becoming the method of choice among educational researchers.

Tests for the Difference between Variances

The standard deviation and its square, the variance, are two statistics for describing the variability of scores obtained from a sample. Just as you might want to determine whether the mean scores for two samples differ significantly, you might want to do a statistical test to determine whether the variances in scores for two samples differ significantly from each other. There are two main reasons for doing this test. The first reason is that most of the commonly used statistical tests—including the t test for the difference between means—are based on the assumption that the variances of the two samples are approximately equal. If the score variances of two samples differ markedly, one of the nonparametric tests discussed later in this chapter should be used instead.

The second reason for testing variance homogeneity between two samples is that your hypothesis might concern the variability of sample scores. For example, you might hypothesize that college graduates are more like one another in scholastic aptitude than college dropouts. The rationale might be that all college graduates are apt to be fairly intelligent but that, for various reasons, both students of high and low aptitude may leave college before graduation. To test this hypothesis in a causal-comparative study, you would administer a measure of scholastic aptitude to a sample of college graduates and a sample of college dropouts. Next you would do a statistical test to determine whether the college graduates have less variable scores on the aptitude measure than do the college dropouts.

The statistical technique used to test whether the observed difference between variances is significant is analysis of variance, which is the same technique used to test for differences between several means. The larger the F ratio, the less likely it is that the variances of the populations from which the samples were drawn are equal. If the F ratio exceeds the alpha level you have set, you would reject the null hypothesis (stating equality of variances) and conclude that the obtained difference between the sample variances is a true one.

You should be aware that several statistical tests are available for comparing the difference between variances. If the two sets of scores are obtained from independent samples, the **test for homogeneity of independent variances** is used to compare the difference between variances in two sets of scores obtained from independent samples. The **test for homogeneity of related variances** is used to compare the difference between variances obtained from repeated measures on a single sample or from two matched samples. The

F maximum test for homogeneity of variance can be used to determine whether the variances of more than two sets of scores differ significantly from one another.

Statistical Analysis: Nonparametric Tests

Advantages and Disadvantages of Nonparametric Tests

The tests of statistical significance that we described in the two previous sections are known as parametric statistics. A parameter describes some aspect of a set of scores for an entire population. **Parametric statistics** are tests of statistical significance that are based upon certain assumptions about population parameters, that is, the shape or variance of the population scores. One such assumption is that the scores in the population are normally distributed about the mean. Another assumption is that the population variances of the comparison groups in one's study are about equal. When large deviations from these assumptions are present in the research data, parametric statistics should not be used. Nonparametric statistical tools should be used instead. **Nonparametric statistics** are tests of statistical significance that do not rely on any assumptions about the shape or variance of population scores.

The use of parametric statistics also is based on the assumption that the scores being analyzed are derived from a measure that has equal intervals. As we explained in Chapter 5, most continuous measures meet this criterion. Measures that yield categorical or rank scores, however, do not have equal intervals, and so one of the nonparametric statistics should be used for data analysis. We discuss the common types of nonparametric statistics in the following sections.

When research data meet the assumption of being interval scores but not the assumptions of normal distribution and variance homogeneity, you still should consider using one of the parametric statistics presented earlier in the chapter. There are three main reasons for recommending the use of parametric statistics in these situations. First, research has shown that moderate departure from the theoretical assumptions has very little effect upon the value of the parametric technique. Second, nonparametric statistics are generally less powerful, that is, they require larger samples in order to yield the same level of statistical significance. Third, for many of the problems encountered in educational research, suitable nonparametric tests are not available.

The Chi-Square Test

The **chi-square** (χ^2) test is a nonparametric statistical test to determine whether research data in the form of frequency counts are distributed differently for different samples. These frequency counts can be placed into two or more categories. The chi-square test was used by Bryan Cook to analyze data resulting from his study of teachers' attitudes toward students with a disability who had been placed in their general education classrooms.[31] This practice is known as *inclusion*, meaning the placement of students with disabilities in regular classrooms, such that the teacher instructs both students with disabilities and students without disabilities.

In Cook's study, 70 elementary teachers were asked to nominate students in their classrooms in response to each of four questions:

1. (Attachment). If you could keep one student another year for the sheer joy of it, whom would you pick?
2. (Concern). If you could devote all your attention to a child who concerns you a great deal, whom would you pick?

31. Cook, B. G. (2001). A comparison of teachers' attitudes toward their included students with mild and severe disabilities. *Journal of Special Education, 34*(1), 203–213.

Touchstones in Research

Coombs, W. T., Algina, J., & Oltman, D. O. (1996). Univariate and multivariate omnibus hypothesis tests selected to control Type I error rates when population variances are not necessarily equal. *Review of Educational Research, 66,* 137–179.

Gibbons, J. D. (1993). *Nonparametric measures of association.* Thousand Oaks, CA: Sage.

TABLE 10.7

Chi-Square Analysis Comparing Nominations of Included Students with Hidden and Obvious Disabilities on Four Teacher Attitudinal Categories

Attitudinal Category	Students with Hidden Disabilities (total $n = 173$) Nominated Students		Students with Obvious Disabilities (total $n = 48$) Nominated Students		χ^2
	n	% of Total n	n	% of Total n	
Attachment	9	5	3	6	
Concern	48	28	16	33	0.41
Indifference	32	18	16	33	3.82*
Rejection	55	32	8	17	3.00*

Note: Cook did not do a chi-square test for the attachment attitude, because some statisticians consider that an expected frequency of at least 10 in each category is needed.

*$p < .05$ (one-tailed test).

Source: Adapted from Table 4 on p. 209 in: Cook, B. G. (2001). A comparison of teachers' attitudes toward their included students with mild and severe disabilities. *Journal of Special Education, 34*(1), 203–213. Copyright © 2001 by PRO-ED, Inc. Reprinted with permission from PRO-ED, Inc.

3. (Indifference). If a parent were to drop by for a conference, whose child would you be least prepared to talk about?
4. (Rejection). If your class was to be reduced by one child, whom would you be relieved to have removed?[32]

Although the phrasing of each question refers to one child, teachers were asked to nominate three children in response to each question. The label in parentheses preceding each question refers to the teacher attitude that the question was considered to measure. For example, a child named in response to question 3 was considered to mean that the teacher had an attitude of indifference toward that child.

The questions were framed such that teachers could nominate either students without a disability or students with a disability in their classroom. Cook's data analysis focused on nominated students who have a disability. These students were further classified as having either a *hidden* or *obvious* disability. Students with a learning disability, attention deficit/hyperactivity disorder, or behavior disorder were categorized as having a hidden disability, because they were not physically distinguishable from students without a disability. Students with mental retardation, autism, hearing impairments, multiple disabilities, orthopedic or visual impairments, and other health impairments were categorized as having an obvious disability, because the disability provides overt cues to individuals who interact with them.

Drawing on several theoretical perspectives, Cook developed several hypotheses, including these two: (1) teachers would be more likely to have an attitude of rejection toward students with a hidden disability than toward students with an obvious disability, and (2) teachers would be more likely to have an attitude of indifference toward students with an obvious disability than toward students with a hidden disability. These hypotheses were tested by the use of the chi-square tests shown in Table 10.7.

32. Ibid., p. 208.

The statistical information shown in Table 10.7 is in the form of *frequency counts*, rather than in the typical form of mean scores and standard deviations. We see, for example, that teachers nominated nine students with hidden disabilities in their classroom as ones toward whom they had an attitude of attachment (i.e., students whom they would keep for another year for the sheer joy of it). We see, too, that these nine students constitute 5 percent of the 173 students with hidden disabilities distributed among the 70 teachers in the sample.

A test of statistical significance, such as the chi-square test, is used to determine whether a null hypothesis can be rejected. In Cook's study, the null hypothesis for, let's say, an attitude of concern is that if he had studied the entire population of elementary teachers, these teachers would nominate the same percentage of students with hidden disabilities and students with obvious disabilities as children about whom they have an attitude of concern. As shown in Table 10.7, the percentages are only slightly different (28% versus 33%), and indeed the chi-square test yields a nonsignificant value. Therefore, the null hypothesis cannot be rejected.

For teacher attitudes of indifference and rejection, the chi-square test yields a significant value. Therefore, the null hypotheses are rejected, and the research hypotheses that there are actual population differences in teachers' attitudes of indifference and rejection toward students with hidden and obvious disabilities are accepted. The directions of the differences are exactly as stated in Cook's two hypotheses.

When the frequency data are grouped into more than four cells, a more complex chi-square test can be done. You also should be aware that when the expected frequency in any cell is less than five, a correction (Yates's correction or the Fisher exact test) needs to be applied to the regular chi-square test. In the process of doing a chi-square test, you also can compute a **phi coefficient** (for a four-cell table) or a **contingency coefficient** (for more than four cells). These correlation coefficients provide an estimate of the magnitude of the relationship between the variables in a chi-square table.[33]

Other Nonparametric Tests

Of the nonparametric tests of significance, chi-square probably is the most frequently used by educational researchers in causal-comparative studies. Other nonparametric tests sometimes are used, particularly when the research data are in the form of rank-order scores or interval scores that grossly violate the parametric test assumptions of normal distribution and homogeneity of variance.

The **Mann-Whitney *U* test** can be used to determine whether the distributions of scores of two independent samples differ significantly from each other. If *U* is statistically significant, it means that the bulk of scores in one population is higher than the bulk of scores in the other population. The two populations are represented by the two independent samples on which the *U* test is made. This test generally is used when the assumption of homogeneity of sample variances underlying the *t* test is grossly violated.[34]

The **Wilcoxon signed rank test** is used to determine whether the distributions of scores for two samples differ significantly from each other when the scores of the samples are correlated (either through matching or because repeated measures are taken on the same sample). The Wilcoxon test is analogous to the *t* test for correlated means except that it is not based on any assumptions about the shape of the score distribution or homogeneity

---

33. The phi coefficient and contingency coefficient are defined in Table 11.3 in Chapter 11.
34. Zimmerman, D. W. (1987). Comparative power of student *t* test and Mann-Whitney *U* test for unequal sample sizes and variances. *Journal of Experimental Education 55,* 171–174. This study showed that even if this assumption *is* violated, when the sizes of the two sample groups are unequal and the smaller sample has the larger variance, the *t* test provides a better test of the null hypothesis than the *U* test.

of variance between the two sets of scores. If more than two groups of subjects are to be compared, a nonparametric one-way analysis of variance (the **Kruskal-Wallis test**) can be used.

Interpretation of Causal-Comparative Findings

The process of interpreting causal-comparative findings can be illustrated by referring to the study of self-regulatory processes discussed earlier in the chapter. You will recall from Table 10.3 that college students who were high test scorers more often stated that they used self-regulatory processes than low-test-scoring college students. We can reasonably infer from this finding that there is a positive relationship between students' use of self-regulatory strategies and their test performance.

Can we reach beyond this conclusion and infer that use of self-regulatory strategies *causes* students to do well on tests? The results are consistent with this interpretation, but because this was a causal-comparative study, other interpretations must be considered as well. For example, it is conceivable that high test scorers performed better than low test scorers on the particular exam used in Kitsantas's study because they had a stronger knowledge base about psychology, and this knowledge enabled them to comprehend the text material covered by the test in greater depth and deploy self-regulatory processes more easily. In this interpretation, a third variable, knowledge about psychology, was responsible for both test performance and use of self-regulatory processes. If this interpretation is true, it means that increasing students' use of self-regulatory processes—without also increasing their background knowledge of psychology—might have no effect on their test performance.

Another interpretation of the findings is that test performance determines the use of self-regulatory processes, rather than the other way around, namely, that the use of self-regulatory processes determines test performance. How could this happen? Suppose that the low test scorers in Kitsantas's study continually score low on tests for reasons they cannot determine. Their continually low test performance might discourage them from experimenting with self-regulatory strategies. High test scorers, in contrast, would be encouraged by their good test performance and therefore seek new ways, including the use of self-regulatory strategies, to improve it.

Two procedures can be used to improve the interpretability of causal-comparative studies. First, as we discussed earlier in the chapter, alternative hypotheses should be formulated and tested whenever possible. Second, the relationships among all the variables in the study can be examined using the technique of *path analysis,* which is discussed in the next chapter.

The most powerful method for demonstrating the causal nature of causal-comparative findings is to do subsequent experiments in which the presumed cause or causes of the outcomes being studied is manipulated. For example, an experiment could be designed in which one group of college students (the treatment group) is trained in self-regulatory processes appropriate to test-taking and another group (the control group) does not receive the training. If self-regulatory processes actually have a causal influence on test performance, we would expect that the treatment group would outperform the control group on tests that they take after the training period. We also would have confidence that providing the training to other students would have similarly positive effects.

We wish to emphasize once again that both causal-comparative research and experiments have advantages. A causal-comparative study is a fairly economical method for identifying possible causes or effects of an important phenomenon. If apparent cause-and-effect relationships are found, they can be tested through controlled experimentation. Experiments typically are more technically demanding and expensive than a causal-comparative study, so they are best employed after the researcher has reason to believe that a causal relationship between two variables exists.

RECOMMENDATIONS FOR
Doing Descriptive and Causal-Comparative Research

1. In planning a descriptive study, select an instrument, or instruments, that will yield the most detailed and valid picture of the phenomena you wish to understand.
2. In planning a longitudinal study, select a sampling design (trend, cohort, panel, or cross-sectional) that is feasible yet will yield valid data about the phenomena you wish to study over time.
3. If you wish to use a panel sampling design in a longitudinal research study, develop procedures that will minimize attrition, inappropriate expectations among panel members, and bias arising from repeated measurements with the same instrument.
4. In planning or interpreting the results of a causal-comparative study, consider whether you can rule out alternative explanations of the cause-and-effect relationships you have found, or expect to find.
5. In analyzing data in a causal-comparative study, determine whether it is most appropriate to use a t test, analysis of covariance, or multivariate analysis of variance.
6. In analyzing data in a causal-comparative study, use a nonparametric test of statistical significance if the data are in the form of frequency counts or if they grossly violate the assumptions underlying parametric tests.

SELF-CHECK TEST

Circle the correct answer to each of the following questions. The answers are provided at the back of the book.

1. A common type of statistic used in descriptive research is a
   a. measure of central tendency.
   b. nonparametric test.
   c. test for the difference between variances.
   d. one-tailed test of statistical significance.

2. A trend study involves
   a. sampling different members of an accessible population at each data-collection point.
   b. collecting data from the same sample of individuals at each data-collection point.
   c. following a specific population of individuals over a period of time.
   d. collecting data about different time periods from all subjects at the same time.

3. The main situation in which a researcher would use a causal-comparative design rather than an experimental design is when
   a. random sampling is not possible.
   b. experimental manipulation is not possible.
   c. use of standardized tests is not possible.
   d. young children are the subjects of the research.

4. One of the main limitations of causal-comparative research is that
   a. it is more expensive than other types of research.
   b. it does not reveal possible causal relationships between variables.
   c. it does not reveal the magnitude of the relationships between variables.
   d. null hypotheses cannot be tested.

5. If the groups to be compared in a causal-comparative study differ on an extraneous variable, the preferred procedure is to
   a. match the groups on the extraneous variable.
   b. match the groups on a standardized intelligence or aptitude test.
   c. use analysis of variance to control for the extraneous variable.
   d. use analysis of covariance to control for the extraneous variable.

6. One of the assumptions that the t test makes about scores obtained in causal-comparative research is that
   a. score variances for the populations under study are equal.
   b. score variances for the populations under study are not equal.
   c. means of the samples are equal.
   d. population means do not differ.

7. If the researcher matches individuals in the groups being studied on a particular characteristic, the appropriate test is the t test for
   a. independent means.
   b. equal variances.
   c. correlated means.
   d. unequal means.

8. If a researcher conducting causal-comparative research is almost certain that any detected change will be in a hypothesized direction, it is appropriate to compute a(n)
   a. analysis of variance.
   b. correlation coefficient.
   c. two-tailed t test.
   d. one-tailed t test.

9. A post hoc method for matching groups on certain variables is the
   a. analysis of covariance.
   b. canonical correlation.
   c. the t test for correlated means.
   d. the t test for independent means.

10. Multivariate analysis of variance is used to detect statistically significant group differences in
   a. vectors of independent variables.
   b. vectors of dependent variables.
   c. correlations between dependent variables.
   d. correlations between independent and dependent variables.

11. An important characteristic of nonparametric statistics is that they
   a. make no assumption about the variance of the population scores.
   b. assume that scores in the population are normally distributed about the mean.
   c. require equal population variances.
   d. can be used only with interval scales of measurement.

12. The purpose of computing a correlational statistic following a t test or analysis of variance is to determine
   a. whether the sample variances are equal.
   b. the magnitude of the relationship between the variables.
   c. the directionality of the observed differences.
   d. all of the above.

CHAPTER 11

Nonexperimental Research: Correlational Designs

OVERVIEW

In this chapter we describe the two purposes for which correlational research designs are used. One purpose is to search for variables, measured at one point in time, that predict a criterion variable measured at a subsequent point in time. Another purpose is to search for possible causal relationships among variables. Various correlational statistics are available to estimate the strength of the prediction or relationship. Bivariate correlational statistics are used when two variables are involved in studying predictions or causal relationships, whereas multivariate correlational statistics are used when three or more variables are involved.

OBJECTIVES

After studying this chapter you should be able to

1. State advantages and disadvantages of correlational research designs.
2. Plot a scattergram and explain its use in correlational research.
3. Draw appropriate inferences from correlation coefficients about the degree, direction, and possible causal nature of relationships between variables.
4. Describe the procedures involved in conducting a study that explores cause-and-effect relationships.
5. Describe the procedures involved in conducting a prediction study.
6. Describe practical uses of prediction studies.
7. Explain the use of Taylor-Russell tables and cross-validation in prediction studies.
8. Select the most appropriate bivariate correlational statistic when correlating two variables.
9. Explain the use of correction for attenuation, correction for restriction in range, and part or partial correlation in correlational research.
10. Select the most appropriate multivariate correlational statistic when correlating three or more variables.
11. Explain the design and purpose of a correlation matrix and a factor analysis.
12. Explain similarities and differences between multiple regression, path analysis, HLM, and structural equation modeling.
13. Explain the use of subgroups and moderator variables to refine a correlational analysis.
14. Interpret the magnitude and statistical significance of correlation coefficients in prediction research and research that explores cause-and-effect relationships.

The Nature of Correlation

Correlational research refers to studies in which the purpose is to discover relationships between variables through the use of correlational statistics. Correlational statistics also are used extensively in test construction and analysis, as we explain in Chapter 7. Because an understanding of a correlation coefficient is essential to what follows, we will briefly discuss its meaning in nonmathematical terms.

Let's start with the notion of individual differences. Suppose everyone had the same level of academic achievement. There would not be much work for researchers to do. Prediction, for example, would be an easy matter because we would be able to make the same, accurate prediction for everyone. There would be no need for developing elaborate measures, either, because in our scenario there is just one achievement level in the population. Yet the fact is that people do vary with respect to this characteristic, and the variations have major personal and social consequences. For example, high academic achievers generally perform a different role in society and view themselves differently than do low academic achievers. If researchers could discover the causes and effects of variability in academic achievement, this knowledge might prove useful in helping both low and high achievers become more personally and academically successful.

Types of Scattergrams

Touchstone in Research

Jacoby, W. G. (1997). *Statistical graphics for univariate and bivariate data.* Thousand Oaks, CA: Sage.

To understand how the correlation coefficient helps us in this kind of investigation, examine the four graphs in Figure 11.1. Each of these graphs is a scattergram. A **scattergram** (also called a **scatter plot**) is a pictorial representation of the correlation between two variables: The scores of individuals on one variable are plotted on the x-axis of a graph and the scores of the same individuals on another variable are plotted on the y-axis. Note that each point on the graph contains two pieces of information, the individual's position with respect to the x-axis and with respect to the y-axis.

Positive Correlation

In graph 1 we see a perfect positive correlation between variable A and variable B. The straight diagonal line, called the *line of best fit,* indicates that each unit of increment in the x-axis variable is accompanied by a unit of increment on the y-axis variable. The correlation, represented by the expression $r = 1.00$, is perfect, because if we know an individual's score on one variable, we can predict perfectly that individual's score on the other variable. For example, consider a hypothetical vocabulary test on which a group of students earned scores varying from 40 to 100. Suppose that students who earned a score of 40 on the vocabulary test had a score of 85 on a test of reading comprehension; those with a vocabulary test score of 41 had a reading comprehension score of 86; and so on through the range of scores, so that students with a vocabulary test score of 100 had a reading comprehension score of 145. If this were the case, there would be a perfect relationship, or correlation, between these two variables. If we know a student's vocabulary score, we can predict perfectly her comprehension score.

Now examine the scattergram in graph 2, which shows a fairly high positive correlation between two variables ($r = .70$). If we know a person's score on the x-axis variable, we cannot predict his score on the y-axis variable perfectly. However, if we follow the straight line (the line of best fit) from the x-axis to where the straight line intersects the y-axis, we can predict his score on the y-axis variable fairly accurately. The person's score on the y-axis probably will fall within a relatively narrow range of scores.

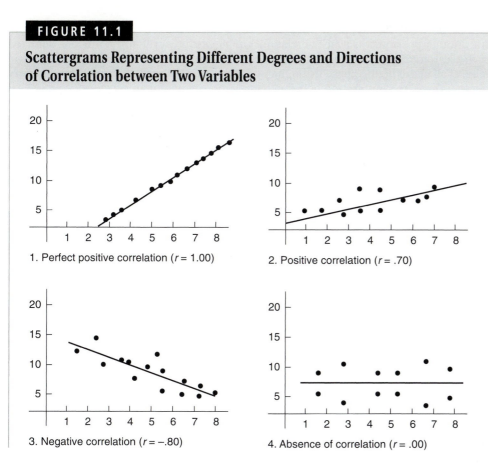

FIGURE 11.1

Scattergrams Representing Different Degrees and Directions of Correlation between Two Variables

1. Perfect positive correlation ($r = 1.00$)

2. Positive correlation ($r = .70$)

3. Negative correlation ($r = -.80$)

4. Absence of correlation ($r = .00$)

Negative Correlation

Another possibility is a negative relationship between two variables, as shown in graph 3. For example, imagine a measure of students' attitude toward school, for which scores can range from 0 (a highly negative attitude) to 10 (a highly positive attitude). If we correlated students' attitudes toward school with their absence rate (number of days during the school year that they did not attend school), we would expect a negative correlation between attitude toward school and absence rate. In other words, we would predict that students with very positive attitudes toward school (let's say a score of 8 or above) would miss very few days of school, and that students with negative attitudes toward school (let's say a score of 3 or below) would have a high number of absences during the school year. If the relationship between attitude toward school and absence rate was perfect, all the points on the scattergram would fall along the line of best fit, just as they did in graph 1. In this case, however, the correlation would be a perfect negative correlation ($r = -1.00$). In graph 3, the negative relationship between the two variables is not perfect, but it is fairly good ($r = -.80$).

Absence of Correlation

Still another possibility is a lack of relationship between two variables, which is depicted by the scattergram in graph 4. Knowing an individual's score on the x-axis variable is of no value at all in predicting her score on the y-axis variable. Using the example of vocabulary test scores and reading comprehension, let us suppose that for any given vocabulary test score there are students with widely varying reading comprehension scores. For example, suppose students with scores of 40 on the vocabulary test have reading comprehension scores ranging from 85 to 145. We would conclude that there is little or no relationship, or correlation, between the two variables. Accurate prediction of reading comprehension scores from vocabulary scores would be impossible.

The Mathematics of Correlation

As we stated above, the line of best fit is the straight line in each of the scattergrams in Figure 11.1. In nonmathematical terms, the **line of best fit** is the line, among all the possible lines that can be drawn across the x- and y-axes, that represents the best prediction of a person's y score from knowing her x score. It can be calculated using the following equation:

$$y = bx + a$$

where y is the variable being predicted, b is the slope of the line (sometimes referred to as the *regression weight*), x is the predictor variable, and a is the point where the line of best fit intersects the y-axis. You will see an elaboration of this basic equation when we discuss multiple regression later in the chapter.

The purpose of the correlation coefficient is to express in mathematical terms the degree and direction of relationship between two (or more) variables. If the relationship between two variables is perfectly positive (for each increment in one variable there is a corresponding increment in the other), the correlation coefficient will be 1.00. If the relationship is perfectly negative, it will be -1.00. If there is no relationship, the coefficient will be 0. If two variables are somewhat related, the coefficients will have a value between 0 and 1.00 (for a positive relationship) or between 0 and -1.00 (for a negative relationship). Thus, the correlation coefficient is a precise way of stating the degree to which one variable is related to another, and the direction of the relationship (positive or negative). To express the idea another way, the correlation coefficient tells us how effectively individuals' scores on one measure (e.g., an intelligence test) can be used to predict their scores on another measure (e.g., an achievement test). If predictions can be made, this suggests (but, as we shall see, does not prove) that the variable measured by the predictor instrument has a causal influence on the variable measured by the other instrument.

The square of a correlation coefficient (r) yields a statistic (r^2) that is called the **explained variance.** For example, the square of a correlation coefficient of .30 is .09. If variable A correlates .30 with variable B, we can say that variable A "explains" 9 percent of the variance in variable B.

The mathematical basis of explained variance is somewhat complicated. A simple way to understand it is to imagine that scores on measure B range from 30 to 70. If A explained none of the variance in B, we could not predict anyone's score on B other than to say that it could be as low as 30 or as high as 70 (a range of 40 points). If A explained all the variance in B, we could predict anyone's score on B perfectly, and so our range of error in any prediction would be 0 points. If A explained 30 percent of the variance in B, we could use A to predict anyone's score within a certain range; for example, our prediction of B might be a range of scores between 40 to 60 (a range of 20 points). In other words, as the explained variance increases, we can use an individual's score on measure A to predict his score on measure B within an increasingly narrow range.

Several types of correlation coefficient are presented in this chapter. Different coefficients are necessary because certain measures are in the form of interval scales or ratio scales (e.g., most measures of intelligence), whereas other measures are in the form of rank orderings (e.g., ranking of teachers in terms of their effectiveness) or dichotomies (e.g., true-false test items). Also, the relationship between the scores on two measures is not always linear, as we shall find in our discussion of the correlation ratio.

Both correlation coefficients and scattergrams express relationships between measured variables. A correlation coefficient is a concise mathematical expression of the relationship, whereas a scattergram provides an easily viewed display of all the data on which the correlation coefficient is based. Researchers often just compute correlation coefficients using a statistical program on a computer. However, you should consider constructing scattergrams as well, particularly if you have reason to think that the relationship is nonlinear (nonlinearity is discussed later in the chapter) or that the sample contains outliers (see Chapter 5).

Correlational Research Design

The basic design in correlational research is very simple, involving nothing more than collecting data on two or more variables for each individual in a sample and computing a correlation coefficient. For example, we might select a group of college freshmen and attempt to predict their first-year grades (variable B) on the basis of their overall Scholastic Aptitude Test (SAT) scores (variable A). Many important studies in education have been done with this simple design. Recent studies have employed more sophisticated correlational techniques in order to include more variables in the data analysis and thereby obtain a clearer picture of the relationships being studied.

As in most research, the quality of correlational studies is determined not by the complexity of the design or the sophistication of analytical techniques, but by the depth of the rationale and theoretical constructs that guide the research design. The likelihood of obtaining an important research finding is greater if the researcher uses theory and the results of previous research to select variables to be correlated with one another.

Correlation and Causality

The correlational approach to analyzing relationships between variables is subject to the same limitations with respect to causal inference as the causal-comparative approach discussed in the preceding chapter. For example, if we found a positive correlation between years of education and level of interest in cultural activities, we might infer that each year of formal schooling is likely to result in—that is, to *cause*—a greater interest in cultural activities.

Two other causal inferences are just as plausible, however. One is that the level of interest in cultural activities determines how much education a student will seek. The other possible inference is that some third variable determines both the amount of education attained and level of interest in cultural activities, thus creating a positive relationship between these two variables. For example, a parents' education is a plausible third variable. Parents who are college graduates might encourage their children to stay in school longer and to develop more cultural interests than parents with less formal education. If this is true, the observed relationship between education and cultural interests is not a cause-and-effect relationship, but rather is the result of their common determination by a third variable.

A correlational relationship between two variables occasionally is the result of an artifact. For example, if we correlate two scales from the same personality inventory, a significant relationship between the scales might be found because both scales contain some of the same items, not because the personality dimensions that they measure are causally related. A statistical technique can be used to correct the correlation coefficient for covariation due to overlapping test items.[1] Also, when raters are used to collect data, a relationship between variables might be found because the same rater scores both variables. This is particularly likely when there is rater bias due to a halo effect (see Chapter 9). For example, we might find correlations between individuals' scores on several "good" traits if raters form an initial positive or negative impression of the individuals being rated. If the impression is positive, they probably will score an individual high on all the traits; if the impression is negative, they probably will assign an individual all low scores. Any correlation found between the traits would be due to this artifact rather than to a true cause-and-effect relationship.

In summary, correlational statistics can be used to explore cause-and-effect relationships between variables, but the obtained results generally do not lead to strong conclusions. A correlation between A and B can mean that A is a determinant of B, that B is a determinant of A, that a third variable X determines both A and B, or that the relationship between A and B is due to an artifact (e.g., the measures of A and B contain some of the same items). Only an experiment can provide a definitive conclusion about a cause-and-effect relationship. Correlation coefficients are best used to measure the degree and direction (i.e., positive or negative) of the relationship between two or more variables and to explore possible causal factors. If a significant relationship between variables is found, their causality can be tested more definitively by using an experimental research design.

Advantages and Uses of Correlational Research

Correlational research designs, like the causal-comparative research designs to which they are closely related, are highly useful for studying problems in education and in the other social sciences. Their principal advantage over causal-comparative or experimental designs is that they enable researchers to analyze the relationships among a large number of variables in a single study. In education and social science, we frequently confront situations in which several variables influence a particular pattern of behavior. Correlational designs allow us to analyze how these variables, either singly or in combination, affect the pattern of behavior. (Path analysis and structural equation modeling, which we discuss later in the chapter, are particularly useful for this purpose.)

Another advantage of correlational designs is that they provide information concerning the degree of the relationship between the variables being studied. This is an advantage over causal-comparative designs. For example, causal-comparative studies of teaching ability often start with the identification of a group of good teachers and a group of ineffective teachers. Comparisons then are made between the two groups on selected dependent variables in order to identify possible causes of the observed differences in teaching ability. Describing one group of teachers as good and another group as ineffective, however, is obviously an artificial dichotomy, because within each of these groups some teachers will certainly be better than others. The differences in degree are ignored in a causal-comparative design. In reality, what we have in this population is not two groups of teachers of distinctly different ability, but a single group ranging in degree of teaching

---

1. This statistical technique is described in: Dahlstrom, W. G., & Welsh, G. S. (1960). *An MMPI handbook: A guide to use in clinical practice and research.* Minneapolis, MN: University of Minnesota Press.

ability from very poor to very good. The correlation coefficient takes into account this range, providing a measure of the degree of relationship over the entire range of teaching ability, or within certain ranges.

Correlational research designs are used for two major purposes: (1) to explore causal relationships between variables and (2) to predict scores on one variable from research participants' scores on other variables. In causal relationship research, the variables can be measured at the same point in time or at different points in time. In prediction research, the variables used for prediction must be measured prior to the measurement of the variable to be predicted.

The design of causal relationship research and prediction research is explained in the next two sections of this chapter. The remainder of the chapter describes the types of correlational statistics that can be used to analyze relational or predictive data. Most of the statistics can be used in either type of research. A few statistical techniques have been developed specifically for prediction research, and these are noted. In the chapters on experimental research designs (Chapters 12 and 13), you will find that the same correlational statistics also can be used to analyze data from experiments.

Planning a Causal Relationship Study

Basic Research Design

The primary purpose of causal relationship studies is to identify the causes and effects of important educational phenomena, such as academic achievement, attitude toward school, teacher morale, leadership style, and the use of particular teaching techniques. This type of research design is especially useful for exploratory studies in areas where little is known. To describe the steps involved in conducting a relationship study, we will use a study by Margaret Hewitt and Susan Homan on the possible effects of test-item readability on students' achievement-test performance.[2]

The Problem

The first step in planning a causal relationship study is to identify specific variables that show promise of being important determinants of the characteristic or behavior pattern being studied. A review of existing research and theory often is helpful in identifying such variables. In the study by Hewitt and Homan, the behavior pattern of interest was students' performance on standardized achievement tests. They reviewed the literature on test validity and made the following observation:

> Although many articles and books discuss the reliability and validity of standardized tests (Resnick & Resnick, 1992; Sacks, 1997; Wiggins, 1989; Wolf, 1993), the issue of validity in terms of readability level of the test items is rarely mentioned. Homan, Hewitt, and Linder (1994) reported that test manuals typically do not provide information about the design principles involved in creating test items and answers, and readability formulas are rarely applied (Drum, Calfee & Cook, 1981).[3]

Based on their literature review, Hewitt and Homan concluded that the readability of test items might affect students' performance on them. If true, the validity of a test item would be compromised, because it is measuring students' ability to read the item rather than whether they have the knowledge or skill that the item is assessing.

---

2. Hewitt, M. A., & Homan, S. P. (2004). Readability level of standardized test items and student performance: The forgotten validity variable. *Reading Research and Instruction, 43*(2), 1–16.
3. Ibid., p. 2.

Hewitt and Homan stated that the purpose of their study was to "demonstrate that students may miss items because of reading problems, not necessarily because of a lack of content knowledge."[4] More specifically, they wished to determine whether the readability of a test item (the independent variable) has a causal effect on students' performance on the item (the dependent variable). If there is no causal relationship between readability and test performance, we would expect the same percentage of students to answer the item correctly whether the item was easy to read or not. If there is a causal relationship, we would expect a higher percentage of students to answer items with easy readability than items with difficult readability.

Selection of Research Participants

The next step in a causal relationship study is to select research participants who can be measured on the variables to be investigated. As we pointed out in our discussion of causal-comparative studies, it is very important to select a group of participants who are reasonably homogeneous. Otherwise, causal relationships between variables might be obscured by the presence of participants who differ widely from each other. If the sample is highly heterogeneous, the researcher should consider forming them into homogeneous subgroups. The technique of moderator analysis, discussed later in the chapter, can be used when subgroups are formed.

Hewitt and Homan chose a large sample of elementary students from a major urban school district for their research study. Their report does not specify the number of schools from which the sample was drawn. Because schools often vary widely in the socioeconomic status and ethnicity of the communities they serve, it would be useful to have this information. However, the researchers did create subgroups by grade level, which creates a certain level of homogeneity in the samples used in the data analysis. Specifically, they formed separate groups of 7,351 third graders, 7,051 fourth graders, and 6,854 fifth graders.

Data Collection

Data for causal relationship studies can be collected by various methods, including standardized tests, questionnaires, interviews, and observational techniques. The only requirement is that the data must be in quantifiable form.

The primary measure used in the study by Hewitt and Homan was the 20-item Social Studies Subtest of the Comprehensive Tests of Basic Skills, Survey, Form A (CTBS), which is administered throughout each school year in April of each year.[5] This measure was analyzed to generate two sets of scores. For each item, the researchers determined its readability level and its difficulty level.

Readability level was measured by the Homan–Hewitt Readability Formula. This formula computes a readability score for an item by measuring the number of difficult words it contains, the number of words having seven or more letters, and sentence complexity (the average number of words in each clause per sentence). The higher the score, the more difficult it is to read.

Item difficulty was measured by computing the percentage of students who successfully answered the item. This percentage was computed for the sample of students drawn from the school district. Another measure of item difficulty was the percentage of a national sample of students who successfully answered the item. (Although the report does not describe the national sample, it most likely is the national norming sample used to determine the characteristics of a standardized test intended for use throughout the United States.)

---

4. Ibid., p. 7.
5. An additional measure was used in the study, but is not discussed here because it was a factor in the primary data analysis.

Data Analysis

In a simple causal relationship study, the data are analyzed by correlating the sample's scores on a measure of the independent variable (the presumed cause) with its scores on a measure of the dependent variable (the presumed effect). In the Hewitt and Homan study, the readability scores for the 20 test items for each subgroup (e.g., third graders) were correlated with the difficulty level of the same 20 items.

The raw data for the correlational analysis for the third-grade group are shown in Table 11.1. The 20 items are identified in the leftmost column and are ordered according to readability level (column 2). The percentage of students in the school district who answered each item correctly is shown in column 3, and the percentage of students in the national sample who answered each item correctly is shown in column 4. For example, we see that item 17 has an easy readability level (2.75), and nearly all the district students (97%) and national-sample students (95%) answered it correctly.

Table 11.1 clearly shows that as items become more difficult to read, fewer students answer them correctly. There are noteworthy exceptions to this generalization, however. For example, item 5 is one of the easiest to read (3.19 on the readability scale), yet only about 50 percent of the two samples could answer it correctly. Another prominent exception is item 9: it is the hardest to read (4.89), but approximately 80% of the two samples answered it correctly.

TABLE 11.1

Difficulty Levels and Readability Levels of the CTBS Social Studies Test Items in the Third-Grade District and National Samples

Item No.	Readability Level	District Item Difficulty	National Item Difficulty
17	2.75	0.97	0.95
16	3.10	0.90	0.88
1	3.11	0.89	0.79
5	3.19	0.57	0.52
6	3.22	0.89	0.81
20	3.25	0.85	0.83
7	3.29	0.80	0.70
15	3.29	0.94	0.94
13	3.60	0.96	0.91
10	3.62	0.87	0.80
18	3.62	0.65	0.60
11	3.77	0.39	0.24
8	3.83	0.35	0.31
2	3.38	0.58	0.45
4	3.86	0.64	0.54
12	4.08	0.51	0.39
3	4.10	0.33	0.34
19	4.47	0.28	0.21
14	4.49	0.49	0.43
9	4.89	0.88	0.79

Source: Adapted from Table 5 on p. 10 in: Hewitt, M. A., & Homan, S. P. (2004). Readability level of standardized test items and student performance: The forgotten validity variable. *Reading Research and Instruction, 43*(2), 1–16. Adapted with permission from the College Reading Association.

TABLE 11.2

Correlations between Test Item Readability and Difficulty Level for Third, Fourth, and Fifth Graders

Grade Level	School District Sample	National Sample
Third graders	−.56	−.58
Fourth graders	−.72	−.62
Fifth graders	−.72	−.62

Note: Alpha levels for tests of statistical significance are not shown because, with such large samples (thousands of students for each calculated correlation coefficient), all the correlation coefficients are statistically significant at a very low alpha level.

Source: Adapted from Tables 2, 3, and 4 in: Hewitt, M. A., & Homan, S. P. (2004). Readability level of standardized test items and student performance: The forgotten validity variable. *Reading Research and Instruction, 43*(2), 1–16. Adapted with permission from the College Reading Association.

These impressions are supported in the statistical analysis involving correlation coefficients, shown in Table 11.2. All the correlations are strongly in the predicted direction. The coefficients have a negative sign, which means that the more difficult an item is to read (high readability score), the fewer the students who can answer it correctly (low percentage of students). Conversely, the easier an item is to read (low readability score), the greater the number of students who can answer it correctly (high percentage of students).

These statistical results support the researchers' hypothesis that the readability of an item has a causal effect on students' ability to answer it correctly. The implicit theory here is that students may have the knowledge or skill being assessed by a test item, but not be able to demonstrate it simply because the item is too difficult to read.

Problems of Interpretation

One advantage of correlational designs is that they permit the researcher to study the relationship between many variables simultaneously. However, this potential advantage can become a weakness if the researcher administers a very large number of measures to a sample of research participants in the hope that some of these measures will turn out to be related to the phenomenon being studied. In the **shotgun approach,** a large number of variables are measured and subjected to correlational analysis even when the researcher has no theoretical basis or commonsense rationale to justify their inclusion.

Although the shotgun approach of correlating many variables with each other sometimes yields significant findings, it should be avoided. First, research participants are inconvenienced and there often is considerable expense when a large number of measures are administered. Furthermore, some of the measures are likely to correlate with the criterion by chance. The only way to identify these chance findings is to repeat the study and determine which findings replicate. The only situation in which the shotgun approach might be justified is when research knowledge is required without regard to cost in an area where previous research is insufficient to form the basis for a more theory-based approach.

A total of six correlation coefficients is shown in Table 11.2. The magnitude of the coefficients, the size of the samples, and the strong rationale for the predicted relationship between the two variables (item readability and item difficulty) strongly suggest that the results are stable and replicable. In fact, the study does include several replications, in that Hewitt and Homan commendably tested their hypothesis both with a local and a national sample of students and at three different grade levels.

Limitations of Causal Relationship Studies

As we explained above, correlations obtained in a causal relationship study cannot establish cause-and-effect relationships between the variables that are correlated. For example, the findings of the study by Hewitt and Homan suggest that the readability level of a test item affects students' ability to answer it correctly. However, it might be that another variable is the actual cause of the observed results. For example, it might be that test items with a more difficult readability level assess more sophisticated knowledge or skills. If this is true, the knowledge and skills assessed by a test item—not its readability—are the actual causes of students' ability to answer it correctly.

A rigorous test of this alternative causal explanation would require an experiment. For example, a researcher might consider some bit of knowledge that students were taught in class and write two test items to assess it: One item would have a more difficult readability level than the other, but both items would test exactly the same knowledge. A sample of students would be randomly assigned to answer one item or the other. If readability level actually affects students' test performance, we would expect that more of the students assigned to respond to the easy-readability item would answer it correctly than would the students assigned to respond to the difficult-readability item. The value of the correlational study by Hewitt and Homan is that it discovered a variable (item readability) that deserves further investigation using controlled experimentation.

Many researchers have criticized causal relationship studies because this type of study breaks down complex abilities, personality characteristics, and behavior patterns into simpler components. Although this atomistic approach is appropriate for many research areas in education and psychology, there is some question whether a complex characteristic, such as text readability, retains its meaning if broken down into its elements. For example, in the study we have been considering, readability of a test item was analyzed into three components: frequency of difficult words, the number of long words, and sentence complexity. Although the researchers presented evidence that these variables relate to readability, this does not mean that each variable is equally important, that they subsume all the important features of readability, or that readability is the same thing for all learners. Correlational research can yield useful findings, but ultimately multiple lines of research and theory building are necessary to develop a full understanding of readability.

Another problem with using correlational statistics to identify variables that may be causally related to complex behavior patterns or abilities is that success in many of the complex activities that interest us probably can be achieved in different ways. For example, a study that attempts to find variables that correlate with success in being a principal might fail because of the lack of any set of characteristics common to all successful principals. In one subgroup of administrators, for example, a domineering personality might be significantly correlated with success, whereas in another subgroup of administrators, who employ different administrative techniques, this characteristic might be negatively correlated with success. We know so little about certain behavior patterns—and many are so highly complex—that only the most careful interpretation of correlational data can provide us with an understanding of the phenomena being studied.

Planning a Prediction Study

Types of Prediction Studies

Educational researchers do many prediction studies, usually with the aim of identifying variables that forecast academic, vocational, and personal success. **Prediction studies**

Touchstone in Research

Schmidt, F., & Hunter, J. (1998). The validity and utility of selection methods in personnel psychology: Practical and theoretical implications of 85 years of research findings. *Psychological Bulletin, 124*, 262–274.

provide three types of information: (1) the extent to which a criterion behavior pattern can be predicted, (2) data for developing a theory about the determinants of the criterion behavior pattern, and (3) evidence about the predictive validity of the test or tests that were correlated with the criterion behavior pattern.

Prediction studies can be differentiated in terms of which of these types of information the researcher is most interested in obtaining. In some studies the emphasis is on a particular criterion (e.g., first-year college grades), and various measures are used to predict this criterion. Those measures that are good predictors can then be applied to practical problems, such as selection of students for college admission. In other studies a similar research design is followed, but the researcher's primary concern is the theoretical significance of the findings. Finally, a researcher can carry out prediction studies for the purpose of test development. The emphasis is on writing test items and determining the test's predictive validity for one or more criteria (see Chapter 7).

Prediction research has made a major contribution to educational practice. Many of these studies have aimed at short-term prediction of the student's performance in a specific course of study, and others have aimed at long-term prediction of general academic success. The findings of these studies have been a great aid to school personnel in identifying the students most likely to succeed in a particular academic environment or course of study. Also, prediction studies provide a scientific basis for efforts to help students plan their academic future. For example, counselors can administer vocational interest tests that have proved effective in predicting success in an occupation and interpret the results to help students select the courses that are most appropriate for their long-term educational and career goals.

Prediction research also can be done to reduce the cost of training new personnel in complex vocational skills. For example, prediction tests used by the U.S. Air Force for pilot training help to eliminate individuals who would fail during the training program. The training is extremely costly, and the cost of training the unsuccessful candidates up to the point of failure must be added to the per-person cost of training successful candidates. A selection process that reduces the number of failures is of great value. Prediction research is done to determine which criteria to incorporate in the selection process.

Basic Research Design

Prediction studies are similar to causal relationship studies in that both involve computing correlations between a complex behavior pattern (the criterion) and variables thought to be related to the criterion. However, in prediction studies the other variables (sometimes called *predictor variables*) are measured some time before the criterion behavior occurs. In contrast, in causal relationship studies the criterion behavior and other variables need not be measured in a particular order, and in practice they often are measured at the same point in time. Also, prediction studies tend to be more concerned with maximizing the correlation between the predictor variables and the criterion, whereas causal relationship studies seek to describe the extent of a relationship, be it high, moderate, or low. As we shall see later in the chapter, correlations obtained in prediction research sometimes can be increased by the use of multiple correlation or moderator analysis.

The Problem

One type of prediction research involves testing the predictive validity of a particular test or self-report measure. An example of this type of research is a prediction study by Robert Bernard, Aaron Brauer, Philip Abrami, and Mike Surkes.[6] The purpose of their study was

6. Bernard, R. M., Brauer, A., Abrami, P. C., & Surkes, M. (2004). The development of a questionnaire for predicting online learning achievement. *Distance Education, 25*(1), 31–47.

to determine the validity of a self-report measure of students' readiness for online learning for predicting their course grades in an online course.

An important aspect of prediction studies is the proper definition of the criterion. Many studies have failed to find predictive relationships because an inadequate criterion was specified. For example, grade-point average (GPA) is sometimes used as a criterion. GPA, however, includes a person's grades in various subjects, such as mathematics, Spanish, and history. Also, the kinds of courses that students take usually change as they progress from the freshman year to the senior year of college. Furthermore, some students select easier courses to take than do other students. These observations suggest that GPA is a shifting, amorphous criterion, and therefore it would be difficult to predict well.

In the study by Bernard and colleagues, the criterion was the students' grade in a course titled *Problem Solving and Academic Strategies*. As the researchers explain: "This grade is a composite of seven assignments that were accomplished during the term, ranging from the simple creation of a study schedule to a more complex essay writing assignment."[7] This description of the criterion suggests that the criterion had the same meaning for all participants and that there was not likely to be a bias in scoring some students' assignments differently from others.

It is worth noting, however, that the course was offered in three different semesters, and the sample included students who took it each semester. If the course content or the assignments changed each semester, the criterion would not be the same for all students in the sample. Shifts in the criterion would make it more difficult to find good predictor variables.

Selection of Research Participants

As we discussed in Chapter 6, it is important to draw research participants from the specific population most pertinent to your study. In the prediction study we have been considering, the researchers were specifically interested in predicting the academic performance of students enrolled in online-learning courses. Therefore, their sample consisted of students who were enrolled in a course that required online learning. The researchers characterized the course as "Web based," but did not describe it in specific detail. Therefore, the reader is left to assume that the course is representative of online courses as they were offered at the time of the study (2002–2003).

Data Collection

Self-report measures, standardized tests, questionnaires, interviews, or observational techniques can be used to measure both the predictor variables and the criterion in a prediction study. Of course, the predictor variables must be measured before the criterion behavior pattern occurs. Otherwise, one cannot claim that a particular test or other measure actually predicted the criterion. In the study by Bernard and colleagues, the primary predictor variables were derived from their review of the literature on the learning characteristics that students need to be successful in an online-learning environment. The researchers developed a questionnaire that measured four variables, each of which was hypothesized to be predictive of success in an online course. The labels for the four predictor variables and two representative questionnaire items for each are shown in Table 11.3. Students' cumulative grade-point average (GPA) was used as another predictor measure. The criterion measure, as we explained above, was students' grades in the online course.

Prediction of behavior that will occur in the near future generally is more accurate than prediction of behavior that will occur in the more distant future. This is because in

7. Ibid., p. 37.

TABLE 11.3

Predictor Variables and Representative Questionnaire Items in a Study of Online-Learning Achievement

Predictor Variable	Representative Questionnaire Items
Confidence in prerequisite skills	1. I possess sufficient computer keyboarding skills for doing online work. 2. I feel comfortable composing text on a computer in an online learning environment.
General beliefs about online learning	1. Learning is the same in class and at home on the Internet. 2. I believe a complete course can be given by the Internet without difficulty.
Self-direction and initiative	1. In my studies, I am self-disciplined and find it easy to set aside reading and homework time. 2. I am able to manage my study time effectively and easily complete assignments on time.
Desire for interaction with others	1. I can collaborate with other students during Internet activities outside of class. 2. As a student, I enjoy working with other students in groups.

Source: Adapted from Table 2 on pp. 38–39 in: Bernard, R. M., Brauer, A., Abrami, P. C., & Surkes, M. (2004). The development of a questionnaire for predicting online learning achievement. *Distance Education, 25*(1), 31–47. Adapted with permission from Taylor & Francis, Ltd. and author Robert Bernard. Journal Web site: http://www.tandf.co.uk/journals

---

short-term prediction, more of the determinants of the behavior being predicted are likely to be present. Furthermore, short-term prediction allows less time for important aspects of the criterion behavior to change or for important new determinants of the criterion behavior to emerge. For example, if we wish to predict the probable success of individuals in management positions, we probably would start with variables that have been found in previous research to be related to later success in management. Our test battery might include measures of such factors as verbal intelligence, social attitudes, emotional maturity, and so on. However, certain variables important to success could not possibly be measured, because they are not present at the time the prediction must be made. For example, a high school senior's ability to work well with superiors in the management hierarchy—a likely determinant of management success—cannot be measured, because the student's future superiors are unknown at the time of prediction.

Data Analysis

The primary method of data analysis in a prediction study is to correlate scores on each predictor measure with the criterion scores. In the study we have been describing, students' scores on the four questionnaire scales of learner characteristics and their GPAs were correlated with their grades in the online course. In addition, their scores on each measure were correlated with their scores on all the other measures. The correlation coefficients are shown in Table 11.4.

Looking at the first data column of Table 11.4, we see how well each predictor measure correlates with students' course grades. The correlation between GPA and course grade is

TABLE 11.4

Correlations between Predictor Measures and Criterion Measure in a Study of Online Learning

Measures[a]	Course Grade	GPA	Skills	Beliefs	Self-Direction	Interaction
Course Grade	1.00					
GPA	+0.68*	1.00				
Skills	+0.04	+0.02	1.00			
Beliefs	+0.19*	−0.14	−0.26*	1.00		
Self-Direction	+0.23*	+0.31*	−0.13	−0.10	1.00	
Interaction	−0.10*	−0.10	−0.32*	−0.28*	−0.05	1.00

*$p < 0.05$ (two-tailed).
[a]N values ranged from 147 to 167, depending on the amount of missing data.

Source: Table 5 on p. 40 in: Bernard, R. M., Brauer, A., Abrami, P. C., & Surkes, M. (2004). The development of a questionnaire for predicting online learning achievement. *Distance Education, 25*(1), 31–47. Adapted with permission from Taylor & Francis, Ltd. and author Robert Bernard. Journal Web site: http://www.tandf.co.uk/journals

substantial ($r = .68$). This finding is typical of that found in many other studies; it supports the commonsense notion that, if students generally do well in their courses, we can predict that they are likely to do well in any particular course.

The first data column also shows that, of the four learner characteristics, self-direction is the best predictor of course grade ($r = .23$). More self-directed students are more likely to do well in an online course; they are also more likely to do well in other courses ($r = .31$ between self-direction and GPA). Students' belief that they can learn effectively from the Internet also predicts, but only slightly ($r = .19$), their grades in the online course. Students' desire to interact with others had a slight, but statistically significant, correlation ($r = −.10$) with course grade. The negative sign means that students with a strong desire to interact with others had a slight tendency to do less well in the online course, whereas students with less desire for interaction had a slight tendency to do well in this learning environment.

The statistics shown in Table 11.4 sometimes are called *bivariate correlational statistics,* because each coefficient expresses the magnitude of relationship between two variables (hence *bi-*variate correlation). This type of statistic is discussed in the next section of the chapter.

Other statistical techniques can be applied to improve predictions from individuals' scores on the predictor variables. The primary technique to maximize prediction is multiple regression, which uses research participants' scores on two or more predictor variables to predict their performance on the criterion variables. (Multiple regression is discussed later in the chapter.) Using multiple regression, Bernard and colleagues found that students' scores on the four predictor measures involving learner characteristics accounted for 8 percent of the variance in their course grades. This means that these four measures had some predictive value, but probably not enough to warrant using them in a practical manner, for example, using students' scores on these measures to decide whom to admit to an online course.

Moderator analysis, also discussed later in the chapter, is another procedure for improving the predictability of a criterion variable. This procedure involves identifying a subgroup for whom the correlation between a criterion and a predictor variable is significantly greater than the correlation for the total sample from which the subgroup was formed.

Statistical Factors in Prediction Research

Group Prediction

The goal of many prediction studies is to develop measures with sufficient predictive validity to be useful in practical selection programs in education or industry. The effectiveness of a measure for selection purposes, however, is not determined solely by its predictive validity. Two other factors influence effectiveness in practical selection. The first factor is the **selection ratio.** This is the proportion of the available candidates who must be selected. A predictive measure gives better results when only the few candidates scoring highest will be chosen than when all but the few who score lowest must be chosen. In other words, as the proportion of candidates who must be chosen decreases, the predictive ability of a measure, or set of measures, increases.

The other factor influencing the effectiveness of a predictive measure is the **base rate,** that is, the percentage of candidates who would be successful if no selection procedure were applied. In educational selection, this might be the percentage of students who succeeded in a particular educational program prior to the use of selective admission. If the base rate percentage is high, the predictive measure will need to have very high validity in order to improve on the success of "natural" selection. For example, if 95 percent of the students typically pass a course, you would be correct 95 percent of the time if you predicted that everyone would pass. It would be difficult to develop a test that would improve on the accuracy of prediction. Predictive measures are most likely to be helpful if the base rate percentage is in the intermediate range, for example, in situations where 25 to 75 percent of the individuals meet the specified criterion.

The **Taylor-Russell Tables** combine three factors: predictive validity, selection ratio, and proportion successful without selection.[8] If these three factors are known, the researcher can predict the proportion of the candidates selected who will be successful when the predictive measure is used.

Shrinkage

In using correlations for prediction, the usual procedure is to select a test or battery of tests that we believe will predict the criterion behavior. These tests are then tried out on a sample in order to determine their actual predictive validity. The correlation between individuals' scores on the test and their later behavior provides an estimate of the predictive validity of the test. This correlation, however, almost certainly will become smaller if we repeat the study with a new sample.

Shrinkage is the tendency for predictive validities to decrease when the research study is repeated. More shrinkage is likely when the original sample is small and the number of predictor variables is large.

Shrinkage is due primarily to the fact that when we initially validate our measures, some of them will yield significant correlations by chance. In fact, we can demonstrate mathematically that if researchers keep adding predictor variables to a multiple regression equation, they eventually will be able to predict each person's score on the criterion measure perfectly. Upon repetition of the study, however, these same predictive relationships, which are based mainly on chance, are not likely to be present. Thus the correlations initially obtained will become smaller.

Because making predictions on the basis of correlations derived from scores for only one sample of individuals is of uncertain value, researchers should conduct a cross-validation of

8. Taylor, H. C., & Russell, J. T. (1939). The relationships of validity coefficients to the practical effectiveness of tests in selection: Discussion and tables. *Journal of Applied Psychology, 23,* 565–578.

predictor variables before using them in practical prediction situations. Thus, after preliminary validation of a test or battery of tests, the predictive validity of each test should be cross-checked with another sample. Those correlations that have dropped to a nonsignificant level should be eliminated.

Bivariate Correlational Statistics

In this section we discuss 10 correlational techniques that can be used to analyze the degree of relationship between two variables. Because two variables are involved, these techniques are called *bivariate* correlational statistics. The form of the variables to be correlated and the nature of the relationship determine which technique is used. Variables in relationship studies are usually expressed in one of five forms, which were described in Chapter 5: continuous score, rank, artificial dichotomy, true dichotomy, and category. Table 11.5 lists 10 bivariate correlational techniques and the conditions under which each is used. We discuss two of them below to illustrate the point that each of these correlational techniques serves a different purpose.

Product-Moment Correlation Coefficient

The **product-moment correlation coefficient (r)** is computed when both variables that we wish to correlate are expressed as continuous scores. (This correlation coefficient sometimes is called a *Pearson r*, because Karl Pearson developed it.) For example, if we administer an intelligence test such as the Wechsler Intelligence Scale for Children and an achievement test such as the Stanford Achievement Test to the same group of students, we will have two sets of continuous scores. The product-moment correlation coefficient r would be the appropriate correlational statistic for determining the magnitude of relationship between students' scores on the two measures.

Product-moment correlation is the most widely used bivariate correlational technique because most educational measures yield continuous scores and because r has a small standard error. In fact, r can be calculated for any two sets of scores, even if one or both measures do not yield scores in continuous form. Researchers frequently compute a correlation matrix in which subjects' scores on a large number of variables are correlated with each other. (The correlation matrix is discussed later in the chapter.) All the correlation coefficients in the matrix usually are product-moment rs, even if the measures yield different types of scores.

Correlation Ratio

In correlational research the usual assumption is that the prediction or relationship being studied is linear. In other words, we assume that a straight line (the line of best fit) best describes the relationship between the two variables. Sometimes, however, the relationship is nonlinear, as in the scattergram shown in Figure 11.2. In this example a curved line rather than a straight line best describes the relationship between the two variables, and therefore leads to better predictions from scores on the x-axis to scores on the y-axis.

Sometimes nonlinear relationships are discovered in correlational studies only after scattergrams have been plotted, but occasionally they are hypothesized to describe the relationship between two variables. For example, some researchers have hypothesized a *curvilinear* relationship between anxiety and intellectual performance. The rationale for this hypothesis is that persons low in anxiety will not be motivated to do well on a performance task and thus will earn low scores. Persons with a moderate amount of

TABLE 11.5

Bivariate Correlational Techniques for Different Forms of Variables

Technique	Symbol	Variable 1	Variable 2	Remarks
Product-moment correlation	r	Continuous	Continuous	The most stable technique, i.e., smallest standard error
Rank-difference correlation *(rho)*	ρ	Ranks	Ranks	A special form of product-moment correlation
Kendall's *tau*	τ	Ranks	Ranks	Preferable to *rho* for samples less than 10
Biserial correlation	r_{bis}	Artificial dichotomy	Continuous	Values can exceed 1; has a larger standard error than r; commonly used in item analysis
Widespread biserial correlation	r_{wbis}	Widespread artificial dichotomy	Continuous	Used when the researcher is interested in persons at the extremes on the dichotomized variable
Point-biserial correlation	r_{pbis}	True dichotomy	Continuous	Yields a lower correlation than r_{bis}
Tetrachoric correlation	r_t	Artificial dichotomy	Artificial dichotomy	Used when both variables can be split at critical points
Phi coefficient	ϕ	True dichotomy	True dichotomy	Used in calculating inter-item correlations
Contingency coefficient	C	Two or more categories	Two or more categories	Comparable to r_t under certain conditions; closely related to chi-square
Correlation ratio, *eta*	η	Continuous	Continuous	Used to detect nonlinear relationships

FIGURE 11.2

Scattergram Representing a Nonlinear Correlation between Two Variables

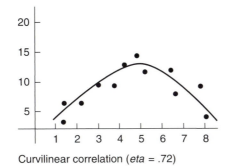

Curvilinear correlation (*eta* = .72)

The product-moment correlation for the same data would be about −.29.

anxiety will be motivated by their anxiety to perform well, and because their anxiety is moderate, it will not disrupt their performance. Therefore, they should earn higher scores than the nonanxious group. By the same reasoning, highly anxious persons should be even more motivated to perform well. If high motivation were the only factor operating, highly anxious persons should earn the highest scores, and the relationship between anxiety and performance would be linear. However, it has been hypothesized that highly anxious persons, though well motivated, are disrupted by their anxiety and thus will earn low performance scores. Consequently, the hypothesized relationship between anxiety and performance is curvilinear, with high- and low-anxiety groups hypothesized to have low performance scores and the middle-anxiety group hypothesized to have high performance scores.

If the scattergrams for research data indicate that the relationship between two variables is markedly nonlinear, the researcher should compute the **correlation ratio** (*eta*). The advantage of the correlation ratio is that it provides a more accurate index of the relationship between two variables than other correlational statistics when the relationship is markedly nonlinear. Other types of correlation coefficients generally underestimate the degree of relationship when nonlinearity exists. A special statistical test can be used to determine whether the *eta* statistic yields a coefficient that is of significantly greater magnitude than the coefficient yielded by a linear correlational statistic.

An alternative to *eta*, especially when several predictor variables are involved, is the technique of multiple regression, which is discussed later in the chapter. This technique can be used to test for nonlinear relationships between variables.[9]

In addition to revealing nonlinear relationships, scattergrams are useful for detecting outliers in research data. (Outliers are discussed in Chapter 5.) The points in the scattergrams in Figure 11.2 are generally clustered near each other. If one of the points was quite far away from the other points in the scattergram, we would have reason to suspect that the research participant represented by that point was an outlier.

---

9. The use of multiple regression to test for nonlinear relationships is illustrated in: Baron, J., & Norman, M. F. (1992). SATs, achievement tests, and high-school class rank as predictors of college performance. *Educational and Psychological Measurement, 52*(4), 1047–1055.

Touchstone in Research

Raju, N. S., & Brand, P. A. (2003). Determining the significance of correlations corrected for unreliability and range restriction. *Applied Psychological Measurement, 27*(1), 52–71.

Adjustments to Correlation Coefficients

The degree of relationship between two variables is most often analyzed using the correlation coefficients described above. In some educational research, however, special circumstances require an "adjustment" of these coefficients. We describe three types of adjustment below.

Correction for Attenuation

When we correlate scores on two measures, the obtained correlation coefficient is lower than the true correlation to the extent that the measures are not perfectly reliable. This lowering of the correlation coefficient due to unreliability of the measures is called *attenuation*. **Correction for attenuation** provides an estimate of what the correlation between the variables would be if the measures had perfect reliability.

Correction for attenuation is not usually applied in prediction studies because we must make predictions on the basis of the measures we have, and the reliability of these measures, even if it is low, must be accepted as a limitation. This correction is sometimes used in exploratory studies, however. These studies often must use crude measures of low reliability, thus lowering the obtained correlation coefficient. The correction for attenuation helps the researcher determine what the relationship between two variables might be if perfect measures of the variables were available.

Correction for Restriction in Range

The **correction for restriction in range** is applied to correlation coefficients when the researcher knows that the range of scores for a sample is restricted on one or both of the variables being correlated. Restriction in range leads to a lowering of the correlation coefficient.

The use of this technique is illustrated in a study by Emily Krohn, Robert Lamp, and Cynthia Phelps.[10] They validated a test of cognitive abilities, the Kaufman Assessment Battery for Children (K-ABC), by correlating children's scores on its various subtests with their scores on a well-established intelligence test, the Stanford-Binet Intelligence Scale (SB). The sample of children was a group of black preschoolers enrolled in a Head Start program.

The standard deviations of the K-ABC and SB for norming groups are 15 and 16, respectively. The standard deviations for the researchers' sample, however, were substantially lower. For example, the sample's standard deviation on the SB was 9.4, which indicates a restricted range of scores relative to the norming group. Therefore, the researchers calculated both the regular correlations (*r*) between students' K-ABC subtest scores and SB total score and the same correlations (*r[cf16]c*) corrected for restriction in range. Each corrected coefficient was found to be larger than the corresponding *r*. For example, the *r* between the Stanford-Binet and the nonverbal subtest of the K-ABC was .41, whereas the *r[cf16]c* was .69.

Use of the correction for restriction in range requires the assumption that the two variables are related to each other linearly throughout their entire range. If the relationship for the total range of scores is nonlinear, the correction for restriction in range is not applicable.

---

10. Krohn, E. J., Lamp, R. E., & Phelps, C. G. (1988). Validity of the K-ABC for a black preschool population. *Psychology in the Schools, 25,* 15–21.

Part and Partial Correlation

Partial correlation is sometimes employed in causal-relationship and prediction studies to rule out the influence of one or more measured variables on a particular relationship or prediction that is being analyzed. In other words, partial correlation removes the influence of variable *A* on variable *B* (the independent or predictor variable) and variable *C* (the criterion variable).

The use of partial correlation is illustrated in Xiaobin Li's study of the relationship between societal factors and variations in teacher salaries among Canadian provinces.[11] The average teacher salaries in 1995 for the 10 provinces that were studied were as follows:

Ontario	$42,758
British Columbia	$38,737
Alberta	$36,390
Manitoba	$36,296
Nova Scotia	$35,530
Newfoundland	$35,253
Quebec	$35,094
Saskatchewan	$33,059
Prince Edward Island	$32,227
New Brunswick	$31,771

These data indicate a spread of almost $11,000 between the highest and lowest provincial salary and also substantial variation within these extremes. The major purpose of the study was to identify variables that might provide a causal explanation for these variations.

Li's review of the research literature resulted in identifying six independent variables that might influence teacher salaries (the dependent variable). The independent variables were population density, family income, farm land price, population growth, teacher supply and demand, and unemployment rate. Li was able to obtain provincial data for each of these variables, for example, average family income in Ontario.

The primary purpose of the statistical analysis was to determine the extent to which each of the six independent variables correlated with the teacher-salary variable. A straightforward analysis would be to simply correlate scores on the measure of each independent variable with the dependent measure (average teacher salary). However, the independent variables also correlated with each other. For example, Li reports a strong correlation ($r = .80$) between family income and population growth. Thus, if we find a positive correlation between family income and teacher salaries, we do not know whether it means that provinces are inclined to pay teacher higher salaries because families in the province have high incomes or because provinces with fast-growing populations need to pay higher teacher salaries, perhaps because they need to attract large numbers of new teachers to accommodate the growing number of students.

Partial correlation provides a statistical approach to removing the influence of one independent variable so that the effect of another independent variable can be studied. This is the approach that Li took. The results of statistical analyses using partial correlation coefficients are shown in Table 11.6.

The one statistically significant result (assuming the conventional alpha level of .05) is the partial correlation coefficient for family income and teacher salaries ($r = .72$). Although the ideal situation would be to partial out the effect of the other five independent

---

11. Li, X. (2002). Variation in average teacher salaries among Canadian provinces and its probable reasons. *Journal of Education Finance, 27*(3), 909–929.

TABLE 11.6

Partial Correlation Coefficients for Six Independent Variables in a Study of Variations in Teacher Salaries

	Density	Family	Land Price	Population Growth	Surplus	Unemployment
Salary	−.24	.72	.55	−.16	.83	.51
p-value	.57	.04	.15	.71	.08	.20
Controlling:	Family income	Land price	Family income	Family income	Family income	Family income
	Land price	Density	Density	Land price	Land price	Land price

Source: Table 2 on p. 917 in: Li, X. (2002). Variation in average teacher salaries among Canadian provinces and its probable reasons. *Journal of Education Finance, 27*(3), 909–929. This article originally appeared in the Winter 2002 *Journal of Education Finance* and is reprinted with permission of the Association of School Business Officials International ® www.asbointl.org. The text herein does not necessarily represent the views or policies of ASBO International, and use of this imprint does not imply any endorsement or recognition by ASBO International and its officers or affiliates.

variables, the small sample size ($n = 10$) did not allow it. Therefore, Li selected two independent variables, average provincial land prices and population density, for reasons explained in the report. The partial correlation of .72 means that provinces with higher family incomes are very likely to pay higher teacher salaries, even when land prices and population densities are held constant.

What does "held constant" mean in this analysis? Consider land prices. If land prices in a province are high and family incomes are also high, families' disposable income is lowered by having higher home mortgage payments and therefore they might not wish to, or be able to, support high teacher salaries. Conversely, if a province's land prices are low and family incomes are also low, their disposable incomes will not be lowered by having high mortgage payments, and so they might be able to support teacher salaries similar to those in high-land-price provinces. Partial correlation provides a statistical method to create a level playing field in which land prices are held constant (i.e., made the same) across the 10 provinces that were studied. When this was done, together with holding population density constant, Li still found a high correlation between family income and teacher salaries. In short, even though Canadian provinces differ in many ways besides family incomes, family income by itself seems to be a primary determinant of teacher salaries.

As explained above, partial correlation removes the influence of one or more measured variables (*A*) on two other variables (*B* and *C*) whose relationship is being analyzed. If a researcher is interested in removing the influence of one or more measured variables (*A*) on just *B* or *C*, the statistical method of part correlation would be used instead of partial correlation. **Part correlation** is a statistic that expresses the degree of relationship between two variables, *A* and *B*, after the effect of a third variable, *C*, on either *A* or *B* (but not both) has been removed.

Multivariate Correlational Statistics

The correlational techniques presented above are used to measure the degree of relationship between two variables. However, many research problems in education involve interrelationships between three or more variables. The multivariate statistics that we present in the following sections allow researchers to measure and study the degree of relationship among various combinations of these variables. Table 11.7 presents a summary of these statistics.

Multivariate correlational statistics have many applications in educational research. Not only are they used to analyze correlational data, but they also are used with increasing frequency in analyzing experimental data. We discuss this latter use of multivariate statistics in Chapters 12 and 13. Furthermore, multivariate correlational statistics can be used in place of, or in addition to, the statistical techniques that are traditionally used in causal-comparative research (see Chapter 10). Thus they need to be carefully studied by anyone considering conducting any of these types of quantitative research. If you plan to use multivariate correlational statistics in a research project, we advise you to consult an expert statistician to ensure that you select the most appropriate technique and apply it correctly.

Multiple Regression

Multiple regression is used to determine the correlation between a criterion variable and a combination of two or more predictor variables. It is one of the most widely used statistical techniques in educational research. The popularity of multiple regression stems from its versatility and the amount of information it yields about relationships among variables. It can be used to analyze data from any of the major quantitative research designs: causal-comparative, correlational, and experimental. It can handle interval, ordinal, or categorical data. And it provides estimates both of the magnitude and statistical significance of relationships between variables.

A Research Example

The use of multiple regression is illustrated in a causal relationship study conducted by Paula Jorde-Bloom and Martin Ford.[12] The purpose of their study was to identify factors that distinguish administrators of early childhood education programs who have adopted the use of microcomputers from administrators who have not. Jorde-Bloom and Ford observed that educational administrators are responsible for deciding which of the innovations that keep appearing in education should be considered for adoption, and for managing the change process after an adoption decision is made. Jorde-Bloom and Ford justified their study in this way:

> an awareness of some of the factors that help explain or predict innovation acceptance may broaden our understanding of how education professionals cope with a changing society.[13]

The researchers hypothesized that an administrator's decision to adopt computers would be influenced by four factors: (1) relevant past experiences, (2) expectancies about what would happen if one decided to adopt computers, (3) openness to change, and (4) presence of support and encouragement from outside the organization. Eight measures of these factors were administered to the sample. They are referred to as *influence variables* in Table 11.8.

The eight influence variables, organized under the four factors, are listed below. Next to each of these variables is a description of the procedure used to measure it.

---

12. Jorde-Bloom, P., & Ford, M. (1988). Factors influencing early childhood administrators' decisions regarding the adoption of computer technology. *Journal of Educational Computing, 4,* 31–47.
13. Ibid., p. 32.

TABLE 11.7

Types of Multivariate Correlational Statistics

Statistic	Use
Canonical correlation	For determining the correlation between a set of criterion variables and a set of predictor variables
Differential analysis	For comparing correlation coefficients obtained from homogeneous subgroups within a sample; can be used to identify moderator variables that improve a measure's predictive validity
Discriminant analysis	For determining the correlation between a set of predictor variables and a criterion variable that is in the form of categories
Factor analysis	For reducing a large number of variables to a small number of factors, with each factor representing a set of variables that are moderately or highly correlated with each other
Hierarchical linear regression	For examining the correlation between a set of predictor variables and a criterion variable at different units of statistical analysis, for example, the relationship between student characteristics and academic achievement at the teacher level, school level, and district level
Logistic regression	For determining the correlation between a dichotomous criterion variable and a set of predictor variables
Multiple linear regression	For determining the correlation between a criterion variable and a set of predictor variables when the correlations are hypothesized to be linear
Nonlinear regression	For determining the correlation between a criterion variable and a set of predictor variables when the correlation is hypothesized to be nonlinear
Path analysis	For testing theories about the hypothesized causal links between a set of variables
Poisson regression	For determining the correlation between a set of predictor variables and a criterion variable that is in the form of a frequency count
Structural equation modeling	For testing theories about hypothesized causal links between variables; yields more valid and reliable measures of the variables to be analyzed than does path analysis
Time-series analysis	For determining whether changes in the data collected on a time-ordered variable (i.e., a variable in which the data can be arranged in chronological order) are chance occurrences or the effect of some intervention

TABLE 11.8

Correlations between Influence Variables and Computer Implementation Variables

Influence Variables	Administrative Use r	Instructional Use r
Computer experience	.74***	.57***
Innovation experience	.19*	.14
Math/science background	.34***	.19*
Self-efficacy	.69***	.61 ***
Consequences of use	.66***	.50***
Innovativeness	.45***	.46***
Professional orientation	.60***	.55***
Outside support	.40***	.31**
Age	.02	.07
Gender	−.20*	−.42***

*$p < .05$
**$p < .01$
***$p < .001$

Source: Adapted from Table 2 on p. 42 in: Jorde-Bloom, P., & Ford, M. (1988). Factors influencing early childhood administrators' decisions regarding the adoption of computer technology. *Journal of Educational Computing Research, 4,* 31–47. Adapted with permission from Baywood Publishing.

Relevant Past Experiences
1. *Computer experience:* 31 questions about the administrator's experience with computer-related technology and microcomputers.
2. *Innovation experience:* 8 questions about experiences with other educational innovations.
3. *Math/science background:* Number of completed high school courses in math and science.

Expectancies
4. *Self-efficacy:* 15 questions about self-perceived ability and confidence to implement computer use.
5. *Consequences of use:* 21 questions about appreciation of computers, computer anxiety, and beliefs about the societal impact of computers.

Openness to Change and Presence of Support
6. *Innovativeness:* 31 questions about one's perceived tendency to innovate.
7. *Professional orientation:* 24 questions about various aspects of the administrator's role, complexity of the organization, on-the-job activities, outside activities, and highest degree obtained.
8. *Outside support:* 10 questions about the support for computer implementation that an administrator has received from spouse, friends, colleagues, or others.

The administrators' age and gender also were viewed as possible influences on the decision to adopt computers and thus were included as influence variables.

A sample of 80 administrators of early childhood programs in the state of Illinois completed the measures described above. They also completed measures of two criterion variables: (1) level of computer implementation for administrative purposes, and (2) level of computer implementation for instructional uses. The measure of each criterion variable assessed how far they had proceeded along a continuum of implementation, from low to high: awareness, active information seeking, assessment, tentative adoption, and institutionalization. These two criterion variables, which are referred to as computer implementation variables in Table 11.8, are listed at the top of the first and second data columns of the table. The intersection of each column and row shows the correlation between each influence variable and each computer implementation variable. For example, the correlation between amount of outside support and level of computer implementation for administrative use is .40, which is statistically significant at the .001 level.

The correlations shown in Table 11.8 form the basis for multiple regression. The purpose of multiple regression in this study is to determine which of the influence variables can be combined to form the best prediction of each criterion variable. In other words, the objective of multiple regression is to use the research participants' scores on some or all of the influence variables to predict their scores on each criterion variable. By contrast, each bivariate correlation coefficient shown in Table 11.8 represents the use of research participants' scores on one influence variable to predict their scores on each criterion variable.

A typical multiple regression will produce many statistics and equations. Only a few of them might appear in the published report of the study. The others can be calculated if appropriate statistics are provided by the authors of the report. We can explain this point further by examining the multiple regression results presented in Table 11.9.

The left side of Table 11.9 lists the variables in the multiple regression analysis. Note that two analyses were carried out, one for each criterion variable. In the first analysis, the criterion variable of level of computer implementation for administrative use was predicted from four influence variables: computer experience, professional orientation, self-efficacy, and math/science background. In the second analysis, the criterion variable labeled level of computer implementation for instructional use was predicted from a similar set of influence variables, but they entered the multiple regression at different steps.

We begin our explanation of Table 11.9 by considering the second data column. It presents the product-moment correlations between each influence variable and the pertinent criterion variable. These correlation coefficients are the same as those that appear in Table 11.8. For example, the correlation between self-efficacy and implementation for instructional use is .61 in Table 11.9. This is the same value as the coefficient shown in Table 11.8 (see the intersection of the fourth row of coefficients and the second data column).

In our explanation of the other parts of Table 11.9, we will concentrate on the multiple regression analysis of the level of computer implementation for administrative use (the top set of rows). You can extend the analysis on your own to the multiple regression results for the level of computer implementation for instructional use.

Steps in a Multiple Regression Analysis

The first step in a multiple regression analysis usually is to compute the correlation between the best single predictor variable and the criterion variable. This procedure yields a multiple correlation coefficient (R), which is shown in the third data column of Table 11.9. Because computer experience is the best predictor, it is the first predictor entered into the multiple regression. Note that the correlation coefficient ($r = .74$) is the same as the multiple correlation coefficient ($R = .74$).

TABLE 11.9

Stepwise Multiple Regression of Influence Variables on Administrators' Level of Computer Implementation

Influence Variables	Beta	Correlation Coefficient (r)	Multiple Correlation (R)	R^2	R^2 Increment
Implementation for Administrative Use					
1. Computer experience	.40	.74	.74	.54	
2. Professional orientation	.30	.60	.81	.66	.12
3. Self-efficacy	.28	.69	.83	.70	.04
4. Math/science background	.20	.34	.86	.73	.03
Implementation for Instructional Use					
1. Self-efficacy	.26	.61	.61	.37	
2. Professional orientation	.28	.55	.69	.47	.10
3. Gender	−.20	−.42	.71	.50	.03
4. Computer experience	.25	.57	.73	.54	.04

Source: Adapted from Tables 3 and 4 on pp. 43–44 in: Jorde-Bloom, P., & Ford, M. (1988). Factors influencing early childhood administrators' decisions regarding the adoption of computer technology. *Journal of Educational Computing Research, 4,* 31–47. Adapted with permisssion from Baywood Publishing.

Unless you specify otherwise, the computer program will start the multiple regression analysis with the most powerful predictor of the criterion variable. In some situations, however, you will want to enter a less powerful predictor first. For example, if the predictor variables can be ordered chronologically, you might want to start the multiple regression analysis by entering the earliest predictor first. Another situation occurs when one of the predictors is well established in the field of education and another predictor is novel. For example, suppose you have developed a new measure of scholastic aptitude and are testing its predictive validity relative to a standard IQ measure. It makes sense to enter IQ scores first in the multiple regression—irrespective of its correlation with the criterion— and then to see how well the new measure improves upon the prediction.

Suppose you have not specified the order in which the predictor variables are to be entered into the multiple regression analysis. In this case, after selecting the best predictor, the computer program will search for the next best predictor of the criterion variable. This second predictor is not chosen on the basis of its product-moment correlation (r) with the criterion. Rather, the second predictor is chosen on the basis of how well it improves upon the prediction achieved by the first variable.

What qualities should a variable have to be a good second predictor? First, it should correlate as little as possible with the first predictor variable. If it correlates substantially with the first variable entered in the multiple regression analysis, there is a possibility that it will explain the same variance in the criterion variable as the first variable. For example, suppose an IQ test and a verbal scholastic aptitude test are used to predict fifth-grade reading achievement. The two predictor variables are likely to correlate highly with each other because they measure the same underlying factor. If IQ scores are entered in the multiple regression first, the verbal aptitude test is unlikely to improve upon the prediction because it mostly explains the same variance in reading achievement as the IQ test. The situation is comparable to using the same IQ scores a second time in an attempt to improve upon the prediction achieved by using them the first time.

The second quality of a good second predictor is obvious: It should correlate as highly as possible with the criterion variable. In short, a good second predictor is one that correlates as little as possible with the first predictor and as highly as possible with the criterion.

Table 11.9 indicates that professional orientation was the second variable entered in the multiple regression analysis to predict administrators' computer implementation for administrative use. The two predictor variables together (computer experience and professional orientation) yield a multiple correlation coefficient (R) of .81, which is shown in the row next to the predictor variable that was last entered into the multiple regression (in this case, professional orientation). This is a moderate improvement upon the prediction achieved by just using computer experience as a predictor ($R = .74$).

At this point you may ask why professional orientation does not improve the prediction more, given that professional orientation on its own correlates .60 with the criterion. Administrators' scores on the measures of computer experience and professional orientation undoubtedly are correlated (in fact, we learned by reading the original research report that the r for these two variables is .38). Because of this overlap in the variance explained by computer experience and professional orientation, professional orientation does not have a chance to improve dramatically upon the prediction made by computer experience, which entered the multiple regression analysis first.

The overlap between two predictor variables, that is, the extent to which they correlate with each other, is called **collinearity.** If the collinearity between the predictor variables is high, only some of the predictor variables will enter the multiple regression analysis as predictors, even though all of them might predict the criterion variable to some extent. Evidently this was the case in Jorde-Bloom and Ford's study. All the influence variables except age correlated significantly with the criterion variable, but only a few of them contributed to the multiple regression analysis.

The third predictor entered in the multiple regression analysis is determined by whether it improves upon the prediction made by the first two predictors. We see in Table 11.9 that self-efficacy slightly improves the multiple correlation coefficient for predicting computer implementation for administrative use, to .83.

The computer program will keep adding predictor variables until there are none left. Each new predictor variable will contribute less to R than the preceding predictor, however, in which case there are rapidly diminishing returns for adding new predictors. A test of statistical significance can be used to limit the number of predictor variables that are used. The researcher can specify in the computer program that new predictor variables are not to be added to the multiple regression analysis unless their contribution to R is statistically significant.

Multiple Correlation Coefficient

At this point we can consider further the meaning of R. The **multiple correlation coefficient** (R) is a measure of the magnitude of the relationship between a criterion variable and some combination of predictor variables. The value of R will increase with each variable that enters the multiple regression analysis. Thus, we see in the top portion of Table 11.9 that the value of R to predict administrative use gradually increases from .74 to .86 as each predictor variable is added. The value of .86 represents the best prediction one can make of level of computer implementation for administrative use from the influence variables listed in Table 11.8. The value of R can range from 0.00 to 1.00; negative values are not possible. The larger the R, the better the prediction of the criterion variable.

Coefficient of Determination

If R is squared, it will yield a statistic known as the **coefficient of determination** (R^2). The fourth data column of Table 11.9 shows the R^2 coefficients corresponding to the Rs in the third data column. For example, the topmost R^2 coefficient is .54, which is the square of the corresponding R coefficient (.74). R^2s expresses the amount of variance in the criterion variable that is explained by a predictor variable or combination of predictor variables.

The final data column of Table 11.9 presents the R^2 increments for the multiple regression analysis. An R^2 increment is a statistic that expresses the additional variance in the criterion variable that can be explained by adding a new predictor variable to the multiple regression analysis. For example, the addition of professional orientation to the analysis explains 12 percent more of the variance in the criterion variable (.66 minus .54 = .12) than can be explained by computer experience alone. Adding self-efficacy to the analysis results in an R^2 increment of just 4 percent, meaning that it explains 4 percent more of the variance in level of computer implementation for administrative use than can be explained by computer experience and professional orientation together.

Two tests of statistical significance are commonly done in multiple regression analysis. One test is done to determine whether the obtained value of R is significantly different from zero. The other test, as we explained above, is done to determine whether the R^2 increment is statistically significant. For example, one could test whether the R^2 of .66 that is obtained by adding professional orientation to the multiple regression analysis is significantly different from the R^2 of .54 obtained without using this variable as a predictor.

The Mathematics of Multiple Regression

The mathematical basis for multiple regression is an equation that links the predictor variable(s) to the criterion variable. Suppose that level of computer implementation for administrative use = Y, computer experience = X_1, professional orientation = X_2, self-efficacy = X_3, and math/science background = X_4. Using C to stand for a constant term, we can state the multiple regression equation as:

$$\hat{Y} = b_1X_1 + b_2X_2 + b_3X_3 + b_4X_4 + C$$

Note that Y has a circumflex above it to indicate that the Y scores are being predicted from the X variables. The predicted values of Y will deviate from research participants' actual Y scores because X_1, X_2, X_3, and X_4 are not perfect predictors. Note, too, that this equation is similar to the equation for the line of best fit for scattergrams depicting bivariate correlation coefficients ($Y = bX + a$), which we presented earlier in the chapter.

Each b value in the multiple regression equation is a regression weight, which can vary from -1.00 to 1.00. A **regression weight** (sometimes called a b weight) is a multiplier term added to each predictor variable in a regression equation in order to maximize the predictive value of the variables. A separate regression weight is calculated for each predictor variable. When each research participant's scores on the predictor variables are multiplied by their respective regression weights and then summed, the result is the best possible prediction of the participant's score on the criterion variable.

Sometimes b weights are converted to beta (B) weights. **Beta weights** are the regression weights in a multiple regression equation in which all the variables in the equation are in standard score form. Some researchers prefer beta weights because they form an absolute scale. For example, a beta weight of + .40 is of greater magnitude than a beta weight of + .30 irrespective of the predictor variable with which it is associated. In contrast, the magnitude of a *b* weight is dependent upon the scale form of the predictor measure with which it is associated.

The magnitude of a predictor variable's beta weight should not be confused with its importance. A predictor variable can be theoretically significant and highly correlated with the criterion, yet have a low beta weight. The beta weight is arbitrary to an extent, because as we explained above, the significance of a predictor variable in a multiple regression equation depends on its correlation with other predictor variables that are entered first.

There are several variations of multiple regression analysis: stepup (also called "forward"), stepdown (also called "backward"), and stepwise. Each variation uses a different procedure for selecting a subset of predictor variables that yields the best prediction of a criterion variable. In **stepup multiple regression,** the predictor that leads to the largest increase in R is added to the current set until the addition no longer leads to a statistically significant increase. In **stepdown multiple regression,** all possible predictor variables are entered into the analysis first, and then, step by step, the variable that results in the smallest decrease in R is deleted until a statistically significant decrease occurs. In **stepwise multiple regression,** both the stepup and the stepdown procedures are combined: Each time a new predictor variable is added to the multiple regression analysis (the stepup method), the computer program doing the analysis checks whether a predictor variable that was included at an earlier step can now be deleted (the stepdown method) because it no longer contributes at a statistically significant level to the multiple regression equation. The title of Table 11.9 indicates that Jorde-Bloom and Ford used the stepwise procedure.

There is still another procedure for selecting a subset of predictor variables, out of all those that were measured, that yields the best prediction of a criterion variable. This procedure involves examining all possible subsets of predictor variables of a given size (e.g., all subsets of three variables in a ten-variable set) to select the subset that yields the best prediction, that is, the largest R^2. Under certain conditions, this procedure will yield a better prediction than the stepup, stepdown, or stepwise procedures.[14]

Types of Multiple Regression

Thus far, we have described the most common type of multiple-regression analysis, sometimes called *ordinary least-squares regression.* This type of regression analysis is used when the measure of the criterion variable is a continuous scale, the measures of the predictor variables are continuous or categorical scales, and the relationship between the predictor variables and the criterion variable is linear. Other types of multiple regression should be considered when different conditions apply. They are shown in Table 11.7.

The decision to use one type of multiple regression rather than another depends on the researcher's purpose for doing the analysis, the form of the data, and whether the assumptions required for its use are satisfied. For example, both discriminant analysis and logistic regression can be used when the measure of the categorical variable is dichotomous. However, discriminant analysis involves more restrictive assumptions. If you are considering multiple regression as a statistical tool for your study, you would be well advised to consult with an expert in this field.

Touchstone in Research

Grimm, L. G., & Yarnold, P. R. (Eds.). (2000). *Reading and understanding more multivariate statistics.* Washington, DC: American Psychological Association. (See also the 1995 edition of this book, titled *Reading and Understanding Multivariate Statistics.*)

14. Thompson, B. (1995). Stepwise regression and stepwise discriminant analysis need not apply here: A guidelines editorial. *Educational and Psychological Measurement, 55,* 525–534.

Cautions in Using Multiple Regression

Multiple regression analysis is sometimes misused by researchers. One common problem is to confuse prediction with explanation. The procedures are relatively straightforward if the purpose is to optimize prediction of a criterion variable. You should be careful, however, if you have a theory that attributes causal significance to the predictor variables. In this situation, you should not confuse the causal significance of a predictor variable with its regression weight or R^2 increment value in a multiple regression equation. If you wish to test a causal theory by using multivariate correlational data, consider path analysis or structural equation modeling (both discussed later in the chapter) rather than multiple regression.

We also caution you to retain a reasonable balance between sample size and the number of predictor variables used. In the extreme case, where sample size equals the number of predictors, R will equal 1.00 (perfect prediction), even if none of the predictors is correlated with the criterion. The multiple regression equation resulting from this analysis almost certainly will yield very poor predictions for a new sample of research participants. A rough rule of thumb is to increase sample size by at least 15 individuals for each variable that will be included in the multiple regression analysis. Using this rule, you would select a sample of at least 45 individuals for a multiple regression analysis involving three predictor variables.

Hierarchical Linear Modeling

We discussed issues relating to the unit of statistical analysis in Chapter 5. These issues arise from the fact that many phenomena of interest to educational researchers involve different levels of individual and organizational functioning. The most common case is that of students in classrooms. Students have characteristics that are independent of the classroom, for example, gender and family socioeconomic status. However, their learning behavior is likely to be affected by other students in the classroom and the teacher to whom they have been assigned. If this were not the case, we could take any sixth-grade student and put him or her in any sixth-grade classroom in the United States and expect the student's learning behavior to remain the same. This expectation is unreasonable if we examine our personal experience with schools and the large body of research evidence demonstrating considerable cross-classroom and cross-school variability.

Another way of describing this phenomenon that we see in the literature uses the concept of **nesting.** We can say that students in Mr. Johnson's classroom are "nested" in the classroom. They are nested, in other words, grouped closely together, such that they are affected by each other's behavior and by Mr. Johnson's behavior. Similarly, down the school hall we might come across Ms. Smith's classroom, and we would say that those students are nested in Ms. Smith's classroom.

Extending the metaphor further, we can say that Mr. Johnson's classroom, Ms. Smith's classroom, and all the other classrooms in the building, or set of interconnected buildings, are nested in the school. By this, we mean that all the classrooms (each with their teacher and students, or in the case of a high school, the classes and teachers who meet in a classroom each day) are grouped in such a way that they are influenced by each other and by school-level factors, such as the school principal's leadership and the school's socioemotional climate.

The nesting effect can be extended to higher levels. For example, we can say that schools are nested in school districts, school districts are nested within educational districts, and educational districts are nested within state departments of education. Sets of data that have this nesting structure sometimes are called *hierarchical data structures*, because the data are arranged in different levels, each at a higher level than the ones below it. For example, we can think of a student's score on an achievement test as a level 1 data

Touchstones in Research

Raudenbush, S. W., & Bryk, A. S. (2001). *Hierarchical linear models: Applications and data analysis methods, Vol. 1*. Thousand Oaks, CA: Sage.

Kreft, I. G., & deLeeuw, J. (1998). *Introducing multilevel modeling*. Thousand Oaks, CA: Sage.

point. This student is one of a group of students in a teacher's classroom, so the teacher is at the next level (level 2) of the hierarchy. The teacher is one of a group of teachers in a school, so the school is at level 3 in the hierarchy.

Hierarchical linear modeling is becoming increasingly accepted as the best statistical approach for understanding and quantitatively estimating these nesting effects. More precisely, **hierarchical linear modeling (HLM)** is a particular statistical software package for determining the effects of predictor variables at different levels of nesting on an outcome variable. (The general approach for analyzing hierarchical data structures is usually called **multilevel modeling,** but HLM is the more frequently used term because of the ubiquitous use of HLM software.) The mathematics of HLM is complex, but we can present a simple version of it here using the principles of multiple regression presented earlier in this chapter. The example that we use comes from research data analyzed by Jason Osborne.[15] The data came from 28,000 eighth-grade students and were collected as part of the National Education Longitudinal Survey.

The dependent variable in the analysis was a combined measure of the students' achievement in mathematics and reading. The predictor variables were (1) students' family socioeconomic status (SES), (2) their locus of control (whether they believe that they can affect their performance or that their performance is due to factors beyond their control), (3) the percentage of ethnic-minority students in the particular student's school, and (4) the percentage of students in the school who receive free lunch, which is an indicator of the poverty level of a school's student population.

Of the four predictor variables, the first two (SES and locus of control) are individual-student characteristics. The second two (percent minority and percent free lunch) are school-level characteristics. As a side note, it is worth considering the fact that SES and locus of control can also be viewed as school-level characteristics. For example, I can average the SES level of all students in the school and characterize the school as, let's say, high, middle, or low SES. I could also retain SES as a student-level characteristic and examine such questions as whether low-SES students in high-SES schools achieve differently from low-SES students in low-SES schools.

Two multiple regression equations are written to express the student-level and school-level predictors. The student-level equation (typically called the level 1 equation) is

$$Y_{ij} = \beta_{0j} + \beta_{1j}(\text{SES}) + \beta_{2j}(\text{locus}) + r_{ij}$$

A separate equation is written for the students in each school. It is similar in meaning to the multiple-regression equation shown in the previous section. In the equation just above, β_{0j} is the school mean achievement on the dependent variable (the mean achievement is calculated from the sample of students in the school); it is equivalent to the constant (C) in a multiple-regression equation. The symbol r_{ij} is the residual, that is, the variance that cannot be explained by the two predictor variables.

The level 2 equations, representing the school-level variables, are

$$\beta_{01} = Y_{00} + Y_{01}(\% \text{ minority}) + Y_{02}(\% \text{ free lunch}) + u_{ij}$$
$$\beta_{1j} = Y_{10} + Y_{11}(\% \text{ minority}) + Y_{12}(\% \text{ free lunch}) + u_{ij}$$

The first of these equations predicts each school's mean achievement using the two school-level factors. (The symbol γ is called *gamma*.) The second equation predicts school slopes representing the correlation between SES and achievement. To understand this equation, suppose that the correlation between students' SES levels and their achievement

15. Osborne, J. W. (2000). Advantages of hierarchical linear modeling. *Practical Assessment, Research & Evaluation, 7*(1). Retrieved December 2, 2005 from http://PAREonline.net/getvn.asp?v=7&n=1

varied from school to school. The second equation would tell us whether the variation in these correlations (i.e., slopes) was affected by the percentage of ethnic-minority students in the school or the percentage of students receiving a free lunch. Another equation of the same type would be written for the predictor variable, locus of control.

Osborne conducted an HLM on the data set. In addition, he did two multiple-regression analyses. In one, he disaggregated the data by using the student as the unit of analysis for all four variables. For example, each student's score on the percent minority variable was the percentage of ethnic-minority students in the student's school; thus, all students in a particular school would have received the same score on that variable. In the other multiple-regression analysis, Osborne aggregated the data to the school level. For example, he calculated the mean SES for all students in a particular school and this constituted the school's score on that variable. The n for this analysis was the number of schools in the sample.

The results of the analysis revealed that each approach yielded different results. Osborne concluded that HLM presented the most valid findings about the relationship between each predictor variable and the dependent variable. Also, he noted that HLM, but not the multiple-regression equations, made it possible to determine whether school-level variables affected individual-level variables' correlation with the dependent variable:

> [T]he analysis revealed significant interactions between SES and both level 2 predictors, indicating that the slope for SES gets weaker as %LUNCH and as %MINORITY increase. Also, there was an interaction between LOCUS and %MINORITY, indicating that as %MINORITY increases, the slope for LOCUS weakens.[16]

Considering just the LOCUS variable, the finding is that internal locus of control, which is a desirable student characteristic and predictive of better student achievement in the HLM analysis, tends to lose its effectiveness if students possessing this characteristic are in schools with a high percentage of ethnic-minority students. The significance of this finding is not obvious, but it seems worthy of further investigation. The important point here is that HLM, but not multiple regression, is capable of identifying these school-level effects on how students' characteristics facilitate or hamper learning. Moreover, HLM is the only statistically unbiased way to model the multiple levels of hierarchically structured data.

HLM is a highly sophisticated approach to data analysis. We have provided an introduction to its purpose and mathematical approach, but there are other features that you will need to learn to use it effectively in a research study or to interpret HLM findings reported in the research literature.

Path Analysis

Path analysis is a method for testing the validity of a theory about causal relationships between three or more variables that have been studied using a correlational research design. Path analysis differs from other multivariate correlational statistics, such as multiple regression, discriminant analysis, canonical correlation, and factor analysis, in that its purpose is to test theories about hypothesized causal links between variables. In contrast, the other multivariate methods that we discussed above are designed to maximize the correlation between various combinations of variables. Occasionally they are used to examine hypotheses about causal relationships between variables, but they are less powerful than path analysis for this purpose.

To illustrate path analysis, we will consider a study by Kathryn Wentzel to determine the causal effects of students' prosocial and antisocial classroom behavior on their academic

Touchstone in Research

Klein, L. (1995). Path analysis. In L. G. Grimm & P. R. Yarnold (Eds.), *Reading and understanding multivariate statistics* (pp. 65–97). Washington, DC: American Psychological Association.

16. Ibid., p. 5.

achievement.[17] Wentzel wished to determine whether such classroom behavior has a direct effect on academic achievement, or if its relationship with achievement is due to its effects on teachers' preferences for students and/or on students' own academically oriented behavior.

Steps in Path Analysis

Path analysis consists basically of three steps. The first step is to formulate hypotheses that causally link the variables of interest. Wentzel posed two alternate hypotheses as to how social behavior and academically oriented behavior might jointly contribute to academic performance:

> The first question addressed was whether prosocial and antisocial behavior were independent predictors of academic outcomes when academic behavior, teachers' preferences, and the background variables were taken into account. Next, I explored the possibility that social behavior was related to achievement indirectly by way of significant relations with academic behavior or teachers' preferences.[18]

After hypotheses are formulated, the next step in path analysis is to select or develop measures of the variables (sometimes called *theoretical constructs* in this context) that are specified by the hypotheses. This step is important, because path analysis will yield invalid results if the measures are not valid representations of the variables. In fact, you might want to identify more than one measure for each variable. Alternate measures of important educational variables often are available. (If alternate measures are administered, LISREL, a method described later in the chapter, can be used instead of path analysis.)

More than 400 sixth- and seventh-grade students and 11 teachers participated in Wentzel's study. Two measures of academic achievement were used as the criterion variables: GPA for the school year, and Basic Scale scores from the Stanford Test of Basic Skills (STBS). Predictor variables included the following student characteristics:

1. Prosocial behavior. Measured by asking students to nominate classmates on sharing/cooperating and helping other students when they have a problem. Each student received a composite score based on the average of the percentage of nominations that he or she received.
2. Antisocial behavior. Measured the same way as for prosocial behavior, except students nominated classmates on starting fights and breaking rules.
3. Academic behavior. An average composite score based on the teacher's rating on a five-point scale of the frequency with which each student (a) shows an interest in schoolwork, (b) works independently, and (c) shows concern with academic evaluation.
4. Preference status. Measured by having the teacher rate on a five-point scale the degree to which he would like to have each of the students in his class again next year.
5. IQ.
6. Family structure.
7. Gender.
8. Ethnicity.
9. Number of days absent from school.

17. Wentzel, K. R. (1993). Does being good make the grade? Social behavior and academic competence in middle school. *Journal of Educational Psychology, 85,* 357–364.
18. Ibid., p. 360.

The third step in path analysis is to compute statistics that show the strength of the relationship between each pair of variables that are causally linked in the hypotheses. Finally, you must interpret the statistics to determine whether they support or refute the theory.

Table 11.10 presents the correlation matrix of all the variables mentioned above. A **correlation matrix** is an arrangement of rows and columns that makes it easy to see how each measured variable in a set of such variables correlates with all the other variables in the set. Note in Table 11.10 that each variable is listed in a separate row of the matrix. Also note that each variable also is listed in a separate column. The correlation between any two variables is given at the point where the row and column corresponding to the variables cross. Only half of a row-by-column matrix is necessary to show the correlation between all possible pairs of variables. That is why the space above the diagonal is blank. Also, the correlation between a variable and itself is not usually shown in a correlation matrix

TABLE 11.10

Intercorrelations among Measures of Students' Academic Achievement, Social Behavior, and Background Characteristics and Teachers' Preferences for Students

Variable	GPA	STBS Scores	Prosocial Behavior	Antisocial Behavior	Academic Behavior	Teacher Preference	IQ	Family Structure	Gender	Ethnicity	Days Absent
GPA	—										
STBS score	.71**	—									
Prosocial behavior	.54**	.38**	—								
Antisocial behavior	−.55**	−.35**	−.31**	—							
Academic behavior	.66**	.39**	.43**	−.49**	—						
Teacher preference	.51**	.30**	.30**	−.54**	.67**	—					
IQ	.61**	.83**	.30**	−.27**	.31**	.23**	—				
Family structure	.32**	.24**	.20**	−.24**	.16*	.12	.18**	—			
Sex	.17**	.09	.23**	−.11	.23**	.15*	−.03	−.01	—		
Ethnicity	−.23**	−.31**	−.16**	.26**	−.16**	−.17**	−.31**	−.23**	.05	—	
Days absent	−.38**	−.21**	−.24**	.20**	−.24**	−.23**	−.15*	−.16*	.04	−.02	—

Note: GPA = grade-point average; STBS = Stanford Test of Basic Skills. Point-biserial correlations were computed for relationships involving family structure, sex, and ethnicity. For these analyses, intact families, girls, and minority status were represented by scores of 1, and single-parent families, boys, and majority status were represented by scores of 0.
*$p < .01$
**$p < .001$

Source: Adapted from Table 1 on p. 360 in: Wentzel, K. R. (1993). Does being good make the grade? Social behavior and academic competence in middle school. *Journal of Educational Psychology, 85,* 357–364. Copyright 1993 by the American Psychological Association. Reprinted with permission from Kathryn R. Wentzel.

because the correlation is always perfect (i.e., 1.00). That is the reason for the dashes that run diagonally left to right in the matrix.

We see in Table 11.10 that both measures of student achievement (GPA and STBS score) are significantly and positively related to prosocial behavior, academically oriented behavior, and teacher preferences for students, and are significantly and negatively related to antisocial behavior. Both measures of achievement also are related significantly to the background variables in the expected directions, except that STBS scores are not related significantly to students' gender.

The fact that social behavior, academically oriented behavior, teacher preferences, and various background behaviors are significantly correlated with student achievement does not mean that any of these variables actually have a causal influence on student achievement. Also, the fact that most of the predictor variables are significantly correlated with each other does not mean that they are determinants of each other. For example, teacher preference correlates significantly with both prosocial ($r = .30$) and antisocial ($r = -.54$) behavior, but this does not mean necessarily that students' prosocial or antisocial behavior causes teachers to like or dislike them.

Partial correlation, which was described earlier in the chapter, could be used to illuminate the causal influences that might be operating to generate these correlations. Path analysis, however, is a more powerful method for this purpose.

Path Analysis Models

You will recall that Wentzel theorized that significant correlations between social behavior and academic outcomes could be explained in part by significant relationships between social behavior and students' own academic behavior, teachers' preferences for students, or both. The hypothesized causal connections between these variables and students' GPA are shown in Figure 11.3. This type of figure is the standard way of representing the contribution of path analysis variables to each other and to a specific outcome.

Note that each variable in the theory is represented in the figure. Also note the use of arrows to connect variables. Each straight arrow indicates a hypothesized causal relationship in the direction of the arrow; for example, prosocial behavior influences academic behavior, prosocial behavior influences GPA, and academic behavior influences GPA. The hypothesis can predict no correlation, a positive correlation, or a negative correlation between the two variables linked by the arrow.

Causal hypotheses are not necessary for all pairs of variables. For example, the lack of an arrow between prosocial behavior and antisocial behavior indicates that Wentzel did not hypothesize a causal relationship between them. In some path analysis diagrams, the lack of a hypothesis is indicated by a curved arrow between the two variables.

Several other features of the path analysis in Figure 11.3 also should be noted. You will observe that all the straight arrows point in one direction. For example, prosocial behavior is hypothesized to influence academic behavior, but academic behavior is not hypothesized to influence prosocial behavior. When a path analysis is ordered in this way, it is said to be based on a recursive model. A **recursive model** is one that considers only unidirectional causal relationships. If variable *A* is hypothesized to influence variable *B*, you cannot also hypothesize that variable *B* influences variable *A*. A **nonrecursive model** would be used instead if the researcher wished to test hypotheses involving reciprocal causation between pairs of variables.

Two types of variables commonly are distinguished in path analysis. **Exogenous variables** are variables that lack hypothesized causes in the path analysis model. Prosocial behavior and antisocial behavior are exogenous variables in Wentzel's study, because no variables are hypothesized to influence them. **Endogenous variables** are variables that

FIGURE 11.3

Path Analysis Depicting Hypothesized Relationships between Prosocial and Social Behavior, Academic Behavior, Teachers' Preferences for Students, and GPA

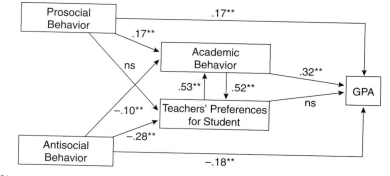

*p < .01
**p < .001

Source: Adapted from Figure 1 on p. 361 in: Wentzel, K. R. (1993). Does being good make the grade? Social behavior and academic competence in middle school. *Journal of Educational Psychology, 85,* 357–364. Copyright 1993 by the American Psychological Association. Adapted with permission from Kathryn R. Wentzel.

have at least one hypothesized cause in the path analysis model. For example, teacher's preferences for students is an endogenous variable, because it is hypothesized to be influenced by students' prosocial and antisocial behavior.

The Mathematics of Path Analysis

At this point in the path analysis, the exogenous and endogenous variables have been identified and measured, and the causal links specified by the researchers' theory have been identified by arrows. The next step is to perform a statistical analysis to determine the strength of association between each set of variables. The mathematical basis of the statistical procedures is complex. Basically the procedures are a form of multiple regression.

The statistical analysis yields a path coefficient for each pair of variables in the path analysis. A **path coefficient** is a standardized regression coefficient indicating the direct effect of one variable on another variable in the path analysis. Because path coefficients are standardized regression coefficients, they have the same meaning as the beta (β) coefficients calculated in multiple regression.

What does the numerical value of a path coefficient mean? The path coefficient can be viewed as a type of correlation coefficient. Like correlation coefficients, path coefficients can range in value from –1.00 to 1.00. The larger the value, the stronger the association between the two variables. The meaning of the path coefficient differs, however, depending on which two variables are being correlated. The path coefficient equals the product-moment coefficient when one variable (variable A) is viewed as dependent on a single cause (variable B) within the path analysis model. Another situation where β equals r is in the case of a variable that is dependent on more than one cause within the path analysis but in which the causes are viewed as independent of each other.

None of the path coefficients in Figure 11.3 satisfies these requirements. In Wentzel's study, academic behavior, teachers' preferences for students, GPA and STBS scores all are hypothesized to have several causes, which in turn are hypothesized to influence each other. Thus, the path coefficients connecting each pair of variables in Figure 11.3 differ from the product-moment correlation coefficients for these pairs of variables shown in Table 11.10. For example, in Table 11.10 we see that antisocial behavior correlates $-.55$ with GPA, $-.49$ with academic behavior, and $-.54$ with teacher preference. However, in Figure 11.3 the path coefficients linking antisocial behavior with these variables are $-.18$ with GPA, $-.10$ with academic behavior, and $-.28$ with teacher preference. These path coefficients are similar to, but not identical to, partial correlation coefficients in that they represent the strength of association between two variables with the effect of other pertinent variables partialed out.

You will note that the path coefficient linking antisocial behavior and GPA ($-.18$ in Figure 11.3) is considerably lower than the product-moment r for the same variables ($r = -.55$ in Table 11.10). This result means that antisocial behavior has some direct effect on GPA, but that part of its effect is indirect. The indirect effect means that part of the effect of antisocial behavior on GPA is due to its effect on academic behavior and teacher preference. The total indirect effect of a variable is equal to the r between it and the dependent variable minus the corresponding path coefficient. For the effect of antisocial behavior on GPA, the direct effect is $-.18$ and the indirect effect is $-.37$ ($-.55$ minus $-.18$). This analysis indicates that the indirect effect of antisocial behavior upon GPA ($-.37$) is substantially more potent than its direct effect ($-.18$).

Path Analysis and Theory Testing

The final step in path analysis is to determine whether the results support the theory. In the research study we have been considering, Wentzel concluded that her theory received some support, but that the results suggested the need for certain modifications in the theory. For example,

> In line with predictions, prosocial and antisocial behavior were . . . related to GPA, by way of their significant relations with academically oriented behavior. . . . Contrary to predictions, teachers' preferences for students did not explain significant relations between social behavior and academic outcomes.[19]

In the discussion section of her article, Wentzl attempts to explain these varied findings, and to pose suggestions for further research.

In summary, the major advantage of path analysis is that it enables the researcher to test causal theories using correlational data. Other multivariate techniques, such as multiple regression and canonical correlation, are not as well suited for this purpose. Path analysis, however, is a delicate technique that requires several conditions in order for it to yield meaningful results. The data need to satisfy certain assumptions, and the results can be misleading if the variables are not well measured, if important causal variables are left out of the theoretical model, or if the sample size is insufficient for the number of variables being considered.[20]

Factor Analysis

Factor analysis is one of the most frequently used techniques in multivariate research, because researchers often measure a large number of variables in a single research project. **Factor analysis** provides an empirical basis for reducing all these variables to a few factors

---

19. Ibid., p. 363.
20. Of these problems, underspecification of the causal model is probably the most serious. This problem is discussed in: Cook, T. D., & Campbell, D. T. (1979). *Quasi-experimentation: Design and analysis issues for field settings*. Chicago: Rand McNally.

by combining variables that are moderately or highly correlated with each other. Each set of variables that is combined forms a **factor,** which is a mathematical expression of the common element in the variables that are combined.

The use of factor analysis is illustrated by a study conducted by Carol Ott, Susan Cashin, and Michael Altekruse.[21] They state that the purpose of their study was "to develop an instrument that could be used to measure baseline campus cigarette use and behavior after exposure to social norms programs and changes in environmental policy."[22]

Their instrument, called the College Tobacco Survey, originally had 88 items. After a review by experts in tobacco prevention, the researchers reduced the instrument to 37 items, of which 15 had to do with beliefs about cigarette smoking and smoking policies. For each item, 11 of which are shown in Table 11.11, respondents indicated their level of agreement with the belief stated in the item. The six points on the rating scale for each item ranged from "strongly agree" to "strongly disagree."

Ott and colleagues did a factor analysis to determine whether the 15 items could be formed into groupings. In other words, they wished to know whether students who agreed with a particular item were also likely to agree or disagree with certain other items. If groupings were found, this would reveal underlying patterns in the disparate items and increase understanding of how students' belief systems about tobacco use are structured.

The factor analysis yielded three factors: (1) peer environment, (2) personal effects, and (3) campus policy endorsement. These factors and the items that can be grouped under them are shown in Table 11.11.

Factor Loadings and Factor Scores

The mathematics of factor analysis basically involves a search for clusters of variables that are all correlated with each other. The first cluster of variables that is identified is called the first factor; it represents the variables that are most intercorrelated. This factor is represented as a score, which is generated for each individual in the sample. Thus it is possible to compute a correlation coefficient between students' factor score and their score on a particular measure of a variable that was entered into the factor analysis. For example, we see in Table 11.11 that item 17 correlates almost perfectly ($r = .938$) with the first factor, peer environment. This correlation coefficient sometimes is called the **loading** of the measure on the factor.

Table 11.11 shows that the first factor includes three survey items (16, 17, 21) that correlate at least .40 with it. (We also can say that the first factor has three items that have loadings of at least .40 with it.) Note that item 21 has a negative correlation ($r = -.488$) with the first factor. This means that students who strongly agree with items 16 and 17 are likely to disagree with item 21.

Table 11.11 contains a note indicating that items with loadings lower than .40 are not shown. This means, for example, that items in the second factor (personal effects) might correlate with the first factor, but these correlations are relatively low (below .40).

Each factor resulting from a factor analysis can be treated as a variable, and each student can be given a score on it, called a **factor score.** The factor scores can be used in subsequent statistical analyses. For example, we could divide college smokers into three groups (heavy, moderate, and nonsmokers), administer the College Tobacco Survey to them, and determine whether they differ significantly from each other on the three factors defined by the 11 items shown in Table 11.11.

Touchstone in Research

Thompson, B. (2004). *Exploratory and confirmatory factor analysis: Understanding concepts and applications.* Washington, DC: American Psychological Association.

21. Ott, C. H., Cashin, S. E., & Altekruse, M. (2005). Development and validation of the College Tobacco Survey. *Journal of American College Health, 53*(5), 231–238.
22. Ibid., p. 231.

TABLE 11.11

Factor Loading for Belief Items in the College Tobacco Survey

| | Factor | | |
Item	1. Peer Environment	2. Personal Effects	3. Campus Policy Endorsement
Places smoke cigarettes with peers			
17. Some time in the next year I will smoke a cigarette.	.938	—	—
16. If one of my close friends were to offer me a cigarette, I would smoke it.	.861	—	—
21. I choose to socialize in a smoke-free environment.	−.488	—	—
Personal appearance			
25. Smoking cigarettes makes teeth yellow.	—	.727	—
23. Smoking cigarettes makes clothes smell bad.	—	.66	—
22. All things being equal, I would rather kiss a nonsmoker.	—	.53	—
24. People who smoke cigarettes have less energy than nonsmokers.	—	.493	—
20. If one of my close friends smoked, I would want to help them quit.	—	.45	—
27. The nicotine in cigarettes can be addictive.	—	.44	—
Smoking permissibility on campus			
19. Smoking should be allowed in the student union.	—	—	.795
18. Smoking should be allowed in the residence halls.	—	—	.729

Note: Items with loadings < .40 were removed.

Source: Adapted from Table 1 on p. 234 in: Ott, C. H., Cashin, S. E., & Altekruse, M. (2005). Development and validation of the College Tobacco Survey. *Journal of American College Health, 53*(5), 231–238. Reprinted with permission from the Helen Dwight Reid Educational Foundation. Published by Heldref Publications, 1319 Eighteenth St., NW, Washington, DC 20036-1802. Copyright © 2005.

Factor analysis is a valuable tool in educational research, but it needs to be used carefully. A frequent caution given to the novice researcher is *GIGO* (garbage in, garbage out), meaning that the factors generated by a factor analysis only are as useful and meaningful as the variables entered into the correlation matrix. Therefore, the researcher should carefully consider the number and types of variables that are to be entered into the factor analysis. If the variables have little or nothing in common conceptually, a factor analysis is inappropriate.

Types of Factor Analysis

Several variations of factor analysis are available. For example, a factor analysis can be done to yield an **orthogonal solution,** meaning that the resulting factors are uncorrelated with each other. An orthogonal solution is desirable if we seek a pure set of factors, with each measuring a construct that does not overlap with constructs measured by other factors. In certain situations, however, it is desirable to do a factor analysis with an **oblique solution,** meaning that factors can be derived that do correlate with each other. For example, a factor analysis of tests of intellectual ability might yield such factors as verbal ability, mathematical ability, logical reasoning ability, listening ability, and so on. These factors are likely to correlate with each other to some extent, because part of each factor measures an underlying construct of general intelligence.

Factor analysis can serve different purposes. An **exploratory factor analysis** is done to determine whether one or more constructs (the *factors* in factor analysis) underlie individuals' scores on a set of measures or on a set of items. For example, suppose you wrote 50 items to measure educators' attitudes toward inservice workshops. Your items might reflect different aspects of workshops (e.g., content, presenters, scheduling, practicality, instructional delivery). You are not sure, though, whether attitude toward workshops is a unitary construct (you either like workshops or don't) or whether it is multifaceted.

You can do an exploratory factor analysis to find out which is the case. For example, you might discover that the attitude items reflect two underlying constructs: attitude toward the workshop format and attitude toward the workshop content. If this is true, you are likely to find educators who like the format of a workshop, but who don't like the content; other educators will dislike the format, but like the content. It is also possible to find that the items reflect more than two underlying constructs or perhaps just one general construct.

Confirmatory factor analysis involves the use of factor analysis to test whether the constructs posited by a theory actually exist and can be distinguished from each other. In other words, confirmatory factor analysis starts with constructs and ends with the confirmation or disconfirmation of their existence, whereas factor analysis starts with data and ends with the discovery of constructs.

Confirmatory factor analysis is illustrated in a study of leadership empowerment conducted by Lee Konzak, Damian Stelley, and Michael Trusty.[23] Based on previous research and theory about leadership, they hypothesized that an empowering leadership style has seven distinct components. (The components are the constructs, or in the language of factor analysis, the hypothesized factors.) The researchers developed items to measure each of the components: (1) delegation of authority; (2) holding staff accountable for outcomes; (3) encouragement of self-directed decision-making; (4) encouragement of self-directed problem solving; (5) sharing information with staff; (6) helping staff secure appropriate training; and (7) coaching for innovative performance. The results of a confirmatory factor analysis supported the existence of all but the problem-solving component. The researchers revised their test items and theory accordingly, and proceeded to conduct another study that tested other hypotheses derived from the theory.

Structural Equation Modeling

A sophisticated method for multivariate correlational analysis has become available in recent years. The method is similar to path analysis, in that it can be used to test theories of causal relationships between variables. It is more powerful than path analysis, however, because it yields more valid and reliable measures of the variables to be analyzed. Because the measures are more valid and reliable, the method provides a more powerful test of causal relationships specified by a theory. This statistical method is called **structural equation modeling.** It also is called **LISREL,** which is the name of the computer program that

---

23. Konzak, L. J., Stelley, D. J., & Trusty, M. L. (2000). Defining and measuring empowering leadership behaviors: Development of an upward feedback instrument. *Educational and Psychological Measurement, 60,* 301–313.

Touchstone in Research

Thompson, B. (2000). Ten commandments of structural equation modeling. In L. G. Grimm & P. R. Yarnold (Eds.), *Reading and understanding more multivariate statistics* (pp. 261–283). Washington, DC: American Psychological Association.

was developed to run it. LISREL is an acronym for *Linear Structural Relationships*. The method has still another name, **latent variable causal modeling,** because it is used to test causal relationships specified by theoretical models, and because, as we shall see below, it involves the measurement of latent variables.

The essential elements of structural equation modeling are illustrated in a study by Suzanne King and Lee Wolfle.[24] The purpose of their study was to identify factors that contribute to the reputation of graduate school departments, as determined by ratings of quality in a national survey. The sample consisted of a large number of university departments of English, French, philosophy, geography, political science, and sociology.

King and Wolfle hypothesized that ratings of a department's quality would be influenced by three factors: size, quality of graduate students, and research productivity of faculty. This causal model is depicted in Figure 11.4. The model is similar to models used in path analysis (for example, see Figure 11.3). Each straight arrow leading to the right indicates a hypothesized causal relationship in the direction of the arrow. For example, department size is hypothesized to influence a department's reputation (labeled "Department Rating" in Figure 11.4). Also, as in path analysis, the curved, double-headed arrows indicate the absence of a hypothesis about how two variables are causally related to each other. For example, the researchers' causal model contained no hypothesis about how department size and graduate student quality would affect each other.

The causal model shown in Figure 11.4 differs from a path analysis in its use of the boxes at the left of the figure. The variables shown in ellipses (size, graduate student quality, and research productivity) are viewed as **latent variables,** which are the theoretical constructs of interest in the model. The rectangles on the left are **manifest variables,** which are the variables that were actually measured by the researchers. Because educational measurement is imprecise, each latent variable ideally is measured by several instruments. The scores obtained from each instrument represent a manifest variable that is conceptually related to one of the latent variables.

We see in Figure 11.4 that the latent variable of department size is represented by three manifest variables: number of faculty members in the department in 1980 (FACNUM); number of graduates of the program between 1976 and 1980 (GRADNUM); and number of full- and part-time doctoral students in 1980 (STUDNUM). Only one manifest variable was used to measure the latent variable of graduate student quality: percentage of graduates who at the time of graduation had definite employment commitments with Ph.D.-granting institutions (EMPPHD). Finally, three manifest variables were used to measure the latent variable of research productivity: number of published articles attributed to faculty members divided by number of faculty in the department (PUBSPER), proportion of faculty with one or more published articles between 1978 and 1980 (MORElPUB), and percentage of faculty members holding research grants from specified agencies between fiscal years 1978 and 1980 (GRANTS).

A similar principle is used in the development of test items. Because a single item seldom is a perfect measure of a construct, researchers combine a variety of items, each of which measures a related aspect of the construct, to form a test. In tests the items usually are summed to yield a total score. In structural equation modeling, however, the measures of the manifest variables are factor analyzed to identify their common variance, that is, the factor that they share in common. Also, the factor analysis tests whether each manifest variable correlates at a sufficiently high level with the factor that will be used to represent the latent variable.

A subsequent step is to compute path coefficients for each arrow leading out from each latent variable. For example, in King and Wolfle's report, path coefficients are reported for the

24. King, S., & Wolfle, L. M. (1987). A latent-variable causal model of faculty reputational ratings. *Research in Higher Education, 27,* 99–105.

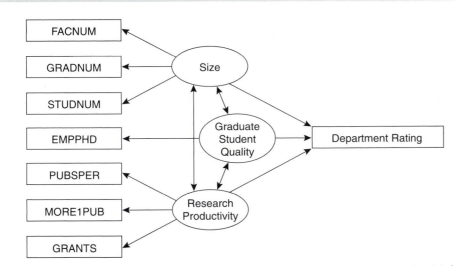

FIGURE 11.4

Latent Variable Causal Model of Factors Affecting Graduate Department Ratings

Source: Adapted from Figure 1 on p. 101 in: King, S., & Wolfle, L. M. (1987). A latent-variable causal model of faculty reputational ratings. *Research in Higher Education, 27*, 99–105. Copyright © 1987 by Springer Science and Business Media. Adapted with permission from Springer Science and Business Media.

ratings of geography departments as follows: .59 for size, .07 for graduate student quality, and .60 for research productivity. Because a larger path coefficient indicates a larger influence, we can conclude that a geography department's size and faculty research productivity have more influence on its reputation than does the quality of its graduate students.

In summary, structural equation modeling is a multivariate correlational method that is used to measure latent variables with maximal reliability and validity, and to test causal theories. It is a powerful method, but difficult to use. Moreover, it requires the satisfaction of several assumptions about the data that are entered into the analysis.

Differential Analysis

Subgroup Analysis in Causal Relationship Studies

In Chapter 10, we stressed the importance of forming homogeneous groups when doing causal-comparative research. The same principle applies to causal relationship studies. The formation of subgroups that are more homogeneous than the total sample might reveal relationships between variables that are obscured when correlations are computed for the total sample.

The first step in subgroup analysis is to ask yourself whether the variables you are correlating with each other might be influenced by a particular factor such as gender, socioeconomic status, or cultural identity. Then select individuals in your sample who have this characteristic (or possess it to a high degree) and recompute the correlation for the two subgroups that result—that is, those having and those not having the characteristic in question (or possessing it to a high degree and possessing it to a low degree). If the resulting correlations are approximately the same, you can conclude that the characteristic in question has

TABLE 11.12		
Correlations between Scholastic Aptitude Test Scores and Grade-Point Average for Different Age Groups		
Age Group	**N**	**r**
18–21	238	.30**
22–25	314	.21*
26–29	72	.41***
30+	121	−.08

$*p < .05$
$**p < .01$
$***p < .001$

Source: Adapted from Table 2 on p. 1043 in: Zeidner, M. (1987). Age bias in the predictive validity of scholastic aptitude tests: Some Israeli data. *Educational and Psychological Measurement, 47*, 1037–1047. Adapted with permission from Sage Publications, Inc.

not contributed to your initial correlation. However, if the two correlations are significantly different, you will have gained new insight into the relationship you are studying.

Moderator Variables in Prediction Studies

Sometimes a test is more effective in predicting the behavior of certain subgroups than the behavior of other subgroups. In this situation we can use differential prediction, which is a form of differential analysis.

The use of differential prediction to improve a test's predictive validity is illustrated in a study by Moshe Zeidner.[25] The purpose of the study was to determine the validity of a scholastic aptitude test for predicting the first-year GPA of students enrolled in an Israeli university. Zeidner expected the aptitude test to be less valid for older students than for younger students. In this instance, students' age is designated a **moderator variable** because it moderates the predictive validity of the test. In other words, Zeidner hypothesized that age would act as a moderator variable for the relationship between aptitude test performance and GPA. He offered the following rationale for this hypothesis:

> Older student candidates may differ from their younger (i.e., late adolescent or early young-adult) counterparts not only in age per se but also in a number of potentially important variables, associated with age or cohort, that might affect test performance. These include: quality of primary and secondary school experience, cultural and social experiences accumulated through the course of day-to-day living, occupational training, and so on. In addition, older examinees, who have long since graduated from high school, may differ from younger examinees on a host of other variables that may also bear on the level of test performance, such as the recency of their test taking experience, test wiseness, test attitudes, motivations and anxieties.[26]

The results of the correlational analysis are shown in Table 11.12. The correlations between aptitude test performance and GPA are positive and statistically significant for the three groups with ages between 18 and 29. The correlation coefficient for the 30+ age group, however, is negative and not statistically significant. Thus the results support Zeidner's hypothesis that aptitude tests have lower predictive validity for older applicants to

25. Zeidner, M. (1987). Age bias in the predictive validity of scholastic aptitude tests: Some Israeli data. *Educational and Psychological Measurement, 47*, 1037–1047.
26. Ibid., p. 1038.

college. Also, the coefficients for the four age groups range from −.08 to .41. Had Zeidner calculated the coefficient for the total sample (i.e., all four age groups combined), the resulting *r* probably would have been in the middle of this range. By using age as a moderator variable, he was able to find subgroups for whom the *r* was higher, notably, students between ages 18 and 21 and those between ages 26 and 29.

Interpretation of Correlation Coefficients

Statistical Significance of Correlation Coefficients

The statistical significance of a correlation coefficient usually indicates whether the obtained coefficient is different from zero at a given level of confidence. (A researcher also could test whether the obtained coefficient is significantly different from some other value of *r*, for example, the value of *r* for a comparison sample.) If the coefficient is not significantly different from zero, the null hypothesis of no difference from zero cannot be rejected. If the coefficient is statistically significant, we can conclude that the relationship between the variables is nonzero. You should keep in mind, however, that the correlation between the variables for the *population* may be greater or less than the correlation coefficient obtained for the sample. If you wish, you can calculate confidence limits to estimate the range of coefficients within which the population coefficient is likely to fall. (Confidence limits are discussed in Chapter 5.)

Most statistics texts include a table from which the statistical significance of a product-moment correlation (*r*) can be determined. The level of statistical significance of a correlation coefficient is determined in large part by the size of the sample upon which the correlation is based. For example, if the sample includes 22 individuals, a product-moment coefficient of .54 is needed to be significant at the .01 level. If 100 individuals are available, however, a correlation of .25 is significant at the .01 level, and with 1,000 individuals a correlation of only .08 is significant at the .01 level.

Statistical significance also depends on whether a one-tailed or two-tailed test is performed. In a two-tailed test, the researcher determines whether the obtained coefficient (ignoring its sign) is either at the positive tail or the negative tail of the normal curve of coefficients that could occur by chance in samples drawn from a population in which *r* = .00. In a one-tailed test, only coefficients on one side of the normal curve distribution are considered, that is, the researcher predicts in advance that the correlation, if significant, will be positive, or that it will be negative.

Causal relationship studies are aimed primarily at gaining a better understanding of the complex skills or behavior patterns being studied, and therefore low correlation coefficients are as meaningful as high coefficients. Prediction studies, however, are designed to forecast certain kinds of future behavior, and therefore require higher correlation coefficients than those usually found in causal relationship studies. In prediction studies, statistical significance is of little consequence because correlation coefficients usually must exceed the specified alpha level (typically, .05) to be of practical value. In other words, practical significance is more important than statistical significance.

Interpreting the Magnitude of Correlation Coefficients

Even correlation coefficients of a low magnitude can have practical significance. This principle is illustrated by a hypothetical situation described by N. L. Gage.[27] Suppose that one

27. Gage, N. L. (1985). *Hard gains in the soft sciences: The case of pedagogy.* Bloomington, IN: Phi Delta Kappa Center on Evaluation, Development, and Research.

TABLE 11.13

Results of a Hypothetical Study of the Relationship between Use of a Specific Teaching Technique and Student Performance

Outcome	Percentage Receiving New Treatment	Percentage Receiving Old Treatment
Good	60	40
Bad	40	60
Total	100	100

Note: Correlation (ϕ) = .20
Percent of Variance Explained = 4 percent

Source: Adapted from Table 1 on p. 12 in: Gage, N. L. (1985). *Hard gains in the soft sciences: The case of pedagogy*. Bloomington, IN: Phi Delta Kappa Center on Evaluation, Development, and Research. Adapted with permission from Phi Delta Kappa International.

variable being investigated is a particular teaching technique. Each teacher in the sample is observed to determine whether he or she uses the technique. The outcome variable is student performance in the teacher's course. Each student is classified as having passed or failed the course. Suppose we obtain the results shown in Table 11.13.

The correlation between the two variables of teaching technique and student performance is only .20. (Note that .20 represents a phi coefficient because both variables are dichotomous.) Although the findings have practical significance, this is a low correlation coefficient. Yet, analysis of the effects of using the technique indicates that it leads to a 50 percent increase in the number of students who pass the course. Specifically, 60 percent of students whose teachers use the technique pass the course, whereas only 40 percent of students whose teachers do not use the technique pass the course. This is a 20 percentage-point difference, which clearly has practical significance.

You should realize that in this example the researcher's purpose was to examine relationships between variables, not to predict one variable from another. We cannot predict the particular students who passed the course and the particular students who failed it. We can examine the possible effect of the teaching technique on the entire group, however. The obtained phi coefficient of .20 tells us that if a teacher uses the technique, a higher percentage of students will pass the course, but not which students. If we wish to predict the particular students who will pass the course, the magnitude of the obtained coefficients must be much higher—generally at least .70. Correlation coefficients of this magnitude are virtually impossible to obtain from a single predictor variable, but they can be achieved by the use of multiple predictor variables that are combined through the technique of multiple regression.

Medical researchers have found that correlations even lower than .20 can have practical significance. For example, Robert Rosenthal cited a medical research study that found a positive relationship between the following two variables: (1) taking aspirin on a regular basis versus taking a placebo, and (2) experiencing versus not experiencing a heart attack.[28] The correlation coefficient for these two variables was only .03. However, this coefficient was considered of such practical importance that the experiment was ended prematurely. The researchers believed that it was unethical to withhold aspirin from the control group

28. Rosenthal, R. (1990). How are we doing in soft psychology? *American Psychologist, 46*, 775–777. See also responses to Rosenthal's article in the October 1991 issue of *American Psychologist*.

any longer. Rosenthal observed that many of the correlation coefficients obtained in the "softer, wilder" sciences such as educational pyschology actually are much larger than those obtained in supposedly more advanced fields such as medical research.

Another point to consider in interpreting the magnitude of correlation coefficients is that many factors influence the behavior patterns and personal characteristics of primary interest to educators. Therefore, the influence of any one factor is not likely to be large. Correlations in the range of .20 to .40 might be all that one should expect to find for many of the relationships between variables studied by educational researchers.

RECOMMENDATIONS FOR

Doing Correlational Research

1. Consider using a correlational research design when you wish to test predictions or explore causal relationships and an experimental design is not feasible.
2. Select a correlational statistic that is appropriate for the scale form of your variables.
3. Explore the possibility that the relationship between the variables in your study is nonlinear.
4. If you have calculated many correlational coefficients in analyzing data from a study, consider the possibility that some of the coefficients will be statistically significant by chance.
5. When doing a prediction study, consider including a cross-validation check to determine the extent of shrinkage in the initial set of correlation coefficients.
6. Consider the use of part or partial correlation to control for variables that provide alternative explanations of observed relationships between the variables of primary interest.
7. If you are exploring causal patterns involving a group of variables, consider path analysis or structural equation modeling as a method for designing the study and analyzing the data.
8. Consider the use of differential analysis to refine your search for predictor variables or causal patterns.
9. Explore not only the statistical significance of obtained correlation coefficients, but also their practical significance.

SELF-CHECK TEST

Circle the correct answer to each of the following questions.
The answers are provided at the back of the book.

1. A perfect negative correlation is represented by a correlation coefficient of
   a. 0.00.
   b. 1.00.
   c. −1.00.
   d. −.50.

2. A major advantage of the correlational method is that it
   a. can be used to study causal relationships.
   b. allows simultaneous study of relationships between a large number of variables.
   c. provides a measure of both the degree and the direction of a causal relationship between two variables.
   d. all of the above.

3. In contrast to relationship studies, prediction studies are more concerned with
   a. testing hypotheses about cause-and-effect relationships.
   b. maximizing the correction for attenuation.
   c. maximizing the correlation of each variable with a criterion.
   d. identifying appropriate criterion measures.

4. If a researcher correlates many variables with each other in a prediction or relationship study, there is an increased risk of
   a. shrinkage.
   b. nonlinearity.
   c. unfavorable selection ratios.
   d. restriction of range in some variables.

5. The correlational statistic most appropriate when both variables are expressed as continuous scores is the
   a. phi coefficient.
   b. rank-difference correlation.
   c. biserial correlation.
   d. product-moment correlation.

6. The calculation of *eta* is useful for
   a. deciding whether to use partial correlation.
   b. deciding whether to do a factor analysis.
   c. correcting for restriction in range.
   d. studying nonlinear relationships between variables.

7. The lowering of a correlation coefficient between two sets of scores due to lack of reliability of the measures is called
   a. attenuation.
   b. restriction in range.
   c. regression.
   d. shrinkage.

8. The process used to rule out the influence of one or more variables upon the criterion behavior pattern is called
   a. multiple regression.
   b. partial correlation.
   c. correction for attenuation.
   d. analysis of variance.

9. The process of determining the maximum correlation between a single criterion variable and a combination of predictor variables is called
   a. canonical correlation.
   b. multiple regression.
   c. structural equation modeling.
   d. path analysis.

10. The purpose of canonical correlation is to determine the magnitude of the relationship between a set of predictor variables and
   a. a set of criterion variables.
   b. a set of exogenous variables.
   c. a set of moderator variables.
   d. the category membership of each individual in a sample.

11. A systematic representation of the correlations between all variables measured in a study is called a
   a. scattergram.
   b. correlation ratio.
   c. path analysis.
   d. correlation matrix.

12. The most powerful of the following correlational techniques for testing causal hypotheses is
   a. factor analysis.
   b. path analysis.
   c. discriminant analysis.
   d. moderator analysis.

13. In factor analysis the term *factor* refers to
   a. product-moment correlations.
   b. test scores.
   c. mathematically derived constructs.
   d. regression equations.

14. Structural equation modeling combines the use of
   a. path analysis and factor analysis.
   b. path analysis and discriminant analysis.
   c. canonical correlation and factor analysis.
   d. differential analysis and factor analysis.

15. If a set of tests predicts a criterion variable better for males than for females, gender is said to be a(n)
   a. predictor variable.
   b. latent variable.
   c. moderator variable.
   d. endogenous variable.

CHAPTER 12

Experimental Research: Designs, Part 1

OVERVIEW

The experiment is the most powerful quantitative research method for establishing cause-and-effect relationships between two or more variables. To yield valid findings, however, experiments must be conducted in a rigorous manner. In this chapter, we describe validity criteria for experiments and other factors that must be considered in designing them. We also explain the most common experimental designs. Additional experimental designs are presented in the next chapter.

OBJECTIVES

After studying this chapter, you should be able to

1. Critically evaluate possible threats to the internal validity of an experiment.
2. Critically evaluate possible threats to the external validity of an experiment.
3. Describe procedures for increasing the generalizability of findings from experiments.
4. Explain how experimenter bias and treatment fidelity can affect the outcome of an experiment.
5. Describe obstacles to maintaining equivalent treatment groups in experiments and how these obstacles can be avoided or overcome.
6. Describe the commonly used experimental designs, including the procedures used in random assignment, formation of experimental and control groups, and pretesting and posttesting procedures.
7. State specific threats to the internal and external validity of common experimental designs.
8. Describe the statistical techniques that typically are used to analyze data yielded by experiments.

Introduction

Of the various quantitative research methods, experiments provide the most rigorous test of causal hypotheses. Although correlational and causal-comparative designs can suggest causal relationships between variables, experimentation is needed to establish whether the observed relationship is one of cause and effect.

Touchstone in Research

Maxwell, S. E., & Delaney, H. D. (2004). *Designing experiments and analyzing data: A model comparison perspective* (2nd ed.). Mahwah, NJ: Erlbaum.

An example of the correlational-experimental loop in research was described by Barak Rosenshine and Norma Furst.[1] They reviewed a set of studies about teaching methods that were conducted over several years at Canterbury University, New Zealand. In a correlational study, the researchers found a significant correlation ($r = .54$) between amount of student learning and the extent to which the teacher followed a student's answer by redirecting the question to another student for comment. In other words, teachers who made extensive use of redirection generally had higher-achieving classes than teachers who made little use of this technique.

This research finding suggests that training teachers in the technique of redirection will improve students' classroom performance. Rosenshine and Furst report, however, that the Canterbury researchers also conducted experiments in which they manipulated teachers' use of redirection. No differences in student learning were found between redirection-present and redirection-absent conditions. Thus, it would have been misleading to advise teachers to make greater use of the redirection technique simply on the basis of correlational evidence. Experiments might corroborate the correlational findings but, then again, they might not, as proved to be the case in the Canterbury research.

Many experiments done by educational researchers have the purpose of testing the effects of various practices (teaching techniques, organization of curriculum, content, instructional programs, etc.) on important outcomes such as student academic achievement and school climate. Therefore, experimental findings about the effectiveness of educational practices sometimes have an impact on the opinions and decisions of policy makers, educators, and other groups. All educational research should be carefully designed and executed, but this is especially true of experiments because of the influence they have on policy and practice.

The number of large-scale experiments in education has been increasing in recent years. For example, in 2005 the U.S. Department of Education issued new regulations that give preference to researchers whose grant applications include requests to do experiments that involve random assignment of students, educators, or other participants to treatment and control groups.[2] Experiments with random assignment (also called *randomized trials*), which we discuss in this chapter, are highly recommended because they provide strong assurance that observed effects are caused by the experimental treatment and not by extraneous variables.

Geoffrey Borman, Robert Slavin, Alan Cheung, Anne Chamberlain, Nancy Madden, and Bette Chambers identified a number of experiments that have had a major impact on contemporary educational practice:

> [T]he randomized longitudinal Tennessee Class Size Study (Finn & Achilles, 1999) led directly to massive class-size reduction initiatives in several states, notably California, and to the Clinton administration's national class-size initiative. The randomized, longitudinal evaluation of the Perry Preschool (Schweinhart, Barnes, & Weikart, 1993) led to substantial expansion of the federal Head Start program and to publicly funded preschool programs in many states and localities.[3]

---

1. Rosenshine B., & Furst, N. (1973). The use of direct observation to study teaching. In R. M. W. Travers (Ed.), *Second handbook of research on teaching* (pp. 122–183). Chicago: Rand McNally.
2. Glenn, D. (2005, March 11). New federal policy favors randomized trials in education research. *Chronicle of Higher Education*, p. A16.
3. Borman, G. D., Slavin, R. E., Cheung, A., Chamberlain, A. M., Madden, N. A., & Chambers, B. (2005). Success for all: First-year results from the national randomized field trial. *Educational Evaluation and Policy Analysis, 27*(1), 1–22. Quote appears on p. 4.

These researchers also cite evidence that the number of experiments in social-science disciplines other than education is increasing rapidly and is having an impact on various social policies developed by legislators and government officials.

Terminology in Experimental Design

Most experiments in education employ some form of the one-variable design. **One-variable experiments** involve the manipulation of a single treatment variable followed by observing the effects of this manipulation on one or more dependent variables.[4] The variable to be manipulated is referred to in this chapter as the **experimental treatment.** It also is called the *independent variable, experimental variable, treatment variable,* or *intervention.* The variable that is measured to determine the effects of the experimental treatment usually is referred to as the *posttest, dependent variable,* or *criterion variable.* In this chapter we use the term **posttest** to describe the measure of the variable that is the intended outcome of the experimental treatment. If a variable is measured before administering the experimental treatment, this measure is called a **pretest.** Many experiments in education involve one group that receives the experimental treatment and one comparison group that does not receive the experimental treatment or receives an alternative treatment. We use the term **control group** to refer to this comparison group.

To understand how these terms are used, consider an experiment to determine the effect of a new reading program on students' reading achievement. The *experimental treatment* would be the introduction of the new reading program into the daily schedule of learning activities of a group of students. The *control group* would receive its regular reading program. The *pretest* would be the measure of students' reading achievement before the new reading program had been introduced into the curriculum. The *posttest* would be the measure of students' reading achievement after they had experienced the new program for a period of time.

Validity Problems in Experiments

The key problem in experimentation is establishing suitable controls so that any change in the posttest can be attributed only to the experimental treatment that was manipulated by the researcher. As we shall see in this chapter, many extraneous variables need to be controlled in order to allow an unequivocal interpretation of experimental data. Various experimental designs can be used depending upon the extraneous variables that you wish to *control,* that is, rule out as possible causes of changes on the posttest.

Although the experiment is a powerful research design, it is not perfect. Even the findings of a well-designed experiment are potentially refutable—a point made by Karl Popper, a philosopher of science whose views we discussed in Chapter 1:

> But what, then, are the sources of our knowledge? The answer, I think, is this: there are all kinds of sources of our knowledge but *none has authority.* . . . I do not, of course, deny that an experiment may also add to our knowledge, and in a most important manner. But it is not a source in any ultimate sense.[5]

As you read this and the next chapter, you will find that many factors can threaten the validity of an experiment. By controlling these factors, a researcher strengthens the power of

---

4. Experiments in which more than one treatment variable is manipulated are called *factorial experiments.* They are discussed in Chapter 13.
5. Popper, K. (1968). *Conjectures and refutations.* New York: Harper Torchbooks. Quote appears on p. 24.

an experiment to demonstrate a cause-and-effect relationship. As Popper observed, however, no single experiment provides an irrefutable demonstration of cause-and-effect, and therefore replications of experiments—especially ones that test alternative causal hypotheses—are desirable.

In the next sections we discuss the main factors that can weaken the power of an experiment. First we discuss potential sources of internal invalidity, that is, the extent to which variables other than the treatment variable provide plausible explanations of the experimental results. Then we discuss factors that affect external validity, that is, the extent to which the experimental findings can be generalized to other settings. Figure 12.1 summarizes the factors affecting both types of validity in order to guide your reading of these sections.

FIGURE 12.1

Factors Affecting the Internal and External Validity of Experiments

Extraneous Variables That Affect Internal Validity
1. History
2. Maturation
3. Testing
4. Instrumentation
5. Statistical regression
6. Differential selection
7. Experimental mortality
8. Selection-maturation interaction
9. Experimental treatment diffusion
10. Compensatory rivalry by the control group
11. Compensatory equalization of treatments
12. Resentful demoralization of the control group

Factors That Affect External Validity

Population Validity
1. The extent to which one can generalize from the experimental sample to a defined population
2. The extent to which personological variables interact with treatment effects

Ecological Validity
1. Explicit description of the experimental treatment
2. Multiple-treatment interference
3. Hawthorne effect
4. Novelty and disruption effects
5. Experimenter effect
6. Pretest sensitization
7. Posttest sensitization
8. Interaction of history and treatment effects
9. Measurement of the dependent variable
10. Interaction of time of measurement and treatment effects

Source: Based on Campbell, D. T., & Stanley, J. C. (1963). *Experimental and quasi-experimental designs for research.* Chicago: Rand McNally; Cook, T. D., & Campbell, D. T. (1979). *Quasi-experimentation: Design and analysis issues for field settings.* Chicago: Rand McNally; and Bracht, G. H., & Glass, G. V (1968). The external validity of experiments. *American Educational Research Journal, 5,* 437–474.

Internal Validity of Experiments

The most difficult task in doing an experiment is to hold constant or eliminate all extraneous variables that might affect the outcome measured by the posttest. If this task is accomplished, the researcher can attribute the observed outcomes (the effect) with a high level of confidence to the treatment variable (the hypothesized cause).

The experimental method was first developed in the physical sciences, where it has been highly useful in the production of knowledge. The success of experiments in this field is due to the fact that physical matter is quite adaptable to study and control in a laboratory. It is doubtful whether the same rigor of experimental control ever can be achieved in the behavioral and social sciences (e.g., psychology, sociology, economics), in which human beings are the focus of experimentation.

Donald Campbell and Julian Stanley wrote a classic paper distinguishing between experimental designs in terms of their internal validity.[6] The **internal validity** of an experiment is the extent to which extraneous variables have been controlled by the researcher, so that any observed effect can be attributed solely to the treatment variable. An **extraneous variable** is any variable other than the treatment variable that can affect the experimental outcome. If extraneous variables are not controlled, we cannot know whether observed changes in the experimental group are due to the experimental treatment or to some extraneous variable.

To demonstrate the importance of controlling for extraneous variables, we will consider an experiment conducted by William Kyle, Jr., Ronald Bonnstetter, and Thomas Gadsden, Jr.[7] As you will see, their study actually is a quasi-experiment (see Chapter 13), because it did not involve random assignment of research participants to the experimental and control groups. However, the study provides a good example of the issues related to internal validity that typically arise in carrying out a field-based experiment in education.

The researchers examined the effects of introducing a new science curriculum into a school district. The curriculum, the well-known Science Curriculum Improvement Study (SCIS), emphasizes an inquiry-oriented, process approach to science. The district's standard curriculum emphasized reading a text, answering questions from it, and completing worksheets—all focused on developing low-level cognitive skills.

During the first year of implementation, SCIS was introduced into six of the 35 elementary schools in the district. At the end of the school year, the researchers administered measures of attitude toward science to teachers and students in these six schools. They also administered the same measures to a sample of teachers who had used the standard science curriculum that year but who would be teaching SCIS the following year and also to their students.

Table 12.1 presents several results of the experiment. There are no significant differences in the percentage of SCIS and non-SCIS teachers who expressed a positive attitude toward science on the various measures. By contrast, a significantly higher percentage of SCIS students expressed a positive attitude toward science on each of the measures. This is a potentially important finding. Can the researchers conclude that the more positive attitudes of SCIS students were caused by students' exposure to SCIS? Similarly, can they

Touchstone in Research

Torgerson, D. J., & Torgerson, C. J. (2003). Avoiding bias in randomized controlled trials in educational research. *British Journal of Educational Studies, 51*(1), 36–45.

---

6. Campbell, D. T., & Stanley, J. C. (1963). *Experimental and quasi-experimental designs for research.* Chicago: Rand McNally.
7. Kyle, W. C., Jr., Bonnstetter, R. J., & Gadsden, T., Jr. (1988). An implementation study: An analysis of elementary students' and teachers' attitudes toward science in process approach vs. traditional science classes. *Journal of Research in Science Teaching, 25,* 103–120.

TABLE 12.1

Percentage of SCIS and Non-SCIS Participants Having Positive Perceptions of Their Science Class

Item	Students			Teachers		
	SCIS[a]	Non-SCIS	χ^2	SCIS	Non-SCIS	χ^2
Science is (was):						
fun	85	53	60.13**	30	35	.41
interesting	88	64	36.24**	45	51	.43
exciting	70	44	33.06**	25	22	1.44
boring	13	35	32.65**	41	38	1.05
Science makes me feel:						
successful	59	45	12.23*	36	32	.38
uncomfortable	11	24	14.30**	31	26	1.08
curious	76	56	21.65**	49	49	.18

[a]SCIS = Science Curriculum Improvement Study

*$p < .01$

**$p < .001$

Source: Adapted from Table 2 on p. 110 in: Kyle, W. C., Jr., Bonnstetter, R. J., & Gadsden, T., Jr. (1988). An implementation study: An analysis of elementary students' and teachers' attitudes toward science in process-approach vs. traditional science classes. *Journal of Research in Science Teaching, 25,* 103–120. Copyright © 1988 National Association for Research in Science Teaching. Reprinted with permission of Wiley-Liss, Inc., a subsidiary of John Wiley & Sons, Inc.

conclude that SCIS did not cause any change in teachers' attitudes toward science? The answers to these questions depend on how well the experiment controlled for extraneous variables.

Campbell and Stanley identified eight types of extraneous variables that can affect the results of experiments. Subsequently, Thomas Cook and Campbell expanded this list to include four more extraneous variables.[8] The resulting 12 extraneous variables are listed in Figure 12.1 and described below in relation to the science curriculum experiment that we are using as an example.

1. *History.* Experimental treatments extend over a period of time, providing opportunity for other events to occur besides the experimental treatment. The students in the experiment we are considering participated in SCIS or the standard science curriculum for an entire school year. Also, the two groups of students were in different schools. Perhaps the SCIS schools had an overall better learning environment than did the non-SCIS schools. As a result of exposure to this environment over the course of a school year, students in SCIS could have developed a more positive attitude toward all their school subjects, not just science. If this were true, the school's learning environment would have produced the attitude effect, not the SCIS curriculum. To avoid this problem in interpreting effects, the researchers need to ensure that the SCIS and non-SCIS schools are similar in all respects except their science curriculum.

8. Cook, T. D., & Campbell, D. T. (1979). *Quasi-experimentation: Design and analysis issues for field settings.* Chicago: Rand McNally.

2. *Maturation.* While the experimental treatment is in progress, physical or psychological changes in the research participants are likely to occur. For example, students might become stronger, more cognitively able, more self-confident, or more independent. In our example, suppose that students in both the SCIS and non-SCIS schools made good gains in the ability to think scientifically. We might be inclined to attribute this gain to exposure to a science curriculum. It also is possible that the research participants—elementary school students—made natural gains in cognitive development that allowed them to think more scientifically. (Piagetian theory, for example, predicts that this type of cognitive maturation occurs.) Thus, it is not clear whether the observed gains are due to the science curriculum or to maturation. To tease out the effects of maturation, it would be necessary to have a control group of children who received no exposure to a science curriculum (or out-of-school science instruction) over the course of a school year. If the SCIS and standard curriculum groups made larger gains on the outcome measure than this control group, it would be reasonable to conclude that the science curriculum—not maturation—led to the growth in the ability to think scientifically.

3. *Testing.* In most educational experiments a pretest is administered, followed by the experimental treatment, and then a posttest is administered. If the two tests are similar, students might show an improvement simply as an effect of their experience with the pretest. In other words, they have become "test-wise." In the science curriculum experiment, this extraneous variable is not a problem because no pretest was administered.

4. *Instrumentation.* A learning gain might be observed from pretest to posttest because the nature of the measuring instrument has changed. In experiments involving observational measurements, instrumentation effects are particularly likely. Observers who assess teachers or students before and after an experimental treatment might be disposed to give more favorable ratings the second time, simply because they expect—consciously or subconsciously—a change to have occurred. Because no pretest was administered in the science curriculum experiment, the extraneous variable of instrumentation is not a threat to its internal validity.

5. *Statistical regression.* Whenever a pretest-posttest procedure is used to assess change as an effect of the experimental treatment, there is the possibility that statistical regression accounts for observed gains in learning. **Statistical regression** is the tendency for research participants whose scores fall at either extreme on a measure to score nearer the mean when the variable is measured a second time.[9] For example, suppose we select a group of students who fall below the 15th percentile on a test of reading achievement. If the same students are tested again on the same or a similar test (i.e., one that is correlated with the first test), their mean score on the second test probably will be higher than on the first test with or without an intervening experimental treatment because of statistical regression. Conversely, if we select another group of students whose initial scores fall above the 85th percentile, these students are likely to earn a lower mean score when retested on a similar measure simply because of statistical regression.

To understand statistical regression, consider the fact that a student who earns a very low score on a test probably does so because of low ability and chance factors (e.g., unlucky guesses, situational stress). When the test is repeated later, the ability factor remains the same, but it is unlikely that these chance factors will work against him as much. Therefore, his score is likely to improve. The same reasoning applies to understanding why students who score very high initially are unlikely to score as well on the second administration.

---

9. A discussion of statistical regression can be found in Campbell and Stanley, *Experimental and quasi-experimental designs*, pp. 180–182. Also see the discussion of gain scores in Chapter 13 of this text.

No premeasures of attitude were administered in the science curriculum study, so it is not possible to determine whether teachers and students in the SCIS and non-SCIS schools had unusually positive or negative attitudes at the start of the experiment. Thus, we have no way of knowing whether differences in their expressed attitudes at the end of the school year reflect a differential statistical regression effect rather than, or in addition to, the effect of the SCIS curriculum.

6. *Differential selection.* In experimental designs in which a control group is used, the effect of the treatment sometimes is confounded by differential selection of research participants for the experimental and control groups. Confounding might have been a major problem in the science curriculum experiment. The researchers do not explicitly state that schools were randomly assigned to the SCIS and non-SCIS treatments. (Random assignment, as we discuss later in the chapter, is the best safeguard against differential selection.)

It is likely that the schools that implemented SCIS in the first year were chosen to do so because in fact they were different from other schools in the district. For example, suppose the SCIS schools were selected to implement this curriculum because their students were more academically able than were students at other schools. If this were true, the observed differences in science attitudes of the SCIS and non-SCIS groups at the end of the school year could be attributed to the fact that different types of students were selected for the two groups, rather than to the effects of the SCIS curriculum.

To continue this line of reasoning, the lack of a difference in science attitudes between SCIS and non-SCIS teachers at the end of the school year might indicate that similar teachers taught at the two groups of schools. In this case, differential selection of teachers would not affect the experimental results. However, because no pretest was administered in this experiment, we do not have information about possible differences between teachers or students in the experimental group and those in the control group that might have existed prior to the experiment. Thus we do not know whether differential selection, rather than SCIS, caused the observed differences between the two student groups on the posttests.

7. *Experimental mortality.* Some research participants might be lost from the experimental or control group because they drop out of the study, miss pretesting or posttesting, or are absent during some sessions. The phenomenon of losing research participants during the course of an experiment is known as **experimental mortality,** or *attrition.* Attrition might result from such factors as illness, participants' resentment about being in what they perceive as the less desirable treatment condition, or their perception that the experiment is too demanding or threatening. Whatever the reason, attrition threatens an experiment's internal validity if it causes differential loss of participants across treatments. For example, suppose low-performing students feel less positively about SCIS and drop out of school in greater numbers during the year as a result. In this case, fewer of these students would complete the posttest measures of science attitudes, thereby artificially inflating the percentage of students with positive attitudes following the experiment.

You can minimize the problem of attrition by randomly assigning students to treatment groups and by making the treatments equally desirable. (A procedure for equating desirability of treatments is described later in the chapter.) Also, you should keep records for each treatment of participants' absenteeism or withdrawal from the experiment.[10] This

---

10. Procedures for analyzing research data to determine the presence of systematic bias in loss of participants from experimental and control groups are described in: Jurs, S. G., & Glass, G. V (1971). The effect of experimental mortality on the internal and external validity of the randomized comparative experiment. *Journal of Experimental Education, 40,* 62–66.

information is not reported for the science curriculum experiment. The researchers stated that 92.3 percent of the total sample of teachers completed the questionnaires that provided the data for Table 12.1. They did not indicate, however, whether the respondents were distributed equally across the experimental and control treatments.

8. *Selection-maturation interaction.* This extraneous variable is similar to differential selection (see number 6 above), except that maturation is the specific confounding variable. Suppose, for example, that the science curriculum study had been done in two different school districts. Further suppose that because of a differential admissions policy, the average age of the experimental group is six months greater than that of the control group. In this case, any group differences in science attitudes can be attributed to the effects of students' ages rather than to the effects of the science curriculum that each group studied.

9. *Experimental treatment diffusion.* If the treatment condition is perceived as highly desirable relative to the control condition, members of the control group may seek access to the treatment condition.[11] Experimental treatment diffusion is especially likely if the experimental and control participants are in close proximity to each other during the experiment. For example, suppose that some teachers in a school building (the treatment group) are assigned to use an innovative, attractive curriculum, whereas other teachers in the same building (the control group) are asked to continue using the standard curriculum. As the experiment progresses, some of the control-group teachers might discuss the new curriculum with treatment-group teachers, even if instructed not to do so. They might even borrow some of the materials and activities to use in their classrooms. Thus, over time the treatment "diffuses" to the control group.

If experimental treatment diffusion occurs, the effect of the experimental treatment on the posttest will be confounded. To avoid this problem, you should try to arrange conditions so that contact between experimental and control groups is minimized. After the experiment is completed, interview some or all of the sample to determine whether experimental treatment diffusion has occurred in any form.

When we examine Table 12.1, we find that many teachers in both groups had negative attitudes and perceptions about their science classes at the end of the school year. For example, about 40 percent of the teachers in both groups stated that science was boring. What we do not know is the percentage of teachers who thought science was boring at the start of the school year. The percentage may have been even higher. If so, the introduction of SCIS reduced the percentage of teachers who found science instruction boring. If the percentage was reduced in the control group as well, this could indicate a treatment diffusion effect.

10. *Compensatory rivalry by the control group.* This extraneous variable is sometimes called the *John Henry effect.* **Compensatory rivalry** involves a situation in which control group participants perform beyond their usual level because they perceive that they are in competition with the experimental group. For example, Gary Saretsky found a marked increase in mathematics achievement in control-group classrooms when they were compared with classrooms in which performance contracting had been introduced.[12] If this phenomenon occurs, the observed difference—or lack of difference—between the experimental treatment and control groups on the posttest can be attributed to the control group's unusual motivation rather than to treatment effects.

---

11. An example of experimental treatment diffusion can be found in: Craven, R. G., Marsh, H. W., & Debus, R. L. (2001). Diffusion effects: Control group contamination threats to the validity of teacher-administered interventions. *Journal of Educational Psychology, 93*(3), 639–645.
12. Saretsky, G. (1972). The OEO P. C. experiment and the John Henry effect. *Phi Delta Kappan, 53,* 579–581.

11. *Compensatory equalization of treatments.* This extraneous variable can come into play if the experimental group receives a treatment that provides goods or services perceived as desirable and administrators attempt to compensate the control group by giving it similar goods and services. If any such actions affect the control group's posttest scores, they would obscure the effects of the experimental treatment. The researchers, instead of comparing the treatment with a no-treatment control condition, are comparing one treatment with another treatment.

Cook and Campbell observed that this problem almost certainly operated in experiments testing the effects of Follow Through and similar compensatory education programs.[13] The control schools usually were given Title I funds for their disadvantaged students in similar amounts to those given to Follow Through schools. Therefore, although the control schools did not have a Follow Through program, they had resources that could be used to purchase similar services for their disadvantaged students.

12. *Resentful demoralization of the control group.* A control group can become discouraged if it perceives that the experimental group is receiving a desirable treatment that is being withheld from it. As a result, its performance on the posttest would be lower than normal. In turn, the experimental treatment would appear to be better than it actually is, because the difference between the posttest scores of the experimental and control groups was artificially increased by the demoralization of the control group.

You will recall that in the science curriculum experiment we have been considering, the control group consisted of teachers who would be implementing SCIS the year following completion of the experiment. Therefore, it seems unlikely that any of the three extraneous variables just described—compensatory rivalry, compensatory equalization, and resentful demoralization—would have affected their teaching performance or attitudes during the course of the experiment.

In summary, we have seen how 12 extraneous variables can threaten the internal validity of an experiment. The science curriculum experiment did not control all these variables, primarily because teachers and students were not randomly assigned to the experimental and control groups and because pretests were not administered. Therefore, the researchers probably drew too strong a conclusion when they stated that, "the nature of the science taught does affect student attitudes toward science."[14] The results are consistent with this conclusion, but they also are consistent with other interpretations involving the operation of extraneous variables.

In summary, the goal in designing an experiment is to create a set of conditions such that any observed changes can be attributed with a high degree of confidence to the experimental treatment rather than to extraneous variables. Random assignment and pretesting and posttesting are central to creating such conditions. Therefore, as you read this chapter and the next chapter, we recommend that you pay particular attention to the experimental designs that incorporate these features.

External Validity of Experiments

External validity is the extent to which the findings of an experiment can be applied to individuals and settings beyond those that were studied. The findings of an educational experiment may be externally valid for one setting, less externally valid for a different setting, and not externally valid at all for some other setting. For example, a researcher might test the effects of illustrations in children's books by taking first-grade children out of their

13. Cook & Campbell, *Quasi-experimentation.*
14. Kyle et al., An implementation study, p. 117.

classrooms in small groups, with each group receiving the same story but different types of illustrations. Perhaps the illustrations, although of acceptable quality, were not created by professional artists who specialize in children's books. Also, the students may have been tested immediately after reading the story, with no intervening discussion of the story. Despite these apparent flaws, the experiment is well controlled in that the same researcher administered all the treatments, used the same interpersonal style with each group, and maintained the same time limits for each of them.

This experiment has good internal validity, but the generalizability of its findings to real classroom conditions—that is, its external validity—is weak.

Glenn Bracht and Gene Glass identified twelve factors that affect an experiment's external validity.[15] The factors are listed in Figure 12.1 and discussed in the following sections.

Population Validity

Population validity concerns the extent to which the results of an experiment can be generalized from the sample that was studied to a specified, larger group. Bracht and Glass distinguished two types of population validity, which are described below.

1. *The extent to which one can generalize from the experimental sample to a defined population.* Suppose you are a teacher seeking to improve your students' reading comprehension. You want to know whether a technology-enriched reading curriculum will lead to greater reading achievement gains than a conventional textbook series. You perform an experiment on a sample of 125 high school students randomly selected from your school. The experiment demonstrates that the technology-enriched curriculum leads to greater achievement gains.

Although you might wish to generalize the findings to the population of "all" students, strictly speaking you can generalize only to the population from which the sample was drawn—namely, high school students in that particular school. Bracht and Glass define the population from which the sample was drawn as the **experimentally accessible population.** The accessible population usually is "local," normally within driving distance of the experimenter's office or laboratory. Assuming that the sample described above was randomly selected, it is valid to generalize the research findings from the 125 participating students to the experimentally accessible population (i.e., all high school students in the school).

Often the researcher or the reader of a research report wishes to generalize from the experimentally accessible population to a still larger group (e.g., all high school students in the United States). The larger group of individuals to whom the research findings are generalized is called the **target population.**[16] Generalizing research findings from the experimentally accessible population to a target population is risky. We must compare the two populations to determine whether they are similar in critical respects. For example, if the experiment was done in a school district composed almost entirely of middle-class suburban families, generalization of the research findings to all U.S. high school students is likely to be invalid.

2. *The extent to which personological variables interact with treatment effects.* In the experiment described above, you do not know whether instructional format interacts with student characteristics. That is, although the technology-enriched reading curriculum was found to be superior to a conventional textbook for high school students, different results

Touchstone in Research

Simmerman, S., & Swanson, H. L. (2001). Treatment outcomes for students with learning disabilities: How important are internal and external validity? *Journal of Learning Disabilities, 34*(3), 221–236.

---

15. Bracht, G. H., & Glass, G. V (1968). The external validity of experiments. *American Educational Research Journal, 5,* 437–474.
16. The distinction between accessible and target populations is also discussed in Chapter 6.

might be obtained with students at different grade levels in high school. If so, the differential effects would limit the generalizability of the experiment's findings.

Student's ability, gender, extraversion-introversion, and anxiety level are examples of other personological variables that might affect the generalizability of findings from experiments. The systematic study of these interactions—called aptitude-treatment interaction (ATI) research—is discussed in the next chapter.

Ecological Validity

Ecological validity concerns the extent to which the results of an experiment can be generalized from the set of environmental conditions created by the researcher to different environmental conditions. If the treatment effects can be obtained only under a limited set of conditions or only by the original researcher, the experimental findings are said to have low ecological validity. The ten factors identified by Bracht and Glass that affect the ecological validity of an experiment are as follows.

1. *Explicit description of the experimental treatment.* The researcher needs to describe the experimental treatment in sufficient detail so that other researchers can reproduce it. Suppose a researcher finds that the discussion method is more effective than the lecture method in promoting positive student attitudes toward doing community service during the summer months. However, the researcher's description of the discussion method is so vague and incomplete that other researchers wishing to replicate the experiment cannot determine whether they are using the method in the same way. In this case, the experimental findings have virtually no generalizability to other settings.

2. *Multiple-treatment interference.* Occasionally a researcher will use an experimental design in which each participant is exposed to more than one experimental treatment. Suppose each participant in an experiment receives three different treatments: A, B, and C. Treatment A is found to produce significantly greater learning gains than treatments B and C. Because of the experimental design that was used, the findings cannot be generalized with confidence to a situation in which treatment A is administered alone. The effectiveness of treatment A may depend on the co-administration of the other two treatments. Whenever it appears that multiple-treatment interference will affect the generalizability of your findings, you should choose an experimental design in which only one treatment is assigned to each research participant.

3. *Hawthorne effect.* The **Hawthorne effect** refers to any situation in which the experimental conditions are such that the mere fact that individuals are aware of participating in an experiment, are aware of the hypothesis, or are receiving special attention improves their performance. In educational research, experimenters often give participating teachers and students special attention. This factor, not the experimental treatment itself, may cause a change in their behavior. Should the Hawthorne effect occur, the external validity of the experiment is jeopardized because the findings might not generalize to a situation in which researchers or others who were involved in the research are not present.

Attempts to manipulate the Hawthorne effect experimentally often have failed to produce evidence of the effect.[17] Even so, it is advisable to minimize special attention given to research participants.

4. *Novelty and disruption effects.* A novel experimental treatment might be effective simply because it is different from the instruction that participants normally receive. If this

17. Adair, J. G. (1984). The Hawthorne effect: A reconsideration of the methodological artifact. *Journal of Applied Psychology, 69,* 334–345.

is true, the results of the experiment have low generalizability, because the treatment's effectiveness is likely to erode as the novelty wears off. The reverse problem occurs with experimental treatments that disrupt normal routine. This type of experimental treatment might be ineffective initially, but with continued use, participants might assimilate the treatment into their routine and find it effective. Thus, the findings of the initial tryout are not generalizable to a condition of continued use.

5. *Experimenter effect.* An experimental treatment might be effective or ineffective because of the particular experimenter, teacher, or other individual who administers the treatment. In this case treatment effects cannot be generalized to conditions in which a different person (often a classroom teacher) administers the treatment. The various ways in which experimenters can influence the administration of a treatment are discussed below in the section on experimenter bias.

6. *Pretest sensitization.* In some experiments, the pretest may react with the experimental treatment and thus affect the research results. If the experiment is repeated without the pretest, different research results are obtained. Let us consider a hypothetical experiment in which this reactive effect might occur. Suppose you are interested in how point of view in a film affects students' attitudes. You might develop a film in which the narrator takes a strongly slanted, positive view of controversial decisions made by a contemporary politician. To assess the effect of the film, you administer a pretest and posttest of students' attitudes toward the politician.

Suppose there is a significant positive shift in students' attitudes, which you attribute to the experimental treatment, that is, the film. Can you generalize this finding and assert that the film will have the same effect when used in other situations? The generalization is not warranted unless you can demonstrate that the pretest has no effect on the experimental treatment. The possibility exists that the pretest activates students' awareness of their attitudes toward this politician and sensitizes them to the narrator's attitude. The sensitization induced by the pretest may interact with the film to produce the attitude shift. In contrast, if they are shown the film alone, students might be more sensitized to learning the facts presented in the film than to adopting the narrator's attitude. Thus, they might show little or no attitude shift because they did not have a set to attend to the narrator's point of view.

Bracht and Glass's review of the literature on pretest sensitization indicates that it is most likely to occur when the pretest is a self-report measure of personality or attitude. A later review of the research on pretest sensitization effects was conducted by Victor Willson and Richard Putnam.[18] They located 32 studies of this phenomenon and did a meta-analysis to determine the average effect size across studies. Willson and Putnam found a substantial effect of pretests on posttest performance. In other words, an experimental group that receives a pretest is likely to perform at a higher level on the posttest than a corresponding experimental group that does not receive a pretest. This effect occurs even when the posttest is different from the pretest. In fact, the meta-analysis revealed that the pretest effect was stronger when the pretest and posttest were different. Furthermore, administration of a pretest usually was found to have a positive effect irrespective of the type of outcome—cognitive, attitudinal, or personality—that was measured.[19]

18. Willson, V. L., & Putnam, R. R. (1982). A meta-analysis of pretest sensitization effects in experimental design. *American Educational Research Journal, 19,* 249–258.
19. In their report on self-report pretest biases operating in experiments involving scarce treatment opportunities, Leona Aiken and Stephen West describe approaches to minimizing the effects of pretest self-report bias on the internal validity of experiments. See: Aiken, L. S., & West, S. G. (1990). Invalidity of true experiments: Self-report pretest biases. *Evaluation Review, 14,* 374–390.

7. *Posttest sensitization.* This source of ecological invalidity is similar to pretest sensitization. The results of an experiment may be dependent upon the administration of a posttest. This can happen if the posttest is a learning experience in its own right. For example, the posttest might cause certain ideas presented during the treatment to "fall into place" for some of the students. When the experiment is repeated without a posttest, the effectiveness of the treatment is diminished. Although posttest sensitization is plausible, it has not been studied to the same extent as its counterpart, pretest sensitization.

8. *Interaction of history and treatment effects.* One can argue that researchers should not generalize beyond the time period in which an experiment was done. An experiment evaluating an innovative educational method might be done at a time when teachers are particularly disenchanted with a corresponding, conventional method. They might be exceptionally motivated to demonstrate the superiority of the new method. At a later time, we might repeat the experiment and find no difference, because teachers no longer see the method as innovative.

9. *Measurement of the dependent variable.* The generalizability of an experiment might be limited by the particular pretest and posttest designed to measure achievement gains or another outcome variable. Suppose the superiority of an online course over a regular course was demonstrated on multiple-choice tests that students took shortly after completing the treatment condition. If the online course is effective only because it facilitates students' ability to take multiple-choice tests, the results of the experiment would not generalize to other measures of the dependent variable. For example, no difference between instructional formats might be found if the pretests and posttests required essays.

10. *Interaction of time of measurement and treatment effects.* Administration of a posttest at two or more points in time may result in different findings about treatment effects. The usual practice is to administer the posttest immediately after the research participants have completed the experimental treatment. Conclusions about treatment effectiveness are based on the results of this posttest administration. If possible, however, it is advisable to administer the same or a parallel posttest several weeks or months later in order to measure retention of learning. Bracht and Glass cite several examples in the research literature in which treatment effects changed from posttest to delayed posttest. The effects may be enhanced, remain the same, or diminish over time.[20]

In designing an experiment, you should identify the real-life educational settings to which you wish to generalize the results of the experiment. Then review the design of the experiment in terms of the two population validity factors and ten ecological validity factors described above. If you see a potential problem, attempt to correct it. If a problem cannot be corrected, it should be noted in the research report as a limit on the generalizability of the research findings.

Representative Design

Some educational researchers, most notably Richard Snow,[21] have criticized conventional experimental design for its artificiality and lack of generalizability. Building on the earlier work of Egon Brunswick, Snow used the label "systematic design" to characterize the typical form of experimentation. In systematic design a few treatment variables and pretest-posttest measures are administered. All other variables are either controlled or ignored. Most of the experiments reported in journals of educational research are based on systematic design principles.

20. Bracht & Glass, External validity, p. 466.
21. Snow, R. E. (1974). Representative and quasi-representative designs for research on teaching. *Review of Educational Research, 44,* 265–291.

The problem with systematic design is that it often produces artificial learning situations and unnatural behavior in the learner. Snow advocates instead the use of *representative design* to combat these problems and also to increase the generalizability of findings from experiments. **Representative design** is a process for planning an experiment so that it accurately reflects both the real-life environments in which learning occurs and the natural characteristics of learners. In this respect, representative design in quantitative research parallels some of the priorities of qualitative researchers, namely, the study of human behavior in natural field settings and an emphasis on the emic perspective (i.e., the primacy of the participants' viewpoint rather than the researcher's viewpoint).

The desirability of representative design is based on a number of assumptions about the learning environment and the human learner. One assumption is that the characteristics of the natural environment are complex and interrelated. We cannot simply choose to vary one environmental characteristic and hold others constant; as one characteristic changes, so do others. We need to study the learning environment as an ecology, in the same way that biologists study the ecology of the natural environment.

Another assumption of representative design is that human beings are active processors of information; they do not react passively to experimental treatments. Therefore, the active nature of learning by humans needs to be considered in designing experiments. A related assumption is that human learners, if allowed, will adjust and adapt to their environment. Systematic experiments are artificial in that they constrain the range of behavior that might be exhibited if the learner were allowed to act naturally.

Finally, representative design assumes that, because the human organism is complex, any experimental intervention is likely to affect the learner in complex ways. An instructional method might be designed only to increase students' knowledge of a specific subject, for example, but the effect may generalize to students' attitudes and also to their knowledge of other subjects. Furthermore, the instructional intervention might be designed primarily to affect short-term performance, but the effects may "radiate out" to affect long-term performance as well.

Snow believes that educational researchers should design experiments to reflect this view of the environment and the learner. That is, experiments should become more *representative* of the natural environment and of research participants as active learners. Snow notes that true representative designs are very difficult to achieve in education, but he suggests compromises that will make experiments more representative. The following are some of his recommendations.

1. When appropriate, conduct the research in the actual educational setting or other environment to which you wish to generalize your findings.

2. Incorporate several environmental variations into the design of the experiment. For example, if the purpose is to evaluate a new instructional method, have not just one teacher but rather a sample of teachers use it. Also, vary the educational setting. For example, an instructional method could be tested in a sample of inner-city schools, suburban schools, and rural schools.

3. Observe what students actually are doing during the experiment. These observations may prove helpful in interpreting the results of the experiment. For example, you might find that the research participants were not attentive to a particular treatment or appeared to be distracted by other events. If the research data later indicated that the treatment was not effective, these observations would be helpful in interpreting the results and in planning future research.

4. A related technique to the one preceding is to observe the social context in which the experiment is being conducted. Certain events that occur in schools or other educational

settings may affect experimental treatments. If such events are observed and recorded, the research findings will be more interpretable.

5. Prepare participants for the experiment. Snow claims that typical practice is for researchers to give research participants brief instructions and perhaps a few minutes of training prior to the start of an experiment. More extensive preparation may be necessary to ensure a smooth transition from participants' current mental set to the one required by the experimental task.

6. Incorporate a control treatment that allows participants to use their customary approaches to learning. Suppose an experiment is designed in which students are formed into dyads and trained to ask questions of each other about curriculum materials. An appropriate control treatment might be to form some students into dyads and allow them to use any procedures they wish to review the same materials. The control group thus forms a naturalistic baseline against which the behavior and learning of the experimental group can be evaluated.

Issues in Designing Experiments

Experimenter Bias

Touchstone in Research

Crawford, J., & Impara, J. C. (2001). Critical issues, current trends, and possible futures in quantitative methods. In V. Richardson (Ed.), *Handbook of research on teaching* (4th ed., pp. 133–173). Washington, DC: American Educational Research Association.

Robert Rosenthal's studies of experimenter bias have made a significant contribution to experimental methodology.[22] **Experimenter bias** refers to researchers' expectations about the outcomes of their experiments that are unintentionally transmitted to participants so that their subsequent behavior is affected. The phenomenon typically occurs outside the awareness of the experimenter. The term *experimenter bias* is not used to refer to situations in which an experimenter, with full awareness of his or her actions and intentions, manipulates participants' behavior or falsifies data in order to yield an expected finding.

Rosenthal and his associates carried out many experiments on experimenter bias, and we shall describe one of the classic ones here.[23] A group of undergraduates was instructed in procedures for running Albino rats through a simple T-maze and for training the rats to solve a discrimination learning problem. The student experimenters were told that, as a result of generations of inbreeding, some rats they would train were "maze-bright" while others were "maze-dull." They were then given instructions regarding expected findings:

> Those of you who are assigned the Maze-Bright rats should find your animals on the average showing some evidence of learning during the first day of running. Thereafter performance should rapidly increase. Those of you who are assigned the Maze-Dull rats should find on the average very little evidence of learning in your rats.[24]

In fact, a homogeneous group of Albino rats (not varying on the dimension of maze brightness or dullness) was randomly assigned to the student experimenters for training. Nevertheless, Rosenthal and Fode found that rats trained by experimenters who thought their rats were maze-bright earned significantly higher learning scores than rats trained by experimenters with the opposite expectancy. The differential learning gains were the result of experimenter bias rather than genetic differences between groups of rats.

Experimenter bias appears to be a major threat to the internal validity of experiments. Thus, you should take steps to avoid the operation of this effect in designing and carrying

22. Rosenthal, R. (1976). *Experimenter effects in behavioral research* (Enlarged ed.). New York: Irvington.
23. Rosenthal, R., & Fode, K. L. (1963). The effect of experimenter bias on the performance of the Albino rat. *Behavioral Science, 8,* 183–189.
24. Ibid., p. 184.

out an experiment. One effective technique is to train naive experimenters to work with the participants. Whenever possible, do not work directly with the research participants yourself. Also, avoid suggesting to the experimenters, directly or indirectly, that one experimental treatment is better than another.

Researchers conceivably can overdo efforts to eliminate experimenter bias. If they go too far in attempts to appear neutral or even skeptical about the experimental treatment, participants might become "turned off" to it. Also, in the interest of appearing neutral, researchers might put the procedure to a test that is too difficult. For example, the experimental treatment might be tried in schools that are experiencing administrative problems. If the initial test is conducted under difficult conditions such as these, it might be labeled ineffective and consequently abandoned.

Generally speaking, it is better initially to identify a set of conditions under which the procedure has a good chance of working. Subsequent experiments can determine the limiting conditions of its effectiveness. Joshua Klayman and Young-Won Ha labeled the approach of testing cases that offer the best chance of supporting one's hypotheses a **positive test strategy**.[25] They demonstrated that under certain conditions, including those in which the purpose of the research is to test hypotheses about new educational programs and methods, researchers should seek instances that support their hypotheses rather than instances that refute them.

Treatment Fidelity

Theodore Barber extended the work of Rosenthal by identifying additional sources of investigator and experimenter bias.[26] The **investigator** is defined as the person who designs the experiment and interprets the data, and the **experimenter** is defined as the person who administers the experimental treatments and collects the data. In many experiments the investigator and experimenter are the same person, but this is not always so. One type of bias identified by Barber occurs when the experimenter fails to follow the exact procedures specified by the investigator for administering the treatments. Barber labeled this type of bias *experimenter failure to follow the protocol effect*, and cited several studies in which it was demonstrated empirically to occur. Other researchers refer to this type of bias as lack of treatment fidelity. **Treatment fidelity** is the extent to which the treatment conditions, as implemented, conform to the researcher's specifications for the treatment.

According to Barber, researchers should try to maximize treatment fidelity and then assess the extent to which they succeeded. This is done too seldom in educational experiments. James Shaver reviewed studies published in the *American Educational Research Journal* for the years 1969 to 1981.[27] He identified 22 reports of teaching methods research in which checking treatment fidelity would have been appropriate. Less than half the reports ($N = 9$) actually made such a check.

Treatment fidelity can be maximized by careful training of the individuals—often teachers—who are to implement the treatment. For example, in the science curriculum experiment that we discussed above, the training of teachers who were to implement SCIS occurred in inservice workshops. From the descriptions provided by the researchers, these workshops appear to have lasted only a few days. This amount of training may not

Touchstone in Research

Gresham, F. M., MacMillan, D. L., Beebe-Frankenberger, M. E., & Bocian, K. M. (2000). Treatment integrity in learning disabilities intervention research: Do we really know how treatments are implemented? *Learning Disabilities Research and Practice, 15,* 198–205.

25. Klayman, J., & Ha, Y-W. (1987). Confirmation, disconfirmation, and information in hypothesis testing. *Psychological Review, 94,* 211–228.
26. Barber, T. (1973). Pitfalls in research: Nine investigator and experimenter effects. In R. M. W. Travers (Ed.), *Second handbook of research on teaching* (pp. 382–404). Chicago: Rand McNally.
27. Shaver, J. P. (1983). The verification of independent variables in teaching methods research. *Educational Researcher, 12(8),* 3–9.

be sufficient to change teacher behavior in the direction of using the process-oriented inquiry approach required by SCIS.

Treatment fidelity can be assessed by first writing precise specifications for the experimental and control treatments. Then the investigator must carefully train the experimenters to follow these specifications. Finally, during the actual experiment the investigator should collect data on the experimenter's behavior to determine the congruence between behavior and treatment specifications. Data on experimenter behavior can be collected by a variety of observational techniques (see Chapter 9).

An example of careful attention to procedures for maximizing and assessing treatment fidelity can be found in an experiment by Lynn Fuchs, Donald Compton, Douglas Fuchs, Kimberly Paulsen, Joan Bryant, and Carol Hamlett.[28] The main purpose of their experiment was to determine the effectiveness of a tutoring program to improve the mathematics achievement of learning-disabled first-graders. Twelve individuals were trained to use the program, which involved following scripted lessons on different mathematical topics. Each tutor worked with several groups of two or three students.

Fuchs and colleagues checked treatment fidelity by the following empirical procedure:

> All tutoring sessions were audiotaped. Tutors did not know which audiotapes would be checked for fidelity. We checked tapes for all 27 tutoring groups for Topic 4 (Day 1 or 2) and Topic 16 (Day 1) by using a checklist that corresponded to the steps included in the lesson's script, with 9–19 items ($M = 12$) per checklist. Each checklist item was marked as observed, not observed, or not applicable. Fidelity was indexed as percentage of items implemented (observed divided by the sum of observed + not observed). A second coder rechecked fidelity for a random sample of 25% of the audiotapes. Agreement between coders was 88.3%. Across tutors and sessions, the percentage of fidelity for the first check was 95.6; for the second check, 93.5.[29]

Although fidelity was not perfect, it was sufficiently high that observed effects on the student learning measures could be attributed to the intervention and not to idiosyncratic interpretations of the intervention by those who implemented it.

To state the matter differently, suppose the researchers found that students in the treatment group did not outperform the control group on the outcome measures. Without treatment-fidelity data, we could not determine whether the intervention was ineffective or whether it was effective, but not in this particular experiment, because the instructors were unable, or unwilling, to implement it as it was designed to be implemented.

Strong versus Weak Experimental Treatments

One of the major challenges in experimental research is to administer a treatment that is strong enough to have a significant effect on the dependent variable. For example, suppose you do an experiment to determine whether a particular teaching method affects student achievement. The experimental design might require a group of teachers to use the method for a period of one week, with student achievement measured at the beginning and end of that time period. Also, there might be a control group of teachers who use a conventional teaching method for the same period of time, with student achievement measured at the same time as for the experimental group.

---

28. Fuchs, L. S., Compton, D. L., Fuchs, D., Paulsen, K., Bryant, J. D., & Hamlett, C. L. (2005). The prevention, identification, and cognitive determinants of math difficulty. *Journal of Educational Psychology, 97*(3), 493–513.
29. Ibid., p. 500.

Suppose no differences are found between the experimental and control groups. Should you conclude that the experimental teaching method does not produce greater achievement gains? Perhaps, but we can raise the criticism that you used a weak treatment. For example, we might argue that the experimental teaching method would have produced greater achievement gains than the control method had it been used for several months or longer.

Of course, as you increase the strength of the treatment, the experiment is likely to increase in complexity, time, and cost. Thus, many educational problems amenable to an experimental approach cannot be tackled by student researchers. These problems require a well-funded and well-staffed research team in order to be investigated properly. Before doing an experiment, you should determine whether you have the resources necessary to design a treatment that will be strong enough to have an effect on student achievement or other dependent variables.

Random Assignment in Experiments

We discussed above the ideas of Campbell and Stanley about factors that affect the internal and external validity of experiments. These researchers also classified types of experimental designs. Table 12.2 presents part of their classification system. You will note that some of the designs are single-group designs, and others are control-group designs with random assignment. As shown in the table, some of the designs have better internal and external validity than others.

The first column of Table 12.2 illustrates each experimental design graphically. For example, the first three designs are single-group designs, meaning that there is no control group. This aspect is illustrated by the fact that for each of these designs the graphic combination of Xs and Os is all on one row. For example, design number 1 involves an experimental treatment (X) followed by a posttest (O), for one group of participants. Design number 2 involves a pretest (the first O), then an experimental treatment (X), and then a posttest (the second O), again for one group of research participants. In design number 3, several pretests (each O before the X) are administered before the experimental treatment, and several posttests (each O after the X) are administered after the experimental treatment.

The control-group designs shown in the second half of Table 12.2 are represented similarly. The main difference is the R at the beginning of each row, indicating that participants are assigned randomly to either the experimental or control group. Random assignment should not be confused with the randomization carried out to select a sample of individuals to participate in one's study (see Chapter 6). Briefly, **randomization** is the use of a sampling procedure that ensures that each person in a defined population has an equal chance of being selected to take part in the study. When conducting an experiment, you need to consider another type of randomization, namely, random assignment of individuals or other sampling units to experimental treatments. **Random assignment** means that each sampling unit (e.g., student, class, school district) has an equal chance of being in each experimental condition. You can use a table of random numbers or similar method to assign each participant by chance to the experimental or control group.[30] Random assignment is the best technique available for assuring initial equivalence between different treatment groups.

Touchstone in Research

Rogers, J. L., Howard, K. I., & Vessey, J. T. (1993). Using significance tests to evaluate equivalence between two experimental groups. *Psychological Bulletin, 113,* 553–565.

30. Random numbers for generating random assignment to experimental groups are available at http:// www.randomizer.org. Retrieved October 11, 2005.

TABLE 12.2

Experimental Designs and Their Potential Sources of Invalidity

Design	Sources of Invalidity	
	Internal	External
Single-group designs		
1. One-shot case study X O	History, maturation, sample selection, and mortality	Interaction of sample selection and X
2. One-group pretest-posttest design O X O	History, maturation, pretesting, instrumentation, interaction of sample selection and other factors	Interaction of testing and X; interaction of sample selection and X
3. Time-series design O O O O X O O O O	History	Interaction of pretesting and X
Control-group designs with random assignment		
4. Pretest-posttest control-group design R O X O R O O	None	Interaction of pretesting and X
5. Posttest-only control-group design R X O R O	Mortality	None
6. Solomon four-group design R O X O R O O R X O R O	None	None

Note: In Campbell and Stanley's tables, some invalidating factors are shown as possible sources of concern in certain designs. Only definite weaknesses in experimental designs are indicated here.
Key: R = Random assignment.
    X = Experimental treatment.
    O = Observation, either a pretest or posttest of the dependent variable.

Source: Adapted from Tables 1, 2, and 3 on pp. 8, 40, and 56, respectively, in: Campbell, D. T., & Stanley, J. C. (1963). *Experimental and quasi-experimental designs for research*. Chicago: Rand McNally. Copyright © 1963 by Houghton Mifflin Company. Adapted with permission from Houghton Mifflin Company.

Treatment-group equivalence is essential to the internal validity of an experiment. To the extent that threats to the internal validity of the experiment are present, the threats should affect each treatment group to an equal extent if the groups are initially equivalent. In this case, differences between groups on the posttest can be attributed with a high degree of confidence to the treatment rather than to extraneous variables.

Random assignment can be achieved easily in brief experiments that occur under laboratory conditions. The situation is more difficult in field experiments conducted in schools, students' homes, or elsewhere. It might be a challenge to obtain participants' cooperation or establish other conditions necessary for random assignment. Furthermore, even if initially equivalent groups are formed through random assignment, the equivalence may break down as the experiment proceeds, for example, by differential attrition in the two groups.

Cook and Campbell identified several specific obstacles to forming and maintaining equivalent treatment groups in field experiments.[31] We turn now to a discussion of some of these obstacles, and consider how they might be avoided or overcome.

1. *Withholding the treatment from the control group.* If one treatment is perceived as more desirable than another, you may encounter strong resistance to the use of random assignment. For example, suppose an experiment is planned to test how the use of computer simulations of science concepts affects middle-school students' achievement. You wish to randomly assign 10 classrooms (the treatment group) to receive the simulation software, and another 10 classrooms (the control group) to continue functioning without the system for the duration of the experiment.

Upon hearing about the proposed experiment, some teachers in the district might wish to have the simulation software in their classrooms. They might view it as innovative and exciting—a real plus for their school and classroom. Some of them might even solicit parent support and lobby central office administrators to be in the group to receive the simulation software. Such teachers are likely to express resistance to being in the control group. In short, they might oppose the use of random assignment to allocate what is perceived as a scarce and valuable resource.

If you ignore teachers' protests and carry out the experiment as originally planned, the experiment is likely to involve one or more of the internal validity threats described above: compensatory rivalry by the control group, compensatory equalization of treatments, or resentful demoralization of the control group. Therefore, you should attempt to find a solution that addresses the protests while at the same time maintaining the integrity of the experiment.

One solution is to tell the control-group participants that they will receive the treatment after the experiment is concluded. In the example above, the 20 teachers and their principals could be told that 10 of the teachers will receive the software the first year, and the other 10 teachers will receive it the second year.

Educators usually are amenable to this solution. The major difficulty with it obviously is that it creates additional work for the researcher. The length of the experiment is effectively doubled. You can save a great deal of effort simply by not collecting data during the administration of the treatment to the control group. On the other hand, if you do collect data, you will have a replication of the experiment. The first treatment group can be compared with the control group, and the control group can be compared with itself (before and after receiving the treatment).

One of the authors of this book (W. Borg) developed another solution that will work in certain situations.[32] This solution involves giving the control-group participants an alternative treatment that they perceive as equally desirable to the experimental treatment. This treatment should be similar in both duration and format to the experimental treatment, but it should be concerned with a different set of dependent variables. For example, Walter Borg and Frank Ascione did an experiment to test the effectiveness of an inservice education program that they developed to improve teachers' classroom management

---

31. Cook & Campbell, *Quasi-experimentation.* Some of the obstacles to treatment-group equivalence identified by Cook and Campbell are not listed here because they are discussed elsewhere in this chapter.
32. Borg, W. (1984). Dealing with threats to internal validity that randomization does not rule out. *Educational Researcher, 13*(10), 11–14.

skills.[33] The experimental group participated in the inservice program, while the control group participated in an equally desirable program of similar format but addressed to a different set of skills, namely, teaching skills to improve students' self-concept.

2. *Faulty randomization procedures.* A defect in the researcher's random-assignment procedures can result in nonequivalent treatment groups. Cook and Campbell cite the famous case of the 1969 military draft lottery. Each day of the year was put on a slip of a paper, and the slips were put into an urn. The order in which the slips were drawn out of the urn determined the order in which draft-age males would be drafted into military service. For example, if February 12 was drawn first, men with that birth date would be drafted first. Evidently the urn was not shaken well, because the slips of days put into it last (those of October, November, and December) remained near the top and were drawn out first. The solution to the problem is obvious, namely, to use a procedure such as a table of random numbers that thoroughly randomizes all the birth dates.

Another problem that might occur in attempts to assign groups randomly to treatment conditions is that participants may not believe the researcher's statement that the assignment to a treatment group was random. This problem is more likely if the researcher is well known to participants and they have reason to believe that the researcher is positively or negatively biased toward some participants. To avoid this problem, we suggest you have a credible witness observe the random-assignment process. For example, if teachers in a school district are to be assigned to treatment groups, you might ask a representative of the teachers association to observe the assignment process.

Suppose that by examining available data about the sample, you discover that, although randomly constituted, the groups obviously are not equivalent. For example, one group might have a disproportionate number of males, students from a particular grade level, or students with high scholastic aptitude scores. If nonequivalence occurs at the time of random assignment, you have two alternatives. First, you can start again with the total sample and redo the random assignment procedures. Hopefully, a second or third attempt at randomization will result in treatment-group equivalence on known dimensions.

The second alternative is to stratify the total sample on the factor or factors for which equivalence is desired. (Stratification procedures are discussed in Chapter 6.) After the total sample has been stratified, individuals can be randomly assigned within strata to treatment groups. This procedure ensures treatment group equivalence on the stratified factors.

3. *Small sample size.* The probability that random assignment will produce initially equivalent treatment groups increases as the size of the sample in each group increases. For example, equivalent groups will more likely result if 100 individuals are randomly assigned to two treatment groups ($N = 50$ per group) than if 10 individuals are assigned to these two groups ($N = 5$ per group).

There are several solutions to the problem of randomly assigning a small sample to two or more treatment groups. One obvious solution is to attempt to increase the sample size. The additional expenditure of resources is worthwhile if the result is equivalent treatment groups, and consequently, more interpretable research results. Another solution is to use matching procedures, which are discussed later in the chapter.

The third solution is to consider whether one or more treatment groups can be eliminated. Suppose, for example, that you are interested in testing the relative effectiveness of four training variations to alleviate an unusual learning disorder. You can locate a sample of only 16 students having the disorder. If the students are randomly assigned to the four

33. Borg, W. R., & Ascione, F. R. (1982). Classroom management in elementary mainstreaming classrooms. *Journal of Educational Psychology, 74,* 85–95.

treatments, there will be only four students per treatment group. Even if there are true differences between treatments, the statistical power will be so low that the null hypothesis of no difference between treatments probably will not be rejected. In this situation you should consider comparing only the two most theoretically interesting or most promising treatments, in which case there would be eight students per treatment group.

4. *Intact groups.* Although not mentioned by Cook and Campbell, the frequent need to use intact groups in educational research poses an obstacle to random assignment. An **intact group** is a set of individuals who must be treated as members of an administratively defined group rather than as individuals. For example, most school classes are intact groups. The intact group usually is defined in terms of a particular grade level, teacher, and classroom (e.g., the fourth-grade class taught by Ms. Jones in Room 16).

Suppose that you wish to do an experiment in which the individual student is the appropriate sampling unit. You have available a sample of 50 fourth-grade students: 25 from a classroom in school A and 25 from a classroom in school B. Random assignment requires that each student be assigned, by chance, to the experimental or control group. School administrators and teachers, however, usually require that you deal with students as members of an intact group. Thus, all students in a classroom must be given the same treatment in order to preserve the intact classroom group.

Given this situation, you can opt to increase the number of classrooms in the sample and institute one treatment condition per classroom. This procedure should result in an experiment with good internal validity if (1) classrooms are randomly assigned to the experimental and control groups, (2) the issue of the appropriate unit of statistical analysis (see Chapter 5) is carefully addressed, and (3) the other obstacles to random assignment described above are avoided.

In practice, random assignment of classrooms to experimental and control groups is often difficult. If classrooms in several schools are involved, one classroom in a school may be assigned by chance to the experimental group, whereas another classroom in the same school is assigned by chance to the control group. Some administrators tend to view all the teachers and students in a school as a whole, however, and want everyone in the school to be treated the same way. Therefore, they might press you to assign one treatment per school. For example, students in the fourth-grade class of school A might be assigned to the treatment condition (a new instructional method designed to improve learning) and students in the fourth-grade class of school B might be assigned to the no-treatment control condition.

This procedure preserves the integrity of the public school structure. This solution however, creates other problems. Consider, for instance, what would happen if students in school A came from predominantly middle-class families and students in school B came from lower-class families. Because academic achievement is correlated with social class, students in school A are more likely to have high posttest achievement scores than students in school B, with or without the instructional treatment. Thus we could not conclude on the basis of the findings that the instructional treatment is superior to conventional instruction. An equally plausible interpretation is that the differential achievement gain results from initial differences in the treatment groups.

The preceding illustrations typify the thorny problems that researchers can encounter in doing a field experiment in which random assignment to experimental treatments is not possible because the research participants are members of intact groups. Nonetheless, it is possible to design an experiment in which the limitations of nonrandom assignment are partially or wholly overcome. Campbell and Stanley refer to experimental designs that do not involve random assignment of participants to treatment conditions as "quasi-experiments," to distinguish them from "true" experiments, which involve random assignment of research participants to treatment conditions. In the next chapter we will discuss procedures for developing equivalence between intact groups receiving different experimental treatments.

Single-Group Designs

The One-Shot Case Study

The **one-shot case study design** hardly qualifies as an experimental design. In this design an experimental treatment is administered, and then a posttest is administered to measure the effects of the treatment. As Table 12.2 shows, this design has low internal validity. Suppose we select a group of students, give them remedial instruction (the experimental treatment), and then administer a measure of achievement (the posttest). How can we determine the influence of the treatment on the posttest? The answer is that we cannot. The students' scores on the posttest could be accounted for by their regular school instruction or by maturation, as well as by the treatment. Also, the fact that students were tested only once makes it impossible to measure any changes in their performance. Without a measure of change, we cannot even determine whether the students' achievement improved over time, regardless of whether this change was due to the treatment or to some other variable. In short, the one-shot case study, although relatively simple to carry out, yields meaningless findings. At the very least, researchers who are limited to studying a single group of individuals should use the experimental design we describe next.

One-Group Pretest-Posttest Design

The **one-group pretest-posttest design** involves three steps: (1) administration of a pretest measuring the dependent variable; (2) implementation of the experimental treatment (independent variable) for participants; and (3) administration of a posttest that measures the dependent variable again. The effects of the experimental treatment are determined by comparing the pretest and posttest scores.

The one-group pretest-posttest design was used in an experiment conducted by Eleanor Semel and Elisabeth Wiig.[34] Their purpose was to determine whether a new training program, based on an auditory processing model, would improve the language skills of learning-disabled children. The sample consisted of 45 elementary school students who were diagnosed as learning disabled in language because they scored two or more grades below age-grade expectation in two or more academic areas, one of them being reading.

All children in the sample received the training program, which was provided 30 minutes daily for 15 weeks. We might reasonably expect that the children, though language disabled, would make some language gains over this long a time period even without special instruction. Realizing this, the researchers made a generous estimate of gains that might be expected due to regular instruction (i.e., history), maturation, and so on; then they judged the effectiveness of the training program by whether it exceeded this estimate. Semel and Wiig explained their reasoning and procedures as follows:

> standardized and age referenced tests were used as pre- and posttraining measures. In fact, then, the standardization samples were considered to be acceptable as a substitute for a control group. A rigid criterion of performance gains (+6 months) was set for the magnitude of gains which could be considered educationally significant. In reality, children with language-learning disabilities would not be expected to gain language skills at the rate expected for children with normal language development.[35]

34. Semel, E. M., & Wiig, E. H. (1981). Semel Auditory Processing Program: Training effects among children with language-learning disabilities. *Journal of Learning Disabilities, 4,* 192–196.
35. Ibid., pp. 195–196.

TABLE 12.3

Pretest and Posttest Results for Students Receiving a Language Training Program

Test	Pretest *M* (1)	Posttest *M* (2)	Age-Level Gain (in months) (3)	Percentage of Students with Gains > 6 mos. (4)
1. ITPA[a] Grammatic Closure	17.51	23.09	15.48	75.57% (χ^2 = 11.76**)
2. DTLA[b]: Auditory Attention Span for Unrelated Words	32.67	37.68	15.73	68.92% (χ^2 = 6.42*)
3. DTLA: Auditory Attention Span for Related Syllables	30.89	39.29	10.13	51.13% (χ^2 = .02)
4. DTLA: Verbal Opposites	19.44	23.64	7.27	37.79% (χ^2 = 2.68)
5. DTLA: Verbal Absurdities	.96	5.36	22.00	71.13% (χ^2 = 8.02**)
6. Carrow Elicited Language Inventory	36.12	40.00	30.37[c]	76% (χ^2 = 8.76**)

[a]Illinois Test of Psycholinguistic Ability
[b]Detroit Tests of Learning Aptitude
[c]This score is the mean percentile gain using the percentile norms for this measure.
*$p < .05$
**$p < .01$

Source: Adapted from text on pp. 194–195 in: Semel, E. M., & Wiig, E. H. (1981). Semel Auditory Processing Program: Training effects among children with language-learning disabilities. *Journal of Learning Disabilities, 4,* 192–196.

The same battery of language proficiency tests was administered before and after the training program. The performance of the students on the pretest and posttest measures is shown in Table 12.3. Mean raw score gains were found on each of the measures (see data columns 1 and 2). To determine whether the gains were educationally and statistically significant, the researchers first converted students' raw scores on each measure to an age-level equivalent. The pretest age-level equivalent then was subtracted from the posttest age-level equivalent to yield an age-level gain score. The mean age-level gain on each measure for the total sample is shown in data column 3 of Table 12.3.

Next the researchers determined the percentage of students whose age-level gain on a particular measure was more than six months. These percentages are shown in the last column of Table 12.3. For example, 76 percent of the students made age-level gains of more than six months on the Illinois Test of Psycholinguistic Ability (ITPA) Grammatic Closure Subtest. The researchers tested whether these percentages were significantly different from a "chance" figure of 50 percent. The chi-square test revealed that more students made gains of +6 months than could be expected if this were a chance event.

The researchers used the one-group pretest-posttest design in this experiment because the school system in which it was conducted did not permit differential services for its students. The absence of a control group was not a serious threat to the internal validity of the experiment, however, because the researchers were able to make a good estimate of expected pretest-posttest gains due to extraneous factors. The gains of the experimental group thus could be evaluated against estimated gains under normal, nonexperimental conditions in which such extraneous factors would be operating.

The one-group pretest-posttest design is especially appropriate when you are attempting to change a characteristic that is very stable or resistant to change. For example, if I participate in an experimental program to learn how to speak Ukrainian (an out-of-the-ordinary behavior), the likelihood that extraneous factors account for the change is small. Similarly, if an experimenter trains a bird to say a few human words, we would hardly dismiss the results as due to extraneous factors.

In summary, the one-group pretest-posttest design is most justified when extraneous factors can be estimated with a high degree of certainty, or can safely be assumed to be minimal or nonexistent.

Statistical analysis The data in the Semel and Wiig study were analyzed by chi-square tests that determined whether an observed measure of pre- and post-test gains (+6 months age-level gain) differed significantly from a chance distribution of gain, that is, a 50-50 split. If the data are in the form of continuous scores, a *t* test for correlated means would be used instead. This test determines whether the difference between the pretest and posttest mean is statistically significant.

If the scores on either the pretest or posttest show marked deviation from the normal distribution, a nonparametric test of statistical significance should be used. These tests are described in Chapter 10.

Time-Series Design

Touchstone in Research

Ostrom, C. W., Jr. (1990). *Time series analysis: Regression techniques* (2nd ed.). Thousand Oaks, CA: Sage.

In the **time-series design** a single group of research participants is measured at periodic intervals, with the experimental treatment administered between two of these intervals. The effect of the experimental treatment, if any, is indicated by a discrepancy in the measurements before and after its appearance.

Campbell and Stanley classify the time-series experiment as a single-group design (see Table 12.2) because it involves a single group of research participants, all of whom receive the experimental treatment. The procedures used to maximize the internal validity of this type of experimental design and to analyze the data are similar to those used in single-case designs. Therefore, we will discuss the time-series design in relation to single-case designs in Chapter 13.

Control-Group Designs with Random Assignment

Touchstone in Research

Boruch, R., de Moya, D., & Snyder, B. (2002). The importance of randomized field trials in education and related areas. In F. Mosteller & R. Boruch (Eds.), *Evidence matters: Randomized trials in education research* (pp. 50–79). Washington, DC: Brookings Institution.

We discuss in this section two of the experimental designs shown in Table 12.2: the pretest-posttest control-group design (number 4); and the posttest-only control group design (number 5). These are among the most commonly used designs in educational research. We also describe two variations on these designs: the pretest-posttest control-group design with matching; and the one-variable multiple-condition design.

The statistical techniques used to analyze data resulting from these and other experimental designs are often the same as those used in causal-comparative designs. We explain these statistical techniques (e.g., the *t* test and analysis of variance) in Chapter 10. Therefore, you may find it helpful to refer to Chapter 10 for more information about the statistical techniques to which we refer in this chapter and Chapter 13.

The Solomon four-group design also is shown in Table 12.2 (number 6), but we will defer our discussion of it until the next chapter. This is because the Solomon four-group design is a factorial design. To understand how it works you need to understand the logic of factorial design, a topic that is covered in Chapter 13.

Pretest-Posttest Control-Group Design

Almost any study that can be conducted with a single-group design can be carried out more satisfactorily with a control-group design. The essential difference between the single-group design and control-group design is that the latter employs at least two groups of research participants, one of which is called the control group. The **control group** is a group of research participants who receive either no treatment, or an alternate treatment to that given the experimental group, in order to assess the effect of extraneous factors on participants' posttest performance.

In a control-group design the goal is to keep the experiences of the experimental and control groups as identical as possible, except that the experimental group is exposed to the experimental treatment. If extraneous variables have brought about changes between the pretest and posttest, these will be reflected in the scores of the control group. Thus, the posttest change of the experimental group beyond the change that occurred in the control group can be safely attributed to the experimental treatment.

If properly carried out, the pretest-posttest control-group design effectively controls for the eight threats to internal validity originally identified by Campbell and Stanley: history, maturation, testing, instrumentation, statistical regression, differential selection, experimental mortality, and selection-maturation interaction. Nevertheless, the external validity of this design might be affected by an interaction between the pretest and the experimental treatment (pretest sensitization in Figure 12.1). That is, the experimental treatment might produce significant effects only because a pretest was administered. When it is tried on a group that has not been pretested, the treatment might not work as well. If you think that your experimental treatment is likely to be affected by pretesting, you should use the posttest-only control-group design or the Solomon four-group design.

The following steps are involved in using a pretest-posttest control-group design: (1) random assignment of research participants to experimental and control groups, (2) administration of a pretest to both groups, (3) administration of the treatment to the experimental group but not to the control group, and (4) administration of a posttest to both groups. The experimental and control groups must be treated as nearly alike as possible except for the treatment variable. For example, both groups must be given the same pretest and posttest, and they must be tested at the same time.

In some experiments, the control group takes only the pretest and posttest and receives no treatment. In other experiments, however, you might want to administer an alternative experimental treatment to the control group. For example, as we discussed above, you might administer an equally desirable but different treatment to the control group. This design feature enables you to avoid the remaining four threats to internal validity identified by Cook and Campbell, namely, experimental treatment diffusion, compensatory rivalry by the control group, compensatory equalization of treatments, and resentful demoralization of the control group.

If the control group receives a treatment rather than being in a no-treatment condition, researchers sometimes refer to it as a *comparison group* rather than a control group. Another option is to refer to the two groups by labels that describe the two treatment conditions, for example, the *computer lab group* and the *computer-in-classroom group*.

The pretest-posttest control-group design was used in a study of reading remediation by Benita Blachman, Christopher Schatschneider, Jack Fletcher, David Francis, Sheila Clonan, Bennett Shaywitz, and Sally Shaywitz.[36] They conducted an experiment to determine

Touchstones in Research

Dugard, P., & Todman, J. (1995). Analysis of pre-test post-test control group designs in educational research. *Educational Psychology, 15,* 181–198.

Mok, M., & Wheldall, K. (1995). Some reservations about the use of analysis of covariance in educational research: A response to Dugard and Todman. *Educational Psychology, 15,* 199–202.

---

36. Blachman, B. A., Schatschneider, C., Fletcher, J. M., Francis, D. J., Clonan, S. M., Shaywitz, B. A., & Shaywitz, S. E. (2004). Effects of intensive reading remediation for second and third graders and a 1-year follow-up. *Journal of Educational Psychology, 96*(3), 444–461.

the effectiveness of a reading-remediation program for second- and third-graders with reading disabilities. They stated their purpose more specifically, as follows:

> In this study our goals were to (a) evaluate an intervention for second- and third-grade students with poor word-level skills; (b) monitor their progress for 1 year after the intervention ended to investigate whether gains were maintained; and (c) determine which areas of reading and spelling, if any, demonstrated long-term gains.[37]

Blachman and colleagues argued that children with reading difficulties at these grade levels need a strong intervention, because otherwise they are likely to be poor readers in later grades and into adulthood.

The experimental treatment consisted of 50 minutes of one-to-one tutoring by a teacher certified in either reading or special education. The tutoring sessions occurred five days per week for nearly an entire school year. The mean number of tutoring sessions was 126. This tutoring replaced any remedial reading instruction that the students otherwise would have received. Children in the control condition received whatever remedial reading instruction was provided by their school, for example, reading instruction in a resource classroom. Children in both the treatment and control condition also continued to receive whatever reading instruction was offered in their regular classroom during the school year.

A critical feature of a pretest-posttest control-group experiment is random assignment of participants to the treatment and control conditions. The children who participated in the Blachman experiment came from second- and third-grade classrooms in 11 schools in four school districts. According to the report, these children "were randomly assigned within schools, grade, and gender to treatment and control groups (e.g., if there were 2 second-grade boys at a given school, 1 was randomly assigned to the treatment group and 1 was randomly assigned to the control group)."[38] This means that stratification, a procedure described in Chapter 6, was used as part of random assignment. Stratification in this experiment helped to ensure that the treatment and control groups included an approximately equal number of students from each school and grade level and also an approximately equal number of boys and girls.

Blachman and colleagues administered a wide range of measures to determine (1) the initial equivalence of the treatment and control groups in ability and academic achievement and (2) the effects of the treatment variable (intensive one-to-one tutoring). The primary measures—those directly related to reading-related skills and the experimental design—are listed in the leftmost column of Table 12.4 and in the note below the table. The skills that they measured are as follows:

- WRMT Basic Skills Cluster. A composite measure of children's decoding skill using their scores on the WRMT Word Identification and Word Attack subtests.
- WRMT Word Identification. Measures word-recognition skill by having children read words from a graded word list.
- WRMT Word Attack. Measures children's skill in reading decodable nonwords.
- WRAT Spelling. Measures children's ability to write single words from dictation.
- GORT Quotient. An overall measure of reading ability derived from subtest scores.
- GORT Accuracy. Measures children's reading accuracy on timed reading passages.
- GORT Rate. Measures children's reading rate on timed reading passages.
- GORT Comprehension. Measures children's skill in responding to questions about the content of reading passages.

37. Ibid., p. 445.
38. Ibid., p. 446.

TABLE 12.4

Descriptive Statistics, Tests of Statistical Significance, and Effect Sizes for Experiment on the Effects of One-to-One Tutoring in Reading

Measure	Treatment[a]			Control[a]			F	P	d[c]
	M	SD	M[b]	M	SD	M[b]			
Pretest									
WRMT Basic Skills Cluster	81.89	6.99		82.38	6.22		0.09	0.7642	
WRMT Word Identification	82.81	6.83		83.97	6.45		0.56	0.4740	
WRMT Word Attack	83.30	8.69		81.97	7.32		0.46	0.4984	
WRAT Spelling	82.08	6.52		81.44	6.95		0.16	0.6930	
GORT Reading Quotient	73.08	8.08		74.03	7.01		0.27	0.6063	
GORT Reading Accuracy	77.43	6.30		78.91	6.81		0.86	0.3541	
GORT Reading Rate	76.62	5.66		78.13	5.79		1.19	0.2800	
GORT Reading Comprehension	78.24	11.56		78.75	10.00		0.04	0.8474	
Posttest									
WRMT Basic Skills Cluster	88.32	12.60	88.62	78.88	9.59	78.53	33.64	0.0001	1.69
WRMT Word Identification	88.65	12.09	89.33	80.38	9.83	79.59	30.58	0.0001	1.31
WRMT Word Attack	90.16	14.07	89.67	80.03	9.46	80.61	13.10	0.0006	0.89
WRAT Spelling	92.22	8.48	92.03	82.81	9.57	83.03	21.62	0.0001	1.13
GORT Reading Quotient	84.92	11.28	85.18	77.78	10.25	77.48	10.24	0.0021	0.78
GORT Reading Accuracy	87.57	13.00	88.07	80.63	10.83	80.04	8.82	0.0041	0.72
GORT Reading Rate	84.05	8.88	84.60	77.97	8.41	77.34	15.84	0.0002	0.96
GORT Reading Comprehension	89.73	11.96	89.80	83.75	11.29	83.67	5.06	0.0275	0.55
Follow-up									
WRMT Basic Skills Cluster	87.57	11.68	87.82	79.56	11.29	79.27	16.24	0.0001	0.97
WRMT Word Identification	87.30	10.94	87.87	79.63	11.03	78.97	18.75	0.0001	1.05
WRMT Word Attack	89.46	12.06	88.97	82.34	13.08	82.91	5.34	0.0243	0.56
WRAT Spelling	90.59	9.95	90.35	83.56	9.42	83.84	11.02	0.0015	0.81
GORT Reading Quotient	84.84	11.64	85.22	79.94	12.23	79.50	5.52	0.0218	0.57
GORT Reading Accuracy	81.89	12.93	82.37	78.91	14.59	78.36	1.56	0.2151	0.30
GORT Reading Rate	82.43	12.51	83.10	75.78	9.76	75.01	11.09	0.0014	0.81
GORT Reading Comprehension	92.57	11.64	92.67	90.00	12.89	89.88	1.02	0.3163	0.24

Note: WRMT = Woodcock Reading Mastery Tests—Revised; WRAT = Wide Range Achievement Test 3; GORT = Gray Oral Reading Tests—Third Edition; [a]Treatment group $n = 37$; control group $n = 32$. [b]Means adjusted by pretest. [c]d = Cohen's measure of effect size.

Source: Adapted from Table 1 on p. 447 in: Blachman, B. A., Schatschneider, C., Fletcher, J. M., Francis, D. J., Clonan, S. M., Shaywitz, B. A., & Shaywitz, S. E. (2004). Effects of intensive reading remediation for second and third graders and a 1-year follow-up. *Journal of Educational Psychology, 96*(3), 444–461. Used with permission from Benita A. Blachman.

Each of these measures was administered to each student in the experiment at three times: (1) as a pretest at the start of the school year, prior to the start of the experimental tutoring program; (2) as a posttest at the end of the school year, after the experimental tutoring program; and (3) as a follow-up test at the end of the following school year, during which time the experimental treatment ceased and instead students in both the treatment and control groups received the regular reading instruction (which in some cases also included remedial instruction) provided by the school.

Statistical aanalysis The first step in analyzing data from a pretest-posttest control-group experiment is to compute descriptive statistics. As shown in Table 12.4, mean scores were computed for the pretest, posttest, and follow-up test for both groups on each measure.

The next step is to test the statistical significance of observed differences in the mean scores of the treatment and control groups. One approach is analysis of covariance (ANCOVA), which we discuss in Chapter 10. Another approach is to do a two-way analysis of variance for repeated measures. This statistical technique is discussed in Chapter 13, in the section on factorial designs. Still another approach is hierarchical linear modeling,[39] also discussed in Chapter 13.

Blachman and colleagues chose to use ANCOVA to test the statistical significance of their observed effects. ANCOVA adjusted the posttest scores for differences between the treatment and control groups on the corresponding pretest. Because the experiment involved a 1-year follow-up in which all the outcome measures were re-administered, ANCOVA also was used to adjust the follow-up test scores in the same manner.

The adjusted mean scores derived from the ANCOVAs are shown in the third and sixth data columns (M^b) of Table 12.4. The adjustment factor is illustrated by students' scores on the GORT reading-rate test. The pretest mean for the treatment group (76.62) was lower than that for the control group (78.13). Even though the students were randomly assigned to the treatment and control groups, differences of this sort can occur by chance. In this case, the treatment group started out at a slight disadvantage relative to the control group.

When we examine the adjusted posttest means, it is apparent how ANCOVA works to eliminate these pretest differences. The posttest mean for the treatment group (84.05) was adjusted upward by ANCOVA (84.60), whereas the posttest mean for the control group (77.97) was adjusted downward (77.34). ANCOVA determines whether these two adjusted posttest means (not the actual posttest means) differ significantly from each other. If you examine the follow-up means for the same test, you will find that ANCOVA adjusted them similarly.

The results of the ANCOVAs are shown in the seventh and eighth data columns of Table 12.4. The ANCOVAs yielded a significant F value for all but two of the comparisons (GORT follow-up reading accuracy and reading comprehension). Blachman and colleagues also included a measure of effect size (rightmost data column) for each comparison. Although they did not interpret the practical significance of the observed effect sizes, it would be reasonable to conclude that they are substantial. For example, an effect size of 1.00 means that a student who is in the 50th percentile in the treatment group would be in the 84th percentile of the control-group score distribution. Differences between the adjusted means of the two groups yielded effect sizes that approached or exceeded 1.00.

---

39. For an example of hierarchical linear modeling in a pretest-posttest control-group experiment, see: Borman, G. D., Slavin, R. E., Cheung, A., Chamberlain, A. M., Madden, N. A., & Chambers, B. (2005). Success for all: First-year results from the national randomized field trial. *Educational Evaluation and Policy Analysis, 27*(1), 1–22.

Blachman and colleagues reached the following conclusions based on their statistical analyses:

> The major findings are that the treatment children, who participated in an intensive, systematic, and explicit program that emphasized the phonologic and orthographic connections in words and text-based reading, showed significantly greater gains than the control children on measures of both real word and nonword reading, reading rate, passage reading, and spelling and, for the most part, maintained these gains at a 1-year follow-up.[40]

This conclusion follows in a straightforward manner from the ANCOVA analyses and effect sizes shown in Table 12.4.

Matching A variation on the pretest-posttest control-group design is the use of the matching technique to obtain additional precision in statistical analysis of the data.[41] **Matching** refers to the selection of research participants for the experimental and control groups in such a manner that they are closely comparable on a pretest that measures either the dependent variable or a variable that is highly correlated with the dependent variable. (Matching also is used in causal-comparative research; see Chapter 10.) Matching is most useful in studies where small samples are to be used and when large differences between the experimental and control group on the dependent variable are not expected. Under these conditions, the small differences that do occur are more likely to be detected if sampling errors are reduced by the use of matching.

Posttest-Only Control-Group Design

This design is similar to the pretest-posttest control-group design except that pretests of the dependent variable are not administered to the experimental and control groups. The steps involved in the **posttest-only control-group design** are as follows:

1. Randomly assign research participants to the experimental and control groups.
2. Administer the treatment to the experimental group and no treatment or an alternative treatment to the control group.
3. Administer the posttest to both groups.

This design is recommended when you are unable to locate a suitable pretest, or when there is a possibility that a pretest has an effect on the experimental treatment. Before choosing this experimental design, you should consider three possible disadvantages of not administering a pretest of the dependent variable. First, random assignment may not be fully successful in eliminating initial differences between the experimental and control groups. If initial differences still exist, any differences found on the posttest can be attributed to them rather than to the effect of the experimental treatment. Because random assignment is most effective in equating groups when large numbers of research participants are involved, the posttest-only control-group design is best employed when you can enlist a large sample.

The second disadvantage of not administering a pretest is that you cannot form subgroups to determine whether the experimental treatment has a different effect on individuals at different levels of the variables measured by the pretest.

---

40. Blachman, et al., Effects of intensive reading, pp. 454–455.
41. An example of this experimental design is reported in: Rivera, E., & Omizo, M. M. (1980). The effects of relaxation and biofeedback on attention to task and impulsivity among male hyperactive children. *Exceptional Child, 27,* 41–51.

The third disadvantage of not administering a pretest occurs when there is differ-ential attrition during the course of the experiment. For example, if participants in the control and experimental groups drop out of the experiment before it is over, any differ-ences on the posttest may be due to the differential characteristics of the dropouts of the two groups, rather than the experimental treatment. Thus, the posttest-only control-group design should not be used when considerable attrition of research participants during the course of the study is likely.

The posttest-only control-group design was used in a study of teacher enthusiasm by Brian Patrick, Jennifer Hisley, and Toni Kempler.[42] The purpose of their experiment was to test the hypothesis that teacher enthusiasm has a positive effect on students' en-thusiasm and intrinsic desire to learn. (In the report of their study, they referred to stu-dents' enthusiasm as "psychological vitality.") They derived their hypothesis from the research literature on intrinsic motivation, self-determination theory, and teacher en-thusiasm during instruction. They also conducted an exploratory correlational study to test the hypothesis.

The results of this correlational study lent support to the hypothesis:

> A teacher who is perceived to have a dynamic, enthusiastic style, then, tends to have students who report being highly intrinsically motivated regarding the subject matter as well as feeling energized in class.[43]

At the same time, the researchers noted the inherent limitation of correlational research with respect to cause-and-effect inferences:

> . . . because the data were strictly correlational, there is no way to determine the causal direc-tion of the relationship between enthusiasm and our outcome measures. Although it is tempt-ing to assume that an enthusiastic teacher produces intrinsically motivated students, it is perhaps equally plausible to draw the converse conclusion.[44]

Therefore, Patrick, Hisley, and Kempler designed a second study, a pretest-posttest con-trol-group experiment, to determine whether teacher enthusiasm has a direct causal effect on student's intrinsic motivation to learn and psychological vitality.

The research participants were 60 students at a small liberal arts college. The students were randomly assigned to the experimental and control conditions. The procedures used in the experiment were designed to mask the purpose of the study. In other words, the stu-dents knew that they were participating in an experiment, but did not know that the vari-ables being investigated were teacher enthusiasm, instrinsic motivation, and psychological vitality.

Each student who received the experimental treatment (labeled the "high-enthusi-asm" condition) engaged individually in a laboratory session. The session involved sev-eral procedures, including a seven-minute lecture on the principles of biofeedback; following the lecture, administration of questionnaires to measure the student's intrinsic motivation to learn about the lecture topic and other matters; and a concluding, 5-minute free-choice activity in which the student could read articles about biofeedback or general-interest magazines (*Time* and *National Geographic*). During the lecture component, the instructor exhibited six indicators of enthusiasm that had been used in previous research

42. Patrick, B. C., Hisley, J., & Kempler, T. (2000). "What's everybody so excited about?": The effects of teacher en-thusiasm on student intrinsic motivation and vitality. *Journal of Experimental Education, 68,* 217–236.
43. Ibid., p. 225.
44. Ibid., p. 226.

on teacher enthusiasm: "(1) vocal delivery with variation in pace, volume, and intonation; (2) eyes that open wide and 'light up'; (3) demonstrative gesturing; (4) frequent large body movements; (5) facial expression of emotion; and (6) a high level of overall energy and vitality."[45]

Students in the control group (labeled the "low-enthusiasm" condition) participated in exactly the same activities as students in the experimental group, with one exception. During the seven-minute lecture, the instructor displayed a relative absence of the six indicators of enthusiasm.

The dependent variables and their measurement in this study are as follows:

1. *Perception of instructor enthusiasm.* The participants completed six items on which they rated the instructor's enthusiasm using a 7-point Likert-type scale. Sample item: "The instructor was very enthusiastic and energetic."
2. *Psychological vitality.* The measure included seven items, which participants rated on a 7-point Likert-type scale. Sample item: "Right now, I feel energized."
3. *Intrinsic motivation (free-choice).* Each participant was observed through a one-way mirror during the free-choice activity. The number of seconds they spent demonstrating interest in the biofeedback articles was recorded.
4. *Intrinsic motivation (self-reported).* The measure included three items which each participant rated on a 7-point Likert-type scale. The measure was administered after the lecture and again after the free-choice activity.

The researchers did not provide a rationale for not including a pretest measure of any of these variables. However, we can infer from their description of their procedures that they were concerned about not revealing the purpose of the experiment to the participants. Pretests of intrinsic motivation or psychological vitality might well have sensitized participants to these variables, and this sensitization would likely have affected their behavior during the experiment and responses to the posttest measures. Also, attrition was not an issue in this experiment, so pretest data would not be necessary to check for differential attrition (a threat to internal validity that we explained earlier in the chapter) and its effects on the data.

Statistical analysis Table 12.5 shows the mean score of participants in the high-enthusiasm and low-enthusiasm groups on each of the posttest measures of the dependent variables. Because there are only two groups, the mean score differences can be tested for statistical significance by a *t* test. Table 12.5 shows instead *F* values, which indicate that the researchers chose to do ANOVAs. However, when two groups are compared, a *t* test and ANOVA yield identical results. Therefore, it is of no consequence that the researchers chose to do ANOVAs rather than *t* tests.

The researchers' decision to measure the participants' perception of their instructor's enthusiasm is a desirable design feature of their experiment. It provides a check of treatment fidelity, which we explained earlier in the chapter. As you can see in Table 12.5, students in the high-enthusiasm group rated their instructor much higher on enthusiasm than did students in the low-enthusiasm group, and this difference was statistically significant. It is also apparent that the researchers' hypothesis was strongly supported: the two groups' mean scores on three of the four measures of intrinsic motivation and

45. Ibid., pp. 227–228.

TABLE 12.5

Effects of Manipulation of Teacher Enthusiasm

Variable	Enthusiasm Condition		F	p
	High *M*	Low *M*		
Perception of instructor enthusiasm	6.18	3.56	125.56	.001
Intrinsic motivation				
Free-choice behavior	133.77	93.70	1.47	*ns*
Self-report				
Postlecture	5.63	4.87	9.26	.004
Post-free-choice period	5.68	5.09	5.30	.025
Psychological vitality	4.11	3.54	4.94	.03

Note: $n = 30$ participants per condition. Free-choice behavior was measured from 0 to 300 seconds. All other variables were measures on a 7-point Likert-type scale.

Source: Adapted from Table 6 on p. 231 in: Patrick, B. C., Hisley, J., & Kempler, T. (2000). "What's everybody so excited about?": The effects of teacher enthusiasm on student intrinsic motivation and validity. *Journal of Experimental Education, 68*, 217–236. Reprinted with permission from the Helen Dwight Reid Educational Foundation. Published by Heldref Publications, 1319 Eighteenth St., NW, Washington, DC 20036-1802. Copyright © 2000.

psychological vitality yielded statistically significant differences; and the difference between their mean scores on the fourth measure (free-choice behavior), while not statistically significant, was in the hypothesized direction.

One-Variable Multiple-Condition Design

The one-variable multiple-condition design is a simple extension of the control-group designs that we have presented thus far. Each of these designs involves random assignment of a sample to *two* groups, but each one can be extended to include *three or more* groups. We call such extensions **one-variable multiple-condition designs.** The *one-variable* designation indicates that the groups differ on only one variable, which is the type of treatment they receive. The *multiple-condition* designation indicates that more than two treatment conditions are involved.

For example, consider the experiment on teacher enthusiasm that we described above. The researchers studied the effects of two levels of the variable of teacher enthusiasm: high and low. If they wished, however, they could distinguish additional levels of enthusiasm (e.g., moderate enthusiasm, extremely high enthusiasm, and extremely low enthusiasm). Each level would be represented by a separate group of participants in the experimental design. There would still be a single treatment variable in the design, but there would be three or more groups depending on how many levels of the variable are to be studied.

Statistical analysis Multiple-condition experiments generally yield three or more mean scores, or similar descriptive statistics. Therefore, the usual test of statistical significance in these experiments is univariate or multivariate analysis of variance, univariate or multivariate analysis of covariance, or a nonparametric equivalent.

RECOMMENDATIONS FOR

Doing Experiments

1. Try to maximize the experiment's internal validity: Consider all the extraneous variables that might affect the posttest variables, and then take steps to eliminate them from the experimental design.

2. Try to maximize the experiment's population validity: Identify the population to which you wish to generalize your findings, and then select a sample that will permit those generalizations.

3. Try to maximize the experiment's ecological validity: Identify the real-life conditions in which the intervention will be used, and then create a "representative design" that approximates those conditions.

4. Consider whether the experiment is susceptible to experimenter bias, and if it is, design the experiment to minimize that bias.

5. In designing an experiment, include procedures for checking treatment fidelity.

6. Design a strong form of the experimental intervention (i.e., the treatment variable) in order to make a fair test of its effectiveness.

7. Whenever possible, use an experimental design that includes at least one control condition and random assignment of research participants to the conditions.

SELF-CHECK TEST

Circle the correct answer to each of the following questions. The answers are provided at the back of the book.

1. A posttest in an experiment is sometimes called the
a. dependent variable.
b. experimental treatment.
c. experimental variable.
d. treatment variable.

2. An experiment in which extraneous variables are controlled is said to be
a. internally reliable.
b. internally valid.
c. externally valid.
d. externally reliable.

3. If students' scores tend to move toward the mean upon retesting, _____ is said to have occurred.
a. experimental mortality
b. statistical regression
c. maturation
d. reactive effect of pretesting

4. If the experimental treatment is affected by the administration of the pretest, the _____ of the experiment would be weakened.
a. internal validity
b. internal reliability
c. external validity
d. external reliability

5. Representative design of experiments assumes that
a. the learning environment is a complex, interrelated ecology.
b. the human learner is an active processor of information.
c. the intended effects of an experimental intervention may radiate out to affect other aspects of performance.
d. all of the above.

6. Researchers often give participating teachers and students special attention that, though not part of the experimental treatment, may cause change. This phenomenon has been called the
   a. Hawthorne effect.
   b. John Henry effect.
   c. effect of multiple-treatment interference.
   d. reactive effect of experimentation.

7. A useful technique to minimize the effects of experimenter bias upon the outcome of an experiment is for the researcher to
   a. train naive experimenters to collect the data from research participants.
   b. select experimenters who have prior experience in doing research on the problem being investigated.
   c. fully disclose the purpose of the study to the experimenters.
   d. all of the above.

For questions 8–10, use the following key:
   R = random assignment
   X = experimental treatment
   O = observation (pretest or posttest)

8. O   X   O
   describes the:
   a. one-group pretest-posttest design.
   b. one-shot case study.
   c. pretest-posttest control-group design.
   d. posttest-only control-group design.

9. R   O   X   O
      O   O
   describes the
   a. posttest-only control-group design.
   b. Solomon two-group design.
   c. counterbalanced design.
   d. pretest-posttest control-group design.

10. R   X   O
           O
   is a useful design if
   a. no control group is available.
   b. a large sample is available.
   c. it is thought the pretest will have an effect on the experimental treatment.
   d. it is thought that the posttest has exceptional construct validity.

CHAPTER 13

Experimental Research: Designs, Part 2

OVERVIEW

This chapter describes the principles of experimental research design that were introduced in Chapter 12 as they apply to three other types of experimental design: quasi-experimental, factorial, and single-case designs. Quasi-experimental designs are used when random assignment of research participants to experimental and control groups is not possible. Factorial designs, in contrast to the one-treatment-variable designs described in Chapter 12, involve simultaneous manipulation of two or more treatment variables. Single-case designs involve intensive study of the effects of a treatment on a single individual or group. Because educational experiments often involve the measurement of achievement gains or other types of change, we include a discussion of this type of measurement.

OBJECTIVES

After studying this chapter, you should be able to

1. Describe how to reduce initial group differences that occur due to nonrandom assignment of research participants to experimental and control treatments.
2. Describe methods and statistical procedures used in the static-group comparison and nonequivalent control-group designs.
3. Describe the major potential threats to the internal validity of quasi-experimental designs.
4. Classify into five types the independent variables that appear in factorial research designs.
5. Explain the purpose, design, and statistical analysis procedures of basic factorial experiments.
6. Describe the methods, purposes, and features of single-case experimental designs.
7. Describe several variations of A-B-A and multiple-baseline designs in single-case experiments, and indicate the most appropriate statistical techniques for analyzing the data yielded by these designs.
8. State several threats to the internal validity and external validity of single-case experiments.
9. Describe problems in using gain scores to measure change, and state two statistical techniques for solving these problems.

Quasi-Experimental Designs

Touchstones in Research

Reichardt, C. S., & Mark, M. M. (1998). Quasi-experimentation. In L. Bickman & D. J. Rog (Eds.), *Handbook of applied social research methods* (pp. 193–228). Thousand Oaks, CA: Sage.

Shadish, W. R., Cook, T. D., & Campbell, D. T. (2002). *Experimental and quasi-experimental designs for generalized causal inference.* Boston: Houghton Mifflin.

We explain in Chapter 12 that random assignment of research participants to experimental and control groups greatly strengthens the internal validity of experiments. Random assignment, however, often is not possible, especially in field studies. Campbell and Stanley refer to experiments that lack random assignment as **quasi-experiments.**[1] This type of experiment, if carefully designed, yields useful knowledge. However, you should be aware of the special problems that can arise when individuals are not assigned randomly to groups and the steps you can take to solve them.

Table 13.1 summarizes the quasi-experimental designs that are discussed in this chapter. The list is not exhaustive, but it does illustrate the range of design options that are available to educational researchers.

Static-Group Comparison Design

The **static-group comparison design** has two characteristics: Research participants are not randomly assigned to the two treatment groups; and a posttest, but no pretest, is administered to both groups. The steps involved in using this experimental design are identical to the posttest-only control-group design described in Chapter 12, except for the absence of random assignment.

The main threat to internal validity in this design is that posttest differences between groups can be attributed to characteristics of the groups other than the experimental conditions to which they were assigned. For example, suppose that faculty members of one university department are given the experimental treatment and the posttest, and faculty members in another department at the same university are given only the posttest. If differences on the posttest are found, it can be argued that those differences are due to pre-existing differences between faculty members in the two departments rather than the effect of the experimental treatment.

The static-group comparison design produces an inherently weak experiment. If you are planning to use it, consider the possibility of administering a pretest to the subjects. With this additional factor, the experiment becomes a nonequivalent control-group design and allows much stronger inferences concerning the effect of the experimental treatment on the posttest. This design is discussed in the next section.

Statistical analysis The data yielded by a static-group comparison design can be analyzed by doing a *t* test of the difference between the posttest mean scores of the experimental and control groups. If the scores deviate considerably from the normal distribution, a nonparametric test (most likely the Mann-Whitney *U* test) should be used instead.

Nonequivalent Control-Group Design

The most commonly used quasi-experimental design in educational research is the **nonequivalent control-group design.** In this design, research participants are not randomly assigned to the experimental and control groups, and both groups take a pretest and a posttest. Except for random assignment, the steps involved in this design are the same as for the pretest-posttest experimental control-group design described in Chapter 12.

It also is possible to use a nonequivalent control-group design involving more than two groups. Furthermore, it is possible to have all groups receive a treatment, rather than having one group in a no-treatment control condition. The only essential features of this

---

1. Campbell, D. T., & Stanley, J. C. (1963). *Experimental and quasi-experimental designs for research.* Chicago: Rand McNally.

TABLE 13.1

Summary of the Experimental Designs Described in Chapter 13

Quasi-experimental Designs

Static-group comparison design
   X O
     O
Nonequivalent control-group design
O X O
O   O

Solomon Four-Group Design

R O X O
R O   O
R   X O
R   O

Counterbalanced Experiments

Group 1 R O X_1 X_2 O
Group 2 R O X_2 X_1 O

Factorial Designs

Two-factor experiments
R O X_1 Y_1 O
R O X_1 Y_2 O
R O X_2 Y_1 O
R O X_2 Y_2 O
Three-factor experiments
R O X_1 Y_1 Z_1 O
R O X_1 Y_1 Z_2 O
R O X_1 Y_2 Z_1 O
R O X_1 Y_2 Z_2 O
R O X_2 Y_1 Z_1 O
R O X_2 Y_1 Z_2 O
R O X_2 Y_2 Z_1 O
R O X_2 Y_2 Z_2 O

Single-Case Designs

A-B designs
A B
A B A
A B A B
Multiple-baseline designs
A B B B A
A A B A B

Key: R = random assignment
    X, Y, Z = Experimental treatments
    $X_1/X_2/X_3$ = Levels of treatment X
    $Y_1/Y_2/Y_3$ = Levels of treatment Y
    $Z_1/Z_2/Z_3$ = Levels of treatment Z
    O = observation, either a pretest or posttest
    A = measurement during baseline condition
    B = measurement during treatment condition

particular design, then, are nonrandom assignment of research participants to groups and administration of a pretest and posttest to all groups. An example of this experimental design is described in Chapter 12. It is the evaluation of the Science Curriculum Improvement Study by William Kyle, Ronald Bonnstetter, and Thomas Gadsden, Jr.

Statistical analysis The main threat to the internal validity of a nonequivalent control-group experiment is the possibility that group differences on the posttest are due to pre-existing group differences rather than to a treatment effect. Analysis of covariance (first discussed in Chapter 10) frequently is used to handle this problem. Analysis of covariance statistically reduces the effects of initial group differences by making compensating adjustments to the posttest means of the two groups. If you plan to use this statistical technique, you should check whether your data satisfy its assumptions.

Factorial Designs

Touchstones in Research

Jaeger, R. M., & Bond, L. (1996). Quantitative research methods and design. In D. C. Berliner & R. C. Calfee (Eds.), *Handbook of educational psychology* (pp. 877–898). New York: Macmillan.

Keppel, G., & Wickens, T. D. (2004). *Design and analysis: A researcher's handbook*. East Rutherford, NJ: Prentice Hall.

Winer, B. J., Brown, D. R., & Michaels, K. M. (1991). *Statistical principles in experimental design* (3rd ed.). New York: Macmillan.

The classic single-treatment-variable experiment aims at holding constant all elements of the experimental situation except the treatment variable. This is the aim of the experiments described in Chapter 12 and the two quasi-experimental designs described in this chapter. In most educational situations, however, the experimental treatment cannot realistically be considered in isolation from other factors. For example, a professional development program for administrators might not be effective for everyone. There may be reason to believe that its effectiveness depends upon whether an educator is fairly new to administration or highly experienced. Factorial experiments make it possible to examine this possibility.

A **factorial experiment** is an experiment in which the researcher determines the effect of two or more independent treatment variables (i.e., factors)—both singly and in interaction with each other—on a dependent variable. The effect of each independent variable on the dependent variable is called a **main effect.** The interaction of the effect of two or more independent variables on the dependent variable is called an **interaction effect.**

Two-Factor Experiments

The simplest type of factorial experiment involves a 2×2 design. The expression 2×2 means that two variations of one factor (A1 and A2) and two variations of another factor (Bl and B2) are manipulated at the same time. This factorial design requires the formation of four treatment groups, with each group receiving a different combination of the two factors: A_1B_1, A_1B_2, A_2B_1, and A_2B_2. Research participants should be randomly assigned to the four treatment groups. If random assignment procedures are not used, the design is a quasi-experiment. The data resulting from a factorial quasi-experiment are very difficult to interpret, because of the difficulty in disentangling main effects and interaction effects from possible initial differences among participants in the different treatment groups.

Example of a Two-Factor Experiment

An example of a two-factor experiment is a study of evaluative threat during instruction by Dawson Hancock.[2] In reviewing the research literature, he found that although evaluation of learning generally increases student achievement, certain evaluation practices—such as instructor emphasis on competition for grades, strictness of rule enforcement, and severity of punishment for rule infractions—have a negative effect on student achievement. Hancock also found evidence that the evaluative threat is particularly debilitating for students with the attribute of high test anxiety. The purpose of his study was to replicate and extend these previous research findings:

> In this study, I sought to replicate previous findings regarding the impact of the learner characteristic, test anxiety, and of the classroom variable, threat of evaluation, on achievement by postsecondary students. More important, because most ATI research has focused on the effects of the individual and situational variables on student achievement, I expanded this research by examining the influence of the variables on postsecondary students' motivation to learn.[3]

You will note that Dawson characterized this line of inquiry as ATI (attribute-treatment-interaction) research, a type of factorial experimentation that we consider later in this chapter.

---

2. Hancock, D. R. (2001). Effects of test anxiety and evaluative threat on students' achievement and motivation. *Journal of Educational Research, 94*, 284–290.
3. Ibid., p. 285.

Hancock used a standardized instrument, the Test Anxiety Inventory, to measure the test anxiety of 61 graduate students enrolled in a research methods course. Students whose scores were above the median were classified as high in test anxiety, and students whose scores were below the median were classified as low in test anxiety. The course professor taught two sections of the course, one with a high level of evaluative threat and the other with a low level of evaluative threat. In the high-evaluative-threat condition, the professor created (1) a climate of competition by such means as having the class break into groups to compete with one another and (2) strict rule enforcement and severe punishment for rule infraction (e.g., lowering a student's grade for getting homework in late).

Approximately equal numbers of high and low test-anxious students were assigned to each course section. Thus, the experiment involved a 2 × 2 factorial design: evaluative threat (high vs. low) and test anxiety (high vs. low).

Statistical analysis The first step in analyzing the results of a factorial experiment is to compute descriptive statistics for each group that represents a particular combination of factors. The mean and standard deviation of the achievement scores of students in each cell of the factorial design for the experiment on evaluative threat are shown in Table 13.2. (Achievement was measured by a professor-made, criterion-referenced test administered after 12 lessons, which marked the end of the experiment.) In addition to these descriptive statistics, Table 13.2 shows the overall column and row means. For example, we see that the mean achievement test score for low-test-anxiety students, ignoring the effect of level of evaluation threat, is 91.77.

The next step in analyzing the results of a factorial experiment is to do an analysis of variance (ANOVA), analysis of covariance (ANCOVA), or multiple regression analysis to determine whether the difference between mean scores within each factor and the interaction between the factors are statistically significant. The main effect for the factor of test anxiety was not statistically significant in the analysis of variance (ANOVA); in other words, the mean achievement score of the high test-anxious group (90.00) did not differ significantly from the mean achievement score of the low test-anxious group (91.77). The main effect for the factor of evaluative threat, however, was statistically significant: The mean

TABLE 13.2

Descriptive Statistics for an Experiment on Evaluative Threat and Test Anxiety

| | Threat of evaluation | | | | | |
| | Low | | High | | Overall | |
Treatment group	*M*	*SD*	*M*	*SD*	*M*	*SD*
Achievement						
Low test anxiety	91.93	2.52	91.60	3.67	91.77	3.09
High test anxiety	92.20	3.95	87.94	3.86	90.00	4.40
Overall	92.07	3.26	89.71	4.14	90.87	3.89

Source: Adapted from Table 1 on p. 287 in: Hancock, D. R. (2001). Effects of test anxiety and evaluative threat on students' achievement and motivation. *Journal of Educational Research, 94,* 284–290. Reprinted with permission from the Helen Dwight Reid Educational Foundation. Published by Heldref Publications, 1319 Eighteenth St., NW, Washington, DC 20036-1802.

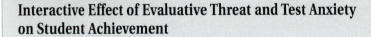

FIGURE 13.1

Interactive Effect of Evaluative Threat and Test Anxiety on Student Achievement

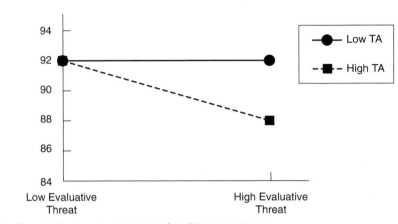

Note: The vertical axis represents scores on the achievement posttest.

Source: Adapted from Figure 1 on p. 288 in Hancock, D. F. R. (2001). Effects of test anxiety and evaluative threat on students' achievement and motivation. *Journal of Educational Research, 94,* 284–290. Reprinted with permission from the Helen Dwight Reid Educational Foundation. Published by Heldref Publications, 1319 Eighteenth St., NW, Washington, DC 20036-1802. Copyright © 2001.

achievement-test score of students in the high-threat condition (89.71) was significantly lower than the mean score of students in the low-threat condition (92.07).

In addition, the ANOVA yielded a statistically significant interaction between the two factors of evaluative threat and test anxiety. The interaction effect is illustrated in Figure 13.1. Students with low test anxiety achieved equally well under either high evaluative threat or low evaluative threat. However, students with high test anxiety suffered a decrement in achievement if they experienced high evaluative threat. They achieved just as well as low-test-anxious students, though, if they experienced low evaluative threat.

The dependent variable of learning motivation was measured by an instrument based on expectancy theory, which specifies learning motivation as a function of the extent to which particular learning outcomes are valued and one's perception that one can master the learning outcome. Hancock obtained findings on this dependent variable similar to those for the dependent variable of academic achievement. Students with high and low test anxiety did not differ in their motivation to learn, and motivation to learn was lower for students in the high-evaluative-threat condition than for students in the low-evaluative-threat condition. However, there was a statistically significant interaction effect: If students learned the course material under conditions of low evaluative threat, their motivation to learn was not affected by their level of test anxiety; in contrast, if they learned the course material under conditions of high evaluative threat, students with high test anxiety, but not students with low test anxiety, suffered a decrement in motivation to learn.

These findings are much more informative than the findings that would be obtained in a simple experimental comparison of levels of evaluative threat during instruction. Therefore, we recommend that if you plan to do an experiment to test the effects of an educational practice, you consider whether the practice will have a systematic differential effect for certain types of individuals.

Solomon Four-Group Design

The **Solomon four-group design** is a special case of a factorial design. It is used to achieve three purposes: (1) to assess the effect of the experimental treatment relative to the control treatment, (2) to determine the presence of pretest sensitization, and (3) to assess the interaction between pretest and treatment conditions.[4]

Example of a Solomon Four-Group Experiment

The Solomon four-group design was used in an experiment by Rosaland Edwards.[5] The main purpose of the experiment was to determine the effect of performance standards on motor skill development in elementary school children. Edwards hypothesized that "an individual with a difficult, specific standard or goal, but one that is attainable, will have a higher level of performance than an individual with no standards or with an easy, non-specific goal.[6]

The experiment involved eight intact fourth-grade and fifth-grade classes, which were assigned to the four groups (two classes per group) of the Solomon design. Students in all groups were taught the motor skill of making a hockey flip shot. This skill involves using a hockey stick to shoot a floor hockey ball through a target 0.31 meters square, 25 centimeters from the floor, and located 1.86 meters from the shooting line. All students participated in a total of six two-minute sessions distributed evenly over two days.

The students in the two experimental treatment groups (groups 1 and 3) were given a performance standard to attain by their teacher. This standard was to make two more successful shots per session than they had averaged the previous day. Based on pilot study results, this standard was considered difficult but attainable. The two control groups (groups 2 and 4) participated in similar practice sessions, but without explicit performance standards.

The pretest consisted of having each student take 45 shots at the target. The student received two points for hitting the hockey ball through the target hole, one point if the hockey ball traveled in the air and hit the target, and zero points otherwise. The pretest score was the total points accumulated in 45 attempts.

Edwards was concerned that the pretest might function as a treatment in its own right. Therefore, for the two experimental groups, one (group 1) received a pretest and the other (group 3) did not. Similarly, for the two control groups, one (group 2) received a pretest and the other (group 4) did not. The inclusion of a pretest factor in the experimental design allowed Edwards to test the effects of the pretest on measures of the dependent variables.

Two dependent variables were measured. First, the behavior of the students during the practice sessions in the instructional phase of the experiment was assessed. The primary measure of student behavior was the total number of shots (called trials) each student took at the target during the six two-minute practice sessions. The other dependent variable, flip-shot skill, was measured by a posttest that was identical in form and scoring to the pretest.

Statistical analysis The Solomon four-group experiment can be viewed as a 2×2 factorial design. The two factors are pretest (present or absent) and treatment (performance

Touchstone in Research

Braver, M. C. W., & Braver, S. L. (1988). Statistical treatment of the Solomon Four-Group Design: A meta-analytic approach. *Psychological Bulletin, 104*(1), 150–154.

---

4. You will recall from the preceding chapter that pretest sensitization is a possible threat to the ecological validity of an experiment. Different results might occur if a pretest is administered to the experimental and control groups than if a pretest is not administered.
5. Edwards, R. (1988). The effects of performance standards on behavior patterns and motor skill achievement in children. *Journal of Teaching in Physical Education, 7*, 90–102.
6. Ibid., p. 90.

TABLE 13.3

Analysis of Variance Results for Solomon Four-Group Experiment on Motor Skill Development

Source	Posttest Scores F	Trials F
Treatment (T)	25.19*	13.51*
Pretest (P)	___ a	___ a
T × P interaction	___ a	18.14*

a The F values were not included in the report, only the fact that they were not statistically significant.
*p < .05

Source: Adapted from text on pp. 95–96 in: Edwards, R. (1988). The effects of performance standards on behavior patterns and motor skill achievement in children. Journal of Teaching in Physical Education, 7, 90–102.

standards present or absent). In the experiment we have been considering, the researcher first did a multivariate analysis of variance (MANOVA) on the two dependent measures—practice trials and posttest score—considered together. Then she did a separate, or univariate, ANOVA for each dependent measure.

The results of the two ANOVAs are shown in Table 13.3. The only factor with a statistically significant effect on students' posttest scores was the treatment variable (standards present or absent). Students receiving performance standards earned a significantly higher mean score ($M = 15.58$) than students not receiving performance standards ($M = 12.58$).

Two conditions had a statistically significant effect on the number of trial shots that students took during the practice sessions. First, students given performance standards had significantly more trials ($M = 70$) than students not given performance standards ($M = 54$). Second, a significant interaction was found between the pretest and the treatment variable. This interaction is illustrated in Figure 13.2. We see that the pretest had a modest effect on the control group: Pretested students had about 10 more trials on average (i.e., took 10 more hockey shots) than did nonpretested students. The pretest, however, had a dramatic effect on the treatment group: Pretested students had about 30 fewer trials on average than did nonpretested students.

To understand this effect, consider the fact that the treatment group with a pretest had both a performance standard and a pretest experience to guide their behavior. Evidently, the pretest experience had more of an effect, because their trial frequency was more similar to the control group that had a pretest than it was to the other treatment group, which also had a performance standard but no pretest experience. Edwards cautioned other researchers to be careful about using pretests in studies of motor skill development because they can mask the effects of instruction.

If a pretest effect seems likely, you can use either a posttest-only control-group design (see Chapter 12) or a Solomon four-group design. The latter is the more powerful experimental design, but it requires a rather large sample and much researcher effort. The effort is justified, however, if there is a high probability that pretesting will have an effect on the experimental treatment and you wish to measure this effect.

FIGURE 13.2

Plot of Effect of Interaction between Pretest and Treatment on Number of Trials in Motor Skills Experiment

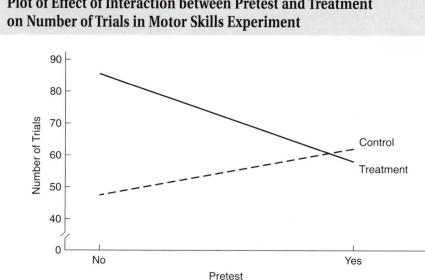

Source: Adapted from Figure 1 on p. 96 in: Edwards, R. (1988). The effects of performance standards on behavior patterns and motor skill achievement in children. *Journal of Teaching in Physical Education, 7*(2), 90–102. Copyright © 1988 by Human Kinetics Publishers, Inc. Adapted with permission from Human Kinetics (Champaign, IL).

Variations in Factorial Experiments

The design and analysis of factorial experiments is a complicated matter. You can choose from many factorial designs. The choice of a design and method of statistical analysis depends on various conditions:

1. The number of independent variables (i.e., factors)
2. Whether the independent variables differ in manipulability
3. Whether the factors are fixed or random
4. Whether research participants receive repeated measures of the same variable
5. Whether there are unequal numbers of research participants in each treatment group
6. The scale and distribution properties of scores on the dependent variables
7. The need for a covariate to compensate for initial differences between treatment groups
8. Whether each research participant is assigned to more than one treatment condition

Several of these variations are discussed below.

Three-Factor Experiments

A factorial experiment is not necessarily limited to the manipulation of two factors. Reports of experiments involving three factors can be found in research journals. Experiments involving more than three factors can be designed, but developing all the treatment variations would be difficult and a large sample would be required for the data analyses to have adequate statistical power. (Statistical power is explained in Chapter 5.)

To illustrate a three-factor experiment, we will create a hypothetical example based on Hancock's study of evaluative threat and test anxiety, which involved a two-factor experiment. Suppose we theorize that lower-division college students (i.e., freshmen and sophomores) are more susceptible to evaluative threat and test anxiety than upper-division college students (i.e., juniors and seniors). Our reasoning is that upper-division students have had more time than lower-division students to learn how to cope effectively with their test anxiety and with professors who have an intimidating instructional style.

If this is true, we would predict the same results as those found by Hancock, but only for lower-division students. The ANOVA would yield seven F values: (1) the main effect for the factor of evaluative threat (ET); (2) the main effect for the factor of test anxiety (TA); (3) the main effect for the factor of college status (CS); (4) the ET $\times$ TA interaction; (5) the ET $\times$ CS interaction; (6) the TA $\times$ CS interaction; and (7) the ET $\times$ TA $\times$ CS interaction. The critical test of our prediction would be the seventh F value, that for the ET $\times$ TA $\times$ CS effect. We would expect to find that lower-division students with high test anxiety suffer an achievement-test decrement under conditions of high evaluative threat, but upper-division students would not suffer this decrement irrespective of their test-anxiety level, nor would lower-division students with low test anxiety. Furthermore, we would expect that all groups (high- and low-test anxiety, lower and upper division) would perform about the same under conditions of low evaluative threat.

It is reasonable to examine three-way interactions in three-factor experiments if they are used to test theoretical predictions. Otherwise, they are difficult to interpret. The main effects and two-way interactions are simpler to comprehend and typically easier to interpret.

Manipulability of Independent Variables

Touchstone in Research

Cronbach, L. J., & Snow, R. E. (1981). *Aptitudes and instructional methods: A handbook for research on interactions.* New York: Irvington.

The key feature of an experiment is that a particular variable is subjected to *manipulation*. In other words, there is an intervention of some sort (e.g., use of a particular curriculum or instructional method) by the researchers or by individuals whom they have trained. In the case of the factorial experiment that we presented above, high and low evaluative threat constituted the intervention. The instructor deliberately varied his instructional behavior to create these two conditions.

The other factor in this experiment was students' test anxiety. This variable was not manipulated, meaning that the researcher did not employ an intervention that elevated some students' test anxiety and lowered other students' test anxiety. Rather, he measured students' existing level of test anxiety and used their scores on the measure to form them into high- and low-test-anxiety groups.

In fact, factors in an experiment (also called independent variables) can vary in manipulability.

Campbell and Stanley developed a useful classification of the types of independent variables that might appear in an educational experiment along this dimension of manipulability, from high to low:

1. Manipulated variables, such as teaching method, assignable at will by the experimenter.
2. Potentially manipulable aspects, such as school subject studied, that the experimenter might assign in some random way to the individuals being studied, but rarely does.
3. Relatively fixed aspects of the environment, such as school attended or family's socioeconomic level, not under the direct control of the experimenter but serving as explicit bases for stratification in the experiment.

4. Organismic characteristics of individuals, such as age, height, weight, and sex.
5. Response characteristics of individuals, such as scores on various tests.[7]

Campbell and Stanley observed that the experimenter's primary interest is usually in manipulating class 1 variables. Variables in classes 3, 4, and 5 are used to group research participants in order to determine how generalizable the effects of manipulated variables are. For example, suppose your primary independent variable is a new teaching method. In addition, you are interested in grouping students by intelligence level (a class 5 variable, because intelligence usually is determined by a test score) in order to determine whether the teaching method is effective for students of all intelligence levels or just for students of a particular intelligence level. This type of experimental design sometimes is called aptitude-treatment interaction (ATI) research.

Aptitude-treatment interaction research, also called *ATI research,* is research designed to determine whether the effects of different instructional methods are influenced by the cognitive or personality characteristics of learners. It does not assume that one instructional method is better than another, nor that students with certain characteristics are better learners than others. Instead, ATI research is based on the assumption that these two factors (instructional method and learner characteristics) can interact in ways that affect learning outcomes. In ATI research, these interactions are revealed by designing factorial experiments similar to the experiment on evaluative threat that we described above.

An ATI experiment usually has two independent variables. The first independent variable might be teaching method, type of curriculum material, learning environment, or a similar instructional variable. The other independent variable is a student characteristic, such as an aptitude, personality dimension, level of academic achievement, or learning style.

The initial focus of ATI research was on *aptitudes,* hence the label "aptitude-treatment interaction." Subsequently, the label "attribute-treatment interaction" was introduced, to indicate that a wide range of learner characteristics—not just aptitudes—can interact with instructional methods.[8] Attribute variables correspond to the last two types of independent variables (classes 4 and 5) in Campbell and Stanley's classification described above: organismic characteristics and response characteristics.

Fixed and Random Factors

The third condition listed at the start of this section—whether the factors are considered fixed or random—requires some explanation. A **fixed factor** is an independent variable whose values will not be generalized beyond the experiment. Some fixed factors exhaust all possible values of the variable, for example, school graduation status. If this is a factor in the experiment, there are two values (also called *levels*): graduate and non-graduate. There is no other graduation status to which generalizations can be made.

Other factors are not exhaustive, but are considered so for purposes of the experiment. For example, the researcher might have a factor, marital status, with two values: married or not married. Generalizations from the research findings will only be made to individuals at those two levels, even though additional values of marital status can be differentiated (e.g., engaged to be married, once-married and divorced, twice-married and divorced). The treatment variable is typically a fixed factor, because researchers usually do not wish to generalize beyond the intervention, or interventions, being studied.

---

7. Campbell & Stanley, *Experimental and quasi-experimental designs*, p. 200.
8. The significance of this broader label is explained in: Tobias, S. (1976). Achievement-treatment interactions. *Review of Educational Research, 46,* 61–74.

A **random factor** is an independent variable whose values will be generalized beyond the experiment. For example, suppose the treatment variable is a new teaching method and the researcher wishes to know whether different teachers obtain different outcomes when using it. The researcher might select five teachers to use the method with the intent of having this sample represent a population of teachers. In this case, each teacher can be incorporated into the experimental design as a value of a *teacher* factor. The result is a 2 × 5 design: The first factor is fixed and has two levels (treatment group versus control group), and the second factor is random and has five levels (teacher 1, teacher 2, teacher 3, teacher 4, teacher 5).

The distinction between fixed and random factors is important, because it affects the statistical techniques used to analyze data resulting from the experiment.

Assignment of Participants to Multiple Treatments

The eighth condition in the list of variations in factorial experiments involves assigning each research participant to more than one treatment condition. For example, suppose we are interested in whether students' on-task behavior in a classroom is affected by 30-second "stretch breaks." Specifically, we wish to know whether no stretch break, one stretch break, two stretch breaks, or three stretch breaks during a 50-minute class period have differential effects on their on-task behavior. One way to conduct the experiment would be to randomly assign 40 classes of students to these four treatment conditions. Another approach would be to select a much smaller number of classes (let's say, 10 to 15) and have them experience each treatment condition on different days.

The advantage of assigning participants to several treatments is that the experiment can be done with a smaller sample. Thus, recruitment of participants is easier, and the costs of conducting the experiment might be reduced. Another advantage is that statistical analysis of the data is more sensitive because each participant is "matched" with himself across treatments.

If individuals participate in more than one treatment, the effect of a treatment can become confounded with its order of administration relative to the other treatments. An **order effect** is the influence that the placement of a treatment in the administration of several treatments has on a dependent variable. For example, an order effect can occur if research participants become fatigued by participating in several treatments. They may do less well on the posttest associated with the last-administered treatment, not because this treatment is less effective, but because they are fatigued from responding to the demands of the previously administered treatments.

Counterbalanced designs are used to avoid the problems of interpretation due to order effects. In a **counterbalanced experiment,** each participant is administered several treatments, but the order of administering the treatments is varied across participants to eliminate the possible confounding of order effects with treatment effects.

To summarize, there are many factorial designs, each suited to a different purpose. It is useless to develop a research hypothesis and to carefully execute the experiment unless you first choose the proper factorial design. If you are planning a factorial experiment, we advise you to read a textbook on experimental design and to consult an expert in the area of factorial design and statistical analysis.

Single-Case Designs

A **single-case experiment,** sometimes called a *single-subject experiment* or a *time-series experiment,* is one that involves the intense study of one individual, or of more than one individual treated as a single group. As Thomas Kratochwill explains, single-case designs "involve the intense analysis of behavior in single organisms.[9] This type of experiment is illustrated in Table 12.5, where it is called a *time-series design*.

The single-case experiment is well suited to research on behavior modification. **Behavior modification** is a specialization within psychology that seeks to change the behavior of individuals by applying experimentally validated techniques such as social and token reinforcement, fading, desensitization, and discrimination training.[10] As an educational strategy, behavior modification is used extensively in such applications as classroom management, skill development, and training of individuals with disabilities. It also is employed widely in counseling, psychotherapy, institutional caretaking, and in drug research. Reports of single-case experiments of interest to educators appear in various journals, especially the *Journal of Applied Behavior Analysis*.

Single-case experiments should not be equated with the case-study method of investigation (see Chapter 14). Both focus on one case, yet they differ greatly in design and purpose. Single-case designs use several procedures to achieve experimental control as conceptualized within the quantitative research tradition: checks on the reliability of the experimenter's observations of the research participant's behavior, frequent observations of the behaviors targeted for change, description of the treatment in sufficient detail to permit replication, and replication of treatment effects within the experiment. In contrast, case studies explore a much broader treatment (typically, a large-scale program), are carried out in a field setting, and rely heavily on qualitative data.

Some researchers consider the single-case experiment to be a watered-down, easier version of one of the group designs presented earlier in this chapter and in Chapter 12. This is not true. Researchers who work with single-case designs are as concerned with problems of internal validity and external validity as researchers who do control-group experiments. Most single-case designs are rigorous and time-consuming, and they may involve as much data collection as a design involving experimental and control groups.

Example of a Single-Case Experiment

The methods used in a single-case experiment are illustrated in a study conducted by Michelle Duda, Glen Dunlap, Lise Fox, Rochelle Lentini, and Shelley Clarke.[11] The purpose of the experiment was to evaluate the effectiveness of a method known as *positive behavior support* when used to help young children in community preschools.

The initial step in positive behavior support is functional assessment, which involves the collection of data to understand the functions served by an individual's behavior (e.g., a child might engage in crying behavior to get an adult's attention) and the environmental variables that maintain this behavior. The second step in positive behavior support is to develop interventions that target the person's behavior to change it in a desirable direction.

Duda and colleagues reviewed the literature on positive behavior support and found it to be effective with a variety of populations and in a variety of settings. However, they found a lack of research on positive behavior support with young children in community preschools, and therefore they conducted the experiment described here.

Touchstone in Research

Franklin, R. D., Allison, D. B., & Gorman, B. S. (Eds.). (1997). *Design and analysis of single-case research*. Mahwah, NJ: Erlbaum.

Kennedy, C. H. (2005). *Single-case designs for educational research*. Boston: Pearson.

Kratochwill, T. R., & Levin, J. R. (Eds.). (1992). *Single-case research design and analysis*. Mahwah, NJ: Erlbaum.

---

9. Kratochwill, T. R. (1992). Single-case research design and analysis: An overview. In T. R. Kratochwill & J. R. Levin (Eds.), *Single-case research design and analysis* (pp. 1–14). Mahwah, NJ: Erlbaum. Quote appears on p. 11.
10. There are many publications on the educational applications of behavior-modification techniques, including Wielkiewicz, R. J. (1986). *Behavior management in the schools: Principles and procedures* (2nd ed.). Boston: Allyn & Bacon.
11. Duda, M. A., Dunlap, G., Fox, L., Lentini, R., & Clarke, S. (2004). An experimental evaluation of positive behavior support in a community preschool program. *Topics in Early Childhood Special Education, 24*(3), 143–155.

The intervention was tried with two children, one of whom was Vanessa, a 3-year-old girl with Down syndrome. Vanessa exhibited various problem behaviors, including aggressiveness when she did not get her way, off-task behavior, disruption of other children, and mouthing of objects. The researchers developed an intervention based on four hypotheses derived from a functional assessment of Vanessa's behavior:

1. The typical function of Vanessa's behavior was to obtain attention.
2. When provided with opportunities to be successful and obtain positive feedback (e.g., touch, back rub, "high five"), Vanessa's rate of problem behavior would decrease.
3. When provided with a high rate of predictability and clear expectations (e.g., beginning and end of a task), Vanessa's problem behavior would decrease.
4. Vanessa's engagement would be enhanced if she were to sit at the curve of a horseshoe seating arrangement and next to an adult who could provide prompting and redirection.[12]

The effectiveness of the intervention was determined by collecting observational data on Vanessa's behavior during two activities: opening circle and planning. Opening circle started the day and included a group activity such as sharing a book or singing a song. Planning followed the opening circle and consisted of a brief physical activity, such as dancing or playing with puppets. These activities were videotaped and scored at 10-second intervals for the occurrence of engagement (appropriate behavior) and problem behavior (turning away from the activity, disruption of others, engagement in nonrelevant activities, mouthing of objects, leaving the designated area).

Figure 13.3 presents graphs showing the results of the single-case experiment with Vanessa. The x-axis marks each class session, and the y-axis shows the two dependent variables: the percentage of 10-second intervals during which Vanessa was observed to be appropriately engaged and the percentage of 10-second intervals during which she exhibited problem behaviors. The top graph is for observations during opening circle, and the bottom graph is for the planning period.

Examining the top graph, we see the percentages of engagement and problem behavior for six sessions with no intervention. This phase of the single-case experiment is called a **baseline** because it shows the child's behavior prior to the experimental treatment. The baseline is similar in purpose to a pretest in the experimental designs presented in Chapter 12 and the first part of this chapter.

Sessions 7 through 11 in the top graph of Figure 13.3 mark the implementation of the experimental treatment (positive behavior support). Inspection of the graph shows that Vanessa's engagement rate improves dramatically over baseline and that her problem behavior decreases just as dramatically. These data are similar to a posttest in the experimental designs presented in Chapter 12 and the first part of this chapter.

In the next baseline period (sessions 12 and 13), the experimental treatment was stopped. The act of withdrawing a treatment after a research participant has become accustomed to it sometimes is called **extinction** by behavioral researchers.

The final phase of the experiment involved reintroduction of the experimental treatment. As in the first treatment phase, Vanessa's task engagement was high, and the incidence of problem behaviors was low. These data are similar to a follow-up posttest in group experimental designs.

The bottom graph in Figure 13.3 shows a similar pattern of results during the baseline and treatment phases of the planning part of the observed preschool sessions. Also, highly

12. Ibid., pp. 145–146.

FIGURE 13.3

Percentages of Observed Intervals of Engagement and Problem Behavior in a Single-Case Experiment on Positive Behavior Support

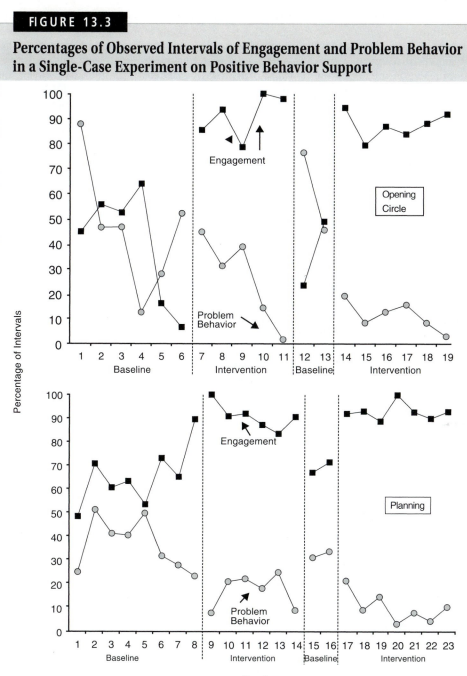

Source: Adapted from Figure 1 on p. 150 in: Duda, M. A., Dunlap, G., Fox, L., Lentini, R., & Clarke, S. (2004). An experimental evaluation of positive behavior support in a community preschool program. *Topics in Early Childhood Special Education, 24*(3), 143–155. Copyright © 2004 by PRO-ED, Inc. Adapted with permission from PRO-ED, Inc.

similar results were obtained for the other child, who constituted a separate case in the experiment.

A single-case experiment typically yields the type of data graphed in Figure 13.3. The researcher must examine the data and decide whether they indicate that the treatment had an effect on the dependent variable. This decision usually is made in two ways. One approach is simply to make a visual examination of the form of the graphed data. The following statement about Figure 13.3 by Duda and colleagues illustrates this approach:

> Data illustrating Vanessa's behavior during the opening circle activities (top graph . . .) indicate a higher rate of engagement and lower rates of problem behaviors during the two intervention conditions relative to the two baseline phases. A similar pattern was observed during the planning activities (bottom graph). In other words, both dependent variables showed systematic changes that were associated with the introduction and withdrawal of the assessment-based intervention.[13]

The other approach to determining a treatment effect is to organize the data so that they can be analyzed using a conventional test of statistical significance. For example, a t test can be employed to compare the pooled mean of the two baseline phases and the pooled mean of the two treatment phases.

An experiment involving baseline-treatment-extinction-treatment phases is one of many single-case designs. In the following sections we describe general features of single-case design, steps to follow in using some of the more common designs, and statistical techniques for analyzing single-case data.

General Design Considerations

Single-case experiments should be designed to have high internal validity. As is true of group designs, the internal validity of a single-case design is a function of the researcher's ability to rule out factors other than the treatment variable as possible causes of changes in the dependent variable. In control-group experiments, internal validity is achieved primarily by random assignment of research participants to the experimental-treatment and control conditions. Because $N = 1$ in single-case research, random assignment and control groups are not possible. Internal validity is achieved by other design techniques, which are described below. These techniques are not exclusive to single-case designs, but are especially important to them.

Reliable Observation

Single-case designs typically require many observations of behavior. If the observations are unreliable, they will obscure treatment effects. Therefore, certain procedures should be followed in making observations, particularly careful training of observers, operational definition of the behaviors to be observed, periodic checks of observer reliability, and control of observer bias. When appropriate, you can consider measurement of behavioral products (e.g., the number of problems solved in a school assignment) as a substitute for observation of behavior. These procedures are discussed in the content-analysis section in Chapter 9 and in books about single-case design.

The simplest procedure is to target one or two behaviors for repeated observation throughout the experiment. For example, the child's rate of engagement and problem behaviors were the only behaviors that were observed in the experiment on positive behavior support. It is possible to monitor additional behaviors, but observational procedures become increasingly complicated as each new behavior is added to the research design.

13. Ibid., p. 418.

Repeated Measurement

In the typical group experimental design, data are collected at two points in time: before (pretest) and after (posttest) the experimental treatment. Single-case designs require many more measurements, because the behavior of an individual can vary greatly even within short time intervals. Consider the fact that the experiment on positive behavior support had four phases: baseline, treatment, second baseline, and second treatment. If the child's engagement and problem behaviors were only once in each phase, it would be impossible to interpret whether variations in these behaviors were a function of the treatment variable or of other naturally occurring events. The use of frequent measurements provides a clearer, more reliable description of how the child's behavior naturally varies and how it varies in response to the treatment condition. Furthermore, statistical significance tests of single-case data are more powerful if many measurements of the dependent variable are available.

Because of the need for repeated measurements in a single-case design, it is important to standardize the measurement procedure. Preferably, each measurement occasion would involve the same observers, the same instructions to the research participant, and the same environmental conditions. Otherwise, treatment effects are likely to be contaminated with measurement effects.

Description of Experimental Conditions

The researcher should provide a precise description of each experimental condition that would be important if one wished to replicate the experiment. Some single-case designs require re-introduction of the baseline and the treatment variable. For example, the baseline and treatment conditions appeared twice in the experiment on positive behavior support. If the conditions involving the baseline or the treatment variable are not specified precisely, they will be difficult to replicate within the experiment. As a consequence, the internal validity of the experiment is threatened. Furthermore, imprecise specification makes it difficult for other researchers to replicate the experiment, thus threatening the external validity of the experiment.

Baseline and Treatment Stability

The baseline in single-case designs is the natural frequency of the target behavior before introduction of the experimental variable. If the occurrence of the target behavior did not vary at all during the period of observation, it would be easy to assess the effect of the treatment variable. Yet most behaviors vary. If the variation is too great, you will have difficulty in separating treatment effects from naturally occurring changes in the research participant's behavior.

To counter the effects of natural fluctuations, you can set a standard for determining when a baseline has stabilized, for example, no more than a 5 percent range of variation from the mean over a period of 10 observations. There are occasions, though, when this type of standard is inappropriate. For example, suppose you plan to use an experimental intervention with a person whose behavior is systematically worsening or improving. If the person's behavior is systematically improving during the baseline period, you are faced with a difficult problem. If the person continues to improve during the treatment phase, one could argue that the continued improvement was due to some condition that existed during the baseline period rather than to a treatment effect. In this situation you should consider withholding the treatment variable until baseline improvement has peaked and then stabilized.

The same need for stability applies to the treatment phase of a single-case design. Suppose that you planned four treatment sessions. No effects appear after the first three sessions, but improvement is apparent after the fourth session. Should you discontinue treatment, as planned? It probably is advisable in this situation to continue treatment until a stable, interpretable pattern of treatment effects has emerged.

Length of Baseline and Treatment Phases

As a general rule, there should be approximately the same length of time and number of measurements in each phase of a single-case design. Otherwise, the imbalance complicates the statistical analysis and interpretation of treatment effects. In some situations, however, this rule of equal phases conflicts with the need to maintain baseline or treatment conditions until a stable pattern of measurements has emerged. You also may need to maintain baseline or treatment conditions longer than intended because of institutional or ethical factors. One way to overcome this problem is to do several pilot studies to explore baseline and treatment conditions in the setting that interests you. The knowledge that you acquire can be used to design a more rigorous experiment in which baseline and treatment conditions are equalized in duration and number of measurements.

A-B-A Designs

A-B-A designs are used in single-case or single-group experiments having one treatment. The A stands for the baseline condition, and the B stands for the treatment. We discuss two of these designs below. There are various other A-B-A designs, including several for investigating interaction effects involving treatments.

A-B Design

The **A-B design** is the simplest of the single-case designs. The researcher begins by selecting a participant for the experiment, one or more target behaviors, measures of the target behaviors, and an experimental treatment. Then the target behavior is measured repeatedly during the baseline period (A). Finally, the experimental treatment (B) is administered while the researcher continues to measure the target behavior.

The A-B design is low in internal validity.[14] If the difference between the means of the A measurements and the B measurements is statistically significant, we can conclude that a reliable change occurred from the baseline phase to the treatment phase. Attributing the change to a treatment effect is difficult, however, because the influence of other factors cannot be ruled out. These factors might be other events occurring during the treatment phase, or the effects of testing during the baseline period. The A-B design should be used only when no suitable alternative is available, or when the researcher intends it as a pilot study to be followed by an experiment using a more rigorous design.

A-B-A and A-B-A-B Designs

The **A-B-A design** follows the same steps as the A-B design, except that a second baseline condition is added. The second baseline typically involves *withdrawal* of the treatment, as in the experiment on positive behavior supports. You can also bring about *reversal* of the treatment in the second baseline condition. For example, in the experiment on positive behavior supports, the researcher might reduce the rate of task predictability and create deliberately vague expectations.

The A-B-A design has high internal validity. If the target behavior changes as expected in each phase of the experiment, one can conclude that the changes were due to the effect of the treatment variable. However, one difficulty with this design is that the experiment

---

14. The uses and internal validity problems of the A-B design are discussed in: Campbell, D. T. (1969). Reforms as experiments. *American Psychologist, 24,* 409–429.

ends on a negative note, because the treatment (presumably positive in nature) is withdrawn or reversed. This condition may be ethically unacceptable to the researcher and to others involved in the experiment.

The A-B-A-B design overcomes the ethical issue of ending on a negative note that may arise with the A-B-A experiment. In the **A-B-A-B design,** the experiment concludes after reintroduction of the treatment variable (B). The experiment on positive behavior support described above exemplifies this design. Each of the four phases of the A-B-A-B design were present: initial period of baseline observation, initial introduction of the treatment variable, withdrawal or reversal of the treatment variable (second baseline), and re-introduction of the treatment variable.

A limitation of this design, and of all baseline designs, is that the observed treatment effect is dependent upon the particular baseline conditions included in the experiment. Assuming that a reliable A-B change is found, we can conclude only that the effect will occur reliably for that set of conditions. Therefore, the baseline conditions must be described precisely. This restriction is similar to the pretest sensitization problem in group designs that include a pretest (see the discussion of internal validity in Chapter 12). Reliable treatment effects found in such designs cannot be presumed to be independent of the particular pretest that was used to discover the effects.

Multiple-Baseline Designs

Time-series designs (A-B-A) generally use the natural occurrence of the target behavior as a control condition for assessing treatment effects. In contrast, **multiple-baseline designs** are experiments in which conditions other than the naturally occurring target behavior are used as controls for assessing treatment effects. Administration of these conditions approximates the use of a control group to improve the internal validity of a group experiment.

Multiple-baseline designs generally are used when reinstatement of baseline conditions in an A-B-A type design is not possible. This problem might occur if the researcher is unable to withdraw or reverse the treatment for ethical reasons. Also, it might not be possible to demonstrate a treatment effect using an A-B-A design. That is, the target behavior might not return to the pretreatment baseline rate after the treatment is withdrawn or reversed. If this occurs, we cannot conclude that the treatment had an effect, even though the target behavior changed reliably from the initial baseline phase to the treatment phase. As an alternative, we can use a multiple-baseline design to investigate the effects of the treatment.

Example of a Multiple-Baseline Experiment

In one of the more commonly used multiple-baseline designs, two or more individuals are used to control for extraneous variables in assessing treatment effects. This was the case in an experiment conducted by Randi Sarokoff and Peter Sturmey.[15] The purpose of their experiment was to determine the effectiveness of a training procedure to help special-education teachers acquire skill in a method of teaching children with autism. The method, called *discrete-trial teaching,* has ten components:

> The teacher making eye contact with student for at least 1 s contiguous to delivery of a verbal instruction, giving no verbal instruction until the child showed the readiness response of being still, delivering instructions with clear articulation once and matching the instruction for that program, implementing the predetermined correction procedure within 3 to 5 s of the verbal

15. Sarokoff, R. A., & Sturmey, P. (2004). The effects of behavioral skills training on staff implementation of discrete-trial teaching. *Journal of Applied Behavior Analysis, 37*(4), 535–538.

direction after failure of the student to respond, providing appropriate and immediate reinforcement for correct responses, using behavior-specific praise, recording data following each trial, and placing a 5-s inter-trial interval between trials.[16]

Discrete-trial teaching can be used to teach children with autism such basic skills as matching (e.g., displaying three items and giving the child one corresponding identical item, which the child matches by placing it on the correct item in the three-item display).

The researchers' multiple-baseline design can be understood by examining the data for teacher 1 in Figure 13.4. The x-axis represents the sessions during which the teacher had an opportunity to use discrete-trial teaching. Each session lasted approximately 5 minutes and included 10 opportunities to use discrete-trial teaching. The y-axis represents

FIGURE 13.4

The Percentage of Correct Implementation of the Discrete-Trial Teaching Method in a Single-Case Experiment on Teacher Training

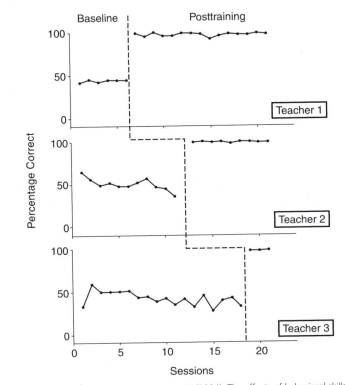

Source: Figure 1 on p. 537 in: Sarokoff, R. A., & Sturmey, P. (2004). The effects of behavioral skills training on staff implementation of discrete-trial teaching. Journal of Applied Behavior Analysis, 37(4), 535–538. Reprinted with permisssion from the Journal of Applied Behavior Analysis and Randi A. Sarokoff.

16. Ibid., p. 536.

the percentage of the 10 components of discrete-trial teaching that the teacher used correctly during the session.

During the baseline period of six sessions, teacher 1 was given a written set of definitions of the components of discrete-trial teaching and instructed to use this method to the best of his or her ability. Inspection of Figure 13.4 shows that teacher 1 consistently used about half of the components of discrete-trial teaching in the baseline sessions. Teacher 1 then participated in the experimental treatment, which involved the experimenter reviewing the definitions, giving feedback on the teacher's baseline performance, providing opportunity for the teacher to practice the components, providing feedback to the teacher after each practice session, and modeling correct performance for the teacher.

Figure 13.4 shows teacher 1's use of the 10 components of discrete-trial teaching for 15 sessions following training. The teacher's performance was consistently near perfect.

It would not make sense to determine whether the experimental treatment was solely responsible for this posttraining effect by reinstating the baseline design, as one would in an A-B-A single-case experiment. Instead, teacher 2 acted as a control for teacher 1 by the researcher extending the number of baseline sessions for teacher 2. Inspection of Figure 13.4 indicates that teacher 2's use of the 10 components of discrete-trial teaching was never much higher than 50 percent and was starting to decline below that level at the same time that teacher 1's performance was nearly perfect following the experimental treatment.

In a similar manner, teacher 2's performance rose to a perfect or near-perfect level following training. To rule out extraneous variables as an explanation for this effect, teacher 3's baseline sessions were extended well into teacher 2's posttraining sessions. The comparison provided a replication for the treatment-baseline effect observed for teachers 1 and 2.

The experiment that we just described used one of various multiple-baseline designs that are available for different situations that arise in single-case experiments. Some of these designs involve the use of multiple target behaviors or multiple stimulus settings to provide baseline control, whereas the design discussed above used multiple research participants to provide baseline control.

Statistical Analysis of Single-Case Data

Many researchers rely exclusively on raw data and a few descriptive statistics for interpreting the results of single-case experiments. Figures 13.3 and 13.4 are typical graphical data plots of single-case data. The abscissa (horizontal line) represents units of time, and the ordinate (vertical line) represents units of the target behavior. Each data point is plotted separately on the graph, and the data points may be connected by lines. Vertical broken lines are used to indicate the transition from one phase to another (e.g., from baseline to treatment).

Using the graphical data plot, you can analyze within each phase the data points for the mean level of the target behavior and the direction of the slope, if any. Also, you can compare adjacent phases for changes in mean level, slope, and level between the last data point for one phase and the first data point for the next phase.

Some researchers also recommend determining the magnitude of a treatment effect by computing the percentage of nonoverlapping data.[17] This percentage is the number of treatment data points that exceed the highest (or lowest, if appropriate) baseline data

Touchstone in Research

Todman, J. B., & Dugard, P. (2001). *Single-case and small*-n *experimental designs: A practical guide to randomization tests.* Mahwah, NJ: Erlbaum.

17. Scruggs, T. E., Mastropieri, M. A., & Casto, G. (1987). The quantitative synthesis of single-subject research: Methodology and validation. *Remedial and Special Education, 8,* 24–33. These researchers also recommend calculating the percentage of nonoverlapping data as a measure of effect size for meta-analyses of single-case experiments. Several articles criticizing this recommendation appear in the same issue of the journal.

FIGURE 13.5

Plots of Identical Data Using Different Ordinal Scales

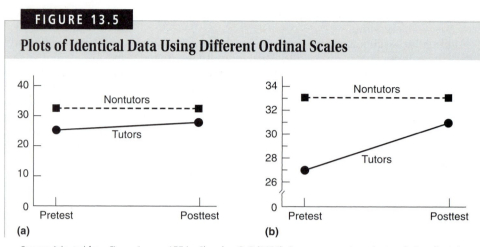

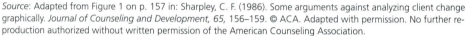

Source: Adapted from Figure 1 on p. 157 in: Sharpley, C. F. (1986). Some arguments against analyzing client change graphically. *Journal of Counseling and Development, 65,* 156–159. © ACA. Adapted with permission. No further reproduction authorized without written permission of the American Counseling Association.

point, divided by the total number of treatment data points. For example, in Figure 13.4, all of the data points for the teachers' treatment phase are higher (the desired direction) than the highest data point in the preceding baseline. Therefore, the percentage of nonoverlapping data is 100 percent.

The use of visual analysis of graphs to interpret treatment effects in single-case experiments has been criticized.[18] One criticism is that the ordinal scale of a graph can be modified to accentuate or mask treatment effects. For example, the same data are plotted in plot a and plot b of Figure 13.5, yet the two graphs give quite different impressions of the magnitude of the treatment effect. Another criticism of visual analysis is that empirical studies have shown low inter-rater reliability in the use of visual analysis to determine whether or how much of a treatment effect occurred.[19]

The alternative to visual analysis is the use of inferential statistics. For example, in the experiment on positive behavior support the researchers could have used a *t* test to compare the pooled mean of the two baseline phases and the pooled mean of the two treatment phases. This use of traditional inferential statistics has been criticized, however.[20] One criticism is that inferential statistics are not appropriate to the logic of the single-case experiment, which involves intensive study of the individual rather than of samples from populations. Another criticism is that inferential statistics involve the assumption that the observations are independent of one another. This assumption is seldom satisfied in

---

18. Sharpley, C. F. (1986). Some arguments against analyzing client change graphically. *Journal of Counseling and Development, 65,* 156–159.
19. DeProspero, A., & Cohen, S. (1979). Inconsistent visual analyses of intrasubject data. *Journal of Applied Behavior Analysis, 12,* 573–579; Jones, R. R., Vaught, R. S., & Weinrott, M. (1978). Time-series analysis in operant research. *Journal of Applied Behavior Analysis, 11,* 277–283.
20. Bass, R. F. (1987). The generality, analysis, and assessment of single-subject data. *Psychology in the Schools, 24,* 97–104.

single-case experiments. The behavior that is observed in any given session probably is dependent on the behavior that occurred in previous sessions. The technical term for this phenomenon is **serial dependency.** Time-series statistics can be used to determine the extent of serial dependency in data from a single-case experiment, plus the presence of a treatment effect. The computations for this statistical technique are complex, however, and many data points are necessary to yield interpretable results.

In summary, researchers can be misled both by visual analysis and by inferential statistics in interpreting data from single-case experiments. Therefore, you need to exercise good judgment in using either or both of these techniques. Good judgment requires both a technical grasp of the techniques and a thorough understanding of relevant theory, previous research findings, and circumstances surrounding the conduct of the experiment. Incorporating replications into the design of the experiment, as in the teacher training experiment described above, also promotes sound interpretations of treatment effects.

External Validity of Single-Case Designs

One of the major criticisms directed at single-case designs is that they have low external validity, that is, the findings cannot be generalized beyond the one case in the experiment. The same critics are likely to look with favor on the traditional group experiment, because they believe that the findings can be generalized from the sample to the population from which it was drawn. Nevertheless, as we observe in Chapter 6, many studies that employ samples—including group experiments—do not involve random selection of the sample from a defined population. Rather, the particular sample is chosen because it is readily accessible, and then the results are generalized through logical inference to a larger population having similar characteristics.

In balance, it appears that both single-case and group experiments can be criticized on similar grounds for limited external validity. The real issue is how to increase the external validity of each type of experiment, rather than rejecting one type in favor of the other. The recommendations for improving the external validity of group experiments discussed earlier in the chapter also apply to single-case experiments.

Other Experimental Designs

We have presented the main designs used in experimental research in this and the preceding chapter. Our presentation, however, is by no means exhaustive. For example, we consider several factorial designs, but there are many others. Also, Campbell and Stanley discuss additional experimental designs that have application to some educational research problems.[21]

In selecting from among the experimental designs that are available, you should try to choose a design that will give the clearest picture of the effect of the experimental treatment, unconfounded by the effect of such variables as history, maturation, and so forth. Another important objective is to select a design that will yield results that can be generalized to other situations in which you are interested. This is not an easy task, especially if you plan to do your experiment in a natural field setting and individuals in this setting seek to place constraints on your preferred design.

---

21. Campbell & Stanley, *Experimental and quasi-experimental designs.*

TABLE 13.4					

Average Gains of Students on Posttests, Classified According to Pretest Standing

Test	Low Group	Low-Middle Group	Middle Group	High-Middle Group	High Group
Critical thinking in social science	6.89	5.48	3.68	4.20	2.26
Science reasoning and understanding	6.26	5.16	2.93	2.04	0.31
Humanities participation inventory	18.00	5.05	4.94	1.39	−2.07
Analysis of reading and writing	5.33	2.89	1.81	1.22	0.25
Critical thinking	6.68	4.65	3.47	2.60	1.59
Inventory of beliefs	9.09	5.31	4.65	3.32	1.01
Problems in human relations	3.19	1.67	1.31	1.51	−0.36

Source: Table 1 on p. 60 in: Diederich, P. B. (1956). Pitfalls in the measurement of gains in achievement. *School Review, 64*, 59–63. Copyright 1956 University of Chicago Press. Reprinted with permission from the University of Chicago Press.

Measurement of Change

Gain Scores

Touchstone in Research

Russell, M. (2000). Summarizing change in test scores: Shortcomings of three common methods. *Practical Assessment, Research & Evaluation, 7*(5). Retrieved October 15, 2005, from http://ericae. net/pare/getvn. asp?v=7&n=5

Basically, all experiments are attempts to determine the effect of one or more independent variables on one or more dependent variables. In educational research the independent variable often is a new educational practice or product, and the dependent variable often is a measure of student achievement, attitude, or self-concept. If the independent variable has an effect, the effect should be reflected as a *change* between students' scores on the measure that was administered prior to the experimental treatment (the pretest) and their scores on the measure administered after it ends (the posttest). The posttest score minus the pretest score is called a **gain score** (also called a *change* or *difference* score). For example, if a student's initial score on a measure of achievement was 50 and the student's score rose to 65 after administration of the experimental treatment, the gain score would be 15. There are serious difficulties, however, in using gain scores to determine the effects of an experimental treatment.

These difficulties can be illustrated by considering a study of achievement gains from the beginning to the end of the freshman year of college conducted by Paul Dressel and Lewis Mayhew.[22] Table 13.4 lists gains made by students from nine colleges on various tests of achievement. The gain scores are presented separately for subgroups that were formed on the basis of their pretest scores on each test. There clearly is a strong inverse relationship between pretest score and achievement gain. For example, on the test of critical thinking in social science, the students whose scores were lowest at the beginning of the year made considerably larger gains (6.89 points) than the students whose scores were initially highest (an average gain of 2.26 points).

How are we to interpret such data? Do the data mean that students with low initial achievement are likely to learn more (as measured by their change scores) than students

---

22. Dressel, P. L., & Mayhew, L. B. (1954). *General Education: Explorations in evaluation.* Washington, DC: American Council on Education. A table of their statistical results is reproduced in Diederich, P. B. (1956). Pitfalls in the measurement of gains in achievement. *School Review, 64*, 59–63. Deiderich's table is shown in Table 13.4.

with initially high achievement? Although this interpretation might be correct, the inverse relationship between pretest scores and achievement gain scores is more likely to be an artifact produced by measurement error.

The following are five problems of interpretation when raw gain scores (posttest scores minus pretest scores) are used to measure the amount of change that has occurred in individuals as the result of an intervention or a natural growth process.

1. *Ceiling effect.* A **ceiling effect** occurs when the range of difficulty of the test items is limited, and therefore scores at the higher end of the possible score continuum are artificially restricted. For example, suppose that a pretest and posttest each include 100 items, but the items fail to measure the entire range of achievement possible on the dimension being measured. As a result, a student who answers 90 items correctly on the pretest can improve her score by only 10 points on the posttest. In contrast, a student with a score of 40 on the pretest can make a potential gain of 60 points. Thus, the ceiling effect places a restriction on the distribution of gain scores across levels of initial ability.

The tests used in Dressel and Mayhew's study might have been subject to a ceiling effect. Students in the high-middle and high groups might have scored near the ceiling of the pretest. Thus, they could earn only a minimal gain score when they took the posttest.

2. *Regression toward the mean.* **Regression toward the mean** (also called *statistical regression*) is a statistical phenomenon describing the tendency for research participants who score either very high or very low on a measure to score nearer the mean when the measure is re-administered.[23] The greater gains made by low achievers in Dressel and Mayhew's study cited above were most likely due to statistical regression. The regression effect occurs because of errors of measurement in the pretest and posttest, and because the tests are correlated with each other.

3. *Assumption of equal intervals.* Use of gain scores assumes equal intervals at all points of the test, yet this assumption almost never is valid for educational measures. For example, on a 100-item test a gain from 90 to 95 points is assumed to be equivalent to a gain from 40 to 45 points. In fact, it probably is much more difficult to make a gain of 5 points when one's initial score is 90 (because of ceiling and regression effects) than when one's initial score is 40. If the test measures knowledge of word definitions, for example, a student whose initial score is 40 could earn 5 more points by learning the meaning of easy, frequently used words, but a student with the initially high score of 90 would have to learn the meanings of difficult, rarely used words to improve his score.

4. *Different types of ability.* With the exception of factorially pure tests, a given score on a test may reflect different types and levels of ability for different students. For example, a mathematics achievement test might include a variety of subtests measuring addition, subtraction, mathematical reasoning, algebra, and so on. Two students might earn the same score on the test, yet this score probably reflects a different pattern of strengths and weaknesses in the two. For example, one student might be weak in subtraction but strong in mathematical reasoning, while the other student might be strong in subtraction but weak in reasoning. The two students might earn the same gain score after a period of time because they overcame their respective deficiencies. Thus, the gain score for the first student reflects improvement in subtraction, whereas the gain score for the second student

---

23. The regression effect is discussed in Chapter 12 as a threat to the internal validity of an experiment. It is possible to get significant achievement gains in an initially low-achievement group of students even if the experimental treatment has no effect because of the regression effect.

reflects improvement in mathematical reasoning. Because the gain scores are not equivalent in meaning, it is questionable to compare them in statistical analyses.

5. *Low reliability.* Still another difficulty with gain scores is that they usually are not reliable.[24] The higher the correlation between pretest and posttest scores, the lower the reliability of the change scores. Also, the reliability of change scores is affected by the degree of unreliability of the pretest and posttest scores themselves.

Statistical Analysis of Change

Touchstone in Research

Linn, R. L. (1986). Quantitative methods in research on teaching. In M. C. Wittrock (Ed.), *Handbook of research on teaching* (3rd ed., pp. 92–118). New York: Macmillan.

Gain scores are problematic, as we explained above, yet some measure of change is necessary if the researcher is to compare the effects of different experimental treatments. Although the limitations of gain scores cannot be overcome entirely, statistical procedures are available for overcoming some of them.

Multiple Regression

A common technique is multiple regression (see Chapter 11), in which students' posttest CTSS scores (test of critical thinking in social science in Table 13.4) are the dependent variable and pretest CTSS scores and, let's say, high school GPA scores are the predictor variables. Pretest CTSS scores are entered first into the prediction equation. A slight variation is to do the multiple regression using only the pretest CTSS scores as a predictor variable. The resulting multiple regression equation can be used to compute a predicted posttest CTSS score for each student. These scores are called *residual gain scores*, or *adjusted gain scores*. Students' high school GPA scores then can be correlated with the residual gain scores.

Analysis of Covariance and t Tests

The other situation in which gain scores are used is in the analysis of mean gain. Suppose you administer an achievement pretest to two groups: One group is to receive an experimental treatment and the other is to serve as a control group. If research participants have been assigned randomly to the two groups, the groups should have equivalent mean pretest scores. If this is the case, you can use *t* tests to determine the statistical significance of the mean gain scores.

Occasionally the mean pretest scores will differ significantly by chance even when subjects have been assigned randomly to treatment groups. Also, when quasi-experimental designs are used, pretest means might differ considerably. To adjust for initial differences in pretest means, analysis of covariance should be used. This statistical technique permits you to attribute observed gains to the effect of the experimental treatment rather than to differences in initial scores. For example, analysis of covariance could be applied to the data in Table 13.4. By using this statistical technique, we could compare the mean achievement gain scores of each of the five subgroups *as if* they had all earned the same mean achievement score at the beginning of the freshman year. As we discussed in Chapter 10, the raw data first need to be examined to determine whether they satisfy certain assumptions underlying analysis of covariance.

Analysis of Variance for Repeated Measures

Still another approach for determining the statistical significance of change is **analysis of variance for repeated measures.** This statistical technique is used to determine

---

24. Gain scores are reliable under a limited set of circumstances. See: Gupta, J. K., Srivastava, A. B. L., & Sharma, K. K. (1988). On the optimum predictive potential of change measures. *Journal of Experimental Education, 56,* 124–128.

whether the pretest-posttest difference for the experimental group is reliably different from the pretest-posttest difference for the control group. The occasions on which the measure of the dependent variable is administered (pretest and posttest) are considered one factor, and the experimental and control treatments are the other factor. The *F* ratios for the two factors (sometimes called *main effects*) are not of particular interest in this analysis of variance. For example, it is not informative for someone to compare the mean of all the pretest scores with the mean of all the posttest scores, ignoring whether the scores are from experimental or control students. Of interest instead is the interaction between time of measurement and treatment. That is, we are interested in whether the difference between the two groups is greater on the posttest than it is on the pretest. If the experimental treatment has the intended effect and if random assignment is successful in producing equivalent groups, we would expect the following results: no statistically significant difference between the treatment and control group on the pretest, but a statistically significant difference favoring the treatment group on the posttest.

This type of statistical analysis is illustrated in a study conducted by Roger Azevedo and Jennifer Cromley.[25] The purpose of their experiment was to determine whether an experimental treatment that trained college students in techniques of self-regulated learning would enhance their ability to learn in a hypermedia environment. In a hypermedia environment, students are exposed to information in varied forms, such as text, graphics, animation, and video; and they can access this information as they wish, meaning that they are not confined to the typical linear format of text.

The control group of 68 college students was told to learn as much as possible about the human body's circulatory system by accessing information in a hypermedia environment about this topic. The experimental group of 63 students was given the same learning task, but beforehand they received a 30-minute session that instructed them in how to self-regulate their learning in a hypermedia environment (e.g., think about what they already know about the topic prior to accessing and studying new information). Students in both groups took a pretest that had three parts: (1) a task in which they matched 16 words with their definitions, (2) a task in which they had to label 20 components on a color picture of the heart, and (3) two tasks that required them to draw and describe as much as possible about the path of blood throughout the human body. The posttest was identical to this pretest.

The descriptive statistics resulting from the experiment are shown in Table 13.5. Inspection of the table shows that both the treatment and control group made gains from pretest to posttest on each measure. The primary question of interest, though, is whether the treatment group (i.e., those who received training in self-regulated learning) made greater gains than the control group. This question was answered by a 2 × 2 repeated measures analysis of variance (ANOVA) for each measure.

The ANOVA revealed a statistically significant main effect of time ($F = 191.78$, $p < .05$) for the mental-models measure. This analysis examines whether students' scores at pretest and posttest differ significantly from each other, irrespective of whether they are in the treatment or control group. In other words, the pretest mean for all students (6.0) is compared with their posttest mean (9.52). (In calculating these means, we took into account the unequal sample size of each group). We can conclude, then, that all students, irre-

25. Azevedo, R., & Cromley, J. G. (2004). Does training on self-regulated learning facilitate students' learning with hypermedia? *Journal of Educational Psychology, 96*(3), 523–535.

TABLE 13.5								

Pretest and Posttest Statistics in Experiment on Training in Self-Regulated Learning in a Hypermedia Environment

| | SRL Training Condition (n = 63) | | | | Control Condition (n = 68) | | | |
| | Pretest | | Posttest | | Pretest | | Posttest | |
Learning Measure	M	SD	M	SD	M	SD	M	SD
Essay and flow diagram (mental models)	6.0	2.9	10.4	2.2	6.0	2.8	8.7	2.7
Matching (%)	60.8	26.7	82.0	17.0	54.9	26.3	73.0	22.3
Labeling (%)	5.5	9.0	38.1	18.6	4.3	9.3	23.6	18.9

Note: SRL = self-regulated learning.

Source: Table 1 on p. 528 in: Azevedo, R., & Cromley, J. G. (2004). Does training on self-regulated learning facilitate students' learning with hypermedia? *Journal of Educational Psychology, 96*(3), 523–535. Reprinted with permission from Roger Azevedo.

spective of the group to which they were assigned, made a significant gain in their mental models of the human circulatory system from pretest to posttest. This is not a surprising finding, as both groups received some form of instruction.

Azevedo and Cromley do not report the ANOVA main effect for treatment, probably because it is not a meaningful comparison. It involves comparing the mean scores of the treatment and control group, ignoring whether the individual scores came from the pretest or the posttest. Yet the entire purpose of the experiment calls for analyses that distinguish between pretest and posttest scores.

The ANOVA yielded a statistically significant effect for the interaction between condition and time ($F = 10.714$, $p < .05$). To determine the nature of the interaction, the researchers did two t tests, one a comparison of the pretest means for the two groups, the other a comparison of their posttest means. They found that the two groups did not differ significantly on the pretest ($t = .02$, $p > .05$), but did so on the posttest ($t = 3.9$, $p < .05$). We can conclude, then, that both groups had similar mental models of the human circulatory system at the outset of the experiment, but the treatment group had a more complete mental model at its conclusion.

Azevedo and Cromley did the same ANOVA for repeated measures on the data for the matching test and labeling test. They found a significant interaction effect for the labeling test, but not for the matching test.

ANOVA for repeated measures yielded interpretable results in this experiment, because identical measures were used for the pretest and posttest. However, if the pretest was different from the posttest, an alternative statistical method—most likely, ANCOVA or multiple regression—would have been required.

RECOMMENDATIONS FOR

Doing Experiments

1. If a nonequivalent control-group design is your only option, attempt to make the experimental and control groups as similar as possible and use the posttest measure also as a pretest measure.
2. In designing an experiment, attempt to increase its usefulness by including not one, but several factors that you have reason to believe have a direct or interactive effect on the outcome variables.
3. If you have reason to believe that the experimental treatment will have different effects for different types of individuals, design the experiment to allow for the identification of aptitude-treatment interactions.
4. Use the Solomon four-group design if you have a particular interest in knowing whether administration of a pretest has an effect on the outcome variable.
5. In designing a single-case experiment, consider doing pilot studies to determine whether baseline stability or treatment stability is likely to be an issue in detecting treatment effects.
6. In analyzing gain-score data, consider which of the following approaches is most suitable: multiple regression, analysis of covariance, or analysis of variance for repeated measures.

SELF-CHECK TEST

Circle the correct answer to each of the following questions. The answers are provided at the back of the book.

1. The distinguishing characteristic of the nonequivalent control-group design is that
   a. no pretest is administered to the control group.
   b. research participants are not randomly assigned to the experimental and control groups.
   c. the experimental group participates in a treatment intervention different from the one in which the control group participates.
   d. all threats to internal validity are controlled by this design.
2. The difference between group means in a nonequivalent control-group design usually is tested for statistical significance by
   a. a *t* test on the posttest means.
   b. the *t* distribution for the correlation between pretest and posttest scores.
   c. analysis of covariance on the posttest means.

   d. separate *t* tests of the pretest-posttest difference for the experimental group and for the control group.
3. Factorial designs are used in order to
   a. control for the effects of nonrandom assignment to treatments.
   b. collect data that can be entered into a factor analysis.
   c. control for statistical regression.
   d. test for the interaction of several variables in the same experiment.
4. A $2 \times 2 \times 2 \times 2$ factorial design indicates an experiment with
   a. two dependent variables.
   b. four dependent variables.
   c. two independent variables.
   d. four independent variables.

5. Which of the following variables is most experi-mentally manipulable?
   a. student ability
   b. teaching method
   c. socioeconomic level of community in which a school is located
   d. instructors' teaching experience

6. The effect of a pretest on the dependent variable in an experiment is best investigated using a(n)
   a. Solomon four-group design.
   b. counterbalanced design.
   c. aptitude-treatment-interaction design.
   d. A-B-A design.

7. Research on aptitude-treatment interaction seeks to discover whether
   a. aptitudes can be increased through appropriate intervention.
   b. certain instructional methods are better than others.
   c. certain students learn better under one instruc-tional method than under another instructional method.
   d. the relationship between aptitude and achieve-ment can be predicted.

8. Counterbalanced experiments are designed to con-trol for the effects of
   a. statistical regression.
   b. order of treatment administration.
   c. maturation.
   d. aptitude-treatment interaction.

9. Within-case replication of the treatment variable is possible with
   a. the A-B design.
   b. the A-B-A design.
   c. the A-B-A-B design.
   d. all of the above.

10. Multiple-baseline designs are used instead of A-B-A designs when
   a. only one individual is included in the experiment.
   b. reinstatement of baseline conditions is not possible.
   c. reinstatement of treatment conditions is not possible.
   d. an intervention occurs during the baseline conditions.

11. Data yielded by single-case experiments often are analyzed to determine
   a. change in the mean performance level from one phase of the experiment to another.
   b. change in the performance level between the last data point in one phase and the first data point in the next phase.
   c. change in the slope from one phase of the ex-periment to another.
   d. all of the above.

12. The higher the correlation between pretest and posttest scores
   a. the lower the reliability of the change scores.
   b. the higher the reliability of the change scores.
   c. the more difficult will be prediction of posttest scores based on pretest scores.
   d. the lower the validity of the posttest scores.

13. When doing an analysis of variance for repeated measures, the researcher is most interested in
   a. the main effect for treatment.
   b. the main effect for testing occasion.
   c. the interaction between treatment and time of testing.
   d. the interaction between treatment and multiple baselines.

PART V

Approaches to Qualitative Research

Qualitative research in education and other social science disciplines has undergone rapid growth and change. The productivity of qualitative researchers is evidenced by the proliferation of new journals, books, and professional associations representing various traditions of qualitative inquiry. Each tradition is marked by distinctive interests, theories, issues, and methods of investigation. In this part of the book we describe approaches to qualitative research that have particular relevance for the study of educational phenomena.

Chapter 14 focuses on case study research, currently the most widely used approach to qualitative inquiry in education. In conducting case studies, researchers collect intensive data about particular instances of a phenomenon, and they seek to understand each instance on its own terms and in its own context.

Chapter 15 provides an overview of specialized traditions of qualitative research. These traditions were developed by researchers in academic disciplines such as anthropology, linguistics, philosophy, psychology, and sociology, but they are being used increasingly by educational researchers. We consider fifteen of these traditions, classified into three types: those involving the study of individual's lived experience, those involving the study of society and culture, and those involving the study of language and communication.

Chapter 16 considers historical research, which is a sixteenth research tradition and one of the oldest and most fully developed of the qualitative research traditions. It is given special treatment partly because the methods of historical research cut across the three categories, or types of traditions, described in Chapter 15. In describing it, we show that while historians conduct their investigations using primarily qualitative methods, they sometimes use quantitative methods also. This blending of qualitative and quantitative methods can increasingly be found in case study research and other qualitative research traditions as well.

CHAPTER 14

Case Study Research

OVERVIEW

A good case study brings a phenomenon to life for readers and helps them understand its meaning. We start this chapter by discussing the general characteristics of case studies and the various purposes they serve. The remaining sections of the chapter concern the procedures involved in conducting, interpreting, and reporting a case study.

OBJECTIVES

After studying this chapter, you should be able to

1. Describe the typical characteristics of a case study.
2. Describe the various purposes that a case study can serve.
3. Explain the meaning of thick description, constructs, themes, patterns, and judgments in case study research.
4. Explain the basic difference between selecting a quantitative research design and a qualitative research design.
5. Describe the five components in Joseph Maxwell's model of qualitative research design.
6. Discuss the advantages and disadvantages of a multiple-case design as compared to a single-case design.
7. Describe the issues that researchers face in gaining entry to the field study site.
8. Explain the potential benefits and drawbacks of a researcher's personal involvement in the collection of data in case study research.

9. Describe the kinds of personal information researchers can provide to facilitate participants' and readers' understanding of their case study.
10. Explain factors to consider in deciding when to stop collecting case study data.
11. Compare the purposes and procedures of interpretational, structural, and reflective data analysis.
12. Explain several strategies that can be used to ensure the quality and rigor of case study findings.
13. Explain how case study researchers deal with the issue of applying their findings to other cases.
14. Explain how reflective reporting and analytic reporting of case study research differ.
15. Describe the main advantages and disadvantages of case study research.

Importance of Case Study in Qualitative Research

We focus on case study in this chapter because in education it is probably the most widely used approach to qualitative inquiry. Furthermore, case study design represents a basic form of qualitative research. It can be used to study almost any topic or type of phenomenon, with the entire range of data collection and analytic methods used by qualitative researchers. Its basic elements also appear in the more specialized approaches to qualitative research, called *qualitative research traditions,* covered in Chapters 15, 16, and 18. Such traditions (e.g., ethnography, semiotics, and historical research) differ from case study in that they focus on particular types of phenomena and use special methods in the study of those phenomena. Learning the case study approach should make it easier for you to understand the purposes and methods of these other approaches to qualitative research.

Another reason for beginning with case study is that, for more than most forms of qualitative inquiry, researchers with a positivist epistemological orientation have contributed a great deal to the literature on case study design. In this chapter we will cover both case study conducted with an interpretive epistemological orientation and that carried out by researchers with a positivist orientation. Some of the sources we cite in this chapter address qualitative research generally, because we see them as relevant to case study in particular. Case study can also play a role in mixed-methods research, and we include examples of case studies reflecting this approach.

Characteristics of Case Studies

We define case study research as (a) the in-depth study of (b) one or more instances of a phenomenon (c) in its real-life context that (d) reflects the perspective of the participants involved in the phenomenon. These characteristics have been present in the best, though not in all, examples of qualitative case study research in education that we have encountered. Below we analyze a specific case study in education in relation to these four characteristics. To explain the characteristics of a case study, we will use as an example a study reported by John Wills.[1] The author indicates that it was part of a larger ethnographic investigation of the lessons and activities surrounding celebration of the Martin Luther King holiday in elementary classrooms, conducted in 1999. The abstract states:

> This study examines the interpretive practices and cultural texts that shape what teachers and students remember and forget during the annual observance of the King holiday in two second-grade classrooms.[2]

Study of Particular Instances

A case study is done to shed light on a **phenomenon,** which is a process, event, person, or other item of interest to the researcher. Examples of phenomena are programs, curricula, roles, and events. In Wills's case study, the phenomenon being studied is "the constitutive work of teachers and students as they jointly interpret, represent, and narrate the past."[3]

Once the phenomenon of interest is clarified, the researcher can select a case for intensive study. A **case** is a particular instance of the phenomenon. Wills's case for this case study was two second-grade classrooms in a suburban elementary school in New York. Students in these classrooms were mostly Caucasian, with a few African American students or

1. Wills, J. (2005). "Some people even died": Martin Luther King, Jr., the civil rights movement and the politics of remembrance in elementary classrooms. *International Journal of Qualitative Studies in Education, 18*(1), 109–131.
2. Ibid., p. 109.
3. Ibid., p. 113.

Touchstones in Research

Glesne, C. (1999). *Becoming qualitative researchers: An introduction* (2nd ed.). New York: Addison Wesley Longman.

Hays, P. A. (2004). Case study research. In K. deMarrais & S. D. Lapan (Eds.), *Foundations for research: Methods of inquiry in education and the social sciences* (pp. 217–234). Mahwah, NJ: Erlbaum.

Merriam, S. B. (1998). *Qualitative research and case study applications in education* (2nd ed.). San Francisco: Jossey-Bass.

students with parents from other nations. Unfortunately, the author gives no further details about the school or community, or even the size of these two classrooms.

In a case study, the **unit of analysis** is the aspect of the phenomenon that will be studied across one or more cases. While Wills does not differentiate the students in the two classrooms, his published report includes descriptions of and quotes from both classroom teachers, Mrs. Peterson and Mrs. Thompson (pseudonyms rather than real names). The unit of analysis thus appears to be the classrooom, which includes a teacher and her students. The researcher chose to study two specific cases within that unit of analysis: Mrs. Peterson and her class and Mrs. Thompson and her class.

Any phenomenon has many aspects. Therefore, the researcher will need to select a focus for investigation. The **focus** is the aspect, or aspects, of the case on which data collection and analysis will concentrate. The focus of a case study can be a specific topic, a particular thesis or proposition to be argued and defended (similar to a research hypothesis), or a theme, which is an overarching concept or theoretical formulation that has emerged from the data analysis. Selection of a focus depends on the audience that the case study will address and the message that the researcher wants to convey. The focus of Wills's study is the process of remembrance related to a specific historical figure, Martin Luther King, Jr., as enacted in two specific second-grade classrooms.

To illustrate these distinctions further, suppose we are interested in how school leaders facilitate mandated curriculum reforms. We decide to study a particular curriculum reform mandated by the Oregon Department of Education and implemented by all Oregon school districts. In this example, the *phenomenon* is curriculum reform implementation, the *case* to be studied is the curriculum reform implemented in Oregon, the *focus* is the study of leadership behavior that facilitates curriculum reform implementation, and the *unit of analysis* is Oregon school districts. Given this unit of analysis, we might select a sample of ten school districts in which to collect data. We could study this phenomenon, though, without defining a unit of analysis. For example, we might decide to study the process by which the Oregon Department of Education developed the curriculum reform. The process might be holistic and embedded in various operations of the department. Thus, the case would not be reducible to any smaller unit of analysis.

Some researchers select a case for study simply because it is interesting or available. If so, the larger significance of the case might be difficult to discern. However, if the case is conceptualized as an example of a broader phenomenon, the case's significance can be seen in terms of the light it sheds on that phenomenon. The notion of focus can help you keep in mind that a typical case has many aspects, and that a case study probably will be more manageable and meaningful if you concentrate on just a few of the aspects. Finally, the decision to define a unit of analysis and sample within it can help make your data collection more manageable and yet allow you to make meaningful generalizations from your data analyses.

In-Depth Study of the Case

In a case study, a substantial amount of data is collected about the specific case (or cases) selected to represent the phenomenon. These data usually are in the form of words, images, or physical objects, and some quantitative data may be collected as well. Often data are collected over an extended time period, and several methods of data collection are used.

In his quest to determine the politics of remembrance surrounding the Martin Luther King, Jr., holiday in these two second-grade classrooms, Wills's collection of data was based on this statement of the research problem:

> How do teachers and students mobilize culturally available tools—metaphors, modes of discourse, popular understandings of historical figures and events—and texts—textbooks, literature

and popular film—to create narrative accounts of the past . . . that represent historical figures and events in particular ways and not others?[4]

Wills engaged in nonparticipant observation of each class in session by videotaping lessons and activities. He conducted formal interviews with the teachers and some of the students. He collected copies of student work and of all the curricular materials that were used during the study of the King holiday. Wills describes Mrs. Peterson's class discussion of King being refused service in a shoe store in Atlanta as a boy:

> Mrs. Peterson: How do you think Martin and his father felt? Alpa?
> Alpa: They were really sad 'cause, that's wrong.
> Emily: Annoyed.
> Mrs. Peterson: Bill?
> Bill: Discouraged.[5]

Wills describes how the teacher focused the discussion on King's likely feelings during the incident and did not pursue comments relating to the morality and injustice of Caucasian people's discriminative acts. He reports:

> Through this analysis I was also able to understand how the use of various cultural texts to produce specific representations of the past was mediated by a larger commemorative narrative privileged in mainstream US society, the curricular frame of conflict resolution, the particular concerns and teaching philosophies of these two teachers, and the mundane realities of classroom life.[6]

Two months after these classrooms had finished their unit on King, Wills returned to the school and conducted a whole-class discussion with the students about what they had learned from the unit. Several students volunteered that they had seen a television movie, "Selma, Lord Selma," which depicted the violent response to the protests against discrimination that King led in the South. Wills noted the contrast between students' depiction of the violence and injustice shown in the movie and the emphasis on conflict resolution, nonviolent protest, and peace that the teachers had emphasized in their treatment of King's history.

Study of a Phenomenon in Its Real-Life Context

Jerome Kirk and Marc Miller define qualitative research as an approach to social science research that involves "watching people in their own territory and interacting with them in their own language, on their own terms."[7] Typically, but not always, case studies involve fieldwork in which the researcher interacts with study participants in their natural settings. Even in instances where fieldwork is not done, the goal still is to learn about the phenomenon from the perspective of those in the field.

Robert Yin also emphasizes the importance of studying a phenomenon in its real-life context.[8] He observes that case studies typically involve investigation of a phenomenon for which the boundaries between the phenomenon and its context are not clearly evident. Yin argues that these boundaries should be clarified as part of the case study.

Many case studies in education are conducted in classrooms or other locations within schools. Such sites are real-life or natural in the sense that they are where the particular actors participating in the phenomenon of public education normally are found. The researcher

Touchstone in Research

Yin, R. K. (1998). The abridged version of case study research. In L. Bickman & D. J. Rog (Eds.), *Handbook of applied social research methods* (pp. 229–259). Thousand Oaks, CA: Sage.

---

4. Ibid.
5. Ibid., p. 116.
6. Ibid., p. 113.
7. Kirk, J., & Miller, M. L. (1986). *Reliability and validity in qualitative research.* Thousand Oaks, CA: Sage.
8. Yin, R. K. (2003). *Case study research: Design and methods* (3rd ed.). Thousand Oaks, CA: Sage.

does not take the participants to a laboratory. With respect to the larger context of teacher and student life, however, classrooms are in many ways artificial and constrained environments. This artificial, constrained quality is reflected in the excerpts of classroom dialogue included in Wills's article. We wonder what different conceptions of the King holiday might have emerged if Wills had observed and talked with some of the students and the teachers on the actual holiday, outside the school context, when they were with friends or family members. The boundaries of this case are clearly the students' and teachers' official roles as students and teachers and do not reflect their lives beyond the classroom.

Representation of Emic and Etic Perspectives

One characteristic of case studies is an effort to portray truthfully the *etic* perspective of the researchers as well the *emic* perspective of the research participants. To reflect the *emic* perspective of the research participants, Wills takes several approaches. He includes many comments from students during the classroom discussions. He carefully describes the constraints operating in Mrs. Peterson's and Mrs. Thompson's classrooms that limited their opportunity to pursue students' comments about the meaning of the events involving King's life. These included late starts to class due to a snowstorm, interruptions to class, and the tight schedule of class activities.

In his teacher interviews Wills also seeks to gain understanding of the teachers' seeming reluctance to address any issues of violence and injustice. He shares a quote from Mrs. Peterson's interview that helps explain why such issues were largely ignored by the teachers:

> I think you have to be careful not to take it too far, too serious, because they have a fear that is hard to address with them, because they don't have years of experience . . . . yet address some of the feelings that they can relate to.[9]

Wills comments that Mrs. Peterson's "continual deflection of students' comments back to the issue of how Martin and his father felt when they were discriminated against is both sensible and understandable, given this concern with her students' well-being."[10] He also notes that "Mrs. Thompson's effort to be upbeat, to focus on how things are getting better . . . provides some understanding of her deflection, or redirection" of the students' discussion of the violence they saw in the TV movie.[11]

Wills's *etic*, or professional, perspective, is also strongly asserted in his case study. The published report of the case study includes Notes on Contributor, describing Wills as an assistant professor of education at the University of California, Riverside, and stating his research interests as the interpretation and narration of history in K–12 classrooms.

Wills's professional perspective is clearly reflected in his analysis of the broader meaning of the classroom dialogue he provides in his report and the theory he draws on to explain it. For example, Wills cites works concerning the issue of whether culture has a greater effect when it is most strongly internalized or when it is on the outside, that is, not deeply internalized or even meaningful to the individuals being studied. He notes that the social rules of remembrance that operate in institutional settings like classrooms cause students' cultural repertoires to be structured in culturally sanctioned ways:

> To the extent that the politics of remembrance in classrooms mirrors the collective memory of mainstream society, students will likely find themselves retelling the story of King and his ad-

---

9. Wills, 'Some people even died', p. 135.
10. Ibid., p. 125.
11. Ibid.

vocacy of non-violent change year after year while *not remembering* the discriminatory practices and violence of Whites in our shared past.[12]

Wills concludes that the time constraints operating in classrooms, the teachers' desires
to avoid controversy or upsetting students, and strong cultural norms defining King's significance as a spokesman for nonviolence led to an avoidance of the issue of conflict and a
centering on the theme of conflict resolution in relation to the King holiday. Through his interpretation of individual children's statements and teacher comments and through analyses such as the above, Wills clearly seeks to represent the emic perspective of both the
teachers and students in his case study, along with the etic perspective of the researcher.

This purpose reflects an interpretive (as contrasted with a positivist) stance. As we explain in Chapter 1, interpretive research seeks to study the local, immediate meanings of
social actions for the actors involved in them. The researcher's task is to figure out how to
view the phenomenon as the participants view it. The participants' viewpoint is called the
emic perspective. Typically, the researcher obtains this perspective through direct observation of the participants (sometimes called "insiders") as they behave naturally in the
field, and through informal conversations with them. The conversations typically include
questions such as, "How did you feel when _____?," "What did you think about when
_____?," and "Why did you _____?"

At the same time, case study researchers generally maintain their own perspective as
investigators of the phenomenon. Their viewpoint as outsiders, which is called the **etic**
perspective, helps them make conceptual and theoretical sense of the case, and to report
the findings so that their contribution to the research literature is clear.

Purposes of Case Studies

Researchers generally do case studies for one of three purposes: to produce detailed descriptions of a phenomenon, to develop possible explanations of it, or to evaluate the phenomenon. We describe each of these purposes below.

Description

In a case study whose purpose is description, the researcher attempts to depict a phenomenon and conceptualize it. The depiction can focus on various phenomena, such as
the meanings that the research participants ascribe to their life and environment, contextual factors that influence their lives, a series of events and their possible outcomes, or the
new or unusual in society. A good depiction will provide what is called a **thick description**
of the phenomenon, that is, statements that re-create a situation and as much of its context as possible, accompanied by the meanings and intentions inherent in that situation.
The term *thick description*, first used by anthropologists to refer to a complete, literal description of a cultural phenomenon,[13] is now used in qualitative research generally. A good
example of thick description, in our opinion, is the opening statements in a report about
a high school dropout by the educational anthropologist Harry Wolcott:

> "I guess if you're going to be here, I need to know something about you, where you're from, and
> what kind of trouble you are in," I said to the lad, trying not to reveal my uncertainty, surprise,
> and dismay at his uninvited presence until I could learn more about his circumstances. It
> wasn't much of an introduction, but it marked the beginning of a dialogue that lasted almost
> two years from that moment. Brad (a pseudonym, although as he noted, using his real name

---

12. Ibid., p. 127.
13. Geertz, C. (1973). *The interpretation of cultures: Selected essays.* New York: Basic Books.

wouldn't really matter, since "no one knows who I am anyway") tersely stated his full name, the fact that his parents had "split up" and his mother was remarried and living in southern California, the local address of his father, and that he was not at present in any trouble because he wasn't "that stupid." He also volunteered that he had spent time in the state's correctional facility for boys, but quickly added, "it wasn't really my fault."

It was not our meeting itself that was a surprise; it was that Brad already had been living at this remote corner of my steep and heavily wooded 20-acre home-site on the outskirts of town for almost five weeks.[14]

In creating thick description, the researcher looks for constructs that bring order to the descriptive data and that relate these data to other research findings reported in the literature. A **construct** is a concept that is inferred from observed phenomena and that can be used to explain those phenomena. For example, Wolcott uses the constructs *education, school, deviant person, deviant act,* and *opportunity* to interpret dropout phenomena as manifested by Brad.

Researchers also can add depth to their descriptions by searching for themes present in the phenomena. We define **themes** as salient, characteristic features of a case. For example, if a student—Sally—fails to turn in her homework on time on one occasion, it can be regarded as an isolated event. If Sally habitually fails to turn in her homework when it is due, we can say that this behavior is characteristic of her; it is a noteworthy theme. If Sally also delays doing household chores and getting ready for family outings, we might see a broader theme in her behavior, namely, procrastination.

The Wills study illustrates the search for themes in case study data, relating to "the interpretive practices and cultural texts that shape what teachers and students remember and forget during the annual observance of the King holiday."[15] These themes include the blending of fact and fiction in the treatment of historical events in classrooms, normative rules that guide students' discourse and indicate what they should remember and what they can or must forget, and classroom management concerns that constrain attending to controversial issues. Another important theme involved the *occlusion* of memory that such treatment tends to produce in students, that is, not amnesia but "blockage, an issue of the salience and accessibility of collective memories that may still be available in various social sites of memory."[16]

Explanation

Some case study research aims to provide explanations for the phenomena that were studied. We refer to these explanations as **patterns,** meaning that one type of variation observed in a case study is systematically related to another observed variation. If the researcher does not claim that one variation has a causal effect on the other, we describe it as a **relational pattern.** If causality is claimed, it is a **causal pattern.**

An example of a causal pattern can be found in David Thomas's case study of the dynamics of cross-race relationships between protégés and their mentors or sponsors in a large telecommunications company.[17] He interviewed both the senior and junior members of 18 such pairs. In all but two pairs, the senior member was white and the junior member was African American.

14. Wolcott, H. F. (1994). *Transforming qualitative data: Description, analysis, and interpretation.* Thousand Oaks, CA: Sage. Quote appears on p. 68.
15. Wills, 'Some people even died', p. 109.
16. Ibid., p. 127.
17. Thomas, D. A. (1993). Racial dynamics in cross-race developmental relationships. *Administrative Science Quarterly, 38,* 169–194.

The members of each pair had formed an association in order to develop a relationship that would foster the professional development of the junior member of the pair. Thomas found that the relationships that developed were of two types, consistent with previous research. In a *sponsor*-protégé relationship, the senior member provided only instrumental career support (e.g., advocacy for promotions and performance feedback). By contrast, in a *mentor*-protégé relationship, the senior member provided not only instrumental career support, but also psychosocial support (e.g., role modeling, counseling, and friendship).

Thomas sought to identify the factors that led to one or the other type of developmental relationship between each cross-race pair. First, he examined the strategies that individuals used for managing the racial difference between the senior and junior member. Thomas found that individuals used one of two general strategies. The *denial and suppression* strategy involved a preference for not directly addressing the racial difference between the senior and junior member, while the *direct engagement* strategy involved a preference for directly addressing (i.e., communicating about) the racial difference.

Thomas initially expected that the relationship between a junior and senior member would develop into a mentor-protégé relationship only when both parties preferred and used the strategy of direct engagement. Instead, he found that when both parties preferred the same strategy—whether direct engagement or denial and suppression—the relationship between the junior and senior member was more likely to develop into a mentor-protégé relationship than a sponsor-protégé relationship.

Thomas's findings led him to develop a theoretical model of racial dynamics in developmental relationships. The model posits that strategies for managing racial differences have an effect on the type of relationship that develops between the junior and senior member of cross-race pairs. This, then, is a causal pattern: Agreements in preference for the strategy used to manage the racial difference, whether through denial and suppression or through direct engagement, are presumed to have an effect on variations in relationships (mentor-protégé vs. sponsor-protégé).

Evaluation

Chapter 17 describes several qualitative approaches to evaluation, including responsive evaluation, fourth-generation evaluation, quasi-legal models of evaluation, and expertise-based evaluation. In each approach, the researcher conducts a case study and makes evaluative judgments. In addition, the researcher might create a thick description of the phenomenon being evaluated and identify salient constructs, themes, and patterns. Case studies whose purpose is evaluation are being done with increasing frequency, because educational programs that receive government funding are required to undergo formal evaluation. For example, a recent case study by Xin Liang and Kim Creasy involves an analysis of how teachers conduct classroom assessment in Web-based graduate education courses.[18] The authors identified common assessment strategies and suggested changes to promote greater learner autonomy.

Designing a Case Study

Standard designs for quantitative research studies have evolved over a period of decades as researchers gained experience in using this approach to inquiry. In planning and executing a new quantitative study, the researcher can look to these standard designs for a

---

18. Liang, X., & Creasy, K. (2004). Classroom assessment in Web-based instructional environment: Instructors' experience. *Practical Assessment, Research & Evaluation, 9*(7). Retrieved June 21, 2005, from http://pareonline.net/getvn.asp?v=9&n=7

Touchstones in Research

Hatch, J. A. (2002). *Doing qualitative research in education settings.* Albany: State University of New York.

Silverman, D. (2004). *Doing qualitative research: A practical handbook.* Thousand Oaks, CA: Sage.

suitable "blueprint" of methods and sequential steps that, if employed properly, will yield the desired type of knowledge about the problem being investigated.

This is not true of case study design. Consistent with qualitative research in general, the design of each case study is determined by the researcher conducting the study and is specific to the phenomenon being studied. In Alan Peshkin's view, the essence of case study design is interpretation, because the researcher's interpretive acts give "importance, order, and form" to the study.[19] These interpretive acts occur throughout the course of the study:

> Interpretation has to do with the confluence of questions, images, and ideas that are the starting point of my inquiry, or the conceptualizing of my study.
> Interpretation has to do with where I choose to look to see that something is going on with regard to my conceptualization, or the situating of my study.
> Interpretation has to do with the judgment of what to collect that provides documentation for what I think is going on, or the instantiating of my study and the further focusing of its field of inquiry.
> Interpretation has to do with what to select for writing that establishes or affirms what I have identified that has gone on, or the composing of the elements of my research study.
> Finally, interpretation has to do with a perspectival accounting for what I have learned, or the shaping of the meanings and understandings of what has gone on from some point of view . . . .[20]

In this view of case study design, the researcher's interpretive skill—acquired through study, apprenticeship, and experience—determines the specific features of the design. In this view, too, case study design is not an event, but an emergent process that occurs throughout the case study.

Joseph Maxwell presents a more explicit model of case study design, but one consistent with Peshkin's emphasis on interpretation.[21] The full design model is shown in Figure 14.1. Its central features are the five components (goals, conceptual frameworks, research questions, methods, and validity), shown in ovals and linked by lines illustrating their connectivity. Maxwell stresses that the upper triangle of this model (goals, conceptual framework, and research questions) should be closely integrated, as should the lower triangle (research questions, methods, and validity). He sees the connections among the model components as "rubber bands": flexible, able to stretch and bend to some extent, but exerting tensions on different components that impose "constraints which, if violated, make the design ineffective."[22] The factors surrounding the five components are not integral to case study design, but rather are influences on, or outcomes of, the research.

Maxwell's model includes issues that are framed as questions, which will help you create a design that has importance, order, and form.

Table 14.1 summarizes eight goals that Maxwell asserts qualitative research can help achieve. We see them as relevant not only to case studies, but also to other approaches to qualitative research (see Chapters 15 to 18) and to mixed-methods research.

In this and the next sections of the chapter, we present a set of relatively discrete, sequential steps for doing a case study. We take this approach for two purposes: to provide a simplified process for doing a case study, and as a basis for comparing case study design with other research designs. In reality, the steps may overlap and be retraced in the course

---

19. Peshkin, A. (2000). The nature of interpretation in qualitative research. *Educational Researcher, 29*(9), 5–9. Quote appears on p. 9.
20. Ibid.
21. Maxwell, J. A. (2005). *Qualitative research design: An interactive approach* (2nd ed.). Thousand Oaks, CA: Sage.
22. Ibid., p. 6

FIGURE 14.1

Contextual Factors Influencing a Research Design

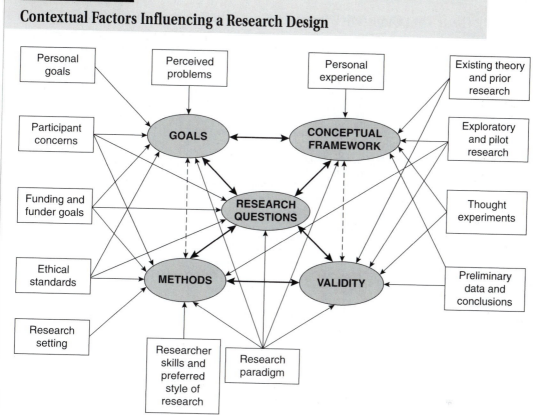

Source: Figure 1.2 on p. 6 in: Maxwell, J. A. (2005). *Qualitative research design: An interactive approach* (2nd ed.). Thousand Oaks, CA: Sage. Copyright © 2005 by Sage Publications. Reprinted with permission from Sage Publications, Inc.

of doing a case study. Also, the methods that we describe within each step are not prescriptive. Selection of specific methods is subordinate to the larger agenda of respecting the unique features of the case, keeping interpretation at the center of the case study, and creating a research design that has coherence and value.

Formulating a Research Problem

The first step in planning a case study is to identify a problem that interests you and that is worthy of study. Often the research problem is grounded in the researcher's personal experience with a particular type of student, instructional program, or other phenomenon.

Once identified, the research problem needs to be translated into explicit questions or objectives. The following are two examples from published case studies.

Swidler, S. A. (2000). Notes on a country school tradition: Recitation as an individual strategy. *Journal of Research in Rural Education, 16*, 8–21.

The researcher used an ethnographic, symbolic-interpretive perspective to study a rural one-teacher school in Nebraska.

TABLE 14.1
Goals That Qualitative Research Can Help Researchers Achieve

1. To grasp the *meaning* that events, situations, experiences, and actions have for participants in the study, which is part of the reality that researchers want to understand.
2. To understand the particular *context* within which the participants are operating and its influence on their actions. In addition to the context in which one's research participants are embedded, qualitative researchers also take into account the contextual factors that influence the research itself (shown in Figure 14.1).
3. To identify *unanticipated* phenomena and influences that emerge in the setting and to generate new grounded theories about such aspects.
4. To grasp the *process* by which events and actions take place that lead to particular outcomes.
5. To develop *causal explanations* based on process theory (which involves tracing the process by which specific aspects affect other aspects), rather than variance theory (which involves showing a relationship between two variables, as in quantitative research).
6. To generate *results and theories* that are understandable and experientially credible, both to the participants in the study and to others.
7. To conduct *formative evaluations,* designed to improve practice, rather than merely to assess the value of a final program or product.
8. To engage in *collaborative and action research* with practitioners and research participants.

Source: Text on pp. 22–25 in: Maxwell, J. A. (2005). *Qualitative research design: An interactive approach* (2nd ed.). Thousand Oaks, CA: Sage.

> *Research problem:* "The present study was undertaken to look at the practices of some of the remaining one-teacher schools, what might be learned from them, and if or how we might capture a glimpse of 'our future in this remaining piece of our past' (Geyer, 1995)." (p. 9).

Huberman, M., & Middlebrooks, S. (2000). The dilution of inquiry: A qualitative study. *Qualitative Studies in Education, 18*(1), 281–304.

> The researchers conducted a qualitative case study of inquiry-based science education at the upper-primary and middle-school levels in six American settings.
> *Research problem:* " 'Inquiry' or 'discovery' science . . . has been notoriously difficult to enact in classrooms . . . . One resulting trend is the watering down or 'dilution' of original designs, even among enthusiastic educators. That process is mirrored in a multiple-case study of *The Voyage of the Mimi*, one of eight innovations nested within a national, then international study." (p. 281).

Selecting a Case

In this section, we describe in general terms the process of selecting a case or cases. To deepen your understanding of the case selection process, you also should study Chapter 6, which describes many specialized sampling techniques.

The key issue in selecting a case is the decision concerning what you want to be able to say something about at the end of the study. Thus, specifying the case is somewhat comparable to the process in quantitative research of specifying the population to which the results obtained from a sample will be generalized. For example, Sister Paula Kleine-Kracht introduced her study of instructional leadership in a high school with this statement of the research problem:

> There are, however, few examinations of secondary schools in which a principal deliberately chooses to cultivate other members' instructional leadership and decides to personally

influence instruction in an indirect way. The following case study is an examination of just such a situation.[23]

In this study, then, the general phenomenon under investigation was instructional leadership. The case was a particular instance (the principal of one high school) of a particular type of instructional leadership, namely, the facilitation of staff members' instructional leadership activities. The findings of the case study might generalize to other principals and might have implications for other manifestations of instructional leadership.

As we explain in Chapter 6, cases in qualitative research are selected by a purposeful sampling process. The particular case to be studied might be selected for various purposes, such as the following: The case is typical; it reflects the phenomenon of interest to an extreme extent; it is a deviant case of special interest; it is politically important.

As we explained earlier in this chapter, the nature of some cases makes it possible to define a unit of analysis that can be sampled. In this situation, the researcher's next decision is to select a sample within the unit of analysis. For example, suppose that the unit of analysis is a group of individuals who share a particular characteristic of interest to the researcher. If the researcher cannot study all these individuals, he will need to consider which ones have experiences or perceptions that give them special value as data sources. There were two such units of analysis in Kleine-Kracht's study of indirect instructional leadership: principals and division chairpersons. Kleine-Kracht selected one school principal from among those who potentially could have been studied. The principal's school had five division chairpersons, each responsible for a different part of the school's curriculum. Kleine-Kracht decided to select the entire sample of chairpersons to study, although she could have selected only one or a few chairpersons within this unit of analysis.

Yin proposes that the decision to study multiple cases should be based on replication logic, which is explained in Chapter 6. According to this logic, two or more cases are studied because the researcher predicts the same results for each case (i.e., literal replication), or expects the results to differ for different cases consistent with specific theoretical propositions (i.e., theoretical replication). Our review of published case studies suggests that replication logic is not commonly used, despite its usefulness for testing theoretical propositions.

Although a multiple-case design frequently is used in case study research, Wolcott argues that the study of multiple cases reduces the total attention that can be given to any one of them, and thus serves to weaken rather than to strengthen the study.[24] He expresses a strong preference for studying just one case in depth, especially when the researcher is not experienced in this type of research. Wolcott suggests that more experienced researchers could be left with the responsibility for aggregating and comparing case studies dealing with similar phenomena, and, when appropriate, to discover whatever systematic relationships they may reveal.

Defining the Role of the Case Study Researcher

Quantitative researchers and qualitative researchers perform similar roles in designing and planning a research study, obtaining necessary institutional review and approval, and obtaining permissions from the site or sites in which the research will be conducted. Once they begin collecting data, however, their roles are quite different. Quantitative researchers

23. Kleine-Kracht, P. (1993). Indirect instructional leadership: An administrator's choice. *Educational Administration Quarterly, 29,* 187–212. Quote appears on p. 187.
24. Wolcott, H. F. (1992). Posturing in qualitative inquiry. In M. D. LeCompte, W. L. Millroy, & J. Preissle (Eds.), *Handbook of qualitative research in education* (pp. 3–52). San Diego: Academic Press.

specify precise procedures for data collection and analysis. They tend to play a limited role in data collection (e.g., administering questionnaires), or they may even use assistants for this purpose.

The role of qualitative researchers, including case study researchers, in data collection is more complex. The researcher is the primary "measuring instrument." This means that she carries out data collection and becomes personally involved in the phenomenon being studied. Thus, the researcher is likely to interact closely with research participants, attend social events in the field setting, and use empathy and other psychological processes to grasp the meaning of the phenomenon as it is experienced by individuals and groups in the setting. Few of these procedures are standardized or can be specified in advance of data collection.

Gaining Entry

Identifying appropriate sites and working with "gatekeepers" to obtain necessary permissions are critical steps in a case study. If not done properly, the researcher may have to abort the study. Also, first impressions created at a site can set the tone for the entire relationship between the researcher and field participants. Issues involved in gaining entry include:

1. identifying people within the field setting with whom to make your initial contact;
2. selecting the best method of communication (e.g., telephone, letter, or personal visit) to deliver your request;
3. deciding how to phrase your request (e.g., focusing on the site's opportunity to contribute to research or on personal benefits to site participants); and
4. being prepared to answer questions and address concerns that might arise both before and after permission is granted.

Margot Ely and her colleagues describe their experiences, and those of their students in a course on qualitative research, in gaining entry and conducting research in field settings.[25] One student's log described her challenges in gaining entry into the field site generally and also into the specific settings she wished to observe and with the specific individuals she wished to interview. The student described her use of the log and her support group (small groups into which students were formed for the duration of the research course) to confront her fears and define her research problem, which involved the experience of aging. She carried out a "dress rehearsal" by visiting a relative who lived in a nursing home, and then identified a different nursing home as a potential site. Unable to find a personal contact who could introduce her, the student made a cold call on the receptionist. She obtained the names of the social service director and the volunteer coordinator, both of whom appeared to be appropriate gatekeepers to approach. Prepared to make a detailed "sales pitch" when she spoke with the director of social work, the student was stunned when she was readily accepted: "You look surprised. Being near a university, we often have students doing research here."[26]

Some of the other students in the qualitative research course had more difficulty gaining entry into the field settings that they initially had selected, and some decided to try elsewhere. Ely and her colleagues note, however, that with common sense and sensitivity researchers can turn around sticky situations and enter successfully and discreetly.

25. Ely, M., Anzul, M., Friedman, T., Garner, D., & Steinmetz, A. M. (1991). *Doing qualitative research: Circles within circles.* New York: Falmer.
26. Ibid., p. 20.

Once you gain entry into a field setting, you will need to enlist the cooperation of the case study participants. Your success will depend on how you present yourself. The student whose nursing home experience we described above recorded this episode in her log:

> If you seem to be fulfilling a role which is aversive to them, friendship and cooperation can evaporate in a flash. I encountered this temporarily when a venerable and very articulate 94-year-old man whom I wanted to interview discovered I had training as a psychologist. He said, "Well, you'll no doubt need to speak to someone else. I'm not a patient." I had to make it clear that I hoped to speak to him as an equal, to be enlightened by his perspective, and not as a psychologist interviewing a patient.[27]

The researcher's appearance also can affect her relationship with the individuals or groups being studied. Consider, for example, the case study by Cathy Evans and Donna Eder involving observations of middle school students during lunch period.[28] (This case study is further described in Chapter 9.) For this phase of their study, the researchers and their assistants sought to fit in with the young people they wanted to observe. Therefore, they dressed and spoke informally and were careful not to react negatively to students' language or behavior, even when they found it disturbing. When interacting with school personnel in other phases of their research, however, the research team dressed and acted as adult professionals.

Addressing Ethical Issues

Data collection in case study research poses various ethical problems. An interviewee might experience unexpected emotional difficulty as a result of expressing deeply held and perhaps controversial beliefs and feelings to an interviewer. Individuals might reveal personal information in the presence of a researcher who is in a participant observer role that they would not share with someone perceived to be an outsider. Analysis of personal documents or artifacts might pose ethical issues unless they are willingly surrendered for research purposes. Even when the researcher takes steps to protect the privacy of case study participants, there often are clues in a case study report that make it possible to identify field sites and particular individuals within them.

David Flinders identifies four types of ethics that can provide a basis for viewing and resolving these and other issues that arise in qualitative research.[29] In **utilitarian ethics,** researchers judge the morality of their decisions and actions by considering the consequences. The most desirable consequence is to produce the greatest good for the greatest number of people. According to Flinders, utilitarian ethics are difficult to apply in case study research because it is difficult to predict the consequences of a case study while it is in progress.

In **deontological ethics,** researchers judge the morality of their decisions and actions by referring to absolute values, such as honesty, justice, fairness, and respect for others. Flinders observes that from a utilitarian perspective, deception in qualitative research could be justified if it could be demonstrated that it did not harm the participants physically or in some other ways. However, deception could not be justified from a deontological perspective. The reason is that deception violates basic values of treating others fairly and with respect.

Touchstones in Research

de Laine, M. (2000). *Fieldwork, participation and practice: Ethics and dilemmas in qualitative research.* Thousand Oaks, CA: Sage.

Christians, C. G. (2005). *Ethics and politics in qualitative research.* In N. K. Denzin & Y. S. Lincoln (Eds.), *The Sage handbook of qualitative research* (3rd ed., pp. 139–164). Thousand Oaks, CA: Sage.

---

27. Ibid., p. 25.
28. Evans, C., & Eder, D. (1993). "NO EXIT": Processes of social isolation in the middle school. *Journal of Contemporary Ethnography, 22,* 139–170.
29. Flinders, D. J. (1992). In search of ethical guidance: Constructing a base for dialogue. *International Journal of Qualitative Studies in Education, 5,* 101–115.

In **relational ethics,** researchers judge the morality of their decisions and actions by the standard of whether these decisions and actions reflect a caring attitude toward others. Nel Noddings states that an ethics of caring "takes fidelity to persons as primary and directs us to analyze and evaluate all recommendations in light of our answers to questions concerning the maintenance of community, the growth of individuals, and the enhancement of subjective aspects of our relationship."[30] Relational ethics require, among other things, that the case study researcher be a sensitive, fully engaged member of the participants' community rather than a detached observer.

The fourth basis for considering the morality of a qualitative research study is ecological ethics. In **ecological ethics,** researchers judge the morality of their decisions and actions in terms of the participants' culture and the larger social systems of which they are part. Thus, whereas the other three ethical perspectives would consider each case study participant as an individual, ecological ethics would consider the participant as a member of a larger cultural and social system. Flinders observes that even a straightforward request such as, "Will you take part in this research?" can mean different things to different people. Depending on the person's cultural background, the request can be perceived as coercive by one individual and as an opportunity to collaborate by another individual. Sex-typed language in a case study report may be viewed as neutral by some readers, but as offensive by others. Data-collection activities may be ethical insofar as the individual participant in a work setting is concerned, but the activities can unfairly disrupt his colleagues' work. An ecological perspective helps avoid these problems by reminding the researcher to consider the larger implications of his local decisions and actions.

Ethical standards for case study research continue to be actively studied and debated. Therefore, if you plan to do case study research, you will need to develop your own ethical perspective. For guidance, we recommend that you review the above ethical perspectives, your institutional review board's standards (see Chapter 3), the unique circumstances of the field setting that you wish to study, and your personal values.

Collecting Case Study Data

Case study researchers might begin a case study with one method of data collection and gradually shift to, or add, other methods. Use of multiple methods to collect data about a phenomenon can enhance the validity of case study findings through a process called *triangulation,* which we explain later in the chapter.

The entire range of data collection methods described in Part III can be used in case study research. As noted earlier, mixed-methods research, in which both qualitative and quantitative research data are collected, is receiving increased attention and respect within the educational research community. Denzin and Lincoln view such research as part of the scientifically based research movement "that takes qualitative research methods out of their natural home, which is within the critical, interpretive framework . . ." and treats them as auxiliary and hence subordinate to quantitative methods.[31] In our view, the use of quantitative methods as auxiliary to qualitative research is an equally valuable strategy, as when enthnographers make counts of specific features of cultural life. Case study researchers

---

30. Noddings, N. (1986). Fidelity in teaching, teacher education, and research for teaching. *Harvard Educational Review, 56,* 496–510. Quote appears on p. 510.
31. Denzin, N. K., & Lincoln, Y. S. (2005). Introduction: The discipline and practice of qualitative research. In N. K. Denzin & Y. S. Lincoln (Eds.), *The Sage handbook of qualitative research* (3rd ed., pp. 1–32). Thousand Oaks, CA: Sage. Quote appears on p. 9.

need to understand and consider using mixed methods in their research studies.[32] For example, consider Claude Goldenberg's case study of the mismatch between a teacher's expectations and the actual reading achievement of two of her first-grade students.[33] Goldenberg carried out qualitative observation of each child's classroom behaviors, as illustrated by these observational notes in the research report:

> Marta and her group are with the aide, who is giving the children instructions for playing lotto. Marta looks at her lotto cards and smiles. She is sitting quietly . . . . Marta looks at what the boy next to her is doing . . . . Marta then begins to giggle as the aide shows the next picture. She looks at the boy next to her and they giggle together. One girl gives a response to the aide's question and Marta begins to laugh. "Ya, Marta," the aide says. ("Enough, Marta.")[34]

In addition, Goldenberg administered two quantitative measures (standardized tests of reading achievement) to each child.

Data from both types of measures yielded several key findings in this case study. While the teacher initially had low expectations about Marta's academic progress, the teacher told the researcher she spent time with Marta and her mother to encourage greater effort from Marta on reading activity. By year's end, Marta was reading at least at grade level (as measured by the reading tests), and the teacher described Marta as her "wonder child." In contrast, another Hispanic student in the same class, Sylvia, about whom the teacher initially had positive expectations, remained in a low reading group. According to Goldenberg, "in essence, Sylvia stagnated. She was never prompted, as was Marta, to change her work habits."[35]

Personal Involvement in the Data-Collection Process

A type of personal involvement debated among case study researchers is the extent to which they should disclose their personal experiences, feelings, or beliefs to field participants during data collection. For example, when interviewing school personnel about special education policies at the school, is it appropriate for a researcher to discuss her own experience working with students in special education, how she felt about this work, and what she believes is the best approach to helping such students? Another issue is the extent to which researchers should include personal experiences, feelings, and beliefs in the research report.

On the issue of personal disclosure to one's case study participants, Daphne Patai describes hearing a well-known historian, Michael Frisch, relate his experience reviewing tapes of research interviews he had conducted.[36] The historian noted that despite all the roadblocks he inadvertently created (which presumably included providing information about himself), most interviewees remained determined to tell him what was important to them and patiently returned to their own themes. This anecdote suggests that personal disclosure may have less effect than one might imagine.

32. Rihoux, B. (2003). Bridging the gap between the qualitative and quantitative worlds? A retrospective and prospective view on qualitative comparative analysis. *Field Methods, 15*(4), 351–365; Scholz, R. W., & Tietje, O. (2001). *Embedded case study methods: Integrating quantitative and qualitative knowledge.* Thousand Oaks, CA: Sage.
33. Goldenberg, C. (1992). The limits of expectations: A case for case knowledge about teacher expectancy effects. *American Educational Research Journal, 29,* 517–544.
34. Ibid., pp. 528–529.
35. Ibid., p. 537.
36. Patai, D. (1994, February 23). Sick and tired of scholars' noveau solipsism. *The Chronicle of Higher Education,* p. A52.

On the issue of personal disclosure in research reports, Patai cites examples of disclosures that she considered excessive or inappropriate:

> Are we really expected to take seriously—and read "generously"—the anthropologist Ruth Behar's claim (in her book *Translated Woman: Crossing the Border With Esperanza's Story,* Beacon Press, 1993) that her struggles to get tenure at an American university should be seen as parallel to the struggles of Esperanza, a Mexican street peddler? Or, to take a different type of example of telling or claiming too much, do readers really benefit from the feminist scholar Nancy K. Miller's description of her father's penis, to which she devotes the closing chapter of her book *Getting Personal* (Routledge, 1991)?[37]

Patai concludes that such intensely personal beliefs and characteristics do not have as much effect on research findings as researchers may believe and therefore are better left out of research reports.

In a report discussing the value of sharing one's subjectivity as a researcher, Alan Peshkin offers an opposing view.[38] Peshkin urges researchers to seek out their subjectivity systematically while their research is in progress, so that they can better determine how it might be shaping their inquiry and research outcomes. While carrying out fieldwork in a multiethnic high school in a community to which he gave the pseudonym *Riverview,* Peshkin undertook a subjectivity audit of himself. A **subjectivity audit** involves taking notes about situations connected to one's research that arouse strong positive or negative feelings. The outcome was a list of different aspects of himself, which he described as "discretely characterized I's," reflecting areas in which the researcher's own beliefs and background influenced his perceptions and actions in the research setting. For example, Peshkin discovered the *Ethnic Maintenance I* based on his identity as a Jew, an aspect of his subjectivity that approves of individuals maintaining their ethnicity. Peshkin's *Justice-Seeking I* was aroused by repeated experiences of hearing both residents and nonresidents of Riverview denigrate the community. According to Peshkin, such denigration reflected the fact that until recently Riverview was the only town in a large California county where African Americans were able to establish residence.

Another issue concerns researchers' personal involvement in their research interpretations, sometimes in the face of objective evidence that their views are incorrect. For example, Deborah Lipstadt, a professor at Emory University, decries what she perceives as a growing assault on historical truth:

> We're in a day and age in which I can make any claim I want. I can say I believe the Buffalo Bills won the Super Bowl. Then I say that it's my opinion and I have a right to it, and you're supposed to back off.[39]

As with most aspects of case study research, there are few firm rules about how much personal involvement or disclosure by a researcher is appropriate. Our view is that if self-disclosure passes a certain point, case study participants and readers of the report will view it as a distraction, or they might question the researcher's qualifications and the trustworthiness of the study's findings. On the other hand, brief comments by the researcher about her background and experiences relevant to the case study may facilitate readers' understanding of the findings.

37. Ibid.
38. Peshkin, A. (1988). In search of subjectivity—one's own. *Educational Researcher, 17*(7), 17–21.
39. Leo, J. (1994, February 28). The junking of history. *U.S. News & World Report,* p. 17.

Analyzing Data during Data Collection

Data collection is emergent in case study research. By this we mean that what the researcher learns from data collected at one point in time often is used to determine subsequent data-collection activities. Therefore, a case study researcher needs to spend time analyzing the data, at least informally, while data collection still is in progress. Two strategies can facilitate this process: making records of field contacts and thinking "finish-to-start."

Making records of field contacts Matthew Miles and A. Michael Huberman recommend that case study researchers use standard forms to summarize data-collection events.[40] The completed forms can reveal missing information and thus indicate the need for further data collection. They also can suggest promising directions for subsequent stages of data collection and analysis. One such form is a **contact summary sheet,** on which the researcher summarizes what was learned from each field observation or interview. The form can be predesigned for recording the specific details in which the researcher is interested, for example, the people, events, or situations involved in the contact, the most interesting or problematic aspects of the contact, or ideas about where the researcher should focus attention during the next contact.

Figure 14.2 is an example of a contact summary form used in a case study. The researcher first summarized eight salient points from the contact, which are coded as "Themes/Aspects" in the right column of the figure. Some of these points probably were taken from the researcher's field notes, and others might have come to the researcher's mind while reviewing the notes. In this case, the contact summary sheet was used in a systematic fashion. That is, the researcher treated each point as a data chunk and coded it, using a theme coding system.

The contact summary sheet is not a substitute for the researcher's field notes relating to the field contact. The field notes should be comprehensive and primarily descriptive. In contrast, a contact summary sheet is brief and focuses on what was learned from the field contact that will guide subsequent data-collection activities.

A **document summary form** serves a purpose similar to a contact summary sheet. The researcher writes a brief summary of each document that has been examined, noting the type of document, its uses, a summary of its contents, and ideas about other documents that should be obtained and studied.

Thinking "finish-to-start" Harry Wolcott advises researchers learning how to do qualitative research to work "start-to-finish" but to think "finish-to-start."[41] This approach involves thinking through one's entire research project at the very beginning. Wolcott recommends doing this thinking as soon as a problem has been formulated and necessary agreements have been obtained, but before beginning fieldwork. He suggests that the researcher make tentative decisions at that point about the form in which the completed account will be presented (e.g., monograph, journal article, or project report). Also, the researcher should try to predetermine the relative emphasis that will be given to thick description and to analysis and interpretation of constructs, themes, and patterns:

> if you plan to go heavy on description (a good way to hedge your bet if you entertain doubts about your sophistication at analysis or interpretation), recognize from the outset that rich detail may be critical and you had better not rely solely on "headnotes" for it. Be thinking

40. Miles, M. B., & Huberman, A. M. (1994). *Qualitative data analysis: An expanded sourcebook* (2nd ed.). Thousand Oaks, CA: Sage.
41. Wolcott, *Transforming qualitative data,* p. 404.

FIGURE 14.2

Contact Summary Form: Salient Points in Contact, with Theme Codes Assigned

Contact Summary

Type of contact:

| Mtg. | Principals | Ken's office | 4/2/76 | Site | Westgate |
| | Who, what group | place | date | | |

| Phone | _____ | _____ | _____ | Coder | MM |
| | With whom, by whom | place | date | | |

| Inf. Int. | _____ | _____ | _____ | Date coded | 4/18/76 |
| | With whom, by whom | place | date | | |

1. Pick out the most salient points in the contact. Number in order on this sheet and note page number on which point appears. Number point in text of write-up. Attach theme or aspect to each point. Invent themes where no existing ones apply and asterisk those. Comment may also be included in double parentheses.

Page	Salient Points	Themes/Aspects
1	1. Staff decisions have to be made by April 30.	Staff
1	2. Teachers will have to go out of their present grade-level assignment when they transfer.	Staff/Resource Mgmt.
2	3. Teachers vary in their willingness to integrate special education students into their classrooms—some teachers are "a pain in the elbow."	*Resistance
2	4. Ken points out that tentative teacher assignment lists got leaked from the previous meeting (implicitly deplores this).	Internal Communic.
2	5. Ken says, "Teachers act as if they had the right to decide who should be transferred." (would make outcry)	Power Distrib.
2	6. Tacit/explicit decision: "It's our decision to make." (voiced by Ken, agreed by Ed)	Power Distrib./Conflict Mgmt.
2	7. Principals and Ken, John, and Walter agree that Ms. Epstein is a "bitch."	*Stereotyping
2	8. Ken decides not to tell teachers ahead of time (now) about transfers ("because then we'd have a fait accompli").	Plan for Planning/Time Mgmt.

Source: Adapted from Figure 4.2 on p. 54 in: Miles, M. B., & Huberman, A. M. (1994). *Qualitative data analysis: An expanded sourcebook* (2nd ed.). Thousand Oaks, CA: Sage. Copyright © 1994 by Sage Publications. Reprinted with permission from Sage Publications, Inc.

about possibilities for presenting detailed vignettes and make sure you are recording such events at an adequate level of detail . . . probably including an abundance of direct quotations.[42]

The finish-to-start approach thus helps researchers anticipate the types of data that should be collected, and in what depth.

42. Ibid.

Ending Data Collection

The decision about when to end the data-collection stage of a case study involves both practical and theoretical considerations. Time and budgetary constraints, or the observation that the participants' patience is running thin, are among the practical considerations that can prompt a decision to end data collection. As to theoretical considerations, Yvonna Lincoln and Egon Guba identify four criteria for determining when it is appropriate to end data collection.[43] The criteria assume that the data have been coded into categories, but they are applicable to other forms of data analysis as well. (Category coding is discussed later in the chapter.) The four criteria are as follows:

1. *Exhaustion of sources.* Data sources (e.g., key informants, institutional files) can be recycled and tapped many times, but at some point it should become clear that little more information of relevance will be gained from further engagement with them.
2. *Saturation of categories.* Eventually, the categories used to code data appear to be definitively established. When continuing data collection produces only tiny increments of new information about the categories in comparison to the effort expended to get them, the researcher can feel confident about ending data collection.
3. *Emergence of regularities.* At some point, the researcher encounters sufficient consistencies in the data that she develops a sense of whether the phenomena represented by each construct occur regularly or only occasionally.
4. *Overextension.* Even if new information still is coming in, the researcher might develop a sense that the new information is far removed from the central core of viable categories that have emerged, and does not contribute usefully to the emergence of additional viable categories.

Analyzing Case Study Data

Data analysis in a quantitative research study is a relatively straightforward process. Suppose the study involves 100 participants and scores on ten variables for each participant—in all, 1,000 bits of numerical data. All these data can be entered into a computer file without much difficulty, and a software program will quickly perform the statistical analyses.

In contrast, even a modest case study will generate a great many pages of observational notes, interview transcripts, and documents obtained from the field setting. Suppose there are 200 such pages, each containing 250 words. That totals 50,000 words. How do you analyze all those words in order to produce significant, meaningful findings?

Renata Tesch reviewed various approaches that have been used to analyze case study data.[44] She classified them into three types: interpretational analysis, structural analysis, and reflective analysis. Each type is explained below. Straightforward techniques are now available for using word processors to analyze and display qualitative data.[45]

43. Lincoln, Y. S., & Guba, E. G. (1985). *Naturalistic inquiry.* Beverly Hills, CA: Sage.
44. Tesch, R. (1990). *Qualitative research: Analysis types and software tools.* New York: Falmer.
45. La Pelle, N. (2004). Simpifying qualitative data analysis using general purpose software tools. *Field Methods, 16*(1), 85–108; Ryan, G. W. (2004). Using a word processor to tag and retrieve blocks of text. *Field Methods, 16*(1), 109–130. Also see Ryan, G., & Bernard, H. L. (2000). Data management and analysis methods. In N. K. Denzin & Y. S. Lincoln (Eds.), *Handbook of qualitative research* (2nd ed., pp. 769–802). Thousand Oaks, CA: Sage; Weitzman, E. A. (2000). Software and qualitative research. In N. K. Denzin & Y. S. Lincoln (Eds.), *Handbook of qualitative research* (2nd ed., pp. 803–820). Thousand Oaks, CA: Sage.

Touchstones in Research

Atkinson, P., & Delamont, S. (2005). Analytic perspectives. In N. K. Denzin & Y. S. Lincoln (Eds.), *Sage handbook of qualitative research* (3rd ed., pp. 821–840). Thousand Oaks, CA: Sage.

Fetterman, D. M. (2002). Web surveys to digital movies: Technological tools of the trade. *Educational Researcher, 31*(6), 29–37.

Our discussion of data analysis emphasizes verbal data. However, visual images—photographs, drawings, paintings, cartoons, film, and the like—are another important data source in some case studies. While the procedures described below are generally applicable to visual images, you should be aware that qualitative researchers have developed special techniques for their analysis.[46]

Interpretational Analysis

Interpretational analysis is the process of examining case study data closely in order to find constructs, themes, and patterns that can be used to describe and explain the phenomenon being studied. For example, suppose researchers are studying a new U.S. history curriculum. They have available a set of documents written by the curriculum developers (the teacher's edition of the textbook, technical reports, advertisements, etc.), as well as transcripts of interviews with parents whose children are studying the curriculum.

In analyzing these data, suppose the researchers find that both the developers and the parents make frequent reference to the curriculum's intended goals. Further analysis reveals that two goals are particularly salient to both groups: (1) development of multicultural sensitivity, and (2) development of pride in one's country. One finding of the study, then, is the discovery of these particular goals (which we call *constructs*) as central to this particular curriculum. Suppose further analysis reveals that the curriculum developers most frequently mention multicultural sensitivity as a goal of the curriculum, while parents view national pride as an essential curriculum goal, but one not sufficiently emphasized in this curriculum. This, then, is a discovery about a possibly significant *pattern:* The salience of a particular curriculum goal depends on whether one is a developer or a parent.

Interpretational analysis helps researchers achieve insights such as those in our hypothetical example. The procedures of interpretational analysis can be carried out either manually or by computer. Because of the advantages of computer analysis, we will describe the procedures as they would be carried out with software programs that are available for this purpose.

Segmenting the Database

The first step in interpretational analysis is to compile all the case study data into a computer database. Handwritten notes need to be typed and formatted as computer files. Documents and other previously typed materials can be transformed into computer files by using a computer scanner. Even photographs and other graphic materials can be prepared as computer files in this manner. However, to analyze graphic materials by the procedures described below, you would need to prepare verbal descriptions of their salient features.

The resulting computer database (i.e., all the computer files containing the case study data) now can be manipulated by software programs designed to perform interpretational analyses. The researcher starts by having the software program assign a number to each line of text in the database. Next the researcher breaks the text into meaningful segments. A **segment** (also called a *meaning unit* or *analysis unit*) is a section of the text that contains one item of information and that is comprehensible even if read outside the context in which it is embedded. For example, in the analysis of interview and questionnaire data, it is common to make each question plus the participant's response a separate segment.

---

46. These techniques are described in: Harper, D. (2005). What's new visually. In N. K. Denzin & Y. S. Lincoln (Eds.), *Handbook of qualitative research* (3rd ed., pp. 747–762). Thousand Oaks, CA: Sage; Rose, G. (2001). *Visual methodologies: An introduction to the interpretation of visual materials.* Thousand Oaks, CA: Sage; Van Leeuwen, T. V., & Jewitt, C. (2001). *The handbook of visual analysis.* Thousand Oaks, CA: Sage.

A segment can be any length: a phrase within a sentence, a sentence, a paragraph, or even several pages of text. The researcher identifies each segment by indicating the line number on which it begins and the line number on which it ends.

Developing Categories

One of the most critical steps of interpretational data analysis is developing a set of categories that adequately encompass and summarize the data. The researcher must decide what is worth taking note of in each segment of the database. For example, Michael Ann Rossi did a study of elementary school teachers who had been prepared by staff of the California Mathematics Project to help their colleagues effect reforms in mathematics instruction at the local school level.[47] What was of interest to Rossi in her database of interviews, questionnaire responses, and documents was the facilitation strategies that these teacher-leaders used.

To be more precise, we would state that facilitation strategies were a *category* in Rossi's data analysis. A **category** is a construct that refers to a certain type of phenomenon mentioned in the database. (A construct is a concept that is inferred from observed phenomena, for example: self-esteem, cooperation, memory.) A category can be expressed numerically: It is either absent (a value of 0) or present (a value of 1) in any observed phenomenon. This numerical expression is called a *variable* by quantitative researchers, and sometimes by qualitative researchers as well.

Researchers need to develop a category label and definition for each type of phenomenon in the database that is to be analyzed. Also, they need to consider whether a particular category can be analyzed into subtypes. In Rossi's case study the broad category of *facilitation strategy* was analyzed into 15 subcategories, each of which refers to a different type of facilitation strategy. Subcategories also can represent different degrees or levels of a construct. For example, *perceived helpfulness of a facilitation strategy* might be conceptualized as a category with three subcategories: very helpful, helpful, and not helpful. Subcategories, as we explain below, are useful for detecting relational and causal patterns in case study data.

How do you establish a list of categories for coding the segments in your database? One approach is to use a list of categories developed by other researchers. Rossi used this approach in her study of facilitation strategies. Her list was developed by Matthew Miles and his colleagues for case studies of change agents in education, and subsequently modified by other researchers doing related studies. Examples of the categories are: coaching of individuals, developing a support structure, resource linking, supporting the client emotionally, and training groups.

The other approach is to develop your own categories. You will need to study your data carefully in order to identify significant phenomena, and then determine which phenomena share sufficient similarities that they can be considered instances of the same construct. This construct becomes a category in your category system. You will need to define the category, give it a label, and specify guidelines that you and others can use to determine whether each segment in the database is or is not an instance of the category.

This process of category development is consistent with the principles of grounded theory.[48] Case study researchers who use these principles derive their categories directly from their data rather than from theories developed by other researchers. In other words, the categories are "grounded" in the particular set of data that you collected. Furthermore, the categories seek to explain the phenomena that are observed as well as to describe them.

47. Rossi, M. A. (1993). The California Mathematics Project: Empowering elementary teachers to be leaders and change agents in mathematics reform. *Dissertation Abstracts International, 54*(09), 3314A. (UMI No. 9305218)
48. Strauss, A. L., & Corbin, J. M. (1998). *Basics of qualitative research: Techniques and procedures for developing grounded theory* (2nd ed.). Thousand Oaks, CA: Sage.

Because of this emphasis on explanation, the categories are considered theoretical. However, even if the categories are purely descriptive, the procedures used in grounded theory are applicable. Therefore, if you intend to develop your own categories, we recommend that you study the principles of grounded theory construction.

Coding Segments

After selecting or developing a category system, the researcher uses it to code each segment in the computer file. It is necessary to examine each segment and decide whether the phenomenon it describes fits one of the categories in the category system. If it does, the researcher types an abbreviation for the category (e.g., a number or acronym) next to the segment. A segment might contain no instances of any category in one's system, or it might contain instances of several categories, in which case the segment would be coded with the abbreviation for each category.

An example of multiple coding is provided in a case study by one of the authors (J. Gall). She interviewed students enrolled in *Careers Plus*, a program designed to assist people age 50 and over to resume work or change careers.[49] The segment to be coded involved the researcher's question and the student's reply:

> Researcher: At this point, what are your reasons for being in the Careers Plus program?
> Student: To get back to work and to be with people again. I was going to church, but wasn't participating in any activities . . . not a part of . . . . Coming to Careers Plus, I got active. [The instructor] called on me a lot in [class]; I think he liked to see me cry. I'm a crier.

The segment was coded as an instance of four categories:

1. Goals/reasons for being in or staying in program: Work
2. Goals/reasons for being in or staying in program: Be with people
3. Learning activities provided by the program: Career exploration class
4. Obstacles to career change: Isolation

This example illustrates that a single segment can provide various types of information of interest to a researcher, and that the information is retrievable through multiple coding.

In the process of coding your segments, you might find that some of your categories are ambiguous or that some segments contain information that is not codable using your category system. If this happens, you will need to revise the category system and then recode all the segments. Researchers typically revise their category system several times before feeling satisfied with it.

Grouping Category Segments

Touchstone in Research

Charmaz, K. (2005). Grounded theory in the 21st century: Applications for advancing social justice studies. In N. K. Denzin & Y. S. Lincoln (Eds.), *The Sage handbook for qualitative research* (3rd ed., pp. 507–535). Thousand Oaks, CA: Sage.

Suppose that the database for a case study contains 500 segments and the category system includes 20 categories (1–20). After coding all the segments, the researcher next would bring together all the segments that were tagged with the Category 1 code. (The process would be repeated for the other 19 categories as well.) Software programs designed for qualitative data analysis can perform this function. For example, if 15 segments were tagged with the Category 1 code, the program would compile all these segments for display on the computer screen, or they can be printed out.

The 15 segments with the Category 1 code are now conveniently grouped together. However, they are decontextualized, that is, they have been removed from their location in the interview transcript, field notes, or other document. This is not a serious problem, however, because each segment includes its line numbers. (You will recall that the software

49. Carried out at a local community college, Gall's case study was a "prototype" that was written up informally and not published.

program numbers each line of text in the database.) Thus, you can easily locate each segment in the database of interview transcripts, field notes, and documents. In addition, you might consider developing and applying several categories to help you situate a segment easily after it is removed from its location in the database. For example, suppose the study included five cases (C1, C2, C3, C4, C5), and the data for each case were derived from either an interview with the individual's colleague (COL) or supervisor (SUP), or from observation notes (OBS). Thus, the first segment for Category 1 might have the supplemental context codes (C2, COL), the second segment might be coded (C5, OBS), and so on. In this way, the researcher is easily reminded of the segment's location in the database.

When you examine as a group all 15 segments that were coded with the Category 1 code, you have an opportunity to reconsider whether the construct corresponding to that category is sensible. You might find, for example, that the content of some segments corresponds to the construct as you have defined it, but the content of other segments does not. The solution to this problem is to redefine the construct and perhaps to develop new categories.

In our hypothetical example, the grouping process will yield 20 displays of grouped segments, one for each of the 20 categories. The researcher most likely will print out each display for convenience. Now the displays can be compared to determine whether the categories overlap, whether some categories are confusing or irrelevant to the study, and whether some categories are of particular importance.

Barney Glaser and Anselm Strauss, the developers of the grounded-theory approach in qualitative research, coined the term **constant comparison** to refer to this continual process of comparing segments within and across categories.[50] (Keep in mind that each category refers to a separate construct and that, ultimately, what is important is the constructs, not the categories used in data analysis.) The term *constant* highlights the fact that the process of comparison and revision of categories is repeated until satisfactory closure is achieved. Using constant comparison, the researcher clarifies the meaning of each category, creates sharp distinctions between categories, and decides which categories are most important to the study. Although the method of constant comparison refers specifically to the development of constructs that are linked together by a theory, it is applicable to the development of purely descriptive constructs as well.

Strauss and Corbin claim that when using grounded-theory principles to determine categories, the researcher should collect data to the point of theoretical saturation. **Theoretical saturation** occurs when no new data are emerging relevant to an established coding category, no additional categories appear to be necessary to account for the phenomena of interest, and the relationships among categories appear to be well established.

By applying the method of constant comparison, the researcher should arrive at a set of well-defined categories with clear coding instructions. As a final check on the category system, the inter-rater reliability of coding should be determined. (Procedures for computing inter-rater reliability statistics are described in Chapter 9.) Demonstration that the category system can be used with high inter-rater reliability enhances the credibility of the case study findings, and it also encourages other researchers to apply the category system in their own case studies.

Drawing Conclusions

The discovery of constructs in qualitative data can be a significant outcome of a case study. Discovery of themes also is important. (You will recall that earlier in the chapter we defined

50. Glaser, B. G., & Strauss, A. L. (1967). *The discovery of grounded theory: Strategies for qualitative research*. Chicago: Aldine.

themes as salient, characteristic features of a case.) For example, Kleine-Kracht used the data from her case study of instructional leadership in a high school (described earlier in the chapter) to identify four themes in effective principals' instructional leadership. One such theme is that "the division chairs are curricular experts."[51] This theme emerged from several sources: data in which the principal stated that he expected the division chairs to be catalysts for instructional leadership and that he had selected them on that basis; a description of the chairs' considerable knowledge of instruction; and data indicating that teachers readily accept the division chairs as instructional leaders.

If the researcher uses a multiple-case design, the generalizability of constructs and themes across cases can be checked. This process might involve noting whether a particular theme observed in one case also is present in other cases. A more sophisticated check would involve determining whether the particular phenomena that were coded as manifestations of a construct in one case are similar to similarly coded phenomena in other cases.

Multiple-case data also can be analyzed to detect relational or causal patterns. The researcher's constructs can be thought of as variables. Each case can be given a score on each variable, typically: 0 = absent and 1 = present; or 0 = absent, 1 = present to a moderate degree, and 2 = present to a high degree. If the scores on one variable across all the cases systematically covary with scores on another variable, the researcher can infer a relational or causal pattern. Suppose, for example, that the researcher has collected data on ten schools, each constituting a separate case. She finds that the school staffs vary in their confidence in the school administrators, and they also vary in their willingness to try out a state-sponsored educational innovation. Suppose the data analysis reveals that cases (i.e., schools) with a high confidence level tend to have high willingness, whereas cases with a low confidence level tend to have low willingness. Given this result, the researcher would be justified in inferring the following pattern, which possibly is causal: Confidence in school administrators facilitates willingness to experiment.[52]

Patterns can be discovered within a single case as well as in multiple-case analysis. For example, suppose that a researcher observed one child extensively in various settings: a mathematics class, a language arts class, the school playground, at home while doing homework, and at home while playing. The researcher also has collected data on the child's state of mind (thoughts and emotions) in these different settings. These data can be analyzed to determine whether there is a relationship between the settings and the child's state of mind. We might find, for example, that the child feels tense and unfocused in academic work settings, but relaxed and fully engaged while playing. This is a relational pattern within a single case. If the researcher can invoke or develop a theory to explain this relationship, we would characterize it as a causal pattern.

Various software programs for Macintosh and PC computers are available to perform the various data analysis procedures described above.[53] The procedures also can be performed manually, but it is prohibitively time consuming. You can write line numbers on the master copy of your interview transcripts, field notes, and other text materials; make a new

51. Kleine-Kracht, Indirect instructional leadership, p. 209.
52. Other types of procedures that can be used to determine relational and causal patterns in case study data are described in: Miles & Huberman, *Qualitative data analysis*. For a discussion of the legitimacy of the use of qualitative research for causal explanation, see: Maxwell, J. A. (2004). Causal explanation, qualitative research, and scientific inquiry in education. *Educational Researcher, 33*(2), 3–11.
53. Boyatzis, R. E. (1998). *Transforming qualitative information: Thematic analysis and code development.* Thousand Oaks, CA: Sage; Strauss, A., & Corbin, J. (1998). *Basics of qualitative research: Techniques and procedures for developing grounded theory* (2nd ed.). Thousand Oaks, CA: Sage. See also La Pelle, Simplifying qualitative data analysis; Ryan, Using a word processor.

copy of these materials; mark the new copy into segments; cut out each segment and paste it onto a 3 × 5 card; write a category code (or codes) on each card; group cards having the same category code; and examine the groupings using the method of constant comparison.

These manual procedures will be exceedingly time consuming if your text materials are extensive. Therefore, many case study researchers plan their data-collection procedures with an eye toward eventually entering them into computer files for manipulation by software designed for interpretational analysis.

Structural Analysis

Structural analysis is the process of examining case study data for the purpose of identifying patterns inherent in discourse, text, events, or other phenomena. To understand how structural analysis differs from interpretational analysis, consider the following example, which consists of a segment of conversation between a Spanish teacher and one of her students:

Teacher: What does *la casa* mean?
Student: House.
Teacher: That's right. *La casa* means house.

A conversation analyst (see Chapter 15) examining this interaction might note certain features of it, such as:

1. The sequence of speakers within this instructional event was teacher, student, teacher.
2. Each of the teacher's utterances contained more words than the student's utterance.
3. Four Spanish words were uttered.
4. Three words (*la, casa, house*) were uttered twice, and the other six words were uttered once.

The conversation analyst then might examine whether each of these observed phenomena are present in other samples of discourse in this teacher's classroom or in other teachers' classrooms.

This example illustrates the essential feature of structural analysis, namely, that the researcher looks for patterns *inherent* in the data. Very little, if any, inference is required. In contrast, a researcher using interpretational analysis overlays a structure of meaning on the data. For example, suppose the researcher is investigating how students receive feedback in the classroom. The above interaction might be considered a segment, and it might be coded as an instance of feedback because of the utterance, "That's right. *La casa* means house." This classification of the utterance is an inference from the data by the researcher.

Structural analysis is used in conversation analysis, ethnoscience, and other qualitative research traditions. Here are a few examples of the types of educational phenomena that might be investigated in case studies that are based on these traditions: how students' speech patterns change over the course of schooling, the sequence of events in children's stories, how the various parts of textbooks are organized, how curriculum experts conceptualize the high school mathematics curriculum, how teachers and students interact with each other during a lesson, and movement patterns within a school building.

Two types of software programs useful in doing structural analyses of case study data are text retrievers and textbase managers.[54] **Text retrievers** are software programs that

54. Weitzman, E. A. (1999). Analyzing qualitative data with computer software. *Health Services Research.* Retrieved July 4, 2005, from http://www.findarticles.com/p/articles/mi_m4149/is_5_34/ai_58451874

operate on individual words and fixed sequences of words (e.g., a phrase such as *bill of rights*). These programs can perform such tasks as listing all words in a document, indicating where each word occurs in the document, and counting how many times each word occurs. **Textbase managers** are software programs that allow the researcher to format a document into fields, code each field, and then retrieve all fields with a given code. For example, if the document is a transcript of a discussion among five educators, each utterance by any of them, no matter how long or short, can be formatted as a field. Next, each field can be assigned one or more codes, such as a code indicating which of the five educators made the utterance. Finally, all fields that have been assigned a given code can be retrieved for display. This feature enables the researcher to retrieve all utterances made by any one of the educators. You may have noticed that text retrievers and textbase managers are similar to software programs for interpretational analysis. Fields, for example, are similar to segments. However, the programs for interpretational analysis have capabilities that those for structural analysis lack.

A textbase manager can search for sequence patterns in a document. Suppose the document is the transcript of the discussion among the five educators mentioned above. This computer program, for example, could identify and compile all sequences in which educator B made a statement that was followed by a statement made by educator D. The identification of such sequences, and their frequency, might reveal interpersonal dynamics that have theoretical or practical implications.

Reflective Analysis

Interpretational analysis and structural analysis involve explicit procedures that are performed in a somewhat prescribed sequence. In contrast, **reflective analysis** is a process in which the researcher relies primarily on intuition and judgment in order to portray or evaluate the phenomenon being studied.

Reflective analysis is associated with several qualitative research traditions, including educational connoisseurship and criticism (see Chapter 17) and phenomenology (see Chapter 15). We believe, however, that reflective analysis also could be used in basic case studies or case studies that draw on other qualitative research traditions. Its use involves a decision by the researcher to rely on her own intuition and personal judgment to analyze the data rather than on technical procedures involving an explicit category classification system.

Some case studies, especially those associated with ethnographic traditions (see Chapter 14), involve a collaborative effort by a team of researchers. In this situation, the reflective analyses are formed through a dynamic process that is likely to involve conflict, negotiation, and ambiguity and that may result in unusually rich interpretations of the data. Judith Wasser and Liora Bresler suggest the concept of the **interpretive zone** to characterize this process: "In the interpretive zone, researchers bring together their different kinds of knowledge, experience, and beliefs to forge new meanings through the process of the joint inquiry in which they are engaged."[55]

One way to understand reflective analysis is to compare it with artistic endeavors. The artist reflects on phenomena and then portrays them in such a way as to reveal both their surface features and essences, a process called *connoisseurship*. Many case study researchers engage in similar reflections and portrayals. Reflective analysis is ideally suited for generating thick description, but it also can lead to the discovery of constructs, themes, and patterns.

---

55. Wasser, J. D., & Bresler, L. (1996). Working in the interpretive zone: Conceptualized collaboration in qualitative research teams. *Educational Researcher, 25*(5), 5–15. Quote appears on p. 13.

The other side of artistic portrayal is criticism. Literary critics, for example, study a literary work in order to develop an appreciation of its aesthetic elements and "message," but also to make critical judgments about its artistic merit. Many case studies conducted by educational evaluators (see Chapter 17) are conducted for similar purposes. These evaluative studies help educators and policy makers understand the features and purposes of educational programs, products, and methods, and also to appreciate their strengths and weaknesses. Just as a literary critic develops reflective ability with experience, so must an educational evaluator build up a store of experience in order to use reflective analysis wisely.

Because reflective analysis is largely subjective, it is not possible to specify standard procedures for doing this type of data analysis. Apprenticeship with an experienced researcher, followed by considerable practice, is essential. However, a few guidelines from hermeneutics (see Chapter 15) might be generally applicable. In doing reflective analysis from a hermeneutical perspective, the researcher carefully examines and then re-examines *all* the data that have been collected. As this process continues, certain features of the phenomenon are likely to become salient. The researcher then should develop an understanding of these features by themselves and in relation to each other. In other words, the analysis should account for as much as possible of the phenomenon being studied. An interpretation or criticism that applies to some of the data should not be contradicted by other data.

Ensuring the Quality and Rigor of Qualitative Research

The growth of qualitative research has been accompanied by burgeoning interest in the topic of research validity. Egon Guba and Yvonna Lincoln explain that in research guided by an interpretive epistemological orientation, "Terms such as credibility, transferability, dependability, and confirmability replace the usual positivist criteria of internal and external validity, reliability, and objectivity."[56]

Many different conceptions exist of the characteristics that reflect the quality of qualitative research.[57] In addition, some qualitative research traditions have evolved their own conceptions of validity. Models of validity for cultural studies research and for critical ethnography are summarized in Chapter 15, for historical research in Chapter 16, and for practitioner research in Chapter 18. Qualitative researchers generally reserve selection of the criteria for determining the soundness of their research to themselves, depending on the topics, methods, audiences, and performers of the research.[58]

Below we summarize various methods and procedures described in the research literature that we consider relevant for ensuring the quality and rigor of qualitative research.[59] Strategies 1 to 5 primarily reflect meeting the needs of users, including research

56. Guba, E. G., & Lincoln. Y. S. (1994). Competing paradigms in qualitative research. In N. K. Denzin & Y. S. Lincoln (Eds.), *Handbook of qualitative research* (pp. 105–117). Thousand Oaks, CA: Sage.
57. Guba, E. G., & Lincoln, Y. S. (2005). Paradigmatic controversies, contradictions, and emerging confluences. In N. K. Denzin & Y. S. Lincoln (Eds.), *The Sage handbook of qualitative research* (3rd ed., pp. 191–215).
58. For example, Lomawaima, K. T., & McCarty, T. L. (2002). Reliability, validity, and authenticity in American Indian and Alaska Native Research. (ERIC Digest, No. ED470951). Available from http://www.eric.ed.gov
59. Particular strategies in this list are further discussed in: Altheide, D. L., & Johnson, J. M. (1998). Criteria for assessing interpretive validity in qualitative research. In N. K. Denzin & Y. S. Lincoln (Eds.), *Collecting and interpreting qualitative materials* (pp. 283–312). Thousand Oaks, CA: Sage; Maxwell, *Qualitative research design;* Merriam, S. B. (1988). *Case study research in education: A qualitative approach.* San Francisco: Jossey-Bass; Miles, M. B., & Huberman, A. M. (1994). *Qualitative data analysis;* Yin, *Case study research.*

participants; strategies 6 to 10 reflect primarily thoroughness of data collection; and strategies 11 to 17 reflect primarily the use of sound research methods.

These strategies are not add-ons to be considered only after a study has been designed, is in progress, or is nearing completion. Instead they are key ingredients of successful qualitative research (including case study research) that need to be built into the research design. Maxwell emphasizes that such strategies are essential to "ruling out validity threats and increasing the credibility of your conclusions."[60] Use of such strategies will increase not only the quality and rigor of qualitative research but also its impact within and beyond education.

Strategies to Meet Users' Needs

1. *Usefulness.* Make the case study useful to readers. Make it a goal to enlighten the individuals who read the case study or to further the emancipation of research participants, readers of the report, and possibly other groups. Julie Kaomea's case study of indigenous studies in elementary schools in Hawaii reflects this strategy.[61] The abstract states that the article "challenges educators and educational researchers to think closely about how they might serve as allies in Indigenous struggles for self-determination."[62]

2. *Participatory models.* Involve participants in all phases of the research from conceptualization of the study to writing the final report.

3. *Chain of evidence.* Build clear, meaningful links between research questions, raw data, and the findings. Make an **audit trail** that documents the research process, covering, for example, source of and method of recording raw data, data reduction and analysis products, data reconstruction and synthesis products, process notes, and information about the development of instruments. Include representative samples of materials in the report, and keep study materials for several years to permit inspection by others.

4. *Truthfulness and reporting style.* Be honest and straightforward. Use an authentic reporting style so as to achieve **verisimilitude,** a style of writing that draws readers so closely into subjects' worlds that these can be palpably felt. Include direct quotes from research participants and descriptions of specific, concrete events that were observed. Use appropriate language and literary genres.

5. *Quasi-statistics.* Provide simple numerical results that can be readily derived from the data to support conclusions of an implicit quantitative nature (e.g., describing a finding as typical, rare, or extreme). Use quasi-statistics to test and support claims and assess the amount of evidence that bears on them.

Strategies to Ensure Thorough Data Collection

6. *Triangulation of data sources, analysts, or theories.* Vary the methods used to generate findings and see if they are corroborated across these variants. If inconsistent or contradictory findings occur, see if they can be reconciled within some explanatory framework. Laurel Richardson proposes the term **crystallization** instead of triangulation, in recognition of the truth that the mixed-genre texts of qualitative research can have "an infinite variety of shapes,

60. Maxwell, *Qualitative research design*, p. 109.
61. Kaomea, J. (2005). Indigenous studies in the elementary curriculum: A cautionary Hawaiian example. *Anthropology and Education Quarterly, 36*(1), 24–42.
62. Ibid., p. 24.

substances, transmutations . . . . Crystals grow, change, alter . . . ."[63] Ovadia Aviram's case study of an Israeli boarding school for Jewish youth illustrates the process of corroborating or reconciling the findings from one data-collection method with another data-collection method.[64] Aviram's direct observations of how staff members treated and talked about students produced data that were highly incongruent with what staff members had reported in interviews and informal conversations with the researcher. Aviram explained these discrepancies as due to the staff's use of "generating appearances," a strategy of maintaining a necessary illusion to the outside world that the boarding school represents a benign environment for students and staff.

7. *Contextual completeness.* Describe the context in which case study phenomena are set: the history, physical setting, environment, number of participants, activities, schedules and temporal order of events, division of labor, routines and variations, significant events and their origins and consequences, members' perceptions and meanings, social rules and basic patterns of order. Demonstrate sensitivity to a setting's **multivocality,** meaning that in many settings participants do not speak with a unified voice. Incorporate **tacit knowledge,** the "largely unarticulated, contextual understanding that is often manifested in nods, silences, humor, and naughty nuances."[65]

8. *Long-term observation.* Gather data over a long period of time and make repeated observations to increase the reliability of case study findings.

9. *Rich data.* Collect rich data, including interview transcripts and detailed notes or recordings of observations, that are detailed and varied enough to provide a full and revealing picture of what is going on.

10. *Representativeness check.* To determine whether a finding is typical of the field setting from which it was obtained, make sure that the sample was selected so as to avoid overreliance on accessible or elite informants. Consider how unusual occurrences or the researcher's presence or absence on specific occasions might have skewed the findings.

Strategies Reflecting Sound Research Design

11. *Coding checks.* Use low-inference descriptors and mechanical means to record data. If data segments have been coded into categories, check the inter-rater reliability of the coding process or seek agreement among observers on the nature of the events being recorded.

12. *Disconfirming case analysis.* Use extreme cases (outliers) to test findings derived from typical cases, and look for negative evidence that would directly disconfirm the researchers' interpretations.

13. *Member checking.* Ensure representation of the emic perspective by **member checking,** which involves having research participants review statements in the report for accuracy and completeness. Correct factual errors and, if necessary, collect more data to reconcile discrepancies, rewrite the report, or include contrasting views.

63. Richardson, L. (2000). Writing: A method of inquiry. In N. K. Denzin & Y. S. Lincoln (Eds.), *Handbook of qualitative research* (2nd ed., pp. 923–948). Thousand Oaks, CA: Sage. Quote appears on p. 6.
64. Aviram, O. (1993). Appearance and reality in a stressful educational setting: Practices inhibiting school effectiveness in an Israeli boarding school. *International Journal of Qualitative Studies in Education, 6,* 33–48.
65. Altheide, D. L., & Johnson, J. M. (1998). Criteria for assessing interpretive validity in qualitative research. In N. K. Denzin & Y. S. Lincoln (Eds.), *Handbook of qualitative research* (pp. 485–499). Thousand Oaks, CA: Sage. Quote appears on p. 492.

14. *Intervention and pattern matching.* Make an informal intervention even if the case lacks a formal treatment, and check whether the patterns in the data correspond to predictions drawn from the theoretical propositions underlying the intervention. For example, say that a case study is done of a curriculum designed to strengthen students' motivation and self-concept. The theory underlying the curriculum predicts that students who experience the curriculum will receive certain benefits. If the pattern of expected benefits is observed in case study participants, the researcher's inference that the curriculum caused the benefits has passed a critical test of rigor.

15. *Comparison.* Compare the same setting at different times to address the *counterfactual* of what would have happened without the presence of the presumed cause, and make less formal comparisons to other settings to contribute to the interpretability of the results.

16. *Peer examination.* Ask colleagues to comment on the findings as they emerge and to review a draft of the case study report.

17. *Researcher reflection.* As researchers, demonstrate sensitivity in relating to the situation being studied, and discuss role relationships and the researcher's assumptions, world view, theoretical orientation, and positionality toward the phenomenon being investigated.

A *researcher identity memo* and its addendum, presented in Maxwell's book on qualitative research design, shows that researchers can begin this reflection process very early in their work.[66] The memo author, Barbara Noel, writes of her personal interest in the topic of educational reform in Bolivia. She tells of her bicultural parents and the deep effect that being bilingual has had on her life. She describes how she relates to the struggle of Bolivians forced to use another culture's language in school: "I mostly feel angry as I write about these issues. In a way it is this anger and the subsequent passion for justice that drove me to the field of intercultural, bilingual education." [67] Her addendum, written later after further reflection, notes:

> While my empathy might help me perceive subtle and important motivations for my informants' responses and behavior . . . I also identified a pattern of behavior I engage in which is to get overly involved with a project so that my emotional connection takes over. I lose my focus and change my role from the one I had objectively started out with. Having identified this pattern, I can, in a way, construct an overhead camera to monitor my actions that might often blink a bright red light to indicate overheating.[68]

It is clear that this researcher will continue to reflect and reorient her positionality as needed as her research work unfolds.

Positivist Conceptions of the Validity and Reliability of Case Study Research

Some major proponents of qualitative case study research reflect a positivist epistemological orientation in their assessment of the quality and rigor of such research.

66. Barbara Noel's researcher identity memo in: Maxwell, *Qualitative research design*, pp. 28–30. Quote appears on p. 29.
67. Ibid., p. 29.
68. Ibid., p. 31.

Yin exemplifies this type of case study researcher.[69] He judges the quality of case study design by three types of validity criteria and one reliability criterion:

1. **Construct validity** is the extent to which a measure used in a case study correctly operationalizes the concepts being studied.
2. **Internal validity** is the extent to which the researcher has demonstrated a causal relationship between X and Y by showing that other plausible factors could not have caused Y. The criterion of internal validity is not applicable to descriptive case study research, because it does not seek to identify causal patterns in phenomena.
3. **External validity** is the extent to which the findings of a case study can be generalized to similar cases.
4. **Reliability** is the extent to which other researchers would arrive at similar results if they studied the same case using exactly the same procedures as the first researcher.

Yin recommends some of the same strategies listed earlier (e.g., chain of evidence and pattern matching) to judge the quality of a case study design. The types of evidence needed for making determinations of validity and reliability are described in Chapter 7 of this book. The concepts of internal and external validity are further explained in Chapter 12.

Determining the Applicability of Case Study Findings

Although each case in case study research is viewed as unique, most researchers or users of qualitative research also have the goal of determining the extent to which the findings of a case study, or of any qualitative research study, are applicable to other cases or settings. In quantitative research, generalization from a sample to a population is the goal, and it is based largely on the selection of random samples and the use of inferential statistics and determination of effect size (see Chapters 4, 5, and 6 for explanations of meta-analysis, effect size, and sampling, respectively). The term **applicability,** rather than *generalizability,* is more appropriate for this goal of qualitative research because it is based on different processes and types of evidence.

A variety of positions exist, however, about whether applicability exists and, if so, how to determine it. Robert Stake takes the position that "How we learn from the singular case is related to how the case is like and unlike other cases we do know, mostly by comparison."[70] Consistent with interpretive epistemology, Stake recommends comparison based on cases, not on variables.[71]

One approach to increasing the applicability of case study findings involves the selection of specific purposeful sampling strategies (described in Chapter 6) to increase the probability that the findings will apply to other cases also representing the phenomenon being studied. For example, one might study a case that is typical of the phenomenon. If an atypical case is selected because it is of particular interest, it might be possible to select a typical case for study as well. Finally, if a unit of analysis has been defined, a random sample within this unit of analysis could be sampled. For example, if researchers are studying the effects of an experimental instructional method being used in a particular teacher's classroom (the case), they might select a random sample of the teacher's students for intensive data collection and analysis.

69. Yin, *Case study research*.
70. Stake, R. (2005). Qualitative case studies. In N. K. Denzin & Y. S. Lincoln, *The Sage handbook of qualitative research* (3rd ed., pp. 443–466). Thousand Oaks, CA: Sage. Quote appears on p. 454.
71. Qualitative comparative analysis, a strategy that uses both quantitative and qualitative methods, is described in Rihoux, *Bridging the gap*.

Another approach to assessing applicability is through the comparison of cases or settings in relation to an existing theory. By contrast, Yin argues that generalizing from case studies is appropriate and is "a matter of analytical generalization (using single or multiple cases to illustrate, represent, or generalize to a theory.)"[72] Yin argues that case studies can be generalized to theoretical propositions, rather than to populations and universes as in quantitative research. He cites Jane Jacobs's book, *The Death and Life of Great American Cities*.[73] While based on New York City, the chapter topics and examples cover broader issues in urban planning, such as the role of neighborhood parks, sidewalks, and mixed-uses public spaces, which represent a theory of urban planning. Yin also notes that replication logic (described in Chapter 6) and a multiple-case design allow the researcher to strengthen or broaden the analytic generalizations, "because the multiple cases were designed to 'replicate' each other . . . ."[74] Sally Hutchinson, by contrast, expresses the view that research based on grounded theory probably is not replicable, and therefore presumably would not apply to other cases or settings: "Grounded theory depends on the interaction between the data and the creative processes of the researcher. It is highly unlikely that two people would come up with the exact same theory."[75]

Davydd Greenwood and Morten Levin address determination of the applicability of case study findings in relation to action research, which they view as "an active process of reflection in which involved actors must make up their minds whether the previous knowledge makes sense in the next context or not and begin working on ways of acting in the new context."[76] Greenwood and Levin's emphasis on reflection on context and anticipation of action as the basis for applicability prefigures still another approach to determining applicability, which is the extent to which the ultimate target of such research, that is, the consumers of the research, view it as relevant to their situation and needs. This approach places the responsibility for determining applicability on the "consumers" of the findings rather than on the researchers. Sandra Wilson uses the term **reader/user generalizability** to indicate that it is the responsibility of each reader or user of case study research to determine the applicability of the findings in their own situations.[77]

Researchers can use several strategies to help readers of a case study report determine the generalizability of findings to their particular situation or to other situations. First, researchers should provide a thick description of the participants and contexts that comprise the case, so that readers who are interested in applying the findings can determine how similar they are to the situation of interest to them. Second, researchers should address the issue of whether the selected case is representative of the general phenomenon being investigated. The use of multiple-case design allows researchers to conduct a cross-case analysis to determine generalizability across the cases that were studied.

Reporting a Case Study

Some ambiguity exists as to whether a particular piece of research should or should not be considered a case study. We identified most of the case studies cited in this chapter through

72. Yin, *The abridged version of case study research*, p. 239.
73. Jacobs, J. (1961). *The death and life of great American cities.* New York: Random House.
74. Yin, *The abridged version of case study research*, p. 240.
75. Hutchinson, S. A. (1988). Education and grounded theory. In R. R. Sherman & R. B. Webb (Eds.), *Qualitative research in education: Focus and methods* (pp. 123–140). London: Falmer Press. Quote appears on p. 132.
76. Greenwood, D. J., & Levin, M. (2005). Reform of the social sciences and universities through action resrarch. In N. K. Denzin & Y. S. Lincoln (Eds.), *The Sage handbook of qualitative research* (3rd ed., pp. 43–64). Thousand Oaks, CA: Sage. Quote appears on p. 55.
77. Wilson, S. (1979). Explorations of the usefulness of case study evaluations. *Evaluation Quarterly, 3,* 446–459.

database searches using *case study* as a keyword (see Chapter 4). However, when we read some of the resulting reports, we found that some used the term *case study* in their reports, while others did not, and we often had to search carefully to find any mention of the term. Several reports indicated that the reported study was part of a larger study or ethnography. Some mentioned previous reports related to the topic with which the current case study was concerned. Such statements reflect the fact that, over time, a researcher may do and report a number of case studies on the same topic. Harry Wolcott's research on Brad, the "sneaky kid," is a well-known example.[78]

Our review of published case studies indicates that they generally follow one of two reporting styles—what we choose to call *reflective reporting* and *analytic reporting*. Elements of either style can appear in the other, but generally the characteristics of one style are dominant. We describe the two styles below, but first we consider the researcher's decision about which case or cases will be reported for a specific case study.

Finalizing Definition of the Case

Case study research is unique in that it is not until the phase of writing up or otherwise reporting the research that the researchers finalize their identification of the specific case or cases that the study concerns. When the researcher has collected "thick" data about various aspects of the phenomenon being studied, it is possible to define the case in different ways. For example, consider Rossi's study of teachers (she called them teacher-leaders) who had participated in the California Mathematics Project. Instead of focusing on the teacher-leaders, she might have focused on data that she had collected about the project (its history, project directors, summer training programs, etc.) and specific facilitation events for which the teacher-leaders were responsible. However, Rossi decided to focus on one particular aspect, namely, the change-agent role of the teacher-leaders. Also, although she started collecting data on three teacher-leaders, she eventually decided to exclude one of them because of unusual circumstances pertaining to that individual. Thus, decisions about which cases and which aspect of the cases to report were not finalized until well after her dissertation proposal had been approved and data collection was underway.

Deciding which case, or cases, to report can be difficult, because technological tools like computers, videotape equipment, and photocopy machines tempt researchers to generate ever more data. The researcher must sort through the data and report only those cases and aspects of them that have the greatest bearing on the questions that interest her. Wolcott makes the point this way:

> The critical task in qualitative research is not to accumulate all the data you can, but to "can" (i.e., get rid of) most of the data you accumulate. That requires constant winnowing, including decisions about data not worth entering in the first place, regardless of how easy that might be to do. The trick is to discover essences and then to reveal those essences with sufficient context, yet not become mired trying to include everything that might possibly be described.[79]

Because case selection can occur late in the research process, Wolcott argues that case study is not a research design or method, but rather an outcome of qualitative research that the researcher chooses at the stage of preparing the report.[80]

78. Wolcott, H. F. (1990). *Writing up qualitative research.* Newbury Park, CA: Sage; Wolcott, H. F. (1994). *Transforming qualitative data: Description, analysis, and interpretation.* Thousand Oaks, CA: Sage; Wolcott, H. F. (2002). *Sneaky kid and its aftermath: Ethics and intimacy in fieldwork.* Walnut Creek, CA: AltaMira.
79. Wolcott, H. F. (2001). *Writing up qualitative research,* p. 44.
80. Wolcott, *Transforming qualitative data.*

Reflective Reporting

As we explained earlier in the chapter, some case study researchers rely heavily or exclusively on reflective analysis of their data rather than on interpretational or structural analysis. These researchers most likely will prefer to write their dissertations or other reports using a reflective reporting style. The two primary characteristics of **reflective reporting** are the use of literary devices to bring the case alive for the reader and the strong presence of the researcher's voice in the report.

Authors of literary works, of course, tell stories. In reflective reporting, we find that the researcher often weaves case study data into a story. It is this type of researcher that Wolcott apparently has in mind when he argues that the ability to be a storyteller, rather than disdain for number crunching, should be regarded as the distinguishing characteristic of qualitative researchers.[81] Among the ways Wolcott suggests for organizing and presenting a case study as a story are: (1) relating events in chronological order; (2) focusing the story on a critical or key event; (3) recounting the events through the eyes of different participants whose perspectives may differ considerably; and (4) reporting a "day-in-the-life," for example, a reconstruction of the first day of fieldwork, or a typical day in the life of a case study participant.

Table 14.2 presents the headings for Wolcott's case study of a school dropout, which we mentioned earlier in the chapter. The story of Brad (the "sneaky kid") starts in present time, and then recounts earlier events in his life as appropriate. Much of the story is organized around broader and narrower themes, one of which is "in the chute," a phrase used to describe individuals whose experiences appear to be leading them toward prison. Wolcott states that he arranged the story sequence this way so that "the reader meets Brad on his own ground, first through a recounting of major events and everyday aspects of his life, next through important dimensions of his worldview."[82] The researcher's voice is heard clearly in the last two sections, where Wolcott presents his interpretation and summary of the case. Wolcott states that the reason for this sequencing is that, "By the time readers arrive at the point where I offer *my* thoughts as to what might be done [about school dropouts], I want to be sure they have a sufficient background to form their own assessment of Brad and his circumstances."[83]

Wolcott's life history of a "sneaky kid" illustrates two principles of reflective reporting. First, the organization of the report highlights what the researcher has learned from the data analysis. Second, the researcher keeps the reader in mind in deciding how to present what he has learned.

The researcher can use various literary devices within the framework of storytelling to bring the case alive for the reader and to convey his point of view as the researcher and narrator of the report. Direct quotes of remarks by the case study participants are particularly effective because they clarify the emic perspective, that is, the meaning of the phenomenon from the point of view of the participants. Much of Wolcott's report consists of direct quotes of statements by Brad, for example:

> I guess being sneaky means I always try to get away with something. There doesn't have to be any big reason. I used to tell the kid I was hanging around with, "I don't steal stuff because I need it. I just like to do it for some excitement."[84]

81. Wolcott, *Writing up qualitative research.*
82. Wolcott, *Transforming qualitative data,* p. 64.
83. Ibid.
84. Ibid., p. 77.

TABLE 14.2

Organization of a Published Case Study Involving Reflective Reporting

Adequate Schools and Inadequate Education

The Life History of a Sneaky Kid

_____*

The Cultural Context of a Free Spirit
The Life History of a Sneaky Kid
   "In the Chute"
      On the loose
      Getting busted
      Second-rate jobs and second-rate apartments
      A new life
      "Picking up" what was needed
      The bicycle thief
      Being sneaky
      I don't have to steal, but
      Breaking and entering
      Inching closer to the chute
      I'm not going to get caught
      Home is the hunter
      Growing up
      Getting paid for dropping out
      Hiding out from life
   Worldview: "Getting My Life Together"
      A job—that's all that makes you middle class
      Building my own life
      Being by myself
      Friends
      I've been more places and done more things
      Some personal standards
      Moderation: Getting close enough, going "medium" fast
      Putting it all together
   Formal Schooling
Adequate Schools and Inadequate Education: An Interpretation Summary

*The report starts with an introductory section that does not have a heading.

Source: Headings for "The Life History of a Sneaky Kid" in: Wolcott, H. F. (1994). _Transforming qualitative data_. Thousand Oaks, CA: Sage. Copyright © 1994 by Sage Publications. Reprinted with permission of Sage Publications, Inc.

Some case study researchers have used more dramatic methods for conveying their findings. Laura Richardson cites examples of case studies that have been reported in the form of fiction, poetry, drama, oral readings, comedy and satire, and visual presentations.[85] In one of her own studies, she wrote a poem to convey her understanding of an unmarried

85. Richardson, Writing: A method of inquiry.

mother whom she had studied. The poem uses only the mother's language, as arranged by Richardson. The first lines of the poem are as follows:

The most important thing
to say   is that
I grew up in the South.
Being Southern shapes
aspirations   shapes
what you think you are
and what you think you're going to be.

(When I hear myself, my Ladybird
kind of accent on tape, I think, OH Lord.
You're from Tennessee.)[86]

The use of these dramatic forms to represent case study findings has been called the **performance turn** in qualitative research. Norman Denzin observes that whereas a standard written text involves one-way transmission of findings from the researcher to the reader, the performance turn intends a dynamic interaction between researcher and audience to co-create meaning:

Through the act of coparticipation, these works bring audiences back into the text, creating a field of shared emotional experience. The phenomenon being described is created through the act of representation . . . . A good performance text must be more than cathartic, it must be political, moving people to action and reflection.[87]

Richardson observes that case study researchers who use these unconventional genres typically have a postmodern sensibility. As we explained in Chapter 1, postmodernism casts doubt on all claims to authoritative methods of inquiry and reporting, including mainstream scientific reports. A postmodernist, therefore, would be inclined to view poetry to be just as legitimate a genre for reporting case study findings as the standard journal article format used by quantitative researchers.

Analytic Reporting

An analytic reporting style is appropriate when the researcher has emphasized interpretational or structural analysis of case study data and has conceptualized the study from a positivist or postpositivist perspective. The major characteristics of **analytic reporting** are an objective writing style (i.e., the researcher's voice is silent or subdued) and a conventional organization of topics to be covered: introduction, review of literature, methodology, results, and discussion. This is essentially the same style and organization used to report quantitative research studies (see Chapter 2).

Suppose a case study researcher has done data analyses to identify constructs, themes, and patterns in the phenomena that have been studied. Suppose further that this researcher used a multiple-case design. Should the researcher report the results for each construct, theme, and pattern across all the cases that have been studied? Or should she report each case by itself and show how the constructs, themes, and patterns are manifested in that particular case? If the former approach is used, the construct, theme, or pattern is highlighted;

86. Richardson, L. (1992). The consequences of poetic representation: Writing the other, rewriting the self. In C. Ellis & M. G. Flaherty (Eds.), *Investigating subjectivity: Research on lived experience* (pp. 125–140). Newbury Park, CA: Sage. Quote appears on p. 126. Reprinted with permission from Sage Publications, Inc.
87. Denzin, N. K. (2000). The practices and politics of interpretation. In N. K. Denzin & Y. S. Lincoln (Eds.), *Handbook of qualitative research* (2nd ed., pp. 897–922). Thousand Oaks, CA: Sage.

TABLE 14.3

Matrix Display of Teachers' Experience in Using a New Educational Practice

User	Feelings/Concerns	How Innovation Looked	What Was User Doing Most?	Problems
Vance	More comfortable with style of teaching and with having kids outside	Still useful, giving good direction and helpful ideas, activities	Working through materials Giving, participating in env'l educ workshops Working with community Off-campus site work	Time too limited for tasks to be done
Drew	Concern with growing number of nonachievers in forestry/ecology class	Too discovery-oriented for kids without biology basics; lecture style more appropriate	Adapting materials and lessons to growing nonachiever population Off-campus site work	Dealing with more nonachievers successfully
Carroll	Excitement with new activities, expanding science program	Same as first year	Working with community Giving, participating in env'l educ workshops Off-campus site work	Overextended activity commitment

Source: Table 7.3 on p. 179 in: Miles, M. B., & Huberman, A. M. (1994). *Qualitative data analysis: An expanded sourcebook* (2nd ed.). Thousand Oaks, CA: Sage. Copyright © 1994 by Sage Publications. Reprinted with permission from Sage Publications, Inc.

however, the reader does not get a holistic understanding of each case. Conversely, if the latter approach is used, the reader sees each case as a whole, but it is difficult to make cross-case comparisons with respect to particular constructs, themes, or patterns.

We have found that a combination of the two approaches works well. First, the data analysis results for each case are reported, including sufficient thick description so that the participants, events, and context come alive for the reader. Next, a cross-case analysis is given, which notes consistencies and differences in constructs, themes, and patterns across the cases that have been studied.

As in quantitative research reports, tables and figures are an effective way to present the results of case study analyses. A useful sourcebook of various display formats for this purpose was prepared by Miles and Huberman.[88] They distinguish between two types of display formats: a matrix and a network. A **matrix** is a table that has defined rows and columns. Table 14.3 is an example of a matrix in their sourcebook, taken from a case study of school improvement and change. It represents in summary form the experiences of three teachers who are attempting to implement a new educational practice.

A **network** is a figure for displaying bits of information, each in a separate "node," and links that show how the bits of information relate to each other. Figure 14.3 is an example of a network in Miles and Huberman's sourcebook, taken from case studies of university students. The left part of the figure shows a sequence of experiences of a student who had temporarily left the university. Each box (a "node") contains a separate experience. The right part of the figure shows a different set of nodes, each containing a force or forces moving the student to the next experience.

Displays such as those shown in Table 14.3 and Figure 14.3 can be helpful in two ways. First, they help researchers organize the results of a data analysis and plan the next stage

88. Miles & Huberman, *Qualitative data analysis*.

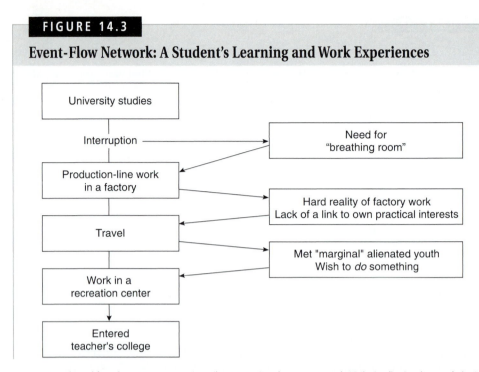

FIGURE 14.3

Event-Flow Network: A Student's Learning and Work Experiences

Source: Adapted from box 5.2 on p. 114 in: Miles, M. B., & Huberman, A. M. (1994). *Qualitative data analysis: An expanded sourcebook* (2nd ed.). Thousand Oaks, CA: Sage. Copyright © 1994 by Sage Publications. Adapted with permission from Sage Publications, Inc.

of analysis. Second, displays can be used in the case study report to present research findings so that they are easily comprehended by the reader. Miles and Huberman's sourcebook contains many examples of matrices and networks that are suitable for various purposes in case study research.

Advantages and Disadvantages of Case Study Research

Now that you have read about case study research, you are in a position to appreciate its advantages over quantitative research. One of them is that the case study researcher, through a process of thick description, can bring a case to life in a way that is not possible using the statistical methods of quantitative research. Thus, readers of case study reports may have a better basis for developing theories, designing educational interventions, or taking some other action than they would have from reading only quantitative research reports. Also, thick description helps readers to compare cases with their own situations. These comparisons are more difficult to make when reading reports of quantitative research, which typically provide only statistical analyses and sparse verbal descriptions of the situations that were studied. Furthermore, a good case study report will reveal the researcher's perspective, thus enabling readers to determine whether the researcher's perspective on the phenomenon is similar to theirs.

There are situations in which a researcher wishes to learn about a particular individual, for example, an outlier who does not fit the general trend. The case study method is ideally suited to investigating outliers and other unusual phenomena. Quantitative research designs are better suited for identifying general trends in populations.

Another advantage of case studies is their emergent quality. As researchers collect data and gain insight into particular phenomena, they can change the case on which the study will focus, adopt new data-collection methods, and frame new research questions. In contrast, quantitative research designs are difficult to change once they are set in motion.

The main disadvantage of case studies is the difficulty of generalizing the findings to other situations, although limited generalizations can be made using the procedures that we described in this chapter. Another disadvantage is that ethical problems can arise if it proves difficult in the report to disguise the identity of the organization or individuals that were studied. Also, case studies are very labor-intensive, and they require highly developed language skills in order to identify constructs, themes, and patterns in verbal data and to write a report that brings the case alive for the reader. For those willing to do the intense work of learning and applying the qualitative case study approach, however, the results can contribute a great deal to the field of educational research and practice.

RECOMMENDATIONS FOR
Doing Case Studies

1. In designing a case study, identify the phenomenon to be studied, the focus, and the unit of analysis.
2. Consider how you will represent the emic and etic perspectives.
3. Maintain awareness of your interpretive process as you design and conduct the case study.
4. Address issues involving goals, conceptual framework, research questions, methods, and validity in creating your case study design.
5. Devote sufficient time for gaining entry, making contacts, and establishing rapport with research participants in order to establish the trust needed to collect rich, reliable data.
6. Consider using a contact summary sheet and document summary sheet to keep track of the data-collection process.
7. If appropriate, use software specifically designed for qualitative data analysis.
8. Consider whether interpretational, structural, or reflective analysis is best suited for making sense of your data.
9. Of the many strategies for improving case study research, choose those that are best aligned with the theoretical orientation and purposes of the study.
10. Consider how you will approach the issue of the applicability of case study findings in reporting your case study.
11. Decide whether a reflective or an analytic style is most appropriate for reporting your case study.
12. Before writing a report of your case study, identify the case or cases on which your report will focus.

SELF-CHECK TEST

Circle the correct answer to each of the following questions.
The answers are provided at the back of the book.

1. In case study research, in-depth study of the case typically requires
   a. a long-term period of data collection.
   b. a substantial amount of data to represent the phenomenon.
   c. ongoing researcher reflection.
   d. all of the above.

2. The unit of analysis in a case study is
   a. the population from which the case is drawn.
   b. the type of term selected for structural analysis.
   c. the database segment selected for category analysis.
   d. an aspect of a phenomenon that is sampled from possible cases.

3. The term *emic perspective* refers to
   a. a positivist researcher's view of the phenomenon being studied.
   b. an interpretive researcher's view of the phenomenon being studied.
   c. the research participants' view of the phenomenon being studied.
   d. the reader's view of the phenomenon being studied.

4. Marty habitually failing to turn in his homework on time represents a(n) _____ in case study research.
   a. construct
   b. evaluation
   c. theme
   d. thick description

5. Case study researchers generate causal explanations primarily based on
   a. observation of relational patterns.
   b. interpretations of the relationships observed between variations in studied phenomena.
   c. variance theory.
   d. unanticipated phenomena and influences.

6. The cases in case study research typically are selected by
   a. researcher interpretation.
   b. convenience sampling.
   c. replication logic.
   d. purposeful sampling.

7. Experts generally agree that researcher bias in case studies is best handled by
   a. honestly revealing one's possible biases and being willing to have them disconfirmed.
   b. using data-collection methods that rule out the possibility of researcher bias.
   c. using several researchers and seeking consensus in their conclusions.
   d. not studying phenomena in which the researcher has a personal interest.

8. Thick description in case study research refers to
   a. a comprehensive, literal depiction of a phenomenon and its meaning.
   b. description of a phenomenon from both an emic and etic perspective.
   c. the use of triangulation in writing up case study findings.
   d. reliance on reflective analysis in writing a case study report.

9. In grounded theory, constructs are derived primarily from
   a. a pre-existing theory about the phenomenon being studied.
   b. reflections by the case study participants.
   c. the data that have been collected.
   d. all of the above.

10. The case study finding that there is an association between the amount of structure in teachers' lessons and how teachers think about students' learning processes is an example of a
    a. construct.
    b. theme.
    c. thick description.
    d. pattern.

11. In interpretational data analysis, the researcher
    a. searches for the meaning inherent in the data.
    b. imposes meaning on the data.
    c. searches for naturally occurring segments in the data.
    d. typically uses categories developed by other researchers.

12. Reliance on the researcher's intuition and judgment to portray the phenomenon being studied is characteristic of _____ analysis in case study research.
a. structural
b. reflective
c. interpretational
d. causal

13. The use of low-inference descriptors and mechanical means to record data is part of the strategy to ensure the quality and rigor of qualitative research known as

a. chain of evidence.
b. contextual completeness.
c. coding checks.
d. member checking.

14. Reflective reporting of a case study tends to rely heavily on
a. presentation of structural data analyses.
b. an objective writing style.
c. formats developed for use in reporting quantitative research studies.
d. the use of literary devices.

CHAPTER 15

Qualitative Research Traditions

OVERVIEW

Qualitative researchers in anthropology, psychology, and other academic disciplines have developed various ways to study human behavior. Their methods, theories, and accumulated findings constitute distinctive research traditions. In this chapter we explore these traditions and describe how they are or might be used in educational research. Some traditions are particularly well-suited to the investigation of people's inner experience, others to the investigation of social and cultural phenomena, and still others to the investigation of communication phenomena such as speech and text. Having a basic understanding of such qualitative research traditions will enable you to think more broadly about your research problem and consider a variety of appropriate methods for studying it.

OBJECTIVES

After studying this chapter, you should be able to

1. Describe the characteristics of a qualitative research tradition.
2. Describe the types of phenomena that cognitive psychologists investigate and the research methods that they use.
3. Explain the purpose of phenomenological research and the steps involved in conducting a phenomenological study.
4. Explain the similarities and differences between phenomenographic research and phenomenology.
5. Describe the types of educational phenomena that might be investigated by the life history approach.
6. State the goals of the research traditions of symbolic interactionism and action research.
7. Describe the characteristics of ethnography and the steps involved in conducting an ethnographic study.
8. Explain some unique issues of ethnographic research.
9. Explain the goals and underlying assumptions of the cultural studies and critical-theory research traditions.
10. Describe the types of investigations conducted by researchers who work within the cultural studies and critical-theory research traditions.
11. Describe the purpose and techniques of ethnomethodological research.
12. State the goals of narrative analysis, ethnographic content analysis, and the ethnography of communication.
13. Explain the goals, assumptions, and basic concepts of hermeneutical analysis.
14. Explain the goals, assumptions, and basic concepts of semiotic research.
15. Explain the basic principles of structuralism and poststructuralism, and describe the types of phenomena that might be investigated using these approaches.

Qualitative Research Traditions in Educational Research

This chapter provides an overview of the major qualitative traditions that have been used in educational research. You are likely to encounter one or more of them in your reviews of the research literature. Knowledge of these traditions can help you formulate questions to guide your research, develop methods for collecting and analyzing your research data, and identify relevant theory to which you might connect your findings. Your research will have added meaning and significance if it is grounded within an established research tradition.

Evelyn Jacob described a **qualitative research tradition** as "a group of scholars who agree among themselves on the nature of the universe they are examining, on legitimate questions and problems to study, and on legitimate techniques to seek solutions."[1] (Jacob's use of the term *scholars* subsumes researchers as well as theorists and writers of research reviews.) In this book we use the term *tradition* also to refer to the body of research and theory generated by these scholars. Norman Densin and Yvonna Lincoln describe the field of qualitative research as currently defined by "a series of tensions, contradictions, and hesitations."[2] In education, the phenomena of interest to qualitative researchers (and what is not of interest?) continue to change and expand, as do the methods for studying such phenomena. As described by Margaret Eisenhart:

> What's different now is that everyday life, including life in schools, seems to be faster paced, more diverse, more complicated, more entangled than before. The kinds of personal and social relationships, exchanges, and networks we participate in seem to be taking new forms, tying together otherwise disparate people, and demanding some new ways of thinking about what to research and how to do it.[3]

While directed to the tradition of ethnography in which Eisenhart works, her statements apply to the research endeavor generally, and are perhaps most obvious when one turns to a discussion of qualitative research traditions.

Qualitative research in education has roots in many academic disciplines, including the social sciences (e.g., anthropology, sociology, and psychology), the humanities (e.g., art, literature, and philosophy), and interdisciplinary studies. Qualitative research also has been influenced by the postmodern approach to inquiry. Postmodernists reject the objectivist orientation to scientific endeavor that is privileged by the entrenched power structure of the professional research establishment.

Consider the research tradition of ethnography, which we discuss in more detail later in the chapter. Researchers who work within this research tradition are interested in the nature of culture and how it functions, and they have developed specialized methods to pursue their inquiries. Their research has produced a body of knowledge about different aspects of culture, including school cultures and the role of education in different world cultures. The ethnographers who produced this knowledge share a common interest in particular phenomena, methods of investigation, and theoretical concepts. Yet there is also a growing variety in the phenomena, methods of investigation, and even the theoretical concepts used by researchers who describe their work as ethnography. An understanding of qualitative research traditions will help you understand both the commonalities among, and differences between, various traditions and the disciplinary foundations of specific qualitative research studies you encounter.

Touchstone in Research

Lancy, D. F. (2001). *Studying children and schools: Qualitative research traditions.* Prospect Heights, IL: Waveland.

1. Jacob, E. (1987). Qualitative research traditions: A review. *Review of Educational Research, 57,* 1–50. Quote appears on pp. 1–2.
2. Denzin, N. K., & Lincoln, Y. S. (2005). Introduction: The discipline and practice of qualitative research. In N. K. Denzin & Y. S. Lincoln (Eds.), *Sage handbook of qualitative research* (3rd ed., pp. 1–32). Thousand Oaks, CA: Sage. Quote appears on pp. 26–27.
3. Eisenhart, M. (2001). Educational ethnography past, present, and future: Ideas to think with. *Educational Researcher, 30*(8), 16–27. Quote appears on p. 24.

The Characteristics of Qualitative Research Traditions

We recommend that you keep in mind the characteristics of qualitative research traditions when carrying out literature searches to guide your research. Traditions are complex and multifaceted, so to identify literature relevant to the traditions that interest you, you need to understand how they are structured. We summarize their main characteristics next.

First, traditions usually are derived from particular wide-scale philosophical formulations and theories and from the writings of the particular individuals who have espoused them. For example, postmodernism is often associated with Jean-Francois Lyotard, whose book *The Postmodern Condition* was published in 1984.[4]

Second, traditions tend to blend with or borrow from each other. Some develop many adherents or branch out into subspecializations. Others, like event structure analysis, remain on the periphery or fade out of use. Over time, traditions change to reflect researchers' embrace of different philosophical and scientific paradigms, along with shifts in the broader social context in which scientific endeavor is pursued. Researchers who share adherence to a tradition still may disagree on epistemological assumptions and other matters. While such transformations enrich the resultant research, they also make it difficult to find unambiguous examples of research traditions. For example, the tradition known as the *ethnography of communication* is based on the research tradition of ethnography, but connected specifically to the study of language, a key feature of cultural life.

Third, a qualitative research tradition usually includes both a focus on a particular phenomenon or class of phenomena and a selected research approach for studying such phenomena. The phenomenon of lived experience, for example, is investigated differently by cognitive psychologists than by phenomenologists or in other research traditions concerned with lived experience. One can study a particular topic—say, the ritual and significance of graduation from college—from the perspective of various traditions, each of which sheds light on different aspects of the phenomenon.

Finally, the forms of writing and representation used in the postmodern inquiries that predominate at this moment tend to be dynamic, problematic, open ended, and complex. With respect to qualitative research traditions, each can have a variety of labels, although one may be prominent in the research literature. For example, the tradition called *ethnoscience* involves the study of a culture's semantic systems for the purpose of revealing the cognitive structure of the culture,[5] and is also known as *cognitive ethnography* and *cognitive anthropology*.

These characteristics suggest the unique contributions that specific qualitative research traditions can make, both to basic research about the teaching and learning process and to applied research about educational systems and structures. They also reflect the challenge that faces the researcher seeking to understand the many traditions relevant to educational research. Here we will discuss a selected sample of such traditions, including some that have been widely used to study educational phenomena and some that hold promise for greater use in educational research.

Table 15.1 presents 15 qualitative research traditions organized into three categories. The traditions within each category are related in that they study similar phenomena. Some focus on understanding the nature of lived experience (type I), others seek to understand cultural and social phenomena (type II), and still others seek to understand language and communication phenomena (type III). Some have played a major role in

---

4. Lyotard's role in postmodernism is discussed in: Crotty, M. (1998). *The foundations of social research*. Thousand Oaks, CA: Sage.
5. Werner, O., & Schoepfle, G. M. (1987). *Systematic fieldwork*, Vols. 1 & 2. Thousand Oaks, CA: Sage.

TABLE 15.1

Qualitative Research Traditions Grouped by Type of Phenomena Investigated

Research Tradition	Involves the Study of
I. Investigation of Lived Experience	
1. Cognitive psychology	Mental structures and processes used by individuals in different situations
2. Phenomenology	Reality as it appears to individuals
3. Phenomenographic research	Individuals' conceptualizations of reality
4. Life history research	Individuals' life experiences from their perspective
II. Investigation of Society and Culture	
1. Symbolic interactionism	The influence of social interactions on social structures and individuals' self-identity
2. Action research	Practitioners' self-reflective efforts to improve the rationality and justice of their work
3. Ethnography	Characteristic features and patterns of a culture
4. Cultural studies and critical-theory research	Contestation of oppressive power relationships in a culture
5. Ethnomethodology	The rules that underlie everyday social interactions
III. Investigation of Language and Communication	
1. Narrative analysis	Organized representations and explanations of human experience
2. Ethnographic content analysis	The content of documents in cultural perspective
3. Ethnography of communication	Use of speech in the social life of members of a cultural group
4. Hermeneutics	The process by which individuals arrive at the meaning of a text
5. Semiotics	Signs and the meanings they convey
6. Structuralism and poststructuralism	The systemic properties of language, text, and other phenomena

educational research, while others rarely have been applied to education but have the potential for greater application.

How can Table 15.1 help you? Suppose you have identified a particular problem for investigation, for example, how to help high school students with personal issues that hamper their motivation in school. A study of the traditions listed in Table 15.1 will reveal several that might appeal to you, for example, an ethnography of low-income families of high school students, a critical-theory analysis of the effects of internalized oppression on such students, or a study of the semiotics (signs and their meanings) operating in teen gangs.

The following sections describe each of the qualitative research traditions listed in Table 15.1. We discuss several of them in detail in order to develop your understanding of each of the three types of qualitative research traditions. Others are described briefly, but in sufficient detail to help you determine their possible relevance to your research interests.

Keep in mind that the list of qualitative research traditions in Table 15.1 is not exhaustive. The field of qualitative research is undergoing rapid growth and continual reconceptualization. New traditions may blend with existing ones, and can be identified by more than one label. Also, our list does not include historical research, a strong qualitative research tradition (see Chapter 16) used to study many of the phenomena listed in Table 15.1 as they occurred in the past. It also does not include case study, which has been identified as a tradition by some scholars, but which we treat as a basic form of qualitative research (see Chapter 14).[6]

Traditions Involving Investigation of Lived Experience

The study of inner experience has been neglected and even disparaged by researchers who adhere to positivist epistemology. The behavioral psychologist B. F. Skinner claimed that the human mind was a "black box" that could not be studied by scientific methods.[7] Qualitative researchers reject this claim. They have developed research traditions that focus on the inner experience of people in general, of particular types of people (e.g., experts as compared to novices in a field of inquiry), or of individuals as they interact with each other. We describe four of these traditions below: cognitive psychology, phenomenological research, phenomenography, and life history research.

Cognitive Psychology

Touchstones in Research

Bruning, R. H., Norby, M. M., Ronning, R. R., & Schraw, G. J. (2004). *Cognitive psychology and instruction.* Upper Saddle River, NJ: Pearson/Merrill/Prentice Hall.

Eysenck, M. W., & Keane, M. T. (2005). *Cognitive psychology: A student's handbook.* New York: Psychology Press.

According to Kenneth Strike, "the majority of educators view psychology as the central discipline of education."[8] In fact, psychology has had a major influence on educational research and practice. Most notably, educators make extensive use of the tests developed by psychologists (e.g., intelligence tests and vocational aptitude tests). The design and scoring of these tests reflect the strongly quantitative orientation of traditional psychological research.

In the past thirty years, various qualitative traditions have gained a foothold in psychology. One tradition in particular has had a major impact on educational theory and practice. This tradition is **cognitive psychology,** which we define as the study of the structures and processes involved in mental activity, and of how these structures and processes are learned or how they develop with maturation.

The study of such cognitive phenomena as perception, memory, attention, thinking, and problem solving has been part of psychology since its inception. However, from about 1930 to 1960 the behaviorist tradition in psychology overshadowed the study of these cognitive phenomena. Consciousness and cognition were relegated to Skinner's unknowable "black box," which was presumed to be situated between a tangible stimulus and an individual's observable response. Skinner in particular argued for a discipline of psychology that would formulate principles of behavioral control and learning without invoking mentalistic constructs such as memory and motivation.

Both the cognitive theorists who preceded Skinner and the cognitive psychologists and cognitive scientists who succeeded him claimed that it is not possible to develop a complete view of human behavior without studying the internal mental and perceptual processes of

---

6. For a treatment of case study as a tradition, see: Lancy, D. F. (2001). *Studying children and schools: Qualitative research traditions.* Prospect Heights, IL: Waveland.
7. Skinner, B. F. (1953). *Science and human behavior.* New York: Macmillan.
8. Strike, K. A. (1994). Epistemology and education. In T. Husén & T. N. Postlethwaite (Eds.), *International encyclopedia of education* (2nd ed., pp. 1996–2001). London: Pergamon.

specific individuals. Most cognitive psychologists assume that there are physical structures in the human brain that determine brain functioning and activity, and that the activity of such physical structures in turn leads to the development of specific cognitive structures and processes. Cognition can be conceptualized broadly as the operation of these structures and processes. As research into brain function and mental activity has expanded, the study of cognition has gained renewed respectability and priority within psychological and educational research.

Educational researchers who work within the tradition of cognitive psychology have investigated various phenomena, including teacher thinking, students' learning processes, and the motivation to learn. Some of their research involves case studies that are grounded in either a positivist or interpretive approach to inquiry. To illustrate this type of research, we present below a study on expert versus novice thinking.

A Study of Differences in the Knowledge Structures of Experts and Novices

In this research study, Samuel Wineburg asked working historians and high-performing high school seniors to think aloud as they reviewed and evaluated primary sources all related to the same event in American history.[9] Other researchers previously had done research on cognitive differences between experts and novices in other fields (e.g., mathematics and chess) in order to identify the cognitive structures, processes, and progressive changes involved in complex thinking. Wineburg wished to extend this line of research to the domain of history, an important subject in education.

Eight historians from universities in an urban area and eight high school students from the same area were the research participants. Four of the historians (the "non-Americanist" historians) had specializations other than American history, and thus were expected to have much less knowledge of this domain of knowledge and inquiry than the other four ("Americanist") historians. A 12-item pretest verified that the groups differed in their knowledge of American history, with the average number of terms correctly identified on the pretest being 10 for the Americanist historians, 4.25 for the non-Americanist historians, and 1.8 for the students.

Each research participant individually was presented eight documents and three paintings concerning the battle of Lexington, which marked the start of the American Revolution in 1775. The participants responded to a fixed set of tasks: (1) to read each document aloud and to "think aloud," that is, to say everything that came to mind as they read; (2) to think aloud as they reviewed each painting, then give a date to each painting and select the most accurate one; and (3) to rank the eight documents in terms of their trustworthiness. All sessions were audiotaped, and transcripts were prepared. Unlike most qualitative research, Wineburg's study was carried out in a laboratory setting and involved individuals responding to a contrived set of tasks. Nevertheless, the tasks were designed to simulate those that historians encounter in the course of their work.

The procedure of thinking aloud that Wineburg's subjects used is called protocol analysis.[10] **Protocol analysis** involves asking individuals to state all their thoughts as they carry out a challenging task, so that the researcher can obtain a holistic overview of their cognitive activity as recorded in their verbal reports. Wineburg used recommended procedures for protocol analysis to ensure that the data obtained would be as valid a reflection of the research participants' thoughts as possible.

9. Wineburg, S. S. (1991). Historical problem solving: A study of the cognitive processes used in the evaluation of documentary and pictorial evidence. *Journal of Educational Psychology, 83,* 73–87.
10. Ericsson, K. A., & Simon, H. A. (1993). *Protocol analysis: Verbal reports as data* (rev. ed.). Cambridge, MA: Bradford.

The transcript for each individual was divided into a protocol for the tasks involving the paintings and a protocol for the tasks involving the documents. The painting protocols were separated into coding units consisting of independent subject/predicate clauses. Based on the researcher's analysis, these coding units were grouped into four categories. *Description* included simple descriptive statements. *Reference* included statements that related the paintings to each other, to certain documents, or to a "mental model" of the historical event that the individual had generated. *Analysis* included statements related to the viewpoint or intentions of the painting or its artist, and unprompted estimates of the dates of the paintings. *Qualification* included statements that qualified other statements (e.g., statements pointing out shortcomings in the paintings or in pictorial sources generally). The document protocols were analyzed by a somewhat different procedure and yielded different types of categories.

Some of the most interesting findings of Wineburg's study involve individual comments. For example, a data table in the research report compares the responses of one historian and one student who both selected the same painting as the most accurate depiction of the historical event. As Wineburg notes, the historian made many references to corroborative information in the documents in explaining her selection, stated qualifications about the painting's accuracy, and made her choice with seeming hesitancy and tentativeness. The student, by contrast, was described as confidently choosing the same picture, and as having chosen that painting as most accurate partly because it included details that were *not* mentioned in any of the documents.

Wineburg contrasted his findings with those of earlier expert-novice research, in which differences were explained in terms of the number and organization of *problem templates,* that is, preset mental structures for solving problems in a specific subject.[11] In the theory underlying such research, successful performance depends both on possession of the appropriate problem template and on activation and confirmation of an appropriate knowledge structure involving available *schemata* (i.e., internal conceptual structures to which the individual relates each new experience). In contrast, Wineburg concluded from his findings that expertise seems to rest not on bringing an available problem template to the task, but rather on constructing a context-specific schema tailored to the specific historical event being studied. Given an unfamiliar event, the non-Americanist historians responded much as the Americanist historians: Both groups "puzzled about discrepancies, they compared the pictures with the written documents, they corroborated and discorroborated key features, and they tried to represent what could and what could not be known."[12] Their learning activity reflected not so much the availability of appropriate problem-solving strategies as it did the belief systems they had about history and historical research—for example, that a document is only as trustworthy as its author and its function make it. In contrast, students treated the tasks as simple and unambiguous, reflecting the noncritical manner in which they had been taught history.

Wineburg's study has some characteristics of quantitative research. For example, the author reported that historians' painting protocols contained significantly more statements overall (based on a Mann-Whitney U test) than the students' protocols. Spearman *rho* correlations and Kendall's coefficients of concordance also were computed, and they showed that the level of agreement among the historians in their rankings of the documents' trustworthiness was much higher than that among the students.

11. This research is summarized in: Chi, M. T. H., Glaser, R., & Farr, M. J. (1988). *The nature of expertise.* Hillsdale, NJ: Erlbaum.
12. Wineburg, Historical problem solving, p. 83.

Wineburg concluded from his study that "able high school students can know a lot about history but still have little idea of how historical knowledge is constructed."[13] This interpretation of the research findings was based both on qualitative and quantitative data. While Wineburg sought to validate and generalize the findings through the use of inferential statistics, he also sought to clarify the emic perspective of the individuals studied.

Phenomenology

Phenomenology is the study of the world as it appears to individuals when they lay aside the prevailing understandings of those phenomena and revisit their immediate experience of the phenomena. As such, phenomenology shares the goal of other qualitative research traditions to understand how individuals construct reality.

Touchstone in Research

Moustakas, C. (1994). *Phenomenological research methods.* Thousand Oaks, CA: Sage.

In doing a phenomenological study, the researcher is intimately connected with the phenomena being studied and comes to know himself within his experiencing of these phenomena. In this respect, phenomenological research is the antithesis of quantitative research, which seeks to detach the researcher's self from the phenomena being studied through the use of objective methods of data collection and analysis.

Phenomenology originated as a philosophical movement founded by Edmund Husserl.[14] He believed that the starting point for knowledge was the self's experience of *phenomena,* which are the various sensations, perceptions, and ideations that appear in consciousness when the self focuses attention on an object. Husserl formulated various processes—described by such exotic terms as *epoche, transcendental-phenomenological reduction, imaginative variation,* and *noesis*— for preparing oneself to experience a phenomenon, for having the experience and recording it, and for analyzing it. Psychologists reformulated these processes into procedures that are more standardized and more closely aligned with the terminology of case study research. The following is a brief account of these procedures as they are used in planning and conducting a phenomenological investigation.

1. *Identify a topic of personal and social significance.* The researcher should select a topic that will engage her both intellectually and emotionally. For example, K. LaCourse decided to investigate the topic of how people describe and experience time. Her rationale for studying this topic included the following statement:

> The study of time beckons to me, I think, because issues of time are prominent in my own life. I have strong feelings about time. I love life, and since in so many ways time is life, I love my time. I put careful thought into how I will use it, and I jealously guard against excessive intrusions into my time by others. I have always seen time as a precious commodity . . . And yet so often I feel I am in conflict with time. There is a lack of clarity within me as to the meaning of time in my life and how I can best live in harmony with it. I am puzzled, intrigued, and frustrated by time, and challenged to learn more about it. It is this challenge that leads me to consider studying time.[15]

It is important for a phenomenological researcher to be invested in the topic in this way because she will be collecting data on her own experience of the phenomenon as well as the experiences of her research participants.

2. *Select appropriate participants.* Husserl acknowledged the possibility of intersubjective communication and knowledge. Through a process of empathy, an individual can come to know another person and check whether his experience of a phenomenon corresponds with another's experience of it. Thus, participants in a phenomenological study can work as

---

13. Ibid., p. 84.
14. Husserl, E. (1931). *Ideas: General introduction to pure phenomenology.* London: George Allen & Unwin.
15. LaCourse, K. (1991). *The experience of time.* Unpublished manuscript, Center for Humanistic Studies, Detroit, MI.

co-researchers with the primary investigator and help with the process of "sifting out intrusive phrases void of meaning . . . exposing and eliminating errors which here too are possible, as they are in every sphere in which validity counts for something."[16] The essential criteria for selecting participants is that they have experienced the phenomenon being studied and share the researcher's interest in understanding its nature and meanings.

3. *Interview each participant.* In phenomenology the goal is to describe things as they are, not as the participant (or the researcher) typically, and automatically, interprets things based on past experience. Therefore, both the researcher and the research participants must "bracket" their understandings and seek to discover things themselves as they are directly experienced. The meaning or essence of the phenomenon must be understood first from the unique experience of the individual. Phenomenological researchers generally conduct at least one long interview with each participant in order to obtain a comprehensive description of their experience of the phenomenon being studied. The interview process is relatively unstructured, but focused on eliciting all aspects of the experience.

4. *Analyze the interview data.* Data analysis in phenomenological research generally follows the procedures of reflective analysis (see Chapter 14). The interview data for each case are broken into segments, and the researcher looks for meaning units and themes in the segments. The researcher then synthesizes the findings for each individual and checks the synthesis with the individual. This is the basis for a textural description of the phenomenon.

A **textural description** is an account of an individual's intuitive, prereflective perceptions of a phenomenon from every angle. The following is an excerpt from a textural description for a patient at a sleep disorder clinic who participated in a phenomenological study of the experience of insomnia:

> The experience of insomnia for Jim is one of restless fluctuation from an initial falling asleep to a sudden awakening. Wanting desperately to sleep but to no avail, he is "propelled into being awake"; imprisoned by wakefulness. This kind of being awake is powerful and charged with distress. "It's like being plugged in or amped . . . bug eyed." The growing fatigue becomes every bit as confining as the wakefulness. Sleep is nowhere to be found; there is just this experience of being "simultaneously fatigued, mentally and physically, but absolutely wide awake."[17]

Data analysis also involves comparing the meaning units and themes discovered for specific cases and synthesizing the findings across individuals. This is the basis for a structural description of the phenomenon.

A **structural description** is an account of the regularities of thought, judgment, imagination, and recollection that underlie the experience of a phenomenon and give meaning to it. The following is a structural description that synthesizes the findings for 25 participants in a phenomenological study of the experience of being "left out":

> Experiencing ourselves as left out evokes an intensely disquieting and painful emotional storm. Previously taken for granted meanings of who we are for others, and who they are for us, are sundered from their past familiar anchors, and now become highly questionable. The smooth reciprocity of self-other relations gives way, and we are confronted by a disturbing negativity. This negativity expresses itself as a tear in the unfolding tapestry of mutual recognition between ourselves and the others. This gap may be a fissure or an abyss, but it discloses an essential break in our connectedness with others.[18]

16. Husserl. *Ideas,* p. 256.
17. Copen, R. (1993). Insomnia: A phenomenological investigation. *Dissertation Abstracts International, 53,* 6542B. (UMI No. 9311957) Quote appears on p. 58.
18. Aanstoos, C. M. (1987). A descriptive phenomenology of the experience of being left out. In F. J. van Zuuren, F. J. Wertz, & B. Mook (Eds.), *Advances in qualitative psychology: Themes and variations* (pp. 137–155). Berwyn, PA: Swets North America.

Phenomenological research has several advantages as an approach to qualitative research. First, it can be used to study a wide range of educational phenomena, for example, how students experience the process of studying and test-taking, how teachers experience a classroom lesson, and how policy makers experience meetings about school reform proposals. Second, the interview process used to collect phenomenological data is wide-ranging, and therefore it is capable of detecting many aspects of experience that may prove to be important with no further analysis, or as variables in subsequent qualitative or quantitative studies. Finally, the procedures of phenomenological inquiry are relatively straightforward. For individuals who are able to suspend judgment and think afresh about any phenomenon, then, it seems likely that less training would be required to do a phenomenological study than would be required to do a study using the methods of a qualitative research tradition such as ethnography or semiotics, for which a great deal of new learning is required.

Phenomenographic Research

Touchstones in Research

Dall' Alba, G., & Hasselgren, B. (eds.). (1996). *Reflections on phenomenography: Toward a methodology?* Göteborg, Sweden: Acta Universitatis Gothoburgensis.

Richardson, J. T. E. (1999). The concepts and methods of phenomenographic research. *Review of Educational Research, 69*(1), 53–82.

Like phenomenological researchers, phenomenographers are interested in studying how reality appears to people, rather than the objective nature of reality. The difference between the two research traditions is that **phenomenographic research** is a specialized method for describing the different ways in which people conceptualize the world around them. For example, different teachers might have various conceptions of what causes students to misbehave in class. A phenomenographer would study a group of teachers to develop a classification of these different conceptions. The method of investigation usually involves interviewing people—in this case, a group of teachers—to determine how and why they would handle a problem posed by the researcher. In contrast, a phenomenological researcher would be concerned with each teacher's total experience of student misbehavior. The phenomenological experience might include the teachers' conception of student misbehavior, but also the teachers' feelings, reflections, and associations with other life experiences.

Phenomenographic research originated at the University of Gothenburg in Sweden. An example of a phenomenographic study is an investigation of university physicists' and fourth-year physics students' ways of talking about physics in order for someone else to make sense of it.[19] Through interviews with each research participant, the researchers identified four different "outcome spaces" used by students to describe proposed solutions to the barrier problem, a problem in quantum physics, and used by physicists to describe their research foci. The researchers characterized these outcome spaces as A. "Expounding in bits," a form of exposition that no listener would be able to make sense of; B. "Expounding in a single perspective," which gives a single explanation that does not reveal the speaker's referent to the problem; C. "Expounding in multiple perspectives," which allows the listener to broaden his view of the problem, and D. "Expounding through contextualization," which helps the listener see relationships between the present topic and other possible problems and research topics. The researchers found that category A was absent from the physicists' expositions, whereas category D was rarely found in the students' expositions.

In offering pedagogical advice the researchers argue that "to support the constitution of nuanced, integrated knowledge objects, expositions of the type in category D have clear

---

19. Ingerman, A., & Booth, S. (2003). Expounding on physics: A phenomenographic study of physicists talking of their physics. *International Journal of Science Education, 25*(12), 1489–1508.

strengths over those of category C, which have strengths over those of category B."[20] They also mention learning situations where expositions of the type of category B might be preferred. The researchers concluded that the four qualitatively distinct ways of expounding on physics constitute "an outcome space where there is a successive shift towards coherent structure and multiple referent domains."[21]

In other investigations as well, phenomenographers have found that there is a limited number of different ways in which people conceptualize a problem or situation. Phenomenographic research is similar to the method that Jean Piaget used in his investigations of how young children understand the world about them. Thus, this research method could be used to investigate individuals' thinking, developmental changes in thinking, and changes in thinking that occur as a result of instruction. Like phenomenological research, phenomenographic research can be used to study virtually any aspect of natural or social reality about which individuals have formed some conception.

Life History Research

Life history is the study of the life experiences of individuals from the perspective of how these individuals interpret and understand the world around them. It is not a unified research tradition. Researchers in different academic disciplines—literature, history, anthropology, psychology, feminist and minority studies—do life history studies for different purposes and with different research methods.[22] Depending upon the researcher, a life history might be called a *biography*, a *life story*, an *oral history*, a *case study*, a *testimonio*, or a *portrait*.[23] Researchers who choose to write about themselves might call their report an *autobiography* or a *memoir*.

Various methods can be used to collect and analyze data for a life history. Researchers traditionally have analyzed materials written by or about the individual being studied, for example, diaries, correspondence, and professional writings. More recent work has focused on the use of interviewing and direct observation, and on the use of narrative research methodology. (We discuss narrative research later in the chapter.)

In education, life history has become a popular approach for studying teacher development.[24] A study by Petra Munro illustrates this line of research.[25] Her life histories of three women teachers were guided by the following research questions:

> [H]ow do women teachers resist the naming of their experiences by others, which distorts and marginalizes their realities? How do they construct themselves as subjects despite the fictions constructed about women teachers?[26]

To answer these questions, she conducted extensive interviews with the research participants (she referred to them as "life historians"); the interviews were tape-recorded and

Touchstones in Research

Atkinson, R. (2002). The life story interview. In J. F. Gubrium & J. A. Holstein (Eds.), *Handbook of interview research: Context & method* (pp. 121–140). Thousand Oaks, CA: Sage.

Cole, A. L., & Knowles, J. G. (2001). *Lives in context: The art of life history research.* Walnut Creek, CA: AltaMira.

Tierney, W. G. (2000). Undaunted courage: Life history and the postmodern challenge. In N. K. Denzin & Y. S. Lincoln (Eds.), *Handbook of qualitative research* (2nd ed., pp. 537–553). Thousand Oaks, CA: Sage.

20. Ibid., p. 1507.
21. Ibid., p. 1489.
22. The varied approaches to life history research are described in: Chase, S. E. (2005). Narrative inquiry: Multiple lenses, approaches, voices. In N. K. Denzin & Y. S. Lincoln (Eds.), *Sage handbook of qualitative research* (3rd ed., pp. 651–679). Thousand Oaks, CA: Sage.
23. Beverley, J. (2005). *Testimonio*, subalternity, and narrative authority. In N. K. Denzin & Y. S. Lincoln (Eds.), *Sage handbook of qualitative research* (3rd ed., pp. 547–557). Thousand Oaks, CA: Sage; Lawrence-Lightfoot, S. & Davis, J. H. (1997). *The art and science of portraiture.* San Francisco: Jossey-Bass.
24. See, for example: Goodson, I. (Ed.). (1992). *Studying teachers' lives.* New York: Teachers College Press.
25. Munro, P. (1998). *Subject to fiction: Women teachers' life history narratives and the cultural politics of resistance.* Buckingham, England: Open University Press.
26. Ibid., p. 3.

transcribed. In addition, she interviewed individuals who knew them (colleagues, administrators, and students), observed one of them teaching, analyzed personal and school documents, and administered a questionnaire concerning their work and family history.

Munro offered the following explanation for her choice of life history as a research approach: " . . . I was drawn to life history and narrative inquiry because of its potential to highlight gendered constructions of power, resistance, and agency . . . ."[27] In turn, the themes of power, resistance, and agency were grounded in several qualitative research traditions that we discuss later in the chapter: critical theory (specifically, various feminist theories) and poststructuralism. These research traditions provided interpretive frameworks for analyzing her research data. However, the frameworks do not constitute a neutral, authoritative basis for interpretation. The study is permeated by Munro's strong self-reflexive challenging of the interpretive frameworks and her co-creation of the meanings of the teachers' lives. (Reflexivity in research is explained in Chapter 1.)

Each life history is accorded a separate chapter in Munro's account of her study. The teacher's life is told more or less chronologically and organized into phases that the researcher considered significant. For example, the life history of Bonnie, a 46-year-old social-studies teacher, has these phases (the labels are those used by the researcher):

Finding a fit. Bonnie described her early validation for her intellectual abilities, especially in history, and the influence that her father's authoritarianism and argumentative nature had on her approach to social issues.

The do-gooder. While going to college, Bonnie took time off to participate in a government volunteer program in which she helped poor black people in the South. After returning to college, she helped pay for her tuition by working as a waitress, during which time she participated in a union strike. Her experience as an activist and advocate shaped her view of what it means to be a teacher.

Learning to teach: "finding a fit." Bonnie chose teaching as a profession in part because she did not find many other alternatives open to her. Her activism and advocacy became expressed by her strong interest in her local teacher's association.

Becoming an advocate for women teachers. In 1990 Bonnie began her 21st year as a high school social-studies teacher. She had been president of her local teachers association and was still a strong advocate for teachers' rights, with special concern about unjust and sexist behavior toward women teachers.

A pain to administrators. In 1990 Bonnie became the department chair of an all-male social studies department. Her approach to administration is based on judicious use of authority and constructive confrontation, which reflects her early experiences with her father.

Munro concluded Bonnie's life history with her own reflections, including the following: "Bonnie's story spoke to my understanding of how women teachers traverse from the world of the classroom, where we create the space to enact our own realities, to the world outside the classroom, in which we are too often left with no voice at all."[28]

After presenting the three life histories, Munro provided a final set of reflections that related the histories to her theoretical concerns. One of these reflections is as follows:

The ongoing negotiation of gendered subjectivity evident in the life history narratives presented here suggests that women's experiencing of gender is not monolithic or grounded in understandings of gender as inevitable. . . . [A]s I learned from Agnes, Cleo and Bonnie, resistance is not an 'act' but a movement, a continual displacement of others' attempts to name our realities.[29]

27. Ibid., p. 7.
28. Ibid., p. 107.
29. Ibid., p. 125.

This study of women teachers demonstrates how the research tradition of life history can make visible for the reader the inner experiences of an individual or a group of individuals. These revelations have implications that extend well beyond the particular lives that are studied. In the study described above, the life histories of three teachers raise questions about changing conceptions of gender identity (both male and female) and the role of gender in the education profession.

Traditions Involving Investigation of Society and Culture

Touchstones in Research

Tedlock, B. (2005). The observation of participation and the emergence of public ethnography. In N. K. Denzin & Y. S. Lincoln (Eds.), *Sage handbook of qualitative research* (3rd ed., pp. 467–481). Thousand Oaks, CA: Sage.

Zou, Y., & Trueba, E. T. (Eds.). (2002). *Ethnography and schools: Qualitative approaches to the study of education*. Lanham, MD: Rowman & Littlefield.

Eisenhart, M. (2001). Changing conceptions of culture and ethnographic methodology: Recent thematic shifts and their implications for research on teaching. In V. Richardson (Ed.), *Handbook of research on teaching* (4th ed., pp. 209–225). Washington, DC: American Educational Research Association.

Many qualitative researchers focus their investigations on how individuals become affiliated with particular groups and organizations (e.g., school classes, work teams, church congregations, countries, or entire societies) and the way in which these social entities influence human thought and behavior. Other researchers focus on the cultural characteristics of specific groups and organizations. The term **culture** refers to all the ways of living (e.g., values, customs, rituals, and beliefs) that are developed by a group of human beings and transmitted from one generation to another, or from current members to new members.

We discuss in the following sections three qualitative research traditions that focus on societal and cultural phenomena: ethnography, cultural studies, and ethnomethodology. Besides these three traditions, there are other qualitative research traditions that also examine societal and cultural phenomena, including symbolic interactionism and action research. **Symbolic interactionism,** which is a sociological research tradition, involves the study of how individuals engage in social transactions and how these transactions contribute to the creation and maintenance of social structures and the individual's self-identity.[30] Using the methods of symbolic interactionism, Gary Alan Fine was able to identify and describe the various social realities that comprise Little League baseball: It is a social structure for learning this particular sport, but also a structure for socialization into "male culture" and an environment for learning the lore and slang of sport.[31]

Action research is a type of self-reflective investigation that professional practitioners undertake for the purpose of improving the rationality and justice of their work. We describe this type of research in Chapter 18.

Ethnography

Ethnography involves intensive study of the features of a given culture and the patterns in those features. If an ethnography has been done well, readers of the final report should be able to understand the culture even though they may not have directly experienced it.

Ethnography was originally developed by anthropologists, but it has since been used, with adaptations, by researchers in other disciplines, including sociology and psychology.[32] In the 1960s and 1970s, many educational researchers who had become disenchanted with positivism turned to ethnography as an alternative approach. The widespread acceptance of ethnography within educational research has in turn led many educational

---

30. Charon, J. M. (2000). *Symbolic interactionism: An introduction, an interpretation, an integration* (7th ed.). Paramus, NJ: Prentice Hall.
31. Fine, G. A. (1987). *With the boys: Little League baseball and preadolescent culture*. Chicago: University of Chicago Press.
32. Some of these adaptations are described in: Wolcott, H. F. (1992). Posturing in qualitative inquiry. In M. D. LeCompte, W. L. Millroy, & J. Preissle (Eds.), *Handbook of qualitative research in education* (pp. 3–52). San Diego: Academic Press.

researchers to study and use the other qualitative research traditions discussed in this chapter. Because of the seminal influence of ethnography on educational research, we provide an extensive description of it below.

Nobuo Shimahara identified three major foci of: ethnographic research: discovering cultural patterns in human behavior, conveying the emic perspective of cultural members, and studying the real-life settings in which culture is manifested.[33] With respect to its focus on cultural patterns, ethnographers seek to find commonalities in the beliefs, customs, and lifestyles that characterize a group of individuals living in proximity and identifying as a group, tribe, or society—that is, the group's **culture.** They are less interested in the idiosyncrasies of individual human beings. Instead, ethnographers view each individual as a "document" that provides information about the larger culture. Cultural patterns that are discovered through ethnographic research then can be used to predict and explain the behavior of other members of the culture.

With respect to the emic perspective, many ethnographers prior to the 1920s *assumed* that their representations about the members' culture were accurate, rather than seeking to *confirm* those representations through member checking. Since that time, increased emphasis on participant observation of events in daily life and on the collection of first-person, native, or insider accounts has provided a firmer scientific basic for ethnographic understanding of the emic perspective.[34] Some ethnographers, however, represent primarily their own etic (outsider's) perspective in their research. In doing so, they use their own terminology and categories to describe the culture. It also is possible to include both perspectives, as demonstrated in the examples of ethnographic research presented later in this section.

Ethnographers focus on studying the real-life settings in which culture is manifested, generally avoid introducing any type of contrived situation into a setting, and pay attention to all aspects of it that reveal cultural patterns. If ethnographers were studying a teacher's classroom as a microculture, they would note carefully the behavior of the teacher, the students, and any other persons in the classroom; they would then relate this behavior to the physical environment of the classroom (e.g., furniture, wall decor, and intercom system) and to other relevant settings (e.g., the playground, teacher's lounge, and school counselor's office). All these observations, in turn, would be related to data on the culture members' emic perspectives of these settings.

The term *culture* originated with efforts to assist the growth of an organism (as in agriculture). Thus, culture was implicitly associated with an evolutionary model that assumed that so-called "native" cultures represented earlier stages of cultural evolution, while "civilized" Western cultures represented advanced stages. Later anthropologists rejected this elitist notion, arguing that the peoples of the world are grouped into many cultures, each with unique characteristics and positive qualities. From this view arose the idealized notion of a culture as a pattern of traditions, symbols, rituals, and artifacts, all of which together relate systematically to each other so as to form an integrated whole. Murray Wax noted that in fact anthropologists have found culture to be a hodge-podge of overlapping qualities, described by one scholar as "a thing of shreds and patches."[35] With the rapid cultural diffusion that has resulted from the modern technology of production, transportation,

33. Shimahara, N. (1988). Anthroethnography: A methodological consideration. In R. R. Sherman & R. B. Webb (Eds.), *Qualitative research in education: Focus and methods* (pp. 76–89). New York: Falmer.
34. Schwandt, T. A. (2001). *Dictionary of qualitative inquiry* (2nd ed.). Thousand Oaks, CA: Sage.
35. Wax, M. (1993). How culture misdirects multiculturalism. *Anthropology and Education Quarterly, 24,* 99–115. Quote appears on p. 101.

and communication, early anthropological conceptions of plural, distinct, historically homogeneous cultures now are both scientifically misleading and educationally irrelevant. Wax commented that anthropologists are documenting the emergence of a "global cultural ecumene" that transcends and blends elements of many cultures.

Nonetheless, ethnographers still believe that what makes human beings unique as a species is the influence of culture in their lives, and that the most important difference between groups of people is their culture. Culture allows a particular group or society to live together and thrive through a system of shared meanings and values, but that same system often leads them to oppose, and even war against, other groups with different shared meanings and values. Thus the influence of culture is both positive and negative.

Ethnographers regard certain aspects of human culture as central to understanding life in a particular society. These aspects include social organization, economic patterns, family structure, religious practices and beliefs, political relationships, and ceremonial behavior. Ethnographers assume that these and other aspects of a culture are interrelated, from which it follows that a researcher cannot develop an understanding of one aspect of a culture without studying the other aspects to which it is related.

Anthropologists generally believe that ethnography should always have at least an implicit cross-cultural perspective—a belief that sets anthropology apart from other social science disciplines.[36] For some ethnographers, the comparative study of cultures is their primary purpose. This branch of anthropology is called **ethnology:** It involves the development of theories of culture based on comparisons of ethnographic data collected from different cultures.

A key issue for educational ethnographers is the question of whether learning is better viewed primarily as a process of cultural transmission or of cultural acquisition. Research on **cultural acquisition** puts the focus on how individuals seek to acquire, or to avoid acquiring, the concepts, values, skills, and behaviors that are reflected in the common culture. For example, John Ogbu developed a model of education and caste based on his ethnographic research.[37] The model claims that U.S.-born members of minority groups who have suffered a long history of economic discrimination in the United States tend to withhold their investment in education because they do not perceive it as having any economic payoff.

Research on **cultural transmission,** by contrast, puts the focus on how the larger social structure intentionally intervenes in individuals' lives in order to promote or, in some cases, to discourage, learning of particular concepts, values, skills, or behaviors. George Spindler and Louise Spindler observed that the more individual focus of cultural acquisition makes it all too easy to slip into a "blame the victim" interpretation of individuals' learning problems.[38] The Spindlers expressed concern that a preoccupation with cultural acquisition could cause researchers to lose ethnography's unique perspective on how societies use their cultural resources to organize the conditions and purposes of learning.

A similar issue is found in other qualitative research traditions. If one believes that culture, language, and social institutions shape the individual, this belief implies that individuals are relatively passive players in social life. If, by contrast, one believes that individuals shape their own destiny, this belief is difficult to reconcile with the regularities

36. Spindler, G., & Spindler, L. (1992). Cultural process and ethnography: An anthropological perspective. In M. D. LeCompte, W. L. Millroy, & J. Preissle (Eds.), *Handbook of qualitative research in education* (pp. 53–92). San Diego: Academic Press.
37. Ogbu, J. U. (1978). *Minority education and caste: The American system in cross-cultural perspective.* New York: Academic Press.
38. Spindler & Spindler, Cultural process and ethnography, p. 60.

observed in social life. It seems likely that both views have some validity, so the task of ethnography and other qualitative research traditions is to determine how cultural factors and human agency interact with each other to co-determine social life. Some qualitative researchers use the term **agency** to refer to the assumed ability of individuals to shape the conditions of their lives.

Phenomena Studied by Ethnographers

Ethnography had its beginnings in studies of what were then called *non-Western* or *native* cultures carried out by anthropologists such as Bronislaw Malinowski studying the native peoples of New Guinea and the Trobriand Islands during World War I[39] and Margaret Mead conducting fieldwork in New Guinea to describe the process of growing up in Manus society.[40]

Today most ethnographers study subcultures within their own country or in other developed countries. This shift reflects both the rapid colonization and destruction of non-Western cultures and researchers' growing rejection of totalistic conceptions of human phenomena. Ethnography increasingly recognizes the local, specific, and time-bound nature of a given cultural phenomenon and the need to conduct research from this perspective. Examples of this type of research are George Spindler and Louise Spindler's comparative ethnographic study of two schools and their communities in Germany and the United States[41] and a study by Sandra Mathison and Melissa Freeman of the effects of state-mandated testing on fourth-grade teachers in two elementary schools in upstate New York.[42] The study of small cultural units such as these sometimes is called **microethnography.** The corresponding term for the study of large cultural units (e.g., the country Burma) is **macroethnography.** Still another unit of study is the self. Research having this focus is called **autoethnography.** Autoethnography has been defined as "an autobiographical genre of writing and research that displays multiple layers of consciousness, connecting the personal to the cultural."[43]

Doing an Ethnographic Study

We next give examples of the phases of a typical ethnographic research study.

Formulating a research problem and selecting a case. To formulate a research problem, the ethnographer defines an aspect of culture to be explored. Howard Becker noted the tendency of ethnographers to capitalize on accidental or forced circumstances in selecting cases.[44] Malinowski's study of the Trobriand Islanders in New Guinea was occasioned, or at least lengthened, by the advent of World War I and his detention on the islands in the status of an enemy alien.

Often the problem is formulated first, and then a setting is selected that fits the problem. Margaret Mead was interested in studying the relationship between spontaneous animism (i.e., a belief in the existence of spirits that appears to develop naturally and independently of any external influence) and the thinking processes of young children.

39. Malinowski, B. (1922). *Argonauts of the Western Pacific.* New York: Dutton.
40. Mead, M. (1930). *Growing up in New Guinea: A comparative study of primitive education.* New York: William Morrow.
41. Spindler & Spindler, Cultural process and ethnography.
42. Mathison, S., & Freeman, M. (2003). Constraining elementary teachers' work: Dilemmas and paradoxes created by state mandated testing. *Education Policy Analysis Archives, 11*(34). Retrieved July 31, 2005 from http://epaa.asu.edu/epaa/v11n34/#_edn2
43. Ellis, C., & Bochner, A. P. (2000). Autoethnography, personal narrative, reflexivity. In N. K. Denzin & Y. S. Lincoln (Eds.), *Handbook of qualitative research* (2nd ed., pp. 733–768). Thousand Oaks, CA: Sage. Quote appears on p. 739.
44. Becker, H. S. (1993). Theory: The necessary evil. In D. J. Flinders & G. E. Mills (Eds.), *Theory and concepts in qualitative research* (pp. 218–229). New York: Teachers College Press.

She selected Melanesia "because it is an area which contains many relatively unspoiled primitive groups and has been conspicuous in ethnological discussions as a region filled with the phenomena usually subsumed under the head of 'Animism.'" [45] Mead selected the Manus tribe for reasons such as the availability of some texts in the native language and of a school boy willing to act as interpreter.

A more recent example of choosing a setting that fits the problem is provided by the selection of two schools by Sandra Mathison and Melissa Freemen to investigate the effects of state-mandated testing on teachers' professionalism.[46] The two schools were in districts that were participating in a National Science Foundation-funded teacher-enhancement project aimed at providing professional development in science to elementary and middle school teachers. The project emphasized helping teachers better prepare students for the New York State fourth- and eighth-grade science tests.

Each of these examples illustrates ethnography's traditional goal of making the familiar strange.[47] This goal involves looking at a cultural phenomenon from the perspective of an outsider, and then seeking to understand the phenomenon from the perspective of insiders. You can achieve this goal by immersing yourself in a culture far different from your own, as in the case of the ethnographic studies of Malinowski and Mead. You also can achieve it by studying a subculture in your own community with which your are unfamiliar, as in Harry Wolcott's study of a youth who had rejected many of the educational and social values espoused by the researcher himself and most of his associates.[48]

Ethnography sometimes is carried out in a familiar setting, of course, particularly when researchers study schools in which they have worked or that at least are similar to those that they themselves attended. In this case researchers must use other means to gain an "outsider's" perspective. For example, Joyce Henstrand described her use of theory to reflect on her findings while conducting an ethnography of the school in which she was teaching.[49] This approach enabled her to step back from her teacher role and focus on her researcher role.

Gaining entry The process of gaining entry varies greatly depending on the nature of the research problem and the requirements of the case. In an ethnographic study of a school principal, Wolcott summarized his approach as follows:

> I spent weeks searching for a suitable and willing subject, and I did not request formal permission from the school district to conduct the study until I had the personal permission and commitment of the selected individual.[50]

As Wolcott's example illustrates, gaining entry might involve several levels of access and sign-off, from the individual to the institutional level. Mead, by contrast, described a less formal, but perhaps even more demanding, strategy. First, she established residence in a thatched house on piles in the center of one of the Manus villages. Then Mead sought to fit herself into the Manus culture for a long period of time in order to gain entry into the daily activities and conversations of the native people. This involved learning the Manus

45. Mead, *Growing up in New Guinea,* p. 289.
46. Mathison & Freeman, Constraining elementary teachers' work.
47. Spindler, G., & Spindler, L. (1982). Roger Harker and Schoenhausen: From the familiar to the strange and back again. In G. Spindler (Ed.), *Doing the ethnography of schooling* (pp. 21–43). New York: Holt, Rinehart, & Winston.
48. Wolcott, H. F. (1994). *Transforming qualitative data: Description, analysis, and interpretation.* Thousand Oaks, CA: Sage.
49. Henstrand, J. (1993). Theory as research guide: A qualitative look at qualitative inquiry. In D. J. Flinders & G. E. Mills (Eds.), *Theory and concepts in qualitative research* (pp. 83–102). New York: Teachers College Press.
50. Wolcott, *Transforming qualitative data,* p. 118

language, playing the children's games, attending feasts, and learning how to avoid violating the hundreds of name taboos in their culture.

Collecting data Ethnographers use the full range of qualitative data-collection techniques and, when appropriate, quantitative techniques. Mead observed the Manus children at play and at home. She collected children's spontaneous drawings, created the first time they ever held a pencil. Mead observed all public events in the village of 210 members, recording conversations and writing her interpretations in the native language. She avoided technical terms, writing "in the field of the novelist."[51] Mead used record sheets to classify material from her notes. For example, the household record sheet included headings for the house owner's children by each marriage, who financed his marriages, and what marriages he was financing. The child's record sheet included headings for what the child chewed, the geographical range of play, and chosen companions. Mead made a detailed analysis of the composition of the Peri population in the Manus tribe, for example, how many married couples, widows, and widowers there were and the average number of children per married couple.

Wolcott's ethnography of the school principal made use of official school notices, quantitative records, and census data for the community in which the school was located. He also collected "time and motion" data, recording what the principal was doing, where, and with whom, at 60-second intervals over a carefully sampled two-week period at school.

Early in the study, Wolcott used primarily participant observation, "shadowing" the principal's everyday activities while making continuous entries in a notebook. Wolcott explained that his intent was to create a precedent for constant note-taking so that people would become comfortable with it. He never returned to the school until he had completed his notes from the last visit. His longhand notes were typed onto 8×5 cards, each card describing a single event. To avoid becoming "overidentified" with the principal, he visited often with teachers and staff members. He also was able to include within the scope of his observations visits with the principal's family at home, the principal's errands and community activities around town, and special social events.

Only after he had spent over half a year at the school did Wolcott add interviewing as a data-collection method. He conducted and taped several one-hour interviews with the principal (e.g., about the principal's forecast of the coming school year, his family life, and what had occurred at the school since Wolcott's last visit). Individual interviews also were conducted with 13 faculty and two staff members about their perceptions of the principal as a school administrator. All fifth- and sixth-grade students were asked to write brief, anonymous comments about the principal. Wolcott concluded his fieldwork by distributing a 10-page questionnaire to all faculty and staff: "The questionnaire was particularly valuable in enabling me to obtain systematic data about the staff, as I could see no point in holding a long taped interview with each of the twenty-nine members of the regular and part-time staff."[52]

In their study of how high-stakes state-mandated student testing challenges teacher professionalism, Mathison and Freeman carried out a year-long ethnographic field study of two elementary schools in upstate New York during the 2001–2002 school year.[53] Their fieldwork focused on fourth-grade classrooms, where the testing burden primarily lies. They spent at least one day per week in each school observing classrooms, talking with administrators

51. Mead, *Growing up in New Guinea*, p. 292.
52. Wolcott, *Transforming qualitative data*, p. 123.
53. Mathison & Freeman, Constraining elementary teachers' work.

and teachers at every grade level, and attending school meetings and events. A focus group interview with teachers and one with parents were conducted, as were individual interviews with building and district administrators. Their online report of their ethnography of two schools includes a poem constructed of teachers' comments on their frustration with the testing and its effects, including this segment:

> What this test is testing is good
> Kids should be able to read a passage
> And respond to it in writing
> There's nothing wrong with that
> What's wrong is the way the adults in the world
> Take the scores and report them[54]

The array of data-collection strategies used by ethnographers continues to expand with modern technology and a growing acceptance of both quantitative and qualitative data. For example, Spindler and Spindler used the Instrumental Activities Inventory (IAI) in their comparative study of a German and a U.S. elementary school. The IAI is a set of line drawings depicting traditional and modernized ways of life that is used to evoke individuals' lifestyle preferences. Spindler and Spindler used statistical techniques to analyze individuals' choices, and the rationales for their choices, of the groups whose lifestyles they preferred. Gender and age were found to be the strongest influences on life choices.

Spindler and Spindler also used film and photographs as evocative stimuli in interviews, showing films of the German classroom to the U.S. students and teachers and vice versa. The Spindlers then interviewed the research participants about what they saw in their own classrooms and in those of the "other," and how they interpreted what they saw. They also implemented an exchange of correspondence between the German and U.S. teachers and between the German and U.S. students. Regarding this activity, they commented:

> These kinds of solicited documents are useful as an expression of the native point of view. An exchange of this sort must be regarded as a research device—that is, a situation created by the ethnographers.[55]

Thus, although ethnography is considered to be a naturalistic method of inquiry, we see that ethnographers can invent new methods if they will help them gain further insights into the phenomena they are studying.

Analyzing and interpreting data As we explained in Chapter 14, data analysis in qualitative research usually begins while the data are being collected, and affects subsequent data-collection efforts. Alan Peshkin's book *Permissible Advantage* explores in depth a private, elite, college-preparatory high school, examining the moral choices made by participants of an exceptionally wealthy school and what the very existence of such a privileged school indicates about U.S. society.[56] In interpreting his ethnographic findings, Peshkin documents the excellence of Edgewood Academy not to extol its success but, rather, to call attention to what is available to its students that is not available to most students in the United States. He cites data to illustrate the cliché "the rich get richer," in terms of the cultural capital students arrive with and the expansion of that capital during and after their education there. Peshkin points out that those few students from the working (or even

54. Ibid, Abstract, paragraph 3. Reprinted with permission of Sandra Mathison.
55. Spindler & Spindler, Roger Harker and Schoenhausen, p. 80.
56. Peshkin, A. (2000). *Permissible advantage: The moral consequences of elite schooling.* Mahwah, NJ: Erlbaum.

middle) class who are recruited to foster Edgewood's diversity tend to forget their roots, reflecting the potentially high price families and communities may pay when the social mobility of their children is significantly enhanced. Affluence and academic achievement are described as the two most relevant factors in the academy, and advantage offers center stage, both in terms of what the school offers and the lifelong doors it opens to the wider world for its graduates. Peshkin's interpretation focuses on justice denied, not through conscious, planful efforts to shortchange other children, but because injustice occurs as the result of imagined limitations of resources and means.

Reporting the case study   Mathison and Freeman engaged a number of teachers and the principals at each school as peer debriefers who continually checked the researchers' understandings as they read draft reports. Their report includes the following comment reflecting the peer debriefers perspective:

> These teachers wonder if policy makers and politicians have any sense of children's individual differences and the centrality of that concept to teaching *and* learning.[57]

Ethnographers, with their concern for thick description and conveying the emic perspective, tend to weave particularly rich stories. Margaret Mead described an interaction between a six-year-old child, Popoli, and his father:

> [H]e whines out in the tone which all Manus natives use when begging betel nut: "A little betel?" The father throws him a nut. He tears the skin off with his teeth and bites it greedily. "Another," the child's voice rises to a higher pitch. The father throws him a second nut, which the child grasps firmly in his wet little fist, without acknowledgement. "Some pepper leaf?" The father frowns. "I have very little, Popoli." "Some pepper leaf." The father tears off a piece of a leaf and throws it to him. The child scowls at the small piece. "This is too little. More! More! More!" His voice rises to a howl of rage.[58]

Marion Dobbert described an ethnographic report as having five parts: (1) statement of the study questions and the situations and problems that led to them, (2) description of the background research and theory used to refine the study questions and design the study, (3) detailed review of the study design, (4) presentation of the data, and (5) explanation of the findings.[59] Dobbert described the presentation of data as the "heart and soul" of the report. To her, this presentation should be a detailed description of the social scene under investigation, presented in organized fashion and based on a low-level (i.e., descriptive or low-inference) categorical analysis of data.

Dobbert identified various formats for ethnographic reporting. Some formats reflect the insider's view (e.g., a typical biography or modal personality viewpoint). Other formats reflect the outsider's or "scientific" view (e.g., an ecological or structural emphasis). Still others (e.g., the community within a community and historical approach) can take either an insider's or an outsider's view. Recently, some ethnographers have turned their field notes or completed reports into theatre performances.[60]

To do a complete ethnography of a culture or an aspect of a culture is a major undertaking, as our examples illustrate. Often a single report represents only one aspect of the

57. Mathison & Freeman, Constraining elementary teachers' work, Conclusions, paragraph 3.
58. Mead, *Growing up in New Guinea*, pp. 20–21.
59. Dobbert, M. (1984). *Ethnographic research: Theory and application for modern schools and societies.* New York: Praeger.
60. Alexander, B. K. (2005). Performance ethnography: The reenacting and inciting of culture. In N. K. Denzin & Y. S. Lincoln (Eds.), *Sage handbook of qualitative research* (3rd ed., pp. 411–441). Thousand Oaks, CA: Sage.

total case study. The individual report thus contributes to, rather than itself constituting, the ethnography. The case might be revisited repeatedly, as in the Spindlers' decades-long comparative study of German and U.S. elementary schools, or different aspects of the phenomenon might be studied at a later time.

Issues Facing Ethnography

The third edition of the *Sage Handbook of Qualitative Research* demonstrates ethnography's central and expanding role in qualitative research, with eight chapters including the term *ethnography* in their titles.[61] As ethnography continues to evolve, it reflects most of the strengths and weaknesses of any qualitative research tradition. Its diverse data-collection and analysis methods, in-depth study of phenomena in their real-life context, and concern for the emic perspective help researchers weave coherent patterns from the diverse elements of the complex cultures in today's world. Nonetheless, questions have been raised as to ethnography's ability to meet the standards of quality and rigor that we discussed in Chapter 14. Some would argue with these standards, but if ethnographers hope to have an impact on social science and educational practice, they must address them. We mention several specific issues next.

While the emic perspective helps the reader or viewer or listener understand culture as a unique social reality, it does not provide a strong basis for discovering regularities of social life. For example, if a researcher writes a good ethnography describing a particular school district, it will help us understand that district, but not other school districts. An etic perspective, in which the researcher develops her own categories for understanding a culture, might provide a better basis for cross-cultural research and the discovery of cross-cultural commonalities. However, these categories might distort our understanding of any particular culture.

Another issue is whether ethnography should subscribe to the goal of the natural sciences to develop universal laws or to the goal of the humanities to understand the unique and particular case. Some ethnographers attempt to pursue both goals in their research.

Another issue concerns the reporting of ethnographic findings. Critics argue that ethnographic reports represent a genre of writing that imposes a particular order on cultural phenomena, an order that may not accurately reflect the culture being described. Clifford Geertz, for example, claims that ethnographies are "fiction" in that they are not the culture itself, but rather a story told by the author using various literary conventions and devices.[62] Some feminist theorists argue that classic ethnographies reflect a privileged male discourse that involves non-reciprocal relationships with, and distance from, the members of the culture being studied.[63] Some ethnographers therefore adopt a "dialogic" stance in which they conduct their research as a collaboration between the researcher and the members of the culture being studied.

If you plan to do ethnographic research, you will need to become well versed in the literature on these issues and decide what stance to take on them. Also, keep in mind that it requires a lengthy apprenticeship to learn how to do ethnography well, and the data-collection process for an ethnographic study can take many months, or even longer.

61. Denzin, N. K., & Lincoln, Y. S. (Eds.). (2005). *Sage handbook of qualitative research* (3rd ed.). Thousand Oaks, CA: Sage.

62. Geertz, C. (1973). *The interpretation of cultures: Selected essays.* New York: Basic Books.

63. Stanley, L., & Wise, S. (1983). *Breaking out: Feminist consciousness and feminist research.* London: Routledge & Kegan Paul.

Cultural Studies and Critical-Theory Research

More than any other qualitative research tradition, cultural studies reflects a blending of disciplinary traditions and methods of study. According to Paula Saukko:

> The distinctive feature of cultural studies is the way in which it combines a hermeneutic focus on lived realities, a (post)structuralist critical analysis of discourses that mediate our experiences and realities, and a contextualist/realist investigation of historical, social, and political structures of power.[64]

Saukko explains that cultural studies is wedded to the idea that social structures of power constitute the bottom line against which the meaning and effectiveness of any discourse or experience should be evaluated. It has been an active field of inquiry in Europe since the 1960s and is becoming increasingly popular in the United States.

Cultural studies has been described as a branch of critical theory.[65] **Critical theory** began in the 1920s with the work of scholars at the Institute of Social Research in Frankfurt, Germany, and, in recent years, it has become closely associated with the work of Jurgen Habermas, who also works in Germany. The investigations of Habermas are primarily theoretical and concern large-scale social structure, whereas researchers who characterize their work as cultural studies tend to be more empirically oriented and concerned with small-scale social structures. There is much overlap between cultural studies and critical theory, however, and the two terms sometimes are used synonymously. Cultural studies in education can be regarded as one form of the field known as **anti-oppressive education,** which involves constantly looking beyond what is taught and learned in order to trouble education and educational research.[66] **Troubling** means to question and expose the assumptions that underlie widely accepted but oppressive cultural practices maintained by traditional educational operations.

Thus, educational researchers who work within the **cultural studies** tradition analyze the power relationships that are ignored or taken for granted by most educators, but that are central to the operation of educational institutions. Their analyses are guided by a commitment to advocate for a more just distribution of power than that operating in the present educational system, which is seen as perpetuating social oppression based on ethnicity, class, gender, sexuality, and other cultural categories applied to individuals.

Assumptions of the Cultural Studies Tradition

Joe Kincheloe and Peter McLaren list seven basic assumptions that are accepted by a criticalist, that is, "a researcher or theorist who attempts to use her or his work as a form of social or cultural criticism."[67] We explain these assumptions below, paraphrasing them to foster understanding and giving examples of their implications for educational research.

1. *Every society systematically gives privileges to certain cultural groups and oppresses other cultural groups.* When a cultural group possesses **privilege,** its members enjoy

Gaztambide-Fernandez, R. A., Harding, H., & Sorde-Marti, T. (Eds.), (2004). *Cultural studies and education: Perspectives on theory, methodology, and practice.* Cambridge, MA: Harvard Education.

Kincheloe, J. L. (2004). *Critical pedagogy primer.* New York: Peter Lang.

Morrow, R. A., & Brown, D. D. (1994). *Critical theory and methodology: Interpretive structuralism as a research program.* Thousand Oaks, CA: Sage.

64. Saukko, P. (2005). Methodologies for cultural studies. In N. K. Denzin & Y. S. Lincoln (Eds.), *Sage handbook of qualitative research* (3rd ed., pp. 343–356). Thousand Oaks, CA: Sage. Quote appears on p. 343.

65. Fiske, J. (1994). Audiencing: Cultural practice and cultural studies. In N. K. Denzin & Y. S. Lincoln (Eds.), *Handbook of qualitative research* (pp. 189–198). Thousand Oaks, CA: Sage.

66. Kumashiro, K. (2002). *Troubling education: Queer activism and anti-oppressive pedagogy.* New York: Routledge Falmer.

67. Kincheloe, J. L., & McLaren, P. (2005). Rethinking critical theory and qualitative research. In N. K. Denzin & Y. S. Lincoln (Eds.), *Sage handbook of qualitative research* (3rd ed., pp. 303–342). Thousand Oaks, CA: Sage. Quote appears on p. 304.

greater power, resources, and life opportunities than the members of other cultural groups. Such privilege is reinforced primarily through hegemony and internalized oppression.

Hegemony refers to the ways in which privileged cultural groups maintain domination of other groups through various cultural agencies that exert power. In a workshop attended by J. Gall, one of the authors, McLaren, pinpointed the political, criminal justice, and educational systems as cultural agencies with particular impact in supporting hegemony.[68] **Internalized oppression** refers to the process by which oppressed individuals unwittingly help maintain their lack of privilege through thoughts and actions consistent with their lesser social status. **Reproduction** of the oppression occurs as new members who are born to or join the culture accept the preexisting patterns of cultural inequity.

The dominant culture exercises hegemony by framing the experiences of individuals through a steady stream of "terms of reference" (e.g., cliches about "the good life," media images, and stories) against which individuals conceive and evaluate their own reality. For McLaren hegemony thus involves "a struggle in which the powerful win the consent of those who are oppressed, with the oppressed unknowingly participating in their own oppression."[69]

2. *The oppression experienced by an individual is an interactive combination of the various oppressions generated in response to all that individual's nonprivileged identities.* Critical theorists claim that conducting research on only one form of oppression at the expense of others (e.g., class oppression vs. racism) obscures the interconnections among them. To understand and combat oppression, it is necessary to examine all the cultural categories that are used to separate and oppress different groups, and to consider their joint operation and effects. For example, to understand why a student is resistant and defiant in school, a teacher must consider the student's ethnic identity, gender, and social class background, as well as other cultural characteristics (e.g., being identified as sensorily deprived, learning disabled, or gay).

3. *Cultural texts (including but not limited to language) are probably the most powerful means of expressing and maintaining differences in privilege.* Besides language, any discourse, object, or event has communicative value and can thus be analyzed as a **text.** An individual's awareness is both expanded and constrained by the language that is available for encoding his experience. The formal and informal language in classrooms or instructional programs involving different forms of discourse (e.g., sex education focused on abstinence only versus sex education including discussion of responsible sexual practices) are examples of how educators use language that maintains or contests hegemony.

The concept of voice is used by critical theorists to study particular expressions of domination and oppression. **Voice** refers to the phenomenon in which people occupying particular social categories or identities are either silenced, empowered, or privileged through the operation of various discourses that maintain or contest dominant and subordinate cultures in a society.[70]

Henry Giroux, an educator, argues that voice "provides a critical referent for analyzing how students are made voiceless in particular settings by not being allowed to speak, or how students silence themselves out of either fear or ignorance regarding the strength and

68. McLaren, P. (2003, February). Critical pedagogy in the age of neoliberal globalization: The domestication of political agency and the struggle for socialist futures. In the Center for Critical Theory and Transnational Studies, *Transnationalism, ethnicity, and the public sphere.* Workshop presented at the University of Oregon, Eugene, OR.

69. McLaren, P. (1994). *Life in schools: An introduction to critical pedagogy in the foundations of education.* New York: Longman. Quote appears on p. 182.

70. For an analysis of voice in research on teachers, see: Hargreaves, A. (1996). Revisiting voice. *Educational Researcher, 25*(1), 12–19.

possibilities that exist in the multiple languages and experience that connect them to a sense of agency and self-formation."[71] In her book on critical pedagogy, Joan Wink gives dozens of examples of how teachers' use of language can empower or disempower different students every day.[72]

4. *Every human act, creation, or communication can be interpreted in relation to the cultural context of capitalist production and consumption.* This assumption means, for example, that how a textbook author (the signifier) writes a textbook (the signified) often involves basic economic considerations, and will vary at different times. Thus, the form and content of most textbooks reflect the values of the dominant culture and are consistent with standards derived from a capitalist value framework.

Viewing most of the texts in education and research as problematic (that is, tending to misrepresent individuals' lived experience), criticalists thus subject texts to **deconstruction,** a process originating in philosophy and literary criticism that asserts that a text has no definite meaning, that words can refer only to other words, and that "playing" with a text can yield multiple, often contradictory interpretations of it. Let's consider examples of violence in schools, ranging from frequent mild events to rare, extreme events. In a deconstruction of such occurrences, Kincheloe and McLaren note:

> If we view the violence we find in classrooms not as random or isolated incidents created by aberrant individuals willfully stepping out of line in accordance with a particular form of social pathology, but as possible narratives of transgression and resistance, then this could indicate that the "political unconscious" lurking beneath the surface of everyday classroom life is not unrelated to practices of race, class, and gender oppression but rather intimately connected to them.[73]

5. *All thought is mediated by socially and historically constructed power relations.* In the context of education, this assumption implies that the beliefs and activities of students, teachers, and other groups involved in education are inevitably affected by their experiences with power and dominance, both within and outside the educational system. Particular beliefs and activities can only be understood in reference to the unique context in which they occur.

Any text can be subjected to contextual analysis to determine how it reflects power relations. For example, McLaren argues that multiculturalism, a movement aimed at improving relationships among students of different cultures and their conformance to society's educational expectations, is still largely a mainstream, progressive agenda, so, while exceedingly important, it is conceptually and politically compromised from the start.[74]

6. *Facts can never be isolated from the domain of values and prevailing assumptions about what is valued.* Critical theorists reject the notion that research about teaching and learning can ever be a neutral or value-free process. Like other qualitative researchers, they question the very notion of objective reality, regarding so-called social reality as constructed by each individual and thereby open to many interpretations and modifiable through human action. Critical theorists argue that educational concepts such as achievement, reason, standards, and freedom are categories constructed by and serving the interests of certain privileged groups in the educational hierarchy.

71. Giroux, H. A. (1992). Resisting difference: Cultural studies and the discourse of critical pedagogy. In L. Grossberg, C. Nelson, & P. Treichler (Eds.), *Cultural studies* (pp. 199–212). New York: Routledge. Quote appears on pp. 205–206.
72. Wink, J. (2000). *Critical pedagogy: Notes from the real world* (2nd ed.). New York: Addison Wesley Longman.
73. Kincheloe & McLaren, Rethinking critical theory and qualitative research, p. 306.
74. McLaren, Critical pedagogy in the age of neoliberal globalization.

7. *Mainstream research practices help reproduce systems of oppression that are based on class, race, gender, and other cultural categories.* Much educational research has been guided by positivism and carried out primarily by middle- and upper-class white males. Critical theorists claim that this type of research thus rests on assumptions about truth, science, and good that have been accepted as universal, but which in fact have served to maintain the oppression of groups who represent other cultural categories. Critical theorists particularly oppose educational research that focuses on prediction and control for the purpose of maximizing educational productivity. Such research reflects the operation of **instrumental rationality,** which involves a preoccupation with means or technology over ends or purposes. Rex Gibson claimed that the IQ testing movement is a key example of the shortcomings and injustices that instrumental rationality effects:

> Instrumental rationality is the cast of thought which seeks to dominate others, which assumes its own rightness to do so, and which exercises its power to serve its own interests. Coldly following its narrow principle of efficiency and applying a crude economic yardstick, its results are all too obvious . . . the interests least served are those of comprehensive schools and pupils from working class homes.[75]

This and other assumptions of the cultural studies tradition are helpful in stimulating critical reflection about mainstream educational practice and research.

Methods of Inquiry

Touchstone in Research

Carspecken, P. F., & Walford, G. (Eds.). (2001). *Critical ethnography and education.* Oxford, UK: Elsevier Science.

The cultural studies tradition draws upon methods used in a wide range of other research traditions, including sociology, semiotics, literary criticism, history, philosophy, psychoanalysis, and anthropology. If there is any method that is common to research and theory-building in the cultural studies tradition, it is critique—critique of the researcher's own perspective and values, critique of methodology, and critique of the phenomena being studied.

Paula Saukko has recommended three forms of validity, corresponding to three methods of inquiry that should be integrated within cultural studies research.

1. *Dialogic/hermeneutic validity* involves methods to ensure sensitivity to the lived realities of informants.
2. *Self-reflexive/poststructuralist validity* involves efforts to expose the politics embedded in the discourses through which realities are constructed and perceived.
3. *Contextual validity*, which most closely mirrors traditional forms of validity, concerns ways to make sense of historical and social reality accurately and truthfully.[76]

Saukko provides detailed examples of research studies that fail to address one or more of the bases for these validities and argues that this failure limits critical understanding of the phenomena addressed. She also describes a more successful example of an ethnography on pro-life and pro-choice women, noting that its study of "two ways of experiencing female caring . . . enables the reader to relate to the contrasting realities of both of these groups of women and to comprehend them, even if not necessarily accepting them."[77]

Because cultural studies draws upon a wide range of other research traditions, having a broad education in the humanities and social sciences will help you investigate an

75. Gibson, R. (1986). *Critical theory and education.* London: Hodder & Stoughton. Quote appears on pp. 8–9.
76. Saukko, Methodologies for cultural studies.
77. Ibid., p. 349.

educational problem using the cultural studies approach. In addition, you will need to develop expertise in the particular methodology you plan to use for data collection or conceptual analysis. An example is Philip Carspecken's model of critical ethnography, designed to generate "validity truth claims" that are supportable.[78] It involves five stages: monological data collection, preliminary reconstructive analysis, dialogical data generation, discovery of system relationships, and seeking of explanations through social-theoretical models. Carspecken uses this model to evaluate an educational program intended to develop inner-city elementary students' self-esteem and conflict-resolution skills. Kincheloe and McLaren applaud Carspecken's work, while noting that recent innovations in critical ethnography have created "new hybridic possibilities for cultural critique . . . opened up by the current blurring and mixing of disciplinary genres—those that emphasize experience, subjectivity, reflexivity, and dialogical understanding."[79]

Another promising method for use in cultural studies and critical-theory research is critical discourse analysis (CDA). In a recent review of the literature on CDA in education, Rebecca Rogers, Elizabeth Malancharuvil-Berkes, Melissa Mosley, Diane Hui, and Glynis O'Garro Joseph chart the findings from 46 CDA studies and offer suggestions for future research.[80]

Focus on Issues Relevant to Education

Researchers who work within the cultural studies tradition have investigated a wide variety of social problems and phenomena, all of which are either relevant to or grounded in educational contexts. For example, they have studied situations that raise issues of social justice for females,[81] racial and ethnic groups,[82] and members of other groups who experience oppression in schools and other educational settings.

Study of educational programs and systems Many cultural studies researchers have studied educational systems outside the academy in which they work. J. Anyon studied the schools' **hidden curriculum,** which refers to the indirect instruction in attitudes and habits that is continually transmitted by the ways in which schools are structured and classroom instruction is organized.[83] Anyon found that schools with a student population from a predominantly working-class background emphasized instructional practices aimed at teaching students the attitudes and habits of factory workers (e.g., blind obedience, discipline, tolerance for repetitive tasks, and respect for authority). In contrast, schools with students from upper socioeconomic classes emphasized instructional practices aimed at helping students become leaders, problem solvers, questioners of authority, and creative organizers of their own work.

Michelle Fine's study of sex education and school-based health clinics illustrates the concern of cultural studies for the relationship between gender and class in how students

78. Carspecken, P. F. (1996). *Critical ethnography in educational research: A theoretical and practical guide.* New York: Routledge.
79. Kincheloe & McLaren, Rethinking critical theory and qualitative research, p. 330.
80. Rogers, R., Malancharuvil-Berkes, E., Mosley, M., Hui, D., & O'Garro Joseph, G. (2005). Critical discourse analysis in education: A review of the literature. *Review of Educational Research, 75*(3), 365–416.
81. For a review of the history, current conceptions, and emerging possibilities of feminist qualitative research, see: Olesen V. (2005). Early millennial feminist qualitative research: Challenges and contours. In N. K. Denzin & Y. S. Lincoln (Eds.), *Sage handbook of qualitative research* (3rd ed., pp. 235–278). Thousand Oaks, CA: Sage.
82. A powerful example of critical and performance ethnography of, for, and about blackness in Africa and America is: Madison, D. S. (2005). Critical ethnography as street performance: Reflections of home, race, murder and justice. In N. K. Denzin & Y. S. Lincoln (Eds.), *Sage handbook of qualitative research* (3rd ed., pp. 537–546). Thousand Oaks, CA: Sage.
83. Anyon, J. (1980). Social class and the hidden curriculum of work. *Journal of Education, 162,* 67–92; see also Apple, M. (1979). *Ideology and curriculum.* London: Routledge & Kegan Paul.

are educated for adulthood.[84] In her ethnographic research, Fine found that female students, particularly low-income ones, have little access to school-based health clinics and sexuality information. Fine found three prevailing discourses of female sexuality in the public school system: (1) It is talked about as essentially violent and coercive, (2) it is associated with victimization, because males are characterized as potential predators, and (3) discussion of females' sexual decision making is centered on the value of premarital abstinence. All three discourses discourage adolescent females from sexual activity, despite research findings reviewed by Fine indicating that adolescent females generally engage in responsible sex practices (e.g., ensuring the use of contraceptives).

Fine described a fourth possibility: the discourse of desire that would acknowledge the possibility of sexual entitlement and responsibility among female students. Fine found that this discourse "remains a whisper inside the official work of U.S. public schools."[85] Fine noted, "How can we ethically continue to withhold educational treatments we know to be effective for adolescent women?"[86] A more recent study of female sexuality in two school sites by Lois Weis and Fine honors "instances of forceful pedagogy that deliberately and directly challenge inequity" and create "buried moments" of "interruption . . . within deeply reproductive educational settings."[87]

Theory Building in Cultural Studies

The cultural studies tradition emphasizes use of theory to explain society and emancipate its participants. Therefore, the development of theory—called "critical theory" in this tradition—is a central preoccupation of cultural studies researchers. Here we summarize a form of critical theory focused on education, describe practices that have been uncovered in critical race theory with implications for education, and give an example of how critical scholars have addressed the phenomenon of knowledge production and distribution in society.

Border pedagogy   Henry Giroux described several assumptions of cultural studies in relation to critical pedagogy.[88] Giroux took as his starting point the assumption that U.S. public education is in crisis. He saw this condition reflected most clearly in the contrast between rhetoric that equates U.S. culture with democracy in its ultimate form and such indicators as low voter participation, growing illiteracy rates among the general population, and an increasingly prevalent view that social criticism and social change are irrelevant to the meaning of American democracy.

Giroux proposed a liberatory theory of "border pedagogy" to replace what he described as the "politics of difference" that characterizes much of the current dialogue about educational problems and solutions. For Giroux the term *border* reflects the notion of permeable, changing boundaries to describe differences between individuals and groups, as opposed to the rigid, "either-or" nature of conventional social categories.

84. Fine, M. (1988). Sexuality, schooling, and adolescent females: The missing discourse of desire. *Harvard Educational Review, 58,* 29–53.
85. Ibid., p. 33.
86. Ibid., p. 50.
87. Weis, L., & Fine, M. (2003). Extraordinary conversations in public schools. In G. Dimitriadis & D. Carlson (Eds.), *Promises to keep: Cultural studies, democratic education, and public life* (pp. 95–123). New York: Routledge Falmer. Quote appears on p. 121.
88. Giroux, H. A. (1988). Critical theory and the politics of culture and voice: Rethinking the discourse of educational research. In R. R. Sherman & R. B. Webb (Eds.), *Qualitative research in education: Focus and methods* (pp. 190–210). New York: Falmer; Giroux, H. A. (1992). Resisting difference.

In Giroux's theory, difference is linked to a broader politics, and schools and pedagogy are organized around a sense of purpose that makes difference central to a critical notion of citizenship and democratic public life. This concept of difference is postmodern in that it recognizes the need to acknowledge the particular, the heterogeneous, and the multiple, and it views the political community as a diverse collection of subcommunities in flux. Within this framework, educators are seen as obliged to give students the opportunity to analyze how the dominant culture creates borders "saturated in terror, inequality, and forced exclusions," and to construct new pedagogical borders where difference becomes the intersection of new forms of culture and identity.[89]

Giroux's border pedagogy would have students no longer study unified subjects but rather the "borderlands" between diverse cultural histories, as sites for both critical analysis and as a potential source of experimentation, creativity, and possibility. Students would explore power, explicitly seeking to grasp how forms of domination are historically and socially constructed. Teachers would use their authority to aid students in emancipation from such domination. Students would learn to read cultural texts critically, to discover the discursive codes and ideological interests that underlie them.

Giroux sees the ultimate outcome of this pedagogy as "nothing less than providing the conditions for educators and their students to become knowledgeable and committed actors in the world."[90] He views this outcome as quite different from that captured in other theoretical discourses, which he feels tend to foster despair rather than hope in their criticism of the current state of education.

Critical race theory In discussing the moral activist role of critical race theory scholarship, Gloria Ladson-Billings and James Donnor describe in detail ways in which the dominant order "distorts the realities of the Other in an effort to maintain power relations that continue to disadvantage those who are excluded from that order."[91] The Other to which they refer is people of color, the racialized residents of the United States who have experienced and continue to experience colonial oppression. Critical race theory views racism as a permanent fixture of American life, which "appears both normal and natural to people in this society."[92] Among the racist cultural practices that they see as permeating U.S. society are the following, all of which we see as having major implications for education and educational research.

1. A racialized identity that collapses distinctions between ethnic groups composed of myriad national and ancestral origins and forces groups into essentialized and totalized units (such as Latinos, Native Americans, African Americans, and Asian Americans) that are perceived to have little or no internal variation

2. The double consciousness (described in relation to *liminal space of alterity, divided self,* and *wide-angle vision*) of scholars excluded from the center, who must continually maintain awareness of both their identity as a member (albeit honorary or momentary) of the mainstream academic culture and of their imposed (be it self-imposed or imposed by the larger culture) racialized identity

89. Giroux, Resisting difference, p. 209.
90. Giroux, Critical theory, p. 208.
91. Ladson-Billings, G., & Donnor, J. (2005). The moral activist role of critical race theory scholarship. In N. K. Denzin & Y. S. Lincoln (Eds.), *Sage handbook of qualitative research* (3rd ed., pp. 279–301). Thousand Oaks, CA: Sage. Quote appears on p. 281.
92. Ladson-Billings, G. (2000). Racialized discourses and ethnic epistemologies. In N. K. Denzin & Y. S. Lincoln (Eds.), *Handbook of qualitative research* (2nd ed., pp. 257–277). Quote appears on p. 264.

3. The operation of a moral vacuum, in which liberal whites situate themselves as saviors of the oppressed while simultaneously maintaining their white-skin privilege, as when U.S. President Clinton ended welfare and took other actions that disproportionately harmed people of color
4. Promulgation of the fiction of color-blindness to eliminate distinctions that reveal disparities among whites and people of color in school achievement, incarceration, income levels, health concerns, and other social and civic concerns, effectively erasing the races while maintaining the social, political, economic, and cultural status quo
5. Appropriating cultural forms from communities of color (e.g., rap music and hip hop) while maintaining oppression of the members of those communities

Ladson-Billings and Donnor see **critical race theory** as a scholarly effort not limited to old notions of race, but rather as a new analytic rubric for considering difference and inequity using multiple methodologies and displacement of taken-for-granted norms around unequal binaries. They describe the work of organic intellectuals like Grace Lee Boggs, who are rewriting the traditions of teaching–learning from a grassroots perspective.[93] They touch on the need for a reconstructed university system, while noting that movements in this direction so far "still represent a very small crack in the solid, almost frozen traditions of the university."[94] They suggest that

> the challenge for those of us in the academy is not how to make those outside the academy more like us, but rather to recognize the "outside the academy" identities that we must recruit for ourselves in order to be more effective researchers on behalf of people who can make use of our skills and abilities as we learn to be "at home" in the wider world.[95]

While the many charges against "whites" addressed by Ladson-Billings and Donnor are understandable and justified, we nonetheless assert that the first cultural practice described above also applies to whites. That is, individuals who express, or are assigned, the label of whites also are assigned a racialized identity that collapses distinctions between our national and ancestral origins and are viewed as people of no color who have little or no internal variation (other than our perceived privilege). In the spirit of Giroux's critique of the "politics of difference" described above, we urge educational researchers interested in cultural studies to explore race and ethnicity in ways that recognize the oppression involved with every racialized classification of individuals and to address in their work all three of the validities and methods of inquiry described by Saukko in their work.

Knowledge production and distribution   Cultural studies scholars readily engage in discussion and critique of major public events, deconstructing their meaning and giving a different take on their cultural significance that is either ignored or cloaked in mainstream educational and media messages. Here we provide a recent example, involving knowledge production and distribution in the world today. In their discussion of critical research, 9/11, and the effort to make sense of the American empire in the 21st century, Kincheloe and McLaren assert that:

93. Boggs, G. L. (2003a, January). We must be the change. Paper based on a presentation at the University of Michigan 2003 Martin Luther King Symposium, Ann Arbor, MI. Retrieved August 18, 2005, from http://www.boggscenter.org/ideas/speeches/mlkspe.shtml; Boggs, G. L. (2003b, February). A paradigm shift in our concept of education. In the Center for Critical Theory and Transnational Studies, *Transnationalism, ethnicity, and the public sphere.* Workshop presented at the University of Oregon, Eugene, OR. An earlier presentation of this material is available from the Grace Lee Boggs Center Web site, http://www.boogscenter.org/edsumm.htm
94. Ladson-Billings & Donnor, The moral activist role, p. 295.
95. Ibid., p. 298.

The way knowledge is produced and transmitted in the United States by a corporatized media and an increasingly corporatized/privatized educational system is one of the central political issues of our time.[96]

We would argue that it is also a central educational issue.

Kincheloe and McLaren see the United States today as "an epistemological empire based on a notion of truth that undermines the knowledges produced by those outside the good graces and benevolent authority of the empire."[97] They describe the bombing of the World Trade Center and the Pentagon on September 11, 2001, as

a profound shock to millions of Americans who obtain their news and worldviews from the mainstream, corporately owned media and their understanding of American international re- lations from what is taught in most secondary schools and in many colleges and universities. . . . These Americans . . . have not been informed by their news sources of the societies that have been undermined by covert U.S. military operations and economic policies.[98]

The authors also describe the erasure of history and one-sided analysis contained in a cri- tique of U.S. educators by the Thomas B. Fordham Foundation titled *September 11: What Our Children Need to Know*.[99]

Strengths and Weaknesses of Cultural Studies

The assumptions and methods of cultural studies have provoked considerable criticism from educators and researchers representing other traditions. To some critics, the decon- structionism that is characteristic of cultural studies makes groundlessness "the only con- stant recognized by this sensibility."[100] In other words, these critics believe that cultural studies researchers and theorists are hypercritical. Taken to an extreme, deconstruction- ism leads to a sense of hopelessness rather than hope for emancipation. However, most theorists and researchers in the cultural studies tradition fulfill its emancipatory agenda, suggesting fresh directions for educators to explore in order to better meet the needs of tra- ditionally underserved students. Most political conservatives would still find cultural stud- ies disturbing because of its challenges to the corporate and political status quo. Thus it is important for researchers in this tradition to document the bases for their criticisms, be ready to defend them if necessary, and seek partners and allies in working toward eman- cipation.

Another limitation of cultural studies and critical theory involves the dense, complex writing and speaking style of many scholars in this tradition. Gibson notes such charac- teristics as "turgidness, unnecessarily complex sentence structures, a preference for their own neologisms (newly-coined words), and an almost willful refusal to attempt to com- municate directly and clearly with the lay reader. . . . The impression conveyed is of 'cliquishness,' or exclusion; of insiders writing only for insiders."[101]

We believe that the publications and presentations of scholars in the cultural studies and critical theory tradition have become somewhat clearer as this tradition has gained a stronger position in qualitative research. In fact, some of this work is written with a power

96. Kincheloe & McLaren, Rethinking critical theory and qualitative research, p. 332.
97. Ibid., p. 307.
98. Ibid., pp. 330–331.
99. Fordham Foundation (2002). *September 11: What our children need to know.* Retrieved August 18, 2005, from http://www.edexcellence.net/institute/publication/publication.cfm?id=65
100. Spretnak, C. (1991). *States of grace: The recovery of meaning in the postmodern age.* New York: HarperCollins. Quote appears on p. 13.
101. Gibson, *Critical theory and education*, pp. 16–17.

and punch that is badly needed in the educational research literature. Nonetheless, scholars need to strive for clarity to make their work accessible to educators or others unfamiliar with this tradition. Readers also have a responsibility to put in the effort to find and read such works, effort that we personally have found to be highly worthwhile.

Ethnomethodology

Touchstone in Research

Coulon, A. (1995). *Ethnomethodology.* Thousand Oaks, CA: Sage.

Think about the first time you encountered a new situation as a learner, for example, starting a new job. You probably received some formal instruction, but much informal learning occurred as well, such as how to talk to your supervisor, what to do when you made a mistake, how to interact with coworkers and clients, what constitutes proper and improper product, and more generally, how to make sense of the workplace so that you understand it in the same way that others in this social environment do. Ethnomethodology is the study of such matters. More precisely, **ethnomethodology** is the study of the techniques that individuals use to make sense of everyday social environments and to accomplish the tasks of communicating, making decisions, and reasoning within them.

Ethnomethodologists reject the sociological view that human actors passively carry out prescribed actions on the basis of internalized social norms. They seek to examine how various aspects of the life-world are produced, experienced, or accomplished interactionally and discursively.[102] Like phenomenologists, ethnomethodologists are concerned with how social reality *appears* to individuals, not with the objective features of social reality. They differ in that phenomenological researchers primarily are concerned with the individual's interpretations of reality, whereas ethnomethodologists are interested in how groups of individuals develop intersubjective interpretations of reality.

The method of data analysis in ethnomethodology is similar to what we described as *reflective analysis* in Chapter 14. Ethnomethodologists use intuition and judgment to understand how individuals in a local social setting make sense of the setting and work together to create a shared social reality. They also have a reflexive orientation, which means that they reflect on how their research methods influence the phenomena they are studying. In other words, the act of research itself involves sense-making and the construction of social reality. Thus, an ethnomethodologist needs to describe not only how his research participants make sense of and construct their local social reality, but also how he himself went about making sense of and constructing a representation of this sense-making, constructive process.

The increased blending of different cultures within educational systems makes it important for researchers to investigate how members of each culture navigate and negotiate the complex interpersonal interchanges that occur in and around such systems. Deborah Hwa-Froelich and Carol Westby carried out an ethnomethodological study to examine how Head Start staff and families make sense of their roles in children's learning.[103] They sought to discover the differing beliefs and resultant behaviors of Head Start teachers and immigrant parents of Southeast Asian children related to goals for students' learning and the definition and appropriate treatment of learning disabilities. Ten children from nine Southeast Asian families and four Head Start staff members participated in the study, which included semistructured interviews with each staff member; observation of three families during conferences with staff; observations of each child at Head Start

---

102. Schwandt, *Dictionary of qualitative inquiry.*
103. Hwa-Froelich, D. A., & Westby, C. E. (2003). Frameworks of education: Perspectives of Southeast Asian parents and Head Start staff. *Language, Speech, and Hearing Services in Schools, 34*(4), 299–319.

during meals, center time, and outdoor play; and content analysis of literature routinely given to parents.

The authors used the constructs of organizational culture, independence–interdependence, and power–distance relationships to help make sense of the themes derived from their coding of the data. Their interpretations of the assumptions and beliefs of Head Start staff included the following: Becoming independent of adults is a key learning goal for every student; second-language learners do not have learning problems and simply need more time to learn; and because Asian children do not misbehave in school, they do not have learning problems. The inferred assumptions and beliefs of Southeast Asian parents included: It is better to keep a child home who has trouble learning than to lose face at school, an important goal for students' learning is to obey adults, and it is better to avoid conflict with staff by listening politely and not expressing disagreement. The researchers concluded that major disagreements in the values and beliefs of staff and parents existed, and could cause conflict and misunderstanding. They proposed that Head Start staff needed to develop skills related to cultural constructs and cross-cultural communication strategies to be able to work effectively with children and parents of different cultures.

Traditions Involving Investigation of Language and Communication

Qualitative researchers have made extensive studies of language and communication because they are central features of social life. The term *communication,* as we use it here, refers to speech, documents (e.g., textbooks, newsletters, and memos), and media productions (e.g., instructional videotapes and hypermedia CD-ROMs). Communication involves the use of language, which can be viewed as a system of signs. Signs can take many forms, for example, spoken and written words, but also a person's wink, a flagpole at the front of a school building, and the color of a traffic signal. From this perspective, anything in the social environment is a "text" that can be read and interpreted.

Qualitative researchers have different interests in studying communication. Some are curious about the nature of the communicative act. They address such questions as, How does language work? How do individuals obtain meaning from text? What are the different meanings of a text for different individuals? What factors influence the act of communicating? Other qualitative researchers are interested in the actual content of the communication because of what it might reveal about some phenomenon of interest to them. For example, ethnographers might analyze documents found in a field setting for what they reveal about the culture being studied. You will find, then, that some of the qualitative research traditions that we describe below emphasize the form, whereas others emphasize the content, of communication.

First we summarize several qualitative research traditions involving language and communication that may be relevant to your research interests. (Methods for qualitative analysis of texts are also described in Chapter 9.) Then we describe in more detail three qualitative research traditions that have figured prominently in the study of communication: hermeneutics, semiotics, and structuralism.

Many acts of communication take the form of telling stories, folktales, anecdotes, and so forth in a variety of formats, such as stage plays, oral story telling, novels, and film. These communicative acts are *narratives,* which we define as the use of a communication format to organize interpretive representations and explanations of personal and social experience. Researchers have used the methods of various disciplines to study the characteristics

Touchstone in Research

Silverman, D. (2000). Analyzing talk and text. In N. K. Denzin & Y. S. Lincoln (Eds.), *Handbook of qualitative research* (2nd ed., pp. 821–834). Thousand Oaks, CA: Sage.

of narratives and how they are constructed through interpretive acts by the speaker or writer. The methods include **discourse analysis,** which is the study of the interpretive processes that individuals use to produce accounts of reality;[104] **conversation analysis,** which is the study of the implicit rules governing the speech acts between two or more people;[105] **sociolinguistics,** which is the study of the effects of social characteristics such as age, socioeconomic status, and ethnicity on language use; and **narratology,** which is the study of literary narratives. The methods developed by cognitive psychologiststs, ethnomethodologists, and scholars in other research traditions involving the study of lived experience also have been used to study narratives. These methods have collectively been called **narrative inquiry.**[106] Educational researchers recently have begun using the methods of narrative research to study the social organization of the lives of teachers, students, and other groups.[107]

Anthropologists have developed several qualitative research traditions that focus on the study of a culture's communication patterns. For example, one could study the terms that a culture uses to describe food in order to determine how the members of the culture conceptualize eating behavior. **Ethnographic content analysis** involves the examination of the content of documents found in field settings as reflections of social interactions in the culture.[108] In contrast, quantitative content analysis (see Chapter 9) involves the study of the content of documents without consideration of the social and cultural context in which they were produced. Finally, the **ethnography of communication** involves the study of how members of a cultural group use speech in their social life.

Hermeneutics

Touchstone in Research

Gallagher, S. (1992). *Hermeneutics and education.* Albany, NY: State University of New York Press.

The term *hermeneutics* originally meant the interpretation of sacred texts. In contemporary philosophy and the social sciences, **hermeneutics** has come to refer to the study of the process by which individuals arrive at the meaning of any text. The term *text* can refer to a document (e.g., a curriculum guide), but it also can refer to social customs, cultural myths, and anything else containing a message that can be "read." Thus, researchers could use hermeneutic principles to interpret a school reform report (e.g., the No Child Left Behind Act, described at http://www.ed.gov/nclb/landing.jhtml?src=pb), a school site council meeting, the clothing worn by students, or a school district's policy on teacher recruitment and retention.

The hermeneutic tradition in philosophy provides much of the theoretical basis for the interpretive perspective that underlies most qualitative research. The term *interpretive* highlights the centrality of interpretation in qualitative research. Because interpretation is at the heart of hermeneutics, it is little wonder that it has had so much influence on qualitative researchers.

Hermeneutic theorists claim that there is no objective reality and, therefore, no possibility of developing correct knowledge about reality. Instead, we develop interpretations of the world. It follows from this assumption that an author starts by forming an interpretation

104. Potter, J. (1997). Discourse analysis as a way of analyzing naturally-occurring talk. In D. Silverman (Ed.), *Qualitative research: Theory, method and practice* (pp. 144–160). London: Sage.
105. Zimmerman, D. H. (1988). On conversation: The conversation analytic perspective. In J. A. Anderson (Ed.), *Communication yearbook 11* (pp. 406–432). Thousand Oaks, CA: Sage.
106. Chase, Narrative inquiry. Criteria for determining the research value of narratives are described in: Connelly, E. M., & Clandin, D. J. (1990). Stories of experience and narrative inquiry. *Educational Researcher, 19*(5), 2–14.
107. For an example, see: Lieblich, A., & Josselson, R. (Eds.). (1997). *The narrative study of lives,* Vol. 5. Thousand Oaks, CA: Sage.
108. Altheide, D. L. (1987). Ethnographic content analysis. *Qualitative Sociology, 10,* 65–77.

of some aspect of the world and then expresses that interpretation as a text through a medium (e.g., a textbook or instructional videotape) that uses conventions (e.g., a table of contents) which themselves are socially constructed through interpretive acts. The reader subsequently comprehends the text by a process of interpretation, which involves an attempt to re-experience the author's interpretive act. According to hermeneutic theorists, then, the author and the reader are each engaged in interpretive processes. There is no way of knowing the world objectively outside the interpretive act.

Hermeneutic theorists have devoted much effort to the problem of why and how humans are capable of interpretation. They have developed concepts and methods that can aid in the interpretation of texts. One such principle is the **hermeneutic circle,** which describes a continuous process of alternating between interpreting the meaning of each part of the text and the text as a whole. Interpretation of the text as a whole helps in interpretation of the parts, and vice versa.

Other hermeneutic principles are illustrated in a study of the deliberations of a curriculum development team by Elaine Atkins, a researcher who also was a member of the team.[109] The team was formed to construct a new general studies curriculum at the local community college. It included members of three previous teams that had developed competing proposals, none of which was acceptable to the college's administrators. The charge given to the new team was to develop a "unified" proposal.

Atkins tape-recorded all 20 meetings held by the team, each lasting about five hours, for the following research objective:

> I wanted to go back and learn more about how we had managed to arrive at the agreements that we had struggled with so hard. I also wanted to locate the places where we had never been able to reach accord. I wanted to identify the points of synthesis or fusion, to see under what conditions genuine dialogue had taken place, and to find where agreement had been blocked.[110]

Using a hermeneutic perspective, Atkins started her "story" of the research project by analyzing her own role in the curriculum development process in order to understand how her prejudices and values might affect her reflections.

She then drew on Hans-Georg Gadamer's hermeneutic concept of "fused horizon" to understand the unfolding work of the curriculum development team.[111] Gadamer assumes that each participant in a dialogue will argue his own opinions and prejudices, but that it is nonetheless possible for each of them to perceive the other participants as authentic beings whose opinions and prejudices can be recognized and translated into terms that each one can comprehend. If participants are willing, they can engage in a hermeneutic conversation in which, by a process of argument and counterargument, they achieve a common language. The ultimate goal is for all participants to have their separate points of view—their separate *horizons* in Gadamer's terminology—recede into the background, so that one human community of thought and action—*fused horizons*—results.

Atkins observed that the team members spent much time in their first few meetings arguing for their positions and against competing positions. They gradually converged on two possible approaches to the general studies curriculum. From that point, Atkins found that the dialogue alternated between fused and separate horizons of understanding, as illustrated by her interpretations of what was happening at different points in the process:

109. Atkins, E. (1990). From competing paradigms to final consensus: A case study of the deliberations of a conflict-prone curriculum group. *Journal of Curriculum and Supervision, 5,* 308–327.
110. Ibid., p. 310.
111. Gadamer, H. (1975). *Truth and method* (G. Barden & J. Cumming, Trans.). New York: Seabury Press.

Time 1. We reached an uneasy compromise, but the same argument sporadically resurfaced, was periodically quelled, and continued to give shape to the resulting curriculum plan.[112]

Time 2. As we came to realize that both agendas [approaches to the general studies curriculum] would be the shaping forces or dual platform for the new curriculum, that neither team would ever let up, we began to look for ways to provide a unified front to the rest of the faculty and administration.[113]

Time 3. At this point, we were all in consonance, partly because we knew the time had come for a political compromise and partly because we now saw the two approaches as phases in a cycle of intellectual investigation, each phase having a powerful place in academic life. The dialectic again shifted: The conflict became one of emphasis rather than polarity.[114]

Atkins supported her interpretations with relevant excerpts of dialogue from the group meetings.

This study illustrates how hermeneutic concepts and methods help clarify the meaning of a text, in this case, an ongoing dialogue in a work group. A noteworthy feature of the hermeneutic analysis is that the researcher's interpretive process focused on the text itself. That is to say, the researcher's key concepts of argument, conflict, and compromise were grounded in the text rather than imposed on it by Atkins's personal perspective or someone else's theory. In reading the report, we sense that the emic perspective of the development team was revealed in an authentic, credible manner.

Semiotics

Touchstone in Research

Gottdiener, M., Boklund-Lagopoulos, K., & Lagopoulos, A. P. (Eds.). (2003). *Semiotics.* Thousand Oaks, CA: Sage.

A moment's reflection will reveal that we convey messages to each other and to ourselves through a system of signs. Language is one such system, but there are others as well—for example, mathematical symbols, musical notation, photographs, road signs, nonverbal gestures. **Semiotics** is the study of sign systems, in particular, the study of how objects (e.g., letters of the alphabet) come to convey meaning and how sign systems relate to human behavior. The importance of the study of signs becomes clear with the realization that a message doesn't exist until it has become coded in the form of signs. This coding process affects the nature of the message that is delivered. Thus, to understand any setting in which messages are transmitted back and forth (for example, classroom instruction), we need to understand the sign system in which those messages have been coded. In other words, it is important to study not only *what* is said or written, but *how* it is said or written. According to semioticists, messages do not represent an objective reality. Rather, messages are a social construction based on the use of sign systems: "At the heart of semiotics is the realization that the whole of human experience, without exception, is an interpretative structure mediated and sustained by signs."[115]

Semioticists have developed various concepts and techniques for studying sign systems and their relationship to human behavior. The most basic concepts are signifier, signified, and sign. A **signifier** is a word, sound, or image that is intended to convey meaning. A **signified** is the meaning conveyed by the object. Together, the signifier and signified constitute a **sign.** A real example of a sign is a **referent.** For example, the expression H_2O is a signifier, and the signified is water. This expression and its meaning together constitute a sign.

---

112. Atkins, From competing paradigms to final consensus, p. 317.
113. Ibid., p. 322.
114. Ibid., p. 325.
115. Deely, J. (1990). *Basics of semiotics.* Bloomington, IN: Indiana University Press. Quote appears on p. 5.

Water flowing from a faucet would be a referent for this sign. The sign H_2O is one of many such signs in chemical notation, which constitutes a sign system. Semioticists are interested in the study of such systems, including the analysis of the elements of the system and how they are used to convey meaning.

Patricia Mellencamp's book, *High Anxiety,* involves a cultural studies analysis of films, media events, and situation comedies involving women, in which she includes the semiotic environment in the object of study.[116] In the view of John Frow and Meaghan Morris, Mellencamp "stretches fine-grained readings of [these texts] to grasp the nexus of 'catastrophe, scandal, age, and comedy' that is organized *socioeconomically* around women in U.S. media culture."[117]

Although semiotics is a strong research tradition in some academic disciplines, it has not been used widely in education. However, it seems to have considerable promise for the study of education because so many educational phenomena involve sign systems used to impart information, which affect what and how students learn.[118]

Structuralism and Poststructuralism

Structuralism is an approach to investigation that focuses on the systemic properties of phenomena, including relationships among elements of a system. For example, this textbook can be viewed as a system that contains various elements organized into a particular structure: chapters, name index, footnotes, pages, headings, quotations, and so on. According to structuralist theory, the meaning of each of these elements can be determined only by examining its relationship to the other elements of the system. For example, the subject index only has meaning in relation to certain words that appear in the chapters.

Structuralism as a qualitative research tradition originated in linguistics with the work of Ferdinand de Saussure and was further developed by researchers in other disciplines, including Jean Piaget in psychology, Basil Bernstein in sociology, Claude Levi-Strauss in anthropology, and Jacques Derrida and Roland Barthes in literary and media studies.[119] As with other qualitative research traditions, the methods of a structuralist inquiry depend upon the particular researcher. Nevertheless, Gibson identified six principles of structuralism, described below.[120]

1. *The whole is greater than the sum of its parts.* To understand the operation of a system, one cannot merely study its elements and their relationships to each other. This is because the elements and their relationships are governed by the system as a whole. For example, a textbook has an overarching instructional design that is more than its constituent chapters and front and back matter. Similarly, a social group is more than its individual members and how each interacts with the others. There is a sense of a group that exists independently of individual members and that influences the actions of each individual within the group.

Touchstones in Research

Caws, P. (1997). *Structuralism updated.* Amherst, MA: Prometheus.

Martusewicz, R. A. (2001). *Seeking passage: Post-structuralism, pedagogy, ethics.* New York: Teachers College Press.

---

116. Mellencamp, P. (1992). *High anxiety: Catastrophe, scandal, age, and comedy.* Bloomington: Indiana University.

117. Frow, J., & Morris, M. (2000). Cultural studies. In N. K. Denzin & Y. S. Lincoln (Eds.), *Handbook of qualitative research* (2nd ed., pp. 315–346). Thousand Oaks, CA: Sage.

118. The use of semiotics to understand various aspects of special education is explored in: Rogers, L. J., & Swadener, B. B. (Eds.). (2001). *Semiotics and disability: Interrogating categories of difference.* Albany, NY: State University of New York Press. An example of its application in educational administration is: Everhart, R. B. (1991). Semiotics as an orientation to administrative practice. *Educational Administration Quarterly, 27,* 358–377.

119. The work of these researchers is discussed in: Gibson, R. (1984). *Structuralism and education.* London: Hodder & Stoughton.

120. Ibid.

2. *Social reality exists not in things, but in their relationships.* To understand this principle, consider language. If we want to know what a particular word in a language means (e.g., *teacher*), we must define it in terms of—that is, in relation to—other words. According to structuralists, words do not point to an independent, objective reality. Rather, "language is elevated to the supreme definer of reality."[121]

Saussure conceptualized speech and text as the visible, transitory manifestations of an invisible, permanent system, which he referred to as *langue* (in English, *language*). Thus, dictionaries and grammar texts represent the elements and rules of writing and speech, but they do not capture all the subtle properties of the whole (i.e., *langue*). Similarly, we study a culture's myths, rituals, laws, and institutions in an effort to understand it. While all these elements are manifestations of the culture, there is an invisible "system" of culture beyond these elements that determines its meaning.

3. *The individual is a subordinate element of various systems.* Structuralists question the notion of the humanistic individual "as an autonomous, free, and transparently self-conscious subject that is the fount of all knowledge and moral and political agency."[122] Rather, individuals are shaped by the various systems of which they are members. Thus, individuals rarely create language, but rather language defines individuals and what they are capable of communicating.

4. *Systems have self-regulating mechanisms that ensure their survival.* According to structuralists, systems have a homeostatic capacity, which ensures that they maintain their integrity despite forces toward change. For example, the codification of the English language must deal with new social and technological developments that call for new words, new meanings for existing words, or the discarding of existing words. The English language thus is constantly changing, yet it retains a recognizable systemic integrity across time.

5. *Social reality is better understood by current "snapshots" than by historical analysis.* Saussure argues that meaning resides in the relationships between words, as these relationships exist at a particular point in time. Therefore, he views historical analysis as irrelevant to understanding current meanings. According to Saussure, the elements of a language are arbitrary signs and therefore can change meaning across speakers, settings, and time. For example, the word *screen* signifies one thing in interior design and quite another in computer design.

6. *Structures are subject to transformation, but according to the laws of the system.* Structuralists believe that systems follow laws that direct the flow of change among their elements and relationships. Mathematics provides a good example of this principle. The equation $4 + 3 = 7$ can be transformed into the equation $3 + 4 = 7$, but not into the equation $3 + 7 = 4$, because of the existence of mathematical laws that govern acceptable and unacceptable transformations. Similarly, the languages of the world change over time, but structuralists believe that the nature of these changes is constrained by universal laws.

The six structuralist principles described above are based on the assumption that it is possible to find meaning in the systemic properties of a phenomenon. A radical version of structuralism, called **poststructuralism** is a postmodernist approach to the study of systems, especially language as a system, that denies the possibility of finding any inherent meaning in them. Thus, a poststructuralist would make no distinction between the plays of Shakespeare and a comic book. Both are systems of signs that can be studied,

121. Ibid., p. 21.
122. Peters, M. A., & Burbules, N. C. (2004). *Poststructuralism and educational research.* Lanham, MD: Rowman & Littlefield.

but neither has a greater claim to truth than the other. Also, there is no one objective, true interpretation of a literary work or text:

> Texts can be read in many ways: each text contains within itself the possibility of an infinite set of structures, and to privilege some by setting up a system of rules to generate them is a blatantly prescriptive and ideological move.[123]

The value of the poststructuralist approach, in the eyes of its proponents, is that it stimulates people to question deeply the assumptions they most take for granted about what they consider to be true or authoritative. This questioning of assumptions by poststructuralists has extended into analyses of scientific reporting. Specifically, poststructuralists question the impersonal, third-person voice in which many research reports (especially those within the quantitative research tradition) are written. Laurel Richardson suggests that this questioning opens up new possibilities for scientific writing:

> [P]oststructuralism suggests two important things to qualitative writers: First, it directs us to understand ourselves reflexively as persons writing from particular positions at specific times; and second, it frees us from trying to write a single text in which we say everything at once to everyone. Nurturing our own voices releases the censorious hold of 'science writing' on our consciousness, as well as the arrogance it fosters in our psyche: Writing is validated as a method of knowing.[124]

As we stated above, structuralism as an approach to inquiry has influenced the work of researchers in a variety of social and human science disciplines. In education, the most notable influence has been on Piaget and other researchers who seek to understand intellectual development in terms of underlying mental structures and the rules of transformation of these structures (e.g., Piaget's principles of assimilation and accommodation). It is surprising that structuralism has not had more influence on the study of curriculum materials, because both structuralism and poststructuralism have had a significant influence on the study of literature and media. Education also has many systemic structures (e.g., grade levels, levels of schooling, personnel hierarchies, courses of study) that would seem amenable to structuralist analysis.

Gibson provides several examples of what might be learned about educational phenomena through structural analysis.[125] One involves the analysis of a teacher's science lesson in a class of young children. Gibson demonstrates how the teacher's actions are shaped by a mental structure characteristic of scientific thinking. The structure constrains her interactions with the children, such that any child's response that does not fit the structure is either ignored or redirected.

In their book *Poststructuralism and Educational Research*, Michael Peters and Nicholas Burbules summarize the work of three exemplars of poststructuralist research in education: Henry Giroux's critical pedagogy, Patti Lather's poststructuralist feminist praxis in education, and Stephen Ball's critical ethnography.[126] Their description reflects the diversity of poststructuralism, but highlights its focus on the notion that individuals are constructed by the language available to them, cultural critique, efforts toward emancipation, and the central role of education and educational research in any such efforts.

123. Culler, J. (1975). *Structuralist poetics: Structuralism, linguistics, and the study of literature.* Ithaca, NY: Cornell University Press. Quote appears on p. 242.
124. Richardson, L. (2000). Writing: A method of inquiry. In N. K. Denzin & Y. S. Lincoln (Eds.), *Handbook of qualitative research* (2nd ed., pp. 923–948). Thousand Oaks, CA: Sage. Quote appears on p. 929.
125. Gibson, Structuralism and education, Chapter 8.
126. Peters & Burbules, *Poststructuralism and educational research.*

RECOMMENDATIONS FOR

Designing a Study Based on a Qualitative Research Tradition

1. Read basic sources explaining the most prominent qualitative research traditions (e.g., ethnography, action research, critical-theory research) until you are able to grasp the present and potential influence of such traditions on education.
2. Carefully analyze the type of phenomenon you plan to investigate (lived experience, society and culture, or language and communication) and the types of research traditions associated with it.
3. In reviewing possible qualitative research traditions to guide your study, consider how well the theoretical assumptions and methods of each one match your own theoretical and methodological preferences.
4. If you select a particular qualitative research tradition to guide your research, immerse yourself in it—including an apprenticeship with an expert, if possible—so that you can make appropriate and insightful use of the tradition.

SELF-CHECK TEST

Circle the correct answer to each of the following questions.
The answers are provided at the back of the book.

1. A textural description is an account of
   a. a think-aloud or stimulated-recall interview.
   b. an individual's prereflective perceptions of a phenomenon.
   c. an individual's interpretation or recall of a phenomenon.
   d. an individual's interpretation of a text.

2. The assertion that a text has no definite meaning is characteristic of
   a. semiotics.
   b. deconstruction.
   c. ethnomethodology.
   d. ethnoscience.

3. The study of how individuals fail to grasp the intended meaning of signs would be of particular interest to researchers who specialize in
   a. the ethnography of communication.
   b. ethnographic content analysis.
   c. semiotics.
   d. poststructuralism.

4. The formal learning experiences of individuals from early childhood through adulthood probably would be of most interest to
   a. life history researchers.
   b. phenomenographers.
   c. ethnographers.
   d. critical-theory researchers.

5. Differences in the thinking processes of experts and novices would be of particular interest to
   a. phenomenological researchers.
   b. semioticists.
   c. cognitive psychologists.
   d. ethnomethodologists.

6. The theory of border pedagogy was developed within the research tradition of
   a. structuralism.
   b. poststructuralism.
   c. cultural studies.
   d. the ethnography of education.

7. The assertion that language determines an individual's actions is fundamental to
   a. hermeneutics.
   b. semiotics.
   c. phenomenology.
   d. structuralism.

8. The concept of cultural acquisition refers to
   a. the individual's learning of his culture.
   b. the process of assimilating members of immigrant populations into a culture.
   c. the role that social structures play in teaching cultural norms and values.
   d. the process by which a culture develops new norms and values.

9. Hegemony refers to
   a. emancipatory methods as conceptualized by critical theorists.
   b. a conception of social justice advocated by critical theorists.
   c. disparities among the emic perspectives of members of a society's privileged groups.
   d. the domination of subordinate groups by a society's privileged groups.

10. The hermeneutic circle is a process for
   a. determining the implicit rules of social interaction.
   b. resolving hegemonic disputes.
   c. analyzing the ethnographic content of a sign-signifier relationship.
   d. arriving at an interpretation of a text.

11. Compared to classic ethnographies, today's ethnographies put greater emphasis on the _____ perspective.
   a. emic
   b. humanistic
   c. etic
   d. phenomenographic

CHAPTER 16

Historical Research

OVERVIEW

Historical research helps educators understand the present condition of education through analysis of the past. It also helps them imagine and judge the likelihood of alternative future scenarios in education. In this chapter we explain how historical research is conducted, from identifying a problem to study through identifying, evaluating, and synthesizing historical data. We emphasize the interpretive processes that historians of education use in conducting their research.

OBJECTIVES

After studying this chapter, you should be able to

1. Describe major differences between contemporary and nineteenth-century historical research.
2. State several purposes for doing historical research in education.
3. List the major stages in a historical research study.
4. Describe five types of problems or topics that prompt historical inquiry in education.
5. Describe how documents, quantitative records, oral recordings, and relics are used as primary historical sources.
6. Distinguish between preliminary, primary, and secondary sources of historical information, and provide an example of each.
7. Describe several procedures that a researcher might use to record information from historical sources.
8. Describe the characteristics of a historical document that one examines in carrying out external criticism.
9. State examples of questions that a historical researcher might ask in carrying out internal criticism of historical data.
10. Distinguish between subjectivity and bias in the reporting of historical events.
11. Explain the statement, "History means interpretation."
12. Describe how the use of particular concepts can affect historical interpretation.
13. Explain the problems of interpretation that are involved in making causal inferences from historical evidence.
14. Describe several different approaches to organizing the report of a historical research study.

Importance of Historical Research in Education

The British historian E. H. Carr answered the question "What is history?" by stating, "it is a continuing process of interaction between the historian and his facts, an unending dialogue between the present and the past."[1] Consistent with Carr's view, we define **historical research** as a process of systematically searching for data to answer questions about a phenomenon from the past to gain a better understanding of the foundation of present institutions, practices, trends, beliefs, and issues in education.

C. H. Edson identified four similarities between historical investigation and other qualitative research methodologies: (1) emphasis on the study of context, (2) the study of behavior in natural rather than in contrived or hypothetical settings, (3) appreciation of the wholeness of experience, and (4) the centrality of interpretation in the research process.[2] Historical research is generally considered a type of qualitative research, even though some historians also use quantitative research methods as we show later in the chapter.

With respect to its epistemological orientation, historical research tends to be positivist rather than purely interpretive. That is, historians acknowledge fallibility and bias in human observation, but nonetheless believe that it is possible through careful analysis and multiple sources of evidence to discover what actually happened during a given time period with respect to the phenomenon being investigated.[3]

Interpretation plays a central role in historical research. Such research necessarily deals with events that occurred prior to the historian's decision to study them. Therefore, historians must rely on records of events that were made by others, such as journalists, court reporters, diarists, or photographers. The recording of the event involves an interpretive act because the biases, values, and experiences of those who recorded the event will cause them to attend to some details and omit others. Thus, the data provided by historical sources are cloaked in interpretation even before a historian retrieves them for study. Historians add another layer of interpretation by the way they choose to emphasize or ignore particular data and how they organize data into categories and patterns. For this reason historical reports are not literal accounts of the past, but rather what the historian Joan Burstyn calls "constructed reality."[4]

The central role of interpretation in contemporary historical research contrasts with the form of historical research that was most popular in the nineteenth century, namely research based on the notion that "history consists of the compilation of a maximum number of irrefutable and objective facts."[5] Reflecting that view, nineteenth-century histories often consisted of multivolume compilations of details about either broad topics (e.g., a history of the Western world, a history of the United States) or limited topics (e.g., a study of the French Revolution or the Spanish-American War). Contemporary historians tend to dismiss these writings as merely historical chronicles. Their own writings tend to be shorter, and they subordinate historical facts to an interpretive framework within which facts, meaning, and significance are attributed to specific occurrences, documents, or relics.

Historical research in education differs from other types of educational research in that most historians typically *discover* their data through a search of historical sources

Touchstones in Research

Donato, R., & Lazerson, M. (2000). New directions in American educational history: Problems and prospects. *Educational Researcher, 29*(8), 4–15.

McCulloch, G., & Richardson, W. (2000). *Historical research in educational settings.* Philadelphia: Open University.

---

1. Carr, E. H. (1967). *What is history?* New York: Random. Quote appears on p. 35.
2. Edson, C. H. (1986). Our past and present: Historical inquiry in education. *The Journal of Thought, 21*, 13–27.
3. For an example of historical research conducted within an interpretive framework (specifically, semiotics), see: Nye, D. E. (1983). *The invented self: An anti-biography, from documents of Thomas A. Edison.* Odense, Denmark: Odense University Press.
4. Burstyn, J. N. (1987). History as image: Changing the lens. *History of Education Quarterly, 27*, 167–180.
5. Carr, *What is history?*, p. 14.

such as diaries, official documents, and relics. In historical research, the evidence usually is available before the historian formulates a thesis, selects a topic, or designs a research plan. (There are exceptions to this rule, however, as in the oral history-based study of a high school in south Texas, described later in the chapter.) In contrast, most other types of educational research require the researcher to *create* data. For example, a researcher creates data when she makes observations or administers tests to determine the effectiveness of an instructional program.

Subject Matter of Historical Research

Arthur Moehlman and his colleagues at the University of Texas developed a classification scheme to describe the range of historical research found in the educational literature.[6] Their goal was to provide a means for computer storage and retrieval of the growing mass of bibliographical materials and original documents relevant to the history of education.

Table 16.1 presents the 11 major categories in the classification system developed by Moehlman and his colleagues. We also include an example of published historical research for each category. The classification system illustrates the wide range of topics and concerns that interest historians of education. You may find the system helpful in clarifying the particular historical problem that you might wish to study.

Impact of Historical Education

Histories of education serve several important purposes. Some historians, referred to as **antiquarians,** value the study of the past for its own sake. Antiquarians become intrigued with a particular historical period and spend their careers documenting the events and objects that make that period distinctive. They seem to have little concern for the relevance of their discoveries to present-day scholars or students.

By contract, Sol Cohen, an educational historian, argues that "the historian's goal resembles that of the therapist—to liberate us from the burden of the past by helping us to understand it."[7]

The past is of great interest to both educational researchers and educational practitioners, for many reasons. Below we summarize some important ways in which educators use historical research methods and findings in their work.

A Subject in the Curriculum

History is a standard part of social studies in most school curricula, reflecting education stakeholders' belief that students need to know about previous events and their meaning if they are to participate in local and world events as informed citizens. Some also believe that study of the past provides guidance to help individuals make sense of life and form moral judgments. To fulfill such goals, however, teachers need to deepen their own understanding of history so that they can correct or supplement the often stereotyped and shallow interpretations present in most textbook accounts of historical events.

Greater understanding of how historians arrive at and modify their interpretations could help schools better teach students about both history and the historical interpretation process. Historians of education have had perhaps their greatest influence on educational practice through their involvement in the training of educators, because most teachers are required to take coursework in the history of education.

6. Moehlman, A. H., Van Tassel, D., Goetzmann, W. H., & Everett, G. D. (1969). *A guide to computer-assisted research in American education.* Austin: University of Texas.
7. Cohen, S. (1976). The history of the history of American education, 1900–1976: The uses of the past. *Harvard Educational Review, 46,* 298–330.

| TABLE 16.1 |

System for Classifying Literature on the History of Education

1. Bibliographies relating to educational history. Example: Brickman, W. W., & Zepper, J. T. (1992). *Russian and Soviet education, 1731–1989: A multilingual annotated bibliography*. New York: Garland.
2. General educational history. Example: Rury, J. L. (2001). *Education and social change: Themes in the history of American schooling*. Mahwah, NJ: Lawrence Erlbaum Associates.
3. History of educational legislation (e.g., taxation, bonds, school land boards and districts, equalization programs, curriculum, state-supported schools and universities, court cases). Example: Tyack, D. B. (1987). *Law and the shaping of public education, 1785–1954*. Madison, WI: University of Wisconsin Press.
4. Historical biographies of major contributors to education. Example: Kakar, S. (1970). *Frederick Taylor: A study in personality and innovation*. Cambridge: MIT Press.
5. History of major branches of education, e.g., school accreditation and attendance laws, curriculum, enrollment, finance, goals, organization and administration, personnel, community education, and instructional methods and materials. Example: Cuban, L. (1993). *How teachers taught* (2nd ed.). New York: Teachers College Press.
6. Institutional history of education (e.g., correspondence schools, kindergarten, elementary school, secondary school, colleges and universities, vocational schools, military education, and research organizations). Example: Knowles, M. S. (1994). *A history of the adult education movement in the United States* (Rev. ed.). Huntington, NY: Krieger.
7. Cultural history of education (e.g., ethnology, anthropology, sociology, and technology). Example: Button, H. W., & Provenzo, E. F., Jr. (1989). *History of education and culture in America* (2nd ed.). Englewood Cliffs, NJ: Prentice-Hall.
8. History of educational planning and policy. Example: Ravitch, D. (2000). *Left back: A century of failed school reform*. New York: Simon and Schuster.
9. Historical critiques of education. Example: Carnoy, M. (1994). *Faded dreams: The politics and economics of race in America*. New York: Cambridge University Press.
10. Comparative history of international education. Example: Silver, H. (1983). *Education as history*. London: Methuen.
11. History of contemporary problems in education. Example: Butchart, R. E. (1988). Outthinking and outflanking the owners of the world: A historiography of the African American struggle for education. *History of Education Quarterly, 28*, 333–366.

Source: Adapted from Moehlman, A. H., Van Tassel, D., Goetzmann, W. H., & Everett, G. D. (1969). *A guide to computer-assisted research in American education*. Austin: University of Texas.

A Foundation for Developing New Knowledge and Policies Related to Education

Historical research is relevant to every topic that an educator wishes to study or help others understand. In the words of Norman Denzin and Yvonna Lincoln, qualitative researchers "always think reflectively and historically, as well as biographically."[8]

Most researchers benefit from the study of past findings and methods of investigation to develop the most fruitful ideas for new research on a topic. Many research reports involve the investigation of a phenomenon as it existed at various times in the past and as it exists today.[9] Moreover, educational researchers almost invariably include in their research reports a review of the literature related to their research topic. Review of past research is critical to give both researchers and readers a historical foundation to understand the topic and a rationale for the design of a new study. Without a literature review, researchers would

8. Denzin, N. K., & Lincoln, Y. S. (2005). Part III: Strategies of inquiry. In N. K. Denzin & Y. S. Lincoln (Eds.), *Sage handbook of qualitative research* (3rd ed., pp. 375–386). Thousand Oaks, CA: Sage. Quote appears on p. 375.
9. A recent treatment of feminist qualitative research illustrates thoughtful inclusion of the historical perspective related to the topic of feminism: Olesen, V. (2005). Early millennial feminist qualitative research: Challenges and contours. In N. K. Denzin & Y. S. Lincoln (Eds.), *Sage handbook of qualitative research* (3rd ed., pp. 235–278). Thousand Oaks, CA: Sage.

be likely to test hypotheses that previously had been shown to be unproductive, re-invent questionable research methodology, "discover" what was already found by previous researchers, and continue to make the same methodological errors as their predecessors. Indeed, without continually updated historical reviews of the research literature, scientific progress would be impossible. In doing your own literature searches, we suggest that you include the keyword *history* to locate historical studies on any topic you wish to investigate.

Similarly, for educational practitioners, study of the history underlying the many educational activities, institutions, and policies operating today helps them understand and make better choices about the teaching–learning process and how to improve it. For example, in campaigning for a bond issue, educators who are ignorant of past legislative actions affecting the budget for their school district might repeat mistakes of their predecessors, or they might create questionable arguments based on inaccurate assumptions about the past.

A Variable Affecting the Validity of Research Findings

History is one type of extraneous variable that Donald Campbell and Julian Stanley identified as important for experimental researchers to control to maximize the validity of experiments.[10] In this context, history refers to specific events other than the intended treatment that occur between the beginning and end of an experiment and therefore could be responsible for changes in the outcome of interest instead of the experimental treatment (see Chapter 12). For example, suppose that a greater number of students took driver education in 1999 than in 2000 in a particular school, after the school instituted a new driver education program. Increased enrollment might be due to the program. However, suppose that a well-publicized traffic accident in which several students were involved occurred in the school community during 1999. In this case, knowledge of the accident could have led parents to pressure their children to take driver education or made students concerned enough to enroll on their own. The accident and its aftermath are an example of history that could have affected the rate of enrollment.

A Basis for Evaluating Educational Programs

In evaluation research (see Chapter 17), knowledge of the history of a current educational phenomenon often is necessary to assess the value or meaning of the phenomenon. A specialized form of historical research that also has an evaluative flavor is **revisionist history,** the goal of which is to sensitize educators to past practices that may have been regarded as benevolent, but have had unjust aims and effects. For example, Michael Katz's study of educational innovation in mid-nineteenth century Massachusetts demonstrates how it functioned to serve dominant economic interests and to thwart democratic aspirations.[11] Many people tend to view past events with a more detached perspective than they do the present, so Katz's study may more readily reveal problems and hidden agendas associated with schooling than would a study of current practices.

A Tool in Planning the Future

Still another purpose of historical research is to help educators define and evaluate alternative future scenarios involving a particular educational phenomenon. If we know how an individual or group has acted in the past, we can predict with a certain degree of confidence how they will act in the future. For example, we can make a good prediction of how

10. Campbell, D. T., & Stanley, J. C. (1963). *Experimental and quasi-experimental designs for research*. Chicago: Rand McNally.
11. Katz, M. B. (1968). *The irony of early school reform: Educational innovation in mid-nineteenth century Massachusetts*. Cambridge, MA: Harvard University Press.

a legislator will vote on an upcoming education bill by doing research on his past voting record. As in other types of educational research, however, prediction rarely is perfect. New social, political, or economic conditions continually arise, thus creating discontinuities in educational practices. In Oregon, for example, the passage in 1991 of Measure 5, a voter-approved initiative, fundamentally changed the basis for funding public schools. After that, previous practices in Oregon education no longer served as a basis for accurate projections of school curriculum, staffing patterns, and organization in Oregon schools.

A type of research called **futurology** specifically examines what the future of a particular phenomenon is likely to be. Some futurological studies are based on surveys of current trends; others use simulation and gaming strategies to generate various future scenarios. The predictions are based largely on statistical logic or reasoning derived from the study of past events.

Despite its documented value, some educational researchers think that historical methodology is irrelevant to their work. They align themselves with the physical and social sciences and consider history as part of the humanities. This view is questionable, because all researchers are historians to some extent. In doing research, they must review the literature to determine what past theoretical work and previous studies have been done on a particular problem. Also, the validity of past research findings about education depends on the degree to which the context in which they were obtained has remained constant or has changed. Furthermore, the search for relevant documents (journal articles, technical reports, unpublished manuscripts, etc.) and interpretation of their significance are tasks that characterize the work of both empirical researchers and historians. Thus the study of historical methodology should help you to become a better researcher, whether or not you choose to do a study that is primarily historical.

Historiography and the Stages of Historical Research

Historiography involves the study of the various steps and procedures that historians have used in their research. We recommend that before undertaking a historical research study you read several historiographical works and also study the historiography of particular educational historians. Reports of their studies often include a historiographical section.

In a series of lectures on historiography, Carr provides the following description of how a historian engages in research:

> Laymen . . . sometimes ask me how the historian goes to work when he writes history. The most common assumption appears to be that the historian divides his work into two sharply distinguishable phases or periods. First, he spends a long preliminary period reading his sources and filling his notebooks with facts; then, when this is over, he puts away his sources, takes out his notebooks, and writes his book from beginning to end. This is to me an unconvincing and unplausible picture. For myself, as soon as I have got going on a few of what I take to be the capital sources, the itch becomes too strong and I begin to write—not necessarily at the beginning, but somewhere, anywhere. Thereafter, reading and writing go on simultaneously. The writing is added to, subtracted from, re-shaped, cancelled, as I go on reading. The reading is guided and directed and made fruitful by the writing: the more I write, the more I know what I am looking for, the better I understand the significance and relevance of what I find.[12]

Educational researchers conducting historical research, as well as those using other methodologies such as experimentation, often use procedures similar to those Carr described.

---

12. Carr, *What is history?*, pp. 32–33.

For example, as a first step, a quantitative researcher might formulate a few tentative hypotheses and plan a research study for testing them. After reviewing the literature and conducting pilot studies, the researcher might decide to make further changes in the hypotheses and research design. Then, after the formal study has been completed, the researcher might formulate new hypotheses not anticipated at the outset that can be tested by the available data.

The next sections of the chapter describe the stages of a typical historical study. Keep in mind that additions to or variations in this sequence might be justified by the particular research questions being asked, the circumstances of the search for historical data, and the interpretive framework that is used to understand the data.

Defining a Problem for Historical Research

As with other types of educational research, the first step in planning a historical study is to define the problem to be investigated. The range of possibilities is large, as David Tyack aptly stated: "One of the appeals of history of education to its scholars is that it gives a lifelong fishing license to study almost any topic."[13] A review of problems and topics studied by other educational historians can help you refine your question or suggest another, more interesting question.

Mark Beach classified the problems and topics that prompt historical inquiry into five types, which we explain in the following paragraphs.[14]

1. *Social issues.* Current social issues are the most popular source of historical problems in education. For example, school policies toward students and families of differing sexual orientations, prevention of student violence, closing the achievement gap among students of differing ethnicities, and the effects of standardized testing on teachers and students are recent social issues that historical research might illuminate.

2. *Study of specific individuals, educational institutions, and social movements.* In the past two decades, historical studies of the educational experiences of minority groups and women have been prominent, as have studies of higher education and teaching. These studies often are motivated by the desire to fill in gaps about what is known about the past. Bernard Bailyn, a historian of the American colonial period, offers the following rationale for this type of research:

> The motivation here is to learn something new and to present this new information; but the precise issues are not defined. There are no specific questions and no hypothetical answers. Thus the motivation for writing a narrative of a battle may be simply to discover what happened in it; to find out how it was that the victors won it. Or, again, one decides to do research and write about Wilson's Administration because we are ignorant of it, and any thorough, clear narrative of it will be valuable because it fills an important gap, an evident vacuum.[15]

Even when a history of an educator, institution, or movement is readily available, however, researchers need to determine whether the history adequately explores the events in which they are interested. In fact, the gaps in knowledge of the past that a researcher discovers from reviewing an incomplete or one-sided history often provide the basis for a historical study.

13. Tyack, D. (2000). Reflections on histories of U.S. education. *Educational Researcher, 29*(8), 19–20. Quote appears on p. 20.
14. Beach, M. (1969). History of education. *Review of Educational Research, 39,* 561–576.
15. Bailyn, B. (1969). The problems of the working historian. In A. S. Eisenstadt (Ed.), *The craft of American history.* New York: AHM Publishing. Quote appears on pp. 202–203.

3. *Exploration of relationships between events.* This type of historical inquiry in education involves an attempt to interpret ideas or events that previously were not viewed or treated as related, but which subsequently have been revealed to reflect possible relationships. For example, a researcher might review various histories of textbook publishing and discover separate, unrelated histories of school curriculum for the same time period. The researcher might decide to review these separate histories in order to detect relationships and raise questions that did not concern the original historians. These perceived relationships and questions can provide the basis for an original historical inquiry. For example, the historian might relate a decision by textbook publishers to begin producing student consumables as a supplement to classroom texts to subsequent changes in school curriculum over a particular time period.

4. *Syntheses of data.* This related type of historical inquiry occurs when the researcher attempts to synthesize old data collected by different historians or to merge old data with new historical facts. For example, a historian may discover the existence of documents written at the time of important events that were not known to other historians who had done research on these events. Thus, the historian who made the discovery can contribute to our understanding of these events by analyzing these new documents to see whether they reinforce existing interpretations of the events, or lead to new interpretations.

5. *Reinterpretation of past events.* As we explained above, revisionist historians do critiques of existing histories by subjecting them to new—and sometimes politically radical—interpretive frameworks. An example is research on the Holocaust in Europe during World War II. Historians have extensively documented the atrocities of the Holocaust. However, some individuals have tried to rewrite history and claim that the Holocaust did not occur.[16]

As in any type of research, you should start by reviewing the literature and talking with experienced researchers before attempting to define problems or topics for historical inquiry. In the process of doing so, you may find that other historians have formulated important problems and questions for future investigation. For example, Guadalupe San Miguel, Jr. reviewed the status of historical research on Chicano education in 1986.[17] He concluded his review by identifying questions that had not yet been answered by historians, including the following:

> First, little is known about the roots and evolution of the Mexican American commitment to education referred to in several of the studies. Who in the community, for instance, supported education, what type of education, and for what purposes? . . . Second, we do not know who attended school nor for how long they attended . . . Finally, new studies comparing and contrasting the educational experiences of Mexican Americans with other minority and immigrant groups are needed. It is unclear yet the extent to which the educational experiences of Mexican Americans were similar or dissimilar to historically dispossessed groups such as blacks and native Americans, or to other language minority groups of European descent.[18]

Questions such as these, formulated by an experienced historian, can be very helpful in identifying a problem for your own study.

An important criterion to consider when deciding on a problem or topic for historical research is whether key sources that you wish to investigate are available and interpretable.

---

16. Lipstadt, D. E. (1993). *Denying the Holocaust: The growing assault on truth and memory.* New York: Free Press.
17. San Miguel, G., Jr. (1986). Status of the historiography of Chicano education: A preliminary analysis. *History of Education Quarterly, 26,* 523–536.
18. Ibid., pp. 535–536.

For example, would you want to select a problem for historical study that required extensive use of documents that are available only in Spanish if you do not read this language? Or what would you do if it proved to be difficult to access key documents you need, such as classified records in government archives?

Studying Historical Sources

Formulating a Search Plan

Historians need to have some idea of what they are looking for before beginning a search for sources that will provide the needed data. Otherwise, they are likely to search aimlessly and overlook important sources of relevant information. Philip C. Brooks suggests the following approach for initiating a search for historical sources:

> Resourcefulness and imagination are essential in the preliminary exploration as well as in the later actual study. One can suppose that certain kinds of sources would exist if he thinks carefully about his subject, the persons involved, the government or institutions concerned, and the kinds of records that would naturally grow out of the events that he will be studying. He should ask himself who would have produced the useful documents in the transaction he is concerned with. What would be the expected flow of events? What kinds of records would have been created? What would be the life history of the documents, from their creation through current use, filing, temporary storage, and eventual retention in a repository where he can consult them? What kinds of materials would one expect to be kept rather than discarded?[19]

The selection of sources from which to obtain historical data of interest cannot be determined entirely in advance. You should create a tentative search plan, however, and revise it as your interpretive framework develops. Changes in the plan will occur as a particular historical source reveals other pertinent sources whose existence you may not have anticipated.

As we explained in Chapter 4, researchers use three basic types of sources in a literature search: preliminary, secondary, and primary sources. In that chapter, we also described sources of each type that generally are applicable to educational research. In the following sections, we describe sources of each type that are specific to historical research.[20]

Searching Preliminary Sources

A **preliminary source** is an index to secondary and primary sources. Preliminary sources include **bibliographies,** which are lists of source materials available on a given topic or field of study. Most preliminary sources in the field of history are indexes of secondary sources, but some list primary sources as well. A literature search for a historical study usually begins with an examination of preliminary sources.

Many of the general preliminary sources described in Chapter 4 are useful for doing a search of historical literature. In addition, there are more specialized preliminary sources for this purpose. Appendix D lists examples of these preliminary sources, including bibliographies of bibliographies, bibliographies of biographies, directories of historical societies, and general indexes to historical publications.

---

19. Brooks, P. C. (1969). *Research in archives: The use of unpublished primary sources.* Chicago: University of Chicago Press. Quote appears on pp. 19–20.
20. Our discussion of primary and secondary sources is based on traditional historiographical definitions of these terms. For a different view of the nature of historical sources, based on a semiotic analysis, see: Nye, *The invented self.* Nye classifies sources on two dimensions: private (e.g., diaries) versus public (e.g., newspaper articles), and whether the "text" is in a natural, found order (e.g., a residence) or a translated order (e.g., a museum).

Reading Secondary Sources

In historical research, **secondary sources** are documents in which individuals give an account of an event at which they were not present. Authors of secondary source documents base their accounts on descriptions or records of historical events that were prepared by others. Thus, most reports of historical research are secondary sources because the historian rarely is a direct witness to the events described. Instead, the report usually is based on the historian's current interpretation of primary sources and other secondary sources.

Appendix D lists commonly used secondary sources in historical research. These sources include biographies, history encyclopedias, geographical reference works, and statistical sourcebooks containing historical information.

Studying Primary Sources

In historical research, a **primary source** is a record (e.g., a diary, a relic, a map, or a set of test scores) that was generated by people who personally witnessed or participated in the historical events of interest. Virtually any object or verbal record that one can imagine can be a primary source for use in historical research.

Primary sources provide the ultimate basis for the information included in historical reports. **Historical facts** can be defined as data that the historian regards as true (i.e., valid) and relevant to the description or interpretation of the phenomenon being investigated. An important issue in doing historical research is whether to cite facts obtained from another historian's research report without personally checking the primary sources from which they were derived. In deciding whether to check these sources, you should consider such factors as the other historian's reputation, the original historian's interpretive framework, and whether it is feasible to gain access to the primary source documents. If you choose to report another historian's statements of facts without further check, we recommend that you cite the other historian's report as the source for the historical facts cited in your study.

Four types of primary sources in historical research are (1) written documents or records, (2) quantitative records, (3) oral records, and (4) relics. The most common type is written or printed materials, sometimes called *documents* or *records*. (Documents and records are described in greater detail in Chapter 9.) These materials take varied forms, such as diaries, memoirs, legal records, court testimony, newspapers, periodicals, business records, notebooks, yearbooks, diplomas, committee reports, memos, institutional files, and tests. They may include handwritten, typed, and printed material, published and unpublished material, material prepared for the public record, and material intended for private use.

The distinction between intentional and unpremeditated documents is important to consider when evaluating the authenticity and genuineness of a source. **Intentional documents,** such as memoirs and yearbooks, are written to serve as a record of the past. **Unpremeditated documents,** such as memos and teacher-prepared tests, are prepared to serve an immediate purpose, with no expectation that they might be used as a historical record at a later time.

Quantitative records, which provide numerical information about an educational phenomenon, are another type of primary source. Census records, school budgets, school attendance records, test scores, and other compilations of numerical data can be valuable sources of data for historical researchers.

Touchstones in Research

Errante, A. (2000). But sometimes you're not part of the story: Oral histories and ways of remembering and telling. *Educational Researcher, 29*(2), 16–27.

Yow, V. R. (2005). *Recording oral history: A guide for the humanities and social sciences.* Walnut Creek, CA: AltaMira.

Taylor, H. A., Cook, T., & Dodds, G. (Eds.). (2003). *Imagining archives: Essays and reflections by Hugh A. Taylor.* Boulder: netLibrary (Ebook).

Another important type of primary source is oral records of people speaking. Ballads, tales, songs, and other forms of spoken language preserve a record of events for posterity. Also, some historians personally conduct oral interviews of individuals who witnessed or participated in events of potential historical significance. These interviews typically are recorded and then transcribed to provide a written record. The branch of historical research involving spoken language is known as **oral history.** Columbia University initiated an oral history program in the 1940s, which includes records of interviews with thousands of individuals who supplied many hours of recollections.[21] The Oral History Association is an organization of historians interested in this type of research.[22] The U.S. Department of Health and Human Services (HHS) has determined that oral history interviewing projects do not involve the type of research defined by HHS regulations and are therefore excluded from Institutional Review Board oversight and review (see Web site http:// omega.dickinson.edu/organizations/oha/org_irb. html).

Relics are a fourth type of primary source. **Relics** include any object whose physical or visual properties provide information about the past. School buildings, school equipment, architectural plans for school physical plants, textbooks, and instructional devices are examples of objects that can be studied by historians as relics of past practice.

Some primary source materials can be classified as both documents and relics, depending on how they are used in a historical study. For example, in a study of the printing methods used in producing textbooks, a specific textbook would be classified as a relic, because one of its physical properties is being examined. On the other hand, the same textbook could be treated as a document in a study of how textbooks of different periods covered a particular topic in mathematics, because the information contained in the textbook is now the focus of study. This information can be studied by various methods, some of which we described in Chapters 6, 9, and 15.

Primary sources of historical information (e.g., diaries, manuscripts, and school records) sometimes are contained in archives (also referred to as *repositories*). **Archives** are special locations where public documents can be stored, preserved in good condition, and accessed with careful monitoring. For example, in reprinting a historical study in their other research text, the authors of this book needed to obtain permission from the Bancroft Library at the University of California, Berkeley, to reprint an inmate's original drawing depicting a boring class for inmates at San Quentin during the Hoyle era.[23]

Many repositories of primary sources relate to education, including university libraries and the files of various public and private organizations. Repositories vary in the ease of access provided to primary sources. The holdings of official archives usually are well indexed, and an archivist might be available to assist a historian in conducting a research project. In other situations, historians are on their own and must learn the filing system that was used. Many records are stored on microfilm or microfiche, which require special equipment for viewing. Some of this equipment has photocopying capability. *ArchivesUSA*® is a current directory of over 5,000 repositories and nearly 150,000 collections of primary source material stored in locations in the United States.

21. Crawford, C. W. (1974). Oral history—the state of the profession. *Oral History Review, 2,* 1–9. Information on Columbia University's Oral History Research Office is available at http://www.columbia.edu/cu/lweb/indiv/oral/

22. Oral History Association, University of Vermont, Burlington. The association has several publications, including the *Oral History Review,* published annually.

23. Justice, B. (2000). "A college of morals": Educational reform at San Quentin Prison, 1880–1920. *History of Education Quarterly, 40,* 279–301.

Regularly updated, the database is available by annual subscription at http://archives. chadwyck.com.

Researchers who wish to study an organization's quantitative data almost certainly will need to enlist the aid of a staff member to interpret them. For example, numerical data often are on printouts generated from computer software prepared specifically for the institution's needs. These data may be difficult to interpret unless a staff member explains the computer program to the researcher.

The search for primary historical sources is time-consuming but exciting, because you are dealing with the ultimate "stuff" from which history is made. Your search will be manageable if you have defined the research problem carefully and prepared a systematic search plan. Keep in mind, too, that preliminary sources (listed in Appendix D) can guide you to relevant primary sources.

Recording Information from Historical Sources

In examining a primary or secondary source, the historical researcher might not know what information will prove useful at a later phase of the study. The interpretational phase of the study may involve searching for new facts that were not viewed as relevant earlier in the study. Deciding what information to abstract from a historical source becomes even more critical when the source is not easily accessible. For example, you may need to travel to archives, which usually do not allow their materials to leave the premises. Thus the researcher needs to decide then and there what information to record for later use.

Before deciding what information to record, you will need to deal with two issues. First is whether the materials—especially primary sources—will be accessible. Institutional records often are made available for study, but this does not mean that anyone can examine them. You might need to make a formal request for permission to study the records. Some documents may be inaccessible, or may be accessible for study only under certain conditions.

The other issue concerns the types of material that can be copied or reproduced in a report. An institution might allow you to examine documents but not quote directly from them, allow only certain portions to be copied, or require formal permission to quote from any document.

You might want to reproduce documents that are considered "literary property," for example, a series of essays or speeches that could at a later time be published for profit. In this situation you need to take care not to infringe on someone's actual or potential copyright. Under the doctrine of fair use established by the U.S. Congress, you can quote short passages of a primary or secondary source without infringing copyright. The fair use doctrine of the U.S. Copyright Office, dated June 1999 (retrieved August 25, 2005), can be found at http://www.copyright.gov/fls/fl102.html.

Many historical researchers routinely photocopy documents for later study. Some repositories have photocopying facilities for this purpose. Photocopying has limitations, however. It might not be possible to photocopy old historical documents, because exposure to the photocopying process could damage them. Some documents, especially newspaper clippings, do not photocopy well. Special photographic techniques might be needed to reproduce oversize documents, maps, and charts.

Scanning is an important technological advance in the copying of documents. A scanner can transform the printed material (either words or images) into a computer file that can be reformatted by word processing software. The computer file can be coded and analyzed using computer programs of the type described in Chapter 14, and can be printed in hard copy form.

Recording and Analyzing Quantitative Data

Touchstones in Research

Burton, O. V., & Finnegan, T. (1990). Teaching historians to use technology: Databases and computers. *International Journal of Social Education, 5,* 23–35.

Darcy, R., & Rohrs, R. C. (1995). *A guide to quantitative history.* Westport, CT: Greenwood.

Quantitative history is a branch of historical research that uses numerical data and statistical methods of data analysis to study representative samples or a complete population in order to make broad, well-grounded generalizations. This approach to historical research has become prevalent because historical conclusions based on large amounts of carefully selected quantitative data usually are regarded as more generalizable than conclusions based on case studies. Furthermore, quantitative techniques make it easier for historians to study the "common man," that is, average citizens. In contrast, older historical studies tended to focus on a small number of men and women who held prominent positions in society. H. Warren Button commented on the emergence of the "common-man" approach to historical research:

> A part of the advantage of quantification in social and educational history is that it allows historians to follow a recent interest, an interest in the history of the common man—no depreciation [sic] intended—"history from the bottom up"—grassroots history. Records for history in this vein are likely to be thin and fragmentary; for coherence it is necessary to mine every source. For instance, for a quantitative study of Buxton, a black antebellum haven in Ontario, it is necessary to assemble data from perhaps fifteen thousand entries in the census manuscripts of 1861, 1871, and 1881; from town auditors' accounts, and church records.[24] The research necessity for compilation and statistical treatment, by unfortunate paradox, produces history almost without personalities, even without names. Still, this new history has and will produce new understandings and will counterweight our long-standing concern for "the better sort."[25]

A quantitative history project requires the ability to use sampling techniques, to define and measure variables, and to conduct statistical analyses. If you plan to do this type of study, you should refer to the parts of this book covering quantitative research and to specialized works on quantitative history.

In carrying out historical research involving quantitative data, you should think carefully about the kinds of data that are necessary to the investigation. Some quantitative information of interest to you might never have been recorded. If recorded, the data might be incomplete or inaccurate in critical aspects. It is unwise to record whatever data you happen to come across, because you might wind up with lots of data that will be time-consuming to analyze but of little value to your study's purpose.

Once the relevant data have been discovered through a search of quantitative historical records, you can analyze them using descriptive statistics. If the data were collected from samples representing defined populations, you also can do tests of statistical significance. See Chapter 5 for procedures for calculating descriptive or inferential statistics that apply to quantitative data.

Evaluation of Historical Sources

The ultimate value of a historical study is determined in large part by the researcher's ability to judge the authenticity and validity of the historical sources that come to light in the process of doing the study. Evaluation of the authenticity of historical sources and of the

---

24. Nenno, B. H. Dissertation in progress, State University of New York at Buffalo; cited in Button, 1979.
25. Button, H. W. (1979). Creating more usable pasts: History in the study of education. *Educational Researcher, 8*(5), 3–9.

validity of the information contained in them usually is referred to as **historical criticism.**
It is a complex, sophisticated process, as Jacques Barzun and Henry Graff observe:

> [Historical criticism] relies on attention to detail, on common-sense reasoning, on a developed
> "feel" for history and chronology, on familiarity with human behavior, and on ever enlarging
> stores of information. Many a "catch question" current among schoolboys calls forth these
> powers in rudimentary form—for instance the tale about the beautiful Greek coin just discov-
> ered and bearing the date "500 B.C." Here a second's historical reflection and reasoning is
> enough for verification: the "fact" is readily rejected.[26]

The following discussion of historical criticism is directed toward the evaluation of documents, although the principles that we describe apply also to the evaluation of quantitative records, oral records, and relics.

External Criticism

External criticism is the process of determining whether the apparent or claimed origin
of a historical document (author, place, date, and circumstances of publication) corresponds to its actual origin. In engaging in historical criticism, the researcher asks such
questions about a document as: Is it genuine? Is it the original copy? Who wrote it? Where?
When? Under what conditions? Many factors must be considered in answering these questions. We can suggest only a few here.

A historical source might be genuine or it might be forged. A **forgery** is a fabrication
claimed to be genuine, that is, the document was written by someone other than the person whose name appears as author.

You never can be completely certain about the genuineness of historical sources. All
you can do is generate and test alternative hypotheses about each source. For example, you
can hypothesize that a particular document was written by a subordinate in the organization rather than the person designated as the author. As this and other hypotheses are
shown to be untenable, you increase the probability—although never to the point of absolute certainty—that the source *is* genuine. If your evaluation of a historical source leads
you to doubt its genuineness, you should note this in your research report.

The existence of variant sources can be a problem in judging the genuineness of a primary source. **Variant sources** are documents that have been altered in some way from the
original document. For example, in going through the files of an educational institution, you
might discover file copies (i.e., copies stored in the organization's official records) of internal memoranda or emails that relate to the topic you are studying. However, it is possible
that the message was not distributed in exactly the same form to all its intended recipients.
Perhaps the writer added a personal note to one recipient's copy of the memo. Thus, you
might find a slightly different version of the memo in the recipient's files than the version in
the official file. In this situation, both versions of the message can be considered original primary sources, each of which reveals relevant, but different, information about a past event.

Variant sources present a special challenge in working with documents predating the
introduction of the typewriter (circa 1880). Copies of these documents, called manuscripts,
were written in longhand and often contained minor errors. In working with such a manuscript, you should make an effort to determine whether it is the only version or whether
copies were made. If other copies are known to exist, you can attempt to locate them and
compare their content.

26. Barzun, J., & Graff, H. F. (1992). *The modern researcher* (5th ed.). New York: Harcourt Brace Jovanovich. Quote appears on p. 99.

Touchstones in Research

Kaestle, C. (1992).
Standards of evidence
in educational history:
How do we know
when we know?
*History of Education
Quarterly, 32,*
361–366.

Wineburg, S. (1991).
Historical problem solv-
ing: A study of the
cognitive processes
used in the evaluation
of documentary and
pictorial evidence.
*Journal of Educational
Psychology, 83,* 73–87.

Authorship of a document usually is listed on the document itself. This indicator is not always reliable, however. Some publications, especially recorded speeches, are ghostwritten by a speech writer rather than written by the person who delivers the speech. In other cases, an author will use a pseudonym to conceal his identity. Barzun and Graff cited the example of a historian who spent 35 years in an attempt to identify the author of a series of unsigned installments in a periodical at the time of the Civil War.[27] If a document has multiple authors, it might be impossible to determine who wrote the parts of it that are of particular relevance to your study.

The place of origin of a document often is apparent from where it is stored, or from indications in the document itself. The date when it was written might be indicated on the document, or if not, the date might be ascertained from statements in the document or from its sequential location in a set of records or files. Dates on a document must be viewed critically, because people often make innocent but misleading errors. For example, at the start of a new year it is not uncommon for someone to make the mistake of entering the previous year.

Knowledge of the conditions under which a document was prepared is helpful in determining its nature and usefulness to the problem under investigation. For example, if you are studying documents from a particular institution, you could study the institution's organization chart and operating procedures. This knowledge would help you understand the purpose of certain documents and for whom they were intended. Having this knowledge during the early stages of the study might help you limit your search to the most useful institutional documents that are available.

Internal Criticism

Internal criticism involves evaluating the accuracy and worth of the statements contained in a historical document. In engaging in internal criticism, researchers ask such questions as: Is it probable that people would act in the way described by the writer? Is it physically possible for the events described to have occurred this close together in time? Do the budget figures mentioned by the writer seem reasonable? In answering these questions, they need to be careful not to reject a statement just because the event or situation described appears improbable. Most people can recall several highly improbable events that have occurred in their lives.

Internal criticism is more complex than external criticism because it includes the historian's judgment about the truth of the statements in a historical source and also an evaluation of the person who wrote them. For example, it is important to know whether the writer was a competent observer of the events to which she refers. Many studies in psychology have demonstrated that eyewitnesses can be extremely unreliable, especially if they are emotionally aroused or under stress at the time of the event. Even under conditions in which little emotional involvement exists, some individuals are much more competent observers than others.

If the events were of a technical nature (e.g., a legal proceeding involving the dismissal of a school administrator), it would be important to know the writer's expertise relating to these events. An individual with limited expertise might be inclined to overlook or misinterpret certain details of the situation. There also is the matter of the writer's truthfulness. If the writer had a personal stake in the events being observed, he might be motivated to distort or lie about what happened.

Even if witnesses are competent and truthful, they probably still will give different versions of events that took place. One only needs to read accounts of an event (e.g., a school board meeting) in different newspapers to discover how widely witnesses' perceptions can

27. Ibid., p. 107.

vary. This does not mean that one witness is correct and the others are wrong. Nor is the reverse necessarily true, that because the majority of witnesses agree in their accounts they are correct, or that a witness who made a different set of observations is mistaken or lying.

Should you come across widely differing accounts of an event, your reaction might be to think there is no objective historical truth, and that all accounts are equally valid or equally false. Carr questions this view: "It does not follow that, because a mountain appears to take on different shapes from different angles of vision, it has objectively either no shape at all or an infinity of shapes."[28] According to Carr, the task of the historian is to combine one or more witnesses' accounts, admittedly subjective, and to interpret them (also a subjective process) in an attempt to discover what actually happened.

Although all accounts of historical events are subjective, it does not follow that every account reflects bias. A **bias** is a set to perceive events in such a way that certain types of facts are habitually overlooked, distorted, or falsified. The person who has strong motives for wanting a particular version of a described event to be accepted usually can be expected to produce biased information.

Many biased reports of events can be traced to people's tendency to make a story more dramatic or to exaggerate their role in events. Biased reports also can occur when the social or political position of individuals requires them to make socially acceptable statements, even if they do not honestly feel that way. For example, a school principal we know was questioned about internal difficulties with particular teachers and classified staff at her school. The principal made claims about high staff morale and cohesiveness at her school. Such claims probably were made to avoid compounding the problem and to guard against putting the speaker in a negative light. For similar reasons, some people in public life prefer to make conciliatory statements about their political opponents, even when such statements have little or no relation to their true feelings.

The opposite approach has emerged in political campaigns, a tendency to "blast" one's opponent regardless of the verifiability of one's statements. For example, suppose that you have located a school memo written by the school superintendent in which he describes a dispute that occurred between him and a member of the school board. You might suspect that the superintendent would present his side of the argument in the most favorable light, to alter his position subconsciously to agree with facts that have become apparent since the meeting, or to omit an opponent's statements that have merit.

Historians often must examine such factors as the ethnic background, political party, religious affiliation, and social status of an observer in an effort to appraise the likelihood of bias. The use of emotionally charged language, whether positive or negative, is one sign of commitment to a particular position on an issue.

If you find a discrepancy between someone's public and private statements, this does not necessarily mean that the public statements have no value as historical evidence. Rather, the discrepancy itself is evidence about the person making the statement, and about the social environment in which she functioned.

Interpretation in Historical Research

Use of Concepts to Interpret Historical Information

As in other types of qualitative research, researchers doing historical research develop concepts to organize and interpret the data that they have collected. **Concepts** are terms that can

---

28. Carr, *What is history,* pp. 30–31.

be used to group individuals, events, or objects that share a common set of attributes. For example, without a concept such as *progressive education,* a great many historical phenomena that share common characteristics might be seen as separate and lacking in significance.

Concepts, however, also place limits on the historical researcher's interpretation of the past. For example, a researcher conducting a historical study of teaching might assume that the defining attribute of the concept of *teaching* is "paid work done by someone who holds a state certificate signifying completion of a college-level teacher education program." This definition of teaching will cause the researcher to study certain individuals from a certain historical period but exclude others—for example, teacher aides, school volunteers, resource personnel—who would be considered to be teaching if a different definition of the concept were used.

Thus one needs to use care in selecting and defining the concepts used in historical research. At the least, you should determine the definition of each concept to determine whether it applies to the historical phenomena you wish to study. If necessary, you should provide definitions of important concepts in the research report. Many educational terms have become part of the everyday vernacular (e.g., intelligence, test, curriculum), but if such terms are defined, it will be clear to readers what they mean in the particular context of the research study.

Recent historical research has made much use of concepts from other disciplines. T. C. R. Horn and Harry Ritter made the following observation about this development:

> In general, the trend has been to look primarily to the "social sciences"—sociology, economics, political science, psychology, and anthropology—for new ideas, and lately to statistics and mathematics; to a lesser degree, historians have turned to "humanistic" disciplines such as language studies, poetics, literary criticism, and philosophy.[29]

Horn and Ritter found that all the historical studies that had won major prizes in a recent year drew upon conceptual frameworks from other disciplines. The use of concepts from other disciplines brings to mind the various qualitative research traditions described in Chapter 15, many of which are based on the same disciplines to which Horn and Ritter refer. Historical research can build on one or more of these traditions. For example, the historical study of a high school walkout, described at the end of this chapter, uses oral history in its methodology and critical-theory research in its interpretations, and it utilizes the concept of micro–macro integration derived from sociology.

Interdisciplinary concepts are useful tools. However, you should be familiar with how these concepts are defined in the discipline from which they originate to ensure that they are used appropriately in your study. For example, in applying the concept of *bureaucracy* to the public school system that developed in the United States during the mid-nineteenth century, Michael Katz defined it with reference to the definition set forth by Carl Friedrich, a sociologist.[30]

Historians as Interpreters

In discussing internal criticism, we noted that witnesses to an event will report different impressions based on their competence, personal position, and relationship to an event. According to Carr, the historian is in a similar situation:

> The facts are really not at all like fish on the fishmonger's slab. They are like fish swimming about in a vast and sometimes inaccessible ocean; and what the historian catches will depend

29. Horn, T. C. R., & Ritter, H. (1986). Interdisciplinary history: A historiographical review. *The History Teacher, 19,* 427.
30. Katz, M. B. (1987). *Reconstructing American education.* Cambridge, MA: Harvard University Press.

partly on chance, but mainly on what part of the ocean he chooses to fish in and what tackle he chooses to use—these two factors being, of course, determined by the kind of fish he wants to catch. By and large, the historian will get the kind of facts he wants. History means interpretation.[31]

If you choose to do historical research, you will first need to clarify your own values, beliefs, and experience concerning the topic that you are investigating, because they allow you to "see" certain aspects of past events and not others. As you become aware of your own inter-pretational framework, you also will have increased sensitivity to the possible interpretational leanings of other historians who have conducted research on the same or similar topics.

Because history involves interpretation, historians constantly are rewriting the past as their interests and concerns change. The last half century of historical research in education has seen the emergence of revisionist historians (also known as *reconstructionist historians*). These researchers take a vastly different view of educational history than the conventional or popular view. They believe that some past educational practices reflect particular political, economic, religious, or other motivations rather than rationality, justice, good will, or pedagogical considerations:

> [Reconstructionist] Historians of education are questioning stereotyped notions of the words *reform* and *progressive* and are thinking in terms of the *irony* of school reform. Historians of education are now ready to examine the public schools as instruments of social control. Historians of education are now disclosing phenomena long hidden by official pieties: the maltreatment of immigrants and ethnic groups, the discriminatory treatment of women and minority groups, the connections between schools and politics and between education and social stratification.[32]

Sometimes revisionist historians are extreme in their reinterpretations of history, for example, claiming that the Holocaust never occurred. By contrast, researchers in the cultural studies and critical-theory research tradition (see Chapter 15) seek to apply a critical orientation toward educational practice that generates historical explanations for controversial or unjust educational practices that greatly differ from conventional, mainstream interpretations.

In contrast to the reconstructionists, historians who conducted educational research before the 1960s tended to examine the past for evidence of how American education contributed to the improvement of our society and students' lives. Another common tendency of educational historians up until recent times was discussed by Bernard Bailyn in a landmark historical study published in 1960.[33] Bailyn observed that until that time most historians of American education had interpreted education predominantly as a process of formal schooling. He urged historians to overcome this bias so that they could view education as not only what occurs in formal school settings, but rather all the ways that are used to transmit a culture to future generations.[34] Partly as a result of Bailyn's influence, educational historians have enlarged their perspective to conduct research on many non-school influences that affect the socialization and learning of young people and adults.

31. Carr, *What is history?*, p. 26.
32. Cohen, *History of the history,* p. 329.
33. Bailyn, B. (1970; reprint of 1960 ed.). *Education in the forming of American society: Need and opportunities for study.* Chapel Hill, NC: University of North Carolina Press.
34. A powerful example of the historical analysis of nonschool influences on education can be found in: Glanders, T. (2000). *Origins of mass communications research during the American Cold War: Educational effects and contemporary implications.* Mahwah, NJ: Erlbaum.

In interpreting their data, historians need to be careful to avoid a type of bias known as presentism. **Presentism** is the interpretation of past events based on concepts and perspectives that originated in more recent times. For example, there has been much interest in the phenomenon referred to as *school choice*. In some communities school choice refers to the fact that parents can send their children to any public school in the school district in which they live, not only to the one nearest their home. In other communities, school choice may take the form of proposals to provide tuition vouchers to parents who opt to send their children to private schools instead of to state-supported public schools. The historical researcher who is interested in this phenomenon might look for evidence of how earlier educators gave parents choices about their children's education. These earlier educators might have used a term similar to *school choice*, but it might have meant something quite different then—for example, whether school attendance should be compulsory or voluntary. The historian needs to discover how various concepts were used in their own time and settings, rather than attach present meanings to them.

Causal Inference in Historical Research

An essential task of historical research consists of investigating the causes of past events. As Carr states, "The study of history is a study of causes."[35] Examples of causal questions that guide many historical studies are: What forces and events gave rise to the intelligence-testing movement? Why did U.S. educators adopt so readily the British open-classroom approach several decades ago? How did the role of school principal originate in U.S. public schools?

Causal inference in historical research is the process of reaching the conclusion that one set of events brought about, directly or indirectly, a subsequent set of events. Historians cannot prove that one past event caused another, but they can make explicit the assumptions that underlie their attributions of causality in sequences of historical events.

Some historians make the assumption that humans act similarly across cultures and across time. Thus, they might use a currently accepted causal pattern to explain an apparently similar pattern in the past. For example, a historian might find an instance in nineteenth-century U.S. education when many students at a particular college stopped attending classes and made criticisms of the school's administration that were reported in the news media. Say that the historian also discovered that this event was preceded by administrative rulings at the college that restricted students' privileges. The historian might infer—perhaps correctly—that these rulings led to a student revolt, his reasoning being that a similar chain of events precipitated student protests in many U.S. colleges in the 1960s.

Historians generally believe, however, that historical events are unique. Most would argue that history does not repeat itself. Thus occurrences at one point in time can be used to illuminate, but not to explain, occurrences at another point in time. Even historians who see past occurrences as a guide to later events must be wary of presentism, which we described above as interpreting events from an earlier time period in terms of concepts having different meanings at a later time period.

Historians have emphasized various types of causes in their attempts to explain past events. They have attributed historical events of catastrophic or far-reaching significance to the actions of certain key persons (the "great man" view of history), to the operation of powerful ideologies, to advances in science and technology, or to economic, geographical, sociological, or psychological trends.

---

35. Carr, *What is history?*, p. 113.

Some historians take an eclectic view and explain past events in terms of a combination of factors. David Tyack's study of compulsory education illustrates well this view of causal patterns in past phenomena.[36] Tyack views the rise of compulsory education as a remarkable part of U.S. educational history. The first, or symbolic, stage (1850–1890), involved the building of a broad base of elementary schools that attracted growing numbers of children. Most states passed compulsory attendance laws, but the laws were unenforced. According to Tyack, little attention was paid to "the organizational apparatus necessary to compel students into classrooms."[37] The second, or bureaucratic, stage began shortly before the turn of the twentieth century. During this period school systems grew in size and complexity, new forms of bureaucratic control emerged, and ideological conflict over compulsion diminished. Attendance laws, tracking of truants, and the labeling of school-leavers as dropouts became routine by the 1950s.

The question arises, Why did schooling in the United States gradually become compulsory under force of law? Tyack examined five causal interpretations to see how well each answered this question. For example, the ethnocultural interpretation argues that compulsory education came about because of the belief that it would inculcate a single "correct" standard of behavior, especially among the nineteenth-century immigrants from southern and eastern Europe who were provoking much concern among certain religious and ethnic groups already established in this country. Another interpretation, drawn from the economic theory of human capital, states that compulsory schooling grew out of a belief that education would improve the productivity and predictability of the work force. Tyack cites the noted educator Horace Mann, who called education "the most prolific parent of material riches."[38]

Each of Tyack's five interpretations explains some of the historical evidence, leaves other evidence unexplained, and suggests new lines of research. In Tyack's view, alternative interpretations help the historian "gain a more complex and accurate perception of the past and a greater awareness of the ambiguous relationship between outcome and intent—both of the actors in history and of the historians who attempt to recreate their lives."[39]

The more we learn about the antecedents of a historical event, the more likely we are to discover possible alternative causes of the event. Therefore, it probably is more defensible to identify an antecedent event as *a* cause rather than *the* cause. Moreover, historians, by their choice of language, can convey their interpretation of the certainty of the causal link ("It is highly likely that . . ." or "It is possible that . . .") and the strength of the causal link ("It was a major influence . . ." or "It was one of many events that influenced . . .").

Generalizability of Historical Evidence

Like other qualitative researchers, historians cannot study all the individuals, settings, events, or objects that interest them. Instead, they usually study only one case or a few instances of the phenomenon of interest. The case that is studied is determined partly by the availability of sources. For example, suppose a historian studied the diaries, correspondence, and other written records of elementary school teachers in the 1800s in order to understand teaching conditions during that time. The study necessarily will be limited to teachers whose writings have been preserved and to which the historian can gain access.

---

36. Tyack, D. B. (1976). Ways of seeing: An essay on the history of compulsory schooling. *Harvard Educational Review, 46,* 55–89.
37. Ibid., p. 60.
38. Ibid., p. 79.
39. Ibid., p. 89.

The historian needs to keep in mind, too, that teachers who were interested in making written records of their work may not be typical of teachers in general. One way to determine whether similar results would be found for other types of teachers is to examine how teachers in different circumstances viewed their teaching experience. For example, did teachers who wrote about their work for publication describe similar conditions as teachers who wrote about their work in private diaries and correspondence?

Another potential problem in historical interpretation involves the accuracy of historical data related to a single individual. For example, the historian might come across a document in which an educator expressed an opinion about a particular educational issue. This does not mean that the educator held the same opinion at a later or earlier time. The historian needs to look for more data that will help her decide whether the expressed opinion was characteristic of this educator.

As in any research project, historical research findings are strengthened by increasing the size of the data set on which they are based. Therefore, it is advisable to conduct an extensive search for primary and secondary sources related to the topic. If the evidence is limited to only a few sources, researchers should exercise restraint in the generality of their interpretations. For example, it may be necessary to make a statement like, "Teachers in rural schools of 50 or fewer students during the period 1860 to 1870 . . ." rather than "Teachers during the period 1860 to 1870 . . ." Quantitative history, which we described earlier in the chapter, is better suited than traditional historical research for making the latter generalization.

Writing a Historical Research Report

Reports of historical research do not have a standard format. The particular problem or topic being investigated and the historian's disciplinary orientation (e.g., feminist, literary, psychological) determines how the presentation of findings will be organized.

One obvious method of organization is to present the historical facts in chronological order. Thus, in a dissertation each chapter might cover a discrete period of time in the life of an individual, the history of an institution, or an educational movement. The other obvious method of organization is to present historical conclusions according to a specific case, topic, or theme. For example, if the purpose of the study was to examine how different school districts came to establish a kindergarten program, the dissertation might have a separate chapter for each school district included in the study.

For some studies, however, neither of the above methods of organization is satisfactory. Suppose the researcher's purpose is to describe the development of a particular university. The researcher could organize the dissertation chronologically, with each chapter devoted to a different time period. But such an approach might obscure certain themes that have continuity across time periods (e.g., the development of the university's relationship to the state government as a prime research contractor, the growth of the university's graduate school, and the construction and revision of the university's undergraduate curriculum). Thematic continuity could be achieved by having a separate chapter for each aspect of the university's development, but then a sense of the institution's unity and overall state of development at particular points in time would be lost. Also, it would be difficult for the researcher to show how various aspects of the university's development influenced and related to one another.

A possible solution to this problem is to combine the chronological and thematic approaches. Each chapter might cover a discrete time period, but the internal organization of the chapters could be thematic. Ultimately, the decision to use a particular organizational approach depends upon the questions that the historical researcher has chosen to ask.

The majority of the report probably will consist of discussion of the researcher's interpretations of the data obtained through a search of preliminary, secondary, and primary sources. In addition, the researcher might wish to have a separate section that reviews other historians' interpretations of the same or similar phenomena. The methodology used in the study, that is, its historiography, might be described in a separate section, especially if the historical sources posed unusual problems of external or internal criticism or if the historian employed unusual or controversial historiography.

The wording must be considered carefully in writing the report, because choice of words reflects the researcher's interpretational framework. We noted above, for example, how the use of certain words can convey differences in the presumed probability of a causal relationship between past events. Adjectives have particular interpretational significance. Suppose that the researcher decides to describe a particular institution as a *major* university. Does the use of this adjective reflect the researcher's own admiration of the institution or the common judgment of other educators? The researcher needs to think carefully about the reasons for using this particular word in describing the research study. Concepts and descriptions with strong affective or value connotations should be substantiated by indicating the sources on which they are based, as well as the researcher's reasoning that led to their use. With such grounding, colorful terms rescue a historical research report from dullness and help it meet its responsibility to reconstruct the past so that it comes alive for the reader.

Examples of Historical Research in Education

To illustrate the steps involved in carrying out historical research, we describe two historical studies below. They provide an introduction to the design of historical research, which you should supplement through your own search for historical sources.

A Micropolitical Perspective on the Education of Mexican Americans in a South Texas Community

A recent study based on oral history, carried out by Miguel Guajardo and Francisco Guajardo, illustrates the extent to which the hidden curriculum of cultural reproduction (described in Chapter 15) permeated schools in south Texas before, during, and for a long time after the 1954 *Brown* v. *Board of Education* decision requiring school desegregation throughout the United States.[40] Their study puts the story of the Edcouch-Elsa High School walkout of 1968 and its impact on the educational systems in south Texas into the broader context of the widespread provision of unequal educational opportunities for nonwhite ethnic groups in U.S. schools.

The authors are two brothers who moved from Mexico to the Edcouch-Elsa community as children, became school teachers in the community, and are now professors of educational leadership at universities in Texas. Most of the data used in the article were collected between 1997 and 2002 as part of the Llano Grande Oral History Collection, which is maintained by the Llano Grande Center for Research and Development, a nonprofit organization at Edcouch-Elsa High School. With the help of current students and teachers, the authors conducted more than 200 oral histories of elders, walkout participants, and other members of the local community. The interviews of each participant were

---

40. Guajardo, M. A., & Guajardo, F. J. (2004). The impact of *Brown* on the brown of south Texas: A micropolitical perspective on the education of Mexican Americans in a south Texas community. *American Educational Research Journal, 41*(3), 501–526.

taped and transcribed, and "many of the stories therein are embedded as part of the curriculum design for classes at Edcouch-Elsa High School."[41]

The authors note that they straddle the fence between insider and outsider status, but have seldom felt like outsiders. As indigenous researchers, they are committed to sharing and collecting stories for the purpose of giving power to the stories and the people who tell them. Through photographs and quotations they tell the story of the conditions in Edcouch, Elsa, and neighboring rural communities going back to the 1920s that set the stage for the walkout in 1968. They bring alive the experiences of Mexican Americans in this community, for example, that of José Tamez, born in 1942 "in Elsa, before Elsa was Elsa."[42]

> . . . when it rained we had to walk a long distance to catch the bus . . . . One rainy day my father walked with us to the bus stop because he wanted to ask the bus driver to drive closer to our home. . . . When my father asked the bus driver, the driver said, "No! Mexicans aren't supposed to get educated anyway. You are meant to work in the fields."[43]

The authors use the theoretical framework of micro–macro integrative theory to analyze their data, constructing a constant communication between the local (micro) realities and the driving forces of the *Brown* decision at the macro (national) level. They use many personal stories, newspaper photographs, and previously published historical accounts of Hidalgo County (where Edcouch-Elsa is situated) to document the "systemic patterns of cultural reproduction of Anglo America" that kept school segregation and discrimination in place from the 1920s into the 1960s in their community. They also describe both micro and macro events that formed the backdrop for the student walkout, including (in roughly chronological order):

- The Zamora family's successful protest to U.S. President Roosevelt in 1942 after daughter Rosie was initially denied enrollment to the educationally and physically superior Red Brick elementary school in Edcouch (previously only Anglo children had attended this school, while Mexican American children attended a run-down wood-frame school in nearby Elsa)
- Efforts by Mexican Americans to gain representation on the Edcouch-Elsa school board, which increased after their experiences on the battlefields in World War II
- Student and family dismay over the demeaning actions of a teacher, Greta Davison, who in 1968 discouraged Edcouch-Elsa High School students who were Mexican American, like Alicia Tamez and A student Raúl Alaniz, from applying to college, instead recommending secretarial school to Alicia and the military to Raúl
- Héctor Ramírez's experience on a Detroit automobile assembly line in 1968 before his senior year in high school, where he experienced the power of labor unions in addressing unsatisfactory working conditions
- Walkouts in East Los Angeles in 1968 by Mexican American college students demanding civil rights and organizing student demonstrations

The authors report the following:

> On the morning of November 14, 1968, at precisely 8:10, a number of Mexican American student protesters stormed out of the classrooms chanting "Walkout! Walkout!" thus igniting a massive student boycott of Edcouch-Elsa High School. More than 150 students followed as they chanted phrases of protest against what they charged was an unjust educational system.

41. Ibid., p. 503.
42. Ibid., p. 506.
43. Ibid., pp. 506, 510.

The Edcouch-Elsa High School Walkout of 1968 became the tipping point . . . in a shift of power from White (Anglo-American) to brown (Mexican American) in south Texas. After decades of a dominant segregationist culture throughout the region, Mexican American high school students in this agricultural community forcefully challenged the power structure in the schools and in the community at large.[44]

The article describes how walkout leaders were jailed and arrested, resulting in a jailside protest late into the night until they were released. In their discussion the authors comment that the adoption of a new policy, such as the *Brown* decision, does not always equate to change. Noting that resistance across the country increased after the *Brown* decision, they assert that "appropriate representation and advocacy are important if Latino communities are to exercise the power to affect policy and affect change."[45] They further argue that their research

teaches us that people who are most affected by policy should be part of creating it, just as they should be part of defining it. Equally important, those who research the policy (such as our high school student researchers) should have a stake in how the past is told, and how the future is shaped.[46]

With respect to generalizability, the authors' treatment of macro forces operating during this historical period demonstrates the relevance and possible applicability of their findings to other schools serving students of different ethnicities. In addition, this historical study illustrates clearly the ongoing educative and emancipatory function that historical research can serve.

Politics and the Pendulum: A Historical Analysis of Whole Language

Researchers who are not primarily historians often undertake historical analysis of a phenomenon in order to offer a different perspective from what prevailed in previous research literature. Such analyses involve primarily a review of the literature and presentation of the authors' own perspective. Some journals contain many "Reply" articles of this sort, inspired by disagreement with the original author's interpretation.

Paula Wolfe and Leslie Poynor undertook such a historical analysis to challenge the characterization of whole-language instruction in a previous publication.[47] The previous article, by Steven Stahl, "likened to the swings of a pendulum" the rise and decline of this educational innovation.[48] The authors cite Stahl's article as reflective of a mischaracterization of "the historical case of whole language in particular and the process of educational innovation in general."[49]

Wolfe and Poynor begin their historical analysis by quoting from C. Edelsky, B. Altwerger, and B. Flores's book on whole language, which states that "there is the current general tendency in the culture to use metaphors that turn human life into machines or packages."[50] In their analysis they explain the theoretical basis and goals of whole-language instruction and deconstruct the pendulum metaphor.

44. Ibid., p. 506.
45. Ibid., p. 523.
46. Ibid., p. 522.
47. Wolfe, P., & Poynor, L. (2001). Politics and the pendulum: An alternative understanding of the case of whole language as educational innovation. *Educational Researcher, 30*(1), 15–20.
48. Stahl, S. (1999). Why innovations come and go (and mostly go): The case of whole language. *Educational Researcher, 28*(8), 13–22.
49. Wolfe & Poynor, Politics and the pendulum, p. 15.
50. Edelsky, C., Altwerger, B., & Flores, B. (1991). *Whole language: What's the difference?* Portsmouth: Heinemann. Quote appears on p. 39.

To help clarify the historical controversy involving whole language versus other forms of reading instruction, we provide here a definition of whole-language instruction from a meta-analysis comparing whole-language, basal, and eclectic modes of instruction:

> Whole language instruction [places] emphasis on (1) whole pieces of literature and functional language as opposed to abridgments, adaptations, or segmented texts; (2) individual students' choice as opposed to teacher-sponsored whole-class assignments; and (3) integrated language experiences as opposed to direct instruction in isolated skill sequences.[51]

The authors argue that the rise and fall of this theoretical and pedagogical movement "more closely resembles a sociopolitical movement inextricably linked to conflicts over hegemonic control" than a pendulum swing.[52] They analyze its history in U.S. education with D. McAdam's political process model of the generation and decline of social movements, involving four factors.[53]

Expanding Political Opportunities

Wolfe and Poynor assert that in the mid to late 1970s broad social processes were restructuring the goals of public schooling and generally questioning "the way it is" with respect to values, traditions, and politics. While basal reading series had dominated reading instruction since 1928 and were still dominant in the early 1960s, whole-language advocates now experienced expanding political opportunities (the first factor in McAdam's model).

Shared Cognitions

The second factor, shared cognitions, is necessary to move from opportunity to action, arising when people attach subjective meaning to the situation and see change as possible. According to Wolfe and Poynor, the grassroots origins of the whole-language movement likely began around 1976, based on a talk regarding the theory and practice of early reading given by two whole-language scholars at a conference at the University of Pittsburgh. As researchers and practitioners shared their insights, "a change in practice and belief for an increasing number of teachers" regarding whole language occurred.[54] This was followed by development of local whole-language support groups, which allowed teachers to share their subjective meanings, break the isolation typical of the teaching profession, and develop shared cognitions about what was possible in reading instruction. In 1981, members of these local support groups began attending annual meetings of the National Council of Teachers of English and the International Reading Association, and in 1989 representatives formed the international network of the Whole Language Umbrella, with more than 3,000 members.

Mobilization of Indigent Organization Resources

The third factor involves mobilization of the resources of organizations supportive of the new movement. Spurred by the local support groups and the Umbrella, an official of Heinemann Educational Books (HEB) met with educators to investigate "literacy education," and by 1982 the HEB literacy education catalog included several whole-language texts. Wolfe and Poynor note that "these early publications marked the beginning of an active campaign to publish whole language texts and to distribute those texts that had been difficult to purchase in the United States."[55]

51. Jeynes, W. H., & Littell, S. W. (2000). A meta-analysis of studies examining the effect of whole language instruction on the literacy of low-SES students. *Elementary School Journal, 101*(1), 21–33.
52. Wolfe & Poynor, Politics and the pendulum, p. 15.
53. McAdam, D. (1999). *Political process and the development of black insurgency, 1930–1970* (2nd ed.). Chicago: University of Chicago.
54. Wolfe & Poynor, Politics and the pendulum, p. 16.
55. Ibid.

Shifting Response of Other Organized Groups to the Movement

Wolfe and Poynor argue that the movement's grassroots nature had a downside for whole language in the response of other organized groups (McAdam's fourth factor). Specifically, the educational establishment defined whole language more as a method than as an alternative theoretical stance on learning, which "allowed researchers, such as Stahl, to describe the process of innovation as the swing between two radical end points of the methodological pendulum."[56] Whole language then became subject to quantitative testing, "as components can be tested while 'theories' cannot."[57] In this way, opponents of whole language could dismiss any nonscientific (i.e., qualitative) research connected to this movement as simply "advertisement," along with a declaration that whole language does not work. Once the evaluation of whole language was taken over by scientific "experts," according to the authors, "control over both the implementation and research of those methodologies [was] taken out of the hands of teachers . . . ."[58]

According to Wolfe and Poynor, whole language had begun to exert political and economic pressure on the "big business of education," and this pressure led to the movement away from whole-language instruction. They argue that, while whole language in the 1980s was not viewed as a threat by the educational mainstream, as teachers took charge of their own classrooms and formed their own organizations, it became "an enormous threat to the existing power structure and hierarchy of schools."[59] The authors note that at this point the many teachers and researchers favorable to whole language missed a key opportunity to identify whole language as a critical pedagogy and a movement for educational and social justice. "Instead, publishing companies 'absorbed the surface of whole language and sold it back to teachers' (P. Shannon, personal communication, September 23, 2000), undermining the theoretical, pedagogical, and sociopolitical nature of the movement."[60]

Wolfe and Poynor then further critique Stahl's use of the pendulum metaphor, rejecting its implication that there can be any neutral (i.e., nonpolitical) middle ground between two political "extremes" or that the status quo necessarily represents "best practice." They describe the decline of the whole-language movement in the 1990s as marked by increasingly overt attacks by researchers, the popular media, and the religious right, who claimed that it "didn't work" and failed to address the needs of economically, culturally, and linguistically diverse children. They assert, "In that whole language was first co-opted and then attacked we argue that Stahl's conception of innovation as failing largely because it had 'swung too far' seems simplistic and perhaps politically motivated."[61]

The authors warn against the sense of inevitable failure that the pendulum-swing metaphor implies toward innovation, noting that such metaphors can lead educators to abdicate responsibility to work for significant change in the structure of schooling. They conclude:

> We must not allow this new story [of whole language as a critical and liberatory theory and pedagogy], in which the inevitable presence of politics in schooling is acknowledged and made central, to be masked or silenced by reductionist metaphors.[62]

---

56. Ibid.
57. Ibid.
58. Ibid., p. 17.
59. Ibid.
60. Ibid.
61. Ibid., p. 19.
62. Ibid.

Whatever one's personal viewpoint on whole language, the authors' use of theory, documentation of significant events in the history of the whole-language movement, and descriptions of the pro and con standpoints surrounding this movement provide a rich model of historical analysis.

RECOMMENDATIONS FOR

Doing Historical Research

1. Before selecting a problem to investigate, determine whether you will be able to access the necessary primary and secondary sources.
2. Instead of relying exclusively on secondary sources, try to confirm and extend your findings by checking relevant primary sources.
3. Subject your historical data to external and internal criticism.
4. Consider whether and how your personal values and experience influenced your selection and interpretation of historical data.
5. Avoid presentism in interpreting events from another historical era.
6. Even if your interpretations focus on a single cause of a historical phenomenon, consider the ways in which other factors might have influenced it.
7. Keep in mind any limits that your data impose on the generalizations you wish to make about a historical phenomenon.
8. In reporting your historical facts and interpretations, organize them into meaningful chronological or thematic patterns.

SELF-CHECK TEST

Circle the correct answer to each of the following questions. The answers are at the back of the book.

1. In historical research, the written and printed materials recorded for the purpose of preserving information about historical phenomena are called
   a. documents and records.
   b. artifacts and relics.
   c. secondary sources.
   d. preliminary sources.
2. In historical research, physical objects preserved from the period being studied are called
   a. primary documents.
   b. secondary documents.
   c. secondary sources.
   d. relics.
3. In historical research, the literature review
   a. is a relatively minor part of the research process.
   b. provides the research data.
   c. is conducted after the data-collection stage.
   d. all of the above.
4. The procedure for determining whether a source of historical data is genuine is termed
   a. internal criticism.
   b. external criticism.
   c. external validation.
   d. causal inference.

5. Internal criticism of a document
   a. focuses on the information that it contains.
   b. includes an evaluation of the writer's motives and values.
   c. is assisted by obtaining other accounts of the same events.
   d. all of the above.

6. Presentism is defined as
   a. the belief that the present is more important than the historical past.
   b. the use of contemporary concepts to interpret past events.
   c. the belief that an understanding of the present is not aided by the study of past events.
   d. the set of assumptions underlying revisionist history.

7. Causal inference in historical research is a process by which a historian
   a. narrows the cause of a historical phenomenon to one set of factors.
   b. uses internal criticism to establish causal links between documents written at different points in time.
   c. uses interpretation to ascribe causality to a sequence of historical events.
   d. identifies past events that can be used to explain events that occurred later.

8. Reports of historical research
   a. usually are organized chronologically.
   b. usually are organized thematically.
   c. can be organized either chronologically or thematically.
   d. are organized in the same way as reports of experimental research.

9. Bernard Bailyn's book about the meaning of the concept of education as it applies to learning within American society contributed to historical research by its
   a. focus on nonschool influences on learning as legitimate topics for historical research in education.
   b. use of the "liberal reform" framework for re-interpreting historical events in education.
   c. development of a new theory of causal inference in historical research.
   d. external criticism of historical sources.

10. Quantitative analysis of historical data is useful for
   a. determining the generalizability of historical findings.
   b. studying the lives of common individuals.
   c. the study of large samples of populations.
   d. all of the above.

PART VI

Applications of Research

Educational researchers generally conduct studies for the purpose of description or prediction, or as a test of the effects of an intervention. The ultimate goal of their efforts is the development of theories that explain educational phenomena.

The methods developed by researchers for these purposes also can be used in the two applications of research that are described in the final two chapters of this book: evaluation research in Chapter 17 and action research in Chapter 18.

With respect to evaluation research, there is a continuing need for this application of educational research. For example, educators who are funded by government agencies to develop innovative programs typically must conduct evaluations to answer such questions as whether the programs are cost-effective, better than available alternatives, and acceptable to different stakeholder groups. Their primary goal in doing evaluation research is to make judgments of worth, value, and utility about specific programs rather than to develop encompassing theories. You will find in Chapter 17 how various research methods described in earlier chapters can be applied to educational evaluation. You also will find that evaluation research involves distinctive questions and issues that do not arise in other types of educational research.

Research methods also find application in action research, which involves investigations by practitioners to improve their own effectiveness, that of the organization in which they work, or education as a whole. Unlike academic research, action research tends to be less formal. However, it has the considerable advantage that the research-into-practice gap is much smaller, because practitioners formulate their own research problem and collect data in their immediate work site. Chapter 18 describes the various procedures for doing an action-research project.

CHAPTER 17

Evaluation Research

OVERVIEW

Evaluation research in education is particularly important to policy makers (e.g., school board members), program managers (e.g., school superintendents and university administrators), and curriculum developers (e.g., teachers and research and development specialists). This chapter describes the procedures for conducting evaluation research. We describe criteria for judging the quality of an evaluation study, and various quantitative and qualitative approaches to evaluation. The chapter concludes with a discussion of the role of evaluation research in educational research and development (R&D), which is a research-based approach to developing new programs and materials to improve education.

OBJECTIVES

After studying this chapter, you should be able to

1. Describe the major purposes of educational evaluation.
2. State major differences between evaluation research and other types of educational research.
3. Describe procedures that clarify the reasons for doing a particular evaluation study and identifying stakeholders.
4. Describe procedures that delineate the components of a program to be evaluated.
5. Explain the difference between the divergent and convergent phases in selection of questions that an evaluation study is designed to answer.
6. Identify several factors involved in creating an evaluation design but not a research design.
7. Describe procedures for collecting and analyzing evaluation data.

8. Explain how the reporting of an evaluation study typically differs from the reporting of a research study.
9. Describe several quantitative approaches to evaluation and the primary characteristics of each.
10. Describe several qualitative approaches to evaluation and the primary characteristics of each.
11. Describe the steps of the educational R&D cycle.
12. State two benefits of defining behavioral objectives for use in educational R&D.
13. Describe the advantages and disadvantages of doing an educational R&D project as your thesis or dissertation study compared to a more basic research study.

The Role of Evaluation in Education

Educational evaluation is the process of making judgments about the merit, value, or worth of educational programs. (We use the term *program* in this chapter as a generic label for the various phenomena—methods, materials, organizations, individuals, etc.—that are the focus of educational evaluation). This type of inquiry has grown remarkably since 1965, when the U.S. government mandated that all educational programs receiving federal funding must spend a portion of those funds on program evaluation.[1] Several research and development centers in the United States focus on the investigation of evaluation methodology,[2] and several social science journals specialize in evaluation.[3] Many school districts have established departments of evaluation, and a large number of educational researchers have moved into the field of evaluation research because of the widespread demand for evaluation services.

Why has educational evaluation attracted so much interest? The main reason is that evaluation has become an important component of policy analysis and program management.

With respect to policy analysis, evaluation research yields important data about the costs, benefits, and limitations of various program alternatives.[4] Policy analysts can use these data to prepare position papers, which are then reviewed by individuals with decision-making authority, such as board members and government officials.

With respect to the political process, evaluation findings are used to create advocacy for or against particular pieces of legislation and budget applications. Proponents and opponents of state-mandated testing of all students, site-based management, and other educational movements often cite data from evaluations of such phenomena, which shows the extent to which evaluation research can affect the political process. Quasi-legal approaches to evaluation, discussed later in the chapter, illustrate the potential political orientation of evaluation.

Evaluation research has also become an increasingly important component of program management. Cost-benefit evaluations (also called "efficiency evaluations") are done to determine whether programs are producing benefits that justify their costs. Another use of evaluations is to hold managers accountable for producing results. Evaluations also are done to help managers make sound decisions related to program design, personnel, and budget.

Relationship between Evaluation and Research

Are evaluation studies the same as research? Is an educational researcher qualified to fill a position involving program evaluation? Our answer to the first question would be: They are both similar and different. To the second question: Yes, but an educational researcher probably would need to acquire additional training.

Educational research and educational evaluation overlap to a great extent. In practice, evaluators use most of the same research designs, measurement tools, and data analysis techniques that constitute the methodology of educational research. For this reason, we

Touchstones in Research

Baker, E. L., & Niemi, D. (1996). School and program evaluation. In D. C. Berliner & R. C. Calfee (Eds.), *Handbook of educational psychology* (pp. 926–944). New York: Macmillan.

Rossi, P. H., Lipsey, M. W., & Freeman, H. E. (2004). *Evaluation: A systematic approach* (7th ed.). Thousand Oaks, CA: Sage.

---

1. McLaughlin, M. W. (1975). *Evaluation and reform: The Elementary and Secondary Education Act of 1965/Title I.* Cambridge, MA: Ballinger.
2. For example: the National Center for Research on Evaluation, Standards, and Student Testing (CRESST) at UCLA, and the Evaluation Center at Western Michigan University.
3. See, for example, *Evaluation Review, Educational Evaluation and Policy Analysis,* and *Evaluation and Program Planning.*
4. The role of evaluation research in policy analysis is explained in: Fowler, F. C. (2000). *Policy studies for educational leaders: An introduction.* Upper Saddle River, NJ: Merrill.

refer to evaluation studies as *evaluation research.* Nonetheless, evaluation differs from other types of research in several ways.

First, an evaluation study usually is initiated by someone's need for a *decision* to be made concerning policy, management, or political strategy. The purpose of the evaluation study is to collect data that will facilitate this decision. By contrast, the purpose of a research study, broadly stated, is to develop an understanding of a particular phenomenon. Of course, the findings of a research study also can be used to guide decision making, while an evaluation can develop understanding of a particular phenomenon.

Second, research and evaluation also differ in the extent to which the findings are generalized. Evaluation typically is done for a very specific purpose. Decision makers might be interested in how well their particular program works, and thus they commission a site-specific evaluation study to collect data relevant to their special concerns. By contrast, researchers are more likely to be interested in discovering generalizable relationships among variables or in discovering the meaning that individuals or groups ascribe to social reality. Researchers recruit a particular group of educators or students to participate in their study, but they typically view them as samples of larger populations to which the findings will be generalized, or as cases for replicating findings relevant to a theory. Again, the difference is not pure: Some evaluation studies are designed to yield widely generalizable findings, and some basic research has limited generalizability.

Third, evaluation and research differ in their judgments of value. Evaluation studies are designed to yield data concerning the worth, merit, or value of educational phenomena. Their findings tend to be stated in such phrases as "This reading program is superior to the other program with respect to . . . " or "The teachers in this district thought that this new approach to in-service training was superior to the existing approach because . . . " By contrast, researchers design their studies to discover the essential characteristics of educational phenomena. Their findings tend to be couched in such phrases as "It appears that variable X has an influence on variable Y," or "Using a grounded theory approach, we discovered that counselors attribute at-risk students' behavior to two types of motivation." Educators may make value judgments and decisions based on such research findings, but this is a secondary use of the findings.

The next section of the chapter describes procedures for conducting an evaluation study. You will find that most of the procedures and terminology are the same as those described in other chapters of the book because, as we stated above, educational evaluators draw extensively on the methodology of educational research.

Touchstones in Research

Worthen, B. R., Sanders, J. R., & Fitzpatrick, J. L. (2004). *Program evaluation: Alternative approaches and practical guidelines* (3rd ed.). Boston: Allyn & Bacon.

Posavac, E. J., & Carey, R. G. (2003). *Program evaluation: Methods and case studies.* Upper Saddle River, NJ: Prentice Hall.

Steps in Program Evaluation

An evaluation study follows essentially the same steps as those involved in doing a research study. Several additional factors must be considered, however, depending upon the evaluation approach that is used. These factors are highlighted below, using as an example an evaluation study conducted by David Strahan, Jewell Cooper, and Martha Ward.[5] The purpose of the evaluation was to evaluate the middle schools in one school district in order to guide school improvement plans.

Although our description of steps in evaluation refers mostly to *program* evaluation, the steps are applicable to other kinds of evaluation, too. In fact, the evaluation study that

5. Strahan, D., Cooper, J., & Ward, M. (2001). Middle school reform through data and dialogue: Collaborative evaluation with 17 leadership teams. *Evaluation Review, 25,* 72–99.

we use as an example focused on the effectiveness both of the schools' programs and their organizational structures.

Clarifying the Reasons for an Evaluation

An evaluation study can be initiated because of the evaluator's personal interest in doing it, because another individual or an agency requested it, or because the evaluator's personal interests and an agency's need for evaluation coincide.

If you conduct an evaluation to answer questions primarily of interest to you, you will need only to clarify for yourself why the study is being done. Such was the case in a study described later in the chapter in the section on expertise-oriented evaluation. That study was motivated by the researcher's interest in using the method of educational criticism to illuminate certain aspects of fourth-grade classroom instruction.

In the case of the middle-school evaluation that we are using as an example, the evaluation was initiated by school-district administrators. They invited a research team from the University of North Carolina at Greensboro to collaborate with the district's research office and middle schools in identifying critical issues at the middle-school level (e.g., interdisciplinary teaming and school safety), collecting evaluative data relating to those issues, and using the data to develop school improvement plans.

When an evaluation is requested, the evaluator should consider probing to determine *all* the reasons for the evaluation request. Evaluations can be requested because they are required by an accreditation board or a funding agency. Such evaluations usually are legitimate.

Evaluations also can be requested for more dubious reasons. Someone might want to use evaluation to "shape up" the behavior of program staff; in this case, the evaluation serves a watchdog function. Someone might want the evaluator to gather evidence to justify an already-made decision to terminate a program or reduce its funding or to gather information that will reflect unfavorably on certain members of the program staff. If staff members perceive that such purposes underlie an evaluation, they may work to sabotage the evaluator's efforts.

To determine the legitimacy of an evaluation request, evaluators need to spend time interviewing key individuals to determine whether the request is reasonable and ethical. Evaluation experts recommend that you refuse to conduct an evaluation if any breach of ethics has occurred or is likely to occur. The ethics of evaluation are discussed further in the section on criteria of a good evaluation study.[6] (Research ethics in general are the subject of Chapter 3.)

Selecting an Evaluation Model

Selecting an appropriate evaluation model requires careful deliberation, as there are many models from which to choose. By one account, nearly 60 different evaluation models were developed between 1986 and 1996.[7] In one meta-evaluation, 22 models were compared.[8]

---

6. Examples of ethical problems faced by evaluators are discussed in Kimmel, A. J. (1988). *Ethics and values in applied social research.* Newbury Park, CA: Sage. One such problem involves breaching confidentiality in order to report behavior of a client that appears to be illegal, and another involves difficulties in defining the evaluator's appropriate role as an expert witness.
7. Worthen, B. R., Sanders, J. R., & Fitzpatrick, J. L. (1997). *Program evaluation: Alternative approaches and practical guidelines* (2nd ed.). New York: Addison Wesley Longman.
8. Stufflebeam, D. L. (2001). *Evaluation models.* San Francisco: Jossey-Bass.

The models, or *approaches* as some evaluation experts prefer to call them, differ on various dimensions, among them being:

- the purpose of the evaluation and the questions being asked
- the methods for collecting data
- the relationship between the evaluator, the administrators overseeing the evaluation, and the individuals in the program or organization being evaluated

Later in the chapter we present a range of evaluation approaches to illustrate the options that are available to you. In addition, we recommend that you review the literature to identify other evaluation approaches and to determine whether a particular model is appropriate for the type of evaluation you plan to do.

Example of Collaborative Evaluation

In the middle-school study, Strahan, Cooper, and Ward selected the collaborative-evaluation model to guide their evaluation process. **Collaborative evaluation** is "any evaluation in which there is a significant degree of collaboration or cooperation between evaluators and stakeholders in planning and/or conducting the evaluation."[9] Thus, the individuals being evaluated are active participants in deciding the direction and uses of the evaluation, rather than passive objects of study. The collaborative-evaluation model is similar in certain respects to the responsive-evaluation model described later in the chapter.

Identifying Stakeholders

A **stakeholder** is anyone involved in the program being evaluated or who might be affected by or interested in the findings of the evaluation. It is important to identify stakeholders at the outset of an evaluation study. They can help you clarify the reasons why the study was requested, questions that should guide the evaluation, choice of research design, interpretation of results, and how the findings should be reported and to whom.

Ignoring some types of stakeholders can have serious political consequences. Specific groups or individuals can sabotage the evaluation process or discredit the results if they perceive the evaluator to have shortchanged their desire for involvement. However, you do not need to involve all stakeholders to the same extent. Some stakeholders wish simply to be kept informed, whereas others may want to influence the questions that guide the study and the evaluation design.

The middle-school evaluation that we are using as an example was comprehensive and collaborative, so there were many stakeholders. District administrators had a stake in ensuring that the 17 middle schools submitted a formal school improvement plan each year and that the plan included school safety and the use of the results of state-mandated achievement tests. The district's research office had a stake in ensuring the validity and utility of the district-wide survey instrument used to collect data about the perceptions of teachers, students, and parents concerning the schools' effectiveness. A leadership team for each school, consisting of teachers, parents, administrators, and a university evaluator/facilitator, was responsible for the school improvement plan. The leadership teams themselves were important stakeholders in the evaluation process. Each team occasionally solicited interview and questionnaire data from the students, teachers, and parents at the school, who were also stakeholders.

---

9. Cousins, J. B., Donohue, J. J., & Bloom, G. A. (1996). Collaborative evaluation in North America: Evaluators' self-reported opinions, practices, and consequences. *Evaluation Practice, 17,* 207–226. Quote appears on p. 210.

Deciding What Is to Be Evaluated

One of the first tasks that confronts the evaluator is **program delineation,** which is the process of identifying the most important characteristics of the program to be evaluated. It is not uncommon for those working in a program to know only program aspects that affect them directly. Unless all program components are delineated, an important component might be overlooked in the evaluation process.

Following program delineation, the program should be analyzed to determine which components to include in the evaluation study. Program components can be grouped into the following categories: program goals, program resources, and program procedures, program management, and program outcomes. These categories are useful for designing an evaluation study irrespective of the evaluation model that is used.

Program Goals

Judgments about the merit of program goals are central to most evaluation studies. A **goal** is the purpose, effect, or end point that the program developer is attempting to achieve. If a program does not have goals, or if the goals are not perceived as worthwhile, it is difficult to imagine how the program itself can have merit.

Some programs have carefully specified goals. In other programs the evaluator must infer the goals that the developer has in mind. Once the program goals have been identified, the evaluator may be asked by stakeholders to determine the extent to which the program actually achieves its intended goals. In *formative evaluation* of a program (described later in the chapter), the assigned task may be to help the developers determine what the goals of the program should be. Then in subsequent *summative evaluation* of the program (also described later in the chapter), an evaluator seeks to determine the extent to which the program meets its goals.

The goals of the middle-school evaluation study were school-improvement goals. Because the study covered several years, evaluation data from one year, presented in individual reports to the 17 leadership teams, shaped the improvement goals for the following year. For example, Strahan, Cooper, and Ward observed that: ". . . all of the 17 teams used the information from their first-year reports as one of several considerations in refining their school improvement plans for the second year."[10] The report information included student-achievement results on state-mandated tests and results of interviews and questionnaires administered to various stakeholder groups.

The evaluators' analysis of the second-year improvement plans revealed the following:

> . . . all 17 teams identified priority goals for instructional improvement in math and writing, 16 of the teams in reading. All 17 teams identified school safety as another priority for improvement. The other areas for improvement that the teams targeted most frequently were advisory programs/character education (15), schoolwide discipline (15), and parental involvement (15).[11]

We can conclude that these goals have merit in the eyes of a wide range of stakeholders, because they in fact generated the data used to create the goals. This appears to be one benefit of the collaborative-evaluation model.

Resources and Procedures

Resources are the personnel, equipment, space, and other cost items needed to implement program procedures. Stakeholders might want to know the answers to such questions as:

10. Strahan, et al., Middle school reform, p. 84.
11. Ibid.

Are our present resources sufficient to operate the program as intended by its developers? Is the program too expensive? Are there hidden costs in the program? Will the program take away resources needed by other programs? Each of these questions requires the evaluator to focus on program resources.

Procedures are the techniques, strategies, and other processes used in conjunction with resources to achieve program goals. Examples of evaluation questions that concern program procedures are "How long did teachers need to use the materials before students mastered the content?" "Did teachers have difficulty in using the constructivist approach to science teaching?" "To what extent did teachers actually use the constructivist approach?" Answers to these questions usually require close and repeated observation of the program in operation.

Evaluation of program resources and procedures is especially helpful for understanding the observed effects of a program. Suppose a new instructional program is observed to have negligible effects on student achievement. Decision makers might choose to discontinue the program because the evaluation results were negative. Yet the program may have been ineffective because needed materials did not arrive on time, or because teachers experienced many interruptions that reduced the total time allotted to program implementation. If the evaluator had collected data on these resource and procedural problems, the decision makers might have chosen an alternative course of action, for example, to remove the "bugs" from the program and try it again. In fact, collection of data on all three aspects of a program that we have discussed so far—goals, resources, and procedures—is important in any type of formative evaluation. Decisions about program revision can be made more effectively if developers know how well the existing program is working, and why.

Program Management

Most programs have a management system to monitor resources and procedures so that they are used effectively to achieve program goals. We might think that management only operates in large-scale programs, such as a system of secondary education or curriculum coordination in a school district. Yet many curriculum programs contain built-in management procedures to monitor students' instructional progress (e.g., daily quizzes and end-of-unit tests). We also could broaden the concept of management to include self-management (e.g., teachers monitoring their own classroom teaching in order to improve their on-the-job performance).

Some evaluation studies focus on management systems in response to such questions as "Is the management system ensuring the effective use of program resources? Is the management system as efficient as it can be?" "Are the management procedures being used as intended by the program developers?" Each of these questions requires the evaluator to design research that delineates the management system and examines its operation in practice.

In the middle-school evaluation study, the leadership team at each of the 17 schools was the key element in the management system used by the school district to bring about school improvement. The evaluators did not make judgments about the leadership teams other than noting that the school principals claimed that "the leadership teams are establishing clearer priorities and monitoring progress more systematically than they were several years ago."[12] It should be that the collaborative evaluation model is not as well suited

12. Ibid., p. 97.

to collecting data about management systems as are other evaluation models, especially the CIPP model described later in the chapter.

Program Outcomes

Typically a major concern, in the evaluation of either an existing program or a newly established one, is to evaluate program outcomes. We introduce this key program component in the section on collecting and analyzing evaluation data and cover it in detail in subsequent descriptions of different approaches to evaluation.

Identifying Evaluation Questions

We stated in Chapter 2 that a research problem can be stated in the form of questions, hypotheses, or objectives. The same range of formats can be used in evaluation studies, although it is most common to state questions.

Lee Cronbach distinguished two phases in selecting questions for an evaluation study.[13] The **divergent phase** involves generating a comprehensive list of questions, issues, concerns, and information needs that might be addressed in the evaluation study. (Note that issues, concerns, and information needs can be rephrased subsequently as questions to maintain a consistent format.) As the evaluator, you should invite all stakeholders to contribute to this list. In addition, you can suggest possible questions for study. The particular approach to evaluation that you have chosen to guide your study also can prompt ideas for questions. For example, in the section on formative and summative evaluation later in the chapter, we include a checklist for evaluating educational products. Stakeholders could be asked to nominate some or all of the checklist items for inclusion in the study. The items, which we have stated in the form of questions, could be added to the list of questions generated by other means.

The second of Cronbach's two phases is the **convergent phase.** It involves reducing the initial list of evaluation questions to a manageable number. This phase is necessary because of the expense involved in answering various evaluation questions. The evaluator, in collaboration with significant stakeholders, must winnow the list to the most important questions that can be answered with available resources.

The report of the middle-school evaluation study indicates that four questions guided the collaborative evaluation:

1. When provided support for gathering data, what issues do middle-school leadership teams choose to explore?
2. How do they use this information to set priorities for school improvement?
3. How do they monitor progress toward these priorities?
4. How does the collaborative evaluation process inform the revision of the district-wide Middle School Survey?[14]

The evaluators do not explain the process used to generate these questions, but it seems likely—given the nature of the questions and the evaluation model used—that they were generated collaboratively by district educators and the evaluation team.

As an evaluation study proceeds, new questions are likely to arise in the minds of the evaluator and stakeholders. Some of the evaluation models described later in the chapter—especially the qualitative models—explicitly acknowledge this possibility. If possible, you

13. Cronbach, L. J. (1982). *Designing evaluations of educational and social programs.* San Francisco: Jossey-Bass.
14. Strahan, Cooper, & Ward. Middle school reform, p. 77. The Middle School Survey was a questionnaire developed by the district's research office to determine stakeholders' perceptions about the middle schools.

should set aside time and other resources that can be used for answering important questions that arise after data collection begins.

Developing an Evaluation Design and Time Line

Many evaluation studies are similar to research studies in design, execution, and reporting. Thus, any of the research procedures described in the preceding chapters can be incorporated into the design of an evaluation study. Evaluation studies, however, present several issues that do not arise in research studies.

One issue is whether the evaluation should be done by an internal evaluator or an external evaluator. An **internal evaluator** is a staff member of the program that is being evaluated. For example, some students do thesis or dissertation projects in which they evaluate some aspect of the school in which they teach. They might do the evaluation while they are on leave to work on their degrees, but even in this situation they function as internal evaluators.

An **external evaluator** is not in the regular employ of the program but is employed specifically to do the evaluation. This person sometimes is called a *third-party evaluator* or *evaluation contractor*.

Most types of evaluation can be done by an internal evaluator, especially when the evaluation findings will be used to guide program management and decision making.[15] Summative evaluation, which is described more fully later in the chapter, is best done by an external evaluator. The purpose of summative evaluation is to determine the merits of a fully operational program and possibly to compare it with a competing program. The evaluator is obliged to represent the interests of the consumers to whom the evaluation study will be reported, or of the external agency that is sponsoring the evaluation. An external evaluator is in a much better position than an internal evaluator to represent these interests. Even so, either an internal evaluator or an external evaluator could be pressured to bias an evaluation design to produce particular results. If such pressure became too intense, the evaluator's only recourse would be to terminate the evaluation on ethical grounds.

Many evaluation studies involve an experimental or quasi-experimental design, because often the primary question is how well the program works, that is, achieves its intended outcomes. (The program is the experimental treatment.) A common issue in this situation is how much internal and external validity should be built into the evaluation design. More resources are required to include a control group and other experimental design features that increase one's confidence that observed effects are attributable to the program and that the effects are generalizable. Program staff, however, might not always be willing to pay the costs needed to improve the experiment's validity.

Resolution of this issue usually depends on who is in control of the evaluation process. Some evaluators do evaluation studies out of personal interest, as was true in McCutcheon's study using the method of educational connoisseurship and criticism described later in the chapter. These evaluators can design more or less rigorous studies, as they choose. When you are doing a study that involves collaboration with stakeholders, the situation is different. You must be sensitive to the quality of information that will satisfy the stakeholders' needs, and to budgetary constraints. This may mean designing a less rigorous study than you might wish.

---

15. For a detailed discussion of the special duties and concerns of internal evaluators, see: Love, A. J. (1991). *Internal evaluation: Building organizations from within.* Newbury Park, CA: Sage.

In designing an evaluation study, you should be aware that evaluation activities can be both beneficial and harmful. Gene Glass described this problem as a paradox.[16] On the one hand, persons involved in a program appear to do best when they feel they are valued unconditionally and do not have an evaluator watching over their shoulder. On the other hand, Glass observed, "it appears that people move truer and more certainly toward excellence to the extent that they clarify their purposes, measure the impact of their action, judge it, and move on—in a few words, evaluate their progress."[17] The perils of evaluation involve not only people, but the program itself. A program might be of high quality, but a poor evaluation can cause others to misjudge it and contribute to its downfall. A program might have great potential, but a negative evaluation while it is under development could lead administrators to withdraw its funding. Furthermore, evaluation activities use resources that could be allocated to support further program development.

The beneficial and harmful effects of evaluation are difficult to reconcile. Some evaluators recommend that you weigh all possible consequences of a planned evaluation activity. You should determine that the potential benefits outweigh the potential harm before you make a decision to proceed with the evaluation. Also, you should design the study to minimize potentially harmful effects. One way to accomplish this goal is to involve significant stakeholders in the design of the study, as was done in the middle-school evaluation study that we are describing. For example, they can assist in selecting or developing measures that reflect the outcomes most likely to be achieved by the program. Including measures suggested by stakeholders can make the evaluation less threatening to them. Such measures may reveal effects that cast a more positive light on the program.

An important issue to consider is time. Many research studies have no time constraints for completion. Not so with evaluation studies. If stakeholders are involved, they usually want the final report by a certain date. In these situations, the evaluator will need to create a time line as part of the evaluation design to ensure that the study is completed by the requested date.[18] One advantage of creating a detailed time line is that it can be used to identify and document the resources needed to complete a study by the requested date. You may need this information later, for example, to convince stakeholders to increase resources if it appears that a specified deadline cannot be met using the resources originally budgeted for the study.

Collecting and Analyzing Evaluation Data

Data collection and analysis in both evaluation studies and research studies are similar. For example, the middle-school evaluation study primarily involved a descriptive design in which stakeholder perceptions and student achievement were measured each school year. Among the data-collection instruments were the following:

1. The Comprehensive Middle School Survey, a questionnaire that was administered district-wide to measure stakeholder perceptions of various elements of middle schools, such as differentiated instruction, advisor/advisee programs, block scheduling/flexible scheduling, interdisciplinary teaming, school safety and discipline, and parent involvement
2. State-mandated end-of-grade achievement tests, to assess program outcomes

---

16. Glass, G. V (1975). A paradox about excellence of schools and the people in them. *Educational Researcher, 4*(3), 9–13.
17. Ibid., p. 12.
18. For a project evaluation matrix for planning educational evaluations that includes a time line, see: Old, B. M., & Miller, R. L. (1997). A measure of success. *ASEE Prism, 7*, 24–29.

3. Unstructured interviews
4. Informal questionnaires developed for local school use
5. The School Climate and Safety Survey, a questionnaire that measures teachers' and students' perceptions of school safety

In addition, the evaluators worked with the district's research office to revise the Comprehensive Middle School Survey to make it more usable by stakeholders. Factor analysis and structural equation modeling (see Chapter 11) were employed to make the questionnaire shorter and to produce scores for clusters of related items.

Reporting Evaluation Results

A typical research study will yield a single report, for example, a master's thesis, doctoral dissertation, or technical report. A condensed version of the report subsequently might be presented as a paper at a professional conference or published as a journal article.

The reporting of an evaluation study sometimes is more complicated because various types of stakeholders are involved, and each has different information needs. In the middle-school evaluation study, the evaluators collaborated with each school leadership team to produce a school improvement plan that reported analyses of evaluative data and actions to be undertaken based on the analyses. These reports were forwarded to district administrators for their review, and undoubtedly they were shared with other stakeholders as well. In addition, it appears that various informal reports were prepared for internal use by individuals directly involved in the collaborative-evaluation process. Finally, the evaluators prepared a journal article to share their findings with the broader community of evaluation researchers.

If you do an evaluation study of a program for a master's or doctoral degree, you might need to communicate your findings in several forms to meet the needs of the program's administrators and other stakeholders. In addition, you will need to report the results in a thesis or dissertation. Your thesis or dissertation committee probably will require you to use the same format as for reporting a research study. For example, you might need to write an extensive review of the literature, which generally is not found in program evaluation reports.

Your thesis or dissertation should include a discussion of how the evaluation findings were used. This is a matter of considerable interest to evaluation experts. In fact, research has been done on how evaluation findings actually are utilized by decision makers.[19]

Another common feature of evaluation studies reported as theses or dissertations is a discussion of the larger significance of the study. For example, your study's findings might have theoretical significance or might serve as a replication of previous findings on the same problem. If so, you should discuss the study from these perspectives.

Many evaluation projects can be viewed as case studies of the application of a particular evaluation model. If appropriate, the discussion section of your thesis or dissertation should consider the study from this perspective. You can discuss your ideas about the model's applicability to the situation you studied, the shortcomings of the model, and how any problems you encountered might be overcome in future studies. In this way, you can contribute to the improvement of evaluation methodology in education. This perspective is present in the concluding section of the journal article reporting the middle-school evaluation. Strahan and his colleagues identify observed benefits of the cooperative-evaluation model,

19. An example of such a study is: Siegel, K., & Tucker, P. (1985). The utilization of evaluation research: A case analysis. *Evaluation Review, 9,* 307–328.

including the fact that, "Participants in this project seem to be finding ways to complement the 'participatory' involvement of primary stakeholders with perspectives from 'external evaluators'."[20]

At the same time, the authors note as a limitation of their study that, "it is too early to assess the extent to which these practices will result in changes in schooling that are substance [sic] and sustained."[21] They also provide a helpful caution for prospective users of the collaborative-evaluation model: "[O]pportunities for participants to discuss evaluation information and reflect together on this information are essential to collaboration."[22]

Finally, the discussion section of your thesis or dissertation should include a brief meta-evaluation. A **meta-evaluation** is an evaluation of an evaluation.[23] Researchers are obligated to include in their reports a discussion of weaknesses in their research design or in the execution of the study that might affect the validity of the findings. Evaluators have a similar obligation. Professional organizations have published criteria for evaluation research that can be used to judge the adequacy of your own study. These criteria are discussed next.

Criteria for Effective Evaluation Research

Program Evaluation Standards

The *Standards for Evaluation of Educational Programs, Projects, and Materials,* originally published in 1981 and revised in 1994 with the title *Program Evaluation Standards,* provides an authoritative list of criteria for evaluation research.[24] The 30 standards described in the report can be helpful if you intend to do evaluation research for your thesis or dissertation project. You can use the standards as criteria for judging the soundness of your evaluation design and for judging previous evaluation studies in your area of interest.[25]

The standards were developed by the Joint Committee on Standards for Educational Evaluation. The Joint Committee, under the direction of well-known evaluator Daniel Stufflebeam, represented many important organizations in education, including the American Association of School Administrators, American Educational Research Association, American Federation of Teachers, American Personnel and Guidance Association, and National School Boards Association. Several hundred educators nationwide were involved in developing and field-testing the standards. The standards were designed for use in judging the quality of educational evaluations, just as the *Standards for Educational and Psychological Testing* (see Chapter 7) were developed for judging the quality of tests.

The standards were developed for several reasons. First, there was a growing awareness that the technical quality of some evaluation studies was poor and that some studies were insensitive to the entity being evaluated. Another reason was to protect the process of evaluation from being corrupted by individuals or groups with ulterior motives. As we noted in the introduction, educational evaluation usually involves political considerations.

Touchstone in Research

Evaluation Center at Western Michigan University. (n.d.). *Evaluation checklist project.* Retrieved September 13, 2005 from http://www.wmich.edu/evalctr/checklists/

---

20. Strahan, et al., Middle school reform, p. 97.
21. Ibid., pp. 97–98.
22. Ibid., p. 97.
23. A well-designed example of a meta-evaluation is: Mattingly, D. J., Prislin, R., McKenzie, T. L., Rodriguez, J. L., & Kayzar, B. (2002). Evaluating evaluations: The case of parent involvement programs. *Review of Educational Research, 72*(4), 549–576.
24. The Joint Committee on Standards for Educational Evaluation (J. R. Sanders, Chair). (1994). *The program evaluation standards* (2nd ed.). Thousand Oaks, CA: Sage. The standards can also be viewed at http://www.wmich.edu/evalctr/jc/ retrieved October 3, 2005.
25. Another important set of standards was developed by the American Evaluation Association: American Evaluation Association. (1995). Guiding principles for evaluators. In W. R. Shadish, D. L. Newman, M. A. Scheirer, and Wye, C. (Eds.), *New directions for program evaluation,* No. 66 (pp. 19–26). San Francisco: Jossey-Bass.

In the absence of standards, evaluators or clients are more likely to attempt to bend the evaluation process to produce results that reflect their biases and self-interests. Third, the Joint Committee felt that a published set of standards might improve the professionalism of educational evaluation. Also, the Joint Committee found that no adequate standards were available at the time they began their work.

The Joint Committee concluded that a good evaluation study satisfies four important criteria: utility, feasibility, propriety, and accuracy. Table 17.1 presents a definition of each

TABLE 17.1

Criteria and Related Standards for Effective Evaluation

Utility: The extent to which the evaluation is informative, timely, and useful to the affected persons.

1. *Stakeholder identification.* All the groups affected by the evaluation should be identified.
2. *Evaluator credibility.* The evaluator should be competent and trustworthy.
3. *Information scope and selection.* The information to be collected should pertain directly to the evaluation questions and stakeholder concerns.
4. *Values identification.* The evaluators' basis for making value judgments from the obtained results should be made clear.
5. *Report clarity.* The evaluators' report should be comprehensive and easily understood.
6. *Report timeliness and dissemination.* Evaluation reports, including interim reports, should be disseminated to users in a timely manner.
7. *Evaluation impact.* The evaluation should be conducted so as to encourage appropriate action by the stakeholders.

Feasibility: The extent to which the evaluation design is (a) appropriate to the setting in which the study is to be conducted and (b) cost-effective.

1. *Practical procedures.* The evaluation procedures should be practical and minimally disruptive to participants.
2. *Political viability.* The evaluators should obtain the cooperation of affected interest groups and keep any of them from subverting the evaluation process.
3. *Cost effectiveness.* The benefits produced by the evaluation should justify the resources expended on it.

Propriety: The extent to which the evaluation is conducted legally and ethically.

1. *Service orientation.* The evaluation should help stakeholders meet the needs of all their clients and the larger society as well.
2. *Formal agreements.* The formal parties to the evaluation should state their obligations and agreements in a written contract.
3. *Rights of human subjects.* The rights and welfare of persons involved in the evaluation should be protected.
4. *Human interactions.* Evaluators should show respect in their interactions with persons involved in the study.
5. *Complete and fair assessment.* The strengths and weaknesses of the entity being evaluated should be explored completely and fairly.
6. *Disclosure of findings.* Individuals with a legal right to know and those affected by the results should be informed about the evaluation results.
7. *Conflict of interest.* If a conflict of interest should arise, it should be treated openly and honestly.
8. *Fiscal responsibility.* Expenditure of resources for the evaluation should be prudent and ethically responsible.

(Continued)

Accuracy: The extent to which the evaluation produces valid, reliable, and comprehensive information for making judgments of the evaluated program's worth.

1. *Program documentation.* All pertinent aspects of the program being evaluated should be described in detail.
2. *Context analysis.* Aspects of the program's context that affect the evaluation should be described in detail.
3. *Described purposes and procedures.* The evaluation's purposes and procedures should be described in detail.
4. *Defensible information sources.* Sources of data should be described in sufficient detail that their adequacy can be judged.
5. *Valid information.* The data-collection procedures should yield valid interpretations.
6. *Reliable information.* The data-collection procedures should yield reliable findings.
7. *Systematic information.* The evaluation data should be reviewed and corrected, if necessary.
8. *Analysis of quantitative information.* Analysis of quantitative data in an evaluation study should be thorough and should yield clear interpretations.
9. *Analysis of qualitative information.* Analysis of qualitative data in an evaluation study should be thorough and should yield clear interpretations.
10. *Justified conclusions.* Evaluators should provide an explicit justification for their conclusions.
11. *Impartial reporting.* Evaluation reports should be free of bias and of the personal feelings of any of those connected to the evaluation.
12. *Meta-evaluation.* The evaluation should be subjected to formative and summative evaluation using this list of standards.

Source: Adapted from Joint Committee on Standards for Educational Evaluation (J. R. Sanders, Chair). (1994). *The program evaluation standards* (2nd ed.). Thousand Oaks, CA: Sage.

criterion and lists the specific standards that the committee formulated to operationalize each of them. Each standard is listed below the criterion to which it most closely relates. Helpful case studies that illustrate each standard are presented in the Joint Committee's report. The various models of evaluation described in this chapter reflect many of these standards.

Daniel Stufflebeam identified several difficulties that arose in attempts to apply the original (1981) version of the standards.[26] He noted trade-offs in applying the standards. For example, efforts to produce valid and reliable information and develop firm conclusions (accuracy standards 5, 6, and 10) often were found to impede the production of timely reports (utility standard 6). In research on efforts to apply the standards, other problems identified include limited utility outside the United States and in the case of large-scale, government-sponsored studies, inappropriateness to some evaluation problems, lack of detail to guide specific design decisions, and inadequate attention to internal self-evaluations.

Bruce Thompson analyzed the 1994 version of the program evaluation standards and found that the main focus of the Joint Committee was optimizing the instrumental use of evaluation research.[27] Instrumental use refers to the application of an evaluation study's findings to make a go/no-go decision about whether to continue or terminate a program. Thompson noted that there are other types of use, but they were not a direct

26. Stufflebeam, D. L. (1991). Professional standards and ethics for evaluators. In M. W. McLaughlin & D. C. Phillips (Eds.), *Evaluation and education: At quarter century. Ninetieth yearbook of the National Society for the Study of Education: Part II* (pp. 249–282). Chicago: NSSE.
27. Thompson, B. (1994). The revised *Program Evaluation Standards* and their correlation with the evaluation use literature. *Journal of Experimental Education, 63,* 54–81.

focus of the Joint Committee's work. One such type is conceptual use, which refers to the influence of evaluation research findings on how stakeholders think about their program. For example, evaluation research can lead stakeholders to reframe the goals for their program. Another type is symbolic use, which refers to the use of evaluation research findings for purposes beyond those of judging or improving the program. For example, program administrators might commission an evaluation study in order to satisfy their funding agency, or they might use evaluation findings to rationalize decisions that were made for reasons that have little to do with the findings.

Thompson's analysis suggests that whether and how an evaluation study is used are the ultimate criteria for judging its worth. However, there are various ways in which evaluation research findings can be used. If you are planning to do an evaluation study, you should work with the stakeholder groups to determine what the desired uses of the findings are. After deciding on these uses, you then can analyze whether the evaluation design is likely to facilitate them.

Personnel Evaluation Standards

The same Joint Committee that produced the *Program Evaluation Standards* described above also developed standards for evaluation of educational personnel, called the *Personnel Evaluation Standards.*[28] These 21 standards involve the same four criteria specified for the program evaluation standards. The *Personnel Evaluation Standards* have been used for various purposes, including assessing the quality of evaluation systems for teachers[29] and for superintendents.[30]

Other Standards for Educational Evaluation

Stufflebeam has developed a newer set of comprehensive guidelines for use in the evaluation of educational or other service organizations.[31] The document recommends that organizations institutionalize one approach for program, client, and personnel evaluation. It includes checklists defining 18 requirements of a sound evaluation system and describing 10 components of a fully functional evaluation system.

In light of recent social problems, such as inadequate response of governmental agencies to Hurricane Katrina, this evaluation model has much to recommend it. For example, requirement 13, *Assure reciprocity in evaluating all staff,* noting that organizations too often focus personnel evaluation on line personnel such as teachers, recommends that equitable attention be given to evaluation of policy makers and administrators as well as line and support staff. Continuing work on this evaluation model can be accessed at the Western Michigan University Evaluation Center Web site. This Web site has a wealth of publications on the evaluation of many aspects of education.[32]

28. Stufflebeam, D. L. (1988). *The personnel evaluation standards: How to assess systems for evaluating educators.* Thousand Oaks, CA: Corwin.
29. Peterson, K. D., Stevens, D., & Ponzio, R. C. (1998). Variable data sources in teacher education. *Journal of Research and Development in Education, 31,* 123–132.
30. Stufflebeam, D. L. (1994). The troubled state of superintendent performance evaluations. *School Administrator, 51*(11), 12–17.
31. Stufflebeam, D. L. (1997). Strategies for institutionalizing evaluation: Revisited. Occasional paper series #18 of the Evaluation Center, Western Michigan University. Retrieved September 30, 2005, from Web site http://www.wmich.edu/evalctr/ pubs/ops/
32. The Evaluation Center Publications, retrieved October 2, 2005, from Web site http://www.wmich.edu/ evalctr/pubs/ ecpub.htm#Evaluation%20Reports

Also, a booklet is being circulated by the U.S. Institute of Education Sciences to help education practitioners evaluate educational practices supported by rigorous evidence.[33] Describing experimental research involving randomized controlled trials as the gold standard for establishing what works, it provides three steps for evaluating educational interventions. Its recommendations are currently the subject of considerable controversy in educational research, especially among qualitative researchers.[34]

Like educational research, educational evaluation takes diverse forms. This is because evaluators over time have developed different purposes, philosophies, and methodologies for evaluation. These differences gradually led to the development of various approaches to evaluation research. The remaining sections of this chapter describe a number of important quantitative and qualitative approaches to evaluation research.[35] If you are planning to do evaluation studies, you should review these approaches to determine which best suits your purpose and your philosophical orientation to research.

Quantitative Approaches to Evaluation

The quantitative approaches described below rely primarily on positivist methods of inquiry. They emphasize objective measurement, representative sampling, experimental control, and the use of statistical techniques to analyze data.

Evaluation of the Individual

Evaluation research can be traced back at least to the early 1900s, when the performance testing movement began. Binet's intelligence test was published in 1904, and group ability testing began during World War I. Evaluation primarily involved the assessment of individual differences in student intelligence and school achievement. Test results were used for assigning course grades and for selecting students into different ability tracks, special services, or advanced educational programs.

This model of evaluation still is widely followed in American education and has been extended to the systematic evaluation of teachers, administrators, and other school personnel. As in the assessment of students, personnel evaluation focuses on measurement of individual differences, and judgments are made by comparing the individual with a criterion or a set of norms.

Objectives-Based Evaluation

Ralph Tyler's work on curriculum evaluation in the 1940s brought about a major change in educational evaluation.[36] Tyler's view was that the curriculum should be organized around explicit objectives and that its success should be judged on the basis of how well students achieve these objectives. This model marked a shift from a concern with evaluating individual students to a concern with evaluating the curriculum. In doing so, the model acknowledged

33. U.S. Department of Education Institute of Education Sciences National Center for Education Evaluation and Regional Assistance (2003). *Identifying and implementing educational practices supported by rigorous evidence: A user friendly guide.* Washington, DC: Institute of Education Science. Retrieved October 2, 2005, from Web site http://www.ed.gov/ rschstat/research/pubs/rigorousevid/rigorousevid.pdf
34. Smith, J. K., & Hodkinson, P. (2005). Relativism, criteria, and politics. In N. K. Denzin & Y. S. Lincoln, *Sage handbook of qualitative research* (3rd ed., pp. 915–932). Thousand Oaks, CA: Sage.
35. Worthen, B. R., Sanders, J. R., & Fitzpatrick, J. L. (1997). *Educational evaluation: Alternative approaches and practical guidelines* (2nd ed.). New York: Addison Wesley Longman.
36. Tyler, R. W. (1949). *Basic principles of curriculum and instruction: Syllabus for Education 360.* Chicago: University of Chicago Press.

that students might perform poorly not because of lack of innate ability, but because of weaknesses in the curriculum.

Tyler's model has had an important influence on subsequent developments in educational evaluation. The National Assessment of Educational Progress originated in the 1960s under Tyler's leadership. This federal program continues to collect data on the academic achievement of American youth. Many state testing programs collect similar data using this program's methods. The increasing practice of competency testing of students and teachers is another outgrowth of the Tyler model.[37] Evaluation of student competencies has reached unprecedented levels with the implementation of the No Child Left Behind Act in 2002.[38]

Educational evaluators have developed other evaluation models that support Tyler's emphasis on measurement of explicit objectives as the basis for determining an educational program's merit. For example, Malcolm Provus developed **discrepancy evaluation,** which involves assessment of discrepancies between the objectives of an educational program and students' actual achievement of the objectives.[39] The resulting information about discrepancies can be used to guide program management decisions.

Another objectives-based approach is cost analysis.[40] Evaluators use **cost analysis** to determine either: (1) the relationship between the costs of a program and its benefits when both costs and benefits can be calculated in monetary terms (called the *cost-benefit ratio*); or (2) the relationship between the costs of various interventions relative to their measured effectiveness in achieving a desired outcome (called *cost-effectiveness*).[35] Alternative programs can be compared to determine which is most cost-effective, that is, which promotes the greatest benefits for each unit of resource expenditure.

If you are planning a study of students' achievement of instructional objectives, one of your major concerns will be the measurement of those objectives. To facilitate measurement, it is helpful to state objectives in behavioral terms, meaning that the program outcomes are stated as behaviors that anyone, including evaluators, can observe in a program participant.[41] This type of objective, commonly called a **behavioral objective,** usually has three components: statement of the program objective as an observable, behavioral outcome; criteria for successful performance of the behavior; and the situational context in which the behavior is to be performed. Here is an example of a behavioral objective: Given a set of 20 single-digit multiplication problems, the learner will be able to solve them by writing the correct answer beneath each problem in less than three minutes with no more than two errors.

37. For a retrospective discussion of the Tyler approach to program evaluation, see: Tyler, R. W. (1991). General statement on program evaluation. In M. W. McLaughlin & D. C. Phillips (Eds.), *Evaluation and education: At quarter century. Ninetieth yearbook of the National Society for the Study of Education: Part II* (pp. 3–17). Chicago: NSSE.

38. See the No Child Left Behind (NCLB) Web site, http://www.ed.gov/nclb/landing. jhtml?src=pb. For discussions of evaluation issues involved in implementing NCLB, see: Linn, R. L. (2005). Test-based educational accountability in the era of No Child Left Behind. CSE Report 651; and Mintrop, H., & Trujillo, T. (2005). Corrective action in low-performing schools: Lessons for NCLB implementation from state and district strategies in first-generation accountability systems—updated version. CSE Report 657; from http://www.cresst.org

39. Provus, M. (1971). *Discrepancy evaluation for educational program improvement and assessment.* Berkeley, CA: McCutchan.

40. Levin, H. M., & McEwan, P. J. (2000). *Cost-effectiveness analysis: Methods and applications* (2nd ed.). Thousand Oaks, CA: Sage; Hummel-Rossi, B., & Ashdown, J. (2002). The state of cost-benefit and cost-effectiveness analyses in education. *Review of Educational Research, 72*(1), 1–30.

41. Procedures for writing behavioral objectives are explained in many sources; see Mager, R. F. (1997). *Preparing instructional objectives: A critical tool in the development of effective instruction* (3rd ed.). Atlanta, GA: Center for Effective Performance.

Behavioral objectives have been criticized on the grounds that they reduce education to a matter of teaching only that which can be stated and measured in the language of behavioral objectives. Of course, behavioral objectives, like any other technique, can be misused. Used appropriately, however, they simplify the task of developing suitable instruments—especially domain-referenced instruments—to measure the learner's achievement of an objective.

Another issue in objectives-based evaluation is determination of which objectives to measure. Evaluators often rely on the program's developers or subject-matter specialists to make this decision. Michael Scriven, however, argued that evaluators should not know the program goals in advance, because they might become co-opted by them and thus over-look other effects of the program, especially adverse side effects.[42] Scriven suggested that to avoid this problem, evaluators should conduct research to discover the actual effects of the program in operation, which may differ markedly from the program developers' stated goals. This strategy for evaluation has come to be known as **goal-free evaluation.**

Although goal-free evaluation has merit, there are many situations in which an evaluator is expected to collect evaluative data about specific program goals. Even in these situations, however, the evaluator can attend to the stated goals but also remain alert to the possibility that the program may have actual effects (both beneficial and adverse) quite different from those intended by program developers.

An example in education of this phenomenon is the evaluations of DISTAR, Direct Instructional System for Teaching and Remediation, an academic program intended to develop the cognitive skills of low-income disadvantaged children. Although most of the evaluation research on this program has focused on measurement of cognitive skills, self-concept instruments were routinely administered to students involved in the evaluation as well. The evaluation findings demonstrate that DISTAR not only fosters students' cognitive development but also has a positive effect on self-esteem.[43]

Needs Assessment

In evaluation research a **need** can be defined as a discrepancy between an existing set of conditions and a desired set of conditions. For example, suppose an educator makes the assertion, "We need to place more emphasis on developing elementary students' competence in science." The educator is saying in effect that there is a discrepancy between the existing science curriculum and the desired curriculum, as evidenced by problems in many students' learning of science concepts. This statement of need reflects a judgment about the present merit of the curriculum. Also, note that assessment of this need provides a basis for setting objectives for curriculum or program development. Because we consider needs assessment to be closely related to objectives-based models of evaluation, we are treating it as a quantitative approach. Nevertheless, qualitative needs assessments also are conducted in education.[44]

42. Scriven, M. (1973). Goal-free evaluation. In E. R. House (Ed.), *School evaluation: The politics and process* (pp. 319–328). Berkeley, CA: McCutchan.

43. Stebbins, L. B., St. Pierre, R. G., Proper, E. C., Anderson, R. B., & Cerva, T. R. An evaluation of follow through. (1978). In T. D. Cook, M. L. Del Rosario, K. M. Hennigan, M. M. Mark, & W. M. K. Trochim (Eds.), *Evaluation Studies Review Annual, Vol. 3* (pp. 571–610). Beverly Hills, CA: Sage. When very complex programs such as DISTAR are evaluated, many factors tend to vary at each site and it is thus impossible to determine the extent to which the designated intervention accounts for the specific set of outcomes observed. For a discussion of this phenomenon in relation to the Comer School Development Program, see: Cook, T. D., Murphy, R. F., & Hunt, H. D. (2000). Comer's School Development Program in Chicago: A theory-based evaluation. *American Educational Research Journal, 37*(2), 535–597.

44. Altschud, J. W., & Witkin, B. R. (2000). *From needs assessment to action: Transforming needs into solution strategies.* Thousand Oaks, CA: Sage.

Example of Needs Assessment

Quantitative research methods enable researchers to measure the precise *extent* of discrepancy between an existing state and a desired state. An example of such a quantitative needs assessment is a study by Thomas Pierce, Deborah Deutsch Smith, and Jane Clarke.[45] The purpose of their study was to update and expand existing databases on the supply and demand of special education doctoral graduates for filling faculty positions at institutions of higher education (IHEs) in the United States. The discrepancy between the number and types of available doctoral graduates and the number of available faculty positions was viewed as a measure of the need for leadership personnel in special education.

The target population for this study was 85 IHEs listed in *The National Directory of Special Education Personnel Preparation Programs* as having doctoral programs in special education. An abbreviated form of the questionnaire used in the survey is shown in Table 17.2. It includes questions to expand the knowledge base concerning the supply and demand of doctoral level leadership personnel.

TABLE 17.2

Abbreviated Survey Questionnaire to Assess Need for Special Education Leadership Personnel

Special Education Doctoral Survey

1. How many doctoral students are enrolled in your doctoral program in special education for the 1990–1991 academic year?
2. Of this number how many do you expect to graduate in 1990–1991?
3. Of the expected special education doctoral graduates for 1990–1991, in what disability area is their concentration (place number on line):
4. Of those listed in #3 above, are any expected graduates trained for leadership positions in more than one exceptionality area? If so please list number and combination (For example, one individual is qualified in both BD and LD).
5. In your estimation is your currently enrolled doctoral student body: larger than last year; smaller than last year; about the same as last year?
6. If you searched for new faculty last year (1989–1990) please respond to the following. (Surveyed rank, tenure track, disability area, and reason for search.) (If not skip to question #7.)
   Approximately how many applicants did you receive, and how many were qualified? (Separate for multiple positions using position letter above.)
   Did you hire? If no, why not?
7. If you anticipate faculty vacancies or new positions during the next three years (1990–1993), fill out the following (chart included estimated number, disability area, and reason for search).
8. On the following chart please include information requested about each doctoral graduate for the past two years. (Chart included categories on student's name, current position, place of employment, type of agency, emphasis area, and ethnicity.)

Source: Adapted from Table 1 on p. 177 of: Pierce, T. B., Smith, D. D., & Clarke, J. (1992). Special education leadership: Supply and demand revisited. *Teacher Education and Special Education, 15*, 175–182. Adapted with permission from *Teacher Education and Special Education*.

45. Pierce, T. B., Smith, D. D., & Clarke, J. (1992). Special education leadership: Supply and demand revisited. *Teacher Education and Special Education, 15*, 175–182.

TABLE 17.3

Survey Results from Needs Assessment on Special Education Leadership Personnel: Ethnicity of Doctoral Students

Student Group	1988–89	1989–90	Total 1988–90
Anglo students	73	69	142
Students of color			
Black	4	9	13
Hispanic	3	1	4
Asian	4*	10**	14
Native American	2	0	2
Total students of color	13	20	33
Unknown	9	0	9
Total, all students	95	89	184

*Includes 2 students from other countries
**Includes 6 students from other countries

Source: Adapted from Table 2 on p. 177 in: Pierce, T. B., Smith, D. D., & Clarke, J. (1992). Special education leadership: Supply and demand revisited. *Teacher Education and Special Education, 15,* 175–182. Adapted with permission from *Teacher Education and Special Education*.

The questionnaire was sent to the department chairperson of each IHE, and after one month was followed up with a letter. The sample consisted of 55 returned questionnaires, which represents a 65 percent response rate. Simple tallies were made, and percentages were calculated for each item on the questionnaire. In cases of no response, the item for that questionnaire was not entered in the database.

A total of 221 doctoral students were found to have graduated from the 55 institutions in the sample during the two-year period 1988–1990. Responses were obtained concerning the ethnicity of 184 of these doctoral students. As shown in Table 17.3, 18 percent of these graduate students ($33 \div 184$) were reported to be students of color, or 14 percent ($25 \div 176$) if the eight students from other countries are eliminated from the calculations.

The researchers also obtained data on the positions taken by the 221 doctoral students who graduated from institutions in the sample during the two-year period 1988–1990. Only 38 percent took permanent IHE positions. Twenty-five percent took positions with state or local education agencies, 5 percent went into private practice, 4 percent remained unemployed, and the remaining 28 percent took other types of positions.

Respondents identified 55 available positions at their institutions during the 1989–1990 academic year, of which 80 percent were tenure-track positions. Fifteen of the 55 positions

(27 percent) remained unfilled at the time of the survey. When asked to indicate why they did not hire individuals for the advertised positions, the most frequently cited reason was inappropriate qualifications or unacceptability of applicants. Respondents also predicted their institution's need for faculty for the next three academic years (1990–1993), and the reasons for this need. A total of 71 openings was projected, and the most common reason (45 percent) was to fill positions vacated through retirements.

The survey results highlight the need to resupply faculties that are diminishing due to retirements and vacancies. Besides the general problem of inadequately qualified candidates, the researchers commented on the low percentage of ethnic minorities among doctoral graduates: "special education appears to have a very limited pool of future applicants who come from culturally and linguistically diverse backgrounds."[46] They also observed that the total pool of graduates of doctoral programs in special education is declining.

The survey by Pierce and his co-researchers provides useful information to faculty and administrators in special education at IHEs concerning the need for new faculty, and the size and characteristics of the pool of graduates available to fill this need. This information could be used in designing recruitment or retention programs for doctoral students who have the characteristics desired of special education faculty members.

Limitations of Needs Assessment

Despite its appeal, needs assessment has some limitations. One involves the definition of *need*. Exactly what is a *desired* set of conditions? J. Roth identified five types of desired states: ideals, norms, minimums, desires (wants), and expectations.[47] A need can be a discrepancy between an actual state and any one of these five desired states. For example, the goal of a college education for all citizens who desire one (an ideal desired state) is certainly a different kind of desired state from the goal of basic skill in reading for all children (a minimum desired state).

Many needs assessments do not make clear the degree to which the desired states that are being determined are viewed as urgent or optional. For example, the study concerning special education leadership supply and demand did not address the level of urgency of the need for more doctoral graduates from culturally and linguistically diverse backgrounds. A percentage comparison of the ethnic backgrounds of students served by special education with those of doctoral students graduating from the sample institutions would have helped pinpoint the urgency of recruiting doctoral students from various ethnic groups to better serve the needs of special education students.

Another limitation of needs assessment is that the values underlying stated needs often are not clearly articulated. It is helpful to determine quantitatively the extent to which certain groups view particular elements of education (e.g., small class size, compulsory school prayer, computer-assisted instruction) as needs. These quantitative expressions of need just scratch the surface, though. Personal values and standards are important determinants of needs, and they too should be assessed to develop a thorough understanding of needs among the groups being studied.

A potential problem with quantitative methods of evaluation generally is that such methods rarely explore fully the differences among different types of stakeholders in their perceptions of worth. In the needs assessment of special education leadership, for example, the researchers obtained only the perspective of university administrators concerning the need. The researchers accepted the judgments of their survey respondents (chair-

---

46. Ibid., p. 181.
47. Roth, J. (1977). Needs and the needs assessment process. *Evaluation News, 5,* 15–17.

persons of special education departments at institutions of higher education) as to the qualifications of doctoral graduates who interviewed for available positions at those institutions. The researchers did not examine the possibility that different chairpersons—or different faculty members within a chairperson's department—might have had different notions about the applicants' qualifications.

You also should be aware that needs-assessment data usually are reported as group trends. Individual differences in stated needs should also be explored. For example, in the study on special education leadership needs, a helpful feature of the data analysis was the number of doctoral graduates of various ethnic backgrounds (shown in Table 17.3.)

A needs assessment is a feasible evaluation project to do as a master's or doctoral study. The primary requirement is having a measure of the target group's current behavior or achievement and a standard against which to compare it. If you are interested in doing curriculum development as part of your professional career, you might consider doing a needs assessment in a curriculum content area that particularly interests you.

Context–Input–Process–Product (CIPP) Evaluation

The approaches described above are designed to provide "arm's length" evaluations of programs, meaning that the evaluator serves as the primary decision maker in determining the specifics of what it is to be evaluated and how to evaluate it. In other approaches to evaluation, evaluators work more closely with the staff of ongoing programs or programs under development. They usually become interested in how they can contribute to the process of program management and program development. Evaluators often collect data to help program managers make critical decisions.

The **CIPP model** was formulated by Daniel Stufflebeam and his colleagues to show how evaluation can contribute to the decision-making process in program management.[48] CIPP is an acronym for the four types of phenomena that are typically evaluated by users of this evaluation model: **C**ontext, **I**nput, **P**rocess, and **P**roduct. Each type of phenomenon involves a different set of decisions that are made in the planning and operation of an evaluation.

Each type of evaluation requires three broad tasks to be performed: delineating the kinds of information needed for decision making, obtaining the information, and synthesizing the information so that it is useful in making decisions. The first and third steps (delineation and synthesis) should be done as a collaborative effort between evaluator and decision maker. The second step, obtaining the information, is a technical activity that can be delegated primarily to the evaluator.

Context evaluation involves the identification of problems and needs that occur in a specific educational setting, which provides an essential basis for developing objectives whose achievement results in program improvement.

Input evaluation involves the collection of information to make judgments about the resources and strategies needed to accomplish program goals and objectives and to determine constraints, such as whether certain resources are unavailable or too expensive. It also involves determining how well a particular strategy is likely to achieve program goals, whether certain strategies are legally or morally acceptable, and how best to utilize personnel as resources. Input evaluation requires the evaluator to have a wide range of

---

48. The CIPP model is described in: Stufflebeam, D. L., & Shinkfield, A. J. (1985). *Systematic evaluation: A self-instructional guide to theory and practice.* Boston: Kluwer-Nijhoff. See also: Stufflebeam, D. L. (2003). The CIPP model for evaluation. In T. Kellaghan & D. L. Stufflebeam (Eds.), *International handbook of educational evaluation* (pp. 31–62). Boston: Kluwer.

knowledge about possible resources and strategies, as well as knowledge about research on their effectiveness in achieving different types of program outcomes.

Process evaluation involves the collection of evaluative data to monitor the program in day-to-day operation. For example, you might keep attendance records on a school district's staff development program based on voluntary participation. If attendance data reveal deviations from what was anticipated (for example, a decline in teachers' attendance at training sessions over time), program decision makers can take action based on their appraisal of the data. Without such a record-keeping system, the program might deteriorate before decision makers became aware of such operational problems. Another function of process evaluation is to keep records of program events over a period of time. These records might prove useful at a later time in detecting strengths and weaknesses of the program that account for its observed outcomes.

Product evaluation involves determining the extent to which the goals of the program have been achieved. In this type of evaluation, measures of the goals are developed and administered, and the resulting data are used to make decisions about continuing or modifying the program.

You may have noted that the CIPP model incorporates elements of objectives-based evaluation and needs assessment, which were described previously. It also resembles formative and summative evaluation, which are described below in our discussion of educational research and development. The CIPP model is distinguished by its comprehensiveness, the fact that it is an ongoing process, and its purpose of guiding the decision-making process in program management. Although used primarily in quantitative evaluation research, it can be adapted for evaluation research from a qualitative perspective.

The CIPP model has proved useful in guiding the work of evaluation staffs in school districts and governmental agencies. To complete all four stages would be difficult in a thesis or dissertation project, so one of the other models described above might be preferable. Nevertheless, you might do an evaluation study involving collaboration with an agency that uses the CIPP model or one similar to it. In this case you should be familiar with the model, so that you can determine how your study fits into the agency's total evaluation process and the kinds of data and other resources that might be available to you.

Qualitative Approaches to Evaluation

The approaches to evaluation described above, while useful, are not suited for addressing several important aspects of evaluation. The objectives-based approaches, for example, tend to take a program's objectives or observed effects as givens. They do not offer much guidance as to why particular objectives are valued or why certain stakeholders agree or do not agree on the worth of certain objectives.

The politics of evaluation also are not given serious attention in most quantitative approaches. Various groups with a stake in the outcome of an evaluation study may try to influence the evaluation process. As the evaluator, should you resist these political influences or try to incorporate them into the design of an evaluation study? Another problem is that evaluations may do more harm than good under certain conditions. As we stated above, most people do not like being evaluated, so the evaluation process itself might hamper the very performance that is being assessed. How can evaluators work with clients so that the evaluation produces the most benefit and the least harm?

To address these questions and others, researchers have developed approaches to evaluation that rely heavily on the qualitative research approaches that we described in Part V.

Touchstones in Research

House, E. R. (2005). Qualitative evaluation and changing social policy. In N. K. Denzin & Y. S. Lincoln (Eds.), *Sage handbook of qualitative research* (3rd ed., pp. 1069–1081). Thousand Oaks, CA: Sage.

Smith, J. K., & Hodkinson, P. (2005). Relativism, criteria, and politics. In N. K. Denzin & Y. S. Lincoln (Eds.), *Sage handbook of qualitative research* (3rd ed., pp. 915–932). Thousand Oaks, CA: Sage.

Patton, M. Q. (2002). *Qualitative research and evaluation methods* (3rd ed.). Thousand Oaks, CA: Sage.

These approaches to evaluation differ most clearly from quantitative methods in not assuming that objective criteria exist for judging the worth of an educational program. Rather, qualitative approaches are based on the assumption that the worth of an educational program depends heavily on the values and perspectives of those doing the judging. Therefore, the selection of the individuals and groups to be involved in the evaluation is critical.

In their concern for grasping the emic perspective, qualitative researchers thus put special emphasis on the examination of different stakeholders' perceptions of worth. For example, suppose that a qualitative evaluation researcher has carried out a study of the need for more special education faculty, as Pierce and his colleagues did in the quantitative study we described earlier. Most likely this researcher will have used more open-ended methods to ask about the desired qualifications of special education leadership personnel. The researcher might also have sought to examine the need as perceived by such stakeholder groups as faculty members, university students in special education, practicing special education teachers, or families receiving special education school services. The qualitative approaches to evaluation described next all emphasize the importance of mining the perspectives of all relevant stakeholder groups with respect to the program or phenomenon being evaluated. In the process, they utilize a variety of data-collection methods, with emphasis on the qualitative data-collection methods described in Chapters 8, 9, and 14.

Responsive Evaluation

Robert Stake pioneered the qualitative approach to educational evaluation.[49] His approach, called **responsive evaluation,** focuses on addressing the concerns and issues of stakeholders. A concern is any matter about which stakeholders feel threatened, or any claim that they want to substantiate. An issue is any point of contention among stakeholders. Concerns and issues provide a much wider focus for evaluation than do the behavioral objectives that are the primary focus of some quantitative approaches to evaluation.

Example of Responsive Evaluation

Egon Guba and Yvonna Lincoln identify four major phases that occur in a responsive evaluation: (1) initiating and organizing the evaluation, (2) identifying key issues and concerns, (3) gathering useful information, and (4) reporting results effectively and making recommendations.[50] They describe a responsive evaluation of the governance structure of a particular school system. The focus of the evaluation was whether this school system's governance structure was open to inputs from various stakeholder groups in establishing school policy.

During the first phase, stakeholders were identified. They included school board members, school administrators, school teachers, students and their parents, the mayoral staff of the city in which the school system was located, and influential members of the community. During this phase, Guba and Lincoln recommend that the evaluator and client negotiate an evaluation contract that specifies such matters as identification of the

49. Stake, R. E. (1967). The countenance of educational evaluation. *Teachers College Record, 68,* 523–540; Stake, R. E. (1978). The case study method in social inquiry. *Educational Researcher, 7*(2), 5–8. A more recent discussion of responsive evaluation by its originator is provided in: Stake, R. E. (1991). Retrospective on "The countenance of educational evaluation." In M. W. McLaughlin & D. C. Phillips (Eds.), *Evaluation and education: At quarter century* (pp. 67–88). Chicago: University of Chicago Press.
50. Guba, E. G., & Lincoln, Y. S. (1981). *Effective evaluation: Improving the usefulness of evaluation results through responsive and naturalistic approaches.* San Francisco: Jossey-Bass.

entity to be evaluated, the purpose of the evaluation, rights of access to records, and guarantees of confidentiality and anonymity.

During the second phase, several key issues and concerns were identified through interviews with stakeholders. Key issues included whether formulation of school policy should be centralized or decentralized, whether policy should be formulated by professionals or by lay groups, and whether the school board should be elected or appointed. The concerns included perceptions of citizen lockout from decision making (for example, the school board was accused of having eliminated the elementary art education program despite parental opposition to the move), and of arrogation of power by a small elite (for example, members of the school staff said that they felt they had little say in school affairs). Such issues and concerns express the different underlying values of different stakeholders. For example, some—but by no means all—stakeholders were found to place great value on a high-quality curriculum, a rational decision-making process, equality of representation in decision making, and accountability.

In the third phase, the evaluators collected more information about the issues, concerns, and values identified by the stakeholders. They also collected descriptive information about the entity being evaluated (the school system's governance structure) and about standards that would be used in making judgments about this entity. Such information can be collected through various methods, including naturalistic observation, interviews, questionnaires, and standardized tests. For example, in the evaluation of the school system's governance structure, some stakeholders were concerned that the school board had disposed of the elementary art education program despite parental opposition. The evaluator could reconstruct this occurrence (i.e., formulate a tentative description of what occurred) to determine whether the information substantiates their concern.

The final phase of a responsive evaluation is to prepare reports of results and recommendations. Frequently a case study format (see Chapter 14) is used in such reports, but when appropriate, a traditional research format (see Chapter 2) can be used. A responsive evaluation report will contain extensive descriptions of the issues and concerns identified by stakeholders. Guba and Lincoln also recommend that the evaluator—in negotiation with the stakeholders—make judgments and recommendations based on the gathered information. In this particular respect, their model is similar to the collaborative-evaluation model, which we described earlier in the chapter.

Emergent Design

Unlike the other types of evaluation research described above, evaluators doing a responsive evaluation do not specify a research design at the outset of their work. Instead, responsive evaluators use an **emergent design,** meaning that the design of the research changes as the evaluators gain new insights into the concerns and issues of stakeholders. For example, Guba and Lincoln describe the sampling techniques in emergent as compared to traditional research design:

> Sampling is almost never representative or random but purposive, intended to exploit competing views and fresh perspectives as fully as possible. Sampling stops when information becomes redundant rather than when subjects are representatively sampled.[51]

This view of sampling is consistent with the purposeful sampling methods of qualitative research described in Chapter 6.

---

51. Ibid., p. 276.

Fourth-Generation Evaluation

Since their book on responsive evaluation appeared, Guba and Lincoln further conceptualized their approach to evaluation and renamed it *fourth-generation evaluation*.[52] The 12 steps of fourth-generation evaluation are shown in Figure 17.1. According to Guba and Lincoln, these steps are not necessarily linear:

> Rather, the chart indicates progression only in a general way; it is the case that frequent back and forth movement, sometimes involving jumps over multiple steps, is not only possible but desirable.[53]

You will note that the chart makes reference to hermeneutic circles as part of the evaluation process. Hermeneutics is a qualitative research tradition that we described in Chapter 15. A **hermeneutic circle** is a process of interpretation that involves interpreting the meaning of each part of a text and the text as a whole. Interpretation of the text as a whole helps interpretation of the parts and vice versa. In the context of responsive evaluation, the *text* would be all the materials and data that have been collected as part of the evaluation study.

Responsive evaluation and fourth generation evaluation represent important developments in educational evaluation. However, the student who is considering using one of these approaches for a thesis or dissertation study must understand that these types of evaluation are usually complex, and are best carried out by a team of evaluators rather than by an individual working alone. Members of a team can act as a check on each other and ensure that a comprehensive picture of the entity being evaluated is formed. Also, the responsive evaluator should be conversant with a variety of research designs ranging from formal experiments to ethnographic inquiry. The reason for this requirement is that emergent design requires the selection of different research methodologies depending upon the phenomenon being investigated at a particular point in the evaluation.

If you plan to use the responsive or fourth-generation approach to evaluation as a guide for your thesis or dissertation study, you should consider finding an experienced team of evaluators with whom you can work. Perhaps the team already is engaged in planning or conducting a responsive evaluation study. You could then select one set of issues as a focus for your project.

Quasi-Legal Models of Evaluation

Adversary evaluation and judicial evaluation are two approaches to evaluation modeled on procedures derived from the field of law.

Adversary Evaluation

Adversary evaluation is distinguished by the use of a wide array of data; the hearing of testimony; and, most importantly, an adversarial approach, meaning that the two sides present positive and negative judgments, respectively, about the program being evaluated. [54]

The following are the four stages of adversary evaluation: (1) generating a broad range of issues concerning the program by surveying various stakeholders; (2) reducing the issues to a manageable number, e.g., through priority ranking by a group of volunteers; (3) formation of two opposing evaluation teams, each of which prepares an argument

---

52. Guba, E. G., & Lincoln, Y. S. (1989). *Fourth generation evaluation.* Thousand Oaks, CA: Sage.
53. Ibid., p. 185.
54. Wolf, R. L. (1975). Trial by jury: A new evaluation method. *Phi Delta Kappan, 57*, 185–187.

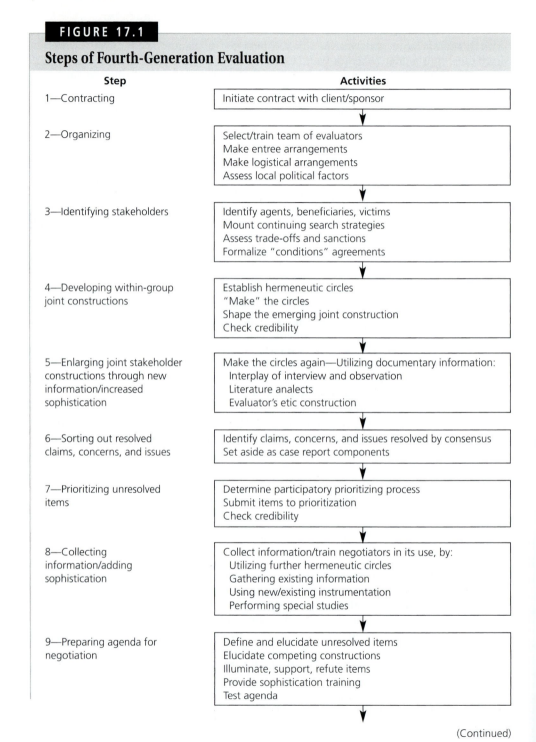

FIGURE 17.1

Steps of Fourth-Generation Evaluation

Step	Activities
1—Contracting	Initiate contract with client/sponsor
2—Organizing	Select/train team of evaluators Make entree arrangements Make logistical arrangements Assess local political factors
3—Identifying stakeholders	Identify agents, beneficiaries, victims Mount continuing search strategies Assess trade-offs and sanctions Formalize "conditions" agreements
4—Developing within-group joint constructions	Establish hermeneutic circles "Make" the circles Shape the emerging joint construction Check credibility

5—Enlarging joint stakeholder constructions through new information/increased sophistication	Make the circles again—Utilizing documentary information:
	    Interplay of interview and observation
	    Literature analects
	    Evaluator's etic construction

6—Sorting out resolved claims, concerns, and issues	Identify claims, concerns, and issues resolved by consensus Set aside as case report components
7—Prioritizing unresolved items	Determine participatory prioritizing process Submit items to prioritization Check credibility

8—Collecting information/adding sophistication	Collect information/train negotiators in its use, by:
	    Utilizing further hermeneutic circles
	    Gathering existing information
	    Using new/existing instrumentation
	    Performing special studies

9—Preparing agenda for negotiation	Define and elucidate unresolved items Elucidate competing constructions Illuminate, support, refute items Provide sophistication training Test agenda

(Continued)

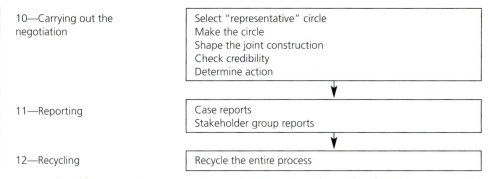

10—Carrying out the negotiation	Select "representative" circle Make the circle Shape the joint construction Check credibility Determine action
11—Reporting	Case reports Stakeholder group reports
12—Recycling	Recycle the entire process

Source: Adapted from Figure 7.1 on pp. 186–187 in: Guba, E. G., and Lincoln, Y. S. (1989). *Fourth generation evaluation*. Thousand Oaks, CA: Sage. Copyright © 1989 by Sage Publications. Reprinted by permission of Sage Publications, Inc.

either in favor of or in opposition to the program on each issue; and (4) conduct of prehearing sessions and a formal hearing, in which the adversarial teams present their cases before those who must make a decision about the program.

Adversary evaluation was used by the National Institute of Education to evaluate minimum competency testing programs at a time when there was considerable controversy about this form of testing.[55] Two teams argued the merits of these programs before a hearings officer, who arbitrated disagreements over qualifications of witnesses and admissibility of testimony. The jury feature, sometimes recommended for adversary evaluation, was not included.

Adversary evaluation has proved useful in exposing strengths and weaknesses of programs and in raising questions that need to be answered. However, evaluators also have discovered that adversary evaluation has shortcomings.[56] Its results can be biased if one of the evaluation teams is more skilled in argumentation than the other. Some evaluators have modified elements of the model to deal with such problems.[57] However, other problems with this approach are built into the evaluation design, and hence are not easily modified. First of all, by its very nature adversary evaluation promotes a combative, "innocent vs. guilty" approach to program evaluation, which may contribute to further opposition among different types of stakeholders. Second, adversary evaluation requires a great deal of time and a large number of people, and thus is very expensive. These problems may explain why very few adversary evaluations can be found in the educational research literature.

Judicial Evaluation

The **judicial evaluation** model simulates the use of legal procedures for the purpose of promoting broad understanding of a program, clarifying the subtle and complex nature of the educational issues it raises, and producing recommendations and policy guidelines

55. Thurston, P., & House, E. R. (1981). The NIE adversary hearing on minimum competency testing. *Phi Delta Kappan, 63,* 87–89.
56. Popham, W. J., & Carlson, D. (1977). Deep dark deficits of the adversary evaluation model. *Educational Researcher, 6*(6), 3–6. See also: Thurston, P. (1978). Revitalizing adversary evaluation: Deep dark deficits or muddled mistaken musings. *Educational Researcher, 7*(7), 3–8.
57. See, for example, Wood, K. C., Peterson, S. E., De Gracie, J. S., & Zaharis, J. K. (1986). The jury is in: Use of a modified legal model for school program evaluation. *Educational Evaluation and Policy Analysis, 8,* 309–315.

that lead to institutional growth and/or improved practice.[58] Unlike adversary evaluation, the judicial evaluation model does not involve a debate between two evaluation teams, with victory or persuasion the desired outcome.

In judicial evaluation, a public presentation of the data is made, following the format of hearings in a court of law. A panel comprised of policy makers, citizens, and other interested stakeholders is convened to hear the evidence. Case presenters call witnesses who present their views in order to make a case relative to a given issue. All witnesses may be subjected to two phases of direct examination and cross examination by two case presenters. As in a court of law, opening and closing arguments are presented. After all evidence is presented, the panel deliberates and makes its recommendations.

Judicial evaluation has proved useful in both formative and summative evaluations of educational programs. While a full-fledged judicial evaluation tends to be expensive and time consuming, the procedure can be scaled down without sacrificing its essential quasi-legal nature.

Expertise-Based Evaluation

The use of experts to make judgments about the worth of an educational program is a time-honored and widely used method of evaluation, called **expertise-based evaluation.** For example, most institutional programs are reviewed periodically by accreditation boards composed of individuals with considerable knowledge and professional experience related to the phenomena with which the institution is concerned. Commissions that include such experts, along with laypersons who wish to contribute to efforts to improve educational programs, often are used to appraise the status of some aspect of the educational enterprise. An example is the National Commission on Excellence in Education, which produced the influential report *A Nation at Risk.*[59] If you do a thesis or dissertation project, its quality will be judged by a panel of professors who are in a similar role, because of their presumed expertise. Expertise-based evaluation has taken a new form with the rapid growth in the use of qualitative research traditions in education. Educational anthropologists, for example, can use the qualitative research method of ethnography to evaluate, as well as to describe, the phenomena that interest them.

Educational Connoisseurship and Criticism

A specific form of expertise-based evaluation is educational connoisseurship and criticism, which was developed by Elliott Eisner, an art educator.[60] This approach involves two aspects: connoisseurship and criticism. The first aspect, **connoisseurship,** is the process of appreciating (in the sense of becoming aware of) the qualities of an educational program and their meaning. To perform this role well, the connoisseur must have expert knowledge of the program being evaluated as well as of other relevant programs. This expertise is similar to that of an art critic who has a special appreciation of a work of art because of intensive study of related works of art and of art theory. An educational connoisseur will be aware of more nuances of an educational program than will a novice educator or lay person. The second aspect, educational **criticism,** is the process of describing and evaluating that which has been appreciated.

58. Wolf, R. L. (1990). Judicial evaluation. In H. J. Walberg & G. D. Haertel (Eds.), *The international encyclopedia of educational evaluation* (pp. 79–81). New York: Pergamon.
59. National Commission on Excellence in Education. (1983). *A nation at risk: The imperative for educational reform.* Washington, DC: U. S. Government Printing Office.
60. Eisner, E. W. (2002). *The educational imagination: On the design and evaluation of school programs* (3rd ed.). Upper Saddle River, NJ: Prentice Hall.

The quality of educational connoisseurship and criticism depends heavily on the expertise of the evaluator. This condition also is a prominent feature of the other qualitative approaches to evaluation described above. Educational criticism differs from responsive evaluation and quasi-legal approaches to evaluation, however, in that it tends to be a solitary endeavor, and the questions that motivate the inquiry usually are set by the evaluator alone rather than in conjunction with stakeholders.

Example of Expertise-Based Evaluation

Gail McCutcheon used the method of educational connoisseurship and criticism in a case study of a fourth-grade classroom.[61] The purpose of the study was to answer several questions about the classroom: What is going on here? Is it worth doing? Was it done well? What are children likely to learn as a result? Notice that several of the questions call for description, and several clearly call for evaluation.

McCutcheon did six weeks of fieldwork in the teacher's classroom, collecting data by means of observation, videotaping, interviews, and inspection of student work. The descriptive part of her report uses a literary style to capture certain qualities of the teacher's classroom. The opening paragraph of the report exemplifies her writing style:

> Myriad sounds, smells, and sights greet the newcomer to Mr. Clement's room. The squeal of a guinea pig and the scrabbling of rats in their wire cages mingle with the voices of children as they discuss their private lives and schoolwork. Penny wants to know whether Maria and Freddie like each other because they sit together. Laura asks Mr. Clement if she may go to the library as another girl returns triumphantly, holding up *Mrs. Piggle Wiggle,* apparently a treasure. The smells of guinea pigs, rats, clean wood shavings, school disinfectant, and a freshly peeled orange intermix. Randy is eating raisins.[62]

Later parts of the report are evaluative, as illustrated by the following comments:

(1) In this lesson, then, children had the opportunity to learn many things—things about the solar system, construction, visual problem-solving, self-control, and social interaction. We might wonder, though, whether responsibility for decision-making, planning socially, and self-control are worthwhile lessons . . . don't children learn these responsibilities anyway—in the home, the community, and school without so much emphasis being placed upon them?[63]

(2) When school is seen as an integral part of children's lives, children may be more likely to apply school learning and to consider doing schoollike things at home. A more unified life may make schooling seem more relevant. The less formal setting of this classroom and Mr. Clement's acknowledging the existence of children's personal interests may work toward this end.[64]

Note that the first evaluative comment is critical, whereas the second is complimentary. An evaluator needs to be sensitive to both the strengths and the weaknesses of the program being evaluated.

This study illustrates how educational connoisseurship and criticism can illuminate the nature and value of a program—in this case, fourth-grade instruction—in a way that would be difficult to accomplish using quantitative evaluation methods. According to Guba and Lincoln, this approach to educational evaluation was the first model to break cleanly with the traditional quantitative research paradigm.[65]

61. McCutcheon, G. (1978). Of solar systems, responsibilities, and basics: An educational criticism of Mr. Clement's fourth grade. In Willis, G. (Ed.), *Qualitative evaluation: Concepts and cases in curriculum criticism* (pp. 188–205). Berkeley, CA: McCutchan.
62. Ibid., p. 192.
63. Ibid., p. 199.
64. Ibid., p. 202.
65. Guba & Lincoln (1989), *Fourth generation evaluation.*

At the same time, the credibility of the findings from educational connoisseurship and criticism is entirely dependent on the expertise of the researcher-critic. Therefore, it would be desirable to replicate the findings by additional case studies, preferably carried out by other researcher-critics. Alternatively, the findings could be considered tentative knowledge claims and further tested for soundness with quantitative research methods.

If you are planning to do an evaluation study using educational connoisseurship and criticism, you first should make a careful study of this approach and the related qualitative approaches that we described in Part V. Also, you should determine whether you have sufficient expertise about the educational phenomenon that you intend to describe and evaluate. This means being knowledgeable about other programs, past and present, that are similar to the one you will study. You should keep in mind that expertise is one of the most important qualifications of an educational critic, just as it is one of the most important qualifications of a literary or art critic.

Empowerment Evaluation

Empowerment evaluation is a recent form of evaluation in which a community uses self-evaluation and reflection to improve its programs.[66] Communities conduct their own evaluation, with an external evaluator acting as coach and facilitator. A variety of technological tools are used to facilitate communication, data collection, and analysis.

This evaluation approach, which is primarily but not exclusively qualitative, is guided by a set of 10 principles: (1) improvement, (2) community ownership, (3) inclusion, (4) democratic participation, (5) social justice, (6) community knowledge, (7) evidence-based strategies, (8) capacity building, (9) organizational learning, and (10) accountability.[67]

The evaluation process includes three key steps:

1. Establishing the mission or vision of the community, with the evaluator serving as coach or critical friend.
2. Taking stock, which involves an assessment of the community baseline, or where it is in its efforts.
3. Planning for the future, which involves developing goals, strategies, and evidence. Traditional evaluation methods, such as interviews and surveys, are used cyclically to test whether strategies are working and to allow the community to make midcourse corrections. To measure growth or change over time, the community then conducts another assessment of its activities and compares the findings to the initial baseline assessment.

Example of Empowerment Evaluation

Through the Digital Village Program a computer company provided technology to help three communities "across the digital divide."[68] Videoconferencing allowed people at sites remote from an American Indian reservation to participate in mission building, taking stock, and priority setting, and itself represented documentation of the group's accomplishments. At other sites digital photographs were used to document problems with student discipline in schools and to demonstrate the positive impact of distributing laptop computers to students and teachers.

66. Fetterman, D. M. (2001). *Foundations of empowerment evaluation.* Thousand Oaks, CA: Sage.
67. Fetterman, D. M., & Wandersman, A. (Eds.). (2004). *Empowerment evaluation principles in practice.* New York: Guilford.
68. Fetterman, D. M. (n.d.). Empowerment evaluation's technological tools of the trade. Harvard Family Research Project, beyond basic training, *The Evaluation Exchange,* 8–9; retrieved October 6, 2005, from http://www.stanford.edu/~davidf/documents/HarvardEvalExch.pdf Also see: Fetterman, D. M. (2002). Web surveys to digital movies: Technological tools of the trade. *Educational Researcher, 31*(6), 29–37.

Educational Research and Development

Evaluation plays a key role in educational research and development (R&D). **Research and development** is an industry-based development model in which the findings of research are used to design new products and procedures, which then are systematically field-tested, evaluated, and refined until they meet specified criteria of effectiveness, quality, or similar standards. Beginning in the 1960–1970 decade, the U.S. government sought to foster educational research and development as a means to reduce the gap between research and practice through funding of educational R&D centers at major universities and independent educational R&D laboratories.[69] The Institute of Education Sciences, established in 2002, is currently the research arm of the Department of Education, with responsibility for federal funding of educational R&D.[70] A survey of research and development expenditures at universities and colleges from the National Science Foundation showed academic R&D expenditures rising 17 percent between 2001 and 2003, with the medical and biological sciences receiving one-half of the total funding.[71] Of a total of $1.4 billion in non-science and engineering R&D funds for 2003, the largest amount ($0.6 billion) supported education research, which represents slightly over 1 percent.[72] Educational R&D holds great promise for improving education because it involves a close connection between systematic program evaluation and program development.

Touchstones in Research

Borg, W. R. (1987). The educational R & D process: Some insights. *Journal of Experimental Education, 55,* 181–188.

Organization for Economic Cooperation and Development. (1995). *Educational research and development: Trends, issues and challenges.* Paris: OECD.

R&D Model

A widely used model of educational research and development is the systems approach model designed by Walter Dick, Lou Carey, and James Carey, which is shown in Figure 17.2. Ten steps are included in this version of the R&D cycle.[73] Step 1 involves the identification of goals for the instructional program or product, which often includes a needs assessment. Steps 2 and 3 may occur in either order, or simultaneously. In step 2, an instructional analysis is undertaken to identify the specific skills, procedures, and learning tasks that are involved in reaching the goals of instruction. Step 3 is designed to identify the learners' entry-level skills and attitudes, the characteristics of the instructional setting, and the characteristics of the settings in which the new knowledge and skills will be used. Step 4 involves translating the needs and goals of instruction into specific performance objectives. Performance objectives (described earlier in the chapter as behavioral objectives) provide a means for communicating about the goals of the instructional program or product at different levels with different types of stakeholders. They also provide the basis for precise planning of assessment instruments, instructional strategies, and instructional materials.

During step 5, assessment instruments are developed. These instruments should be directly related to the knowledge and skills specified in the performance objectives. In step 6 a specific instructional strategy is developed for assisting learners with their efforts to achieve each performance objective. Step 7 involves the development of instructional materials,

69. For a critical account of U.S. federal funding of educational research and development through the 1990s, see: Vinovskis, M. A. (2001). *Revitalizing federal education research and development: Improving the R&D centers, regional educational laboratories, and the "new" OERI.* Ann Arbor: University of Michigan.

70. For current information, see the Institute of Education Sciences Web site, retrieved October 2, 2005, from http://www.ed.gov/about/offices/list/ies/index.html

71. Jankowski, J. E. (2005). Academic R&D doubled during past decade, reaching $40 billion in FY 2003. InfoBrief NSF 05-315, Division of Science Resources Statistics. Arlington, VA: National Science Foundation; retrieved October 4, 2005, from http:///www.nsf.gov/statistics/infbrief/nsf05315

72. Ibid.

73. Dick, W., Carey, L., & Carey, J.O. (2005). *The systematic design of instruction* (6th ed.). New York: Allyn & Bacon. Another R&D model is presented in: Gagné, R. M., Briggs, L. J., & Wager, W. W. (1992). *Principles of instructional design* (3rd ed.). New York: Holt, Rinehart and Winston.

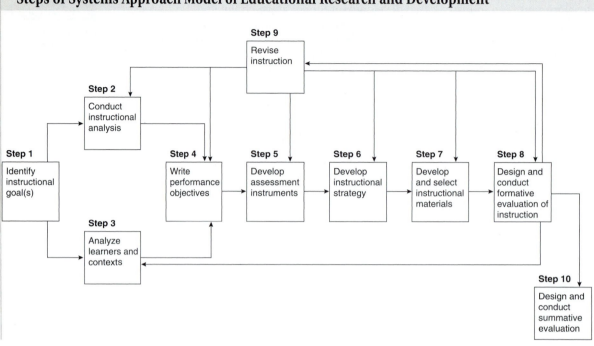

FIGURE 17.2

Steps of Systems Approach Model of Educational Research and Development

Source: Adapted from Figure 6 on pp. xxii–1 in: Dick, W., Carey, L., & Carey, J. O. (2005). *The systematic design of instruction* (6th ed.). New York: Allyn & Bacon. Published by Allyn and Bacon, Boston, MA. Copyright © 2005 by Pearson Education. Adapted with permission from the publisher.

which may include print materials such as textbooks and teacher training manuals, or other media such as interactive video systems. If the instructional strategy involves a teacher, lesson plans or guidelines for instruction by this person also would be developed as part of step 7.

Formative and Summative Evaluation

Steps 8, 9, and 10 of Dick, Carey, and Carey's model involve the distinction between formative evaluation and summative evaluation formulated by Michael Scriven.[74] He observed that, in practice, evaluation serves two distinct functions. Program developers conduct **formative evaluation** while the program or product is under development, in order to support the process of improving its effectiveness. In some situations, formative evaluation findings may result in a decision to abort further development, so that resources are not wasted on a program that has little chance of ultimately being effective. **Summative evaluation**

---

74. Scriven, M. (1967). The methodology of evaluation. In R. E. Stake (Ed.), *Curriculum evaluation*, American Educational Research Association Monograph Series on Evaluation, No. 1 (pp. 39–83). Chicago: Rand McNally. In a more recent publication, Scriven discusses ten common fallacies he has observed in interpretation of the concepts of formative and summative evaluation: Scriven, M. (1991). Beyond formative and summative evaluation. In M. W. McLaughlin & D. C. Phillips (Eds.), *Evaluation and education: At quarter century. Ninetieth yearbook of the National Society for the Study of Education: Part II* (pp. 19–64). Chicago: NSSE.

is conducted to determine how worthwhile the final program is, usually in comparison to other competing programs. This type of evaluation usually is done by individuals other than the program developers, similar to the manner in which the Consumers Union (the publisher of *Consumer Reports*), conducts comparative evaluations of many types of competing commercial products.

Scriven created a 12-item checklist for use in summative evaluation of educational products or programs. The following questions summarize the statements of considerations and 4-point rating scale Scriven provides for each checklist item.[75]

1. How great is the need for the product?
2. How large and important is the market for the product?
3. How generalizable are the results of field tests of the product?
4. Did the field tests result in good data on samples of all relevant user groups?
5. How thorough was the cost analysis for the product?
6. How good is the evidence on the long-term effects of the product?
7. Were side-effects of the product diligently sought?
8. Were relevant ethical, professional, and research standards applied during the product development process?
9. Was the research design used in the field trial sufficiently rigorous to determine that the product was the actual cause of any observed effects?
10. How rigorous was the comparison between the product and its competitors?
11. How appropriate were the statistical analyses of field-test results, and if statistical significance tests were done, did they yield significant results?
12. How great is the educational significance of the product?

Unfortunately, most educational programs and products are developed without the type of rigorous evaluation recommended by Scriven.[76] For example, textbook publishers spend minimal time on summative evaluation of print materials, with the exception of expert reviews.

In Dick, Carey, and Carey's model, formative evaluation (step 8) is conducted throughout the development process, and its results are used to revise (step 9) the R&D product or program during any of the first seven stages—that is, to revise the instructional goals, instructional analysis, analysis of learners and contexts, performance objectives, assessment instruments, instructional strategy, and/or instructional materials in ways that appear desirable based upon the formative evaluation results.

Dick and his colleagues recommend a three-level process of formative evaluation: (1) trying out prototype materials one-on-one (i.e., one evaluator working with one learner); (2) a small group tryout with six to eight students; and (3) a field trial with a whole class of learners. This phase of evaluation relies heavily on qualitative data-collection methods, for example, interviewing and observation by the developer. Based upon the preliminary results the educational program is modified and further developed, and then tried out with a larger (although still somewhat small) number of learners. The evaluation again involves primarily qualitative methods, although quantitative methods (e.g., performance tests or self-report ratings) also might be used. Based on these results, the program is refined and expanded further, and then subjected to a field trial in a situation fairly close to the context

75. Scriven, M. (1974). Standards for the evaluation of educational programs and products. In G. D. Borich (Ed.), *Evaluating educational programs and products.* Englewood Cliffs, NJ: Educational Technology. A slightly different version of the checklist (the one that we describe) is available at http://www.wmich.edu/evalctr/checklists/
76. Komoski, K. (1985). Instructional materials will not improve until we change the system. *Educational Leadership,* 42(7), 31–37.

in which it ultimately will be used (e.g., with a regular-size class of learners). At this point, the evaluation tends to be quantitative in nature, involving tests and other measures to determine the extent to which the program is achieving its intended objectives.

When the product or program has been taken through the entire development process, it is subjected to summative evaluation. Summative evaluation is listed as step 10 of this model. The authors comment, however, that it is "not part of the design process," because it "usually does not involve the designer of the instruction but instead involves an independent evaluator."[77]

Example of R&D Evaluation

Educational R&D projects require substantial resources. It is highly unlikely that a graduate student will be able to find the financial and personnel support to complete a major R&D project. In fact, educational R&D is beyond the capabilities of most school districts.

If you plan to do an R&D project for a thesis or dissertation, you should keep these cautions in mind. It is best to undertake a small-scale project that involves a limited amount of original instructional design. Also, unless you have substantial financial resources, you will need to avoid expensive instructional media, such as film and synchronized slide-tape. Another way to scale down the project is to limit development to just a few steps of the R&D cycle.

Joanna Dunlap carried out an educational research and development project involving the addition of problem-based learning (PBL) to a university colleague's capstone course in software engineering.[78] Dunlap, from the School of Education, collaborated with the course instructor to design the capstone course, a required, 16-week undergraduate course that is the final course in software engineering. The collaborators first conducted a front-end analysis to determine what the course needed to achieve in the program and what students needed to know and be able to do to meet the expectations of the profession and needs of employers. Then they considered the types of learning experiences students received prior to the capstone course and the content and skills covered by those experiences. Dunlap notes:

> This analysis defined a clear gap that the capstone course needed to bridge—primarily, to help students apply what they had learned in their more didactically oriented courses to professional problems of practice. . . . the PBL approach was appropriate for use with computer science students because it closely aligned with the software development life cycle (SDLC) approach to software engineering problems . . . an approach followed in one form or another by most software engineering professionals—instead of introducing a new approach.[79]

Dunlap's article deals primarily with the formative evaluation of the course itself, giving less attention to the type of instructional materials, if any, used by the instructor or students. However, her article includes a table listing the four phases of the model of PBL used in the course and the instructional activities used to teach each phase. Students addressed the problem of responding to an RFP (request for proposal) from a construction company that involved developing a Web-based project-planning application for the company. The four phases of PBL were (1) respond to the RFP, (2) conduct detailed software analysis, (3) develop software design solution, and (4) implement and test software solution. The PBL element of the course was threefold, focusing on the instructional strategies of authentic activities, collaboration, and reflection. For example, in phase 2, also called solution

77. Dick, Carey, & Carey, *Systematic design,* p. 8.
78. Dunlap, J. C. (2005). Problem-based learning and self-efficacy: How a capstone course prepares students for a profession. *Educational Technology Research and Development, 53*(1), 65–85.
79. Ibid., pp. 67–68.

design, the first activity is described as "Based on action plans, students engage in self-directed study to gather information that will help them respond to the requirements in the RFP."[80] In phase 3, solution development, the final activity is described as, "When the group believes it has enough knowledge to write a response to the client's RFP, it finalizes the RFP and submits it to the client."[81] These examples illustrate the focus on authentic activities and collaboration. The reflection aspect of PBL involved the students' generation of journals describing their learning experience.

Dunlap's evaluation corresponds to what Dick and his colleagues describe as a field trial of the R&D instructional program, carried out in the actual learning context where the program will be taught. They add, "But the question remains about whether the learner can use the new skills in what we have called the *performance context*—the site where the skills are ultimately required."[82] The entire thrust of Dunlap's formative evaluation is to test whether the capstone course, with its emphasis on PBL, was perceived by students as having prepared them for actual work as software engineers. This focus corresponds closely to the performance context mentioned by Dick and his colleagues.

Evaluation included an analysis of students' guided journal output, generated prior to, during, and after the four phases of PBL, and a pretest and posttest administration of a self-efficacy scale measuring students' confidence and self-judgment as to their ability to organize and implement actions needed to perform effectively as software engineers.

Students' journals showed changes in both students' confidence regarding their software development abilities and changes in their professional identity. Journal excerpts showed that at the beginning of the course, 29 of the 31 students expressed concerns about whether they were prepared to be software developers in the real world. While working on the construction company project, 30 students began expressing changes in their self-confidence with regard to software development. For example, "I've learned a lot over the last three weeks. . . . This class is more like in a [sic] real world."[83] By the end of the course, 27 students indicated that the course had prepared them to deal with the demands of actual software development. For example, "I feel that if I was hired right now by a firm that I'd be able to go in there and get right to work. I'm definitely ready."[84]

Dunlap also notes that "twenty-two students reported that they found the instructor's use of authentic problems of practice very effective. . . ."[85] She also notes that all the students in the course "received a grade of B or higher, based on client evaluations, so students' perceived achievement was in line with their actual performance."[86]

Students also rated their perceived self-efficacy on a 10-item self-efficacy measure by checking a 4-point scale ranging from 1 (low) to 4 (high) for each item. Thus their total score could vary from 10 (10 times 1) to 40 (10 times 4). The pre-PBL mean score was 22.07 ($SD = 4.55$, $N = 31$), and the post-PBL mean score was 37.90 ($SD = 2.57$, $N = 31$), which represents a significant increase in students' perceived self-efficacy [$t(30 \text{ df}) = 27.88$; $p < .0001$].

Dunlap concludes that through "authentic activities, collaboration, and reflection, the PBL experience gave the computer science students in this study the opportunity to engage in vicarious learning and increase their performance accomplishments by successfully working through a complex software development project."[87] She recommends that

---

80. Ibid., p. 69.
81. Ibid.
82. Dick, Carey, & Carey, *Systematic design,* p. 292.
83. Dunlap, Problem-based learning, p. 75.
84. Ibid.
85. Ibid., p. 78.
86. Ibid., p. 77.
87. Ibid., p. 79.

future course design efforts provide for students to be involved in authentic problem-solving activities throughout their academic programs, not just as a final step.

If you are considering an R&D project for your thesis or dissertation study, you should give careful consideration to the time required to plan and carry out such a project. The considerable time required for an R&D project is worthwhile if you are interested in making a contribution that will lead to an immediate tangible improvement in educational practice.

In the case of the R&D project described above, the developer was able to make a contribution to a colleague's educational practice and to suggest future R&D efforts to build a worthwhile instructional strategy (PBL) into other phases of the target audience's educational program. The results of this pilot test contributed new knowledge, and raised new questions, about the effects of problem-based learning on students' performance skills and perceived self-efficacy.

If you decide to carry out educational R&D for a master's or doctoral degree, you and your advisor will need to consider the appropriate scope of the proposed R&D product or program and also which steps of the R&D cycle you need to complete for the effort to constitute an acceptable study. To truthfully represent the R&D process, your project should include at least one stage of formative or summative evaluation.

RECOMMENDATIONS FOR

Doing an Evaluation Research Study or an R&D Evaluation

When doing an evaluation research study:
1. Explore the various reasons that may underlie an individual's or agency's request for an evaluation study.
2. Identify the significant stakeholders who are involved in the program to be evaluated.
3. As a step in deciding the particular aspects that will be the actual focus of evaluation, delineate all possible aspects of the program that might be evaluated.
4. Remain open to new evaluation questions that arise as the evaluation process proceeds.
5. Be alert to the possibility of unintended positive or negative side effects of the program being evaluated.
6. Consider preparing different reports of an evaluation study to meet the needs of different stakeholder groups and of the professional evaluation community.
7. Consider which of the various quantitative or qualitative models of evaluation is best suited for your study.
8. Use the *Program Evaluation Standards* or another set of recognized standards in designing your evaluation study and in judging its adequacy once completed.

When doing an R&D evaluation:

9. Draw upon pertinent research findings and research-based principles of instructional design in designing a new educational program or product.

10. Determine at the outset whether there is a sufficient need for the program or product and whether effective competitors already exist.

11. State the program or product objectives in a form that enables them to be evaluated clearly.

12. Use methods of formative evaluation at each step of the development process.

13. Consider ending or redesigning an R&D project if the results of a formative evaluation support one of these decisions.

14. Consider having an external evaluator do a summative evaluation of its quality if the project results in a completed version of the program or product.

15. Consider doing a formative or summative evaluation as a part of another group's R&D project if you are interested in R&D and do not have the resources to develop your own program or product.

SELF-CHECK TEST

Circle the correct answer to each of the following questions. The answers are provided at the back of the book.

1. Educational evaluation can be used to improve
   a. program management.
   b. policy analysis.
   c. political decision making.
   d. all of the above.

2. Evaluation research is most similar to other types of research in its concern with
   a. providing information to facilitate decision making.
   b. using systematic procedures to collect and analyze data.
   c. obtaining findings that apply to a wider audience than those studied in the research.
   d. collecting data to shed light on the worth or value of educational phenomena.

3. Compared to an internal evaluator, an external evaluator generally
   a. is less concerned with identification of stakeholders affected by the program being evaluated.
   b. is more likely to be biased toward the program being evaluated.

   c. is more likely to do a qualitatively oriented evaluation than a quantitatively oriented evaluation.
   d. is in a better position to do a summative evaluation of a program.

4. A basic principle of goal-free evaluation is that
   a. the evaluation design should not have goals.
   b. the evaluator should be given free rein to determine goals for the program.
   c. the evaluator should not know in advance the decisions that need to be made about the program.
   d. the evaluator should not know in advance the program goals.

5. Objectives-based evaluation is used primarily to
   a. determine how well a program is achieving its objectives.
   b. compare the performance of individual students with group norms.
   c. determine appropriate objectives for an educational program.
   d. help decision makers identify their objectives for doing an evaluation study.

6. In the Context-Input-Process-Product (CIPP) model of evaluation, close collaboration between evaluators and program decision makers is required for every stage *except* to:
   a. delineate the kinds of information needed for decision making.
   b. synthesize obtained information so that it is maximally useful in making decisions.
   c. obtain information as to the extent to which the goals of the program have been achieved.
   d. determine whether an evaluation should be carried out.

7. Unlike judicial evaluation, adversary evaluation is characterized by
   a. the use of various data sources.
   b. a reliance on human testimony.
   c. pro and con arguments.
   d. a quasi-legal orientation.

8. In evaluation research, a discrepancy between an existing condition and a desired condition is called
   a. a standard.
   b. a need.
   c. a cost-benefit.
   d. a concern.

9. An emergent design in evaluation research is specified
   a. before the stakeholders are identified.
   b. at the time that program delineation occurs.
   c. as the evaluation process occurs.
   d. after concerns have been identified, through the use of the CIPP model.

10. The method of educational connoisseurship and criticism depends heavily on
   a. stakeholders' opinions of the program being evaluated.
   b. the evaluator's prior understanding of the type of program being evaluated.

   c. program managers' judgments of the program being evaluated.
   d. all of the above.

11. Qualitative approaches to evaluation differ from quantitative models primarily in their
   a. concern for identifying needs that should be addressed.
   b. assumption of the availability of objective criteria to judge program worth.
   c. concern for the values and perspectives of different stakeholders.
   d. use of external evaluators to determine program worth.

12. Educational research and development (R&D) differs from other approaches to developing instructional programs because it
   a. places heavy emphasis on evaluation as a basis for program revision.
   b. focuses on maximizing the marketability of the educational program being developed.
   c. avoids the use of qualitative data to make decisions about program revision.
   d. does not depend on needs assessment to define instructional goals.

13. The typical sequence in formative evaluation of an educational program during an R&D cycle involves
   a. starting with a small number of learners and moving toward a field trial with a whole group of learners.
   b. starting with test sites that approximate real-life conditions and moving toward sites that provide more experimental control.
   c. starting with an emphasis on quantitative research methods and moving toward an emphasis on qualitative research methods.
   d. all of the above.

CHAPTER 18

Action Research

OVERVIEW

Action research has played a growing role in the field of education in recent years because of its promise for improving educators' practice, strengthening the connection between research and practice, and improving the justice of education's impact on society. This chapter describes the purposes that action research projects can serve, the unique features of action research, and the stages of a typical action research project. The chapter discusses five criteria for determining the credibility and trustworthiness of action research projects. We provide suggestions for designing action research that helps practitioners reduce discrepancies between their espoused theories and theories-in-action, and suggest strategies for dealing with the unique ethical issues in action research.

OBJECTIVES

After studying this chapter, you should be able to

1. Understand how action research compares to other forms of research.
2. Explain the main purposes for which educators carry out action research.
3. Explain the cyclical nature of action research.
4. Explain the importance of data collection and analysis as a basis for action in action research.
5. Explain the role of reflection in action research.
6. Describe the typical stages of an action research project.
7. Apply five criteria for determining the credibility and trustworthiness of an action research project.
8. Understand how action research helps inform practitioners' theories-in-action.
9. Understand how to address unique ethical issues arising in action research.

Characteristics of Action Research

Action research in education is a form of applied research whose primary purpose is to increase the quality, impact, and justice of education professionals' practice. We use the term *action research* to include what is sometimes called *practitioner research,*[1] *teacher*

---

1. Zeichner, K. M., & Noffke, S. E. (2001). Practitioner research. In V. Richardson (Ed.), *Handbook of research on teaching* (4th ed., pp. 298–330). Washington, DC: American Educational Research Association.

TABLE 18.1

Typical Differences between Formal Research and Action Research

Aspect of Research	How Approached in Formal Research	How Approached in Action Research
Researcher experience/training	Considerable knowledge of, and training in conduct of, research	Practical experience, with minimal knowledge or experience in research
Research purpose	To produce generalizable knowledge	To solve a problem or achieve a goal in current practice
Research focus	Based on review of previous research	Based on current problems or goals in practice
Basis for research	Extensive literature review of primary sources	Limited literature review of secondary sources
Approach to: Sampling	Random or representative sample	Convenience sample of own students/clients
Research design	Rigorous control, long time frame	Casual procedures, emergent design, short time frame
Use of measures	Measures evaluated and pretested	Convenient measures
Data analysis	Use of statistical significance tests or in-depth qualitative analysis	Focus on raw data and practical significance
Reporting of results	Published report, journal article, or presentation at professional conference	Informal sharing with colleagues, publication through online networks
Application of results	Emphasis on theoretical implications, contribution to knowledge base in education and research	Emphasis on practical significance, contribution to practice

Touchstones in Research

Reason, P., & Bradbury, H. (Eds.). (2001). *Participative inquiry and practice.* Thousand Oaks, CA: Sage.

Hendicks, C. (2006). *Improving schools through action research: A comprehensive guide for educators.* Boston: Pearson.

research,[2] *insider research,*[3] and (usually when carried out by teacher educators on their own practice) *self-study research.*[4] Teachers conduct much of the action research in education, and this chapter sometimes refers specifically to teacher research in explaining the characteristics of action research.

Action research may utilize any of the research methods described in other chapters of this book and often involves collaboration with colleagues, clients, or professional researchers (typically, university professors). It also may have other purposes in addition to improving practice, as we describe later in the chapter.

Table 18.1 provides a convenient summary of the typical differences between action research and the formal research that is designed to produce generalizable knowledge of the type reported in academic journals. It should be noted, however, that action research often has some of the characteristics of formal research and might be published in academic

2. Cochran-Smith, M., & Lytle, S. L. (1999). The teacher research movement: A decade later. *Educational Researcher, 28*(7), 15–25.
3. Kemmis, S., & McTaggart, R. (2000). Participatory action research. In N. K. Denzin & Y. S. Lincoln (Eds.), *Handbook of qualitative research* (2nd ed., pp. 567–605). Thousand Oaks, CA: Sage.
4. Zeichner & Noffke, Practitioner research.

journals or presented at professional conferences. More typically, action research projects are publicly reported in online action research journals or Web sites of various action research networks.[5] These reports enable other practitioners, whether or not they carry out their own action research, to benefit from the knowledge generated by action researchers.

Purposes for Conducting Action Research

The topics and methods of action research are virtually unlimited. It is important for practitioners to consider their purposes for undertaking action research so that they are more likely to produce results consistent with those purposes. In an effort to clarify the varied motivations that underlie action research endeavors, Kenneth Zeichner and Susan Noffke define three dimensions—personal, professional, and political—to reflect the varied purposes for which action research may be carried out.[6] Here, using teacher research as the form of action research, we summarize the examples that the authors give to clarify each dimension. We find some overlap between the dimensions, which you may notice in the author's examples. In fact, Zeichner and Noffke describe the dimensions as "interwoven categories . . . for illuminating emphases" within action research.[7]

Personal Purposes for Action Research

Action research with a primarily personal motivation has as its central purpose the improvement of the researcher's practice. Thus the focus is on the teacher and the teacher's own students. Specific purposes might include the following:

- to develop a greater understanding of individual students' thoughts and actions
- to develop a deeper understanding of teachers' experiences with particular educational innovations
- to provide teachers an opportunity for personal examination and generation of theory
- to produce heightened self-awareness in practitioners, including clarification of their assumptions about education and recognition of contradictions between their espoused ideas and actual classroom practice
- to examine the impact of the research process on practitioners
- to conduct research as an individual learning process that values experiential knowledge

In summary, action research done for personal purposes is intended to promote greater self-knowledge, fulfillment, and professional awareness among practitioners.

Professional Purposes for Action Research

Action research that is carried out primarily for professional purposes typically involves practitioners:

- engaging in action research as a form of staff development.
- seeking to legitimize their role as producers of knowledge and contributors to the literature on educational research and theory.
- developing networks of practitioners engaged in action research to promote their colleagueship and professionalism.

---

5. For a summary of Internet resources supporting teacher research networks, see: Hobson, D., & Smolin, L. (2001). Teacher researchers go online. In Burnaford, G., Fischer, J., & Hobson, D. (Eds.), *Teachers doing research* (2nd ed., pp. 83–118). Mahwah, NJ: Erlbaum.
6. Zeichner & Noffke, Practitioner research.
7. Ibid, p. 307.

Action research undertaken for professional purposes, then, typically involves teachers' efforts to extend their research beyond the classroom. It enables practitioners to study, and seek to influence directly, the social and institutional contexts in which they work, rather than depending on analyses of their work contexts by outsiders. According to Zeichner and Noffke, such action research helps bridge the gap between theory and practice, but without fundamentally altering the relationship between the educational research and practice communities.

Political Purposes for Action Research

Action research can explicitly address political purposes by:

Touchstone in Research

Freedman, S. W., Simons, E. R., Kalnin, J. S., & Casareno, A. (1999). *Inside city schools: Investigating literacy in multicultural classrooms.* New York: Teachers College Press.

- seeking to make one's own teaching practices more humane and just.
- providing full participation in the research process of all those who are affected by it.
- embracing an overt agenda of social change, with a commitment to promote economic and social justice through collaborative efforts to increase educational opportunities and outcomes for all constituents. Typical efforts address issues of gender, class, cultural equity, and voice in education.[8]

Zeichner and Noffke claim that "all forms of educational research embody particular [political] stances, either to maintain existing lines of power and privilege or to transform them along more just and caring lines."[9] However, action research that is explicitly carried out with a political purpose is intended to bring about fundamental social change toward the goal of greater social justice for all. In the process, action researchers seek to emancipate themselves as well from existing limits to expression of their voice and to take actions that challenge the status quo with respect to their professional identities.

In reading action research reports, we suggest that you consider the researcher's stated purpose or purposes for carrying out the research. In addition, we recommend that you consider the three purposes (personal, professional, and political) that we describe above to make your own analysis of why a particular action research project was carried out or what purposes it served, whether intended or not. As action researchers gain greater knowledge and research experience, some may narrow their purpose, while others may broaden their focus to address varied purposes. If you plan to carry out an action research project, we suggest that you reflect on your own purposes early in your planning.

Cyclical Nature of Action Research

Various models of action research exist. Some focus on the types of participants in and goals of action research, while others define specific steps (or stages) of the process. Some conceptions of action research treat it as having a definite beginning and end, similar to most formal research projects.[10] Action research projects that are carried out for a dissertation or course assignment may fit this pattern, particularly because writing up the project tends to require the completion of an activity and a summary report of the results. However, when carried out by practitioners as part of their everyday work, action research is more likely to be ongoing and typically cyclical in nature.

8. Other approaches for addressing these issues are cultural studies and critical theory, which are described in Chapter 15.
9. Zeichner & Noffke, Practitioner research, p. 309.
10. Noffke, S. E. (1997). Professional, personal, and political dimensions of action research. In M. W. Apple (Ed.), *Review of research in education* (vol. 22, pp. 305–343). Washington, DC: American Educational Research Association.

FIGURE 18.1

Cyclical Nature of Action Research

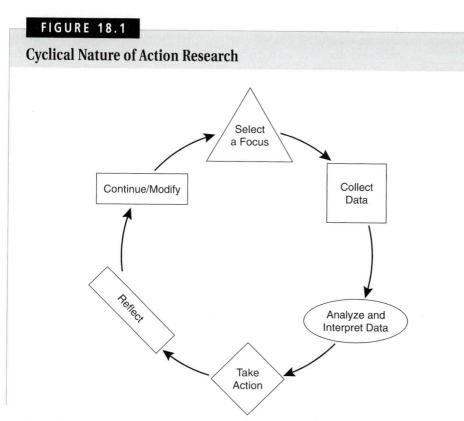

Source: Figure 1.10 on p. 27 in: Glanz, J. (1998). *Action research: An educational leader's guide to school improvement.* Norwood, MA: Christopher-Gordon. Permission granted by the publisher.

The reason for this cyclicity is that action researchers: (a) do not always carry out the stages of action research in the same order, (b) may return to an earlier stage as their research progresses, and (c) may continue going through the stages rather than bringing the research to an end. In fact, if action researchers systematically collect information on the effectiveness of their practice or of changes in it, and then continue or further modify their practice based on their findings and reflections, action research can become a natural component of practice.

Jeffrey Glanz analyzes the process of an action research project into six steps: (1) selecting a focus, (2) collecting data, (3) analyzing and interpreting the data, (4) taking action, (5) reflecting, and (6) continuing or modifying one's actions, which in turn leads to a new focus for another round of action research. The steps are illustrated in Figure 18.1. Later in the chapter we use Glanz's model,[11] along with a seventh step, reporting the research, to describe the stages of a specific action research project.

11. Glanz, J. (1998). *Action research: An educational leader's guide to school improvement.* Norwood, MA: Christopher-Gordon.

In designing an action research project, you need to think about your starting point. Once you choose a focus, most likely you will start by either trying a new action prior to collecting data or by first collecting data on the impact of your practice prior to taking any new action. Once the action research cycle is in motion, researchers typically move back and forth between experimenting with new practices and collecting more data, using the latter to inform and guide the former. Sometimes data collection itself represents a new action, because it can significantly modify the way in which action researchers carry out their practice. For example, James Lytle conducted action research in the district where he had just become the superintendent.[12] The project involved collaborative research designed "to lead a group of urban principals and a group of middle management support staff toward the design of demonstrably effective educational organizations."[13]

As the new superintendent, Lytle first reviewed performance evaluation reports on students from the previous school year and then visited 800 classrooms in September and October to develop "first impressions."[14] From November through February he conducted a second round of visits, focusing on classrooms and subjects in which failure rates were high. He made extended field notes on 30 classrooms, which he shared with principals and other administrators. He did not share these notes with the teachers he had observed, however, because the observations were largely critical. Lytle discovered, as John Goodlad had found years before,[15] that:

> A great deal of classroom activity was boring, repetitive, unengaging, and vapid. It seemed intended primarily to kill time. But I also heard a recurrent lament from the teachers: the children they were teaching were different, they said, from the ones they had taught five and 10 years earlier; their emotional needs were so great that the teachers felt constantly torn between teaching the curriculum and tending to their students' problems.[16]

Lytle ended the school year by conducting discussions with the teachers whose classrooms he had visited, inviting them in grade-level groups of sixteen to eighteen teachers. Two-thirds of the teachers accepted the invitations. He proposed that during the second school year the principals conduct a study "as a way of deepening our shared understanding of why students behave and perform as they do."[17] The study put the principals themselves in the role of action researchers. Each principal shadowed one student from his or her school, collecting varied forms of data and then in small teams writing a report of their findings, which they shared with the entire group. Four focus groups of principals met to discuss final report card grades from the previous school year. Then all the principals in the district agreed to study themselves as a way of better understanding the principalship. Working in pairs, they created an ethnography of their partners.

Lytle noted discernible improvements in student performance over the three-year period of his action research project, although "it would be inappropriate to claim a causal relationship between the administrative development activities of the regional office and student performance."[18] Nonetheless, Lytle's report of the expanding data-collection

12. Lytle, J. H. (1996). The inquiring manager: Developing new leadership structures to support reform. *Phi Delta Kappan, 77,* 664–670.
13. Ibid, p. 664.
14. Ibid, p. 666.
15. Goodlad, J. I. (1984). *A place called school: Prospects for the future.* New York: McGraw-Hill.
16. Lytle, The inquiring manager, p. 666.
17. Ibid, p. 667.
18. Ibid, p. 670.

process makes it clear that his fostering of other school administrators' participation in data collection was itself a major new action, or set of actions, on the superintendent's part, designed to transform the exercise of leadership in the district.

Before describing the stages of action research in relation to specific research projects, we briefly summarize next two foci that we consider critical to action research: the collection and analysis of data as a basis for action, and the use of reflection as part of the research process.

Focus on Data Collection and Analysis as a Basis for Action

Most educational practitioners seek to refine and improve their practice in various ways. For example, they might use trial and error, get ideas from colleagues, or try out a strategy they hear about at a professional meeting. These strategies can be a good starting point for the improvement of practice, but action research takes them further by including a process of systematic data collection and analysis.

Touchstone in Research

Mills, G. E. (2000). *Action research: A guide for the teacher researcher.* Upper Saddle River, NJ: Prentice Hall.

Some qualitative researchers claim that action research involves the collection of qualitative data only.[19] However, the various action research reports that we have read include qualitative, quantitative, or both types of data. Davydd Greenwood and Morten Levin emphasize this feature of action research by stating:

> . . . action research is inherently multimethod research, including scientific experiments, quantitative social research, and qualitative research methods from as many disciplines as necessary to address the problem at hand. Effective action research cannot accept an a priori limitation to one or another research modality.[20]

An example of "multimethod" action research is the study by Thomas Scott and Michael O'Sullivan of students' use of the Internet to get information for social studies assignments.[21] This action research project was carried out in the high school where Scott served as a social studies teacher and O'Sullivan as the instructional media coordinator and librarian. Their published research report presents questionnaire results on the percentage of students reporting use of the Internet daily (25 percent) or weekly (3 percent), use of the Internet specifically as a research tool to collect information for assignments (42 percent), and use of search engines (74 percent) and online databases (7 percent).

Another finding of their action research project was that 262 of the 309 respondents (nearly 85 percent) evaluated their Internet search skills as either excellent or good. Scott and O'Sullivan did not accept these quantitative findings as the whole story, however, noting that, ". . . as our qualitative data will show, many students expressed difficulties navigating Web sites."[22] The researchers analyzed qualitative data from essays written by student volunteers after they completed an assignment that involved use of the Internet in a search for information on a specific social studies topic and each student's evaluation of the three top Web sites identified in the search.

19. See, for example: Zeni, J. (Ed.). (2001). *Ethical issues in practitioner research.* New York: Teachers College Press.
20. Greenwood, D. J., & Levin, M. (2000). Reconstructing the relationships between universities and society through action research. In N. K. Denzin & Y. S. Lincoln (Eds.), *Handbook of qualitative research* (2nd ed., pp. 85–106). Thousand Oaks, CA: Sage.
21. Scott, T. J., & O'Sullivan, M. (2000). The internet and information literacy: Taking the first step toward technology education in the social studies. *The Social Studies,* May/June, 121–125.
22. Ibid, p. 122.

Despite the students' high regard for the Internet's value to learning, the essays reveal their frustration over constraints in usage (e.g., difficulty in navigating and the time that it took). A student who had researched the topic of the Boxer Rebellion observed:

> The Internet search told me a lot about the Internet. . . . The first page just told me that the Boxer Rebellion originated in China. It had no depth on the subject. My second site wanted to sell me a book on it. . . . The third was just junk, it was someone trying to get people to rebel against wearing boxer shorts.[23]

The qualitative essay data also revealed students' eventual discovery of effective Internet search strategies.

Both quantitative and qualitative data were central to Scott and O'Sullivan's recommendations about how social studies teachers should develop students' information literacy. They urge social studies teachers "to develop their students' ability to question, think critically, and use inquiry to determine truth from falsehood" by developing a curriculum "infused with lessons that examine the ideological, ethical, cultural, and scientific relationship of technology to our daily lives . . . [and] whether technological change and innovation are shared equitably on a national and international basis."[24]

The data collected to generate these recommendations exemplify the type of knowledge that action research can provide to other practitioners. One could argue, however, that they are written in a form that approaches a claim to generalizable knowledge, which is typically not associated with action research findings (see Table 18.1). As in case study research, both the design of an action research study and the way in which it is reported can affect its applicability to other educational settings. Efforts to study typical cases, or to select a random sample within the group that the researcher studies, increase the likelihood of wider applicability. Ultimately, the readers' interpretation determines whether the findings reported in an action research study fit their situation. Scott and O'Sullivan's action research report provides two kinds of information to help readers make this determination: first, the inclusion of descriptive quantitative statistics (student percentages) that are easy to compare in different settings, and second, the provision of a rich, thick description of their qualitative findings.

Focus on Reflection

Action research emphasizes reflection as an important part of the research cycle. **Reflection** is a process in which practitioners step back from the fast-paced and problematic world of practice to ponder and share ideas about the meaning, value, and impact of their practice. From such reflection, practitioners make new commitments, discover new topics to explore, and gain new insights into the strengths and weaknesses of their current practices.

David Hobson describes reflection as "a process of making sense of one's experience and telling the story of one's journey."[25] He claims that action research gives teachers an opportunity to perceive their world more freshly by reflecting on it and thus "to render the familiar strange."[26] Such reflection corresponds to what Donald Schön calls *reflection-on-action*, which consists of reflection after the event, as opposed to *reflection-in-action*, which is undertaken in the midst of the action.[27]

23. Ibid, p. 124.
24. Ibid, p. 125.
25. Hobson, D. (2001). Action and reflection: Narrative and journaling in teacher research. In Burnaford, G., Fischer, J., & Hobson, D. (Eds.), *Teachers doing research* (2nd ed., pp. 7–27). Mahwah, NJ: Erlbaum. Quote appears on p. 8.
26. Ibid.
27. Schön, D. A. (1983). *The reflective practitioner.* San Francisco: Jossey-Bass.

TABLE 18.2

Suggestions for Keeping an Action Research Journal

1. Use $8^{1}/_{2}"\times 11"$ pages and put them in a 3-ring binder so that pages can be removed, added, or rearranged. For ease of carrying, you might prefer a $6"\times 9"$ binder, blank lesson plan book, post-it note pad, or spiral-bound notebook.
2. Date and time each entry to facilitate viewing developmental processes over time. Start each entry on a new page, so that the pages can be grouped to reflect recurring patterns or reconstruct sequences.
3. Make time for journaling by picking a regular time free of interruption, or writing in class while your students are writing.
4. Use descriptive writing to record directly observed/experienced details for later review.
5. Use reflective writing to comment, associate, and make meaning.
6. Use double-entry journal writing with a description in one column and reflection in the other column.
7. Keep a daily log to help reveal priorities, what absorbs your attention, and what continuing issues predominate.
8. Name each important teacher you have known, and describe each one. Look for commonalities; describe the steppingstones in your experience of teaching and reflect on your development over time.
9. Examine the materials you have been reading and bring the results of your investigations into your journal.
10. Develop a "journal of the journals," going back through your entire journal to seek themes and highlight passages, and have a friend read aloud the lines you have highlighted.
11. Ask your students to turn in "exit slips" at the end of each class reflecting on their learning, questions, and expectations.

Source: Adapted from Hobson, D. (2001). Action and reflection: Narrative and journaling in teacher research. In Burnaford, G., Fischer, J., & Hobson, D. (Eds.), *Teachers doing research* (2nd ed., pp. 7–27). Mahwah, NJ: Erlbaum.

Hobson views autobiographical narrative as being at the heart of reflection in teacher action research:

Narrative asks the question: What does this research have to do with me?

... Our narratives include our insights, searches for meaning, and the connectedness we find in the world ... Looking at our own autobiographies, reliving our own experiences with inequity, power, and authority in schools, offers us the opportunity to inform ourselves further and move forward to change situations in which today's students experience injustice.[28]

Hobson also recommends that teacher researchers keep a journal, a "*written record of practice*," to help them evaluate their experiences.[29] Table 18.2 summarizes Hobson's suggestions for keeping an action research journal as a basis for reflection.

The reflections that occur through autobiographical narrative and journaling help action researchers throughout the research process: to identify problems of practice that deserve systematic attention via action research, to highlight issues or assumptions in their own beliefs about teaching and learning, and to suggest personally relevant interpretations of the data they collect. Hobson uses an action research project by Rick Moon, a physical education teacher and teacher researcher, to illustrate these uses of reflection.[30] Moon found

28. Hobson, Action and reflection, p. 14; also see Chapter 15, where narrative research is discussed.
29. Ibid, p. 19.
30. Moon, R. (2001). The personal and the professional: Learning about gender in middle school physical education. In Burnaford, G., Fischer, J., & Hobson, D. (Eds.), *Teachers doing research* (2nd ed., pp. 151–156). Mahwah, NJ: Erlbaum.

himself observing the girls and boys in his classes more closely after the birth of his first daughter, and reflected on his old beliefs about gender differences:

> [Prior to] the birth of my daughters, . . . I concentrated solely on male athletics . . . though I helped score or officiate some of the girls' athletic competitions, I realize now that I did not have much respect for them.[31]

To illustrate his prefeminist orientation, Moon shares an excerpt he prepared for a notebook that he turned in to the male instructor of a physical education class Moon took while in college:

> Our society is being taken over by women who won't allow their children to play any rough sports and condemn any fighting. . . . It is our job as PE teachers to teach combativeness, roughness, and physical contact to students, without causing serious injury, in order to prevent women and sissies from taking over our society.[32]

Moon adds, "My teacher responded to this with the words: 'And don't ever forget it!' "[33]

Moon's action research involved studying gender equity in his own classroom. His report of his reflections includes memories of his own college years and the birth of his first daughter; experiences working with his male and female students; imagining his second daughter shattering gender stereotypes in the future; and his personal insight that "to be a man today and to be married, and to be a father, requires rethinking the images one holds."[34]

By including these reflections in his action research report, Moon not only documented his own personal growth, but also possibly helped fellow practitioners on their own reflective journey.

For a more in-depth treatment of the meanings and implications of practitioner reflection, Lynn Fendler traces the genealogy of reflection in teacher education, noting that "common practices of reflection (journal writing and autobiographical narratives) may have unintended and undesirable political effects."[35]

Stages of Action Research

To illustrate the stages of an action research project, we will refer to a study conducted by Susan Green, Clair Britt, and Patsy Parker on promoting literacy in a kindergarten classroom.[36] At the time of this research, Green was a faculty member at Winthrop University and university liaison to Cotton Belt Elementary, Britt was a Winthrop University student doing an internship at Cotton Belt, and Parker was a teacher at Cotton Belt. This school is a rural pre-K–5 professional development school associated with Winthrop University, located in South Carolina. The three authors collaborated to complete a meaningful action research project during Britt's one-semester internship at the school. Using Glanz's model (see Figure 18.1), we present the stages in the order in which they were completed.

Selecting a Focus

The researchers decided to explore how to entice children to visit the kindergarten classroom's reading center more frequently, which had often been the least-used center compared to

31. Ibid, p. 151.
32. Ibid, pp. 151–152.
33. Ibid, p. 152.
34. Hobson, Action and reflection, p. 16.
35. Fendler, L. (2003). Teacher reflection in a hall of mirrors: Historical influences and political reverberations. *Educational Researcher, 32*(3), 16–25. Quote appears on p. 23.
36. Green, S. K., Britt, C., & Parker, P. (2002). When do they choose the reading center? Promoting literacy in a kindergarten classroom. *Reading Horizons, 43*(2), 103–113.

"the more active play of the block center and housekeeping [center]."[37] (The three other centers available in the classroom are the writing, art, and computer centers.) While some children happily spent time reading and sharing books with friends, others never chose to pick up a book. The researchers agreed that participation in the reading center was a concrete indicator of children's motivation to read and that watching patterns of attendance at the reading center could provide them insights to encourage more reading.

Taking Action

Green and her colleagues decided to put activities in place that might promote visits to the reading center. They tested three approaches to get books into children's hands. One activity was presented each day, and every third day they started again with the first activity. On day 1, called "Read To" day, Ms. B introduced a book during early morning group time, telling the children about the book and indicating that she would be in the reading center later to read it to them. During center time, the children could first listen to the story if they chose the reading center and then look at other books or move to another center. On day 2, "On Tables" day, baskets of specially selected books were placed on the tables before the children entered the classroom in the morning. At the beginning of the day they could sit at the tables and look at books. On day 3, "In Centers" day, the book baskets were placed in five of the six centers during center time, so children could stop and read if they wished or could incorporate the books into their other center activities. For example, they could read to a doll in the housekeeping center, use tracing paper to trace words or illustrations from books in the writing or art centers, or look at books about construction and vehicles in the building center. This three-day alternating pattern was implemented for 13 weeks.

Collecting Data

The researchers devised a chart listing all students' names with dates and the alternating daily activities across the top. Ms. B noted with a check when each student used books to meet the objective of each of the three daily activities (e.g., listening to the story on "Read To" day, reading at the tables on "On Tables" day, or incorporating books into other center activities on "In Centers" day. She entered a star whenever students visited the reading center and read books in addition to, or sometimes instead of, the daily activities.

Analyzing and Interpreting the Data

The researchers met at least once every two weeks to look at the data Ms. B was collecting. After two weeks they found that more stars were generated on "Read To" day than on the other two days (9 versus 4 or 5). They reported: "The children seemed to be spending more free time at the reading center on the days that Ms. B read to them."[38]

Continuing or Modifying Action

The researchers now had data to answer their initial research question, but "We also checked which children had no stars."[39] This represents a new direction, in which the researchers sought to influence the children most in need of developing their literacy skills. They found that after two weeks three of the four students judged to be lowest in literacy skills had no stars.

---

37. Ibid., p. 105.
38. Ibid., p. 107.
39. Ibid.

They reported,

> Our discovery led Ms. B to focus on the interests of these children, hand picking books for "Read To" days that suited their interests.[40]

They described finding specific books for individual students' interest in racing, dogs, and pizza and books with unusual visual characteristics or wonderful rhythm or literary devices that

> encouraged children to go to the reading center for a closer look and to read their favorite passages.[41]

They also developed a list of titles that they found piqued the interest of reluctant kindergarten students, which they included as a table in their research report. Later data analyses showed increased use of the reading center, particularly on the "Read To" days (a median of three children per day, compared to a median of one child per day on the "On Tables" and "In Centers" days). The researchers also continued to focus on the three students with the lowest literacy skills (the fourth had moved away three weeks into the project). The authors found more books specific to these reluctant readers' interests and encouraged them to reread books and not give up after one try or take favorite books home. They note:

> Our focus on them paid off because we found that by the end of the project these students visited the reading center voluntarily a total of 16 times. . . . For comparison purposes, we found that three other randomly chosen boys (who had stronger literacy skills) visited the reading center a total of ten times during the project.[42]

The researchers also found that changing books in the baskets and in the reading center helped keep students' interest, so they began doing so every two weeks. They also brainstormed ideas for how to maintain the "Read To" days after Ms. B finished her internship. As a result, the classroom teacher obtained the help of a fifth-grade student who read to the kindergarten children twice a week, and a special sign-up sheet was designed on which children could keep track of their own visits to the reading room.

Reflection

The researchers reported that one implication of this project "is the importance of collecting data and using it to make some decisions about what goes on in a classroom."[43] They added, "Collecting the data forced us to reflect. We found it made us think about ways to encourage children to enjoy reading and books."[44] They conclude that among the most important applications of this project will be their future effort to conduct action research with the more reluctant learners and to integrate the teaching of children with the state standards for reading.

Reporting Action Research

To achieve the purposes of action research we described earlier (personal, professional, or political), action researchers also need to share their research with others. Reporting might be in the form of informal sharing with colleagues, a presentation to the local community or at professional meetings, publication in an online action research journal,[45] or

---

40. Ibid.
41. Ibid.
42. Ibid., p. 110.
43. Ibid., p. 111.
44. Ibid.
45. *Networks* is an example of an online action research journal, retrieved October 17, 2005, from http://education.ucsc.edu/faculty/gwells/networks/

TABLE 18.3

Example of Sonata-Form Case Writing with Sidenotes

So I start to explain. *If you want to go to college, you have to start planning now. You have to decide what you want to take your senior year and make sure you have the courses that you need for those next year. Have you thought about your senior year classes?*

There is a long pause. Jaime's reply is reluctant. "No, Mrs. Wallace," then he adds, "We don't do that." I wait for elaboration. *We?* I finally ask. "That's what guerros do," he appends. He misreads the confusion that must be evident on my face, and explains the word. "The guerros. White people. Look around, Miss. White people are the ones who go around talking about their senior classes in their freshman year. Mexicans don't do that."[6]	[6]Signithia Fordham and John Ogbu (1992) identified this exact dynamic in their article "Black Students' School Success" (1992). Fordham elaborated on the dynamic in her book, *Blacked Out.* Nancy Dibble's classroom experience corroborated Fordham and Ogbu's finding among a group of three Mexican American students. It is this experience upon which this case study is based.

Source: From Acting White section, paragraph 2 of: Dibble, N., & Rosiek, J. (2002). White out: A case study introducing a new citational format for teacher practical knowledge research. *International Journal of Education & the Arts, 3*(5). Retrieved October 19, 2005, from http://ijea.asu.edu/v3n5/ Reprinted with permission from the *International Journal of Education & the Arts.*

an article in a hard-copy refereed journal, as was the case for the study by Green and her colleagues on promoting reading literacy in kindergarteners, which was reported in the journal *Reading Horizons.*

In our reviews of the studies in online or print sources listed as action research in preliminary source databases, we found that such studies run the gamut from very simple descriptions of a single action taken by one or more practitioners to sophisticated research studies conducted by practitioners, academics, and community representatives that present a good deal of qualitative data, quantitative data, or data of both types, and have widespread and long-range applications and goals. Thus the reporting style for action research will necessarily vary to suit its purposes and scope.

A new style of report writing that action researchers might consider is the **sonata-form case study** with sidenotes.[46] Written in the first person in present tense, the sonata-form case study is designed to evoke the lived experience of teaching (or other form of practice) and is viewed as hypothetical fiction. In the example in Table 18.3, a teacher's comments appear on the left side and the comments of her research collaborator from a university appear on the right side. This reporting style is designed to allow the differing forms of discourse of these two types of participants to expand and reinforce each other, with neither form privileged.

Credibility and Trustworthiness of Action Research

In this section we describe five validity criteria proposed by Gary Anderson and Kathryn Herr for use in evaluating the credibility and trustworthiness of action research studies.[47] For each criterion we also provide an example of an action research study that we believe

46. Dibble, N., & Rosiek, J. (2002). White out: A case study introducing a new citational format for teacher practical knowledge research. *International Journal of Education & the Arts, 3*(5). Retrieved October 15, 2005, from http://ijea.asu.edu/v3n5/

47. Anderson, G. L., & Herr, K. (1999). The new paradigm wars: Is there room for rigorous practitioner knowledge in schools and universities? *Educational Researcher, 28*(5), 12–21, 40. For other sets of criteria for evaluating action research, see: Zeichner & Noffke, Practitioner research; Melrose, M. J. (2001). Maximizing the rigor of action research: Why would you want to? How could you? *Field Methods, 13*(2), 160–180.

addresses that criterion well. All these studies happen to involve collaboration between practitioners and academics, although our intention in their selection was to identify a variety of clearly described, well-designed, recent studies that include actions involving documented improvements in educator's practice, their effect on clients, or both.

In designing action research studies or reading others' studies, we agree with Zeichner and Noffke's recommendation that practitioners not rely solely on existing models, but instead develop and apply their own criteria to improve and evaluate research quality.[48]

Outcome Validity

Outcome validity involves the extent to which actions occur that lead to a resolution of the problem under study or to the completion of a research cycle that results in action. Ellen Agosta, Janet Graetz, and Margo Mastropieri's study of teacher–researcher partnerships to improve the social behavior of a 6-year-old boy with autism reflects this criterion.[49] The teacher read Robert a social story with words and pictures designed to remind him about appropriate circle-time behavior, and trained observers recorded instances of Robert's screaming before, during, and after the intervention was applied. Charts in the report show consistent reductions in the target behavior and increases in the amount of time Robert sat quietly during circle-time class activities.

Process Validity

Process validity addresses the adequacy of the processes used in different phases of research, such as data collection, analysis, and interpretation, and whether triangulation of data sources and methods was used to guard against bias. The study by Green and her colleagues that we discussed earlier to illustrate the stages of action research addressed this criterion simply yet effectively.[50] The report presents quantitative data showing patterns of book use and reading center participation at the beginning and end of the research project. It also contains detailed descriptions of how the researchers analyzed and addressed the needs of individual children, particularly reluctant readers, and how they modified the action plan after the teacher intern completed her internship.

Democratic Validity

Democratic validity indicates the extent to which the research is done in collaboration with all parties who have a stake in the problem under investigation and to which multiple perspectives and interests are taken into account. Belinda Gimbert and Dean Cristol reported on a study involving integrating technology into the early childhood education curriculum to enhance pre-K–2 children's technological competencies.[51] Three university faculty members from two universities worked with five classroom teachers in developing curriculum units involving technology. The authors note that the classroom teachers' voices "resonate throughout each case" in the report:[52] Matt on "Animals in the Wild for Preschoolers," Jennifer on "Plants for Kindergartners [sic]," Deb on "First-graders and Puppetry," Judi on "Dinosaurs in a Primary Classroom," and Cathy on "Technology and Mathematics

48. Zeichner & Noffke, Practitioner research.
49. Agosta, E., Graetz, J. E., & Mastropieri, M. A. (2004). Teacher–researcher partnerships to improve social behavior through social stories. *Intervention in School and Clinic, 39*(5), 276–287.
50. Green, et al., When do they choose the reading center?
51. Gimbert, B., & Cristol, D. (2004). Teaching curriculum with technology: Enhancing children's technological competence during early childhood.
52. Ibid., p. 208.

Competencies and Second-Graders in a Computer Technology Laboratory." Each case describes the software used in the curriculum unit, teacher and student activities, and the teacher's goals for the unit. Every teacher identified "professional sharing and collegial support *in the classroom*" from adults with technological competence as essential inputs for their and their students' development.[53]

Catalytic Validity

Catalytic validity examines the degree to which the action research energizes the participants so that they are open to transforming their view of reality in relation to their practice, and highlights the emancipatory potential of practitioner research. Mary Lou Morton and Nancy Williams, two university professors, report on their action research in a small charter school "created by the university and the local school district to serve traditionally marginalized students of poverty living within the city limits."[54] The authors sought to help school faculty and staff move toward the school's goal of "creating more equitable learning situations for students who have come from lives of poverty and the challenges with which that leaves them and their families."[55] Specifically, they sought to facilitate students' literacy achievement by helping teachers use more transdisciplinary methods of teaching. To the degree desired by each of the seven K–3 teachers, the authors provided resource books relevant to themes the teachers wished to develop, demonstrated transdisciplinary teaching, and worked with teachers individually in their classrooms. They give detailed descriptions of how each teacher gradually accepted help and incorporated interactive, hands-on activities more closely attuned to the children's real-world experiences and interests.

Dialogic Validity

Dialogic validity is an assessment of the degree to which the research promotes a reflective dialogue among all the participants in the research, to generate and review the action research findings and interpretations. William Gaudelli and William Fernekes carried out action research to describe and evaluate the social studies curriculum concerning global human rights in an affluent, high-achieving suburban high school.[56] At the time of this study, Gaudelli was an assistant professor of social studies education at a university, and Fernekes was a teacher and the social studies department chair at the high school. The world history–world cultures course was developed in response to state graduation requirements in 1989–1990, is taught by several teachers, and is taken by all high school seniors. The authors indicate that for controversial issues, such as how government-sponsored torture is addressed, faculty have discussed these issues and come to general agreement on how to treat them. The authors also note that each teacher of the course has considerable latitude in how to teach the course and needs to "be sensitive to student feedback and willing to make curricular adjustments accordingly."[57] The report includes comments and reflections from other teachers of the course. Another aspect of dialogic validity is shown by citations to other work by both authors, who have written about and presented papers on global education to their professional peers.

53. Ibid., pp. 213–214.
54. Morton, M. L., & Williams, N. L. (2002). Apples, bats and transdisciplinary teaching: Collaborative action research in literacy at an urban charter school. In P. E. Linder & M. B. Sampson (Eds.), *Celebrating the faces of diversity: The twenty-third yearbook, a peer reviewed publication of the College Reading Association* (pp. 151–168). Commerce, TX: College Reading Association.
55. Ibid., p. 166.
56. Gaudelli, W., & Fernekes, W. R. (2004). Teaching about global human rights for global citizenship. *The Social Studies, 95*(1), 16–26.
57. Ibid., p. 20.

Reducing Discrepancies between Practioners' Espoused Theories and Theories-in-Action

Touchstone in Research

Robinson, V. M., & Lai, M. K. (2006). *Practitioner research for educators: A guide to improving classrooms and schools.* Thousand Oaks, CA: Corwin.

The theory of action developed by Chris Argyris and Richard Schön provides a conceptual foundation for strengthening the design and hence the outcomes of action research.[58] Argyris and Schön claim that a major challenge in the professional development of teachers and other practitioners involves fostering the discovery of discrepancies between an individual's **espoused theory** (that is, one's beliefs about how one deals with problems of practice) and the individual's **theory-in-action** (that is, what one actually does in practice). For example, a teacher might say that he believes in gender equity, but in practice he might invariably select girls to carry out mundane classroom tasks. If practitioners are actively committed to improving their practice through action research, it is likely that they will be motivated to take steps to reduce such discrepancies when they discover them. They can do so either by bringing their actions more into line with their espoused beliefs, or by clarifying what they are truly committed to and then initiating actions consistent with those commitments.

Practitioners can collect data that directly help them explore areas where what they say they believe and what they actually do may be discrepant. For example, a teacher could set up a videotape recorder in her classroom and videotape herself as she carries out a lesson—a type of research that gained prominence in the development and evaluation of a form of teacher training known as *microteaching.*[59] She could then compare her espoused theory and her theory-in-action by observing the videotape and filling out an observation scale to assess the extent to which she carried out the actions that she intended to carry out. She could also ask others, particularly her teaching colleagues, to observe and give her feedback and then compare it to her own observations or those of outsiders.

Argyris and Schön suggest that a practitioner's theory-in-action is best determined through observations made by others. Stephen Kemmis and Robin McTaggart, however, claim that reliance on the interpretations of observers who are "outsiders"—typically academics—would disempower teachers and would support the view that outsider research is more valid than teacher research.[60]

We would argue that both perspectives are valuable to action researchers. As described earlier, practitioners should use reflection to discover any discrepancies between their beliefs and their actions. However, we also see the value of comparing their perceptions with those of others whose opinions they value, such as colleagues, administrators, or staff development specialists.

Practitioner–Academic Collaboration

All or most of the examples of action research presented in this chapter involve collaboration between school practitioners and university professors. We do not, however, accept the labels of *insider* and *outsider* to describe these two types of educators, because both types engage in practice in their own work settings and also are capable of carrying out research in their own and other settings. Recently, Greenwood and Levin have called for university academics to work with practitioners from varied settings, in real-world contexts, as true equals, for the desired outcome not only of practitioners gaining university credit

58. Argyris, C., & Schön, D. A. (1974). *Theory in practice: Increasing professional effectiveness.* San Francisco: Jossey-Bass.
59. MacLeod, G. (1995). Microteaching in teacher education. In L. W. Anderson (Ed.), *International encyclopedia of teaching and teacher education* (2nd ed., pp. 573–577). Tarrytown, NY: Elsevier Science.
60. Kemmis & McTaggart, Participatory action research.

for their learning, but also to transform the roles of, interdepartmental relationships among, and administrative structures governing university academics.[61]

Ethical Issues in Action Research

In Chapter 3, we described general policies and practices designed to ensure the ethical conduct of research studies. Because action research is so closely intertwined with practice, action researchers may face additional ethical issues in reconciling their role of researcher with their traditional role of serving students and other clients. In 1995 the U.S. Office for Protection from Research Risks (OPRR) directed that all research—including action research studies of commonly accepted educational settings and involving normal educational practices—needs to be examined by an institutional review board (IRB).[62] We suggest that you contact your institution's IRB to determine whether it is using these regulations and if so, what procedures you need to follow.

Jane Zeni argues that action research does not fit the typical IRB model, because "action researchers pursue a question through an often meandering route, finding appropriate data sources along the way."[63] Her guide to ethical decision making poses questions to help researchers to address the unique ethical problems of action research.[64]

Many of the questions in Zeni's guide are similar to those asked in a typical IRB review, for example: "What is your time frame? Is this a one-shot project or do you anticipate several cycles? Have you done a preliminary study?"[65] Others help action researchers address the unique ethical issues that are likely to be most challenging to them. In Zeni's experience, these unique ethical issues typically involve (a) participation and collaboration in the research and (b) presentation or publication of the research report. Examples of questions dealing with participation and collaboration issues are: "Does your inquiry focus on people with less power than you?" and "How does your project demonstrate mutual respect and justice?"[66] Examples of questions dealing with presentation and publication issues are: "What do your students know of your research? Who told them? What are the risks to them or their families of their knowing (or not knowing) what you write or collect?"[67]

Zeni argues that dialogue with others about such ethical issues will help action researchers build "covenants of trust" with colleagues as well as with those who participate in or read their research.[68] Taking time to address the questions in Zeni's guide will help action researchers build such a covenant of trust with their own research collaborators, participants, and audience.

Ivor Pritchard's analysis of the relationship between practitioner research and institutional review boards also addresses ethical issues in action research.[69] Pritchard points out discrepancies in how practitioners, ethicists, and IRB members view such issues and gives suggestions for improving their relationships.

61. Greenwood, D. J., & Levin, M. (2005). Reform of the social sciences, and of universities through action research. In N. K. Denzin & Y. S. Lincoln (Eds.), *Sage handbook of qualitative research* (3rd ed., pp. 43–64). Thousand Oaks, CA: Sage.
62. Anderson, P. V. (1998). Simple gifts: Ethical issues in the conduct of person-based composition research. *College Composition and Communication, 49*(1), 63–89. Subsequently OPRR was reorganized as the Office of Human Research Protections (OHRP).
63. Zeni, J. (2001) Epilogue: A guide to ethical decision making for insider research. In Zeni, J. (Ed.), *Ethical issues in practitioner research* (pp. 153–165). New York: Teachers College Press. Quote appears on p. 153.
64. Ibid.
65. Ibid, p. 157.
66. Ibid, p. 159.
67. Ibid, p. 163.
68. Ibid, p. 161.
69. Pritchard, I. A. (2002). Travelers and trolls: Practitioner research and institutional review boards. *Educational Researcher, 31*(3), 3–13.

RECOMMENDATIONS FOR

Doing Action Research

1. When designing an action research project, determine the personal, professional, and political purposes you want the project to serve.
2. Choose data-collection methods—qualitative, quantitative, or both—that will best help you answer your research question.
3. Build reflection into your action research process through autobiographical narrative and journaling.
4. After taking action, decide whether and how you wish to continue or modify your action research project.
5. Design and report your action research project in a way that helps other practitioners determine the extent to which your findings fit their situation.
6. Apply the criteria described in the chapter for credibility and trustworthiness to your own or others' action research projects, and identify any other criteria that you consider important.
7. When interpreting your action research findings, seek to reduce discrepancies between your espoused theory and your theory-in-action through reflection, data collection, and feedback from others.
8. Carefully address the unique ethical issues involved in designing and carrying out an action research project.

SELF-CHECK TEST

Circle the correct answer to each of the following questions.
The answers are provided at the back of the book.

1. Action research differs most from other forms of educational research in its emphasis on
   a. obtaining knowledge to apply to one's local situation.
   b. generation of generalizable findings.
   c. collaboration between researchers.
   d. analysis of qualitative data about one's students.
2. An action research project concerned mainly with promoting colleagueship among practitioners best represents the _____ purpose of action research.
   a. personal
   b. professional
   c. political
   d. instrumental

3. Action research differs most from typical professional practice in its
   a. concern for fostering students' learning.
   b. concern for discovering generalizable knowledge.
   c. promotion of practitioners' professional development.
   d. systematic collection of data as a guide to improving practice.
4. Which of the following is *not* recommended for increasing the generalizability of an action research study's findings?
   a. studying cases that are unique
   b. studying a random sample within the group of interest
   c. providing statistical results that can be compared across settings
   d. providing a rich, thick description of any qualitative findings

5. The chapter recommends that action researchers use an action research journal primarily for the purpose of
   a. recording data to be analyzed for the research project.
   b. saving drafts of the action research report.
   c. maintaining their schedule for carrying out each stage of research.
   d. reflecting on the strengths and weaknesses of their current practice.

6. Attempts to take into account the views of all parties who have a stake in the problem being investigated improve the _____ validity of an action research project.
   a. outcome
   b. process
   c. democratic
   d. dialogic

7. Discrepancies between an action researcher's espoused theory and theory-in-action can be reduced by all of the following *except*
   a. using a narrative form of reporting.
   b. obtaining the observations of outsiders.
   c. collecting data to explore areas where discrepancies may exist.
   d. reflecting on his or her research findings.

8. A unique ethical issue faced by action researchers involves the decision whether to
   a. do a preliminary study.
   b. make students aware of the types of data being collected.
   c. use quantitative research methods.
   d. obtain permission from an institutional review board.

9. For their action research projects to be considered successful, practitioners need to
   a. receive extensive preparation to develop research knowledge and skills.
   b. focus on professional purposes for doing the project.
   c. describe the generalizability of their results.
   d. apply the findings to their own practice.

SELF-CHECK TEST ANSWERS

Chapter 1. The Nature of Educational Research
1. d   2. c   3. b   4. b   5. a   6. d   7. d   8. b   9. a   10. b

Chapter 2. The Research Process: From Proposal to Final Report
1. c   2. a   3. d   4. b   5. c   6. a   7. c

Chapter 3. Ethics and Site Relations in Educational Research
1. d   2. c   3. d   4. a   5. d   6. a   7. b   8. c   9. c   10. a   11. d   12. c   13. b

Chapter 4. Reviewing the Literature
1. d   2. b   3. b   4. a   5. c   6. a   7. c   8. b   9. d   10. c   11. d   12. d

Chapter 5. Statistical Techniques
1. c   2. a   3. b   4. d   5. a   6. d   7. a   8. d   9. b   10. b

Chapter 6. Selecting a Sample
1. d   2. a   3. b   4. d   5. c   6. a   7. a   8. c   9. b   10. b   11. c   12. c   13. d   14. d
15. b

Chapter 7. Collecting Research Data with Tests and Self-Report Measures
1. a   2. c   3. b   4. b   5. b   6. c   7. d   8. b   9. c   10. d   11. d   12. d   13. a

Chapter 8. Collecting Research Data with Questionnaires and Interviews
1. c   2. b   3. b   4. c   5. d   6. d   7. a   8. a   9. b   10. b   11. c   12. b   13. b   14. d
15. c   16. b   17. d

Chapter 9. Collecting Research Data through Observation and Content Analysis
1. b   2. b   3. d   4. a   5. c   6. d   7. a   8. b   9. c   10. a   11. d

Chapter 10. Nonexperimental Research: Descriptive and Causal-Comparative Designs
1. a   2. a   3. b   4. c   5. d   6. a   7. c   8. d   9. a   10. b   11. a   12. b

Chapter 11. Nonexperimental Research: Correlational Designs
1. c   2. d   3. c   4. a   5. d   6. d   7. a   8. b   9. b   10. a   11. d   12. b   13. c   14. a
15. c

Chapter 12. Experimental Research: Designs, Part 1
1. a   2. b   3. b   4. c   5. d   6. a   7. a   8. a   9. d   10. c

Chapter 13. Experimental Research: Designs, Part 2
1. b   2. c   3. d   4. d   5. b   6. a   7. c   8. b   9. c   10. b   11. d   12. a   13. c

Chapter 14. Case Study Research
1. d   2. d   3. c   4. c   5. b   6. d   7. a   8. a   9. c   10. d   11. b   12. b   13. c   14. d

Chapter 15. Qualitative Research Traditions
1. b   2. b   3. c   4. a   5. c   6. c   7. d   8. a   9. d   10. d   11. a

Chapter 16. Historical Research
1. a   2. d   3. b   4. b   5. d   6. b   7. c   8. c   9. a   10. d

Chapter 17. Evaluation Research
1. d   2. b   3. d   4. d   5. a   6. c   7. c   8. b   9. c   10. b   11. c   12. a   13. a

Chapter 18. Action Research
1. a   2. b   3. d   4. a   5. d   6. c   7. a   8. b   9. d

Questions for Evaluating Quantitative Research Reports

The following are questions to use in evaluating each section of a quantitative research report. For each question we identify the type of information you will need to look for in the report to answer the question, and we provide a sample answer. The examples are drawn from our experience in evaluating quantitative research studies.

Introductory Section

1. Are the research problems or findings unduly influenced by the researchers' institutional affiliations, beliefs, values, or theoretical orientation?

    Information needed. Find the researchers' institutional affiliation. (This information usually appears beneath the title of the report or at the end.) Also, locate any information in the report that indicates their beliefs about education, values, or theoretical orientation.

    Example. Most of the researchers' prior work has advocated cognitive models of learning. Therefore, they may have biased their experiment so that the cognitively oriented teaching method came out better than the behaviorally oriented teaching method.

2. Do the researchers demonstrate undue positive or negative bias in describing the subject of the study (an instructional method, program, curriculum, person, etc.)?

    Information needed. Identify any adjectives or other words that describe an instructional method, program, curriculum, person, and so on in clearly positive or negative terms.

    Example. The researchers described the group of students as difficult to handle, unmotivated, and disorganized. No evidence was presented to support this characterization. This description in the absence of evidence may indicate a negative attitude toward the children who were studied.

3. Is the literature review section of the report sufficiently comprehensive? Does it include studies that you know to be relevant to the problem?

    Information needed. Examine the studies mentioned in the report. Note particularly if a recent review of the literature relevant to the research problem was cited or if the researchers mentioned an effort to make their own review comprehensive.

    Example. The researchers stated the main conclusions of a previously published comprehensive literature review on the instructional program that they intended to study. They demonstrated clearly how their study built on the findings and recommendations of this review.

Source: Adapted from pages 534–538 in: Gall, J. P., Gall, M. D., & Borg, W. R. (2005). *Applying educational research* (5th ed.). New York: Pearson/Allyn & Bacon.

4. Is each variable in the study clearly defined?

Information needed. Identify all the variables (also called constructs) that were studied. For each variable, determine if and how it is defined in the report.

Example. One of the variables is intrinsic motivation, which is defined in the report as the desire to learn because of curiosity. This definition is not consistent with other definitions, which state that intrinsic motivation is the desire to learn because of the satisfaction that comes from the act of learning and from the content being learned.

5. Is the measure of each variable consistent with how the variable was defined?

Information needed. Identify how each variable in the study was measured.

Example. The researchers studied self-esteem but did not define it. Therefore, it was not possible to determine whether their measure of self-esteem was consistent with their definition.

6. Are research hypotheses, questions, or objectives explicitly stated, and if so, are they clear?

Information needed. Examine each research hypothesis, question, or objective stated in the report.

Example. The researcher stated one general objective for the study. It was clearly stated, but did not give the reader sufficient understanding of the specific variables that were to be studied.

7. Do the researchers make a convincing case that a research hypothesis, question, or objective was important to study?

Information needed. Examine the researchers' rationale for each hypothesis, question, or objective.

Example. The researchers showed how the hypothesis to be tested was derived from a theory. They also showed that if the hypothesis was confirmed by the study it would add support to the validity of the theory, which is currently being used in the design of new reading curricula.

Methods Section

8. Did the sampling procedures produce a sample that is representative of an identifiable population or your local population?

Information needed. Identify the procedures that the researchers used to select their sample.

Example. The researchers selected several classes (not randomly) from one school. The only information given about the students was their average ability and gender distribution. I cannot tell from this description whether the sample is similar to students in our schools.

9. Did the researchers form subgroups to increase understanding of the phenomena being studied?

Information needed. Determine whether the sample was formed into subgroups, and if so, why.

Example. The researchers showed the effects of the instructional program for both boys and girls; this information was helpful. However, they did not show the effects for different ethnic subgroups. This is an oversight because the program might have a cultural bias that could have an adverse effect on some ethnic subgroups.

10. Is each measure in the study sufficiently valid for its intended purpose?

Information needed. Examine any evidence that the researchers presented to demonstrate the validity of each measure in the study.

Example. The XYZ Test was used because it purportedly predicts success in vocational education programs. However, the researchers presented evidence from only one study to support this claim. That study involved a vocational education program that was quite different from the one they investigated.

11. Is each measure in the study sufficiently reliable for its intended purpose?

Information needed. Examine any evidence that the researchers presented to demonstrate the reliability of each measure in the study.

Example. The researchers had observers rate each student's on-task behavior during Spanish instruction in a sample of 30 classrooms. Inter-observer reliability was checked by having pairs of observers use the rating system in the same 5 classrooms. The pairs typically agreed on 90 percent of their ratings, which indicates good reliability.

12. Is each measure appropriate for the sample?

Information needed. Determine whether the researchers reported the population for whom the measure was developed.

Example. The ABC Reading Test was developed 20 years ago for primary grade students. The current study also involves primary grade students, but the test may no longer be valid, because students and the reading curriculum have changed considerably over the past 20 years.

13. Were the research procedures appropriate and clearly stated so that others could replicate them if they wished?

Information needed. Identify the various research procedures that were used in the study and the order in which they occurred.

Example. The researchers administered three research tests during one class period the day before the experimental curriculum was introduced. The tests, though brief, may have overwhelmed the students so that they did not do their best work. Also, some aspects of the experimental curriculum (e.g., the types of seatwork activities) were not clearly described, and the researchers did not indicate how soon the final research tests were administered after the curriculum was completed.

Results Section

14. Were appropriate statistical techniques used, and were they used correctly?

Information needed. Identify any statistical techniques described in the report.

Example. The researchers calculated the mean score for students' performance on the five tests that were administered. However, they did not give the range of scores (i.e., lowest score and highest score). This would be helpful information, because they studied a highly heterogeneous group of students.

Discussion of Results

15. Do the results of the data analyses support what the researchers conclude are the findings of the study?

Information needed. Identify what the researchers considered to be the major findings of the study.

Example. The researchers concluded that the experimental treatment led to superior learning compared to the control treatment, but this claim was true for only two of the four criterion measures used to measure the effects of the treatments.

16. Did the researchers provide reasonable explanations of the findings?

Information needed. Identify how the researchers explained the findings of the study and whether alternative explanations were considered.

Example. The researchers concluded that the narrative version of the textbook was less effective than the traditional expository version. Their explanation was that the story in the narrative version motivated students to keep reading, but that it also distracted them from focusing on the factual information that was included on the test. They presented no evidence or theoretical rationale to support this explanation, although it seems plausible.

17. Did the researchers draw reasonable implications for practice and future research from their findings?

Information needed. Identify any implications for practice and future research that the researchers drew from their findings.

Example. The researchers claimed that teachers' morale would be higher if administrators would provide more self-directed staff development. However, this recommendation is based only on their questionnaire finding that teachers expressed a desire for more self-directed staff development. The researchers are not justified in using this bit of data to claim that teachers' morale will improve if they get the kind of staff development they prefer.

Questions for Evaluating Qualitative Research Reports

The following are questions to use in evaluating each section of a qualitative research report. For each question, we identify the type of information you will need to look for in the report to answer the question, and we provide a sample answer. The examples are drawn from our experience in evaluating qualitative research studies.

Introductory Section

1. Do the researchers explain their experience, orientation, and expectations relevant to the problem being investigated and indicate how these factors might affect the results?

   Information needed. Check for information about the researchers' institutional affiliation and position. Also look for comments or use of language that might reflect their beliefs, values, or theoretical orientation related to the research topic.

   Example. The researcher has been a high school coach for many years. This gives him empathy toward school athletes, but possible biases about such students' experience. The researcher expresses many judgments, both positive and negative, about the effects of athletics on students and admits to having strong opinions about the value of athletic experience for students.

2. Is the research being carried out in a real-life setting?

   Information needed. Determine whether the research will be conducted in the setting or settings in which research participants typically are found.

   Example. To study parenting styles, the researchers obtained permission to visit students' homes during the dinner hour and to observe after-dinner study sessions while parents interact with their school-age children.

3. If appropriate, do the researchers tie their research to a particular qualitative research tradition?

   Information needed. Determine whether any research traditions are mentioned as a basis for the study and, if so, whether each tradition is used appropriately in the definition of the research problem and in the collection, analysis, and interpretation of the data.

   Example. The research is described as an ethnography of college students living in a dorm. One researcher, a dorm advisor, played a participant–observer role, which ethnographers commonly assume when immersing themselves in the culture that they investigate. The report includes a thick description, with observations of and quotations from students to depict their study habits and forms of entertainment. The researchers use a theory of student culture to interpret their data.

Research Procedures

4. Was purposeful sampling used to select research participants, and was the type of sampling appropriate to the research question or topic?

   Information needed. Examine how the researchers define the phenomenon of interest and whether they used an appropriate purposeful sampling strategy to select the case or cases studied in the research.

   Example. The purpose of the research is stated as "to add to understanding of school–university partnerships." The researchers chose to study a case of this phenomenon involving the university where they are employed, which appears to be a convenience sample. Convenience is generally not a recommended strategy for selecting cases for study. The researchers should have stated what made this case information-rich for the purposes of their study.

5. Does each data-collection method to be used in the study appear to be suited for its intended purpose?

   Information needed. Examine any evidence that the researchers present to demonstrate the trustworthiness of the data that will result from the data-collection procedures to be used in the study.

   Example. The researcher's goal is to carry out a life history of a famous educator. He plans to read many biographies about this individual and to interview a number of practicing educators who knew him well. He will check the credibility of the statements in his report by having several people who were involved in some of the events described review a draft of the report. This plan appears to be well designed to produce a life history of high quality and rigor.

6. Is the time frame for data collection sufficient to allow in-depth study of the case or question being researched?

   Information needed. Identify the time period over which data will be collected on specific participants or events in the setting and the amount of time that the researchers plan to spend in the setting. If documents are to be analyzed, determine how extensive the search for documents was and how they will be analyzed.

   Example. The researchers want to learn how elementary teachers establish classroom management procedures at the beginning of the school year. They plan to observe each teacher in one school every day for the first three weeks, which is a good procedure. However, they will observe only the first hour of class time, because they assume that class routines will be explained at that time. The trustworthiness of the data resulting from this limited time sample may be questionable.

7. Will strategies be used to ensure consistency across observers or other data collectors to demonstrate a fit between the data and what occurs in the setting under study?

   Information needed. Examine any evidence that the researchers provide to demonstrate agreement among observers in their observations or in any codings of the data.

   Example. Two researchers developed a category system for coding field data related to teacher burnout. Each researcher independently coded the segments into which interview transcripts, field notes, documents, and other materials had been divided. They calculated the mean percentage of agreement across segments on each coding variable and found that no mean percentage fell below 80 percent.

8. Will quantitative data be obtained if appropriate to understanding the research problem?

   Information needed. Identify quantitative comments as to expected research findings, for example, "more than," "significant," "extremely," "not very much," and examine whether quantitative measures will be used to document such comments with data such as means and standard deviations.

Example. The researchers studied three teacher aides and made such comments as "They spent most of their time helping individual children and passing out or collecting papers." Time is difficult to estimate accurately but is easily quantified, so the researchers should have collected data in which observers coded each teacher aide's classroom activities into categories. Then the researchers could have recorded the time spent in each activity.

Research Results

9. Was an emergent design used in the research study?

Information needed. Determine whether the researchers specified a preliminary plan for the research, but modified the plan as needed in response to analysis of data early in the study.

Example. In a study of the power distribution among staff in a middle school, the researcher conducted interviews of selected administrators. When she analyzed the data, she sensed she was missing key aspects of power, so she added observations of administrators interacting with teachers, students, or parents. Her examination of findings at various stages of the research helped her determine whether more data needed to be collected and the research participants on whom she should focus.

10. Was there adequate triangulation/crystallization of sources, data-collection methods, and researcher perspectives to confirm the findings?

Information needed. See whether various data-collection methods or sources of data were used and compared to confirm or clarify the key findings of the study.

Example. The researchers found that school textbook adoption committees were generally frustrated with their task because textbook publishers provided scanty written information, and they rarely could question publishers' representatives in person. This frustration was documented by quotes from interviews of committee members, researcher field notes during committee meetings, and letters written by the committee chair to school and state department administrators.

11. Was the research designed and carried out with sufficient clarity and quality that it would be possible to replicate the study?

Information needed. Determine whether the report makes clear each research procedure used in the study and the order in which they occurred.

Example. The researchers' data-collection and analysis procedure involved (1) asking students questions as they attempted to solve various math problems and (2) using structural analysis to identify patterns inherent in their discourse. The math problems and questions are provided in the report, and the researchers explain the particular types of responses and sequencing of responses they used to analyze the data. Thus the study should be replicable.

12. Did the researchers obtain and report sufficient data and do adequate member checking to clarify the emic perspective of the various types of research participants involved?

Information needed. Determine whether the report includes sufficient quotations or summary comments from the research participants to clarify their perspective and whether the researchers checked the findings with members before finalizing the report.

Example. The researcher noted how the two teachers in his study responded to certain types of student comments about racial violence in society and ignored others. He provided three quotations from each teacher and discussed his interpretation of the teachers' perspectives. However, he did not appear to do any member checking with the teachers to ensure that he conveyed their perspectives accurately.

13. Did the researchers clarify their own etic perspective with respect to the findings?

Information needed. Check whether the researchers summarized their personal reactions to the findings or compared their perspective on the phenomenon studied to those of research participants.

Example. The researcher notes that she, like the women she studied, had an eating disorder. She comments that she later questioned her decision not to study such women in a treatment context, because her work might have had more impact on treatment had she done so. She does not reveal her own perspective on how the eating disorder affected her. Thus the etic perspective is not entirely clear.

Discussion of Results

14. Did the researchers provide reasonable interpretations of the findings?

Information needed. Identify how the researchers interpreted the findings of the study and whether alternative interpretations were considered.

Example. The researchers found that peer coaching did not improve the achievement of students who were coached at the school that they studied. They attributed its failure to the lack of a supportive context, especially low collegiality among the students. Another plausible explanation, which they did not consider, is that the peer coaches may not have been adequately trained for their roles.

15. Are the researchers' conclusions supported by evidence?

Information needed. Examine the researchers' conclusions and how each of them was supported by the data analyses.

Example. According to the report, most teachers in the study complained that standardized testing requirements made it impossible for them to teach students in a way that kept students motivated. The researcher used this finding to argue that standardized testing in the schools he studied should be eliminated. Given the current emphasis nationally on standardized testing, he should have provided other sources of evidence to support this radical conclusion.

16. Does the research report make clear the extent to which the findings can be applied to other settings?

Information needed. Look for statements about how the research findings might be applied to other settings or types of research participants and the rationale provided to justify such statements.

Example. The case study documented major changes in one teacher's views about school reform following completion of an in-service program in which the teacher conducted collaborative action research with other teachers. The researchers speculated that such in-service experience would have a similar impact on teachers with similar length of experience, skills, and motivation as the case teacher.

17. Did the researchers draw reasonable implications for practice and future research?

Information needed. Identify any implications for practice and future research noted by the researchers and whether they appear justified by the research findings.

Example. The researchers found that students who volunteer for community service derive many benefits from the experience. Therefore, they encouraged all educators to support students' participation in community service programs. This recommendation appears to be reasonable given the research findings.

APPENDIX C

Preliminary and Secondary Sources: Tests and Self-Report Measures

Assessment of Exceptional Students: Educational and Psychological Procedures

Taylor, R. L. (2005). *Assessment of exceptional students: Educational and psychological procedures* (7th ed.). Boston: Allyn & Bacon.

Comprehensive Handbook of Psychological Assessment: Behavioral Assessment

Hersen, M., Haynes, S. N., & Heiby, E. M. (Eds.). (2004). *Comprehensive handbook of psychological assessment: Behavioral assessment* (Vol. 3). Hoboken, NJ: Wiley.

Comprehensive Handbook of Psychological Assessment: Industrial and Organizational Assessment

Hersen, M., & Thomas, J. C. (Eds.). (2004). *Comprehensive handbook of psychological assessment: Industrial and organizational assessment* (Vol. 4). Hoboken, NJ: Wiley.

Comprehensive Handbook of Psychological Assessment: Intellectual and Neuropsychological Assessment

Goldstein, G., & Beers, S. R. (Eds.). (2004). *Comprehensive handbook of psychological assessment: Intellectual and neuropsychological assessment* (Vol. 1). Hoboken, NJ: Wiley.

Comprehensive Handbook of Psychological Assessment: Personality Assessment

Hilsenroth, M. J., Segal, D. L., & Hersen, M. (Eds.). (2004). *Comprehensive handbook of psychological assessment: Personality assessment* (Vol. 2). Hoboken, NJ: Wiley.

Dictionary of Behavioral Assessment Techniques

Herson, M., & Bellack, A. S. (Eds.). (2002). *Dictionary of behavioral assessment techniques.* Clinton Corners, NY: Percheron. Includes hundreds of measures of a wide variety of problems and disorders that occur in children, adolescents, adults, and senior citizens.

Directory of Unpublished Experimental Mental Measures

Goldman, B. A., & Mitchell, D. F. (2003). *Directory of unpublished experimental mental measures* (Vol. 8). Washington, DC: American Psychological Association.

Encyclopedia of Social Measurement

Kempf-Leonard, K. (Ed.). (2004). *Encyclopedia of social measurement* (Vols. 1–3). Washington, DC: American Psychological Association.

ETS (Educational Testing Service) TestLink

TestLink includes the ETS Test Collection and the ETS Tests in Microfiche. The Test Collection, the largest compilation of psychological tests in the world, is available online (http://www.ets.org/testcoll/index.html) and contains more than 25,000 tests and other measurment instruments developed from the early 1900s to the present. Tests in Microfiche is a database of tests designed for research purposes and tests that are not commercially available, that can be ordered directly from ETS.

Handbook of Classroom Assessment: Learning, Adjustment, and Achievement

Phye, G. D. (Ed.). (1996). *Handbook of classroom assessment: Learning, adjustment, and achievement.* San Diego, CA: Academic Press.

Handbook of Family Measurement Techniques

Touliatos, J., Perlmutter, B. F., Straus, M. A., & Holden, G. W. (Eds.). (2000). *Handbook of family measurement techniques* (Vols. 1–3). Thousand Oaks, CA: Sage.

Health and Psychosocial Instruments

This electronic source (www.ovid.com/site/catalog; click on Databases) lists unpublished measures that have been used in studies reported in journals.

Measures of Personality and Social Psychological Attitudes

Robinson, J. P., Shaver, P. R., & Wrightsman, L. S. (Eds.) (1991). *Measures of personality and social psychological attitudes.* San Diego, CA: Academic Press.

Mental Measurements Yearbook

Plake, B., & Spies, R. (Eds.). (2005). *Mental measurements yearbook* (16th ed.). Lincoln, NE: Buros Institute of Mental Measurements, University of Nebraska Press. Each new edition includes tests that are new or revised since the previous yearbook or that have generated 20 or more new references in the literature. Provides extensive information about each test and, for many of them, critical reviews. See also *Test Reviews Online* and *Tests in Print* in this appendix.

Psychware Sourcebook

Krug, S. E. (1993). *Psychware sourcebook* (4th ed.). Champaign, IL: MetriTech. Describes more than 500 computer-based products for assessment in education, psychology, and business.

Test Critiques

Keyser, D. J., & Sweetland, R. C. (Eds.). (1984–current). *Test critiques* (Vols. 1–11). Austin, TX: Pro-Ed. Provides extensive information about each of hundreds of widely used measures. Updated regularly.

Test Reviews Online

An electronic version of the *Mental Measurements Handbook* series is available online at http://buros.unl.edu/buros/jsp/search.jsp. It provides information on nearly 4,000 commercially available tests, including critical reviews of over 2,000 tests conducted by the Buros Institute, publishers of the *Mental Measuments Yearbook*. Free information about each test is provided; critical reviews are fee-based.

Tests: A Comprehensive Reference for Assessments in Psychology, Education, and Business

Maddox, T. (Ed.). (2003). *Tests: A comprehensive reference for assessments in psychology, education, and business* (5th ed.). Austin, TX: Pro-Ed.

Tests in Print

Buros Institute (2006). *Tests in print* (7th ed.). Lincoln, NE: Buros Institute of Mental Measurements, University of Nebraska Press. A comprehensive index of tests reviewed in all editions of the *Mental Measurements Yearbook* and other sourcebooks about tests. See also *Test Reviews Online* and *Mental Measurements Yearbook* in this appendix.

Preliminary and Secondary Sources on the History of Education

I. Preliminary Sources

Preliminary sources are indexes to various types of publications and other information. The following is a list of important preliminary sources used by historians of education. We provide a brief bibliographic citation for the hard-copy version. Some of them are also available in one or more electronic versions. A research librarian or university library catalog can help you identify and access these versions. (One good library catalog, accessible via the Web, is that of the Library of Congress: http://catalog.loc.gov.)

A. Bibliographies of Bibliographies

Fritze, R. H., Coutts, B. E., & Vyhnanek, L. A. (2004). *Reference sources in history: An introductory guide* (2nd ed.). Santa Barbara, CA: ABC-CLIO.

Norton, M. B. (1995). *The American Historical Association's guide to historical literature* (3rd ed.). New York: Oxford University Press. This preliminary source not only is a bibliography of bibliographies, but it also includes historiographical essays on each section topic.

B. Bibliographies of Biographies

Biography and genealogy master index (Vols. 1–2). (2006). Farmington Hills, MI: Gale.

Current biography cumulated index: 1940–2005. (2006). New York: Wilson.

Matthew, H. C. G., & Harrison, B. (2004). *Oxford dictionary of national biography.* New York: Oxford University Press.

C. Directories of Historical Societies

Many historical societies have been formed in order to advance the historical study of particular regions, time periods, and topics. The following is an example of a directory of these societies:

American Association for State and Local History Staff. *Directory of historical organizations in the United States and Canada* (15th ed.). Walnut Creek, CA: AltaMira.

D. General Indexes to Historical Publications

America: History and life. Online preliminary source that indexes publications about the United States and Canada from prehistory to the present. Information about this index is at http://www.abc-clio.com/academic

Historical abstracts. Online preliminary source that indexes publications about the history of the world, except for the United States and Canada, from 1450 to the present. Information about this index is at http://www.abc-clio.com/academic

E. Newspaper Reference Sources

United States newspaper program. (n.d.). A national effort by the states and the federal government to index and preserve on microfilm newspapers published in the United States from the eighteenth century to the present. Information about this program and its resources is at http://www.neh.gov/projects/usnp.html/

F. Indexes to Nonpublished Primary Sources

The following are several preliminary sources that are useful for accessing various types of primary sources, such as unpublished manuscripts, oral histories, films, and archival materials:

Directory of genealogical and historical libraries, archives and collections in the US and Canada 2002. Boulder, CO: Iron Gate.

National archives. A federal agency that preserves and indexes documents and materials created in the course of business conducted by the U.S. government. Information about this agency is at http://www.archives.gov/about/

National Historical Publications and Records Commission. (1988). *Directory of archives and manuscript repositories in the United States* (2nd ed.). Phoenix, AZ: Oryx.

National union catalog of manuscript collections. A program to index archival and manuscript collections in U.S. repositories. Information about this program is at http://www.loc.gov/coll/numc/

Smith, A. (1988). *Directory of oral history collections.* Phoenix, AZ: Oryx.

II. Secondary Sources

Secondary sources are publications in which the author describes other individuals' research studies, theories, and opinions. Many of these secondary sources are reviews of the literature on a particular historical topic. In this section, we list important secondary sources relating to the history of education. However, the list is not exhaustive, and some of the sources might go into new editions. Therefore, we recommend you check the currency of the edition. Electronic versions of *Books in Print* and the Library of Congress catalog (http://catalog.loc.gov) are useful for this purpose.

A. Biographies

There are a great many biographical dictionaries. To learn what is available, you can look in *Books in Print* or in a university library catalog under the title *Biographical Dictionary.* Some examples are:

American men and women of science (22nd ed.). (2004). Farmington Hills, MI: Gale.

Bowling, L. (2005). *Shapers of the great debate on the great society: A biographical dictionary.* Westport, CT: Greenwood.

Grattan-Guinness, I. (2003). *Companion encyclopedia of the history and philosophy of the mathematical sciences* (Vols. 1–2). Baltimore: Johns Hopkins University Press.

Meyner, N. E. (2001). *Biographical dictionary of Hispanic Americans* (2nd ed.). New York: Facts on File.

Nash, G. B. (2003). *Encyclopedia of American history.* New York: Facts on File.

Ohles, F., Ohles, S. M., & Ramsay, J. G. (1997). *Biographical dictionary of modern American educators.* Westport, CT: Greenwood.

B. History Encyclopedias

History encyclopedias contain articles that summarize what is known about particular historical topics. The articles usually contain a reference list, which can guide you to other relevant sources. Two examples are:

Bacon, D. C., Davidson, R. H., & Keller, M. (1995). *Encyclopedia of the United States Congress.* New York: Simon & Schuster.

Thernstrom, S. A., Orlov, A., & Handlin, O. (Eds.). (1980). *Harvard encyclopedia of American ethnic groups.* Cambridge, MA: Harvard University Press.

C. Geographical Reference Works

Geographical reference works provide data about the history and characteristics of geographical locations. An example is:

Merriam-Webster's geographical dictionary (3rd ed., rev.) (2005). Springfield, MA: Merriam-Webster.

D. Statistical Sourcebooks

Statistical sourcebooks contain many tables of numerical data arranged by topic area, as well as introductory essays that provide bibliographic information about other sources on the topic. Three major sources of U.S. government statistical data are

Carter, S. B., and others. (2006). *Historical statistics of the United States: Earliest times to the present.* New York: Cambridge University Press.

U.S. Bureau of the Census (1989). *Historical statistics of the United States: Colonial times to 1970.* New York: Cambridge University Press. Available only as a CD-ROM.

U.S. Bureau of the Census (1878 to date). *Statistical abstract of the United States.* Washington, DC: U.S. Government Printing Office.

A-B design. A type of single-case experiment in which the researcher institutes a baseline condition (A), followed by the treatment (B). The target behavior is measured repeatedly during both conditions.

A-B-A design. A type of single-case experiment in which the researcher institutes a baseline condition (A), administers the treatment (B), and institutes a second baseline condition (A). The target behavior is measured repeatedly during all three conditions.

A-B-A designs. Any single-case experiment that has at least one baseline condition (designated A) and one treatment condition (designated B).

A-B-A-B design. A type of single-case experiment in which the researcher institutes a baseline condition (A), administers the treatment (B), institutes a second baseline condition (A), and then readministers the treatment (B). The target behavior is measured repeatedly during all four conditions.

Accessible population. All the members of a set of people, events, or objects that feasibly can be included in the researcher's sample.

Achievement test. A type of performance test intended to measure an individual's knowledge of specific facts, as well as the individual's capability to perform higher-cognitive processes, such as reasoning and problem-solving, in a particular subject area.

Acquiescence bias. In testing, a type of response set in which individuals agree with items irrespective of their content.

Action research. A type of applied research, the purpose of which is the improvement of education professionals' own practice.

Adversary evaluation. A type of evaluation research that is characterized by the use of a wide array of data and the hearing of testimony, and that has opportunities for individuals with opposing opinions to present positive and negative judgments about the program being evaluated.

Age equivalent. A type of derived score that represents a given raw score on a measure as the average age of individuals in the norming group who earned that score.

Agency. In qualitative research, the assumed ability of individuals to shape the conditions of their lives.

Alpha. See *Cronbach's alpha coefficient.*

Alpha level. The level of statistical significance that is selected prior to data collection for rejecting a null hypothesis.

Alternate-form reliability. An approach to estimating test reliability in which individuals' scores on one version of a test are correlated with their scores on a different version of the test.

Analysis of covariance (ANCOVA). A procedure for determining whether the difference between the mean scores of two or more groups on one or more dependent variables is statistically significant, after controlling for initial differences between the groups on one or more extraneous variables. When the groups have been classified on several independent variables (called *factors*), the procedure can be used to determine whether each factor and the interactions between the factors have a statistically significant effect on the dependent variable, after controlling for the extraneous variable.

Analysis of variance (ANOVA). A procedure for determining whether the difference between the mean scores of two or more groups on a dependent variable is statistically significant. When the groups have been classified on several independent variables (called *factors*), the procedure can be used to determine whether each factor and the interactions between the factors have a statistically significant effect on the dependent variable.

Analysis of variance for repeated measures. A procedure for determining whether the difference between the mean pretest-posttest gain score of the experimental group and that of the control group is statistically significant.

Analysis unit. See *segment.*

Analytic induction. In qualitative research, the process of inferring themes and patterns from an examination of data.

Analytic reporting. In a qualitative research report, the use of an objective writing style (i.e., the researcher's voice is silent or subdued) and other conventions typical of quantitative research reporting.

Anti-oppressive education. A critical form of pedagogy that involves constantly looking beyond what is taught and learned in order to question and expose oppression.

Antiquarian. An individual who studies the past for its own sake with little concern for its relevance to present-day issues and happenings.

Applicability. The extent to which the findings of a qualitative research study are applicable to other cases or settings.

Aptitude test. A measure of abilities that are assumed to be relevant to future performance in a specific type of skill or an area of achievement.

Aptitude-treatment interaction (ATI) experiment (or *attribute-treatment interaction experiment*). A type of experiment that is designed to determine whether instructional methods or other interventions have different effects for different types of individuals.

Archive (or *repository*). A facility for storing documents so that they are preserved in good condition, and access to them can be carefully monitored.

Artifact. See *material culture*.

Artificial dichotomy. A categorical variable with only two values, which are formed from continuous scores (e.g., classifying a student as low-achieving if his test score is below 30 and as high-achieving if his test score is above 70).

Attitude. A measure of an individual's viewpoint or disposition toward a particular person, thing, or idea.

Attribute-treatment interaction experiment. See *aptitude-treatment interaction experiment.*

Attrition. The loss of research participants from a sample over a period of time.

Audit trail. In a literature review, an account of all the procedures and decision rules that were used by the reviewer. In qualitative research, the process of documenting the materials and procedures used in each phase of a study.

Autoethnography. An approach to qualitative research that involves autobiography and investigation of multiple levels of individual consciousness in relation to cultural phenomena.

B **weight.** See *beta weight.*

b **weight.** See *regression weight.*

Bar graph. A diagram that shows the relationship between two measures, one of which yields categorical scores.

Baseline. In a single-case experiment, the research participant's natural behavior pattern in the absence of the experimental treatment. In prediction research, the percentage of individuals who actually will achieve a particular outcome if no prediction procedure is applied.

Behavior modification. The use of such techniques as social and token reinforcement, fading, desensitization, and discrimination training for the purpose of changing an individual's behavior patterns.

Behavioral objective. A statement of a program goal that includes three components: an observable behavior that serves as an indicator of goal attainment, criteria for successful performance of the behavior, and the situational context in which the behavior is to be performed.

Beta weight (or *B weight*). A multiplier term added to each predictor variable in a multiple regression equation after the predictor variables have been converted to standard score form.

Bias. A set to perceive events or other phenomena in such a way that certain facts are habitually overlooked, distorted, or falsified. In sampling, a procedure that results in a sample that is not representative of the target population.

Bibliography. A type of preliminary source that lists publications on a given topic or field of study.

Bivariate correlation coefficient. Any type of statistic that describes the magnitude of the relationship between two variables.

Boolean operator. A method based on Boolean algebra for searching an electronic database for records that contain two or more designated keywords (by using an AND operator), that contain any of two or more designated keywords (by using an OR operator), or that contain at least one designated keyword but not another designated keyword (by using a NOT operator); the term "connector" is sometimes used instead of "operator."

Canonical correlation. A type of multiple regression analysis involving the use of two or more measured variables to predict a composite index of several criterion variables.

Case. In qualitative research, a particular instance of a phenomenon of interest to the researcher.

Case study research. The in-depth study of instances of a phenomenon in real-life settings and from the perspective of the participants involved in the phenomenon.

Catalytic validity. A judgment about the credibility of an action research project based on the extent to which the project causes stakeholders to transform their view of reality in relation to their professional practice.

Categorical variable. A characteristic that has been measured as a nominal scale.

Category. In qualitative research, a construct that is used to classify a certain type of phenomenon in the database.

Causal inference. Based on the results of a data analysis, the conclusion that one set of events brought about, directly or indirectly, a subsequent set of events.

Causal pattern. In case study research, an inference that particular phenomena within a case or across cases are systematically related to each other and that the relationship is one of cause-and-effect.

Causal-comparative research. A type of quantitative investigation that seeks to discover possible causes and effects of a personal characteristic (e.g., self-esteem or academic success) by comparing individuals in whom it is present with individuals in whom it is absent or present to a lesser degree.

CD-ROM. An acronym for *Compact Disk-Read Only Memory,* a computer device for storing and providing easy access to a large amount of information (e.g., an index to the education literature).

Ceiling effect. A situation in which the test has a limited range of difficulty, with most test items so difficult that many testees earn a very low score, or with most items so easy that many testees earn the maximum score or a score close to it.

Centroid. The mean of the vector scores for all the individuals classified as members of a particular group in a multivariate analysis of variance.

Chain of evidence. In qualitative research, the validation of a study's findings by demonstrating clear, meaningful links among the study's research questions, the raw data, the data analysis, and the findings.

Chain sample. See *snowball sample.*

Chart essay. A verbal and visual format for describing the findings of a research study so that they are easily understood by policy makers and practitioners.

Chi-square (χ^2) test. A nonparametric test of statistical significance that is used when the research data are in the form of frequency counts for two or more categories.

CIJE. See *Current Index to Journals in Education.*

CIPP model. A type of evaluation that is designed to support the decision-making process in program management. CIPP is an acronym for the four types of educational evaluation included in the model: Context evaluation, Input evaluation, Process evaluation, and Product evaluation.

Citation (or *bibliographic citation* or *reference*). The information about a document that one would need in order to locate it, usually including author, title, publication date, publisher, and, in the case of journal articles, page numbers and volume number.

Closed-form item. A question that permits a response only from among prespecified response options (e.g., a multiple-choice question).

Cluster sample. A group of research participants that is formed by selecting naturally occurring groups (i.e., clusters) in the population. See also *multistage-cluster sample.*

Coding. A method of data analysis in qualitative research in which segments of data are assigned to one or more categories.

Coefficient of determination (R^2). A mathematical expression of the amount of variance in the criterion variable that is explained in a multiple regression analysis by a predictor variable or a combination of predictor variables.

Coefficient of equivalence. A measure of the alternate-form reliability of a test, based on the magnitude of the relationship between individuals' scores on two parallel versions of the same test.

Coefficient of internal consistency. See *split-half reliability correlation coefficient.*

Coefficient of stability. A measure of the alternate-form reliability of a test, based on the magnitude of the relationship between individuals' scores on two forms of the same test on two different testing occasions.

Cognitive anthropology. See *ethnoscience.*

Cognitive ethnography. See *ethnoscience.*

Cognitive psychology. The study of the structures and processes involved in mental activity and of how these structures and processes are learned or develop with maturation.

Cohort longitudinal research. A type of investigation in which changes in a population over time are studied by selecting a different sample at each data-collection point from a population that remains constant.

Collaborative evaluation. Any form of evaluation in which there is a significant degree of cooperative effort between evaluators and stakeholders in the planning and conduct of the evaluation.

Collinearity. The degree of correlation between any two variables that are to be used as predictors in a multiple regression analysis.

Combination/mixed purpose sampling. A form of purposeful sampling involving a change from one sampling strategy to another as data collection progresses, in order to serve multiple research purposes.

Command file. In statistical analysis, a list of the computer software instructions that are used to perform a particular analysis.

Compensatory rivalry (or *John Henry effect*). In experiments, a situation in which control group participants perform beyond their usual level because they perceive that they are in competition with the experimental group.

Complete-observer role. In qualitative research, the observer's maintenance of a posture of detachment while collecting research data in a field setting.

Complete-participant role. In qualitative research, the observer's assumption of the role of group member while collecting research data about it.

Computer-adaptive testing. An approach to measurement in which the difficulty level of test items presented to a particular test-taker is matched by the computer to the test-taker's ability level as judged from performance on earlier test items.

Computer-assisted telephone interview. A type of interview in which the interviewer uses a computer to assist in gathering information while conducting a telephone interview.

Concepts. In qualitative research, terms that can be used to group individuals, events, or objects that share a common set of attributes.

Concurrent evidence (also called *concurrent validity*). The extent to which individuals' scores on a new test correspond to their scores on an established test of the same construct that is administered at approximately the same point in time.

Confidence interval. All the values within the range defined by the confidence limits of a sample statistic.

Confidence limits. As determined from sample statistics, an upper value and lower value that are likely to contain the actual population parameter (e.g., the population mean is likely to be between 2.3 and 4.7).

Confirmation survey interview. In qualitative research, a type of interview that is used to confirm the findings obtained from data that were collected by other methods.

Confirmatory factor analysis. The use of factor analysis to test hypotheses about the latent traits (also called *factors*) that underlie a set of measured variables.

Confirming and disconfirming case sample. A group of cases that is selected for the purpose of validating the findings of previous research.

Connoisseurship and criticism. A type of expertise-based evaluation involving appreciation of the phenomenon being evaluated (connoisseurship), along with assessment of the strengths and weaknesses of the phenomenon (criticism).

Consequences-of-testing evidence of test validity. The extent to which the values and consequences associated with test scores are consistent with the decisions made about individuals based on their test scores.

Consequential validity. See *consequences-of-testing evidence of test validity.*

Constant comparison. In the grounded theory approach, a process for analyzing qualitative data to identify categories, to create sharp distinctions between categories, and to decide which categories are theoretically significant.

Constitutively defined construct. A concept that is defined by reference to other concepts.

Construct. A concept that is inferred from commonalities among observed phenomena and that can be used to explain those phenomena. In theory development, a concept that refers to a structure or process that is hypothesized to underlie particular observable phenomena.

Constructivism. An epistemological doctrine that asserts a reality that is socially constructed and transmitted to members of a society by various social agencies and processes.

Construct validity. In case study research, the extent to which a measure used in a case study correctly operationalizes the concepts being studied.

Contact summary sheet. A brief form that is designed by the researcher for summarizing what was learned from each data-collection event and what types of data need to be collected next.

Content analysis. The study of particular aspects of the information contained in a document, film, or other form of communication.

Content-related evidence of test validity. The extent to which the items in a test represent the domain of content that the test is designed to measure.

Content validity. See *content-related evidence of test validity.*

Context evaluation. In the CIPP model of evaluation research, the identification of problems and needs that are occurring in a specific educational setting.

Contingency coefficient. A measure of the magnitude of the relationship between two variables in a chi-square analysis, when at least one of the variables has more than two categories.

Continuous recording. The recording of everything that is observed in an event, with the observations organized in chronological sequence.

Continuous score. A value of a measure that forms an interval or ratio scale with an indefinite number of points along its continuum.

Control group. In an experiment, a group of research participants who receive no treatment or an alternate treatment so that the effect of extraneous variables can be determined.

Convenience sample. A group of cases that are selected simply because they are available and easy to access.

Convergent evidence. Support for the validity of test-score interpretations that comes from positive correlations between a sample's scores on the test and their scores on other measures that are hypothesized to measure the same construct.

Convergent phase. The phase of an evaluation study in which the initial list of evaluation questions is reduced to a manageable number to ensure that the most important questions can be addressed with available resources.

Conversation analysis. The study of the implicit rules governing the speech acts between two or more people.

Correction for attenuation. A statistical procedure for estimating how much greater the correlation coefficient for two measured variables would be if the measures had perfect reliability.

Correction for restriction in range. A statistical procedure for estimating how much greater the correlation coefficient would be if the range of scores on one or both measured variables in a sample was extended to represent the full range of scores in the population.

Correlation coefficient. A mathematical expression of the direction and magnitude of the relationship between two measured variables.

Correlation matrix. An arrangement of correlation coefficients in rows and columns that makes it easy to see how each of a set of measured variables correlates with all the other variables.

Correlation ratio (*eta*). A mathematical expression that provides a more accurate index of the magnitude of the relationship between two measured variables than other correlational statistics when the relationship is markedly nonlinear.

Correlational research. A type of investigation that seeks to discover the direction and magnitude of the relationship among variables through the use of correlational statistics.

Cost analysis. In evaluation research, the determination of either (1) the relationship between the costs of a program and its benefits when both costs and benefits can be calculated in monetary terms (called the *cost-benefit ratio*), or (2) the relationship between the costs of various interventions relative to their measured effectiveness in achieving a desired outcome (called *cost-effectiveness*).

Cost-benefit ratio. See *cost analysis.*

Cost-effectiveness. See *cost analysis.*

Counterbalanced experiment. A type of experiment in which each research participant receives several treatments, but the order of administering the treatments is varied across participants to eliminate the possibility of an order effect.

Criterion sample. A group of cases that satisfy particular specifications or standards.

Criterion-referenced measurement. An approach to testing in which an individual's score on a test is interpreted by comparing it to a prespecified standard of performance.

Criterion-referenced measurement reliability. A measure of the consistency with which a measure accurately estimates each individual's level of mastery of the test domain, usually reported as the percentage of agreement with which different forms of the measure classify testees as those who reached the criterion and those who did not.

Criterion-related observer reliability. The extent to which the scores assigned by a trained observer agree with those assigned by an expert observer.

Criterion-related validity. Types of validity (specifically, predictive and concurrent validity) that involve an explicit standard against which claims about a test can be judged.

Critical race theory. A body of scholarship that explores how the life experiences of people of color are distorted and oppressed through power relations maintained by the dominant order, that is, "whites," and advocates strategies for material and social transformation of this condition.

Critical theory. The formulation of principles designed to clarify the power relationships and forms of oppression existing in a society or culture, and thus to serve as a guide to efforts to emancipate its members from those forms of oppression.

Critical-case sample. A single case that provides a crucial test of a theory, program, or other phenomenon.

Criticism. See *connoisseurship and criticism.*

Cronbach's alpha coefficient (α). A measure of the internal consistency of a test containing items that are not scored dichotomously, based on the extent to which test-takers who answer a given test item one way respond to other items in a similar way.

Cross-sectional longitudinal research. A type of investigation in which changes in a population over time are studied by collecting data at one point in time, but from samples that vary in age or developmental stage.

Crystallization. The use of mixed genres and methods to produce qualitative research of high quality that deconstructs the traditional ideas of validity and triangulation and provides a deepened, complex understanding of phenomena.

Cultural acquisition. The process by which individuals develop the concepts, values, skills, and behaviors associated with the culture in which they are raised.

Cultural studies. A branch of critical theory that involves the study of power relationships and forms of oppression in a culture in order to help emancipate its members from those forms of oppression.

Cultural transmission. The process by which cultural institutions intervene in individuals' lives to shape their learning or nonlearning of specific features of life in the culture.

Culture. The sum total of ways of living (e.g., values, customs, rituals, and beliefs) that are built up by a group of human beings and that are transmitted from one generation to another or from current members to newly admitted members.

Current Index to Journals in Education (CIJE). An index to articles in hundreds of education-related journals. Published monthly by ERIC.

Database. A collection of information, such as literature citations or a sample's scores on various measures, that has been organized for easy searching and analysis, typically by a computer.

Deception. The act of creating a false impression in the minds of research participants through such procedures as withholding information, providing false information, creating false intimacy, or using accomplices.

Deconstruction. The assertion that any text has no definite meaning and therefore no authority, that words can refer only to other words, and that "playing" with a text can yield multiple, often contradictory interpretations.

Dehoaxing. If a research study involves deception, a type of debriefing in which the researcher must convince all deceived participants that they were in fact deceived, so that the deception will have no continuing harmful effect on them.

Democratic validity. A judgment about the credibility of an action research project based on the extent to which the perspectives and interests of all stakeholders were taken into account.

Deontological ethics. In research, judgments about the morality of one's research decisions and actions by reference to absolute values (e.g., honesty, justice, and respect for others).

Dependent variable. A variable that the researcher thinks occurred after, and as a result of, another variable (called the *independent variable*). In a hypothesized cause-and-effect relationship, the dependent variable is the effect.

Derived score. A transformation of a raw score (e.g., age equivalents) to reveal the individual's performance relative to a norming group.

Descriptive observational variable (or *low-inference variable*). A variable that requires little inference on the part of an observer to determine its presence or level.

Descriptive research. In quantitative research, a type of investigation that measures the characteristics of a sample or population on prespecified variables. In qualitative research, a type of investigation that involves providing a detailed portrayal of one or more cases.

Descriptive statistics. Mathematical techniques for organizing, summarizing, and displaying a set of numerical data.

Descriptor. In a preliminary source, a term that is used to classify all documents that contain information about the topic denoted by the term.

Desensitization. If a research study involves deception, a type of debriefing in which the researcher helps all deceived participants cope with any negative perceptions about themselves that the deception induced.

Deviance bias. In testing, a type of response set in which an individual answers items to create the appearance of being atypical or abnormal.

Deviant-case sample. See *extreme-case sample.*

Diagnostic test. A type of measure that is used to identify a student's strengths and weaknesses in a particular school subject.

Dialogic validity. A judgment about the credibility of an action research project based on the extent to which colleagues shared in the development of the practitioner/researcher's findings and interpretations.

Dichotomy. A categorical variable that has only two values.

Differential item functioning. A feature of a test item whereby individuals of equal ability but from different subgroups (e.g., males and females) do not have the same probability of earning the same score on the item.

Directional hypothesis. A type of prediction that the researcher makes on the basis of theory or speculation and that is tested by collecting and analyzing data. The prediction specifies the direction of the relationship (positive or negative) expected between two measured variables, or

which research group will score higher on the measured variable.

Disconfirming case sample. See *confirming and disconfirming case sample.*

Discourse analysis. The study of the interpretive processes that individuals use to produce their accounts of reality.

Discrepancy evaluation. A type of evaluation research that involves the investigation of discrepancies between the objectives of a program and students' actual achievement of the objectives.

Discrete score. A value of a measure that forms a nominal scale with only a finite number of values between any two points on the scale.

Discriminant analysis. A type of multiple regression analysis involving the use of two or more measured variables that yield continuous scores to predict a single criterion variable that is categorical in nature.

Discriminant evidence. Support for the validity of test-score interpretations that comes from negative correlations between a sample's scores on the test and their scores on other measures that are hypothesized to measure a different construct.

Divergent phase. The phase of an evaluation study in which a comprehensive list of questions, issues, concerns, and information needs that might be addressed in the evaluation is generated.

Document summary form. A brief form that is designed by the researcher for summarizing what was learned from examining a particular document and ideas about other documents that should be obtained and studied.

Domain-referenced measurement. A type of criterion-referenced measurement that assesses how well an individual performs on a sample of items that represents a well-defined content area.

Dual publication. The unethical practice of publishing more than one report about the same research results in order to create an exaggerated impression of a researcher's productivity.

Duncan's multiple-range test. A type of *t* test for multiple comparisons.

Duration recording. The measurement of the amount of time that various observational variables occur during an event (e.g., a classroom lesson).

Ecological ethics. In research, judgments about the morality of one's research decisions and actions in terms of the participants' culture and the larger social systems of which they are a part.

Ecological validity. The extent to which the results of an experiment can be generalized from conditions in the research setting to particular naturally occurring conditions.

Educational connoisseurship and criticism. See *connoisseurship and criticism.*

Educational evaluation. The process of making judgments about the merit, value, or worth of an educational program, method, or other phenomenon.

Educational Resources Information Center (ERIC). A federally funded agency that provides many information resources to the education community, including a database of citations for education-related journals and reports.

Effect size. A statistical measure of the strength of an observed difference between groups on a test or other instrument or the strength of an observed relationship between two or more measured variables.

Emancipatory action research. A type of self-reflective investigation that professional practitioners undertake for the purpose of improving the rationality and justice of their work.

Emergent design. In qualitative research, the researchers' specification of a preliminary plan for the research and subsequent modification of the plan as needed in response to the analysis of data early in the study. In responsive evaluation, the practice of changing the design of an evaluation as the evaluator gains new insights into the concerns and issues of the stakeholders.

Emic perspective. The research participants' perceptions and understanding of their social reality.

Empowerment evaluation. A type of evaluation in which a community uses self-evaluation and reflection to improve its programs, with an external evaluator acting as coach and facilitator.

Endogenous variable. In a path analysis model, a variable for which there is another variable in the model that is hypothesized to influence it.

Epistemology. The branch of philosophy that studies the nature of knowledge and the process by which knowledge is acquired and validated.

ERIC. See *Educational Resources Information Center.*

Error of central tendency. The tendency for an observer to rate all or most of the individuals at or near the midpoint of an observational scale.

Error of leniency. The tendency for an observer to assign high ratings to the majority of research participants even when they differ considerably on the variable being measured.

Espoused theory. In the theory of action, professionals' beliefs about how they deal with problems of practice.

Eta. See *correlation ratio.*

Ethnographic content analysis. In anthropology, the study of the content of documents found in field settings as reflections of the local culture.

Ethnography. The in-depth study of the features of life in a given culture and the patterns in those features.

Ethnography of communication. In anthropology, the study of how members of a cultural group use speech in their social life.

Ethnology. In anthropology, the study of similarities and differences among cultures.

Ethnomethodology. In sociology, the study of the techniques that individuals use to make sense of their everyday social life and to accomplish the tasks of communicating, making decisions, and reasoning in social situations.

Etic perspective. The researcher's conceptual and theoretical understanding of the research participants' social reality.

Evaluative observational variable. A variable that requires an observer both to make an inference from behavior to a construct that is presumed to underlie the behavior and an evaluative judgment.

Evidence-based practice. An approach used by practitioners in education and other professions to make decisions on behalf of their clients based on the best available research, rather than solely on their own experience and beliefs.

Ex post facto research. A term from Latin (meaning "from that which is done afterward") that refers to correlational or causal-comparative research because, in these types of investigation, causes are studied after they presumably have exerted their effect on the variable of interest.

Exogenous variable. In a path analysis model, a variable for which there is no other variable in the model that is hypothesized to influence it.

Experimental mortality. The loss of research participants from an experiment while it is in progress.

Experimental treatment. See *treatment variable.*

Experimentally accessible population. A defined population, usually local in nature, from which it is feasible for the researcher to draw a sample to participate in an experiment.

Experimenter bias. In experiments, a situation in which the researcher's expectations about what will occur are unintentionally transmitted to the research participants so that their behavior in the experiment is affected. Also, a situation in which the researcher's expectations affect data collection and data analysis.

Expertise-based evaluation. The use of experts to make judgments about the worth of an educational program.

Explained variance (r^2). In correlation, a statistic that specifies the percentage of the variance in variable X that can be predicted from the variance in variable Y. The greater the value of r^2, the greater the amount of explained variance.

Exploratory data analysis. A method for discovering patterns in a set of scores.

Exploratory factor analysis. An approach to factor analysis in which the researcher has no prior hypotheses about the latent variables (also called *factors*) that might underlie a set of measured variables.

External criticism. In historical research, the determination of whether the apparent or claimed origin (author and place, date, and circumstances of publication) of a historical document corresponds to its actual origin.

External evaluator (or *third-party evaluator* or *evaluation contractor*). An individual who is employed to evaluate a program, but is not a member of the program's staff.

External validity. The extent to which the results of a research study can be generalized to individuals and situations beyond those involved in the study.

Extinction. In a single-case experiment or the practice of behavior modification, the act of withdrawing a treatment after a research participant has become accustomed to it.

Extraneous variable. In experiments, any aspect of the situation, other than the treatment variable, that can influence the dependent variable and that, if not controlled, can make it impossible to determine whether the treatment variable is responsible for any observed effect on the dependent variable.

Extreme-case sample (or *deviant-case sample*). A group of cases that are highly unusual manifestations of the phenomenon being investigated.

Extreme-groups technique. In causal-comparative research, the procedure of selecting comparison groups that are at the minimum and maximum of a score distribution on variable X.

F maximum test for homogeneity of variance. A procedure for determining whether the observed difference among the variances of scores of more than two groups on variable X is statistically significant.

Face validity. The extent to which a casual, subjective inspection of a test's items indicates that they cover the content that the test is claimed to measure.

Factor. In a factor analysis of a set of variables, a mathematical expression of a feature shared by a particular subset of the variables.

Factor analysis. A statistical procedure for reducing a set of measured variables to a smaller number of variables (called *factors* or *latent variables*) by combining variables that are moderately or highly correlated with each other.

Factor score. The score earned by each individual on a particular factor identified in a factor analysis.

Factorial experiment. A type of experiment in which the researcher studies how two or more treatment variables (called *factors* in this context) affect a dependent variable either independently or in interaction with each other.

Fixed factor. In experimental designs, an independent variable whose values will not be generalized beyond the experiment.

Focus. In case study research, the aspects of a phenomenon on which data collection and analysis will concentrate.

Focus group interview. A type of interview involving an interviewer and a group of research participants, who are free to talk with and influence each other in the process of sharing their ideas and perceptions about a defined topic.

Forgery. In historical research, a document or relic that is claimed to be genuine, but that actually is a deception.

Formative evaluation. A type of evaluation that is done while a program is under development in order to improve its effectiveness, or to support a decision to abort further development so that resources are not wasted on a program that has little chance of ultimately being effective.

Frequency-count recording. Measurement of the number of times that each observational variable occurs during an event (e.g., a classroom lesson).

Futurology. A type of research whose goal is prediction of what the future of a particular phenomenon is likely to be.

Gain score (or *change score* or *difference score*). An individual's score on a test administered at one point in time minus that individual's score on a test administered at an earlier time.

General interview guide approach. A type of interview in which a set of topics is planned, but the order in which the topics are covered and the wording of questions is decided as the interview proceeds.

Generalizability. The extent to which the findings of a quantitative research study can be assumed to apply not only to the sample studied, but also to the population that the sample represents.

Generalizability coefficient. In generalizability theory, a measure of test reliability that considers the joint effect of all the sources of measurement error that have been investigated.

Generalizability theory. An approach to conceptualizing and assessing the relative contribution of different sources of measurement error to a set of test scores.

Goal-free evaluation. A type of evaluation research in which the evaluator investigates the actual effects of a program without being influenced by prior knowledge of the program's stated goals.

Grade equivalent. A type of derived score that represents a given raw score on a measure as the average grade level of individuals in a norming group who earned that score.

Grounded theory. An approach to theory development that involves deriving constructs and laws directly from the immediate data that the researcher has collected rather than drawing on an existing theory.

Group test. A test that is administered at the same time to all the members of a group to be tested.

Halo effect. The tendency for the observer's early impressions of an individual being observed to influence the observer's ratings of all variables involving the same individual.

Hawthorne effect. An observed change in research participants' behavior based on their awareness of participating in an experiment, their knowledge of the researcher's hypothesis, or their response to receiving special attention.

Hegemony. The maintenance of domination of subordinate groups by privileged groups through its cultural agencies (e.g., governmental bodies and public school systems).

Hermeneutic circle. An interpretation of a text by the process of alternating between interpreting the meaning of each part of the text and the meaning of the text as a whole.

Hermeneutics. A field of inquiry that seeks to understand how individuals develop interpretations of texts.

Hidden curriculum. The knowledge, values, and behaviors that are taught tacitly by the way in which schools are structured and classroom instruction is organized.

Hierarchical linear modeling (or *HLM* or *multilevel modeling*). A statistical technique for analyzing the relationship between predictor variables and a criterion variable when each bit of data reflects several nested categories, such as students' test scores being "nested" within the students' classroom and also within their school; HLM makes it possible to determine the effect of each nested category (e.g., classroom and school) and their interactions on the predictor-criterion relationship.

High-inference variable. See *inferential observational variable.*

Histogram. A diagram that shows the relationship between two measured variables both of which yield continuous scores.

Historical criticism. See *internal criticism* and *external criticism.*

Historical facts. Data that historical researchers regard as true, that is, valid, and relevant to the description or interpretation of the phenomenon being investigated.

Historical research. The study of past phenomena for the purpose of gaining a better understanding of present institutions, practices, trends, and issues.

Historiography. The study of the methods that historians use in their research.

Homogeneous-case sample. A group of cases that are similar in that they represent one defined point of variation in the phenomenon being studied.

Hypothesis. The researcher's prediction, derived from a theory or from speculation, about how two or more measured variables will be related to each other.

Independent variable. A variable that the researcher thinks occurred prior in time to, and had an influence on, another variable (called the *dependent variable*). In a hypothesized cause-and-effect relationship, the independent variable is the cause.

Individual-referenced measurement. An approach to testing in which an individual's score on a test at one point in time is interpreted in relation to the same individual's performance on it at other points in time.

Individual test. A test that is administered to one individual at a time.

Inferential observational variable (or *high-inference variable*). A variable that requires the observer to make an inference from behavior to a construct that is presumed to underlie the behavior.

Informal conversational interview. In qualitative research, a type of interview that relies entirely on the spontaneous generation of questions during natural interaction, such as occurs in participant observation in a field setting.

Informed consent. The ethical and legal requirement that a researcher tell all potential research participants about the study's procedures, the information that they will be asked to disclose to the researcher, and the intended uses of that information.

Input evaluation. In the CIPP model of evaluation research, judgments about the resources and strategies needed to accomplish program goals and objectives.

Institutional review board (IRB). A committee that is established by an institution to ensure that participants in any research proposed by individuals affiliated with the institution will be protected from harm.

Instrumental rationality. In action research, an overriding focus on method and efficiency of professional practice over goals and purposes.

Intact group. A collection of persons who must be studied as members of a previously defined group (e.g., a classroom) rather than as individuals.

Intelligence quotient (IQ). A single global score from an intelligence test that estimates an individual's overall intellectual performance.

Intelligence test. A performance test that provides an estimate of an individual's general intellectual level by sampling performance on a variety of intellectual tasks.

Intensity case sample. A group of cases that manifest the phenomenon of interest to a considerable degree, but not to an extreme degree.

Intentional documents. In historical research, writings (e.g., memoirs and yearbooks) that have the explicit purpose of serving as a record of the past.

Interaction effect. In experiments, a situation in which the effect of a treatment variable on a dependent variable is influenced by one or more other treatment variables.

Internal consistency. An approach to estimating test reliability that examines the extent to which individuals who respond one way to a test item tend to respond the same way to other items on the test.

Internal criticism. An evaluation of the accuracy and worth of the statements contained in a historical document.

Internal evaluator. An individual who plays a role in evaluating a program while also employed as a member of the program's staff.

Internalized oppression. The process by which oppressed individuals unwittingly help maintain their lack of privilege through thoughts and actions consistent with their lesser social status.

Internal-structure evidence of test validity. The extent to which the relationship between specific test items is consistent with test-score interpretations.

Internal validity. In experiments, the extent to which extraneous variables have been controlled by the researcher, so that any observed effects can be attributed solely to the treatment variable. In qualitative research, the extent to which the researcher has demonstrated a causal relationship between two phenomena by showing that other plausible factors could not have caused the relationship.

Internet. A worldwide network of computers that enables network members to communicate with each other and to access electronic information resources by computer.

Inter-observer reliability. The extent to which different observers demonstrate agreement in their observations of the same events.

Interpretational analysis. The process of examining qualitative data to identify constructs, themes, and patterns that can be used to describe and explain the phenomenon being studied.

Interpretive research (or *qualitative research*). The study of the immediate and local meanings of social actions to the actors involved in them.

Interpretive validity. The extent to which the knowledge claims (i.e., interpretations) resulting from a qualitative study satisfy four criteria: they have useful consequences; they take context into account; they acknowledge the researcher's role in the study; and they are accepted as authentic—by readers.

Interpretive zone. In case-study research, the process of making sense of data through collaborative inquiry by a group of researchers.

Inter-tester reliability. A measure of a test's internal consistency based on the extent of agreement between the scores assigned by different administrators or scorers of a test.

Interval recording. The recording of observational variables at given time intervals (e.g., making an observation every three seconds).

Interval scale. A measure (e.g., a thermometer) that lacks a true zero point and for which the distance between any two adjacent points is the same.

Interview. A form of data collection involving direct interaction between the researcher and the research paricipant, using oral questions by the interviewer and oral responses by the participants.

Interview guide. A measure that specifies the questions to be asked of each research participant, the sequence in which they are to be asked, and guidelines for what the interviewer is to say at the opening and closing of the interview.

Intra-observer reliability. The extent to which an observer makes consistent recordings of observational variables while viewing a videotape or listening to an audiotape of an event on several occasions.

Item analysis. A set of procedures for determining the difficulty, the validity, and the reliability of each item in a test.

Item-characteristic curve. A mathematical function describing the relationship between test-item performance and the underlying ability.

Item-characteristic curve theory. See *item-response theory*.

Item-difficulty index. For each item on a test, the number of individuals who answered it correctly divided by the total number of individuals taking the test.

Item-reliability coefficient. The correlation between individuals' responses to a particular item on a test and their total test score.

Item-response theory (or *latent trait theory* or *item-characteristic curve theory*). An approach to test construction based on the assumptions that: (1) an individual's performance on a test item reflects a single ability; (2) individuals with different amounts of that ability will perform differently on the item; and (3) the relationships between the variables of ability and item performance can be represented as a mathematical function.

Item statistic. A number that represents some property of individual items in a measure.

Item-validity coefficient. The correlation between individuals' responses to a particular item on a test and their total score on a criterion measure.

John Henry effect. See *compensatory rivalry*.

Judicial evaluation model. A type of evaluation research that simulates the use of legal procedures for the purpose of promoting broad understanding of a program, clarifying the issues raised by the program, and producing recommendations and policy guidelines that lead to improvements in the program.

Key informant interview. A type of interview in which the researcher collects data from individuals who have special knowledge or perceptions that would not otherwise be available to the researcher.

Keyword. A word, or set of words, that is entered into an electronic search engine with the request that the search engine find all records, such as journal titles, that contain the word or set of words; similar to the "Find" function in a word-processing program such as Microsoft Word.

Kruskal-Wallis test. A nonparametric procedure for determining whether the observed difference between the distribution of scores for more than two groups on a measured variable X is statistically significant.

Kuder-Richardson formulas. Measures of the internal consistency of tests whose items have only two response options (e.g., yes or no).

Lake Wobegon phenomenon. See *test score pollution*.

Latent trait. An unobservable characteristic that is hypothesized to explain observed behavior.

Latent trait theory. See *item-response theory.*

Latent variable. In structural equation modeling, an unmeasured variable that is hypothesized to underlie a set of measured variables (called *manifest variables*).

Law (or *scientific law*). A generalization about a causal, sequential, or other type of relationship between two or more constructs.

Life history. The study of the experiences of individuals during different phases of their lives and the way in which they conceptualize these experiences in order to give meaning to their lives.

Likert scale. A measure that asks individuals to check their level of agreement with various statements about an attitude object (e.g., strongly agree, agree, undecided, disagree, or strongly disagree).

Limit field. In an electronic version of a preliminary source, a classification category (e.g., the year of publication) that can be specified in order to limit the search to publications belonging to that category.

Line of best fit. In correlational statistics, the line on a scattergram that represents the best prediction of each person's Y score from their X score.

LISREL. An acronym for *Linear Structural Relationships,* which is a computer program for structural equation modeling.

Literal replication. In case study research, the process of repeating a research study with a different case and hypothesizing that the case will yield results that are similar to those of a previously studied case.

Loading. In factor analysis, the degree and direction of the correlation between a measured variable and a particular factor.

Logistic regression. A type of multiple regression analysis involving the use of two or more measured variables yielding continuous or categorical scores to predict a criterion variable that is categorical in nature.

Longitudinal study. A type of investigation that involves describing changes in a sample's characteristics over a specified period of time.

Low-inference variable. See *descriptive observational variable.*

M. See *mean.*

Macroethnography. In anthropology, the study of large cultural units, such as a national culture.

Main effect. In experiments, the influence of a treatment variable by itself (i.e., not in interaction with any other variable) on a dependent variable.

Manifest variable. In structural equation modeling, a measured variable that is hypothesized to indicate an underlying, unmeasured variable (called a *latent variable*).

Mann-Whitney *U* test. A nonparametric procedure for determining whether the observed difference between the distribution of scores for each of two groups on a measured variable X is statistically significant. The procedure is used when there is no relationship between the two sets of scores and when the assumptions underlying the t test for independent means are grossly violated.

Matching. A procedure that equates two or more groups on the extraneous variable Z at the outset of a study so that it can be ruled out as an influence on any relationship between X and Y that is later observed.

Material culture (or *artifact*). The various objects created by members of a past or present culture that can be studied as reflections of that culture.

Matrix. In a qualitative research report, a type of table that has defined rows and columns for reporting the results of data analyses and other information.

Maximum-variation sample. A group of cases that represent the full range of variation in the phenomenon to be studied.

Mean (*M*). A measure of central tendency calculated by dividing the sum of the scores in a set by the number of scores.

Meaning unit. See *segment.*

Measure of central tendency. A single numerical value (e.g., the mean) that is representative of an entire set of scores.

Measurement error. In classical test theory, the difference between an individual's true score on a test and the scores that the individual actually obtains on it when it is administered over a variety of conditions.

Median. A measure of central tendency corresponding to the middle point in a distribution of scores.

Member checking. In qualitative research, the process of having research participants judge the accuracy and completeness of statements made in the researcher's report.

Meta-analysis. The use of particular statistical procedures to identify trends in the statistical results of a set of studies concerning the same research problem.

Meta-evaluation. In evaluation research, a review of the weaknesses in the evaluation design or in the execution of the evaluation that might affect the validity of the findings.

Microethnography. In anthropology, the study of small cultural units, such as subcultures that exist within a country.

Mixed methods research. A type of research in which quantitative and qualitative methodologies are combined and used in a single investigation.

Mixed-purpose sampling. See *combination/mixed purpose sampling.*

Mode. A measure of central tendency corresponding to the most frequently occurring score in a distribution of scores.

Moderator variable. In predictive research, a variable Z that affects the extent to which variable X predicts variable Y, such that the correlation between X and Y for some values of Z will be different than the correlation between X and Y for other values of Z.

Multimethod research. See *mixed methods research.*

Multiple-baseline designs. A type of single-case experiment in which conditions other than baseline incidence of the target behavior are used to control for extraneous variables.

Multiple-case study design. A form of case study research in which the unit of analysis is at least two individuals or two instances of a phenomenon, selected either to be similar or different in some way of interest to the researchers.

Multiple correlation coefficient (R). A mathematical expression of the magnitude of the relationship between a criterion variable and some combination of predictor variables in a multiple regression analysis.

Multiple regression. A statistical procedure for determining the magnitude of the relationship between a criterion variable and a combination of two or more predictor variables.

Multistage cluster sample. A type of cluster sample that is formed first by selecting clusters and then by selecting individuals within these clusters. See also *cluster sample.*

Multivariate analysis of variance (MANOVA). A procedure that has the same purpose as analysis of variance, except that that the dependent variable is a composite index (called a *vector*) of two or more measured variables. The procedure is useful only when the measured dependent variables are correlated with each other.

Multivariate correlation. Any statistical analysis (e.g., multiple regression or factor analysis) that expresses the relationship among three or more variables.

Multivocality. A situation in which the participants in a culture or societal group do not speak with a unified voice, but rather have diverse points of view and interests.

Narrative inquiry. A representation and explanation of social reality that is communicated through various story structures (e.g., folktales and anecdotes). A collective term for the methods developed by scholars in various qualitative research traditions involving the study of lived experience and narratives.

Narrative analysis (or *narratology*). The study of folktales, plays, anecdotes, and other narrative forms by methods developed in cognitive psychology, ethnomethodology, conversation analysis, and other disciplines.

Narratology. See *narrative analysis.*

NCE score. See *normal curve equivalent score.*

Need. In evaluation research, a discrepancy between an existing set of conditions and a desired set of conditions.

Network. In a qualitative research report, a type of figure for displaying bits of information, each in a separate "node," and links that show how they relate to each other.

Nominal scale. A measure in which numbers represent categories that have no order or quantitative value (e.g., coding French students as "1," Italian students as "2," and Norwegian students as "3").

Nonequivalent control-group design. A type of experiment in which research participants are not randomly assigned to the experimental and control groups, and in which each group takes a pretest and a posttest.

Nonlinear multiple regression. A type of multiple regression analysis that is used to detect curvilinear relationships between the predictor variables and the criterion variable.

Nonparametric test of statistical significance. A type of test of statistical significance that does not make assumptions about the distribution and form of scores on the measured variable.

Nonprobability sampling. A form of sampling in which individuals are selected not by chance, but by some other means.

Nonproportional stratified random sample. A stratified random sample in which the number of individuals in one or more subgroups in the sample is not in proportion to their representation in the population.

Nonreactive measure. See *unobtrusive measure.*

Nonreactive observation. Collection of data based on observation of individuals in real-life contexts and in which individuals do not know that they are being observed. The study of material objects to gain insights about individuals' behavior.

Nonrecursive model. An application of path analysis that allows the researcher to test hypotheses involving reciprocal causation between pairs of variables.

Norm-referenced measurement. An approach to testing in which an individual's score on a test is interpreted by comparing it to the scores earned by a norming group.

Normal curve (or *normal probability curve*). A distribution of scores that form a symmetrical, bell-shaped curve when plotted on a graph.

Normal curve equivalent (NCE) score. A type of standard score with a distribution that has a mean of 50 and a standard deviation of 21.06; the scores are continuous and have equality of units.

Norming group. A large sample (ideally one that is representative of a well-defined population) whose scores on a test provide a set of standards against which the scores of subsequent individuals who take the test can be referenced.

Null hypothesis. A prediction that no relationship between two measured variables will be found, or that no difference between groups on a measured variable will be found.

Objective reality. The view that features of the external environment exist independently of the beliefs and perceptions of individuals.

Objectives-referenced measurement. A type of criterion-referenced measurement that assesses how well an individual performs on a sample of items that measure achievement of specific instructional objectives.

Objectivity. In testing, the extent to which scores on a test are undistorted by the biases of those who administer and score it.

Oblique solution. In factor analysis, a procedure that is used to generate factors that possibly are correlated with each other.

Observer bias. See *observer effect.*

Observer contamination. A situation in which the observer's awareness of certain information about an individual or setting to be observed influences the observer's recording of data involving that individual on the variables being studied.

Observer drift. The tendency for an observer gradually to redefine the observational variables during data collection, with the consequence that the data that the observer collects during the latter stages of data collection do not match the definitions that were learned during training.

Observer effect. Any action or bias of an observer that weakens the validity or reliability of the data that the observer collects.

Observer omission. The failure of an observer to record the occurrence of a behavior that fits one of the categories in the observational schedule.

Observer–participant role. In qualitative research, the observer's maintenance of a posture of detachment while collecting research data in a setting, but with casual interaction with the individuals or groups being studied as necessary.

Observer personal bias. The occurrence of errors in observational data due to personal characteristics of the specific observer.

One-group pretest-posttest design. A type of experiment in which all participants are exposed to the same conditions: measurement of the dependent variable (pretest), implementation of the experimental treatment, and another measurement of the dependent variable (posttest).

One-shot case study design. A type of experiment in which an experimental treatment is administered and then a posttest is administered to measure the effects of the treatment.

One-tailed test of statistical significance. A mathematical procedure for determining whether a null hypothesis that specifies the direction of the difference between two groups (or other prediction involving only one tail of a probability distribution) can be rejected at a given alpha level.

One-variable experiment. An experiment in which a single treatment variable is manipulated to determine its effect on one or more dependent variables.

One-variable multiple-condition designs. A type of experiment in which there is one treatment variable, but more than two experimental groups (e.g., an experimental-treatment group and several control groups, each controlling for a different extraneous variable).

Online search. The use of an on-site computer and telephone hook-up to interact with an off-site computer containing an electronic version of a preliminary source such as *ERIC*.

Open-form item. A question that permits research participants to make any response they wish (e.g., an essay question).

Operational-construct sample. See *theory-based sample*.

Operationally defined construct. A concept that is defined by specifying the activities used to measure or manipulate it.

Opportunistic sampling. A form of sampling in which findings from one case inform the researcher's selection of the next case for study.

Oral history. The use of oral interviews of individuals who witnessed or participated in particular events as sources of data about the past; also, the use of ballads, tales, and other forms of spoken language as sources of data about the past.

Order effect. In experiments where each research participant receives more than one treatment, the influence of the order in which the treatments are administered on the dependent variable.

Ordinal scale. A measure in which numbers represent a rank ordering of individuals or objects on some variable.

Orthogonal solution. In factor analysis, a procedure that is used to generate factors that are uncorrelated with each other.

Outcome validity. A judgment about the credibility of an action research project based on the extent to which new actions lead to a resolution of the problem that prompted the project.

Outlier. A research participant or other unit of analysis whose score on a measure differs markedly from the other scores in the sample or population.

p. See *probability value*.

Panel longitudinal research. A type of investigation in which changes in a population over time are studied by selecting a sample at the outset of the study and then collecting data from the same sample throughout the duration of the study.

Parameter. Any number that describes a characteristic of a population's scores on a measure.

Parametric test of statistical significance. A type of test of statistical significance that makes certain assumptions about the distribution and form of scores on the measured variable.

Paraphragiarism. Borrowing of another author's writing (e.g., extended paraphrases or one-to-one correspondence in the expression of ideas) to such an extent as to constitute representation of the other's work as one's own.

Part correlation coefficient. A statistic that expresses the magnitude of the relationship between two measured variables (X and Y) after the influence of another measured variable on either X or Y (but not on both) has been removed.

Partial correlation coefficient. A statistic that expresses the magnitude of the relationship between two measured variables (X and Y) after the influence of one or more other measured variables on both X and Y has been removed.

Partial publication. The unethical practice of writing separate articles about different aspects of a research study, rather than one article that presents the study as a coherent whole, in order to create an exaggerated impression of a researcher's productivity.

Participant construct interview. In qualitative research, a type of interview that is used to learn how respondents structure their physical and social world.

Participant–observer role. In qualitative research, the observer's assumption of a meaningful identity within the group being observed, but that does not involve engaging in activities that are at the core of the group's identity.

Path analysis. A statistical method for testing the validity of a theory about causal links between three or more measured variables.

Path coefficient. In a path analysis, a standardized regression coefficient that expresses the degree of direct effect of one measured variable on another measured variable.

Pattern. In case study research, an inference that particular phenomena within a case or across cases are systematically related to each other. See also *relational pattern* and *causal pattern*.

Pattern matching. The process of validating a causal inference from patterns in qualitative data by demonstrating that the patterns are consistent with predictions drawn from theoretical propositions.

Pearl building. The process of constructing a new literature search using descriptors obtained from document citations in the current literature search.

Pearson *r*. See *product-moment correlation coefficient*.

Percentile. A type of rank score that represents a given raw score on a measure as the percentage of individuals in the norming group whose score falls below that score.

Performance assessment (or *authentic assessment* or a *alternative assessment*). An approach to evaluating individuals by examining their performance on complex, complete, real-life tasks that have intrinsic value.

Performance test. Any of a class of tests designed to measure intellectual capacity or to diagnose an individual's strengths and weaknesses, on which the testee's presumed goal is to obtain the highest possible score.

Performance turn. An approach to qualitative research in which the researcher and an audience engage in dynamic interaction to co-create the meaning of a case study.

Personality inventory. A type of measure that assesses a variety of personality traits, typically in a self-report, paper-and-pencil format.

Personality measure. Any of a class of tests designed to measure personal characteristics of individuals, on which the testee's presumed goal is to give an accurate picture of the specific personal characteristic that the test involves.

PERT. See *Program Evaluation* and *Review Technique*.

Phenomenographic research. The study of the different ways in which people conceptualize the world around them.

Phenomenology. The study of the world as it appears to individuals when they lay aside the prevailing understandings of phenomena and revisit their immediate experience of those phenomena.

Phenomenon. A process, event, person, document, or other thing of interest to the researcher. In phenomenology, a sensation, perception, or ideation that appears in consciousness when the self focuses attention on an object.

Phi coefficient. A measure of the magnitude of the relationship between two dichotomous variables in a chi-square analysis.

Pilot study. A small-scale, preliminary investigation that is conducted to develop and test the measures or procedures that will be used in a research study.

Plagiarism. The direct lifting of another individual's words for use in one's own report.

Poisson regression. A type of multiple regression that is used when the measure of the criterion variable yields a frequency count.

Politically important case sample. A group of cases that are selected because they are of particular interest to the agency funding the study or some other influential constituency.

Population validity. The extent to which the results of a study can be generalized from the sample that participated in it to a particular population.

Portfolio. In performance assessment, a purposeful collection of a student's work that records the student's progress in mastering a subject domain (e.g., writing in multiple genres) along with the student's personal reflections on his or her progress.

Positive test strategy. The decision to evaluate the effectiveness of a program, method, or other intervention under a set of conditions that are likely to provide the best possible opportunity for the intervention to succeed.

Positivism. The epistemological doctrine that physical and social reality is independent of those who observe it, and that observations of this reality, if unbiased, constitute scientific knowledge.

Positivist research. See *quantitative research*.

Postmodernism. A broad social and philosophical movement that questions the rationality of human action, the use of positivist epistemology, and any human endeavor (e.g., science) that claims a privileged position with respect to the search for truth or that claims progress in its search for truth.

Postpositivism. An epistemological doctrine that asserts an objective reality, but one that cannot be known from a value-free perspective and with absolute certainty.

Poststructuralism. The study of phenomena as systems, with the assumption that these systems have no inherent meaning.

Posttest. A measure that is administered following an experimental or control treatment or other intervention in order to determine the effects of the intervention.

Posttest-only control-group design. A type of experiment that includes three phases: random assignment of research participants to the experimental and control groups; administration of the treatment to the experimental group and either no treatment or an alternative treatment to the control group; and administration of a measure of the dependent variable to both groups.

Practice-oriented material culture. Objects that are created by members of a past or present culture for particular uses (e.g., tools used in building houses), which also may have personal associations and symbolic meanings.

Precontact. An initial message sent to a sample of potential questionnaire respondents in which the researchers identify themselves, discuss the purpose of the study, and request cooperation.

Prediction research. A type of investigation that seeks to predict future events, conditions, or accomplishments from variables measured at an earlier point.

Predictive validity. See r*elationship-to-other-variables evidence of test validity.*

Preliminary source. An index to, or bibliography of, secondary-source and primary-source literature on particular topics.

Presentism. A type of bias in historical research in which past events are interpreted with concepts and perspectives that originated in more recent times.

Pretest. A measure that is administered prior to an experimental treatment or other intervention.

Primary source. A document (e.g., a journal article or a book) written by an individual who actually conducted the research study, developed the theory, witnessed the events, or formulated the opinions described in the document.

Privilege. The possession of greater power, resources, and life opportunities by the members of certain cultural groups than those of other cultural groups. To assign such advantages to certain cultural groups.

Proactive action research. A type of action research in which practitioners first try out a procedure, and then collect and analyze data to determine whether the procedure is achieving its intended purpose.

Probability sampling. A procedure for drawing a sample from a population such that each individual in the population has a known chance of being selected.

Probability value (*p*). The likelihood that a statistical result was obtained by chance.

Process evaluation. In the CIPP model of evaluation research, the collection of evaluative data once the program has been designed and put into operation.

Process validity. A judgment about the credibility of an action research project based on the adequacy of the processes used in different phases of the project.

Product evaluation. In the CIPP model of evaluation research, the determination of the extent to which the goals of the program have been achieved.

Product-moment correlation coefficient (or *r* or *Pearson r*). A mathematical expression of the direction and magnitude of the relationship between two measures that yield continuous scores.

Program delineation. In evaluation research, the process of identifying the salient characteristics of the program to be evaluated.

Program Evaluation and Review Technique (PERT). In the context of research studies, a planning technique that is used to identify the activities to be accomplished, the order in which they need to be accomplished, and the estimated time to accomplish each activity, in order to complete a study on schedule.

Progressive discourse. The practice of seeking to advance scientific understanding of physical and social reality by giving all individuals the right to criticize a research study or the methods of scientific inquiry, and if the criticism proves to have merit, revising a theory, interpretations of findings, or methods accordingly.

Projective technique. A measure that provides amorphous stimuli and freedom of response, on the assumption that this approach will reveal an individual's inner thoughts, fantasies, and unique structuring of reality.

Proportional stratified random sample. A stratified random sample in which the proportion of each subgroup in the sample is the same as their proportion in the population.

Protocol analysis. In cognitive psychology, a method that involves asking individuals to state all their thoughts as they carry out a challenging task, so that the researcher can obtain a holistic overview of their cognitive activity as recorded in their verbal reports.

Purposeful sampling. The process of selecting cases that are likely to be "information-rich" with respect to the purposes of a qualitative research study.

Qualitative research (or *constructivist research*). Inquiry that is grounded in the assumption that individuals construct social reality in the form of meanings and interpretations, and that these constructions tend to be transitory and situational. The dominant methodology is to discover these meanings and interpretations by studying cases intensively in natural settings and by subjecting the resulting data to analytic induction.

Quantitative history. The collection and statistical analysis of quantitative data from the past to investigate historical phenomena, especially the characteristics of a population.

Quantitative records. In historical research, compilations of numerical data (e.g., census records and school budgets) that are used as sources of data about the past.

Quantitative research (or *positivist research*). Inquiry that is grounded in the assumption that features of the social environment constitute an objective reality that is relatively constant across time and settings. The dominant methodology is to describe and explain features of this reality by collecting numerical data on observable behaviors of samples and by subjecting these data to statistical analysis.

Quasi-experiment. A type of experiment in which research participants are not randomly assigned to the experimental and control groups.

Questionnaire. A measure that presents a set of written questions to which all individuals in a sample respond.

R. See *multiple correlation coefficient.*

r. See *product-moment correlation coefficient.*

R^2. See *coefficient of determination.*

R^2 **increment.** The additional variance in the criterion variable that can be explained by adding a new predictor variable to a multiple regression analysis.

Random assignment. The process of assigning individuals or groups (e.g., classrooms) to the experimental and control treatments such that each individual or group has an equal chance of being in each treatment.

Random factor. In experimental designs, an independent variable whose values will be generalized beyond the experiment.

Random purposeful sample. In qualitative research, a group of cases that are selected by random sampling methods for the purpose of establishing that the selection of cases was not biased.

Random sample (or *simple random sample*). A group of research participants that is formed such that all members of the accessible or target population have an equal and independent chance of being selected. By "independent" is meant that the selection of one individual for the sample has no effect on the selection of any other individual.

Range. A measure of the amount of dispersion in a distribution of scores; it is expressed as the lowest and highest scores in the distribution.

Rank score. The relative position of a person or object on an ordinal scale (e.g, a student with the fifth highest grade point average in a class is assigned a rank score of 5).

Ratio scale. A measure (e.g., a yardstick) that has a true zero point and for which the distance between any two adjacent points is the same.

Rational equivalence. An approach to estimating a test's internal consistency, typically involving the application of the Kuder-Richardson formulas.

Raw score. An individual score on a measure as determined by the scoring key, without any further statistical manipulation.

Reactive observation. Collection of data based on observation of individuals in real-life contexts and in which individuals know that they are being observed.

Reader/user generalizability. In qualitative research, the view that the generalizability of a study's findings is not an inherent feature of the findings, but rather a judgment by individuals as to whether the findings are applicable to their particular situation.

Recursive model. An application of path analysis that considers only unidirectional causal relationships, such that if variable X is hypothesized to influence variable Y, it is not also possible to hypothesize that variable Y influences variable X.

Refereed journal. A journal in which the articles that appear were first evaluated by a panel of acknowledged experts to assure that they merit publication.

Reflection. In action research, a process in which practitioners step back from the problematic world of practice and ponder and share ideas about the meaning, value, and impact of their work.

Reflective analysis. In qualitative research, a process in which the researcher relies primarily on intuition and judgment in order to portray or evaluate the phenomena being studied.

Reflective reporting. In a qualitative research report, the use of a writing style that is characterized by literary devices and the strong presence of the researcher's voice.

Reflexivity. In qualitative research, the researcher's act of focusing on himself or herself as a constructor and interpreter of the social reality being studied.

Regression toward the mean. See *statistical regression*.

Regression weight (or *b weight*). A multiplier term added to each predictor variable in a multiple regression equation in order to maximize the predictive value of the variables. When an individual's scores on the predictor variables are multiplied by their respective regression weights and then summed, the result is the best possible prediction of the individual's score on the criterion variable.

Relational ethics. In research, judgments about the morality of one's research decisions and actions by the standard of whether these decisions and actions reflect a caring attitude toward others, including the research participants.

Relational pattern. In case study research, an inference that particular phenomena within a case or across cases are systematically related to each other, but that the relationship is not necessarily causal.

Relationship-to-other-variables evidence of test validity. The extent to which test scores either predict or are related to scores on another measure in a manner that is consistent with the nature of the other measure.

Reliability. In case study research, the extent to which other researchers would arrive at similar results if they studied the same case using exactly the same procedures as the first researcher. In classical test theory, the amount of measurement error in the scores yielded by a test.

Reliability decay. The tendency for the observational data recorded during the later stages of data collection to be less reliable than the observational data collected during earlier stages.

Relic. In historical research, any object whose physical properties provide information about the past.

Replication. The process of repeating a research study with a different group of research participants using the same or similar conditions, for the purpose of increasing confidence in the original study's findings.

Replication logic. The use of theory to determine other cases to which the findings of a case study can be generalized.

Repository. See *archive*.

Representative design. The planning of experiments so that they reflect accurately both the real-life environments in which the phenomena being studied occur and the research participants' natural behavior and cognitive processes in those environments.

Reproduction. The process by which new members who are born to or join a culture accept the preexisting patterns of cultural inequity.

Research and development (R&D). The use of research findings to design new products and procedures, followed by the application of research methods to field-test, evaluate, and refine the products and procedures until they meet specified criteria of effectiveness, quality, or similar standards.

Research tradition. A line of research and theory established by investigators who share an interest in certain phenomena, make the same epistemological assumptions, and use similar methodologies in their studies.

Resources in Education (RIE). An index to papers presented at education conferences and reports of ongoing research studies, studies sponsored by federal research programs, and projects conducted by local education agencies. Published monthly by ERIC.

Response-processes evidence of test validity. The extent to which the processes used by test-takers in taking a test are consistent with the particular construct or constructs that the test purportedly measures.

Response set. In observational data collection, the tendency for an observer to make a rating based on a generalized disposition about the rating task rather than on the basis of the actual behavior of the individuals who are observed. In testing, a predisposition to give the same type of answer to some or all the items in a test rather than an answer to each item based on careful consideration of that item's content.

Responsive action research. A type of action research in which practitioners first collect and analyze data, and then use their findings to develop a new procedure to improve their effectiveness.

Responsive evaluation. A type of evaluation research that focuses on the concerns and issues affecting stakeholders.

Revisionist history. The study of past practices that appear to have had unjust aims and effects, but that have continued into the present and thus require reform; also, the correction of presumably inaccurate interpretations of the past.

RIE. See *Resources in Education.*

Risk-benefit ratio. In a proposed research study, the balance between the level of risk of physical, psychological, or legal harm to which participants may be exposed and the potential contribution of the research findings.

Rotated descriptor display. In the *Thesaurus of ERIC Descriptors,* a presentation of each descriptor (e.g., *achievement*) and all other descriptors that share any word in common with it (e.g., *academic achievement*).

Rubric. In performance assessment, a scale for measuring different levels of proficiency demonstrated in students' portfolios.

Sampling. The process of selecting members of a research sample from a defined population, usually with the intent that the sample accurately represent that population.

Sampling error. The amount of deviation of a sample statistic from its population value.

Sampling frame. A list of all members of the population from which a sample will be drawn.

Scattergram (or *scatterplot*). A graph of the correlation between two variables, such that the scores of individuals on one variable are plotted on the *x* axis of the graph and the scores of the same individuals on another variable are plotted on the *y* axis.

Scatter plot. See *scattergram.*

Scheffé test. A type of *t* test for multiple comparisons.

Scientific realism. The philosophical doctrine that there is an objective reality comprised of layers of causal structures, some of which are hidden from view, and which interact with each other to produce effects that may or may not be observable.

SD. See *standard deviation.*

Search engine. Specialized computer software that has various features for helping users sort through a database to identify documents, Web sites, or other items that satisfy user-specified criteria.

Secondary source. A document (e.g., a journal article or a book) written by an individual who did not actually do the research, develop the theories, witness the events, or formulate the opinions described in the document.

Segment (or *meaning unit* or *analysis unit*). In qualitative research, a section of a text that contains one item of information and that is comprehensible for purposes of data analysis even if read outside the context in which it is embedded.

Selection ratio. In prediction research, the proportion of the available individuals who will be chosen for a given position or role.

Self-concept. A personality measure focused on the set of cognitions and feelings that an individual has about himself or herself.

Self-report measure. A paper-and-pencil instrument whose items yield numerical scores from which inferences can be made about various aspects of self.

Semantic differential scale. A measure that asks individuals to rate an attitude object on a series of bipolar adjectives (e.g., fair-unfair, valuable-worthless, hot-cold).

Semiotics. The study of sign systems, in particular, the study of how objects (e.g., letters of the alphabet) come to convey meaning and how sign systems affect human behavior.

Semistructured interview. A type of interview in which the interviewer asks a series of structured questions and then probes more deeply with open-ended questions to obtain additional information.

Serial dependency. In single-case or time-series experiments, which involve multiple observations of a target behavior over time, a situation in which each observed occurrence of the behavior is influenced by the immediately preceding observed occurrence.

Shotgun approach. A type of quantitative investigation that involves studying a large number of variables simply because they are interesting or easily measured, rather than because the variables relate to theoretical constructs of relevance to the investigation.

Shrinkage. In prediction research, the tendency for correlation coefficients obtained in the original prediction study to have smaller values when the study is repeated with a new sample.

Sign. In semiotics, a signifier and what is signified by it (i.e., what it means).

Signified. In semiotics, the meaning conveyed by an object.

Signifier. In semiotics, an object (e.g., the expression H_2O) that is intended to convey meaning.

Simple random sample. A group of individuals drawn by a procedure in which all the individuals in the defined population have an independent and approximately equal chance of being selected as a member of the group.

Single-case experiment (or *single-subject experiment* or *time-series experiment*). A type of experiment in which a particular behavior of an individual or a group is measured at periodic intervals, and the experimental treatment is administered one or more times between those intervals.

Single-case study design. A form of case study research in which either the unit of analysis is a single individual or a single instance of a phenomenon, or in which several instances of the same phenomenon are collectively studied as one case.

Single-subject experiment. See *single-case experiment*.

Skewed distribution. A set of scores that form a nonsymmetrical curve when plotted on a frequency graph.

Snowball sample (or *chain sample*). A group of cases that are selected by asking one person to recommend someone else suitable as a case of the phenomenon of interest, who then recommends another person who is a suitable case or who knows of other potential cases; the process continues until the desired sample size is achieved.

Social desirability set. In testing, a type of response set in which individuals answer items in such a way as to cast themselves in a favorable light or as they think a "good" person would, rather than as to reveal their true feelings and beliefs.

Sociolinguistics. The study of the effects of social characteristics such as age, socioeconomic status, and ethnicity on language use.

Solomon four-group design. A type of experiment involving two treatment groups and two control groups, so that the researcher can determine the effect of both the treatment variable and the pretest on the dependent variable.

Sonata-form case study. A type of qualitative research report written in first person, present tense that is designed to evoke the lived experience of teaching or other form of practice and is viewed as hypothetical fiction.

Spearman-Brown prophecy formula. A correction to the split-half reliability correlation coefficient to adjust for the fact that this coefficient only represents the reliability of half the test that was administered.

Split-half reliability correlation coefficient (or *coefficient of internal consistency*). The magnitude of relationship between individuals' scores on two parts of a test, which usually are formed by placing all odd-numbered items in one part and all even-numbered items in another part.

SPSS. See *Statistical Package for the Social Sciences*.

Stakeholder. In evaluation research, anyone who has a role in the program being evaluated or who might be affected by or interested in the findings of the evaluation.

Standard deviation (SD). A measure of the extent to which the scores in a distribution deviate from their mean.

Standard error of measurement. A statistic that is used to estimate the probable range within which an individual's true score on a test falls.

Standard score. A type of derived score that uses standard deviation units to indicate an individual's performance relative to the norming group's performance.

Standardized open-ended interview. A type of interview involving a predetermined sequence and wording of the same set of questions to be asked of each respondent.

Standardized test. A test for which procedures have been developed to ensure consistency in administration and scoring across all testing situations.

Stanine. A type of standard score with a distribution that has a mean of 5 and a standard deviation of 2; the scores are continuous and have equality of units.

Static-group comparison design. A type of experiment in which research participants are not randomly assigned to the two treatment groups, and in which each group takes a posttest, but no pretest.

Statistic. Any number that describes a characteristic of a sample's scores on a measure.

Statistical inference. A set of procedures for determining whether the researcher's null hypothesis can be rejected at a given alpha level.

Statistical Package for the Social Sciences (SPSS). A comprehensive, integrated collection of computer programs that is available for managing, analyzing, and displaying data.

Statistical power. The probability that a particular test of statistical significance will lead to the rejection of a false null hypothesis.

Statistical power analysis. A procedure for determining the likelihood that a particular test of statistical significance will be sufficient to reject a false null hypothesis.

Statistical regression (or *regression toward the mean*). The tendency for research participants who score either very high or very low on a measure to score nearer the mean when the measure is re-administered.

Statistical significance. See *test of statistical significance.*

Statistics. Mathematical techniques for summarizing or analyzing numerical data.

Stem-and-leaf display. A condensed graphical presentation of the scores of all the members of a sample or population on a particular measure.

Stenomask. A sound-shielded microphone attached to a portable tape recorder that is worn on a shoulder strap. The device enables an observer to speak into the microphone while an activity is occurring without people nearby being able to hear the dictation.

Stepdown multiple regression. A type of multiple regression analysis in which the entire set of measured predictor variables is entered into a prediction equation, and then, step-by-step, the variable that results in the smallest decrease in R is deleted until a statistically significant decrease occurs.

Stepup multiple regression. A type of multiple regression analysis in which, from among a set of measured predictor variables, the one that leads to the largest increase in R is next added to the prediction equation. This process is repeated until there are no variables left in the set that would lead to a statistically significant increase.

Stepwise multiple regression. A type of multiple regression analysis in which a set of measured predictor variables first is used to construct a prediction equation using stepup multiple regression, and then this equation is subjected to stepdown multiple regression.

Stratified-purposeful sample. A group of cases that represent defined points of variation (e.g., average, above average, and below average) in the phenomenon being studied.

Stratified random sample. A group of research participants that is formed by identifying subgroups with certain characteristics in the population (e.g., males and females) and then drawing a random sample of individuals from each subgroup. See also *proportional stratified random sample* and *nonproportional stratified random sample.*

Strong inference. The testing of plausible alternative hypotheses.

Structural analysis. The process of examining qualitative data to identify patterns that are inherent features of discourse, text, events, or other phenomena.

Structural description. In phenomenology, an account of the regularities of thought, judgment, imagination, and recollection that underlie the experience of a phenomenon and give meaning to it.

Structural equation modeling (or *latent variable causal modeling*). A statistical procedure for testing the validity of a theory about the causal links among variables, each of which has been measured by one or more different measures.

Structuralism. The study of phenomena as systems, with particular emphasis on the meaning of the relationships between the elements of a system.

Structured interview. A type of interview in which the interviewer asks a series of closed-form questions that either have yes-no answers or can be answered by selecting from among a set of short-answer choices.

Subjectivity audit. A process in which the researcher systematically records and reviews his or her subjective perceptions and feelings while a study is in progress to assess how they may be affecting the research design or outcomes.

Summative evaluation. A type of evaluation that is conducted to determine the worth of a fully developed program, especially in comparison with competing programs.

Survey interview. In qualitative research, a type of interview that is used to supplement the data that have been collected by other methods.

Survey research. The use of questionnaires or interviews to collect data about the characteristics, experiences, knowledge, or opinions of a sample or a population.

Symbolic interactionism. In sociology, the study of how individuals engage in social transactions and how these transactions create and maintain social structures and individual self-identity.

Systematic random sample. A group of individuals obtained by taking every "nth" individual from a list containing the defined population.

t **distribution.** A probability distribution that is used to determine the level of statistical significance of an obtained *t* value for the difference between two sample means or other statistic.

T **score.** A type of standard score with a distribution that has a mean of 50 and a standard deviation of 10; the scores are continuous and have equality of units.

t **test.** A test of statistical significance that is used to determine whether the null hypothesis that two sample means come from identical populations can be rejected.

t **test for a single mean.** A procedure for determining whether the difference between a sample mean and a population mean on a measured variable is statistically significant.

t **test for correlated means.** A procedure for determining whether an observed difference between the means of two groups on variable X is statistically significant. The procedure is used when there is a relationship between the two sets of scores.

t **test for homogeneity of independent variances.** A procedure for determining whether the observed difference between the variances of scores of two groups on variable X is statistically significant. The procedure is used when there is no relationship between the two sets of scores.

t **test for homogeneity of related variances.** A procedure for determining whether the observed difference between the variances of scores of two groups on variable X is statistically significant. The procedure is used when there is a relationship between the two sets of scores.

t **test for independent means.** A procedure for determining whether the observed difference between the means of two groups on variable X is statistically significant. The procedure is used when there is no relationship between the two sets of scores.

t **test for multiple comparisons.** Following an analysis of variance that yields significant effects involving three or more groups, a procedure for determining whether the difference between the means of any two of the groups is statistically significant.

Tacit knowledge. Implicit meanings that the individuals being studied either cannot find the words to express or that they take so much for granted that they do not explicate them either in everyday discourse or in research interviews.

Target population (or *universe*). The population (typically very large and geographically dispersed) that is represented by the experimentally accessible population (usually local and relatively small).

Taylor-Russell tables. A summary list of computations that enables one to predict the proportion of individuals who will be successful on a given outcome when a test with a known degree of predictive validity for that outcome is administered to those individuals at an earlier point in time.

Technical rationality. The view that professional practice should be based directly on knowledge and theory generated by the research community.

Test. A structured performance situation that can be analyzed to yield numerical scores, from which inferences are made about how individuals differ in the construct measured by the test.

Test manual. A booklet provided by the publisher of a test that provides information to help prospective test users determine whether the test is appropriate to their purposes and, if so, how to use the test.

Test norms. For a particular test, the scores of a large group, typically converted to percentiles or another type of derived score, to which the scores of subsequent test-takers are compared.

Test of statistical significance. A mathematical procedure for determining whether a null hypothesis can be rejected at a given alpha level.

Test reliability. The extent to which there is measurement error present in the scores yielded by a test.

Test score pollution (or the *Lake Wobegon phenomenon*). An increase in the average score on a test over time such that norms for the test are no longer meaningful.

Test–retest reliability. An approach to estimating test reliability in which individuals' scores on a test administered at one point in time are correlated with their scores on the same test administered at another point in time.

Test validity. See *validity*.

Text. Any object, event, discourse, or element of language that can be analyzed in terms of its communicative value.

Text base managers. Software programs that facilitate structural analysis by formatting a document into fields, coding each field, and retrieving all fields with a given code.

Text retrievers. Software programs that facilitate structural analysis by performing such tasks as listing all words in a document, indicating where each word occurs in the document, and counting how many times each word occurs.

Textural description. In phenomenology, an account of individuals' intuitive, prereflective perceptions of a phenomenon from various perspectives.

Theme. In case study research, an inference that a feature of a case is salient and characteristic of the case.

Theoretical construct. A concept, embedded within a theory, that is inferred from observed phenomena and related to other concepts in the theory.

Theoretical replication. In case study research, the process of repeating a research study with a different case and hypothesizing that the case will yield a different result than was obtained with the previously studied case.

Theoretical saturation. In the grounded theory approach, the point in data collection when the researcher concludes that no new data are emerging to call into question established coding categories, no additional categories are necessary to account for the phenomena of interest, and the relationships between categories are well established.

Theory. An explanation of the commonalities and the relationships among observed phenomena in terms of the causal structures and processes that are presumed to underlie them.

Theory-based sample (or *operational construct sample*). A group of cases that exemplify a particular construct in a theory.

Theory-in-action. In the theory of action, the actual behavior of professionals as they engage in their work.

Thesaurus of ERIC Descriptors. A published list of the terms that are used to classify *CIJE* and *RIE* documents. Researchers can use these terms to identify documents on a particular topic.

Thick description. In qualitative research, a richly detailed report that re-creates a situation and as much of its context as possible, along with the meanings and intentions inherent in that situation.

Thurstone scale. A measure that requires individuals to express agreement or disagreement with a series of statements about an attitude object.

Time-series analysis. A statistical technique for analyzing changes in an observed variable over time.

Time-series design. A type of experiment in which a single group of research participants is measured at periodic intervals, and the experimental treatment is administered between two of these intervals.

Time-series experiment. See *single-case experiment.*

Time-series statistics. A mathematical procedure for determining the extent of serial dependency in data from a single-case or time-series experiment, and whether observed changes in a target behavior represent a treatment effect.

Treatment fidelity. The extent to which the implementation of an experimental or control treatment adheres to the researcher's specifications.

Treatment variable (or *independent variable* or *experimental treatment*). In experimental research, the variable to be manipulated in order to determine its effect on one or more dependent variables.

Trend longitudinal research. A type of investigation in which changes in a population over time are studied by selecting a different sample at each data-collection point from a population that does not remain constant.

Triangulation. The use of multiple data-collection methods, data sources, analysts, or theories as corroborative evidence for the validity of qualitative research findings.

Troubling. The pedagogical process of questioning and exposing the assumptions that underlie widely accepted but oppressive cultural practices that are maintained by traditional educational operations.

True dichotomy. A categorical variable that has only two natural values (e.g., male and female).

True score. In classical test theory, the actual amount of the characteristic measured by the test (e.g., ability, attitude, personality trait) that the test-taker possesses.

Truncation. In the use of an electronic version of a preliminary source, a procedure that enables the user to identify all publications that have been classified by various terms (e.g., *parent, parents, parenting,* and *parenthood*) having a common root (*parent*).

Tukey's honestly significant difference test. A type of *t* test for multiple comparisons.

Two-tailed test of statistical significance. A mathematical procedure for determining whether a null hypothesis that does not specify the direction of the difference between the two groups (or any other null hypothesis involving both tails of a probability distribution) can be rejected at a given alpha level.

Type I error. The rejection of the null hypothesis when it is true.

Type II error. The acceptance of the null hypothesis when it is false.

Typical case sample. A group of cases that represent the middle range of the phenomenon to be studied.

Unit of analysis. In case study research, the aspect of the phenomenon that will be studied across a sample of cases.

Unit of statistical analysis. The element (e.g., the individual student vs. the class of students) that is the basis for selecting a research sample.

Unobtrusive measure (or *nonreactive measure*). A procedure for measuring variables by using data that are found naturally in a field setting and that can be collected without field participants' awareness.

Unpremeditated documents. In historical research, writings (e.g., memos and teacher-prepared tests) that have an immediate purpose, with no expectation that they might be used as a historical record at a later time.

Unstructured interview. A type of interview in which the interviewer does not use a detailed interview guide, but instead asks situationally determined questions that gradually lead respondents to give the desired information.

Utilitarian ethics. Judgments about the morality of one's research decisions and actions by the standard of the consequences of those decisions and actions.

Validity. In testing, the appropriateness, meaningfulness, and usefulness of specific inferences made from test scores. In qualitative research, the extent to which the research uses methods and procedures that ensure a high degree of research quality and rigor.

Variability. The amount of dispersion in a distribution of scores; the greater the variability of a set of scores, the more they deviate from their mean.

Variable. A quantitative expression of a construct (e.g., academic motivation) that can vary in quantity or quality in observed phenomena.

Variance. A measure of the extent to which scores in a distribution deviate from the mean; it is calculated by squaring the standard deviation of the score distribution.

Variant source. In historical research, a document that has been altered in some way from the original document.

Vector. A single mathematical expression that represents an individual's scores on two or more dependent variables in a multivariate analysis of variance.

Verisimilitude. In qualitative research, a style of writing that draws readers emotionally into the research participants' world and leads them to perceive the research report as credible and authentic.

Voice. In critical theory, the condition of particular social categories of individuals being silenced, empowered, or privileged by dominant groups in a society.

Vulnerable population. Any category of individuals (e.g., disabled students, pregnant women, prisoners) who are more susceptible to risk than the general population as a result of participation in a research study.

Web questionnaire. A questionnaire administered and responded to on the Internet that allows automatic recording of raw data.

Wilcoxon signed rank test. A nonparametric procedure for determining whether the observed difference between the distributions of scores for two groups on a measured variable X is statistically significant. The procedure is used when the two sets of scores are correlated and when the assumptions underlying the t test for correlated means is grossly violated.

z **score.** A type of standard score with a distribution that has a mean of zero and a standard deviation of 1.00; the scores are continuous and have equality of units.

NAME INDEX

SUBJECT INDEX